Teacher's Edition

SC

HOLT McDOUGAL

WORLD HISTORY

Ancient Civilizations

Through the Renaissance

Stanley M. Burstein
Richard Shek

HOLT McDOUGAL

 HOUGHTON MIFFLIN HARCOURT

Authors

Dr. Stanley M. Burstein

Dr. Stanley M. Burstein is Professor Emeritus of Ancient History and former Chair of the Department of History at California State University, Los Angeles. Dr. Burstein received his B.A., M.A., and Ph.D. degrees from the University of California at Los Angeles. The author of more than 100 books, articles, and chapters on ancient history, Dr. Burstein co-authored *The Ancient World: Readings in Social and Cultural History* (Englewood Cliffs, 2002). His specialties include ancient Greek history, Greek and Roman Egypt, and Kush. Dr. Burstein has served as president of the Association of Ancient Historians and was a member of the Educational Testing Service Task Force for Development of the AP World History Course.

Dr. Richard Shek

Dr. Richard Shek is Professor of Humanities and Religious Studies at California State University, Sacramento. A native of China, Dr. Shek received his B.A. in Tokyo, Japan, and he received his M.A. and a Ph.D. in history from the University of California at Berkeley. His specialties are East Asian cultural and religious history. The author of numerous publications on Confucianism, Daoism, Buddhism, and popular religion in China and Japan, Dr. Shek co-edited *Heterodoxy in Late Imperial China: Essays in Inquiry* (University of California Press, 2004). Dr. Shek was inducted into the International Educators' Hall of Fame in 1999.

Printed in the U.S.A.

ISBN 978-0-547-96329-7

2 3 4 5 6 7 8 9 10 2266 19 18 17 16 15 14 13

4500407709 ^ B C D E F G

Program Consultants

Contributing Author

Kylene Beers
Senior Reading Researcher
School Development Program
Yale University
New Haven, Connecticut

A former middle school teacher, Dr. Beers has turned her commitment to helping struggling readers into the major focus of her research, writing, speaking, and teaching. She is the former editor of the National Council of Teachers of English literacy journal *Voices from the Middle* and has also served as NCTE president. Her published works include *When Kids Can't Read: What Teachers Can Do* (Heinemann, 2002).

General Editor

Frances Marie Gipson
Secondary Literacy
Los Angeles Unified School District
Los Angeles, California

In her current position, Frances Gipson guides reform work for secondary instruction and supports its implementation. She has designed curriculum at the district, state, and national levels. Her leadership of a coaching collaborative with UCLA's Subject Matter Projects evolved from her commitment to rigorous instruction and to meeting the needs of diverse learners.

Senior Literature and Writing Specialist

Carol Jago
English Department Chairperson
Santa Monica High School
Santa Monica, California

An English teacher at the middle and high school levels for 26 years, Carol Jago also directs the Reading and Literature Project at UCLA. She has been published in numerous professional journals and has authored several books, including *Cohesive Writing: Why Concept Is Not Enough* (Boynton/Cook, 2002). She became president of the National Council of Teachers of English (NCTE) in 2010.

Consultants

John Ferguson, M.T.S., J.D.
Senior Religion Consultant
Assistant Professor
Political Science/Criminal Justice
Howard Payne University
Brownwood, Texas

Rabbi Gary M. Bretton-Granatoor
Religion Consultant
Director of Interfaith Affairs
Anti-Defamation League
New York, New York

J. Frank Malaret
Senior Consultant
Dean, Downtown and West Sacramento Outreach Centers
Sacramento City College
Sacramento, California

Kimberly A. Plummer, M.A.
Senior Consultant
History-Social Science Educator/Advisor
Holt McDougal

Andrés Reséndez, Ph.D.
Senior Consultant
Assistant Professor
Department of History
University of California at Davis
Davis, California

Reviewers

Academic Reviewers

Jonathan Beecher, Ph.D.
Department of History
University of California, Santa Cruz

Jerry H. Bentley, Ph.D.
Department of History
University of Hawaii

Elizabeth Brumfiel, Ph.D.
Department of Anthropology
Northwestern University
Evanston, Illinois

Eugene Cruz-Uribe, Ph.D.
Department of History
Northern Arizona University

Toyin Falola, Ph.D.
Department of History
University of Texas

Sandy Freitag, Ph.D.
Director, Monterey Bay History and Cultures Project
Division of Social Sciences
University of California, Santa Cruz

Yasuhide Kawashima, Ph.D.
Department of History
University of Texas at El Paso

Robert J. Meier, Ph.D.
Department of Anthropology
Indiana University

Marc Van De Mieroop, Ph.D.
Department of History
Columbia University
New York, New York

M. Gwyn Morgan, Ph.D.
Department of History
University of Texas

Robert Schoch, Ph.D.
CGS Division of Natural Science
Boston University

David Shoenbrun, Ph.D.
Department of History
Northwestern University
Evanston, Illinois

Educational Reviewers

Henry John Assetto
Twin Valley High School
Elverson, Pennsylvania

Julie Barker
Pittsford Middle School
Pittsford, New York

Michael Bloom
Ross School
Ross, California

Anthony Braxton
Herbert H. Cruickshank Middle School
Merced, California

Robert Crane
Taylorsville High School
Salt Lake City, Utah

Katherine A. DeForge
Marcellus High School
Marcellus, New York

Mary Demetrion
Patrick Henry Middle School
Los Angeles, California

Charlyn Earp
Mesa Verde Middle School
San Diego, California

Yolanda Espinoza
Walter Stiern Middle School
Bakersfield, California

Tina Nelson
Deer Park Middle School
Randallstown, Maryland

Don Polston
Lebanon Middle School
Lebanon, Indiana

Robert Valdez
Pioneer Middle School
Tustin, California

Contents

UNIT 2 Mesopotamia, Egypt, and Kush

UNIT 3 Civilization in India and China

UNIT 4 Foundations of Western Ideas

UNIT 5 The Roman World

UNIT 6 Islamic and African Civilizations

UNIT 7 Empires of Asia and the Americas

UNIT 8 Renewal in Europe

Available @

- Reading Like a Historian
- Geography and Map Skills Handbook
- Economics Handbook
- Facts about the World

References

HISTORY™ is the leading destination for revealing, award-winning, original non-fiction series and event-driven specials that connect history with viewers in an informative, immersive and entertaining manner across multiple platforms. HISTORY is part of A&E Television Networks (AETN), a joint venture of Hearst Corporation, Disney/ABC Television Group and NBC Universal, an award-winning, international media company that also includes, among others, A&E Network™, BIO™, and History International™.

HISTORY programming greatly appeals to educators and young people who are drawn into the visual stories our documentaries tell. Our Education Department has a long-standing record in providing teachers and students with curriculum resources that bring the past to life in the classroom. Our content covers a diverse variety of subjects, including American and world history, government, economics, the natural and applied sciences, arts, literature and the humanities, health and guidance, and even pop culture.

The HISTORY website, located at **www.history.com**, is the definitive historical online source that delivers entertaining and informative content featuring broadband video, interactive timelines, maps, games, podcasts and more.

"We strive to engage, inspire and encourage the love of learning..."

Since its founding in 1995, HISTORY has demonstrated a commitment to providing the highest quality resources for educators. We develop multimedia resources for K–12 schools, two- and four-year colleges, government agencies, and other organizations by drawing on the award-winning documentary programming of A&E Television Networks. We strive to engage, inspire and encourage the love of learning by connecting with students in an informative and compelling manner. To help achieve this goal, we have formed a partnership with Houghton Mifflin Harcourt.

In addition to premium video-based resources, **HISTORY** has extensive offerings for teachers, parents, and students to use in the classroom and in their in-home educational activities, including:

- ***The Idea Book for Educators*** is a biannual teacher's magazine, featuring guides and info on the latest happenings in history education to help keep teachers on the cutting edge.

- **HISTORY Classroom (www.history.com/classroom)** is an interactive website that serves as a portal for history educators nationwide. Streaming videos on topics ranging from the Roman aqueducts to the civil rights movement connect with classroom curricula.

- **HISTORY email newsletters** feature updates and supplements to our award-winning programming relevant to the classroom with links to teaching guides and video clips on a variety of topics, special offers, and more.

- **Live webcasts** are featured each year as schools tune in via streaming video.

- **HISTORY Take a Veteran to School Day** connects veterans with young people in our schools and communities nationwide.

In addition to **HOUGHTON MIFFLIN HARCOURT**, our partners include the *Library of Congress*, the *Smithsonian Institution, National History Day, The Gilder Lehrman Institute of American History,* the *Organization of American Historians*, and many more. HISTORY video is also featured in museums throughout America and in over 70 other historic sites worldwide.

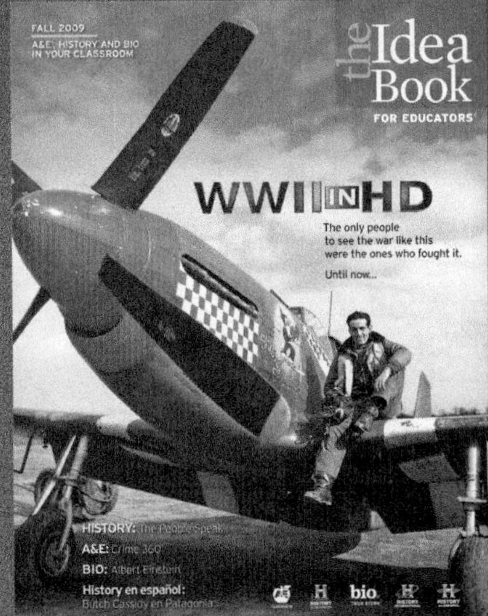

The Idea Book for Educators

Classroom resources that bring the past to life

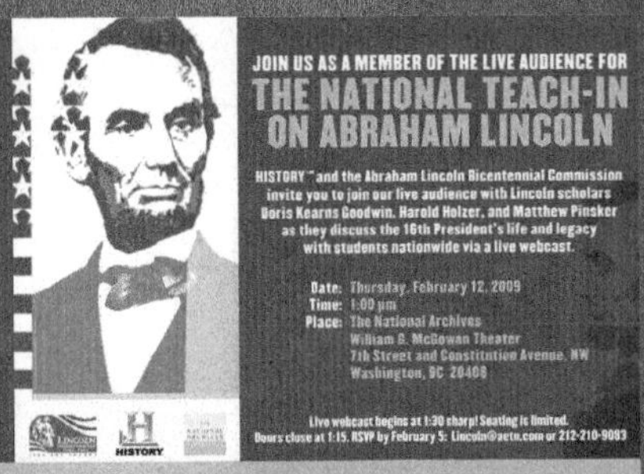

Live webcasts

HISTORY Take a Veteran to School Day

Inspire students with the story...

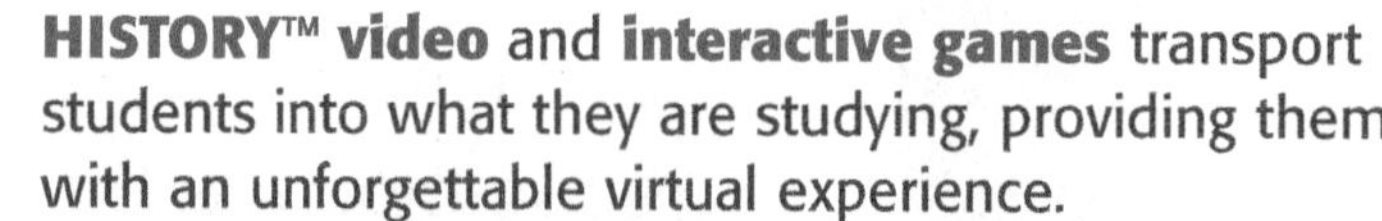

HISTORY™ video and **interactive games** transport students into what they are studying, providing them with an unforgettable virtual experience.

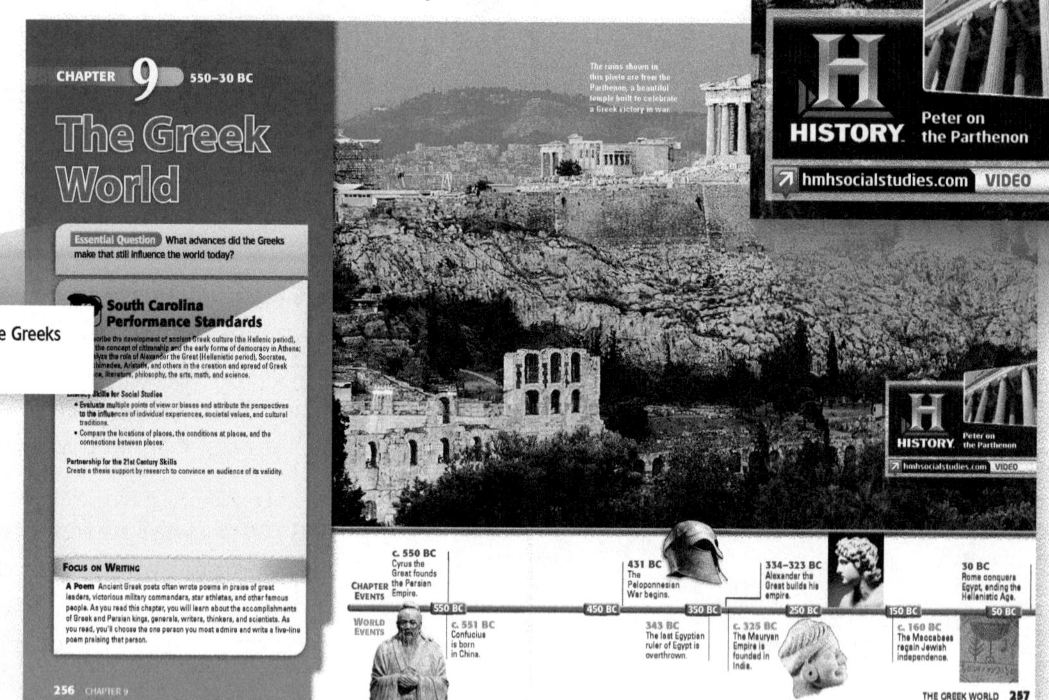

Essential Question What advances did the Greeks make that still influence the world today?

The **Essential Question,** at the beginning of each chapter, engages students by connecting people, places and events and setting the main purpose for reading.

Compelling stories told with dynamic visuals bring people, places and events to life, grabbing students' interest to stimulate and encourage learning.

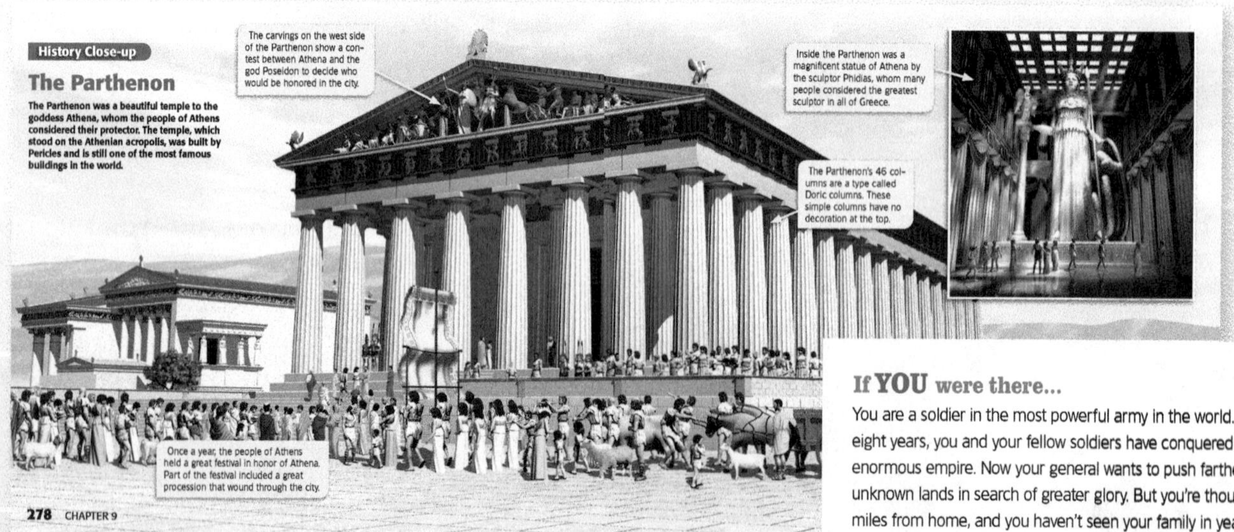

History Close-up
The Parthenon
The Parthenon was a beautiful temple to the goddess Athena, whom the people of Athens considered their protector. The temple, which stood on the Athenian acropolis, was built by Pericles and is still one of the most famous buildings in the world.
The carvings on the west side of the Parthenon show a contest between Athena and the god Poseidon to decide who would be honored in the city.
Inside the Parthenon was a magnificent statue of Athena by the sculptor Phidias, whom many people considered the greatest sculptor in all of Greece.
The Parthenon's 46 columns are a type called Doric columns. These simple columns have no decoration at the top.
Once a year, the people of Athens held a great festival in honor of Athena. Part of the festival included a great procession that wound through the city.
278 CHAPTER 9

If YOU were there...

You are a soldier in the most powerful army in the world. In just eight years, you and your fellow soldiers have conquered an enormous empire. Now your general wants to push farther into unknown lands in search of greater glory. But you're thousands of miles from home, and you haven't seen your family in years.

Do you agree to go on fighting? Why or why not?

& HISTORY

Connect to 21st century learners...

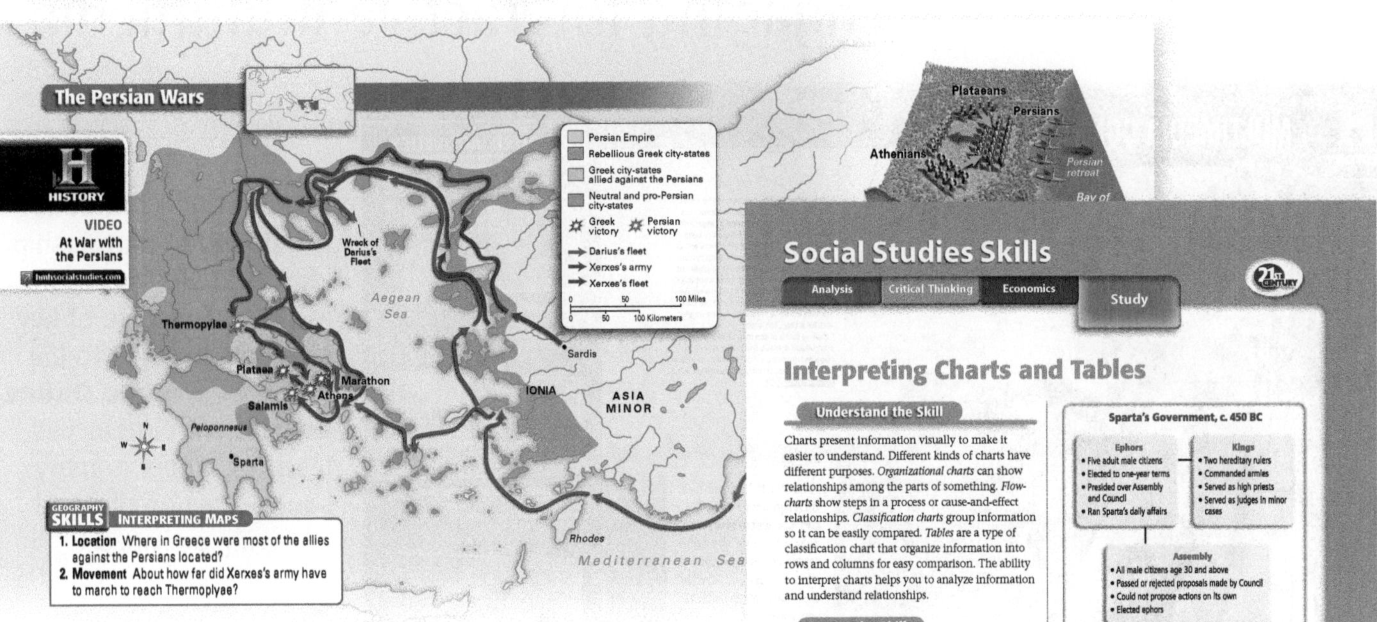

Holt McDougal Social Studies programs are organized to help students connect to the content and develop skills. The Student Editions are designed with:

- **Main Ideas, Big Idea, Key Terms and People,** and **Taking Notes** that prepare students to learn with focused success
- **Section sub-headings** tied to the Main Ideas that provide an outline for reading
- **Maps, visuals, charts,** and **documents** that make content accessible to all students
- **21st Century Skills** that require students to apply what they know

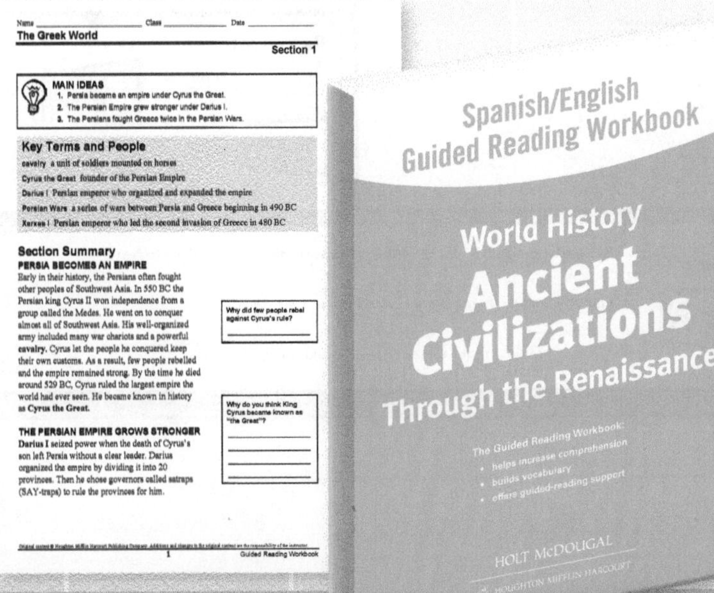

Guided Reading Workbooks (English and Spanish) help guide students as they read, take notes while reading adapted-level summaries, practice skills with an activity, and assess their understanding of content.

Experience
engaging interactive multimedia...

Multimedia Connections, developed in partnership with HISTORY™, provide in-depth coverage of key concepts brought to life in the **Interactive Online Edition** with interactive features, video, primary source documents, and engaging activities.

Power Presentations with Media Gallery DVD-ROM allows teachers to show, edit, and create dynamic multimedia presentations using interactive maps, informative graphics, and fine art and engages students with games and puzzles.

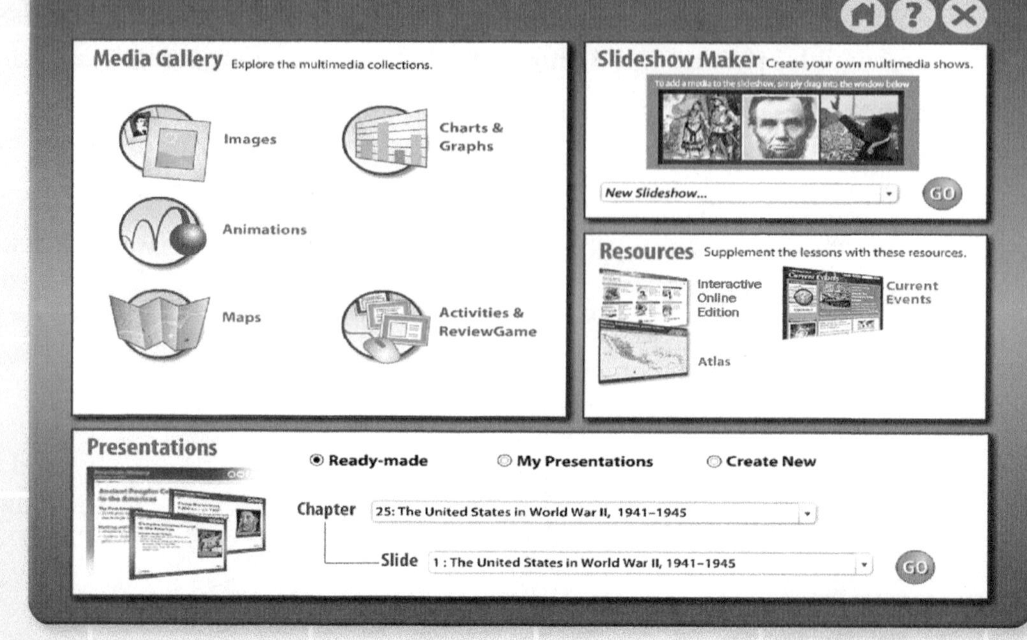

Imagine

easy-to-access, digital content...

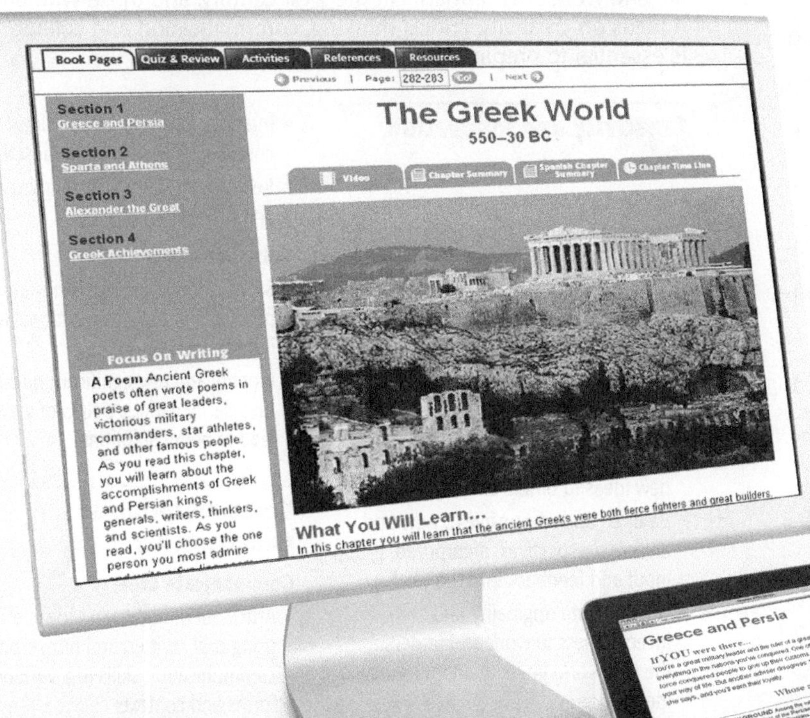

The **Interactive Online Edition** is an interactive textbook that links the content of the Student Edition with the world of enhanced features such as activities, interactive maps, and assessments.

Premium Interactive Online Edition contains everything included in the Interactive Online Edition and:

- Additional chapter-based, interactive **Multimedia Connections** with HISTORY™ video, primary sources and maps for both the teacher and the student.
- **eReader files** of the Student Edition are also included for download to any mobile device.

The **Teacher One Stop** includes everything you need to plan, present, and assess—all on one convenient DVD. Easy to use, editable resources include:

- Reading Support
- Assessment
- Teacher Resources
- Chapter Resource Files
- Lesson Plans
- Videos
- Interactive Teacher's Edition
- Enrichment Activities
- Skill Development Activities
- Examview Assessment Suite
- MindPoint Quiz Show
- Calendar Planner
- PuzzleMaker
- State Specific Resources

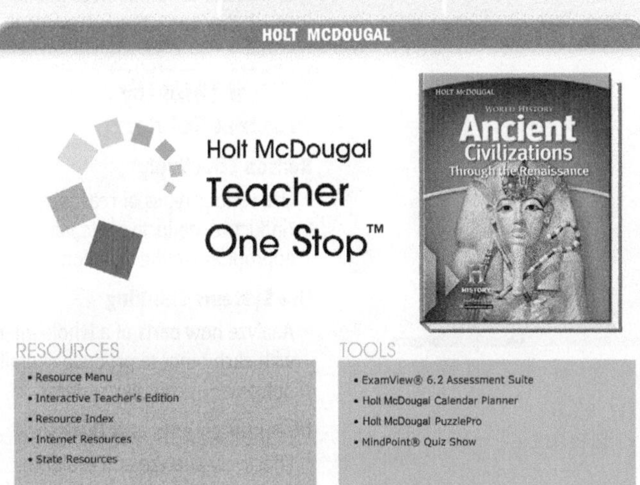

PROGRAM HIGHLIGHTS

Partnership for **21st Century Skills**

The Partnership for 21st Century Skills is the leading advocacy organization focused on infusing 21st century skills into education. The organization brings together the business community, education leaders, and policy makers to define a powerful vision for 21st century education to ensure every child's success as citizens and workers in the 21st century by providing tools and resources to help facilitate and drive change.

A listing of the 21st century skills (P21) outlined by the Partnership is provided here. As an Affiliate of the Partnership, Houghton Mifflin Harcourt helps support the teaching of these skills.

Throughout this book skills lessons that can be used to support the instruction of the P21 framework are indicated by this logo.

For more information about the Partnership for 21st Century Skills, visit www.p21.org

Learning and Innovation Skills

Learning and innovation skills increasingly are being recognized as those that separate students who are prepared for a more and more complex life and work environments in the 21st century, and those who are not. A focus on creativity, critical thinking, communication and collaboration is essential to prepare students for the future.

Creativity and Innovation

Think Creatively

- Use a wide range of idea creation techniques (such as brainstorming)
- Create new and worthwhile ideas (both incremental and radical concepts)
- Elaborate, refine, analyze and evaluate their own ideas in order to improve and maximize creative efforts

Work Creatively with Others

- Develop, implement and communicate new ideas to others effectively
- Be open and responsive to new and diverse perspectives; incorporate group input and feedback into the work
- Demonstrate originality and inventiveness in work and understand the real world limits to adopting new ideas
- View failure as an opportunity to learn; understand that creativity and innovation is a long-term, cyclical process of small successes and frequent mistakes

Implement Innovations

- Act on creative ideas to make a tangible and useful contribution to the field in which the innovation will occur

Critical Thinking and Problem Solving

Reason Effectively

- Use various types of reasoning (inductive, deductive, etc.) as appropriate to the situation

Use Systems Thinking

- Analyze how parts of a whole interact with each other to produce overall outcomes in complex systems

Make Judgments and Decisions

- Effectively analyze and evaluate evidence, arguments, claims and beliefs
- Analyze and evaluate major alternative points of view
- Synthesize and make connections between information and arguments
- Interpret information and draw conclusions based on the best analysis
- Reflect critically on learning experiences and processes

Solve Problems

- Solve different kinds of non-familiar problems in both conventional and innovative ways
- Identify and ask significant questions that clarify various points of view and lead to better solutions

Communication and Collaboration

Communicate Clearly

- Articulate thoughts and ideas effectively using oral, written and nonverbal communication skills in a variety of forms and contexts
- Listen effectively to decipher meaning, including knowledge, values, attitudes and intentions
- Use communication for a range of purposes (e.g. to inform, instruct, motivate and persuade)
- Utilize multiple media and technologies, and know how to judge their effectiveness a priori as well as assess their impact
- Communicate effectively in diverse environments (including multi-lingual)

Collaborate with Others

- Demonstrate ability to work effectively and respectfully with diverse teams
- Exercise flexibility and willingness to be helpful in making necessary compromises to accomplish a common goal
- Assume shared responsibility for collaborative work, and value the individual contributions made by each team member

Information, Media and Technology Skills

People in the 21st century live in a technology and media-suffused environment, marked by various characteristics, including: 1) access to an abundance of information, 2) rapid changes in technology tools, and 3) the ability to collaborate and make individual contributions on an unprecedented scale. To be effective in the 21st century, citizens and workers must be able to exhibit a range of functional and critical thinking skills related to information, media and technology.

Information Literacy

Access and Evaluate Information

- Access information efficiently (time) and effectively (sources)
- Evaluate information critically and competently

Use and Manage Information

- Use information accurately and creatively for the issue or problem at hand
- Manage the flow of information from a wide variety of sources
- Apply a fundamental understanding of the ethical/legal issues surrounding the access and use of information

Media Literacy

Analyze Media

- Understand both how and why media messages are constructed, and for what purposes
- Examine how individuals interpret messages differently, how values and points of view are included or excluded, and how media can influence beliefs and behaviors
- Apply a fundamental understanding of the ethical/legal issues surrounding the access and use of media

Create Media Products

- Understand and utilize the most appropriate media creation tools, characteristics and conventions
- Understand and effectively utilize the most appropriate expressions and interpretations in diverse, multi-cultural environments

ICT (Information, Communications and Technology) Literacy

Apply Technology Effectively

- Use technology as a tool to research, organize, evaluate and communicate information
- Use digital technologies (computers, PDAs, media players, GPS, etc.), communication/networking tools and social networks appropriately to access, manage, integrate, evaluate and create information to successfully function in a knowledge economy
- Apply a fundamental understanding of the ethical/legal issues surrounding the access and use of information technologies

Life and Career Skills

Today's life and work environments require far more than thinking skills and content knowledge. The ability to navigate the complex life and work environments in the globally competitive information age requires students to pay rigorous attention to developing adequate life and career skills.

Flexibility and Adaptability

Adapt to Change

- Adapt to varied roles, job responsibilities, schedules and contexts
- Work effectively in a climate of ambiguity and changing priorities

Be Flexible

- Incorporate feedback effectively
- Deal positively with praise, setbacks and criticism
- Understand, negotiate and balance diverse views and beliefs to reach workable solutions, particularly in multi-cultural environments

Initiative and Self-Direction

Manage Goals and Time

- Set goals with tangible and intangible success criteria
- Balance tactical (short-term) and strategic (long-term) goals
- Utilize time and manage workload efficiently

Work Independently

- Monitor, define, prioritize and complete tasks without direct oversight

Be Self-directed Learners

- Go beyond basic mastery of skills and/or curriculum to explore and expand one's own learning and opportunities to gain expertise
- Demonstrate initiative to advance skill levels towards a professional level
- Demonstrate commitment to learning as a lifelong process
- Reflect critically on past experiences in order to inform future progress

Social and Cross-Cultural Skills

Interact Effectively with Others

- Know when it is appropriate to listen and when to speak
- Conduct themselves in a respectable, professional manner

Work Effectively in Diverse Teams

- Respect cultural differences and work effectively with people from a range of social and cultural backgrounds
- Respond open-mindedly to different ideas and values
- Leverage social and cultural differences to create new ideas and increase both innovation and quality of work

Productivity and Accountability

Manage Projects

- Set and meet goals, even in the face of obstacles and competing pressures
- Prioritize, plan and manage work to achieve the intended result

Produce Results

- Demonstrate additional attributes associated with producing high quality products including the abilities to:
  - Work positively and ethically
  - Manage time and projects effectively
  - Multi-task
  - Participate actively, as well as be reliable and punctual
  - Present oneself professionally and with proper etiquette
  - Collaborate and cooperate effectively with teams
  - Respect and appreciate team diversity
  - Be accountable for results

Leadership and Responsibility

Guide and Lead Others

- Use interpersonal and problem-solving skills to influence and guide others toward a goal
- Leverage strengths of others to accomplish a common goal
- Inspire others to reach their very best via example and selflessness
- Demonstrate integrity and ethical behavior in using influence and power

Be Responsible to Others

- Act responsibly with the interests of the larger community in mind

Explanation of Correlation The following document is a correlation of Holt McDougal *World History: Ancient Civilizations Through the Renaissance* to the South Carolina Grade-Level Standards for Social Studies: Grade 6, including the Social Studies Literacy Skills for the Twenty-First Century: Grades 6-8. The correlation provides a cross-reference between the content in the South Carolina standards and representative page numbers where that content is taught or assessed.

The references contained in this correlation reflect Holt McDougal's interpretation of the Social Studies Indicators outlined in the South Carolina curriculum.

Key to References

PREFIX	EXPLANATION
SE	Student's Edition

Holt McDougal *World History: Ancient Civilizations Through the Renaissance* correlated to the

South Carolina Grade-Level Standards for Social Studies: Grade 6

STANDARD 6-1
The student will demonstrate an understanding of the development of the cradles of civilization as people moved from a nomadic existence to a settled life.

ENDURING UNDERSTANDING
The first humans were nomads who continually traveled in search of food. As these hunter-gatherers developed better ways of doing things, they began to develop into the world's earliest civilizations. Civilized societies have established written languages, permanent structures, forms of government, dependence on agriculture, and specializations of labor. These societies have also developed customs such as formal religions and traditions in family structure, food, and clothing that have endured. To understand how early civilizations evolved, the student will utilize the knowledge and skills set forth in the following indicators:

INDICATORS		PAGE REFERENCES
6-1.1	Explain the characteristics of hunter-gatherer groups and their relationship to the natural environment.	SE: 32–34, 36–39, 45–46
6-1.2	Explain the emergence of agriculture and its effect on early human communities, including the domestication of plants and animals, the impact of irrigation techniques, and subsequent food surpluses.	SE: 40–43, 45–46, 55–57, 79

INDICATORS		PAGE REFERENCES
6-1.3	Compare the river valley civilizations of the Tigris and Euphrates (Mesopotamia), the Nile (Egypt), the Indus (India), and the Huang He (China), including the evolution of written language, government, trade systems, architecture, and forms of social order.	SE: 54–59, 60–64, 65–66, 68–69, 73, 76–77, 79–80, 86–95, 96–98, 99–100, 102–103, 104–106, 110–111, 113, 116, 123, 126–131, 142–145, 147–148, 151, 154, 162–165, 166–168, 171
6-1.4	Explain the origins, fundamental beliefs, and spread of Eastern religions, including Hinduism (India), Judaism (Mesopotamia), Buddhism (India), and Confucianism and Taoism (China).	SE: 130–132, 133–135, 136–139, 140–141, 144–145, 153–154, 169–171, 188–189, 194, 202–207, 208–213, 214–219, 221, 222
STANDARD 6-2 **The student will demonstrate an understanding of life in ancient civilizations and their contributions to the modern world.**		
ENDURING UNDERSTANDING **The foundations of government, science, technology, and the arts are legacies of ancient civilizations. To understand that the contributions of these ancient civilizations have endured and are evident in our society today, the student will utilize the knowledge and skills set forth in the following indicators:**		
6-2.1	Describe the development of ancient Greek culture (the Hellenic period), including the concept of citizenship and the early forms of democracy in Athens.	SE: 229–223, 236–241, 243–245, 253–254, 263–265, 266–271
6-2.2	Analyze the role of Alexander the Great (Hellenistic period), Socrates, Plato, Archimedes, Aristotle, and others in the creation and spread of Greek governance, literature, philosophy, the arts, math, and science.	SE: 272–276, 277–282, 283, 285–286
6-2.3	Describe the development of Roman civilization, including language, government, architecture, and engineering.	SE: 296–299, 302–307, 308–313, 314–316, 327–328, 347MC1–347MC2
6-2.4	Describe the expansion and transition of the Roman government from monarchy to republic to empire, including the roles of Julius Caesar and Augustus Caesar (Octavius).	SE: 297–299, 322–326, 328, 329, 345

INDICATORS		PAGE REFERENCES
6-2.5	Explain the decline and collapse of the Roman Empire and the impact of the Byzantine Empire, including the Justinian Code and the preservation of ancient Greek and Roman learning, architecture, and government.	SE: 339–343, 346
6-2.6	Compare the polytheistic belief systems of the Greeks and the Romans with the origins, foundational beliefs, and spread of Christianity.	SE: 242–245, 334–338, 345–346

STANDARD 6-3
The student will demonstrate an understanding of changing political, social, and economic cultures in Asia.

ENDURING UNDERSTANDING
Asian cultures were developing in ways both similar to and different from those in other parts of the world. The cultures of China, India, Japan, and the Middle East influenced each other's growth and development as well as that of the rest of the world. To understand the contributions of Asian societies that have endured and are evident in our society today, the student will utilize the knowledge and skills set forth in the following indicators:

INDICATORS		PAGE REFERENCES
6-3.1	Summarize the major contributions of the Chinese civilization from the Qin dynasty through the Ming dynasty, including the golden age of art and literature, the invention of gunpowder and woodblock printing, and the rise of trade via the Silk Road.	SE: 172–177, 178–183, 184–185, 186–189, 190–191, 193–194, 410–413, 414–416, 417–419, 420–423, 424–426, 427–429, 433–434
6-3.2	Summarize the major contributions of the Japanese civilization, including the Japanese feudal system, the Shinto traditions, and works of art and literature.	SE: 442–443, 444–445, 446–450, 452–453, 454–459, 461–462, 512–515
6-3.3	Summarize the major contributions of India, including those of the Gupta dynasty in mathematics, literature, religion, and science.	SE: 130–135, 136–141, 142–146, 147–151, 154
6-3.4	Explain the origin and fundamental beliefs of Islam and the geographic and economic aspects of its expansion.	SE: 354–357, 358–361, 362–367, 373

STANDARD 6-4
The student will demonstrate an understanding of the changing political, social, and economic cultures in Africa and the Americas.

ENDURING UNDERSTANDING
African and American cultures were developing independently in ways similar to and different from those in other parts of the world. These cultures also influenced the development of the rest of the world. To understand that the contributions of African and American cultures have endured and are evident in our society today, the student will utilize the knowledge and skills set forth in the following indicators:

INDICATORS		PAGE REFERENCES
6-4.1	Compare the major contributions of the African civilizations of Ghana, Mali, and Songhai, including the impact of Islam on the cultures of these kingdoms.	SE: 386–389, 390–393, 394–395, 402
6-4.2	Describe the influence of geography on trade in the African kingdoms, including the salt and gold trades.	SE: 380–382, 384–385, 386–388
6-4.3	Compare the contributions and the decline of the Maya, Aztec, and Inca civilizations in Central and South America, including their forms of government and their contributions in mathematics, astronomy, and architecture.	SE: 468–473, 474–478, 479–483, 484–485, 487–488
6-4.4	Explain the contributions, features, and rise and fall of the North American ancestors of the numerous Native American tribes, including the Adena, Hopewell, Pueblo, and Mississippian cultures.	SE: 602–607

STANDARD 6-5
The student will demonstrate an understanding of the Middle Ages and the emergence of nation-states in Europe.

ENDURING UNDERSTANDING
Political systems are made up of the people, practices, and institutions that use power to make and enforce decisions. Feudalism during the Middle Ages in Europe was a political and economic system in which control of land was the main source of power. To understand feudalism and its relationship to the development of the European nation-states, the student will utilize the knowledge and skills set forth in the following indicators:

INDICATORS		PAGE REFERENCES
6-5.1	Explain feudalism and its relationship to the development of European monarchies and nation-states, including feudal relationships, the daily lives of peasants and serfs, and the economy under the manorial system.	SE: 506–511, 512–515, 518, 542

INDICATORS		PAGE REFERENCES
6–5.2	Explain the effects of the Magna Carta on European society, its effect on the feudal system, and its contribution to the development of representative government in England.	SE: 540-541, 543, 552
6-5.3	Summarize the course of the Crusades and explain their effects on feudalism and their role in spreading Christianity.	SE: 528–532, 551
6-5.4	Explain the role and influence of the Roman Catholic Church in medieval Europe.	SE: 500–502, 518, 524–527, 533–539, 552, 546–549
6-5.5	Summarize the origins and impact of the bubonic plague (Black Death) on feudalism.	SE: 543, 544–545, 552

STANDARD 6-6

The student will demonstrate an understanding of the impact of the Renaissance, the Reformation, and the Age of Exploration on Europe and the rest of the world.

ENDURING UNDERSTANDING

The Renaissance, the Reformation, and the Age of Exploration were times of great discovery and learning that affected the way individuals viewed themselves and the world around them. To understand the connections among the Renaissance, the Reformation, and the exploration of the world, the student will utilize the knowledge and skills set forth in the following indicators:

INDICATORS		PAGE REFERENCES
6-6.1	Summarize the contributions of the Italian Renaissance, including the importance of Florence, the influence of humanism and the accomplishments of the Italians in art, music, literature, and architecture.	SE: 558–564, 580
6-6.2	Identify key figures of the Renaissance and the Reformation and their contributions (e.g., Leonardo da Vinci, Michelangelo, Johannes Gutenberg, John Calvin, and Martin Luther).	SE: 562–564, 566–568, 571–572, 575
6-6.3	Explain the causes, events, and points of contention and denominational affiliations (of nations) of the Reformation and the Catholic Reformation (Counter Reformation).	SE: 569–575, 580

INDICATORS		PAGE REFERENCES
6-6.4	Compare the economic, political, and religious incentives of the various European countries to explore and settle new lands.	SE: 478, 593–594, 598–601
6-6.5	Identify the origin and destinations of the voyages of major European explorers.	SE: 478, 482–483, 593–596
6-6.6	Explain the effects of the exchange of plants, animals, diseases, and technology throughout Europe, Asia, Africa, and the Americas (known as the Columbian Exchange).	SE: 478, 597–599

LITERACY SKILLS FOR SOCIAL STUDIES	
Explain change and continuity over time and across cultures.	SE: This standard is addressed throughout the text. For example, see pages 9, 21, 45, 135, 194, 286, 305, 413, 423, 504, 580
Interpret parallel time lines from different places and cultures.	SE: 2–3, 24–25, 50–51, 82–83, 120–121, 156–157, 198–199, 224–225, 256–257, 290–291, 318–319, 346, 350–351, 376–377, 394, 406–407, 436–437, 464–465, 492–493, 520–521, 554–555, 584–585
Identify and explain the relationships among multiple causes and multiple effects.	SE: This standard is addressed throughout the text. For example, see pages 84–85, 113, 116, 168, 346, 434, 462, 477, 488, 580
Evaluate multiple points of view or biases and attribute the perspectives to the influences of individual experiences, societal values, and cultural traditions.	SE: 268, 395, 552, 580
Analyze evidence, arguments, claims, and beliefs.	SE: This standard is addressed throughout the text. For example, see pages 73, 97, 129, 151, 170, 240, 251, 280, 300, 305, 335
Select or design appropriate forms of social studies resources to organize and evaluate social studies information.	SE: This standard is addressed throughout the text. For example, see pages 11, 17, 22, 27, 34, 39, 43, 57, 64, 69, 77, 89, 100, 106, 113, 154, 222, 252, 254, 286, 292–293, 316, 320–321, 378–379, 578, 580
Interpret Earth's physical and human systems by using maps, mental maps, geographic models, and other social studies resources.	SE: This standard is addressed throughout the text. For example, see pages 14–15, 18–19, 55, 58, 61, 78, 87, 98, 125,129, 161, 203, 206, 217, 229, 264, 295, 298, 314, 330–331, 400, 411, 432, 458, 497, 501, 550

INDICATORS	PAGE REFERENCES
Compare the locations of places, the conditions at places, and the connections between places.	**SE:** This standard is addressed throughout the text. For example, see pages 14–15, 17, 54–55, 86–87, 124–126, 160–161, 228–230, 294–295, 354–355, 380–382, 440–441, 496–499
Explain his or her relationship to others in the global community.	**SE:** H8–H9
Understand responsible citizenship in relation to the state, national, and international communities.	**SE:** H8–H9
Explain how political, social, and economic institutions are similar or different across time and/or throughout the world.	**SE:** This standard is addressed throughout the text. For example, see pages 134, 240–241, 245, 266–271, 304, 326–328, 335, 398, 419, 457, 512–515, 537, 599
Explain how the endowment and development of productive resources affects economic decisions and global interactions.	**SE:** This standard is addressed throughout the text. For example, see pages 189, 190–191, 230–233, 384–385, 486
Apply economic decision making to understand how limited resources necessitate choices.	**SE:** 76, 194, 402, 486, 488
Explain why trade occurs and how historical patterns of trade have contributed to global interdependence.	**SE:** This standard is addressed throughout the text. For example, see pages 76–77, 187–189, 190–191, 229–233, 384–385, 488, 593–594, 597–601
Examine the costs and the benefits of economic choices made by a particular society and explain how those choices affect overall economic well-being.	**SE:** This standard is addressed throughout the text. For example, see pages 41–43, 56–57, 76–77, 97–98, 111, 430, 459, 473, 486, 488, 509–511, 558–561, 593–601
Explain the use of a budget in making personal economic decisions and planning for the future.	**SE:** H8–H9
Explain how entrepreneurship and economic risk-taking promotes personal and social economic development in the past and the present.	**SE:** H8–H9, 600–601

INDICATORS	PAGE REFERENCES
Partnership for the 21st Century Skills	
Elaborate and refine ideas in order to improve and maximize creative efforts.	**SE:** 2, 22, 24, 46, 47WW1–47WW2, 82, 116, 117WW1–117WW2, 195WW1–195WW2, 224, 254, 256, 286, 287WW1–287WW2, 318, 346, 347WW1–347WW2, 403WW1–403WW2, 406, 434, 489WW1–489WW2, 554, 580, 582–583, 611WW1–611WW2
Articulate his or her own thoughts and ideas and those of others objectively through speaking and writing.	**SE:** 47WW1–47WW2, 50, 80, 117WW1–117WW2, 156, 194, 195WW1–195WW2, 287WW1–287WW2, 290, 316, 347WW1–347WW2, 350, 374, 376, 402, 403WW1–403WW2, 406, 434, 436, 462, 464, 488, 489WW1–489WW2, 520, 552, 582–583, 584, 610, 611WW1–611WW2
Demonstrate the ability and willingness to make compromises to accomplish a common team goal.	**SE:** H8–H9, 608
Create a thesis supported by research to convince an audience of its validity.	**SE:** 47WW1–47WW2, 195WW1–195WW2, 287WW1–287WW4, 347WW1–347WW2, 489WW1–489WW2, 611WW1–611WW2
Literacy in History/Social Studies, Science, and Other Technical Subjects	
Cite specific textual evidence to support the analysis of primary and secondary sources.	**SE:** This standard is addressed throughout the text. For example, see pages 71, 114, 116, 123, 185, 250–251, 300–301, 337, 426, 447, 571
Integrate information from a variety of media sources with print or digital text in an appropriate manner.	**SE:** 80, 154, 195MC1–195MC2, 254, 255MC1–255MC2, 347MC1– 347MC2, 374, 463MC1–463MC2, 489MC1–489MC2, 518, 553MC1–553MC2

South Carolina Skills Scope and Sequence

* Denotes 21st Century Skill
♦ Denotes ELA Common Core Standard

READING AND CRITICAL THINKING SKILLS	HM World History, Ancient Civilizations through the Renaissance, South Carolina Edition	HM Geography, South Carolina Edition	HM The Americans, South Carolina Edition	HM Psychology: Principles in Practice	HM Sociology: The Study of Human Relationships
Taking Notes with Graphic Organizers*	p. 74, 114, 194, 232	p. 26, 116, 235, 344, 502	p. 25, 205, 317, 446, 537, 666, 774, 869, 1093	p. 4, 106, 178, 257, 320, 431	p. 4, 95, 141, 186, 260, 342
Finding Main Ideas* ♦	p. 54, 88, 108, 240, 298, 352, 392	p. 13, 122, 213, 507, 661	p. R2, 96, 357, 488, 578, 694, 847, 1075	p. S1, 6, 69, 107, 258, 309, 433, 509	p. S1, 27, 101, 190, 221, 283, 344
Summarizing/Paraphrasing* ♦	p. 31, 161, 180, 183, 273	NA	p. R4, 7, 135, 312, 423, 596, 713, 878	p. 17, 70, 160, 263, 312, 425, 520	p. 14, 111, 172, 224, 358
Sequencing Events/Chronological Order* ♦	p. 26, 39, 161, 301, 355	p. 230–231, 432–433	p. R3, 918, 964, 1010	p. 73, 181	p. 22, 120, 235
Categorizing/Organizing Information*	p. 69, 79, 106, 205	p. 153, 357, 331, 397	p. . 150, 544, 902	p. 14, 310, 462	p. 47, 237
Analyzing Causes and Effects*	p. 59, 103, 119, 242, 360	p. 47, 171, 307, 531, 631	p. R7, 22, 330, 476, 809	p. S2, 337, 449	p. S2, 41, 118, 128, 191
Comparing and Contrasting* ♦	p. 11, 187, 311	p. 164, 459, R3	p. R8, 17, 247, 327, 641, 922, 1051	p. 24, 137, 318, 447	p. 7, 116, 210, 278, 418
Identifying Problems and Solutions/ Analyzing Costs and Benefits*	p. 280	p. 97, 243, 457	p. R5, 116, 384, 567, 975	p. S3	p. S3
Making Inferences and Predictions*	p. 29, 126, 142, 335, 343	p. 29, 130, 315, 572	p. R10, R20, 9, 417, 599, 656, 910	p. 99	p. 249
Making Generalizations*	p. 68, 94, 185, 337	p. 9, 153, 301, 639	p. R21, 10, 235, 518, 631, 725, 833, 902	p. 26, 176, 347, 474	p. 73, 172
Drawing Conclusions* ♦	p. 86, 92, 107, 146, 207, 256	p. 58, 215, 359, 490, 739	p. R18, 258, 415, 582, 677, 787	p. S4, 21, 83, 260	p. S4, 9, 113, 219
Evaluating/Asking and Using Questions*	p. 57, 116, 176, 183	p. 243, 397	p. 104, 223, 342, 450, 514, 633	p. 149, 414	p. 18, 140
Analyzing Point of View/Forming and Supporting Opinions* ♦	p. 100, 155, 191	p. 162, 378	p. R17, 62	p. 527	p. 120, 252
Distinguishing Fact from Opinion*	p. 224	p. 729	p. R9	NA	NA
Recognizing Bias, Propaganda, and Stereotypes* ♦	p. 20, 406	NA	p. R15	NA	NA
Identifying, Using, and Analyzing Primary and Secondary Sources*	H1–H9, p. 114	p. 182, 255, 329, 395	p. R22, S8, S10	p. S9, S10	p. S9, S10
Understanding Specialized Vocabulary, Word Origins or Parts*	p. H12–H13, 4, 252	p. 37, 155, 705	p. 26, 274, 512, 797	p. S16, 306, 519	p. 115, 252, 327

READING AND CRITICAL THINKING SKILLS	HM World History, Ancient Civilizations through the Renaissance, South Carolina Edition	HM Geography, South Carolina Edition	HM The Americans, South Carolina Edition	HM Psychology: Principles in Practice	HM Sociology: The Study of Human Relationships
Using Context Clues and Supporting Details* ◆	H1–H9, p. 114	p. 77, 82, 86, 90, 95	p. R2, 933	p. 21, 71, 79, 83, 88	p. 211, 217, 224
Linking Past to Present*	p. 33, 154, 271, 344	p. 150, 436, 578	p. 99, 234, 370, 414, 526, 644, 824, 945	p. 89, 246	p. 220, 236, 255
Connecting to Literature / Using Prior Knowledge/Setting a Purpose for Reading/Re-Reading* ◆	p. 72–73, 206, 330, 444	p. 86, 173, 227, 432	p. 246, 430, 664, 834, 968, 1080	p. 96, 101, 106, 111	p. 136, 141, 146, 158, 162, 168

GEOGRAPHIC LITERACY AND STATISTICAL ANALYSIS SKILLS	HM World History, Ancient Civilizations through the Renaissance, South Carolina Edition	HM Geography, South Carolina Edition	HM The Americans, South Carolina Edition	HM Psychology: Principles in Practice	HM Sociology: The Study of Human Relationships
Interpreting Maps / Creating Maps	p. H7, H14–H17, 18–19, 80	p. 80, 142, 204, 554, 720	p. R25, R32, 39, 268, 437, 1060	NA	p. 19, 149, 223, 328, 429
Interpreting Charts, Tables, Lists, Graphs, and Statistics	p. 68, 187, 310, 329, 418	p. 82, 234, 377, 686	p. R27, R28, S14, S16, S18	p. S6, S7	p. S6, S7
Analyzing Political Cartoons and Images	p. 43	S12–S13	p. R24, S12, 315	p. S11	p. S11
Interpreting Diagrams/Cartograms	p. 174	p. 38, 733	p. 60–61, 933	p. 20, 36, 69, 74	p. 41, 64, 166
Using Longitude, Latitude, Scale, Elevation, and Projection	p. H14–H17, H18–H19, 227	p. 6, 17, 18–19	p. S20, A4, A16, A20	NA	NA
Connecting Ideas to Geography and Geographer's practices (fieldwork, labs, experiments)	p. 60–61, 212, 260, 364	p. 509	p. R31, 727, 138, 286, 440, 572, 856, 1052	p. 90, 150, 440	p. 130, 226, 388

* Denotes 21st Century Skill
♦ Denotes ELA Common Core Standard

RESEARCH, WRITING, AND PRESENTATION SKILLS	HM World History, Ancient Civilizations through the Renaissance, South Carolina Edition	HM Geography, South Carolina Edition	HM The Americans, South Carolina Edition	HM Psychology: Principles in Practice	HM Sociology: The Study of Human Relationships
Formulating Historical Questions *	p. 426	p. 124, 349	p. R12	NA	NA
Conducting Research* ♦	p. 350	p. 262, 334	p. 189	p. 293, 385	p. 79, 161, 403
Outlining*	p. 322	p. 359	p. R34	p. 329. 557	p. 176–177
Constructed Response / Extended Response / Essay* ♦	p. 52, 259, 282, 314, 424	p. S30, S32, 591	p. S26, S28, R34	p. 29	p. 83
Learning to Write/Writing Process* ♦	p. 48–49, 136–137	p. 215, 331, 359	p. R34	p. 125, 153, 185, 269	p. 83, 179, 363
Creating a Oral Presentation (Speech or Debate)*	p. 187, 198	p. 229	p. R36	p. 219, 387, 430, 514	p. 159, 225, 331

MEDIA AND INTERNET SKILLS	HM World History, Ancient Civilizations through the Renaissance, South Carolina Edition	HM Geography, South Carolina Edition	HM The Americans, South Carolina Edition	HM Psychology: Principles in Practice	HM Sociology: The Study of Human Relationships
Using a Search Engine/Database*	p. 183, 219	p. R15	p. 65	p. 433, 435	p. 64, 188, 371
Evaluating Internet Sources* ♦	p. 350–351	p. 151, 172, 209, 369	p. R29, 533	p. S15	p. S14
Doing Internet Research/ WebQuests* ♦	p. 19, 214	p. 77, 331	p. 91, 333, 635	p. 57, 258, 353, 433, 481, 570	p. 101, 209, 385, 406
Analyzing Visual Media (Television, Film/Video, Internet)*	p. 25, 119	p. 551	p. R23, 837, 1033	p. 3, 157, 213, 305	p. 53
Creating a Multimedia Presentation*	p. 222	p. 25, 254, 605	p. R37	p. 443	p. 179

TEST-TAKING STRATEGIES AND SKILLS	HM World History, Ancient Civilizations through the Renaissance, South Carolina Edition	HM Geography, South Carolina Edition	HM The Americans, South Carolina Edition	HM Psychology: Principles in Practice	HM Sociology: The Study of Human Relationships
Multiple Choice	p. 47, 83, 117, 135	p. S6	p. S6, 33, 301, 805, 995	p. 494	p. 204
Primary Source	p. H3, 9, 15, 38, 192, 355	p. S8, 182, 328, 470, 535, 603, 670, 736	p. 42, 224, 371, 447, 538, 652, 714, 867, 965	p. S9	p. S9, 253, 317
Secondary Source	p. H4	p. S10	p. R22	p. S10	p. S10
Political Cartoon	NA	p. S12	p. 233, 560, 699	NA	NA
Charts	p. 68, 187, 329, 418	p. S14, 147, 250, 377, 561, 686	p. 115, 285, 398, 428, 585, 706	p. 83, 179, 308, 433, 508, 598	p. 39, 127, 201, 263, 361, 425
Line and Bar Graphs	NA	p. S16, 69, 266, 313, 443, 546, 596, 629, 670, 737	p. 175, 216, 320, 540, 622, 714, 812, 867, 929, 1015	p. 31, 133, 203, 290, 448, 572, 611	p. 51, 289, 374, 428
Pie Graphs	NA	p. S20, 140, 348	p. 81, 251, 335, 648, 832, 929	p. S6, 10, 329	p. 40, 133, 222
Political Maps	p. H20–H25	p. S22, A4–A5, A20–A21	p. S20, A4, A16, A20	NA	NA
Thematic Maps	p. H20–H25	p. S26, A10–A11. A12–A13, 22–33	p. S22, 67, 227, 1053	p. S8	p. S8, 85, 123, 181, 220, 365
Time Lines	p. 24–25, 52–53, 372, R18–R23	p. 137, 230, 362, 455, 568, 652, 727	p. 126, 334, 438, 786, 881, 970, 1104, 1112	p. xxii–xxiii	p. 64, 116, 235, 348, 380
Document-Based Questions/Essays	p. 75, 192, 335	p. S34	p. S30	NA	NA
Project-Based Assessment	p. 118, 250, 348	p. 31	p. 373, 479	p. 300–301, 416–417	p. 50, 106, 228, 361

Become an Active Reader

Did you ever think you would begin reading your social studies book by reading about reading? Actually, it makes better sense than you might think. You would probably make sure you learned some soccer skills and strategies before playing in a game. Similarly, you need to learn some reading skills and strategies before reading your social studies book. In other words, you need to make sure you know whatever you need to know in order to read this book successfully.

Tip #1

Use the Reading Social Studies Pages

Take advantage of the two pages on reading at the beginning of every chapter. Those pages introduce the chapter themes; explain a reading skill or strategy; and identify key terms, people, and academic vocabulary.

Themes

Why are themes important? They help our minds organize facts and information. For example, when we talk about baseball, we may talk about types of pitches. When we talk about movies, we may discuss animation.

Historians are no different. When they discuss history or social studies, they tend to think about some common themes: Economics, Geography, Religion, Politics, Society and Culture, and Science and Technology.

Reading Skill or Strategy

Good readers use a number of skills and strategies to make sure they understand what they are reading. These lessons will give you the tools you need to read and understand social studies.

Key Terms, People, and Academic Vocabulary

Before you read the chapter, review these words and think about them. Have you heard the word before? What do you already know about the people? Then watch for these words and their meanings as you read the chapter.

Gives you practice in the reading skill or strategy.

Tells which theme or themes are important in the chapter

Explains a skill or strategy good readers use

Identifies the important words in the chapter.

Tip #2

Read like a Skilled Reader

You will never get better at reading your social studies book—or any book for that matter—unless you spend some time thinking about how to be a better reader.

Skilled readers do the following:

- They preview what they are supposed to read before they actually begin reading. They look for vocabulary words, titles of sections, information in the margin, or maps or charts they should study.
- They divide their notebook paper into two columns. They title one column "Notes from the Chapter" and the other column "Questions or Comments I Have."
- They take notes in both columns as they read.
- They read like **active readers**. The Active Reading list below shows you what that means.
- They use clues in the text to help them figure out where the text is going. The best clues are called signal words.

  Chronological Order Signal Words: *first, second, third, before, after, later, next, following that, earlier, finally*

  Cause and Effect Signal Words: *because of, due to, as a result of, the reason for, therefore, consequently*

  Comparison/Contrast Signal Words: *likewise, also, as well as, similarly, on the other hand*

READING SOCIAL STUDIES

Active Reading

Successful readers are **active readers**. These readers know that it is up to them to figure out what the text means. Here are some steps you can take to become an active, and successful, reader.

Predict what will happen next based on what has already happened. When your predictions don't match what happens in the text, re-read the confusing parts.

Question what is happening as you read. Constantly ask yourself why things have happened, what things mean, and what caused certain events.

Summarize what you are reading frequently. Do not try to summarize the entire chapter! Read a bit and then summarize it. Then read on.

Connect what is happening in the part you're reading to what you have already read.

Clarify your understanding. Stop occasionally to ask yourself whether you are confused by anything. You may need to re-read to clarify, or you may need to read further and collect more information before you can understand.

Visualize what is happening in the text. Try to see the events or places in your mind by drawing maps, making charts, or jotting down notes about what you are reading.

Tip #3

Pay Attention to Vocabulary

It is no fun to read something when you don't know what the words mean, but you can't learn new words if you only use or read the words you already know. In this book, we know we have probably used some words you don't know. But, we have followed a pattern as we have used more difficult words.

READING SOCIAL STUDIES

Key Terms and People

At the beginning of each section you will find a list of key terms or people that you will need to know. Be on the lookout for those words as you read through the section.

Much of Egyptian religion **afterlife**, or life after death. Th believed that the afterlife

The Afterlife
Osiris, god of the underworld, waited to judge the souls of the dead.
The god Anubis weighed each dead person's heart against the feather of truth. If they weighed the same amount, the person was allowed into the underworld.

Religion and Egyptian Life

The ancient Egyptians had strong religious beliefs. Worshipping the gods was a part of their everyday lives. Many Egyptian religious customs focused on what happened after people died.

The Gods of Egypt

Like Mesopotamians, Egyptians practiced polytheism. Before the First Dynasty, each village worshipped its own gods. During the Old Kingdom, however, Egyptian officials tried to give some sort of structure to religious beliefs. Everyone was expected to worship the same gods, though how they worshipped the gods might differ from one region of Egypt to another.

The Egyptians built temples to the gods all over the kingdom. The temples collected payments from both the government and worshippers. These payments allowed the temples to grow more influential.

Over time, certain cities became centers for the worship of certain gods. In Memphis, for example, people prayed to Ptah, the creator of the world.

The Egyptians had gods for nearly everything, including the sun, the sky, and the earth. Many gods mixed human and animal forms. For example, Anubis, the god of the dead, had a human body but a jackal's head. Other major gods included

- Re, or Amon-Re, the sun god
- Osiris, the god of the underworld
- Isis, the goddess of magic, and
- Horus, a sky god, god of the pharaohs

Emphasis on the Afterlife

Much of Egyptian religion focused on the **afterlife, or life after death.** The Egyptians believed that the afterlife was a happy place. Paintings from Egyptian tombs show the afterlife as an ideal world where all the people are young and healthy.

The Egyptian belief in the afterlife stemmed from their idea of *ka* (KAH), or a person's life force. When a person died, his or her *ka* left the body and became a spirit. The *ka*, however, remained linked to the

CHAPTER 4

The griots' stories were both entertaining and informative. They told of important past events and of the accomplishments of distant ancestors. For example, some stories explained the rise and fall of the West African empires. Other stories described the actions of powerful kings and warriors. Some griots made their stories more lively by acting out the events like scenes in a play.

In addition to stories, the griots recited **proverbs**, or short sayings of wisdom or truth. They used proverbs to teach lessons to the people. For example, one West African proverb warns, "Talking doesn't fill the basket in the farm." This proverb reminds people that they must work to accomplish things. It is not enough for people just to talk about what they want to do.

In order to tell their stories and proverbs, the griots memorized hundreds of names and events. Through this memorization process the griots passed on West African history from generation to generation. However, some griots confused names and events in their heads. When this happened, the facts of some historical events became distorted. Still, the griots' stories tell us a great deal about life in the West African empires.

West African Epics

Some of the griot poems are epics—long poems about kingdoms and heroes. Many of these epic poems are collected in the *Dausi* (DAW-zee) and the *Sundiata*.

The *Dausi* tells the history of Ghana. Intertwined with historical events, though, are myths and legends. One story is about a seven-headed snake god named Bida. This god promised that Ghana would prosper if the people sacrificed a young woman to him every year. One year a mighty warrior killed Bida. As the god died, he cursed Ghana. The griots say that this curse caused the empire of Ghana to fall.

The *Sundiata* is about Mali's great ruler. According to the epic, when Sundiata was still a boy, a conqueror captured Mali and killed Sundiata's father and 11 brothers.

hmhsocialstudies.com
ANIMATED HISTORY
Modern Griots

ACADEMIC VOCABULARY
process a series of steps by which a task is accomplished

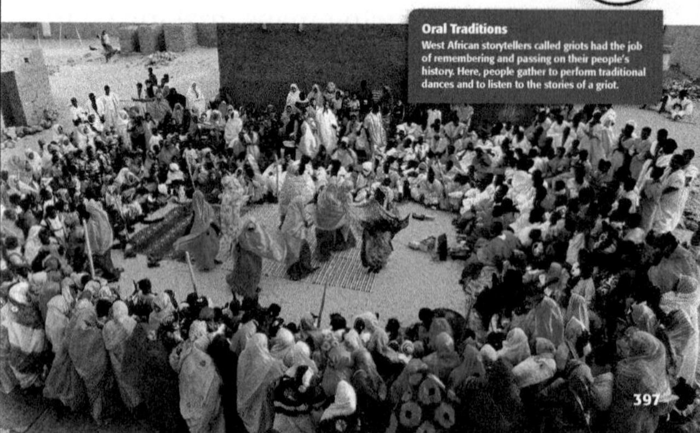

Oral Traditions
West African storytellers called griots had the job of remembering and passing on their people's history. Here, people gather to perform traditional dances and to listen to the stories of a griot.

397

ACADEMIC VOCABULARY

process a series of steps by which a task is accomplished

Academic Vocabulary

When we use a word that is important in all classes, not just social studies, we define it in the margin under the heading Academic Vocabulary. You will run into these academic words in other textbooks, so you should learn what they mean while reading this book.

Words to Know

As you read this social studies textbook, you will be more successful if you know or learn the meanings of the words on this page. There are two types of words listed here. The first list contains academic words, the words we pointed out at the bottom of the previous page. These words are important in all classes, not just social studies. The second list contains words that are special to this particular topic of social studies, world history.

Academic Words

acquire	to get
affect	to change or influence
agreement	a decision reached by two or more people in a group
aspect	part
authority	power or influence; right to rule
classical	referring to the cultures of ancient Greece and Rome
competition	a contest between two rivals
conflict	an open clash between two opposing groups
consequences	effects of a particular event or events
contracts	binding legal agreements
defend	to keep secure from danger
development	creation; the process of growing or improving
distribute	to divide among a group of people
efficient	productive and not wasteful
establish	to set up or create
features	characteristics
function	work or perform
ideals	ideas or goals that people try to live up to
influence	change, or have an effect on
innovation	a new idea, method, or device
logical	reasoned, or well thought out
method	a way of doing something
motive	reason for doing something
neutral	not engaged in either side
opposition	the act of opposing or resisting
policy	rule, course of action
primary	main, most important
principles	basic beliefs, rules, or laws
procedure	the way a task is accomplished
process	a series of steps by which a task is accomplished
purpose	the reason something is done
rebel	to fight against authority
role	a part or function; assigned behavior
strategy	a plan for fighting a battle or war
structure	the way something is set up or organized
values	ideas that people hold dear and try to live by
vary	to be different

Social Studies Words

AD	also CE, refers to dates after Jesus's birth
BC	also BCE, refers to dates before the birth of Jesus of Nazareth
BCE	refers to "Before Common Era," dates before the birth of Jesus of Nazareth
CE	refers to "Common Era," dates after Jesus's birth
century	a period of 100 years
civilization	the culture characteristic of a particular time or place
climate	the weather conditions in a certain area over a long period of time
culture	the knowledge, beliefs, customs, and values of a group of people
custom	a repeated practice; tradition
economy	the system in which people make and exchange goods and services
era	a period of time
geography	the study of the earth's physical and cultural features
physical features	the features on the land's surface, such as mountains and rivers
politics	government
region	an area with one or more features that make it different from surrounding areas
resources	materials found on the earth that people need and value
society	a group of people who share common traditions
trade	the exchange of goods or services

How to Make This Book Work for You

Studying history will be easy for you using this textbook. Take a few minutes to become familiar with the easy-to-use structure and special features of this history book. See how this textbook will make history come alive for you!

Unit

Each chapter of this textbook is part of a Unit of study focusing on a particular time period. Each unit opener provides an illustration, usually showing a young person of the period, and gives you an overview of the exciting topics that you will study in the unit.

Chapter

Each Chapter includes a chapter-opener introduction with a time line of important events, a Social Studies Skills activity, Chapter Review pages, and a Standardized Test Practice page.

Reading Social Studies These chapter level reading lessons give you skills and practice that you can use to help you read the textbook. Within each chapter there is a Focus on Reading note in the margin on the page where the reading skill is covered. There are also questions in the Chapter Review activity to make sure that you understand the reading skill.

Social Studies Skills The Social Studies Skills lessons give you an opportunity to learn and use a skill that you will most likely use again. You will also be given a chance to make sure that you understand each skill by answering related questions in the Chapter Review activity.

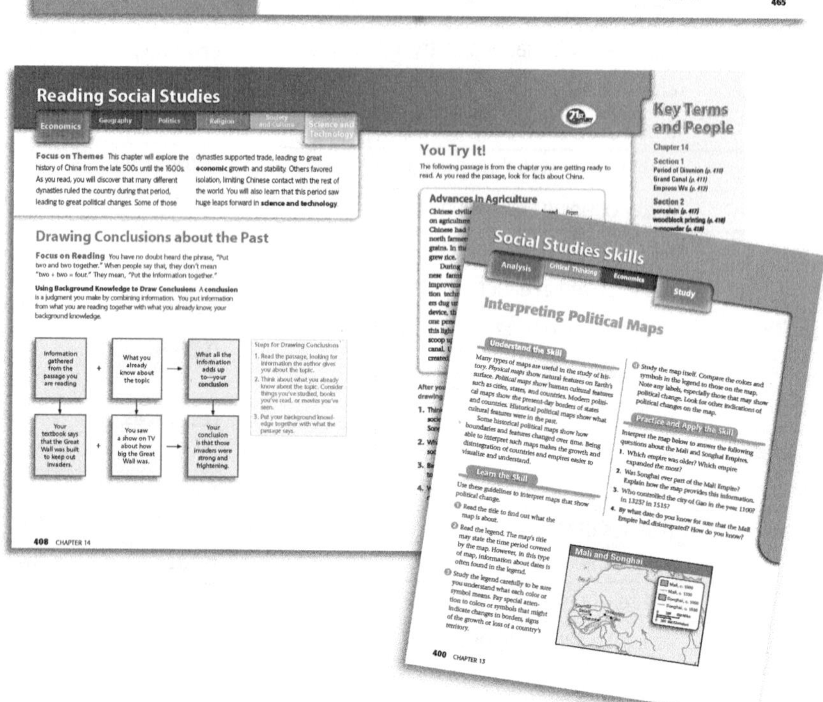

Section

The Section opener pages include Main Idea statements, an overarching big idea statement, and Key Terms and People. In addition, each section includes the following special features.

If You Were There . . . introductions begin each section with a situation for you to respond to, placing you in the time period and in a situation related to the content that you will be studying in the section.

Building Background sections connect what will be covered in this section with what you studied in the previous section.

Short sections of content organize the information in each section into small chunks of text that you shouldn't find too overwhelming.

Taking Notes suggestions and online graphic organizers help you read and take notes on the important ideas in the section.

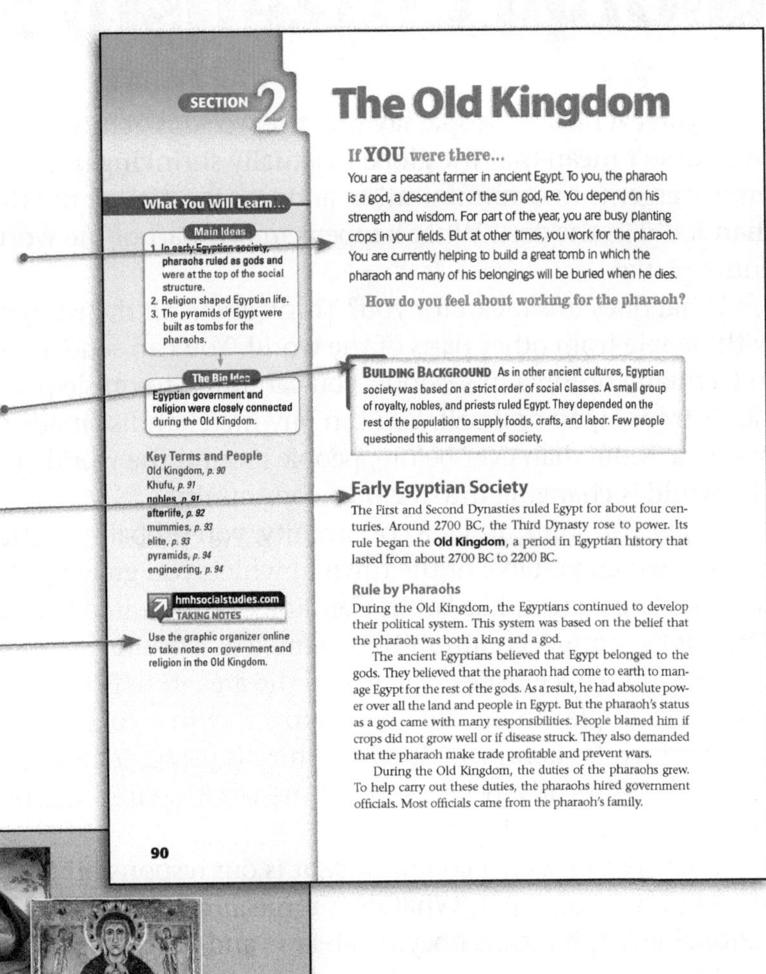

SECTION 2

What You Will Learn...

Main Ideas

1. In early Egyptian society, pharaohs ruled as gods and were at the top of the social structure.
2. Religion shaped Egyptian life.
3. The pyramids of Egypt were built as tombs for the pharaohs.

The Big Idea

Egyptian government and religion were closely connected during the Old Kingdom.

Key Terms and People

Old Kingdom, *p. 90*
Khufu, *p. 91*
nobles, *p. 91*
afterlife, *p. 92*
mummies, *p. 93*
elite, *p. 93*
pyramids, *p. 94*
engineering, *p. 94*

hmhsocialstudies.com TAKING NOTES

Use the graphic organizer online to take notes on government and religion in the Old Kingdom.

The Old Kingdom

If YOU were there...

You are a peasant farmer in ancient Egypt. To you, the pharaoh is a god, a descendent of the sun god, Re. You depend on his strength and wisdom. For part of the year, you are busy planting crops in your fields. But at other times, you work for the pharaoh. You are currently helping to build a great tomb in which the pharaoh and many of his belongings will be buried when he dies.

How do you feel about working for the pharaoh?

BUILDING BACKGROUND As in other ancient cultures, Egyptian society was based on a strict order of social classes. A small group of royalty, nobles, and priests ruled Egypt. They depended on the rest of the population to supply foods, crafts, and labor. Few people questioned this arrangement of society.

Early Egyptian Society

The First and Second Dynasties ruled Egypt for about four centuries. Around 2700 BC, the Third Dynasty rose to power. Its rule began the **Old Kingdom**, a period in Egyptian history that lasted from about 2700 BC to 2200 BC.

Rule by Pharaohs

During the Old Kingdom, the Egyptians continued to develop their political system. This system was based on the belief that the pharaoh was both a king and a god.

The ancient Egyptians believed that Egypt belonged to the gods. They believed that the pharaoh had come to earth to manage Egypt for the rest of the gods. As a result, he had absolute power over all the land and people in Egypt. But the pharaoh's status as a god came with many responsibilities. People blamed him if crops did not grow well or if disease struck. They also demanded that the pharaoh make trade profitable and prevent wars.

During the Old Kingdom, the duties of the pharaohs grew. To help carry out these duties, the pharaohs hired government officials. Most officials came from the pharaoh's family.

90

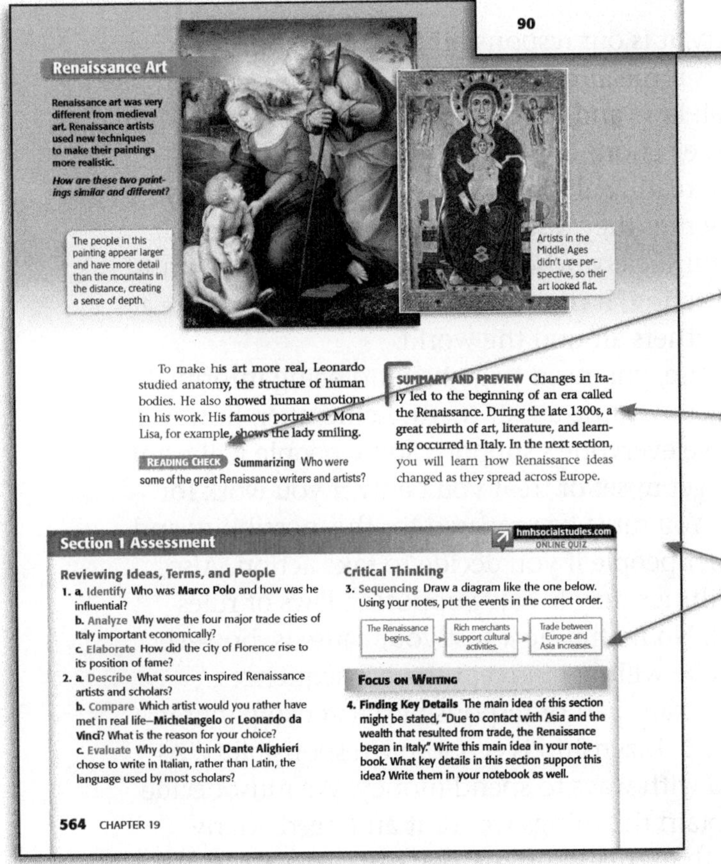

Renaissance Art

Renaissance art was very different from medieval art. Renaissance artists used new techniques to make their paintings more realistic.

How are these two paintings similar and different?

The people in this painting appear larger and have more detail than the mountains in the distance, creating a sense of depth.

Artists in the Middle Ages didn't use perspective, so their art looked flat.

To make his art more real, Leonardo studied anatomy, the structure of human bodies. He also showed human emotions in his work. His famous portrait of Mona Lisa, for example, shows the lady smiling.

READING CHECK **Summarizing** Who were some of the great Renaissance writers and artists?

SUMMARY AND PREVIEW Changes in Italy led to the beginning of an era called the Renaissance. During the late 1300s, a great rebirth of art, literature, and learning occurred in Italy. In the next section, you will learn how Renaissance ideas changed as they spread across Europe.

Section 1 Assessment

hmhsocialstudies.com ONLINE QUIZ

Reviewing Ideas, Terms, and People

1. a. Identify Who was **Marco Polo** and how was he influential?
   b. Analyze Why were the four major trade cities of Italy important economically?
   c. Elaborate How did the city of Florence rise to its position of fame?
2. a. Describe What sources inspired Renaissance artists and scholars?
   b. Compare Which artist would you rather have met in real life—**Michelangelo** or **Leonardo da Vinci**? What is the reason for your choice?
   c. Evaluate Why do you think **Dante Alighieri** chose to write in Italian, rather than Latin, the language used by most scholars?

Critical Thinking

3. Sequencing Draw a diagram like the one below. Using your notes, put the events in the correct order.

The Renaissance begins.
Rich merchants support cultural activities.
Trade between Europe and Asia increases.

Focus on Writing

4. **Finding Key Details** The main idea of this section might be stated, "Due to contact with Asia and the wealth that resulted from trade, the Renaissance began in Italy." Write this main idea in your notebook. What key details in this section support this idea? Write them in your notebook as well.

564 CHAPTER 19

Reading Check questions end each section of content so that you can test whether or not you understand what you have just studied.

Summary and Preview To connect what you have just studied in the section to what you will study in the next section, we include the Summary and Preview.

Section Assessments The section assessment boxes provide an opportunity for you to make sure that you understand the main ideas of the section. We also provide assessment practice online!

Global Citizenship

Have you ever heard people say that the world is getting smaller? Obviously, this doesn't mean that the globe is actually shrinking. It means that, because of improvements in communication and transportation, the world seems smaller than it did in the past. What happens in one part of the world can affect the entire planet.

What does this mean for you? Think about all the ways you can interact with people from other parts of the world. You can send an e-mail to a student in Germany or India in seconds. You can listen to music performed by the latest bands from Japan or Brazil. You can buy merchandise made in Africa or South America. More than ever before, people around the world are coming together. The world is changing into a global community.

When you think about a community, you probably picture the neighborhood in which you live or the town in which you grew up. You probably don't consider larger areas, like South Carolina or the United States, to be communities, but they are. A community is defined as a group of people with common interests or characteristics. The size of the area in which they live means nothing. For example, Americans are tied together in a community by a shared love of the principles upon which our country is based, including freedom, equality, and justice. Similarly, people around the world share a desire for peace, prosperity, and equality for all people.

As citizens of such a community, it is our responsibility to do our parts to preserve and promote it. What does it mean to do your part? On the state and national levels, it means obeying all laws and paying taxes to pay for government programs. It means voting in elections and making well-informed decisions. On a broader scale, it means treating all people equally and respectfully, regardless of where they live or whether they disagree with you about issues. It means doing nothing that will harm society, whether a large thing like committing a crime or a small thing like littering. It means working together to create a better future, for ourselves and for others around the world.

In order to work for a better future, you need to go beyond being informed about issues. You have to try to do something about them. Remember, however, that few changes to society will have everyone's support. Some people will want things to stay the same. They may get upset or treat you badly if you work for changes with which they disagree. You must be prepared for this possibility and be willing to compromise with other people if you decide to take action. Also, remember that efforts to improve things may involve opposing laws or rules that you think need to be changed. No matter how just your cause is, however, if you break laws or rules you must be willing to accept the consequences.

Political involvement is an important part of responsible citizenship, but it is not the only part. Also key to good citizenship is economic responsibility. As consumers, we are constantly faced with ways to spend money. We must decide how to use our money wisely to obtain the things we want and need. Many people are tempted to spend more than they should, often on things they don't really need. They may need help making good economic decisions.

One way to make good financial decisions is to prepare a budget, or a plan for how you will spend your money. A budget lists your total income, or how much money you have available to spend in a given period. It also lists your anticipated expenses for the same period. By comparing how much money you have with how much you will spend, a good budget can help you make better use of your money.

Making good use of your money does not, however, mean that you should avoid spending money altogether. In fact, calculated risks can lead to great financial benefits. For example, many people choose to invest money in stocks, which can be risky. Such investments, however, support companies and can lead to the creation of new products and jobs. In addition, those who invest in stocks can potentially make large amounts of money—or they can lose their entire investment.

Among those who take the greatest economic risks are entrepreneurs, or people who start their own businesses. Inspired by an idea for a product or new way of doing business, an entrepreneur spends his or her own money to create a business. He or she knows that a new business risks failure, but at the same time, it has the potential to be a great success. Throughout history, big-thinking entrepreneurs have created products that reshaped the societies in which they lived. For example, in the 1400s a German goldsmith named Johann Gutenberg borrowed money to build a new device he had invented. That device was the printing press, and it changed Europe forever. The light bulb, the modern automobile, the personal computer—all are the creations of entrepreneurs, and our lives would be very different without them.

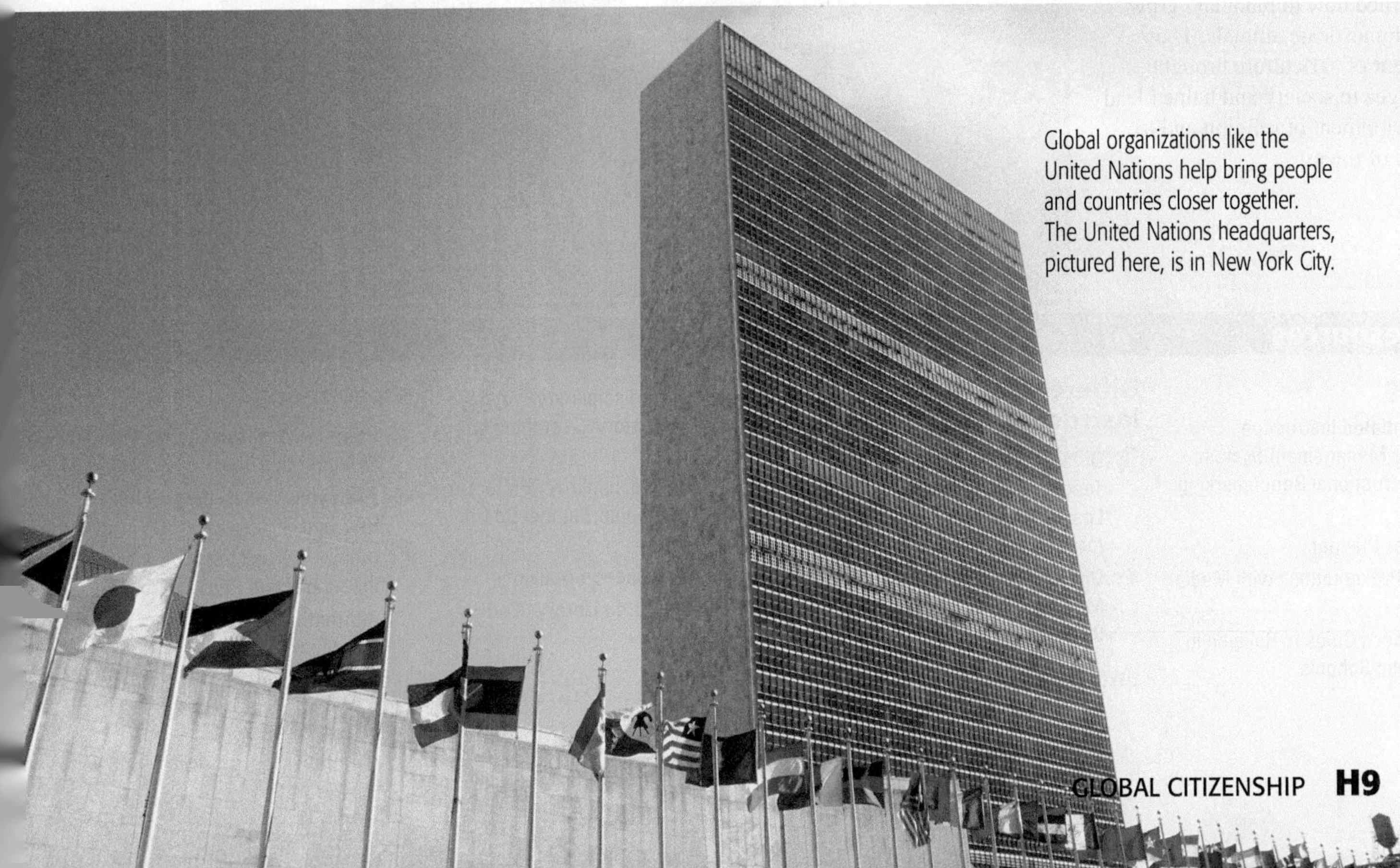

Global organizations like the United Nations help bring people and countries closer together. The United Nations headquarters, pictured here, is in New York City.

Unit Preview

Introduce the Unit

Share the information in the chapter overviews with students.

Chapter 1 The textbook begins by looking at why and how people study the past. Historians and archaeologists, people who study objects of the past, use many tools and methods to learn about the past. Understanding the past helps people to understand the world today better. History also helps people make better decisions for the future. Geography, the study of the earth's physical and cultural features, has influenced history. Learning about geography contributes to the study of history by providing additional clues about where people lived and what the area was like.

Chapter 2 Historians call the time before there was writing prehistory. Scholars study prehistoric peoples by examining the objects they left behind. Prehistoric people learned to make simple tools, to use fire, to use language, and to make art. Scholars believe the earliest people lived in what is now East Africa. Over time, people moved out of Africa as Earth's climates changed. As people moved, they learned to adapt to new environments. In time, people learned how to plant and grow food and domesticate animals. The development of agriculture brought great changes to society and helped lead to the development of religion and to the growth of towns.

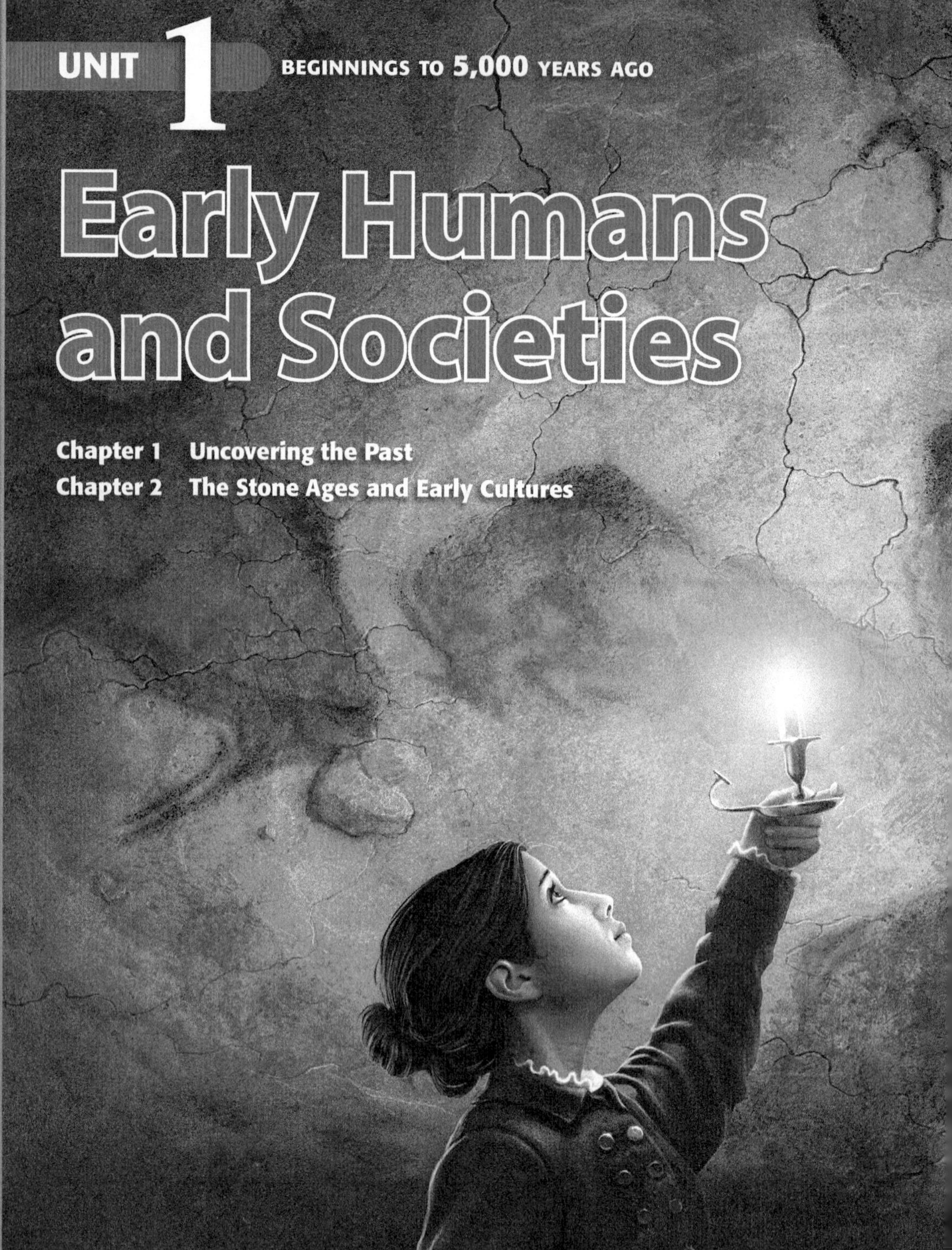

UNIT 1
BEGINNINGS TO 5,000 YEARS AGO
Early Humans and Societies
Chapter 1 Uncovering the Past
Chapter 2 The Stone Ages and Early Cultures

Unit Resources

Planning

- Differentiated Instruction Teacher Management System: Unit Instructional Benchmarking Guides
- TOS Calendar Planner
- Power Presentations with Media Gallery
- A Teacher's Guide to Religion in the Public Schools

Differentiating Instruction

- Differentiated Instruction Teacher Management System: Lesson Plans for Differentiated Instruction
- Differentiated Instruction Modified Worksheets and Tests CD-ROM

Enrichment

- **CRF 1:** Economics and History Activity: Economics and History
- **CRF 1:** Interdisciplinary Project: Studying History: Searching for Roots
- **CRF 2:** Interdisciplinary Project: The First People: Flannel Board Story
- Civic Participation Activities
- Primary Source Library CD-ROM

Assessment

- Progress Assessment System Solution: Unit Test
- TOS ExamView Assessment Suite: Unit Test
- Online Assessment Program, in the Interactive Student Edition
- Alternative Assessment Handbook

The **Differentiated Instruction Teacher Management System** provides a planning and instructional benchmarking guide for this unit.

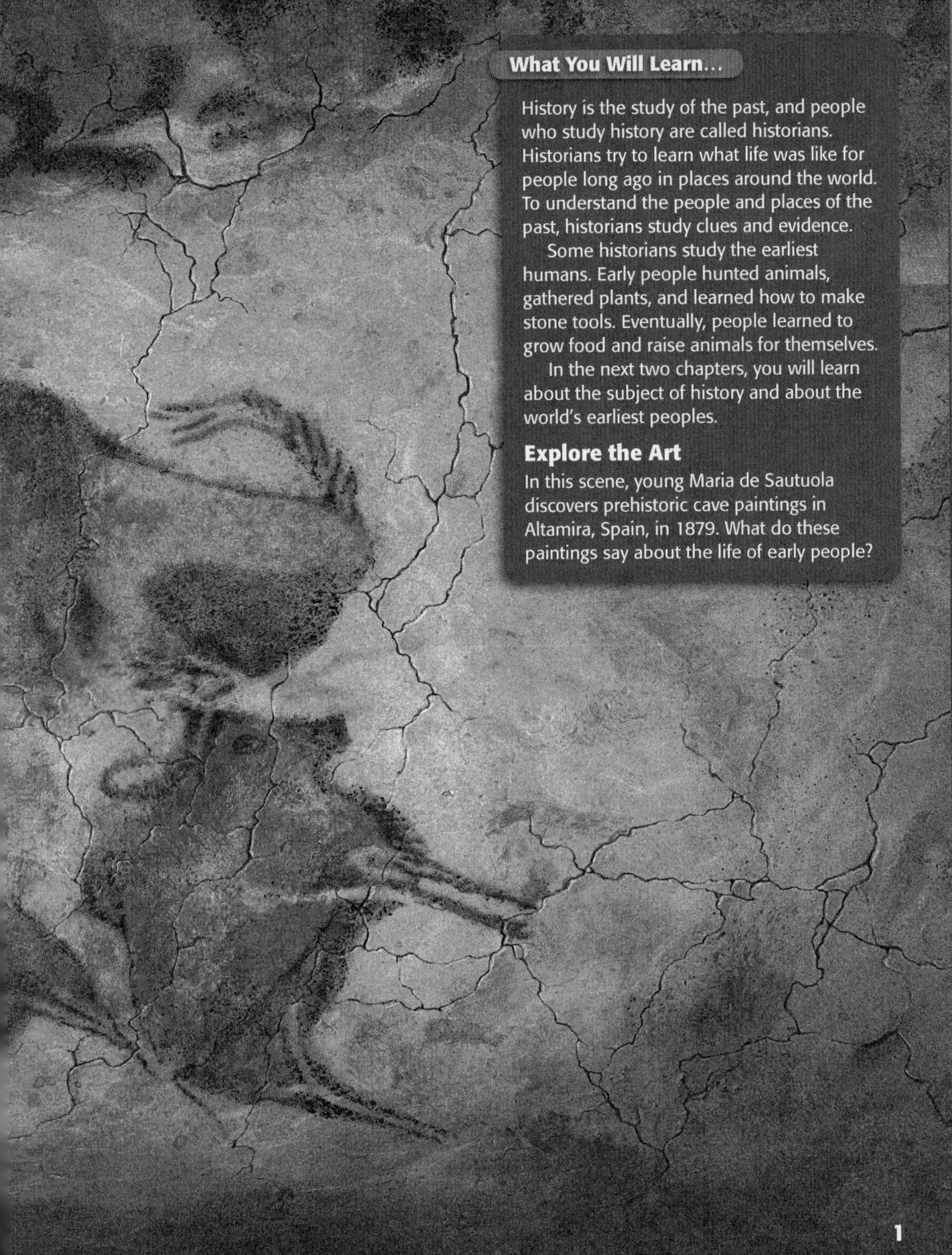

What You Will Learn...

History is the study of the past, and people who study history are called historians. Historians try to learn what life was like for people long ago in places around the world. To understand the people and places of the past, historians study clues and evidence.

Some historians study the earliest humans. Early people hunted animals, gathered plants, and learned how to make stone tools. Eventually, people learned to grow food and raise animals for themselves.

In the next two chapters, you will learn about the subject of history and about the world's earliest peoples.

Explore the Art

In this scene, young Maria de Sautuola discovers prehistoric cave paintings in Altamira, Spain, in 1879. What do these paintings say about the life of early people?

1

Unit Preview

Connect to the Unit

Activity History in Popular Culture Ask students to describe what they know about the Stone Ages. Make a list of their answers, and have students explain where they learned the information. Discuss with students how popular depictions of the past often mix accurate and inaccurate information. Then lead a discussion about how historians and archaeologists learn about the past.

During the study of the unit, have students work as a class to create a large collage on butcher paper that shows depictions of prehistory in popular culture. Students might collect comic strips, pictures of famous characters, movie posters or ads, and images from TV shows or books. Use the mural to help students understand the difference between accurate sources of historical information and popular depictions of history. In addition, point out the popularity of history as cultural entertainment.

LS Interpersonal, Visual/Spatial

Explore the Art

In 1879, Maria de Sautuola and her father, an amateur archaeologist, were exploring the cave pictured at left. While he looked for fossilized bones, Maria wandered into a side cavern. When she looked up she was amazed to see red, black, and violet paintings of bulls covering the ceiling. Today, the images, which are actually bison, remain the earliest known examples of prehistoric cave paintings. The Altamira cave has since been named a World Heritage Site.

About the Illustration

This illustration is an artist's conception based on available sources. However, historians are uncertain exactly what this scene looked like.

Democracy and Civic Education

At Level

Research Required

Responsibility: Finding Information

Background For a representative democracy to operate effectively, citizens need to be informed about political issues and history. Knowing where to find different types of information and how to conduct research is an essential skill—and a useful one in studying history.

1. Organize students into small groups. Assign each group a public issue and a historical topic. Contact the school librarian and set up a time to have students learn about library resources and other sources for finding information.
2. Have each group make a list of possible sources of information for each of the group's assigned topics. Have the groups share their findings with the class.
3. Then have the groups combine their findings to create an Information and Research Guide.

LS Interpersonal, Verbal/Linguistic

Alternative Assessment Handbook, Rubrics 1: Acquiring Information; and 14: Group Activity

Civic Participation Activities

Answers

Explore the Art *that they had the skill to make tools for drawing, that they were interested in keeping records of animals for reasons we can only speculate about, that they used this cave perhaps as a dwelling or place for holding rituals*

Chapter 1 Planning Guide

Uncovering the Past

Overview	Instructional Resources	
CHAPTER 1 **Essential Question:** Why do scholars study the people, events, and ideas of long ago? **Focus on the Essential Question Podcast**	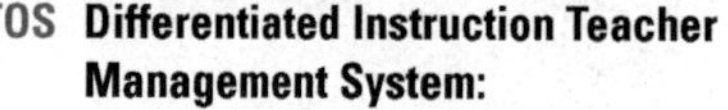 **TOS Differentiated Instruction Teacher Management System:** • Instructional Benchmarking Guides • Lesson Plans for Differentiated Instruction 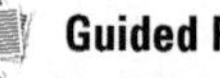 **Guided Reading Workbook** **Chapter Resource File:** • Chapter Review Activity • Focus on Writing Activity: A Job Description • Social Studies Skills Activity: Recognizing Personal Conviction and Bias	**TOS Calendar Planner** **Power Presentations with Media Gallery** **Differentiated Instruction Modified Worksheets and Tests CD-ROM** **Primary Source Library CD-ROM for World History** **Interactive Skills Tutor CD-ROM** **Student Edition on Audio CD Program** **Video:** Cult of Djedfre
Section 1: **Studying History** **The Big Idea:** Historians use many kinds of clues to understand how people lived in the past.	**TOS Differentiated Instruction Teacher Management System:** Section 1 Lesson Plan   **Guided Reading Workbook:** Section 1 **Chapter Resource File:** • Vocabulary Builder Activity, Section 1 • Biography Activity: Howard Carter • Biography Activity: Jean-François Champollion • Interdisciplinary Project: Studying History: Searching for Roots • Literature Activity: "Who Cares About Great Uncle Edgar?" • Primary Source Activity: *The Discovery of the Tomb of King Tutankhamen*, by Howard Carter • Primary Source Activity: Photographs from King Tutankhamen's Tomb	**Daily Bellringer Transparency:** Section 1  **Internet Activity:** Primary vs. Secondary
Section 2: **Studying Geography** **The Big Idea:** Physical geography and human geography contribute to the study of history.	**TOS Differentiated Instruction Teacher Management System:** Section 2 Lesson Plan   **Guided Reading Workbook:** Section 2 **Chapter Resource File:** • Vocabulary Builder Activity, Section 2 • Economics and History Activity: Economics and History • History and Geography Activity: Human Communities	 **Daily Bellringer Transparency:** Section 2  **Map Transparency:** Studying Maps

Chart Key:

SE Student Edition  Presentation Resource  MP3 Audio

TOS Teacher One Stop  DVD/CD-ROM 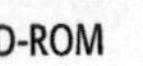 HISTORY™

Printable Resource

Program Resources available on TOS and @ 

Review, Assessment, Intervention

- **Quick Facts Transparency:** Uncovering the Past Visual Summary
- **Spanish Chapter Summaries Audio CD Program**

- **Quiz Game CD-ROM**
- **Progress Assessment Support System (PASS):** Chapter Test
- **Differentiated Instruction Modified Worksheets and Tests CD-ROM:** Modified Chapter Test
- TOS **ExamView® Assessment Suite (English/Spanish)**
- **Online Assessment Program**, in the Interactive Student Edition

---

- **PASS:** Section 1 Quiz
- **Online Quiz:** Section 1

- **Alternative Assessment Handbook**

- **PASS:** Section 2 Quiz
- **Online Quiz:** Section 2
- **Alternative Assessment Handbook**

Supporting Resources

- Multimedia Classroom Global History Series
- Global History Teacher's Guide

Maps Globes Graphs Level F

- Student Workbook
- Teacher's Guide

Social Studies Trade Library Collections

- Premier Secondary World History Trade Collection
- NCSS Middle School Trade Collection

History's Impact

World History Video Program

- **Archaeology**

For more information or to purchase go to 

Power Presentations with Media Gallery

Power Presentations with Media Gallery are visual presentations of each chapter's main ideas. Presentations can be customized by including Quick Facts charts, images from the text, and video clips.

Differentiating Instruction

How do I address the needs of varied learners?

The Target Resource acts as your primary strategy for differentiated instruction.

ENGLISH-LANGUAGE LEARNERS & STRUGGLING READERS

Interactive Skills Tutor CD-ROM

The Interactive Skills Tutor CD-ROM contains lessons that provide additional practice for 20 different critical thinking skills.

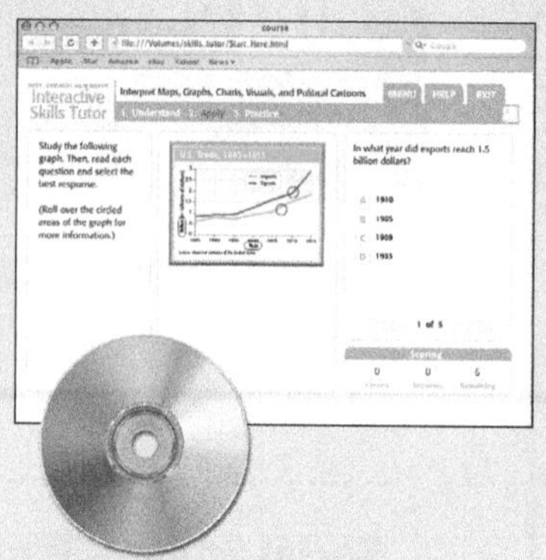

Additional Resources

Differentiated Instruction Teacher Management System: Lesson Plans for Differentiated Instruction

Chapter Resource File:

- Vocabulary Builder Activities
- Social Studies Skills Activity: Recognizing Personal Conviction and Bias

Quick Facts Transparencies: Uncovering the Past Visual Summary

Student Edition on Audio CD Program

Spanish/English Guided Reading Workbook

SPECIAL NEEDS LEARNERS

Differentiated Instruction Modified Worksheets and Tests CD-ROM

- Vocabulary Flash Cards
- Vocabulary Builder Activities
- Chapter Review Activity
- Chapter Test

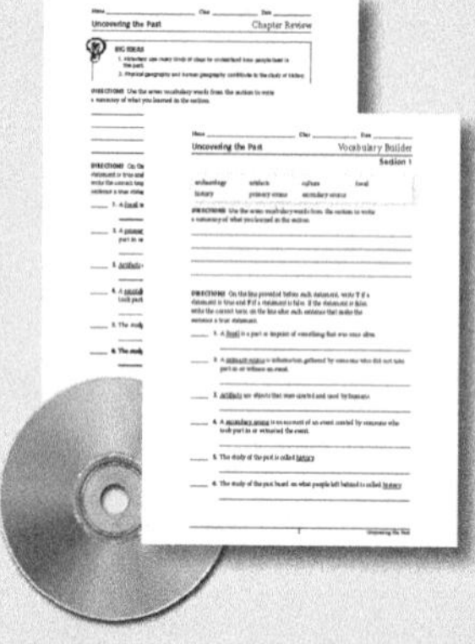

Additional Resources

Differentiated Instruction Teacher Management System: Lesson Plans for Differentiated Instruction

Guided Reading Workbook

Chapter Resource File: Social Studies Skills Activity: Recognizing Personal Conviction and Bias

Student Edition on Audio CD Program

Interactive Skills Tutor CD-ROM

ADVANCED/GIFTED-AND-TALENTED STUDENTS

Primary Source Library CD-ROM for World History

The Library contains longer versions of quotations in the text, extra sources, and images. Included are point-of-view articles, journals, diaries, historic fiction, and political documents.

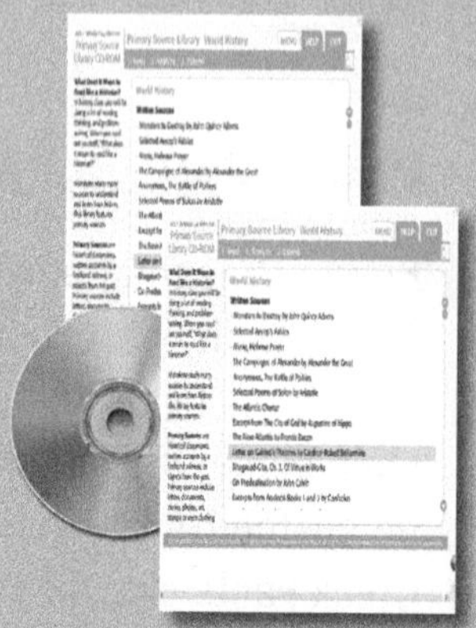

Additional Resources

Differentiated Instruction Teacher Management System: Lesson Plans for Differentiated Instruction

Chapter Resource File:

- Focus on Writing Activity: A Job Description
- Literature Activity: "Who Cares About Great Uncle Edgar?"

Document-Based Questions Activities

Differentiated Activities in the Teacher's Edition

- Linking Geography and History, p. 16
- Learning from Maps, p. 19

Teacher One Stop™

How can I manage the lesson plans and support materials for differentiated instruction?

With the Teacher One Stop, you can easily organize and print lesson plans, planning guides, and instructional materials for all learners. The Teacher One Stop includes the following materials to help you differentiate instruction:

- Interactive Teacher's Edition
- Calendar Planner and pacing guides
- Editable lesson plans
- All reproducible ancillaries in Adobe Acrobat (PDF) format
- ExamView Assessment Suite (English & Spanish)
- Transparency and video previews

Differentiated Activities in the Teacher's Edition

- Back and Forth in Time, p. 7
- Mapping Your School, p. 15

Interactive Student Edition

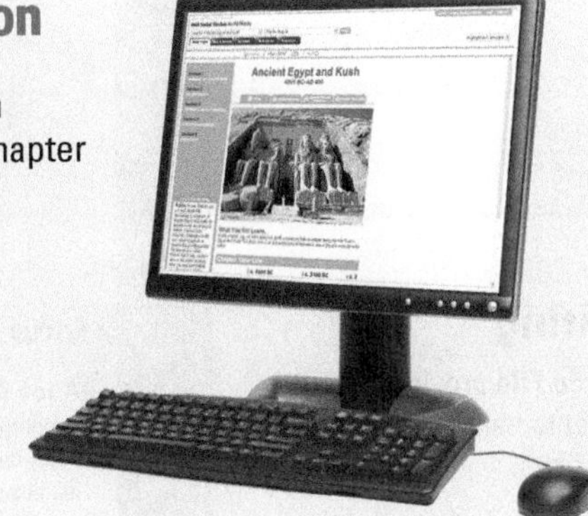

Complete online student edition with interactive multimedia support for chapter content assessment and reporting

- Interactive Maps and Notebook
- Graphic Organizers
- Standardized Test Prep
- Online Homework Practice and Research Activities
- Current Events
- Chapter-based Internet Activities
- Animated History Activities
- and more!

Differentiated Activities in the Teacher's Edition

- History on the Front Page, p. 9
- Day in the Life, p. 13

• Chapter Preview •

Essential Question

Introduce the Essential Question

- Explain that historians and archaeologists use a variety of clues to study past civilizations.
- Point out that understanding the past can help people better understand the present and plan for the future.
- Discuss how geography can help shape a place's history.

CHAPTER 1

Uncovering the Past

Essential Question Why do scholars study the people, events, and ideas of long ago?

South Carolina Performance Standards

Literacy Skills for Social Studies

- Explain change and continuity over time and across cultures.
- Interpret parallel time lines from different places and cultures.
- Evaluate multiple points of view or biases and attribute the perspectives to the influences of individual experiences, societal values, and cultural traditions.
- Analyze evidence, arguments, claims, and beliefs.
- Interpret Earth's physical and human systems by using maps, mental maps, geographic models, and other social studies resources.
- Explain how political, social, and economic institutions are similar or different across time and/or throughout the world.

Partnership for the 21st Century Skills
Elaborate and refine ideas in order to improve and maximize creative efforts.

Focus on Writing

A Job Description What is the job of a historian? an archaeologist? a geographer? In this chapter you will read about the work of people who study the past—its events, its people, and its places. Then you will write a job description to include in a career-planning guide.

2 CHAPTER 1

Focus on Writing

The **Chapter Resource File** provides a Focus on Writing worksheet to help students create their job descriptions.

CRF: Focus on Writing Activity: A Job Description

Key to Differentiating Instruction

Below Level
Basic-level activities designed for all students encountering new material

At Level
Intermediate-level activities designed for average students

Above Level
Challenging activities designed for honors and gifted and talented students

Standard English Mastery
Activities designed to improve standard English usage

LS Learning Styles

Introduce the Chapter

At Level

History is Happening!

1. Call on students to suggest a recent event that will probably appear in history books, such as a major scientific advance, a terrorist act, a peaceful change of government, or similar event.
2. Then ask students why people of the future should know about the event. Students may reply, for example, that knowledge of the event could serve as a warning, inspire other people to fight for justice, or help cure diseases. Discuss how understanding the event could help people of the future avoid mistakes. Encourage students to think of specific ways this could work.
3. Point out that history, archaeology, and geography help people learn about the past. Learning about the past then helps us understand the present and predict the future. Students will learn more about the importance of history, archaeology, and geography in this chapter. **LS Verbal/Linguistic**

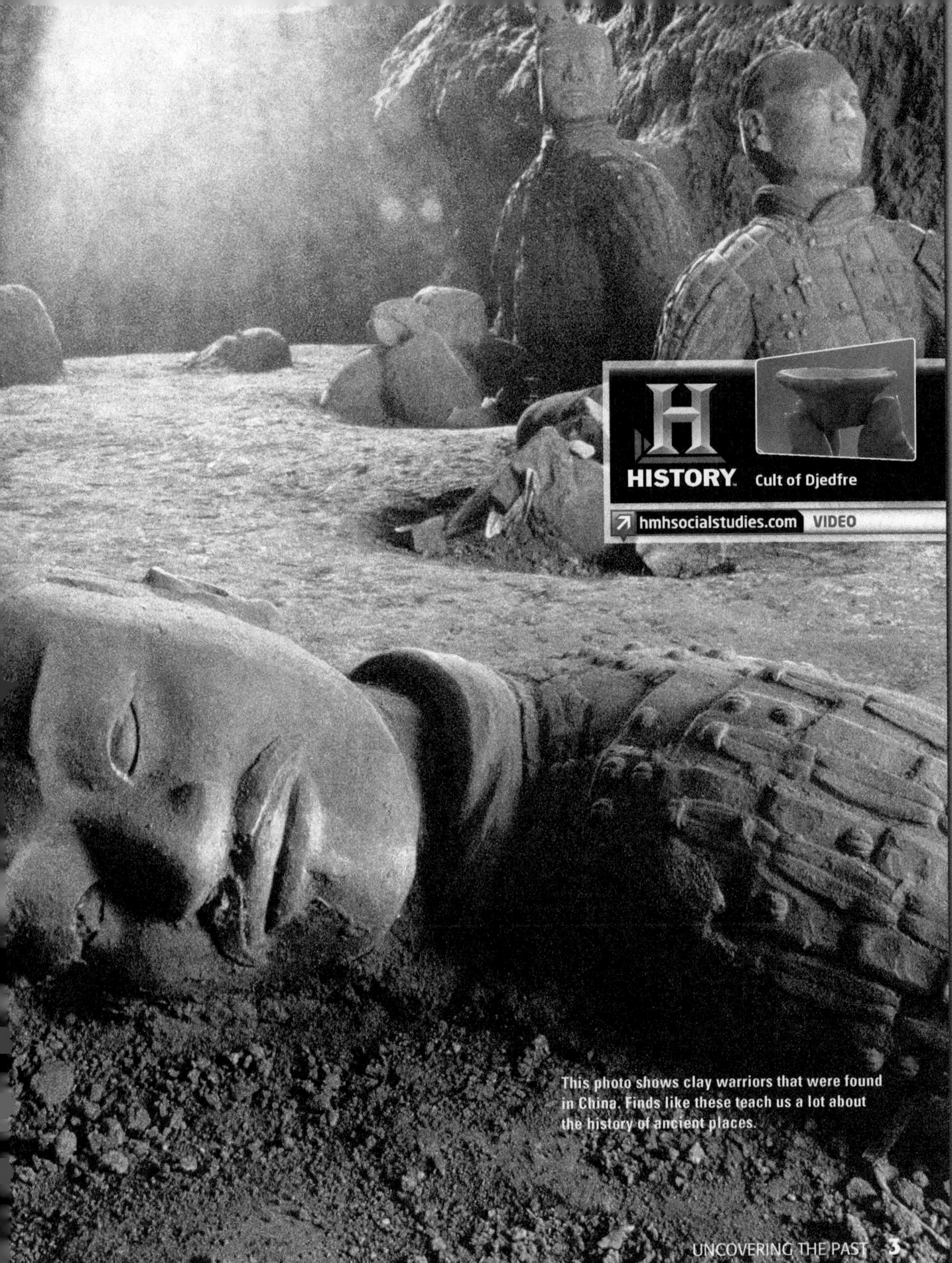

This photo shows clay warriors that were found in China. Finds like these teach us a lot about the history of ancient places.

• Chapter Preview •

Explore the Picture

Archaeology Of the three history-related careers you will learn about in this chapter—historian, archaeologist, and geographer—an archaeologist is the person most likely to study these life-size clay warriors. Archaeologists learn about people based on the objects they leave behind.

Analyzing Visuals What might these clay warriors tell you about life in China during the time that they were made? *possible answers—The military was an important segment of society; perhaps warriors were honored; possibly soldier statues were buried with leaders for protection in the afterlife.* What task may an archaeologist have to perform with broken objects such as these? *repair or reassemble them*

hmhsocialstudies.com
Teacher Resources

Analyzing Visuals

Asking Historical Questions Because students are just beginning their study of world history, they have more questions than answers. Ask each student to write down at least one question about the clay warriors in the picture. *Examples: How big are they? Who made them? How old are they? Where were they found?* Solicit students' questions. Point out that historians ask similar questions. Challenge students to distinguish between questions that can be answered by examining the statues directly and those that require different kinds of inquiry.

Other People, Other Places

Egyptian Pyramids Explain to students that just as the Chinese honored an emperor with an impressive tomb guarded by these warriors, the Egyptians also built giant structures, the pyramids, to honor their powerful rulers. Tell students they will learn more about these pyramids in a later chapter. Have students imagine that they live in ancient times. Ask them what items might be placed in their own tombs that could be discovered thousands of years later.

Reading Social Studies

Understanding Themes

Tell students that there are many themes that are repeated throughout history. Point out to students the themes listed across the page. Ask students to discuss what each theme might mean and how it might be related to the study of history. Tell students that this chapter will focus on the themes of society and culture and science and technology.

Specialized Vocabulary of History

Focus on Reading Review with students the specialized history vocabulary terms on this page. Check to see that the students understand the terms. Have students write a paragraph in which they use each of the terms listed. Ask volunteers to read their paragraphs to the class. Then have students brainstorm other specialized vocabulary that is used in history. Examples might include *civilization*, *empire*, *historian*, or *constitution*.

Reading Social Studies

Economics | Geography | Politics | Religion | **Society and Culture** | **Science and Technology**

Focus on Themes This chapter sets the stage for reading the rest of the book. In it you will learn the definitions of many important terms. You will learn how studying history helps you understand the past and the present. You will also read about the study of geography and learn how the world's physical features affected when and where civilization began. Finally, you will begin to think about how **society and culture** and **science and technology** have interacted throughout time.

Specialized Vocabulary of History

Focus on Reading Have you ever done a plié at the barre or sacked the quarterback? You probably haven't if you've never studied ballet or played football. In fact, you may not even have known what those words meant.

Specialized Vocabulary Plié, barre, sack, and quarterback are **specialized vocabulary**, words that are used in only one field. History has its own specialized vocabulary. The charts below list some terms often used in the study of history.

Terms that identify periods of time	
Decade	a period of 10 years
Century	a period of 100 years
Age	a long period of time marked by a single cultural feature
Era	a long period of time marked by great events, developments, or figures
Ancient	very old, or from a long time ago

Terms used with dates	
circa or **c.**	a word used to show that historians are not sure of an exact date; it means "about"
BC	a term used to identify dates that occurred long ago, before the birth of Jesus Christ, the founder of Christianity; it means "before Christ." As you can see on the time line below, BC dates get smaller as time passes, so the larger the number the earlier the date.
AD	a term used to identify dates that occurred after Jesus's birth; it comes from a Latin phrase that means "in the year of our Lord." Unlike BC dates, AD dates get larger as time passes, so the larger the number the later the date.
BCE	another way to refer to BC dates; it stands for "before the common era"
CE	another way to refer to AD dates; it stands for "common era"

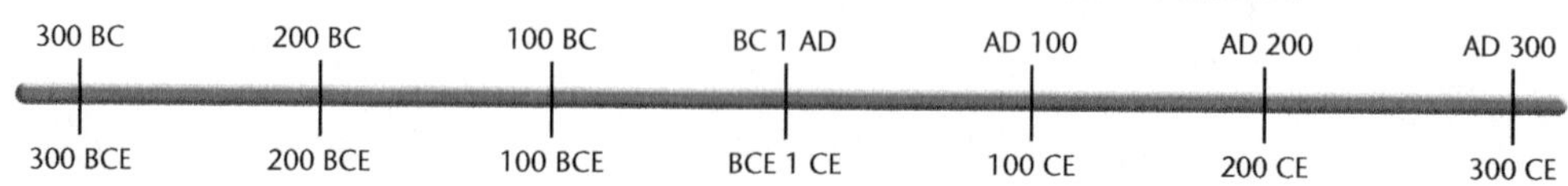

Reading and Skills Resources

Reading Support

- Guided Reading Workbook
- Student Edition on Audio CD
- Spanish Chapter Summaries Audio CD Program

Social Studies Skills Support

- Interactive Skills Tutor CD-ROM

Vocabulary Support

- **CRF:** Vocabulary Builder Activities
- **CRF:** Chapter Review Activity
- Differentiating Instruction Modified Worksheets and Tests CD-ROM:
  - Vocabulary Flash Cards
  - Vocabulary Builder Activity
  - Chapter Review Activity
- **TOS** Holt McDougal PuzzleView

You Try It!

As you read this textbook, you will find many examples of specialized vocabulary terms that historians use. Many of these terms will be highlighted in the text and defined for you as key terms. Others may not be highlighted, but they will still be defined. For some examples, read the passage below. Learning these words as you come across them will help you understand what you read later in the book. For your own reference, you may wish to keep a list of important terms in your notebook.

Vocabulary in Context

We must rely on a variety of sources to learn history. For information on the very first humans, we have fossil remains. A **fossil** is a part or imprint of something that was once alive. Bones and footprints preserved in rock are examples of fossils.

As human beings learned to make things, by accident they also created more sources of information for us. They made what we call **artifacts**, objects created by and used by humans. Artifacts include coins, arrowheads, tools, toys, and pottery.

From Chapter 1, page 10

Answer the following questions about the specialized vocabulary of history.

1. What is a fossil? What is an artifact? How can you tell?
2. Were you born in a BC year or an AD year?
3. Put the following dates in order: AD 2000, 3100 BC, 15 BCE, AD 476, AD 3, CE 1215
4. If you saw that an event happened c. AD 1000, what would that mean?

Key Terms

Chapter 1

Section 1
history *(p. 6)*
culture *(p. 7)*
archaeology *(p. 7)*
fossil *(p. 10)*
artifacts *(p. 10)*
primary source *(p. 10)*
secondary source *(p. 10)*

Section 2
geography *(p. 12)*
landforms *(p. 12)*
climate *(p. 12)*
environment *(p. 13)*
region *(p. 15)*
resources *(p. 16)*

Academic Vocabulary

Success in school is related to knowing academic vocabulary—the words that are frequently used in school assignments and discussions. In this chapter, you will learn the following academic words:

values *(p. 8)*
features *(p. 14)*

As you read Chapter 1, keep a list in your notebook of specialized vocabulary words that you learn.

Reading Social Studies

Key Terms and People

Preteach these words by instructing students to create a Double Door FoldNote. Have students label the two doors *History Terms* and *Geography Terms.* Read the key terms aloud and have students write the term under the appropriate side of the FoldNote. Ask students to discuss the meanings of the words, and define any terms that they do not understand.

LS Verbal/Linguistic, Visual/Spatial

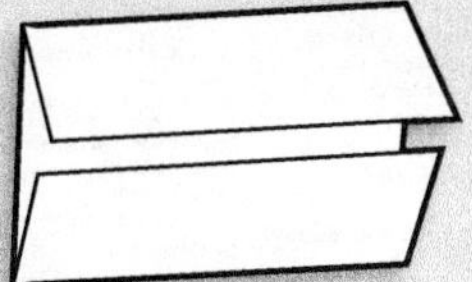

Focus on Reading

See the **Focus on Reading** questions in this chapter for more practice on this reading social studies skill.

Reading Social Studies Assessment

See the **Chapter Review** at the end of this chapter for student assessment questions related to this reading skill.

Teaching Tip

Explain to students that specialized vocabulary words can often have double meanings. In other words, the words have a different meaning when applied to a specialized field than they might to someone outside of that field. For instance, the word *check* means something completely different to a person in the banking industry than it does to someone who plays hockey. Have students try to identify other words used in the study of history or geography that have double meanings.

Answers

You Try It! 1. *fossil—part of or imprint of something that was once alive; artifact—object created and used by humans; the words immediately following* artifact *and* fossil *reveal their meaning;* **2.** *AD;* **3.** *3100 BC, 15 BCE, AD 3, AD 476, CE 1215, AD 2000;* **4.** *It happened about 1,000 years after Jesus's birth.*

Preteach

Bellringer

If YOU were there . . . Use the **Daily Bellringer Transparency** to help students answer the question.

Daily Bellringer Transparency, Section 1

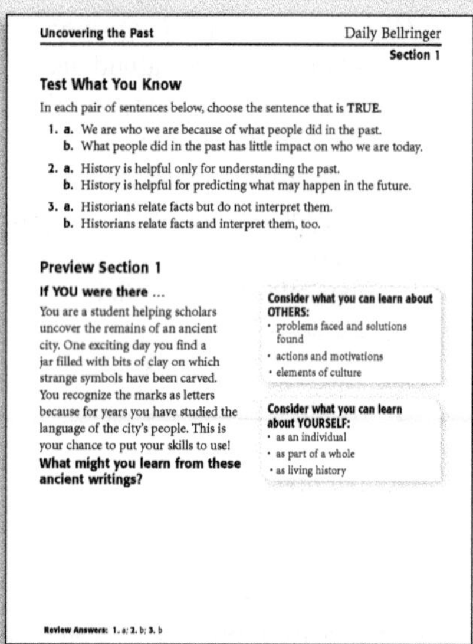

Uncovering the Past Daily Bellringer

Section 1

Test What You Know

In each pair of sentences below, choose the sentence that is TRUE.

1. **a.** We are who we are because of what people did in the past.
   b. What people did in the past has little impact on who we are today.
2. **a.** History is helpful only for understanding the past.
   b. History is helpful for predicting what may happen in the future.
3. **a.** Historians relate facts but do not interpret them.
   b. Historians relate facts and interpret them, too.

Preview Section 1

If YOU were there ...

You are a student helping scholars uncover the remains of an ancient city. One exciting day you find a jar filled with bits of clay on which strange symbols have been carved. You recognize the marks as letters because for years you have studied the language of the city's people. This is your chance to put your skills to use!

What might you learn from these ancient writings?

Consider what you can learn about OTHERS:
- problems faced and solutions found
- actions and motivations
- elements of culture

Consider what you can learn about YOURSELF:
- as an individual
- as part of a whole
- as living history

Review Answers: 1. a; 2. b; 3. b

Academic Vocabulary

Review with students the high-use academic term in this section.

values ideas that people hold dear and try to live by (p. 8)

Taking Notes

Have students use the graphic organizer online to take notes on the section. This activity will prepare students for the Section Assessment, in which they will complete a graphic organizer that builds on the information using the Critical Thinking Skill: Categorizing.

SECTION 1

Studying History

What You Will Learn...

Main Ideas

1. History is the study of the past.
2. We can improve our understanding of people's actions and beliefs through the study of history.
3. Historians use clues from various sources to learn about the past.

The Big Idea

Historians use many kinds of clues to understand how people lived in the past.

Key Terms

history, *p. 6*
culture, *p. 7*
archaeology, *p. 7*
fossil, *p. 10*
artifacts, *p. 10*
primary source, *p. 10*
secondary source, *p. 10*

Use the graphic organizer online to take notes about the clues historians use to understand the past.

If YOU were there...

You are a student helping scholars uncover the remains of an ancient city. One exciting day you find a jar filled with bits of clay on which strange symbols have been carved. You recognize the marks as letters because for years you have studied the language of the city's people. This is your chance to put your skills to use!

What might you learn from the ancient writings?

BUILDING BACKGROUND Last year you learned about our country's past. Now you begin a study of world history, which started many centuries before the history of the United States. You will find that we learn about world history in many ways.

The Study of the Past

The people of the ancient world didn't build skyscrapers, invent the automobile, or send spaceships to Mars. But they did remarkable things. Among their amazing feats were building huge temples, inventing writing, and discovering planets. Every step we take—in technology, science, education, literature, and all other fields—builds on what people did long ago. We are who we are because of what people did in the past.

What Is History?

History is the study of the past. A battle that happened 5,000 years ago and an election that happened yesterday are both parts of history.

Historians are people who study history. Their main concern is human activity in the past. They want to know how people lived and why they did the things they did. They try to learn about the problems people faced and how they found solutions.

6

Teach the Big Idea

At Level

Studying History

1. **Teach** Ask students the questions in the Main Idea boxes to teach this section.
2. **Apply** Ask students to imagine that they are historians who are living in the year 2999 writing about the young people of the early 2000s. Call on students to describe how their generation should be remembered. Topics may include music, food, clothing, education, entertainment, and others. Write their comments for students to see.
   LS **Verbal/Linguistic**
3. **Review** Have students review their comments and list the most important points that a future historian might want to know about this generation.
4. **Practice/Homework** Ask students to use the information to list items for a time capsule for portraying their generation.
   LS **Intrapersonal**

Historians are interested in how people lived their daily lives. How and where did they work, fight, trade, farm, and worship? What did they do in their free time? What games did they play? In other words, historians study the past to understand people's **culture**—the knowledge, beliefs, customs, and values of a group of people.

What Is Archaeology?

An important field that contributes much information about the past is **archaeology** (ahr-kee-AH-luh-jee). It is the study of the past based on what people left behind. Archaeologists, or people who practice archaeology, explore places where people once lived, worked, or fought. The things that people left in these places may include jewelry, dishes, or weapons. They range from stone tools to huge buildings.

Modern technology, including computers and satellite imagery, has allowed archaeologists to more easily locate and study objects from the past.

Archaeologists examine the objects they find to learn what they can tell about the past. In many cases, the objects that people left behind are the only clues we have to how they lived.

READING CHECK **Comparing** How are the fields of history and archaeology similar?

Studying the Past

Historians and archaeologists study the people and places of the past. For example, by studying the remains of an ancient Egyptian temple (right), they can learn about the lives of the ancient Egyptians (left).

Direct Teach

Main Idea

❶ The Study of the Past

History is the study of the past.

Define Who are historians? *people who study history*

Describe What kinds of information contribute to an understanding of people's culture? *their knowledge, beliefs, customs, and values*

Draw Conclusions What might the discovery of an ancient people's dishes tell us about how they lived? *possible answers—materials that were available, level of technological skill, artistic taste, how many different kinds of food and drink they had, and so on*

- **CRF:** Primary Source: *The Discovery of the Tomb of King Tutankhamen* by Howard Carter
- **CRF:** Primary Source: Photographs from King Tutankhamen's Tomb

Info to Know

Tools of the Trade In their excavations, archaeologists use tools that are common in American homes, but they use those items differently. Archaeologists use ladles, spoons, dustpans, and paintbrushes to move small amounts of dirt that cover artifacts. To remove larger amounts of dirt and rubble, archaeologists use shovels and trowels.

History Humor

What is the definition of an archaeologist? *A person whose career is in ruins!*

Collaborative Learning

Below Level

Back and Forth in Time

1. Organize the class into small groups.
2. Have students study the photo on this page to describe and write down the differences between the two sides of the monument. Then ask students to write down possible answers to this question: "How did historians and archaeologists figure out what the temple may have looked like?"
3. As a class, discuss students' responses. Accept all feasible answers. Then invite students to look through this book for other examples of ancient sites. Ask students to pose questions that historians and archaeologists may ask about those same sites. **LS Interpersonal, Visual/Spatial**

- Alternative Assessment Handbook, Rubric 14: Group Activity

Answers

Reading Check *Both study people and places of the past.*

Direct Teach

Main Idea

❷ Understanding Through History

We can improve our understanding of people's actions and beliefs through the study of history.

Identify Name two groups of Americans who might interpret our country's history differently. *Native Americans, European settlers, Asian immigrants, enslaved Africans, and others*

Summarize How does history help citizens around the world know their own countries better? *It teaches people about their past, how their government came into being, their nation's triumphs and tragedies, and the experiences people have been through together.*

Predict What may tomorrow's history books say about today's world? *Answers will vary.*

Activity Holidays and History Have students select a nonreligious U.S. holiday and write a paragraph about how that holiday helps us to remember our country's history. Examples include Veterans' Day, Thanksgiving, Presidents' Day, or Independence Day. **LS Verbal/Linguistic**

CRF: Literature Activity: "Who Cares About Great Uncle Edgar?"

Info to Know

The Father of History Herodotus was a Greek author who lived during the 400s BC. He has been called the Father of History for attempting the first real historical narrative. Herodotus's great work is an account of Greece's wars with Persia. Inserted into the history are amusing short stories, dialogue, and speeches. Readers still study the works of Herodotus for insights into the ancient world.

Understanding through History

ACADEMIC VOCABULARY
values ideas that people hold dear and try to live by

There are many reasons why people study history. Understanding the past helps us to understand the world today. History can also provide us with a guide to making better decisions in the future.

Knowing Yourself

History can teach you about yourself. What if you did not know your own past? You would not know which subjects you liked in school or which sports you enjoyed. You would not know what makes you proud or what mistakes not to repeat. Without your own personal history, you would not have an identity.

History is just as important for groups as it is for individuals. What would happen if countries had no record of their past? People would know nothing about how their governments came into being. They would not remember their nation's great triumphs or tragedies. History teaches us about the experiences we have been through as a people. It shapes our identity and teaches us the **values** that we share.

Knowing Others

Like today, the world in the past included many cultures. History teaches about the cultures that were unlike your own. You learn about other peoples, where they lived, and what was important to them. History teaches you how cultures were similar and how they were different.

History also helps you understand why other people think the way they do. You learn about the struggles people have faced. You also learn how these struggles have affected the way people view themselves and others.

Understanding the World

History can help us understand the world around us. For example, why do these buildings in San Francisco look the way they do? The answer is history. These buildings are in a neighborhood called Chinatown, where Chinese immigrants began settling in the 1800s.

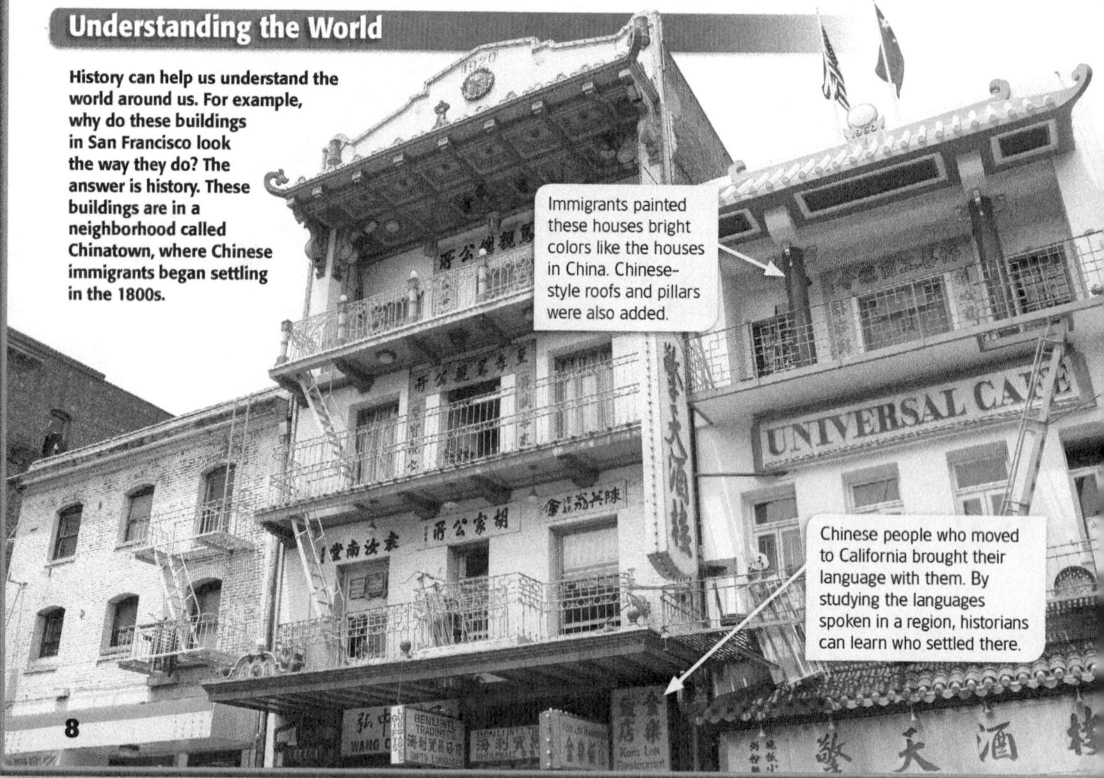

Immigrants painted these houses bright colors like the houses in China. Chinese-style roofs and pillars were also added.

Chinese people who moved to California brought their language with them. By studying the languages spoken in a region, historians can learn who settled there.

Social Studies Skill: Developing Personal Participation Skills

History on TV **At Level**

1. Ask students to imagine that they are media producers who want to start a new television cable channel. The student "producers" will propose a channel devoted to interesting young people in history.
2. Organize the class into pairs. Have each pair create a proposal for the new cable channel to be presented to financial investors. Students may create any one of a range of products for their proposals—posters, letters, or dialogues, for example—to discuss the importance of history for young people.
3. Call on volunteers to present their work to the class. Then lead a discussion on how students could apply this imaginary proposal to real-world issues about learning history. **LS Interpersonal**

Alternative Assessment Handbook, Rubric 29: Presentations

For example, Native Americans, European settlers, enslaved Africans, and Asian immigrants all played vital roles in our country's history. But the descendants of each group have a different story to tell about their ancestors' contributions.

Learning these stories and others like them that make up history can help you see the viewpoints of other peoples. It can help teach you to respect and understand different opinions. This knowledge helps promote tolerance. History can also help you relate more easily to people of different backgrounds. In other words, knowing about the past can help build social harmony throughout the world today.

Knowing Your World

History can provide you with a better understanding of where you live. You are part of a culture that interacts with the outside world. Even events that happen in other parts of the world affect your culture. History helps you to understand how today's events are shaped by the events of the past. So knowing the past helps you figure out what is happening now.

History is concerned with the entire range of human activities. It is the record of humanity's combined efforts. You might be surprised by how much some of these efforts from the distant past resemble our lives today. Throughout history, people have lived, worked, dreamed, and played, just as people do today. They have fought wars, created art, and questioned the decisions of their leaders. In other words, history is not just a story of change over time, but a tale of continuity. History can teach us how things remain the same across years and cultures.

History also promotes good decision-making skills. A famous, often repeated saying warns us that those who forget their past are doomed to repeat it. This means that people who ignore the results of past decisions often make the same mistakes over and over again.

Individuals and countries both benefit from the wisdom that history can teach. Your own history may have taught you that studying for a test results in better grades. In a similar way, world history has taught that providing young people with education makes them more productive when they become adults.

Historians have been talking about the value of history for centuries. More than 2,000 years ago a great Greek historian named Polybius wrote:

> "The purpose of history is not the reader's enjoyment at the moment of perusal [reading it], but the reformation [improvement] of the reader's soul, to save him from stumbling at the same stumbling block many times over."
>
> –Polybius, from *The Histories, Book XXXVIII*

FOCUS ON READING What does the word *century* mean?

READING CHECK **Summarizing** What are some benefits of studying history?

Primary Source

BOOK

History Makers

One way to study history is to study the "big names" of the past, the people whose lives and actions shaped the times and places in which they lived. In this passage from a collection of essays, historian Barbara W. Tuchman explains why some historians focus their attention on such people.

> "They are the captains and kings, saints and fanatics, traitors, rogues and villains, pathfinders and explorers, thinkers and creators, even, occasionally, heroes. They are significant—if not necessarily admirable . . . they *matter*. They are the actors, not the acted upon, and are consequently that much more interesting."
>
> –Barbara W. Tuchman, from *Practicing History: Selected Essays*

ANALYSIS SKILL ANALYZING PRIMARY SOURCES

What words does the author use to make history sound interesting?

Direct Teach

Main Idea

❷ Understanding Through History

We can improve our understanding of people's actions and beliefs through the study of history.

Recall How is history a study of both continuity and change? *because historians study both how things remain the same over time and how they change*

Compare How is the saying about forgetting the past similar to the view of Greek historian Polybius? *Both stress that learning from the past can prevent future mistakes.*

Teaching Tip

Interpreting History Have students read the Barbara W. Tuchman quote. Point out that people have different opinions about which historical figures fall into the groups that Tuchman describes. For example, some people may label a powerful ruler a hero, while others feel that ruler was a villain. Emphasize that people interpret history differently, but that students should first gather accurate information.

Critical Thinking: Analyzing Information

Above Level

Prep Required

History on the Front Page

1. Provide pages from the national and international sections of daily newspapers to students. Be sure that all students have at least one complete newspaper story.
2. Ask students to skim their pages to find a complete story about an important event. Students should read the story carefully.
3. Have students either take notes on the historical background of the event as reported in the story or, if such background is missing, write down questions about the event's history that would make the story more meaningful.
4. Call on students to describe their events and either their notes or questions.

LS Intrapersonal, Verbal/Linguistic

Answers

Analyzing Primary Sources *possible answers—captains, kings, saints, fanatics, traitors, rogues, villains, pathfinders, explorers, thinkers, creators, heroes, significant, admirable, matter, actors*

Reading Check *helps us understand the world today and make better decisions in the future; helps us know ourselves, others, and our world*

Direct Teach

Main Idea

3 Using Clues

Historians use clues from various sources to learn about the past.

Define What is a fossil? *a part or imprint of something that was once alive*

Draw Conclusions How do fossils and artifacts help teach us about the past? *Fossil remains teach us about the first humans, and artifacts teach us about the tools and objects used by humans in the past.*

Predict What are some things that historians of tomorrow may use as primary sources? *possible answers—recordings of televised speeches, digital photographs, a soldier's letters home, and so on*

CRF: Biography Activity: Howard Carter

CRF: Biography Activity: Jean-François Champollion

hmhsocialstudies.com

Online Resources
Activity: Primary vs. Secondary

Connect to Science

Tree-Ring Dating Archaeologists have many methods available to them for determining the age of artifacts. To find the age of wooden objects they may use dendrochronology, or dating by tree-ring growth. Because the growth of annual rings reflects climate conditions, scientists can correlate growth patterns with particular years. In the United States, dendrochronology is particularly useful in the Southwest, because the dry climate there preserves wood well.

Clues from the Past

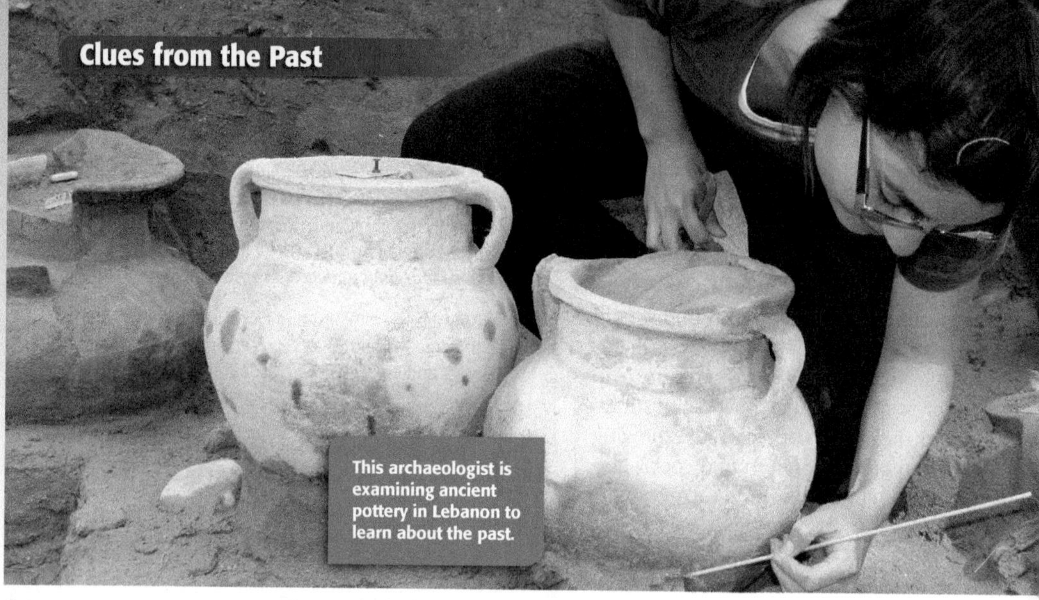

This archaeologist is examining ancient pottery in Lebanon to learn about the past.

Using Clues

We must rely on a variety of sources to learn history. For information on the very first humans, we have fossil remains. A **fossil** is a part or imprint of something that was once alive. Bones and footprints preserved in rock are examples of fossils.

As human beings learned to make things, by accident they also created more sources of information for us. They made what we call **artifacts**, objects created by and used by humans. Artifacts include coins, arrowheads, tools, toys, and pottery. Archaeologists examine artifacts and the places where the artifacts were found to learn about the past.

Sources of Information

About 5,000 years ago, people invented writing. They wrote laws, poems, speeches, battle plans, letters, contracts, and many other things. In these written sources, historians have found countless clues about how people lived. In addition, people have recorded their messages in many ways over the centuries. Historians have studied writing carved into stone pillars, stamped onto clay tablets, scribbled on turtle shells, typed with typewriters, and sent by computer.

Historical sources are of two types. A **primary source** is an account of an event created by someone who took part in or witnessed the event. Treaties, letters, diaries, laws, court documents, and royal commands are all primary sources. An audio or video recording of an event is also a primary source.

A **secondary source** is information gathered by someone who did not take part in or witness an event. Examples include history textbooks, journal articles, and encyclopedias. The textbook you are reading right now is a secondary source. The historians who wrote it did not take part in the events described. Instead, they gathered information about these events from different sources.

Critical Thinking: Finding Main Ideas

At Level

Primary and Secondary Sources

Research Required

1. Ask students to select a newsworthy event in recent history—one that an adult they know has experienced or witnessed. Examples include a severe weather event or an election.
2. Next, have students use primary and secondary sources to learn more about the event. Suggest that they interview a parent or another adult for the primary source and read published accounts for the secondary sources. Point out that a newspaper article can be a primary source if the reporter witnessed the event directly, and that either type of source can be biased.
3. Have each student write a paragraph comparing the information from the two types of sources for similarities and differences.
LS Interpersonal, Verbal/Linguistic,

Alternative Assessment Handbook, Rubric 30: Research

Written records, like this writing from a tomb in Egypt, are valuable sources of information about the past.

Sometimes, archaeologists must carefully reconstruct artifacts from hundreds of broken pieces, like they did with this statue of an Aztec bat god from Mexico.

Sources of Change

Writers of secondary sources don't always agree about the past. Historians form different opinions about the primary sources they study. As a result, historians may not interpret past events in the same way.

For example, one writer may say that a king was a brilliant military leader. Another may say that the king's armies only won their battles because they had better weapons than their enemies did. Sometimes new evidence leads to new conclusions. As historians review and reanalyze information, their interpretations can and do change.

READING CHECK **Contrasting** How are primary and secondary sources different?

SUMMARY AND PREVIEW We benefit from studying the past. Scholars use many clues to help them understand past events. In the next section you will learn how geography connects to history.

Section 1 Assessment

hmhsocialstudies.com ONLINE QUIZ

Reviewing Ideas, Terms, and People

1. a. **Identify** What is **history**?
   b. **Explain** What kinds of things do historians try to discover about people who lived in the past?
   c. **Predict** What kinds of evidence will historians of the future study to learn about your **culture**?
2. a. **Describe** How does knowing its own history provide a group with a sense of unity?
   b. **Elaborate** Explain the meaning of the phrase, "Those who forget their past are doomed to repeat it."
3. a. **Identify** What is a **primary source**?
   b. **Explain** How did the invention of writing affect the sources on which historians rely?
   c. **Elaborate** Could a photograph be considered a primary source? Why or why not?

Critical Thinking

4. **Categorizing** Using your notes, identify four types of clues to the past and give at least two examples of each.

clues

Focus on Writing

5. **Understanding What Historians Do** What is the difference between a historian and an archaeologist? Take notes about the work these people do.

Direct Teach

MISCONCEPTION ALERT

It's Not Over Yet! Some students may think that all the great archaeological discoveries have been made, and nothing remains to be found. It's not true! Point out that the clay warriors in the chapter opener photo were just found in 1974. Although the imperial tomb they guard has been located with some certainty, it has not yet been opened. If ancient written sources are accurate, archaeologists will see amazing things when they finally excavate the tomb.

Every year, archaeologists announce more remarkable finds. New technologies are helping in the search for evidence of past civilizations and peoples.

Review & Assess

Close

Briefly review the benefits, the challenges, and the methods of studying history.

Review

Online Quiz, Section 1

Assess

SE Section 1 Assessment

PASS: Section 1 Quiz

Alternative Assessment Handbook

Reteach/Classroom Intervention

Guided Reading Workbook, Section 1

Interactive Skills Tutor CD-ROM

Section 1 Assessment Answers

1. **a.** the study of the past
   b. how they lived and their knowledge, beliefs, customs, and values
   c. possible answers—television broadcasts, newspapers, books, films, videos, CDs
2. **a.** possible answer—It teaches them about the experiences they have been through as a people and about the values they share.
   b. possible answer—Studying history helps people keep from making the same mistakes that people made in the past.
3. **a.** a firsthand account of an event
   b. It provided them with many more types of records.
   c. possible answer—yes; shows a firsthand account of an event
4. fossils, artifacts, primary sources of information, secondary sources of information
5. Students' answers will vary, but should mention that archaeologists primarily study artifacts that people have left behind whereas historians gather information from sources including writings by witnesses to events.

Answers

Reading Check *Primary sources provide a firsthand account of an event, while secondary sources include information gathered by someone who did not witness the event.*

Preteach

Bellringer

If YOU were there . . . Use the **Daily Bellringer Transparency** to help students answer the question.

Daily Bellringer Transparency, Section 2

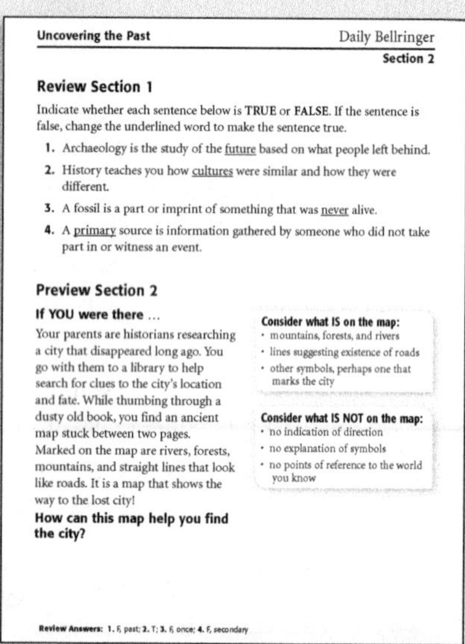

Uncovering the Past — Daily Bellringer — Section 2

Review Section 1

Indicate whether each sentence below is TRUE or FALSE. If the sentence is false, change the underlined word to make the sentence true.

1. Archaeology is the study of the <u>future</u> based on what people left behind.
2. History teaches you how <u>cultures</u> were similar and how they were different.
3. A fossil is a part or imprint of something that was <u>never</u> alive.
4. A <u>primary</u> source is information gathered by someone who did not take part in or witness an event.

Preview Section 2

If YOU were there . . .

Your parents are historians researching a city that disappeared long ago. You go with them to a library to help search for clues to the city's location and fate. While thumbing through a dusty old book, you find an ancient map stuck between two pages. Marked on the map are rivers, forests, mountains, and straight lines that look like roads. It is a map that shows the way to the lost city!

How can this map help you find the city?

Consider what IS on the map:
- mountains, forests, and rivers
- lines suggesting existence of roads
- other symbols, perhaps one that marks the city

Consider what IS NOT on the map:
- no indication of direction
- no explanation of symbols
- no points of reference to the world you know

Review Answers: 1. F, past; 2. T; 3. F, once; 4. F, secondary

Academic Vocabulary

Review with students the high-use academic term in this section.

features characteristics (p. 14)

Taking Notes

Have students use the graphic organizer online to take notes on the section. This activity will prepare students for the Section Assessment, in which they will complete a graphic organizer that builds on the information using the Critical Thinking Skill: Comparing and Contrasting.

SECTION 2

Studying Geography

What You Will Learn...

Main Ideas

1. Geography is the study of places and people.
2. Studying location is important to both physical and human geography.
3. Geography and history are closely connected.

The Big Idea

Physical geography and human geography contribute to the study of history.

Key Terms

geography, *p. 12*
landforms, *p. 12*
climate, *p. 12*
environment, *p. 13*
region, *p. 15*
resources, *p. 16*

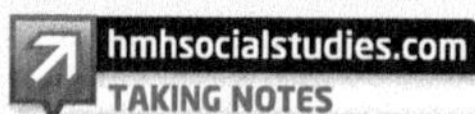

Use the graphic organizer online to take notes on physical geography and human geography.

If YOU were there...

Your parents are historians researching a city that disappeared long ago. You go with them to a library to help search for clues to the city's location and fate. While thumbing through a dusty old book, you find an ancient map stuck between two pages. Marked on the map are rivers, forests, mountains, and straight lines that look like roads. It is a map that shows the way to the lost city!

How can this map help you find the city?

BUILDING BACKGROUND You have read how historians and archaeologists help us learn about the past. Another group of scholars—geographers—also contribute to our study of history.

Studying Places and People

When you hear about an event on the news, the first questions you ask may be, "Where did it happen?" and "Who was there?" Historians ask the same questions about events that happened in the past. That is why they need to study geography. **Geography** is the study of the earth's physical and cultural features. These features include mountains, rivers, people, cities, and countries.

Physical Geography

Physical geography is the study of the earth's land and features. People who work in this field are called physical geographers. They study **landforms**, the natural features of the land's surface. Mountains, valleys, plains, and other such places are landforms.

Physical geographers also study **climate**, the pattern of weather conditions in a certain area over a long period of time. Climate is not the same as weather. Weather is the conditions at a specific time and place. If you say that your city has cold winters, you are talking about climate. If you say it is below freezing and snowing today, you are talking about the weather.

Teach the Big Idea

At Level

Studying Geography

1. **Teach** Ask students the questions in the Main Idea boxes to teach this section.
2. **Apply** Write *Physical Geography* and *Human Geography* for students to see, spacing the phrases so that more words and phrases can be added to create a web. Call on students to suggest words and phrases that add details and examples to the two basic terms. For example, *landforms, climate,* and *location* could be added to the *Physical* side. Challenge students to add details specific to your state. **LS Visual/Spatial**
3. **Review** Next, ask students to imagine that they are studying your state's history this year. Ask how the details on the web could enhance their study of the state's history.
4. **Practice/Homework** Ask students to create a similar web of the physical and human geography of their neighborhood. **LS Visual/Spatial**

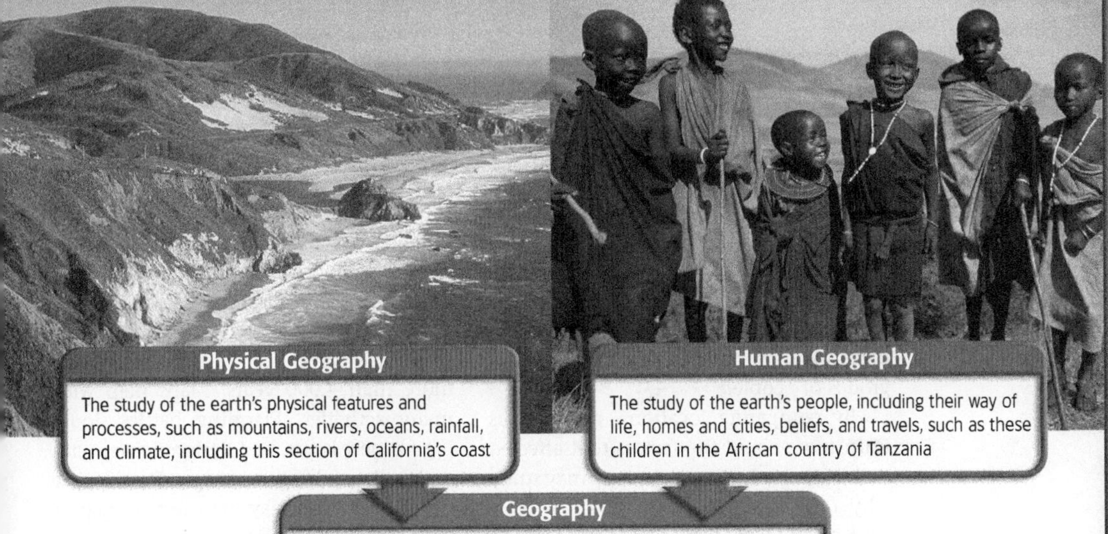

Physical Geography

The study of the earth's physical features and processes, such as mountains, rivers, oceans, rainfall, and climate, including this section of California's coast

Human Geography

The study of the earth's people, including their way of life, homes and cities, beliefs, and travels, such as these children in the African country of Tanzania

Geography

The study of the earth's physical and cultural features

Climate affects many features of a region. For example, it affects plant life. Tropical rain forests require warm air and heavy rain, while a dry climate can create deserts. Climate also affects landforms. For example, constant wind can wear down mountains into flat plains.

Although climate affects landforms, landforms can also affect climate. For example, the Coast Ranges in northern California are mountains parallel to the Pacific coast. As air presses up against these mountains, it rises and cools. Any moisture that the air was carrying falls as rain. Meanwhile, on the opposite side of the range, the Central Valley stays dry. In this way, a mountain range creates two very different climates.

Landforms and climate are part of a place's environment. The **environment** includes all the living and nonliving things that affect life in an area. This includes the area's climate, land, water, plants, soil, animals, and other features.

Human Geography

The other branch of geography is human geography—the study of people and the places where they live. Specialists in human geography study many different things about people and their cultures. What kind of work do people do? How do they get their food? What are their homes like? What religions do they practice?

Human geography also deals with how the environment affects people. For example, how do people who live near rivers protect themselves from floods? How do people who live in deserts survive? Do different environments affect the size of families? Do people in certain environments live longer? Why do some diseases spread easily in some environments but not in others? As you can see, human geographers study many interesting questions about people and this planet.

READING CHECK **Summarizing** What are the two main branches of geography?

Direct Teach

Main Idea

1 Studying Places and People

Geography is the study of places and people.

Define What is geography? *the study of the earth's physical and cultural features*

Summarize What are some examples of physical features? *possible answers—mountains, rivers, valleys, plains, oceans*

Contrast What is the difference between climate and weather? *Weather is the conditions at a specific time and place; climate is the weather conditions in a certain area over a longer period of time.*

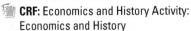

CRF: Economics and History Activity: Economics and History

CRF: History and Geography Activity: Human Communities

Info to Know

Global Warming A main component of physical geography seems to be changing: global temperatures are rising. But what is the cause? Many scientists say that human activities are to blame. They say that carbon dioxide in the atmosphere is creating a greenhouse effect, which is raising average temperatures worldwide. Some people say, however, that temperature changes may be caused by natural factors.

Critical Thinking: Finding Main Ideas

At Level

Research Required

Day in the Life

1. Review with students how physical and human geographers study the earth's features and how environments affect people.
2. Then have each student select a country he or she may like to visit someday. Have students research landforms, climate, and other environmental conditions in their chosen countries. Ask each student to write a short "Day in the Life of . . . " account about what it may be like to live in that country. Have students include information about the area's physical and human geography.
3. Ask for volunteers to present their essays to the class. LS **Verbal/Linguistic**

Alternative Assessment Handbook, Rubric 30: Research and 37: Writing Assignments

Answers

Reading Check *physical geography and human geography*

Direct Teach

Main Idea

❷ Studying Location

Studying location is important to both physical and human geography.

Define What does *location* mean? *the exact description of where something is*

Summarize What are some activities that would use maps? *possible answers—exploring lands, finding one's way in unfamiliar surroundings, planning a new community, and plotting military actions*

Draw Inferences What are some regions within the United States? *possible answers—Southwest, New England, Midwest, Gulf Coast, and so on*

Activity **An Original Map** Have students create a physical map of a fictional country. Caution students that their maps should describe a possible landscape. For example, rivers must flow from high elevations to lower elevations.

Teaching Tip

California Climates
Have students use Internet sources to check weather reports from the California cities shown on the maps. Point out that only by using many weather reports over a long period of time can one make generalizations about a location's climate.

Answers

Studying Maps **1.** *mountains, deserts, rivers, valley; Sierra Nevada;* **2.** *highland, marine, Mediterranean, semiarid, desert; possible answers—highland climate in the highest mountains, marine climate near coast, desert climate in Mojave Desert, semiarid in Central Valley*

ACADEMIC VOCABULARY
features characteristics

Studying Location

Both physical and human geographers study location. Location is the exact description of where something is. Every place on Earth has a specific location.

No two places in the world are exactly alike. Even small differences between places can lead to major differences in how people live. That is why geographers try to understand the effects that different locations have on human populations, or groups of people.

By comparing locations, geographers learn more about the factors that affected each of them. For example, they may study why a town grew in one location while a town nearby got smaller.

Learning from Maps

To study various locations, geographers use maps. A map is a drawing of an area. Some maps show physical **features**. Others show cities and the boundaries of states or countries. Most maps have symbols to show different things. For example, large dots often stand for cities. Blue lines show where rivers flow. Most maps also include a guide to show direction.

People have been making maps for more than 4,000 years. Maps help with many activities. Planning battles, looking for new lands, and designing new city parks all require good maps. On the first day of class, you may have used a map of your school to find your classrooms.

Studying Maps

By studying and comparing maps, you can see how a place's physical and human features are related.

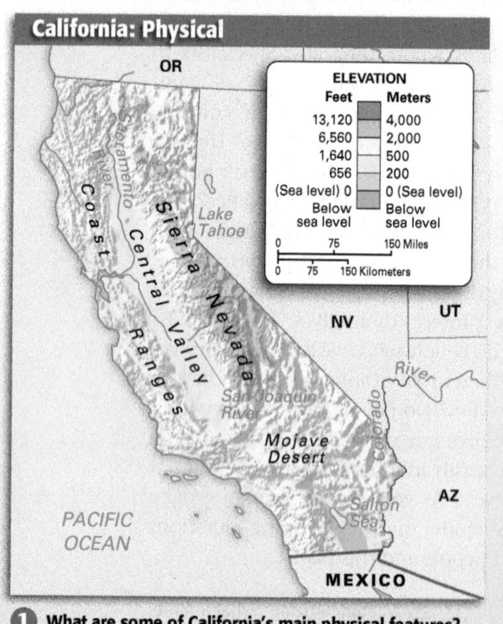

❶ What are some of California's main physical features? Where are the state's highest mountains?

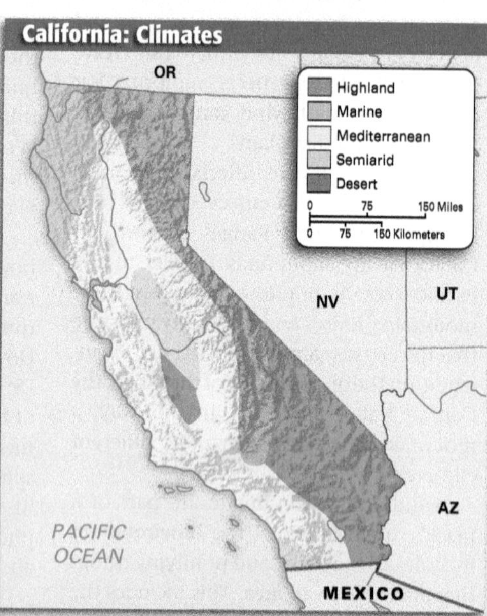

❷ What climates are found in California? How are the climate regions related to California's physical features?

Collaborative Learning: Where in the World?

At Level

Learning about Regions

Research Required

1. Organize the class into small groups. Ask each group to select a region somewhere in the world and conduct research about the region's physical and human characteristics. Students should concentrate on physical characteristics, however. Next, have each group write five characteristics of its region but not identify the region by name.
2. Have all students open this book to the atlas at the back to help them find the regions.
3. Play a "Where in the World?" game. Have each group read its list of characteristics. Challenge the rest of the class to name or describe the region.
4. Discuss the characteristics of any regions not identified. **LS Interpersonal, Visual/Spatial**

Alternative Assessment Handbook, Rubric 14: Group Activity, and 30: Research

Learning about Regions

Learning about regions is another key part of studying geography. A **region** is an area with one or more features that make it different from surrounding areas. These features may be physical, such as forests or grasslands. There may also be differences in climate. For example, a desert area is a type of region. Physical barriers such as mountains and rivers often form a region's boundaries.

Human features can also define regions. An area with many cities is one type of region. An area with only farms is another type. Some regions are identified by the language that people there speak. Other regions are identified by the religion their people practice.

READING CHECK **Categorizing** What are some types of features that can identify a region?

Primary Source

BOOK

What Geography Means

Some people think of geography as the ability to read maps or name state capitals. But as geographer Kenneth C. Davis explains, geography is much more. It is related to almost every branch of human knowledge.

"Geography doesn't simply begin and end with maps showing the location of all the countries of the world. In fact, such maps don't necessarily tell us much. No—geography poses fascinating questions about who we are and how we got to be that way, and then provides clues to the answers. It is impossible to understand history, international politics, the world economy, religions, philosophy, or 'patterns of culture' without taking geography into account."

–Kenneth C. Davis, from *Don't Know Much About Geography*

ANALYSIS SKILL **ANALYZING PRIMARY SOURCES**

Why does the writer think that geography is important?

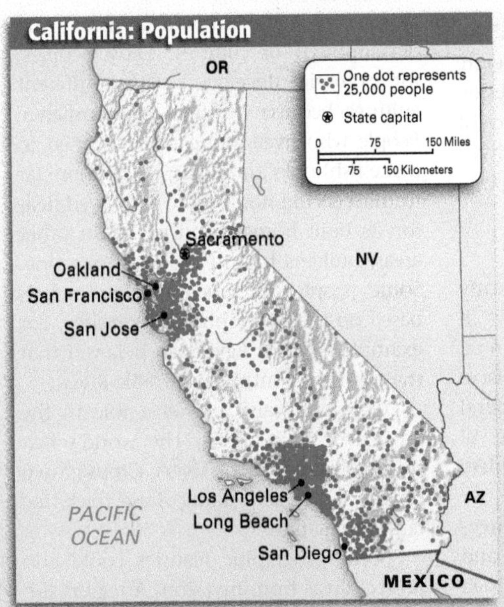

3 **Where are California's two main population centers? What kind of climate is found in these areas?**

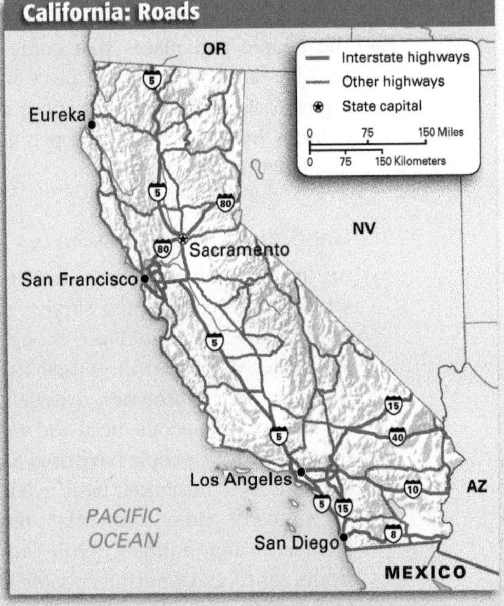

4 **How are California's roads related to its physical features? How are they related to its population centers?**

Direct Teach

Main Idea

2 Studying Location

Studying location is important to both physical and human geography.

Define What is a region? *an area with one or more features that make it different from surrounding areas*

Describe What are some human features that can define a region? *number of cities, an area with many farms, language, religion*

Evaluate Would all people define a region the same way? Why or why not? *possible answer—no, because people interpret both physical and human features differently*

Map Transparency: Studying Maps

Connect to Geography

Ancient Maps People have been making maps for a very long time. The oldest known map is a Babylonian clay tablet that dates from about 2500 BC. People who did not yet have a written language also made diagrams of their world. For example, early Arctic Inuit, Native Americans, and some Pacific Islanders all made maps.

Critical Thinking Activity: Interpreting Maps

Below Level

Standard English Mastery **Prep Required**

Mapping Your School

1. On a sheet of butcher paper, draw a rough map of the area surrounding your school. Label the school on the map.
2. Call on students to mark on the map main roads and local landmarks, such as places of worship and favorite restaurants or stores.
3. When all the students have marked information on the map, ask each student to write at least one sentence making a generalization about the map's information.

Example: *The restaurants are located near each other on a main street.*

4. Then have students use the thesaurus or dictionaries to add appropriate adjectives and descriptive phrases to their sentences.

LS Visual/Spatial

Alternative Assessment Handbook, Rubric 20: Map Creation

Answers

Analyzing Primary Sources *because it poses fascinating questions and affects so many other aspects of the world*

Studying Maps 3. *Los Angeles and San Francisco; Mediterranean;* **4.** *fewer major roads in the desert and mountains; more roads in population centers*

Reading Check *physical features such as mountains, forests, and rivers; human features such as religion or language*

Direct Teach

Main Idea

❸ Geography and History

Geography and history are closely connected.

Recall What are three aspects of human life that geography affects? *resources, cultures, history*

Draw Conclusions Why can present-day people live in places that lack resources valued by early humans? *possible answers—Irrigation brings water to dry areas; modern transportation brings resources from far away.*

Evaluate How do you think physical geography has affected your community? your state? *Answers will vary but should be logical.*

Activity Connecting Geography and History Have students review the maps of fictional countries that they created earlier. Ask each student to imagine how the physical geography of the "country" might affect its development. Instruct students to write brief essays in which they describe those effects.

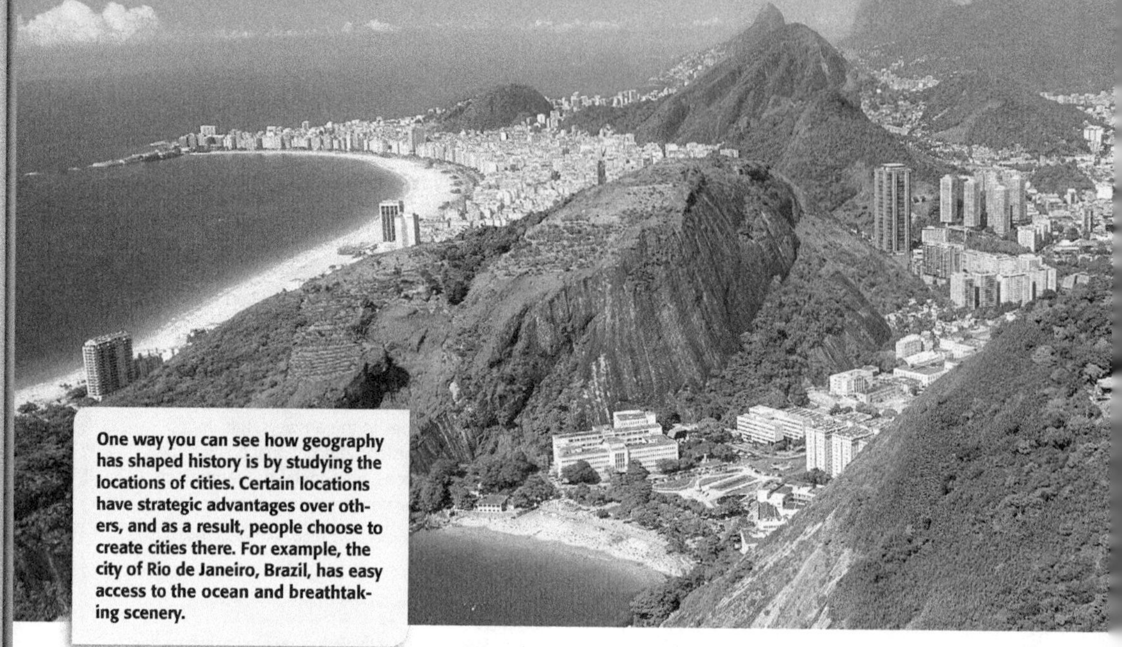

One way you can see how geography has shaped history is by studying the locations of cities. Certain locations have strategic advantages over others, and as a result, people choose to create cities there. For example, the city of Rio de Janeiro, Brazil, has easy access to the ocean and breathtaking scenery.

Geography and History

Geography gives us important clues about the people and places that came before us. Like detectives, we can piece together a great deal of information about ancient cultures by knowing where people lived and what the area was like.

Geography Affects Resources

An area's geography was critical to early settlements. People could survive only in areas where they could get enough food and water. Early people settled in places that were rich in **resources**, materials found in the earth that people need and value. All through history, people have used a variety of resources to meet their basic needs.

In early times, essential resources included water, animals, fertile land, and stones for tools. Over time, people learned to use other resources, including metals such as copper, gold, and iron.

Geography Shapes Cultures

Geography also influenced the early development of cultures. Early peoples, for example, developed vastly different cultures because of their environments. People who lived along rivers learned to make fishhooks and boats, while those far from rivers did not. People who lived near forests built homes from wood. In other areas, builders had to use mud or stone. Some people developed religious beliefs based on the geography of their area. For example, ancient Egyptians believed that the god Hapi controlled the Nile River.

Geography also played a role in the growth of civilizations. The world's first societies formed along rivers. Crops grown on the fertile land along these rivers fed large populations.

Some geographic features could also protect areas from invasion. A region surrounded by mountains or deserts, for example, was hard for attackers to reach.

Differentiating Instruction

Struggling Readers — Below Level

1. Copy the diagram shown for students to see, omitting the blue answers.
2. Help students fill in the diagram with information from this section that shows how geography relates to history.
3. Then ask students to provide examples for each of the circles shown on the diagram.
4. Review the link between geography and history to conclude the activity.

LS **Visual/Spatial**

Geography — *Climate and physical features affect human geography.* — *How and where people live varies, depending on geography.* — *Different cultures arise, based on physical geography.* — *Geography affects events—past and future.* — **History**

environments in positive and negative ways. People have planted millions of trees. They have created new lakes in the middle of deserts. But people have also created wastelands where forests once grew and built dams that flooded ancient cities. This interaction between humans and their environment has been a major factor in history. It continues today.

READING CHECK **Summarizing** In what ways has geography shaped human history?

SUMMARY AND PREVIEW The field of geography includes physical geography and human geography. Geography has had a major influence on history. In the next chapter you will learn how geography affected the first people.

Geography Influences History

Geography has helped shape history and has affected the growth of societies. People in areas with many natural resources could use their resources to get rich. They could build glorious cities and powerful armies. Features such as rivers also made trade easier. Many societies became rich by trading goods with other peoples.

On the other hand, geography has also caused problems. Floods, for example, have killed millions of people. Lack of rainfall has brought deadly food shortages. Storms have wrecked ships, and with them, the hopes of conquerors. In the 1200s, for example, a people known as the Mongols tried to invade Japan. However, most of the Mongol ships were destroyed by a powerful storm. Japanese history may have been very different if the storm had not occurred.

The relationship between geography and people has not been one-sided. For centuries, people have influenced their

Section 2 Assessment

hmhsocialstudies.com
ONLINE QUIZ

Reviewing Ideas, Terms, and People

1. a. **Define** What is **geography**?
   b. **Summarize** What are some of the topics included in human geography?
2. a. **Describe** Identify a **region** near where you live, and explain what sets it apart as a region.
   b. **Predict** How might a map of a city's **landforms** help an official who is planning a new city park?
3. a. **Recall** Where did early peoples tend to settle?
   b. **Compare and Contrast** How could a river be both a valuable **resource** and a problem for a region?

Critical Thinking

4. **Comparing and Contrasting** Using your note-taking chart, compare and contrast physical and human geography.

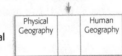

Physical Geography	Similarities	Human Geography

Focus on Writing

5. **Understanding What Geographers Do** In this section you learned how geographers contribute to the study of history. What is the difference between a physical geographer and a human geographer?

Direct Teach

Main Idea

3 Geography and History

Geography and history are closely connected.

Recall How did a weather event affect Japan's history in the 1200s? *Mongol ships on their way to conquer Japan were destroyed by a deadly storm.*

Summarize How were some societies made richer by the geographic makeup of their region? *more natural resources, access to trade routes*

Review & Assess

Close

Call on volunteers to examine the photo on these pages to describe how geography has affected the development of Rio de Janeiro.

Review

Online Quiz, Section 2

Assess

SE Section 2 Assessment

PASS: Section 2 Quiz

Alternative Assessment Handbook

Reteach/Classroom Intervention

Guided Reading Workbook, Section 2

Interactive Skills Tutor CD-ROM

Section 2 Assessment Answers

1. **a.** the study of the Earth's physical and cultural features
   b. what work people do, how they get their food, the homes they live in, religions they practice
2. **a.** Answers will vary but should display an understanding of the concept of a region.
   b. possible answers—A map would show areas that have trees for shade, water for activities, or areas that might not be desirable for building a park, such as steep hills or swamps.
3. **a.** in areas rich in natural resources
   b. Rivers could provide water and access to trade routes; flooding can destroy settlements or leave them open to invasion.
4. Physical—earth's land and features; Human—people and the places where they live
5. Physical geographer—studies earth's land and features; Human geographer—studies people and the places where they live

Answers

Reading Check *possible answers—Areas rich in resources thrived, access to rivers made trade possible, and events associated with physical geography have changed history.*

History and Geography

Info to Know

Teotihuacán Teotihuacán is located about 30 miles northeast of what is now Mexico City. The city reached its height in the 500s AD. At that time, it was probably the sixth-largest city in the world, with an estimated population of 125,000. The city covered some eight square miles. It contained pyramids, temples, plazas, palaces, and more than 2,000 residential buildings. Many of the people who lived there were farmers or craftspeople. Others were merchants, nobles, or priests. Sometime in the 600s or 700s, a fire destroyed much of Teotihuacán. The event led to the city's swift decline, and it was soon abandoned.

Much of the information in the map at right is based on the Teotihuacán Mapping Project, done in the 1960s and 1970s.

City of the Gods Centuries after the abandonment of Teotihuacán, Aztec travelers came across the ruins. The Aztec believed the place to be holy and the birthplace of the gods. As a result, they named it Teotihuacán, which means "City of the Gods" in the Aztec language. The city's original name and the language its residents spoke remain unknown.

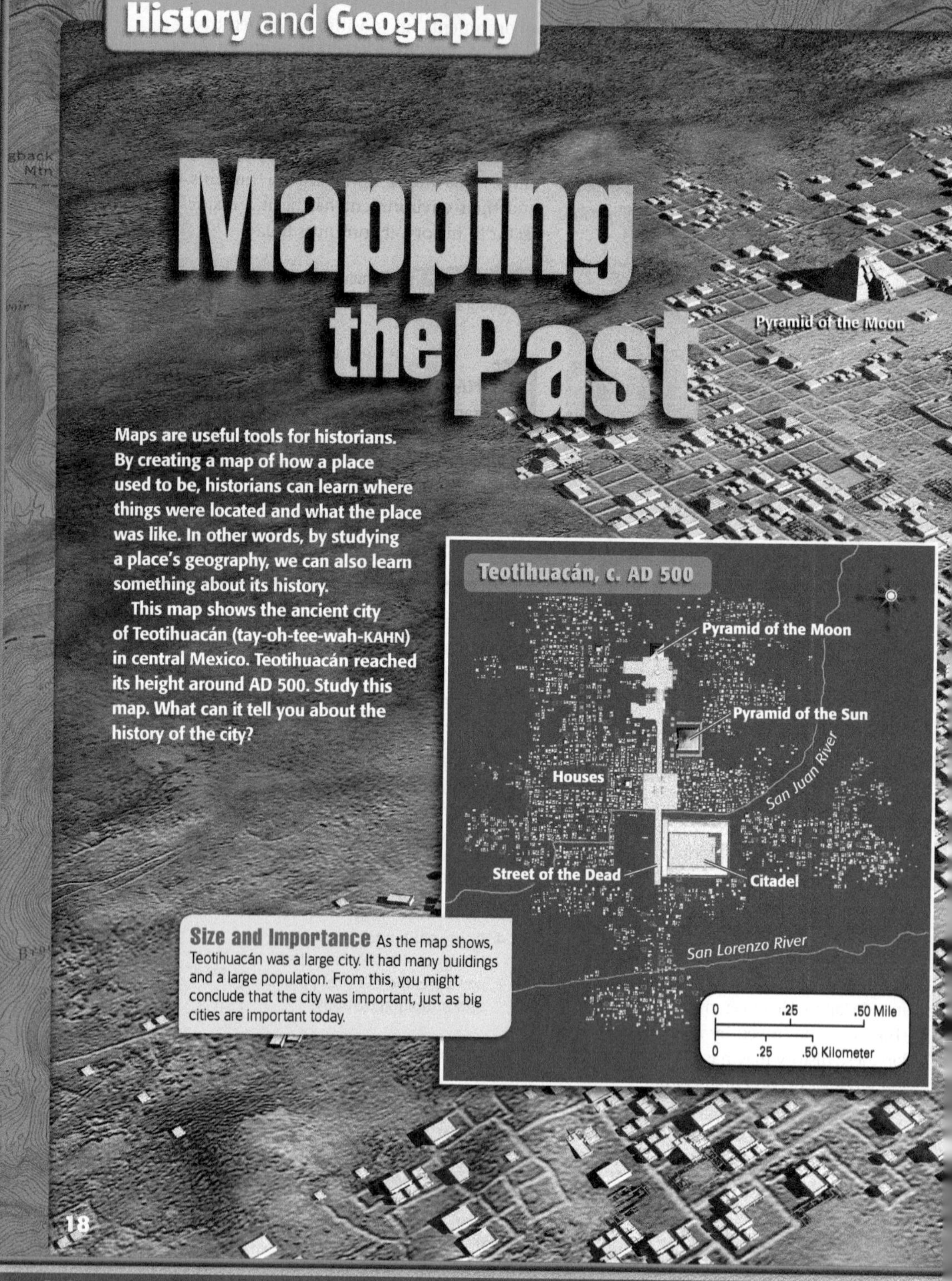

History and Geography
Mapping the Past
Pyramid of the Moon
Maps are useful tools for historians. By creating a map of how a place used to be, historians can learn where things were located and what the place was like. In other words, by studying a place's geography, we can also learn something about its history.
This map shows the ancient city of Teotihuacán (tay-oh-tee-wah-KAHN) in central Mexico. Teotihuacán reached its height around AD 500. Study this map. What can it tell you about the history of the city?
Teotihuacán, c. AD 500
Pyramid of the Moon
Pyramid of the Sun
Houses
San Juan River
Street of the Dead
Citadel
San Lorenzo River
0 .25 .50 Mile
0 .25 .50 Kilometer
Size and Importance As the map shows, Teotihuacán was a large city. It had many buildings and a large population. From this, you might conclude that the city was important, just as big cities are important today.
18

Social Studies Skill: Interpreting Maps

At Level

Detectives in Time

1. Have students examine the map to see what they can learn about the city of Teotihuacán and the people who lived there. Have students consider the following questions:
   - Approximately how big was the area of the city in 500 AD?
   - Why might people have settled there? What natural resources are apparent?
   - How spaced out are the dwellings? Do they appear to have yards or gardens?
   - Why do you think the river's course was changed? How many people and what sort of equipment might such a project have involved?
2. Discuss what the answers reveal about the people and city of Teotihuacán.
3. Then encourage students to ask their own questions about the information on the map. Explain that this process of forming questions based on maps is one way that historians work. **LS Visual/Spatial**

Alternative Assessment Handbook, Rubric 21: Map Reading

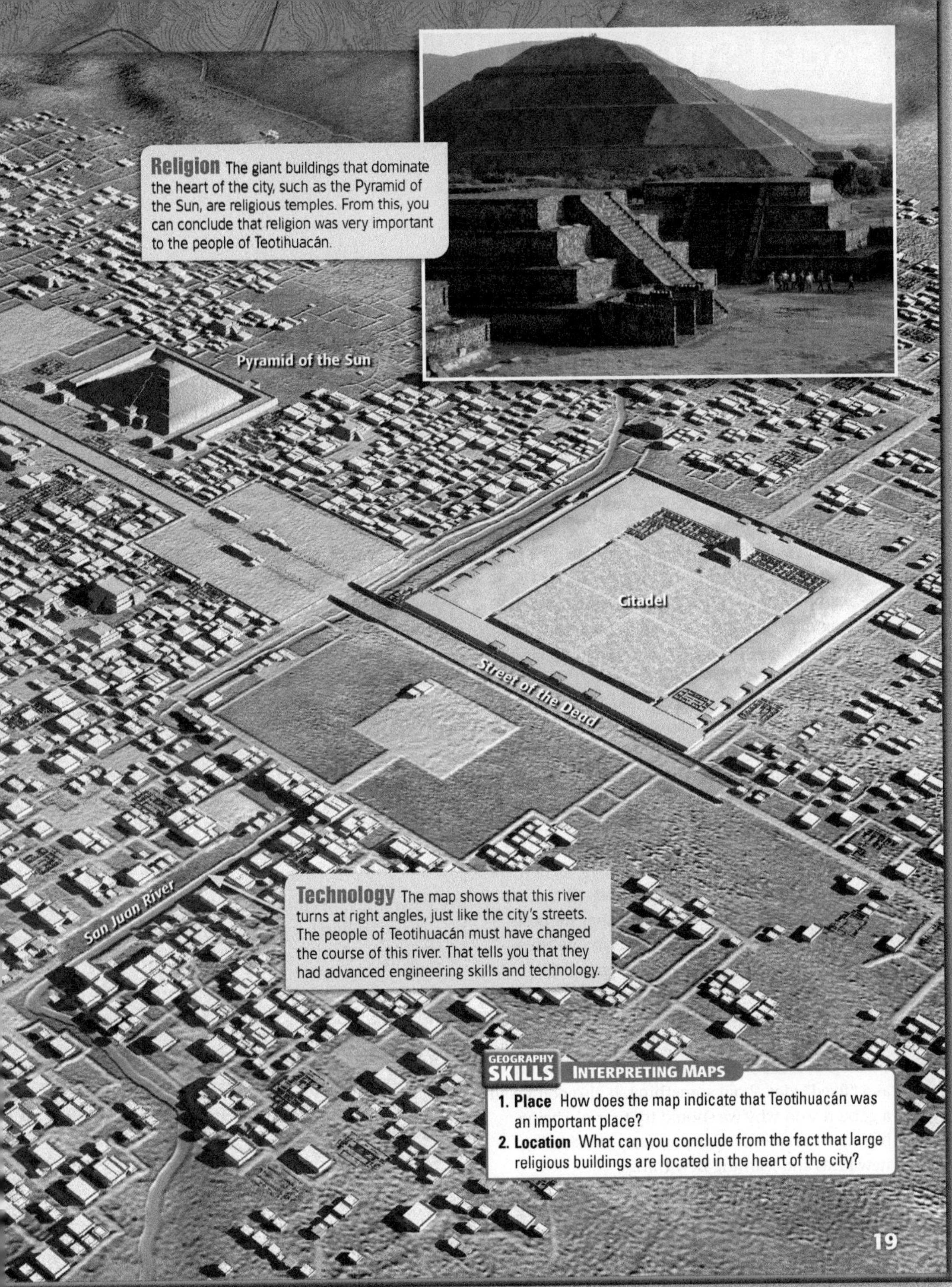

Religion The giant buildings that dominate the heart of the city, such as the Pyramid of the Sun, are religious temples. From this, you can conclude that religion was very important to the people of Teotihuacán.
Pyramid of the Sun
Citadel
Street of the Dead
San Juan River
Technology The map shows that this river turns at right angles, just like the city's streets. The people of Teotihuacán must have changed the course of this river. That tells you that they had advanced engineering skills and technology.
GEOGRAPHY SKILLS INTERPRETING MAPS
1. Place How does the map indicate that Teotihuacán was an important place?
2. Location What can you conclude from the fact that large religious buildings are located in the heart of the city?
19

Differentiating Instruction

Struggling Readers **Below Level**

1. To help students understand how historians learn from maps, draw the following chart for students to see. Complete the chart as you explain each point.
2. Then, encourage students to point out other significant or interesting features in the map and suggest what they might mean.

LS Visual/Spatial

Alternative Assessment Handbook, Rubrics 7: Charts; and 21: Map Reading

What the Map Shows	What We Can Learn
Size: *large city with many temples, buildings, homes*	*large population; probably important city*
Religion: *pyramids, or religious temples, at key sites in the city*	*religion very important to the people*
Technology: *pyramids, buildings, rerouted river*	*had advanced engineering skills, large labor force*

History and Geography

Connect to Civics

Early City Planning Teotihuacán was carefully planned. The Street of the Dead, the main axis of the city, runs north-south and points directly at the mountain Cerro Gordo. (The road is slightly off of true north.) On each side of the street, structures are arranged in grids, often in symmetrical layouts. Ask students how a carefully planned city could contribute to civic pride.

Info to Know

Mistaken Interpretations The names of structures in Teotihuacán reveal more about the people who named them than about their original purposes. For example, the Aztec thought the ruined buildings along the city's central road were burial sites. As a result, they named the road the Street of the Dead. Later, Spaniards mistook other ruins for a fortress and named it the Citadel. This large space was more likely used for rituals.

Linking to Today

Pyramids of Teotihuacán Archaeologists continue to dig and discover new finds at Teotihuacán. Recent excavations at the Pyramid of the Moon uncovered the skeletons of three high-ranking priests or officials. The figures were discovered seated cross-legged with their hands clasped in front of them. Their bodies were adorned with collars, ear and nose rings, and possibly headdresses. The archaeologists also found jade stones, figurines, animal remains, and carved seashells in the pyramid.

Draw Conclusions What might this discovery tell us about the culture of Teotihuacán? *possible answers—had a class structure, ceremonies for the deceased, and belief in an afterlife*

Answers

Interpreting Maps 1. *It was a large city with many buildings and a large population, and therefore likely an important city.* **2.** *Religion was important to the city's residents.*

Social Studies Skills

Recognizing Bias

Activity **Bias in the News**

Materials: photocopies of newspaper pages

1. Pass out photocopies of the editorial page and the front page from a local newspaper. Have students contrast the articles that appear on each page. Guide students in determining that the front-page news coverage is mainly objective reporting of facts. The editorial page likely contains many opinionated items.
2. Next, have students examine the editorials and letters to the editor. Ask students to identify any biases the writers might hold. How are these biases shaping the writers' viewpoints and opinions? See if students can find examples of stereotyping or prejudice.
3. Then assign students one editorial or letter to the editor. Have each students create a three-column chart listing the verifiable statements, or facts; the unverifiable statements, or opinions; and any examples of bias. Review students' charts as a class.
LS Verbal/Linguistic

Alternative Assessment Handbook, Rubric 7: Charts

Interactive Skills Tutor CD-ROM, Lesson 20: Evaluate Sources of Information for Authenticity, Reliability, and Bias

Social Studies Skills

Analysis | Critical Thinking | Economics | Study

Recognizing Bias

Understand the Skill

Everybody has convictions, or things that they strongly believe. However, if we form opinions about people or events based only on our beliefs, we may be showing bias. Bias is an idea about someone or something based solely on opinions, not facts.

There are many types of bias. Sometimes people form opinions about others based on the group to which that person belongs. For example, some people might believe that all teenagers are selfish or that all politicians are dishonest. These are examples of a type of bias called *stereotyping.* Holding negative opinions of people based on their race, religion, age, gender, or similar characteristics is known as *prejudice.*

We should always be on guard for the presence of personal biases. Such biases can slant how we view, judge, and provide information. Honest and accurate communication requires people to be as free of bias as possible.

Learn the Skill

As you read or write, watch out for biases. One way to identify a bias is to look for facts that support a statement. If a belief seems unreasonable when compared to the facts, it may be a sign of bias.

Another sign of bias is a person's unwillingness to question his or her belief if it is challenged by evidence. People sometimes cling to views that evidence proves are wrong. This is why bias is defined as a "fixed" idea about something. It also points out a good reason why we should try to avoid being biased. Our biases can keep us from considering new ideas and learning new things.

You will meet many peoples from the past as you study world history. Their beliefs, behaviors, and ways of life may seem different or strange to you. It is important to remain unbiased and to keep an open mind. Recognize that "different" does not mean "not as good."

Understand that early peoples did not have the technology or the accumulation of past knowledge that we have today. Be careful to not look down on them just because they were less advanced or might seem "simpler" than we are today. Remember that their struggles, learning, and achievements helped make us what we are today.

The following guidelines can help you to recognize and reduce your own biases. Keep them in mind as you study world history.

1. When discussing a topic, try to think of beliefs and experiences in your own background that might affect how you feel about the topic.
2. Try to not mix statements of fact with statements of opinion. Clearly separate and indicate what you *know* to be true from what you *believe* to be true.
3. Avoid using emotional, positive, or negative words when communicating factual information.

Practice and Apply the Skill

Professional historians try to be objective about the history they study and report. Being *objective* means not being influenced by personal feelings or opinions. Write a paragraph explaining why you think being objective is important in the study of history.

Social Studies Skills Activity: Recognizing Bias

Recognizing Bias in Primary and Secondary Sources **At Level**

1. Read the textbook's definitions of primary and secondary sources aloud for students.
   - **primary source:** an account of an event created by someone who took part in or witnessed the event
   - **secondary source:** information gathered by someone who did not take part in or witness an event
2. Ask students to list examples of each type of source (primary—diaries, editorials, letters, newspaper articles, photographs, political cartoons; secondary—biographies, encyclopedias, history textbooks, and monographs). Then discuss with students the bias that might be inherent in each example (e.g., the letters of a military commander and the journal of a soldier will reflect different viewpoints and perspectives on a conflict).
LS Interpersonal, Verbal/Linguistic

Alternative Assessment Handbook, Rubric 11: Discussions

Answers

Practice and Apply the Skill
Answers will vary, but students should note that biases will influence the ways in which people interpret events in history. Thus, historians need to remain objective when they interpret events and try to view the events within the context of the period.

CHAPTER 1

Chapter Review

History's Impact
▶ **video series**
Review the video to answer the focus question:
What is an artifact, and how can it help an archaeologist learn about history?

Visual Summary

Use the visual summary below to help you review the main ideas of the chapter.

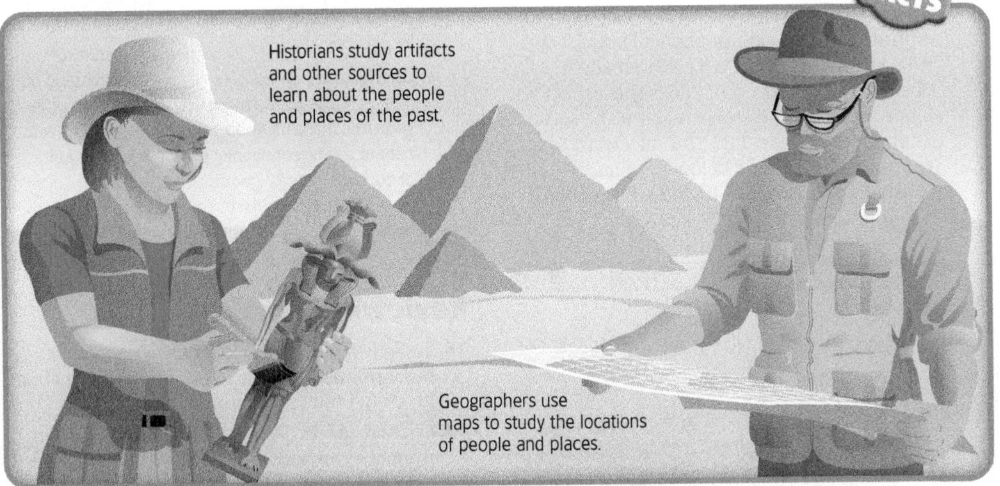

QUICK FACTS
Historians study artifacts and other sources to learn about the people and places of the past.
Geographers use maps to study the locations of people and places.

Reviewing Vocabulary, Terms, and People

For each statement below, write T if it is true or F if it is false. If the statement is false, write the correct term that would make the sentence a true statement.

1. History is the study of the past based on what people left behind.
2. Knowledge, beliefs, customs, and values of a group of people are part of their environment.
3. A handwritten letter from a soldier to his family would be considered a primary source.
4. Geography is the study of the past, whether recent or long ago.
5. Your state probably has many different landforms, such as mountains, plains, and valleys.
6. Weather changes from day to day, but a location's climate does not change as often.
7. Values are ideas that people hold dear and try to live by.

Comprehension and Critical Thinking

SECTION 1 *(Pages 6–11)*

8. **a. Describe** What is history? What is archaeology? How do the two fields work together?
   b. Make Inferences Why may a historian who is still alive disagree with conclusions drawn by a historian who lived a hundred years ago?
   c. Evaluate Do you think primary sources or secondary sources are more valuable to modern historians? Why?

SECTION 2 *(Pages 12–17)*

9. **a. Identify** What are the two main branches of geography, and how does each contribute to our understanding of history?
   b. Analyze If you were asked to divide your state into regions, what features would you use to define those regions? Why?
   c. Predict How might a long period of severe heat or cold affect the history of a city or region?

Answers

Visual Summary

Review and Inquiry Have students use the visual summary to discuss details related to the professions of historian and geographer.

Quick Facts Transparency: Uncovering the Past Visual Summary

Reviewing Vocabulary, Terms, and People

1. F; archaeology
2. F; culture
3. T
4. F; history
5. T
6. T
7. T

Comprehension and Critical Thinking

8. **a.** study of the past; study of the past based on what people left behind; possible answer—Each field can help the other fill in the blanks in what they know.
   b. possible answer—New information or new interpretations can lead historians to draw new conclusions.
   c. possible answers—primary, because they are from eyewitnesses; secondary, because they draw from many sources, and even eyewitnesses are not completely reliable

Review and Assessment Resources

Review and Reinforce

- SE Chapter Review
- **CRF:** Chapter Review Activity
- Quick Facts Transparency: Uncovering the Past Visual Summary
- Spanish Chapter Summaries Audio CD Program
- Online Chapter Summaries in Six Languages
- TOS Holt McDougal PuzzleView
- Quiz Game CD-ROM

Assess

- SE Standardized Test Practice
- PASS: Chapter Test, Forms A and B
- Alternative Assessment Handbook
- TOS ExamView Assessment Suite, Chapter Test
- Differentiated Instruction Modified Worksheets and Tests CD-ROM: Chapter Test
- Online Assessment Program, in the Interactive Student Edition

Reteach/Intervene

- Guided Reading Workbook
- Differentiated Instruction Teacher Management System: Lesson Plans
- Differentiated Instruction Modified Worksheets and Tests CD-ROM
- Interactive Skills Tutor CD-ROM

hmhsocialstudies.com
Chapter Resources

Answers

9. **a.** physical, human; physical—Landforms, climate, resources, and other aspects of physical geography affect where and how people live; human—Culture affects how people make history.

b. Answers will vary, but students should make logical choices among physical features such as mountains and rivers and human factors such as language or ways of making a living.

c. possible answers—could affect ability to raise food, to transport goods to or from markets, to support a tourist industry, to help vulnerable people survive, and so on

Using the Internet

10. Go to hmhsocialstudies.com to access a rubric for this activity.

Social Studies Skills

11. an idea about someone or something based solely on opinion

12. A conviction is a strong belief; a bias is an opinion based only on beliefs.

13. so that they can accurately report the past and be open to new ideas; identify their own beliefs, avoid emotional language

14. Responses will vary.

Reading Skills

15. history, culture, artifacts, values, history or geography

Using the Internet 

10. Activity: Describing Artifacts Archaeologists study the past based on what people have left behind. Using your online textbook, explore recent archaeological discoveries. Select one artifact that interests you and write a short article about it. Write your article as if it will be printed in a school magazine. Describe the artifact in detail: What is it? Who made it? Where was it found? What does the artifact tell archaeologists and historians about the society or culture that created it? You may want to create a chart like the one below to organize your information. If possible, include illustrations with your article.

Artifact	
What is it?	
Who made it?	
Where was it found?	
What does it tell us?	

hmhsocialstudies.com

Social Studies Skills 

Recognizing Bias Answer the following questions about personal convictions and bias.

11. What is bias?

12. What is the difference between a personal conviction and a bias?

13. Why do historians try to avoid bias in their writing? What methods might they use to do so?

14. Do you think it is possible for a historian to remove all traces of bias from his or her writing? Why or why not?

Reading Skills

15. Specialized Vocabulary of History Read the following passage in which several words have been left blank. Fill in each of the blanks with the appropriate word that you learned in this chapter.

> "Although ________ is defined as the study of the past, it is much more. It is a key to understanding our ________, the ideas, languages, religions, and other traits that make us who we are. In the ________ left behind by ancient peoples we can see reflections of our own material goods: plates and dishes, toys, jewelry, and work objects. These objects show us that human ________ has not changed that much.

Reviewing Themes

16. Society and Culture How may a historian's description of a battle reveal information about his or her own society or culture?

17. Science and Technology If hundreds of years from now archaeologists study the things we leave behind, what may they conclude about the role of technology in American society? Explain your answer.

Focus on Writing 

18. Writing Your Job Description Review your notes on the work of historians, archaeologists, and physical and human geographers. Choose one of these jobs and write a description of it. You should begin your description by explaining why the job is important. Then identify the job's tasks and responsibilities. Finally, tell what kind of person would do well in this job. For example, a historian may enjoy reading and an archaeologist may enjoy working outdoors. When you have finished your description, you may be able to add it to a class or school guide for career planning.

Reviewing Themes

16. possible answer—may reveal how the historian's society or culture viewed war in general or that particular battle, depending on who participated and who won; may also reveal what qualities the historian's society admired in a leader or in warriors

17. possible answer—Technology was important not just for business and basic communication, but also for entertainment.

Focus on Writing

18. Rubric Students' job descriptions should:

- explain why the job is important.
- describe the tasks and responsibilities of the job.
- end by telling what kind of person would be good for the job.
- use correct grammar, punctuation, spelling, and capitalization.

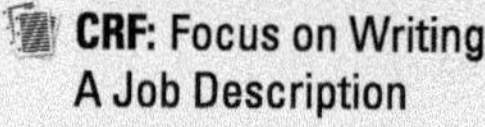

CRF: Focus on Writing: A Job Description

22 CHAPTER 1

CHAPTER 1

Standardized Test Practice

DIRECTIONS: Read each question, and write the letter of the best response.

1

The object with ancient writing that is shown in this photo is a

A primary source and a resource.
B primary source and an artifact.
C secondary source and a resource.
D secondary source and an artifact.

2 Which of the following is the *best* reason for studying history?

A We can learn the dates of important events.
B We can learn interesting facts about famous people.
C We can learn about ourselves and other people.
D We can hear stories about strange things.

3 The study of people and the places where they live is called

A archaeology.
B environmental science.
C human geography.
D history.

4 Which of the following subjects would interest a physical geographer the *least*?

A a place's climate
B a mountain range
C a river system
D a country's highways

5 The type of evidence that an archaeologist would find most useful is a(n)

A artifact.
B primary source.
C secondary source.
D landform.

6 Which statement *best* describes the relationship between people and natural environments?

A Natural environments do not affect how people live.
B People cannot change the environments in which they live.
C Environments influence how people live, and people change their environments.
D People do not live in natural environments.

7 Each of the following is a primary source *except*

A a photograph.
B a diary.
C a treaty.
D an encyclopedia.

Answers

Standardized Test Practice

1. B
Break Down the Question Point out to students who missed the question that the writing on the artifact contributes to its being a primary source. It is also an artifact because it was left behind by an ancient people, the Egyptians.

2. C
Break Down the Question Although the other three choices are not totally wrong, C is the best answer because it includes all the choices.

3. C
Break Down the Question This question requires students to recall factual information. Refer students who miss it to Section 2.

4. D
Break Down the Question Because highways are not natural physical features, they would be of the least interest to a physical geographer.

5. A
Break Down the Question Although an archaeologist may value primary and secondary sources, he or she gets more information from artifacts. Landforms are not relevant in this case.

6. C
Break Down the Question This question requires students to recall the close relationship of history and geography. Refer students who miss it to Section 2.

7. D
Break Down the Question All the choices except D are primary sources.

Intervention Resources

Reproducible

- Guided Reading Workbook
- Differentiated Instruction Teacher Management System: Lesson Plans

Technology

- Quick Facts Transparency: Uncovering the Past Visual Summary
- Differentiated Instruction Modified Worksheets and Tests CD-ROM
- Interactive Skills Tutor CD-ROM

Tips for Test Taking

Take It All In Encourage students to preview the test to get a mental map of their tasks:

- Know how many questions there are.
- Know where to stop.
- Set time checkpoints.
- Do the easy sections first; easy questions can be worth just as many points as hard ones.

Chapter 2 Planning Guide

The Stone Ages and Early Cultures

Overview	Instructional Resources	
CHAPTER 2 **Essential Question:** How did humans' ways of living change as they interacted and adapted? **Focus on the Essential Question Podcast**	TOS **Differentiated Instruction Teacher Management System:** • Instructional Benchmarking Guides • Lesson Plans for Differentiated Instruction **Guided Reading Workbook** **Chapter Resource File:** • Chapter Review Activity • Focus on Writing Activity: A Storyboard • Social Studies Skills Activity: Identifying Central Issues	TOS **Calendar Planner** **Power Presentations with Media Gallery** **Differentiated Instruction Modified Worksheets and Tests CD-ROM** **Primary Source Library CD-ROM for World History** **Interactive Skills Tutor CD-ROM** **Student Edition on Audio CD Program** **Video:** Stone Age Tools
Section 1: **The First People** **The Big Idea:** Prehistoric people learned to adapt to their environment, to make simple tools, to use fire, and to use language.	TOS **Differentiated Instruction Teacher Management System:** Section 1 Lesson Plan **Guided Reading Workbook:** Section 1 **Chapter Resource File:** • Vocabulary Builder Activity, Section 1 • Biography Activity: Donald Johanson and Tim White • Biography Activity: The Leakey Family • Interdisciplinary Project: The First People: Flannel Board Story • Literature Activity: *Boy of the Painted Cave*, by Justin Denzel • Primary Source Activity: The Discovery of Chauvet Cave	**Daily Bellringer Transparency:** Section 1 **Map Transparency:** Early Hominid Sites **Quick Facts Transparency:** Early Hominids **Internet Activity:** Archaeology Article **Internet Activity:** Mary Leakey Sketch
Section 2: **Early Human Migration** **The Big Idea:** As people migrated around the world they learned to adapt to new environments.	TOS **Differentiated Instruction Teacher Management System:** Section 2 Lesson Plan **Guided Reading Workbook:** Section 2 **Chapter Resource File:** • Vocabulary Builder Activity, Section 2	**Daily Bellringer Transparency:** Section 2 **Map Transparency:** Early Human Migration **Animated History:** Early Human Migration
Section 3: **Beginnings of Agriculture** **The Big Idea:** The development of agriculture brought great changes to human society.	TOS **Differentiated Instruction Teacher Management System:** Section 3 Lesson Plan **Guided Reading Workbook:** Section 3 **Chapter Resource File:** • Vocabulary Builder Activity, Section 3 • History and Geography Activity: Agriculture and Animals • Primary Source Activity: Objects from Çatal Hüyük	**Daily Bellringer Transparency:** Section 3 **Map Transparency:** Early Domestication

Chart Key:

SE Student Edition
TOS Teacher One Stop
Printable Resource
 Presentation Resource
DVD/CD-ROM
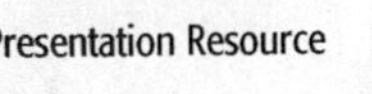
 MP3 Audio
HISTORY™

Program Resources available on TOS and @ hmhsocialstudies.com

Review, Assessment, Intervention

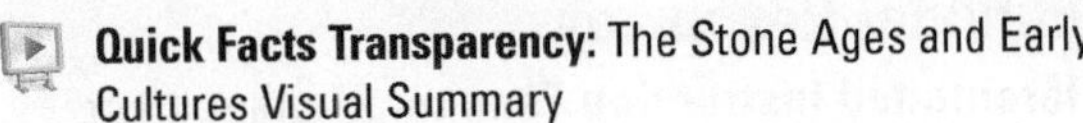

- **Quick Facts Transparency:** The Stone Ages and Early Cultures Visual Summary
- **Spanish Chapter Summaries Audio CD Program**
- **Quiz Game CD-ROM**
- **Progress Assessment Support System (PASS):** Chapter Test
- **Differentiated Instruction Modified Worksheets and Tests CD-ROM:** Modified Chapter Test
- TOS **ExamView® Assessment Suite (English/Spanish)**
- **Online Assessment Program,** in the Interactive Student Edition

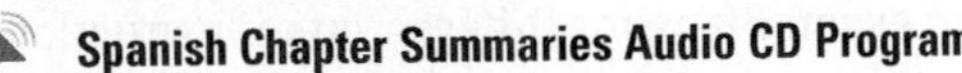
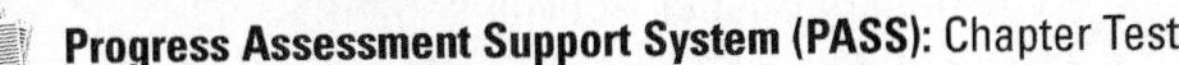

- **PASS:** Section 1 Quiz
- **Online Quiz:** Section 1
- **Alternative Assessment Handbook**

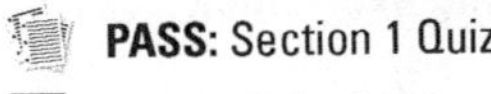

- **PASS:** Section 2 Quiz
- **Online Quiz:** Section 2
- **Alternative Assessment Handbook**

- **PASS:** Section 3 Quiz
- **Online Quiz:** Section 3
- **Alternative Assessment Handbook**

Supporting Resources

- Multimedia Classroom Global History Series
- Global History Teacher's Guide

Maps Globes Graphs Level F

- Student Workbook
- Teacher's Guide

Social Studies Trade Library Collections

- Premier Secondary World History Trade Collection

History's Impact

World History Video Program

- **Early Migrations to North America**

For more information or to purchase go to hmhsocialstudies.com

Power Presentations with Media Gallery

Power Presentations with Media Gallery are visual presentations of each chapter's main ideas. Presentations can be customized by including Quick Facts charts, images from the text, and video clips.

Differentiating Instruction

How do I address the needs of varied learners?

The Target Resource acts as your primary strategy for differentiated instruction.

ENGLISH-LANGUAGE LEARNERS & STRUGGLING READERS

Interactive Skills Tutor CD-ROM

The Interactive Skills Tutor CD-ROM contains lessons that provide additional practice for 20 different critical thinking skills.

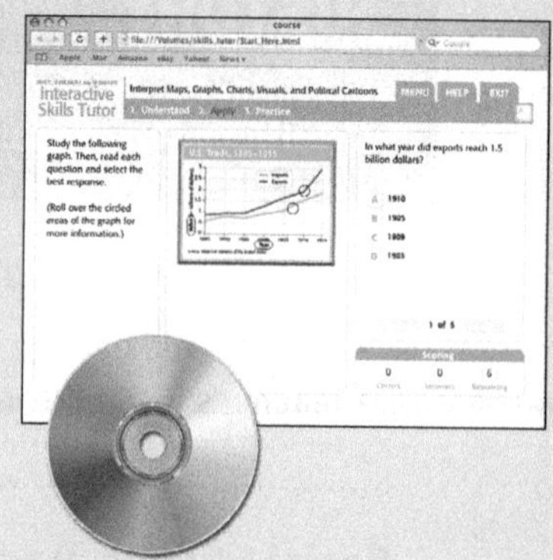

Additional Resources

Differentiated Instruction Teacher Management System: Lesson Plans for Differentiated Instruction

Chapter Resource File:

- Vocabulary Builder Activities
- Social Studies Skills Activity: Identifying Central Issues

Quick Facts Transparencies:

- Early Hominid Sites
- The Stone Ages and Early Cultures Visual Summary

Student Edition on Audio CD Program

Spanish/English Guided Reading Workbook

SPECIAL NEEDS LEARNERS

Differentiated Instruction Modified Worksheets and Tests CD-ROM

- Vocabulary Flash Cards
- Vocabulary Builder Activities
- Chapter Review Activity
- Chapter Test

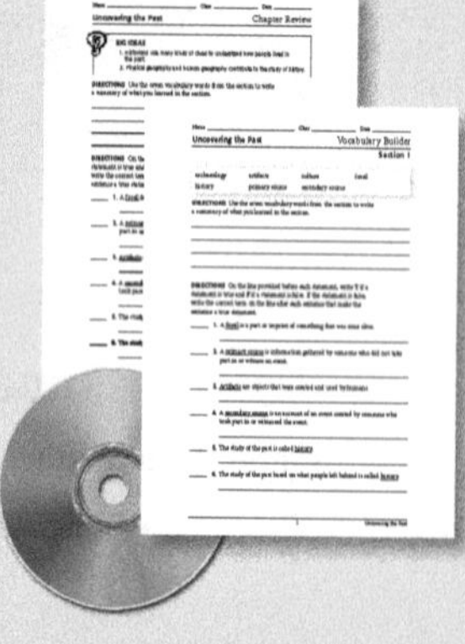

Additional Resources

Differentiated Instruction Teacher Management System: Lesson Plans for Differentiated Instruction

Guided Reading Workbook

Chapter Resource File: Social Studies Skills Activity: Identifying Central Issues

Student Edition on Audio CD Program

Interactive Skills Tutor CD-ROM

ADVANCED/GIFTED-AND-TALENTED STUDENTS

Primary Source Library CD-ROM for World History

The Library contains longer versions of quotations in the text, extra sources, and images. Included are point-of-view articles, journals, diaries, historical fiction, and political documents.

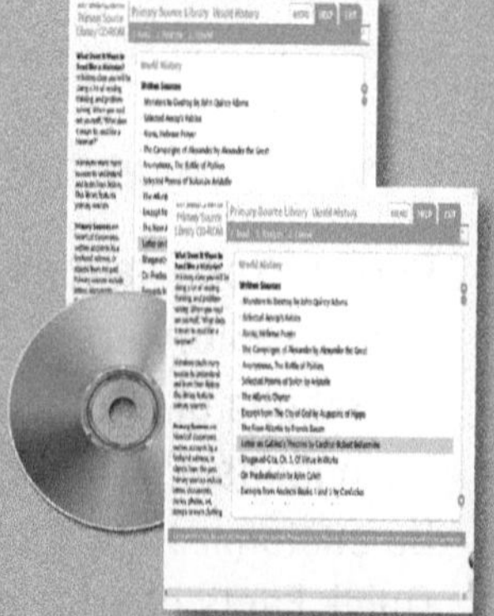

Additional Resources

Differentiated Instruction Teacher Management System: Lesson Plans for Differentiated Instruction

Chapter Resource File:

- Focus on Writing Activity: A Storyboard
- Literature Activity: *Boy of the Painted Cave*, by Justin Denzel

Document-Based Questions Activities

Differentiated Activities in the Teacher's Edition

- Drawing a Map of Africa, p. 29
- Organizing Ideas, p. 44

Teacher One Stop™

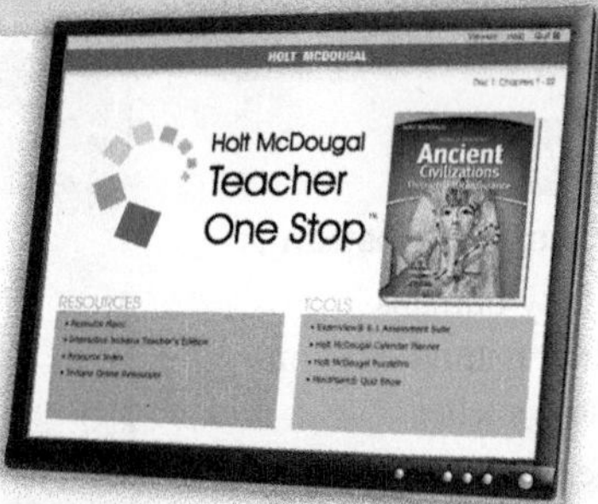

How can I manage the lesson plans and support materials for differentiated instruction?

With the Teacher One Stop, you can easily organize and print lesson plans, planning guides, and instructional materials for all learners. The Teacher One Stop includes the following materials to help you differentiate instruction:

- Interactive Teacher's Edition
- Calendar Planner and pacing guides
- Editable lesson plans
- All reproducible ancillaries in Adobe Acrobat (PDF) format
- ExamView Assessment Suite (English & Spanish)
- Transparency and video previews

Differentiated Activities in the Teacher's Edition

- Describing Tools for a Time Capsule, p. 30
- Creating a Mural, p. 41

Interactive Student Edition

Complete online student edition with interactive multimedia support for chapter content assessment and reporting

- Interactive Maps and Notebook
- Graphic Organizers
- Standardized Test Prep
- Online Homework Practice and Research Activities
- Current Events
- Chapter-based Internet Activities
- Animated History Activities
- and more!

Differentiated Activities in the Teacher's Edition

- Exploring the Role of Chance in History, p. 31
- Researching Archaeological Sites, p. 35

• Chapter Preview •

Essential Question

Introduce the Essential Question

- Point out that early humans depended on their natural environment for food and shelter.
- Explain that the shift from hunting and gathering to agriculture led to the development of larger, more permanent human settlements.
- Discuss how surpluses and labor specialization allowed complex villages to develop and how humans' lives changed as a result.

Focus on Writing

The **Chapter Resource File** provides a Focus on Writing work sheet to help students organize and write their poem.

CRF: Focus on Writing Activity: A Storyboard

Key to Differentiating Instruction

Below Level

Basic-level activities designed for all students encountering new material

At Level

Intermediate-level activities designed for average students

Above Level

Challenging activities designed for honors and gifted and talented students

Standard English Mastery

Activities designed to improve standard English usage

LS Learning Styles

CHAPTER 2 | 5 MILLION YEARS AGO–5,000 YEARS AGO

The Stone Ages and Early Cultures

Essential Question How did humans' ways of living change as they interacted and adapted?

South Carolina Performance Standards

6-1.1 Explain the characteristics of hunter-gatherer groups and their relationship to the natural environment; **6-1.2** Explain the emergence of agriculture and its effect on early human communities, including the domestication of plants and animals, the impact of irrigation techniques, and subsequent food surpluses.

Literacy Skills for Social Studies

- Evaluate multiple points of view or biases and attribute the perspectives to the influences of individual experiences, societal values, and cultural traditions.

Partnership for the 21st Century Skills

Articulate his or her own thoughts and those of others objectively through speaking and writing.

FOCUS ON WRITING

A Storyboard Prehistoric humans did not write. However, they did carve and paint images on cave walls. In the spirit of these images, you will create a storyboard that uses images to tell the story of prehistoric humans. Remember that a storyboard tells a story with simple sketches and short captions.

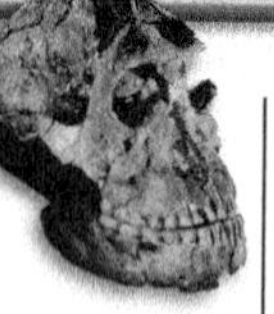

4–5 million Early humanlike creatures called Australopithecus develop in Africa.

5 MILLION YEARS AGO

2.6 million Hominids make the first stone tools.

Introduce the Chapter

At Level

Focus on the Stone Age

1. Ask students to describe ways in which Stone Age people are shown today in movies, comic strips, television programs, video games, or other media. List students' suggestions for the class to see.
2. Discuss whether these productions show early peoples as stupid or smart, capable or clumsy, aggressive or peaceful.
3. Then challenge students to consider how well they would do if they faced the same challenges that Stone Age peoples faced.
4. Point out that in this chapter, students will learn that early peoples developed remarkable skills in order to survive. **LS Verbal/Linguistic**

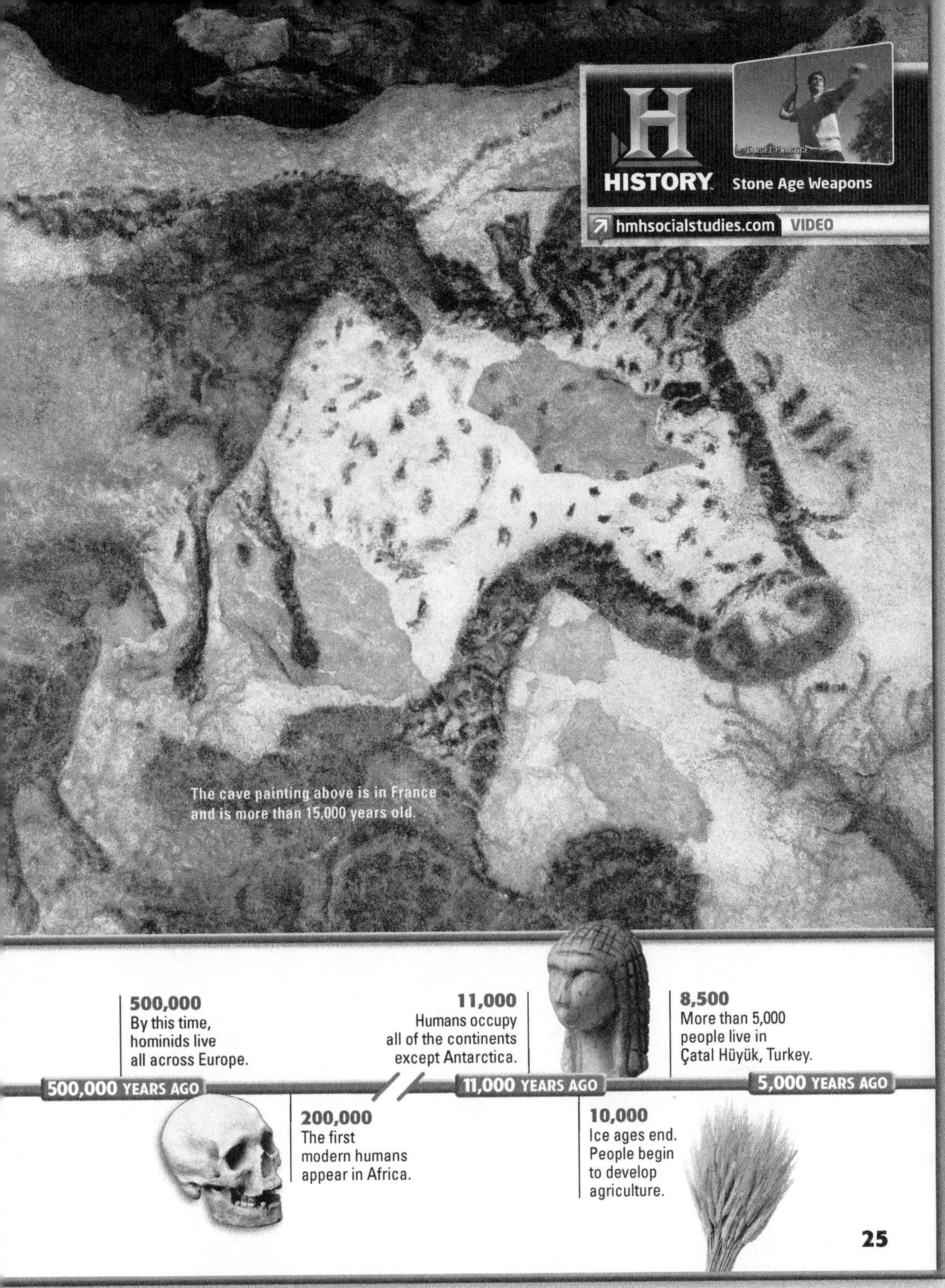
HISTORY
Stone Age Weapons
hmhsocialstudies.com VIDEO
500,000
By this time, hominids live all across Europe.
500,000 YEARS AGO
200,000
The first modern humans appear in Africa.
11,000
Humans occupy all of the continents except Antarctica.
11,000 YEARS AGO
10,000
Ice ages end. People begin to develop agriculture.
8,500
More than 5,000 people live in Çatal Hüyük, Turkey.
5,000 YEARS AGO
25

The cave painting above is in France and is more than 15,000 years old.

Chapter Preview

Explore the Picture

Lascaux Cave Paintings The paintings shown at left are in a cave in France. They were created 17,000 to 15,000 years ago. Some 600 painted and drawn animals adorn the walls of this cave. Four teenage boys discovered the cave by accident in 1940, and the site was opened to the public in 1948. Because they were exposed to artificial lighting, damp air, and people, the paintings began to deteriorate. In 1963 the cave was closed to the public. A partial replica was created and made available to tourists.

Analyzing Visuals What details can you identify in the paintings of the animals? *possible answers—spots on the cow, horse's mane*

hmhsocialstudies.com
Teacher Resources

Explore the Time Line

1. About when did the first modern humans appear in Africa? *200,000 years ago*
2. When did the Ice Ages end? *10,000 years ago*
3. About how many years passed between the end of the Ice Ages and Çatal Hüyük's growth into a large town? *1,500 years*
4. Why does the time line have breaks in it? *because it covers such a long period of time that it would take up several pages otherwise*

MISCONCEPTION ALERT

Multiple Ice Ages Some students may be under the impression that there was just one long period when the ice sheets advanced. Explain to students that there were several ice ages, however; these periods of glacial action date back hundreds of millions of years. Some scientists think that eventually we will enter another Ice Age.

Reading Social Studies

Understanding Themes

Introduce the themes of this chapter by asking students to imagine that it is thousands of years ago, and they live in a very small group in the wilderness. Their group is responsible for finding its own food, making its own clothing, building its own shelters, and protecting itself. Ask students what kind of geography would best be suited for survival. Have students describe the type of society and culture that might develop in these circumstances.

Chronological Order

Focus on Reading Ask each student to write one or two paragraphs that summarize their typical school day. Have students write their summaries in chronological order, from the time they wake up in the morning until they go to sleep. Ask students to exchange summaries. Have each student circle words or phrases they find that signal chronological order. Then have students use those words to create a sequence chain that tracks the events of a typical day.

Reading Social Studies

Economics | Geography | Politics | Religion | Society and Culture | Science and Technology

Focus on Themes In this chapter you will learn about the earliest humans and how they lived. You will read about scientists who work constantly to learn more about this mysterious time. As you read, you will see the beginnings of human **society and culture**—the making of tools, the use of fire, and the creation of language. You will also read about the **geography** of the world and how it shaped where and how early people lived.

Chronological Order

Focus on Reading History, just our like our lives, can be seen as a series of events in time. To understand history and events, we often need to see how they are related in time.

Understanding Chronological Order The word **chronological** means "related to time." Events discussed in this history book are discussed in **sequence**, in the order in which they happened. To understand history better, you can use a sequence chain to take notes about events in the order they happened.

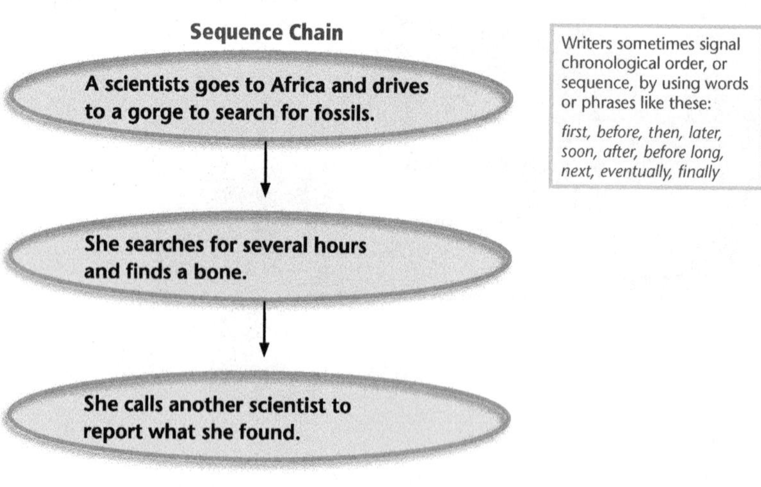

Sequence Chain
A scientists goes to Africa and drives to a gorge to search for fossils.
She searches for several hours and finds a bone.
She calls another scientist to report what she found.
Writers sometimes signal chronological order, or sequence, by using words or phrases like these:
first, before, then, later, soon, after, before long, next, eventually, finally

Reading and Skills Resources

Reading Support

- Guided Reading Workbook
- Student Edition on Audio CD
- Spanish Chapter Summaries Audio CD Program

Social Studies Skills Support

- Interactive Skills Tutor CD-ROM

Vocabulary Support

- **CRF:** Vocabulary Builder Activities
- **CRF:** Chapter Review Activity
- Differentiated Instruction Modified Worksheets and Tests CD-ROM:
  - Vocabulary Flash Cards
  - Vocabulary Builder Activity
  - Chapter Review Activity

TOS Holt McDougal PuzzleView

You Try It!

The following passage is from the chapter you are about to read. Read the sentences carefully and think about order of events.

Scientists Study Remains

From Chapter 2, pages 28–29

One archaeologist who made important discoveries about prehistory was Mary Leakey. In 1959 she found bones in East Africa that were more than 1.5 million years old. She and her husband, Louis Leakey, believed that the bones belonged to a hominid, an early ancestor of humans . . .

In 1974 anthropologist Donald Johanson found the bones of another early ancestor . . . Johanson named his find Lucy. Tests showed that she lived more than 3 million years ago . . .

In 1994 anthropologist Tim White found even older remains. He believes that the hominid he found may have lived as long as 4.4 million years ago.

After you read the sentences, answer the following questions.

1. Complete the time line below with information about scientists from the passage you just read?

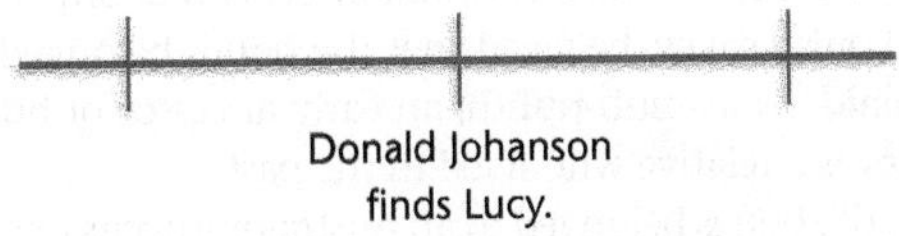
Donald Johanson
finds Lucy.

2. Each of the scientists discussed in the passage found the bones of people who lived at different times. Make another time line that shows the order in which these people lived. What do you notice about this order compared to the order in which the bones were found?

Key Terms and People

Chapter 2

Section 1
prehistory *(p. 28)*
hominid *(p. 28)*
ancestor *(p. 28)*
tool *(p. 30)*
Paleolithic Era *(p. 31)*
society *(p. 33)*
hunter-gatherers *(p. 33)*

Section 2
migrate *(p. 36)*
ice ages *(p. 36)*
land bridge *(p. 36)*
Mesolithic Era *(p. 38)*

Section 3
Neolithic Era *(p. 41)*
domestication *(p. 41)*
agriculture *(p. 42)*
megaliths *(p. 42)*

Academic Vocabulary

Success in school is related to knowing academic vocabulary—the words that are frequently used in school assignments and discussions. In this chapter, you will learn the following academic words:

distribute *(p. 33)*
development *(p. 42)*

As you read Chapter 2, look for words that indicate the order in which events occurred.

Reading Social Studies

Key Terms and People

Preteach these words by instructing students to create a time line. Have them list on the time line *Paleolithic Era, Mesolithic Era,* and *Neolithic Era.* Write the key terms for the class to see, mixing up the order in which they appear in the chapter. Have students select the terms that they believe represent each era and write these terms under the appropriate era. Discuss the meanings of each term with the students. Then have students correct their time lines, placing the key terms under the appropriate era. **LS Verbal/Linguistic**

Focus on Reading

See the **Focus on Reading** questions in this chapter for more practice on this reading social studies skill.

Reading Social Studies Assessment

See the **Chapter Review** at the end of this chapter for student assessment questions related to this reading skill.

Teaching Tip

To help students understand the larger context of world history chronology, have them keep a world time line that identifies the various civilizations and cultures and lists what events happened at what time. You might even post a large world time line for students to see. As the class covers different events, add them to the time line.

Answers

You Try It! 1. *1959, Mary Leakey finds bones in East Africa; 1974, Donald Johanson finds Lucy, 1994, Tim White finds hominid remains.* **2.** *possible answer—technology has improved with time, making it possible to judge the age of remains or to locate bones;* **3.** *remains found by Tim White, 4.4 million years old; Lucy, 3 million years old; bones found by Mary Leakey, 1.5 million years old*

Preteach

Bellringer

If YOU were there. . . Use the **Daily Bellringer Transparency** to help students answer the question.

Daily Bellringer Transparency, Section 1

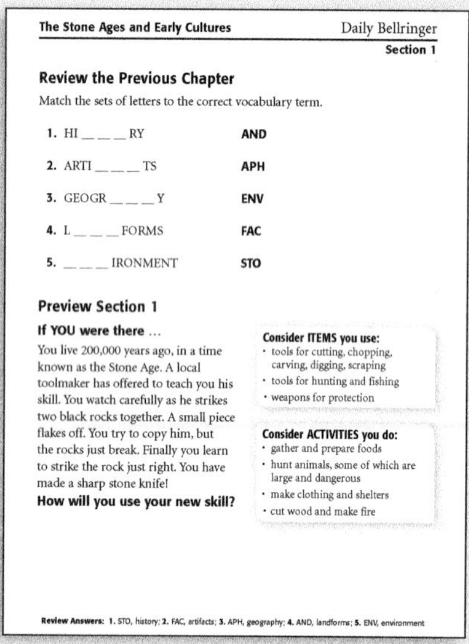

The Stone Ages and Early Cultures Daily Bellringer

Section 1

Review the Previous Chapter

Match the sets of letters to the correct vocabulary term.

1. HI ___ RY	**AND**
2. ARTI ___ TS	**APH**
3. GEOGR ___ Y	**ENV**
4. L ___ FORMS	**FAC**
5. ___ IRONMENT	**STO**

Preview Section 1

If YOU were there ...

You live 200,000 years ago, in a time known as the Stone Age. A local toolmaker has offered to teach you his skill. You watch carefully as he strikes two black rocks together. A small piece flakes off. You try to copy him, but the rocks just break. Finally you learn to strike the rock just right. You have made a sharp stone knife!

How will you use your new skill?

Consider ITEMS you use:
- tools for cutting, chopping, carving, digging, scraping
- tools for hunting and fishing
- weapons for protection

Consider ACTIVITIES you do:
- gather and prepare foods
- hunt animals, some of which are large and dangerous
- make clothing and shelters
- cut wood and make fire

Review Answers: **1.** STO, history; **2.** FAC, artifacts; **3.** APH, geography; **4.** AND, landforms; **5.** ENV, environment

Academic Vocabulary

Review with students the high-use academic term in this section.

distribute to divide among a group of people (p. 33)

CRF: Vocabulary Builder Activity, Section 1

Taking Notes

Have students use the graphic organizer online to take notes on the section. This activity will prepare students for the Section Assessment, in which they will complete a graphic organizer that builds on the information using the Critical Thinking Skill: Evaluating.

SECTION 1

The First People

What You Will Learn...

Main Ideas

1. Scientists study the remains of early humans to learn about prehistory.
2. Hominids and early humans first appeared in East Africa millions of years ago.
3. Stone Age tools grew more complex as time passed.
4. Hunter-gatherer societies developed language, art, and religion.

The Big Idea

Prehistoric people learned to adapt to their environment, to make simple tools, to use fire, and to use language.

Key Terms

prehistory, *p. 28*
hominid, *p. 28*
ancestor, *p. 28*
tool, *p. 30*
Paleolithic Era, *p. 31*
society, *p. 33*
hunter-gatherers, *p. 33*

hmhsocialstudies.com TAKING NOTES

Use the graphic organizer online to take notes on the advances made by prehistoric humans.

If YOU were there...

You live 200,000 years ago, in a time known as the Stone Age. A local toolmaker has offered to teach you his skill. You watch carefully as he strikes two black rocks together. A small piece flakes off. You try to copy him, but the rocks just break. Finally you learn to strike the rock just right. You have made a sharp stone knife!

How will you use your new skill?

BUILDING BACKGROUND Over millions of years early people learned many new things. Making stone tools was one of the earliest and most valuable skills that they developed. Scientists who study early humans learn a lot about them from the tools and other objects that they made.

Scientists Study Remains

Although humans have lived on the earth for more than a million years, writing was not invented until about 5,000 years ago. Historians call the time before there was writing **prehistory**. To study prehistory, historians rely on the work of archaeologists and anthropologists.

One archaeologist who made important discoveries about prehistory was Mary Leakey. In 1959 she found bones in East Africa that were more than 1.5 million years old. She and her husband, Louis Leakey, believed that the bones belonged to an early **hominid** (HAH-muh-nuhd), an early ancestor of humans. An **ancestor** is a relative who lived in the past.

In fact, the bones belonged to an Australopithecus (aw-stray-loh-PI-thuh-kuhs), one of the earliest ancestors of humans. In 1974 anthropologist Donald Johanson (joh-HAN-suhn) found bones from another early ancestor. He described his discovery:

> "We reluctantly headed back toward camp ... I glanced over my right shoulder. Light glinted off a bone. I knelt down for a closer look... Everywhere we looked on the slope around us we saw more bones lying on the surface."
>
> –Donald Johanson, from *Ancestors: In Search of Human Origins*

Teach the Big Idea

At Level

The First People

1. **Teach** Ask students the questions in the Main Idea boxes to teach this section.
2. **Apply** Ask each student to choose a time period from the section and to imagine that he or she lived during that time. Have students create drawings to show what daily life was like. Students should include topics such as available tools, food, and activities in their drawings. **LS Visual/Spatial**
3. **Review** Display and discuss the drawings.
4. **Practice/Homework** Ask students to imagine they are archaeologists who have discovered their drawings. Have each student write a paragraph about what an archaeologist might conclude about prehistoric life based on the drawings. Students should base the conclusions on the information in the section. **LS Verbal/Linguistic**

Alternative Assessment Handbook, Rubric 40: Writing to Describe

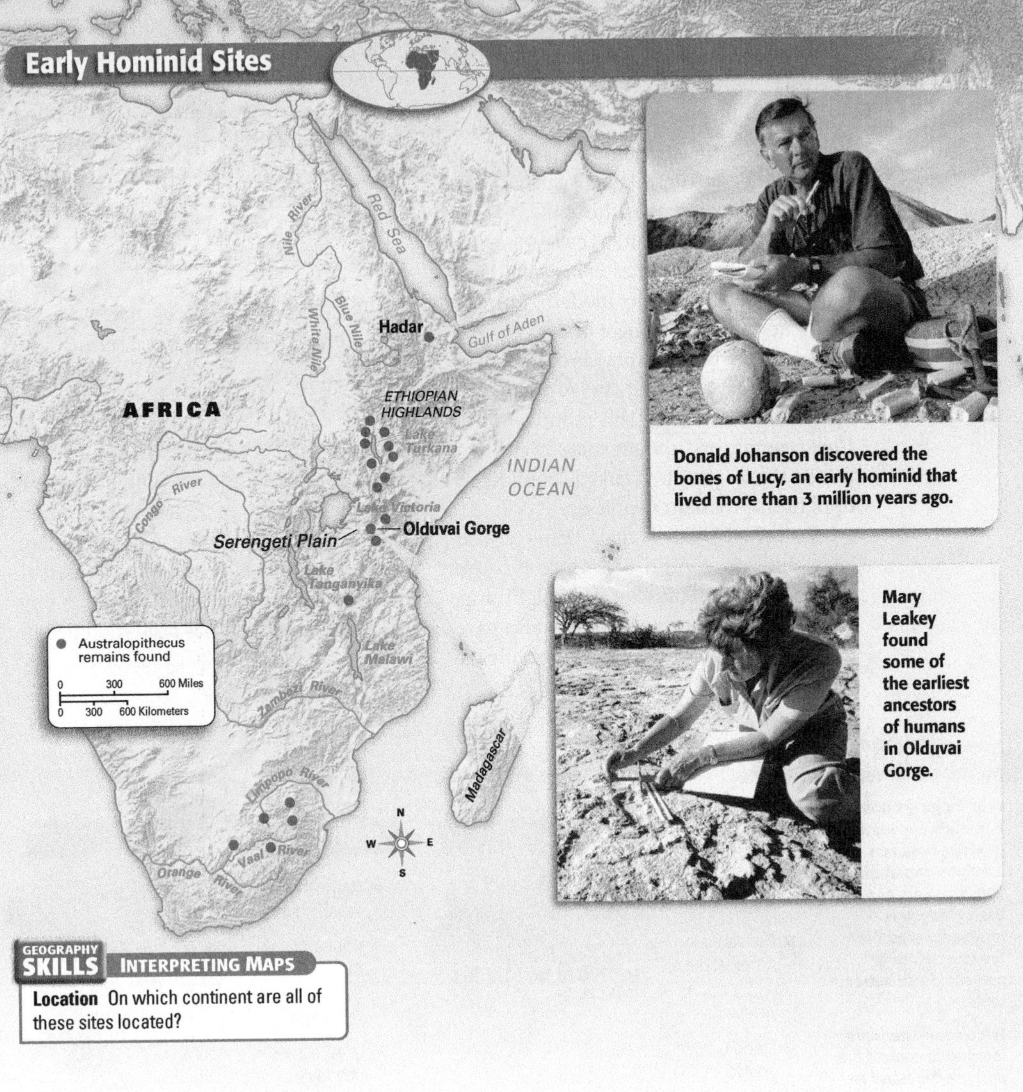

Donald Johanson discovered the bones of Lucy, an early hominid that lived more than 3 million years ago.

Mary Leakey found some of the earliest ancestors of humans in Olduvai Gorge.

GEOGRAPHY SKILLS INTERPRETING MAPS

Location On which continent are all of these sites located?

Johanson named his find Lucy. Tests showed that she lived more than 3 million years ago. Johanson could tell from her bones that she was small and had walked on two legs. The ability to walk on two legs was a key step in human development.

In 1994 anthropologist Tim White found even older remains. He believes that the hominid he found may have lived as long as 4.4 million years ago. But some scientists disagree with White's time estimate. Discoveries of ancient bones give us information about early humans and their ancestors, but not all scientists agree on the meaning of these discoveries.

READING CHECK **Drawing Inferences** What can ancient bones tell us about human ancestors?

Direct Teach

Main Idea

1 Scientists Study Remains

Scientists study the remains of early humans to learn about prehistory.

Recall What did Donald Johanson conclude by examining the bones of the hominid called Lucy? *that she was small and had walked on two legs*

Draw Conclusions What can the Leakeys' discoveries tell us about prehistory? *Hominids lived many years ago and were ancestors of humans.*

Make Judgments Why do you think some scientists do not agree that Tim White's discovery is 4.4 million years old? *It's difficult to determine the age of extremely old remains.*

- **CRF:** Biography Activity: Donald Johanson and Tim White
- **CRF:** Interdisciplinary Project: The First People: Flannel Board Story
- Map Transparency: Early Hominid Sites

hmhsocialstudies.com

Online Resources
Activity: Archaeology Article

Linking to Today

A Family Tradition Mary and Louis Leakey's granddaughter, Louise, is also an anthropologist. In 1999 Louise and her mother, Meave Leakey, discovered a 3.5-million-year-old fossil skull at a site in Kenya. Some scholars believe this fossil may represent another early hominid group.

Differentiating Instruction

English-Language Learners

Reaching Standards

1. Have students study the map shown on this page. Point out the map legend.
2. After students discuss the map, have them draw their own maps of Africa and create their own symbols for various features, such as bodies of water, mountain ranges, and early hominid sites. For example, students might draw a bone to represent a hominid site. In addition, students should provide a title and compass rose for their maps.
3. Call on volunteers to display their maps and explain their legends and symbols. **LS Visual/Spatial**

- Alternative Assessment Handbook, Rubric 20: Map Creation
- Map Transparency: Early Hominid Sites

Answers

Interpreting Maps *Africa*

Reading Check *They can teach us about human development and early human physical appearances.*

Direct Teach

Main Idea

❷ Hominids and Early Humans

Hominids and early humans first appeared in East Africa millions of years ago.

Recall When do many scientists believe the first modern humans appeared? *about 200,000 years ago*

Compare What characteristic did *Homo erectus* have that modern humans also have? *the ability to walk upright*

Make Inferences How did fire help protect *Homo erectus* from wild animals? *Animals were probably afraid of fire, so* Homo erectus *could use fire to keep dangerous animals away.*

Activity **Early Human Time Line** Have each student construct a time line showing when *Homo habilis, Homo erectus,* and *Homo sapiens* most likely first appeared.

- Alternative Assessment Handbook, Rubric 36: Time Lines
- **CRF:** Biography Activity: The Leakey Family
- Quick Facts Transparency: Early Hominids

hmhsocialstudies.com

Online Resources
Activity: Mary Leakey Sketch

Hominids and Early Humans

Later groups of hominids appeared about 3 million years ago. As time passed they became more like modern humans.

Focus on Reading
Dates in a text can help you keep events in order in your mind.

In the early 1960s Louis Leakey found hominid remains that he called *Homo habilis*, or "handy man." Leakey and his son Richard believed that *Homo habilis* was more closely related to modern humans than Lucy and had a larger brain.

Scientists believe that another group of hominids appeared in Africa about 1.5 million years ago. This group is called *Homo erectus*, or "upright man." Scientists think these people walked completely upright like modern people do.

Scientists believe that *Homo erectus* knew how to control fire. Once fire was started by natural causes, such as lightning, people used it to cook food. Fire also gave them heat and protection against animals.

Eventually hominids developed characteristics of modern humans. Scientists are not sure exactly when or where the first modern humans lived. Many think that they first appeared in Africa about 200,000 years ago. Scientists call these people *Homo sapiens*, or "wise man." Every person alive today belongs to this group.

Reading Check **Contrasting** How was *Homo erectus* different from *Homo habilis*?

Stone Age Tools

The first humans and their ancestors lived during a long period of time called the Stone Age. To help in their studies, archaeologists divide the Stone Age into three periods based on the kinds of tools used at the time. To archaeologists, a **tool** is any handheld object that has been modified to help a person accomplish a task.

Early Hominids — Quick Facts

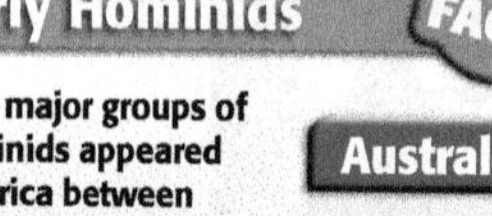

Four major groups of hominids appeared in Africa between 5 million and about 200,000 years ago. Each group was more advanced than the one before it and could use better tools.

Which early hominid learned to control fire and use the hand ax?

Australopithecus

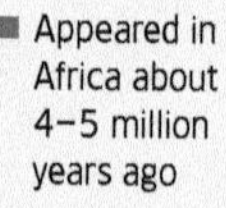

- Name means "southern ape"
- Appeared in Africa about 4–5 million years ago
- Stood upright and walked on two legs
- Brain was about one-third the size of modern humans

Homo habilis

- Name means "handy man"
- Appeared in Africa about 2.4 million years ago
- Used early stone tools for chopping and scraping
- Brain was about half the size of modern humans

An early Stone Age chopper

Critical Thinking: Drawing Inferences

Below Level

A Time Capsule

1. Review the definition of the word *tool*. Then discuss with students how discovering tools of our early ancestors helps us understand how early humans lived.
2. Ask students to propose three present-day tools that they would put in a time capsule to teach future generations about today's society. Discuss an example, such as a ballpoint pen, which tells later generations that we used writing.
3. Have students write short descriptions of what their items say about modern society.
4. Ask volunteers to read their lists and descriptions aloud. **LS Visual/Spatial**

- Alternative Assessment Handbook, Rubric 11: Discussions

Answers

Early Hominids *Homo erectus*

Reading Check *Unlike Homo habilis, Homo erectus walked completely upright and could control fire.*

The first part of the Stone Age is called the **Paleolithic** (pay-lee-uh-LI-thik) **Era**, or Old Stone Age. It lasted until about 10,000 years ago. During this time people used stone tools.

The First Tools

Scientists have found the oldest tools in Tanzania, a country in East Africa. These sharpened stones, about the size of an adult's fist, are about 2.6 million years old. Each stone had been struck with another rock to create a sharp, jagged edge along one side. This process left one unsharpened side that could be used as a handle.

Scientists think that these first tools were mostly used to process food. The sharp edge could be used to cut, chop, or scrape roots, bones, or meat. Tools like these, called choppers, were used for about 2 million years.

Later Tools

Over time people learned to make better tools. For example, they developed the hand ax. They often made this tool out of a mineral called flint. Flint is easy to shape, and tools made from it can be very sharp. People used hand axes to break tree limbs, to dig, and to cut animal hides.

People also learned to attach wooden handles to tools. By attaching a wooden shaft to a stone point, for example, they invented the spear. Because a spear could be thrown, hunters no longer had to stand close to animals they were hunting. As a result, people could hunt larger animals. Among the animals hunted by Stone Age people were deer, horses, bison, and elephantlike creatures called mammoths.

READING CHECK **Summarizing** How did tools improve during the Old Stone Age?

Homo erectus

- Name means "upright man"
- Appeared in Africa about 2–1.5 million years ago
- Used early stone tools like the hand ax
- Learned to control fire
- Migrated out of Africa to Asia and Europe

A hand ax

Homo sapiens

- Name means "wise man"
- Appeared in Africa about 200,000 years ago
- Migrated around the world
- Same species as modern human beings
- Learned to create fire and use a wide variety of tools
- Developed language

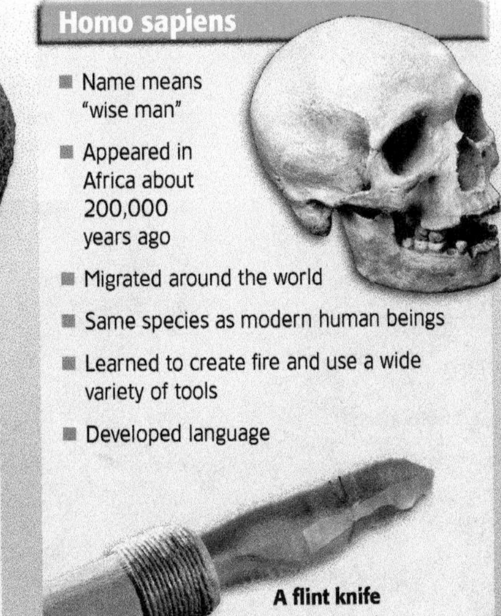

A flint knife

Direct Teach

Main Idea

❸ Stone Age Tools

Stone Age tools grew more complex as time passed.

Define How did people make the tools we call choppers? *They struck one stone with another to create a sharp, jagged edge on one side of the chopper.*

Recall Where have the oldest stone tools been found? *Tanzania, in East Africa*

Make Inferences Why do you think hunters with spear-throwers could hunt larger animals? *They didn't need to get as close to the large, dangerous animals.*

Connect to Science

Carbon-14 Dating One of the most common techniques for measuring the age of human remains is called carbon-14 dating. This technique can date organic matter, or matter that used to be alive, that ranges from several hundred years old to about 50,000 years old. To date such materials, scientists measure how much of a type of carbon, carbon-14, in the object has decayed to become nitrogen-14—a process that happens at a regular, measurable rate.

Critical Thinking: Making Predictions

Above Level

Chance and Early People

1. Point out that chance has played a big role in history: in countless instances, events could have happened very differently, but a small incident changed everything.
2. Pair students, and have each pair propose a scenario in which chance could have affected an invention of early humans. Have pairs create brief skits to illustrate the chosen incidents.
3. Call on volunteers to present their skits or discuss their suggested scenarios.
4. Conclude by leading a discussion about the false starts that may have preceded the major steps forward made by early humans. For example, if an early toolmaker cut himself badly making a stone tool, perhaps he would not try to make another.

Alternative Assessment Handbook, Rubric 33: Skits and Reader's Theater

Answers

Reading Check *People learned to use flint to make tools and to attach wooden handles to the tools.*

Direct Teach

History Close-up

Hunter-Gatherers

1. Have students examine the images on this page. Discuss with students what life may have been like for the early hunter-gatherers.
2. Next, have students identify the various activities shown in the illustration. *hunting, painting on cave walls, cooking, gathering food, making tools*
3. Ask students to name some hardships that early hunter-gatherers faced, as suggested by the picture. *possible answers—limited protection from bad weather, limited food supply, had to rely on nearby resources since they only traveled on foot, dangerous animals* LS **Visual/Spatial**

Linking to Today

A New View of Hunter-Gatherers A site in central Texas now shows that some prehistoric people led a fairly settled life. At the 40-acre site, thick layers of earth blackened by cooking fires and countless stone flakes and tools indicate that people had settled there for thousands of years. Other evidence tells archaeologists that a wide range of plants and animals were available in the region. Because there was also a steady water supply along with the food sources, people could stay there for long periods of time instead of moving from place to place.

History Close-up

Hunter-Gatherers

Early people were hunter-gatherers. They hunted animals and gathered wild plants to survive. Life for these hunter-gatherers was difficult and dangerous. Still, people learned how to make tools, use fire, and even create art.

Hunting
Most hunting was done by men. They worked together to bring down large animals.
Art
People painted herds of animals on cave walls.
Gathering
Most gathering was done by women. They gathered food like wild plants, seeds, fruits, and nuts.
Fire
People learned to use fire to cook their food.
Tools
Early people learned to make tools such as this spear for hunting.
ANALYSIS SKILL ANALYZING VISUALS
What tools are people using in this picture?

Critical Thinking: Comparing and Contrasting

At Level

Creating a Venn Diagram

1. Have students examine the picture on this page, paying close attention to the roles that men and women may have played as hunter-gatherers.
2. Draw an example of a Venn diagram for students to see. Use the following labels: *Men's Chores, Women's Chores, Shared Chores.*
3. Next, have students copy the diagram and complete it by using the information shown in the illustration.
4. Review the answers students listed in their Venn diagrams as a class. LS **Visual/Spatial**

Alternative Assessment Handbook, Rubric 13: Graphic Organizers

Answers

Analyzing Visuals *spears*

Hunter-gatherer Societies

As early humans developed tools and new hunting techniques, they formed societies. A **society** is a community of people who share a common culture. These societies developed cultures with languages, religions, and art.

Society

Anthropologists believe that early humans lived in small groups. In bad weather they might have taken shelter in a cave if there was one nearby. When food or water became hard to find, groups of people would have to move to new areas.

The early humans of the Stone Age were **hunter-gatherers**—people who hunt animals and gather wild plants, seeds, fruits, and nuts to survive. Anthropologists believe that most Stone Age hunters were men. They hunted in groups, sometimes chasing entire herds of animals over cliffs. This method was both more productive and safer than hunting alone.

Women in hunter-gatherer societies probably took responsibility for collecting plants to eat. They likely stayed near camps and took care of children.

Language, Art, and Religion

The most important development of early Stone Age culture was language. Scientists have many theories about why language first developed. Some think it was to make hunting in groups easier. Others think it developed as a way for people to form relationships. Still others think language made it easier for people to resolve issues like how to **distribute** food.

Language wasn't the only way early people expressed themselves. They also created art. People carved figures out of stone, ivory, and bone. They painted and carved images of people and animals on cave walls. Scientists still aren't sure why people made art. Perhaps the cave paintings were used to teach people how to hunt, or maybe they had religious meanings.

ACADEMIC VOCABULARY
distribute to divide among a group of people

LINKING TO TODAY

Stone Tools

Did you know that Stone Age people's tools weren't as primitive as we might think? They made knife blades and arrowheads—like the one shown below—out of volcanic glass called obsidian. The obsidian blades were very sharp. In fact, they could be 100 times sharper and smoother than the steel blades used for surgery in modern hospitals.

Today some doctors are going back to using these Stone Age materials. They have found that blades made from obsidian are more precise than modern scalpels. Some doctors use obsidian blades for delicate surgery on the face because the stone tools leave "nicer-looking" scars.

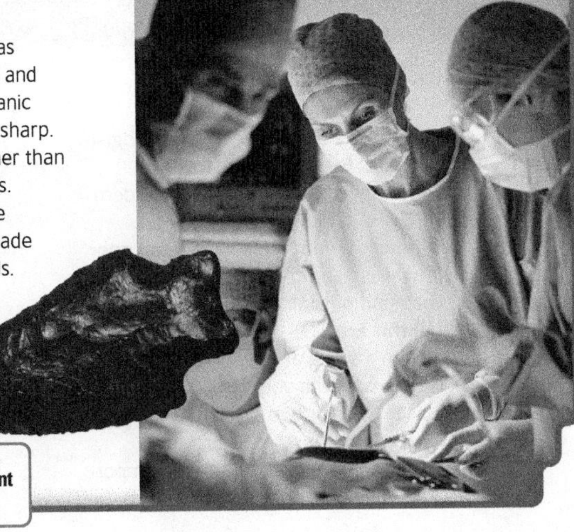

ANALYSIS SKILL ANALYZING INFORMATION

How do you think modern obsidian blades are different from Stone Age ones?

Direct Teach

Main Idea

4 Hunter-gatherer Societies

Hunter-gatherer societies developed language, art, and religion.

Define Who were hunter-gatherers? *early humans who hunted animals and gathered wild plants to survive*

Summarize How did early humans express themselves? *through language and art*

Draw Conclusions Why do you think hunting in groups was safer than hunting alone? *Groups offered protection against dangerous animals.*

CRF: Literature Activity: Boy of the Painted Cave

CRF: Primary Source Activity: The Discovery of Chauvet Cave

Did you know . . .

Early humans used natural dyes from different colors of plants and berries to paint images on cave walls.

Checking for Understanding

True or False Answer each statement *T* if it is true or *F* if it is false. If false, explain why.

1. Historians use the term *prehistory* to refer to the time before there was writing. *T*
2. Scientists think the first tools were developed to use as weapons. *F; think they were developed to process food.*
3. An important development of *Homo erectus* was the ability to control fire. *T*

Collaborative Learning

At Level

Communicating Without Words

Materials: index cards

1. Discuss with students why language was so important to human development.
2. Organize students into pairs. Give one member of each pair a card with the sentence "I am thirsty." on it. Give the other student a card with the sentence "The rains washed away our food." Tell the students not to reveal what is written on their cards.
3. Have one member of each pair try to express what is on the card to the other student without using words. Students can use drawings or body language to make themselves understood. Then have the other student try to express his or her statement.
4. After the activity, ask students to share how successful they were. What frustrations did they experience? Then lead a discussion about the ease or difficulty of communicating without words.

LS Interpersonal, Kinesthetic, Verbal/Linguistic

Alternative Assessment Handbook, Rubric 14: Group Activity

Answers

Linking to Today *They are more precise than modern scalpels and leave "nicer-looking" scars.*

Direct Teach

Info to Know

More Than a Pretty Picture Some cave paintings show not just animals that people hunted but also how predator animals hunted their own prey. For example, 32,000-year-old paintings in a Chauvet cave in France show now-extinct lions watching a herd of bison. The way the painter drew the lions with their heads down and their ears back shows that the artist had carefully observed the lions' behavior. In Africa today, lions pose the same way before rushing at their prey.

CRF: Primary Source Activity: The Discovery of Chauvet Cave

Review & Assess

Close

Have students summarize the important developments of hunter-gatherer societies covered in this section.

Review

Online Quiz, Section 1

Assess

SE Section 1 Assessment

PASS: Section 1 Quiz

Alternative Assessment Handbook

Reteach/Classroom Intervention

Guided Reading Workbook, Section 1

Interactive Skills Tutor CD-ROM

Cave Paintings
Thousands of years ago, early people decorated cave walls with paintings like this one. No one knows for sure why people created cave paintings, but many historians think they were related to hunting.

Why do you think this cave painting may be connected to hunting?

Scholars know little about the religious beliefs of early people. Archaeologists have found graves that included food and artifacts. Many scientists think these discoveries are proof that the first human religions developed during the Stone Age.

READING CHECK **Analyzing** What was one possible reason for the development of language?

SUMMARY AND PREVIEW Scientists have discovered and studied the remains of hominids and early humans who lived in East Africa millions of years ago. These Stone Age people were hunter-gatherers who used fire, stone tools, and language. In the next section you will learn how early humans moved out of Africa and populated the world.

Section 1 Assessment

hmhsocialstudies.com ONLINE QUIZ

Reviewing Ideas, Terms, and People

1. a. **Identify** Who found the bones of Lucy?
   b. **Explain** Why do historians need archaeologists and anthropologists to study **prehistory**?
2. a. **Recall** What is the scientific name for modern humans?
   b. **Make Inferences** What might have been one advantage of walking completely upright?
3. a. **Recall** What kind of **tools** did people use during the **Paleolithic Era**?
   b. **Design** Design a stone and wood tool you could use to help you with your chores. Describe your tool in a sentence or two.
4. a. **Define** What is a **hunter-gatherer**?
   b. **Rank** In your opinion, what was the most important change brought by the development of language?

Critical Thinking

5. **Evaluate** Review the notes in your chart on the advances made by prehistoric humans. Using a graphic organizer like the one here, rank the three advances you think are most important. Next to your organizer, write a sentence explaining why you ranked the advances in that order.

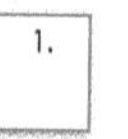

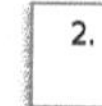

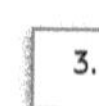

Focus on Writing

6. **Listing Stone Age Achievements** Look back through this section and make a list of important Stone Age achievements. Which of these will you include on your storyboard? How will you illustrate them?

Section 1 Assessment Answers

1. a. Donald Johanson
   b. because there are no written records from the earliest times of human development
2. a. *Homo sapiens*
   b. possible answers—Humans could use their hands, see farther, and perhaps travel faster.
3. a. stone choppers, axes, and spears
   b. Students' tools will vary, but descriptions should be logical.
4. a. a person who hunts animals and gathers wild plants, seeds, fruits, and nuts to survive
   b. possible answers—improved hunting; relationships formed; could more easily solve problems, such as how to distribute food
5. Rankings will vary, but students should justify their answers.
6. Lists and storyboards will vary, but students should support their selections.

Answers

Cave Paintings *shows animals that may have provided meat, hides, and other resources*

Reading Check *made it easier to hunt as a group, distribute food, and establish relationships*

BIOGRAPHY

The Iceman

The Iceman's dagger and the scabbard, or case, he carried it in

Why was a Stone Age traveler in Europe's highest mountains?

When did he live? about 5,300 years ago

Where did he live? The frozen body of the Iceman was discovered in the snowy Ötztal Alps of Italy in 1991. Scientists nicknamed him Ötzi after this location.

What did he do? That question has been debated ever since Ötzi's body was found. Apparently, he was traveling. At first scientists thought he had frozen to death in a storm. But an arrowhead found in his shoulder suggests that his death was not so peaceful. After he died, his body was covered by glaciers and preserved for thousands of years.

Why is he important? Ötzi is the oldest mummified human ever found in such good condition. His body, clothing, and tools were extremely well preserved, telling us a lot about life during the Stone Ages. His outfit was made of three types of animal skin stitched together. He wore leather shoes padded with grass, a grass cape, a fur hat, and a sort of backpack. He carried an ax with a copper blade as well as a bow and arrows.

Drawing Conclusions Why do you think the Iceman was in the Alps?

Scientists examine the Iceman's body in 1991, before it was removed from the glacier.

Biography

Reading Focus Question

Have students consider the basic needs of a person in the Stone Age, such as needs for food and shelter. Ask: What needs might this man have been trying to fill by climbing in the mountains? *possible answers—hunting, looking for materials to make clothing or shelter*

Did You Know . . .

The Iceman may have been hungry when he died. Scientists determined from studying a portion of the Iceman's intestine that he had not eaten within eight hours of his death.

About the Illustration

This illustration of the Iceman is an artist's conception based on available sources. However, historians are uncertain exactly what the Iceman looked like.

Answers

Drawing Conclusions *possible answers—He may have been hunting, escaping from the person or persons who may have killed him, or he could have been exiled from his people.*

Differentiating Instruction

Advanced/Gifted and Talented

Above Level | Research Required

1. Remind students that the Iceman's body was undiscovered for thousands of years. Only when surrounding ice had melted did climbers see the body.
2. Point out that archaeological sites both small and large are still being discovered. On the other hand, some sites are being destroyed. Warfare and rising waters from dam construction are two of the most common causes of this destruction.
3. Organize the class into two large groups—one to research recently discovered archaeological sites and the other to research sites that are being destroyed. Then have each group organize into smaller groups to conduct further research on individual sites within the two broad categories.
4. Ask each small group to prepare a presentation on its chosen site. Students should discuss what information the site may provide or has provided and its current condition. Encourage students to use visual aids to enhance their presentations.

Alternative Assessment Handbook, Rubrics 29: Presentations; and 30: Research

Preteach

Bellringer

If YOU were there. . . Use the **Daily Bellringer Transparency** to help students answer the question.

Daily Bellringer Transparency, Section 2

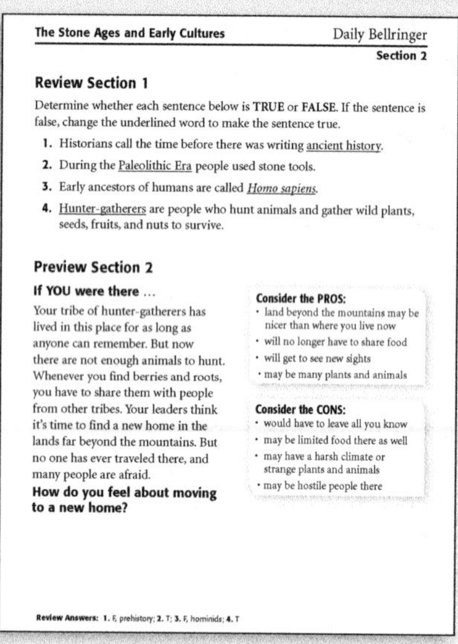

The Stone Ages and Early Cultures — Daily Bellringer — Section 2

Review Section 1

Determine whether each sentence below is TRUE or FALSE. If the sentence is false, change the underlined word to make the sentence true.

1. Historians call the time before there was writing ancient history.
2. During the Paleolithic Era people used stone tools.
3. Early ancestors of humans are called *Homo sapiens*.
4. Hunter-gatherers are people who hunt animals and gather wild plants, seeds, fruits, and nuts to survive.

Preview Section 2

If YOU were there ...

Your tribe of hunter-gatherers has lived in this place for as long as anyone can remember. But now there are not enough animals to hunt. Whenever you find berries and roots, you have to share them with people from other tribes. Your leaders think it's time to find a new home in the lands far beyond the mountains. But no one has ever traveled there, and many people are afraid.

How do you feel about moving to a new home?

Consider the PROS:
- land beyond the mountains may be nicer than where you live now
- will no longer have to share food
- will get to see new sights
- may be many plants and animals

Consider the CONS:
- would have to leave all you know
- may be limited food there as well
- may have a harsh climate or strange plants and animals
- may be hostile people there

Review Answers: 1. F, prehistory; 2. T; 3. F, hominids; 4. T

Building Vocabulary

Preteach or review the following terms:

environment all the living and nonliving things that affect life in an area (p. 38)

pottery dishes and other vessels made from clay (p. 39)

CRF: Vocabulary Builder Activity, Section 2

Taking Notes

Have students use the graphic organizer online to take notes on the section. This activity will prepare students for the Section Assessment, in which they will complete a graphic organizer that builds on the information using the Critical Thinking Skill: Sequencing.

SECTION 2

Early Human Migration

What You Will Learn...

Main Ideas

1. People moved out of Africa as the earth's climates changed.
2. People adapted to new environments by making clothing and new types of tools.

The Big Idea

As people migrated around the world they learned to adapt to new environments.

Key Terms

migrate, *p. 36*
ice ages, *p. 36*
land bridge, *p. 36*
Mesolithic Era, *p. 38*

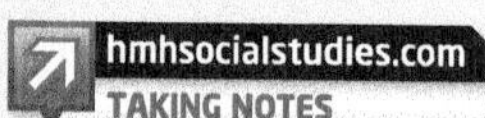

Use the graphic organizer online to take notes on the sequence and paths of migration of early humans.

If YOU were there...

Your tribe of hunter-gatherers has lived in this place for as long as anyone can remember. But now there are not enough animals to hunt. Whenever you find berries and roots, you have to share them with people from other tribes. Your leaders think it's time to find a new home in the lands far beyond the mountains. But no one has ever traveled there, and many people are afraid.

How do you feel about moving to a new home?

BUILDING BACKGROUND From their beginnings in East Africa, early humans moved in many directions. Eventually, they lived on almost every continent in the world. People probably had many reasons for moving. One reason was a change in the climate.

People Move Out of Africa

During the Old Stone Age, climate patterns around the world changed, transforming the earth's geography. In response to these changes, people began to **migrate**, or move, to new places.

The Ice Ages

Most scientists believe that about 1.6 million years ago, many places around the world began to experience long periods of freezing weather. These freezing times are called the **ice ages**. The ice ages ended about 10,000 years ago.

During the ice ages huge sheets of ice covered much of the earth's land. These ice sheets were formed from ocean water, leaving ocean levels lower than they are now. Many areas that are now underwater were dry land then. For example, a narrow body of water now separates Asia and North America. But scientists think that during the ice ages, the ocean level dropped and exposed a **land bridge**, a strip of land connecting two continents. Land bridges allowed Stone Age peoples to migrate around the world.

Teach the Big Idea

At Level

Early Human Migration

1. **Teach** Ask students the questions in the Main Idea boxes to teach this section.
2. **Apply** Organize students into small groups. Ask students to imagine that flooding has forced them to move from dwellings near a river to a colder, mountainous, and rocky environment. Have groups write down ways they could adapt to and survive in this new environment.
LS Interpersonal, Logical/Mathematical
3. **Review** Have volunteers from each group share their suggestions.
4. **Practice/Homework** Have each student write a short journal entry about this imaginary trek from one environment to another, including how people eventually settled in the new environment.
LS Verbal/Linguistic

Alternative Assessment Handbook, Rubric 15: Journals

hmhsocialstudies.com
ANIMATED HISTORY

Early Human Migration

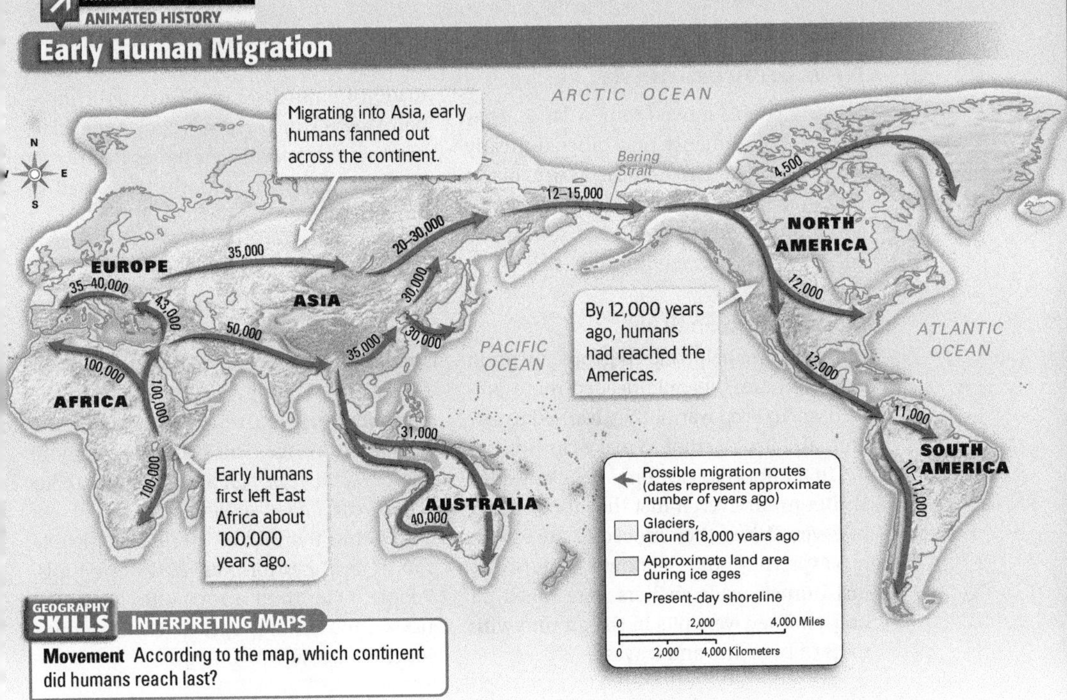

GEOGRAPHY SKILLS INTERPRETING MAPS

Movement According to the map, which continent did humans reach last?

Settling New Lands

Scientists agree that migration around the world took hundreds of thousands of years. Early hominids, the ancestors of modern humans, migrated from Africa to Asia as early as 2 million years ago. From there, they spread to Southeast Asia and Europe.

Later, humans also began to migrate around the world, and earlier hominids died out. Look at the map to see the dates and routes of early human migration.

Humans began to migrate from East Africa to southern Africa and southwestern Asia around 100,000 years ago. From there, people moved east across southern Asia. They could then migrate to Australia. Scientists are not sure exactly how the first people reached Australia. Even though ocean levels were lower then, there was always open sea between Asia and Australia.

From southwestern Asia, humans also migrated north into Europe. Geographic features such as high mountains and cold temperatures delayed migration northward into northern Asia. Eventually, however, people from both Europe and southern Asia moved into that region.

From northern Asia, people moved into North America. Scientists disagree on when and how the first people arrived in North America. Most scholars think people must have crossed a land bridge from Asia to North America. Once in North America, these people moved south, following herds of animals and settling South America. By 9000 BC, humans lived on all continents of the world except Antarctica.

READING CHECK **Analyzing** How did the ice ages influence human migration?

Direct Teach

Main Idea

❶ People Move Out of Africa

People moved out of Africa as the earth's climates changed.

Explain How may Stone Age people have crossed from Asia to North America? *by using a land bridge*

Recall What was one problem that made migrating to northern Asia difficult? *possible answers—high mountains, cold temperatures*

Predict What kind of evidence could provide more information about how people reached Australia? *possible answer—dateable remains of boats that showed people could have crossed open water*

Map Transparency: Early Human Migration

Info To Know

Homo Floresiensis In 2004 archaeologists reported the discovery of a new human species' remains. The bones were found on Flores Island in Indonesia. Called *Homo floresiensis,* this hominid lived as recently as 12,000 years ago. Standing only three feet tall, *Homo floresiensis* was probably related closely to *Homo erectus.* Scientists believe that *Homo erectus* may have migrated to Flores Island by boat and evolved into the smaller species. Such a difficult feat suggests that *Homo erectus* was more intelligent than previously thought.

Critical Thinking: Comparing

Above Level

Migration Throughout History

1. Explain that there are two types of migration—voluntary (to search for better opportunities) and forced (to escape climate changes, war, or other problems).
2. Lead a discussion about whether the migration of early humans was voluntary or forced. *possible answer—either, depending on local circumstances*
3. Have students work in pairs to write one or more verses to a song that early peoples could have sung as they migrated to new lands. Songs should tell about the circumstances of the group's migration. Suggest that students write lyrics to go with a popular or familiar tune.
4. Call on volunteers to perform their songs for the class. **LS Auditory/Musical**

Alternative Assessment Handbook, Rubric 26: Poems and Songs

Answers

Interpreting Maps *South America*

Reading Check *allowed people to cross to the Americas on a land bridge*

Direct Teach

Main Idea

❷ People Adapt to New Environments

People adapted to new environments by making clothing and new types of tools.

Explain Why did early humans build shelters? *because they migrated to colder climates*

Recall What types of shelters did early people use? *caves; when no caves available—pit houses, tents, or structures of wood, stone, clay, or other materials*

Elaborate How did new techniques change the daily lives of Middle Stone Age people? *Hooks, fishing spears, bows and arrows, canoes, and pottery enabled people to find new food sources, store various goods, and travel by water. Keeping dogs helped people hunt more efficiently and warned people of dangerous animals or intruders.*

Info to Know

A Third Theory Some archaeologists propose another origin for the first Americans—Europe. This theory says that early Europeans braved the North Atlantic in boats that may have been like those made by modern Arctic Inuit peoples. Similar spear points have been found in Europe and the Americas, which led some archaeologists to develop the new theory.

People Adapt to New Environments

As early people moved to new lands, they found environments that differed greatly from those in East Africa. Many places were much colder and had strange plants and animals. Early people had to learn to adapt to their new environments.

Clothing and Shelter

Although fire helped keep people warm in very cold areas, people needed more protection. To keep warm, they learned to sew animal skins together to make clothing.

In addition to clothing, people needed shelter to survive. At first they took shelter in caves. When they moved to areas with no caves, they built their own shelters. The first human-made shelters were called pit houses. They were pits in the ground with roofs of branches and leaves.

Later, people began to build homes above the ground. Some lived in tents made of animal skins. Others built more permanent structures of wood, stone, clay, or other materials. Even bones from large animals such as mammoths were used in building shelters.

New Tools and Technologies

People also adapted to new environments with new types of tools. These tools were smaller and more complex than tools from the Old Stone Age. They defined the **Mesolithic** (me-zuh-LI-thik) **Era**, or the Middle Stone Age. This period began more than 10,000 years ago and lasted to about 5,000 years ago in some places.

During the Middle Stone Age, people found new uses for bone and stone tools. People who lived near water invented hooks and fishing spears. Other groups invented the bow and arrow.

Primary Source

POINTS OF VIEW

Views of Migration to the Americas

For many years scientists were fairly certain that the first Americans came from Asia, following big game through an ice-free path in the glaciers.

"Doubtless it was a formidable [challenging] place . . . an ice-walled valley of frigid winds, fierce snows, and clinging fogs . . . yet grazing animals would have entered, and behind them would have come a rivulet [stream] of human hunters."

—**Thomas Canby,**
1979, quoted in *Kingdoms of Gold, Kingdoms of Jade* by Brian M. Fagan

New discoveries have challenged beliefs about the first Americans. Some scientists now are not so sure the first Americans came along an ice-free path in the glaciers.

"There's no reason people couldn't have come along the coast, skirting [going around] the glaciers just the way recreational kayakers do today."

—**James Dixon,**
quoted in *National Geographic,* December 2000

ANALYSIS SKILL ANALYZING PRIMARY SOURCES

Why might a scientist change his or her mind about a long-held belief?

Critical Thinking: Drawing Conclusions

At Level

Views of Migration

1. Read aloud the quote by Thomas Canby. Ask students whether the journey he describes would have been difficult or easy. Ask students to pick out words or phrases from the quote that support their opinions.
2. Then display a map of the Western Hemisphere. Call on volunteers to point out the routes proposed by the two archaeologists in the feature—across land from northwestern Asia (Canby) and by boat from Asia along the Pacific coast (Dixon).
3. Have students write one to three paragraphs about which theory they think is more logical. Remind students to provide reasons to support their opinions.

LS Logical/Mathematical, Verbal/Linguistic

Alternative Assessment Handbook, Rubric 43: Writing to Persuade

Answers

Analyzing Primary Sources *possible answer—New discoveries can provide new information and interpretations.*

A Mammoth House

Early people used whatever was available to make shelters. In Central Asia, where wood was scarce, some early people made their homes from mammoth bones.

The frame was probably covered with animal hides to form a solid roof and walls.
Heavy mammoth bones were used as a frame for the shelter.

In addition to tools, people developed new technologies to improve their lives. For example, some learned to make canoes by hollowing out logs. They used the canoes to travel on rivers and lakes. They also began to make pottery. The first pets may also have appeared at this time. People kept dogs to help them hunt and for protection. Developments like these, in addition to clothing and shelter, allowed people to adapt to new environments.

READING CHECK **Finding Main Ideas**
What were two ways people adapted to new environments?

SUMMARY AND PREVIEW Early people adapted to new environments with new kinds of clothing, shelter, and tools. In Section 3 you will read about how Stone Age peoples developed farming.

Section 2 Assessment

hmhsocialstudies.com ONLINE QUIZ

Reviewing Ideas, Terms, and People

1. a. **Define** What is a **land bridge**?
   b. **Analyze** Why did it take so long for early people to reach South America?
2. a. **Recall** What did people use to make tools in the **Mesolithic Era**?
   b. **Summarize** Why did people have to learn to make clothes and build shelters?

Critical Thinking

3. **Sequencing** Draw the organizer below. Use your notes and sequence chain to show the path of migration around the world.

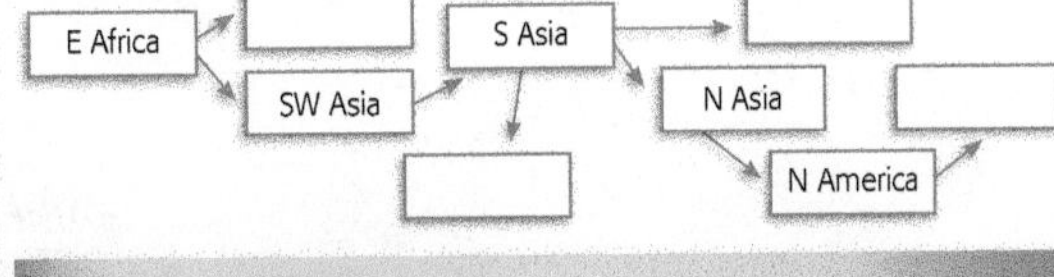

FOCUS ON WRITING

4. **Illustrating** How will you illustrate early migration on your storyboard? Draw some sketches. How does this information relate to your ideas from Section 1?

Direct Teach

Other People, Other Places

Home on the Range People of many places and times have learned how to build shelters from limited resources. The Inuit who live in Arctic regions build domed shelters called igloos from blocks of snow or ice. Nomads of Mongolia create tent-like structures called yurts. A yurt's basic structure is a frame of wooden poles covered with animal skins, textiles, or felt.

Did you know . . .

The last of the mammoths lived on islands off Russia's Arctic coast. They survived until about 4,000 years ago, when pharaohs ruled Egypt.

Review & Assess

Close

Ask students how the picture of the mammoth-bone shelter on this page contrasts with images of prehistoric people that show them as dull-witted.

Review

Online Quiz, Section 2

Assess

SE Section 2 Assessment
PASS: Section 2 Quiz
Alternative Assessment Handbook

Reteach/Classroom Intervention

Guided Reading Workbook, Section 2
Interactive Skills Tutor CD-ROM

Section 2 Assessment Answers

1. a. a strip of land connecting two continents
   b. They had to get across Asia, then across the land bridge into North America, and gradually all the way to South America.
2. a. bone and stone
   b. They moved to climates that were colder than those in East Africa.
3. from East Africa to Europe; Southern Asia to Australia and East Asia; North America to South America
4. Sketches will vary. Students' answers should include the development of clothing, shelter, and tools as early humans migrated and adapted to new environments.

Answers

Reading Check *possible answers—used animal skins for clothing to keep warm; built shelters; developed new hunting tools, such as the bow and arrow or fishing spear*

Preteach

Bellringer

If YOU were there. . . Use the **Daily Bellringer Transparency** to help students answer the question.

Daily Bellringer Transparency, Section 3

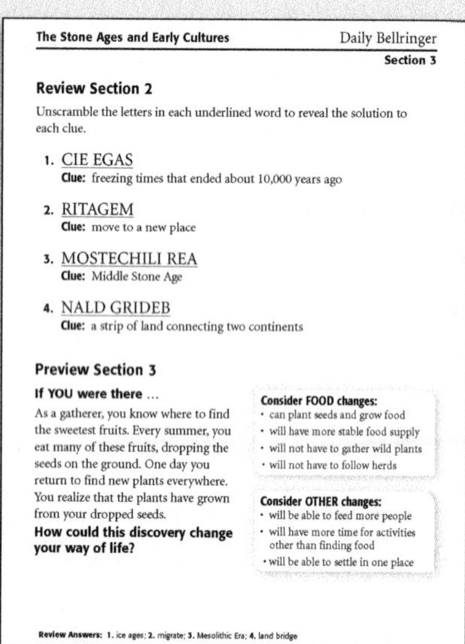

The Stone Ages and Early Cultures — Daily Bellringer
Section 3

Review Section 2

Unscramble the letters in each underlined word to reveal the solution to each clue.

1. CIE EGAS
   Clue: freezing times that ended about 10,000 years ago
2. RITAGEM
   Clue: move to a new place
3. MOSTECHILI REA
   Clue: Middle Stone Age
4. NALD GRIDEB
   Clue: a strip of land connecting two continents

Preview Section 3

If YOU were there ...

As a gatherer, you know where to find the sweetest fruits. Every summer, you eat many of these fruits, dropping the seeds on the ground. One day you return to find new plants everywhere. You realize that the plants have grown from your dropped seeds.

How could this discovery change your way of life?

Consider FOOD changes:
- can plant seeds and grow food
- will have more stable food supply
- will not have to gather wild plants
- will not have to follow herds

Consider OTHER changes:
- will be able to feed more people
- will have more time for activities other than finding food
- will be able to settle in one place

Review Answers: 1. ice ages; 2. migrate; 3. Mesolithic Era; 4. land bridge

Academic Vocabulary

Review with students the high-use academic term in this section.

development creation (p. 42)

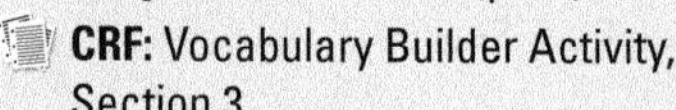

CRF: Vocabulary Builder Activity, Section 3

Taking Notes

Have students use the graphic organizer online to take notes on the section. This activity will prepare students for the Section Assessment, in which they will complete a graphic organizer that builds on the information using the Critical Thinking Skill: Identifying Cause and Effect.

SECTION 3

Beginnings of Agriculture

What You Will Learn...

Main Ideas

1. The first farmers learned to grow plants and raise animals in the New Stone Age.
2. Farming changed societies and the way people lived.

The Big Idea

The development of agriculture brought great changes to human society.

Key Terms

Neolithic Era, *p. 41*
domestication, *p. 41*
agriculture, *p. 42*
megaliths, *p. 42*

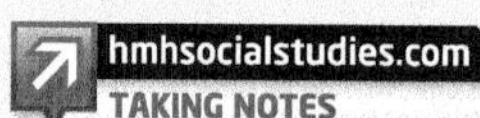

Use the graphic organizer online to take notes on the different changes related to the development of agriculture.

If YOU were there...

As a gatherer, you know where to find the sweetest fruits. Every summer, you eat many of these fruits, dropping the seeds on the ground. One day you return to find new plants everywhere. You realize that the plants have grown from your dropped seeds.

How could this discovery change your way of life?

BUILDING BACKGROUND The discovery that plants grew from seeds was one of the major advances of the late Stone Age. Other similar advances led to great changes in the way people lived.

Early Domestication

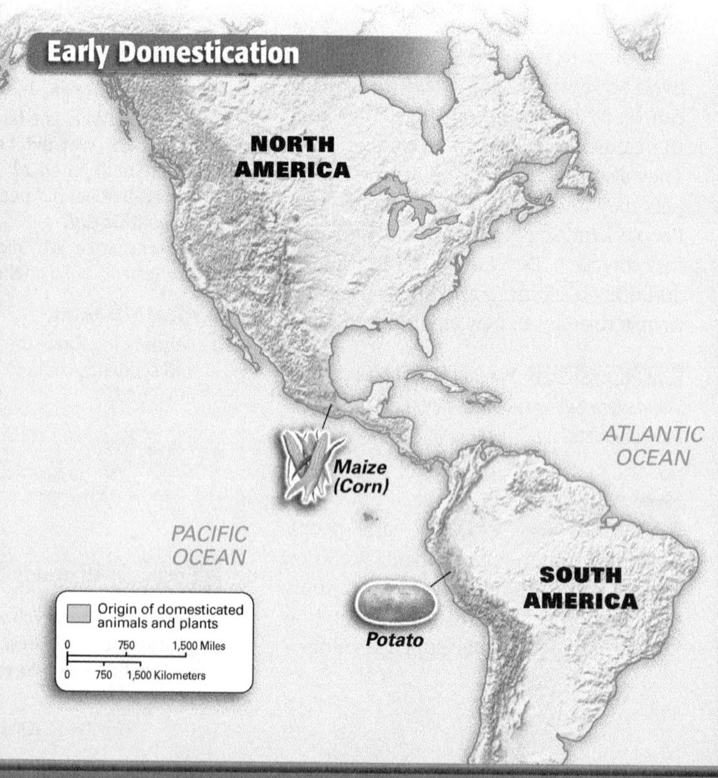

Teach the Big Idea

At Level

Beginnings of Agriculture

1. **Teach** Ask students the questions in the Main Idea boxes to teach this section.
2. **Apply** Draw a circle labeled *Beginnings of Agriculture* for students to see and copy. Call on students to identify basic changes in human societies caused by the development of agriculture. Add these suggestions to create an idea web.
3. **Review** Call on other volunteers to expand the web by suggesting further developments that could have been caused by the basic changes. For example, building megaliths may have inspired new stonecutting techniques.
4. **Practice/Homework** Have students add to their idea webs by connecting elements already suggested and illustrating the webs. **LS Visual/Spatial**

Alternative Assessment Handbook, Rubric 13: Graphic Organizers

History and Geography Activity: Agriculture and Animals

The First Farmers

After the Middle Stone Age came a period of time that scientists call the **Neolithic** (nee-uh-LI-thik) **Era**, or New Stone Age. It began as early as 10,000 years ago in Southwest Asia. In other places, this era began much later and lasted much longer than it did there.

During the New Stone Age people learned to polish stones to make tools like saws and drills. People also learned how to make fire. Before, they could only use fire that had been started by natural causes such as lightning.

The New Stone Age ended in Egypt and Southwest Asia about 5,000 years ago, when toolmakers began to make tools out of metal. But tools weren't the only major change that occurred during the Neolithic Era. In fact, the biggest changes came in how people produced food.

Plants

After a warming trend brought an end to the ice ages, new plants began to grow in some areas. For example, wild barley and wheat plants started to spread throughout Southwest Asia. Over time, people came to depend on these wild plants for food. They began to settle where grains grew.

People soon learned that they could plant seeds themselves to grow their own crops. Historians call the shift from food gathering to food producing the Neolithic Revolution. Most experts believe that this revolution, or change, first occurred in the societies of Southwest Asia.

Eventually, people learned to change plants to make them more useful. They planted only the largest grains or the sweetest fruits. The process of changing plants or animals to make them more useful to humans is called **domestication**.

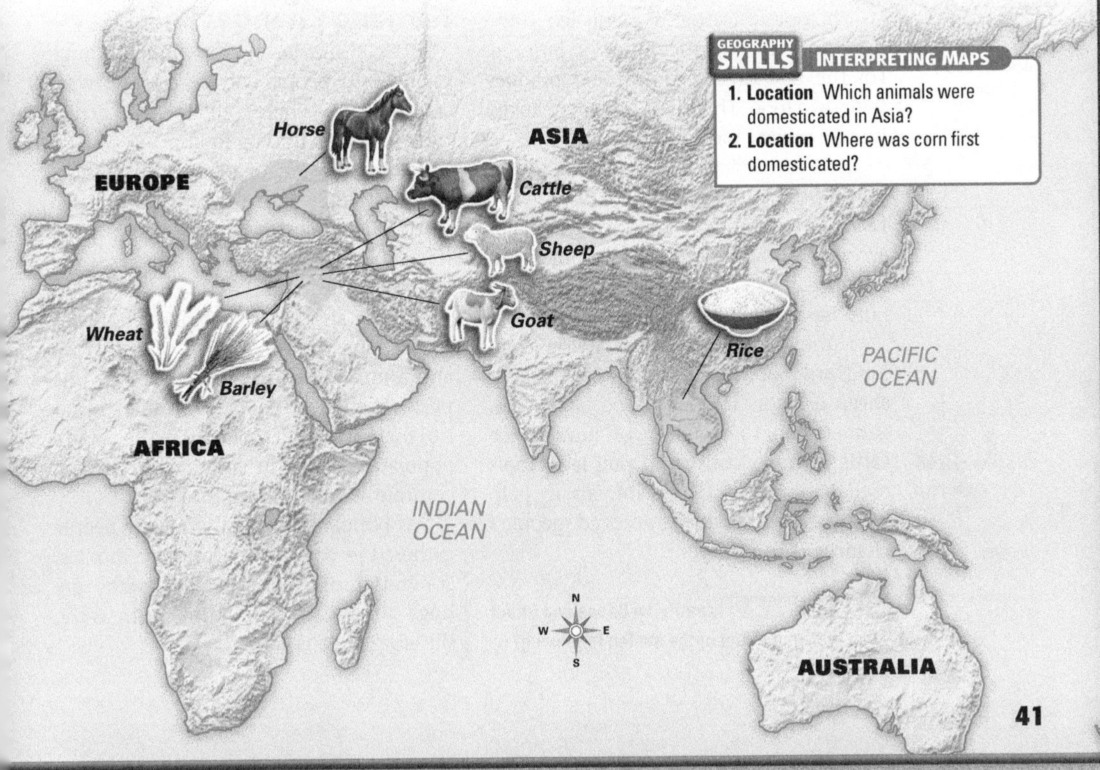

GEOGRAPHY SKILLS INTERPRETING MAPS

1. **Location** Which animals were domesticated in Asia?
2. **Location** Where was corn first domesticated?

Direct Teach

Main Idea

1 The First Farmers

The first farmers learned to grow plants and raise animals in the Stone Age.

Define What was the Neolithic Revolution? *the shift from food gathering to food producing*

Contrast What is the difference between the domestication of plants and simply planting seeds? *Domestication involves changing the plants to make them more useful.*

Rate Which do you think had more significant results—the domestication of plants or of animals? *possible answers—plants, because plants were more important food sources and people could still hunt; animals, because they helped with tasks besides farming, such as pulling loads of building materials.*

History and Geography Activity: Agriculture and Animals

Map Transparency: Early Domestication

Info to Know

Cats and People People domesticated cats not just for catching rats and mice, but also for companionship. In fact, the domestication of cats may have started some 9,500 years ago. This date comes from the earliest known burial of a cat with a human, found in 2004 in Cyprus. Archaeologists have concluded that the cat was the human's pet.

Collaborative Learning

Below Level

Mural of Ancient Farm Community

Materials: butcher paper, art supplies

1. As a class, review what life was like for early farmers. Then organize the class into small groups and have each group create a mural that depicts early farming communities.
2. Have students use Internet or library resources to find images they can include in their murals, such as images of plants, animals, housing, and religious shrines.
3. Display the groups' murals in the classroom. Call on group volunteers to describe what is illustrated in the murals.
LS Interpersonal, Visual/Spatial

Alternative Assessment Handbook, Rubrics 3: Artwork; and 14: Group Activity

Answers

Interpreting Maps 1. *cattle, sheep, goats* **2.** *southern part of North America*

Direct Teach

Main Idea

2 Farming Changes Societies

Farming changed societies and the way people lived.

Define What are megaliths? *huge stones used as monuments*

Identify What gods did people in the Neolithic Age probably believe in? *those associated with the four elements—air, water, fire, and earth—or with animals*

Draw Conclusions How did a change in the use of fire demonstrate human ingenuity? *People learned how to make fire, not just use fire that had been started by natural causes.*

CRF: Primary Source Activity: Objects from Çatal Hüyük

Did you know...

Not all of the changes brought about by agriculture were positive. Although people in farming communities had more food, they did not eat the same variety of foods as hunter-gatherers did. In addition, the presence of animals in or near human communities brought new diseases.

Linking to Today

Major Megaliths A group of huge shaped stones was raised at Stonehenge in southern England starting in about 3100 BC. Neolithic people may have used Stonehenge for predicting the seasons and for religious ceremonies.

History Close-up

An Early Farming Society

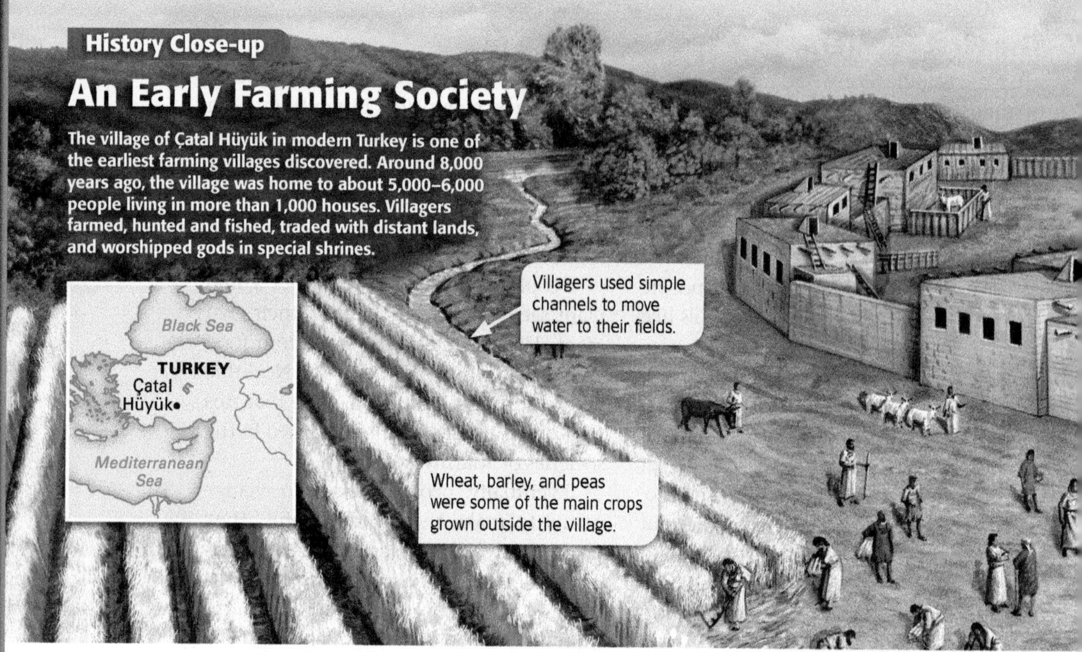

The village of Çatal Hüyük in modern Turkey is one of the earliest farming villages discovered. Around 8,000 years ago, the village was home to about 5,000–6,000 people living in more than 1,000 houses. Villagers farmed, hunted and fished, traded with distant lands, and worshipped gods in special shrines.
Black Sea
TURKEY
Çatal Hüyük
Mediterranean Sea
Villagers used simple channels to move water to their fields.
Wheat, barley, and peas were some of the main crops grown outside the village.

ACADEMIC VOCABULARY
development creation

The domestication of plants led to the development of **agriculture**, or farming. For the first time, people could produce their own food. This development changed human society forever.

Animals

Learning to produce food was a major accomplishment for early people. But learning how to use animals for their own purposes was almost equally important.

Hunters didn't have to follow wild herds anymore. Instead, farmers could keep sheep or goats for milk, food, and wool. Farmers could also use large animals like cattle to carry loads or to pull large tools used in farming. Using animals to help with farming greatly improved people's chances of surviving.

THE IMPACT TODAY One famous megalith, Stonehenge in England, attracts millions of curious tourists and scholars each year.

READING CHECK **Identifying Cause and Effect** What was one effect of the switch to farming?

Farming Changes Societies

The Neolithic Revolution brought huge changes to people's lives. With survival more certain, people could focus on activities other than finding food.

Domestication of plants and animals enabled people to use plant fibers to make cloth. The domestication of animals made it possible to use wool from goats and sheep and skins from horses for clothes.

People also began to build permanent settlements. As they started raising crops and animals, they needed to stay in one place. Then, once people were able to control their own food production, the world's population grew. In some areas farming communities developed into towns.

As populations grew, groups of people gathered to perform religious ceremonies. Some put up megaliths. **Megaliths** are huge stones used as monuments or as the sites for religious gatherings.

Critical Thinking: Summarizing

At Level

A Day in the Life

Standard English Mastery

1. Discuss with students how domestication of plants and animals changed how Neolithic people lived day-to-day.
2. Have each student write a journal entry describing a day in the life of a Neolithic farm family. Ask students to include such details as the crops and animals on the farm. Remind students to use Standard English in their journal entries. Work with individual students as needed.
3. Ask volunteers to read their journal entries to the class.
4. **Extend** To extend the activity, ask students to add another journal entry in which the farmer reflects on stories he or she has heard about what daily life for the local people used to be like before farming. **LS Verbal/Linguistic**

Alternative Assessment Handbook, Rubric 15: Journals

Answers

Reading Check *possible answers—People stopped moving around to find food, populations grew with better control of food production, and towns developed in some areas.*

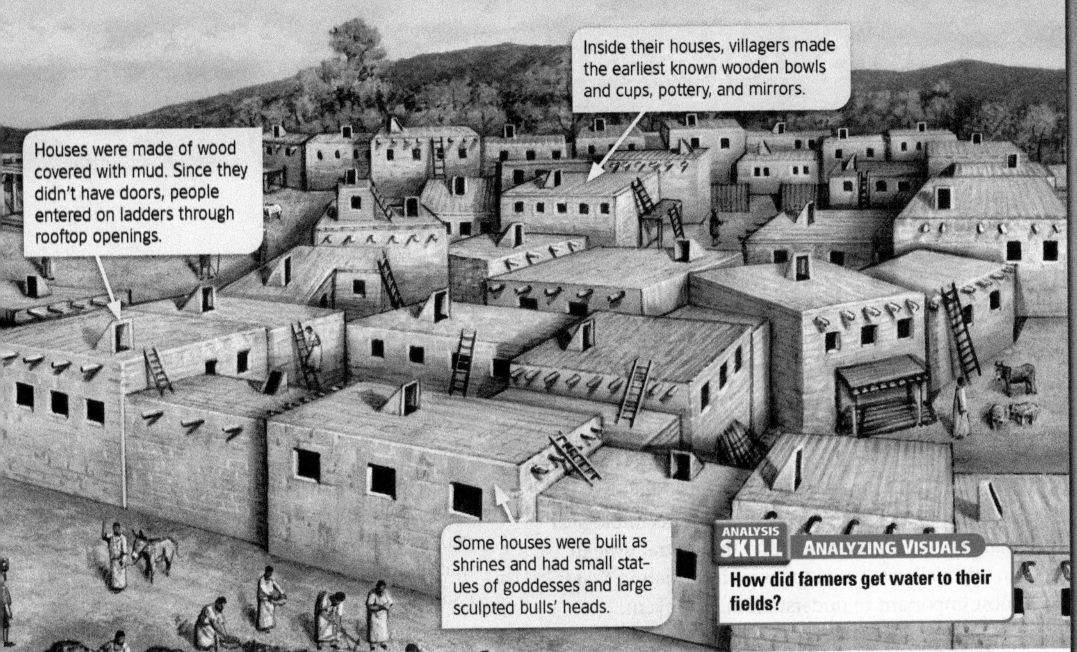

Inside their houses, villagers made the earliest known wooden bowls and cups, pottery, and mirrors.
Houses were made of wood covered with mud. Since they didn't have doors, people entered on ladders through rooftop openings.
Some houses were built as shrines and had small statues of goddesses and large sculpted bulls' heads.

ANALYSIS SKILL **ANALYZING VISUALS**

How did farmers get water to their fields?

Early people probably believed in gods and goddesses associated with the four elements—air, water, fire, and earth—or with animals. For example, one European group honored a thunder god, while another group worshipped bulls. Some scholars also believe that prehistoric peoples also prayed to their ancestors. People in some societies today still hold many of these same beliefs.

READING CHECK **Analyzing** How did farming contribute to the growth of towns?

SUMMARY AND PREVIEW Stone Age peoples adapted to new environments by domesticating plants and animals. These changes led to the development of religion and the growth of towns. In the next chapter you will learn more about early towns.

Section 3 Assessment

hmhsocialstudies.com ONLINE QUIZ

Reviewing Ideas, Terms, and People

1. a. **Define** What is **domestication** of a plant or animal?
   b. **Make Generalizations** How did early people use domesticated animals?
2. a. **Describe** What were gods and goddesses probably associated with in prehistoric religion?
   b. **Explain** How did domestication of plants and animals lead to the development of towns?

Critical Thinking

3. **Identifying Cause and Effect** Copy the graphic organizer at right. Use it to show one cause and three effects of the development of agriculture.

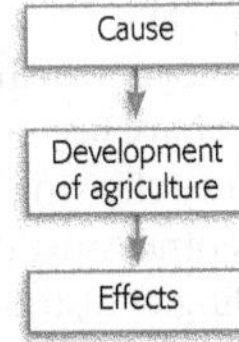

Focus on Writing

4. **Beginnings of Agriculture** Now that you've read about the birth of agriculture, you're ready to plan your storyboard. Look back through your notes from previous sections and the text of this one. Make a list of the events and ideas you will include on your storyboard. Then plan how you will arrange these items.

Direct Teach

Connect to Art

An Artistic First As people settled in villages and towns, they could pursue other tasks besides finding or growing food. Some people could devote more time to art. In Çatal Hüyük, an artist created the first known landscape painting. This painting, which dates from about 6150 BC, shows the town's houses at the foot of an erupting volcano. In fact, there is a similar volcano, now extinct, within sight of Çatal Hüyük.

Review & Assess

Close

Ask students to compare the farming methods of Neolithic times to food production today.

Review

Online Quiz, Section 3

Assess

SE Section 3 Assessment

PASS: Section 3 Quiz

Alternative Assessment Handbook

Reteach/Classroom Intervention

Guided Reading Workbook, Section 3

Interactive Skills Tutor CD-ROM

Section 3 Assessment Answers

1. a. changing a plant or animal to make it more useful to humans
   b. for milk, food, and/or wool; for carrying loads or pulling tools used in farming
2. a. earth, air, fire, and water or animals
   b. People settled in one place to grow crops and tend animals, and better control of food production enabled populations to grow.
3. cause—Warming trend after ice ages caused new plants to grow; effects—could produce own food, easier to farm, new kinds of clothing, populations grew, settlements became towns, religion more organized
4. Notes should include changes in climate, domestication of plants and animals, growth of populations and settlements, and the emergence of religious ceremonies.

Answers

Analyzing Visuals *Farmers used channels to move water to their fields.*

Reading Check *Because people stayed in one place to control food production, towns developed.*

Social Studies Skills

Identifying Central Issues

Activity **Central Issues in the Community** Write the following statement for students to see: *The school district's budget will be cut $300,000 next year.* Tell students this statement is not true but hypothetical. Ask students to identify the most important questions and concerns that people might have in response to this news. Responses might include the following: What will the schools have to cut to lower their budgets—such as teachers, textbooks, art classes, and so on? Will classes be bigger? Will extracurricular activities be cut? Will free lunches be cut? After a brief period of discussion, ask students to identify what all these concerns have in common. Lead students to realize that the central issue involved is how will budget cuts affect educational quality and school life. To extend the activity, have students practice the skill on an article from their school or local newspaper. **LS Logical/Mathematical**

Alternative Assessment Handbook, Rubric 11: Discussions

Interactive Skills Tutor CD-ROM, Lesson 12: Identify Issues and Problems

Social Studies Skills

Analysis | Critical Thinking | Economics | Study

Identifying Central Issues

Understand the Skill

Central issues are the main problems or topics that are related to an event. The issues behind a historical event can be varied and complicated. Central issues in world history usually involve political, social, economic, territorial, moral, or technological matters. The ability to identify the central issue in an event allows you to focus on information that is most important to understanding the event.

Learn the Skill

In this chapter you learned about prehistory. Some of the events you read about may not seem very important. It is hard for people in the computer age to appreciate the accomplishments of the Stone Age. For example, adding wooden handles to stone tools may seem like a simple thing to us. But it was a life-changing advance for people of that time.

This example points out something to remember when looking for central issues. Try not to use only modern-day values and standards to decide what is important about the past. Always think about the times in which people lived. Ask yourself what would have been important to people living then.

The following guidelines will help you to identify central issues. Use them to gain a better understanding of historical events.

1. Identify the subject of the information. What is the information about?
2. Determine the source of the information. Is it a primary source or a secondary source?
3. Determine the purpose of what you are reading. Why has the information been provided?
4. Find the strongest or most forceful statements in the information. These are often clues to issues or ideas the writer thinks are the most central or important.
5. Think about values, concerns, ways of life, and events that would have been important to the people of the times. Determine how the information might be connected to those larger issues.

Practice and Apply the Skill

Apply the guidelines to identify the central issue in the following passage. Then answer the questions.

"What distinguished the Neolithic Era from earlier ages was people's ability to shape stone tools by polishing and grinding. This allowed people to make more specialized tools. Even more important changes took place also. The development of agriculture changed the basic way people lived. Earlier people had been wanderers, who moved from place to place in search of food. Some people began settling in permanent villages. Exactly how they learned that seeds could be planted and made to grow year after year remains a mystery. However, the shift from food gathering to food producing was possibly the most important change ever in history."

1. What is the general subject of this passage?
2. What changes distinguished the Neolithic Era from earlier periods?
3. According to this writer, what is the central issue to understand about the Neolithic Era?
4. What statements in the passage help you to determine the central issue?

Social Studies Skills Activity: Identifying Central Issues

At Level

Guided and Independent Practice

1. Have volunteers read aloud the Section 1 text in this chapter titled "Scientists Study Remains."
2. Have students work as a class to go through the five guidelines and questions listed above in the bottom of the left-hand column and in the top of the right-hand column.
3. Then assign students the text in Section 2 titled "People Adapt to New Environments." Have students work independently to answer the same five questions. Review the answers as a class.
4. **Struggling Readers** Have these students practice the skill first on an easier text, such as a selection from a fourth-grade history book or a selection you write. Once students master the skill, have them apply it to grade-level text. **LS Verbal/Linguistic**

Alternative Assessment Handbook, Rubric 1: Acquiring Information

Answers

Practice and Apply the Skill **1.** *the changes that distinguish the Neolithic Era from earlier ages;* **2.** *people's ability to shape stone tools by polishing and grinding; the development of agriculture;* **3.** *that advances, such as agriculture, greatly changed the way people lived;* **4.** *first, third, fourth, and last sentences*

CHAPTER 2

Chapter Review

History's Impact
▶ video series
Review the video to answer the focus question:
What are some of the theories for how early migration occurred?

Visual Summary

Use the visual summary below to help you review the main ideas of the chapter.

Hominids developed in Africa and learned how to use tools.

Early humans lived as hunter-gatherers.

Humans migrated around the world, adapting to new environments.

Eventually, people learned how to farm and raise animals.

Reviewing Vocabulary, Terms, and People

For each group of terms below, write a sentence that shows how all the terms in the group are related.

1. prehistory
   ancestor
   hominid
2. domestication
   Neolithic Era
   agriculture
3. Paleolithic Era
   tool
   hunter-gatherers
   develop
4. land bridge
   ice ages
   migrate
5. society
   megaliths
   Neolithic Era

Comprehension and Critical Thinking

SECTION 1 *(Pages 28–34)*

6. a. **Recall** What does *Homo sapiens* mean? When may *Homo sapiens* have first appeared in Africa?
   b. **Draw Conclusions** If you were an archaeologist and found bead jewelry and stone chopping tools in an ancient woman's grave, what may you conclude?
   c. **Elaborate** How did stone tools change over time? Why do you think these changes took place so slowly?

SECTION 2 *(Pages 36–39)*

7. a. **Describe** What new skills did people develop to help them survive?
   b. **Analyze** How did global climate change affect the migration of early people?
   c. **Evaluate** About 15,000 years ago, where do you think life would have been more difficult—in eastern Africa or northern Europe? Why?

Answers

Visual Summary

Review and Inquiry Use the visual summary to review the chapter's main ideas. Ask students to provide details about what daily life may have been like for the people shown in the image.

Quick Facts Transparency: The Stone Ages and Early Cultures Visual Summary

Reviewing Vocabulary, Terms, and People

1. possible answer—Hominids, the ancestors of humans, lived during a time we call prehistory.
2. possible answer—During the Neolithic Era, the domestication of plants and animals led to agriculture.
3. possible answer—Hunter-gatherers developed stone tools during the Paleolithic Era.
4. possible answer—People might have migrated across a land bridge to get to North America during the ice ages.
5. possible answer—A Neolithic Era society might have used megaliths in religious ceremonies.

Comprehension and Critical Thinking

6. a. "wise man"; 200,000 years ago
   b. possible answer—that the people who buried her had some form of religion
   c. went from choppers to using flint and having handles; possible answers—because the old tools worked well enough, better materials were not readily

Review and Assessment Resources

Review and Reinforce

SE Chapter Review

CRF: Chapter Review Activity

Quick Facts Transparency: The Stone Ages and Early Cultures Visual Summary

Spanish Chapter Summaries Audio CD Program

Online Chapter Summaries in Six Languages

TOS Holt McDougal PuzzleView

Quiz Game CD-ROM

Assess

SE Standardized Test Practice

PASS: Chapter Test, Forms A and B

Alternative Assessment Handbook

TOS ExamView Assessment Suite, Chapter Test

Differentiated Instruction Modified Worksheets and Tests CD-ROM: Chapter Test

Online Assessment Program, in the Interactive Student Edition

Reteach/Intervene

Guided Reading Workbook

Differentiated Instruction Teacher Management System: Lesson Plans

Differentiated Instruction Modified Worksheets and Tests CD-ROM

Interactive Skills Tutor CD-ROM

Chapter Resources

Answers

available, or early people couldn't communicate well enough to discuss improvements

7. **a.** how to make clothing, build shelters, make more complex tools, find new uses for tools, make canoes and pottery, tame dogs

   b. created land bridge that allowed people to migrate from northern Asia to the Americas

   c. possible answer—northern Europe, because the ice ages would have made survival there difficult

8. **a.** the shift from food gathering to food producing

   b. allowed people to settle down and create towns

   c. possible answers—Stone was readily available and long-lasting; large stone structures could be seen from far away; or building with stone required much labor but few tools.

Reviewing Themes

9. possible answers—People had to learn to make clothes and shelter in cold temperatures; warming brought new plants and the development of farming; ice ages caused land bridges, allowing people to migrate around the world.
10. possible answers—Hunting improved because people could communicate; people formed personal relationships; it became easier to solve problems, such as how to distribute food.

Using the Internet

11. Go to hmhsocialstudies.com to access a rubric for this activity.

Reading and Analysis Skills

12. Paleolithic Era begins. Mesolithic Era begins. Neolithic Era begins.
13. *Homo habilis* appears. *Homo erectus* appears. *Homo sapiens* appears.
14. People make stone tools. People attach wooden handles to tools. People make metal tools.

Social Studies Skills

15. possible answer—Wild almonds are poisonous, so how people figured out that they could eat them is puzzling.
16. how people figured out that they could change poisonous plants into useful plants

Focus on Writing

17. **Rubric** Students' storyboards should:
    - include numbered panels.
    - feature clear but simple sketches.
    - end with a clear summary.

CRF: Focus on Writing: A Storyboard

SECTION 3 *(Pages 40–43)*

8. **a. Define** What was the Neolithic Revolution?

   b. Make Inferences How did domestication of plants and animals change early societies?

   c. Predict Why do you think people of the Neolithic Era put up megaliths instead of some other kind of monuments?

Reviewing Themes

9. **Geography** What were three ways in which the environment affected Stone Age peoples?
10. **Society and Culture** How did the development of language change hunter-gatherer society?

Using the Internet 

11. **Activity: Creating a Skit** In the beginning of the Paleolithic Era, or the Old Stone Age, early humans used modified stones as tools. As the Stone Age progressed, plants and animals became materials for tools too. Use your online textbook to research the development of tools and the use of fire. Then create a skit that tells about an early human society discovering fire, creating a new tool, or developing a new way of doing a task.

hmhsocialstudies.com

Reading Skills 

Understanding Chronological Order *Below are several lists of events. Arrange the events in each list in chronological order.*

12. Mesolithic Era begins.
    Paleolithic Era begins.
    Neolithic Era begins.
13. *Homo sapiens* appears.
    Homo habilis appears.
    Homo erectus appears.
14. People make stone tools.
    People make metal tools.
    People attach wooden handles to tools.

Social Studies Skills 

Identifying Central Issues *Read the primary source passage below and then answer the questions that follow.*

> "Almonds provide a striking example of bitter seeds and their change under domestication. Most wild almond seeds contain an intensely bitter chemical called amygdalin, which (as was already mentioned) breaks down to yield the poison cyanide. A snack of wild almonds can kill a person foolish enough to ignore the warning of the bitter taste. Since the first stage in unconscious domestication involves gathering seeds to eat, how on earth did domestication of wild almonds ever reach that first stage?"
>
> –Jared Diamond, from *Guns, Germs, and Steel*

15. What is the main point of this passage?
16. What does the author suggest is the major issue he will address in the text?

Focus on Writing

17. **Creating Your Storyboard** Use the notes you have taken to plan your storyboard. What images will you include in each frame of the storyboard? How many frames will you need to tell the story of prehistoric people? How will you represent your ideas visually?

    After you have sketched an outline for your storyboard, begin drawing it. Be sure to include all significant adaptations and developments made by prehistoric people, and don't worry if you can't draw that well. If you like, you might want to draw your storyboard in the simple style of prehistoric cave paintings. As the last frame in your storyboard, write a detailed summary to conclude your story.

CHAPTER 2 Standardized Test Practice

DIRECTIONS: Read each question, and write the letter of the best response.

1 Use the map to answer the following question.

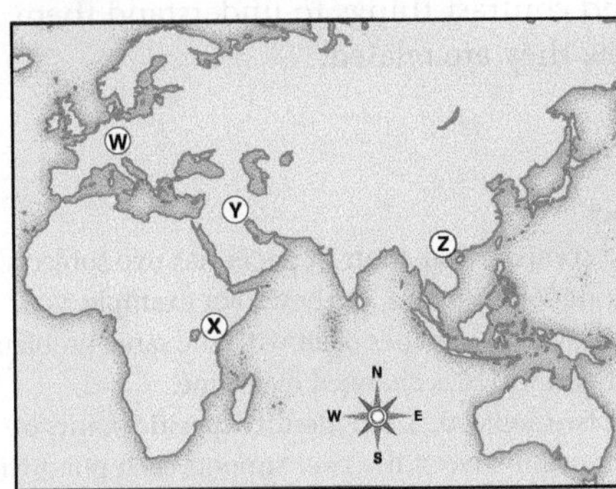

The region in which the first humans lived is shown on the map by the letter

A W.
B X.
C Y.
D Z.

2 The earliest humans lived

A by hunting and gathering their food.
B as herders of sheep and other livestock.
C alone or in pairs.
D in farming villages along rivers and streams.

3 The development of farming brought all of the following changes to the lives of early humans *except*

A the first human-made shelters.
B a larger supply of food.
C the construction of permanent settlements.
D new types of clothing.

4 The region of the world that was likely occupied *last* by early humans was

A northern Asia.
B southern Asia.
C North America.
D South America.

5 Hunter-gatherer societies in the Old Stone Age possessed all of the following *except*

A fire.
B art.
C bone tools.
D religious beliefs.

Connecting with Past Learnings

6 You know that history is the study of people and events from the past. To learn about prehistory, historians would likely study all of the following *except*

A graves.
B journals.
C bones.
D art.

7 A skull from a human who lived during the Neolithic Era would be considered a(n)

A tool.
B artifact.
C fossil.
D secondary source.

Answers

Standardized Test Practice

1. B
Break Down the Question Refer students who missed the question to the map in Section 2.

2. A
Break Down the Question This question requires students to recall the chronology of human development.

3. A
Break Down the Question Remind students that all but one of the answers describe changes to people's lives. Refer students who miss the question to the material titled "Clothing and Shelter" in Section 2.

4. D
Break Down the Question This question requires students to recall information about the land bridge between Asia and the Americas. Refer students who missed the question to the map in Section 2.

5. C
Break Down the Question This question requires that students recall factual information. Refer students who missed the question to the material on the Mesolithic Era in Section 2.

6. B
Break Down the Question Refer students who missed the question to the map in Section 2.

7. C
Break Down the Question This question requires that students recall material covered in the previous chapter about the lack of written information for prehistory.

Intervention Resources

Reproducible

- Guided Reading Workbook
- Differentiated Instruction Teacher Management System: Lesson Plans

Technology

- Quick Facts Transparency: The Stone Ages and Early Cultures Visual Summary
- Differentiated Instruction Modified Worksheets and Tests CD-ROM
- Interactive Skills Tutor CD-ROM

Tips for Test Taking

Study the Directions In order to follow directions, students have to know what the directions are! Have students read all test directions as if they contain the key to lifetime happiness. Then they should read the directions again and study the answer sheet. How is it laid out? Students should determine if they are arranged

A B
C D or A B C D.

Urge students to be sure they know what to do before they make the first mark.

Preteach

Bellringer

Motivate Write the words *cat* and *dog* for students to see. Ask students how the two animals are similar. Then ask students how they are different. Explain that comparing (showing how things are similar) and contrasting (showing how things are different) is one way to learn about events and people in history. Tell students that they will write a paper comparing and contrasting two ancient societies.

Interactive Skills Tutor CD-ROM, Lesson 1: Compare and Contrast

Direct Teach

Writing a Thesis

Make a Point After students have selected the topic of their paper and made lists of similarities and differences, have them examine the lists. Were the two groups or events they compared mainly alike or mainly different? Did certain similarities or differences stand out as significant or influential? Have students write one sentence in answer to each question. Tell students to use the sentences as a starting point for selecting and writing a thesis.

Organizing

Once around the Block Students who use the block style to organize their papers should check that they address the same points in the same order for each topic. Have students use a different color of ink to underline each point they made about the first topic. Then have students use the same colors to underline the points they made about the second topic. The colors and order should match.

Comparing and Contrasting Societies

Assignment
Write a paper comparing and contrasting two early human societies.

Comparing means finding likenesses between or among things. Contrasting means finding differences. You often compare and contrast things to understand them better and see how they are related.

TIP Using a Graphic Organizer
A Venn diagram can help you see ways that the two societies are similar and different.

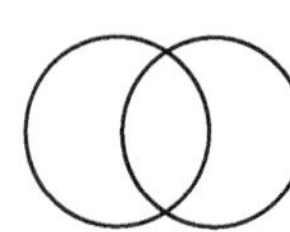

1. Prewrite

Getting Started

Unlike most essays, a compare and contrast paper has two subjects. However, it still has only one big idea, or thesis. For example, your idea may be to show how two societies dealt with the same problem or to show how two human societies changed over time.

Begin by choosing two subjects. Then identify specific points of similarities and differences between the two. Support each point with historical facts, examples, and details.

Organizing Your Information

Choose one of these two ways to organize your points of comparison.

- Present all the points about the first subject and then all the points about the second subject: AAABBB, or block style
- Alternate back and forth between the first subject and the second subject: ABABAB, or point-by-point style

2. Write

This framework will help you use your notes to write a first draft.

A Writer's Framework

Introduction
- Clearly identify your two subjects.
- Give background information readers will need in order to understand your points of comparison between the societies.
- State your big idea, or main purpose in comparing and contrasting these two societies.

Body
- Present your points of comparison in block style or point-by-point style.
- Compare the two societies in at least two ways, and contrast them in at least two ways.
- Use specific historical facts, details, and examples to support each of your points.

Conclusion
- Restate your big idea.
- Summarize the points you have made in your paper.
- Expand on your big idea, perhaps by relating it to your own life, to other societies, or to later historical events.

Differentiating Instruction

Special Needs Learners
Below Level

1. Have special needs learners work in small groups to create Venn diagrams before writing.
2. Have an aide read a short part of a relevant portion of the textbook aloud. Then have the students add the information to their diagrams. Have the aide continue to read the text aloud, stopping frequently to allow students to add to their Venn diagrams. LS **Visual/Spatial**

English-Language Learners
Below Level
Standard English Mastery

1. Have English learners write the drafts for their papers in their primary language.
2. Students should then refer back to these drafts as they write their final papers in English.
3. Before students write in English, review the rules for forming comparative and superlative adjectives and adverbs. Provide guided practice as needed. LS **Verbal/Linguistic**

3. Evaluate and Revise

Evaluating

Use the following questions to discover ways to improve your paper.

Evaluation Questions for a Comparison/Contrast Paper

- Do you introduce both of your subjects in your first paragraph?
- Do you state your big idea, or thesis, at the end of your introduction?
- Do you present two or more similarities and two or more differences between the two societies?
- Do you use either the block style or point-by-point style of organization?
- Do you support your points of comparison with enough historical facts, details, and examples?
- Does your conclusion restate your big idea and summarize your main points?

TIP Help with Punctuation

Use the correct punctuation marks before and after clue words within sentences. Usually, a comma comes before *and, but, for, nor, or, so,* and *yet,* with no punctuation after the word. When they are in the middle of a sentence, clue words and phrases such as *however, similarly, in addition, in contrast,* and *on the other hand* usually have a comma before and after them.

Revising

When you are revising your paper, you may need to add comparison-contrast clue words. They will help your readers see the connections between ideas.

Clue Words for Similarities	Clue Words for Differences
also, another, both, in addition, just as, like, similarly, too	although, but, however, in contrast, instead, on the other hand, unlike

4. Proofread and Publish

Proofreading

Before sharing your paper, you will want to polish it by correcting any remaining errors. Look closely for mistakes in grammar, spelling, capitalization, and punctuation. To avoid two common grammar errors, make sure that you have used the correct form of *–er* or *more* and *–est* or *most* with adjectives and adverbs when making comparisons.

Publishing

One good way to share your paper is to exchange it with one or more classmates. After reading each other's papers, you can compare and contrast them. How are your papers similar? How do they differ? If possible, share papers with someone whose big idea is similar to yours.

Practice and Apply

Use the steps and strategies outlined in this workshop to write your compare and contrast paper.

Reteach

Providing Support

Back It Up Remind students that describing the similarities and differences for each group or period is not enough. Students must also support their descriptions with facts and examples. Have students circle each claim or point they make about each group or period in their papers. Then have students underline the support for each claim or point. If they have not provided support, have them ask themselves, "How do I know this point?" Then have students provide an answer in their papers.

Teaching Tip

Sentence Variety Tell students that comparison-contrast papers can become monotonous because they are highly structured. Explain that the papers will be more enjoyable to read if students vary their sentence structures, such as the way they start sentences. Help students rework, combine, or break sentences as needed to increase variety.

Practice & Apply

Rubric

Students' comparison-contrast papers should

- present a clear statement of the big idea, or main purpose.
- provide historical background to place the topic in context.
- use either block or point-by-point organization.
- provide three points of comparison and support for each one.
- end with a summary and a restatement of the big idea.
- use correct grammar, punctuation, spelling, and capitalization.

Struggling Readers **Below Level**

1. For students who have trouble getting words on paper, write the outline at right for them to see. Explain that the outline shows the question(s) they should answer in each part of their comparison-contrast papers.
2. Have students copy the outline and leave plenty of room to add information below each part. Then have students complete the outline by answering the questions. Encourage students to use complete sentences.

I. **Introduction:** What two things are you comparing and contrasting? What do you want to show by comparing and contrasting them?

II. **Body Paragraphs:** What is one way the two things are alike or different? How do you know? What is a second way? How do you know? What is a third way? How do you know?

III. **Conclusion:** Briefly, what have you stated in your paper? **LS Verbal/Linguistic**

Unit Preview

Introduce the Unit

Share the information in the chapter overviews with students.

Chapter 3 The first civilizations grew up in river valleys in Asia and Africa. Such valleys provided water and fertile land for farming. In the region of the Tigris and Euphrates river valley, the Sumerians developed the world's first civilization. The Sumerians' many advances include the wheel and the first system of writing. After the Sumerians, a series of empires rose and fell in the region. These societies also made advances, such as a written code of law, that still influence civilization today.

Chapter 4 In Africa, two great civilizations developed in the fertile valley of the Nile River. Ancient Egypt rose in northern Africa. Government and religion were closely connected, and Egyptians believed their rulers were gods. A strong belief in the afterlife led to preserving their rulers' bodies as mummies and burying them in pyramids, huge stone tombs with four triangle-shaped sides. The Egyptians developed a rich culture and made lasting achievements in writing, architecture, and art. South of Egypt, the kingdom of Kush developed in a region called Nubia. Kush grew wealthy from trade. Around 1500 BC Egypt conquered Kush. Over the next 500 years, the people of Kush adopted many aspects of Egyptian culture. Kush grew strong and later conquered Egypt. In time, however, Kush weakened and eventually fell to a nearby kingdom.

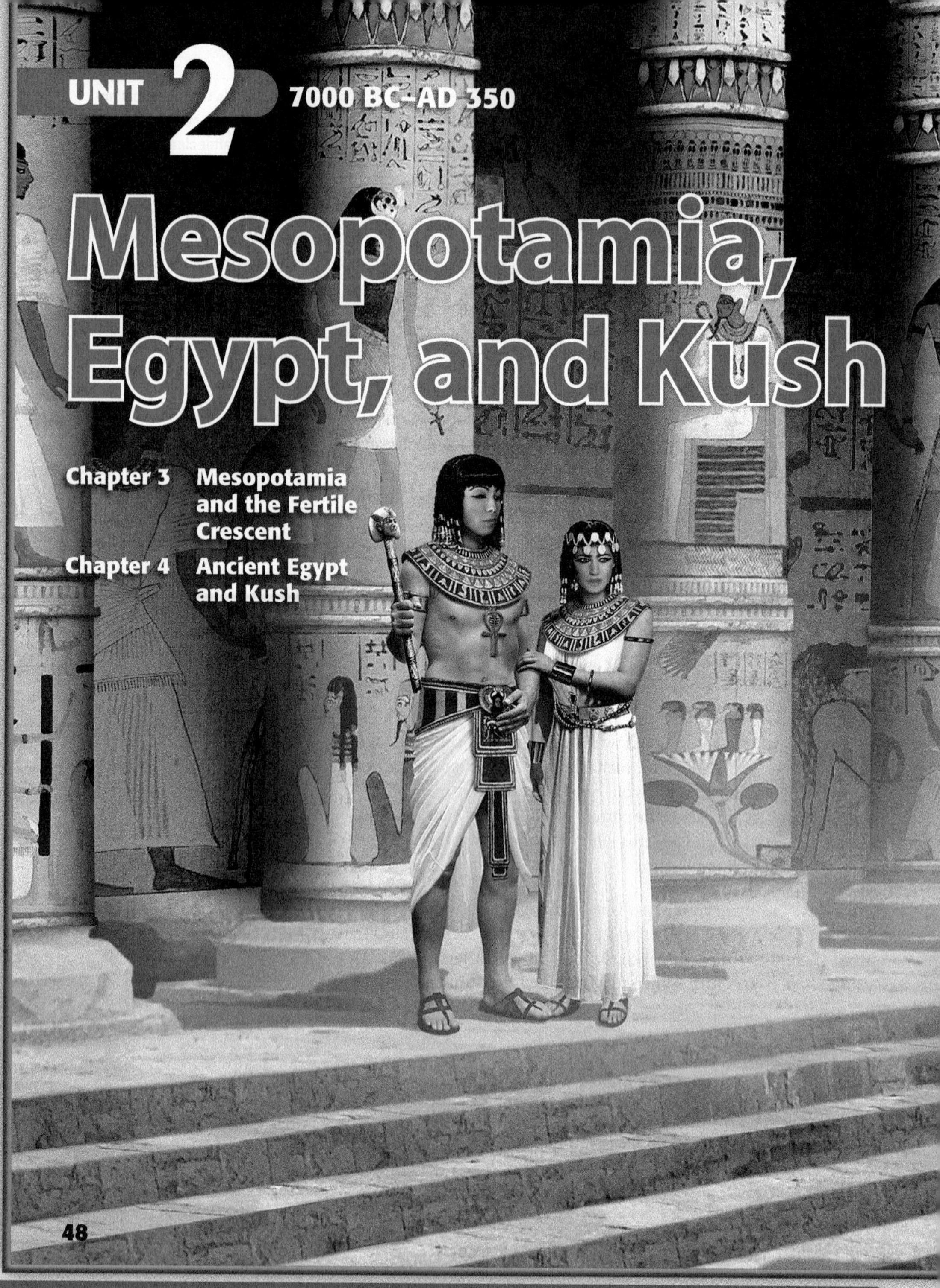

UNIT 2
7000 BC–AD 350
Mesopotamia, Egypt, and Kush
Chapter 3 Mesopotamia and the Fertile Crescent
Chapter 4 Ancient Egypt and Kush
48

Unit Resources

Planning

- Differentiated Instruction Teacher Management System: Unit Instructional Benchmarking Guides
- TOS Calendar Planner
- Power Presentations with Media Gallery
- A Teacher's Guide to Religion in the Public Schools

Differentiating Instruction

- Differentiated Instruction Teacher Management System: Lesson Plans for Differentiated Instruction
- Differentiated Instruction Modified Worksheets and Tests CD-ROM

Enrichment

- **CRF 3:** Economics and History Activity: The First Coins
- **CRF 3:** Interdisciplinary Project: Mesopotamia: The First Writing
- **CRF 4:** Interdisciplinary Project: Egypt: The Afterlife
- Civic Participation Activities
- Primary Source Library CD-ROM

Assessment

- Progress Assessment System Solution: Unit Test
- TOS ExamView Assessment Suite: Unit Test
- Online Assessment Program, in the Interactive Student Edition
- Alternative Assessment Handbook

The **Differentiated Instruction Teacher Management System** provides a planning and instructional benchmarking guide for this unit.

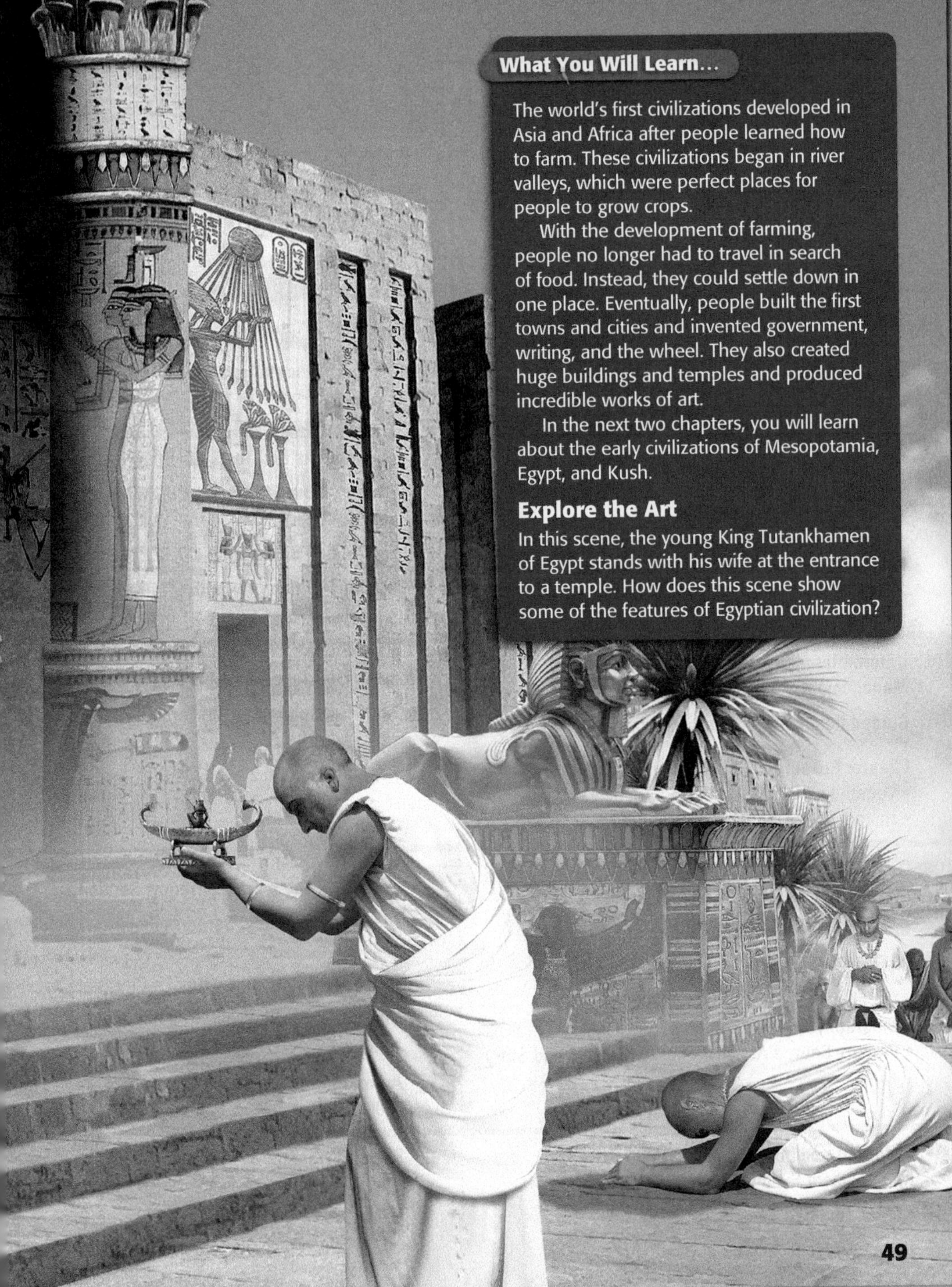

What You Will Learn...

The world's first civilizations developed in Asia and Africa after people learned how to farm. These civilizations began in river valleys, which were perfect places for people to grow crops.

With the development of farming, people no longer had to travel in search of food. Instead, they could settle down in one place. Eventually, people built the first towns and cities and invented government, writing, and the wheel. They also created huge buildings and temples and produced incredible works of art.

In the next two chapters, you will learn about the early civilizations of Mesopotamia, Egypt, and Kush.

Explore the Art

In this scene, the young King Tutankhamen of Egypt stands with his wife at the entrance to a temple. How does this scene show some of the features of Egyptian civilization?

49

Democracy and Civic Education

At Level

Justice: Rule of Law and Hammurabi's Code

Background The earliest known written set of laws is Hammurabi's Code. This set of 282 laws established rule of law in the Babylonian Empire.

1. Explain the term rule of law, under which all members of a society, including rulers, must follow set laws. Discuss the importance of the rule of law for the protection of individual rights and for promoting the common good.
2. Have students work in small groups to develop standards for evaluating laws. Students should decide what justice is and what are just laws. Have students apply their standards to the excerpt from Hammurabi's Code on p. 73. Are these laws just?
3. Have students work as a class to establish a code of school rules. Students should consider a range of specific situations, from running in the halls to fighting. LS **Interpersonal, Verbal/Linguistic**

Alternative Assessment Handbook, Rubrics 11: Discussion; and 14: Group Activity

Civic Participation Activities

Unit Preview

Connect to the Unit

Activity River Valley Civilizations Remind students that the development of farming led to the growth of towns. Explain that in time, towns developed into civilizations, the first of which grew up in river valleys in Asia and Africa. Write the phrase River Valley for students to see. Below the phrase, create a two-column chart and label the columns Advantages and Disadvantages. Ask students to brainstorm why the first civilizations developed in river valleys. Write the responses in the Advantages column. To help students get started, remind them that farming led to population growth and to the development of more complex societies. Then ask students to consider what some of the disadvantages of living in river valleys might be. List the responses in the Disadvantages column. At the end of the unit, have students review the chart and revise it based on what they have learned.
LS **Visual/Spatial**

Explore the Art

In 1922, Howard Carter led a team of archaeologists that located the tomb of King Tutankhamen, or King Tut. King Tut was a pharaoh, or ruler, of ancient Egypt. The tomb had been undisturbed and contained many treasures. As a result, King Tut has become one of the most famous of Egypt's pharaohs, although he was in fact only a minor ruler.

About the Illustration

This illustration is an artist's conception based on available sources. However, historians are uncertain exactly what this scene looked like.

Answers

Explore the Art *shows architecture, clothing styles, jewelry, artifacts, paintings on temple walls, respect shown to king*

Chapter 3 Planning Guide

Mesopotamia and the Fertile Crescent

Overview	Instructional Resources	
CHAPTER 3 **Essential Question:** How did geography influence the development of civilization in Southwest Asia? **Focus on the Essential Question Podcast**	TOS **Differentiated Instruction Teacher Management System:** • Instructional Benchmarking Guides • Lesson Plans for Differentiated Instruction **Guided Reading Workbook** **Chapter Resource File:** • Chapter Review Activity • Focus on Writing Activity: A Poster • Social Studies Skills Activity: Interpreting Physical Maps	TOS **Calendar Planner** **Power Presentations with Media Gallery** **Differentiated Instruction Modified Worksheets and Tests CD-ROM** **Primary Sources Library CD-ROM for World History** **Interactive Skills Tutor CD-ROM** **Student Edition on Audio CD Program**
Section 1: **Geography of the Fertile Crescent** **The Big Idea:** The valleys of the Tigris and Euphrates rivers were the site of the world's first civilizations.	TOS **Differentiated Instruction Teacher Management System:** Section 1 Lesson Plan **Guided Reading Workbook:** Section 1 **Chapter Resource File:** • Vocabulary Builder Activity, Section 1 • History and Geography Activity: A Fertile Land	**Daily Bellringer Transparency:** Section 1 **Map Transparency:** The Fertile Crescent **Animated History:** Fertile Crescent, 2400–1600 BC
Section 2: **The Rise of Sumer** **The Big Idea:** The Sumerians developed the first civilization in Mesopotamia.	TOS **Differentiated Instruction Teacher Management System:** Section 2 Lesson Plan **Guided Reading Workbook:** Section 2 **Chapter Resource File:** • Vocabulary Builder Activity, Section 2 • Biography Activity: Enheduanna • Primary Source Activity: The Sumerian Flood Story	**Daily Bellringer Transparency:** Section 2 **Map Transparency:** Sargon's Empire, c. 2330 BC **Internet Activity:** Drawing of a City-State **Internet Activity:** Sumerian Gods and Goddesses **Animated History:** Sumerian City-States, 2300 BC
Section 3: **Sumerian Achievements** **The Big Idea:** The Sumerians made many advances that helped their society develop.	TOS **Differentiated Instruction Teacher Management System:** Section 3 Lesson Plan **Guided Reading Workbook:** Section 3 **Chapter Resource File:** • Vocabulary Builder Activity, Section 3 • Interdisciplinary Projects: Mesopotamia: The First Writing • Literature Activity: *The Epic of Gilgamesh*	**Daily Bellringer Transparency:** Section 3 **Animated History:** Ziggurat
Section 4: **Later peoples of the Fertile Crescent** **The Big Idea:** After the Sumerians, many cultures ruled parts of the Fertile Crescent.	TOS **Differentiated Instruction Teacher Management System:** Section 4 Lesson Plan **Guided Reading Workbook:** Section 4 **Chapter Resource File:** • Vocabulary Builder Activity, Section 4 • Biography Activity: Hammurabi • Biography Activity: King Nebuchadnezzar • Primary Source Activity: The Code of Hammurabi • Primary Source: Descriptions of the Phoenicians	**Daily Bellringer Transparency:** Section 4 **Quick Facts Transparency:** Hammurabi's Code **Map Transparency:** Babylonian and Assyrian Empires **Map Transparency:** Phoenicia, c. 800 BC

Chart Key:

SE Student Edition
 Presentation Resource
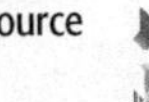 MP3 Audio
TOS Teacher One Stop
 DVD/CD-ROM
HISTORY™
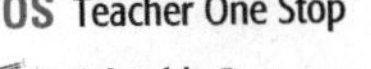 Printable Resource

Program Resources available on TOS and @ hmhsocialstudies.com

Review, Assessment, Intervention

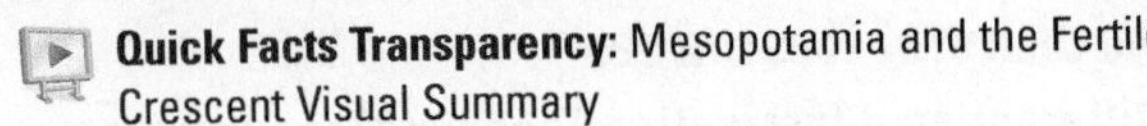

- **Quick Facts Transparency:** Mesopotamia and the Fertile Crescent Visual Summary
- **Spanish Chapter Summaries Audio CD Program**
- **Quiz Game CD-ROM**
- **Progress Assessment Support System (PASS):** Chapter Test
- **Differentiated Instruction Modified Worksheets and Tests CD-ROM:** Modified Chapter Test
- TOS **ExamView® Assessment Suite (English/Spanish)**
- **Online Assessment Program,** in the Interactive Student Edition

- **PASS:** Section 1 Quiz
- **Online Quiz:** Section 1
- **Alternative Assessment Handbook**

- **PASS:** Section 2 Quiz
- **Online Quiz:** Section 2
- **Alternative Assessment Handbook**

- **PASS:** Section 3 Quiz
- **Online Quiz:** Section 3
- **Alternative Assessment Handbook**

- **PASS:** Section 4 Quiz
- **Online Quiz:** Section 4
- **Alternative Assessment Handbook**

Supporting Resources

- Multimedia Classroom Global History Series
- Global History Teacher's Guide

Maps Globes Graphs Level F

- Student Workbook
- Teacher's Guide

Social Studies Trade Library Collections

- Premier Secondary World History Trade Collection
- Ancient World History Trade Collection

History's Impact

World History Video Program

- **Mesopotamian Achievements**

For more information or to purchase go to hmhsocialstudies.com

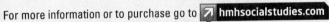

Power Presentations with Media Gallery

Power Presentations with Media Gallery are visual presentations of each chapter's main ideas. Presentations can be customized by including Quick Facts charts, images from the text, and video clips.

CHAPTER 3 PLANNING GUIDE

Differentiating Instruction

How do I address the needs of varied learners?

The Target Resource acts as your primary strategy for differentiated instruction.

ENGLISH-LANGUAGE LEARNERS & STRUGGLING READERS

Interactive Skills Tutor CD-ROM

The Interactive Skills Tutor CD-ROM contains lessons that provide additional practice for 20 different critical thinking skills.

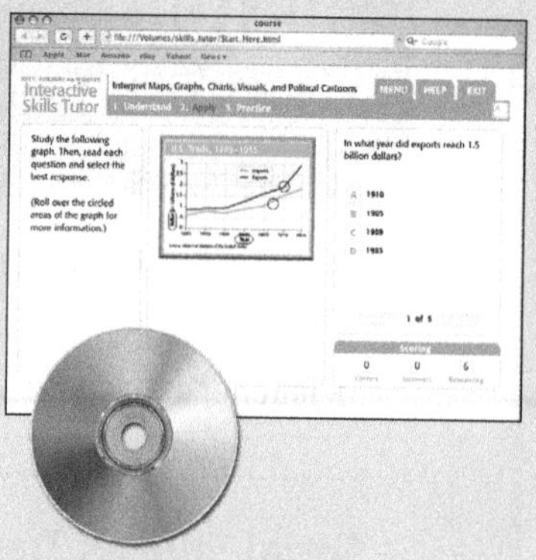

Additional Resources

Differentiated Instruction Teacher Management System: Lesson Plans for Differentiated Instruction

Chapter Resource File:
- Vocabulary Builder Activities
- Social Studies Skills Activity: Interpreting Physical Maps

Quick Facts Transparencies: Mesopotamia and the Fertile Crescent Visual Summary

Student Edition on Audio CD Program

Spanish/English Guided Reading Workbook

SPECIAL NEEDS LEARNERS

Differentiated Instruction Modified Worksheets and Tests CD-ROM

- Vocabulary Flash Cards
- Vocabulary Builder Activities
- Chapter Review Activity
- Chapter Test

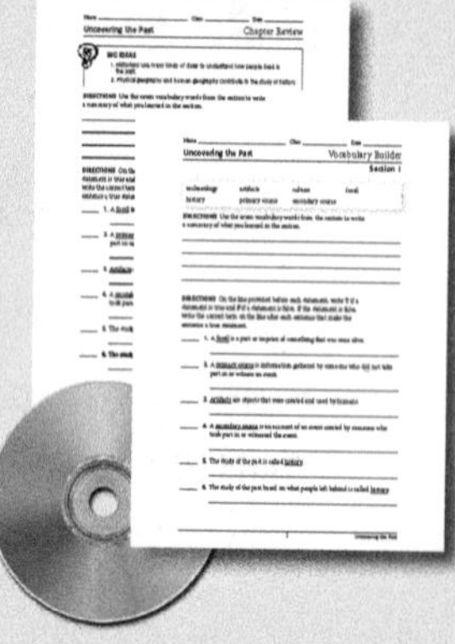

Additional Resources

Differentiated Instruction Teacher Management System: Lesson Plans for Differentiated Instruction

Guided Reading Workbook

Chapter Resource File: Social Studies Skills Activity: Interpreting Physical Maps

Student Edition on Audio CD Program

Interactive Skills Tutor CD-ROM

ADVANCED/GIFTED-AND-TALENTED STUDENTS

Primary Source Library CD-ROM for World History

The Library contains longer versions of quotations in the text, extra sources, and images. Included are point-of-view articles, journals, diaries, historical fiction, and political documents.

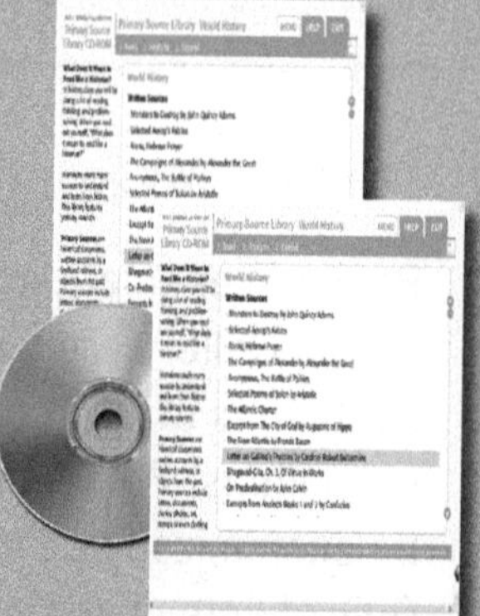

Additional Resources

Differentiated Instruction Teacher Management System: Lesson Plans for Differentiated Instruction

Chapter Resource File:
- Focus on Writing Activity: A Poster
- Literature Activity: *The Epic of Gilgamesh*

Document-Based Questions Activities

Differentiated Activities in the Teacher's Edition

- Learning from Visuals, p. 58
- Creating Pictographs, p. 66

Teacher One Stop™

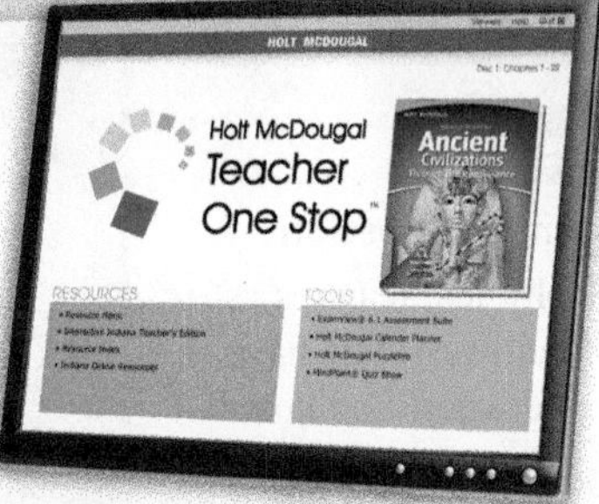

How can I manage the lesson plans and support materials for differentiated instruction?

With the Teacher One Stop, you can easily organize and print lesson plans, planning guides, and instructional materials for all learners. The Teacher One Stop includes the following materials to help you differentiate instruction:

- Interactive Teacher's Edition
- Calendar Planner and pacing guides
- Editable lesson plans
- All reproducible ancillaries in Adobe Acrobat (PDF) format
- ExamView Assessment Suite (English & Spanish)
- Transparency and video previews

Differentiated Activities in the Teacher's Edition

- Making a Collage, p. 67
- Using Visual Aids, p. 78

Interactive Student Edition

Complete online student edition with interactive multimedia support for chapter content assessment and reporting

- Interactive Maps and Notebook
- Graphic Organizers
- Standardized Test Prep
- Online Homework Practice and Research Activities
- Current Events
- Chapter-based Internet Activities
- Animated History Activities
- and more!

Differentiated Activities in the Teacher's Edition

- Linking to Today, p. 58
- Writing Sumerian Numerals, p. 67

Chapter Preview

Essential Question

Introduce the Essential Question

- Explain that the physical features and climate of Southwest Asia have strongly influenced where and how people live.
- Explain that Sumer, an early civilization, developed in Mesopotamia, the land between the Tigris and Euphrates rivers.
- Describe how several great empires rose and fell in the Fertile Crescent, the region stretching from the Persian Gulf northwest up the Tigris and Euphrates and west to the Mediterranean Sea.

Focus on Writing

The **Chapter Resource File** provides a Focus on Writing worksheet to help students organize their writing.

CRF: Focus on Writing Activity: A Poster

Key to Differentiating Instruction

Below Level
Basic-level activities designed for all students encountering new material

At Level
Intermediate-level activities designed for average students

Above Level
Challenging activities designed for honors and gifted and talented students

Standard English Mastery
Activities designed to improve standard English usage

LS Learning Styles

CHAPTER 3 7000–500 BC

Mesopotamia and the Fertile Crescent

Essential Question How did geography influence the development of civilization in Southwest Asia?

South Carolina Performance Standards

6-1.2 Explain the emergence of agriculture and its effect on early human communities, including the domestication of plants and animals, the impact of irrigation techniques, and subsequent food surpluses; **6-1.3** Compare the river valley civilizations of the Tigris and Euphrates (Mesopotamia), the Nile (Egypt), the Indus (India), and the Huang He (China), including the evolution of written language, government, trade systems, architecture, and forms of social order.

Literacy Skills for Social Studies

- Interpret Earth's physical and human systems by using maps, mental maps, geographic models, and other social studies resources.
- Compare the locations of places, the conditions of places, and the connections between places.
- Explain why trade occurs and how historical patterns of trade have contributed to global interdependence.

Focus on Writing

A Letter Most elementary students have not read or heard much about ancient Mesopotamia. As you read this chapter, you can gather information about that land. Then you can write a letter to share some of what you have learned with a young child.

CHAPTER EVENTS

c. 7000 BC Agriculture first develops in Mesopotamia.

7000 BC

WORLD EVENTS

c. 3100 BC Menes becomes the first pharaoh of Egypt.

Introduce the Chapter

At Level

The Development of Cities

1. Ask students to imagine that they are living in a large farming community in ancient times. Remind students that early farming villages were not technologically advanced. As the communities grew more food, their settlements grew in size. Have students discuss what inventions, technology, or organizations would be needed in the community as it grows. Ask students to explain why each item or idea is needed. What might it take to create these advances?
2. Explain to students that they are going to learn about the world's first civilization, Mesopotamia, and how it grew from small farming communities to a civilization with advanced technology and large cities.
3. Ask students to keep track of the new ideas that were developed in Mesopotamia and the impact those new ideas would have on the world. **LS Verbal/Linguistic, Interpersonal**

c. 2350–2330 BC
Sargon of Akkad conquers Mesopotamia and forms the world's first empire.
c. 1770 BC
Hammurabi of Babylon issues a written code of laws.
c. 1000 BC
Phoenicians trade all around the Mediterranean.
2750 BC
2000 BC
1250 BC
500 BC
c. 2300 BC
The Harappan civilization rises in the Indus Valley.
c. 1500 BC
The Shang dynasty is established in China.
c. 965 BC
Solomon becomes king of Israel.
51

This photo shows the partially reconstructed remains of an ancient temple in Mesopotamia.

Chapter Preview

Explore the Picture

Ziggurat at Ur Mesopotamian temples known as ziggurats served as places of worship and were the largest, most important buildings in their cities. The photo here shows one of the most famous Mesopotamian ziggurats, the ziggurat at Ur. The ruins of the ancient Sumerian temple, believed to have been built in about 2100 BC, are located near the present-day city of Nasiriyah, in southeastern Iraq. Attempts at restoring the ziggurat took place in the 1930s, but only the lower level of the temple was restored.

Analyzing Visuals What types of technology or knowledge were probably needed to build this temple? *possible answers—knowledge of architecture, engineering, masonry, surveying*

hmhsocialstudies.com
Teacher Resources

Explore the Time Line

1. About how many years passed between the writing of Hammurabi's code of laws and the establishment of the Shang dynasty? *270*
2. When was the world's first empire established? between *2350 and 2330 BC*
3. Which occurred first, the creation of the Harappan civilization in India or the rise of the Shang dynasty in China? *Harappan civilization*

Info to Know

The Code of Hammurabi One of the oldest known collections of written laws, the Code of Hammurabi contains 282 laws dealing with matters ranging from marriage and divorce to theft and murder. The legal code, engraved on a large stone slab, was discovered in 1901 at the site of the ancient Mesopotamian city of Susa in modern-day Iran. However, historians believe the code of laws originally stood in the temple of Marduk in Babylon.

Reading Social Studies

Understanding Themes

Discuss with students the two key themes of this chapter. Organize the class into small groups. Ask students to imagine that they are members of a culture that has recently adopted a settled, agricultural lifestyle. Have each group discuss what types of technology they might need to function in their villages and cities. Then have students discuss the type of government they might establish in their settlement. Help the class to see that technology and politics were two themes of great importance to early civilizations.

Main Ideas in Social Studies

Focus on Reading Ask students to bring in newspaper or magazine articles that interest them. Have each student read his or her article and select two or three paragraphs to work with. For each paragraph, have students follow the steps listed at right to identify the main idea. Then ask students to find a partner with whom to exchange articles. Have students read the selected paragraphs and identify the main idea for each. When students are finished, have them compare main ideas. Ask students if they each identified the same main idea.

Reading Social Studies

Economics | Geography | **Politics** | Religion | Society and Culture | **Science and Technology**

Focus on Themes Chapter three introduces you to a region in Southwest Asia called Mesopotamia, the home of the world's first civilization. You will read about what made this area one where civilizations could begin and grow. You will learn about one group of people—the Sumerians—and their great **technological** inventions. You will also read about other people who invaded Mesopotamia and brought their own rules of governing and **politics** to the area.

Main Ideas in Social Studies

Focus on Reading Have you ever set up a tent? If you have, you know that one pole provides structure and support for the whole tent. A paragraph has a similar structure. One idea—the **main idea**—provides support and structure for the whole paragraph.

Identifying Main Ideas Most paragraphs written about history include a main idea that is stated clearly in a sentence. At other times, the main idea is suggested, not stated. However, that idea still shapes the paragraph's content and the meaning of all of the facts and details in it.

Identifying Main Ideas

1. Read the paragraph. Ask yourself, "What is this paragraph mostly about?"
2. List the important facts and details that relate to that topic.
3. Ask yourself, "What seems to be the most important point the writer is making about the topic?" Or ask, "If the writer could say only one thing about this paragraph, what would it be?" **This is the main idea of the paragraph.**

Having people available to work on different jobs meant that society could accomplish more. Large projects, such as constructing buildings and digging irrigation systems, required specialized workers, managers, and organization. To complete these projects, the Mesopotamians needed structure and rules. Structure and rules could be provided by laws and government.

Topic: The paragraph talks about people, jobs, and structure.

\+

Facts and Details:

- People working on different jobs needed structure.
- Laws and government provided this structure.

=

Main Idea: Having people in a society work on many different jobs led to the creation of laws and government.

Reading and Skills Resources

Reading Support

- Guided Reading Workbook
- Student Edition on Audio CD
- Spanish Chapter Summaries Audio CD Program

Social Studies Skills Support

- Interactive Skills Tutor CD-ROM

Vocabulary Support

- **CRF:** Vocabulary Builder Activities
- **CRF:** Chapter Review Activity
- Differentiated Instruction Modified Worksheets and Tests CD-ROM:
  - Vocabulary Flash Cards
  - Vocabulary Builder Activity
  - Chapter Review Activity
- **TOS** Holt McDougal PuzzleView

You Try It!

The passage below is from the chapter you are about to read. Read it and then answer the questions below.

Technical Advances

One of the Sumerians' most important developments was the wheel. They were the first people to build wheeled vehicles, including carts and wagons. Using the wheel, Sumerians invented a device that spins clay as a craftsperson shapes it into bowls. This device is called a potter's wheel.

The plow was another important Sumerian invention. Pulled by oxen, plows broke through the hard soil of Sumer to prepare it for planting. This technique greatly increased farm production. The Sumerians also invented a clock that used falling water to measure time.

Sumerian advances improved daily life in many ways. Sumerians built sewers under city streets. They learned to use bronze to make stronger tools and weapons. They even produced makeup and glass jewelry.

Answer the following questions about finding main ideas.

1. Reread the first paragraph. What is its main idea?
2. What is the main idea of the third paragraph? Reread the second paragraph. Is there a sentence that expresses the main idea of the paragraph? What is that main idea? Write a sentence to express it.
3. Which of the following best expresses the main idea of the entire passage?
   - **a.** The wheel was an important invention.
   - **b.** The Sumerians invented many helpful devices.

As you read Chapter 3, find the main ideas of the paragraphs you are studying.

Key Terms and People

Chapter 3

Section 1
Fertile Crescent *(p. 55)*
silt *(p. 55)*
irrigation *(p. 56)*
canals *(p. 56)*
surplus *(p. 56)*
division of labor *(p. 56)*

Section 2
rural *(p. 60)*
urban *(p. 60)*
city-state *(p. 60)*
Gilgamesh *(p. 61)*
Sargon *(p. 61)*
empire *(p. 61)*
polytheism *(p. 62)*
priests *(p. 63)*
social hierarchy *(p. 63)*

Section 3
cuneiform *(p. 65)*
pictographs *(p. 66)*
scribe *(p. 66)*
epics *(p. 66)*
architecture *(p. 68)*
ziggurat *(p. 68)*

Section 4
monarch *(p. 72)*
Hammurabi's Code *(p. 73)*
chariot *(p. 74)*
Nebuchadnezzar *(p. 75)*
alphabet *(p. 77)*

Academic Vocabulary

Success in school is related to knowing academic vocabulary—the words that are frequently used in school assignments and discussions. In this chapter, you will learn the following academic words:

role *(p. 62)*
impact *(p. 63)*

Reading Social Studies

Key Terms and People

This chapter has a lengthy list of key terms. Some will be familiar to students, but others will be new. Read the list aloud so that students will know how to pronounce each term or name. After you read each term, ask volunteers to explain what the term might mean. Correct student suggestions if necessary. Then have students copy the words into a two-column chart labeled *People* and *Terms*. As you prepare to study each section, have students define or identify each term or person in their list.
LS Verbal/Linguistic

Focus on Reading

See the **Focus on Reading** questions in this chapter for more practice on this reading social studies skill.

Reading Social Studies Assessment

See the **Chapter Review** at the end of this chapter for student assessment questions related to this reading skill.

Teaching Tip

Tell students that in order to get the most out of their studying time, they should make sure they understand the main ideas of what they are reading or studying. One way to do this is to be sure that they understand the main idea of a passage before moving on to the next one. Suggest that while they are reading, they stop after every few paragraphs or after every heading and identify that passage's main idea. This will help students become active readers and retain more of what they have read.

Answers

You Try It! 1. *One of the most important Sumerian developments was the wheel.* **2.** *Sumerian advances improved their daily life; no; possible main idea—Sumerians made other important advances.* **3.** *b*

Preteach

Bellringer

If YOU were there . . . Use the **Daily Bellringer Transparency** to help students answer the question.

Daily Bellringer Transparency, Section 1

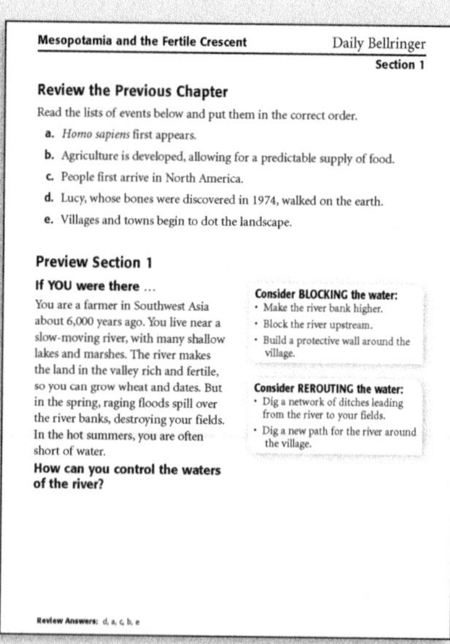
Mesopotamia and the Fertile Crescent — Daily Bellringer, **Section 1**

Review the Previous Chapter

Read the lists of events below and put them in the correct order.

- **a.** *Homo sapiens* first appears.
- **b.** Agriculture is developed, allowing for a predictable supply of food.
- **c.** People first arrive in North America.
- **d.** Lucy, whose bones were discovered in 1974, walked on the earth.
- **e.** Villages and towns begin to dot the landscape.

Preview Section 1

If YOU were there ...

You are a farmer in Southwest Asia about 6,000 years ago. You live near a slow-moving river, with many shallow lakes and marshes. The river makes the land in the valley rich and fertile, so you can grow wheat and dates. But in the spring, raging floods spill over the river banks, destroying your fields. In the hot summers, you are often short of water.

How can you control the waters of the river?

Consider BLOCKING the water:
- Make the river bank higher.
- Block the river upstream.
- Build a protective wall around the village.

Consider REROUTING the water:
- Dig a network of ditches leading from the river to your fields.
- Dig a new path for the river around the village.

Review Answers: d, a, c, b, e

Building Vocabulary

Preteach or review the following terms:

occupations work or ways of making a living (p. 56)

plateau an elevated flatland with a level surface (p. 55)

CRF: Vocabulary Builder Activity, Section 1

Taking Notes

Have students use the graphic organizer online to take notes on the section. This activity will prepare students for the Section Assessment, in which they will complete a graphic organizer that builds on the information using the Critical Thinking Skill: Identifying Cause and Effect.

SECTION 1

Geography of the Fertile Crescent

What You Will Learn...

Main Ideas

1. The rivers of Southwest Asia supported the growth of civilization.
2. New farming techniques led to the growth of cities.

The Big Idea

The valleys of the Tigris and Euphrates rivers were the site of the world's first civilizations.

Key Terms

Fertile Crescent, *p. 55*
silt, *p. 55*
irrigation, *p. 56*
canals, *p. 56*
surplus, *p. 56*
division of labor, *p. 56*

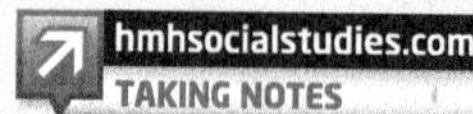

Use the graphic organizer online to list the cause-and-effect relationship between each river valley and the civilization that developed around it.

If YOU were there...

You are a farmer in Southwest Asia about 6,000 years ago. You live near a slow-moving river, with many shallow lakes and marshes. The river makes the land in the valley rich and fertile, so you can grow wheat and dates. But in the spring, raging floods spill over the riverbanks, destroying your fields. In the hot summers, you are often short of water.

How can you control the waters of the river?

BUILDING BACKGROUND In several parts of the world, bands of hunter-gatherers began to settle down in farming settlements. They domesticated plants and animals. Gradually their cultures became more complex. Most early civilizations grew up along rivers, where people learned to work together to control floods.

Rivers Support the Growth of Civilization

Early peoples settled where crops would grow. Crops usually grew well near rivers, where water was available and regular floods made the soil rich. One region in Southwest Asia was especially well suited for farming. It lay between two rivers.

Teach the Big Idea

At Level

Geography of the Fertile Crescent

1. **Teach** Ask students the questions in the Main Idea boxes to teach this section.
2. **Apply** Have each student create a proposal to the United Nations requesting a memorial or historical marker for Mesopotamia. Have students explain why they believe there should be a memorial and what significance Mesopotamia has to history. Remind students to cite specific accomplishments from the section and to use persuasive language in their proposal. **LS Verbal/Linguistic**
3. **Review** Ask students to exchange their completed proposals with one another as a review of the section.
4. **Practice/Homework** Have students draw sketches of what their proposed memorials or markers might look like and where they could be located. **LS Visual/Spatial**

Alternative Assessment Handbook, Rubrics 3: Artwork; and 43: Writing to Persuade

The Land Between the Rivers

The Tigris and Euphrates rivers are the most important physical features of the region sometimes known as Mesopotamia (mes-uh-puh-TAY-mee-uh). Mesopotamia means "between the rivers" in Greek.

As you can see on the map, the region called Mesopotamia lies between Asia Minor and the Persian Gulf. The region is part of a larger area called the **Fertile Crescent**, a large arc of rich, or fertile, farmland. The Fertile Crescent extends from the Persian Gulf to the Mediterranean Sea.

In ancient times, Mesopotamia was actually made of two parts. Northern Mesopotamia was a plateau bordered on the north and the east by mountains. Southern Mesopotamia was a flat plain. The Tigris and Euphrates rivers flowed down from the hills into this low-lying plain.

The Rise of Civilization

Hunter-gatherer groups first settled in Mesopotamia more than 12,000 years ago. Over time, these people learned how to plant crops to grow their own food. Every year, floods on the Tigris and Euphrates rivers brought **silt**, a mixture of rich soil and tiny rocks, to the land. The fertile silt made the land ideal for farming.

The first farm settlements formed in Mesopotamia as early as 7000 BC. Farmers grew wheat, barley, and other types of grain. Livestock, birds, and fish were also good sources of food. Plentiful food led to population growth, and villages formed. Eventually, these early villages developed into the world's first civilization.

READING CHECK **Summarizing** What made civilization possible in Mesopotamia?

The Fertile Crescent

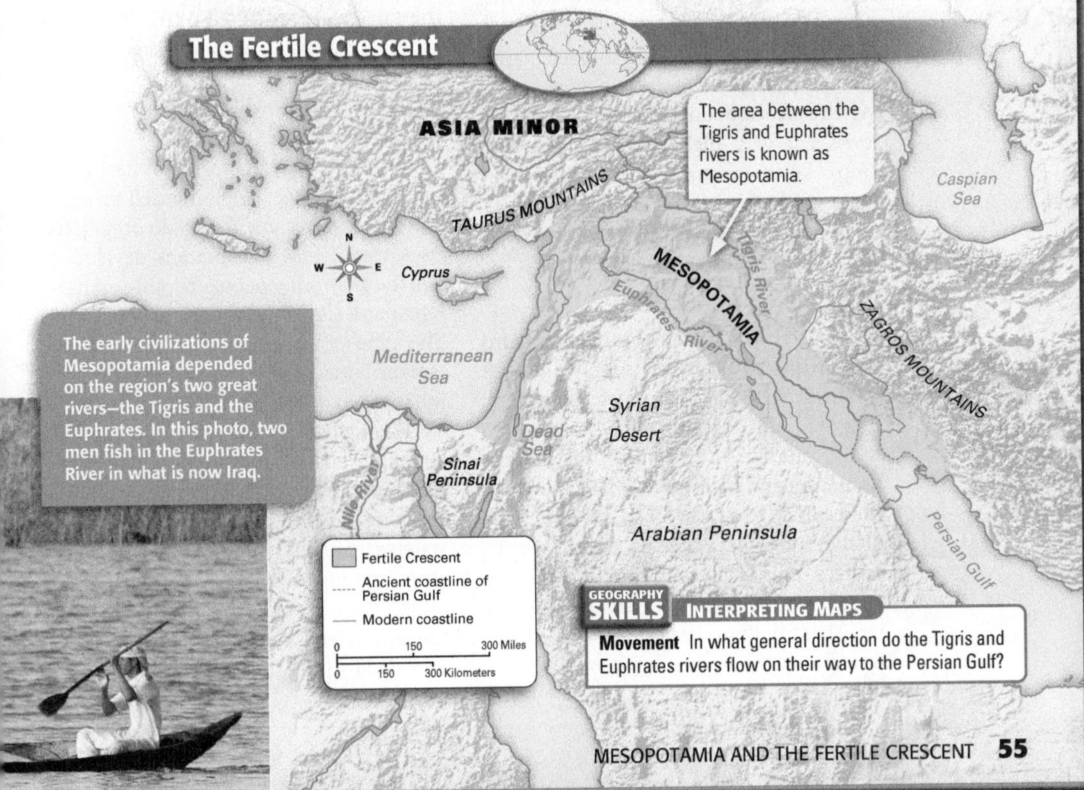

The early civilizations of Mesopotamia depended on the region's two great rivers—the Tigris and the Euphrates. In this photo, two men fish in the Euphrates River in what is now Iraq.

GEOGRAPHY SKILLS INTERPRETING MAPS

Movement In what general direction do the Tigris and Euphrates rivers flow on their way to the Persian Gulf?

Direct Teach

Main Idea

❶ Rivers Support the Growth of Civilization

The rivers of Southwest Asia supported the growth of civilization.

Identify What does *Mesopotamia* mean? On what rivers did Mesopotamia develop? *"between the rivers"; Tigris and Euphrates rivers*

Explain What is the Fertile Crescent? *a large arc of rich farmland extending from the Persian Gulf to the Mediterranean Sea*

Summarize When and how were farming settlements established in Mesopotamia? *By 7000 BC people were growing crops along the Tigris and Euphrates rivers and had formed small settlements there.*

CRF: History and Geography Activity: A Fertile Land

Map Transparency: The Fertile Crescent

Connect to Geography

Mesopotamia's Exotic Rivers The Tigris and Euphrates rivers are considered exotic rivers, meaning that they begin in humid regions and then flow across dry areas. Both rivers begin in the mountains of Asia Minor and flow to the Persian Gulf. Before they reach the Persian Gulf, however, they join together in a single, 120-mile-long channel known as the Shatt al-Arab.

Critical Thinking: Understanding Cause and Effect

Below Level

Cause-and-Effect Posters

1. Discuss with students the reasons why Mesopotamia was the site of the world's first civilization. Ask students why hunter-gatherers might have decided to settle in the Fertile Crescent. Then, discuss with students what the effects were of settlement in Mesopotamia. Encourage students to take notes about the discussion.
2. Have each student briefly sketch a diagram that depicts the causes of settlement in the Fertile Crescent and the results of this settlement. Then, have each student create a poster using illustrations to show the causes and effects of settlement in the Fertile Crescent. Remind students that their posters should be easy to understand.
3. Ask volunteers to share their cause-and-effect posters with the class.
LS Visual/Spatial, Verbal/Linguistic

Alternative Assessment Handbook, Rubrics 3: Artwork; and 6: Cause and Effect

Answers

Interpreting Maps *southeast*

Reading Check *Tigris and Euphrates flooding left a fertile layer of soil for crops, which provided food for early settlements.*

Direct Teach

Main Idea

❷ Farming and Cities

New farming techniques led to the growth of cities.

Explain How did irrigation help farmers? *It provided a way of supplying water to fields and storing water for times of need.*

Analyze What effects did irrigation have on farming settlements? *It made farmers more productive, which led to a food surplus and less need for people to farm, and these in turn led to a division of labor.*

Make Inferences How might big construction projects like the building of canals and large buildings lead to laws and government? *To keep workers organized and following the construction plan, structure and rules were needed, and these would lead to governments and laws.*

Info to Know

Raw Materials The people of Mesopotamia survived on resources provided by the Tigris and Euphrates rivers and the flat plains along the rivers. Wood, stone, and metal were almost nonexistent in the region. Without wood, buildings had to be made of clay bricks. Without stone, roads were difficult to maintain. However, by carefully using their water resources, people had enough vegetables, grains, fish, and livestock.

Irrigation and Civilization

Early farmers faced the challenge of learning how to control the flow of river water to their fields in both rainy and dry seasons.

❶ Early settlements in Mesopotamia were located near rivers. Water was not controlled, and flooding was a major problem.

❷ Later, people built canals to protect houses from flooding and move water to their fields.

Farming and Cities

Although Mesopotamia had fertile soil, farming wasn't easy there. The region received little rain. This meant that the water levels in the Tigris and Euphrates rivers depended on how much rain fell in eastern Asia Minor where the two rivers began. When a great amount of rain fell there, water levels got very high. Flooding destroyed crops, killed livestock, and washed away homes. When water levels were too low, crops dried up. Farmers knew they needed a way to control the rivers' flow.

Controlling Water

To solve their problems, Mesopotamians used **irrigation**, a way of supplying water to an area of land. To irrigate their land, they dug out large storage basins to hold water supplies. Then they dug **canals**, human-made waterways, that connected these basins to a network of ditches. These ditches brought water to the fields. To protect their fields from flooding, farmers built up the banks of the Tigris and Euphrates. These built-up banks held back floodwaters even when river levels were high.

THE IMPACT TODAY

People still build dikes, or earthen walls along rivers or shorelines, to hold back water.

Food Surpluses

Irrigation increased the amount of food farmers were able to grow. In fact, farmers could produce a food **surplus**, or more than they needed. Farmers also used irrigation to water grazing areas for cattle and sheep. As a result, Mesopotamians ate a variety of foods. Fish, meat, wheat, barley, and dates were plentiful.

Because irrigation made farmers more productive, fewer people needed to farm. Some people became free to do other jobs. As a result, new occupations developed. For the first time, people became crafters, religious leaders, and government workers. The type of arrangement in which each worker specializes in a particular task or job is called a **division of labor**.

Having people available to work on different jobs meant that society could accomplish more. Large projects, such as constructing buildings and digging irrigation systems, required specialized workers, managers, and organization. To complete these projects, the Mesopotamians needed structure and rules. Structure and rules could be provided by laws and government.

Collaborative Learning

Below Level

Creating a Farming Community

1. Organize the class into small groups. On a sheet of paper, have each group sketch a small farming community in its early stages. Students may use icons for houses, water, and other features.
2. Have groups introduce irrigation to their community. Ask students what adjustments they need to make to their village. Inform students that their village now has a food surplus. Ask groups how the village might change as a result. Have them add the changes to their drawings.
3. Remind students that one result of a food surplus is the division of labor. Have groups decide how their community will develop as a result and revise their drawings.
4. Drawings should gradually get larger, and students should see that their small community is becoming a city. Ask students what features they think are necessary for their city.

LS Visual/Spatial, Logical/Mathematical

Alternative Assessment Handbook, Rubric 14: Group Activity

3 With irrigation, the people of Mesopotamia were able to grow more food.

4 Food surpluses allowed some people to stop farming and concentrate on other jobs, like making clay pots or tools.

The Appearance of Cities

Over time, Mesopotamian settlements grew in size and complexity. They gradually developed into cities between 4000 and 3000 BC.

Despite the growth of cities, society in Mesopotamia was still based on agriculture. Most people still worked in farming jobs. However, cities were becoming important places. People traded goods there, and cities provided leaders with power bases. They were the political, religious, cultural, and economic centers of civilization.

READING CHECK **Analyzing** Why did the Mesopotamians create irrigation systems?

SUMMARY AND PREVIEW Mesopotamia's rich, fertile lands supported productive farming, which led to the development of cities. In Section 2 you will learn about some of the first city builders.

hmhsocialstudies.com
ANIMATED HISTORY
Fertile Crescent, 2400-1600 BC

Section 1 Assessment

hmhsocialstudies.com ONLINE QUIZ

Reviewing Ideas, Terms, and People

1. a. **Identify** Where was Mesopotamia?
   b. **Explain** How did the **Fertile Crescent** get its name?
   c. **Evaluate** What was the most important factor in making Mesopotamia's farmland fertile?
2. a. **Describe** Why did farmers need to develop a system to control their water supply?
   b. **Explain** In what ways did a **division of labor** contribute to the growth of Mesopotamian civilization?
   c. **Elaborate** How might running large projects prepare people for running a government?

Critical Thinking

3. **Identifying Cause and Effect** Farmers who used the rivers for irrigation were part of a cause-effect chain. Use a chart like this one to show that chain.

Water levels in rivers get too low. → [ ] → [ ] → [ ] → Mesopotamians enjoy many foods.

Focus on Writing

4. **Understanding Geography** Make a list of the words you might use to help young students imagine the land and rivers. Then start to sketch out a picture or map you could use on your poster.

Direct Teach

Linking to Today

Irrigation Irrigation is still a necessary part of farming. In fact, over 50 percent of all farmers today use some form of irrigation for their crops. While many farmers still use canals to direct water onto their fields, they use many other methods as well. Sprinkler irrigation and drip irrigation are two forms widely used in the United States.

Review & Assess

Close

Discuss with students the role that water, and the control of it, played in the development of Mesopotamian civilizations.

Review

Online Quiz, Section 1

Assess

SE Section 1 Assessment
PASS: Section 1 Quiz
Alternative Assessment Handbook

Reteach/Classroom Intervention

Guided Reading Workbook, Section 1
Interactive Skills Tutor CD-ROM

Section 1 Assessment Answers

1. **a.** in Southwest Asia, between the Tigris and Euphrates rivers
   b. It came from the arc of fertile land from the Mediterranean Sea to the Persian Gulf.
   c. annual flooding of the Tigris and Euphrates
2. **a.** When the rivers flooded, crops, livestock, and homes were destroyed. Too little water ruined crops. Farmers needed a stable water supply for farming and raising livestock.
   b. People developed expertise outside of farming; large-scale projects were completed, and laws and government needed to carry out such projects were developed.
   c. Both require specialized workers, organization, planning, and rules.
3. possible answers—build up riverbanks to hold back floodwaters; dig storage basins to hold excess water; build canals to connect the basins to ditches; dig a network of ditches to bring water to fields; use irrigation to water grazing areas for cattle and sheep
4. possible answers—fertile lands, plentiful crops, beautiful rivers

Answers

Reading Check *to protect against damage from too much or too little water and to ensure a stable supply of water for crops and livestock*

History and Geography

Activity **Cause-and-Effect Chart** Ask students to imagine that they are in a boat floating down either the Tigris or Euphrates River in ancient Mesopotamia. What might be some of the sights and activities they see on their trip? *Students might suggest farming, irrigation, and people in boats fishing or traveling like them.* Then have each student create a chart showing the causes and effects of settlement and farming in river valleys as shown along the river during their voyages. *causes—see the introduction text at right; effects—see the captions at right.*

LS Verbal/Linguistic

Alternative Assessment Handbook, Rubrics 6: Cause and Effect; and 7: Charts

Linking to Today

Aswan High Dam Egyptians lived by the flooding cycle of the Nile River for thousands of years. In 1970, however, Egypt built the Aswan High Dam. This dam is 364 feet (111 m.) high and more than two miles (3.2 km.) long at the top. The dam created Lake Nasser. The dam generates large amounts of electricity and provides irrigation to many parts of the Nile River Valley.

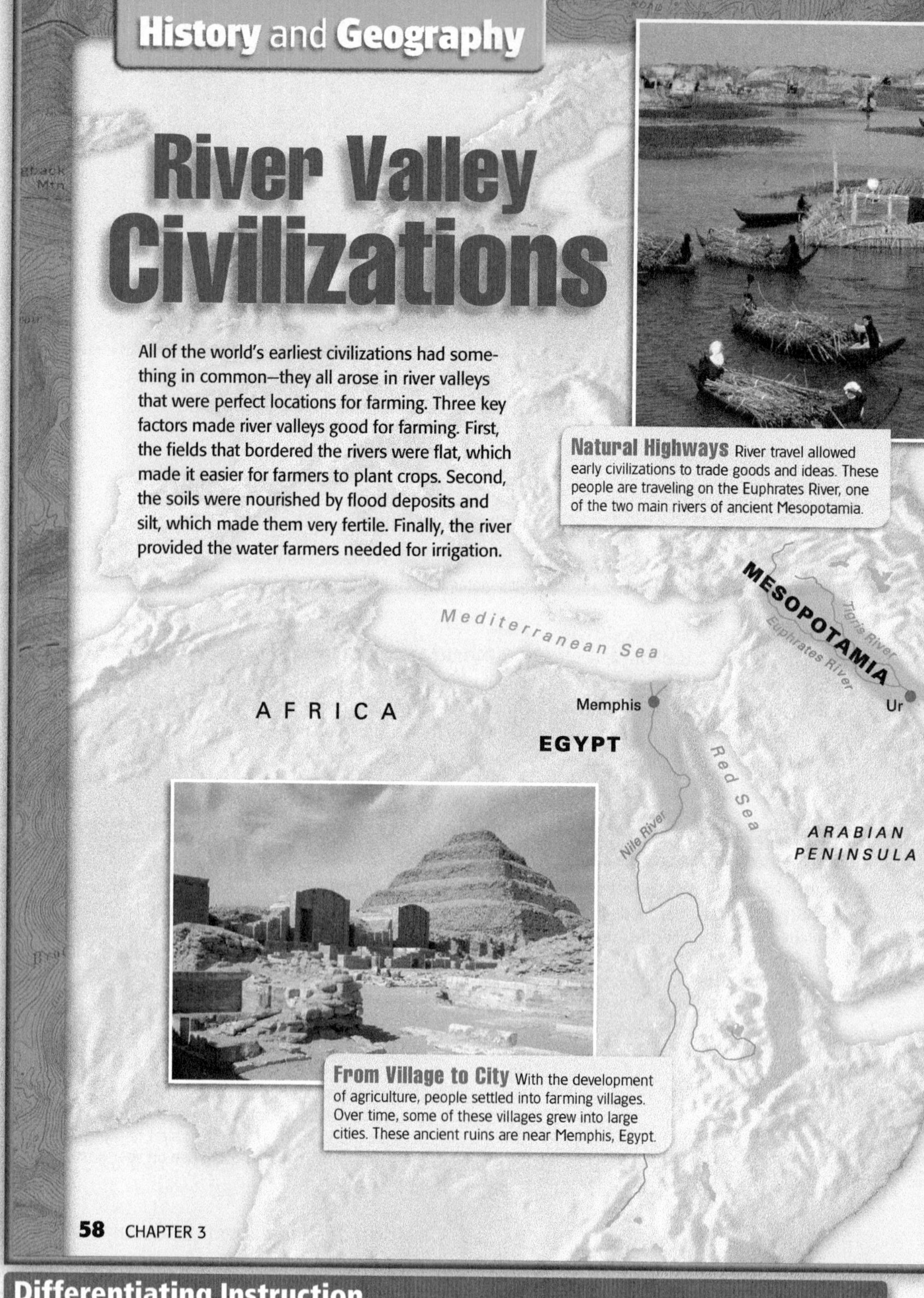

History and Geography
River Valley Civilizations
All of the world's earliest civilizations had something in common—they all arose in river valleys that were perfect locations for farming. Three key factors made river valleys good for farming. First, the fields that bordered the rivers were flat, which made it easier for farmers to plant crops. Second, the soils were nourished by flood deposits and silt, which made them very fertile. Finally, the river provided the water farmers needed for irrigation.
Mediterranean Sea
MESOPOTAMIA
Tigris River
Euphrates River
Ur
AFRICA
Memphis
EGYPT
Red Sea
Nile River
ARABIAN PENINSULA

Natural Highways River travel allowed early civilizations to trade goods and ideas. These people are traveling on the Euphrates River, one of the two main rivers of ancient Mesopotamia.

From Village to City With the development of agriculture, people settled into farming villages. Over time, some of these villages grew into large cities. These ancient ruins are near Memphis, Egypt.

58 CHAPTER 3

Differentiating Instruction

Struggling Readers — Below Level

Learning from Visuals To help struggling readers, have them match the text to the images in the above feature. Read aloud the introduction and each caption. As you do, have students identify images and map elements that correspond to the text, such as cities and river highways. Remind students that this book has many illustrations that can help them learn.

LS Visual-Spatial

Advanced /Gifted and Talented — Above Level

Linking to Today Have students discuss how people rely on rivers today. Write students' responses for the class to see. If you have any rivers in your area, ask students if they know how these rivers are used. Then, encourage volunteers to share ways they have seen rivers being used. Remind students that people around the world are dependent on rivers.

LS Verbal/Linguistic

Alternative Assessment Handbook, Rubric 11: Discussions

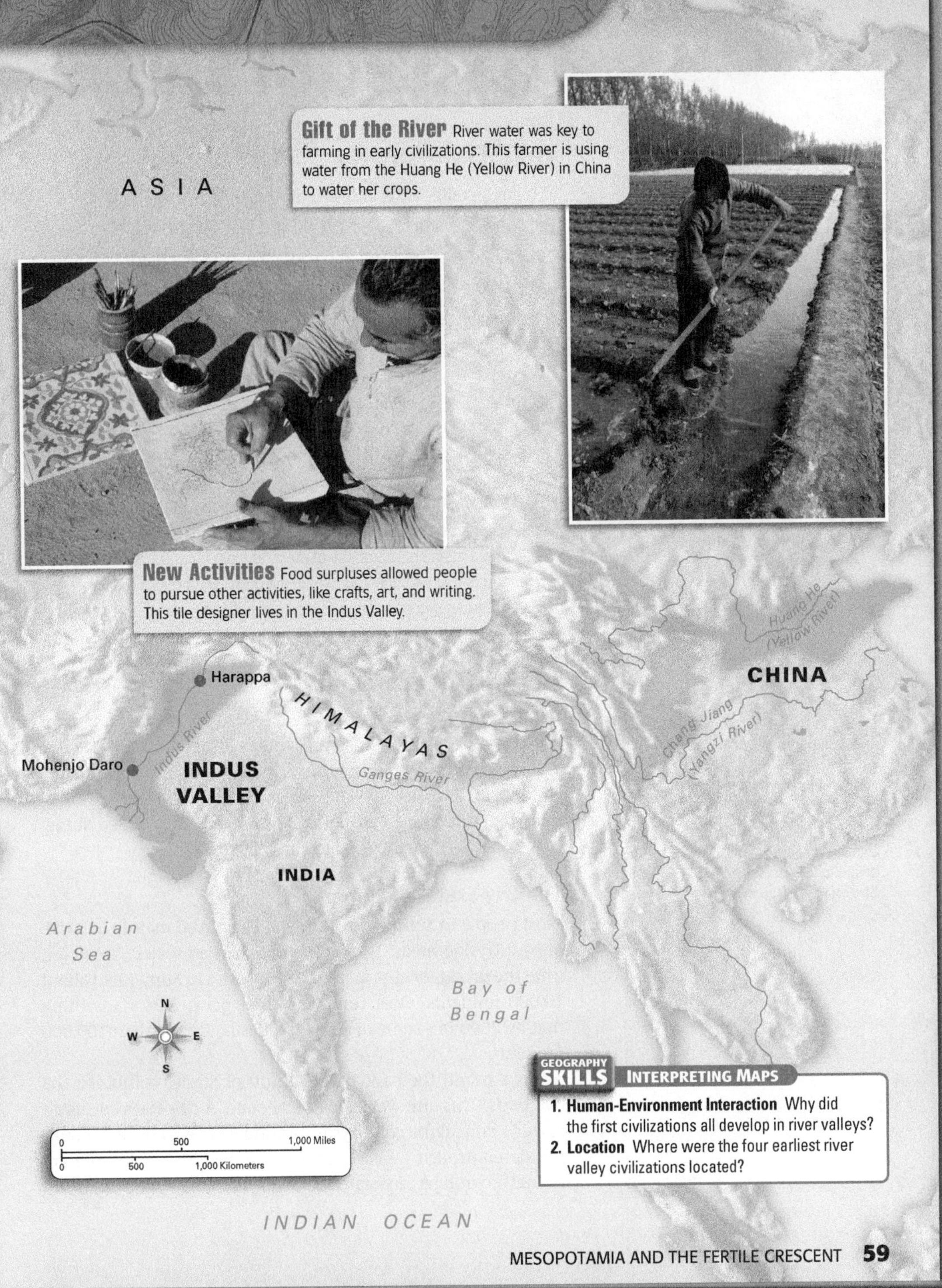

Gift of the River River water was key to farming in early civilizations. This farmer is using water from the Huang He (Yellow River) in China to water her crops.

New Activities Food surpluses allowed people to pursue other activities, like crafts, art, and writing. This tile designer lives in the Indus Valley.

GEOGRAPHY SKILLS INTERPRETING MAPS

1. **Human-Environment Interaction** Why did the first civilizations all develop in river valleys?
2. **Location** Where were the four earliest river valley civilizations located?

History and Geography

Connect to Geography

Human-Environment Interaction If you visit the Indus River Valley today, it will not look like it did 5,000 years ago. Over time, people's presence in the river valley has greatly changed the landscape. One major change has been deforestation, or the widespread cutting down of trees. Few trees grow along the lower Indus River today.

Analyzing Visuals Examine the images on this page. How do they illustrate ways in which people have altered and adapted to river valley environments? *possible answers—altered: built irrigation canals and cities; adapted: used boats for travel*

Activity Researching River Valleys Today Have students create a table with four columns and label the columns *China, Egypt, Indus Valley,* and *Mesopotamia.* In each column have students provide (1) the countries located there today, (2) their capitals, and (3) their populations. A good online source for information is the CIA World Factbook, which can be found at www.cia.gov.
LS Verbal/Linguistic

Collaborative Learning

At Level

Ranking Geographic Regions

1. Draw a chart with four columns and four rows for the class to see. Label the columns *fresh water, flat plain, good soil,* and *transportation.* Label the rows *river valley, seacoast, jungle,* and *desert.*
2. Have the class complete the chart by rating whether each location provides each criteria for settlement and farming. For example, a jungle may provide fresh water and good soil, but it may have poor transportation and does not provide an open flat plain.
3. After students complete the chart, have them discuss how the information relates to the settlement patterns of ancient peoples and why all early civilizations arose in river valleys. **LS Interpersonal, Visual/Spatial**

Alternative Assessment Handbook, Rubric 7: Charts

Answers

Interpreting Maps 1. *because they provided good locations for farming* **2.** *Egypt, Mesopotamia, Indus Valley, and China*

Preteach

Bellringer

If YOU were there . . . Use the **Daily Bellringer Transparency** to help students answer the question.

Daily Bellringer Transparency, Section 2

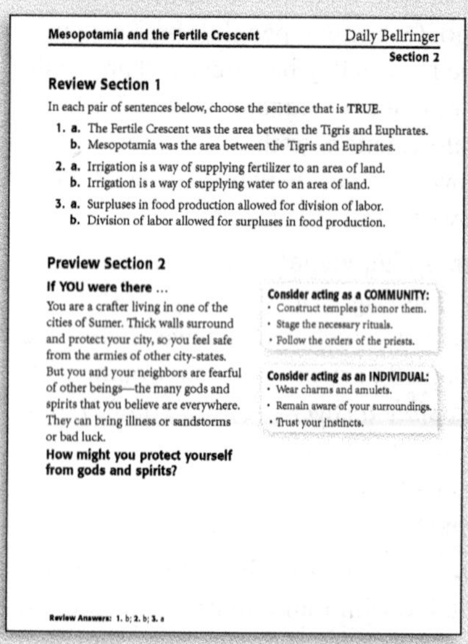

Mesopotamia and the Fertile Crescent Daily Bellringer

Section 2

Review Section 1

In each pair of sentences below, choose the sentence that is TRUE.

1. **a.** The Fertile Crescent was the area between the Tigris and Euphrates.
   b. Mesopotamia was the area between the Tigris and Euphrates.
2. **a.** Irrigation is a way of supplying fertilizer to an area of land.
   b. Irrigation is a way of supplying water to an area of land.
3. **a.** Surpluses in food production allowed for division of labor.
   b. Division of labor allowed for surpluses in food production.

Preview Section 2

If YOU were there ...

You are a crafter living in one of the cities of Sumer. Thick walls surround and protect your city, so you feel safe from the armies of other city-states. But you and your neighbors are fearful of other beings—the many gods and spirits that you believe are everywhere. They can bring illness or sandstorms or bad luck.

How might you protect yourself from gods and spirits?

Consider acting as a COMMUNITY:
- Construct temples to honor them.
- Stage the necessary rituals.
- Follow the orders of the priests.

Consider acting as an INDIVIDUAL:
- Wear charms and amulets.
- Remain aware of your surroundings.
- Trust your instincts.

Review Answers: 1. b; 2. b; 3. a

Academic Vocabulary

Review with students the high-use academic terms in this section.

impact effect, result (p. 63)

role a part or function (p. 62)

CRF: Vocabulary Builder Activity, Section 2

Taking Notes

Have students use the graphic organizer online to take notes on the section. This activity will prepare students for the Section Assessment, in which they will complete a graphic organizer that builds on the information using the Critical Thinking Skill: Summarizing.

SECTION 2

The Rise of Sumer

What You Will Learn...

Main Ideas

1. The Sumerians created the world's first advanced society.
2. Religion played a major role in Sumerian society.

The Big Idea

The Sumerians developed the first civilization in Mesopotamia.

Key Terms and People

rural, *p. 60*
urban, *p. 60*
city-state, *p. 60*
Gilgamesh, *p. 61*
Sargon, *p. 61*
empire, *p. 61*
polytheism, *p. 62*
priests, *p. 63*
social hierarchy, *p. 63*

Use the graphic organizer online to take notes on the Sumerian civilization.

If YOU were there...

You are a crafter living in one of the cities of Sumer. Thick walls surround and protect your city, so you feel safe from the armies of other city-states. But you and your neighbors are fearful of other beings—the many gods and spirits that you believe are everywhere. They can bring illness or sandstorms or bad luck.

How might you protect yourself from gods and spirits?

BUILDING BACKGROUND As civilizations developed along rivers, their societies and governments became more advanced. Religion became a main characteristic of these ancient cultures. Kings claimed to rule with the approval of the gods, and ordinary people wore charms and performed rituals to avoid bad luck.

An Advanced Society

In southern Mesopotamia, a people known as the Sumerians (SOO-MER-ee-unz) developed the world's first civilization. No one knows where they came from or when they moved into the region. However, by 3000 BC, several hundred thousand Sumerians had settled in Mesopotamia, in a land they called Sumer (SOO-muhr). There they created an advanced society.

The City-States of Sumer

Most people in Sumer were farmers. They lived mainly in **rural**, or countryside, areas. The centers of Sumerian society, however, were the **urban**, or city, areas. The first cities in Sumer had about 10,000 residents. Over time, the cities grew. Historians think that by 2000 BC, some of Sumer's cities had more than 100,000 residents.

As a result, the basic political unit of Sumer combined the two parts. This unit was called a city-state. A **city-state** consisted of a city and all the countryside around it. The amount of countryside controlled by each city-state depended on its military strength. Stronger city-states controlled larger areas.

Teach the Big Idea

At Level

The Rise of Sumer

1. **Teach** Ask students the questions in the Main Idea boxes to teach this section.
2. **Apply** Have students create a three-column chart on their own paper. In the first column ask students to write down any headings, subheadings, or important terms from the section. In the second column, have students create as many questions about each term or heading in the first column as they can. Lastly, have students write the answers to their questions in the third column.
   LS Verbal/Linguistic
3. **Review** Have students cover the answer column with a sheet of blank paper as they review the answers to the questions from the section. Students may also quiz a partner.
4. **Practice/Homework** Have students use their charts to create five multiple-choice questions about the section. Remind students to provide an answer key and an explanation of why each answer is correct.
   LS Verbal/Linguistic

Alternative Assessment Handbook, Rubric 37: Writing Assignments

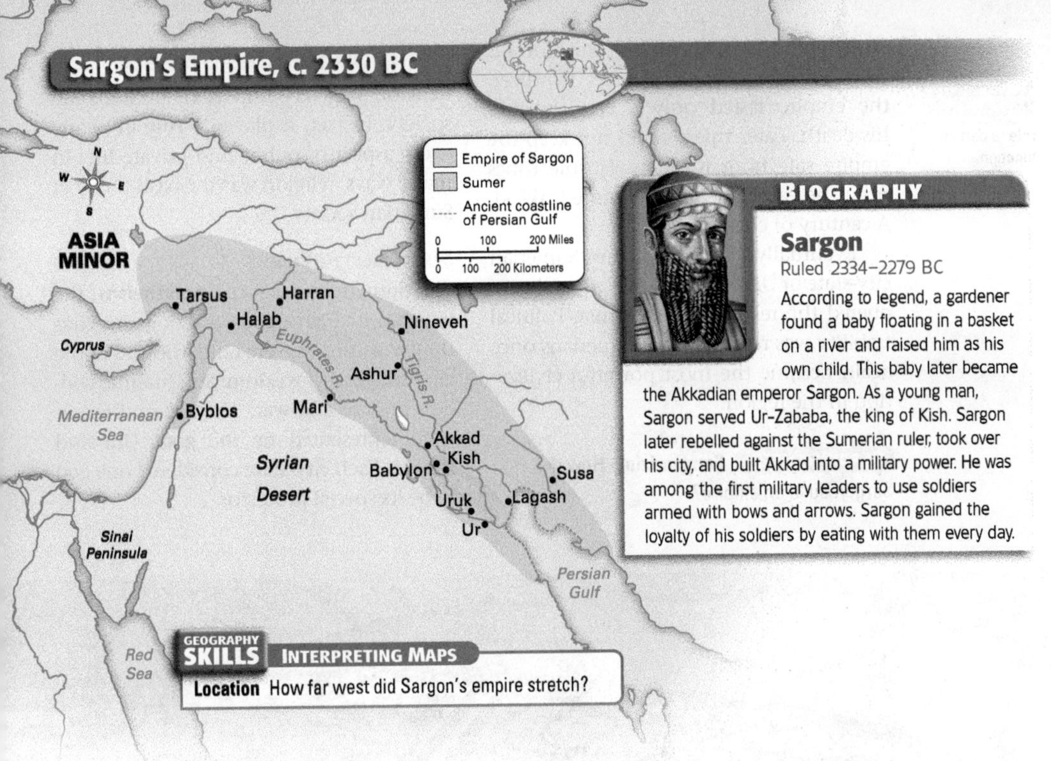

GEOGRAPHY SKILLS INTERPRETING MAPS

Location How far west did Sargon's empire stretch?

BIOGRAPHY

Sargon

Ruled 2334–2279 BC

According to legend, a gardener found a baby floating in a basket on a river and raised him as his own child. This baby later became the Akkadian emperor Sargon. As a young man, Sargon served Ur-Zababa, the king of Kish. Sargon later rebelled against the Sumerian ruler, took over his city, and built Akkad into a military power. He was among the first military leaders to use soldiers armed with bows and arrows. Sargon gained the loyalty of his soldiers by eating with them every day.

City-states in Sumer fought each other to gain more farmland. As a result of these conflicts, the city-states built up strong armies. Sumerians also built strong, thick walls around their cities for protection.

Individual city-states gained and lost power over time. By 3500 BC, a city-state known as Kish had become quite powerful. Over the next 1,000 years, the city-states of Uruk and Ur fought for dominance. One of Uruk's kings, known as **Gilgamesh**, became a legendary figure in Sumerian literature.

Rise of the Akkadian Empire

In time, another society developed along the Tigris and Euphrates. It was created by the Akkadians (uh-KAY-dee-uhns). They lived just north of Sumer, but they were not Sumerians. They even spoke a different language than the Sumerians. In spite of their differences, however, the Akkadians and the Sumerians lived in peace for many years.

That peace was broken in the 2300s BC when **Sargon** sought to extend Akkadian territory. He built a new capital, Akkad (A-kad), on the Euphrates River, near what is now the city of Baghdad. Sargon was the first ruler to have a permanent army. He used that army to launch a series of wars against neighboring kingdoms.

Sargon's soldiers defeated all the city-states of Sumer. They also conquered northern Mesopotamia, finally bringing the entire region under his rule. With these conquests, Sargon established the world's first **empire**, or land with different territories and peoples under a single rule. The Akkadian Empire stretched from the Persian Gulf to the Mediterranean Sea.

hmhsocialstudies.com
ANIMATED HISTORY
Sumerian City-States, 2300 BC

Direct Teach

Main Idea

1 An Advanced Society

The Sumerians created the world's first advanced society.

Recall Where and how did most Sumerians live? *The majority were farmers who lived in the countryside.*

Describe What were city-states, and how did they get along with each other? *the basic political unit of Sumer consisting of a city and the land around it; often fought each other for farmland*

Draw Conclusions How was Sargon able to build the first empire? *He used a permanent army to defeat all the city-states of Sumer.*

Map Transparency: Sargon's Empire, c. 2330 BC

hmhsocialstudies.com
Online Resources
Activity: Drawing of a City-state

Other People, Other Places

Empires and Armies Many other empires besides the Akkadian have risen and fallen. The Roman Empire might be the most famous. It was at its height about 2,000 years after the Akkadian Empire. The British Empire rose another 1,700 years or so after that. One common feature of empires is a strong military. Sargon established the world's first permanent army in his empire. In doing so, he started a military tradition that would be a feature of world powers for thousands of years.

Cross-Discipline Activity: Literature

At Level

Writing an Autobiography

1. Review with students the information regarding Sargon of Akkad, including the biography feature above.
2. Ask each student to imagine that he or she is Sargon of Akkad and that Sargon has been asked to write an autobiography. Have students choose an event or accomplishment from Sargon's life.
3. Have each student write about the event or accomplishment they chose from Sargon's point of view. Students should include what they imagine Sargon might have thought about the event or accomplishment. Ask students to use vivid descriptions and details.
4. Ask volunteers to share their "autobiographies" with the class.

LS Verbal/Linguistic

Alternative Assessment Handbook, Rubric 41: Writing to Express

Answers

Interpreting Maps *from the Persian Gulf to the Mediterranean Sea*

Direct Teach

Main Idea

2 Religion Shapes Society

Religion played a major role in Sumerian society.

Identify What is polytheism? *the worship of many gods*

Explain What kind of powers did Sumerians believe their gods possessed? *power over harvests, floods, illness, health, and wealth*

Make Inferences Why did priests gain high status in Sumer? *because the people believed the priests gained the gods' favor*

CRF: Primary Source Activity: Sumerian Flood Story

hmhsocialstudies.com

Online Resources
Activity: Sumerian Gods and Goddesses

Info to Know

Religion and Government Each city-state in Mesopotamia had a city god and goddess. People built houses for the gods. As the city developed, these houses became large temples, or ziggurats. According to tradition, the ruler of the city, called an *ensi,* was in charge of the temple to the city's god, and the ruler's wife was in charge of the temple to the city's goddess. The people of Mesopotamia believed that the well-being of the city-state depended on the way they treated the gods.

Answers

Reading Check *He was a very capable military leader and used a permanent army to defeat all the city-states of Sumer.*

ACADEMIC VOCABULARY
role a part or function

Sargon was emperor, or ruler of his empire, for more than 50 years. However, the empire lasted only a century after his death. Later rulers could not keep the empire safe from invaders. Hostile tribes from the east raided and captured Akkad. A century of chaos followed.

Eventually, however, the Sumerian city-state of Ur rebuilt its strength and conquered the rest of Mesopotamia. Political stability was restored. The Sumerians once again became the most powerful civilization in the region.

READING CHECK **Summarizing** How did Sargon build an empire?

Religion Shapes Society

Religion was very important in Sumerian society. In fact, it played a **role** in nearly every aspect of public and private life. In many ways, religion was the basis for all of Sumerian society.

Sumerian Religion

The Sumerians practiced **polytheism**, the worship of many gods. Among the gods they worshipped were Enlil, the lord of the air; Enki, god of wisdom; and Inanna, goddess of love and war. The sun and moon were represented by the gods Utu and Nanna. Each city-state considered one god to be its special protector.

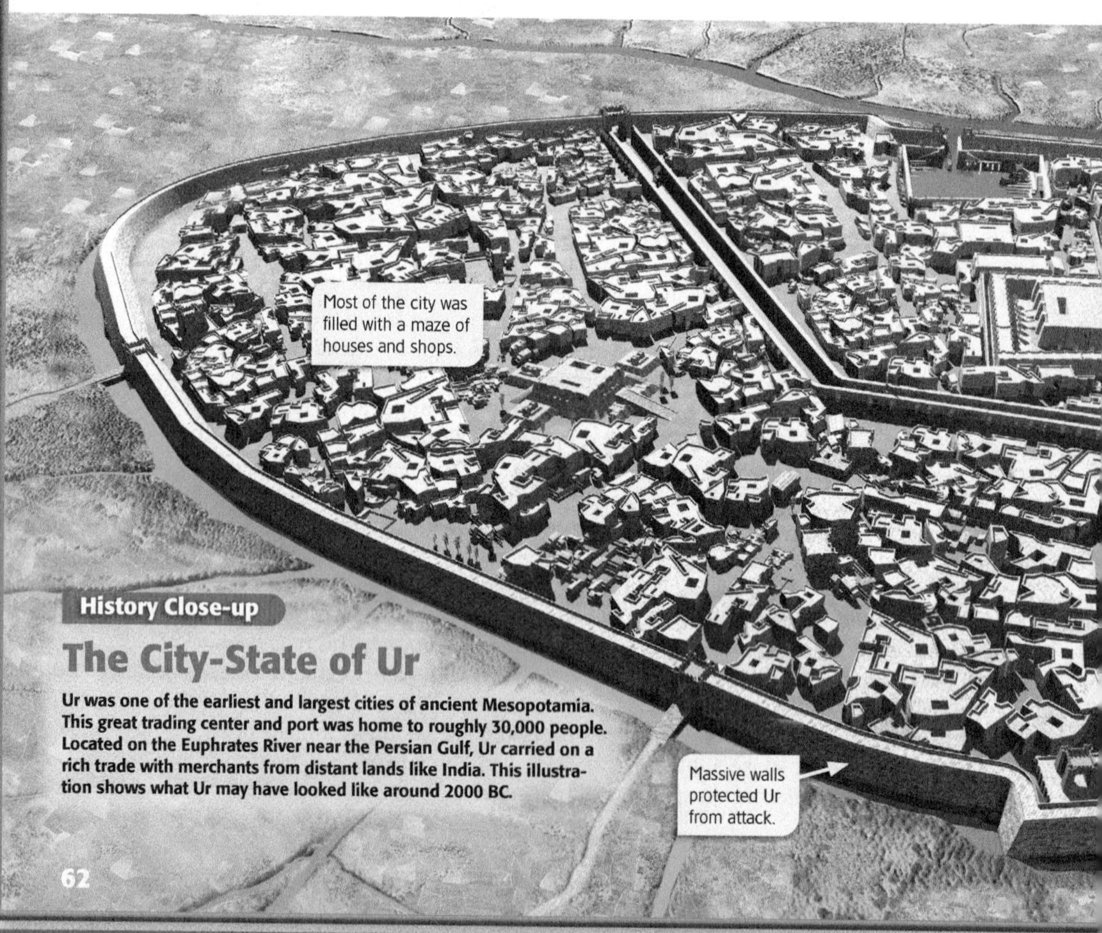
Most of the city was filled with a maze of houses and shops.
Massive walls protected Ur from attack.

History Close-up

The City-State of Ur

Ur was one of the earliest and largest cities of ancient Mesopotamia. This great trading center and port was home to roughly 30,000 people. Located on the Euphrates River near the Persian Gulf, Ur carried on a rich trade with merchants from distant lands like India. This illustration shows what Ur may have looked like around 2000 BC.

62

Differentiating Instruction

Struggling Readers — Below Level

1. To help students learn the major characteristics of Sumer, draw the graphic organizer for students to see. Omit the blue, italicized answers.
2. Have each student copy and complete the graphic organizer. When students are finished, review the answers with the class.
LS Verbal/Linguistic, Visual/Spatial

The Rise of Sumer

Government	Religion	Society
• *originally organized into city-states* • *large empire created by Sargon* • *first permanent army*	• *polytheistic* • *each city had a god as protector* • *gods have enormous power* • *priests interpret wishes of gods* • *everyone must serve and worship gods*	• *kings* • *priests* • *skilled crafters, merchants, and traders* • *laborers and farmers* • *slaves*

The Sumerians believed that their gods had enormous powers. Gods could bring a good harvest or a disastrous flood. They could bring illness, or they could bring good health and wealth. The Sumerians believed that success in every area of life depended on pleasing the gods. Every Sumerian had a duty to serve and to worship the gods.

Priests, people who performed religious ceremonies, had great status in Sumer. People relied on them to help gain the gods' favor. Priests interpreted the wishes of the gods and made offerings to them. These offerings were made in temples, special buildings where priests performed their religious ceremonies.

Sumerian Social Order

Because of their status, priests occupied a high level in Sumer's **social hierarchy**, the division of society by rank or class. In fact, priests were just below kings. The kings of Sumer claimed that they had been chosen by the gods to rule.

Below the priests were Sumer's skilled craftspeople, merchants, and traders. Trade had a great **impact** on Sumerian society. Traders traveled to faraway places and exchanged grain for gold, silver, copper, lumber, and precious stones.

Below traders, farmers and laborers made up the large working class. Slaves were at the bottom of the social order.

ACADEMIC VOCABULARY
impact effect, result

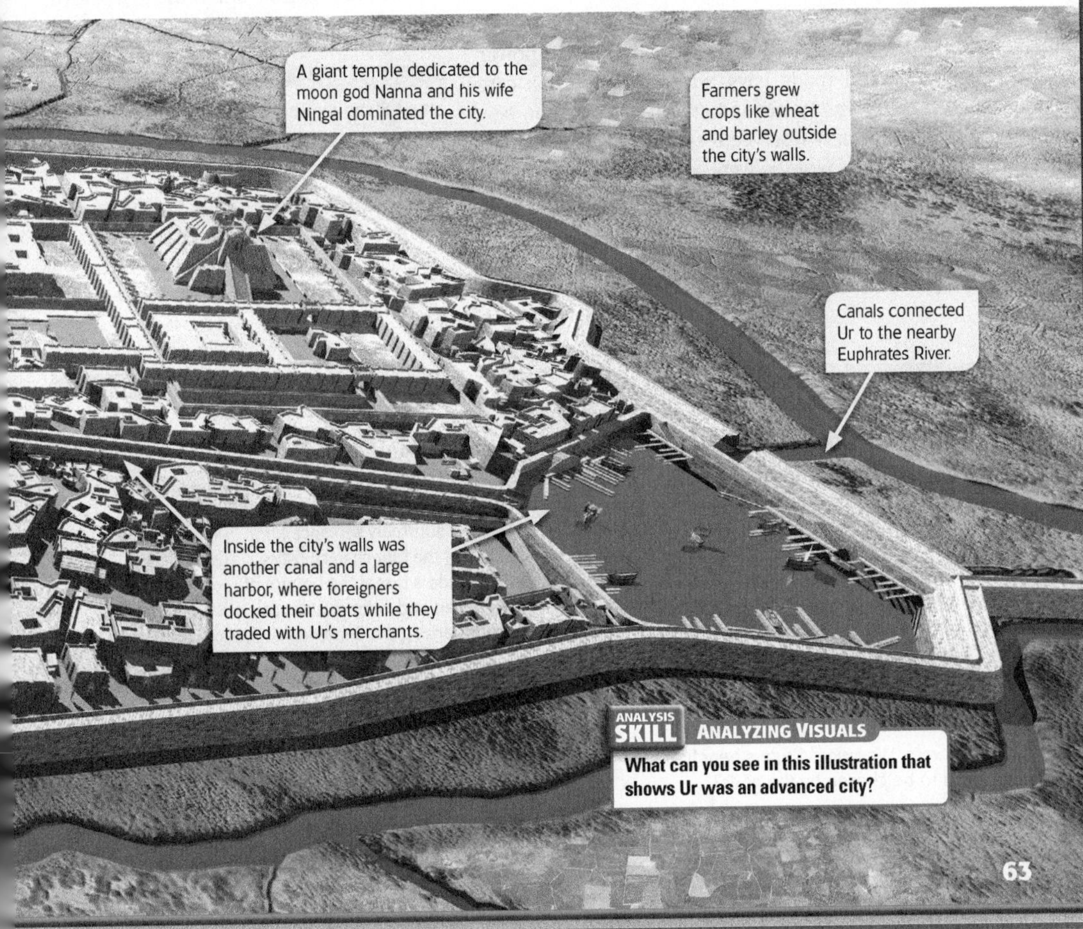
A giant temple dedicated to the moon god Nanna and his wife Ningal dominated the city.
Farmers grew crops like wheat and barley outside the city's walls.
Canals connected Ur to the nearby Euphrates River.
Inside the city's walls was another canal and a large harbor, where foreigners docked their boats while they traded with Ur's merchants.
ANALYSIS SKILL ANALYZING VISUALS
What can you see in this illustration that shows Ur was an advanced city?
63

Direct Teach

History Close-up

The City-State of Ur Review the illustration of Ur with students. Ask the following questions:

Recall What purpose did the wall around the city serve? *protected the city from attack*

Make Inferences Where did the merchants of Ur probably live? *in the city, possibly near their shops or the market*

Elaborate Why do you think the temple is the largest building in Ur? *possible answers—because religion was very important, because many people would visit the temple*

Info to Know

The Discovery of Ur Ur was not discovered until the 1800s. Until that time, people thought references to the city of Ur were mere legend. Excavations in the 1920s indicated that the city was established around 4000 BC. In the 1950s archaeologists found the oldest known written laws at Ur. They dated back to about 2050 BC. Over the years great riches have been found in the ruins, including beautiful gold jewelry, golden weapons, and precious stones.

Critical Thinking: Summarizing

At Level

Illustrated Social Hierarchy

1. Review with students the meaning of the term *social hierarchy*. Ask students to look up the word *hierarchy* in a dictionary. Help students understand that a hierarchy is a ranking of things.
2. Have each student create a list of the social classes in ancient Sumer, along with the jobs or responsibilities of members in each social class. Ask students which classes they think would have more people. Why? Which classes would have fewer people?
3. Then have each student create an illustration that reflects the social classes of Sumer as well as the primary responsibilities of each. One example might be a triangle with a crown in the top level to represent the king.
4. Have students display their social hierarchy illustrations for the class to see.
LS Visual/Spatial, Verbal/Linguistic

Alternative Assessment Handbook, Rubric 3: Artwork

Answers

Analyzing Visuals *massive walls, elaborate buildings, system of canals, and harbors*

Direct Teach

Main Idea

❷ Religion Shapes Society

Religion played a major role in Sumerian society.

Explain Who made up the middle ranks of society? *craftspeople, merchants, and traders*

Make Inferences Why might Enheduanna have had an easier time than other women in becoming a writer? What hurdles might she still have faced? *possible answers—because she was Sargon's daughter and therefore had privileges; still faced ridicule or hostility from men who held powerful positions in society*

CRF: Biography Activity: Enheduanna

Review & Assess

Close

Have students write a short paragraph summarizing the government, religion, and society of Sumer.

Review

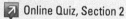

Online Quiz, Section 2

Assess

SE Section 2 Assessment

PASS: Section 2 Quiz

Alternative Assessment Handbook

Reteach/Classroom Intervention

Guided Reading Workbook, Section 2

Interactive Skills Tutor CD-ROM

Sumerian society was divided into different groups. This ancient artifact shows Sumerian leaders celebrating a military victory while a musician plays his instrument.

Men and Women in Sumer

Sumerian men and women had different roles. In general, men held political power and made laws, while women took care of the home and children. Education was usually reserved for men, but some upper-class women were educated as well.

Some educated women were priestesses in Sumer's temples. Some priestesses helped shape Sumerian culture. One, Enheduanna, the daughter of Sargon, wrote hymns to the goddess Inanna. She is the first known female writer in history.

READING CHECK **Analyzing** How did trade affect Sumerian society?

SUMMARY AND PREVIEW In this section you learned about Sumerian city-states, religion, and society. In Section 3, you will read about the Sumerians' achievements.

Section 2 Assessment

hmhsocialstudies.com ONLINE QUIZ

Reviewing Ideas, Terms, and People

1. a. **Recall** What was the basic political unit of Sumer?
   b. **Explain** What steps did **city-states** take to protect themselves from their rivals?
   c. **Elaborate** How do you think Sargon's creation of an **empire** changed the history of Mesopotamia? Defend your answer.
2. a. **Identify** What is **polytheism**?
   b. **Draw Conclusions** Why do you think **priests** were so influential in ancient Sumerian society?
   c. **Elaborate** Why would rulers benefit if they claimed to be chosen by the gods?

Critical Thinking

3. **Summarizing** In the right column of your note-taking chart, write a summary sentence for each of the four characteristics. Then add a box at the bottom of the chart and write a sentence summarizing the Sumerian civilization.

Characteristics	Notes
Cities Government Religion Society	

Summary Sentence:

Focus on Writing

4. **Gathering Information about Sumer** What aspects of Sumerian society will you include on your poster? What important people, religious beliefs, or social developments do you think the students should learn?

Section 2 Assessment Answers

1. **a.** the city-state
   b. built up strong armies and constructed walls around their cities
   c. possible answers—reduced conflicts between city-states, created better chance for civilization to develop in peacetime
2. **a.** the worship of many gods
   b. because people relied on them to gain the gods' favor
   c. People would do what the rulers said because they did not want to offend the gods by disobeying the rulers.
3. Cities—The Sumerians built the world's first cities. Government—They created the first empire. Religion—Religion influenced every aspect of life. Society—Society was very structured. Summary—The Sumerians developed the world's first advanced civilization.
4. Responses will vary but should be consistent with text content.

Answers

Reading Check *It brought important goods like copper and lumber to Sumer and led to greater wealth.*

Sumerian Achievements

SECTION 3

What You Will Learn...

Main Ideas

1. The Sumerians invented the world's first writing system.
2. Advances and inventions changed Sumerian lives.
3. Many types of art developed in Sumer.

The Big Idea

The Sumerians made many advances that helped their society develop.

Key Terms

cuneiform, *p. 65*
pictographs, *p. 66*
scribe, *p. 66*
epics, *p. 66*
architecture, *p. 68*
ziggurat, *p. 68*

hmhsocialstudies.com
TAKING NOTES

Use the graphic organizer online to list the achievements and advances made by the Sumerian civilization.

If YOU were there...

You are a student at a school for scribes in Sumer. Learning all the symbols for writing is very hard. Your teacher assigns you lessons to write on your clay tablet, but you can't help making mistakes. Then you have to smooth out the surface and try again. Still, being a scribe can lead to important jobs for the king. You could make your family proud.

Why would you want to be a scribe?

BUILDING BACKGROUND Sumerian society was advanced in terms of religion and government organization. The Sumerians were responsible for many other achievements, which were passed down to later civilizations.

The Invention of Writing

The Sumerians made one of the greatest cultural advances in history. They developed **cuneiform** (kyoo-NEE-uh-fohrm), the world's first system of writing. But Sumerians did not have pencils, pens, or paper. Instead, they used sharp tools called styluses to make wedge-shaped symbols on clay tablets.

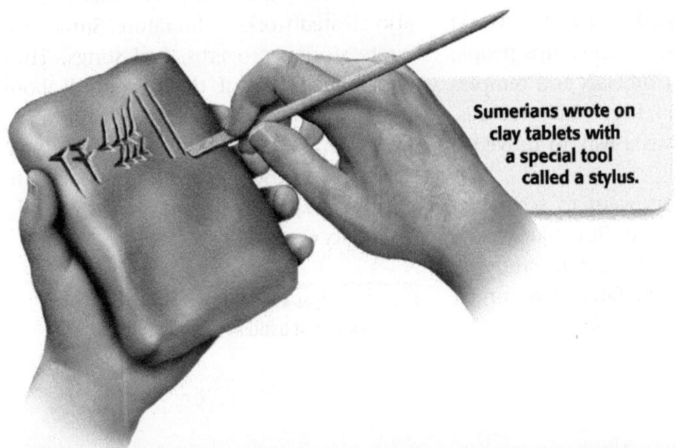

Sumerians wrote on clay tablets with a special tool called a stylus.

Preteach

Bellringer

If YOU were there . . . Use the **Daily Bellringer Transparency** to help students answer the question.

Daily Bellringer Transparency, Section 3

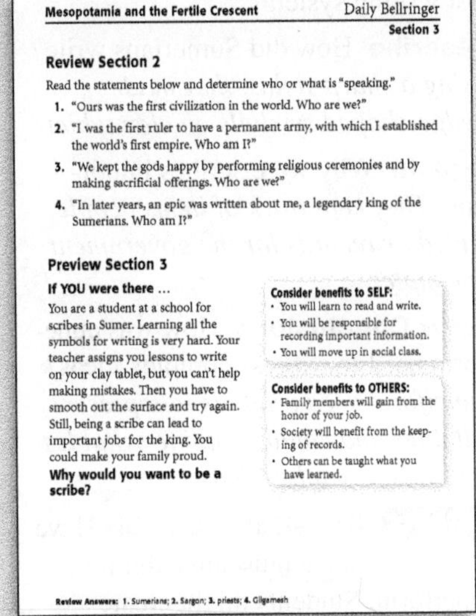

Mesopotamia and the Fertile Crescent — Daily Bellringer, **Section 3**

Review Section 2

Read the statements below and determine who or what is "speaking."

1. "Ours was the first civilization in the world. Who are we?"
2. "I was the first ruler to have a permanent army, with which I established the world's first empire. Who am I?"
3. "We kept the gods happy by performing religious ceremonies and by making sacrificial offerings. Who are we?"
4. "In later years, an epic was written about me, a legendary king of the Sumerians. Who am I?"

Preview Section 3

If YOU were there ...

You are a student at a school for scribes in Sumer. Learning all the symbols for writing is very hard. Your teacher assigns you lessons to write on your clay tablet, but you can't help making mistakes. Then you have to smooth out the surface and try again. Still, being a scribe can lead to important jobs for the king. You could make your family proud.

Why would you want to be a scribe?

Consider benefits to SELF:
- You will learn to read and write.
- You will be responsible for recording important information.
- You will move up in social class.

Consider benefits to OTHERS:
- Family members will gain from the honor of your job.
- Society will benefit from the keeping of records.
- Others can be taught what you have learned.

Review Answers: 1. Sumerians; 2. Sargon; 3. priests; 4. Gilgamesh

Building Vocabulary

Preteach or review the following terms:

catalogue to make an itemized list of (p. 67)

styluses sharp instruments used for writing (p. 65)

CRF: Vocabulary Builder Activity, Section 3

Taking Notes

Have students use the graphic organizer online to take notes on the section. This activity will prepare students for the Section Assessment, in which they will complete a graphic organizer that builds on the information using the Critical Thinking Skill: Identifying Effects.

...ch the Big Idea

At Level

Sumerian Achievements

1. **Teach** Ask students the questions in the Main Idea boxes to teach this section.
2. **Apply** Tell students to draw a table with two long columns. As they read through the chapter, have them list in one column the different Sumerian achievements, such as those in writing, technology, and art. Once they have finished the section, have them fill in the other column, explaining whether we use each achievement in today's world and, if so, how. **LS Visual/Spatial**
3. **Review** As you review the section's main ideas, have students discuss some of the specific achievements, how they were used at the time, and how they are used today.
4. **Practice/Homework** Have students write down five inventions that have been made in the last 20 years and predict whether or not those inventions might still be used 5,000 years from now. **LS Verbal/Linguistic**

Alternative Assessment Handbook, Rubrics 7: Charts; and 37: Writing Assignments

Direct Teach

Main Idea

1 The Invention of Writing

The Sumerians invented the world's first writing system.

Describe How did Sumerians write? *Using a sharp stylus, they made wedge-shaped symbols on clay tablets.*

Explain Why were scribes important? *They kept track of items people traded or records for the government or temples.*

Draw Conclusions How was cuneiform used to express complex ideas? *Cuneiform used symbols to represent syllables and could combine syllables to express complex ideas.*

Activity **Cuneiform Exhibit** Have students create a museum exhibit on cuneiform. Students might create a clay tablet of their own, provide information about cuneiform, or show images of actual cuneiform writing.
LS Visual/Spatial, Verbal/Linguistic

- **CRF:** Literature Activity: *The Epic of Gilgamesh*
- **CRF:** Interdisciplinary Projects: Mesopotamia: The First Writing

Did you know . . .

Sumerian scribes wrote their symbols on wet clay tablets, which were then dried in the sun or in ovens. Though these clay tablets were the standard writing surface in Mesopotamia, wood, metal, and even stone were used occasionally. The more durable of these materials have lasted thousands of years!

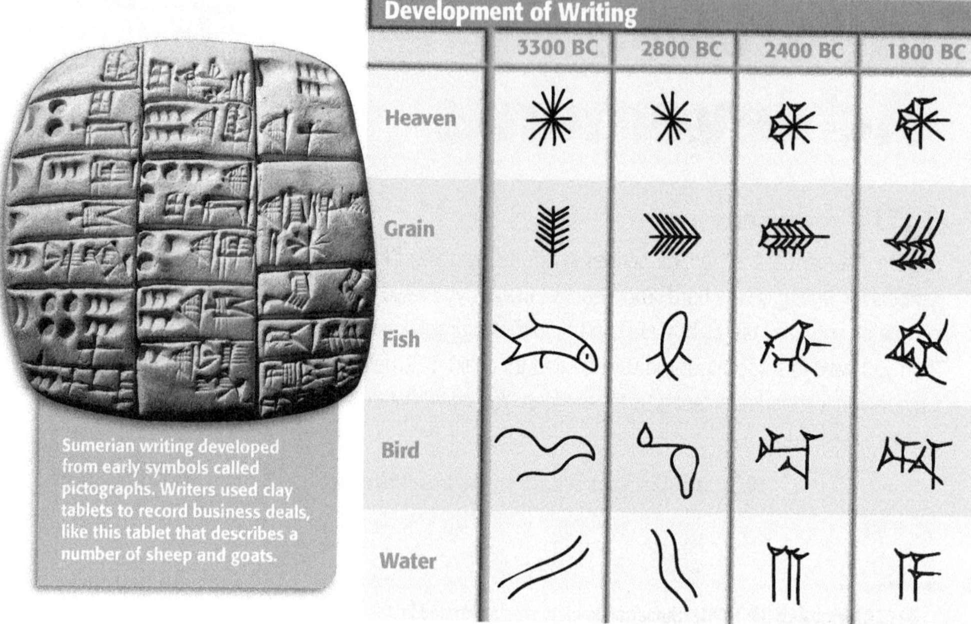

Sumerian writing developed from early symbols called pictographs. Writers used clay tablets to record business deals, like this tablet that describes a number of sheep and goats.

Earlier written communication had used **pictographs**, or picture symbols. Each pictograph represented an object, such as a tree or an animal. But in cuneiform, symbols could also represent syllables, or basic parts of words. As a result, Sumerian writers could combine symbols to express more complex ideas such as "joy" or "powerful."

Sumerians first used cuneiform to keep business records. A **scribe**, or writer, would be hired to keep track of the items people traded. Government officials and temples also hired scribes to keep their records. Becoming a scribe was a way to move up in social class.

Sumerian students went to school to learn to read and write. But, like today, some students did not want to study. A Sumerian story tells of a father who urged his son to do his schoolwork:

> "Go to school, stand before your 'school-father,' recite your assignment, open your schoolbag, write your tablet . . . After you have finished your assignment and reported to your monitor [teacher], come to me, and do not wander about in the street."
>
> –Sumerian essay quoted in *History Begins at Sumer*, by Samuel Noah Kramer

In time, Sumerians put their writing skills to new uses. They wrote works on history, law, grammar, and math. They also created works of literature. Sumerians wrote stories, proverbs, and songs. They wrote poems about the gods and about military victories. Some of these were **epics**, long poems that tell the stories of heroes. Later, people used some of these poems to create *The Epic of Gilgamesh*, the story of a legendary Sumerian king.

READING CHECK **Generalizing** How was cuneiform first used in Sumer?

Differentiating Instruction

English-Language Learners **At Level**

1. Review with students the chart on the development of writing. Discuss with students how pictographs in 3300 BC resembled the objects they expressed. Have students create 10 pictographs for everyday objects or ideas. Ask students to write the English translation next to each pictograph.
2. Remind students that pictographs were only the beginning of the development of writing. Symbols became simpler as people wrote more and more. Have students simplify their pictographs into symbols like those in the chart above.
3. Lastly, have students write only their symbols on a blank sheet of paper. Organize the class into pairs and have students try to guess the meanings of each other's symbols.
LS Visual/Spatial

- Alternative Assessment Handbook, Rubric 3: Artwork

Answers

Reading Check *for keeping business records*

Advances and Inventions

Writing was not the only great Sumerian invention. These early people made many other advances and discoveries.

Technical Advances

One of the Sumerians' most important developments was the wheel. They were the first people to build wheeled vehicles, including carts and wagons. Using the wheel, Sumerians invented a device that spins clay as a craftsperson shapes it into bowls. This device is called a potter's wheel.

The plow was another important Sumerian invention. Pulled by oxen, plows broke through the hard clay soil of Sumer to prepare it for planting. This technique greatly increased farm production. The Sumerians also invented a clock that used falling water to measure time.

Sumerian advances improved daily life in many ways. Sumerians built sewers under city streets. They learned to use bronze to make stronger tools and weapons. They even produced makeup and glass jewelry.

Math and Sciences

Another area in which Sumerians excelled was math. In fact, they developed a math system based on the number 60. Based on this system, they divided a circle into 360 degrees. Dividing a year into 12 months—a factor of 60—was another Sumerian idea. Sumerians also calculated the areas of rectangles and triangles.

THE IMPACT TODAY

Like the Sumerians we use a base-60 system when we talk about 60 seconds in a minute and 60 minutes in an hour.

Sumerian scholars studied science, too. They wrote long lists to record their study of the natural world. These tablets included the names of thousands of animals, plants, and minerals.

The Sumerians also made advances in medicine. They used ingredients from animals, plants, and minerals to produce healing drugs. Items used in these medicines included milk, turtle shells, figs, and salt. The Sumerians even catalogued their medical knowledge, listing treatments according to symptoms and body parts.

READING CHECK **Categorizing** What areas of life were improved by Sumerian inventions?

LINKING TO TODAY

The Wheel

Do you realize how much the achievements of ancient Sumer affect your life today—and every day? For instance, try to imagine life without the wheel. How would you get around? Look at the streets outside. The cars, trucks, and buses you see are all modern versions of Sumerian wheeled vehicles. Wheelchairs, bicycles, and in-line skates all depend on wheels as well. Even modern air travel owes a large debt to the Sumerians. As impressive as jets are, they could never get off the ground without their wheels!

ANALYSIS SKILL **ANALYZING INFORMATION**

Generalizing Why is the wheel so important to modern society?

Direct Teach

Main Idea

❷ Advances and Inventions

Advances and inventions changed Sumerian lives.

Recall What was one of the most important technical developments of Sumer? *the wheel*

Describe What Sumerian advance in mathematics do we use every day when we look at a calendar? *They used a calendar divided into 12 months.*

Evaluate Which invention or advancement of the Sumerians do you think was the most important? Why? *possible answers—the wheel because it enabled faster transportation; a math system because it allowed them to keep track of items and even time*

Other People, Other Places

The Wheel in the Americas One of the most important inventions of all time is that of the wheel. The oldest known wheel dates back to Mesopotamia about 3500 BC, and was likely used for transporting goods on a platform. Civilizations in the Americas, however, did not use the wheel for transportation until the arrival of Europeans in the 1400s.

Differentiating Instruction

Special Needs Learners

Below Level **Prep Required**

Lead the class in a discussion of the inventions of the Sumerians. Ask students how their inventions and ideas have affected our world. Then, have students find images from newspapers and magazines that reflect the contributions of the Sumerians and create a collage. Display the collages in the classroom.

LS Visual/Spatial

Alternative Assessment Handbook, Rubric 8: Collages

Advanced/Gifted and Talented

Above Level **Research Required**

Have students use the library, Internet, or other resources to find the answers to the following: Write the numbers 1–15 in Sumerian numerals; What numeral could Sumerians not express? *0;* Write the number 78 in Sumerian numerals.

Alternative Assessment Handbook, Rubric 30: Research

Answers

Analyzing Information *It is used in most modes of transportation today.*

Reading Check *transportation, agriculture, art, trade, science, medicine, and the military*

Direct Teach

Main Idea

3 The Arts of Sumer

Many types of art developed in Sumer.

Recall What was at the center of most Sumerian cities? *the temple, or ziggurat*

Compare and Contrast How were the homes of rich Sumerians similar to and different from those of most Sumerians? *rich—lived in large, two-story homes with many rooms; most Sumerians—smaller, one-story homes, fewer rooms; both—made of mud bricks, built side-by-side on narrow unpaved streets*

Summarize What different types of art did the Sumerians create? *sculpture, pottery, jewelry, cylinder seals, music, and dance*

Linking to Today

Lost Art Hundreds of thousands of ancient Mesopotamian works of art were housed in the National Museum of Iraq in Baghdad. When the 2003 Iraqi war broke out, museum workers stored many artifacts to protect them from damage. Unfortunately, thousands of pieces were damaged or stolen when thieves looted the museum. In the months following the war, some items were returned, although many priceless items are still missing today.

Sumerian Achievements

The Sumerians' artistic achievements included beautiful works of gold, wood, and stone.

Cylinder seals like this one were carved into round stones and then rolled over clay to leave their mark.

This stringed musical instrument is called a lyre. It features a cow's head and is made of silver decorated with shell and stone.

The Arts of Sumer

The Sumerians' skills in the fields of art, metalwork, and **architecture**—the science of building—are well known to us. The ruins of great buildings and fine works of art have provided us with wonderful examples of the Sumerians' creativity.

Architecture

Most Sumerian rulers lived in large palaces. Other rich Sumerians had two-story homes with as many as a dozen rooms. Most people, however, lived in smaller, one-story houses. These homes had six or seven rooms arranged around a small courtyard. Large and small houses stood side by side along the narrow, unpaved streets of the city. Bricks made of mud were the houses' main building blocks.

hmhsocialstudies.com
ANIMATED HISTORY
Ziggurat

City centers were dominated by their temples, the largest and most impressive buildings in Sumer. A **ziggurat**, a pyramid-shaped temple tower, rose above each city. Outdoor staircases led to a platform and a shrine at the top. Some architects added columns to make the temples more attractive.

The Arts

Sumerian sculptors produced many fine works. Among them are the statues of gods created for temples. Sumerian artists also sculpted small objects out of ivory and rare woods. Sumerian pottery is known more for its quantity than quality. Potters turned out many items, but few were works of beauty.

Jewelry was a popular item in Sumer. The jewelers of the region made many beautiful works out of imported gold, silver, and gems. Earrings and other items found in the region show that Sumerian jewelers knew advanced methods for putting gold pieces together.

Cylinder seals are perhaps Sumer's most famous works of art. These small objects were stone cylinders engraved with designs. When rolled over clay, the designs would leave behind their imprint. Each seal left its own distinct imprint. As a result, a person could show ownership of a container by rolling a cylinder over the container's wet clay surface. People could also use cylinder seals to "sign" documents or to decorate other clay objects.

Collaborative Learning

At Level

Creating a Television Commercial

1. Organize the class into small groups. Then, ask students to imagine that they are the curators of a museum that has a new exhibit titled "Sumerian Achievements."
2. Have each group create a television commercial that promotes the museum exhibit. Commercials should highlight Sumerian achievements discussed in this section and convince people to visit the museum exhibit.
3. Have each group record their commercial or perform it live for the class.

LS Interpersonal, Visual/Spatial

Alternative Assessment Handbook, Rubrics 2: Advertisements; and 29: Presentations

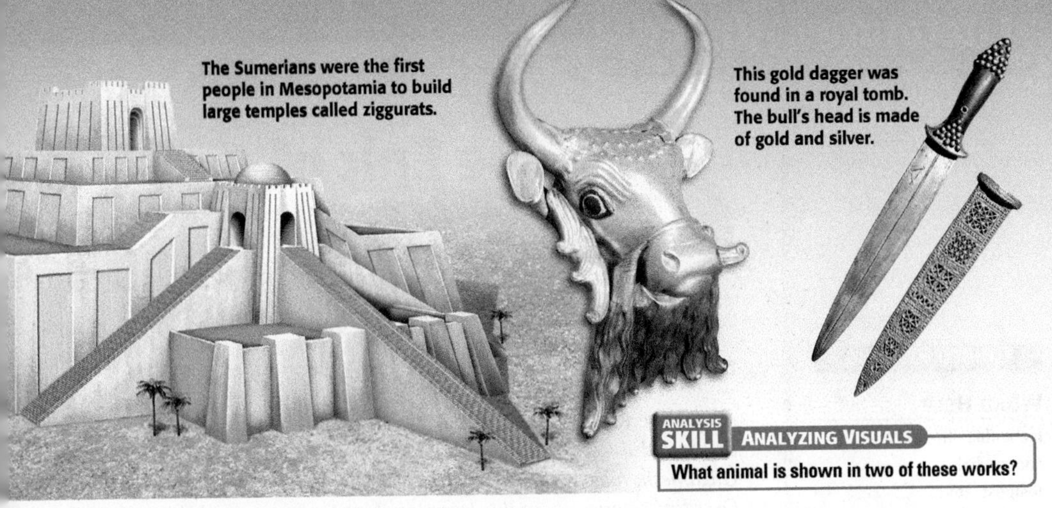
The Sumerians were the first people in Mesopotamia to build large temples called ziggurats.

This gold dagger was found in a royal tomb. The bull's head is made of gold and silver.

ANALYSIS SKILL **ANALYZING VISUALS**

What animal is shown in two of these works?

Some seals showed battle scenes. Others displayed worship rituals. Some were highly decorative, with hundreds of carefully cut gems. They required great skill to make.

The Sumerians also enjoyed music. Kings and temples hired musicians to play on special occasions. Sumerian musicians played reed pipes, drums, tambourines, and stringed instruments called lyres. Children learned songs in school. People sang hymns to gods and kings. Music and dance provided entertainment in marketplaces and homes.

READING CHECK **Drawing Inferences** What might historians learn from cylinder seals?

SUMMARY AND PREVIEW The Sumerians greatly enriched their society. Next you will learn about the later peoples who lived in Mesopotamia.

Section 3 Assessment

hmhsocialstudies.com ONLINE QUIZ

Reviewing Ideas, Terms, and People

1. a. **Identify** What is **cuneiform**?
   b. **Analyze** Why do you think writing is one of history's most important cultural advances?
   c. **Elaborate** What current leader would you choose to write an **epic** about, and why?
2. a. **Recall** What were two early uses of the wheel?
   b. **Explain** Why do you think the invention of the plow was so important to the Sumerians?
3. a. **Describe** What was the basic Sumerian building material?
   b. **Make Inferences** Why do you think cylinder seals developed into works of art?

Critical Thinking

4. **Identifying Effects** In a chart like this one, identify the effect of each Sumerian advance or achievement you listed in your notes.

Advance/ Achievement	Effect

FOCUS ON WRITING

5. **Evaluating Information** Review the Sumerian achievements you just read about. Then create a list of Sumerian achievements for your letter. Would this list replace some of the information you collected in Section 2?

Section 3 Assessment Answers

1. a. world's first writing system made up of wedge-shaped symbols on clay tablets
   b. Writing makes collecting, storing, and sharing information easier and more accurate.
   c. Students should recognize that epics generally deal with heroic people and events.
2. a. wheeled vehicles and the potter's wheel
   b. In Sumerian society, farming was the principal activity. Hence, innovations in farming would be extremely valuable.
3. a. mud bricks
   b. possible answer—Having a beautiful seal may have been a mark of status or a way of expressing one's identity.
4. writing—improved record keeping; allowed works on law, math, and grammar to be written; made literature possible; wheel—improved transportation; improved pottery-making; plow—increased efficiency and farm production
5. Possible responses might include cuneiform, music, advanced architecture, sculpture, science, mathematics.

Direct Teach

Checking for Understanding

True or False Answer each statement *T* if it is true or *F* if it is false. If false, explain why.

1. The Sumerians based their mathematical system on the number 10. *F: the Sumerian system was based on the number 60.*
2. The Sumerians used rubber stamps to show ownership of objects. *F: They used cylinder seals.*
3. Music was illegal in Sumer. *F: The Sumerians enjoyed music, and kings and temples hired musicians on special occasions.*

Review & Assess

Close

Ask students to name Sumerian achievements and describe why they were important.

Review

Online Quiz, Section 3

Assess

SE Section 3 Assessment

PASS: Section 3 Quiz

Alternative Assessment Handbook

Reteach/Classroom Intervention

Guided Reading Workbook, Section 3

Interactive Skills Tutor CD-ROM

Answers

Analyzing Visuals *cattle*

Reading Check *Cylinder seals sometimes show historical events or worship rituals. They also give historians a glimpse of artistic talent and what was valued in the culture.*

Literature in History

The Epic of Gilgamesh

As You Read Ask students what qualities they think a king would need to kill a legendary monster. Remind them that Humbaba was large and powerful. As they read, students should make a list of human qualities that Gilgamesh shows, as well as his godly qualities. *human—he sheds tears, has weak arms, cuts cedars; godly—has support of sun-god, has divine father, kills Humbaba*

Info to Know

The Epic of Gilgamesh There is no one author responsible for *The Epic of Gilgamesh.* In fact, there are many versions and tales about the exploits of Gilgamesh. Sumerian priests may have passed along the stories for generations before they were written down on the clay tablets by scribes. Most of the story has been translated from 12 broken clay tablets. These were found in a royal library at Nineveh. Only by piecing together the different parts of the story do we have the entire epic today.

Info to Know

The God Shamash Shamash, the god of the sun, was one of three main gods in ancient Sumer. Sumerians believed Shamash exerted the power of good over evil and served as the god of justice over the whole universe.

Answers

Guided Reading 1. *He seems afraid; he is crying.* **2.** *eight winds summoned by Shamash*

from The Epic of Gilgamesh

translated by N. K. Sandars

About the Reading The Epic of Gilgamesh *is the world's oldest epic, first recorded—carved on stone tablets—in about 2000 BC. The actual Gilgamesh, ruler of the city of Uruk, had lived about 700 years earlier. Over time, stories about this legendary king had grown and changed. In this story, Gilgamesh and his friend Enkidu seek to slay the monster Humbaba, keeper of a distant forest. In addition to his tremendous size and terrible appearance, Humbaba possesses seven splendors, or powers, one of which is fire. Gilgamesh hopes to claim these powers for himself.*

AS YOU READ **Notice both the human qualities and the godly qualities of Gilgamesh.**

GUIDED READING

WORD HELP

menacing threatening
succor help
tempest storm
felled cut down

Humbaba came from his strong house of cedar. He nodded his head and shook it, menacing Gilgamesh; and on him he fastened his eye, the eye of death. Then Gilgamesh called to Shamash and his tears were flowing, "O glorious Shamash, I have followed the road you commanded but now if you send no succor how shall I escape?" ❶ Glorious Shamash heard his prayer and he summoned the great wind, the north wind, the whirlwind, the storm and the icy wind, the tempest and the scorching wind; they came like dragons, like a scorching fire, like a serpent that freezes the heart, a destroying flood and the lightning's fork. The eight winds rose up against Humbaba, they beat against his eyes; he was gripped, unable to go forward or back. ❷ Gilgamesh shouted, "By the life of Ninsun my mother and divine Lugulbanda my father . . . my weak arms and my small weapons I have brought to this Land against you, and now I will enter your house." ❸

So he felled the first cedar and they cut the branches and laid them at the foot of the mountain. At the first stroke Humbaba blazed out, but still they advanced. They felled seven cedars and cut and bound the branches and laid them at the foot of the mountain, and seven times Humbaba loosed his glory on them. As the seventh blaze died out they reached his lair. He slapped his thigh in scorn. He approached like a noble wild bull roped on the mountain, a warrior whose elbows

❶ Shamash, the sun-god, supports Gilgamesh.
What human emotion seems to seize Gilgamesh here? How can you tell?

❷ ***What stops Humbaba in his tracks?***

❸ Gilgamesh tries to speak and act bravely, but he is terrified by Humbaba's evil glare.

Differentiating Instruction

English-Language Learners — Below Level

Have students illustrate the scene on this page. The drawing should contain Gilgamesh and Humbaba approaching each other. Have students re-read the page, noting how the setting contributes to the character's problems. Encourage students to make the illustration as dramatic as the written story.

Alternative Assessment Handbook, Rubric 3: Artwork

Advanced/Gifted and Talented — Above Level

Tell students that a dialogue is a piece of writing that records people talking. When written, the words are placed in quotation marks. Have students write a half-page dialogue between Gilgamesh and Enkidu that takes place just before this battle and describes the two characters planning their attack. Call on volunteers to read their dialogues.

LS Verbal/Linguistic

Alternative Assessment Handbook, Rubric 37: Writing Assignments

were bound together. The tears started to his eyes and he was pale, "Gilgamesh, let me speak. I have never known a mother, no, nor a father who reared me. I was born of the mountain, he reared me, and Enlil made me the keeper of this forest. Let me go free, Gilgamesh, and I will be your servant, you shall be my lord; all the trees of the forest that I tended on the mountain shall be yours. I will cut them down and build you a palace." . . . ❹

Enkidu said, "Do not listen, Gilgamesh: this Humbaba must die. Kill Humbaba first and his servants after." But Gilgamesh said, "If we touch him the blaze and the glory of light will be put out in confusion, the glory and glamour will vanish, its rays will be quenched." Enkidu said to Gilgamesh, "Not so, my friend. First entrap the bird, and where shall the chicks run then? Afterwards we can search out the glory and the glamour, when the chicks run distracted through the grass."

Gilgamesh listened to the word of his companion, he took the ax in his hand, he drew the sword from his belt, and he struck Humbaba with a thrust of the sword to the neck, and Enkidu his comrade struck the second blow. At the third blow Humbaba fell. Then there followed confusion for this was the guardian of the forest whom they had felled to the ground . . .

When he saw the head of Humbaba, Enlil raged at them. "Why did you do this thing? From henceforth may the fire be on your faces, may it eat the bread that you eat, may it drink where you drink." Then Enlil took again the blaze and the seven splendors that had been Humbaba's: he gave the first to the river, and he gave to the lion, to the stone of execration, to the mountain . . . ❺

O Gilgamesh, king and conqueror of the dreadful blaze; wild bull who plunders the mountain, who crosses the sea, glory to him.

GUIDED READING

WORD HELP

execration a cursing
plunders takes by force

❹ ***What effect does Humbaba hope his words will have on Gilgamesh?***

❺ The angry air-god Enlil curses the heroes for slaying Humbaba. He takes back the monster's powers and gives them to other creatures and elements of nature.

In your opinion, is Gilgamesh more or less heroic for slaying Humbaba and angering Enlil?

Archaeologists think this statue from the 700s BC represents Gilgamesh.

CONNECTING LITERATURE TO HISTORY

1. **Analyzing** In Sumerian culture, the gods' powers were thought to be enormous. According to this story, what roles do gods play in people's lives?
2. **Making Inferences** Violence was common in Sumerian society. How does the character of Gilgamesh suggest that Sumerian society could be violent?

Literature in History

Info to Know

The God Enlil Enlil was not a god that the Sumerians wanted to anger. Sometimes called the Lord of the Air, Enlil was the god not just of the wind and agriculture but also of all energy and force. According to Mesopotamian myth, Enlil played an important role in the creation of man.

Connect to Art

Stylized Art Point out to students that some design elements of the statue shown are stylized. This means that they are not meant to look real, but have been simplified according to a set of rules. Gilgamesh's beard and the lion cub's fur have been stylized. Challenge students to find other examples of stylized art in this book or books on art history. Egyptian art in particular offers several examples.

Modern creative works also exhibit stylized design elements, however. For example, Japanese anime artists draw human characters with unnaturally big eyes.

Cross-Discipline Activity: Literature

At Level

Writing Alternative Endings

1. Organize the class into pairs. Tell students that Gilgamesh's decision to follow Enkidu's advice and kill Humbaba is a "plot point" in the story. Based on Gilgamesh's actions, the plot changes to reflect his choice. That is why it is an important part of the story.
2. Have students create alternate endings to the story, starting at the point where Enkidu advises Gilgamesh to kill Humbaba.
3. Ask students to imagine what would have happened if Gilgamesh had allowed Humbaba to live, and have them write a new ending to this tale.
4. Ask volunteers to share their stories with the class. LS **Verbal/Linguistic**

Alternative Assessment Handbook, Rubrics 14: Group Activity; and 39: Writing to Create

Answers

Guided Reading 4. *Humbaba hopes to persuade Gilgamesh not to kill him.* **5.** *Responses will vary but should be supported with details from the passage.*

Connecting Literature to History
1. *Shamash helps Gilgamesh stop Humbaba by sending powerful winds, and Enlil punishes Gilgamesh for killing Humbaba.* **2.** *Gilgamesh's mindset is one of violence, and this is shown by his actions as he attacks and kills Humbaba.*

Preteach

Bellringer

If YOU were there . . . Use the **Daily Bellringer Transparency** to help students answer the question.

Daily Bellringer Transparency, Section 4

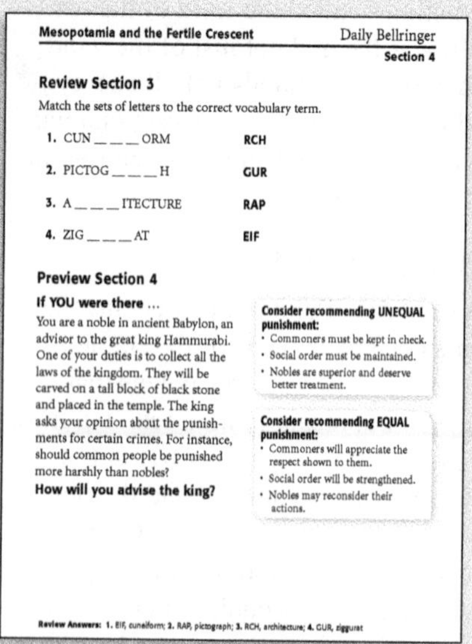

Mesopotamia and the Fertile Crescent — Daily Bellringer **Section 4**

Review Section 3

Match the sets of letters to the correct vocabulary term.

1. CUN _ _ _ ORM	**RCH**
2. PICTOG _ _ _ H	**GUR**
3. A _ _ _ ITECTURE	**RAP**
4. ZIG _ _ _ AT	**EIF**

Preview Section 4

If YOU were there ...

You are a noble in ancient Babylon, an advisor to the great king Hammurabi. One of your duties is to collect all the laws of the kingdom. They will be carved on a tall block of black stone and placed in the temple. The king asks your opinion about the punishments for certain crimes. For instance, should common people be punished more harshly than nobles?

How will you advise the king?

Consider recommending UNEQUAL punishment:
- Commoners must be kept in check.
- Social order must be maintained.
- Nobles are superior and deserve better treatment.

Consider recommending EQUAL punishment:
- Commoners will appreciate the respect shown to them.
- Social order will be strengthened.
- Nobles may reconsider their actions.

Review Answers: 1. EIF, cuneiform; 2. RAP, pictograph; 3. RCH, architecture; 4. GUR, ziggurat

Building Vocabulary

Preteach or review the following terms:

assassin one who kills an important person (p. 74)

looting seizing goods by force, especially in times of war (p. 75)

penalties punishments for a crime or offense (p. 73)

CRF: Vocabulary Builder Activity, Section 4

Taking Notes

Have students use the graphic organizer online to take notes on the section. This activity will prepare students for the Section Assessment, in which they will complete a graphic organizer that builds on the information using the Critical Thinking Skill: Categorizing.

SECTION 4

Later Peoples of the Fertile Crescent

What You Will Learn...

Main Ideas

1. The Babylonians conquered Mesopotamia and created a code of law.
2. Invasions of Mesopotamia changed the region's culture.
3. The Phoenicians built a trading society in the eastern Mediterranean region.

The Big Idea

After the Sumerians, many cultures ruled parts of the Fertile Crescent.

Key Terms and People

monarch, *p. 72*
Hammurabi's Code, *p. 73*
chariot, *p. 74*
Nebuchadnezzar, *p. 75*
alphabet, *p. 77*

Use the graphic organizer online to keep track of the empires of the Fertile Crescent.

If YOU were there...

You are a noble in ancient Babylon, an advisor to the great king Hammurabi. One of your duties is to collect all the laws of the kingdom. They will be carved on a tall block of black stone and placed in the temple. The king asks your opinion about the punishments for certain crimes. For instance, should common people be punished more harshly than nobles?

How will you advise the king?

BUILDING BACKGROUND Many peoples invaded Mesopotamia. A series of kings conquered the lands between the rivers. Each new culture inherited the earlier achievements of the Sumerians. Some of the later invasions of the region also introduced skills and ideas that still influence civilization today, such as a written law code.

The Babylonians Conquer Mesopotamia

Although Ur rose to glory after the death of Sargon, repeated foreign attacks drained its strength. By 2000 BC, Ur lay in ruins. With Ur's power gone, several waves of invaders battled to gain control of Mesopotamia.

The Rise of Babylon

Babylon was home to one such group. That city was located on the Euphrates River near what is today Baghdad, Iraq. Babylon had once been a Sumerian town. By 1800 BC, however, it was home to a powerful government of its own. In 1792 BC, Hammurabi (ham-uh-RAHB-ee) became Babylon's king. He would become the city's greatest **monarch** (MAH-nark), a ruler of a kingdom or empire.

Teach the Big Idea

At Level

Later Peoples of the Fertile Crescent

1. **Teach** Ask students the questions in the Main Idea boxes to teach this section.
2. **Apply** Have students draw a time line that includes the later empires and kingdoms that developed in Mesopotamia. Students should also include a short note about why each civilization was important. Encourage students to share their time lines with the class. **LS Visual/Spatial**
3. **Review** As a review of the section, have students create seven multiple choice questions. Then have students quiz each other with the questions they have created.
4. **Practice/Homework** Have students use their time lines to help them create at least one illustration for every empire or people mentioned in the section. **LS Visual/Spatial**

Alternative Assessment Handbook, Rubrics 3: Artwork; and 36: Time Lines

Hammurabi's Code

Hammurabi was a brilliant war leader. His armies fought many battles to expand his power. Eventually, he brought all of Mesopotamia into his empire, called the Babylonian Empire, after his capital.

Hammurabi's skills were not limited to the battlefield, though. He was also an able ruler who could govern a huge empire. He oversaw many building and irrigation projects and improved Babylon's tax collection system to help pay for them. He also brought much prosperity through increased trade. Hammurabi, however, is most famous for his code of laws.

Hammurabi's Code was a set of 282 laws that dealt with almost every part of daily life. There were laws on everything from trade, loans, and theft to marriage, injury, and murder. It contained some ideas that are still found in laws today. Specific crimes brought specific penalties. However, social class did matter. For instance, injuring a rich man brought a greater penalty than injuring a poor man.

Hammurabi's Code was important not only for how thorough it was, but also because it was written down for all to see. People all over the empire could read exactly what was against the law.

Hammurabi ruled for 42 years. During his reign, Babylon became the most important city in Mesopotamia. However, after his death, Babylonian power declined. The kings that followed faced invasions from people Hammurabi had conquered. Before long, the Babylonian Empire came to an end.

READING CHECK **Analyzing** What was Hammurabi's most important accomplishment?

Primary Source

HISTORIC DOCUMENT

Hammurabi's Code

The Babylonian ruler Hammurabi is credited with putting together the earliest known written collection of laws. The code set down rules for both criminal and civil law, and informed citizens what was expected of them.

196. If a man put out the eye of another man, his eye shall be put out.

197. If he break another man's bone, his bone shall be broken.

198. If he put out the eye of a freed man, or break the bone of a freed man, he shall pay one gold mina.

199. If he put out the eye of a man's slave, or break the bone of a man's slave, he shall pay one-half of its value.

221. If a physican heal the broken bone or diseased soft part of a man, the patient shall pay the physician five shekels in money.

222. If he were a freed man he shall pay three shekels.

223. If he were a slave his owner shall pay the physician two shekels.

–Hammurabi, from the Code of Hammurabi, translated by L. W. King

ANALYZING PRIMARY SOURCES

How do you think Hammurabi's code of laws affected citizens of that time?

Direct Teach

Main Idea

1 The Babylonians Conquer Mesopotamia

The Babylonians conquered Mesopotamia and created a code of law.

Recall When did Hammurabi become Babylon's king? *1792 BC*

Explain How did Hammurabi conquer Mesopotamia? *He expanded his power through military victories.*

Draw Conclusions Why would it have been helpful for people to have the law code written down? *Everyone could know what was against the law. Additionally, laws that are written down cannot change as easily as those that are passed down orally.*

CRF: Biography Activity: Hammurabi

CRF: Primary Source Activity: The Code of Hammurabi

Quick Facts Transparency: Hammurabi's Code

Primary Source

Reading Like a Historian

Hammurabi's Code Help students practice reading this document like a historian. Ask

- What do these laws indicate about the Babylonian system of justice?
- Why do you think the laws treat freed men differently from slaves?

About the Illustration

This illustration of Hammurabi is an artist's conception based on available sources. However, historians are uncertain exactly what Hammurabi looked like.

Differentiating Instruction

Advanced/Gifted and Talented

Above Level

1. Ask students to imagine a world in which there are no written laws. Then have each student write a one-page short story in which two characters in such a world come into conflict. Stories may involve topics such as theft, a fight, or an accidental injury.
2. Students should include a conflict-resolution or judgment scene that shows how a written code of laws helps resolve the situation.
3. Call on volunteers to read their short stories to the class. Then lead a discussion about how the stories illustrate the importance of Hammurabi's Code. LS **Verbal/Linguistic**

Alternative Assessment Handbook, Rubric 39: Writing to Create

Answers

Analyzing Primary Sources *possible answer—They may have obeyed the laws, since punishments were often severe.*

Reading Check *his code of laws*

• Direct Teach •

Main Idea

❷ Invasions of Mesopotamia

Invasions of Mesopotamia changed the region's culture.

Recall Why did the Hittite Kingdom come to an end? *Their king was assassinated, and the kingdom was overrun by the Kassites.*

Identify What military advantages did the Assyrians have? *iron weapons, chariots, and good organization*

Draw Conclusions How do you think the use of chariots by Hittites affected the opposing army's foot soldiers? *possible answer—increased their fear and reduced their effectiveness, because they could not predict from where the enemy would appear next, and the chariots were moving targets*

Map Transparency: Babylonian and Assyrian Empires

Info to Know

The Assyrian Army The Assyrian military was impressive, even by today's standards. Assyrian field armies consisted of 50,000 men, the equal of five modern U.S. divisions. When taking the field for a battle, the army would stretch about a mile and a half across and 100 yards deep! The Assyrian military was also known for its innovations—cavalry, battering rams, and boots for their soldiers.

Invasions of Mesopotamia

Several other civilizations also developed in and around the Fertile Crescent. As their armies battled each other for fertile land, control of the region passed from one empire to another.

The Hittites and Kassites

Focus on Reading
What is the topic of this paragraph? Is the main idea stated in a single sentence?

A people known as the Hittites built a strong kingdom in Asia Minor, in what is today Turkey. Their success came, in part, from two key military advantages they had over rivals. First, the Hittites were among the first people to master ironworking. This meant that they could make the strongest weapons of the time. Second, the Hittites skillfully used the **chariot**, a wheeled, horse-drawn cart used in battle. The chariots allowed Hittite soldiers to move quickly around a battlefield and fire arrows at their enemy. Using these advantages, Hittite forces captured Babylon around 1595 BC.

Hittite rule did not last long, however. Soon after taking Babylon, the Hittite king was killed by an assassin. The kingdom plunged into chaos. The Kassites, a people who lived north of Babylon, captured the city and ruled for almost 400 years.

The Assyrians

Later, in the 1200s BC, the Assyrians (uh-SIR-ee-unz) from northern Mesopotamia briefly gained control of Babylon. However, their empire was soon overrun by invaders. After this defeat, the Assyrians took about 300 years to recover their strength. Then, starting about 900 BC, they began to conquer all of the Fertile Crescent. They even took over parts of Asia Minor and Egypt.

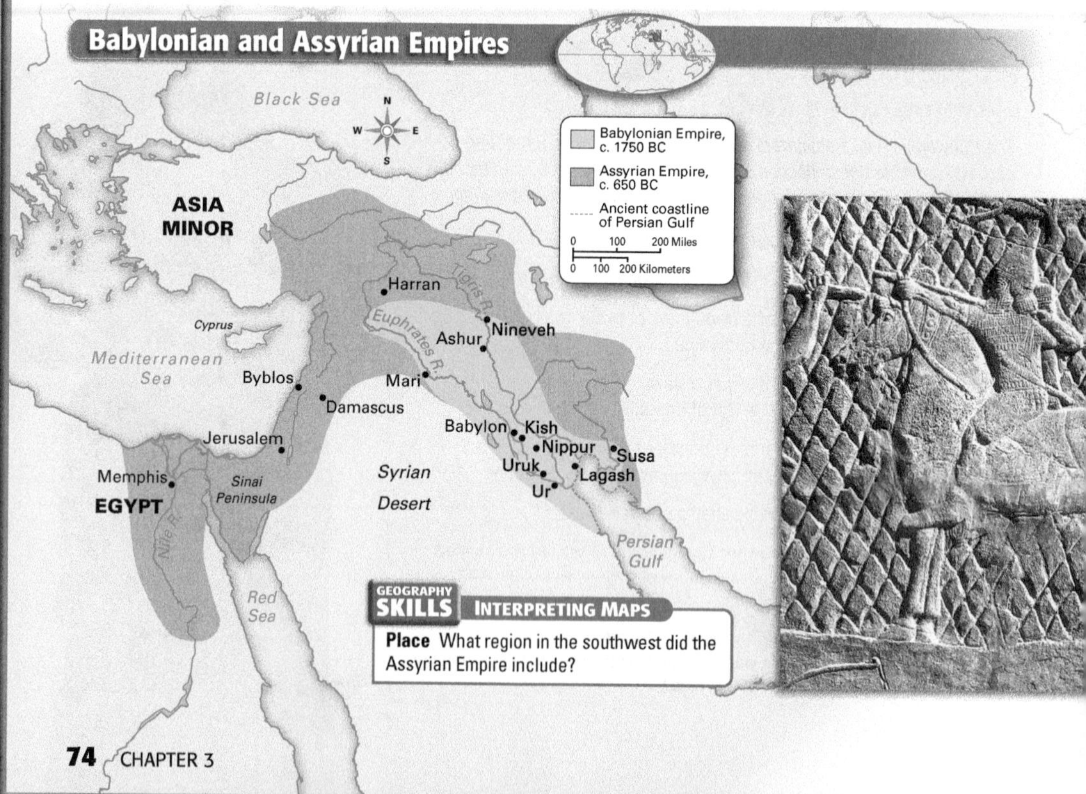

Geography Skills INTERPRETING MAPS
Place What region in the southwest did the Assyrian Empire include?

Differentiating Instruction

Struggling Readers Below Level

1. Have students work in pairs to write a letter from the Hittite king to the leader of Babylon explaining why the Babylonians should surrender. You may wish to pair a student who has good writing skills with a struggling student to complete this activity.
2. Have students include details about the superiority of the Hittite military and what consequences might result from the Babylonians' refusal to surrender.
3. Ask for volunteers to read their letters to the class. LS **Verbal/Linguistic**

Alternative Assessment Handbook, Rubric 37: Writing Assignments

Answers

Interpreting Maps *Egypt*

The key to the Assyrians' success was their strong army. Like the Hittites, the Assyrians used iron weapons and chariots. The army was very well organized, and every soldier knew his role.

The Assyrians were fierce in battle. Before attacking, they spread terror by looting villages and burning crops. Anyone who still dared to resist them was killed.

After conquering the Fertile Crescent, the Assyrians ruled from Nineveh (NI-nuh-vuh). They demanded heavy taxes from across the empire. Areas that resisted these demands were harshly punished.

Assyrian kings ruled their large empire through local leaders. Each governed a small area, collected taxes, enforced laws, and raised troops for the army. Roads were built to link distant parts of the empire. Messengers on horseback were sent to deliver orders to faraway officials.

The Chaldeans

In 652 BC a series of wars broke out in the Assyrian Empire over who should rule. These wars greatly weakened the empire. Sensing this weakness, the Chaldeans (kal-DEE-unz), a group from the Syrian Desert, led other peoples in an attack on the Assyrians. In 612 BC, they destroyed Nineveh and the Assyrian Empire.

In its place, the Chaldeans set up a new empire of their own. **Nebuchadnezzar** (neb-uh-kuhd-NEZ-uhr), the most famous Chaldean king, rebuilt Babylon into a beautiful city. According to legend, his grand palace featured the famous Hanging Gardens. Trees and flowers grew on its terraces and roofs. From the ground the gardens seemed to hang in the air.

The Chaldeans admired Sumerian culture. They studied the Sumerian language and built temples to Sumerian gods.

At the same time, Babylon became a center for astronomy. Chaldeans charted the positions of the stars and kept track of economic, political, and weather events. They also created a calendar and solved complex problems of geometry.

READING CHECK **Sequencing** List in order the peoples who ruled Mesopotamia.

The Assyrian Army
The Assyrian army was the most powerful fighting force the world had ever seen. It was large and well organized, and it featured iron weapons, war chariots, and giant war machines used to knock down city walls.

What kinds of weapons can you see in this carving?

Direct Teach

Main Idea

❷ Invasions of Mesopotamia

Invasions of Mesopotamia changed the region's culture.

Summarize How did the Assyrians rule their empire? *Kings ruled through local leaders who enforced laws and collected taxes; they also punished any resistance to their rule very harshly.*

Describe What advances did the Chaldeans make? *They studied astronomy, weather events, geometry, and economics, and they created a calendar.*

 **CRF:** Biography Activity: King Nebuchadnezzar

Info to Know

The Seven Wonders of the World The Hanging Gardens of Babylon are one of the Seven Wonders of the World. These wonders were ancient structures that inspired awe in historians of ancient Greece. They included the Great Pyramid of Giza, the Statue of Zeus at Olympia, the Temple of Artemis at Ephesus, the Mausoleum at Halicarnassus, the Colossus of Rhodes, and the Lighthouse of Alexandria. Of the seven, only the Great Pyramid still stands.

Critical Thinking: Summarizing

At Level

Creating a Book Jacket

1. Explain to students what a book jacket looks like and what purpose it serves. You might want to show examples.
2. Point out to students that book jackets include the title and a picture or illustration on the front cover, a brief summary of the book's contents on the inside flaps, author and publisher on the spine, and comments about the book's influence on the back cover.
3. Ask students to imagine that they have been asked to design a book jacket for a book titled *Invasions of Mesopotamia.* Draw a sample layout of the elements of a book jacket for students to follow.
4. Ask volunteers to share their finished book jackets with the class.

LS **Visual/Spatial, Verbal/Linguistic**

Answers

Reading Check *Babylonians, Hittites, Kassites, Assyrians, and Chaldeans*

The Assyrian Army *spear, bow and arrow*

Direct Teach

Main Idea

❸ The Phoenicians

The Phoenicians built a trading society in the eastern Mediterranean region.

Identify Where did Phoenician ships sail? *They sailed around the Mediterranean, to Egypt, Greece, Italy, Sicily, and Spain, and through the Straits of Gibraltar into the Atlantic Ocean.*

Explain Why was the Phoenician alphabet an important development? *It made writing much easier and has had a major impact on other languages, including English.*

Draw Conclusions What led the Phoenicians to create a successful sea trade? *Mountains and hostile neighbors blocked overland trade routes, so in order to trade they had to go to sea.*

CRF: Primary Source Activity: Descriptions of the Phoenicians

Map Transparency: Phoenicia, c. 800 BC

Connect to Geography

The Cedars of Lebanon The famous trees are so closely tied to the history of Lebanon that a cedar is featured in the middle of the Lebanese flag. However, because people have been cutting down the big trees for centuries, few traces of the old forests remain. Reforestation efforts have begun, though.

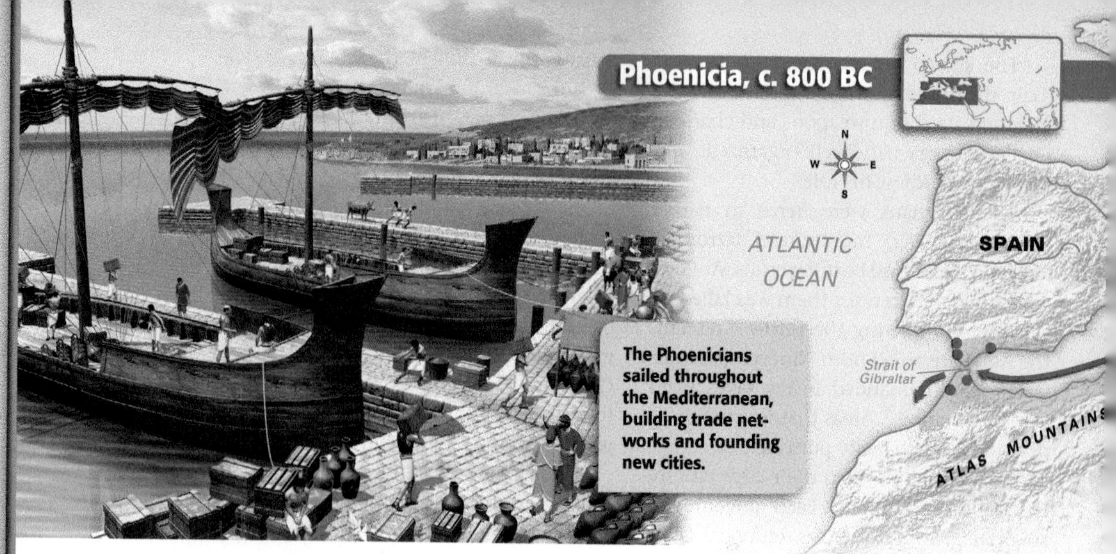

The Phoenicians sailed throughout the Mediterranean, building trade networks and founding new cities.

The Phoenicians

At the western end of the Fertile Crescent, along the Mediterranean Sea, was a land known as Phoenicia (fi-NI-shuh). It was not home to a great military power and was often ruled by foreign governments. Nevertheless, the Phoenicians created a wealthy trading society.

The Geography of Phoenicia

Today the nation of Lebanon occupies most of what was once Phoenicia. Mountains border the region to the north and east. The western border is the Mediterranean.

Phoenicia had few resources. One thing it did have, however, was cedar. Cedar trees were prized for their timber, a valuable trade item. But Phoenicia's overland trade routes were blocked by mountains and hostile neighbors. Phoenicians had to look to the sea for a way to trade.

THE IMPACT TODAY
Because so many cedar trees have been cut down in Lebanon's forests over the years, very few trees remain.

The Expansion of Trade

Motivated by a desire for trade, the people of Phoenicia became expert sailors. They built one of the world's finest harbors at the city of Tyre. Fleets of fast Phoenician trading ships sailed to ports all around the Mediterranean Sea. Traders traveled to Egypt, Greece, Italy, Sicily, and Spain. They even passed through the Strait of Gibraltar to reach the Atlantic Ocean.

The Phoenicians founded several new colonies along their trade routes. Carthage (KAHR-thij), located on the northern coast of Africa, was the most famous of these. It later became one of the most powerful cities on the Mediterranean.

Phoenicia grew wealthy from its trade. Besides lumber, the Phoenicians traded silverwork, ivory carvings, and slaves. Beautiful glass objects also became valuable trade items after crafters invented glassblowing—the art of heating and shaping glass. In addition, the Phoenicians made purple dye from a type of shellfish. They then traded cloth dyed with this purple color. Phoenician purple fabric was very popular with rich people.

The Phoenicians' most important achievement, however, wasn't a trade good. To record their activities, Phoenician

Critical Thinking: Analyzing

At Level

Phoenician Exports

1. Tell students that a nation's exports are the goods and products it sells to other nations.
2. To help students identify the exports of the Phoenicians, copy the graphic organizer for students to see. Omit the blue, italicized answers. Have students copy and complete the graphic organizer on their own paper.
LS Visual/Spatial, Verbal/Linguistic

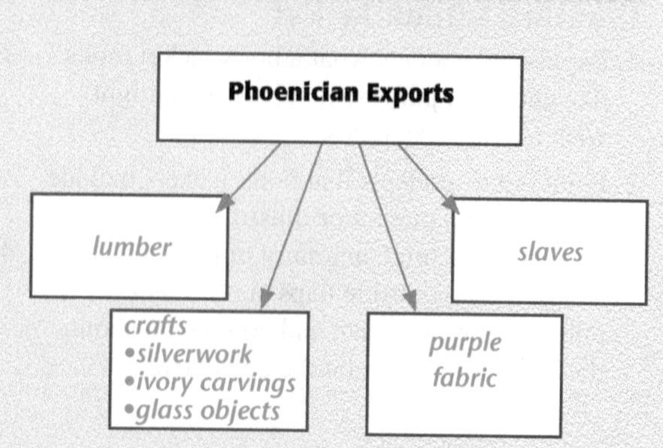

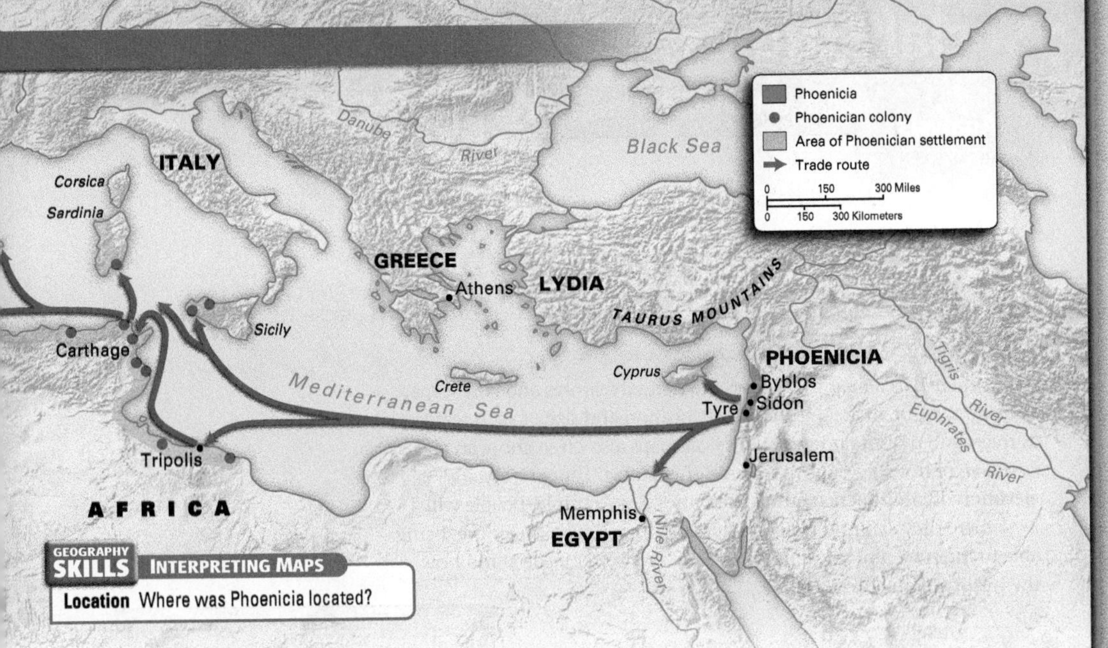

GEOGRAPHY SKILLS INTERPRETING MAPS

Location Where was Phoenicia located?

traders developed one of the world's first alphabets. An **alphabet** is a set of letters that can be combined to form words. This development made writing much easier. It had a major impact on the ancient world and on our own. In fact, the alphabet we use for the English language is based on the Phoenicians', as modified by later civilizations. Later civilizations, including our own, benefited from the innovations passed along by Phoenician traders.

READING CHECK **Finding Main Ideas** What were the main achievements of the Phoenicians?

SUMMARY AND PREVIEW Many different peoples ruled in the Fertile Crescent after the Sumerians. Some made important contributions that are still valued today. In the next chapter you will learn about two remarkable civilizations that developed along the Nile River.

Section 4 Assessment

hmhsocialstudies.com ONLINE QUIZ

Reviewing Ideas, Terms, and People

1. a. **Identify** Where was Babylon located?
   b. **Analyze** What does **Hammurabi's Code** reveal about Babylonian society?
2. a. **Describe** What two advantages did Hittite soldiers have over their opponents?
   b. **Rank** Which empire discussed in this section do you feel contributed the most to modern-day society? Why?
3. a. **Identify** For what trade goods were the Phoenicians known? For what else were they known?
   b. **Analyze** How did Phoenicia grow wealthy?

Critical Thinking

4. **Categorizing** Use your note-taking diagram with the names of the empires. List at least one advance or achievement made by each empire.

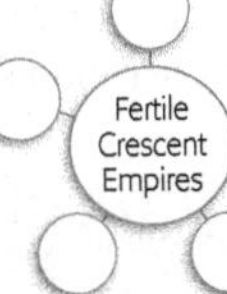

Focus on Writing

5. **Gathering Information about Later Peoples** Several different peoples contributed to civilization in the Fertile Crescent after the Sumerians. Which ones, if any, will you mention in your letter? What will you say?

Section 4 Assessment Answers

1. **a.** on the Euphrates near what is today Baghdad, Iraq
   b. It was based on social hierarchy and showed the importance of class distinctions. It also reveals the significance of business, trade, and family in the Babylonian Empire.
2. **a.** iron weapons and chariots
   b. possible answers: Babylonians—Hammurabi's laws; Chaldeans—restored Sumerian customs, studies in math and astronomy; Phoenicians—an alphabet
3. **a.** lumber, silverwork, ivory carvings, slaves, beautiful glass objects, and purple cloth; development of an alphabet
   b. Phoenicians were expert sailors with a fast fleet of trading ships and had valuable items to trade.
4. Babylonian; Hittite; Assyrian; Chaldean; Phoenician; advances or achievements listed will vary.
5. Answers will vary but should reflect knowledge of section content.

Direct Teach

History Humor

Why did the Phoenician decide to go sailing in his boat? *He had a flat Tyre!*

Teaching Tip

If students have difficulty remembering the order of the civilizations and empires discussed in this chapter, have them write sentences starting with the first letters of the civilizations' names. Sentences may be nonsensical. Here is an example; **S**am (Sumer) **a**nd (Akkad) **B**ob (Babylonian) **h**eard (Hittites) **ka**ngaroos (Kassites) **a**nd (Assyrians) **ch**impanzees (Chaldeans) **p**laying (Phoenicians).

Review & Assess

Close

Discuss with students the order of peoples that ruled Mesopotamia and how each group came to power.

Review

Online Quiz, Section 4

Assess

SE Section 4 Assessment

PASS: Section 4 Quiz

Alternative Assessment Handbook

Reteach/Classroom Intervention

Guided Reading Workshop, Section 4

Interactive Skills Tutor CD-ROM

Answers

Interpreting Maps *at the eastern end of the Mediterranean Sea*

Reading Check *They were expert sailors with fast ships, built outstanding harbors and a vast trade network, and developed an alphabet.*

Social Studies Skills

Interpreting Physical Maps

Activity Reading a Local Physical Map Make copies of a physical map of the city, town, or county where your school is located. Have students describe the area's topography by identifying the different natural features and the landscape. Then ask students how the area's topography might affect the people who live in the area. For example, how might the topography affect industry and business in the area? Have students consider an important industry in your area. Then have students discuss how the topography of your area might have affected early settlers there. Last, have students write one to two paragraphs describing how they think the topography might have affected early people in the area.
LS Verbal/Linguistic, Visual/Spatial

- Alternative Assessment Handbook, Rubric 37: Writing Assignments
- Interactive Skills Tutor CD-ROM, Lesson 6: Interpret Maps, Graphs, Charts, Visuals, and Political Cartoons

Social Studies Skills

Analysis | Critical Thinking | Economics | Study

Interpreting Physical Maps

Understand the Skill

A *physical map* is a map that shows the natural features and landscape, or *topography*, of an area. It shows the location and size of such features as rivers and mountain ranges. Physical maps also often show an area's *elevation*, or how high above sea level the land is. Topography and elevation often influence human activities. For example, people will live where they can find water and defend themselves. Therefore, being able to interpret a physical map can help you better understand how the history of an area unfolded.

Learn the Skill

Follow these steps to interpret a physical map.

1. Read the map's title, distance scale, and legend. These will provide basic information about the map's contents.
2. Note the colors used to show elevation. Use the legend to connect colors on the map to elevations of specific places.
3. Note the shapes of the features, such as how high a mountain range is, how far it stretches, and how long a river is. Note where each feature is in relation to others.
4. Use information from the map to draw conclusions about the effect of the region's topography on settlement and economic activities.

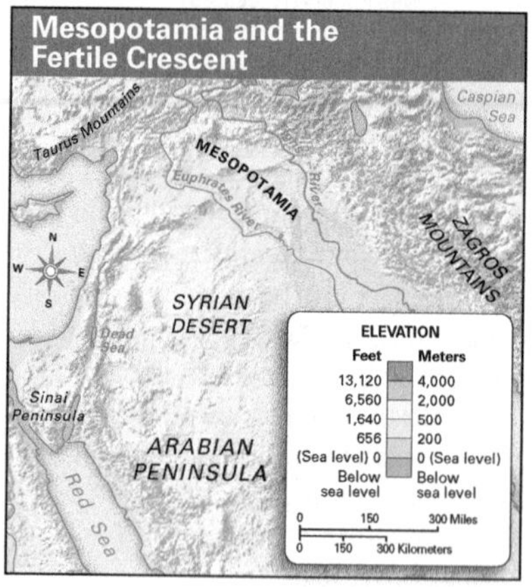

Mesopotamia and the Fertile Crescent

Practice and Apply the Skill

Use the guidelines to answer these questions about the map above.

1. What is the elevation of the western half of the Arabian Peninsula?
2. Describe the topography of Mesopotamia. Why would settlement have occurred here before other places on the map?
3. What feature might have stopped invasions of Mesopotamia?

Social Studies Skills Activity: Interpreting Physical Maps

Special Needs Learners — Below Level

Materials: solid-colored table cloth

Using Visual Aids Lay a table cloth over your desk, a table, or another flat surface in the classroom. Push the table cloth together so that it forms folds and wrinkles similar to those on a physical map. Help students to see how these folds, dips, and flat areas resemble the mountains, valleys, and plains on a physical map. Then show students photographs of mountains and valleys and relate the images to the same features on a physical map.
LS Kinesthetic, Visual/Spatial

English-Language Learners — At Level

Building Geographic Vocabulary English learners might need help with the vocabulary related to physical maps. Write the following terms for students to see: *elevation, landscape, mountain ranges, plains, sea level, topography,* and *valleys.* Help students write definitions for the terms first in their primary language and then in English. **LS Verbal/Linguistic**

- Alternative Assessment Handbook, Rubric 1: Acquiring Information

Answers

Practice and Apply the Skill
1. *between 1,640 (500 m.) and 6,560 (2,000 m.) feet above sea level;* **2.** *fairly flat with two rivers providing good water sources; would be good for agriculture and settlement;* **3.** *possible answers—the desert to the southwest and the mountains to the north and northeast*

CHAPTER 3

Chapter Review

History's Impact
▶ **video series**
Review the video to answer the focus question:
How are Hammurabi's laws and American laws alike and different?

Visual Summary

Use the visual summary below to help you review the main ideas of the chapter.

QUICK FACTS

The early Mesopotamians developed irrigation to grow food.
Food production in Mesopotamia led to the world's first civilization.
Sumerian advances included ziggurats, the wheel, and the first writing system.
Later peoples developed the first written laws and the first empires.

Reviewing Vocabulary, Terms, and People

Using your own paper, complete the sentences below by providing the correct term for each blank.

1. Mesopotamian farmers built ____________ to irrigate their fields.
2. While city dwellers were urban, farmers lived in ____________ areas.
3. The people of Sumer practiced ____________, the worship of many gods.
4. Instead of using pictographs, Sumerians developed a type of writing called ____________.
5. Horse-drawn ____________ gave the Hittites an advantage during battle.
6. The Babylonian king ____________ is famous for his code of laws.
7. Another word for effect is ____________.
8. Sumerian society was organized in ____________, which consisted of a city and the surrounding lands.

Comprehension and Critical Thinking

SECTION 1 *(Pages 54–57)*

9. a. Describe Where was Mesopotamia, and what does the name mean?

b. Analyze How did Mesopotamian irrigation systems allow civilization to develop?

c. Elaborate Do you think a division of labor is necessary for civilization to develop? Why or why not?

SECTION 2 *(Pages 60–64)*

10. a. Identify Who built the world's first empire, and what did that empire include?

b. Analyze Politically, how was early Sumerian society organized? How did that organization affect society?

c. Elaborate Why did the Sumerians consider it everyone's responsibility to keep the gods happy?

Answers

Visual Summary

Review and Inquiry Have students use the visual summary to write a brief paragraph summarizing the important themes depicted in the illustration.

Quick Facts Transparency: Mesopotamia and the Fertile Crescent Visual Summary

Reviewing Vocabulary, Terms, and People

1. canals
2. rural
3. polytheism
4. cuneiform
5. chariots
6. Hammurabi
7. impact
8. city-states

Comprehension and Critical Thinking

9. a. It was located between the Tigris and Euphrates rivers, and the name means " between the rivers" in Greek.

b. They allowed the people to control the flow of the rivers and produce a surplus of food, which freed people to create a civilization.

c. possible answer—yes, because it allows people to focus on building a civilization rather than just surviving

10. a. Sargon; the area between the Tigris and Euphrates rivers and much of Mesopotamia

b. Kings and priests made up the upper class, while the middle class was craftspeople, merchants, and traders and the working class

Review and Assessment Resources

Review and Reinforce

- SE Chapter Review
- **CRF:** Chapter Review Activity
- Quick Facts Transparency: Mesopotamia and the Fertile Crescent Visual Summary
- Spanish Chapter Summaries Audio CD
- Online Chapter Summaries in Six Languages
- TOS Holt McDougal PuzzleView
- Quiz Game CD-ROM

Assess

- SE Standardized Test Practice
- PASS: Chapter Test, Forms A and B
- Alternative Assessment Handbook
- TOS ExamView Assessment Suite, Chapter Test
- Differentiated Instruction Modified Worksheets and Tests CD-ROM, Chapter Test
- Online Assessment Program, in the Interactive Student Edition

Reteach/Intervene

- Guided Reading Workbook
- Differentiated Instruction Teacher Management System: Lesson Plans
- Differentiated Instruction Modified Worksheets and Tests CD-ROM
- Interactive Skills Tutor CD-ROM

hmhsocialstudies.com
Chapter Resources

Answers

consisted of farmers and laborers. Slaves were at the bottom. Priests and the wealthy ruled society, while the working class supported them.

c. The gods had great powers, and in order for the people to lead happy and prosperous lives, everyone had to do their part in keeping the gods happy.

11. a. cuneiform; significant because it is the world's first system of writing

b. similar—students went to school to learn to read and write, they produced makeup and jewelry, enjoyed music; different—their writing was cuneiform, wrote on clay tablets

c. Answers will vary but should display knowledge of chapter content.

12. a. purple dye, founded Carthage, developed an alphabet

b. possible answer—Separately they stood no chance, but by banding together they were able to make an impact.

c. Answers will vary but should be supported by facts.

Reviewing Themes

13. Answers will vary but should display knowledge of chapter content.

14. possible answer—He was the first to institute such a far-reaching and comprehensive structure of laws, which influenced many future societies.

Reading Skills

15. A

16. B

SECTION 3 *(Pages 65–69)*

11. a. Identify What was the Sumerian writing system called, and why is it so significant?

b. Compare and Contrast What were two ways in which Sumerian society was similar to our society today? What were two ways in which it was different?

c. Evaluate Other than writing and the wheel, which Sumerian invention do you think is most important? Why?

SECTION 4 *(Pages 72–77)*

12. a. Describe What were two important developments of the Phoenicians?

b. Draw Conclusions Why do you think several peoples banded together to fight the Assyrians?

c. Evaluate Do you think Hammurabi was more effective as a ruler or as a military leader? Why?

Reviewing Themes

13. Science and Technology Which of the ancient Sumerians' technological achievements do you think has been most influential in history? Why?

14. Politics Why do you think Hammurabi is so honored for his code of laws?

Reading Skills

Identifying Main Ideas *For each passage, choose the letter that corresponds to the main idea sentence.*

15. (A) Sumerians believed that their gods had enormous powers. (B) Gods could bring a good harvest or a disastrous flood. (C) They could bring illness or they could bring good health and wealth.

16. (A) The wheel was not the Sumerians' only great development. (B) They developed cuneiform, the world's first system of writing. (C) But Sumerians did not have pencils, pens, or paper. (D) Instead, they used sharp reeds to make wedge-shaped symbols on clay tablets.

Using the Internet 

17. Activity: Looking at Writing The Sumerians made one of the greatest cultural advances in history by developing cuneiform. This was the world's first system of writing. Through your online book, research the evolution of language and its written forms. Look at one of the newest methods of writing: text messaging. Then write a paragraph explaining how and why writing was developed and why it was important using text-messaging abbreviations, words, and symbols.

hmhsocialstudies.com

Social Studies Skills

Interpreting Physical Maps *Could you use a physical map to answer the questions below? For each question, answer yes or no.*

18. Are there mountains or hills in a certain region?

19. What languages do people speak in that region?

20. How many people live in the region?

21. What kinds of water features such as rivers or lakes would you find there?

Focus on Writing

22. Writing Your Letter Use the notes you have taken to create a plan for your letter. You might want to start with a rough outline of two or three main points. For example, one of your main points might be about the land of Mesopotamia. Another might be about the achievements of the Sumerians.

After you have a good plan in mind, you can start to write your letter. As you write, think about the young student who will be reading the letter. What words will he or she understand? How can you capture the student's interest and keep it? If you think it would help the student to see a map or a drawing, create one and attach it to your letter.

Using the Internet

17. Go to hmhsocialstudies.com to access a rubric for this activity.

Social Studies Skills

18. yes

19. no

20. no

21. yes

Focus on Writing

22. Rubric Students' letters should

- express main points clearly and accurately.
- use appropriate vocabulary.

CHAPTER 3

Standardized Test Practice

DIRECTIONS: Read each question, and write the letter of the best response.

1 Use the map to answer the following question.

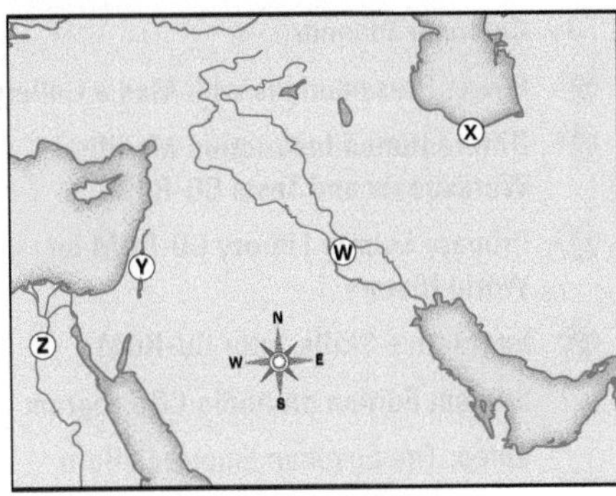

The region known as Mesopotamia is indicated on the map by the letter

A W.
B X.
C Y.
D Z.

2 All of the following ancient civilizations developed in Mesopotamia *except* the

A Akkadians.
B Babylonians.
C Egyptians.
D Sumerians.

3 Which of the following is *not* true of the first writing system?

A It was developed by the Babylonians.
B It began with the use of pictures to represent syllables and objects.
C It was recorded on tablets made of clay.
D It was first used to keep business records.

4 In Sumerian society, people's social class or rank depended on their wealth and their

A appearance.
B religion.
C location.
D occupation.

5 Hammurabi's Code is important in world history because it was an early

A form of writing that could be used to record important events.
B written list of laws that controlled people's daily life and behavior.
C record-keeping system that enabled the Phoenicians to become great traders.
D set of symbols that allowed the Sumerians to communicate with other peoples.

6 What was the most important contribution of the Phoenicians to our civilization?

A purple dye
B their alphabet
C founding of Carthage
D sailing ships

Connecting with Past Learnings

7 In this chapter, you learned about agriculture in Mesopotamia. During what period of prehistory was agriculture first practiced?

A Megalithic Era
B Mesolithic Era
C Paleolithic Era
D Neolithic Era

Answers

Standardized Test Practice

1. A

Break Down the Question Point out that the region labeled Y is part of the Fertile Crescent, but not Mesopotamia. Have students who miss the question review the map in Section 1.

2. C

Break Down the Question Remind students that the word *except* in this question signals that they should identify the false answer choice.

3. A

Break Down the Question Remind students that the word *not* in this question signals that they should identify the false answer choice.

4. D

Break Down the Question This question requires students to recall factual information from Section 2.

5. B

Break Down the Question This question requires students to recall factual information from Section 4.

6. B

Break Down the Question Point out to students that the most lasting contribution from the Phoenicians to our world has been the alphabet.

7. D

Break Down the Question This question requires students to recall factual information from Chapter 20.

Intervention Resources

Reproducible

- Guided Reading Workbook
- Differentiated Instruction Teacher Management System: Lesson Plans

Technology

- Quick Facts Transparency: Mesopotamia and the Fertile Crescent Visual Summary
- Differentiated Instruction Modified Worksheets and Tests CD-ROM
- Interactive Skills Tutor CD-ROM

Tips for Test Taking

I'm Stuck! Give students these tips for when they get stuck on a standardized test. If you come across a question that stumps you, don't get frustrated. First master the question to make sure you understand what is being asked. Then work through the strategies you have already learned. If you are still stuck, circle the question and go on to others. Come back to it later. What if you still have no idea? Practice the 50/50 strategy and make an educated guess.

Chapter 4 Planning Guide

Ancient Egypt and Kush

Overview	Instructional Resources	
CHAPTER 4 **Essential Question:** How was the success of the Egyptian civilization tied to the Nile River? **Focus on the Essential Question Podcast**	TOS **Differentiated Instruction Teacher Management System:** • Instructional Benchmarking Guides • Lesson Plans for Differentiated Instruction **Guided Reading Workbook** **Chapter Resource File:** • Chapter Review Activity • Focus on Writing Activity: A Riddle • Social Studies Skills Activity: Assessing Primary and Secondary Sources	TOS **Calendar Planner** **Power Presentations with Media Gallery** **Differentiated Instruction Modified Worksheets and Tests CD-ROM** **Primary Source Library CD-ROM for World History** **Interactive Skills Tutor CD-ROM** **Student Edition on Audio CD Program** HISTORY **Video:** The Egyptian Empire Is Born
Section 1: **Geography and Ancient Egypt** **The Big Idea:** The water, fertile soils, and protected setting of the Nile Valley allowed a great civilization to arise in Egypt around 3200 BC.	TOS **Differentiated Instruction Teacher Management System:** Section 1 Lesson Plan **Guided Reading Workbook:** Section 1 **Chapter Resource File:** • Vocabulary Builder Activity, Section 1	**Daily Bellringer Transparency:** Section 1 **Map Transparency:** Ancient Egypt HISTORY **Video:** How Does the Nile Measure Up?
Section 2: **The Old Kingdom** **The Big Idea:** Egyptian government and religion were closely connected during the Old Kingdom.	TOS **Differentiated Instruction Teacher Management System:** Section 2 Lesson Plan **Guided Reading Workbook:** Section 2 **Chapter Resource File:** • Vocabulary Builder Activity, Section 2	**Daily Bellringer Transparency:** Section 2 **Internet Activity:** Pyramids HISTORY **Video:** Are Mummies Beef Jerky? **Animated History:** The Great Pyramid
Section 3: **The Middle and New Kingdoms** **The Big Idea:** During the Middle and New Kingdoms, order and greatness were restored in Egypt.	TOS **Differentiated Instruction Teacher Management System:** Section 3 Lesson Plan **Guided Reading Workbook:** Section 3 **Chapter Resource File:** • Vocabulary Builder Activity, Section 3	**Daily Bellringer Transparency:** Section 3 **Map Transparency:** Egyptian Trade, c. 1400 BC HISTORY **Video:** Let's Move a Mountain
Section 4: **Egyptian Achievements** **The Big Idea:** The Egyptians made lasting achievements in writing, architecture, and art.	TOS **Differentiated Instruction Teacher Management System:** Section 4 Lesson Plan **Guided Reading Workbook:** Section 4 **Chapter Resource File:** • Vocabulary Builder Activity, Section 4	**Daily Bellringer Transparency:** Section 4 **Map Transparency:** Phoenicia, c. 800 BC **Internet Activity:** Hieroglyphics
Section 5: **Ancient Kush** **The Big Idea:** The kingdom of Kush, which arose south of Egypt in a land called Nubia, developed an advanced civilization with a large trading network.	TOS **Differentiated Instruction Teacher Management System:** Section 5 Lesson Plan **Guided Reading Workbook:** Section 5 **Chapter Resource File:** • Vocabulary Builder Activity, Section 5	**Daily Bellringer Transparency:** Section 5 **Map Transparency:** Ancient Kush **Internet Activity:** Time Travel to Ancient Kush

Chart Key:

SE Student Edition  Presentation Resource 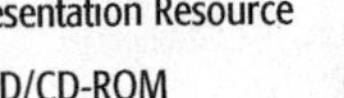 MP3 Audio
TOS Teacher One Stop  DVD/CD-ROM 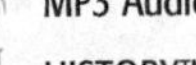 HISTORY™
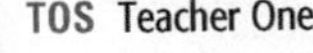 Printable Resource

Program Resources available on TOS and @  hmhsocialstudies.com

Review, Assessment, Intervention

 **Quick Facts Transparency:** Ancient Egypt and Kush Visual Summary

 **Spanish Chapter Summaries Audio CD Program**

 **Quiz Game CD-ROM**

 **Progress Assessment Support System (PASS):** Chapter Test

 **Differentiated Instruction Modified Worksheets and Tests CD-ROM:** Modified Chapter Test

 TOS **ExamView® Assessment Suite (English/Spanish)**

 **Online Assessment Program,** in the Interactive Student Edition

 **PASS:** Section 1 Quiz

 **Online Quiz:** Section 1

 **Alternative Assessment Handbook**

 **PASS:** Section 2 Quiz

 **Online Quiz:** Section 2

 **Alternative Assessment Handbook**

 **PASS:** Section 3 Quiz

 **Online Quiz:** Section 3

 **Alternative Assessment Handbook**

 **PASS:** Section 4 Quiz

 **Online Quiz:** Section 4

 **Alternative Assessment Handbook**

 **PASS:** Section 5 Quiz

 **Online Quiz:** Section 5

 **Alternative Assessment Handbook**

Supporting Resources

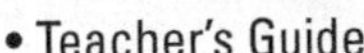

- Multimedia Classroom Global History Series
- Global History Teacher's Guide

Maps Globes Graphs Level F

- Student Workbook
- Teacher's Guide

Social Studies Trade Library Collections

- Premier Secondary World History Trade Collection
- Ancient World History Trade Collection

History's Impact

World History Video Program

- **The Egyptian Pyramids**

For more information or to purchase go to hmhsocialstudies.com

Power Presentations with Media Gallery

Power Presentations with Media Gallery are visual presentations of each chapter's main ideas. Presentations can be customized by including Quick Facts charts, images from the text, and video clips.

Differentiating Instruction

How do I address the needs of varied learners?

The Target Resource acts as your primary strategy for differentiated instruction.

ENGLISH-LANGUAGE LEARNERS & STRUGGLING READERS

Interactive Skills Tutor CD-ROM

The Interactive Skills Tutor CD-ROM contains lessons that provide additional practice for 20 different critical thinking skills.

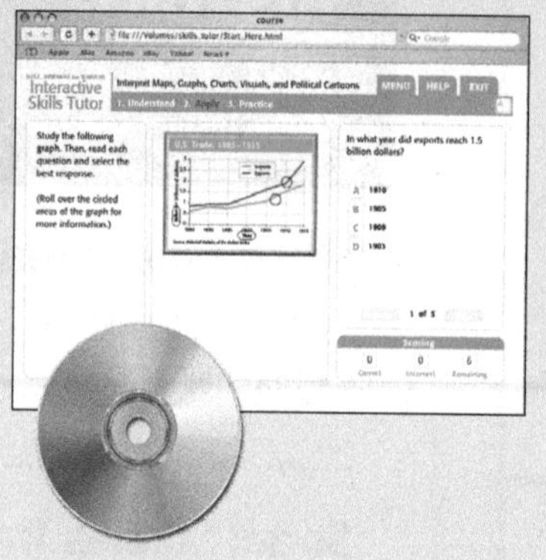

Additional Resources

Differentiated Instruction Teacher Management System: Lesson Plans for Differentiated Instruction

Chapter Resource File:

- Vocabulary Builder Activities
- Social Studies Skills Activity: Assessing Primary and Secondary Sources

Quick Facts Transparencies: Ancient Egypt and Kush Visual Summary

Student Edition on Audio CD Program

Interactive Skills Tutor CD-ROM

Spanish/English Guided Reading Workbook

SPECIAL NEEDS LEARNERS

Differentiated Instruction Modified Worksheets and Tests CD-ROM

- Vocabulary Flash Cards
- Vocabulary Builder Activities
- Chapter Review Activity
- Chapter Test

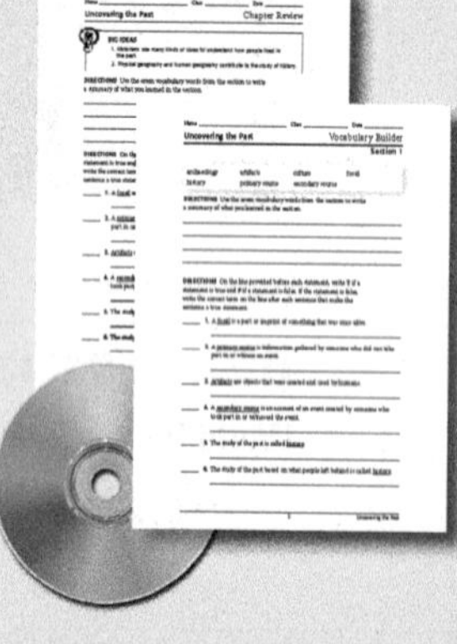

Additional Resources

Differentiated Instruction Teacher Management System: Lesson Plans for Differentiated Instruction

Guided Reading Workbook

Chapter Resource File: Social Studies Skills Activity: Assessing Primary and Secondary Sources

Student Edition on Audio CD Program

Interactive Skills Tutor CD-ROM

ADVANCED/GIFTED-AND-TALENTED STUDENTS

Primary Source Library CD-ROM for World History

The Library contains longer versions of quotations in the text, extra sources, and images. Included are point-of-view articles, journals, diaries, historical fiction, and political documents.

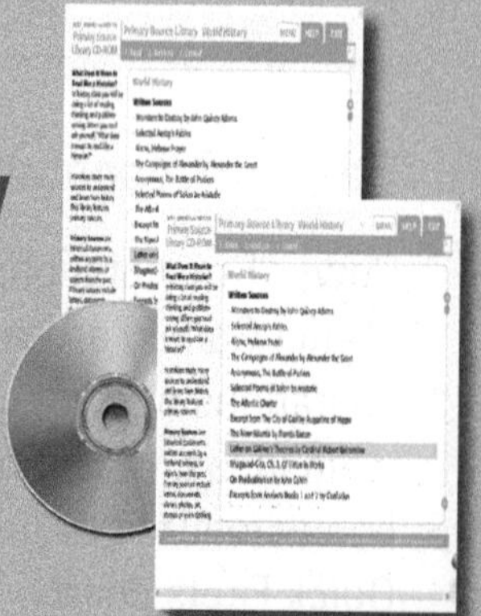

Additional Resources

Differentiated Instruction Teacher Management System: Lesson Plans for Differentiated Instruction

Chapter Resource File:

- Focus on Writing Activity: A Riddle
- Literature Activity: The Egyptian Cinderella

Document-Based Questions Activities

Differentiated Activities in the Teacher's Edition

- Using Graphic Organizers, p. 88
- Comparing Egyptian Society and Modern Society, p. 99
- Rosetta Stone Summary, p. 103
- Charting Natural Resources, p. 109

Teacher One Stop™

How can I manage the lesson plans and support materials for differentiated instruction?

With the Teacher One Stop, you can easily organize and print lesson plans, planning guides, and instructional materials for all learners. The Teacher One Stop includes the following materials to help you differentiate instruction:

- **Interactive Teacher's Edition**
- **Calendar Planner and pacing guides**
- **Editable lesson plans**
- **All reproducible ancillaries in Adobe Acrobat (PDF) format**
- **ExamView Assessment Suite (English & Spanish)**
- **Transparency and video previews**

Differentiated Activities in the Teacher's Edition

- Two New Kingdom Rulers, p. 98
- Designing Stone Carvings, p. 112

Interactive Student Edition

Complete online student edition with interactive multimedia support for chapter content assessment and reporting

- Interactive Maps and Notebook
- Graphic Organizers
- Standardized Test Prep
- Online Homework Practice and Research Activities
- Current Events
- Chapter-based Internet Activities
- Animated History Activities
- and more!

Differentiated Activities in the Teacher's Edition

- Creating Storyboards, p. 92
- Writing and Performing Skits, p. 111

Chapter Preview

Essential Question

Introduce the Essential Question

- Point out that the yearly flood of the Nile River made the area near the river very fertile.
- Talk about the many different crops Egyptian farmers were able to grow, including grains, fruits, vegetables, and flax (which was made into linen cloth).
- Tell students that the Nile was also a valuable mode of transportation. Trade goods and sometimes armies traveled north and south along the river.

CHAPTER 4 4500 BC–AD 400

Ancient Egypt and Kush

Essential Question How was the success of the Egyptian civilization tied to the Nile River?

South Carolina Performance Standards

6-1.3 Compare the river valley civilizations of the Tigris and Euphrates (Mesopotamia), the Nile (Egypt), the Indus (India), and the Huang He (China), including the evolution of written language, government, trade systems, architecture, and forms of social order.

Literacy Skills for Social Studies

- Identify and explain the relationships among multiple causes and multiple effects.
- Interpret Earth's physical and human systems by using maps, mental maps, geographic models, and other social studies resources.
- Compare the locations of places, the conditions at places, and the connections between places.
- Explain how the endowment and development of productive resources affects economic decisions and global interactions.
- Explain why trade occurs and how historical patterns of trade have contributed to global interdependence.

Partnership for the 21st Century Skills

Cite specific textual evidence to support the analysis of primary and secondary sources.

Focus on Writing

Riddles In ancient times, according to legend, a sphinx—an imaginary creature like the one whose sculpture is found in Egypt—demanded the answer to a riddle. People died if they couldn't answer the riddle correctly. After you read this chapter, you will write two riddles. The answer to one of your riddles will be "Egypt." The answer to your other riddle will be "Kush."

Chapter Events

c. 4500 BC Agricultural communities develop in Egypt.

4000 BC

World Events

Focus on Writing

The **Chapter Resource File** provides a Focus on Writing worksheet to help students write their riddles.

CRF: Focus on Writing Activity: A Riddle

Key to Differentiating Instruction

Below Level
Basic-level activities designed for all students encountering new material

At Level
Intermediate-level activities designed for average students

Above Level
Challenging activities designed for honors and gifted and talented students

Standard English Mastery
Activities designed to improve standard English usage

LS Learning Styles

Introduce the Chapter

At Level

Impressions of Egypt

1. Ask students what they already know about ancient Egypt. What books or articles have they read? What photos or movies have they seen? Do they have or have they seen any jewelry that has Egyptian designs? Write responses for students to see.
2. Tell students that some things portrayed in popular culture and in the media are true and some are not. For example, workers on the pyramids have often been portrayed as slaves, but most Egyptologists now think these workers were mostly common people, such as free farmers. Tell students that in their research they may see the term *Egyptologist*, which refers to a person who studies Egyptian antiquities.
3. Tell students that in this chapter they will see how accurately their current knowledge about Egypt reflects ancient Egyptian life. **LS Verbal/Linguistic**

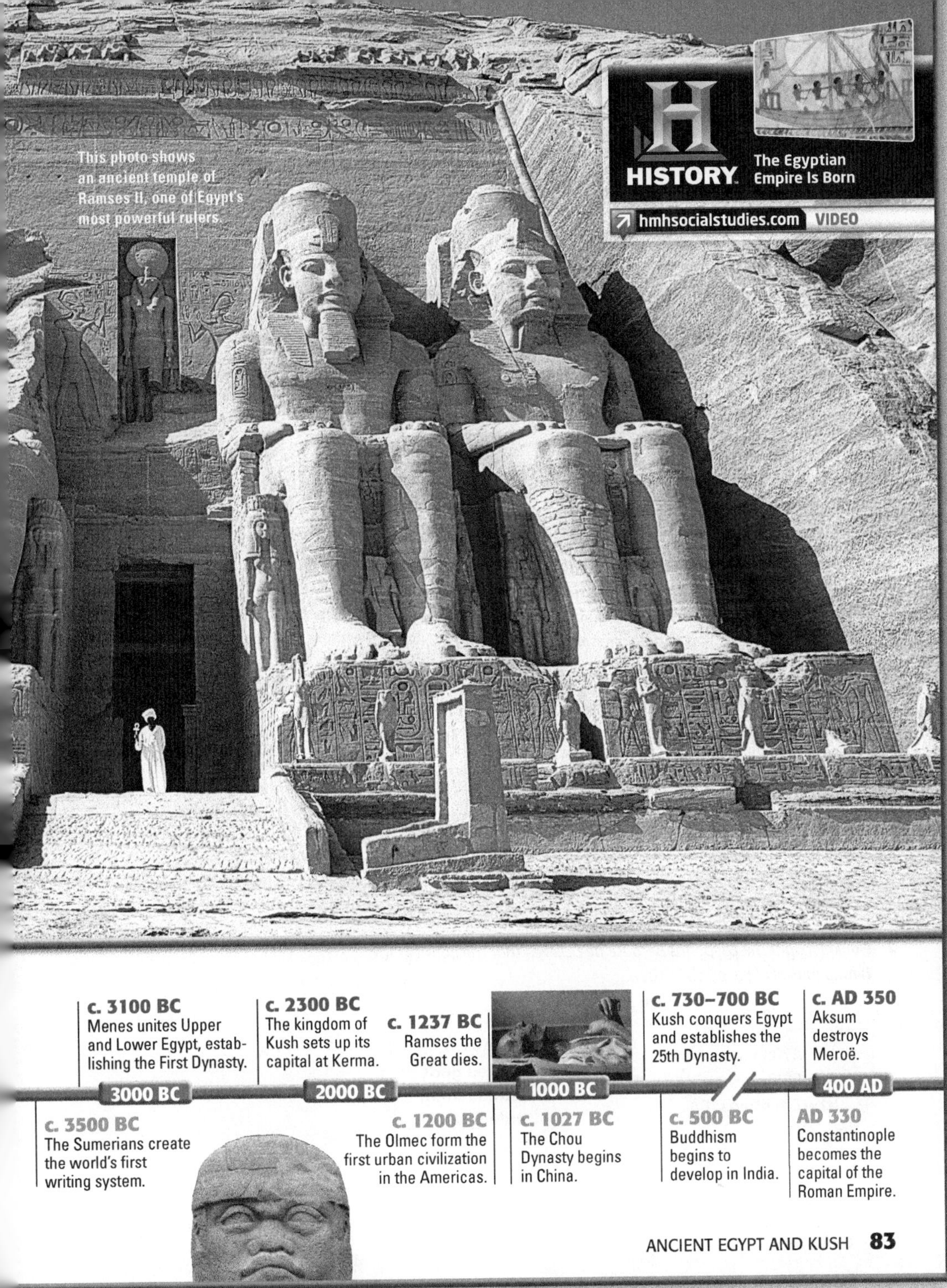

This photo shows an ancient temple of Ramses II, one of Egypt's most powerful rulers.

HISTORY The Egyptian Empire Is Born

hmhsocialstudies.com VIDEO

c. 3500 BC The Sumerians create the world's first writing system.

c. 3100 BC Menes unites Upper and Lower Egypt, establishing the First Dynasty.

3000 BC

c. 2300 BC The kingdom of Kush sets up its capital at Kerma.

2000 BC

c. 1237 BC Ramses the Great dies.

c. 1200 BC The Olmec form the first urban civilization in the Americas.

1000 BC

c. 1027 BC The Chou Dynasty begins in China.

c. 730–700 BC Kush conquers Egypt and establishes the 25th Dynasty.

c. 500 BC Buddhism begins to develop in India.

400 AD

AD 330 Constantinople becomes the capital of the Roman Empire.

c. AD 350 Aksum destroys Meroë.

ANCIENT EGYPT AND KUSH **83**

• Chapter Preview •

Explore the Picture

Ramses the Great This picture shows the entrance to Ramses the Great's temple at Abu Simbel. The entrance is flanked by four 66-foot high statues of the pharaoh. However, the structure you see in the photo is not in its original location. When dam construction on the Nile River threatened to flood the temple, workers cut the entire structure into blocks and rebuilt it on higher ground.

Analyzing Visuals Why may Ramses have had not just one but four statues of himself placed before the temple? *possible answer—to make the entrance more impressive or to emphasize different roles that he had in Egyptian politics and religion*

hmhsocialstudies.com Teacher Resources

Explore the Time Line

1. How many years separate the founding of the first dynasty and the death of Ramses the Great? *about 1,863 years*
2. What was happening in the Americas at about the same time Ramses died? *The Olmec were forming the first urban civilization in the Americas.*
3. What happened in Kush about 20 years after Constantinople became the capital of the Roman Empire? *Aksum destroyed Meroë.*

Info to Know

Beyond the Time Line Although Kush conquered Egypt between 730 and 700 BC, Egyptian history continued long after that date. However, Egypt was never again as powerful or influential as it had been. One after the other, Assyrians, Persians, and Macedonians conquered Egypt. The Egyptians maintained their own distinct culture, though, until about 30 BC. At that time, Rome took control of Egypt, and Egyptian traditions began to change for all time.

Reading Social Studies

Understanding Themes

Two themes, economics and geography, are presented in this chapter. Have students look at a map of Africa and determine where the ancient kingdoms of Egypt and Kush were located. Then have students use the map to draw inferences about the geography of Egypt and Kush. Finally, ask students how trade affected the economy of Egypt and Kush. Have students use the map to determine with what civilizations Egypt and Kush might have traded.

Causes and Effects in History

Focus on Reading Ask students to name examples of something in their community or school that has caused a direct effect. For example, lunch lines may have been so long that the school created two lunch periods. In the community, a lack of open land may have been the motivation for the creation of new parks. Have students look for examples of activities, events, or improvements in their own communities that show cause and effect. Have students write their cause and effect statements using the signal words on this page.

Reading Social Studies

Economics | Geography | Politics | Religion | Society and Culture | Science and Technology

Focus on Themes As you read this chapter, you will learn about the ancient kingdoms of Egypt and Kush. You will see that the **geography** of the areas helped these kingdoms to develop. You will also learn how Egypt conquered and ruled Kush and then how Kush conquered and ruled Egypt. You will learn how the **economies** of these kingdoms, based on trade, grew strong. Finally you will learn about the importance of **religion** to the people of both of these ancient societies.

Causes and Effects in History

Focus on Reading Have you heard the saying, "We have to understand the past to avoid repeating it"? That is one reason we look for causes and effects in history.

Identifying Causes and Effects A **cause** is something that makes another thing happen. An **effect** is the result of something else that has happened. Most historical events have a number of causes as well as a number of effects. You can understand history better if you look for causes and effects of events.

1. *Because the Egyptians had captured and destroyed the city of Kerma, the kings of Kush ruled from the city of Napata.* (p. 109)

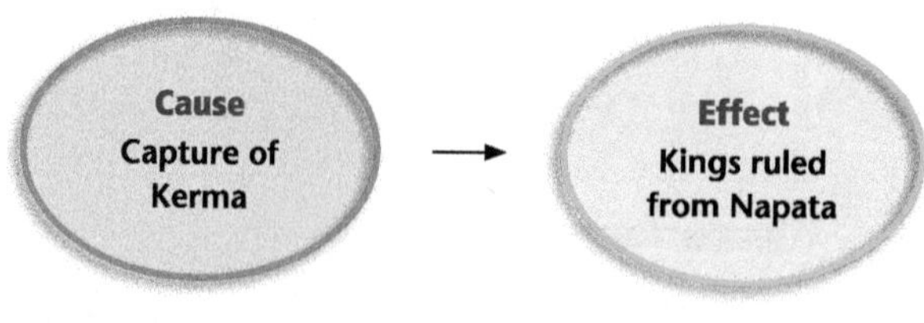

Sometimes writers use words that signal a cause or an effect. Here are some:

Cause—*reason, basis, because, motivated, as*

Effect—*therefore, as a result, for that reason, so*

2. *Piankhi fought the Egyptians because he believed that the gods wanted him to rule all of Egypt.* (p. 110)

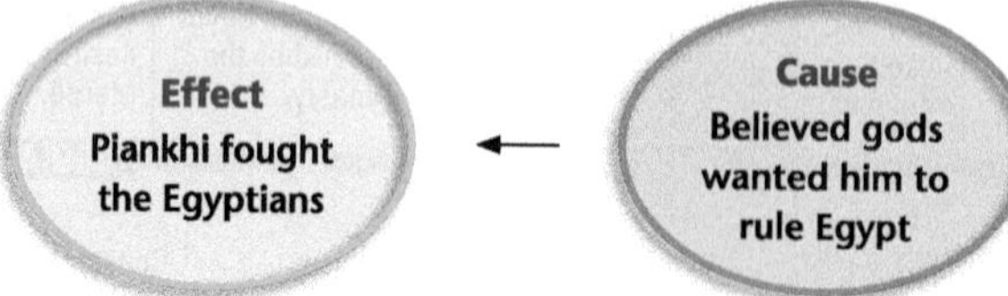

Reading and Skills Resources

Reading Support

- Guided Reading Workbook
- Student Edition on Audio CD
- Spanish Chapter Summaries Audio CD Program

Social Studies Skills Support

- Interactive Skills Tutor CD-ROM

Vocabulary Support

- **CRF:** Vocabulary Builder Activities
- **CRF:** Chapter Review Activity
- Differentiating Instruction Modified Worksheets and Tests CD-ROM:
  - Vocabulary Flash Cards
  - Vocabulary Builder Activity
  - Chapter Review Activity
- TOS Holt McDougal PuzzleView

You Try It!

The following selections are from the chapter you are about to read. As you read each, identify which phrase or sentence describes a cause and which describes an effect.

Finding Causes and Effects

1. "During the mid-1000s BC the New Kingdom in Egypt was ending. As the power of Egypt's pharaohs declined, Kushite leaders regained control of Kush. Kush once again became independent." (p. 109)
2. "A series of inept pharaohs left Egypt open to attack." (p. 109)
3. "The Assyrians' iron weapons were better than the Kushites' bronze weapons. Although the Kushites were skilled archers, they could not stop the invaders (p. 111)
4. "Iron ore and wood for furnaces were easily available, so the iron industry grew quickly." (p. 111)

After you read the sentences, answer the following questions.

1. In selection 1, is "Kush once again became independent" the cause of the Egyptians growing weaker or the effect?
2. In selection 2, what left Egypt open to attack? Is that the cause of why Egypt was easily attacked or the effect?
3. In selection 3, who is using the iron weapons, the Assyrians or the Kushites? What was the effect of using the weapons?
4. In selection 4, does the word *so* signal a cause or an effect?

As you read Chapter 4, look for words that signal causes or effects. Make a chart to keep track of these causes and effects.

Key Terms and People

Chapter 4

Section 1
cataracts *(p. 87)*
delta *(p. 87)*
Menes *(p. 89)*
pharaoh *(p. 89)*
dynasty *(p. 89)*

Section 2
Old Kingdom *(p. 90)*
Khufu *(p. 91)*
nobles *(p. 91)*
afterlife *(p. 92)*
mummies *(p. 93)*
elite *(p. 93)*
pyramids *(p. 94)*
engineering *(p. 94)*

Section 3
Middle Kingdom *(p. 96)*
New Kingdom *(p. 97)*
trade routes *(p. 97)*
Queen Hathepsut *(p. 98)*
Ramses the Great *(p. 98)*

Section 4
hieroglyphics *(p. 102)*
papyrus *(p. 102)*
Rosetta Stone *(p.103)*
sphinxes *(p. 104)*
obelisk *(p. 104)*
King Tutankhamen *(p. 106)*

Section 5
Piankhi *(p. 110)*
trade network *(p. 111)*
merchants *(p. 111)*
exports *(p. 111)*
imports *(p. 111)*
Queen Shanakhdakheto *(p. 113)*
King Ezana *(p. 113)*

Academic Vocabulary
acquire *(p. 91)*
method *(p. 93)*
contracts *(p. 100)*
authority *(p. 113)*

Reading Social Studies

Key Terms and People

Preteach these terms and people to the class. Familiarize students with the key terms and people by having students use the terms in sentences about Egypt and Kush. Then have students rewrite their sentences, leaving blanks where the key term belongs. Have students exchange papers with a partner and fill in the blanks. **LS Verbal/Linguistic**

Focus on Reading

See the **Focus on Reading** questions in this chapter for more practice on reading social studies skills.

Reading Social Studies Assessment

See the **Chapter Review** at the end of this chapter for student assessment questions related to this reading skill.

Teaching Tip

Review the cause-and-effect signal words with students. Ask them to suggest simple sentences that use these signal words. Write the sentences for all students to see, and examine the cause and effect relationship. For example, in the sentence "Because it rained last night, baseball practice was cancelled," the cause is because it rained last night, and the effect is that baseball practice was cancelled. Have students create sentences that use each of the signal words that indicate cause or effect.

Answers

You Try It! 1. *effect;* **2.** *a series of weak pharaohs was the cause of why Egypt was easily attacked;* **3.** *Assyrians; effect was the Kushites could not stop them;* **4.** *effect*

Preteach

Bellringer

If YOU were there . . . Use the **Daily Bellringer Transparency** to help students answer the question.

Daily Bellringer Transparency, Section 1

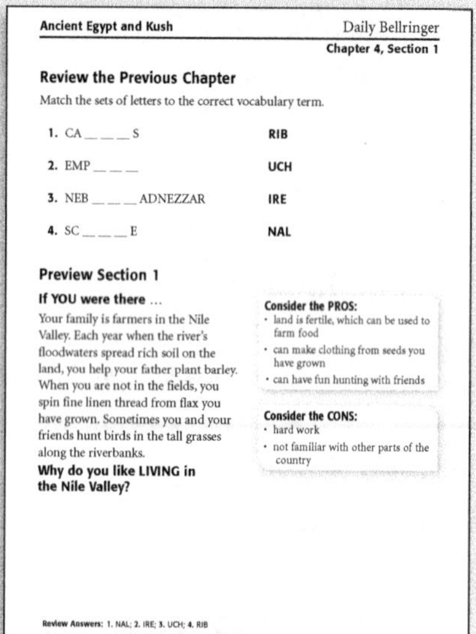

Ancient Egypt and Kush — Daily Bellringer

Chapter 4, Section 1

Review the Previous Chapter

Match the sets of letters to the correct vocabulary term.

1. CA _ _ _ S	**RIB**
2. EMP _ _ _	**UCH**
3. NEB _ _ _ ADNEZZAR	**IRE**
4. SC _ _ _ E	**NAL**

Preview Section 1

If YOU were there ...

Your family is farmers in the Nile Valley. Each year when the river's floodwaters spread rich soil on the land, you help your father plant barley. When you are not in the fields, you spin fine linen thread from flax you have grown. Sometimes you and your friends hunt birds in the tall grasses along the riverbanks.

Why do you like LIVING in the Nile Valley?

Consider the PROS:
- land is fertile, which can be used to farm food
- can make clothing from seeds you have grown
- can have fun hunting with friends

Consider the CONS:
- hard work
- not familiar with other parts of the country

Review Answers: 1. NAL; 2. IRE; 3. UCH; 4. RIB

Building Vocabulary

Preteach or review the following terms:

fertile capable of producing plentiful vegetation (p. 86)

rapids parts of a river where the water is shallow and turbulent (p. 87)

silt finely ground soil deposited by flowing water (p. 87)

CRF: Vocabulary Builder Activity, Section 1

Taking Notes

Have students use the graphic organizer online to take notes on the section. This activity will prepare students for the Section Assessment, in which they will complete a graphic organizer that builds on the information using the Critical Thinking Skill: Comparing and Contrasting.

SECTION 1

Geography and Ancient Egypt

What You Will Learn...

Main Ideas

1. Egypt was called the gift of the Nile because the Nile River gave life to the desert.
2. Civilization developed along the Nile after people began farming in this region.
3. Strong kings unified all of Egypt.

The Big Idea

The water, fertile soils, and protected setting of the Nile Valley allowed a great civilization to arise in Egypt around 3200 BC.

Key Terms and People

cataracts, *p. 87*
delta, *p. 87*
Menes, *p. 89*
pharaoh, *p. 89*
dynasty, *p. 89*

Use the graphic organizer online to take notes on characteristics of the Nile River and the way it affected Egypt.

If YOU were there...

Your family are farmers in the Nile Valley. Each year when the river's floodwaters spread rich soil on the land, you help your father plant barley. When you are not in the fields, you spin fine linen thread from flax you have grown. Sometimes you and your friends hunt birds in the tall grasses along the riverbanks.

Why do you like living in the Nile Valley?

BUILDING BACKGROUND Mesopotamia was not the only place where an advanced civilization grew up along a great river. The narrow valley of the Nile River in Egypt also provided fertile land that drew people to live there. The culture that developed in Egypt was more stable and long-lasting than those in Mesopotamia.

The Gift of the Nile

Geography played a key role in the development of Egyptian civilization. The Nile River brought life to Egypt. The river was so important to people in this region that the Greek historian Herodotus (hi-RAHD-du-tus) called Egypt the gift of the Nile.

Location and Physical Features

The Nile is the longest river in the world. It begins in central Africa and runs 4,000 miles north to the Mediterranean Sea. Egyptian civilization developed along a 750-mile stretch of the Nile in northern Africa.

Ancient Egypt included two regions, a southern region and a northern region. The southern region was called Upper Egypt. It was so named because it was located upriver in relation to the Nile's flow. Lower Egypt, the northern region, was located downriver. The Nile sliced through the desert of Upper Egypt. There, it created a fertile river valley about 13 miles wide. On either side of the Nile lay hundreds of miles of bleak desert.

86

Teach the Big Idea

At Level

Geography and Ancient Egypt

1. **Teach** Ask students the questions in the Main Idea boxes to teach this section.
2. **Apply** Organize the class into pairs. Have each pair write a verse for a national anthem that Menes may have commissioned to celebrate the unification of Upper and Lower Egypt. Verses may focus on any aspect of early Egyptian history as reflected in the section.
3. **Review** Call on volunteers to read their verses. Adventuresome students may want to sing their verses to the tune of a popular song. Discuss any topics not covered by the verses. **LS Verbal/Linguistic, Auditory/Musical**
4. **Practice/Homework** Have each student write another verse for his or her anthem. **LS Verbal/Linguistic, Auditory/Musical**

Alternative Assessment Handbook, Rubric 26: Poems and Songs

As you can see on the map to the right, the Nile rushed through rocky, hilly land south of Egypt. At several points, this terrain caused **cataracts**, or strong rapids, to form. The first cataract, 720 miles south of the Mediterranean, marked the southern border of Upper Egypt. Five more cataracts lay farther south. These rapids made sailing that portion of the Nile very difficult.

In Lower Egypt, the Nile divided into several branches that fanned out and flowed into the Mediterranean Sea. These branches formed a **delta**, a triangle-shaped area of land made of soil deposited by a river. In ancient times, swamps and marshes covered much of the Nile Delta. Some two thirds of Egypt's fertile farmland was located in the Nile Delta.

The Floods of the Nile

Because it received so little rain, most of Egypt was desert. Each year, however, rainfall far to the south of Egypt in the highlands of east Africa caused the Nile to flood. The Nile floods were easier to predict than those of the Tigris and Euphrates rivers in Mesopotamia. Almost every year, the Nile flooded Upper Egypt in midsummer and Lower Egypt in the fall, coating the land around the river with a rich silt.

The silt from the Nile made the soil ideal for farming. The silt also made the land a dark color. That is why the Egyptians called their country the black land. They called the dry, lifeless desert beyond the river valley the red land.

Each year, Egyptians eagerly awaited the flooding of the Nile. For them the river's floods were a life-giving miracle. Without the floods, people never could have settled in Egypt.

READING CHECK **Summarizing** Why was Egypt called the gift of the Nile?

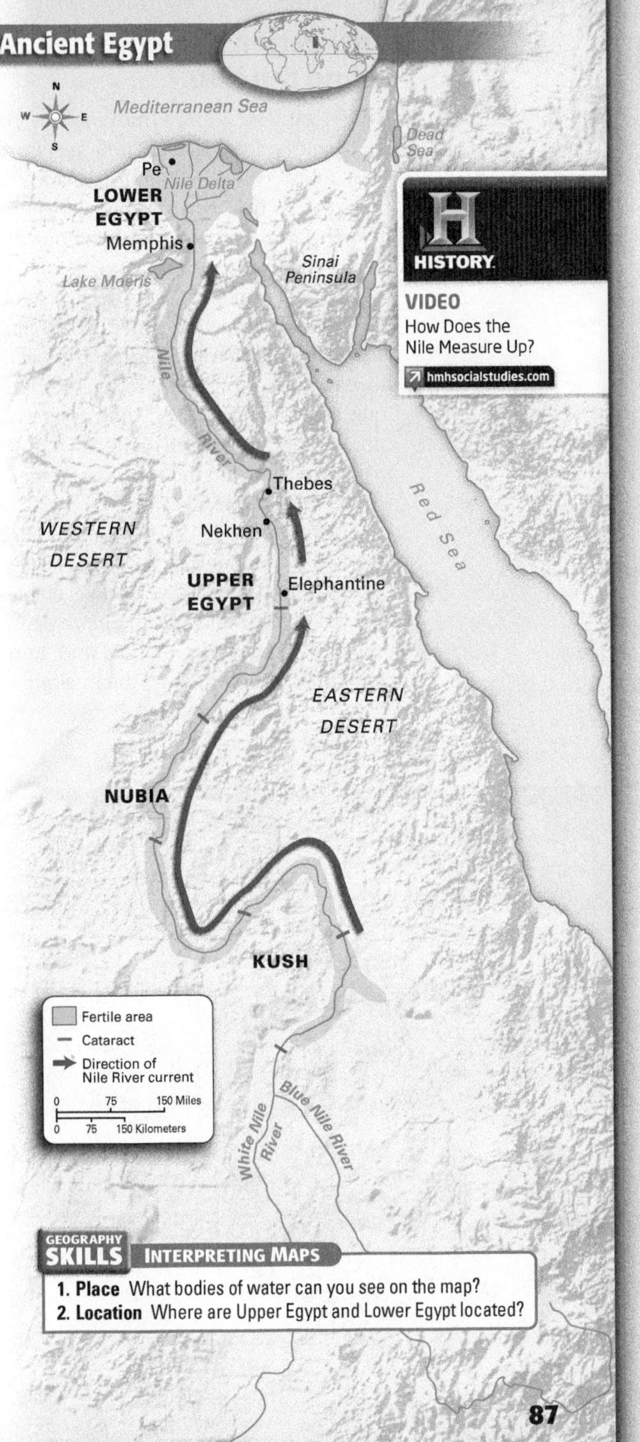

GEOGRAPHY SKILLS **INTERPRETING MAPS**

1. **Place** What bodies of water can you see on the map?
2. **Location** Where are Upper Egypt and Lower Egypt located?

Direct Teach

Main Idea

1 The Gift of the Nile

Egypt was called the "gift of the Nile" because the Nile River gave life to the desert.

Explain Where were Upper Egypt and Lower Egypt? *Upper Egypt—southern Egypt, upriver on the Nile; Lower Egypt—northern Egypt, downriver on the Nile*

Draw Conclusions Why was it important to the Egyptians that the Nile's flooding was consistent? *It provided a bountiful growing season every year, and people knew they could count on a food supply in the future.*

CRF: History and Geography Activity: The Nile's Fertile Shore

Map Transparency: Ancient Egypt

Did You Know . . .

Instead of four seasons, the Egyptian year had only three: *akhet,* when the Nile flooded the valley; *peret,* when the water receded; and *shomu,* when water was scarce.

Interpreting Maps

Ancient Egypt

Location Where is the Nile Delta? *northern Lower Egypt*

Place What is the land to the east and west of the Nile Valley like? *desert*

Collaborative Learning

At Level

A 3-D Map of Ancient Egypt

Materials: plywood or other firm board on which to build map, clay, poster paint

1. Organize students into small groups. Instruct students that each group will use the map on this page to create a map of the Nile Valley and the geographical features surrounding it.
2. Students use clay or a similar material to create their three-dimensional map. They may need to consult additional maps to determine elevations of different geographical features.
3. After the clay has dried, students should color-code and paint their maps. They should also label prominent features such as Upper and Lower Egypt and bodies of water.

LS Visual/Spatial, Kinesthetic

Alternative Assessment Handbook Rubric 14: Group Activity; and 20: Map Creation

Answers

Interpreting Maps **1.** *Nile River, White Nile River, Blue Nile River, Mediterranean Sea, Red Sea, Dead Sea* **2.** *Lower Egypt is in northern Egypt; Upper Egypt is in southern Egypt.*

Reading Check *Without the "gift" of flooding that provided rich soil for crops, civilization could not have developed in Egypt.*

Direct Teach

Main Idea

2 Civilization Develops Along the Nile

Civilization developed after people began farming along the Nile.

Recall How did farmers use the Nile to grow their crops? *They built canals to direct the Nile's water to the fields.*

Predict Why might the ruins of early Egyptian settlements lack evidence of protective walls? *because the desert, bodies of water, and cataracts provided natural protection from many enemies*

CRF: Primary Source Activity: Ancient Egyptian Poem

Linking to Today

Damming the Nile The Aswan High Dam on the Nile was completed in 1971. It was built to generate electricity and make water available year-round to farmers. Although the dam fulfilled these goals, it has caused other problems. Because the Nile no longer drops silt on the fields, Egyptian farmers now have to use millions of tons of expensive chemical fertilizers. In addition, because less silt is deposited there, the Mediterranean coastline is eroding more rapidly.

Analyzing Visuals

Ask students what this artwork reveals about farming in ancient Egypt. *possible answers—Farmers did some work by hand and had simple tools; both men and women worked in the fields.*

Civilization Develops Along the Nile

Hunter-gatherer groups moved into the Nile Valley more than 12,000 years ago. They found plants, wild animals, and fish there to eat. In time these people learned how to farm, and they settled along the Nile in small villages.

As in Mesopotamia, farmers in Egypt developed an irrigation system. They built basins to collect water during the yearly floods and to store this precious resource long afterward. They also built a series of canals that could be used in the dry months to direct water from the basins to the fields where it was needed.

The Nile provided early Egyptian farmers with an abundance of food. The farmers grew wheat, barley, fruits, and vegetables, and raised cattle and sheep. The river also provided many types of fish, and hunters trapped wild geese and ducks along its banks. Like the Mesopotamians, Egyptians enjoyed a varied diet.

In addition to a stable food supply, the Nile Valley offered another valuable advantage. It had natural barriers that made Egypt hard to invade. The desert to the west was too big and harsh to cross. To the north, the Mediterranean Sea kept many enemies away. The Red Sea provided protection against invasion as well. Cataracts in the Nile made it difficult for outsiders to sail in from the south.

Protected from invaders, the villages of Egypt grew. Wealthy farmers emerged as village leaders, and strong leaders gained control over several villages. By 3200 BC, the villages had banded together and developed into two kingdoms. One was called Lower Egypt and the other was called Upper Egypt.

READING CHECK **Summarizing** What attracted early settlers to the Nile Valley?

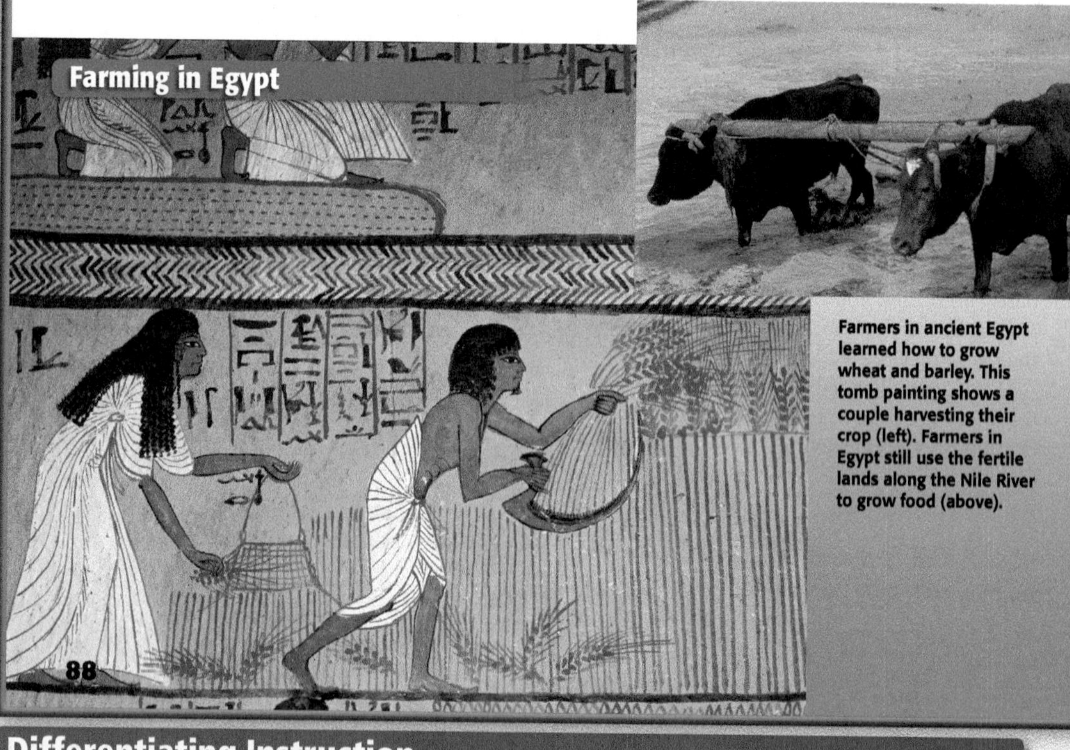

Farming in Egypt

Farmers in ancient Egypt learned how to grow wheat and barley. This tomb painting shows a couple harvesting their crop (left). Farmers in Egypt still use the fertile lands along the Nile River to grow food (above).

Differentiating Instruction

English-Language Learners — Below Level

1. Draw the diagram shown here for students to see, omitting the answers. Have students copy it.
2. Instruct students to fill in the diagram. Below *The Nile provides life,* they should add at least two ways the Nile helped civilization grow. Below *Natural barriers provide protection,* they should add at least three different types of natural barriers that discouraged invaders.
3. Call on students to discuss their graphic organizers to ensure that they have been completed correctly. **LS Visual/Spatial**

Alternative Assessment Handbook, Rubric 13: Graphic Organizers

The Nile provides life.
- *fertile soil for crops*
- *water for people, animals, and irrigation*

Natural barriers provide protection.
- *deserts*
- *cataracts along the Nile*
- *bodies of water*

→ **Growth of Ancient Egypt**

Answers

Reading Check *ability to find and grow plenty of food, natural protection from invasion*

Kings Unify Egypt

The king of Lower Egypt ruled from a town called Pe. He wore a red crown to symbolize his authority. Nekhen was the capital city of Upper Egypt. In this kingdom, the king wore a cone-shaped white crown.

Around 3100 BC a leader named **Menes** (MEE-neez) rose to power in Upper Egypt. He sought to finish what an earlier king, called Scorpion, had started. He wanted to unify Upper and Lower Egypt.

The armies of Menes invaded and took control of Lower Egypt. Menes then united the two kingdoms. He married a princess from Lower Egypt to strengthen his control over the unified country. As Egypt's ruler, Menes wore both the white crown of Upper Egypt and the red crown of Lower Egypt. This symbolized his leadership over the two kingdoms. Later, he combined the two crowns into a double crown.

Historians consider Menes to be Egypt's first **pharaoh** (FEHR-oh), the title used by the rulers of Egypt. The title *pharaoh* means "great house." Menes also founded Egypt's first dynasty. A **dynasty** is a series of rulers from the same family.

Menes built a new capital city at the southern tip of the Nile Delta. The city was later named Memphis. For centuries, Memphis was the political and cultural center of Egypt. Many government offices were located there, and the city bustled with artistic activity.

The First Dynasty lasted for about 200 years. Pharaohs who came after Menes also wore the double crown to symbolize their rule over Upper and Lower Egypt. They extended Egyptian territory southward along the Nile and into southwest Asia. Eventually, however, rivals appeared to challenge the First Dynasty for power. These challengers took over Egypt and established the Second Dynasty.

READING CHECK **Drawing Inferences** Why do you think Menes wanted to rule over both kingdoms of Egypt?

SUMMARY AND PREVIEW Civilization in ancient Egypt began in the fertile, protected Nile River Valley. People there formed two kingdoms that were later united under one ruler. In the next section, you will learn how Egypt grew and changed under later rulers in a period known as the Old Kingdom.

Section 1 Assessment

Reviewing Ideas, Terms, and People

1. a. **Recall** What were the two regions that made up ancient Egypt?
   b. **Make Inferences** Why was the Nile Delta well suited for settlement?
   c. **Predict** How might the Nile's **cataracts** have both helped and hurt Egypt?
2. a. **Describe** What foods did the Egyptians eat?
   b. **Analyze** What role did the Nile play in supplying Egyptians with these foods?
   c. **Elaborate** How did the desert on both sides of the Nile help ancient Egypt?
3. a. **Identify** Who was the first **pharaoh** of Egypt?
   b. **Draw Conclusions** Why did the pharaohs of the First Dynasty wear a double crown?

Critical Thinking

4. **Comparing and Contrasting** Use your notes on the Nile River to complete a Venn diagram like the one shown. List the differences and similarities between the Nile River in Egypt and the Tigris and Euphrates rivers in Mesopotamia.

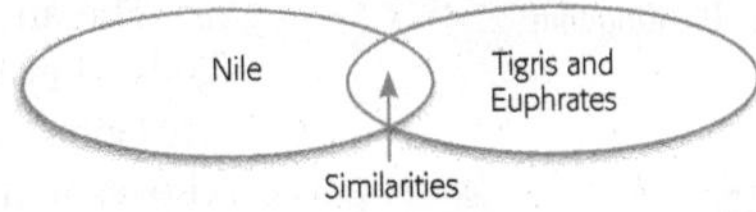

FOCUS ON WRITING

5. **Thinking about Geography and Early History** In this section, you read about Egypt's geography and early history. What could you put into your riddle about geography and historical events that would be a clue to the answer?

Direct Teach

Main Idea

3 Kings Unify Egypt

Strong kings unified all of Egypt.

Define What does the title *pharaoh* mean? *"great house"*

Explain How did the pharaoh's crown display the unification of Egypt? *The pharaoh combined the white crown of Upper Egypt and the red crown of Lower Egypt to symbolize his rule over both lands.*

Analyze Do you think Menes made a good choice in building his capital city at Memphis? Why or why not? *possible answer—yes, because it was in a fertile region, but still had the protection of being inland*

Make Judgments Which part of Egypt—Upper or Lower—do you think was more valuable to a ruler? Why? *possible answer—Lower Egypt had the extremely fertile delta and access to the Mediterranean.*

Review & Assess

Close

Call on volunteers to compose additional questions about the illustrations in this section.

Review

Online Quiz, Section 1

Assess

SE Section 1 Assessment

PASS: Section 1 Quiz

Alternative Assessment Handbook

Reteach/Classroom Intervention

Guided Reading Workbook, Section 1

Interactive Skills Tutor CD-ROM

Section 1 Assessment Answers

1. a. Upper Egypt and Lower Egypt
   b. possible answer—fertile land, abundant wildlife, near the sea
   c. provided protection against invasion, but made travel on the river difficult
2. a. wheat, barley, fruits, vegetables, beef, lamb, fish, goose, and duck
   b. essential role—provided water for crops and animals, fish, homes for wild geese and ducks
   c. provided strong protection against invasion by enemy forces
3. a. Menes
   b. to symbolize the unification of Lower and Upper Egypt
4. Nile—predictable flooding, gentler flooding pattern; Tigris and Euphrates—destructive, unpredictable flooding; Similarities—provided water, irrigation led to increased crop production, silt enriched the soil, civilizations arose on their banks.
5. Answers will vary but should be accurate.

Answers

Reading Check *Ruling over both kingdoms brought greater wealth, status, and power.*

Preteach

Bellringer

If YOU were there . . . Use the **Daily Bellringer Transparency** to help students answer the question.

Daily Bellringer Transparency, Section 2

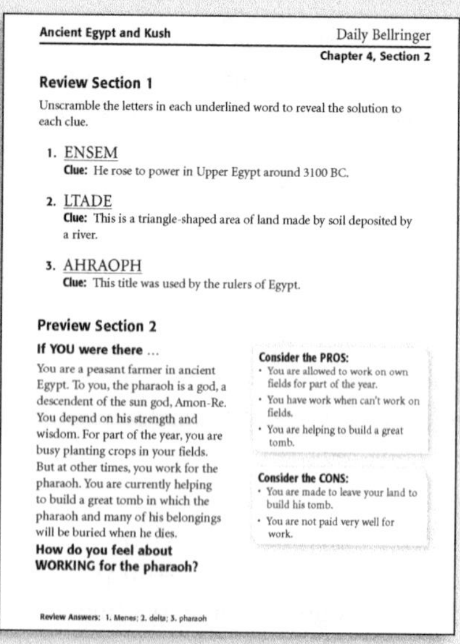

Ancient Egypt and Kush — Daily Bellringer
Chapter 4, Section 2

Review Section 1

Unscramble the letters in each underlined word to reveal the solution to each clue.

1. ENSEM
   Clue: He rose to power in Upper Egypt around 3100 BC.
2. LTADE
   Clue: This is a triangle-shaped area of land made by soil deposited by a river.
3. AHRAOPH
   Clue: This title was used by the rulers of Egypt.

Preview Section 2

If YOU were there ...

You are a peasant farmer in ancient Egypt. To you, the pharaoh is a god, a descendent of the sun god, Amon-Re. You depend on his strength and wisdom. For part of the year, you are busy planting crops in your fields. But at other times, you work for the pharaoh. You are currently helping to build a great tomb in which the pharaoh and many of his belongings will be buried when he dies.

How do you feel about WORKING for the pharaoh?

Consider the PROS:
- You are allowed to work on own fields for part of the year.
- You have work when can't work on fields.
- You are helping to build a great tomb.

Consider the CONS:
- You are made to leave your land to build his tomb.
- You are not paid very well for work.

Review Answers: 1. Menes; 2. delta; 3. pharaoh

Academic Vocabulary

Review with students the high-use academic terms in this section.

acquire to get (p. 91)

method a way of doing something (p. 93)

CRF: Vocabulary Builder Activity, Section 2

Taking Notes

Have students use the graphic organizer online to take notes on the section. This activity will prepare students for the Section Assessment, in which they will complete a graphic organizer that builds on the information using the Critical Thinking Skill: Generalizing.

SECTION 2

The Old Kingdom

What You Will Learn...

Main Ideas

1. In early Egyptian society, pharaohs ruled as gods and were at the top of the social structure.
2. Religion shaped Egyptian life.
3. The pyramids of Egypt were built as tombs for the pharaohs.

The Big Idea

Egyptian government and religion were closely connected during the Old Kingdom.

Key Terms and People

Old Kingdom, *p. 90*
Khufu, *p. 91*
nobles, *p. 91*
afterlife, *p. 92*
mummies, *p. 93*
elite, *p. 93*
pyramids, *p. 94*
engineering, *p. 94*

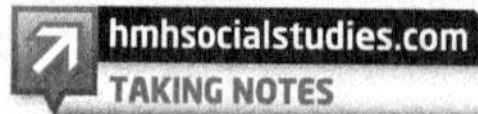

Use the graphic organizer online to take notes on government and religion in the Old Kingdom.

If YOU were there...

You are a peasant farmer in ancient Egypt. To you, the pharaoh is a god, a descendent of the sun god, Re. You depend on his strength and wisdom. For part of the year, you are busy planting crops in your fields. But at other times, you work for the pharaoh. You are currently helping to build a great tomb in which the pharaoh and many of his belongings will be buried when he dies.

How do you feel about working for the pharaoh?

BUILDING BACKGROUND As in other ancient cultures, Egyptian society was based on a strict order of social classes. A small group of royalty, nobles, and priests ruled Egypt. They depended on the rest of the population to supply foods, crafts, and labor. Few people questioned this arrangement of society.

Early Egyptian Society

The First and Second Dynasties ruled Egypt for about four centuries. Around 2700 BC, the Third Dynasty rose to power. Its rule began the **Old Kingdom**, a period in Egyptian history that lasted from about 2700 BC to 2200 BC.

Rule by Pharaohs

During the Old Kingdom, the Egyptians continued to develop their political system. This system was based on the belief that the pharaoh was both a king and a god.

The ancient Egyptians believed that Egypt belonged to the gods. They believed that the pharaoh had come to earth to manage Egypt for the rest of the gods. As a result, he had absolute power over all the land and people in Egypt. But the pharaoh's status as a god came with many responsibilities. People blamed him if crops did not grow well or if disease struck. They also demanded that the pharaoh make trade profitable and prevent wars.

During the Old Kingdom, the duties of the pharaohs grew. To help carry out these duties, the pharaohs hired government officials. Most officials came from the pharaoh's family.

Teach the Big Idea

At Level

The Old Kingdom

1. **Teach** Ask students the questions in the Main Idea boxes to teach this section.
2. **Apply** Ask students to imagine that they have been asked by the government of Egypt to design stamps commemorating the 4,700th anniversary of the Old Kingdom's beginning. Organize the class into three groups—one for each subsection. Then have each student choose a subtopic within that subsection and draw a stamp to illustrate it. LS **Visual/Spatial**
3. **Review** Display the stamps, and call on volunteers to describe their illustrations.
4. **Practice/Homework** Have students write summaries of how the topics they illustrated were related to other aspects of the Old Kingdom. LS **Verbal/Linguistic**

Alternative Assessment Handbook, Rubric 42: Writing to Inform

The most famous pharaoh of the Old Kingdom was **Khufu** (KOO-foo), who ruled in the 2500s BC. Egyptian legend says that he was cruel, but historical records tell us that the people who worked for him were well fed. Khufu is best known for the monuments that were built to him.

The Social Structure

By 2200 BC, Egypt had about 2 million people. At the top of Egyptian society was the pharaoh. Just below him were the upper classes, which included priests and key government officials. Many of these priests and officials were **nobles**, or people from rich and powerful families.

Below the nobles was a middle class of lesser government officials, scribes, craftspeople, and merchants. Egypt's lower class, about 80 percent of the population, was made up mostly of farmers. During flood season, when they could not work the fields, farmers worked on the pharaoh's building projects. Below farmers in the social order were slaves and servants.

Egypt and Its Neighbors

Although well-protected by its geography, Egypt was not isolated. Other cultures had influenced it for centuries. For example, Sumerian designs are found in Egyptian art. Egyptian pottery also reflects styles from Nubia, a region south of Egypt.

During the Old Kingdom, Egypt began trading with its neighbors. Traders returned from Nubia with gold, ivory, slaves, and stone. Traders traveled to Punt, an area on the Red Sea, to acquire incense and myrrh (MUHR). These two items were used to make perfume and medicine. Trade with Syria provided Egypt with wood.

ACADEMIC VOCABULARY
acquire (uh-KWYR) to get

READING CHECK **Generalizing** How was society structured in the Old Kingdom?

Egyptian Society

Pharaoh
The pharaoh ruled Egypt as a god.

Nobles
Officials and priests helped run the government and temples.

Scribes and Craftspeople
Scribes wrote and craftspeople produced goods.

Farmers, Servants, and Slaves
Most Egyptians were farmers. Below them were servants and slaves.

ANALYSIS SKILL ANALYZING VISUALS
Which group helped run the government and temples?

Direct Teach

Main Idea

1 Early Egyptian Society

In early Egyptian society, pharaohs ruled as gods and were at the top of the social structure.

Recall How long did the Old Kingdom last? *about 500 years, from 2700 to 2200 BC*

Drawing Conclusions What responsibilities did the pharaoh have that balanced his high status? *make crops grow, keep people healthy, make trade profitable, prevent wars*

Make Judgments What may be some advantages and disadvantages for such a large segment of the population being farmers, servants, and slaves? *possible answers: advantages—plenty of food and labor; disadvantages—potential for rebellion*

 **CRF:** Biography: Khufu

Primary Source

A Father's Career Advice There is an ancient description of what an Egyptian scribe named Duaf tells his son Khety while taking Khety to be trained as a scribe. Duaf wrote: "I will make you love writing more than your mother, I will show its beauties to you; Now, it is greater than any trade, There is not one like it in the land." Duaf goes on to describe the miseries of the metalworker, carpenter, jeweler, and barber. Ask: Do you think Duaf exaggerated the hardships of the other trades? Why or why not? *possible answer—yes, to make being a scribe sound better*

Critical Thinking: Evaluating

At Level

Being Pharaoh

1. Ask students what advantages pharaohs seemed to have in Egyptian society. Write responses for students to see. *possible responses—believed to be a god, wealth and easy life, monuments honored him*
2. Then ask what disadvantages there were to being a pharaoh. Write these next to the advantages. *possible answers—blamed for crop failure, disease, poor economy, and invasions*
3. Organize students into pairs to discuss with their partners whether or not they would want to be a pharaoh and give specific reasons for their responses.
4. Call on volunteers to share their reasoning with the class.

LS Interpersonal, Logical/Mathematical

Alternative Assessment Handbook, Rubric 11: Discussions

Answers

Analyzing Visuals *nobles, including officials and priests*

Reading Check *pharaoh at the top, nobles, scribes and craftspeople, and farmers, servants, and slaves below*

Direct Teach

Main Idea

2 Religion and Egyptian Life

Religion shaped Egyptian life.

Identify Who was the Egyptian sun god? *Re, or Amon-Re* What else did the main Egyptian gods represent? *underworld, magic, sky*

Evaluate Why might Egyptians have worshipped the gods differently? *possible answer—initial lack of structure in religious beliefs and practices; some gods may have been more important in some regio.*

Describe How did the Egyptians see the afterlife? *as an ideal world where all the people are young and healthy*

CRF: Primary Source Activity: Scene from the Tomb of Nakht

Teaching Tip

Polytheism Remind students that the word *polytheism* means "the worship of more than one god."

Analyzing Visuals

Egyptian Gods Horus was often depicted as a falcon or a man wearing a falcon headress. Egyptians believed that the eyes of Horus were the sun and the moon. Ask students why the Egyptians may have formed this connection between the falcon, the sun, and the moon. *possible answer—because falcons have keen eyesight*

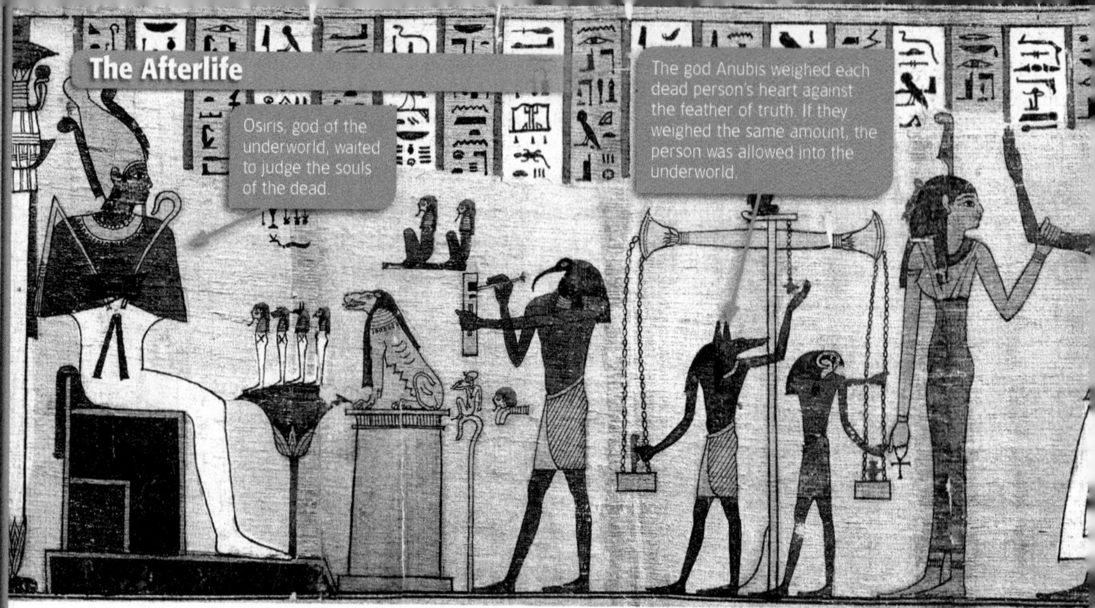

The Afterlife
Osiris, god of the underworld, waited to judge the souls of the dead.
The god Anubis weighed each dead person's heart against the feather of truth. If they weighed the same amount, the person was allowed into the underworld.

Religion and Egyptian Life

The ancient Egyptians had strong religious beliefs. Worshipping the gods was a part of their everyday lives. Many Egyptian religious customs focused on what happened after people died.

The Gods of Egypt

Like Mesopotamians, Egyptians practiced polytheism. Before the First Dynasty, each village worshipped its own gods. During the Old Kingdom, however, Egyptian officials tried to give some sort of structure to religious beliefs. Everyone was expected to worship the same gods, though how they worshipped the gods might differ from one region of Egypt to another.

The Egyptians built temples to the gods all over the kingdom. The temples collected payments from both the government and worshippers. These payments allowed the temples to grow more influential.

Over time, certain cities became centers for the worship of certain gods. In Memphis, for example, people prayed to Ptah, the creator of the world.

The Egyptians had gods for nearly everything, including the sun, the sky, and the earth. Many gods mixed human and animal forms. For example, Anubis, the god of the dead, had a human body but a jackal's head. Other major gods included

- Re, or Amon-Re, the sun god
- Osiris, the god of the underworld
- Isis, the goddess of magic, and
- Horus, a sky god, god of the pharaohs

Emphasis on the Afterlife

Much of Egyptian religion focused on the **afterlife**, or life after death. The Egyptians believed that the afterlife was a happy place. Paintings from Egyptian tombs show the afterlife as an ideal world where all the people are young and healthy.

The Egyptian belief in the afterlife stemmed from their idea of *ka* (KAH), or a person's life force. When a person died, his or her *ka* left the body and became a spirit. The *ka,* however, remained linked to the

Differentiating Instruction

Advanced/Gifted and Talented

Above Level **Research Required**

1. Tell students that there are many stories about the Egyptian gods and their duties and interactions.
2. Organize students into small groups. Have each group conduct research on two or three Egyptian gods. Have them look for specific characteristics and stories about the gods. Then have each group select one god and create a storyboard about the god.
3. Have groups present their storyboards to the class.
4. Then lead a discussion about how these stories might have affected the Egyptians' lives or behavior.

LS Interpersonal, Visual/Spatial

Alternative Assessment Handbook, Rubric 3: Artwork

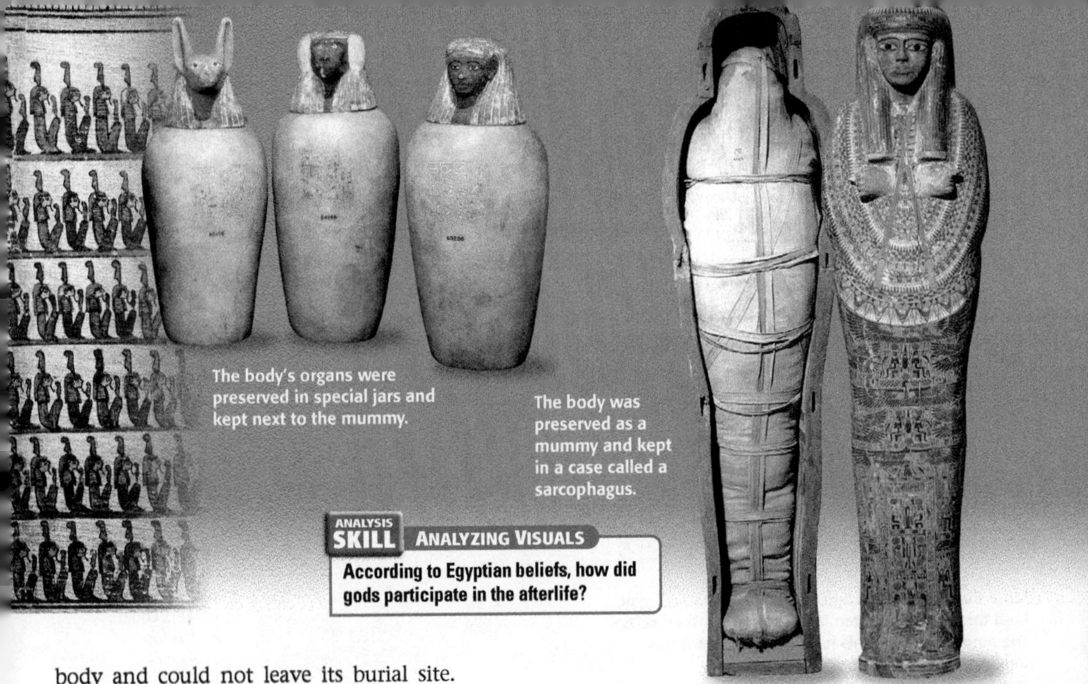

The body's organs were preserved in special jars and kept next to the mummy.

The body was preserved as a mummy and kept in a case called a sarcophagus.

ANALYSIS SKILL ANALYZING VISUALS

According to Egyptian beliefs, how did gods participate in the afterlife?

body and could not leave its burial site. The *ka* had all the same needs that the person had when he or she was living.

To fulfill the *ka's* needs, people filled tombs with objects for the afterlife. These objects included furniture, clothing, tools, jewelry, and weapons. Relatives of the dead were expected to bring food and beverages to their loved ones' tombs so the *ka* would not be hungry or thirsty.

Burial Practices

Egyptian ideas about the afterlife shaped their burial practices. Egyptians believed that a body had to be prepared for the afterlife before it could be buried. This meant the body had to be preserved. If the body decayed, its spirit could not recognize it. That would break the link between the body and spirit. The *ka* would then be unable to receive the food and drink it needed to have a good afterlife.

To keep the *ka* from suffering, the Egyptians developed a <u>method</u> called embalming. Embalming allowed bodies to be preserved for many, many years as **mummies**, specially treated bodies wrapped in cloth. A body that was not embalmed would decay quickly.

Embalming was a complex process that took several weeks. When finished, embalmers wrapped the body with linen cloths and bandages. The mummy was then placed in a coffin. Relatives often wrote magic spells inside the coffin to help the mummy receive food and drink.

Only royalty and other members of Egypt's **elite** (AY-leet), or people of wealth and power, could afford to have mummies made. Peasant families buried their dead in shallow graves at the edge of the desert. The hot dry sand and lack of moisture preserved the bodies naturally.

READING CHECK **Analyzing** How did religious beliefs affect Egyptian burial practices?

VIDEO
Are Mummies Beef Jerky?
hmhsocialstudies.com

ACADEMIC VOCABULARY
method a way of doing something

Direct Teach

Main Idea

2 Religion and Egyptian Life

Religion shaped Egyptian life.

Define What is a mummy? *a preserved body that is wrapped in cloth*

Contrast How was the *ka* different from the body? *The ka was not a physical entity, but rather the person's life force. It left the physical body at death but could not leave the burial site.*

Analyze Why did the Egyptians believe it was important to preserve the physical body? *If the body decayed, the ka would not be able to receive the food and drink it needed.*

Activity **Designing a Sarcophagus** Ask students to imagine that they have been hired to design a sarcophagus for a pharaoh's adult son or daughter. How might the sarcophagus be decorated? Have students examine the image of the sarcophagus on this page. Have students prepare their sketches and have volunteers explain their designs to the class.

Social Studies Skill: Identifying Central Issues

At Level

Prep Required

Museum Exhibit

Materials: art supplies, photos, or illustrations showing Egyptian burial artifacts and tombs

1. Organize students into small groups.
2. Have students imagine they are museum curators planning an exhibit on Egyptian burial practices. Have them create a list of questions their exhibit will answer.
3. Have each group plan and create its exhibit, making sure it answers all of their questions. It should contain drawings or photographs of burial artifacts. Encourage the groups to be creative and rely mainly on graphics, keeping text to a minimum.
4. Display the exhibits for the class to view. **LS Interpersonal, Visual/Spatial**

Alternative Assessment Handbook, Rubric 3: Artwork; and 14: Group Activity

Answers

Analyzing Visuals *judged souls, allowed persons into the underworld*

Reading Check *Believing that the spirit remained linked to the body, Egyptians developed mummification and filled tombs with food and other items the spirit might need in the afterlife.*

Direct Teach

Main Idea

3 The Pyramids

The pyramids of Egypt were built as tombs for the pharaohs.

Recall How many limestone blocks did the Great Pyramid require? *more than 2 million*

Describe What is the shape of a pyramid? *four triangle-shaped walls that meet in a point on top*

Predict How would the invention of large animal-drawn wheeled vehicles have affected pyramid construction? *possible answer—would have made transporting the blocks of stone much easier, cutting labor needs and construction time considerably*

Did You Know . . .

In 1954, archaeologists made an astonishing discovery. Buried at the base of the Great Pyramid was a 144-foot-long wooden boat. The boat may have carried Khufu's body across the Nile to his tomb. Or, it may have been placed there to symbolically carry Khufu to the afterlife.

Linking to Today

Pyramids and Pollution Even though the pyramids have stood for thousands of years, they are not safe from harm. In fact, the stone shows signs of deterioration. Pollution from nearby Cairo and damage done by tourists may be to blame for the problems.

History Close-up

The Great Sphinx has undergone many restorations, including one by pharaoh Tuthmosis IV in about 1400 BC. The pharaoh dreamed that the Sphinx asked him to clear the sand from around it in return for giving the pharaoh power over both Upper and Lower Egypt.

Answers

Focus on Reading *As a result*

The Pyramids

Focus on Reading
What group of words in this paragraph signals an effect?

hmhsocialstudies.com
ANIMATED HISTORY
The Great Pyramid

Egyptians believed that burial sites, especially royal tombs, were very important. As a result, they built spectacular monuments in which to bury their rulers. The most spectacular of all were the **pyramids**, huge stone tombs with four triangle-shaped walls that met in a point on top.

The Egyptians began to build pyramids during the Old Kingdom. Some of the largest pyramids ever constructed were built during this time. Many of these huge structures are still standing. The largest is the Great Pyramid of Khufu near the town of Giza. It covers more than 13 acres at its base and stands 481 feet high. This single pyramid took more than 2 million limestone blocks to build. Historians are still not sure exactly how Egyptians built the pyramids. They are, however, amazing feats of **engineering**, the application of scientific knowledge for practical purposes.

Burial in a pyramid demonstrated a pharaoh's importance. The size was a symbol

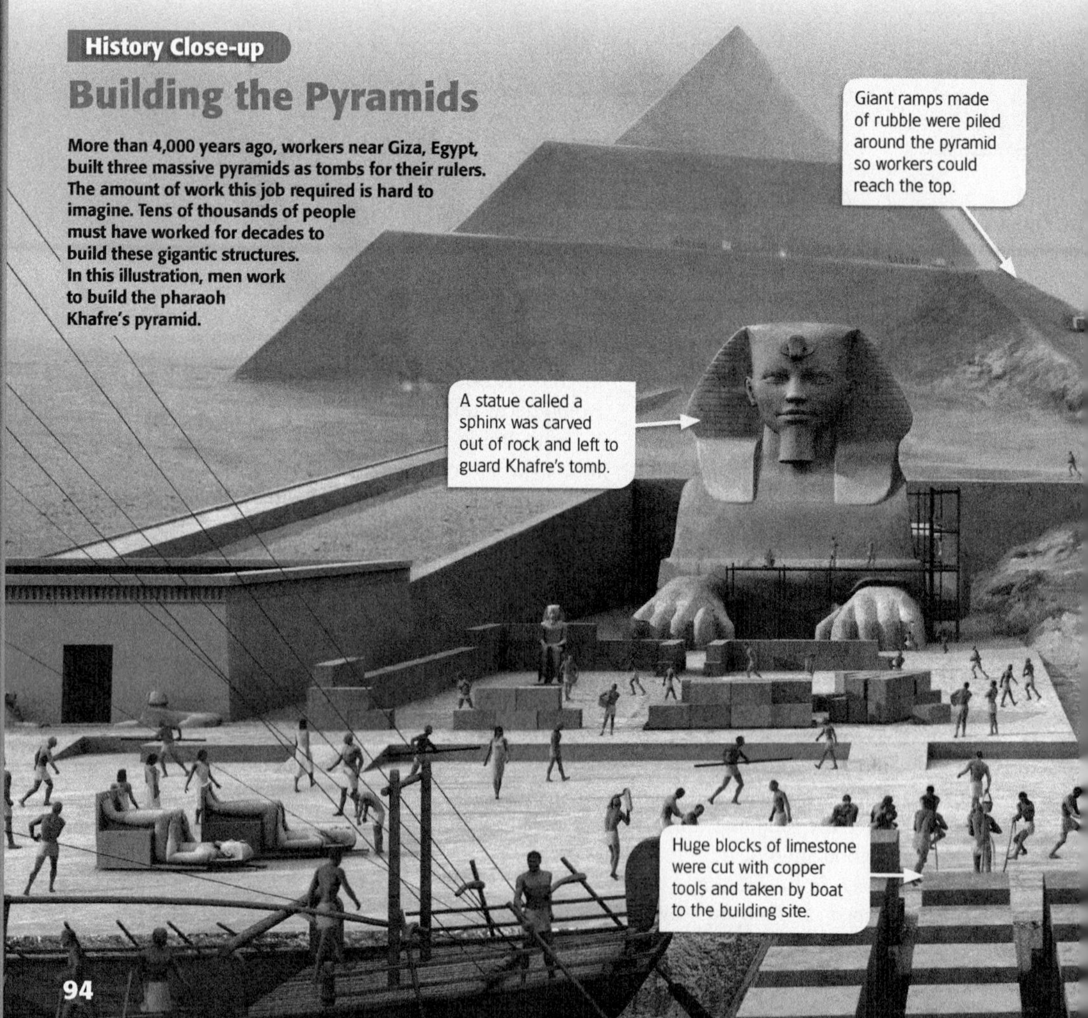

History Close-up
Building the Pyramids
More than 4,000 years ago, workers near Giza, Egypt, built three massive pyramids as tombs for their rulers. The amount of work this job required is hard to imagine. Tens of thousands of people must have worked for decades to build these gigantic structures. In this illustration, men work to build the pharaoh Khafre's pyramid.
Giant ramps made of rubble were piled around the pyramid so workers could reach the top.
A statue called a sphinx was carved out of rock and left to guard Khafre's tomb.
Huge blocks of limestone were cut with copper tools and taken by boat to the building site.
94

Cross-Discipline Activity: Math

Above Level

The Geometry of Pyramids

Research Required

Materials: heavy paper or cardboard, glue or tape

1. Explain to students that the Egyptians would not have been able to build the pyramids without a clear understanding of geometry. To construct a pyramid, each side had to slope upward and inward at exactly the same angle. Builders checked their work often, because even a tiny error in the early stages could mean a big error later.
2. Have students use the Internet and other resources to conduct research on the geometry of pyramid building.
3. Have students build and label models to demonstrate their findings.

LS Logical/Mathematical, Verbal/Linguistic

Alternative Assessment Handbook, Rubric 30: Research

of the pharaoh's greatness. The pyramid's shape, pointing to the skies, symbolized the pharaoh's journey to the afterlife. The Egyptians wanted the pyramids to be spectacular because they believed that the pharaoh, as their link to the gods, controlled everyone's afterlife. Making the pharaoh's spirit happy was a way of ensuring a happy afterlife for every Egyptian.

READING CHECK **Identifying Points of View**
Why were pyramids so important to the people of ancient Egypt?

SUMMARY AND PREVIEW During the Old Kingdom, new political and social orders were created in Egypt, and many of the pyramids were built. In Section 3, you will learn about life in later periods, the Middle and New Kingdoms.

Teams of workers dragged the stones on wooden sleds to the pyramid.

ANALYSIS SKILL **ANALYZING VISUALS**
How did workers get their stone blocks to the pyramids?

Section 2 Assessment

hmhsocialstudies.com ONLINE QUIZ

Reviewing Ideas, Terms, and People

1. a. **Recall** To what does the term **Old Kingdom** refer?
   b. **Analyze** Why was the pharaoh's authority never questioned?
   c. **Elaborate** How did trade benefit the Egyptians?
2. a. **Describe** What did Egyptians mean by the **afterlife**?
   b. **Analyze** Why was embalming important to the Egyptians?
3. a. **Identify** What is **engineering**?
   b. **Elaborate** What does the building of the **pyramids** tell us about Egyptian society?

Critical Thinking

4. **Generalizing** Using your notes, complete this graphic organizer with three statements about the relationship between government and religion in the Old Kingdom.

Government and Religion
1.
2.
3.

FOCUS ON WRITING

5. **Noting Characteristics of the Old Kingdom** The Old Kingdom developed special characteristics related to religion and social structure. Write down any of those characteristics you might want to include in your riddle.

Direct Teach

Main Idea

❸ The Pyramids

The pyramids of Egypt were built as huge tombs for the pharaohs.

Explain Why did the Egyptians want the pyramids to be spectacular? *because they believed their own fate in the afterlife depended on the pharaoh's*

Judge Do you think the Egyptians were gloomy and obsessed by death? Why or why not? *possible answer—no, they were more interested in living forever because they loved life*

hmhsocialstudies.com
Online Resources
Activity: Pyramids

Review & Assess

Close

Ask students to imagine what went through the workers' minds as they built the pyramids.

Review

Online Quiz, Section 2

Assess

SE Section 2 Assessment
PASS: Section 2 Quiz
Alternative Assessment Handbook

Reteach/Classroom Intervention

Guided Reading Workbook, Section 2
Interactive Skills Tutor CD-ROM

Section 2 Assessment Answers

1. a. the 500-year period from 2700 to 2200 BC
   b. The Egyptians thought of him as a god.
   c. possible answer—brought gold, ivory, slaves, and stone from Nubia, incense and myrrh from Punt, and wood from Syria
2. a. life after death
   b. If a body was allowed to decay, the spirit would not be able to recognize it in the afterlife.
3. a. the application of scientific knowledge for practical purposes
   b. possible answer—that Egyptian society was capable of the complex organization and discipline required to build the pyramids
4. possible answers—Pharaoh ruled as a god; nobles and priests helped run government and temples; only elite could afford to have mummies made; lower classes worked on tombs.
5. Answers will vary but should reflect text information.

Answers

Analyzing Visuals *brought to the building site on boats, transported to the pyramids on wooden sleds, hauled up the pyramids on ramps*

Reading Check *because the Egyptians believed that their own afterlife was linked to the eternal life of the pharaoh buried in the pyramid*

Preteach

Bellringer

If YOU were there . . . Use the **Daily Bellringer Transparency** to help students answer the question.

Daily Bellringer Transparency, Section 3

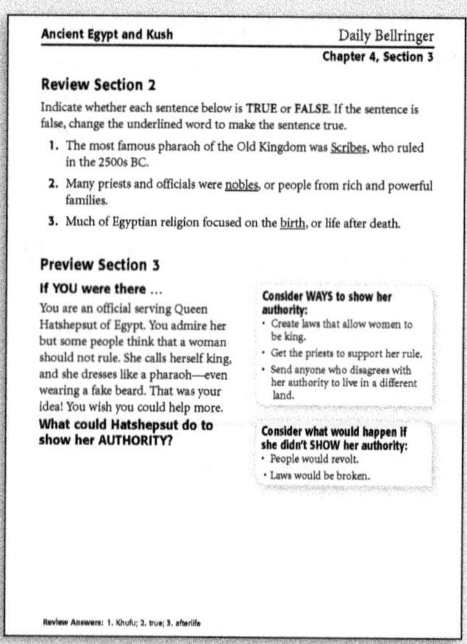

Ancient Egypt and Kush Daily Bellringer

Chapter 4, Section 3

Review Section 2

Indicate whether each sentence below is TRUE or FALSE. If the sentence is false, change the underlined word to make the sentence true.

1. The most famous pharaoh of the Old Kingdom was Scribes, who ruled in the 2500s BC.
2. Many priests and officials were nobles, or people from rich and powerful families.
3. Much of Egyptian religion focused on the birth, or life after death.

Preview Section 3

If YOU were there ...

You are an official serving Queen Hatshepsut of Egypt. You admire her but some people think that a woman should not rule. She calls herself king, and she dresses like a pharaoh—even wearing a fake beard. That was your idea! You wish you could help more.

What could Hatshepsut do to show her AUTHORITY?

Consider WAYS to show her authority:
- Create laws that allow women to be king.
- Get the priests to support her rule.
- Send anyone who disagrees with her authority to live in a different land.

Consider what would happen if she didn't SHOW her authority:
- People would revolt.
- Laws would be broken.

Review Answers: 1. Khufu; 2. true; 3. afterlife

Academic Vocabulary

Review with students the high-use academic terms in this section.

contracts binding legal agreements (p. 100)

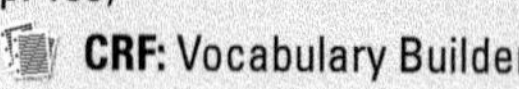

CRF: Vocabulary Builder Activity, Section 3

Taking Notes

Have students use the graphic organizer online to take notes on the section. This activity will prepare students for the Section Assessment, in which they will complete a graphic organizer that builds on the information using the Critical Thinking Skill: Categorizing.

SECTION 3

The Middle and New Kingdoms

What You Will Learn...

Main Ideas

1. The Middle Kingdom was a period of stable government between periods of disorder.
2. In the New Kingdom, Egyptian trade and military power reached their peak, but Egypt's greatness did not last.
3. Work and daily life were different for each of Egypt's social classes.

The Big Idea

During the Middle and New Kingdoms, order and greatness were restored in Egypt.

Key Terms and People

Middle Kingdom, *p. 96*
New Kingdom, *p. 97*
trade routes, *p. 97*
Queen Hatshepsut, *p. 98*
Ramses the Great, *p. 98*

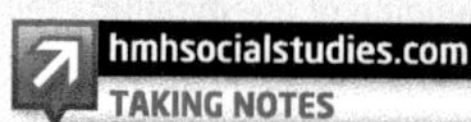

hmhsocialstudies.com
TAKING NOTES

Use the graphic organizer online to take notes on life in Egypt during the Middle and New Kingdoms.

If YOU were there...

You are an official serving Queen Hatshepsut of Egypt. You admire her, but some people think that a woman should not rule. She calls herself king, and she dresses like a pharaoh—even wearing a fake beard. That was your idea! You wish you could help more.

What could Hatshepsut do to show her authority?

BUILDING BACKGROUND The power of the pharaohs expanded during the Old Kingdom. Society was orderly, based on great differences between social classes. But rulers and dynasties changed, and Egypt changed with them. In time, these changes led to new eras in Egyptian history, eras called the Middle and New Kingdoms.

The Middle Kingdom

At the end of the Old Kingdom, the wealth and power of the pharaohs declined. Building and maintaining pyramids cost a lot of money. Pharaohs could not collect enough taxes to keep up with the expenses. At the same time, ambitious nobles used their government positions to take power from the pharaohs.

In time, nobles gained enough power to challenge the pharaohs. By about 2200 BC, the Old Kingdom had fallen. For the next 160 years, local nobles battled each other for power in Egypt. The kingdom had no central ruler. Chaos within Egypt disrupted trade with foreign lands and caused farming to decline. The people faced economic hardship and famine.

Finally, around 2050 BC, a powerful pharaoh named Mentuhotep II defeated his rivals. Once again all of Egypt was united. Mentuhotep's rule began the **Middle Kingdom**, a period of order and stability that lasted until about 1750 BC.

Toward the end of the Middle Kingdom, however, Egypt again experienced internal disorder. Its pharaohs could not hold the kingdom together. There were other problems in Egypt as

Teach the Big Idea

At Level

The Middle and New Kingdoms

1. **Teach** Ask students the questions in the Main Idea boxes to teach this section.
2. **Apply** Have students create time lines for the Middle and New Kingdoms, including those periods' prominent rulers and events. Under each ruler, students should list his or her major accomplishments. LS **Visual/Spatial**
3. **Review** Use the student time lines as well as the map on page 98 to review the events discussed in this section.
4. **Practice/Homework** Have each student write a brief eulogy, or speech to be delivered at a funeral, for either Hatshepsut or Ramses the Great. LS **Verbal/Linguistic**

Alternative Assessment Handbook, Rubric 36: Time Lines; and 37: Writing Assignments

well. In the mid-1700s BC, a group from Southwest Asia called the Hyksos (HIK-sohs) invaded. They used horses, chariots, and advanced weapons to conquer Lower Egypt, which they ruled for 200 years.

The Egyptians did not like being occupied by the Hyksos. The people of Egypt resented having to pay taxes to foreign rulers. Eventually, the Egyptians fought back. In the mid-1500s BC, Ahmose (AHM-ohs) of Thebes drove the Hyksos out of Egypt. Once the Hyksos were gone, Ahmose declared himself king of all Egypt.

READING CHECK **Summarizing** What problems caused the end of the Middle Kingdom?

The New Kingdom

Ahmose's rise to power marked the beginning of Egypt's 18th Dynasty. More importantly, it was the beginning of the **New Kingdom**, the period during which Egypt reached the height of its power and glory. During the New Kingdom, which lasted from about 1550 BC to 1050 BC, conquest and trade brought tremendous wealth to the pharaohs.

Building an Empire

After battling the Hyksos, Egyptian leaders feared future invasions. To prevent such invasions from occurring, they decided to take control of all possible invasion routes into the kingdom. In the process, these leaders turned Egypt into an empire.

Egypt's first target was the homeland of the Hyksos. After taking over that area, the army continued north and conquered Syria. As you can see from the map on the next page, Egypt had taken over the entire eastern shore of the Mediterranean. It had also defeated the kingdom of Kush, south of Egypt. By the 1400s BC, Egypt was the leading military power in the region. Its empire extended from the Euphrates River to southern Nubia.

Military conquests made Egypt rich. The kingdoms it conquered regularly sent treasures to their Egyptian conquerors. For example, the kingdom of Kush in Nubia sent annual payments of gold, leopard skins, and precious stones to the pharaohs. Assyrian, Babylonian, and Hittite kings also sent expensive gifts to Egypt in an effort to maintain good relations.

Growth and its Effects on Trade

Conquest also brought Egyptian traders into contact with more distant lands. Egypt's trade expanded along with its empire. Profitable **trade routes**, or paths followed by traders, developed. Many of the lands that Egypt took over also had valuable resources for trade. The Sinai Peninsula, for example, had large supplies of turquoise and copper.

BIOGRAPHY

Queen Hatshepsut
Ruled c. 1472–1458 BC

Hatshepsut was married to the pharaoh Thutmose II, her half-brother. He died young, leaving the throne to Thutmose III, his son by another woman. Since Thutmose III was still very young, Hatshepsut took over power. Many people did not think women should rule, but Hatshepsut dressed as a man and called herself king. After Hatshepsut died, her stepson took back power and destroyed all of the monuments Hatshepsut had built during her rule.

Analyze Why do you think some Egyptians objected to the idea of being ruled by a woman?

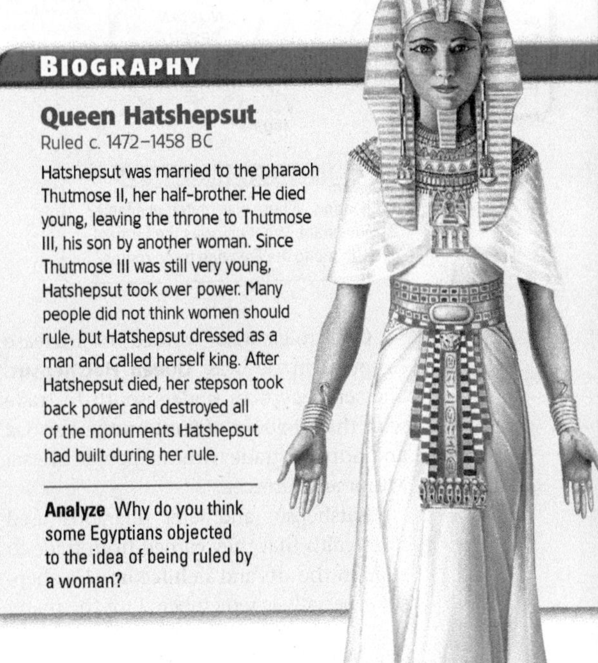

Direct Teach

Main Idea

1 The Middle Kingdom

The Middle Kingdom was a period of stable government between periods of disorder.

Identify Where were the Hyksos from? *Southwest Asia*

Analyze What were two reasons the pharaohs' power declined at the end of the Old Kingdom? *They did not collect enough taxes to cover their expenses, and ambitious nobles took power from the pharaohs.*

Evaluate What may the Hyksos' success indicate about Egypt's level of technological advance? *Although the Egyptians had built pyramids, they may not have had chariots or advanced weapons.*

About the Illustration
This illustration of Hatshepsut is an artist's conception based on available sources. However, historians are uncertain exactly what Hatshepsut looked like.

Info to Know

A Mysterious Death Thutmose III became pharaoh after Hatshepsut's death. The sources are unclear about how she died. According to some historians, Thutmose had her murdered so he could succeed as pharaoh.

Critical Thinking Skills: Interpreting Maps

At Level

Trade Routes of Ancient Egypt

1. Have students examine the map on page 98.
2. Lead a class discussion about the following questions: Which of these routes do you think would have been easier to follow? Which would have been more difficult? Why might particular routes have developed? For example, why does the southernmost route loop southward from the Nile and then back north to Elephantine?
3. Ask students to describe the different routes and challenges traders would have faced along them. Call on volunteers to propose how trade changed both the lives of the Egyptians and the people with whom they traded.
4. Complete the discussion by asking how the Egyptians may have used the products listed in the map legend.
   LS Visual/Spatial, Auditory/Musical

Alternative Assessment Handbook, Rubric 11: Discussions; and 21: Map Reading

Answers

Biography *possible answers—Pharaohs were viewed as gods; she called herself a king; most women worked in the home; it was unusual.*

Reading Check *the decline of the pharaohs' power and the Hyksos invasion*

Direct Teach

Main Idea

❷ The New Kingdom

In the New Kingdom, Egyptian trade and military power reached their peak, but Egypt's greatness did not last.

Identify Who was Hatshepsut? *a female ruler who expanded trade and built great monuments during the New Kingdom*

Analyze What weakened the New Kingdom? *fighting on several fronts, including invasions of the Hittites and the Sea Peoples*

Judge Why do you think leaders of the New Kingdom wanted to control all of the eastern Mediterranean shore? *possible answers—protection from invasion by peoples beyond the region, had valuable resources*

Map Transparency: Egyptian Trade, c. 1400 BC

CRF: Biography: Tiy

CRF: Biography: Akhenaton

Interpreting Maps

Mediterranean Ports Ask students to list the Mediterranean ports visited by Egyptian traders. *Kyrene, Mycenae, Ugarit, Enkomi, Byblos*

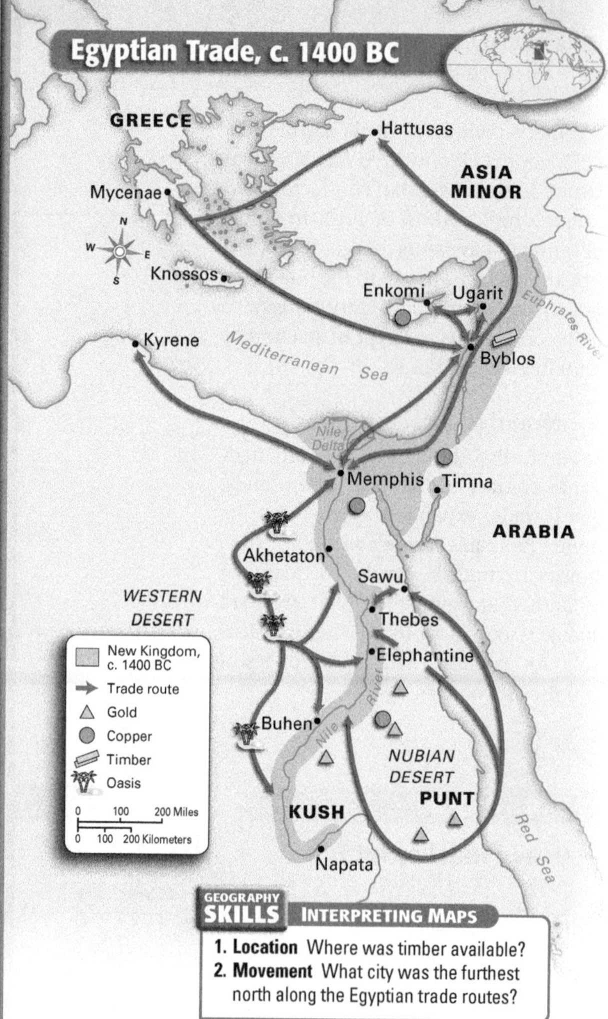

GEOGRAPHY SKILLS INTERPRETING MAPS

1. **Location** Where was timber available?
2. **Movement** What city was the furthest north along the Egyptian trade routes?

One ruler who worked to increase Egyptian trade was **Queen Hatshepsut**. She sent Egyptian traders south to trade with the kingdom of Punt on the Red Sea and north to trade with the people of Asia Minor and Greece.

Hatshepsut and later pharaohs used the wealth that they earned from trade to support the arts and architecture. Hatshepsut especially is remembered for the many impressive monuments and temples built during her reign. The best known of these structures was a magnificent temple built for her near the city of Thebes (THEEBZ).

Invasions of Egypt

Despite its great successes, Egypt's military might did not go unchallenged. In the 1200s BC the pharaoh Ramses (RAM-seez) II, or **Ramses the Great**, came to power. Ramses, whose reign was one of the longest in Egyptian history, fought the Hittites, a group from Asia Minor. The two powers fought fiercely for years, but neither could defeat the other. Ramses and the Hittite leader eventually signed a peace treaty. Afterwards, the Egyptians and the Hittites became allies.

Egypt faced threats in other parts of its empire as well. To the west, a people known as the Tehenu invaded the Nile Delta. Ramses fought them off and built a series of forts to strengthen the western frontier. This proved to be a wise decision because the Tehenu invaded again a century later. Faced with Egypt's strengthened defenses, however, the Tehenu were defeated once more.

Soon after Ramses the Great died, invaders called the Sea Peoples sailed into southwest Asia. Little is known about these people. Historians are not even sure who they were. All we know is that they were strong warriors who had crushed the Hittites and destroyed cities in southwest Asia. Only after 50 years of fighting were the Egyptians able to turn them back.

Egypt survived, but its empire in Asia was gone. Shortly after the invasions of the Hittites and the Sea Peoples, the New Kingdom came to an end. Egypt once again fell into a period of violence and disorder. Egypt would never again regain its power.

READING CHECK **Identifying Cause and Effect** What caused the growth of trade in the New Kingdom?

Critical Thinking: Summarizing

Below Level

Two New Kingdom Rulers

1. Draw the following chart for students to see, omitting the blue answers. Explain that both Hatshepsut and Ramses the Great faced challenges during their reigns, yet they also had many accomplishments.
2. Instruct students to complete the table by listing each leader's challenges and accomplishments. Call on volunteers to share their answers with the class.

LS Visual/Spatial, Verbal/Linguistic

	Queen Hatshepsut	Ramses the Great
Challenges	*husband died, leaving the throne to his son by another wife; objections to rule by a woman*	*had to fight the Hittites, faced invaders from the west*
Accomplishments	*took over as ruler when her husband died, stayed in authority over many objections; increased trade; built many monuments and temples*	*kept the Hittites from conquering Egypt, built forts to strengthen western frontier, built monuments*

Answers

Interpreting Maps 1. *near Byblos* **2.** *Hattusas*

Reading Check *conquest, efforts by Hatshepsut*

Work and Daily Life

Although Egyptian dynasties rose and fell, daily life for Egyptians did not change very much. But as the population grew, society became more complex. A complex society requires people to take on different jobs.

Scribes

Other than priests and government officials, no one in Egypt was more honored than scribes. They worked for the government and for temples. Scribes kept records and accounts for the state. They also wrote and copied religious and literary texts. Scribes did not pay taxes, and many became wealthy.

Artisans, Artists, and Architects

Below scribes on the social scale were artisans whose jobs required advanced skills. Among the artisans who worked in Egypt were sculptors, builders, carpenters, jewelers, metal workers, and leather workers. Most of Egypt's artisans worked for the government or for temples. They made statues, furniture, jewelry, pottery, footwear, and other items.

Architects and artists were also admired in Egypt. Architects designed the temples and royal tombs for which Egypt is famous. Talented architects could rise to become high government officials. Artists, often employed by the state or the temples, produced many different works. Artists often worked in the pharaohs' tombs painting detailed pictures.

Soldiers

After the Middle Kingdom, Egypt created a professional army. The military offered a chance to rise in status. Soldiers received land as payment and could keep treasure they captured in war. Those who excelled could be promoted to officer positions.

Daily Life in Egypt

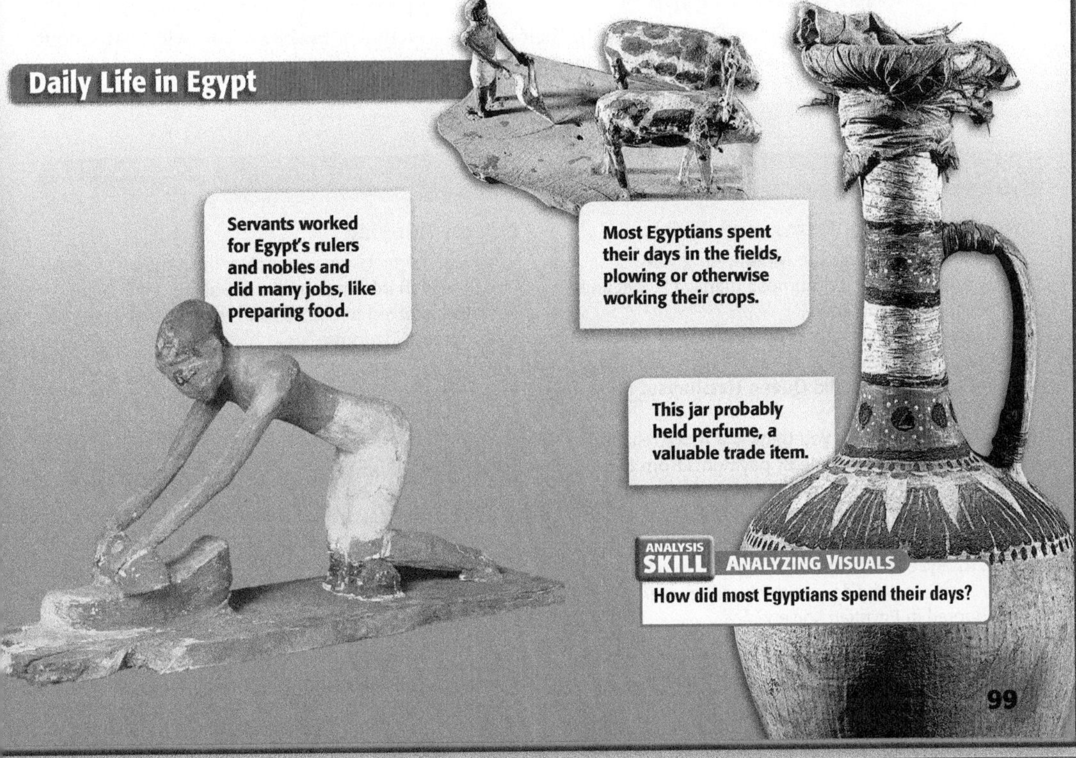

Servants worked for Egypt's rulers and nobles and did many jobs, like preparing food.
Most Egyptians spent their days in the fields, plowing or otherwise working their crops.
This jar probably held perfume, a valuable trade item.
ANALYSIS SKILL ANALYZING VISUALS
How did most Egyptians spend their days?
99

Direct Teach

Main Idea

3 Work and Daily Life

Work and daily life were different for each of Egypt's social classes.

Describe What kinds of writing did scribes do? *kept records and accounts for the state, wrote and copied religious and literary texts*

Analyze Why did the pharaohs value talented architects? *Having well-designed pyramids and temples made the pharaoh powerful and, according to Egyptian religion, ensured a happy afterlife.*

Make Judgments Which of these jobs would you have preferred: scribe, artisan, artist, architect or soldier? Why? *Answers will vary.*

 **CRF:** Biography: Nefertiti

Did You Know . . .

Some Egyptians slept on their backs with their heads placed in wooden headrests to keep their hairstyles neat.

Teaching Tip

Ask students to explain the difference between an artist and an artisan. If they are uncertain, ask a student to look up the terms in a dictionary and report to the class.

Differentiating Instruction

Struggling Readers Below Level Prep Required

Materials: art supplies

1. Lead a discussion comparing each group in Egyptian society with a similar group of people today. For example, compare the methods used by ancient Egyptian farmers and by farmers in the present-day United States.
2. Then have students draw Egyptians from at least three of the following groups at work: government officials, priests, scribes, artists and artisans, architects, traders, soldiers, and farmers. Pictures should be as detailed as possible.
3. Have students display and explain their work. **LS Visual-Spatial**

Alternative Assessment Handbook, Rubric 3, Artwork

Answers

Analyzing Visuals *in the fields, plowing and working on crops*

Direct Teach

Main Idea

3 Work and Daily Life

Work and daily life were different for each of Egypt's social classes.

Identify Who made up the majority of Egypt's population? *farmers and other peasants*

Describe What did slaves in Egypt do? *worked on farms, on building projects, and in households*

Make Inferences How may we have learned about Egyptian toys and games? *artifacts, art showing the toys and games in use*

Review & Assess

Close

Point out that Egyptian children played versions of tug of war, leap frog, and checkers.

Review

Online Quiz, Section 3

Assess

SE Section 3 Assessment

PASS: Section 3 Quiz

Alternative Assessment Handbook

Reteach/Classroom Intervention

Guided Reading Workbook, Section 3

Interactive Skills Tutor CD-ROM

Farmers and Other Peasants

Egypt's farmers and other peasants were toward the bottom of the social scale. They made up the vast majority of Egypt's population. Peasant farmers used wooden hoes or cow-drawn plows to prepare the land before the Nile flooded. After the floodwaters had drained away, they planted seeds. Farmers worked together to gather the harvest.

Farmers had to give crops to the pharaoh as taxes. All peasants, including farmers, were subject to special duty. The pharaoh could demand at any time that people work on projects such as building pyramids, mining gold, or fighting in wars.

ACADEMIC VOCABULARY
contracts binding legal agreements

Slaves

The few slaves in Egypt were considered lower than farmers. They worked on farms, on building projects, and in households. Slaves had some legal rights and in some cases could earn their freedom.

Family Life in Egypt

Most Egyptian families lived in their own homes. Men were expected to marry young so that they could start having children. Most Egyptian women were devoted to their homes and their families. Some, however, had jobs outside the home. A few served as priestesses, and some worked as administrators and artisans. Unlike most women in the ancient world, Egyptian women had certain legal rights. These included the right to own property, make **contracts**, and divorce their husbands.

Children played with toys, took part in ballgames, and hunted. Most boys and girls received an education. At school they learned morals, writing, math, and sports. At age 14, most boys left school to enter their father's profession.

READING CHECK **Categorizing** What types of jobs did people perform in ancient Egypt?

SUMMARY AND PREVIEW Egypt's power and wealth peaked during the New Kingdom. As society became more complex, people in different classes worked at different jobs. Next, you will learn about Egyptian achievements.

Section 3 Assessment

hmhsocialstudies.com ONLINE QUIZ

Reviewing Ideas, Terms, and People

1. a. **Recall** What was the **Middle Kingdom**?
   b. **Analyze** How did Ahmose manage to become king of all Egypt?
2. a. **Identify** Which group of invaders did **Ramses the Great** defeat?
   b. **Describe** What did **Queen Hatshepsut** do as pharaoh of Egypt?
   c. **Predict** What do you think is a more reliable source of wealth—trade or payments from conquered kingdoms? Why?
3. a. **Identify** What job employed the most people in ancient Egypt?
   b. **Analyze** What rights did Egyptian women have?
   c. **Evaluate** Why do you think scribes were so honored in Egyptian society?

Critical Thinking

4. **Categorizing** Using your notes, fill in the pyramids below with information about political and military factors that led to the rise and fall of the Middle and New Kingdoms.

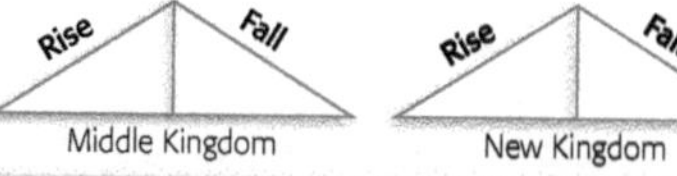

FOCUS ON WRITING

5. **Developing Key Ideas from the Middle and New Kingdoms** Your riddle should contain some information about the later pharaohs and daily life in Egypt. Decide which key ideas you should include in your riddle and add them to your list.

Section 3 Assessment Answers

1. a. a period of order and stability from 2050 to 1750 BC that began after Mentuhotep II defeated his rivals
   b. by driving the Hyksos out of Egypt and declaring himself king
2. a. the Tehenu
   b. increased trade, built many impressive temples and monuments
   c. Students' answers will vary.
3. a. farming
   b. the ability to own property, make contracts, and divorce their husbands
   c. possible answer—because they were involved in religious procedures, which were very important to the Egyptians, and because they portrayed history to later generations
4. Middle: Rise—Mentuhotep consolidates power; Fall—internal conflict, invasion by Hyksos; New: Rise—Ahmose defeats the Hyksos, Egypt becomes an empire through military conquest, trade expands; Fall—invasions by various peoples
5. Students' key ideas will vary.

Answers

Reading Check *priests and priestesses, government officials, scribes, artisans, artists, architects, traders, soldiers, farmers, peasants, slaves*

BIOGRAPHY

Ramses the Great

How Could a Ruler Achieve Fame That Would Last 3,000 Years?

When did he live? the late 1300s and early 1200s BC

Where did he live? As pharaoh, Ramses lived in a city he built on the Nile Delta. The city's name, Pi-Ramesse, means the "house of Ramses."

What did he do? From a young age, Ramses was trained as a ruler and a fighter. Made an army captain at age 10, he began military campaigns even before he became pharaoh. During his reign, Ramses greatly increased the size of his kingdom.

Why is he so important? Many people consider Ramses the last great Egyptian pharaoh. He accomplished great things, but the pharaohs who followed could not maintain them. Both a great warrior and a great builder, he is known largely for the massive monuments he built. The temples at Karnak, Luxor, and Abu Simbel stand as 3,000-year-old symbols of the great pharaoh's power.

Drawing Conclusions Why do you think Ramses built great monuments all over Egypt?

KEY IDEAS

Ramses had a poem praising him carved into the walls of five temples, including Karnak. One verse of the poem praises Ramses as a great warrior and the defender of Egypt.

Gracious lord and bravest king,
savior-guard
Of Egypt in the battle, be our
ward;
Behold we stand alone, in the
hostile Hittite ring,
Save for us the breath of life,
Give deliverance from the
strife,
Oh! protect us Ramses
Miamun!
Oh! save us, mighty king!

—Pen-ta-ur, from *The Victory of Ramses over the Khita*, in *The World's Story*, edited by Eva March Tappan

VIDEO
Let's Move a Mountain
hmhsocialstudies.com

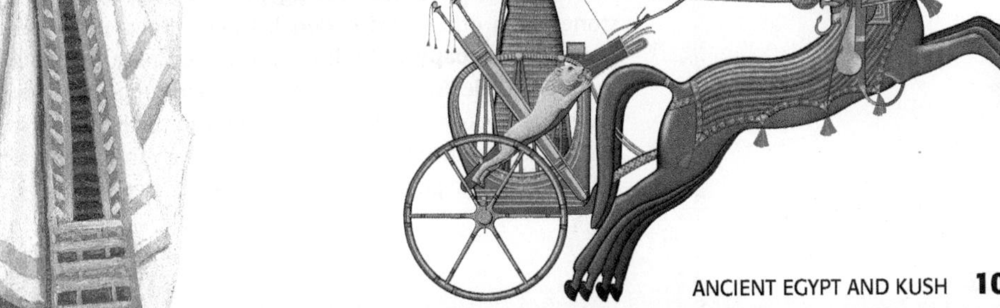

This copy of an ancient painting shows Ramses the Great on his chariot in battle against the Hittites.

Biography

Reading Focus Question

Point out that Ramses was known not just for wartime accomplishments but also for peacetime achievements. Challenge students to name more recent leaders who have achieved lasting fame in both areas. *possible answers—George Washington, Winston Churchill*

Ramses the Warrior

At one point in a famous battle against the Hittites, Ramses and a few of his charioteers appeared to be doomed when they were completely surrounded by Hittite forces. Fortunately, reinforcements arrived in time to save them. Ramses was extremely proud of his stand against the Hittite's larger force. A long poem was written about the battle and scenes from it were carved into several temple walls.

Ramses the Pharaoh

The reign of Ramses was the second-longest in Egyptian history. Ramses II was so popular that nine pharaohs of the 20th dynasty used his name.

Analyzing Visuals

Egyptian Warfare What does this painting tell about Egyptian warfare during the time of Ramses the Great? *that the Egyptians used bows and arrows and fought in two-wheeled chariots with spoked wheels drawn by two horses*

Critical Thinking: Solving Problems

Above Level

Research Required

Saving Abu Simbel

1. Explain to students that in the 1960s, Egypt's leaders decided to control the Nile's annual flood by building the Aswan High Dam. Unfortunately, the lake thus created—Lake Nasser—would flood many Egyptian antiquities, including the temple of Ramses at Abu Simbel. Many organizations worked together to save the Abu Simbel temple.
2. Have students work in pairs to conduct research on this engineering feat and report on their findings.
3. Reports should explain some of the engineering problems that the project presented and how they were solved. Reports may take any form.
4. Challenge students to suggest alternative solutions to the engineering hurdles.

LS Interpersonal, Kinesthetic

Alternative Assessment Handbook, Rubric 30: Research

Answers

Drawing Conclusions *possible answer—to impress possible invaders or rebels with his power, to make sure his fame lasted a long time*

Preteach

Bellringer

If YOU were there . . . Use the **Daily Bellringer Transparency** to help students answer the question.

Daily Bellringer Transparency, Section 4

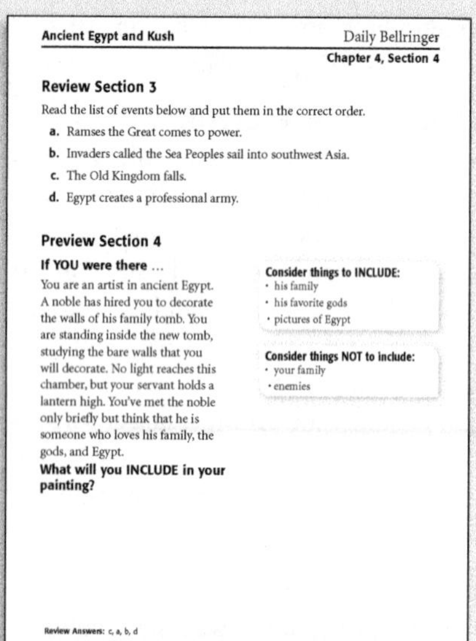

Ancient Egypt and Kush — Daily Bellringer
Chapter 4, Section 4

Review Section 3

Read the list of events below and put them in the correct order.

a. Ramses the Great comes to power.
b. Invaders called the Sea Peoples sail into southwest Asia.
c. The Old Kingdom falls.
d. Egypt creates a professional army.

Preview Section 4

If YOU were there ...

You are an artist in ancient Egypt. A noble has hired you to decorate the walls of his family tomb. You are standing inside the new tomb, studying the bare walls that you will decorate. No light reaches this chamber, but your servant holds a lantern high. You've met the noble only briefly but think that he is someone who loves his family, the gods, and Egypt.

What will you INCLUDE in your painting?

Consider things to INCLUDE:
- his family
- his favorite gods
- pictures of Egypt

Consider things NOT to include:
- your family
- enemies

Review Answers: c, a, b, d

Building Vocabulary

Preteach or review the following term:

lavishly marked by excess or overabundance (p. 104)

CRF: Vocabulary Builder Activity, Section 4

Taking Notes

Have students use the graphic organizer online to take notes on the section. This activity will prepare students for the Section Assessment, in which they will complete a graphic organizer that builds on the information using the Critical Thinking Skill: Summarizing.

SECTION 4

Egyptian Achievements

What You Will Learn...

Main Ideas

1. The Egyptians developed a writing system using hieroglyphics.
2. The Egyptians created magnificent temples, tombs, and works of art.

The Big Idea

The Egyptians made lasting achievements in writing, architecture, and art.

Key Terms and People

hieroglyphics, *p. 102*
papyrus, *p. 102*
Rosetta Stone, *p. 103*
sphinxes, *p. 104*
obelisk, *p. 104*
King Tutankhamen, *p. 106*

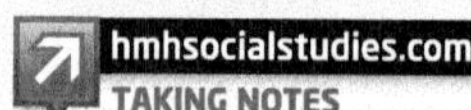

Use the graphic organizer online to take notes on the many achievements of the ancient Egyptians.

If YOU were there...

You are an artist in ancient Egypt. A noble has hired you to decorate the walls of his family tomb. You are standing inside the new tomb, studying the bare walls that you will decorate. No light reaches this chamber, but your servant holds a lantern high. You've met the noble only briefly but think that he is someone who loves his family, the gods, and Egypt.

What will you include in your painting?

BUILDING BACKGROUND The Egyptians had a rich and varied history, but most people today remember them for their cultural achievements, such as their unique writing system. In addition, Egyptian art, including the tomb paintings mentioned above, is admired by millions of tourists in museums around the world.

Egyptian Writing

If you were reading a book and saw pictures of folded cloth, a leg, a star, a bird, and a man holding a stick, would you know what it meant? You would if you were an ancient Egyptian. In the Egyptian writing system, or **hieroglyphics** (hy-ruh-GLIH-fiks), those five symbols together meant "to teach." Egyptian hieroglyphics were one of the world's first writing systems.

Writing in Ancient Egypt

The earliest known examples of Egyptian writing are from around 3300 BC. These early Egyptian writings were carved in stone or on other hard material. Later, the Egyptians learned how to make **papyrus** (puh-PY-ruhs), a long-lasting, paper-like material made from reeds. The Egyptians made papyrus by pressing layers of reeds together and pounding them into sheets. These sheets were tough and durable, yet easy to roll into scrolls. Scribes wrote on papyrus using brushes and ink.

Teach the Big Idea

At Level

Egyptian Achievements

1. **Teach** Ask students the questions in the Main Idea boxes to teach this section.
2. **Apply** Ask students to imagine that they are Egyptians who contributed to the civilization's achievements. For example, a student may imagine herself as the inventor of papyrus or as a temple painter. Have students create book jackets for autobiographies of their chosen characters. The books' titles should be *My Life as* ___ , filling in the chosen role. LS **Visual/Spatial**
3. **Review** Call on students to display and explain their book jackets until all the major achievements have been discussed.
4. **Practice/Homework** Have students write the introductory paragraphs for the blurbs inside their book jackets. LS **Verbal/Linguistic**

Egyptian Writing

Egyptian hieroglyphics used picture symbols to represent sounds.

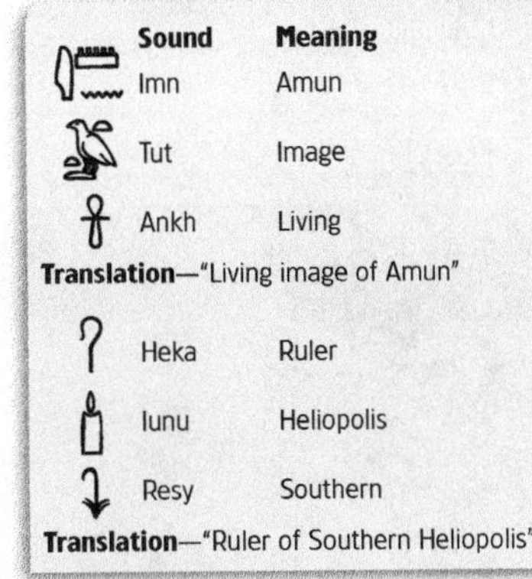

Sound Meaning
Imn Amun
Tut Image
Ankh Living
Translation—"Living image of Amun"

ANALYSIS SKILL ANALYZING VISUALS

What does the symbol for ruler look like?

The hieroglyphic writing system used more than 600 symbols, mostly pictures of objects. Each symbol represented one or more sounds in the Egyptian language. For example, a picture of an owl represented the same sound as our letter *M*.

Hieroglyphics could be written either horizontally or vertically. They could be written from right to left or from left to right. These options made hieroglyphics flexible to write but difficult to read. The only way to tell which way a text is written is to look at individual symbols.

The Rosetta Stone

Historians and archaeologists have known about hieroglyphics for centuries, but for a long time they didn't know how to read them. In fact, it was not until 1799 when a lucky discovery by a French soldier gave historians the key they needed to read ancient Egyptian writing.

That key was the **Rosetta Stone,** a stone slab inscribed with hieroglyphics. In addition to hieroglyphics, the Rosetta Stone had text in Greek and a later form of Egyptian. Because the text in all three languages was the same, scholars who knew Greek figured out what the hieroglyphics said.

THE IMPACT TODAY

An object that helps solve a difficult mystery is sometimes called a Rosetta Stone.

Egyptian Texts

Because papyrus did not decay in Egypt's dry climate, many Egyptian texts survive. Historians today can read Egyptian government and historical records, science texts, and medical manuals. Literary works have also survived. We can read stories, poems, and mythological tales. Some texts, such as *The Book of the Dead,* tell about the afterlife. Others include love poems and stories about gods and kings.

READING CHECK **Comparing** How is our writing system similar to hieroglyphics?

Direct Teach

Main Idea

1 Egyptian Writing

The Egyptians developed a writing system using hieroglyphics.

Explain What did each symbol in the hieroglyphic system represent? *one or more sounds in the Egyptian language*

Analyze What were some advantages of using papyrus? *made of readily available materials, tough, durable, could be rolled into scrolls*

Make Judgments What would it be like to use a language that could be written either up or down, right to left, or left to right? *possible answer—It was more flexible than our system, and the Egyptians were used to it, so it probably caused no problems.*

CRF: Literature: The Egyptian Cinderella

hmhsocialstudies.com

Online Resources

Activity: Hieroglyphics

Connect to Math

The Eye of Horus Hieroglyphic symbols also stood for mathematical concepts. For example, the parts of a drawing of an eye, called the Eye of Horus, stand for various fractions. The symbol comes from an Egyptian myth in which the god Horus suffered an injury to his left eye. The god Thoth healed it, and a drawing of the eye became a powerful symbol. Challenge students to research the Eye of Horus as a mathematical symbol and to explain it to the class.

Differentiating Instruction

English Language Learners

Below Level **Prep Required**

1. Locate and display a photo of the Rosetta Stone. Point out the Egyptian hieroglyphics, the other form of Egyptian (called *demotic*), and the Greek text.
2. Then draw an outline of the Rosetta Stone for students to see, and divide it into three bands.
3. Select a sentence from the students' main native language. Print it in one area. Print the English translation in another area. Write the same English phrase in cursive in the third area. Use the drawing to demonstrate how the Rosetta Stone was deciphered.
4. Ask students to write a paragraph summarizing what they have learned.

LS Visual/Spatial, Verbal/Linguistic

Answers

Analyzing Visuals *possible answer—a shepherd's crook, symbolizing the ruler as a shepherd of his people*

Reading Check *Letters stand for sounds just as hieroglyphic symbols stand for sounds.*

Direct Teach

Main Idea

❷ Temples, Tombs, and Art

The Egyptians created magnificent temples, tombs, and works of art.

Identify What is a sphinx? *imaginary creature with the body of a lion and the head of another animal or a human*

Recall What are the two types of large structures created by the Egyptian architects? *pyramids and temples*

Analyze Why do you think builders placed obelisks at the gates of temples? *possible answer—because they pointed to the sky, leading the way to the afterlife*

Info to Know

Obelisks Most obelisks were carved from red granite. Their pyramid-shaped tops were usually sheathed in electrum, an alloy of gold and silver. Some obelisks weighed more than 100 tons. Because some obelisks have been taken out of Egypt, genuine Egyptian obelisks now stand in London, Rome, and New York City.

Linking to Today

Tourism in Egypt Revenue from tourism accounts for about 25 percent of Egypt's foreign exchange income. The pyramids and temples are major attractions. More than 5 million tourists visit Egypt each year.

Temples, Tombs, and Art

The Egyptians are famous for their architecture and art. The walls of Egypt's magnificent temples and tombs are covered with impressive paintings and carvings.

Egypt's Great Temples

You have already read about the Egyptians' most famous structures, the pyramids. But the Egyptians also built massive temples. Those that survive are among the most spectacular sites in Egypt today.

The Egyptians believed that temples were the homes of the gods. People visited the temples to worship, offer the gods gifts, and ask for favors.

Many Egyptian temples shared similar features. Rows of stone **sphinxes**—imaginary creatures with the bodies of lions and the heads of other animals or humans—lined the path leading to the entrance. The entrance itself was a huge, thick gate. On either side of the gate might stand an **obelisk** (AH-buh-lisk), a tall, four-sided pillar that is pointed on top.

THE IMPACT TODAY
The Washington Monument, in Washington, DC, was built in the shape of an obelisk.

Inside, temples were lavishly decorated, as you can see in the drawing of the Temple of Karnak. Huge columns supported the temple's roof. In many cases, these columns were covered with paintings and hieroglyphics, as were the temple walls. Statues of gods and pharaohs often stood along the walls as well. The sanctuary, the most sacred part of the building, was at the far end of the temple.

The Temple of Karnak is only one of Egypt's great temples. Others were built by Ramses the Great at Abu Simbel and Luxor. Part of what makes the temple at Abu Simbel so impressive is that it is carved out of sandstone cliffs. At the temple's entrance, four 66-foot-tall statues show Ramses as pharaoh. Nearby are some smaller statues of his family.

History Close-up

The Temple of Karnak

The Temple of Karnak was Egypt's largest temple. Built mainly to honor Re, the sun god, Karnak was one of Egypt's major religious centers for centuries. Over the years, pharaohs added to the temple's many buildings. This illustration shows how Karnak's great hall may have looked during an ancient festival.

Karnak's interior columns and walls were painted brilliant colors.

ANALYSIS SKILL ANALYZING VISUALS
What features of Egyptian architecture can you see in this illustration?

Cross-Discipline Activity: Math

Above Level

Measuring a Temple

1. Organize students into small groups.
2. Have students calculate various dimensions of the temple's interior. They should use the priests in the foreground as a basic ruler and estimate that the men were about 5'5" tall.
3. To add interest to the activity, challenge groups to race in making their calculations.
4. Lead a discussion about how the Egyptians built and decorated temples with such stupendous dimensions.

LS Interpersonal, Logical/Mathematical

Answers

Analyzing Visuals *columns covered by paintings and hieroglyphics, high windows*

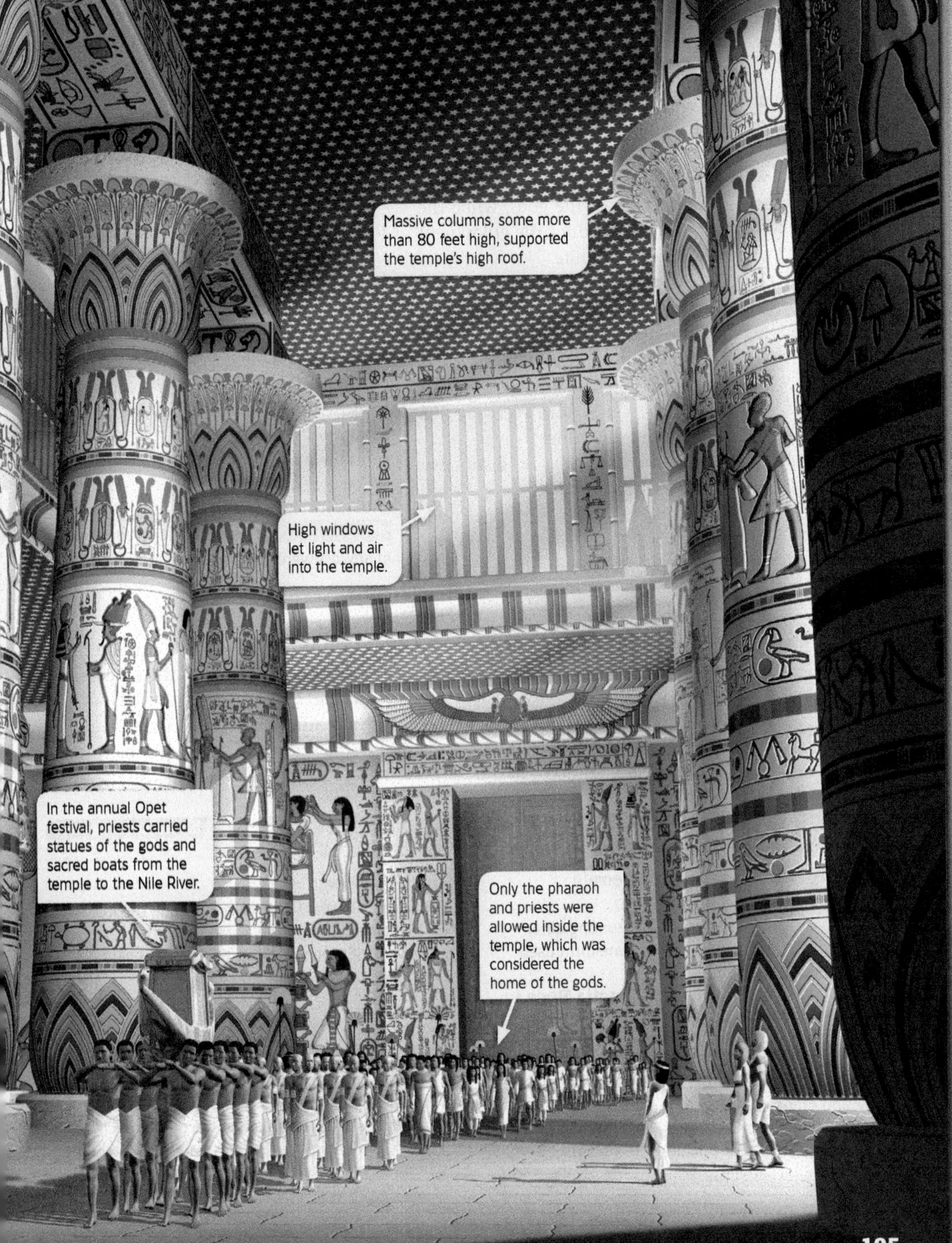

Massive columns, some more than 80 feet high, supported the temple's high roof.
High windows let light and air into the temple.
In the annual Opet festival, priests carried statues of the gods and sacred boats from the temple to the Nile River.
Only the pharaoh and priests were allowed inside the temple, which was considered the home of the gods.
105

Direct Teach

Main Idea

❷ Temples, Tombs, and Art

The Egyptians created magnificent temples, tombs, and works of art.

Identify What was the most sacred part of a temple? *the sanctuary*

Analyze Why do you think many Egyptian temples had rows of sphinxes leading to the entrance? *possible answer—as symbolic protection for the temple*

History Close-up

Analyzing Visuals Opet was the ancient Egyptian festival of the New Year. During this festival, the god Amon and his family made a ritual journey from Karnak to the Temple of Luxor. Scenes from this festival are carved into columns at Luxor.

Cross-Discipline Activity: Arts and the Humanities

At Level

Research Required

The Opet Festival

Materials: art supplies

1. Have students conduct research on the Opet festival, including its purpose and what kinds of ceremonies took place during this time.
2. Have students paint a picture of an event that might have taken place during Opet. They should not simply copy an existing painting, but create an original one based on what they have learned in their research.
3. Encourage students to include as much detail as possible, showing, for example, the kinds of garments and jewelry people would have worn. People should be drawn in the Egyptian style.
4. Display students' paintings. **LS Visual/Spatial**

Alternative Assessment Handbook, Rubric 3: Artwork; and 30: Research

Direct Teach

Main Idea

❸ Temples, Tombs, and Art

The Egyptians created magnificent temples, tombs, and works of art.

Recall Give examples of two common subjects of Egyptian paintings. *events such as the crowning of kings and founding of temples, religious rituals, and scenes from everyday life*

Analyze Why was the discovery of King Tutankhamen's tomb so important? *It had never been disturbed by tomb robbers.*

Elaborate Why do you suppose the Egyptians drew animals realistically but drew people with their heads and legs from the side and their upper bodies and shoulders straight on? *Answers will vary but should be consistent with text information.*

History Humor

What did the young King Tut say when he got scared? *I want my mummy!*

Review & Assess

Close

Have students describe the works of art shown on these pages.

Review

Online Quiz, Section 4

Assess

SE Section 4 Assessment

PASS: Section 4 Quiz

Alternative Assessment Handbook

Reteach/Classroom Intervention

Guided Reading Workbook, Section 4

Interactive Skills Tutor CD-ROM

Answers

Reading Check *paintings and carvings, statues, jewelry, clothing, burial masks, and ivory statuettes*

Egyptian Art

The ancient Egyptians were masterful artists. Egyptians painted lively, colorful scenes on canvas, papyrus, pottery, plaster, and wood. Detailed works also covered the walls of temples and tombs. The temple art was created to honor the gods, while the tomb art was intended for the enjoyment of the dead in the afterlife.

The subjects of Egyptian paintings vary widely. Some paintings show important historical events, such as the crowning of kings and the founding of temples. Others illustrate major religious rituals. Still other paintings show scenes from everyday life, such as farming or hunting.

Egyptian painting has a distinctive style. People's heads and legs are always seen from the side, but their upper bodies and shoulders are shown straight on. In addition, people do not always appear the same size. Important figures such as pharaohs appear huge in comparison to others. In contrast, Egyptian animals were usually drawn realistically.

Painting was not the only art form in which Egyptians excelled. For example, the Egyptians were skilled stoneworkers. Many tombs included huge statues and detailed carvings on the walls.

The Egyptians also made beautiful objects out of gold and precious stones. They made jewelry for both women and men. This included necklaces, collars, and bracelets. The Egyptians also used gold to make burial items for their pharaohs.

Over the years, treasure hunters emptied many pharaohs' tombs. At least one tomb, however, was not disturbed. In 1922 archaeologists found the tomb of **King Tutankhamen** (too-tang-KAHM-uhn), or King Tut. This tomb was filled with treasures, including jewelry, robes, a burial mask, and ivory statues. King Tut's treasures have taught us much about Egyptian burial practices and beliefs.

READING CHECK **Summarizing** What types of artwork were contained in Egyptian tombs?

SUMMARY AND PREVIEW Ancient Egyptians developed one of the best known cultures in the ancient world. Next, you will learn about a culture that developed in the shadow of Egypt—Kush.

Section 4 Assessment

hmhsocialstudies.com ONLINE QUIZ

Reviewing Ideas, Terms, and People

1. a. **Identify** What are **hieroglyphics**?
   b. **Contrast** How was hieroglyphic writing different from our writing today? from cuneiform used by the Mesopotamians?
   c. **Evaluate** Why was finding the **Rosetta Stone** so important to scholars?
2. a. **Describe** What were two ways the Egyptians decorated their temples?
   b. **Analyze** Why were tombs filled with art, jewelry, and other treasures?
   c. **Draw Conclusions** Why do you think pharaohs like Ramses the Great built huge temples?

Critical Thinking

3. **Summarizing** Draw a chart like the one below. Under each heading, write a statement that summarizes Egyptian achievements in that field.

Writing	Architecture	Art

FOCUS ON WRITING

4. **Adding Up What You Know about Egypt** Look at the notes you have taken at the end of each section. Think about what clues you might include when you write your riddle about Egypt.

Section 4 Assessment Answers

1. **a.** the Egyptian writing system
   b. had 600 symbols, rather than the 26 in our alphabet, could be written horizontally or vertically, left to right, or right to left; hieroglyphics represent sounds, rather than actual things
   c. allowed scholars to decipher hieroglyphics
2. **a.** possible answers—columns, obelisks, paintings, hieroglyphics, and statues
   b. The Egyptians believed that the dead enjoyed these items in the afterlife.
   c. possible answers—to worship the gods, display the pharaoh's power and wealth
3. possible answers: Writing—had over 600 symbols, wrote on papyrus; Architecture—temples covered in hieroglyphics, many buildings were built for religious purposes; Art—people drawn in unrealistic way, animals drawn realistically
4. Students' notes will vary, but should reflect section content.

Ancient Kush

SECTION 5

If YOU were there...

You live along the Nile River, where it moves quickly through swift rapids. A few years ago, armies from the powerful kingdom of Egypt took over your country. Some Egyptians have moved here. They bring new customs, and many people are imitating them. Now your sister has a new baby and wants to give it an Egyptian name! This upsets many people in your family.

How do you feel about following Egyptian customs?

BUILDING BACKGROUND Egypt dominated the lands along the Nile, but it was not the only ancient culture to develop along the river. Another kingdom called Kush arose to the south of Egypt. Through trade, conquest, and political dealings, the histories of Egypt and Kush became closely tied together.

The Geography of Early Nubia

South of Egypt, a group of people settled in the region we now call Nubia. These Africans established the first great kingdom in the interior of Africa. We know this kingdom by the name the Egyptians gave it—Kush. The development of Kushite society was greatly influenced by the geography of Nubia, especially the role played by the Nile River.

The ruins of ancient Kushite pyramids stand behind those reconstructed to look the way they did when originally built.

What You Will Learn...

Main Ideas

1. The geography of early Nubia helped civilization develop there.
2. Kush and Egypt traded, but they also fought.
3. Later Kush became a trading power with a unique culture.
4. Both internal and external factors led to the decline of Kush.

The Big Idea

The kingdom of Kush, which arose south of Egypt in a land called Nubia, developed an advanced civilization with a large trading network.

Key Terms and People

Piankhi, *p. 110*
trade network, *p. 111*
merchants, *p. 111*
exports, *p. 111*
imports, *p. 111*
Queen Shanakhdakheto, *p. 113*
King Ezana, *p. 113*

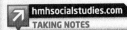

Use the graphic organizer online to take notes on the rise and fall of Kush.

Preteach

Bellringer

If YOU were there . . . Use the **Daily Bellringer Transparency** to help students answer the question.

Daily Bellringer Transparency, Section 5

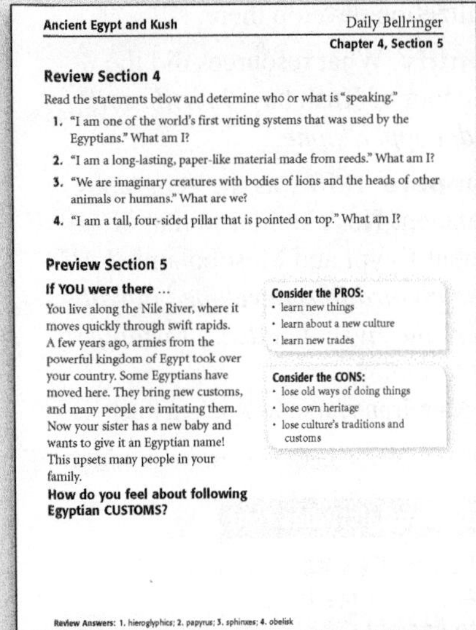

Ancient Egypt and Kush — Daily Bellringer — **Chapter 4, Section 5**

Review Section 4

Read the statements below and determine who or what is "speaking."

1. "I am one of the world's first writing systems that was used by the Egyptians." What am I?
2. "I am a long-lasting, paper-like material made from reeds." What am I?
3. "We are imaginary creatures with bodies of lions and the heads of other animals or humans." What are we?
4. "I am a tall, four-sided pillar that is pointed on top." What am I?

Preview Section 5

If YOU were there ...

You live along the Nile River, where it moves quickly through swift rapids. A few years ago, armies from the powerful kingdom of Egypt took over your country. Some Egyptians have moved here. They bring new customs, and many people are imitating them. Now your sister has a new baby and wants to give it an Egyptian name! This upsets many people in your family.

How do you feel about following Egyptian CUSTOMS?

Consider the PROS:
- learn new things
- learn about a new culture
- learn new trades

Consider the CONS:
- lose old ways of doing things
- lose own heritage
- lose culture's traditions and customs

Review Answers: 1. hieroglyphics; 2. papyrus; 3. sphinxes; 4. obelisk

Academic Vocabulary

Review with students the high-use academic term in this section.

authority power or influence (p. 113)

CRF: Vocabulary Builder Activity, Section 5

Taking Notes

Have students use the graphic organizer online to take notes on the section. This activity will prepare students for the Section Assessment, in which they will complete a graphic organizer that builds on the information using the Critical Thinking Skill: Identifying Cause and Effect.

Teach the Big Idea

At Level

Ancient Kush

1. **Teach** Ask students the questions in the Main Idea boxes to teach this section.
2. **Apply** Help students locate and describe ancient Kush and summarize its relations with Egypt. To do so, have each student plan a billboard advertisement with words and pictures for one of the following purposes: to draw new settlers to Kush, to join the Egyptian army in the conquest of Kush, or to join the Kushite army in the fight for independence from Egypt. Organize the class into three groups to ensure all topics are covered. **LS Verbal/Linguistic, Visual/Spatial**
3. **Review** As you review the section's main ideas, have students discuss the information contained or implied in their billboard ads.
4. **Practice/Homework** Have each student create an ad for one of the other two topics. **LS Verbal/Linguistic, Visual/Spatial**

Alternative Assessment Handbook, Rubric 2: Advertisements

Direct Teach

Main Idea

1 The Geography of Early Nubia

The geography of early Nubia helped civilization develop there.

Identify What resources did the kingdom of Kush have? *fertile soil, gold, copper, stone*

Compare How was the geography of ancient Kush similar to that of ancient Egypt and Mesopotamia? *All three civilizations developed in valleys where the rivers flooded, providing fertile soil.*

Map Transparency: Ancient Kush

Online Resources
Activity: Time Travel to Ancient Kush

Interpreting Maps

Ancient Kush

Movement What was probably the main north-south travel route in Kush? *the Nile River*

Info to Know

Napata A hill in Napata called Barkol was considered a holy mountain and the home of the god Amon. Even after the Kushite capital was moved to Meroë, Napata remained the Kushite religious capital. Royal burials took place there until 315 BC.

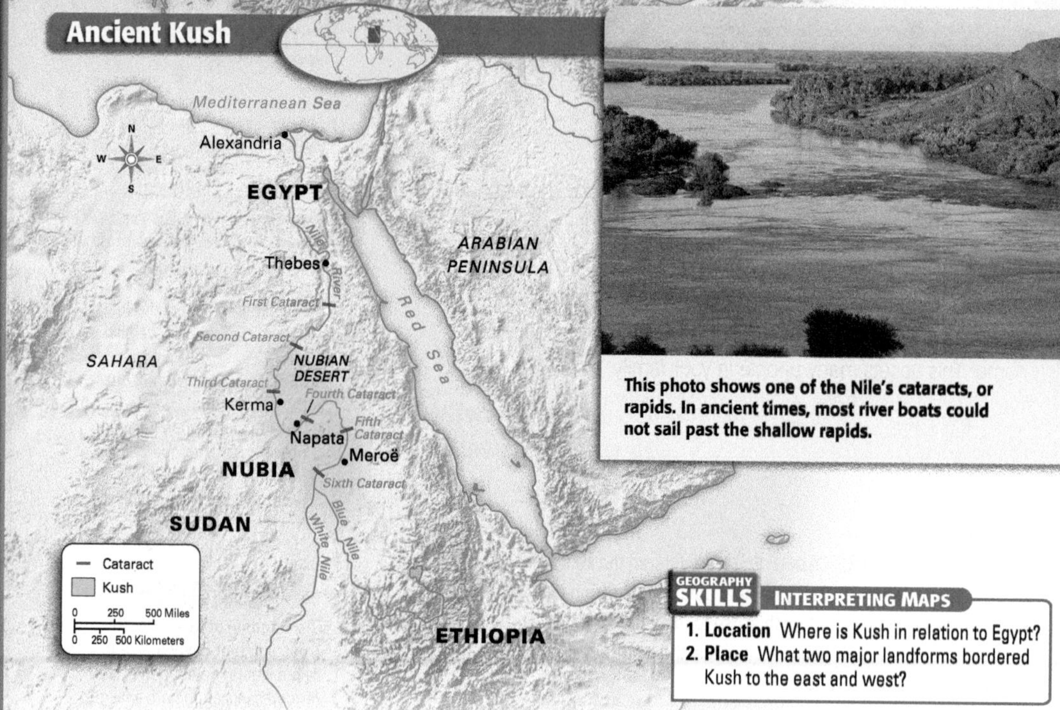

This photo shows one of the Nile's cataracts, or rapids. In ancient times, most river boats could not sail past the shallow rapids.

GEOGRAPHY SKILLS INTERPRETING MAPS

1. **Location** Where is Kush in relation to Egypt?
2. **Place** What two major landforms bordered Kush to the east and west?

The Land of Nubia

Today desert covers much of Nubia, but in ancient times the region was more fertile than it is now. Rain flooded the Nile every year, providing a rich layer of silt to nearby lands. The kingdom of Kush developed in this fertile area.

Ancient Nubia was rich in minerals such as gold, copper, and stone. These resources played a major role in the area's history and contributed to its wealth.

Early Civilization in Nubia

Like all early civilizations, the people of Nubia depended on agriculture for their food. Fortunately for them, the Nile's floods allowed the Nubians to plant both summer and winter crops. Among the crops they grew were wheat, barley, and other grains.

Besides farmland, the banks of the Nile also provided grazing land for livestock. As a result, farming villages thrived all along the Nile by 3500 BC.

Over time some farmers grew richer than others. These farmers became village leaders. Sometime around 2000 BC, one of these leaders took control of other villages and made himself king of the region. His new kingdom was called Kush.

The kings of Kush ruled from their capital at Kerma (KAR-muh). This city was located on the Nile just south of the third cataract. Because the Nile's cataracts made parts of the river hard to pass through, they were natural barriers against invaders. For many years the cataracts kept Kush safe from the more powerful Egyptian kingdom to the north.

Cross-Discipline Activity: Geography

At Level

Elevation Profiles of Kush

1. Display the History and Geography Transparency map titled "Ancient Kush" for students to see.
2. Using a washable marker, draw three horizontal parallel lines across Nubia—near its northern edge, near its southern edge, and at its center. The lines should be parallel to the top of the page.
3. Instruct students to use these lines to draw elevation profiles. An elevation profile is like a cross-sectional or cutaway view of a region.
4. Have each student use the transparency and the above map to create three elevation profiles of Nubia.
5. After students have drawn their elevation profiles, lead a discussion about how the profiles show mountains to the east, the Nile valley, and the river itself. LS **Visual/Spatial**

Alternative Assessment Handbook, Rubric 21: Map Reading

Answers

Interpreting Maps **1.** *south of Egypt* **2.** *Nubian Desert and the Sahara*

As time passed, Kushite society grew more complex. Besides farmers and herders, some Kushites became priests and artisans. Early Kush was influenced by cultures to the south. Later, Egypt played a greater role in Kush's history.

READING CHECK **Finding Main Ideas** How did geography help civilization grow in Nubia?

Kush and Egypt

Kush and Egypt were neighbors. Sometimes the neighbors lived in peace with each other and helped each other prosper. For example, Kush became a major supplier of both slaves and raw materials to Egypt. The Kushites sent materials such as gold, copper, and stone to Egypt. The Kushites also sent the Egyptians ebony, a type of dark, heavy wood, and ivory, the hard white material that makes up elephant tusks.

Egypt's Conquest of Kush

Relations between Kush and Egypt were not always peaceful, however. As Kush grew wealthy from trade, its army grew stronger as well. Egypt's rulers soon feared that Kush would grow even more powerful and attack Egypt.

To prevent such an attack from occurring, the pharaoh Thutmose I sent an army to take control of Kush around 1500 BC. The pharaoh's army conquered all of Nubia north of the Fifth Cataract. As a result, Kush became part of Egypt.

After his army's victory, the pharaoh destroyed Kerma, the Kushite capital. Later pharaohs—including Ramses the Great—built huge temples in what had been Kushite territory.

Effects of the Conquest

Kush remained an Egyptian territory for about 450 years. During that time, Egypt's influence over Kush grew tremendously. Many Egyptians settled in Kush. Egyptian became the language of the region. Many Kushites used Egyptian names and wore Egyptian-style clothing. They also adopted Egyptian religious practices.

A Change in Power

During the mid-1000s BC the New Kingdom in Egypt was ending. As the power of Egypt's pharaohs declined, Kushite leaders regained control of Kush. Kush once again became independent.

We know almost nothing about the history of the Kushites from the time they gained independence until 200 years later. Kush is not mentioned in any historical records that describe those centuries.

The Conquest of Egypt

By around 850 BC Kush had regained its strength. It was once again as strong as it had been before it had been conquered by Egypt. Because the Egyptians had captured and destroyed the city of Kerma, the kings of Kush ruled from the city of Napata. Built by the Egyptians, Napata was on the Nile, about 100 miles southeast of Kerma.

As Kush grew stronger, Egypt was further weakened. A series of inept pharaohs

BIOGRAPHY

Piankhi (PYAN-kee)

c. 751–716 BC

Also known as Piye, Piankhi was among Kush's most successful military leaders. A fierce warrior on the battlefield, the king was also deeply religious. Piankhi's belief that he had the support of the gods fueled his passion for war against Egypt. His courage inspired his troops on the battlefield. Piankhi loved his horses and was buried with eight of his best steeds.

Drawing Conclusions How did Piankhi's belief that he was supported by the gods affect his plans for Egypt?

Direct Teach

Main Idea

❷ Kush and Egypt

Kush and Egypt traded, but they also fought.

Recall What raw materials did Kush sell to Egypt? *gold, copper, stone, ebony, ivory*

Analyze Why did the Egyptians attack Kush? *They feared Kush was getting too powerful and could even attack Egypt.*

Identify Cause and Effect Egypt ruled Kush for about 450 years. How did Egyptian rule affect the people of Kush? *Egyptian language, styles, and religion became widespread in Kush.*

Identify From where did the kings of Kush rule starting in about 850 BC, and why did they rule from there? *from Napata, because the Egyptians had destroyed Kerma*

Checking for Understanding

True or False Answer each statement *T* if it is true or *F* if it is false. If false, explain why.

1. After their invasion of Kush, Egyptian leaders respected Kushite buildings and religion. *F; The Egyptians destroyed Kerma and built temples in what had been Kushite territory.*
2. Kush remained under Egyptian control for 2,000 years. *F; Kush became independent again after about 450 years.*

About the Illustration

This illustration of Piankhi is an artist's conception based on available sources. However, historians are uncertain exactly what Piankhi looked like.

Critical Thinking: Analyzing Information

Below Level

Charting Natural Resources

1. To promote understanding of Kush's trade in raw materials, copy the chart at right for students to see. Omit the blue, italicized answers.
2. Have students copy the chart and complete it by using what they know, by looking at the section's visuals, and by making predictions. Students should also refer back to the sections on Egypt for ideas. **LS Visual/Spatial**

Kush's Exports

Natural Resources	How Might Have Been Used
gold	*coins, jewelry*
copper	*coins, pots, tools*
stone	*pyramids, temples, statues*
ebony	*furniture, decorative items*
ivory	*small statues, jewelry, decorative items*

Answers

Biography *It fueled his passion and made him dedicated to winning. It inspired his troops on the battlefield.*

Reading Check *The flooding Nile provided fertile agricultural land; the river's cataracts served as barriers to invaders.*

Direct Teach

Main Idea

❷ Kush and Egypt

Kush and Egypt traded, but they also fought.

Cause and Effect How did the Assyrians defeat the Kushites? *Their iron weapons were better than the Kushites' bronze weapons.*

Analyze How was Kush able to conquer Egypt? *attacked when Egypt was weak*

Identify Cause and Effect How did the Kush conquest of Egypt change life there? *The Kushites restored some Egyptian cultural practices, such as the use of pyramids, and worked to preserve Egyptian writing.*

CRF: Biography Activity: King Taharqa

Activity Kush's Trade Network Photocopy the map on this page and provide a copy for each student. Supply art materials. Have students draw and cut out symbols for the various products that were traded along the network. Ask students to put the symbols in their places of origin and then to move them along the trade route to their destinations.

LS Kinesthetic, Visual/Spatial

Alternative Assessment Handbook, Rubric 21: Map Reading

CRF: Primary Source Activity: Text Describing the Selection of Aspulta as King of Kush

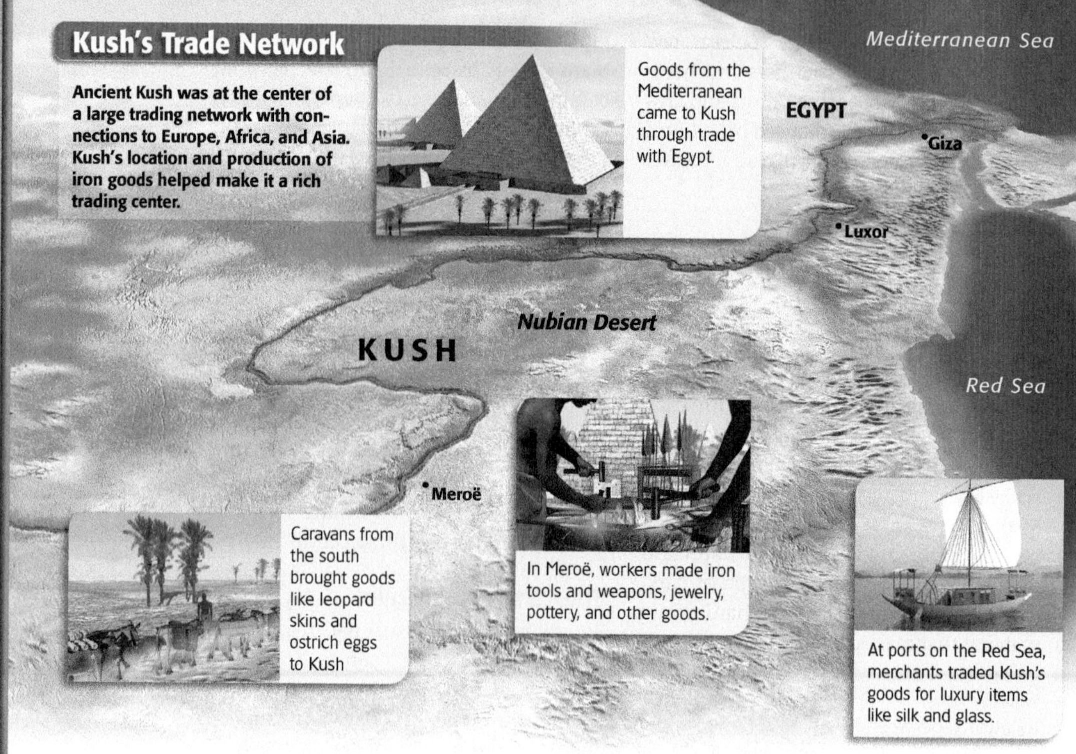

Kush's Trade Network
Ancient Kush was at the center of a large trading network with connections to Europe, Africa, and Asia. Kush's location and production of iron goods helped make it a rich trading center.
Mediterranean Sea
Goods from the Mediterranean came to Kush through trade with Egypt.
EGYPT
Giza
Luxor
Nubian Desert
KUSH
Red Sea
Meroë
Caravans from the south brought goods like leopard skins and ostrich eggs to Kush
In Meroë, workers made iron tools and weapons, jewelry, pottery, and other goods.
At ports on the Red Sea, merchants traded Kush's goods for luxury items like silk and glass.

left Egypt open to attack. In the 700s BC a Kushite king, Kashta, seized on Egypt's weakness and attacked it. By about 751 BC he had conquered Upper Egypt. He then established relations with Lower Egypt.

After Kashta died, his son **Piankhi** (PYAN-kee) continued to attack Egypt. The armies of Kush captured many cities, including Egypt's ancient capital. Piankhi fought the Egyptians because he believed that the gods wanted him to rule all of Egypt. By the time he died in about 716 BC, Piankhi had accomplished this task. His kingdom extended north from Napata to the Nile Delta.

The Kushite Dynasty

After Piankhi died, his brother Shabaka (SHAB-uh-kuh) took control of the kingdom. Shabaka then declared himself pharaoh. This declaration began the 25th Dynasty, or Kushite Dynasty, in Egypt.

Shabaka and later rulers of his dynasty believed that they were heirs of the great pharaohs of Egypt's past. They tried to restore old Egyptian cultural practices and renew faded traditions. Some of these practices and traditions had been abandoned during Egypt's period of weakness. For example, Shabaka was buried in a pyramid. The Egyptians had stopped building pyramids for their rulers centuries before.

The Kushite rulers of Egypt built new temples to Egyptian gods and restored old temples. They also worked to preserve Egyptian writings. As a result, Egyptian culture thrived during the 25th Dynasty.

Collaborative Learning

Above Level

Victory Newspaper

Research Required

1. Have students create an ancient Kushite newspaper covering the conquest of Egypt. First, brainstorm with students possible ideas for articles about the military campaign and occupation of Egypt.
2. Organize students into pairs. Have each team research a topic. One member of each pair should be the researcher and the other the writer. Ask students to write their articles in column format and to include headlines.
3. Have volunteers read their articles to the class. If possible, assemble students' columns into a newspaper format, while discussing with the class the columns placement and importance. Display the completed newspaper.

LS Interpersonal, Verbal/Linguistic

Alternative Assessment Handbook, Rubrics 23: Newspapers; and 30: Research

The End of Kushite Rule in Egypt

The Kushite Dynasty remained strong in Egypt for about 40 years. In the 670s BC, however, the powerful army of the Assyrians from Mesopotamia invaded Egypt. The Assyrians' iron weapons were better than the Kushites' bronze weapons. Although the Kushites were skilled archers, they could not stop the invaders. The Kushites were steadily pushed southward. In just 10 years the Assyrians had driven the Kushite forces completely out of Egypt.

READING CHECK **Analyzing** How did internal problems in Egypt benefit Kush?

Later Kush

After they lost control of Egypt, the people of Kush devoted themselves to agriculture and trade, hoping to make their country rich again. Within a few centuries, the kingdom of Kush had indeed become prosperous and powerful once more.

Kush's Iron Industry

The economic center of Kush during this period was at Meroë (MER-oh-wee), the kingdom's new capital. Meroë's location on the east bank of the Nile helped Kush's economy to grow. Large deposits of gold could be found nearby, as could forests of ebony and other wood. More importantly, the area around Meroë was full of rich iron ore deposits.

In this location, the Kushites developed Africa's first iron industry. Iron ore and wood for furnaces were easily available, so the iron industry grew quickly.

The Expansion of Trade

In time, Meroë became the center of a large **trade network**, a system of people in different lands who trade goods. The Kushites sent goods down the Nile to Egypt. From there, Egyptian and Greek **merchants**, or traders, carried goods to ports on the Mediterranean and Red seas and to southern Africa. These goods may have eventually reached India, and perhaps China.

Kush's **exports**—items sent out to other regions—included gold, pottery, iron tools, slaves, and ivory. Kushite merchants also exported leopard skins, ostrich feathers, and elephants. In return, the Kushites received **imports**—goods brought in from other regions—such as fine jewelry and luxury items from Egypt, Asia, and other lands along the Mediterranean Sea.

Kushite Culture

As Kushite trade grew, merchants came into contact with people from other cultures. As a result, the people of Kush combined customs from other cultures with their own unique Kushite culture.

The most obvious influence on Kushite culture was Egypt. Many buildings in Meroë, especially temples, resembled those in Egypt. Many people in Kush worshipped Egyptian gods and wore Egyptian clothing. Kushite rulers used the title *pharaoh* and were buried in pyramids.

THE IMPACT TODAY More than 50 ancient Kushite pyramids still stand near the ruins of Meroë.

Many elements of Kushite culture were not borrowed. Kushite houses and daily life were unique. One Greek geographer noted some Kushite differences.

> "The houses in the cities are formed by interweaving split pieces of palm wood or of bricks. ...They hunt elephants, lions, and panthers. There are also serpents ... and there are many other kinds of wild animals."
>
> –Strabo, *The Geographies*

In addition to Egyptian gods, the people of Kush worshipped their own gods. They also developed their own written language, Meroitic. Unfortunately, historians are not yet able to understand Meroitic.

Direct Teach

Main Idea

③ Later Kush

Later Kush became a trading power with a unique culture.

Identify What city became the capital and economic center of later Kush? *Meroë*

Recall How did Kush rebuild its economy? *through agriculture and trade*

Make Inferences In what parts of the world might archaeologists find Kushite export items? *Egypt, the Mediterranean and Red seas, southern Africa, possibly India and China*

Identify What Kushite customs were borrowed from other cultures? *Egyptian-style temples, religion, clothing, and pyramids*

Did you know . . .

As early as 4000 BC, people knew how to make iron objects from meteorites. Centuries later, people mastered smelting—heating iron ore in a furnace using charcoal.

Differentiating Instruction

Advanced/Gifted and Talented

Above Level | Research Required

1. Have students conduct research into how ancient peoples made iron. Then organize students into groups of four and have students choose a role from among the following: wood cutter, miner, bellows operator, and blacksmith.
2. Ask each group to write a short skit that explains how iron is made. Skits should be suitable for presentation to elementary school students, as if they were on a field trip to a Kushite iron-making workshop.
3. Have the students perform their skits for the class. Discuss the skits to make sure that students understand the iron-making process. **LS Interpersonal, Kinesthetic**

Alternative Assessment Handbook, Rubrics 30: Research; and 33: Skits and Reader's Theater

Answers

Reading Check *They made Egypt weak and vulnerable to attack from Kush.*

Direct Teach

History Close-up

Rulers of Kush

Activity Ask students these questions to highlight similarities and differences between Kushite and Egyptian culture.

1. Which culture believed their rulers to be gods? *both*
2. How were Kushite pyramids different from Egyptian pyramids? *smaller, different style*
3. How were Kushite queens viewed compared to Egyptian queens? *seem to have been more important*
4. Why did the Kushites and Egyptians carve on stone? *to commemorate important buildings and events*

Linking to Today

Collections of Kushite Artifacts Some of the finest collections of Kushite artifacts are here in the United States. These collections are on display at Boston's Museum of Fine Arts, Philadelphia's University Museum, and Chicago's Oriental Institute Museum. These museums have all participated in archaeological digs in Nubia.

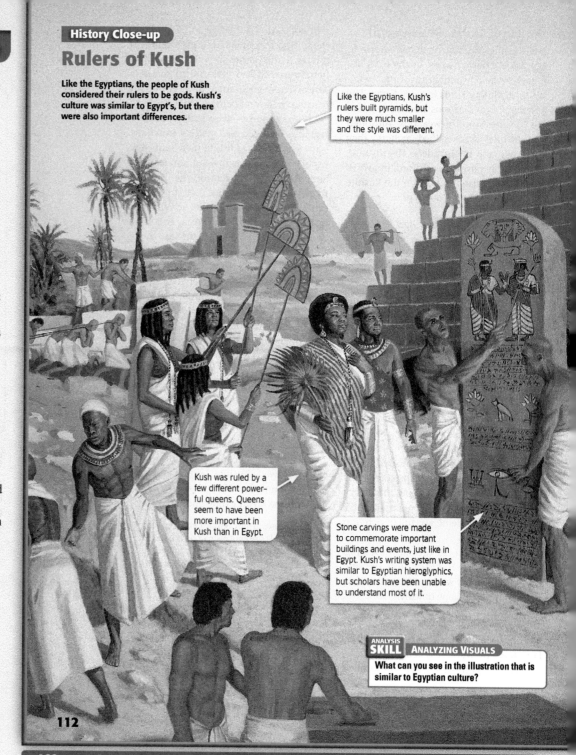

Answers

Analyzing Visuals *pyramids, wigs, clothing and jewelry styles, stone carvings*

History Close-up

Rulers of Kush

Like the Egyptians, the people of Kush considered their rulers to be gods. Kush's culture was similar to Egypt's, but there were also important differences.

Like the Egyptians, Kush's rulers built pyramids, but they were much smaller and the style was different.

Kush was ruled by a few different powerful queens. Queens seem to have been more important in Kush than in Egypt.

Stone carvings were made to commemorate important buildings and events, just like in Egypt. Kush's writing system was similar to Egyptian hieroglyphics, but scholars have been unable to understand most of it.

ANALYSIS SKILL ANALYZING VISUALS

What can you see in the illustration that is similar to Egyptian culture?

112

Differentiating Instruction

Special Needs Learners **Below Level**

Materials: art supplies

Have students design their own stone carvings to represent information about Kush.

1. Discuss with students what they have learned about ancient Kush and its relations with Egypt.
2. Have each student identify two pieces of information they know about ancient Kush.
3. Have students study the stone carving on this page. Tell students to draw on paper a stone carving that uses pictures to relate their two pieces of information. **LS Visual/Spatial**

Alternative Assessment Handbook, Rubric 3: Artwork

Women in Kushite Society

The women of Kush were expected to be active in their society. They worked in the fields, raised children, cooked, and performed other household tasks.

Some Kushite women rose to positions of **authority**. Some served as co-rulers with their husbands or sons. A few women ruled the empire alone. Historians believe that the first woman to rule Kush was **Queen Shanakhdakheto** (shah-nakh-dah-KEE-toh). She ruled from 170 BC to 150 BC.

READING CHECK **Contrasting** How was Kushite culture unlike Egyptian culture?

The Decline of Kush

Kush gradually declined in power. A series of problems within the kingdom weakened its economy. One problem was that Kush's cattle were allowed to overgraze. When cows ate all the grass, wind blew the soil away, causing farmers to produce less food.

In addition, ironmakers used up the forests near Meroë. As wood became scarce, furnaces shut down. Kush produced fewer weapons and trade goods.

Kush was also weakened by a loss of trade. Foreign merchants set up new trade routes that went around Kush. One such trade route bypassed Kush in favor of Aksum (AHK-soom), a kingdom located along the Red Sea in what is today Ethiopia and Eritrea. In the first two centuries AD, Aksum grew wealthy from trade.

By the AD 300s Kush had lost much of its wealth and military might. The king of Aksum took advantage of his former trade rival's weakness. In about AD 350 the Aksumite army of **King Ezana** (AY-zah-nah) destroyed Meroë and took over Kush.

In the late 300s, the rulers of Aksum became Christian. About two hundred years later, the Nubians also converted. The last influences of Kush had disappeared.

READING CHECK **Summarizing** What factors led to the decline of Kush?

SUMMARY AND PREVIEW From their capital at Meroë, the people of Kush controlled a powerful trading network. Next, you will learn about a land that may have traded with Kush—India.

ACADEMIC VOCABULARY

authority power or influence

Much of the population of Ethiopia, which includes what used to be Aksum, is still Christian today.

Section 5 Assessment

hmhsocialstudies.com ONLINE QUIZ

Reviewing Ideas, Terms, and People

1. **a. Recall** On which river did Kush develop?
   b. Evaluate How did Nubia's natural resources influence the early history of Kush?
2. **a. Identify** Who was **Piankhi** and why was he important to the history of Kush?
   b. Analyze What were some elements of Egyptian culture that became popular in Kush?
   c. Draw Conclusions Why is the 25th Dynasty significant in the history of both Egypt and Kush?
3. **a. Describe** What advantages did the location of Meroë offer to the Kushites?
   b. Compare How were Kushite and Egyptian cultures similar?
4. **a. Identify** Who conquered Kush in the AD 300s?
   b. Evaluate What was the impact of new trading routes on Kush?

Critical Thinking

5. **Identifying Cause and Effect** Create a chart like this one. Using your notes, list an effect for each cause.

Cause	Effect
Thutmose I invades Kush.	
Power of Egyptian pharaohs declines.	
Piankhi attacks Egypt.	

FOCUS ON WRITING

6. **Taking Notes on Kush** Review this section and take notes on those people, places, and events that would make good clues for your riddle about Kush.

Section 5 Assessment Answers

1. **a.** the Nile
   b. Nubia's natural resources were in demand in Egypt, so they helped Kush grow in wealth and power.
2. **a.** one of Kush's most successful military leaders; he conquered Egypt
   b. speaking Egyptian, using Egyptian names, wearing Egyptian-style clothing, and adopting Egyptian religious practices
   c. possible answer—because Kushite leaders ruled and restored many ancient Egyptian cultural practices and traditions
3. **a.** nearby gold, ebony and other wood, iron ore deposits
   b. had similar clothing and building styles, used title *pharaoh*, worshipped some similar gods, had some female rulers
4. **a.** Aksum
   b. Kush was weakened by loss of trade.
5. possible answers—Kush becomes part of Egypt; Kushite leaders regain control of Kush; Kush extends to the Nile Delta.
6. Students' answers will vary but should reflect section content.

Direct Teach

Main Idea

4 The Decline of Kush

Both internal and external factors led to the decline of Kush.

Describe Why did agriculture and ironmaking decline in Kush? *Cows ate the grass, and the soil blew away; ironmakers cut down the forests.*

Contrast How were the roles of Kushite women different from women's roles in other cultures? *Unlike in most ancient cultures, women sometimes gained great authority. Some Kushite women rose to high positions in religion and government.*

Analyze How did shifts in trade affect Kush? *New trade routes that went around Kush weakened Kush and its economy further.*

CRF: Literature Activity: The Fall of Meroë

Review & Assess

Close

Call on volunteers to pose questions about the images in this section and on others to suggest answers.

Review

Online Quiz, Section 5

Assess

SE Section 5 Assessment

PASS: Section 5 Quiz

Alternative Assessment Handbook

Reteach/Classroom Intervention

Guided Reading Workbook, Section 5

Interactive Skills Tutor CD-ROM

Answers

Reading Check *Kushite culture differed from Egypt's in its housing, kinds of animals hunted, religion, language, and the role of women.*

Reading Check *With the loss of resources such as fertile soil and forests, Kush's military and economic power declined. New trade routes that bypassed Kush furthered its decline.*

Social Studies Skills

Assessing Primary and Secondary Sources

Activity Have students consider the following scenario: They missed the last football game at their school. They asked several of their friends who attended to describe the game. The students then asked other friends who played in the game to discuss it. The students also read a local newspaper article about the game. Have students discuss how each of these accounts of the game might differ. How might some of the accounts be biased or inaccurate? Why might students want to hear or read all of these accounts? How might the accounts combine to form a more complete picture of the game? Encourage student discussion.

Next, have students discuss the importance of primary and secondary sources in the study of history. Then have each student create a graphic organizer of his or her choosing that illustrates what primary and secondary sources are, the problems with each (such as bias), and how they combine to provide a better picture of history.

LS Verbal/Linguistic, Visual/Spatial

Alternative Assessment Handbook, Rubric 13: Graphic Organizer

Interactive Skills Tutor CD-ROM, Lesson 2: Identify Primary and Secondary Sources; Lesson 17: Interpret Primary Sources

Social Studies Skills

Analysis | Critical Thinking | Economics | Study

Assessing Primary and Secondary Sources

Understand the Skill

Primary sources in history are materials created by people who lived during the times they describe. Examples include letters, diaries, and photographs. *Secondary sources* are accounts written later by someone who was not present. They are designed to teach about or discuss a historical topic. This textbook is an example of a secondary source.

Together, primary and secondary sources can present a good picture of a historical period or event. However, they must be used carefully to make sure that the picture they present is accurate.

Learn the Skill

Here are some questions to ask to help you judge the accuracy of primary and secondary sources.

1. **What is it?** Is it a firsthand account or is it based on information provided by others? In other words, is it primary or secondary?
2. **Who wrote it?** For a primary source, what was the author's connection to what he or she was writing about? For a secondary source, what makes the author an authority on this subject?
3. **Who is the audience?** Was the information meant for the public? Was it meant for a friend or for the writer alone? The intended audience can influence what the writer has to say.
4. **What is the purpose?** Authors of either primary or secondary sources can have reasons to exaggerate—or even lie—to suit their own goals or purposes. Look for evidence of emotion, opinion, or bias in the source. These might influence the accuracy of the account.
5. **Does other evidence support the source?** Look for other information that supports the source's account. Compare different sources whenever possible.

Practice and Apply the Skill

Below are two passages about the military in ancient Egypt. Read them both and use the guidelines to answer the questions that follow.

> "The pharaohs began . . . leading large armies out of a land that had once known only small police forces and militia. The Egyptians quickly extended their military and commercial influence over an extensive region that included the rich provinces of Syria . . . and the numbers of Egyptian slaves grew swiftly."
>
> –C. Warren Hollister, from *Roots of the Western Tradition*

> "Let me tell you how the soldier fares . . . how he goes to Syria, and how he marches over the mountains. His bread and water are borne [carried] upon his shoulders like the load of [a donkey]; they make his neck bent as that of [a donkey], and the joints of his back are bowed [bent]. His drink is stinking water . . . When he reaches the enemy, he is trapped like a bird, and he has no strength in his limbs."
>
> –from *Wings of the Falcon: Life and Thought of Ancient Egypt*, translated by Joseph Kaster

1. Which quote is a primary source, and which is a secondary source?
2. Is there evidence of opinion, emotion, or bias in the second quote? Explain why or why not.
3. Which information is more likely to be accurate on this subject? Explain your answer.

Social Studies Skills: Assessing Primary and Secondary Sources — At Level

Applying the Skill

1. Have students look at the Egyptian tomb painting on p. 88, which shows a couple harvesting their crop. Ask students to look closely at the image and write two questions about Egypt that could be answered from the image.
2. Then have students write two questions about Egypt that would best be answered by a secondary source, such as a history book about Egypt.
3. Have volunteers discuss their questions with the class. Continue the exercise by having students suggest other questions about Egypt that could best be answered by a primary source or a secondary source.
4. **Extend** Have students create a poster that lists the five guidelines for assessing primary and secondary sources and provides an image to illustrate each guideline.

LS Logical/Mathematical, Visual Spatial

Alternative Assessment Handbook, Rubrics 11: Discussions; and 28: Posters

Answers

Practice and Apply the Skill

1. *Hollister quote—secondary;* Wings of the Falcon *quote—primary;* **2.** *yes, emotion and opinion, as the author describes the hardships soldiers face;* **3.** *The first quote provides an objective overall view of the period, but the second illustrates how some soldiers of the time thought and felt about events.*

CHAPTER 4

Chapter Review

History's Impact

▶ **video series**

Review the video to answer the focus question:

What was the original purpose of the pyramids?

Visual Summary

Use the visual summary below to help you review the main ideas of the chapter.

QUICK FACTS

Egypt
Egyptian civilization developed along the Nile River. There, powerful pharaohs ruled a diverse society whose achievements included building impressive pyramids and developing a writing system.

Kush
Kush developed farther south along the Nile. Ruled by their own kings and queens, the Kushites had extensive interaction with the Egyptians and blended Egyptian influences into their own advanced culture.

Reviewing Vocabulary, Terms, and People

For each group of terms below, circle the letter of the term that does not relate to the others. Then write a sentence that explains how the other two terms are related.

1. **a.** cataract
   b. delta
   c. dynasty
2. **a.** afterlife
   b. mummies
   c. engineering
3. **a.** hieroglyphics
   b. Rosetta Stone
   c. obelisk
4. **a.** exports
   b. imports
   c. papyrus

Comprehension and Critical Thinking

SECTION 1 *(pages 86–89)*

5. **a. Describe** Besides crops, what foods did the Nile provide?
   b. Analyze Why did Menes wear a double crown?
   c. Predict What do you think happened in the years when the Nile River did not flood?

SECTION 2 *(pages 90–95)*

6. **a. Identify** In what type of structure were pharaohs buried?
   b. Analyze How were beliefs in the afterlife linked to items placed in tombs?
   c. Elaborate Why did nobles and commoners alike obey the pharaoh?

SECTION 3 *(pages 96–100)*

7 **a. Describe** What factors contributed to Egypt's wealth during the New Kingdom?

Answers

Visual Summary

Review and Inquiry Have students use the visual summary to review the main events, personalities, and achievements of the ancient Egyptians and Kushites.

Quick Facts Transparency: Ancient Egypt and Kush Visual Summary

Reviewing Terms and People

1. **c.** Cataract and delta are features in a river, such as the Nile.
2. **c.** Egyptians created mummies because of their beliefs about the afterlife.
3. **c.** The Rosetta Stone was used to decipher hieroglyphics.
4. **c.** Exports and imports are elements of trade.

Comprehension and Critical Thinking

5. **a.** fish, geese, and ducks
   b. to symbolize the unification of Lower and Upper Egypt
   c. possible answers—People starved because of famine; they depended on food they had stored from the previous season; they traded for food.
6. **a.** pyramids
   b. Items were placed in tombs to fulfill the needs of the buried person's ka.
   c. They believed he was a god.
7. **a.** conquest and trade
   b. become a soldier
   c. invasions by the Sea Peoples and others

Review and Assessment Resources

Review and Reinforce

- SE Chapter Review
- **CRF:** Chapter Review Activity
- Quick Facts Transparency: Ancient Egypt and Kush Visual Summary
- Spanish Chapter Summaries Audio CD
- Online Chapter Summaries in Six Languages
- TOS Holt McDougal PuzzleView

Assess

- SE Standardized Test Practice
- PASS: Chapter Test
- Alternative Assessment Handbook
- TOS ExamView Assessment Suite, Chapter Test
- Differentiated Instruction Modified Material CD-ROM: Chapter Test
- Online Assessment Program, in the Interactive Student Edition

Reteach/Intervene

- Guided Reading Workbook
- Differentiated Instruction Teacher Management System: Lesson Plans
- Modified Material for Struggling Students CD-ROM
- Interactive Skills Tutor CD-ROM

Chapter Resources

Answers

8. **a.** imaginary creature with the body of a lion and the head of another animal or a human
b. hieroglyphics, it had 600 symbols, rather than the 26 in our alphabet. Hieroglyphics could also be written horizontally or vertically, left to right, or right to left. Our writing is horizontal left to right.
c. It was Egypt's largest temple and is lavishly decorated.

9. **a.** in Nubia, south of Egypt along the Nile
b. Egypt feared Kush would grow powerful enough to attack Egypt.
c. Kush ruled Egypt and restored many ancient Egyptian cultural practices and traditions.

Reviewing Themes

10. possible answers—yes, if another reliable source of water were found; no, because the Nile and what it provides are unique

11. Because religious beliefs were such a large part of their cultures, they influenced their government, art, architecture, and almost every aspect of daily life.

12. deposits of iron ore and forests to fuel furnaces

Using the Internet

13. Go to hmhsocialstudies.com to access a rubric for this activity.

---

b. Analyze How might a young Egyptian rise in social status?

c. Elaborate What caused the New Kingdom to fall?

SECTION 4 *(pages 102–106)*

8. a. Identify What is a sphinx?

b. Describe What was the name of the Egyptian system of writing and how does it differ from our system of writing?

c. Elaborate Why is the temple at Karnak so famous?

SECTION 5 *(pages 107–113)*

9. a. Describe Where did Kushite civilization develop?

b. Draw Conclusions Why did Egypt want to gain control of Kush?

c. Evaluate Why was the 25th Dynasty so important for both Kush and Egypt?

Reviewing Themes

10. Geography Do you think that societies like those in Egypt and Kush could have grown up anywhere besides the Nile River Valley? Why or why not?

11. Religion How did religious beliefs shape both Egyptian and Kushite culture?

12. Economics What led to the creation of Africa's first iron industry in Kush?

Using the Internet

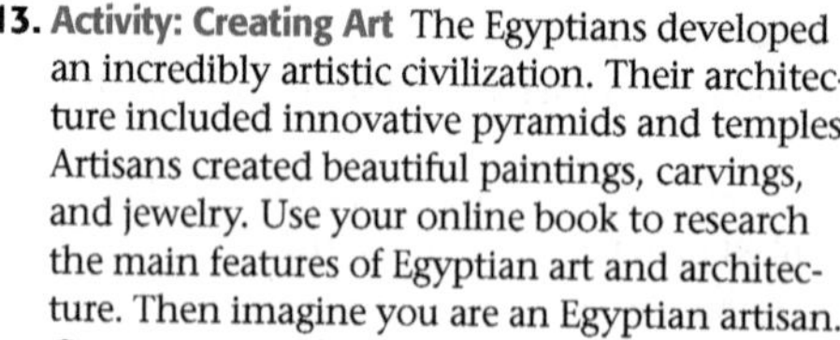

13. Activity: Creating Art The Egyptians developed an incredibly artistic civilization. Their architecture included innovative pyramids and temples. Artisans created beautiful paintings, carvings, and jewelry. Use your online book to research the main features of Egyptian art and architecture. Then imagine you are an Egyptian artisan. Create a piece of art to place inside a pharaoh's tomb. Include hieroglyphics telling the pharaoh about your art.

hmhsocialstudies.com

Reading Skills

Causes and Effects in History Read the following passage and answer the questions.

> Much of Egyptian religion is focused on the afterlife. The Egyptians believed that the afterlife was a happy place. Their belief in the afterlife stemmed from their idea of *ka*, or a person's life force. When a person died, his or her *ka* left the body and became a spirit. The *ka*, however, remained linked to the body and could not leave its burial site. The *ka* had all the same needs that the person had when he or she was living. To fulfill the *ka's* needs, people filled tombs with objects for the afterlife.

14. What is the cause of the Egyptian custom of putting objects in tombs?

15. According to the passage, what is an effect of the Egyptian belief in *ka*?

Social Studies Skills

16. Assessing Primary and Secondary Sources Write three questions you would want to ask about a primary source and three questions you would want to ask about a secondary source that deals with the history of Egypt and Kush.

Focus on Writing

17. Writing Riddles You have all the information you need for your riddles, but you may have to narrow your list of questions. Choose five details about Egypt and five details about Kush. Then, write a sentence about each detail. Each sentence of your riddle should be a statement ending with "me." For example, if you were writing about the United States, you might say, "In the north, Canada borders me." After writing five sentences for each riddle, end each riddle with "Who am I?"

Reading Skills

14. They believed the *ka* had the same needs as a living person.

15. People put objects in tombs for the afterlife.

Social Studies Skills

16. Responses will vary but should display knowledge of both Kush and Egypt.

Focus on Writing

17. Rubric Students' riddles should

- include one about Egypt and one about Kush
- follow the assigned statement structure
- use information from the chapter

CRF: Focus on Writing Activity: A Riddle.

CHAPTER 4 Standardized Test Practice

DIRECTIONS: Read each question and write the letter of the best response.

1

> Oh great god and ruler, the gift of Re,
> God of the Sun.
> Oh great protector of Egypt and its people.
> Great one who has saved us from the horrible Tehenu.
> You, who have turned back the Hittites.
> You, who have fortified our western border to forever protect us from our enemies.
> We bless you, oh great one.
> We worship and honor you, oh great pharaoh.

A tribute such as the one above would have been written in honor of which Egyptian ruler?

A Khufu
B Ramses the Great
C King Tutankhamen
D Queen Hatshepsut

2 **The Nile helped civilization develop in Egypt and Nubia in all of the following ways *except* by**

A providing a source of food and water.
B allowing farming to develop.
C enriching the soil along its banks.
D protecting against invasion from the west.

3 **The most fertile soil in Egypt was located in the**

A Nile Delta.
B desert.
C cataracts.
D far south.

4 **Which of the following statements about the relationship of Egypt and Kush is *NOT* true?**

A Egypt ruled Kush for many centuries.
B Kush was an important trading partner of Egypt.
C Egypt sent the first people to colonize Kush.
D Kush ruled Egypt for a period of time.

5 **How did Egypt influence Kush?**

A Egypt taught Kush how to raise cattle.
B Egypt helped Kush develop its irrigation system.
C Egypt taught Kush to make iron products.
D Kush learned about pyramids from Egypt.

Connecting with Past Learnings

6 **In this chapter, you learned about hieroglyphics, one of the world's first writing systems. In Chapter 3, you read about another ancient writing system called**

A Sumerian.
B Hammurabi.
C ziggurat.
D cuneiform.

7 **In Chapter 3 you read about Sargon I, who first united Mesopotamia under one ruler. Which Egyptian ruler's accomplishments were most similar to Sargon's?**

A King Ezana's
B Khufu's
C Menes's
D Hatshepsut's

Answers

Standardized Test Practice

1. B
Break Down the Question This question requires students to recall the notable features of four pharaohs' reigns. Refer students who miss it to Section 3.

2. D
Break Down the Question Refer students who miss this question to the map in Section 1 and the fact that desert protected against invasion from the west.

3. A
Break Down the Question This question requires students to recall factual information. Refer students who miss it to Section 1.

4. C
Break Down the Question This question requires students to recall that civilization developed independently in Egypt and Kush.

5. D
Break Down the Question Refer students who missed the question to the *Kushite Culture* material in Section 5.

6. D
Break Down the Question This question requires students to recall information from the previous chapter on Mesopotamia.

7. C
Break Down the Question Remind students who missed the question that Menes united Egypt, as Sargon I had united Mesopotamia.

Intervention Resources

Reproducible

- Guided Reading Workbook
- Differentiating Instruction Teacher Management System: Lesson Plans

Technology

- Quick Facts Transparency: Ancient Egypt Visual Summary
- Modified Material for Struggling Students CD-ROM
- Interactive Skills Tutor CD-ROM

Tips for Test Taking

Search for Skips and Smudges Remind students that to avoid losing points on a machine-graded test they should be sure they did not skip any answers, gave only one answer for each question, made the marks dark and within the lines, and erased any smudges. Students should also make sure there are no stray pencil marks, such as from pencil tapping. They should cleanly erase places where they changed their minds.

Preteach

Bellringer

Motivate Ask students to choose one place with which they are very familiar and spend a lot of time, such as their bedroom or their backyard. Have students list each of the five senses. Have them note descriptive details about the place they have chosen next to each sense. Ask: What does the collection of sensory observations tell you about the location? Tell students that in this workshop they will use the same process to write a description of a place in ancient Mesopotamia, Egypt, or Kush.

Direct Teach

Making Generalizations

Begin by Concluding Tell students that if they begin this assignment by gathering several details, they will naturally come to some realization about the place. Ask students to imagine themselves living in the place they are describing. What can they now say about the place or about the people living there? Students' generalization statements can be made from one of these answers.

Teaching Tip

Remembering the Senses A quick way to help students to recall each of the five senses quickly is to remind them that if they touch the sense organs located on their heads, they will have used all five. Ears: *hearing*, eyes: *sight*, nose: *smell*, tongue: *taste*, and the fingers they touched them with: *touch*. Though this is a very simple procedure, it is a time-saver and can be helpful on exams.

A Description of a Historical Place

Assignment
Write a description of a place—a city, village, building, or monument—in ancient Mesopotamia, Egypt, or the Fertile Crescent.

If a picture is worth a thousand words, then a thousand words could add up to a good description. Writers turn to description when they want to explain what a place is like—what you would see if you were there, or what you might hear, smell, or touch.

1. Prewrite

Picking a Subject and a Main Idea

Think about the civilizations of ancient Mesopotamia, Egypt, and the Fertile Crescent. Which civilization seems most interesting to you? What villages, cities, or buildings seem interesting? Select one place and use this textbook, the Internet, or sources in your library to find out more about it.

You also need to decide on your point of view about your subject. For example, was this place scary, exciting, or overwhelming?

Choosing Details

As you conduct your research, look for details to show your readers what it would have been like to actually be in that place.

- **Sensory Details** What color(s) do you associate with your subject? What shape or shapes do you see? What sounds would you hear if you were there? What could you touch—rough walls, dry grass, a smooth, polished stone?
- **Factual Details** How big was this place? Where was it located? When did it exist? If people were there, what were they doing?

When you choose the details to use in your description, think about your point of view on this place. If it was exciting, choose details that will help you show that.

TIP Organizing Details
Organize the details you gather in one of these ways.

- **Spatial Order** Arrange details according to where they are. You can describe things from right to left, top to bottom, or faraway to close up.
- **Chronological Order** Arrange details in the order they occurred or in the order that you experienced them.
- **Order of Importance** Arrange details from the most to least important or vice versa.

2. Write

This framework will help you use your notes to write a first draft.

A Writer's Framework

Introduction	Body	Conclusion
■ Identify your subject and your point of view on it. ■ Give your readers any background information that they might need.	■ Describe your subject, using sensory and factual details. ■ Follow a consistent and logical order.	■ Briefly summarize the most important details about the place. ■ Reveal your point of view about the place.

Differentiating Instruction

English-Language Learners

Below Level

Standard English Mastery

1. Assist English-language learners with the vocabulary of description by offering sample sentences for each sense. Use your classroom as an example. *The room* _smells_ *of new textbooks and the* _scent_ *of sharpened pencils.*
2. Encourage students to use dictionaries to look up words they want to use to be sure their thoughts are translated properly. Check to make sure they choose words appropriate to the description. **LS Verbal/Linguistic**

Advanced/Gifted and Talented

Above Level

1. Suggest that students explain what they sense by making comparisons. Each of these descriptive statements may extend to several sentences. *The smell of wood reminded me of the tree house we had built in the backyard of our old house. Even after we moved out and two years had passed, the smell still reminded me of that special retreat.*
2. Remind students to stay focused on supporting their topic. **LS Verbal/Linguistic**

3. Evaluate and Revise

Evaluating

Use the following questions to discover ways to improve your paper.

Evaluation Questions for a Description of a Place

- Do you immediately catch the reader's interest?
- Do you use sensory and factual details that work together to create a vivid picture of your subject?
- Do you clearly state your point of view or most important idea?
- Is the information organized clearly?
- Do you end the description by summarizing the most important details?

TIP **Showing Location** When describing the physical appearance of something, make sure you use precise words and phrases to explain where a feature is located. Some useful words and phrases for explaining location are *below, beside, down, on top, over, next to, to the right,* and *to the left.*

Revising

We often help others understand or imagine something by making a comparison. Sometimes we compare two things that are really very much alike. For example, "The city grew like San Diego did. It spread along a protected harbor." At other times we compare two things that are not alike. These comparisons are called figures of speech, and they can help your readers see something in an interesting way.

- Similes compare two unlike things by using words such as *like* or *so.* **EXAMPLE** *The city center curved around the harbor like a crescent moon.*
- Metaphors compare two unlike things by saying one is the other. **EXAMPLE** *The city was the queen of the region.*

When you evaluate and revise your description, look for ways you can make your subject clearer by comparing it to something else.

4. Proofread and Publish

- Make sure you use commas correctly with a list of details. **EXAMPLE** *The temple was 67 feet high, 35 feet wide, and 40 feet deep.*
- Share your paper with students who wrote about a similar place. What details do your descriptions share? How are they different?
- Find or create a picture of the place you have described. Ask a classmate or a family member to read your description and compare it to the picture.

Practice and Apply

Use the steps and strategies outlined in this workshop to write your description of a place in ancient Mesopotamia or Africa.

Reteach

Revision

Take Advantage of Technology

Once students finish a paper, they find it almost painful to consider rewriting. Tell students that they are probably better writers than their first draft makes them appear. If they use the spelling and grammar-checking program on a computer, their writing will improve. They will learn to avoid common mistakes as they make their corrections. Remind students that this is not the only step they should use in proofreading their work, as electronic spelling checks are not failsafe. For example, if a student writes *form* and means *from*, the computer would not highlight that as an error.

Teaching Tip

The "I think" Trap

Caution students to avoid using the words "I think" or "In my opinion" in their writing. Remind students that you already know that this is the writer's opinion, as their name is at the top of the page. The same logic can be applied to the "I am going to write about" phrase.

Struggling Readers

Below Level **Standard English Mastery**

1. Guide struggling readers with conducting research on one subject. Print out or photocopy pertinent pages they have chosen. Assist students with highlighting facts that might help them add sensory details.
2. Choose a detail and discuss it before having students write one sentence about the sense to which it refers.
3. Have students write all their sensory detail statements before writing their generalization and category statements for paragraph one.
4. Discuss how their topic is related to the economic problems of the 1930s. Then have students write their final paragraphs. **LS Verbal/Linguistic**

Practice & Apply

Rubric

Students' descriptive essays should

- begin with one generalization about the place.
- have two to four body paragraphs representing specific categories.
- include details using all five senses.
- include details from two or more sources.
- summarize their findings.
- relate their topic to larger issues.
- use correct grammar, punctuation, spelling, and capitalization.

Unit Preview

Introduce the Unit

Share the information in the chapter overviews with students.

Chapter 5 Indian civilization developed and thrived in the Indus River Valley. The Harappan civilization was followed by the Aryans. As Aryan society became more complex, it divided into strict groups. This class system became a central part of Indian society. Two major religions, Hinduism and Buddhism, developed in India. Two great empires also emerged. The Mauryan Empire and the Gupta Empire in turn united much of India. During these empires, Indians made great advances in the arts and science.

Chapter 6 Chinese civilization began in the Huang He and Chang Jiang river valleys. Under the Shang dynasty, people developed a social order and a writing system. The Zhou dynasty succeeded the Shang. This dynasty eventually crumbled, however, and disorder erupted. In response, the new teachings of Confucianism, Daoism, and Legalism emerged. The Qin dynasty unified China with a strong government and a system of standardization. The Han dynasty then created a form of government that valued family, art, and learning. The arts and sciences flourished in China during this period. Trade also expanded, leading to the exchange of products and ideas between China and other cultures. From India, Buddhism came to China and gained many followers.

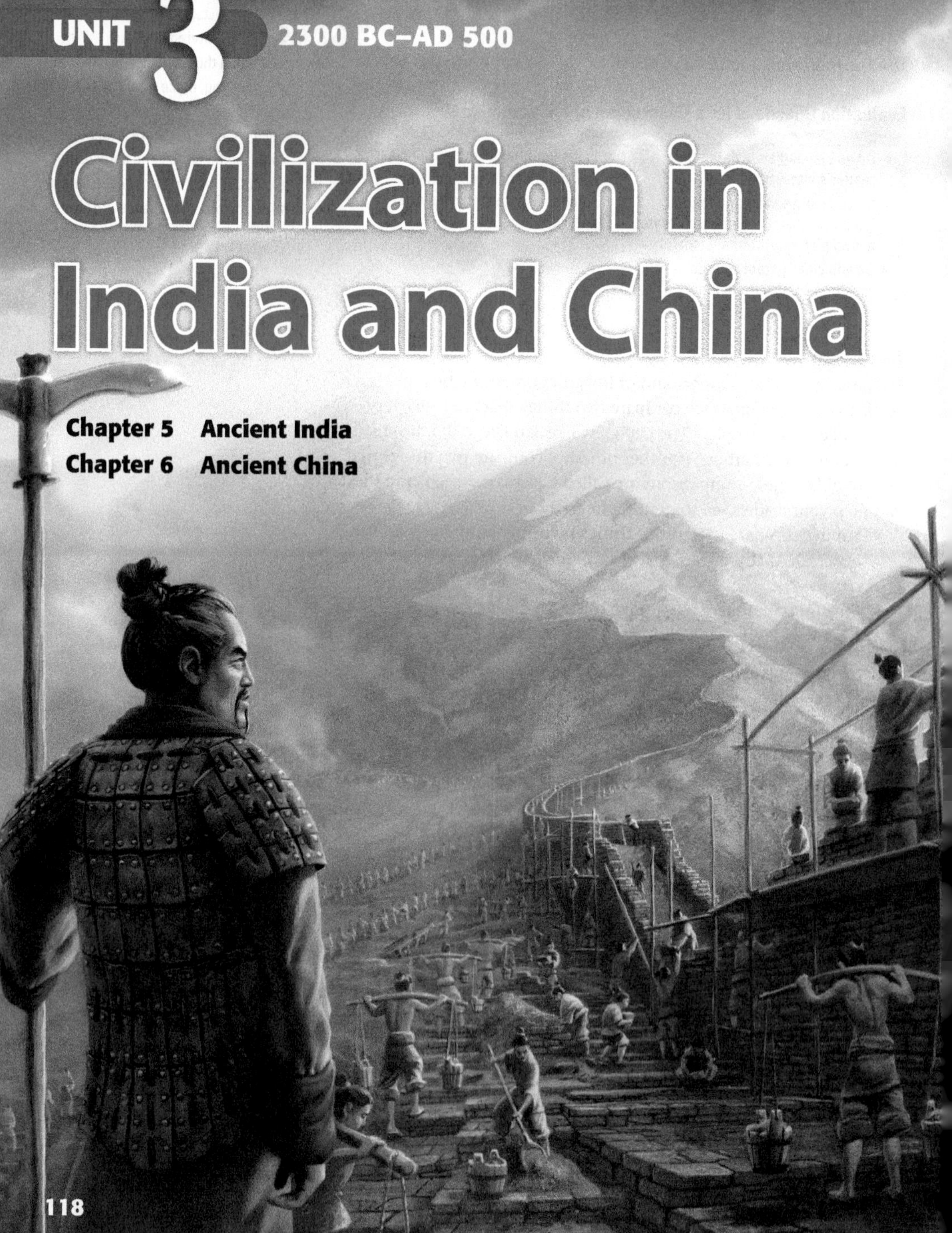

Unit Resources

Planning

- Differentiated Instruction Teacher Management System: Unit Instructional Benchmarking Guides
- TOS Calendar Planner
- Power Presentations with Media Gallery
- A Teacher's Guide to Religion in the Public Schools

Differentiating Instruction

- Differentiated Instruction Teacher Management System: Lesson Plans for Differentiated Instruction
- Differentiated Instruction Modified Worksheets and Tests CD-ROM

Enrichment

- **CRF 5:** Interdisciplinary Project: Ancient India: Aryan Society
- **CRF 6:** Economics and History Activity: The Chinese Economy
- **CRF 6:** Interdisciplinary Project: Ancient China: Dynasty Triptych
- Civic Participation Activities
- Primary Source Library CD-ROM

Assessment

- Progress Assessment System Solution: Unit Test
- TOS ExamView Assessment Suite: Unit Test
- Online Assessment Program, in the Interactive Student Edition
- Alternative Assessment Handbook

The **Differentiated Instruction Teacher Management System** provides a planning and instructional benchmarking guide for this unit.

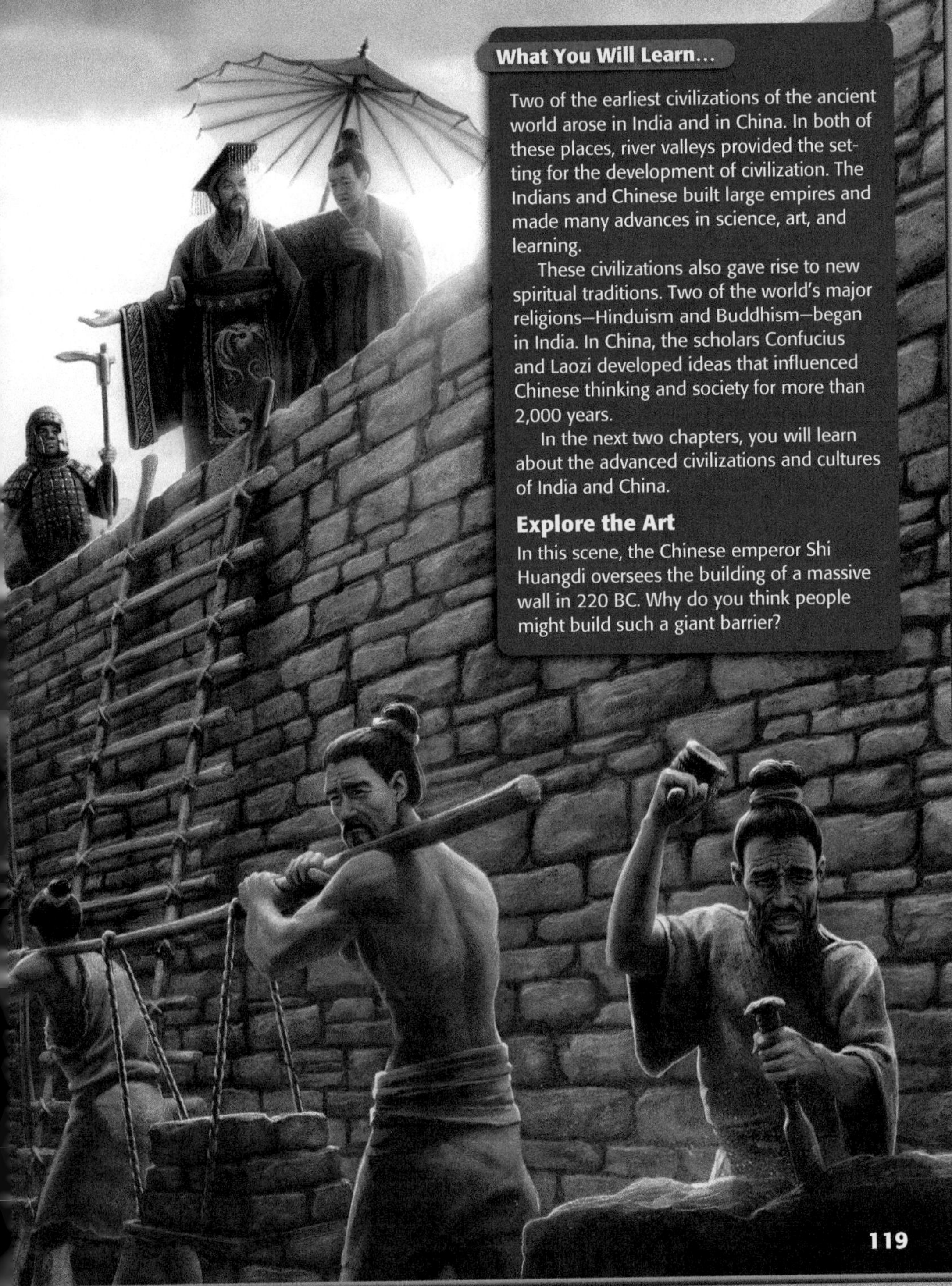

What You Will Learn...
Two of the earliest civilizations of the ancient world arose in India and in China. In both of these places, river valleys provided the setting for the development of civilization. The Indians and Chinese built large empires and made many advances in science, art, and learning.
These civilizations also gave rise to new spiritual traditions. Two of the world's major religions—Hinduism and Buddhism—began in India. In China, the scholars Confucius and Laozi developed ideas that influenced Chinese thinking and society for more than 2,000 years.
In the next two chapters, you will learn about the advanced civilizations and cultures of India and China.
Explore the Art
In this scene, the Chinese emperor Shi Huangdi oversees the building of a massive wall in 220 BC. Why do you think people might build such a giant barrier?
119

Unit Preview

Connect to the Unit

Activity **Comparing and Contrasting China and India** Draw a two-column table for students to see. Label the columns *Similarities* and *Differences.* Ask students how they think India and China are similar to one another. Then ask how they think they are different. Write students' responses in the appropriate columns. As students study this unit, encourage them to refer back to this table and to evaluate their responses.
LS Visual/Spatial

Explore the Art

Chinese emperor Shi Huangdi unified China. He also supported many building projects, including the massive wall pictured at left. This wall formed part of what is now the Great Wall of China. At some 4,500 miles in length, the Great Wall is an enduring example of Chinese ingenuity and engineering.

About the Illustration

This illustration is an artist's conception based on available sources. However, historians are uncertain exactly what this scene looked like.

Democracy and Civic Education

At Level

Justice: Confucianism, Daoism, and Legalism

Research Required

Background The teachings of Confucianism, Daoism, and Legalism emerged in Ancient China in response to a period of political disorder. Each teaching provided different views of life, including views about ideal government and justice.

1. Organize students into small groups. Have each group create a three-column chart and label the columns Confucianism, Daoism, and Legalism. Have group members contrast how the three teachings define ideal government and justice.
2. Have the groups share their responses as you complete a master copy of the chart.
3. Then have the groups conduct research on the court system in their community or state and create charts describing the court system. How does this justice system compare to the concept of justice in each Chinese teaching?
LS Interpersonal, Verbal/Linguistic

Alternative Assessment Handbook, Rubrics 7: Charts; and 11: Discussion

Civic Participation Activities

Answers

Explore the Art *to define their territory and to protect it from hostile invaders by providing a defensive barrier*

Chapter 5 Planning Guide

Ancient India

Overview	Instructional Resources	
CHAPTER 5 **Essential Question:** How do India's rich history and culture affect the world today? **Focus on the Essential Question Podcast**	TOS **Differentiated Instruction Teacher Management System:** • Instructional Benchmarking Guides • Lesson Plans for Differentiated Instruction **Guided Reading Workbook** **Chapter Resource File:** • Chapter Review Activity • Focus on Writing Activity: An Illustrated Poster • Social Studies Skills Activity: Interpreting Diagrams	TOS **Calendar Planner** **Power Presentations with Media Gallery** **Differentiated Instruction Modified Worksheets and Tests CD-ROM** **Student Edition on Audio CD Program** **The World's Music Audio Program**
Section 1: **Geography and Early India** **The Big Idea:** Indian civilization first developed on the Indus River.	TOS **Differentiated Instruction Teacher Management System:** Section 1 Lesson Plan **Guided Reading Workbook:** Section 1 **Chapter Resource File:** • Vocabulary Builder Activity, Section 1 • History and Geography Activity: The Indus River Valley	**Daily Bellringer Transparency:** Section 1 **Map Transparency:** India: Physical **Map Transparency:** Aryan Migrations **Internet Activity:** Ancient India Advertisement **Animated History:** Aryan Migrations
Section 2: **Origins of Hinduism** **The Big Idea:** Hinduism, the largest religion in India today, developed out of ancient Indian beliefs and practices.	TOS **Differentiated Instruction Teacher Management System:** Section 2 Lesson Plan **Guided Reading Workbook:** Section 2 **Chapter Resource File:** • Vocabulary Builder Activity, Section 2 • Primary Source Activity: Gandhi's Autobiography	**Daily Bellringer Transparency:** Section 2 **Quick Facts Transparency:** *The Varnas* **Quick Facts Transparency:** Major Beliefs of Hinduism
Section 3: **Origins of Buddhism** **The Big Idea:** Buddhism began in India and became a major religion.	TOS **Differentiated Instruction Teacher Management System:** Section 3 Lesson Plan **Guided Reading Workbook:** Section 3 **Chapter Resource File:** • Vocabulary Builder Activity, Section 3	**Daily Bellringer Transparency:** Section 3 **Quick Facts Transparency:** The Eightfold Path **Map Transparency:** Early Spread of Buddhism
Section 4: **Indian Empires** **The Big Idea:** The Mauryas and the Guptas built great empires in India.	TOS **Differentiated Instruction Teacher Management System:** Section 4 Lesson Plan **Guided Reading Workbook:** Section 4 **Chapter Resource File:** • Vocabulary Builder Activity, Section 4 • Biography Activities: Candragupta Maurya; Kautilya; Mahinda	**Daily Bellringer Transparency:** Section 4 **Map Transparency:** Mauryan Empire, c. 320-185 BC **Map Transparency:** Gupta Empire, c. 400 **Internet Activity:** Mauryan Leaders
Section 5: **Indian Achievements** **The Big Idea:** The people of ancient India made great contributions to the arts and sciences.	TOS **Differentiated Instruction Teacher Management System:** Section 5 Lesson Plan **Guided Reading Workbook:** Section 5 **Chapter Resource File:** • Vocabulary Builder Activity, Section 5 • Primary Source Activity: The Story of Savitri	**Daily Bellringer Transparency:** Section 5

Chart Key:

SE Student Edition 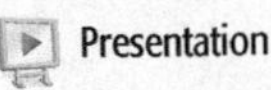 Presentation Resource  MP3 Audio

TOS Teacher One Stop DVD/CD-ROM HISTORY™

Printable Resource

Program Resources available on TOS and @ hmhsocialstudies.com

Review, Assessment, Intervention

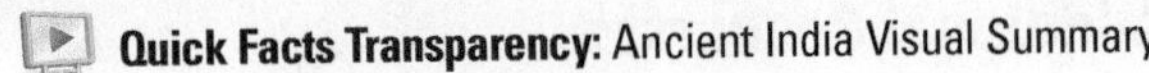

Quick Facts Transparency: Ancient India Visual Summary

Spanish Chapter Summaries Audio CD Program

Quiz Game CD-ROM

Progress Assessment Support System (PASS): Chapter Test

Differentiated Instruction Modified Worksheets and Tests CD-ROM: Modified Chapter Test

TOS **ExamView® Assessment Suite (English/Spanish)**

Online Assessment Program, in the Interactive Student Edition

---

PASS: Section 1 Quiz

Online Quiz: Section 1

Alternative Assessment Handbook

PASS: Section 2 Quiz

Online Quiz: Section 2

Alternative Assessment Handbook

PASS: Section 3 Quiz

Online Quiz: Section 3

Alternative Assessment Handbook

PASS: Section 4 Quiz

Online Quiz: Section 4

Alternative Assessment Handbook

PASS: Section 5 Quiz

Online Quiz: Section 5

Alternative Assessment Handbook

Supporting Resources

- Multimedia Classroom Global History Series
- Global History Teacher's Guide

Maps Globes Graphs Level F

- Student Workbook
- Teacher's Guide

Social Studies Trade Library Collections

- Premier Secondary World History Trade Collection

History's Impact

World History Video Program

- **Buddhism as a World Religion**

For more information or to purchase go to hmhsocialstudies.com

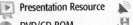

Power Presentations with Media Gallery

Power Presentations with Media Gallery are visual presentations of each chapter's main ideas. Presentations can be customized by including Quick Facts charts, images from the text, and video clips.

Differentiating Instruction

How do I address the needs of varied learners?

The Target Resource acts as your primary strategy for differentiated instruction.

ENGLISH-LANGUAGE LEARNERS & STRUGGLING READERS

Interactive Skills Tutor CD-ROM

The interactive Skills tutor CD-ROM contains lessons that provide additional practice for 20 different critical thinking skills.

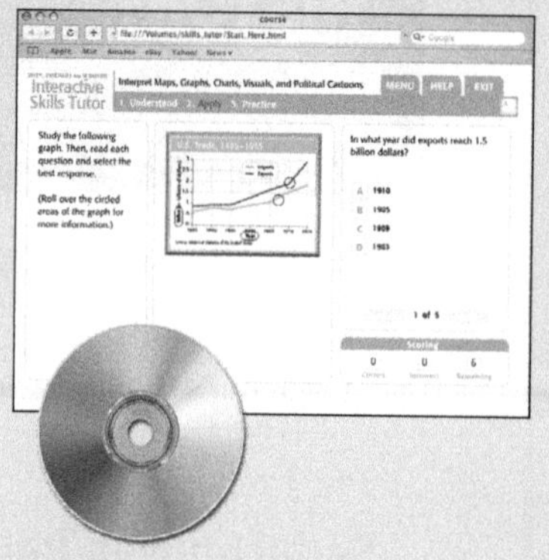

Additional Resources

Differentiated Instruction Teacher Management System: Lesson Plans for Differentiated Instruction

Chapter Resource File:

- Vocabulary Builder Activities
- Social Studies Skills Activity: Interpreting Diagrams

Quick Facts Transparencies: Ancient India Visual Summary

Student Edition on Audio CD Program

Spanish/English Guided Reading Workbook

SPECIAL NEEDS LEARNERS

Differentiated Instruction Modified Worksheets and Tests CD-ROM

- Vocabulary Flash Cards
- Vocabulary Builder Activities
- Chapter Review Activity
- Chapter Test

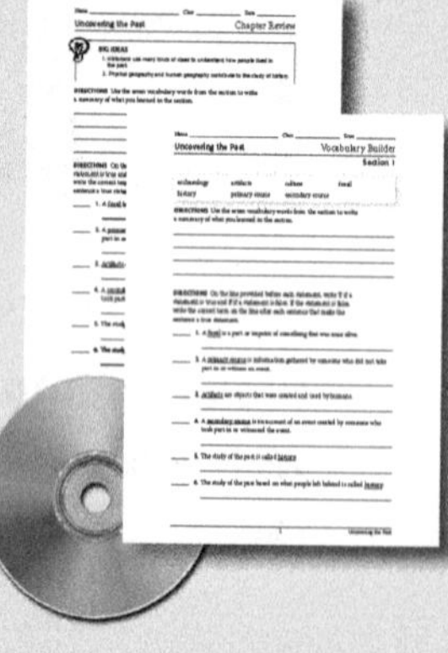

Additional Resources

Differentiated Instruction Teacher Management System: Lesson Plans for Differentiated Instruction

Guided Reading Workbook

Chapter Resource File: Social Studies Skills Activity: Interpreting Diagrams

Student Edition on Audio CD Program

Interactive Skills Tutor CD-ROM

ADVANCED/GIFTED-AND-TALENTED STUDENTS

Primary Source Library CD-ROM for World History

- The Library contains longer versions of quotations in the text, extra sources, and images. Included are point-of-view articles, journals, diaries, historical fiction, and political documents.

Additional Resources

Differentiated Instruction Teacher Management System: Lesson Plans for Differentiated Instruction

Chapter Resource File:

- Focus on Writing Activity: An Illustrated Poster
- Literature Activity: Comparing Literature

Document-Based Questions Activities

Differentiated Activities in the Teacher's Edition

- Building Vocabulary, p. 132
- Designing an Advertisement, p. 150

Teacher One Stop™

How can I manage the lesson plans and support materials for differentiated instruction?

With the Teacher One Stop, you can easily organize and print lesson plans, planning guides, and instructional materials for all learners. The Teacher One Stop includes the following materials to help you differentiate instruction:

- Interactive Teacher's Edition
- Calendar Planner and pacing guides
- Editable lesson plans
- All reproducible ancillaries in Adobe Acrobat (PDF) format
- ExamView Assessment Suite (English & Spanish)
- Transparency and video previews

Differentiated Activities in the Teacher's Edition

- Studying a Map of India, p. 125
- Labeling and Interpreting Maps, p. 144

Interactive Student Edition

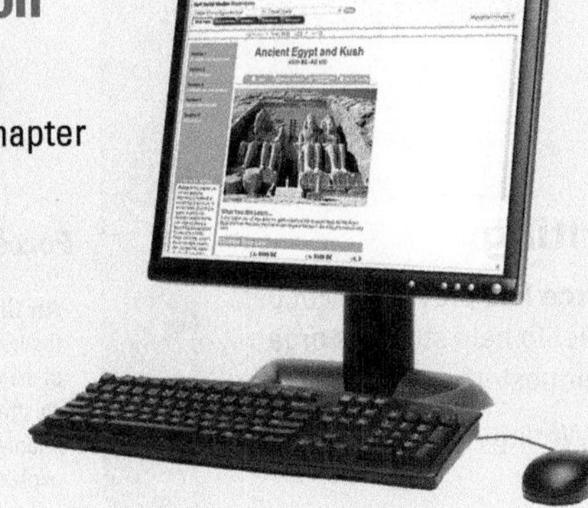

Complete online student edition with interactive multimedia support for chapter content assessment and reporting

- Interactive Maps and Notebook
- Graphic Organizers
- Standardized Test Prep
- Online Homework Practice and Research Activities
- Current Events
- Chapter-based Internet Activities
- Animated History Activities
- and more!

Differentiated Activities in the Teacher's Edition

- Writing a Report, p. 131
- Writing a Newspaper Article, p. 138

• Chapter Preview •

Essential Question

Introduce the Essential Question

- Point out that India's rich history and culture are important parts of the world's cultural legacy.
- Explain that India's literature, religion, drama, and poetry have influenced the world.
- Discuss India's important contributions to the world in mathematics, astronomy, and architecture.

CHAPTER 5 2300 BC–AD 500

Ancient India

Essential Question How do India's rich history and culture affect the world today?

South Carolina Performance Standards

6-1.3 Compare the river valley civilizations of the Tigris and Euphrates (Mesopotamia), the Nile (Egypt), the Indus (India), and the Huang He (China), including the evolution of written language, government, trade systems, architecture, and forms of social order; 6-1.4 Explain the origins, fundamental beliefs, and spread of Eastern religions, including Hinduism (India), Judaism (Mesopotamia), Buddhism (India), and Confucianism and Taoism (China); 6-3.3 Summarize the major contributions of India, including those of the Gupta dynasty in mathematics, literature, religion, and science.

Literacy Skills for Social Studies

- Interpret Earth's physical and human systems by using maps, mental maps, geographic models, and other social studies resources.
- Compare the locations of places, the conditions at places, and the connections between places.

Focus on Writing

An Illustrated Poster Ancient India was a fascinating place. It was the home of amazing cities, the site of strong empires, and the birthplace of major religions. As you read this chapter, think about how you could illustrate one aspect of Indian culture in a poster. When you finish the chapter, you will design such a poster, which will include captions that explain the illustrations you have drawn.

Chapter Events

c. 2300 BC The Harappan civilization develops.

2300 BC

World Events

2200 BC The Old Kingdom ends in Egypt.

Focus on Writing

The **Chapter Resource File** provides a Focus on Writing worksheet to help students organize and create their posters.

CRF: Focus on Writing Activity: An Illustrated Poster

Key to Differentiating Instruction

Below Level

Basic-level activities designed for all students encountering new material

At Level

Intermediate-level activities designed for average students

Above Level

Challenging activities designed for honors and gifted and talented students

Standard English Mastery

Activities designed to improve standard English usage

LS Learning Styles

Introduce the Chapter

At Level

Telling Tales in Ancient India

1. Call on a volunteer to answer this question: If you wanted to teach a friend an important lesson about life, which would be more effective—telling him or her what to do or telling a story that makes the point indirectly?
2. Point out that many people respond better to a story. In ancient India, people told stories, also called fables, that taught important lessons. These fables were collected in a work called the *Panchatantra.* Long ago, this collection was translated into other languages. It influenced many works of literature, including *The Thousand and One Nights,* the source of Sinbad the Sailor tales. Ask students if they are familiar with the Sinbad stories.
3. Tell students that ancient India gave birth to more than fun stories; two of the world's most important religions began there. Tell students they will learn about these topics and more in this chapter. **LS Verbal/Linguistic**

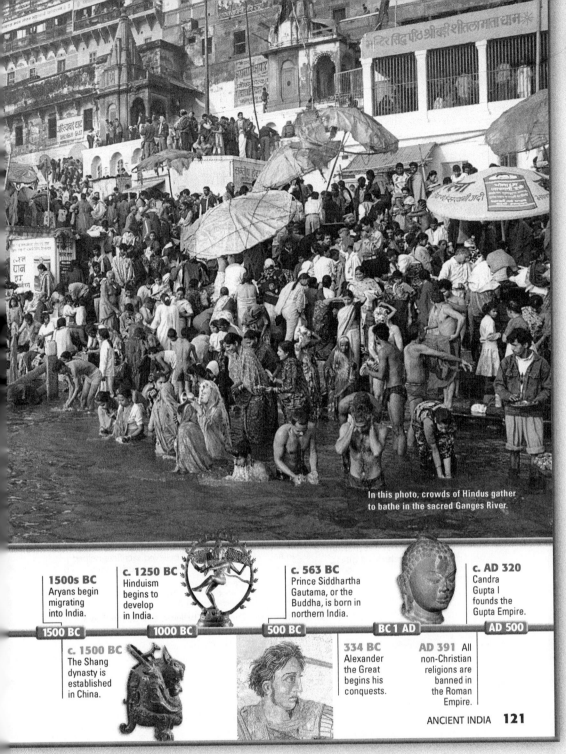

In this photo, crowds of Hindus gather to bathe in the sacred Ganges River.

1500s BC Aryans begin migrating into India.

c. 1250 BC Hinduism begins to develop in India.

c. 563 BC Prince Siddhartha Gautama, or the Buddha, is born in northern India.

c. AD 320 Candra Gupta I founds the Gupta Empire.

1500 BC — 1000 BC — 500 BC — BC 1 AD — AD 500

c. 1500 BC The Shang dynasty is established in China.

334 BC Alexander the Great begins his conquests.

AD 391 All non-Christian religions are banned in the Roman Empire.

• Chapter Preview •

Explore the Picture

The Sacred Ganges River Hindus believe that Ganga (also called Ganges) is the daughter of Himalaya, the mountain god. According to Hindu beliefs, the Ganges River is sacred, and bathing in it will wash away one's sins. Many Hindus ask that after death they be cremated on the banks of the Ganges and their ashes sprinkled on the water.

Analyzing Visuals

Besides bathing in the water, how else do the people in the photo seem to be showing their devotion to Ganga, the Hindu goddess of the river? *drinking the water, placing flowers in the water*

Explore the Time Line

1. About when may the Old Kingdom of Egypt and the Harappan civilization of India have overlapped? *from about 2300 to 2200 BC*
2. What was happening in China about the same time that the Aryans began migrating into India? *The Shang dynasty was established.*
3. How many years elapsed from the time Hinduism began to develop in India and Christianity became the official religion of the Roman Empire? *about 1641 years*

Info to Know

The Case of the Missing Art Information on India's distant past is spotty at best. One reason is that for a long span of time in Indian history there are virtually no examples of painting, sculpture, or other forms of the visual arts. Between the end of the Harappan civilization and the beginning of the Mauryan Empire in the 300s BC, the Aryans dominated India. We have remarkable works of literature from that time, but practically no art. Ask students why they think this may be so.

Reading Social Studies

Understanding Themes

Like other civilizations students have studied thus far, religion played a major role in people's lives in India. Religion also played an important role in the structure of Indian society and culture. As students read the chapter, ask them to look for relationships between religion and society and culture.

Inferences about History

Focus on Reading Ask students if they have ever been able to predict the end of a book or a film. Maybe they figured out who the criminal was in a mystery novel. Ask students to discuss what led them to make the correct inference. Did they read or see clues? Point out to students that making inferences often involves paying careful attention to details, and using prior knowledge about a subject. Discuss with students the inference drawn on this page. Explain to students how the information inside and outside the text led to this inference.

Reading Social Studies

Economics | Geography | Politics | **Religion** | **Society and Culture** | Science and Technology

Focus on Themes This chapter outlines and describes the development of India. You will read about India's first civilization, the Harappan civilization, so advanced that the people had indoor bathrooms and their own writing system. You will also learn about the **society and culture** that restricted who Indian people could talk with or marry. Finally, you will read about the **religions** and empires that united India and about the art and literature that Indians created.

Inferences about History

Focus on Reading What's the difference between a good guess and a weak guess? A good guess is an educated guess. In other words, the guess is based on some knowledge or information. That's what an **inference** is, an educated guess.

Making Inferences About What You Read Making inferences is similar to drawing conclusions. You use almost the same process to make an inference: combine information from your reading—what's "inside the text"—with what you already know—what's "outside the text"—and make an educated guess about what it all means. Once you have made several inferences, you may be able to draw a conclusion that ties them all together.

Steps for Making Inferences
1. Ask a question.
2. Note information "inside the Text."
3. Note information "outside the Text."
4. Use both sets of information to make an educated guess, or inference.

Question: Why did Aryan priests have rules for performing sacrifices?	
Inside the Text	**Outside the Text**
Sacred texts tell how to perform sacrifices.	Other religions have duties only priests can perform.
Priests sacrificed animals in fire.	Many ancient societies believed sacrifices helped keep the gods happy.
Sacrifices were offered to the gods.	

Inference: The Aryans believed that performing a sacrifice incorrectly might anger the gods.

Reading and Skills Resources

Reading Support

- Guided Reading Workbook
- Student Edition on Audio CD
- Spanish Chapter Summaries Audio CD Program

Social Studies Skills Support

- Interactive Skills Tutor CD-ROM

Vocabulary Support

- **CRF:** Vocabulary Builder Activities
- **CRF:** Chapter Review Activity
- Differentiated Instruction Modified Worksheets and Tests CD-ROM:
  - Vocabulary Flash Cards
  - Vocabulary Builder Activity
  - Chapter Review Activity
- **TOS** Holt McDougal PuzzleView

You Try It!

The following passage is from the chapter you are about to read. Read the passage and then answer the questions that follow.

Harappan Achievements

From Chapter 5, p. 128

Harappan civilization was very advanced. Most houses had bathrooms with indoor plumbing. Artisans made excellent pottery, jewelry, ivory objects, and cotton clothing. They used high-quality tools and developed a system of weights and measures.

Harappans also developed India's first writing system. However, scholars have not yet learned to read this language, so we know very little about Harappan society. Historians think that the Harappans had kings and strong central governments, but they aren't sure. As in Egypt, the people may have worshipped the king as a god.

Harappan civilization ended by the early 1700s BC, but no one is sure why.

Answer the following questions to make inferences about Harappan society.

1. Do you think the Harappan language was closely related to the languages spoken in India today? Consider the information inside the text and things you have learned outside the text to make an inference about the Harappan language.
4. What have you just learned about Harappan achievements? Think back to other civilizations you have studied that made similar achievements. What allowed those civilizations to make their achievements? From this, what can you infer about earlier Harappan society?

As you read Chapter 5, use the information you find in the text to make inferences about Indian society.

Key Terms and People

Chapter 5

Section 1
subcontinent *(p. 124)*
monsoons *(p. 125)*
Sanskrit *(p. 129)*

Section 2
caste system *(p. 131)*
Hinduism *(p. 133)*
reincarnation *(p. 133)*
karma *(p. 134)*
Jainism *(p. 134)*
nonviolence *(p. 135)*
Sikhism, *(p. 135)*

Section 3
fasting *(p. 137)*
meditation *(p.137)*
the Buddha *(p. 137)*
Buddhism *(p. 138)*
nirvana *(p. 138)*
missionaries *(p.140)*

Section 4
Candragupta Maurya *(p. 142)*
Asoka *(p. 143)*
Candra Gupta II *(p. 144)*

Section 5
metallurgy *(p. 150)*
alloys *(p. 150)*
Hindu-Arabic numerals *(p. 150)*
inoculation *(p. 150)*
astronomy *(p. 151)*

Academic Vocabulary

Success in school is related to knowing academic vocabulary—the words that are frequently used in school assignments and discussions. In this chapter, you will learn the following academic words:

establish *(p. 144)*
process *(p.150)*

Reading Social Studies

Key Terms and People

Preteach this chapter's key terms and people by assigning one term or person to each student. Have each student define or identify that term. Then have students teach each other the words they learned. Encourage students to keep a list of key terms and people to study.
LS Interpersonal, Verbal/Linguistic

Focus on Reading

See the **Focus on Reading** questions in this chapter for more practice on this reading social studies skill.

Reading Social Studies Assessment

See the **Chapter Review** at the end of this chapter for student assessment questions related to this reading skill.

Teaching Tip

Students may have difficulty learning to make inferences in the activity above. To help students learn how to do this, have students create a T-chart. Ask students to label one column of the chart *Inside the Text,* and the other column *Outside Knowledge.* Then have students pay attention to the details in the reading to complete the first column, and use their own outside knowledge on the subject to complete the second column. Students should then use the information in each column to make an inference.

Answers

You Try It! 1. *No, if Harappan language was similar to modern languages scientists might have learned how to read it.* **2.** *Harappan achievements—lived in cities, bathrooms, indoor plumbing, pottery, cotton clothing, high-quality tools, system of weights and measures, writing system, had an organized society with artisans, builders, priests, and kings; other civilizations—Education, technology, division of labor, wealth, peace, and stability enabled them to make their achievements; Harappans had many of the same characteristics as other advanced societies.*

Preteach

Bellringer

If YOU were there . . . Use the **Daily Bellringer Transparency** to help students answer the question.

Daily Bellringer Transparency, Section 1

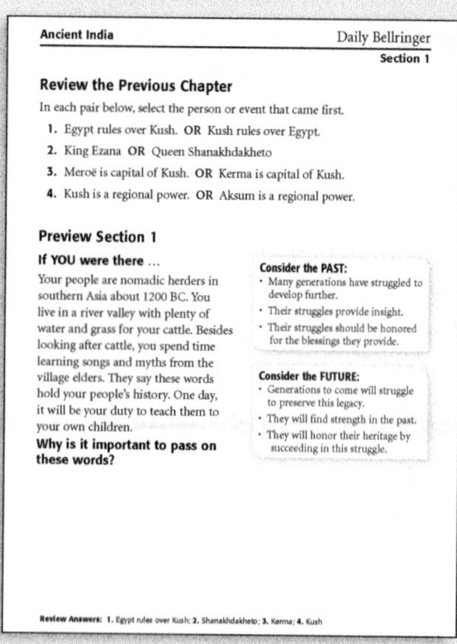

Ancient India — Daily Bellringer, **Section 1**

Review the Previous Chapter

In each pair below, select the person or event that came first.

1. Egypt rules over Kush. **OR** Kush rules over Egypt.
2. King Ezana **OR** Queen Shanakhdakheto
3. Meroë is capital of Kush. **OR** Kerma is capital of Kush.
4. Kush is a regional power. **OR** Aksum is a regional power.

Preview Section 1

If YOU were there ...

Your people are nomadic herders in southern Asia about 1200 BC. You live in a river valley with plenty of water and grass for your cattle. Besides looking after cattle, you spend time learning songs and myths from the village elders. They say these words hold your people's history. One day, it will be your duty to teach them to your own children.

Why is it important to pass on these words?

Consider the PAST:
- Many generations have struggled to develop further.
- Their struggles provide insight.
- Their struggles should be honored for the blessings they provide.

Consider the FUTURE:
- Generations to come will struggle to preserve this legacy.
- They will find strength in the past.
- They will honor their heritage by succeeding in this struggle.

Review Answers: **1.** Egypt rules over Kush; **2.** Shanakhdakheto; **3.** Kerma; **4.** Kush

Building Vocabulary

Preteach or review the following term:

fortress fort (p. 127)

influenced affected (p. 125)

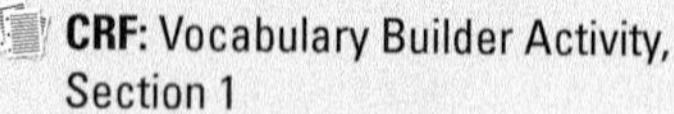

CRF: Vocabulary Builder Activity, Section 1

Taking Notes

Have students use the graphic organizer online to take notes on the section. This activity will prepare students for the Section Assessment, in which they will complete a graphic organizer that builds on the information using the Critical Thinking Skill: Drawing Conclusions.

SECTION 1

Geography and Early India

What You Will Learn...

Main Ideas

1. The geography of India includes high mountains, great rivers, and heavy seasonal rain.
2. Harappan civilization developed along the Indus River.
3. The Aryan migration to India changed the region's civilization.

The Big Idea

Indian civilization first developed on the Indus River.

Key Terms

subcontinent, *p. 124*
monsoons, *p. 125*
Sanskrit, *p. 129*

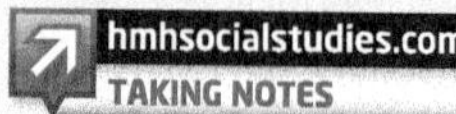

hmhsocialstudies.com
TAKING NOTES

Use the graphic organizer online to take notes on India's geography and its two earliest civilizations, the Harappan and Aryan civilizations.

If YOU were there...

Your people are nomadic herders in southern Asia about 1200 BC. You live in a river valley with plenty of water and grass for your cattle. Besides looking after cattle, you spend time learning songs and myths from the village elders. They say these words hold your people's history. One day, it will be your duty to teach them to your own children.

Why is it important to pass on these words?

BUILDING BACKGROUND Like Mesopotamia and Egypt, India was home to one of the world's first civilizations. Like other early civilizations, the one in India grew up in a river valley. But the society that eventually developed in India was very different from the ones that developed elsewhere.

Geography of India

Look at a map of Asia in the atlas of this book. Do you see the large, roughly triangular landmass that juts out from the center of the southern part of the continent? That is India. It was the location of one of the world's earliest civilizations.

Landforms and Rivers

India is huge. In fact, it is so big that many geographers call it a subcontinent. A **subcontinent** is a large landmass that is smaller than a continent. Subcontinents are usually separated from the rest of their continents by physical features. If you look at the map on the next page, for example, you can see that mountains largely separate India from the rest of Asia.

Among the mountains of northern India are the Himalayas, the highest mountains in the world. To the west are the Hindu Kush. Though these mountains made it hard to enter India, invaders have historically found a few paths through them.

Teach the Big Idea

At Level

Geography and Early India

1. **Teach** Ask students the questions in the Main Idea boxes to teach this section.
2. **Apply** Create a Venn diagram for students to see, with *Geography and the Harappans* and *Geography and the Aryans* as heads for the circles and *Geography and Both Peoples* for the overlap. Have students suggest how geography affected early Indian civilizations. For example, Indus River floods made farming possible for the Harappans, but the monsoons would have affected both peoples. Then discuss other details of the two civilizations.
   LS **Interpersonal, Visual/Spatial**
3. **Review** Have students tell what we do know about these civilizations and why we don't know more about the Harappans.
4. **Practice/Homework** Have students create a chart listing the characteristics of the Harappan and Aryan civilizations.
   LS **Visual/Spatial**

Alternative Assessment Handbook, Rubric 7: Charts

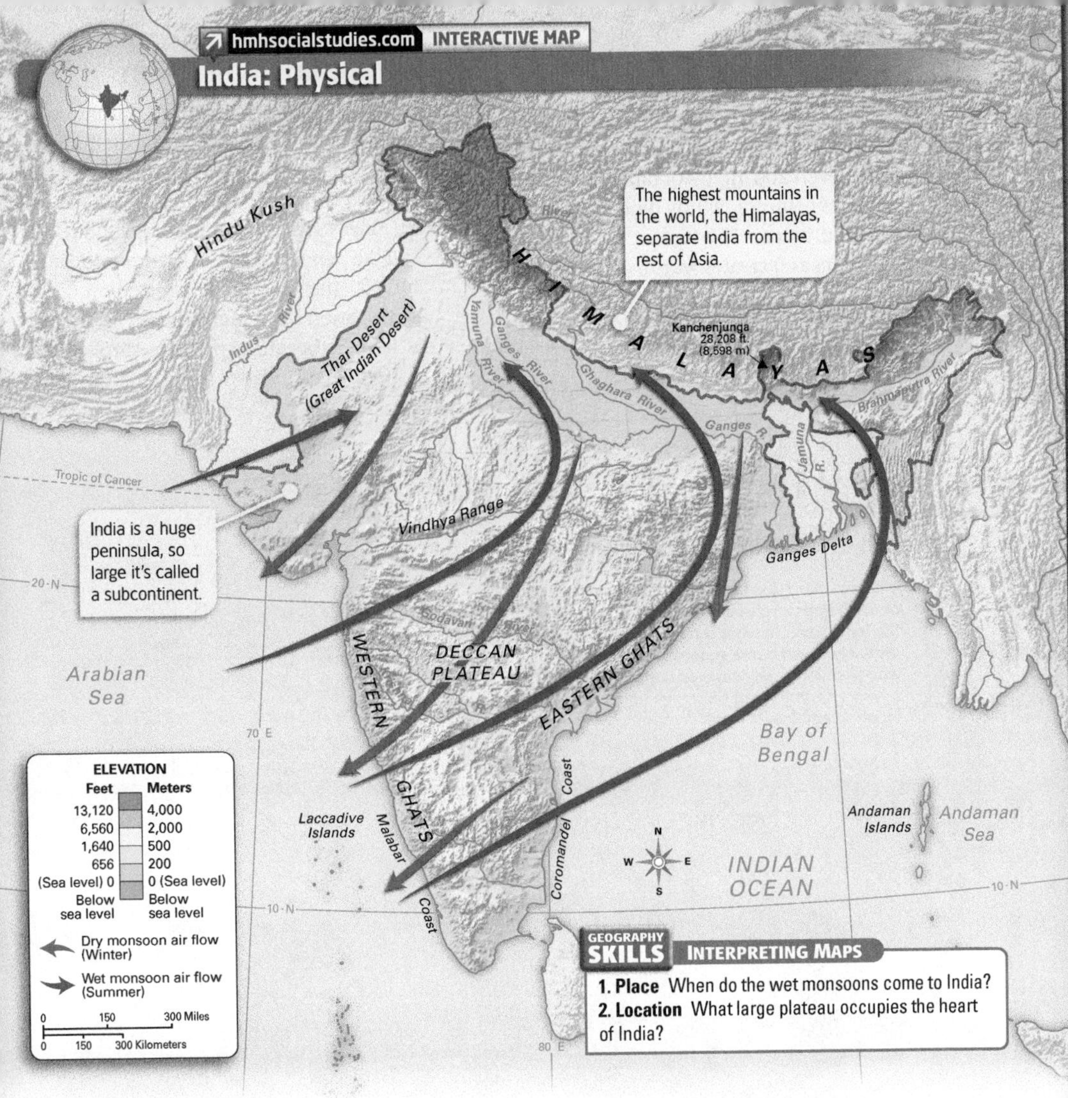

To the west of the Himalayas is a vast desert. Much of the rest of India is covered by fertile plains and rugged plateaus.

Several major rivers flow out of the Himalayas. The valley of one of them, the Indus, was the location of India's first civilization. The Indus is located in present-day Pakistan, west of India. When heavy snows in the Himalayas melted, the Indus flooded. As in Mesopotamia and Egypt, the flooding left behind a layer of fertile silt. The silt created ideal farmland for early settlers.

Climate

Most of India has a hot and humid climate. This climate is heavily influenced by India's **monsoons**, seasonal wind patterns that cause wet and dry seasons.

Direct Teach

Main Idea

❶ Geography of India

The geography of India includes high mountains, great rivers, and heavy seasonal rain.

Describe What is the shape of the Indian subcontinent? *roughly triangular*

Contrast How is the geography of the northeastern part of the subcontinent different from the northwestern? *northeastern—mountainous; northwestern—desert*

Draw Inferences Why may Indian farmers consider the monsoons both a blessing and a curse? *possible answer—The monsoons bring rain for watering fields, but can also cause destructive floods.*

Map Transparency: India: Physical

CRF: History and Geography Activity: The Indus River Valley

Connect to Geography

The Khyber Pass Various invaders have found their way from central Asia through the mountains into India by means of the Khyber Pass. It is a narrow passage 28 miles long on what is now the border between Pakistan and Afghanistan.

Differentiating Instruction

Special Needs Learners Below Level

Materials: outline maps of Indian subcontinent, map pencils

1. Show students a map of India and ask for volunteers to identify major physical features.
2. Give each student a blank map of India and have them label the following on their maps: major rivers and other bodies of water, the entire Indus River Valley, mountain ranges, and plateaus.
3. Instruct students to create a map legend and color-code their maps based on the region's geographical features and the map legend shown.
4. Finally, lead a discussion about how the monsoons affect the subcontinent.

LS Visual/Spatial

Alternative Assessment Handbook, Rubric 20: Map Creation

Answers

Interpreting Maps 1. *in the summer* **2.** *Deccan Plateau*

Direct Teach

Main Idea

❷ Harappan Civilization

Harappan civilization developed along the Indus River.

Identify What were the two main cities of the Harappan civilization? *Harappa and Mohenjo Daro*

Recall When did the Harappan civilization thrive? *between 2300 and 1700 BC*

Analyze What are some explanations for why Harappa and Mohenjo Daro were very similar? *possible answers—People from one of the cities founded the other; communication, travel, and/or trade made Harappan civilization fairly uniform throughout the region.*

hmhsocialstudies.com

Online Resources
Activity: Ancient India Advertisement

History Close-Up

Mohenjo Daro How did the area's physical geography affect the city's defenses? *possible answer—The people of Mohenjo Daro had to build a fortress, since the region's flat landscape didn't provide natural barriers.*

Linking to Today

Pottery Wheel Much of the Harappan pottery seems to have been made on human-powered potters' wheels. This type of machine is still used around the world today.

In the summer, monsoon winds blow into India from the Indian Ocean, bringing heavy rains that can cause terrible floods. Some parts of India receive as much as 100 or even 200 inches of rain during this time. In the winter, winds blow down from the mountains. This forces moisture out of India and creates warm, dry winters.

READING CHECK **Drawing Conclusions** How do you think monsoons affected settlement in India?

Harappan Civilization

Historians call the civilization that grew up in the Indus River Valley the Harappan (huh-RA-puhn) civilization. In addition, many Harappan settlements were found along the Sarasvati River, located southeast of the Indus.

Like other ancient societies you have studied, the Harappan civilization grew as irrigation and agriculture improved. As farmers began to produce surpluses of food, towns and cities appeared in India.

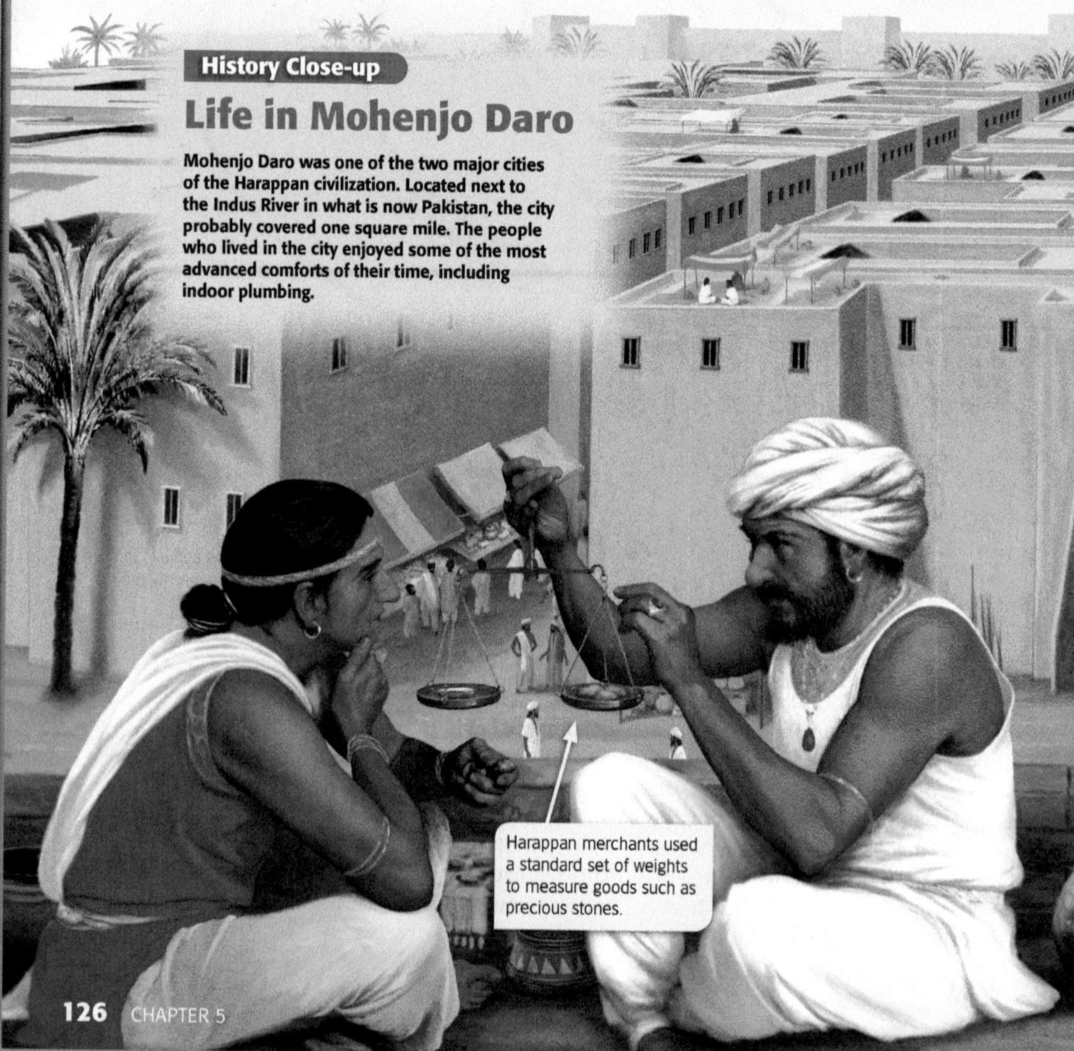

History Close-up
Life in Mohenjo Daro
Mohenjo Daro was one of the two major cities of the Harappan civilization. Located next to the Indus River in what is now Pakistan, the city probably covered one square mile. The people who lived in the city enjoyed some of the most advanced comforts of their time, including indoor plumbing.
Harappan merchants used a standard set of weights to measure goods such as precious stones.
126 CHAPTER 5

Cross-Discipline Activity: Science

Above Level

Understanding Monsoons

Research Required

1. Instruct students to conduct research to learn more about the causes and results of monsoons. Students should use at least two independent, credible sources.
2. Have students prepare presentations on their findings. The presentations should incorporate detailed graphics illustrating wind changes and their effects.
3. Students should give their presentations to the class. **LS Verbal/Linguistic**

Alternative Assessment Handbook, Rubrics 29: Presentations; and 30: Research

Answers

Reading Check *People probably settled where monsoon rains helped farming but tried to avoid places where flooding was common.*

India's First Cities

The Harappan civilization was named after the modern city of Harappa (huh-RA-puh), Pakistan. It was near this city that ruins of the civilization were first discovered. From studying these ruins, archaeologists think that the civilization thrived between 2300 and 1700 BC.

The greatest sources of information we have about Harappan civilization are the ruins of two large cities, Harappa and Mohenjo Daro (mo-HEN-joh DAR-oh). The two cities lay on the Indus more than 300 miles apart but were remarkably similar.

Both Harappa and Mohenjo Daro were well planned. Each stood near a towering fortress. From these fortresses, defenders could look down on the cities' brick streets, which crossed at right angles and were lined with storehouses, workshops, market stalls, and houses. In addition, both cities had many public wells.

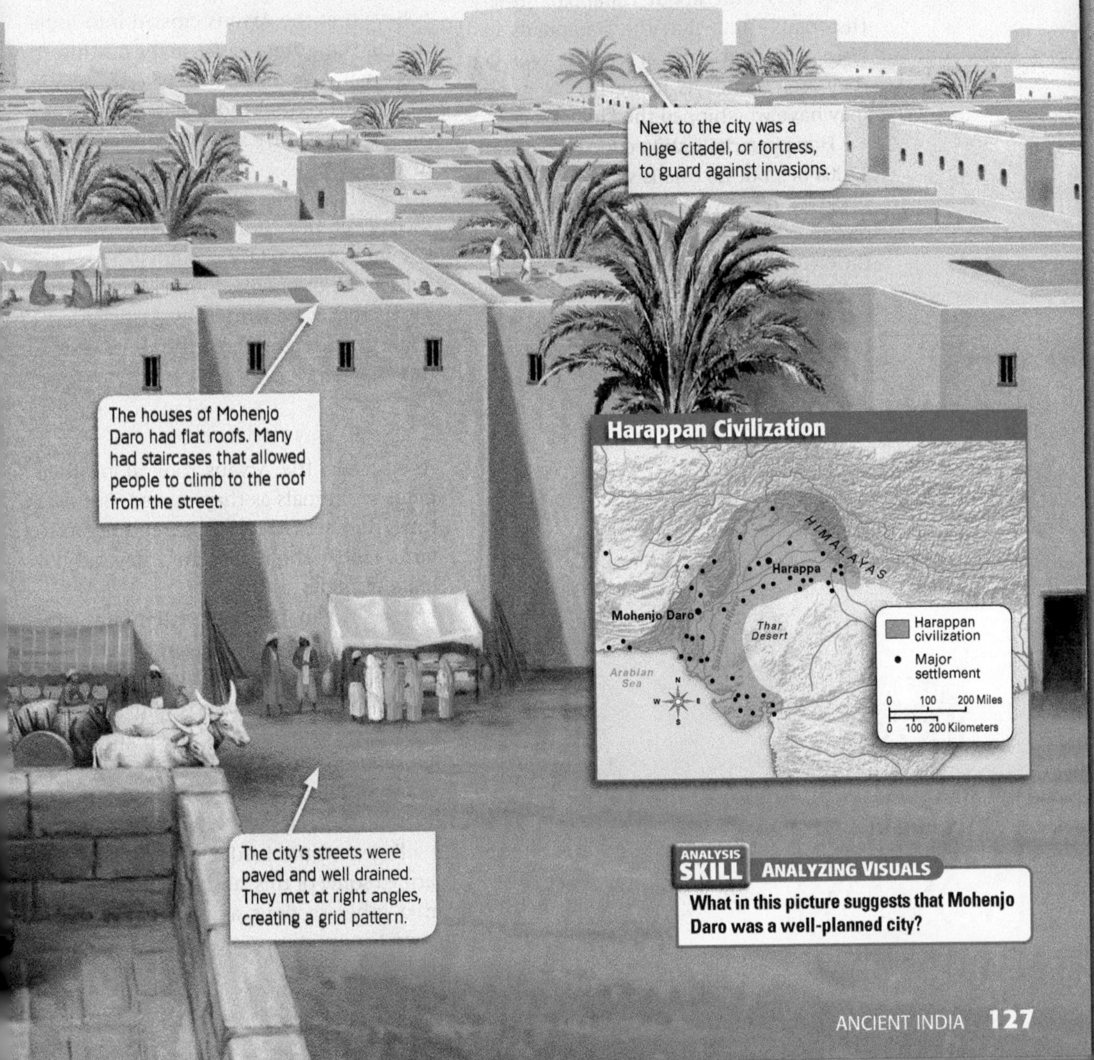

Next to the city was a huge citadel, or fortress, to guard against invasions.
The houses of Mohenjo Daro had flat roofs. Many had staircases that allowed people to climb to the roof from the street.
The city's streets were paved and well drained. They met at right angles, creating a grid pattern.
Harappan Civilization
HIMALAYAS
Harappa
Mohenjo Daro
Thar Desert
Arabian Sea
N
W
E
S
Harappan civilization
Major settlement
0 100 200 Miles
0 100 200 Kilometers

ANALYSIS SKILL **ANALYZING VISUALS**

What in this picture suggests that Mohenjo Daro was a well-planned city?

Direct Teach

Main Idea

❷ Harappan Civilization

Harappan civilization developed along the Indus River.

Recall How do we know about Harappan civilization? *ruins of cities*

Describe What are some characteristics of the cities of Harappa and Mohenjo Daro? *well planned, protected by fortresses, brick streets that crossed at right angles, storehouses, workshops, market stalls, and houses*

Compare Recall what you have learned about Egypt. How does the Harappans' control of the countryside east and west of the Indus River compare to the Egyptians' control of the Nile Valley? *The Harappan civilization was spread across more of the countryside. Egyptian control was limited to a very narrow band along the Nile.*

Did you know . . .

The name *Mohenjo Daro* means "the mound of the dead."

Interpreting Maps

Location What geographical features are south of Harappa? *Sarasvati River, Thar Desert*

Place Note the settlements not on a river. What can we conclude about them? *possible answer—Farms that supported these settlements had sources of water besides rivers.*

Collaborative Learning

At Level

Traveling to a Harappan City

1. Organize students into small groups. Ask students to imagine that they are farmers from the Indus River Valley. One family member has just returned from his or her first journey to the city of Mohenjo Daro or Harappa.
2. Instruct each group to create a skit re-enacting the traveler's return. One group member should be the person who made the journey, while others pretend to be that person's siblings.
3. The brothers and sisters should ask questions about daily life in the city and the achievements of its people. The traveler may wish to create simple drawings showing what the buildings and roads looked like to respond to their questions.
4. Have students present their skits to the class.

LS Interpersonal, Kinesthetic

Alternative Assessment Handbook, Rubric 33: Skits and Reader's Theater

Answers

Analyzing Visuals *Streets were at right angles to each other. Homes were built close together and were protected by a fortress.*

Direct Teach

Main Idea

❸ Aryan Migration

The Aryan migration into India changed the region's civilization.

Identify From where did the Aryans come? *Central Asia*

Compare How was the Aryan civilization different from the Harappan? *The Aryans didn't build cities, didn't have a single ruling authority, and didn't have a written language.*

Evaluate Why are the Vedas so important to historians? *because so much of what we know about the Aryans comes from them*

Other People, Other Places

Indo-European Languages Sanskrit belongs to a language group called the Indo-European languages. Similarities among the Indo-European languages show that they are related. For example, look at these words for the English word *mother:* Sanskrit, *matar;* Greek, *meter;* Latin, *mater;* and Old Irish, *mathair.* The languages listed—and many others—developed from a lost language called Proto-Indo-European. People who lived from Europe to India may have spoken this ancient language between 10,000 and 6,000 years ago.

Harappan Achievements

Harappan civilization was very advanced. Most houses had bathrooms with indoor plumbing. Artisans made excellent pottery, jewelry, ivory objects, and cotton clothing. They developed a system of weights and measures. Traders bought and sold goods from as far away as Egypt and Mesopotamia.

Harappans also developed India's first writing system. However, scholars have not yet learned to read this language, so we know very little about Harappan society. Historians think that the Harappans had kings and strong central governments, but they aren't sure. As in Egypt, the people may have worshipped the king as a god.

Harappan civilization ended by the early 1700s BC, but no one is sure why. Perhaps invaders destroyed the cities or natural disasters, like floods or earthquakes, caused the civilization to collapse.

READING CHECK **Analyzing** Why don't we know much about Harappan civilization?

Harappan Art

Like other ancient peoples, the Harappans made small seals like the one below that were used to stamp goods. They also used clay pots like the one at right as burial urns.

Aryan Migration

Not long after the Harappan civilization crumbled, a new group arrived in the Indus Valley. They were called the Aryans (AIR-ee-uhnz). They were originally from the area around the Caspian Sea in Central Asia. Over time, however, they became the dominant group in India.

Arrival and Spread

The Aryans first arrived in India in the 2000s BC. Historians and archaeologists believe that the Aryans crossed into India through mountain passes in the northwest. Over many centuries, they spread east and south into central India. From there they moved even farther east into the Ganges River Valley.

Much of what we know about Aryan society comes from religious writings known as the Vedas (VAY-duhs). These are collections of poems, hymns, myths, and rituals that were written by Aryan priests. You will read more about the Vedas later in this chapter.

Government and Society

As nomads, the Aryans took along their herds of animals as they moved. But over time, they settled in villages and began to farm. Unlike the Harappans, they did not build big cities.

The Aryan political system was also different from the Harappan system. The Aryans lived in small communities, based mostly on family ties. No single ruling authority existed. Instead, each group had its own leader, often a skilled warrior.

Aryan villages were governed by rajas (RAH-juhz). A raja was a leader who ruled a village and the land around it. Villagers farmed some of this land for the raja. They used other sections as pastures for their cows, horses, sheep, and goats.

Critical Thinking: Making Decisions

At Level

A Raja's Choice

1. Ask students to imagine that they are rajas of small villages. Local herders and farmers have come to the raja to tell him they need more land for their crops and animals. The raja has a choice. He can either go to war against the larger, stronger village nearby to take its land, or he can try to find a peaceful solution to his people's growing needs.
2. Have students work in pairs to decide which plan of action they will take.
3. Have each pair write a brief speech in which the raja explains his decision to the people of his village.
4. Have volunteers share their speeches with the class. LS **Verbal/Linguistic**

Alternate Assessment Handbook, Rubric 35: Solving Problems

Answers

Reading Check *because historians have not been able to read the Harappan language*

Although many rajas were related, they didn't always get along. Sometimes rajas joined forces before fighting a common enemy. Other times, however, rajas went to war against each other. In fact, Aryan groups fought each other nearly as often as they fought outsiders.

Language

The first Aryan settlers did not read or write. Because of this, they had to memorize the poems and hymns that were important in their culture, such as the Vedas. If people forgot these poems and hymns, the works would be lost forever.

The language in which these Aryan poems and hymns were composed was **Sanskrit**, the most important language of ancient India. At first, Sanskrit was only a spoken language. Eventually, however, people figured out how to write it down so they could keep records. These Sanskrit records are a major source of information about Aryan society. Sanskrit is no longer spoken today, but it is the root of many modern South Asian languages.

READING CHECK **Identifying** What source provides much of the information we have about the Aryans?

Aryan Migrations

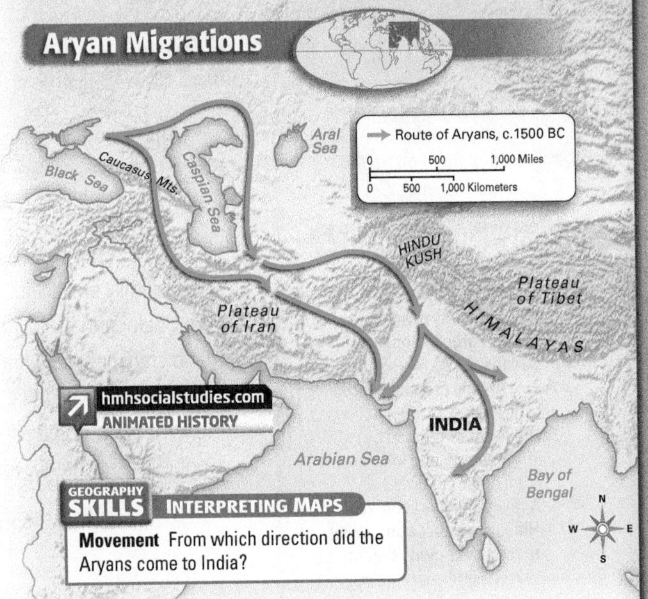

hmhsocialstudies.com ANIMATED HISTORY

GEOGRAPHY SKILLS **INTERPRETING MAPS**

Movement From which direction did the Aryans come to India?

SUMMARY AND PREVIEW The earliest civilizations in India were centered in the Indus Valley. First the Harappans and then the Aryans lived in this fertile valley. In the next section, you will learn about a new religion that developed in the Indus Valley after the Aryans settled there—Hinduism.

Hindi, the most widely spoken Indian language, is based on Sanskrit.

Section 1 Assessment

hmhsocialstudies.com ONLINE QUIZ

Reviewing Ideas, Terms, and People

1. a. **Define** What are **monsoons**?
   b. **Contrast** How does northern India differ from the rest of the region?
   c. **Elaborate** Why is India called a **subcontinent**?
2. a. **Recall** Where did Harappan civilization develop?
   b. **Analyze** What is one reason that scholars do not completely understand some important parts of Harappan society?
3. a. **Identify** Who were the Aryans?
   b. **Contrast** How was Aryan society different from Harappan society?

Critical Thinking

4. **Drawing Conclusions** Using your notes, draw conclusions about the effect of geography on Indian society. Record your conclusions in a diagram like this one.

Geography of India	Harappan society
	Aryan society

Focus on Writing

5. **Illustrating Geography and Early Civilizations** This section described two possible topics for your poster: geography and early civilizations. Which of them is more interesting to you? Write down some ideas for a poster about your chosen topic.

Direct Teach

Main Idea

3 Aryan Migration

The Aryan migration into India changed the region's civilization.

Identify What is Sanskrit? *the most important language of ancient India*

Explain Why did the Aryans memorize their poems and hymns? *because they didn't have a written language*

Map Transparency: Aryan Migrations

Review & Assess

Close

Challenge students to suggest questions they would like archaeologists and historians to find out about the Harappan or Aryan civilizations.

Review

Online Quiz, Section 1

Assess

SE Section 1 Assessment

PASS: Section 1 Quiz

Alternative Assessment Handbook

Reteach/Classroom Intervention

Guided Reading Workbook, Section 1

Interactive Skills Tutor CD-ROM

Section 1 Assessment Answers

1. **a.** seasonal wind patterns that cause wet and dry seasons
   b. Northern India has the Himalayas and a desert. The rest of India is mainly fertile plains and plateaus.
   c. India is very large and separated from the main continent by mountains.
2. **a.** the Indus River Valley
   b. Scholars have yet to learn how to read their language.
3. **a.** people who moved into India from Central Asia
   b. Aryans didn't farm at first, and didn't build large, planned cities; they had no single ruling authority; their villages were led by rajas.
4. Review material under *Harappan Civilization* and *Aryan Migrations* for answers.
5. Responses will vary but should display familiarity with the chosen topics.

Answers

Interpreting Maps *northwest*

Reading Check *the Vedas*

Preteach

Bellringer

If YOU were there . . . Use the **Daily Bellringer Transparency** to help students answer the question.

Daily Bellringer Transparency, Section 2

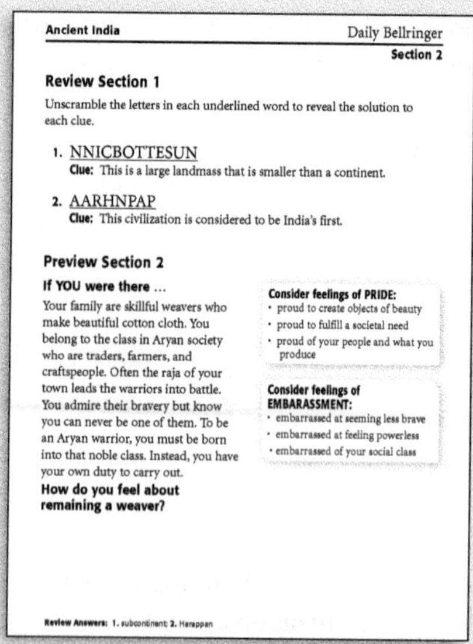

Ancient India — Daily Bellringer — Section 2

Review Section 1

Unscramble the letters in each underlined word to reveal the solution to each clue.

1. NNICBOTTESUN
   Clue: This is a large landmass that is smaller than a continent.
2. AARHNPAP
   Clue: This civilization is considered to be India's first.

Preview Section 2

If YOU were there ...

Your family are skillful weavers who make beautiful cotton cloth. You belong to the class in Aryan society who are traders, farmers, and craftspeople. Often the raja of your town leads the warriors into battle. You admire their bravery but know you can never be one of them. To be an Aryan warrior, you must be born into that noble class. Instead, you have your own duty to carry out.

How do you feel about remaining a weaver?

Consider feelings of PRIDE:
- proud to create objects of beauty
- proud to fulfill a societal need
- proud of your people and what you produce

Consider feelings of EMBARASSMENT:
- embarrassed at seeming less brave
- embarrassed at feeling powerless
- embarrassed of your social class

Review Answers: 1. subcontinent 2. Harappan

Building Vocabulary

Preteach or review the following term:

rituals ceremonies, rites (p. 132)

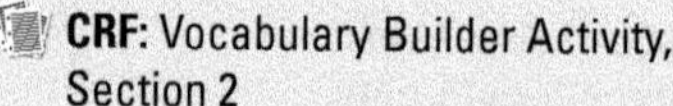

CRF: Vocabulary Builder Activity, Section 2

Taking Notes

Have students use the graphic organizer online to take notes on the section. This activity will prepare students for the Section Assessment, in which they will complete a graphic organizer that builds on the information using the Critical Thinking Skill: Analyzing Causes.

SECTION 2

Origins of Hinduism

What You Will Learn...

Main Ideas

1. Indian society divided into distinct groups under the Aryans.
2. The Aryans practiced a religion known as Brahmanism.
3. Hinduism developed out of Brahmanism and influences from other cultures.
4. A few groups reacted to Hinduism by breaking away to form their own religions.

The Big Idea

Hinduism, the largest religion in India today, developed out of ancient Indian beliefs and practices.

Key Terms

caste system, *p. 131*
Hinduism, *p. 133*
reincarnation, *p. 133*
karma, *p. 134*
Jainism, *p. 134*
nonviolence, *p. 135*
Sikhism, *p. 135*

hmhsocialstudies.com TAKING NOTES

Use the graphic organizer online to take notes on Hinduism. Pay attention to the religion's origins, its teachings, and other religions that developed alongside it.

If YOU were there...

Your family are skillful weavers who make beautiful cotton cloth. You belong to the class in Aryan society who are traders, farmers, and craftspeople. Often the raja of your town leads the warriors into battle. You admire their bravery but know you can never be one of them. To be an Aryan warrior, you must be born into that noble class. Instead, you have your own duty to carry out.

How do you feel about remaining a weaver?

BUILDING BACKGROUND As the Aryans moved into India, they developed a strict system of social classes. As the Aryans' influence spread through India, so did their class system. Before long, this class system was a key part of Indian society.

Indian Society Divides

As Aryan society became more complex, their society became divided into groups. For the most part, these groups were organized by people's occupations. Strict rules developed about how people of different groups could interact. As time passed, these rules became stricter and became central to Indian society.

The *Varnas*

According to the Vedas, there were four main *varnas*, or social divisions, in Aryan society. These *varnas* were:

- Brahmins (BRAH-muhns), or priests,
- Kshatriyas (KSHA-tree-uhs), or rulers and warriors,
- Vaisyas (VYSH-yuhs), or farmers, craftspeople, and traders, and
- Sudras (SOO-drahs), or laborers and non-Aryans.

The Brahmins were seen as the highest ranking because they performed rituals for the gods. This gave the Brahmins great influence over the other *varnas*.

Teach the Big Idea

At Level

Origins of Hinduism

1. **Teach** Ask students the questions in the Main Idea boxes to teach this section.
2. **Apply** Ask students to list people and terms associated with Hinduism. Write responses for students to see. Karma, dharma, nonviolence, and reincarnation may be among the terms suggested. Call on volunteers to describe how the terms listed relate to each other. **LS Verbal/Linguistic**
3. **Review** Review the major beliefs of Hinduism and ask for volunteers to explain each one.
4. **Practice/Homework** Have students pick one of the major beliefs of Hinduism and, using the information provided in this section, draw a picture or diagram to illustrate the belief. **LS Visual/Spatial**

Alternative Assessment Handbook, Rubric 3: Artwork

The Caste System

As the rules of interaction between *varnas* got stricter, the Aryan social order became more complex. In time, each of the four *varnas* in Aryan society was further divided into many castes, or groups. This **caste system** divided Indian society into groups based on a person's birth, wealth, or occupation. At one time, some 3,000 separate castes existed in India.

The caste to which a person belonged determined his or her place in society. However, this ordering was by no means permanent. Over time, individual castes gained or lost favor in society as caste members gained wealth or power. On rare occasions, people could change caste.

Both men and women belonged to castes. Early in the Aryan period, women had most of the same rights as men. They could, for example, own property and receive an education. Over time, however, laws were passed to limit these rights.

By the late Aryan period, a segment of early Indian society had developed that did not belong to any caste. This group was called the untouchables. They could hold only certain, often unpleasant, jobs.

Caste Rules

To keep their classes distinct, the Aryans developed sutras, or guides, which listed all the rules for the caste system. For example, people were not allowed to marry anyone from a different class. It was even forbidden for people from one class to eat with people from another. People who broke the caste rules could be banned from their homes and their castes, which would make them untouchables. Because of these rules, people spent almost all of their time with others in their same class.

READING CHECK **Drawing Inferences** How did a person become a member of a caste?

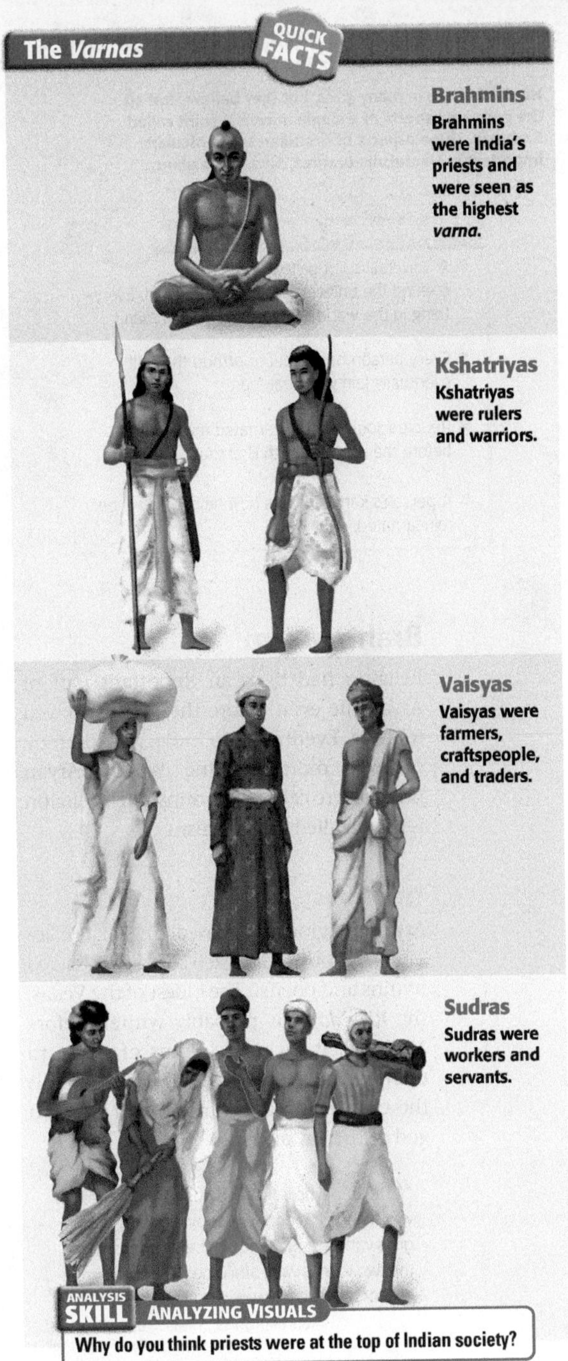

The *Varnas*
QUICK FACTS
Brahmins
Brahmins were India's priests and were seen as the highest *varna.*
Kshatriyas
Kshatriyas were rulers and warriors.
Vaisyas
Vaisyas were farmers, craftspeople, and traders.
Sudras
Sudras were workers and servants.
ANALYSIS SKILL ANALYZING VISUALS
Why do you think priests were at the top of Indian society?

Direct Teach

Main Idea

1 Indian Society Divides

Indian society divided into distinct groups under the Aryans.

Recall What were the four varnas? *Brahmins, Kshatriyas, Vaisyas, and Sudras*

Describe What were some rules described in the sutras? *People couldn't marry anyone or eat with anyone from a different class.*

Explain What could happen to someone who broke caste rules? *They could be banned from their homes and their caste, which would make them untouchables.*

Quick Facts Transparency: The *Varnas*

Info to Know

The Harijans Although of people who didn't belong to any caste were often called untouchables, Mohandas Gandhi called them Harijans, which means "children of God," and worked to raise their status. The Indian constitution of 1949 gave the Harijans legal recognition and rights. Although some members of the group have become powerful political leaders, some discrimination against them still exists.

Did you know . . .

The Brahmins included not only priests, but also teachers and scholars—those who dealt in knowledge and spirituality.

Critical Thinking: Identifying Points of View

Above Level

Research Required

The Caste System

1. Organize students into two groups: one group will report on positive views of the caste system and the other will report on negative views.
2. Have students use library and Internet resources to find differing views of the caste system. Encourage them to find and examine English-language newspapers and magazines from India. Students should pay particular attention to what factors may have influenced the writer's opinions.
3. Ask each group to elect a spokesperson to report its findings to the class. Lead a discussion about how the different points of view about the caste system were expressed.

LS Interpersonal

Alternative Assessment Handbook, Rubric 14: Group Activity

Answers

Analyzing Visuals *possible answer—Priests performed rituals that people believed could make the gods grant their wishes.*

Reading Check *born into it*

Direct Teach

Main Idea

❷ Brahmanism

The Aryans practiced a religion known as Brahmanism.

Identify What is the *Rigveda? the oldest of the Vedas that contained a collection of hymns of praise to many gods*

Recall When was *Rigveda* probably written*? before 1000 BC*

Compare How did the Upanishads differ from other Vedic texts? *The Upanishads were reflections on the Vedas written by religious students and teachers.*

Explain Why did priests place sacrifices into a fire? *They believed the fire would carry the sacrifice to the gods.*

Activity Standard English Mastery

Hymn to Indra Read the excerpt from the hymn to Indra. Remind students that an adjective is a word that describes someone or something. Then have students write down adjectives that the Aryans may have used to describe this god had they spoken English. Encourage students to use a thesaurus or dictionary to find appropriate adjectives. Call on volunteers to share their lists.

Quick Facts Transparency: Major Beliefs of Hinduism

Did you know . . .

Veda means "knowledge" in Sanskrit.

Hindu Gods and Beliefs

Hindus believe in many gods, but they believe that all the gods are aspects of a single universal spirit called Brahman. Three aspects of Brahman are particularly important in Hinduism—Brahma, Siva, and Vishnu.

Major Beliefs of Hinduism (QUICK FACTS)

- A universal spirit called Brahman created the universe and everything in it. Everything in the world is just a part of Brahman.
- Every person has a soul or *atman* that will eventually join with Brahman.
- People's souls are reincarnated many times before they can join with Brahman.
- A person's karma affects how he or she will be reincarnated.

The god Brahma represents the creator aspect of Brahman. His four faces symbolize the four Vedas.

Brahmanism

Religion had been an important part of Aryan life even before the Aryans moved to India. Eventually, in India, religion took on even more meaning. Because Aryan priests were called Brahmins, their religion is often called Brahmanism.

The Vedas

Aryan religion was based on the Vedas. There are four Vedas, each containing sacred hymns and poems. The oldest of the Vedas, the *Rigveda*, was probably written before 1000 BC. It includes hymns of praise to many gods. This passage, for example, is the opening of a hymn praising Indra, a god of the sky and war.

> "The one who is first and possessed of wisdom when born; the god who strove to protect the gods with strength; the one before whose force the two worlds were afraid because of the greatness of his virility [power]: he, O people, is Indra."
>
> –from the *Rigveda*, in *Reading about the World, Volume I*, edited by Paul Brians, et al

Later Vedic Texts

Over the centuries, Aryan Brahmins wrote down their thoughts about the Vedas. In time these thoughts were compiled into collections called Vedic texts.

One collection of Vedic texts describes Aryan religious rituals. For example, it describes how sacrifices should be performed. Priests placed animals, food, or drinks to be sacrificed in a fire. The Aryans believed that the fire would carry these offerings to the gods.

A second collection of Vedic texts describes secret rituals that only certain people could perform. In fact, the rituals were so secret that they had to be done in the forest, far from other people.

The final group of Vedic texts are the Upanishads (oo-PAHN-ee-shads), most of which were written by about 600 BC. These writings are reflections on the Vedas by religious students and teachers.

READING CHECK **Finding Main Ideas** What are the Vedic texts?

Cross-Discipline Activity: Literature

At Level

The Rigveda

Prep Required

1. Organize the class into groups. In advance, locate and duplicate examples from the *Rigveda.* Provide each member of a group the same sample, but give each group a different sample.
2. Have each group discuss the meaning of its sample. Provide dictionaries to help students in the task. Ask students also to find examples of descriptive language in the text.
3. Call on volunteers from each group to report their findings.
4. Extend the activity by asking interested students to locate and listen to a modern composition, *Choral Hymns from the Rig Veda,* by Gustav Holst. Ask them to play selections for the class. **LS Verbal/Linguistic**

Alternative Assessment Handbook, Rubric 14: Group Activity

Answers

Reading Check *sacred hymns and poems, collections of writings by Aryan Brahmins*

Siva, the destroyer aspect of Brahman, is usually shown with four arms and three eyes. Here he is shown dancing on the back of a demon he has defeated.

Vishnu is the preserver aspect of Brahman. In his four arms, he carries a conch shell, a mace, and a discus, symbols of his power and greatness.

Hinduism Develops

The Vedas, the Upanishads, and the other Vedic texts remained the basis of Indian religion for centuries. Eventually, however, the ideas of these sacred texts began to blend with ideas from other cultures. People from Persia and other kingdoms in Central Asia, for example, brought their ideas to India. In time, this blending of ideas created a religion called **Hinduism**, the largest religion in India today.

Hindu Beliefs

The Hindus believe in many gods. Among them are three major gods: Brahma the Creator, Siva the Destroyer, and Vishnu the Preserver. At the same time, however, Hindus believe that each god is part of a single universal spirit called Brahman. They believe that Brahman created the world and preserves it. Gods like Brahma, Siva, and Vishnu represent different aspects of Brahman. In fact, Hindus believe that everything in the world is part of Brahman.

Life and Rebirth

According to Hindu teachings, everyone has a soul, or *atman*, inside them. This soul holds the person's personality, the qualities that make them who they are. Hindus believe that a person's ultimate goal should be to reunite that soul with Brahman, the universal spirit.

Hindus believe that their souls will eventually join Brahman because the world we live in is an illusion. Brahman is the only reality. The Upanishads taught that people must try to see through the illusion of the world. Since it is hard to see through illusions, it can take several lifetimes. That is why Hindus believe that souls are born and reborn many times, each time in a new body. This process of rebirth is called **reincarnation**.

THE IMPACT TODAY

More than 800 million people in India practice Hinduism today. Over the centuries the religion has also spread, mostly through trade and migration. Hinduism is practiced throughout South and Southeast Asia, the Middle East, and the Americas.

Hinduism and the Caste System

According to the traditional Hindu view of reincarnation, a person who has died is reborn in a new physical form.

Direct Teach

Main Idea

3 Hinduism Develops

Hinduism developed out of Brahmanism and influences from other cultures.

Identify According to Hindu belief, what are the three major forms of Brahman? *Brahma the creator, Siva the destroyer, Vishnu the preserver*

Analyze What led to the development of Hinduism? *the blending of the Vedic texts with ideas from other cultures*

Evaluate How may believing that this world is merely an illusion affect one's behavior? *Answers will vary but should reflect logical thinking.*

Connect to Art

Lord of the Dance The bronze statue shown portrays Siva as Nataraja, or Lord of the Dance. Stylized flames surround him. Underfoot is the Demon of Ignorance. According to Hindu belief, during his dance Siva destroys the universe, but it is continually reborn. This statue was made in the 1200s.

Collaborative Learning

At Level

Collages about Hinduism

Materials: art supplies

1. First, review the three major forms of Brahman and the main beliefs of Hinduism.
2. Then organize students into small groups. Have some of the groups create collages combining original illustrations and text to describe the Hindu concept of the three aspects of Brahman. Have other groups create collages about the other main Hindu beliefs.
3. Have volunteers present their collages to the class. **LS Visual/Spatial, Interpersonal**

Alternative Assessment Handbook, Rubric 8: Collages

Direct Teach

Main Idea

3 Hinduism Develops

Hinduism developed out of Brahmanism and influences from other cultures.

Identify What is karma? *the effects that good or bad actions have on a person's soul*

Evaluate Do you think a wealthy Brahmin would want his or her servants to believe in *dharma*? Why or why not? *possible answers—Servants would be more likely to accept their fate in life if they believed in* dharma.

CRF: Primary Source Activity: Mohandas Gandhi's Autobiography

Primary Source

Martin Luther King, Jr. Martin Luther King Jr. described nonviolent resistance as "passive physically but strongly active spiritually; it is nonaggressive physically but dynamically aggressive spiritually." Ask students what they think Dr. King meant by this statement and whether they think Mohandas Gandhi would agree with it. *possible answer—although nonviolent resistance doesn't require physical strength, it does demand a strong spirit; yes, because they both believed in nonviolent protest*

The type of form depends upon his or her **karma**, the effects that good or bad actions have on a person's soul. Evil actions will build bad karma. A person with bad karma will be born into a lower caste or life form.

In contrast, good actions build good karma. People with good karma are born into a higher caste in their next lives. In time, good karma will bring salvation, or freedom from life's worries and the cycle of rebirth. This salvation is called *moksha.*

Hinduism taught that each person had a *dharma,* or set of spiritual duties, to fulfill. Fulfilling one's *dharma* required accepting one's station in life. By teaching people to accept their stations, Hinduism helped preserve the caste system.

READING CHECK **Summarizing** What determined how a person would be reborn?

Groups React to Hinduism

Although Hinduism was widely followed in India, not everyone agreed with its beliefs. Some unsatisfied people and groups looked for new religious ideas. Two such groups were the Jains (JYNZ), believers in a religion called Jainism (JY-niz-uhm), and the Sikhs (SEEKS), believers in Sikhism (SEEK-iz-uhm).

Jainism

Jainism is based on the teachings of a man named Mahavira, who is believed to have been born around 599 BC. Mahavira was raised as a Hindu. As an adult, however, he thought Hinduism put too much emphasis on rituals. Instead of ritual, his teachings emphasize four basic principles: injure no life, tell the truth, do not steal, and own

LINKING TO TODAY

Nonviolence

In modern times, nonviolence has been a powerful tool for social protest. Mohandas Gandhi led a long nonviolent struggle against British rule in India. This movement helped India win its independence in 1947. About 10 years later, Martin Luther King Jr. adopted Gandhi's nonviolent methods in his struggle to win civil rights for African Americans. Then, in the 1960s, Cesar Chavez organized a campaign of nonviolence to protest the treatment of farm workers in California. These three leaders proved that people can bring about social change without using violence. As Chavez once explained, "Nonviolence is not inaction. It is not for the timid or the weak. It is hard work. It is the patience to win."

Mohandas Gandhi (top), Martin Luther King Jr. (above), and Cesar Chavez (right)

ANALYSIS SKILL **ANALYZING INFORMATION**

How did these three leaders prove that nonviolence is a powerful tool for social change?

Differentiating Instruction

Advanced/Gifted and Talented

Above Level | Research Required

1. Have students research the life of Mohandas Gandhi—particularly how his beliefs affected his nonviolent methods of protest. Point out that some of Gandhi's beliefs contrasted with traditional Hindu beliefs. Students should use library and Internet sources.
2. Students should then write brief reports that tell how Gandhi's religious beliefs affected his actions.
3. To extend the activity, have interested students locate descriptions of Gandhi written by British writers during the 1940s and report on how they portrayed him.

LS Verbal/Linguistic

Alternative Assessment Handbook, Rubrics 30: Research; and 42: Writing to Inform

Answers

Analyzing Information *by helping to end British rule in India, winning civil rights for African Americans, improving treatment of farm workers*

Reading Check *their actions during their lifetimes*

no property. In their efforts not to injure anyone or anything, the Jains practice **nonviolence**, or the avoidance of violent actions. The Sanskrit word for this nonviolence is *ahimsa* (uh-HIM-sah). Many Hindus also practice *ahimsa*.

The Jains' emphasis on nonviolence comes from their belief that everything is alive and part of the cycle of rebirth. Jains are very serious about not injuring or killing any creature—humans, animals, insects, or even plants. They do not believe in animal sacrifice, unlike the ancient Brahmins. Because they don't want to hurt living creatures, Jains are vegetarians. They do not eat any food that comes from animals.

Sikhism

Founded centuries later than Jainism, **Sikhism** has its roots in the teachings of the Guru Nanak, who lived in the AD 1400s. The title *guru* is Sanskrit for "teacher." Like Mahavira, Nanak was raised a Hindu but grew dissatisfied with the religion's teachings. He began to travel and came into contact with many other religions, including Islam. His teachings blended ideas from Hinduism with ideas from Islam and other religions. Over time, these teachings were explained and expanded by nine other gurus.

Sikhism is monotheistic. Sikhs believe in only one God, who has no physical form but can be sensed in the creation. For Sikhs, the ultimate goal is to be reunited with God after death. To achieve this goal, one must meditate to find spiritual enlightenment. Because they believe that achieving enlightenment may take several lifetimes, Sikhs also believe in reincarnation. Sikhism teaches that people should live truthfully and treat all people equally, regardless of gender, social class, or any other factor.

Sikhs pray several times each day. They are expected to wear five items at all times as signs of their religion: long hair, a small comb, a steel bracelet, a sword, and a special undergarment. In addition, all Sikh men wear turbans, as do many women.

READING CHECK **Finding Main Ideas**
What are two religions that developed out of Hinduism?

SUMMARY AND PREVIEW You have learned about three religions that developed in India—Hinduism, Jainism, and Sikhism. In Section 3, you will learn about another religion that began there—Buddhism.

Section 2 Assessment

Reviewing Ideas, Terms, and People

1. a. **Identify** What is the **caste system**?
   b. **Explain** Why did strict caste rules develop?
2. a. **Identify** What does the *Rigveda* include?
   b. **Analyze** What role did sacrifice play in Aryan society?
3. a. **Define** What is **karma**?
   b. **Sequence** How did Brahmanism develop into **Hinduism**?
   c. **Elaborate** How does Hinduism reinforce followers' willingness to remain within their castes?
4. a. **Recall** What are the four main teachings of **Jainism**?
   b. **Draw Conclusions** How do you think Guru Nanak's travels influenced the development of **Sikhism**?

Critical Thinking

5. **Analyzing Causes** Draw a graphic organizer like this one. Using your notes, explain how Hinduism developed from Brahmanism, and how Jainism and Sikhism developed from Hinduism.

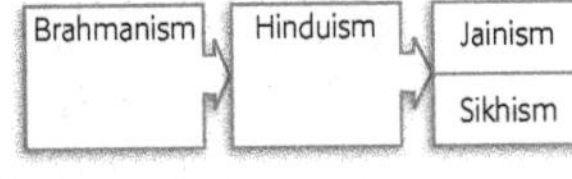

FOCUS ON WRITING

6. **Illustrating Hinduism** Now you have a new possible topic for your poster. How might you explain a complex religion like Hinduism?

Direct Teach

Main Idea

4 Groups React to Hinduism

The Jains and Sikhs reacted to Hinduism by breaking away to form their own religions.

Identify On whose teachings were Jainism and Sikhism based? *Mahavira and Nanak*

Contrast How did Jainism differ from Hinduism? *The Jains placed less emphasis on ritual.*

Explain Why do Sikhs carry special objects with them at all times? *as symbols of their religious faith*

Review & Assess

Close

Review the key terms and other unfamiliar phrases and how they relate to each other.

Review

Online Quiz, Section 2

Assess

SE Section 2 Assessment
PASS: Section 2 Quiz
Alternative Assessment Handbook

Reteach/Classroom Intervention

Guided Reading Workbook, Section 2
Interactive Skills Tutor CD-ROM

Section 2 Assessment Answers

1. a. a social system in which people are divided into groups based on a person's birth, wealth or occupation
   b. to keep the classes distinct
2. a. hymns of praise to many gods
   b. very important to religious ceremonies
3. a. the effects that good or bad actions have on a person's soul
   b. from Vedic texts and ideas from other cultures
   c. Hinduism teaches that if a person accepts their dharma, including their caste, they may be reborn into a higher caste.
4. a. Injure no life, tell the truth, do not steal, and own no property.
   b. possible answer—Travel exposed him to new ideas that helped shape the teachings of Sikhism.
5. Brahmanism—Aryan religion based on the Vedas; Hinduism—blending of the Vedas with ideas from other cultures; Jainism—based on teachings of Mahavira, who wanted less emphasis on rituals; Sikhism—combined beliefs of Hinduism and other religions to form a new belief system
6. Answers will vary but should be accurate.

Answers

Reading Check *Jainism, Sikhism*

Preteach

Bellringer

If YOU were there . . . use the **Daily Bellringer Transparency** to help students answer the question.

Daily Bellringer Transparency, Section 3

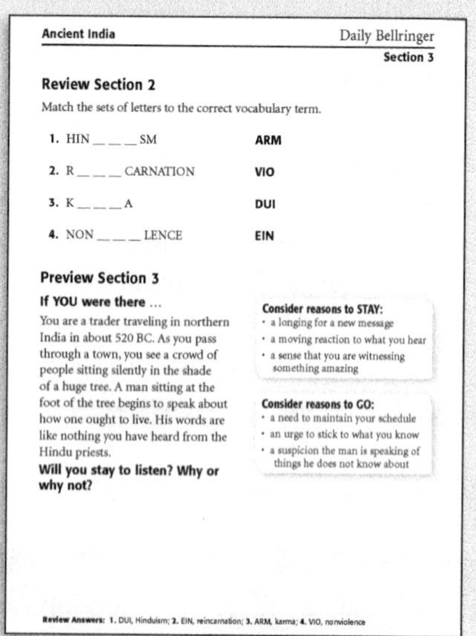

Ancient India — Daily Bellringer, Section 3

Review Section 2

Match the sets of letters to the correct vocabulary term.

1. HIN __ __ __ SM	**ARM**
2. R __ __ __ CARNATION	**VIO**
3. K __ __ __ A	**DUI**
4. NON __ __ __ LENCE	**EIN**

Preview Section 3

If YOU were there ...

You are a trader traveling in northern India in about 520 BC. As you pass through a town, you see a crowd of people sitting silently in the shade of a huge tree. A man sitting at the foot of the tree begins to speak about how one ought to live. His words are like nothing you have heard from the Hindu priests.

Will you stay to listen? Why or why not?

Consider reasons to STAY:
- a longing for a new message
- a moving reaction to what you hear
- a sense that you are witnessing something amazing

Consider reasons to GO:
- a need to maintain your schedule
- an urge to stick to what you know
- a suspicion the man is speaking of things he does not know about

Review Answers: 1. DUI, Hinduism; 2. EIN, reincarnation; 3. ARM, karma; 4. VIO, nonviolence

Building Vocabulary

Preteach or review the following term:

enlightenment clarification, understanding (p. 137)

CRF: Vocabulary Builder Activity, Section 3

Taking Notes

Have students use the graphic organizer online to take notes on the section. This activity will prepare students for the Section Assessment, in which they will complete a graphic organizer that builds on the information using the Critical Thinking Skill: Finding Main Ideas.

SECTION 3

Origins of Buddhism

What You Will Learn...

Main Ideas

1. Siddhartha Gautama searched for wisdom in many ways.
2. The teachings of Buddhism deal with finding peace.
3. Buddhism spread far from where it began in India.

The Big Idea

Buddhism began in India and became a major religion.

Key Terms and People

fasting, *p. 137*
meditation, *p. 137*
the Buddha, *p. 137*
Buddhism, *p. 138*
nirvana, *p. 138*
missionaries, *p. 140*

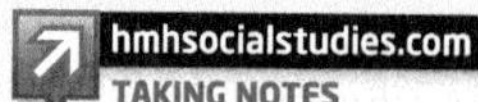

Use the graphic organizer online to take notes on the basic ideas of Buddhism and on Buddhism's spread.

If YOU were there...

You are a trader traveling in northern India in about 520 BC. As you pass through a town, you see a crowd of people sitting silently in the shade of a huge tree. A man sitting at the foot of the tree begins to speak about how one ought to live. His words are like nothing you have heard from the Hindu priests.

Will you stay to listen? Why or why not?

BUILDING BACKGROUND The Jains were not the only ones to break from Hinduism. In the 500s BC a young Indian prince attracted many people to his teachings about how people should live.

Siddhartha's Search for Wisdom

In the late 500s BC a restless young man, dissatisfied with the teachings of Hinduism, began to ask his own questions about life and religious matters. In time, he found answers. These answers attracted many followers, and the young man's ideas became the foundation of a major new religion in India.

The Quest for Answers

The restless young man was Siddhartha Gautama (si-DAHR-tuh GAU-tuh-muh). Born around 563 BC in northern India, near the Himalayas, Siddhartha was a prince who grew up in luxury. Born a Kshatriya, a member of the warrior class, Siddhartha never had to struggle with the problems that many people of his time faced. However, Siddhartha was not satisfied. He felt that something was missing in his life.

Siddhartha looked around him and saw how hard other people had to work and how much they suffered. He saw people grieving for lost loved ones and wondered why there was so much pain in the world. As a result, Siddhartha began to ask questions about the meaning of human life.

Teach the Big Idea

At Level

Origins of Buddhism

1. **Teach** Ask students the questions in the Main Idea boxes to teach this section.
2. **Apply** Organize the class into pairs. Have each pair create a flowchart or another graphic organizer of the students' choosing to show the development of Buddhism from the ideas of Siddhartha Gautama to its influence throughout Asia. Students should add details such as the Four Noble Truths and the steps in the Eightfold Path. LS **Visual/Spatial**
3. **Review** Call on volunteers to present their flowcharts to the class.
4. **Practice/Homework** Have students fill in any missing information on their graphic organizers and write a paragraph describing how the Buddha's teachings differed from Hinduism. LS **Verbal/Linguistic**

Alternative Assessment Handbook, Rubric 13: Graphic Organizers

In this painting, Prince Siddhartha leaves his palace to search for the true meaning of life, an event known as the Great Departure. Special helpers called *ganas* hold his horse's hooves so he won't awaken anyone.

Before Siddhartha reached age 30, he left his home and family to look for answers. His journey took him to many regions in India. Wherever he traveled, he had discussions with priests and people known for their wisdom. Yet no one could give convincing answers to Siddhartha's questions.

The Buddha Finds Enlightenment

Siddhartha did not give up. Instead, he became even more determined to find the answers he was seeking. For several years, he wandered in search of answers.

Siddhartha wanted to free his mind from daily concerns. For a while, he did not even wash himself. He also started **fasting**, or going without food. He devoted much of his time to **meditation**, the focusing of the mind on spiritual ideas.

According to legend, Siddhartha spent six years wandering throughout India. He eventually came to a place near the town of Gaya, close to the Ganges River. There, he sat down under a tree and meditated. After seven weeks of deep meditation, he suddenly had the answers that he had been looking for. He realized that human suffering comes from three things:

- wanting what we like but do not have,
- wanting to keep what we like and already have, and
- not wanting what we dislike but have.

Siddhartha spent seven more weeks meditating under the tree, which his followers later named the Tree of Wisdom. He then described his new ideas to five of his former companions. His followers later called this talk the First Sermon.

THE IMPACT TODAY Buddhists from all over the world still travel to India to visit the Tree of Wisdom and honor the Buddha.

Siddhartha Gautama was about 35 years old when he found enlightenment under the tree. From that point on, he would be called **the Buddha** (BOO-duh), or the "Enlightened One." The Buddha spent the rest of his life traveling across northern India and teaching people his ideas.

READING CHECK **Summarizing** What did the Buddha conclude about the cause of suffering?

Direct Teach

Main Idea

1 Siddhartha's Search for Wisdom

Siddhartha Gautama searched for wisdom in many ways.

Identify Who was Siddhartha Gautama? *a prince who became known as the Buddha*

Describe What did Siddhartha endure before reaching enlightenment? *wandered for several years, didn't wash, fasted, meditated*

Evaluate Of the three things that Siddhartha said caused human suffering, which one do you think causes the most suffering today? Why? *Answers will vary but should display logic and reflection.*

Info to Know

The Great Departure Stories and pictures about events in Siddhartha's life were created by his followers years after his death. According to stories about the Great Departure, Siddhartha had to sneak out of the palace because his father wanted him to be a soldier and ruler, rather than a searcher for religious truths. Ask students: How might the origin of these stories affect their accuracy? *Because followers created the stories, they may not be objective or strictly accurate.*

Critical Thinking: Sequencing

Below Level

Life of the Buddha

1. Have each student create a sequence diagram showing the major events in the Buddha's life. Diagrams may take different forms but should show a clear progression from one event to the next. Encourage students to create a rough draft of their diagrams first to ensure that they have included all the major events in the proper order.
2. Allow interested students to illustrate their sequence diagrams.
3. Call on volunteers to read the steps in their sequence diagrams. Have students revise their diagrams as needed. Display the diagrams for class members to see. LS **Visual/Spatial**

Alternative Assessment Handbook, Rubric 13: Graphic Organizers

Answers

Reading Check *wanting what we do not have, wanting to keep what we like and already have, and not wanting what we dislike but have*

Direct Teach

Main Idea

2 Teachings of Buddhism

The teachings of Buddhism deal with finding peace.

Identify Many of the Buddha's teachings reflect the ideas of which other world religion? *Hinduism*

Recall What are the Four Noble Truths? *See text for answers.*

Analyze What do you think the quote from the Buddha on this page means? *possible answer—People can progress toward enlightenment by responding to bad behavior with good behavior.*

Evaluate What advantage do you think the Buddha saw in following the "middle way"? *possible answer—Extreme behavior of any kind is not helpful or healthy.*

Activity Distinguishing between Hinduism and Buddhism Prepare a list of terms associated with Hinduism and Buddhism. As you read the list to the class, ask with which religion each is associated.

Quick Facts Transparency: The Eightfold Path

Linking to Today

The Buddha's Tree at Bodh Gaya The 80-foot statue shown on this page is near the Buddha's Tree of Wisdom. The original tree died long ago. Over the centuries, it has been replaced many times by offshoots of the Buddha's tree. Authorities have placed signs asking visitors not to take leaves from the tree or soil from the ground surrounding it. Near the tree is a golden platform that, according to tradition, marks the exact spot where Siddhartha Gautama sat while waiting for enlightenment.

Teachings of Buddhism

As he traveled, the Buddha gained many followers, especially among India's merchants and artisans. He even taught his views to a few kings. These followers were the first believers in **Buddhism**, a religion based on the teachings of the Buddha.

The Buddha was raised Hindu, and many of his teachings reflected Hindu ideas. Like Hindus, he believed that people should act morally and treat others well. In one of his sermons, he said:

> "Let a man overcome anger by love. Let him overcome the greedy by liberality [giving], the liar by truth. This is called progress in the discipline [training] of the Blessed."
>
> –The Buddha, quoted in *The History of Nations: India*

Four Noble Truths

At the heart of the Buddha's teachings were four guiding principles. These became known as the Four Noble Truths:

1. Suffering and unhappiness are a part of human life. No one can escape sorrow.
2. Suffering comes from our desires for pleasure and material goods. People cause their own misery because they want things they cannot have.
3. People can overcome desire and ignorance and reach **nirvana** (nir-VAH-nuh), a state of perfect peace. Reaching nirvana frees the soul from suffering and from the need for further reincarnation.
4. People can overcome ignorance and desire by following an eightfold path that leads to wisdom, enlightenment, and salvation.

The chart on the next page shows the steps in the Eightfold Path. The Buddha believed that this path was a middle way between human desires and denying oneself any pleasure. He believed that people should overcome their desire for material goods. They should, however, be reasonable, and not starve their bodies or cause themselves unnecessary pain.

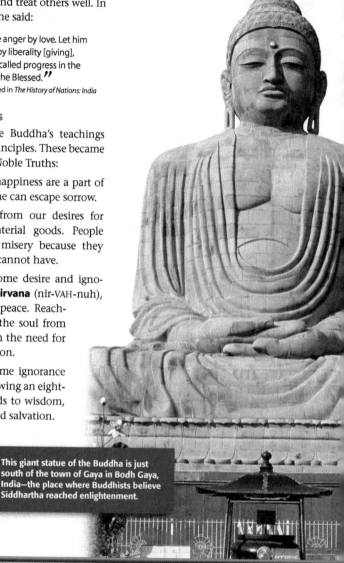

This giant statue of the Buddha is just south of the town of Gaya in Bodh Gaya, India—the place where Buddhists believe Siddhartha reached enlightenment.

Differentiating Instruction

Advanced/Gifted and Talented

Above Level | Research Required

1. Explain to students that some Buddhists become monks and nuns. Read dictionary definitions for both terms.
2. Ask students to imagine that they are newspaper reporters assigned to spend one day with a Buddhist monk or nun and report on their subjects' daily lives.
3. Have students conduct research on Buddhist monks or nuns—either in the present or the past.
4. Then have students write brief newspaper articles describing one day's events in a monk's or nun's life.
5. Encourage students to make their articles as specific as possible. For example, they might discuss the person's chores or the kinds or ceremonies in which he or she participates.

LS Verbal/Linguistic

Alternative Assessment Handbook, Rubric 40: Writing to Describe

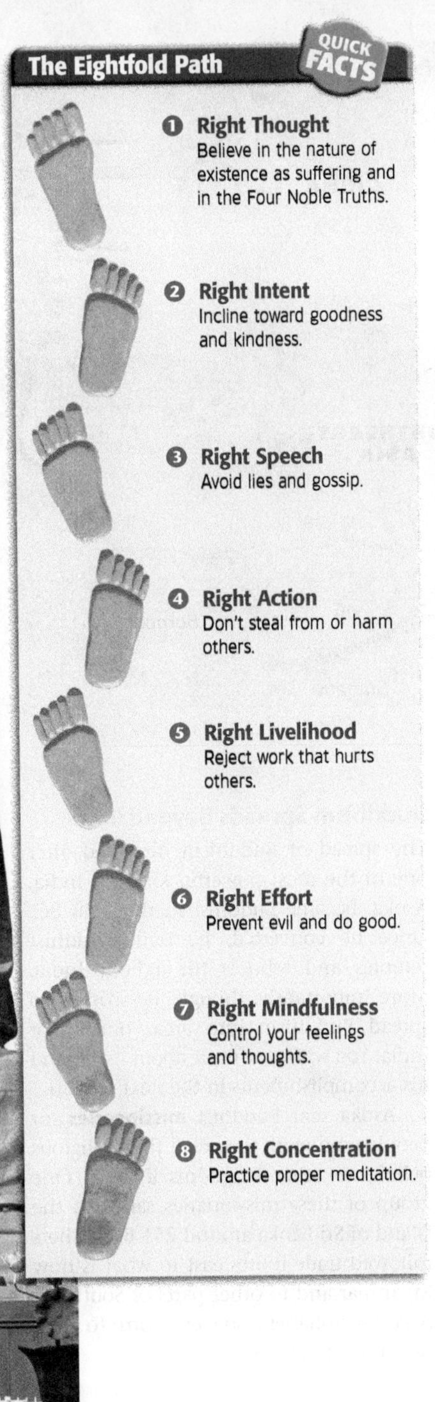
The Eightfold Path
QUICK FACTS
1 Right Thought
Believe in the nature of existence as suffering and in the Four Noble Truths.
2 Right Intent
Incline toward goodness and kindness.
3 Right Speech
Avoid lies and gossip.
4 Right Action
Don't steal from or harm others.
5 Right Livelihood
Reject work that hurts others.
6 Right Effort
Prevent evil and do good.
7 Right Mindfulness
Control your feelings and thoughts.
8 Right Concentration
Practice proper meditation.

Challenging Hindu Ideas

Some of the Buddha's teachings challenged traditional Hindu ideas. For example, the Buddha rejected many of the ideas contained in the Vedas, such as animal sacrifice. He told people that they did not have to follow these texts.

The Buddha challenged the authority of the Hindu priests, the Brahmins. He did not believe that they or their rituals were necessary for enlightenment. Instead, he taught that it was the responsibility of each individual to work for his or her own salvation. Priests could not help them. However, the Buddha did not reject the Hindu teaching of reincarnation. He taught that people who failed to reach nirvana would have to be reborn time and time again until they achieved it.

The Buddha was opposed to the caste system. He didn't think that people should be confined to a particular place in society. Everyone who followed the Eightfold Path properly, he said, would achieve nirvana. It didn't matter what *varna* or caste they had belonged to in life as long as they lived the way they should.

The Buddha's opposition to the caste system won him support from the masses. Many of India's herdsmen, farmers, artisans, and untouchables liked hearing that their low social rank would not be a barrier to enlightenment. Unlike Hinduism, Buddhism made them feel that they had the power to change their lives.

The Buddha also gained followers among the higher classes. Many rich and powerful Indians welcomed his ideas about avoiding extreme behavior while seeking salvation. By the time of his death around 483 BC, the Buddha's influence was spreading rapidly throughout India.

READING CHECK **Comparing** How did Buddha's teachings agree with Hinduism?

Direct Teach

Main Idea

2 Teachings of Buddhism

The teachings of Buddhism deal with finding peace.

Explain What did the Buddha think about the caste system? *He was opposed to it.*

Contrast How is "right thought" different from "right action"? *"Right thought" refers to beliefs, whereas "right action" has to do with how we put beliefs and thoughts into action.*

Evaluate How do you think people reacted to the Buddha's telling them they did not have to accept the Brahmins' authority? *possible answers—The Brahmins would have resented it, while other Hindus may have been relieved.*

Linking to Today

Buddhism in India Many Hindus of India do not see Buddhism as a religion truly separate from Hinduism. Instead, they regard the Buddha as the ninth incarnation of the god Vishnu. As a result, they see Buddhism as a sect within Hinduism.

Checking for Understanding

True or False Answer each statement *T* if it is true or *F* if it is false. If false, explain why.

1. Siddhartha Gautama was raised as a Hindu. *T*
2. The Buddha rejected all Hindu ideas. *F; The Buddha believed in reincarnation.*
3. At the heart of the Buddha's teachings were four guiding principles known as the Four Noble Truths. *T*

Social Studies Skill: Identifying Central Issues

At Level

Buddhism and Hinduism

1. Remind students that some of the Buddha's teachings conflicted with Hinduism, while others agreed with Hindu beliefs.
2. Organize students into pairs. Have each pair write a conversation or argument that a traditional Hindu might have had with a Hindu who has adopted the teachings of the Buddha. For traditional Hindus, students may choose a Brahmin or a person from a lower caste.
3. Call on volunteers to read their arguments or conversations.
4. Finally, lead a class discussion about why Buddhism gained followers among all classes. **LS Interpersonal**

Alternative Assessment Handbook, Rubric 11: Discussions

Answers

Reading Check *Buddha's teachings included reincarnation.*

Direct Teach

Main Idea

❸ Buddhism Spreads

Buddhism spread far from where it began in India.

Identify What are some places to which Buddhism spread? *throughout India, Sri Lanka, Myanmar and other parts of Southeast Asia, near the Himalayas, Central Asia, Persia, Syria, Egypt, China, Korea, Japan*

Explain What is one reason why Buddhism spread quickly? *Buddha's teachings were popular and easy to understand.*

Contrast How are the Theravada and Mahayana branches of Buddhism different? *Theravada—follow the Buddha's teachings exactly; Mahayana—can interpret Buddha's teachings to help them reach nirvana*

Map Transparency: Early Spread of Buddhism

Info to Know

Theravada and Mahayana Theravada and related versions of Buddhism are called Hinayana, or "lesser vehicle" in Sanskrit. Theravada is the older of the two major divisions. Followers trace Theravada traditions all the way back to monks of the first Buddhist community. Theravadins believe that one must become a monk to reach enlightenment. Today, Theravada Buddhism dominates Sri Lanka and Southeast Asia.

Mahayana means "greater vehicle." Mahayanists believe that people who attain enlightenment should stay in the world and help others gain salvation. It is the main form of Buddhism in China, Korea, Japan, and Tibet.

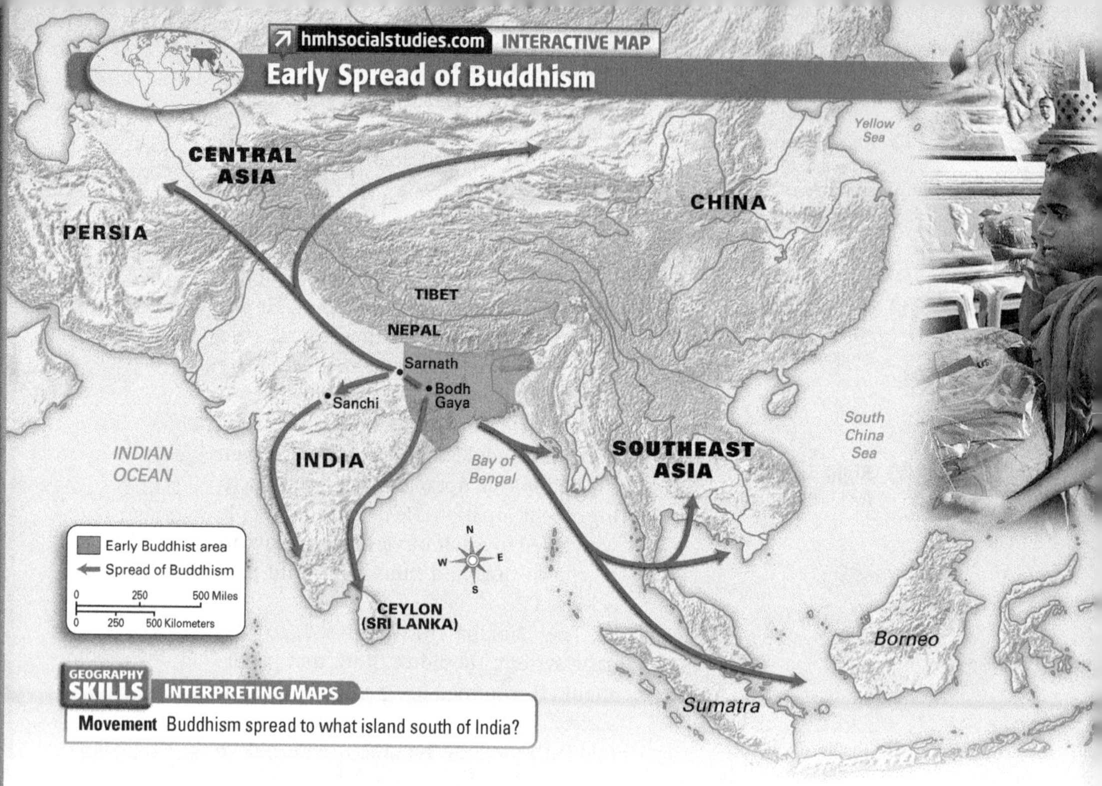

hmhsocialstudies.com INTERACTIVE MAP

Early Spread of Buddhism

GEOGRAPHY SKILLS INTERPRETING MAPS

Movement Buddhism spread to what island south of India?

Buddhism Spreads

Buddhism continued to attract followers after the Buddha's death. After spreading through India, the religion began to spread to other areas as well.

Buddhism Spreads in India

According to Buddhist tradition, 500 of the Buddha's followers gathered together shortly after he died. They wanted to make sure that the Buddha's teachings were remembered correctly.

In the years after this council, the Buddha's followers spread his teachings throughout India. The ideas spread very quickly, because Buddhist teachings were popular and easy to understand. Within 200 years of the Buddha's death, his teachings had spread through most of India.

Buddhism Spreads Beyond India

The spread of Buddhism increased after one of the most powerful kings in India, Asoka, became Buddhist in the 200s BC. Once he converted, he built Buddhist temples and schools throughout India. More importantly, though, he worked to spread Buddhism into areas outside of India. You will learn more about Asoka and his accomplishments in the next section.

Asoka sent Buddhist **missionaries**, or people who work to spread their religious beliefs, to other kingdoms in Asia. One group of these missionaries sailed to the island of Sri Lanka around 251 BC. Others followed trade routes east to what is now Myanmar and to other parts of Southeast Asia. Missionaries also went north to areas near the Himalayas.

Collaborative Learning

At Level

Interviewing a Missionary

1. Ask students to imagine that they lived in Sri Lanka when the first Buddhist missionaries arrived. Then have them imagine what it would have been like had there been television news during that time.
2. Organize students into pairs and instruct each pair to create a skit in which a news commentator interviews a Buddhist missionary.
3. The commentator should create a list of questions for the missionary, such as: Why have you come to Sri Lanka? What is meant by this word "enlightenment"? How do you think your beliefs can help people?
4. Using the information in this section, the missionary responds to these questions. Ask for volunteers to present their skits to the class. LS **Interpersonal**

Alternative Assessment Handbook, Rubric 33: Skits and Reader's Theater

Answers

Interpreting Maps *Ceylon (Sri Lanka)*

Young Buddhist students carry gifts in Sri Lanka, one of the many places outside of India where Buddhism spread.

Missionaries also introduced Buddhism to lands west of India. They founded Buddhist communities in Central Asia and Persia. They even taught about Buddhism as far away as Syria and Egypt.

Buddhism continued to grow over the centuries. Eventually it spread via the Silk Road into China, then Korea and Japan. Through their work, missionaries taught Buddhism to millions of people.

A Split within Buddhism

Even as Buddhism spread through Asia, however, it began to change. Not all Buddhists could agree on their beliefs and practices. Eventually disagreements between Buddhists led to a split within the religion. Two major branches of Buddhism were created—Theravada and Mahayana.

Members of the Theravada branch tried to follow the Buddha's teachings exactly as he had stated them. Mahayana Buddhists, though, believed that other people could interpret the Buddha's teachings to help people reach nirvana. Both branches have millions of believers today, but Mahayana is by far the larger branch.

READING CHECK **Sequencing** How did Buddhism spread from India to other parts of Asia?

SUMMARY AND PREVIEW Buddhism, one of India's major religions, grew more popular once it was adopted by rulers of India's great empires. You will learn more about those empires in the next section.

Section 3 Assessment

hmhsocialstudies.com ONLINE QUIZ

Reviewing Ideas, Terms, and People

1. a. **Identify** Who was **the Buddha**, and what does the term *Buddha* mean?
   b. **Summarize** How did Siddhartha Gautama free his mind and clarify his thinking as he searched for wisdom?
2. a. **Identify** What is **nirvana**?
   b. **Contrast** How are Buddhist teachings different from Hindu teachings?
   c. **Elaborate** Why do Buddhists believe that following the Eightfold Path leads to a better life?
3. a. **Describe** Into what lands did **Buddhism** spread?
   b. **Summarize** What role did **missionaries** play in spreading Buddhism?

Critical Thinking

4. **Finding Main Ideas** Draw a diagram like this one. Use it and your notes to identify and describe Buddhism's Four Noble Truths. Write a sentence explaining how these Truths are central to Buddhism.

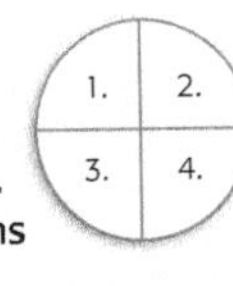

FOCUS ON WRITING

5. **Considering Indian Religions** Look back over what you've just read and the notes you took about Hinduism earlier. Perhaps you will want to focus your poster on ancient India's two major religions. Think about how you could design a poster around this theme.

Direct Teach

Linking to Today

Zen Buddhism Emphasize that the types of Buddhism practiced today vary around the world. One type of Buddhism commonly practiced in Japan is Zen Buddhism. It teaches that enlightenment can be achieved by breaking through the boundaries of everyday logical thought. This process is best achieved by following the guidance of a master. Zen Buddhism has helped shape not just Japan's religious life, but also its culture. Today almost 10 million Japanese follow Zen Buddhism.

Review & Assess

Close

Have students review the Four Noble Truths and the Eightfold Path.

Review

Online Quiz, Section 3

Assess

SE Section 3 Assessment

PASS: Section 3 Quiz

Alternative Assessment Handbook

Reteach/Classroom Intervention

Guided Reading Workbook, Section 3

Interactive Skills Tutor CD-ROM

Section 3 Assessment Answers

1. **a.** Siddhartha Gautama, a prince who found enlightenment; Enlightened One
   b. fasted, didn't bathe, meditated
2. **a.** a state of perfect peace
   b. Buddhists don't believe in sacrifices, the caste system, or that they needed the help of the Brahmins.
   c. It leads them down a path of fulfillment without excess or denial, which then leads to nirvana.
3. **a.** Sri Lanka, Myanmar, other parts of Southeast Asia, Central Asia, Persia, Syria, Egypt, and eventually to China and then Korea and Japan
   b. important role, because they traveled to distant lands to spread Buddhist teachings
4. See page 138 for answers.
5. Students' ideas will vary, but should display familiarity with text content.

Answers

Reading Check *Missionaries traveled to Sri Lanka, Myanmar, other parts of Southeast Asia, Central Asia, Persia, Syria, Egypt, and eventually to China and then Korea and Japan.*

Preteach

Bellringer

If YOU were there . . . Use the **Daily Bellringer Transparency** to help students answer the question.

Daily Bellringer Transparency, Section 4

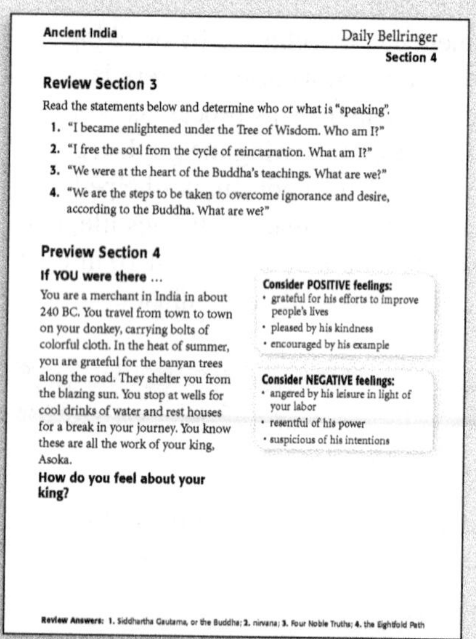

Ancient India Daily Bellringer **Section 4**

Review Section 3

Read the statements below and determine who or what is "speaking".

1. "I became enlightened under the Tree of Wisdom. Who am I?"
2. "I free the soul from the cycle of reincarnation. What am I?"
3. "We were at the heart of the Buddha's teachings. What are we?"
4. "We are the steps to be taken to overcome ignorance and desire, according to the Buddha. What are we?"

Preview Section 4

If YOU were there ...

You are a merchant in India in about 240 BC. You travel from town to town on your donkey, carrying bolts of colorful cloth. In the heat of summer, you are grateful for the banyan trees along the road. They shelter you from the blazing sun. You stop at wells for cool drinks of water and rest houses for a break in your journey. You know these are all the work of your king, Asoka.

How do you feel about your king?

Consider POSITIVE feelings:
- grateful for his efforts to improve people's lives
- pleased by his kindness
- encouraged by his example

Consider NEGATIVE feelings:
- angered by his leisure in light of your labor
- resentful of his power
- suspicious of his intentions

Review Answers: **1.** Siddhartha Gautama, or the Buddha; **2.** nirvana; **3.** Four Noble Truths; **4.** the Eightfold Path

Academic Vocabulary

Review with students the high-use academic term in this section.

establish to set up or create (p. 144)

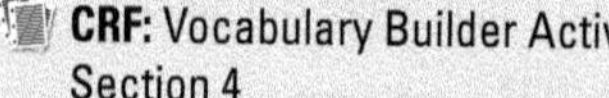

CRF: Vocabulary Builder Activity, Section 4

Taking Notes

Have students use the graphic organizer online to take notes on the section. This activity will prepare students for the Section Assessment, in which they will complete a graphic organizer that builds on the information using the Critical Thinking Skill: Categorizing.

Indian Empires

What You Will Learn...

Main Ideas

1. The Mauryan Empire unified most of India.
2. Gupta rulers promoted Hinduism in their empire.

The Big Idea

The Mauryas and the Guptas built great empires in India.

Key People

Candragupta Maurya, *p. 142*
Asoka, *p. 143*
Candra Gupta II, *p. 144*

Use the graphic organizer online to take notes about the rise and fall of ancient India's two greatest empires.

If YOU were there...

You are a merchant in India in about 240 BC. You travel from town to town on your donkey, carrying bolts of colorful cloth. In the heat of summer, you are grateful for the banyan trees along the road. They shelter you from the blazing sun. You stop at wells for cool drinks of water and rest houses for a break in your journey. You know these are all the work of your king, Asoka.

How do you feel about your king?

BUILDING BACKGROUND For centuries after the Aryan invasion, India was divided into small states. Each state had its own ruler and India had no central government. Then, in the 300s BC, a foreign conqueror, Alexander the Great, took over part of northwestern India. His armies soon left, but his influence continued to affect Indian society. Inspired by Alexander's example, a strong leader soon united India for the first time.

Mauryan Empire Unifies India

In the 320s BC a military leader named **Candragupta Maurya** (kuhn-druh-GOOP-tuh MOUR-yuh) seized control of the entire northern part of India. By doing so, he founded the Mauryan Empire. Mauryan rule lasted for about 150 years.

The Mauryan Empire

Candragupta Maurya ruled his empire with the help of a complex government. It included a network of spies and a huge army of some 600,000 soldiers. The army also had thousands of war elephants and thousands of chariots. In return for the army's protection, farmers paid a heavy tax to the government.

In 301 BC Candragupta decided to become a Jainist monk. To do so, he had to give up his throne. He passed the throne to his son, who continued to expand the empire. Before long, the Mauryas ruled all of northern India and much of central India as well.

Teach the Big Idea

At Level

Indian Empires

1. **Teach** Ask students the questions in the Main Idea boxes to teach this section.
2. **Apply** Have each student place the headings *Mauryan Empire* and *Gupta Empire* at the top of a sheet of paper. Ask half the class to fill in the paper with major events of each empire, along with the dates or approximate dates of those events. The other half of the class should write down details about the empires' societies, cultures, and achievements. **LS Visual/Spatial**
3. **Review** Call on volunteers from the events group to write the main events for all students to see. Have them spread out their entries so that volunteers from the other group can fill in details that they wrote down.
4. **Practice/Homework** Ask each student to write a verse for a national anthem for the Mauryan Empire or the Gupta Empire, using a popular song as the melody. **LS Verbal/Linguistic, Auditory/Musical**

Asoka

Around 270 BC Candragupta's grandson **Asoka** (uh-SOH-kuh) became king. Asoka was a strong ruler, the strongest of all the Mauryan emperors. He extended Mauryan rule over most of India. In conquering other kingdoms, Asoka made his own empire both stronger and richer.

For many years, Asoka watched his armies fight bloody battles against other peoples. A few years into his rule, however, Asoka converted to Buddhism. When he did, he swore that he would not launch any more wars of conquest.

After converting to Buddhism, Asoka had the time and resources to improve the lives of his people. He had wells dug and roads built throughout the empire. Along these roads, workers planted shade trees and built rest houses for weary travelers. He also encouraged the spread of Buddhism in India and the rest of Asia. As you read in the previous section, he sent missionaries to lands all over Asia.

Asoka died in 233 BC, and the empire began to fall apart soon afterward. His sons fought each other for power, and invaders threatened the empire. In 184 BC the last Mauryan king was killed by one of his own generals. India divided into smaller states once again.

FOCUS ON READING What can you infer about the religious beliefs of Asoka's sons?

READING CHECK **Finding Main Ideas** How did the Mauryans gain control of most of India?

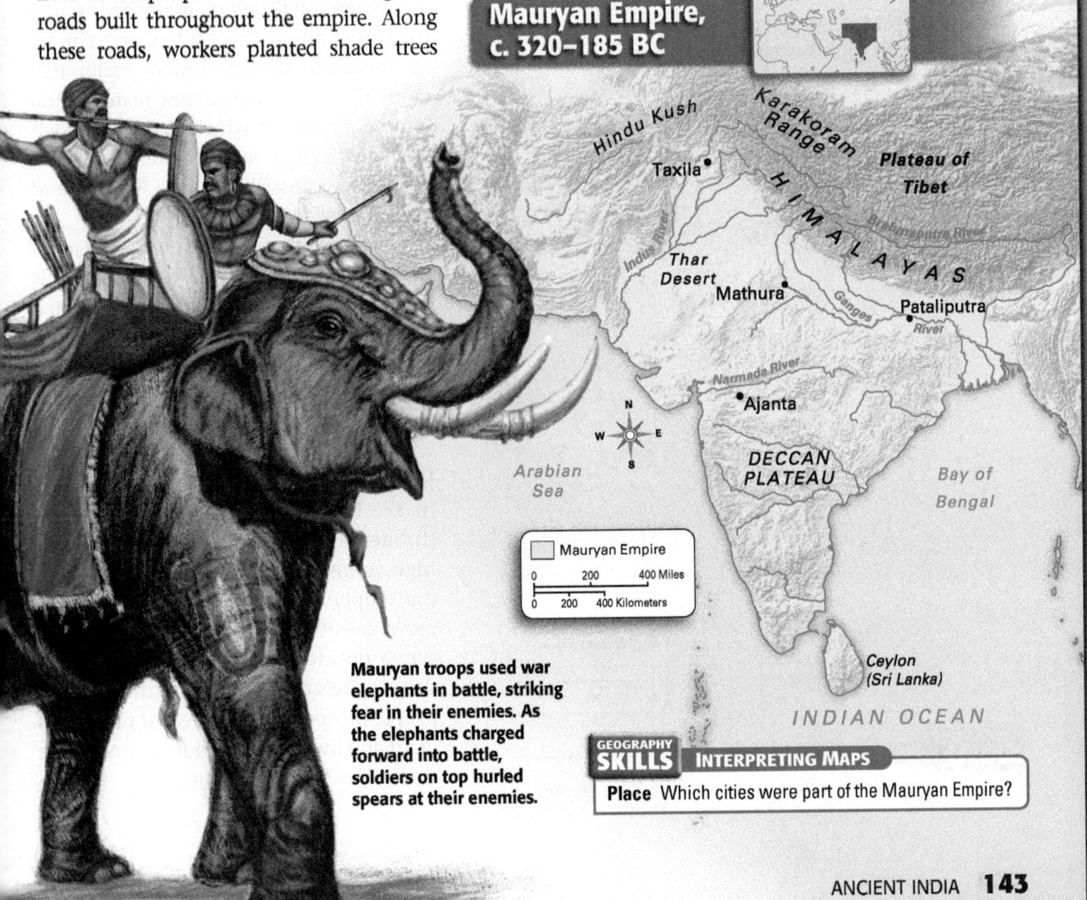

Mauryan troops used war elephants in battle, striking fear in their enemies. As the elephants charged forward into battle, soldiers on top hurled spears at their enemies.

GEOGRAPHY SKILLS INTERPRETING MAPS

Place Which cities were part of the Mauryan Empire?

Direct Teach

Main Idea

1 Mauryan Empire Unifies India

The Mauryan Empire unified most of India.

Identify Who was Candragupta Maurya? *a military leader who seized control of northern India in the 320s BC, founding the Mauryan Empire*

Describe What was Candragupta Maurya's government like? *network of spies, army of 600,000 soldiers along with many elephants and chariots, heavy taxes*

Explain How did becoming a Buddhist change Asoka's behavior? *He worked to improve his people's lives and spread Buddhism.*

- **CRF:** Biography Activity: Candragupta Maurya
- **CRF:** Biography Activity: Kautilya
- **CRF:** Biography Activity: Mahinda
- Map Transparency: Mauryan Empire, c. 320–185 BC

hmhsocialstudies.com

Online Resources
Activity: Mauryan Leaders

Interpreting Maps

Human/Environment Interaction

How may physical geography have limited the spread of the Mauryan Empire? *Mountains limited the spread to the northeast.*

Social Studies Skill: Retrieving and Analyzing Information

Mauryan Time Line

Above Level Research Required

1. Draw a blank time line for students to see. Write 320s BC and 184 BC on the time line. Call on volunteers to tell why those were important years for the Mauryan Empire.
2. Instruct students to create their own time lines titled *History of the Mauryan Empire.* They should start by incorporating information in this section.
3. Then have students conduct additional research on the Mauryan Empire so that they can include at least two facts not presented in this section in their time lines.
4. Display the time lines for other students to see. Lead a discussion about which events seem to be more significant than others. **LS Visual/Spatial**

Alternative Assessment Handbook, Rubrics 30: Research; and 36: Time Lines

Answers

Focus on Reading *Answers will vary but should reflect an understanding of the text.*

Interpreting Maps *Taxila, Mathura, Pataliputra, Ajanta*

Reading Check *by conquering neighboring kingdoms*

Direct Teach

Main Idea

❷ Gupta Rulers Promote Hinduism

Gupta rulers promoted Hinduism in their empire.

Describe What was India like after the fall of the Mauryan Empire? *divided for about 500 years*

Identify Who were Candra Gupta I and Candra Gupta II? *founder of the Gupta Empire; emperor under whom Gupta society reached its high point*

Analyze Why did the Gupta rulers support the caste system? *They believed it would make the empire more stable.*

Predict How do you think India would be different today if the Gupta rulers had not taken over? *possible answer—might be primarily Buddhist*

Activity **Early Indian Empire Tic-Tac-Toe** Have each student write down two questions from this section. Organize the class into two teams: *X*s and *O*s. Have students play a game of tic-tac-toe in which each team member is asked a question and gets to place a mark on the grid when he or she answers correctly. **LS Interpersonal**

Map Transparency: Gupta Empire, c. 400

Other People, Other Places

Trade with Rome For many years, India and the Roman Empire enjoyed a lively trade relationship. In fact, at one point the Romans had built special warehouses just for pepper imported from India. Although trade between Rome and India was sometimes disrupted, by the 300s and 400s it was again strong. Roman coins found in Sri Lanka are evidence of this trade.

Answers

Interpreting Maps *southern and southwestern*

Gupta Rulers Promote Hinduism

After the collapse of the Mauryan Empire, India remained divided for about 500 years. During that time, Buddhism continued to prosper and spread in India, and so the popularity of Hinduism declined.

A New Hindu Empire

ACADEMIC VOCABULARY
establish to set up or create

Eventually, however, a new dynasty was **established** in India. It was the Gupta (GOOP-tuh) dynasty, which took over India around AD 320. Under the Guptas, India was once again united, and it once again became prosperous.

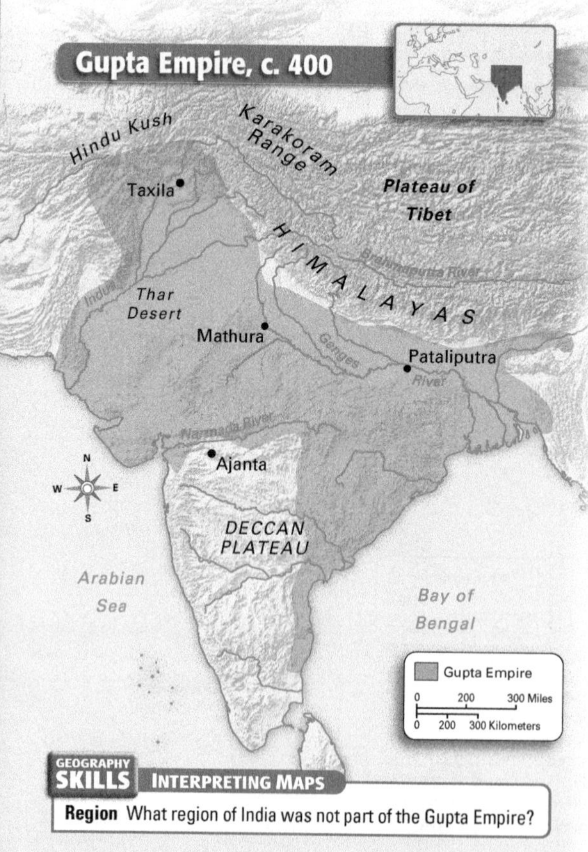

GEOGRAPHY SKILLS **INTERPRETING MAPS**

Region What region of India was not part of the Gupta Empire?

The first Gupta emperor was Candra Gupta I. Although their names are similar, he was not related to Candragupta Maurya. From his base in northern India, Candra Gupta's armies invaded and conquered neighboring lands. Eventually he brought much of the northern part of India under his control.

Candra Gupta was followed as emperor by his son, Samudra Gupta, a brilliant military leader. He continued his father's wars of conquest, fighting battles against many neighboring peoples. Through these wars, Samudra Gupta added more territory to his empire. By the time he died, for example, he had taken control of nearly all of the Ganges River valley.

Indian civilization flourished under the Gupta rulers. These rulers were Hindu, so Hinduism became India's major religion. The Gupta kings built many Hindu temples, some of which became models for later Indian architecture. They also promoted a revival of Hindu writings and worship practices.

Although they were Hindus, the Gupta rulers also supported the religious beliefs of Buddhism and Jainism. They promoted Buddhist art and built Buddhist temples. They also established a university at Nalanda that became one of Asia's greatest centers for Buddhist studies.

Gupta Society

In 375 Emperor **Candra Gupta II** took the throne in India. Gupta society reached its high point during his rule. Under Candra Gupta II, the empire continued to grow, eventually stretching all the way across northern India. At the same time, the empire's economy strengthened, and people prospered. They created fine works of art and literature. Outsiders admired the empire's wealth and beauty.

Differentiating Instruction

Special Needs Learners

Below Level **Prep Required**

1. Organize students into pairs. Provide each student with an outline map of the Indian subcontinent.
2. One member of the pair should draw the area included in the Mauryan Empire on his or her map. The other student should do the same for the Gupta Empire. Students should label the empires' cities and major geographical features.
3. Then have students exchange maps with their partners and draw the outline of the empire not yet recorded on the map.
4. Call on volunteers to describe how the boundaries of the two empires differed. **LS Visual/Spatial**

Alternative Assessment Handbook, Rubric 20: Map Creation

Gupta Art
This Gupta painting of a palace scene shows some of India's different castes. Gupta rulers supported Hinduism and the caste system.

Gupta kings believed the social order of the Hindu caste system would strengthen their rule. They also thought it would keep the empire stable. As a result, the Gupta considered the caste system an important part of Indian society.

Gupta rule remained strong in India until the late 400s. At that time the Huns, a group from Central Asia, invaded India from the northwest. Their fierce attacks drained the Gupta Empire of its power and wealth. As the Hun armies marched farther into India, the Guptas lost hope. By the middle of the 500s, Gupta rule had ended, and India had divided into small kingdoms yet again.

READING CHECK **Summarizing** What was the Gupta dynasty's position on religion?

SUMMARY AND PREVIEW The Mauryas and Guptas united much of India in their empires. Next you will learn about their many achievements.

Section 4 Assessment

hmhsocialstudies.com ONLINE QUIZ

Reviewing Ideas, Terms, and People

1. a. **Identify** Who created the Mauryan Empire?
   b. **Summarize** What happened after **Asoka** became a Buddhist?
   c. **Elaborate** Why do you think many people consider Asoka the greatest of all Mauryan rulers?
2. a. **Recall** What religion did most of the Gupta rulers belong to?
   b. **Compare and Contrast** How were the rulers **Candragupta Maurya** and Candra Gupta I alike, and how were they different?

Critical Thinking

3. **Categorizing** Draw a chart like this one. Fill it with information about India's rulers.

Ruler	Dynasty	Accomplishments

Focus on Writing

4. **Comparing Indian Empires** Another possible topic for your poster would be a comparison of the Mauryan and Gupta empires. Make a chart in your notebook that shows such a comparison.

Direct Teach

Main Idea

2 Gupta Rulers Promote Hinduism

Gupta rulers promoted Hinduism in their empire.

Summarize What led to the decline of the Gupta Empire? *The Huns from Central Asia invaded from the northwest; their armies attacked and marched deep into India.*

Review & Assess

Close

Refer students to the illustration of the Mauryan war elephants. Ask them to describe what it would be like to face these animals in battle.

Review

Online Quiz, Section 4

Assess

SE Section 4 Assessment
PASS: Section 4 Quiz
Alternative Assessment Handbook

Reteach/Classroom Intervention

Guided Reading Workbook, Section 4
Interactive Skills Tutor CD-ROM

Section 4 Assessment Answers

1. a. Candragupta Maurya
   b. Asoka focused on improving the lives of the citizens and spreading Buddhism.
   c. He gave up making war and concentrated instead on improving his people's lives.
2. a. Hinduism
   b. alike—India flourished under their rule; different—Candragupta Maurya became a Jainist monk, and Candra Gupta I was a Hindu.
3. Candragupta Maurya—Mauryan; founded the Mauryan empire, gave up his throne to become a Jainist monk; Asoka—Mauryan; extended Mauryan rule, converted to Buddhism, improved people's lives, spread Buddhism; Candra Gupta I—Gupta; first Gupta emperor, brought much of the northern part of India under control; Candra Gupta II—Gupta; expanded empire, Gupta society at its height
4. Charts will vary but should reflect text content.

Answers

Reading Check *Even though Gupta rulers were Hindus, they supported the beliefs of Buddhism and Jainism.*

Biography

Reading Focus Question

Lead a discussion about decisions students have made that have affected various aspects of their lives. Or, you may prefer that students discuss decisions made by family members, contemporary world leaders, or other figures in world history. Point out that every day people make decisions that have wide-ranging effects. Use a daily newspaper to spark discussion about decisions and their ramifications.

Linking to Today

Stupas Originally, Asoka built eight monuments, or *stupas*, at Sanchi, but only three remain today. In 1989, the entire area was added to UNESCO's World Heritage List.

Info to Know

The Great Stupa The hemispherical shape of this monument, called the Great Stupa, has symbolic meaning. Ask students why this shape might have been chosen for the monument. *It symbolizes the dome of the sky as we look at it from the earth.*

About the Illustration

This illustration of Asoka is an artist's conception based on available sources. However, historians are uncertain exactly what Asoka looked like.

BIOGRAPHY

Asoka

How can one decision change a man's entire life?

When did he live? before 230 BC

Where did he live? Asoka's empire included much of northern and central India.

What did he do? After fighting many bloody wars to expand his empire, Asoka gave up violence and converted to Buddhism.

Why is he important? Asoka is one of the most respected rulers in Indian history and one of the most important figures in the history of Buddhism. As a devout Buddhist, Asoka worked to spread the Buddha's teachings. In addition to sending missionaries around Asia, he built huge columns carved with Buddhist teachings all over India. Largely through his efforts, Buddhism became one of Asia's main religions.

Generalizing How did Asoka's life change after he became Buddhist?

KEY EVENTS

- **c. 270 BC** Asoka becomes the Mauryan emperor.
- **c. 261 BC** Asoka's empire reaches its greatest size.
- **c. 261 BC** Asoka becomes a Buddhist.
- **c. 251 BC** Asoka begins to send Buddhist missionaries to other parts of Asia.

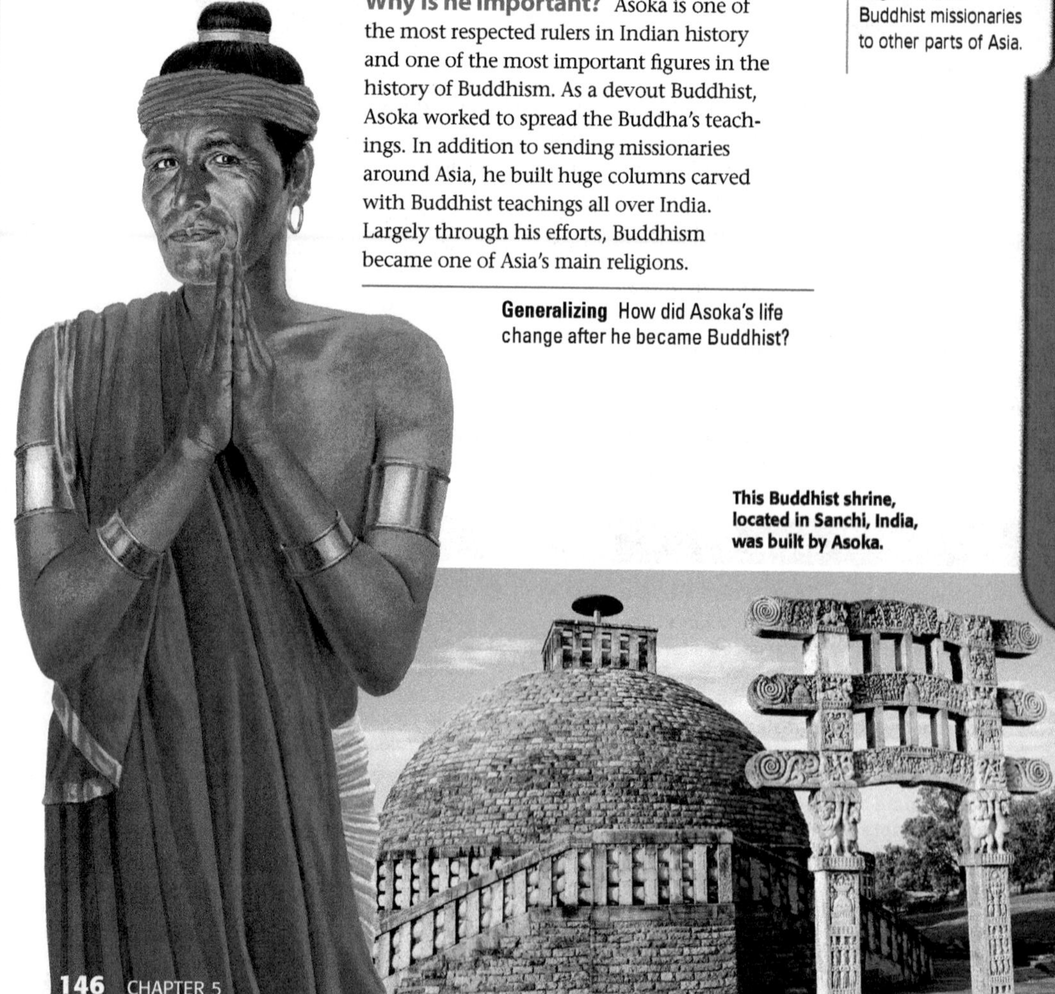

This Buddhist shrine, located in Sanchi, India, was built by Asoka.

Critical Thinking: Solving Problems

At Level

Asoka's Plan for Helping His People

1. Organize students into small groups. Ask students to imagine that they are Asoka's advisers.
2. Tell students that Asoka has called the advisers together to announce his conversion to Buddhism. Asoka has asked them to suggest plans for helping his people.
3. Each group should use what members know about Asoka and India to list specific ideas. Students should not limit themselves to those items mentioned in this section.
4. Then have groups add to their lists by suggesting problems or hurdles that may slow the progress of Asoka's plans. Examples include issues related to physical geography, opposition by local rulers, and so on.
5. Challenge students to suggest ways these problems could be overcome.

LS Interpersonal, Logical/Mathematical

Alternative Assessment Handbook, Rubric 14: Group Activity

Answers

He became a peace-loving ruler dedicated to improving the lives of his people.

Indian Achievements

SECTION 5

If YOU were there...

You are a traveler in western India in the 300s. You are visiting a cave temple that is carved into a mountain cliff. Inside the cave it is cool and quiet. Huge columns rise all around you. You don't feel you're alone, for the walls and ceilings are covered with paintings. They are filled with lively scenes and figures. In the center is a large statue with calm, peaceful features.

How does this cave make you feel?

BUILDING BACKGROUND The Mauryan and Gupta empires united most of India politically. During these empires, Indian artists, writers, scholars, and scientists made great advances. Some of their works are still studied and admired today.

Religious Art

The Indians of the Mauryan and Gupta periods created great works of art, many of them religious. Many of their paintings and sculptures illustrated either Hindu and Buddhist teachings. Magnificent temples—both Hindu and Buddhist—were built all around India. They remain some of the most beautiful buildings in the world today.

Temples

Early Hindu temples were small stone structures. They had flat roofs and contained only one or two rooms. In the Gupta period, though, temple architecture became more complex. Gupta temples were topped by huge towers and were covered with carvings of the god worshipped inside.

Buddhist temples of the Gupta period are also impressive. Some Buddhists carved entire temples out of mountainsides. The most famous such temple is at Ajanta. Its builders filled the caves with beautiful wall paintings and sculpture.

What You Will Learn...

Main Ideas

1. Indian artists created great works of religious art.
2. Sanskrit literature flourished during the Gupta period.
3. The Indians made scientific advances in metalworking, medicine, and other sciences.

The Big Idea

The people of ancient India made great contributions to the arts and sciences.

Key Terms

metallurgy, *p. 150*
alloys, *p. 150*
Hindu-Arabic numerals, *p. 150*
inoculation, *p. 150*
astronomy, *p. 151*

Use the graphic organizer online to take notes on the achievements of ancient India.

Preteach

Bellringer

If YOU were there . . . Use the **Daily Bellringer Transparency** to help students answer the question.

Daily Bellringer Transparency, Section 5

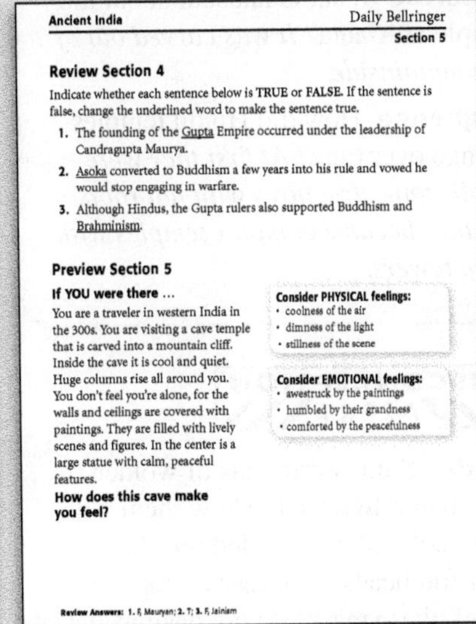

Ancient India — Daily Bellringer **Section 5**

Review Section 4

Indicate whether each sentence below is **TRUE** or **FALSE**. If the sentence is false, change the underlined word to make the sentence true.

1. The founding of the Gupta Empire occurred under the leadership of Candragupta Maurya.
2. Asoka converted to Buddhism a few years into his rule and vowed he would stop engaging in warfare.
3. Although Hindus, the Gupta rulers also supported Buddhism and Brahminism.

Preview Section 5

If YOU were there ...

You are a traveler in western India in the 300s. You are visiting a cave temple that is carved into a mountain cliff. Inside the cave it is cool and quiet. Huge columns rise all around you. You don't feel you're alone, for the walls and ceilings are covered with paintings. They are filled with lively scenes and figures. In the center is a large statue with calm, peaceful features.

How does this cave make you feel?

Consider PHYSICAL feelings:
- coolness of the air
- dimness of the light
- stillness of the scene

Consider EMOTIONAL feelings:
- awestruck by the paintings
- humbled by their grandness
- comforted by the peacefulness

Review Answers: 1. F, Mauryan; 2. T; 3. F, Jainism

Academic Vocabulary

Review with students the high-use academic term in this section.

process a series of steps by which a task is accomplished (p. 150)

CRF: Vocabulary Builder Activity, Section 5

Taking Notes

Have students use the graphic organizer online to take notes on the section. This activity will prepare students for the Section Assessment, in which they will complete a graphic organizer that builds on the information using the Critical Thinking Skill: Categorizing.

Teach the Big Idea

At Level

Indian Achievements

1. **Teach** Ask students the questions in the Main Idea boxes to teach this section.
2. **Apply** Organize students into three groups. Assign one of the subsections—Religious Art, Sanskrit Literature, or Scientific Advances—to each group. Each group should create a poster or mural to illustrate the main points in its subsection. **LS Visual/Spatial**
3. **Review** As each group presents its illustration to the class, go over the concepts and terms related to that subsection.
4. **Practice/Homework** Instruct students to create a chart listing each of this section's three main ideas. Under each main idea, students should list at least two examples that support the idea. **LS Verbal/Linguistic**

Alternative Assessment Handbook, Rubric 3: Artwork

Direct Teach

Main Idea

❶ Religious Art

Indian artists created great works of religious art.

Describe What is unusual about the temple at Ajanta? *It was carved out of a mountainside.*

Sequence How did Hindu temples change over time? *At first they were small stone structures with flat roofs, but they became complex temples with huge towers.*

Bindis Some portrayals of women in Indian religious art show them with small colored dots, called *bindis,* on their foreheads. Contrary to popular belief, these marks do not designate a woman's caste. Depending on where the woman lives, the *bindi* may indicate that she is married. *Bindis* are primarily for decorative purposes, though. Indian women used to apply their *bindis* in powdered form. Now, however, they can buy peel-and-stick *bindis.*

Connect to Art

Teaching with Art Much of the art of India's great temples tells stories about gods. People who could not read the written language could "read" the stories in the sculpture and paintings and learn more about their religion. The carvings on the temple exteriors were especially important because not everyone was allowed inside the temples.

Temple Architecture

This Hindu temple is covered with incredibly detailed carvings and decorations. Many individual sculptures are images of important Hindu gods, like the statue of Vishnu above.

Another type of Buddhist temple was the stupa. Stupas had domed roofs and were built to house sacred items from the life of the Buddha. Many of them were covered with detailed carvings.

Paintings and Sculpture

The Gupta period also saw the creation of great works of art, both paintings and statues. Painting was a greatly respected profession, and India was home to many skilled artists. However, we don't know the names of many artists from this period. Instead, we know the names of many rich and powerful members of Gupta society who paid artists to create works of beauty and significance.

Most Indian paintings from the Gupta period are clear and colorful. Some of them show graceful Indians wearing fine jewelry and stylish clothes. Such paintings offer us a glimpse of the Indians' daily and ceremonial lives.

Artists from both of India's major religions, Hinduism and Buddhism, drew on their beliefs to create their works. As a result, many of the finest paintings of ancient India are found in temples. Hindu painters drew hundreds of gods on temple walls and entrances. Buddhists covered the walls and ceilings of temples with scenes from the life of the Buddha.

Indian sculptors also created great works. Many of their statues were made for Buddhist cave temples. In addition to the temples' intricately carved columns, sculptors carved statues of kings and the Buddha. Some of these statues tower over the cave entrances. Hindu temples also featured impressive statues of their gods. In fact, the walls of some temples, such as the one pictured above, were completely covered with carvings and images.

READING CHECK **Summarizing** How did religion influence ancient Indian art?

Collaborative Learning

Below Level

Describing an Indian Temple

Standard English Mastery

1. Ask students to imagine that they are Indian farmers who are seeing the temple shown on this page, called Kesava Temple, for the first time. Point out that the temple may have been the most spectacular sight the farmer had ever seen.
2. Have each student write down a completion for either of these prompts: "As I approached Kesava Temple, I felt ___" or "As I approached Kesava Temple, I noticed ___." Encourage students to use the text and photos to help them write clear, informative sentences using standard English.
3. Provide a thesaurus or dictionary to those students who need assistance.
4. Call on volunteers to read their sentences. Review them as examples of standard English usage. **LS Verbal/Linguistic**

Answers

Reading Check *Most artists illustrated religious beliefs in their works, many of which can be seen in temples.*

Sanskrit Literature

Sanskrit was the main language of the ancient Aryans. During the Mauryan and Gupta periods, many works of Sanskrit literature were created. These works were later translated into many other languages.

Religious Epics

The greatest of these Sanskrit writings are two religious epics, the *Mahabharata* (muh-HAH-BAH-ruh-tuh) and the *Ramayana* (rah-MAH-yuh-nuh). Still popular in India, the *Mahabharata* is one of the world's longest literary works. It is a story about the struggle between two families for control of a kingdom. Included within the story are many long passages about Hindu beliefs. The most famous is called the *Bhagavad Gita* (BUG-uh-vuhd GEE-tah).

The *Ramayana*, according to Hindu tradition written prior to the *Mahabharata*, tells about a prince named Rama. In truth, the prince was the god Vishnu in human form. He had become human so he could rid the world of demons. He also had to rescue his wife, a princess named Sita. For centuries, the characters of the *Ramayana* have been seen as models for how Indians should behave. For example, Rama is seen as the ideal ruler, and his relationship with Sita as the ideal marriage.

Other Works

Writers in the Gupta period also created plays, poetry, and other types of literature. One famous writer of this time was Kalidasa (kahl-ee-DAHS-uh). His work was so brilliant that Candra Gupta II hired him to write plays for the royal court.

Sometime before 500, Indian writers also produced a book of stories called the *Panchatantra* (PUHN-chuh-TAHN-truh). The stories in this collection were intended to teach lessons. They praise people for cleverness and quick thinking. Each story ends with a message about winning friends, losing property, waging war, or some other idea. For example, the message below warns listeners to think about what they are doing before they act.

> "The good and bad of given schemes
> Wise thought must first reveal:
> The stupid heron saw his chicks
> Provide a mongoose meal."
>
> –from the *Panchatantra*, translated by Arthur William Ryder

Eventually, translations of this collection spread throughout the world. It became popular even as far away as Europe.

READING CHECK **Categorizing** What types of literature did writers of ancient India create?

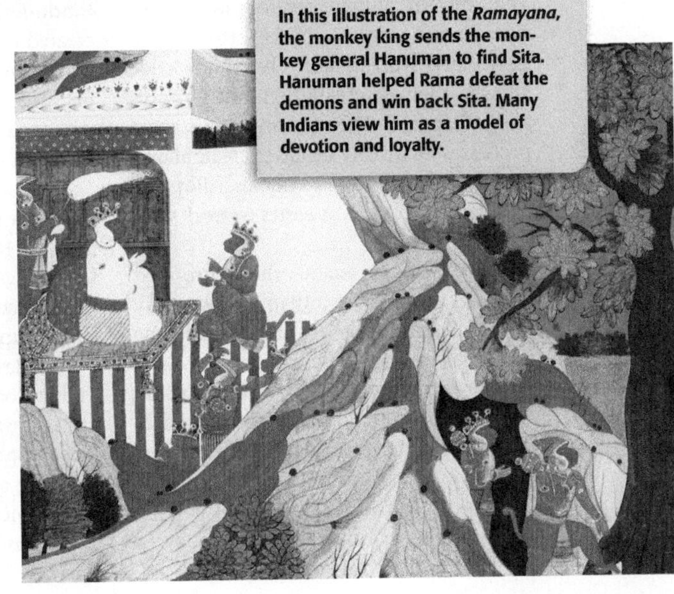

In this illustration of the *Ramayana*, the monkey king sends the monkey general Hanuman to find Sita. Hanuman helped Rama defeat the demons and win back Sita. Many Indians view him as a model of devotion and loyalty.

Direct Teach

Main Idea

❷ Sanskrit Literature

Sanskrit literature flourished during the Gupta period.

Recall Who was Kalidasa? *a brilliant writer of the Gupta period*

Contrast How is the theme of the *Mahabharata* different from the theme of the *Ramayana*? *The* Mahabharata *is about the struggle between two families, while the* Ramayana *is about the ideal love and devotion of a married couple.*

Evaluate How may the *Panchatantra* be similar to Aesop's Fables? *Both teach lessons through stories.*

CRF: Primary Source Activity: The Story of Savitri from India's *Mahabharata*

CRF: Literature Activity: Comparing Buddhist and Hindu Literature

Info to Know

Hanuman The divine monkey chief, Hanuman, serves as a model for Indians for how to practice devotion to a god. He showed his devotion in many ways—by acting as Rama's spy in a demon's kingdom, burning down the demon's city, traveling to the Himalayas to bring healing herbs to Rama's wounded soldiers, and leaping from India to Sri Lanka in a single bound.

The hanuman monkey bears the mythical creature's name. As a result, many Indians view these animals as sacred.

Cross-Discipline Activity: Literature

At Level

Prep Required

Tales from the Panchatantra

1. In advance, locate tales from the *Panchatantra*. Many are available online.
2. Organize the class into groups. Duplicate the tales so that each group has a different one, and each student has a copy of his or her group's tale.
3. Ask each group to study its tale and then present it to the class. Groups may present the tale in the form of a skit. Or, they may elect a student to retell the tale as if he or she were a village elder speaking to the local children.
4. After each performance, lead a discussion about the lesson that the tale provided.

LS Kinesthetic, Interpersonal

Alternative Assessment Handbook, Rubric 33: Skits and Reader's Theater

Answers

Reading Check *religious epics, plays, poems, and fables*

Direct Teach

Main Idea

❸ Scientific Advances

The Indians made scientific advances in metalworking, medicine, and other sciences.

Describe What were some operations that Indian surgeons could perform? *fixing broken bones, treating wounds, removing infected tonsils, reconstructing broken noses, reattaching torn earlobes*

Compare How were metallurgy and alloys connected? *Creating alloys, or mixtures of two or more metals, was a skill within metallurgy that ancient Indians developed.*

Evaluate Why do you think the concept of zero was so important? *Zero acts as a placeholder when using numbers of a specific base such as base 10, allowing mathematicians to make calculations easily.*

Connect to Science

Mystery Solved? Recently, scientists at the Indian Institute of Technology announced that they had figured out why the Iron Pillar has not rusted. They said that phosphorous in the iron had allowed a very thin protective layer of an iron, oxygen, and hydrogen compound to form on the pillar's surface. This film is only one-twentieth of a millimeter thick. Because present-day iron-making processes remove most phosphorous, modern iron rusts more easily.

Indian Science

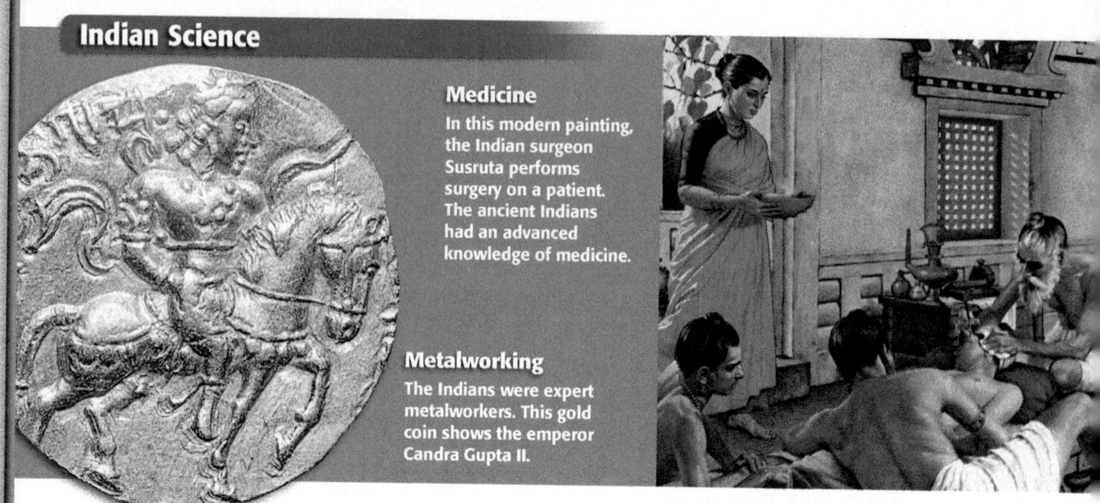

Medicine In this modern painting, the Indian surgeon Susruta performs surgery on a patient. The ancient Indians had an advanced knowledge of medicine.

Metalworking The Indians were expert metalworkers. This gold coin shows the emperor Candra Gupta II.

Scientific Advances

Indian achievements were not limited to art, architecture, and literature. Indian scholars also made important advances in metalworking, math, and the sciences.

Metalworking

The ancient Indians were pioneers of **metallurgy** (MET-uhl-uhr-jee), the science of working with metals. Their knowledge allowed them to create high-quality tools and weapons. The Indians also knew processes for mixing metals to create **alloys**, mixtures of two or more metals. Alloys are sometimes stronger or easier to work with than pure metals.

ACADEMIC VOCABULARY
process a series of steps by which a task is accomplished

Metalworkers made their strongest products out of iron. Indian iron was very hard and pure. These features made the iron a valuable trade item.

During the Gupta dynasty, metalworkers built the famous Iron Pillar near Delhi. Unlike most iron, which rusts easily, this pillar is very resistant to rust. The tall column still attracts crowds of visitors. Scholars study this column even today to learn the Indians' secrets.

Mathematics and Other Sciences

Gupta scholars also made advances in math and science. In fact, they were among the most advanced mathematicians of their day. They developed many elements of our modern math system. The very numbers we use today are called **Hindu-Arabic numerals** because they were created by Indian scholars and brought to Europe by Arabs. The Indians were also the first people to create the zero. Although it may seem like a small thing, modern math wouldn't be possible without the zero.

The ancient Indians were also very skilled in the medical sciences. As early as the AD 100s, doctors were writing their knowledge down in textbooks. Among the skills these books describe is making medicines from plants and minerals.

Besides curing people with medicines, Indian doctors knew how to protect people against disease. The Indians practiced **inoculation** (i-nah-kyuh-LAY-shuhn), or injecting a person with a small dose of a virus to help him or her build up defenses to a disease. By fighting off this small dose, the body learns to protect itself.

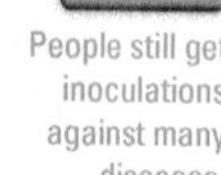

People still get inoculations against many diseases.

Differentiating Instruction

Struggling Readers — Below Level

Materials: art supplies

1. Discuss with students the wide variety of scientific advances made by the people of ancient India.
2. Ask students to imagine that they are metalworkers, doctors, mathematicians, or scientists of ancient India. Have each student design an advertisement that he or she might have placed in the yellow pages of a phone book of the time, had there been such a thing.
3. Ask students to discuss their yellow pages ads. As they do so, review the accomplishments of ancient Indians.
4. Display the ads in the classroom. **LS Visual/Spatial**

Alternative Assessment Handbook, Rubric 2: Advertisements

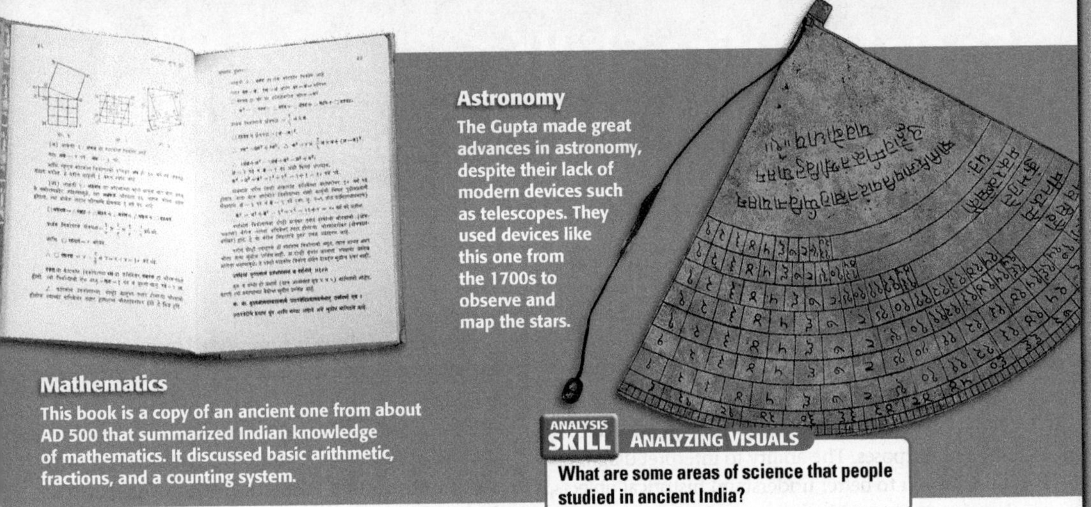

Astronomy
The Gupta made great advances in astronomy, despite their lack of modern devices such as telescopes. They used devices like this one from the 1700s to observe and map the stars.

Mathematics
This book is a copy of an ancient one from about AD 500 that summarized Indian knowledge of mathematics. It discussed basic arithmetic, fractions, and a counting system.

ANALYSIS SKILL ANALYZING VISUALS

What are some areas of science that people studied in ancient India?

For people who were injured, Indian doctors could perform surgery. Surgeons repaired broken bones, treated wounds, removed infected tonsils, reconstructed broken noses, and even reattached torn earlobes! If they could find no other cure for an illness, doctors would cast magic spells to help people recover.

Indian interest in **astronomy**, the study of stars and planets, dates back to early times as well. Indian astronomers knew of seven of the planets in our solar system. They knew that the sun was a star and that the planets revolved around it. They also knew that the earth was a sphere and that it rotated on its axis. In addition, they could predict eclipses of the sun and the moon.

READING CHECK **Finding Main Ideas** What were two Indian achievements in mathematics?

SUMMARY AND PREVIEW From a group of cities on the Indus River, India grew into a major empire whose people made great achievements. In the next chapter, you'll read about another civilization that experienced similar growth—China.

Section 5 Assessment

hmhsocialstudies.com ONLINE QUIZ

Reviewing Ideas, Terms, and People

1. a. **Describe** What did Hindu temples of the Gupta period look like?
   b. **Analyze** How can you tell that Indian artists were well respected?
   c. **Evaluate** Why do you think Hindu and Buddhist temples contained great works of art?
2. a. **Identify** What is the *Bhagavad Gita*?
   b. **Explain** Why were the stories of the *Panchatantra* written?
   c. **Elaborate** Why do you think people are still interested in ancient Sanskrit epics today?
3. a. **Define** What is **metallurgy**?
   b. **Explain** Why do we call the numbers we use today **Hindu-Arabic numerals**?

Critical Thinking

4. **Categorizing** Draw a chart like this one. Identify the scientific advances that fall into each category below.

Metallurgy	Math	Medicine	Astronomy

FOCUS ON WRITING

5. **Highlighting Indian Achievements** Make a list of Indian achievements that you could include on a poster. Now look back through your notes from this chapter. Which will you choose as the subject of your poster?

Direct Teach

Main Idea

3 Scientific Advances

The Indians made scientific advances in metalworking, medicine, and other sciences.

Recall What were some Indian achievements in astronomy? *knew of seven planets, that the sun was a star and that planets revolved around it, the earth was a rotating sphere; could predict eclipses*

Draw Inferences Since the Indians did not have telescopes, how did they become expert astronomers? *possible answer—careful, systematic observation and record-keeping*

Review & Assess

Close

Point out that India had veterinarians also. Doctors who treated horses and elephants were highly respected and valued.

Review

Online Quiz, Section 5

Assess

SE Section 5 Assessment
PASS: Section 5 Quiz
Alternative Assessment Handbook

Reteach/Classroom Intervention

Guided Reading Workbook, Section 5
Interactive Skills Tutor CD-ROM

Section 5 Assessment Answers

1. a. stone structures topped by huge towers, exteriors covered with carvings of the god worshipped inside
   b. Rich and powerful members of Gupta society paid artists to create works of beauty and significance.
   c. possible answer—Religion was important in Indian society, and most art honored the gods. Also, many Indians were illiterate, so art helped explain religious concepts.
2. a. long passage about Hindu beliefs within the *Mahabharata*
   b. They were intended to teach lessons.
   c. possible answer—because they reflect the history of India and are still lively stories
3. a. the science of working with metals
   b. because they were created by Indian scholars and brought to Europe by Arabs
4. See text under *Scientific Advances.*
5. Lists and chosen topics will vary.

Answers

Analyzing Visuals *metallurgy, mathematics, medicine, and astronomy*

Reading Check *Hindu-Arabic numerals; the zero*

Social Studies Skills

Interpreting Diagrams

Activity **Guided Practice**
Materials: photocopies of sample diagrams
Make photocopies of several diagrams. You might ask the librarian to suggest books that contain some diagrams related to the chapter content. Provide each student with copies of the diagrams and go through the diagrams as a class. Have students identify labeled items and other items. Then have each student select one diagram and write a paragraph describing what the diagram shows. Have volunteers read their paragraphs to the class. Correct any student errors. **LS Visual/Spatial**

Alternative Assessment Handbook, Rubric 37: Writing Assignments

Interactive Skills Tutor CD-ROM, Lesson 6: Interpret Maps, Charts, Visuals, and Political Cartoons

Social Studies Skills

Analysis | Critical Thinking | Economics | **Study**

Interpreting Diagrams

Understand the Skill

Diagrams are drawings that illustrate or explain objects or ideas. Different types of diagrams have different purposes. The ability to interpret diagrams will help you to better understand historical objects, their functions, and how they worked.

Learn the Skill

Use these guidelines to interpret a diagram:

1. Read the diagram's title or caption to find out what it represents. If a legend is present, study it as well to understand any symbols and colors in the diagram.
2. Most diagrams include labels that identify the object's parts or explain relationships between them. Study these parts and labels carefully.
3. If any written information or explanation accompanies the diagram, compare it to the drawing as you read.

The diagram below is of the Great Stupa at Sanchi in India, which is thought to contain the Buddha's remains. Like most stupas, it was shaped like a dome.

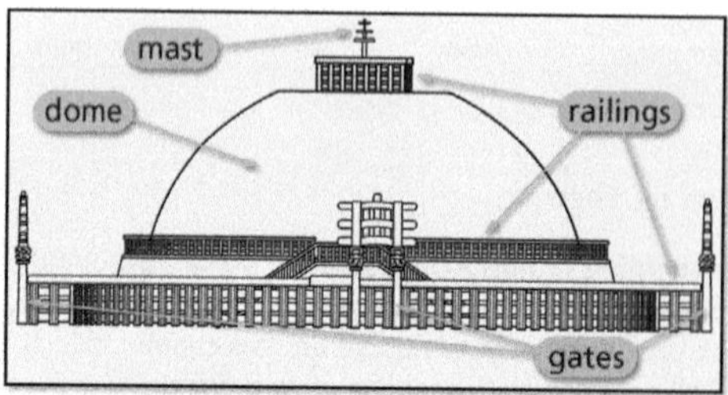

The Sanchi stupa is surrounded by a stone railing with four gates called *torenas*. About halfway up the side of the mound is a second railing next to a walkway. Worshippers move along this walkway in a clockwise direction to honor the Buddha. The stupa is topped by a cube called the *harmika*. Rising from the harmika is a mast or spire. These parts and their shapes all have religious meaning for Buddhists.

Practice and Apply the Skill

Here is another diagram of the Sanchi stupa. Interpret both diagrams on this page to answer the questions that follow.

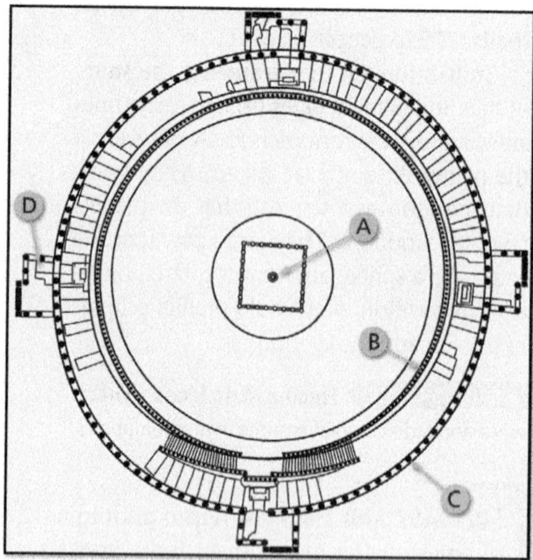

1. Which letter in this diagram labels the *torenas*?
2. What part of the stupa does the letter A label?
3. The walkway and railing are labeled by which letter?

Social Studies Skills Activity: Interpreting Diagrams

At Level

Creating Diagrams

Research Required

Materials: art supplies, poster board

1. Have each student conduct research to find a diagram of a historical structure in India.
2. Each student should create a large copy of the diagram on poster board. Below the diagram, students should provide captions explaining the information in the diagram and providing background information about the structure.
3. Ask for volunteers to share their diagrams with the class. Give other students a chance to interpret the diagrams and to ask questions. Then have volunteers explain their diagrams.
4. Display students' diagrams around the classroom. **LS Visual/Spatial**

Alternative Assessment Handbook, Rubrics 3: Artwork; and 30: Research

Answers

Practice and Apply the Skill **1.** *D;* **2.** *the mast or spire on the* harmika; **3.** *B*

CHAPTER 5

Chapter Review

History's Impact

▶ **video series**

Review the video to answer the focus question:

Who was the historical Buddha, and what are his Four Noble Truths?

Visual Summary

Use the visual summary below to help you review the main ideas of the chapter.

The Harappan civilization began in the Indus River Valley.

Hinduism and Buddhism both developed in India.

Indians made great advances in art, literature, science, and other fields.

Reviewing Vocabulary, Terms and People

Fill in the blanks with the correct term or name from this chapter.

1. _________ are winds that bring heavy rainfall.
2. A _________ is a division of people into groups based on birth, wealth, or occupation.
3. Hindus believe in _________, the belief that they will be reborn many times after death.
4. _________ founded the Mauryan Empire.
5. The focusing of the mind on spiritual things is called _________.
6. People who work to spread their religious beliefs are called _________.
7. People who practice _________ use only peaceful ways to achieve change.
8. _________ converted to Buddhism while he was ruler of the Mauryan Empire.
9. A mixture of metals is called an _________.

Comprehension and Critical Thinking

SECTION 1 *(Pages 124–129)*

10. a. Describe What caused floods on the Indus River, and what was the result of those floods?

b. Contrast How was Aryan culture different from Harappan culture?

c. Elaborate Why is the Harappan culture considered a civilization?

SECTION 2 *(Pages 130–135)*

11. a. Identify Who were the Brahmins, and what role did they play in Aryan society?

b. Analyze How do Hindus believe karma affects reincarnation?

c. Elaborate Hinduism has been called both a polytheistic religion—one that worships many gods—and a monotheistic religion—one that worships only one god. Why do you think this is so?

Answers

Visual Summary

Review and Inquiry Have students use the visual summary to provide details about the chapter's main ideas.

Quick Facts Transparency: Ancient India Visual Summary

Reviewing Vocabulary, Terms, and People

1. monsoons
2. caste system
3. reincarnation
4. Candragupta Maurya
5. meditation
6. missionaries
7. nonviolence
8. Asoka
9. alloy

Comprehension and Critical Thinking

10. a. melting of heavy snows in the Himalayas; left behind layer of silt, making the land ideal for farming

b. Aryan—migrants from Central Asia, small settlements based on family ties, kept livestock and later farmed, each village ruled by a raja, no writing system; Harappan—in the Indus River Valley, created fortified and well-planned cities, may have had a strong central government, created India's first writing system

c. had well-planned cities with technical advances, writing system, division of labor as shown by wide range of objects created

11. a. priests; highest class in Aryan society

Review & Assessment Resources

Review and Reinforce

SE Chapter Review

CRF: Chapter Review Activity

Quick Facts Transparency: Ancient India Visual Summary

Spanish Chapter Summaries Audio CD Program

Online Chapter Summaries in Six Languages

TOS Holt McDougal PuzzleView

Quiz Game CD-ROM

Assess

SE Standardized Test Practice

PASS: Chapter Test, Forms A and B

Alternative Assessment Handbook

TOS Exam View Assessment Suite, Chapter Test

Differentiated Instruction Modified Worksheets and Tests CD-ROM: Chapter Test

Online Assessment Program, in the Interactive Student Edition

Reteach/Intervene

Guided Reading Workbook

Differentiated Instruction Teacher Management System: Lesson Plans

Differentiated Instruction Modified Worksheets and Tests CD-ROM

Interactive Skills Tutor CD-ROM

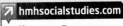

Chapter Resources

Answers

b. Karma determines if you are reborn into a higher or lower caste.

c. Hindus believe in three major gods—Brahma, Siva, and Vishnu. However, they also believe these gods are parts of a universal spirit called Brahman.

12. a. wanting what we like but do not have, wanting to keep what we like and already have, not wanting what we dislike but have

b. Missionaries spread Buddhism across Asia; it split into two major branches.

c. *possible answers*—They were assured that their low social rank was not a barrier to enlightenment and that they had the power to change their lives.

13. a. seized control of northern India and by so doing founded the Mauryan Empire

b. Both unified much of India; Mauryan rulers promoted Buddhism, while Gupta rulers promoted Hinduism.

c. possible answer—Buddhism might not have spread to the rest of Asia, and Hinduism would be even more prevalent in India than it is today.

14. a. Buddhist and Hindu temples, paintings, and sculptures

b. possible answer—Their Hindu beliefs affect how the characters interact.

c. Answers will vary but should display familiarity with the achievements mentioned in this section.

Reviewing Themes

15. Both share belief in reincarnation; Hinduism supported the caste system, while Buddhism did not.

16. defined who one could marry and eat with, along with many other aspects of daily life

Using the Internet

17. Go to hmhsocialstudies.com to access a rubric for this activity.

Reading Skills

18. Answers will vary, but students should infer that there was religious tolerance in ancient India.

Social Studies Skills

19. Diagrams will vary but should follow the general format shown.

Focus on Writing

20. Rubric Students' illustrated posters should:

- present the ideas clearly.
- contain appropriate, accurate, and vivid illustrations.
- have proper labels and captions.
- use correct grammar, punctuation, spelling, and capitalization.

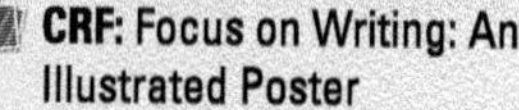
CRF: Focus on Writing: An Illustrated Poster

SECTION 3 *(Pages 136–141)*

12. a. Describe What did the Buddha say caused human suffering?

b. Analyze How did Buddhism grow and change after the Buddha died?

c. Elaborate Why did the Buddha's teachings about nirvana appeal to many people of lower castes?

SECTION 4 *(Pages 142–145)*

13. a. Identify What was Candragupta Maurya's greatest accomplishment?

b. Compare and Contrast What was one similarity between the Mauryas and the Guptas? What was one difference between them?

c. Predict How might Indian history have been different if Asoka had not become a Buddhist?

SECTION 5 *(Pages 147–151)*

14. a. Describe What kinds of religious art did the ancient Indians create?

b. Make Inferences Why do you think religious discussions are included in the *Mahabharata?*

c. Evaluate Which of the ancient Indians' achievements do you think is most impressive? Why?

Reviewing Themes

15. Religion What is one teaching that Buddhism and Hinduism share? What is one idea about which they differ?

16. Society and Culture How did the caste system affect the lives of most people in India?

Using the Internet 

17. Activity: Making a Brochure In this chapter, you learned about India's diverse geographical features and the ways in which geography influenced India's history. Use your online textbook to research the geography and civilizations of India, taking notes as you go. Finally, use the interactive brochure template to present what you have found.

hmhsocialstudies.com

Reading Skills 

18. Inferences about History Based on what you learned about the Gupta period, what inference can you draw about religious tolerance in ancient India? Draw a box like the one below to help you organize your thoughts.

Question:	
Inside the Text:	Outside the Text:
Inference:	

Social Studies Skills

19. Understanding Diagrams Look back over the diagram of the Buddhist temple in the skills activity at the end of this chapter. Using this diagram as a guide, draw a simple diagram of your house or school. Be sure to include labels of important features on your diagram. An example has been provided for you below.

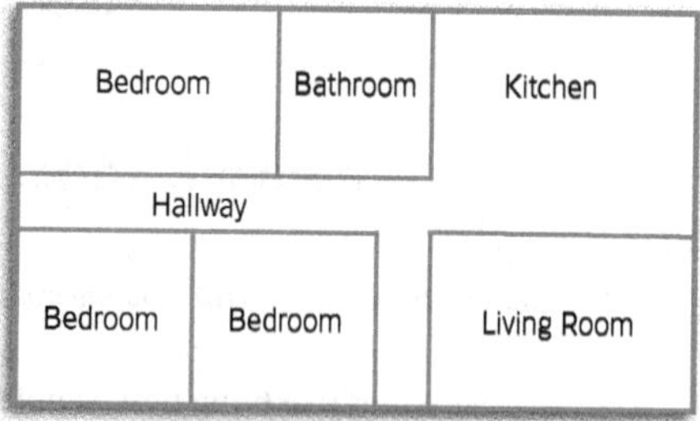

Focus on Writing

20. Designing Your Poster Now that you have chosen a subject for your poster, it's time to create it. On a large sheet of paper or poster board, write a title that identifies your subject. Then draw pictures, maps, or diagrams that illustrate it.

Next to each picture, write a short caption. Each caption should be two sentences long. The first sentence should identify what the picture, map, or diagram shows. The second sentence should explain why the picture is important to the study of Indian history.

Standardized Test Practice

DIRECTIONS: Read each question, and write the letter of the best response.

1 Use the map to answer the following question.

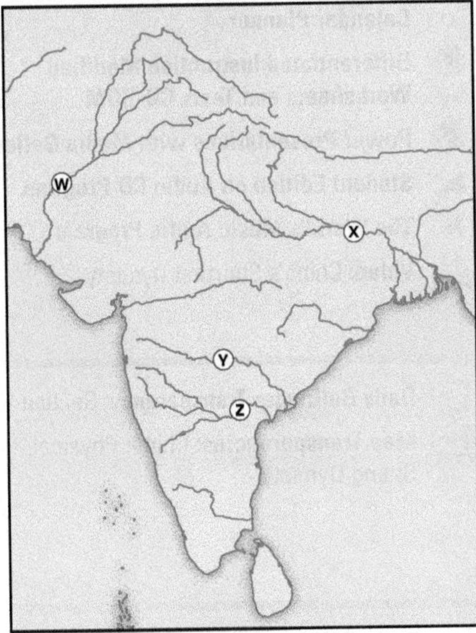

Civilization grew on the Indian subcontinent along the river marked on the map by the letter

A W.
B X.
C Y.
D Z.

2 The people of which *varna* in early India had the hardest lives?

A Brahmins
B Kshatriyas
C Sudras
D Vaisyas

3 What is the *main* goal of people who follow Buddhism as it was taught by the Buddha?

A wealth
B rebirth
C missionary work
D reaching nirvana

4 The Mauryan emperor Asoka is known for all of the following *except*

A expanding the empire across most of India.
B spreading Hinduism.
C working to improve his people's lives.
D practicing nonviolence.

5 Early India's contributions to world civilization included

A developing the world's first calendar.
B creating what is now called algebra.
C inventing the plow and the wheel.
D introducing zero to the number system.

Connecting with Past Learnings

6 In this chapter you learned about two great epics, the *Mahabharata* and the *Ramayana*. Which of the following is also an epic poem that you have studied?

A Hammurabi's Code
B the *Book of the Dead*
C *Gilgamesh*
D the Pyramid Texts

7 As you learned earlier in this course, the ancient Egyptians held elaborate religious rituals. Which of these Indian religions also involved many rituals, including sacrifices?

A Buddhism
B Brahmanism
C Jainism
D Mauryanism

Answers

Standardized Test Practice

1. A
Break Down the Question This question requires students to recall map information. Refer students who miss it to the maps in Section 1.

2. C
Break Down the Question Refer students who miss this question to the diagram in Section 2 and text information about the caste system.

3. D
Break Down the Question Seeking wealth would be a barrier to reaching nirvana. Rebirth can provide a path to nirvana. Missionary work is not a requirement of Buddhism. Refer students who miss the question to review *Teachings of Buddhism.*

4. B
Break Down the Question This question requires students to recall factual information. Asoka spread Buddhism, not Hinduism. Refer students who miss the question to section 4.

5. D
Break Down the Question Although ancient India contributed much to world civilization, the only contribution in this list that is mentioned in the chapter is the introduction of zero.

6. C
Break Down the Question This question requires students to recall information from a previous chapter on Mesopotamia.

7. B
Break Down the Question Refer students who miss the question to Section 2. Remind students that Brahmanism involved many rituals, including sacrifices, led by the Brahmins.

Intervention Resources

Reproducible

- Guided Reading Workbook
- Differentiated Instruction Teacher Management System: Lesson Plans Technology

Technology

- Quick Facts Transparency: Ancient India Visual Summary
- Differentiated Instruction Modified Worksheets and Tests CD-ROM
- Interactive Skills Tutor CD-ROM

Tips for Test Taking

Getting the Full Picture When a question refers to a table or a chart, students should carefully read all the information in the table or chart, including headings and labels, before answering the question. When a question refers to a graph, encourage students to first carefully study the data plotted on the graph to determine any trends or oddities before answering the question.

Chapter 6 Planning Guide

Ancient China

Overview	Instructional Resources	
CHAPTER 6 **Essential Question:** How do the people, events, and ideas that shaped ancient China continue to influence the world? **Focus on the Essential Question Podcast**	TOS **Differentiated Instruction Teacher Management System:** • Instructional Benchmarking Guides • Lesson Plans for Differentiated Instruction **Guided Reading Workbook** **Chapter Resource File:** • Chapter Review Activity • Focus on Speaking Activity: Oral Presentation • Social Studies Skills Activity: Conducting Internet Research	TOS **Calendar Planner** **Differentiated Instruction Modified Worksheets and Tests CD-ROM** **Power Presentations with Media Gallery** **Student Edition on Audio CD Program** **The World's Music Audio Program** **Video:** China's Shortest Dynasty
Section 1: **Geography and Early China** **The Big Idea:** Chinese civilization began with the Shang dynasty along the Huang He.	TOS **Differentiated Instruction Teacher Management System:** Section 1 Lesson Plan **Guided Reading Workbook:** Section 1 **Chapter Resource File:** • Vocabulary Builder Activity, Section 1 • History and Geography Activity: Shang China	**Daily Bellringer Transparency:** Section 1 **Map Transparencies:** China: Physical, Shang Dynasty
Section 2: **The Zhou Dynasty and New Ideas** **The Big Idea:** Confucius and other philosophers taught ways to deal with political and social problems in ancient China.	TOS **Differentiated Instruction Teacher Management System:** Section 2 Lesson Plan **Guided Reading Workbook:** Section 2 **Chapter Resource File:** • Vocabulary Builder Activity, Section 2 • Literature Activity: *The Book of Songs* • Primary Source Activity: The Teachings of Confucius and Laozi	**Daily Bellringer Transparency:** Section 2 **Map Transparency:** Zhou Dynasty **Quick Facts Transparencies:** Zhou Society, Main Ideas of Confucianism **Internet Activity:** Dialogue **Animated History:** Ancient China **Video:** Confucius: Words of Wisdom
Section 3: **The Qin Dynasty** **The Big Idea:** The Qin dynasty unified China with a strong government and a system of standardization.	TOS **Differentiated Instruction Teacher Management System:** Section 3 Lesson Plan **Guided Reading Workbook:** Section 3 **Chapter Resource File:** • Vocabulary Builder Activity, Section 3	**Daily Bellringer Transparency:** Section 3 **Map Transparency:** Qin Dynasty **Quick Facts Transparency:** Emperor Shi Huangdi **Video:** The First Emperor of China **Video:** Omens in Ancient China
Section 4: **The Han Dynasty** **The Big Idea:** The Han Dynasty created a new form of government that valued family, art, and learning.	TOS **Differentiated Instruction Teacher Management System:** Section 4 Lesson Plan **Guided Reading Workbook:** Section 4 **Chapter Resource File:** • Vocabulary Builder Activity, Section 4 • Biography Activities: Liu Bang; Wu-ti	**Daily Bellringer Transparency:** Section 4 **Map Transparency:** Han Dynasty **Internet Activity:** Chinese Art **Animated History:** Han Dynasty
Section 5: **Han Contacts with Other Cultures** **The Big Idea:** Trade routes led to the exchange of new products and ideas among China, Rome, and other peoples.	TOS **Differentiated Instruction Teacher Management System:** Section 5 Lesson Plan **Guided Reading Workbook:** Section 5 **Chapter Resource File:** • Vocabulary Builder Activity, Section 5 • Economics and History: The Chinese Economy	**Daily Bellringer Transparency:** Section 5 **Map Transparency:** The Silk Road

Chart Key:

SE Student Edition  Presentation Resource 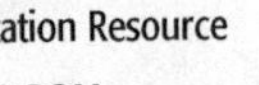 MP3 Audio

TOS Teacher One Stop 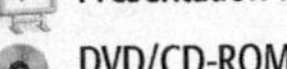 DVD/CD-ROM  HISTORY™

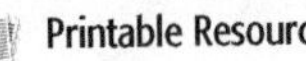 Printable Resource

Program Resources available on TOS and @ hmhsocialstudies.com

Review, Assessment, Intervention

 **Quick Facts Transparency:** Ancient China Visual Summary

 **Spanish Chapter Summaries Audio CD Program**

 **Progress Assessment Support System (PASS):** Chapter Test

 **Differentiated Instruction Modified Worksheets and Tests CD-ROM:** Modified Chapter Test

 TOS **ExamView® Assessment Suite (English/Spanish)**

 **Online Assessment Program,** in the Interactive Student Edition

 **PASS:** Section 1 Quiz

 **Online Quiz:** Section 1

 **Alternative Assessment Handbook**

 **PASS:** Section 2 Quiz

 **Online Quiz:** Section 2

 **Alternative Assessment Handbook**

 **PASS:** Section 3 Quiz

 **Online Quiz:** Section 3

 **Alternative Assessment Handbook**

 **PASS:** Section 4 Quiz

 **Online Quiz:** Section 4

 **Alternative Assessment Handbook**

 **PASS:** Section 5 Quiz

 **Online Quiz:** Section 5

 **Alternative Assessment Handbook**

Supporting Resources

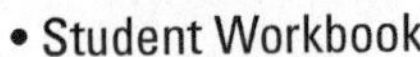

- Multimedia Classroom Global History Series
- Global History Teacher's Guide

Maps Globes Graphs Level F

- Student Workbook
- Teacher's Guide

Social Studies Trade Library Collections

- Premier Secondary World History Trade Collection

History's Impact

World History Video Program

- **Buddhism as a World Religion**

For more information or to purchase go to hmhsocialstudies.com

Power Presentations with Media Gallery

Power Presentations with Media Gallery are visual presentations of each chapter's main ideas. Presentations can be customized by including Quick Facts charts, images from the text, and video clips.

Differentiating Instruction

How do I address the needs of varied learners?
The Target Resource acts as your primary strategy for differentiated instruction.

ENGLISH-LANGUAGE LEARNERS & STRUGGLING READERS

Interactive Skills Tutor CD-ROM

The interactive Skills tutor CD-ROM contains lessons that provide additional practice for 20 different critical thinking skills.

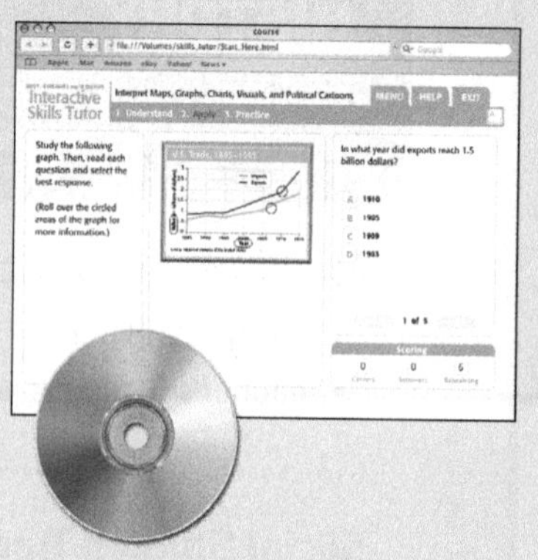

Additional Resources

Differentiated Instruction Teacher Management System: Lesson Plans for Differentiated Instruction

Chapter Resource File:
- Vocabulary Builder Activities
- Social Studies Skills Activity: Conducting Internet Research

Quick Facts Transparencies: Ancient China Visual Summary

Student Edition on Audio CD Program

Spanish/English Guided Reading Workbook

SPECIAL NEEDS LEARNERS

Differentiated Instruction Modified Worksheets and Tests CD-ROM

- Vocabulary Flash Cards
- Vocabulary Builder Activities
- Chapter Review Activity
- Chapter Test

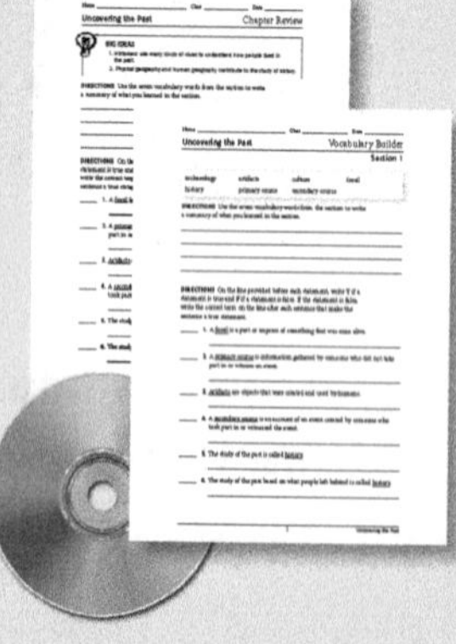

Additional Resources

Differentiated Instruction Teacher Management System: Lesson Plans for Differentiated Instruction

Guided Reading Workbook

Chapter Resource File: Social Studies Skills Activity: Participating in Groups

Student Edition on Audio CD Program

Interactive Skills Tutor CD-ROM

ADVANCED/GIFTED-AND-TALENTED STUDENTS

Primary Source Library CD-ROM for World History

The Library contains longer versions of quotations in the text, extra sources, and images. Included are point-of-view articles, journals, diaries, historical fiction, and political documents.

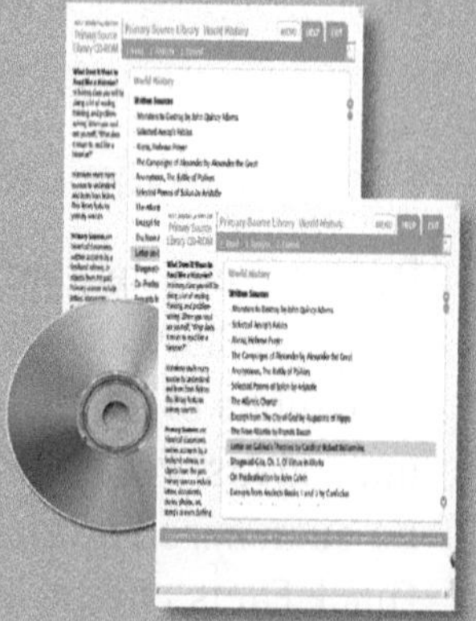

Additional Resources

Differentiated Instruction Teacher Management System: Lesson Plans for Differentiated Instruction

Interactive Reader and Study Guide

Chapter Resource File: Social Studies Skills Activity: Conducting Internet Research

Student Edition on Audio CD Program

Interactive Skills Tutor CD-ROM

Differentiated Activities in the Teacher's Edition

- Understanding the Main Idea, p. 168
- Illustrating a Story with a Cartoon, p. 184

Teacher One Stop™

How can I manage the lesson plans and support materials for differentiated instruction?

With the Teacher One Stop, you can easily organize and print lesson plans, planning guides, and instructional materials for all learners. The Teacher One Stop includes the following materials to help you differentiate instruction:

- **Interactive Teacher's Edition**
- **Calendar Planner and pacing guides**
- **Editable lesson plans**
- **All reproducible ancillaries in Adobe Acrobat (PDF) format**
- **ExamView Assessment Suite (English & Spanish)**
- **Transparency and video previews**

Differentiated Activities in the Teacher's Edition

- Drawing a Chart, p. 164
- Creating a Poster, p. 175

Interactive Student Edition

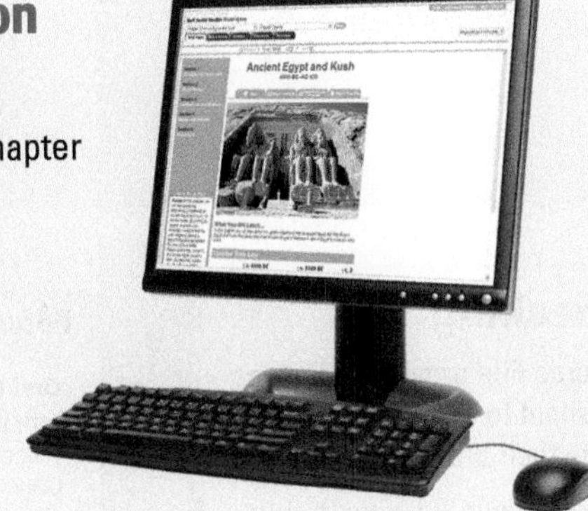

Complete online student edition with interactive multimedia support for chapter content assessment and reporting

- Interactive Maps and Notebook
- Graphic Organizers
- Standardized Test Prep
- Online Homework Practice and Research Activities
- Current Events
- Chapter-based Internet Activities
- Animated History Activities
- and more!

Differentiated Activities in the Teacher's Edition

- Interpreting Poems, p. 182
- Researching Advances in Han China, p. 187

• Chapter Preview •

Essential Question

Introduce the Essential Question

- Discuss the importance of China's ancient dynasties and the dynastic cycle.
- Explain that Chinese philosophies such as Legalism, Confucianism, and Daoism had immediate and lasting effects on China's history.
- Point out that many Chinese innovations are still used in the modern world.

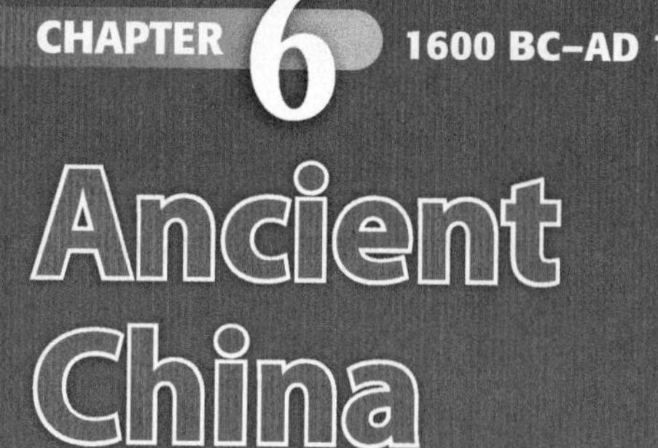

CHAPTER 6 1600 BC–AD 1

Ancient China

Essential Question How do the people, events, and ideas that shaped ancient China continue to influence the world?

South Carolina Performance Standards

6-1.3 Compare the river valley civilizations of the Tigris and Euphrates (Mesopotamia), the Nile (Egypt), the Indus (India), and the Huang He (China), including the evolution of written language, government, trade systems, architecture, and forms of social order; **6-1.4** Explain the origins, fundamental beliefs, and spread of Eastern religions, including Hinduism (India), Judaism (Mesopotamia), Buddhism (India), and Confucianism and Taoism (China); **6-3.1** Summarize the major contributions of the Chinese civilization from the Qin dynasty through the Ming dynasty, including the golden age of art and literature, the invention of gunpowder and woodblock printing, and the rise of trade via the Silk Road.

Literacy Skills for Social Studies

- Interpret Earth's physical and human systems by using maps, mental maps, geographic models, and other social studies resources.
- Compare the locations of places, the conditions at places, and the connections between places.
- Explain why trade occurs and how historical patterns of trade have contributed to global interdependence.

Focus on Speaking

Oral Presentation In this chapter you will read about China's fascinating early years. Choose one person or event from that history. You will then tell your classmates why the person or event was important to the history of China.

CHAPTER EVENTS

c. 1500s BC The Shang dynasty is established in China.

1600 BC

WORLD EVENTS

c. 1480 BC Queen Hatshepsut rules Egypt.

156 CHAPTER 6

Focus on Speaking

The **Chapter Resource File** provides a Focus on Speaking worksheet to help students organize and create their oral presentations.

CRF: Focus on Speaking Activity: Oral Presentation

Key to Differentiating Instruction

Below Level
Basic-level activities designed for all students encountering new material

At Level
Intermediate-level activities designed for average students

Above Level
Challenging activities designed for honors and gifted and talented students

Standard English Mastery
Activities designed to improve standard English usage

LS Learning Styles

Introduce the Chapter

At Level

Focus on China

1. Ask students the following questions: If you were lost in the woods, what could you use to learn which direction is which? On what material is this book printed? What instrument do scientists use to learn about earthquakes that occur far away? What medical procedure uses many tiny needles inserted in a patient's skin?
2. In order, the answers are a compass, paper, seismograph, and acupuncture. Then ask students if they can guess what these questions and answers have in common. *They are all about inventions and innovations created by the Chinese.*
3. Point out that China has one of the world's oldest civilizations and that Chinese civilization has influenced ours in ways that are not always obvious. Tell students they will be introduced to Chinese civilization and its influence in this chapter.

LS Verbal/Linguistic

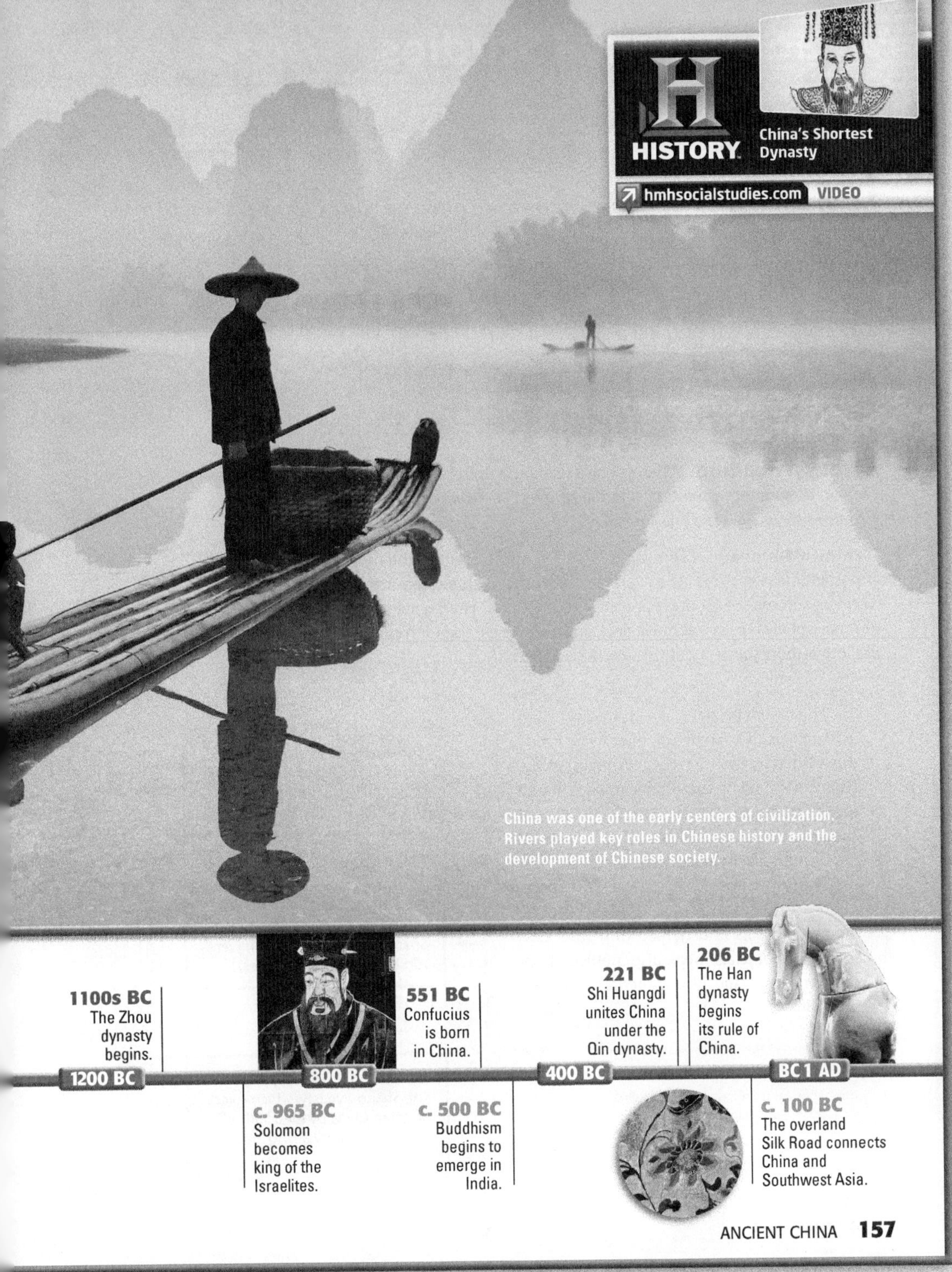
HISTORY
China's Shortest Dynasty
hmhsocialstudies.com VIDEO
China was one of the early centers of civilization. Rivers played key roles in Chinese history and the development of Chinese society.
1100s BC The Zhou dynasty begins.
551 BC Confucius is born in China.
221 BC Shi Huangdi unites China under the Qin dynasty.
206 BC The Han dynasty begins its rule of China.
1200 BC
800 BC
400 BC
BC 1 AD
c. 965 BC Solomon becomes king of the Israelites.
c. 500 BC Buddhism begins to emerge in India.
c. 100 BC The overland Silk Road connects China and Southwest Asia.
ANCIENT CHINA 157

• Chapter Preview •

Explore the Picture

A Chinese Landscape The photo shows unusual formations that have been featured in Chinese paintings for centuries. Point out the odd, steep hills in the background. They are called karst towers and were formed by the erosion of limestone by water. The karst towers attract many tourists.

Analyzing Visuals Ask students what they think the people in the photo are doing. As a hint, point out the birds on the boat in the foreground. Tell students the birds, called cormorants, have been trained to perform a certain task. *The people are fishing. They have trained cormorants to dive into the water for fish. Because a cord is tied around the bird's neck, the cormorant does not swallow the fish but gives it to the fisher. Historians are not sure when cormorant fishing was first practiced in China, but in some parts of the country, the practice—like many traditional Chinese ways of life—goes back several centuries.*

hmhsocialstudies.com
Teacher Resources

Explore the Time Line

1. When did the Shang dynasty begin? *about 1500s BC*
2. How many years passed between Shi Huangdi's unification of China and the beginning of the Han dynasty? *16 years*
3. During which century did both Confucianism and Buddhism emerge? *sixth century BC*
4. Who ruled Egypt while the Shang dynasty ruled China? *Queen Hatshepsut*
5. When did the Silk Road connect China and Southwest Asia? *about 100 BC*

Did you know . . .

The dynasties depicted on this time line are only a few of the 10 major dynasties that have ruled over China. The longest-lasting dynasty in Chinese history was the Zhou, which ruled for some 600 years. The shortest major dynasty was the Qin, which ruled for fewer than 20 years. China's imperial age ended with the overthrow of the Qing dynasty in 1912.

Reading Social Studies

Understanding Themes

This chapter focuses on two themes—politics, and society and culture. Ask students to use their knowledge of other civilizations to make predictions about the political structure in ancient China. Write student predictions for everyone to see. Help students to see which of their predictions are correct or incorrect. Then have students discuss what they may already know about Chinese society and culture. Tell students that this chapter will teach them about the development of China, how its governments were formed, and how its society was organized.

Summarizing Historical Texts

Focus on Reading Have students bring newspaper or magazine articles on topics they find interesting. Then have each student write a brief summary of their article. Ask students to exchange their summary with a partner, and have students critique each other's summaries. Ask students to discuss what mistakes they saw in the summaries and how they might correct those mistakes.

Reading Social Studies

Economics | Geography | **Politics** | Religion | **Society and Culture** | Science and Technology

Focus on Themes This chapter will describe the early development of China—how Chinese civilization began and took shape under early dynasties. You will see how these dynasties controlled the government and **politics**. You will also see how the Chinese, influenced by the philosopher Confucius, established traditions such as the importance of families. They also encouraged art and learning, helping to shape the **society and culture** that would last for centuries in China.

Summarizing Historical Texts

Focus on Reading When you are reading a history book, how can you be sure that you understand everything? One way is to briefly restate what you've read in a summary.

Writing a Summary A **summary** is a short restatement of the most important ideas in a text. The example below shows three steps used in writing a summary. First underline important details. Then write a short summary of each paragraph. Finally, combine these paragraph summaries into a short summary of the whole passage.

The first dynasty for which we have clear evidence is the Shang, which was firmly established by the 1500s BC. Strongest in the Huang He Valley, the Shang ruled a broad area of northern China. Shang rulers moved their capital several times, probably to avoid floods or attack by enemies.

The king was at the center of Shang political and religious life. Nobles served the king as advisors and helped him rule. Less important officials were also nobles. They performed specific governmental and religious duties.

Summary of Paragraph 1
China's first dynasty, the Shang, took power in northern China in the 1500s BC.

Summary of Paragraph 2
Shang politics and religion were run by the king and nobles.

Combined Summary
The Shang dynasty, which ruled northern China by the 1500s BC, was governed by a king and nobles.

Reading and Skills Resources

Reading Support

- Guided Reading Workbook
- Student Edition on Audio CD
- Spanish Chapter Summaries Audio CD Program

Social Studies Skills Support

- Interactive Skills Tutor CD-ROM

Vocabulary Support

- **CRF:** Vocabulary Builder Activities
- **CRF:** Chapter Review Activity
- Differentiated Instruction Modified Worksheets and Tests CD-ROM:
  - Vocabulary Flash Cards
  - Vocabulary Builder Activity
  - Chapter Review Activity

TOS Holt McDougal PuzzleView

You Try It!

The following passage is from the chapter you are about to read. As you read it, think about what you would include in a summary.

Early Settlements

From Chapter 6 p. 162

Archaeologists have found remains of early Chinese villages. One village near the Huang He had more than 40 houses. Many of them were partly underground and may have had straw-covered roofs. The site also included animal pens, storage pits, and a cemetery.

Some of the villages along the Huang He grew into large towns. Walls surrounded these towns to defend them against floods and hostile neighbors. In towns like these, the Chinese left many artifacts, such as arrowheads, fishhooks, tools, and pottery. Some village sites even contained pieces of cloth.

After you read the passage, answer the following questions.

1. Read the following summaries and decide which one is the better summary statement. Explain your answer.
   a) Archaeologists have found out interesting things about the early settlements of China. For example, they have discovered that the Chinese had homes with straw-covered roofs, pens for their animals, and even cemeteries. Also, they have found that larger villages were surrounded by walls for defense. Finally, they have found tools like arrowheads and fishhooks.
   b) Archaeologists have found remains of early Chinese villages, some of which grew into large walled settlements. Artifacts found there help us understand Chinese culture.
2. What are three characteristics of a good summary?

Key Terms and People

Chapter 6

Section 1
jade *(p. 163)*
oracle *(p. 164)*

Section 2
lords *(p. 167)*
peasants *(p. 167)*
Confucius *(p. 169)*
ethics *(p. 169)*
Confucianism *(p. 169)*
Daoism *(p. 170)*
Laozi *(p. 170)*
Legalism *(p. 170)*

Section 3
Shi Huangdi *(p. 172)*
Great Wall *(p. 175)*

Section 4
sundial *(p. 182)*
seismograph *(p. 182)*
acupuncture *(p. 183)*

Section 5
silk *(p. 187)*
Silk Road *(p. 187)*
diffusion *(p. 189)*

Academic Vocabulary

Success in school is related to knowing academic vocabulary—the words that are frequently used in school assignments and discussions. In this chapter, you will learn the following academic words:

vary *(p. 161)*
structure *(p. 168)*
innovation *(p. 182)*
procedure *(p. 187)*

As you read Chapter 6, think about how you would summarize the material you are reading.

Reading Social Studies

Key Terms and People

Preteach the key terms and people from this chapter by asking students what they think each term means or who each person was. Ask the class to identify six of the terms or people about which they know the least. Write the list of six terms for the class to see. Then have each student define or identify the six terms or people. Have students draw an illustration that best represents each term or person.
LS Verbal/Linguistic, Visual/Spatial

Focus on Reading

See the **Focus on Reading** questions in this chapter for more practice on this reading social studies skill.

Reading Social Studies Assessment

See the **Chapter Review** at the end of this chapter for student assessment questions related to this reading skill.

Teaching Tip

Students may think that every fact is an important detail to include in a summary. Remind students that not every fact is important. One way to help students keep to the important details is to have them identify the main idea of each paragraph in a few words. Then instruct students to only underline details that support that main idea. Model this strategy for students by summarizing a paragraph or two as a class.

Answers

You Try It! 1. *Summary B, because it briefly covers the main points of the passage, whereas summary A is too long;* **2.** *It should summarize important details from the passage, be brief, and should cover the entire passage.*

Preteach

Bellringer

If YOU were there . . . Use the **Daily Bellringer Transparency** to help students answer the question.

Daily Bellringer Transparency, Section 1

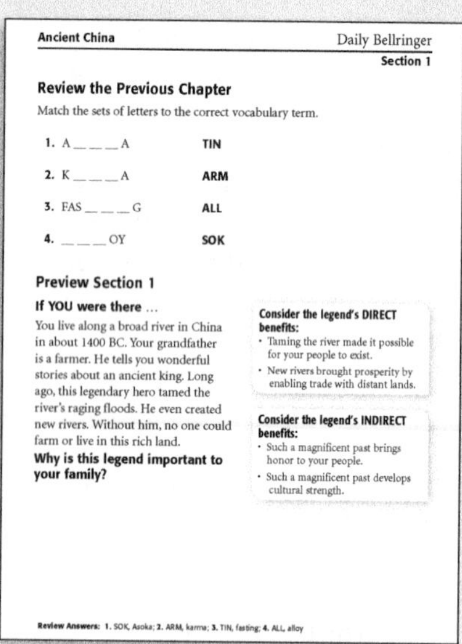

Ancient China — Daily Bellringer
Section 1

Review the Previous Chapter

Match the sets of letters to the correct vocabulary term.

1. A _ _ _ A — **TIN**
2. K _ _ _ A — **ARM**
3. FAS _ _ _ G — **ALL**
4. _ _ _ OY — **SOK**

Preview Section 1

If YOU were there ...

You live along a broad river in China in about 1400 BC. Your grandfather is a farmer. He tells you wonderful stories about an ancient king. Long ago, this legendary hero tamed the river's raging floods. He even created new rivers. Without him, no one could farm or live in this rich land.

Why is this legend important to your family?

Consider the legend's DIRECT benefits:
- Taming the river made it possible for your people to exist.
- New rivers brought prosperity by enabling trade with distant lands.

Consider the legend's INDIRECT benefits:
- Such a magnificent past brings honor to your people.
- Such a magnificent past develops cultural strength.

Review Answers: 1. SOK, Asoka; 2. ARM, karma; 3. TIN, fasting; 4. ALL, alloy

Academic Vocabulary

Review with students the high-use academic term in this section.

vary to be different (p. 161)

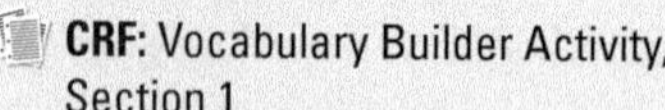
CRF: Vocabulary Builder Activity, Section 1

Taking Notes

Have students use the graphic organizer online to take notes on the section. This activity will prepare students for the Section Assessment, in which they will complete a graphic organizer that builds on the information using the Critical Thinking Skill: Comparing and Contrasting.

SECTION 1

Geography and Early China

What You Will Learn...

Main Ideas

1. China's physical geography made farming possible but travel and communication difficult.
2. Civilization began in China along the Huang He and Chang Jiang rivers.
3. China's first dynasties helped Chinese society develop and made many other achievements.

The Big Idea

Chinese civilization began with the Shang dynasty along the Huang He.

Key Terms

jade, *p. 163*
oracle, *p. 164*

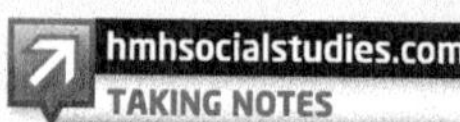

Use the graphic organizer online to take notes on China's geography and its early civilizations.

If YOU were there...

You live along a broad river in China in about 1400 BC. Your grandfather is a farmer. He tells you wonderful stories about an ancient king. Long ago, this legendary hero tamed the river's raging floods. He even created new rivers. Without him, no one could farm or live in this rich land.

Why is this legend important to your family?

BUILDING BACKGROUND Like other river civilizations, the Chinese people had to learn to control floods and irrigate their fields. China's geographical features divided the country into distinct regions.

China's Physical Geography

Geography played a major role in the development of Chinese civilization. China has many different geographical features. Some features separated groups of people within China. Others separated China from the rest of the world.

A Vast and Varied Land

China covers an area of nearly 4 million square miles, about the same size as the United States. One of the physical barriers that separates China from its neighbors is a harsh desert, the Gobi (GOH-bee). It spreads over much of China's north. East of the Gobi are low-lying plains. These plains, which cover most of eastern China, form one of the world's largest farming regions. The Pacific Ocean forms the country's eastern boundary.

More than 2,000 miles to the west, rugged mountains make up the western frontier. In the southwest the Plateau of Tibet has several mountain peaks that reach more than 26,000 feet. From the plateau, smaller mountain ranges spread eastward. The most important of these ranges is the Qinling Shandi (CHIN-LING shahn-DEE). It separates northern China from southern China.

Teach the Big Idea

At Level

Geography and Early China

1. **Teach** Ask students the questions in the Main Idea boxes to teach this section.
2. **Apply** Write the following labels for students to see: China's Physical Geography, Civilization Begins, and First Dynasties. Organize the students into three groups, one for each label. Then have each group work together to identify the key points, concepts, and terms that pertain to their topic. Have each group present these main ideas to the class in the form of a skit.
   LS **Visual/Spatial, Verbal/Linguistic**
3. **Review** As each group presents its skit, have students take notes on the main ideas from their presentation. Students can use these notes as a review of the section.
4. **Practice/Homework** Have each student select a skit other than the one on which he or she worked. Have students write reviews of the skit, making sure to state the main ideas presented. LS **Verbal/Linguistic**

Alternative Assessment Handbook, Rubrics 33: Skits and Reader's Theater; and 37: Writing Assignments

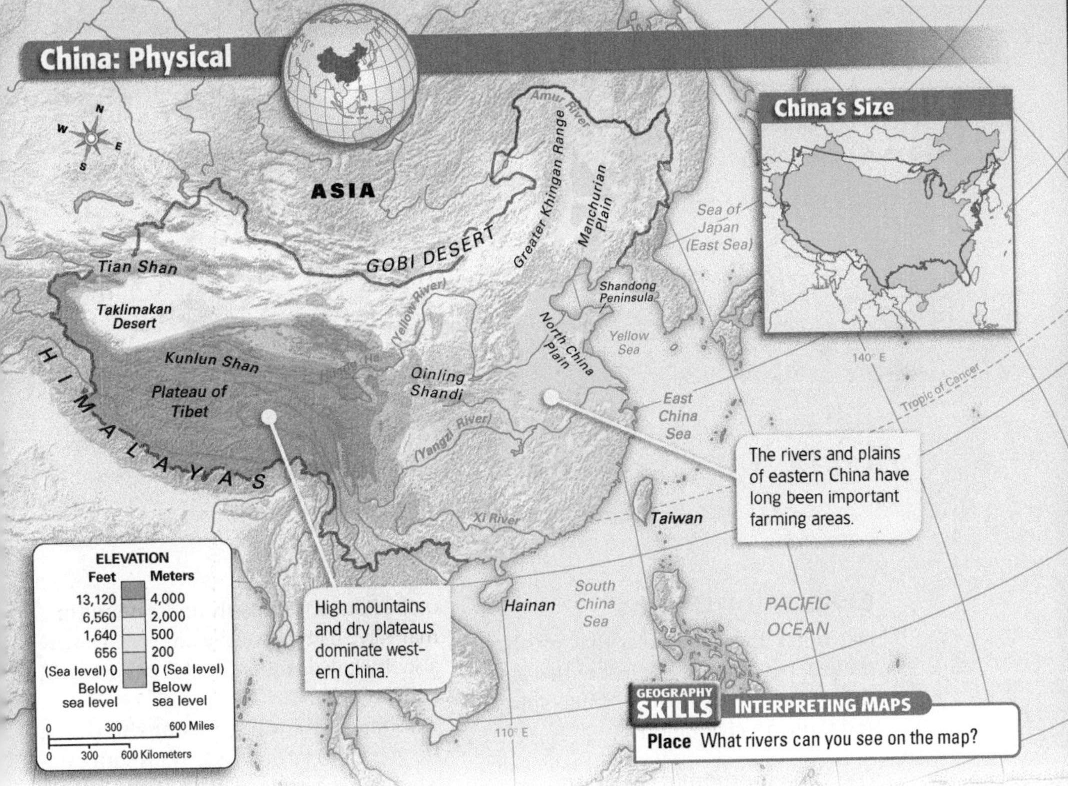

GEOGRAPHY SKILLS INTERPRETING MAPS

Place What rivers can you see on the map?

Weather and temperature patterns **vary** widely across China. In the northeast, the climate is cold and dry. Winter temperatures drop well below 0°F. Rivers there are frozen for more than half of the year. In the northwest, the deserts are very dry. But on the eastern plains of China, heavy rains fall. The tropical southeast is the wettest region. Monsoons can bring 250 inches of rain each year. That's enough water to cover a two-story house!

ACADEMIC VOCABULARY
vary to be different

The Rivers of China

Two great rivers flow from west to east in China. The Huang He, or Yellow River, stretches for nearly 3,000 miles across northern China. The river often floods, and the floods leave behind layers of silt on the surrounding countryside. Because these floods can be very destructive, the river is sometimes called China's Sorrow. Over the years, millions of people have died in Huang He floods.

To the south, the Chang Jiang, or Yangzi River, cuts through central China. It flows from the mountains of Tibet to the Pacific Ocean. The Chang Jiang is the longest river in Asia.

In early China, the two rivers helped link people in the eastern part of the country with those in the west. At the same time, the mountains between the rivers limited contact.

READING CHECK **Summarizing** What geographical features limited travel in China?

Collaborative Learning

Below Level

Travel Poster

Research Required

1. Review the physical map of China and the illustrations in this section with students. Then guide students in a discussion on the geographic features of China.
2. Organize students into pairs and assign each pair a different region of China. Have each pair create a travel poster of their assigned region. Students should research their region and identify their region on a blank outline map of China.
3. Posters should highlight the geography of the region as well as attract travelers. Have students come up with the many things one can do and see in each region. Ask each pair to use illustrations and photos to make their posters appealing.
4. Ask volunteers to present their posters to the class. **LS Verbal/Linguistic, Visual/Spatial**

Alternative Assessment Handbook, Rubric 28: Posters

Direct Teach

Main Idea

1 China's Physical Geography

China's physical geography made farming possible but travel and communication difficult.

Identify What were ancient China's two great rivers? *the Huang He and the Chang Jiang*

Draw Conclusions Why is the Huang He sometimes called China's Sorrow? *It often floods, killing people and destroying land.*

Make Judgments Which region in ancient China do you think would have been the hardest place to live and why? *Answers will vary, but should show understanding of China's geographic features.*

Map Transparency China: Physical

Did you know . . .

The Chang Jiang and the Huang He are the third and fourth longest rivers in the world. The two longest are, in order, the Nile River in Africa and the Amazon River in South America.

Info to Know

China's Isolation Great distances, rugged mountain ranges, and harsh deserts isolated China from other civilizations in India and western Asia. As a result, China developed its own unique culture. The Chinese did adopt some ideas and skills from other peoples, but they were influenced less by other cultures than were any other people in ancient times.

Answers

Interpreting Maps *Chang Jiang, Amur, Huang He, and Xi*

Reading Check *mountains and deserts*

Direct Teach

Main Idea

❷ Civilization Begins

Civilization began in China along the Huang He and Chang Jiang rivers.

Recall How did the floods along the rivers help the Chinese? *They deposited fertile silt, making the land ideal for growing crops.*

Explain What information have burial sites provided about the culture of early China? *information about works of art, differences in social order, and possibly belief in an afterlife*

Draw Conclusions Why do you think some of the homes of the ancient Chinese were partially underground? *possible answers—to keep them cool; to protect from wind*

Info to Know

The Mummies of Ürümqi Archaeologists found very interesting burial sites in the Tarim Basin in far western China in the 1970s. They uncovered dozens of mummies whose origins can be traced to about 2000 BC. Many of these incredibly well-preserved mummies are still dressed in the colorful clothing and woolen hats they wore in life. What is truly remarkable is that the mummies have European facial features.

Geography and Living

China is a large country with many different types of environments.

How do these photos show China's diverse geography?

❶ **In northern China, the Huang He, or Yellow River, has long been the center of civilization. The silt in the river gives it a yellow look.**

Civilization Begins

Like other ancient peoples that you have studied, people in China first settled along rivers. There they farmed, built villages, and formed a civilization.

The Development of Farming

Farming in China started along the Huang He and Chang Jiang. The rivers' floods deposited fertile silt. These silt deposits made the land ideal for growing crops.

As early as 7000 BC farmers grew rice in the middle Chang Jiang Valley. North, along the Huang He, the land was better for growing cereals such as millet and wheat.

Along with farming, the early Chinese people increased their diets in other ways. They fished and hunted with bows and arrows. They also domesticated animals such as pigs and sheep. With more sources of food, the population grew.

Early Settlements

Archaeologists have found remains of early Chinese villages. One village site near the Huang He had more than 40 houses. Many of the houses were partly underground and may have had straw-covered roofs. The site also included animal pens, storage pits, and a cemetery.

Some of the villages along the Huang He grew into large towns. Walls surrounded these towns to defend them against floods and hostile neighbors. In towns like these, the Chinese left many artifacts, such as arrowheads, fishhooks, tools, and pottery. Some village sites even contained pieces of cloth.

Separate cultures developed in southern and northeastern China. These included the Sanxingdui (sahn-shing-DWAY) and Hongshan peoples. Little is known about them, however. As the major cultures along the Huang He and Chang Jiang grew, they absorbed other cultures.

Over time, Chinese culture became more advanced. After 3000 BC people used potter's wheels to make more types of pottery. These people also learned to dig water wells. As populations grew, villages spread out over larger areas in both northern and southeastern China.

Critical Thinking: Drawing Conclusions

At Level

Early Chinese Settlements

1. Discuss with students the early settlements that developed in China. Ask students how the differing climates and geography of China might have led to differences between cultures of the early settlements.
2. Divide the class into small groups and assign each group one of the regions of China. Have groups discuss how the geography of that region might have affected the culture that developed there. Remind students to consider such things as settlement patterns, housing, crops, and clothing.
3. Then have each group create a scrapbook that highlights the culture of a settlement in their region. Have students use illustrations and captions to explain the influence that geography had on forming the culture in that area.
4. Have groups display their scrapbook pages for the class to see.

LS Verbal/Linguistic, Visual/Spatial

Answers

Geography and Living *river valleys with fertile soil in northern China, to southern China's more tropical climate, to the rugged mountains and deserts of western China*

2 Southern China receives more rain than northern China, and farmers can grow several crops of rice a year.

3 Western China's high mountains and wide deserts make travel difficult and isolate China's population centers in the east.

Burial sites have provided information about the culture of this period. Like the Egyptians, the early Chinese filled their tombs with objects. Some tombs included containers of food, suggesting a belief in an afterlife. Some graves contained many more items than others. These differences show that a social order had developed. Often the graves of rich people held beautiful jewelry and other objects made from **jade**, a hard gemstone.

READING CHECK **Generalizing** What were some features of China's earliest settlements?

China's First Dynasties

Societies along the Huang He grew and became more complex. They eventually formed the first Chinese civilization.

The Xia Dynasty

According to ancient stories, a series of kings ruled early China. Around 2200 BC one of them, Yu the Great, is said to have founded the Xia (SHAH) dynasty.

Writers told of terrible floods during Yu's lifetime. According to these accounts, Yu dug channels to drain the water to the ocean. This labor took him more than 10 years and is said to have created the major waterways of north China.

Archaeologists have not yet found evidence that the tales about the Xia are true. However, the stories of Xia rulers were important to the ancient Chinese because they told of kings who helped people solve problems by working together. The stories also explained the geography that had such an impact on people's lives.

The Shang Dynasty

The first dynasty for which we have clear evidence is the Shang, which was firmly established by the 1500s BC. Strongest in the Huang He Valley, the Shang ruled a broad area of northern China. Shang rulers moved their capital several times, probably to avoid floods or attack by enemies.

The king was at the center of Shang political and religious life. Nobles served the king as advisors and helped him rule.

Direct Teach

Main Idea

3 China's First Dynasties

China's first dynasties helped Chinese society develop and made many other achievements.

Recall According to ancient stories, what was the first Chinese dynasty, and who was its founder? *Xia dynasty; Yu the Great*

Analyze Why were the ancient stories about the Xia rulers important? *explained geography that influenced lives and told of kings who helped people solve problems by working together*

Did you know . . .

Until the 1920s historians believed that both the Xia and Shang dynasties were merely the stuff of legends. However, excavations along the Huang He in the 1920s uncovered inscriptions that proved the Shang dynasty was real and even had a capital near modern-day Anyang. This discovery leads some historians to believe that one day evidence will be uncovered that will prove the existence of the Xia dynasty as well.

Cross-Discipline Activity: English/Language Arts

At Level

Writing a Legend

1. Review with students the information on the Xia dynasty. Remind students that much of what we know of the Xia is through ancient stories. Explain to students that many of these ancient stories explain the geography of China or explain how early kings solved problems by working with the people.
2. Discuss with students what types of stories might have been told about the Xia rulers. Possible responses might include the creation of China, the development of social classes, explanations for the creation of mountains or government.
3. Tell students that they will each write a legend that explains some element of early Chinese culture, geography, or government. Have students select a topic and write a one-page story in the form of an ancient legend.
4. Ask volunteers to share their legends with the class. LS **Verbal/Linguistic**

Alternative Assessment Handbook, Rubric 39: Writing to Create

Answers

Reading Check *homes in villages buried partly underground, straw-covered roofs, animal pens, storage pits, cemeteries, walls to protect settlements from flooding and hostile neighbors, water wells*

Less important officials were also nobles. They performed specific governmental and religious duties.

The social order became more organized under the Shang. The royal family and the nobles were at the highest level. Nobles owned much land, and they passed on their wealth and power to their sons. Warrior leaders also had high rank in society. Most people in the Shang ruling classes lived in large homes in cities. These homes generally had wooden frames, clay walls, and thatched roofs.

Artisans settled outside the city walls. Some artisans made weapons. Other artisans made pottery, tools, or clothing. Artisans were at a middle level of importance in Shang society.

Farmers ranked below artisans in the social order. Farmers worked long hours but had little money. Taxes claimed much of what they earned. Slaves, who filled society's lowest rank, were an important source of labor during the Shang period.

The Shang made many advances, including China's first writing system. This system used more than 2,000 symbols to express words or ideas. Although the system has gone through changes over the years, the Chinese symbols used today are based on those of the Shang period.

Shang writing has been found on thousands of cattle bones and turtle shells. Priests had carved questions about the future on bones or shells, which were then heated, causing them to crack. The priests believed they could "read" these cracks to predict the future. The bones were called oracle bones because an **oracle** is a prediction.

In addition to writing, the Shang also made other achievements. Artisans made beautiful bronze containers for cooking and

Shang Dynasty, c. 1500–1050 BC

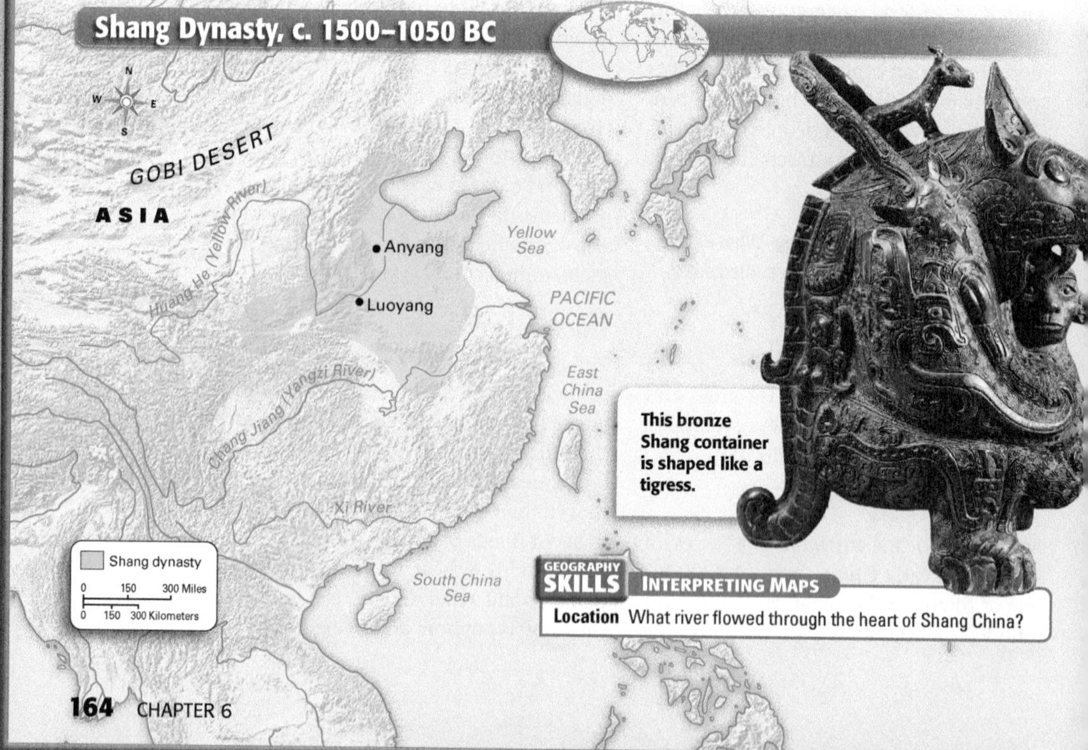

This bronze Shang container is shaped like a tigress.

GEOGRAPHY SKILLS INTERPRETING MAPS

Location What river flowed through the heart of Shang China?

Direct Teach

Main Idea

3 China's First Dynasties

China's first dynasties helped Chinese society develop and made many other achievements.

Summarize What advances were made during the Shang dynasty? *the development of China's first writing system, use of oracle bones, war chariots, the use of bronze, and the development of a calendar*

Make Judgments How difficult would daily life have been for farmers during the Shang dynasty? *Answers will vary but should show knowledge of how farmers worked long and hard, had little money, and occupied a low social rank.*

Activity China's Social Pyramid Have students draw a pyramid showing the social structure during the Shang dynasty.

- **CRF:** History and Geography Activity: Shang China
- Map Transparency: Shang Dynasty, c. 1500–1050 BC

Info to Know

Offerings to Ancestors During the Shang dynasty, people made offerings of food and drink to the spirits of their ancestors at special religious ceremonies. They prepared food for the dead as though they were preparing a large meal for the living. The food was offered to the ancestors in elaborately decorated cauldrons or dishes.

Differentiating Instruction

Special Needs Learners **Below Level**

1. Help students identify the accomplishments of the Shang dynasty by drawing the chart for students to see. Omit the blue, italicized answers.
2. Divide the class into mixed ability pairs. Have each student draw the chart on his or her own paper. Then have students work with their partners to complete the chart.

LS Verbal/Linguistic, Visual/Spatial

Shang Dynasty	
government	*kings ruled, nobles advised*
religion	*king at center of religion, priests used oracle bones to make predictions*
society	*royal family/nobles at highest level, artisans at middle level, farmers, slaves at lower levels*
achievements	*writing system, use of bronze, calendar, war chariots, and bows*

Answers

Interpreting Maps *Huang He*

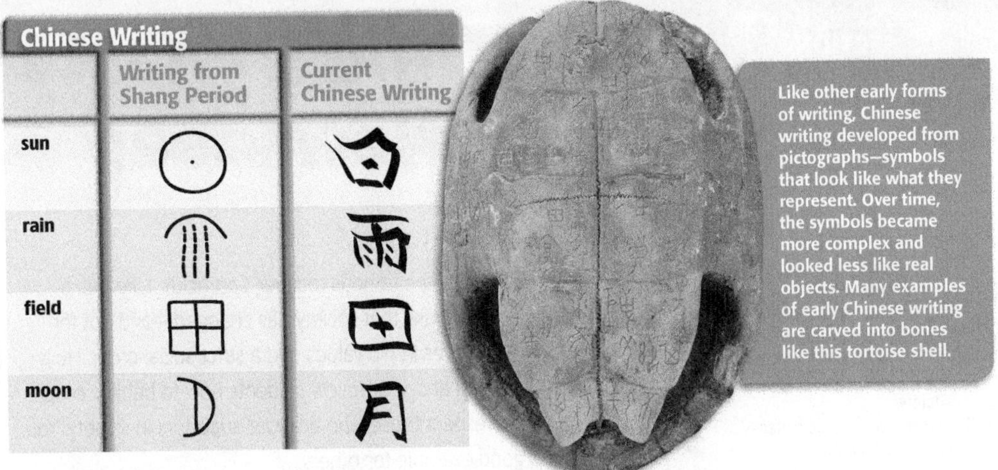

Chinese Writing
Writing from Shang Period
Current Chinese Writing
sun
rain
field
moon
日
雨
田
月

Like other early forms of writing, Chinese writing developed from pictographs—symbols that look like what they represent. Over time, the symbols became more complex and looked less like real objects. Many examples of early Chinese writing are carved into bones like this tortoise shell.

religious ceremonies. They also made axes, knives, and ornaments from jade. The military developed war chariots, powerful bows, and bronze body armor. Shang astrologers also made an important contribution. They developed a calendar based on the cycles of the moon.

READING CHECK **Contrasting** What is a major historical difference between the Xia and Shang dynasties?

SUMMARY AND PREVIEW China is a vast land with a diverse geography. Ancient Chinese civilization developed in the fertile valleys of the Huang He and Chang Jiang. Civilization there advanced under Shang rule. People developed a social order, a writing system, and made other achievements. In the next section you will learn about new ideas in China during the rule of the Zhou dynasty.

Section 1 Assessment

hmhsocialstudies.com ONLINE QUIZ

Reviewing Ideas, Terms, and People

1. a. **Identify** Name China's two major rivers.
   b. **Analyze** How did China's geography affect its development?
2. a. **Identify** In which river valley did China's civilization begin?
   b. **Explain** What made China's river valleys ideal for farming?
   c. **Elaborate** What do Chinese artifacts reveal about China's early civilization?
3. a. **Describe** How do historians know about the Xia dynasty?
   b. **Draw Conclusions** What does the use of **oracle** bones tell us about the early Chinese?

Critical Thinking

4. **Comparing and Contrasting** Draw a chart like this one. Use it and your notes to compare and contrast the Xia and Shang dynasties.

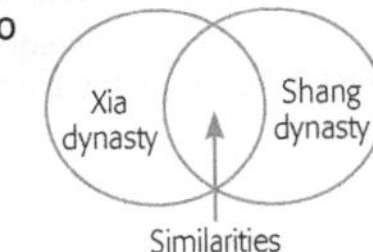

Focus on Speaking

5. **Thinking about Events** Look back over the section to note the important events of China's earliest times. Think about what it is that makes one event more important than another. Write down your ideas in a notebook.

Direct Teach

Did you know . . .

Modern Chinese writing is very complex. While the English alphabet uses 26 letters to spell words, there are more than 1,000 basic characters in the Chinese language. Characters are combined to represent more complex ideas. By some estimates, there are close to 40,000 characters in the Chinese writing system!

Review & Assess

Close

Have students write a short paragraph to summarize the main ideas from this section.

Review

Online Quiz, Section 1

Assess

SE Section 1 Assessment

PASS: Section 1 Quiz

Alternative Assessment Handbook

Reteach/Classroom Intervention

Guided Reading Workbook, Section 1

Interactive Skills Tutor CD-ROM

Section 1 Assessment Answers

1. a. Huang He and Chang Jiang
   b. It made it hard for trade and communication with other civilizations, but Chinese civilizations grew along the rivers, whose fertile soil made farming easier.
2. a. Huang He
   b. the fertile soil along the river banks
   c. They hunted, fished, and used pottery for food and water, made cloth, and established settlements.
3. a. only through ancient stories
   b. They believed in predicting the future and had a written language.
4. Xia dynasty—founded by Yu the Great; information from ancient stories; Shang dynasty—organized social order; many advances including writing system, calendar, and use of bronze; archaeological evidence; Both—along Huang He; had kings
5. Possible responses might include that one event had a greater effect than another or that we have evidence about certain events and not about others.

Answers

Reading Check *Archaeologists have not been able to find any evidence of the Xia dynasty but have found artifacts and other evidence from the Shang dynasty.*

Preteach

Bellringer

If YOU were there . . . Use the **Daily Bellringer Transparency** to help students answer the question.

Daily Bellringer Transparency, Section 2

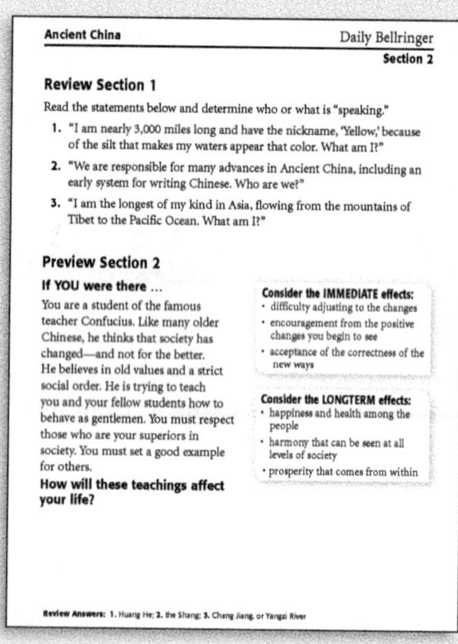

Ancient China — Daily Bellringer **Section 2**

Review Section 1

Read the statements below and determine who or what is "speaking."

1. "I am nearly 3,000 miles long and have the nickname, 'Yellow,' because of the silt that makes my waters appear that color. What am I?"
2. "We are responsible for many advances in Ancient China, including an early system for writing Chinese. Who are we?"
3. "I am the longest of my kind in Asia, flowing from the mountains of Tibet to the Pacific Ocean. What am I?"

Preview Section 2

If YOU were there ...

You are a student of the famous teacher Confucius. Like many older Chinese, he thinks that society has changed—and not for the better. He believes in old values and a strict social order. He is trying to teach you and your fellow students how to behave as gentlemen. You must respect those who are your superiors in society. You must set a good example for others.

How will these teachings affect your life?

Consider the IMMEDIATE effects:
- difficulty adjusting to the changes
- encouragement from the positive changes you begin to see
- acceptance of the correctness of the new ways

Consider the LONGTERM effects:
- happiness and health among the people
- harmony that can be seen at all levels of society
- prosperity that comes from within

Review Answers: 1. Huang He; 2. the Shang; 3. Chang Jiang, or Yangzi River

Academic Vocabulary

Review with students the high-use academic term in this section.

structure the way something is set up or organized (p. 168)

CRF: Vocabulary Builder Activity, Section 2

Taking Notes

Have students use the graphic organizer online to take notes on the section. This activity will prepare students for the Section Assessment, in which they will complete a graphic organizer that builds on the information using the Critical Thinking Skill: Finding Main Ideas.

SECTION 2

The Zhou Dynasty and New Ideas

What You Will Learn...

Main Ideas

1. The Zhou dynasty expanded China but then declined.
2. Confucius offered ideas to bring order to Chinese society.
3. Daoism and Legalism also gained followers.

The Big Idea

The Zhou dynasty brought political stability and new ways to deal with political and social changes in ancient China.

Key Terms and People

lords, *p. 167*
peasants, *p. 167*
Confucius, *p. 169*
ethics, *p. 169*
Confucianism, *p. 169*
Daoism, *p. 170*
Laozi, *p. 170*
Legalism, *p. 170*

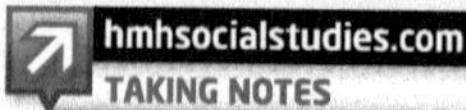

Use the graphic organizer online to take notes on changes that occurred during the Zhou dynasty.

If YOU were there...

You are a student of the famous teacher Confucius. Like many older Chinese, he thinks that society has changed—and not for the better. He believes in old values and a strict social order. He is trying to teach you and your fellow students how to behave properly. You must respect those who are your superiors in society. You must set a good example for others.

How will these teachings affect your life?

BUILDING BACKGROUND The people of the Shang dynasty made many advances, including beautiful metalwork, a writing system, and a calendar. The next dynasty, the Zhou, established other Chinese traditions. Some of these traditions included the importance of family and social order. Later thinkers looked back with admiration to the values of the Zhou period.

The Zhou Dynasty

In the 1100s BC the leaders of a people who came to be known as the Zhou (JOH) ruled over a kingdom in China. They joined with other nearby tribes and attacked and overthrew the Shang dynasty. The Zhou dynasty lasted longer than any other dynasty in Chinese history.

Time Line

The Zhou Dynasty

1200 BC — 800 BC — 400 BC

1100s BC The Zhou dynasty begins.

771 BC Invaders reach the Zhou capital.

551 BC Confucius is born.

481 BC Civil war spreads across China during the Warring States period.

166

Teach the Big Idea

At Level

The Zhou Dynasty and New Ideas

1. **Teach** Ask students the questions in the Main Idea boxes to teach this section.
2. **Apply** Divide the class into small groups. Then have each group create a brochure that summarizes the period of the Zhou dynasty. Ask students to include an interesting title page, a section on Zhou government, its rise and fall from power, society, and the three main philosophies. Remind students to create illustrations to enliven their brochures. LS **Verbal/Linguistic, Visual/Spatial**
3. **Review** As you review each main idea, have volunteers from different groups read aloud the information they used in their brochures.
4. **Practice/Homework** Have each student create a time line of the Zhou dynasty with at least 10 events. LS **Verbal/Linguistic**

Alternative Assessment Handbook, Rubrics 36: Time Lines; and 37: Writing Assignments

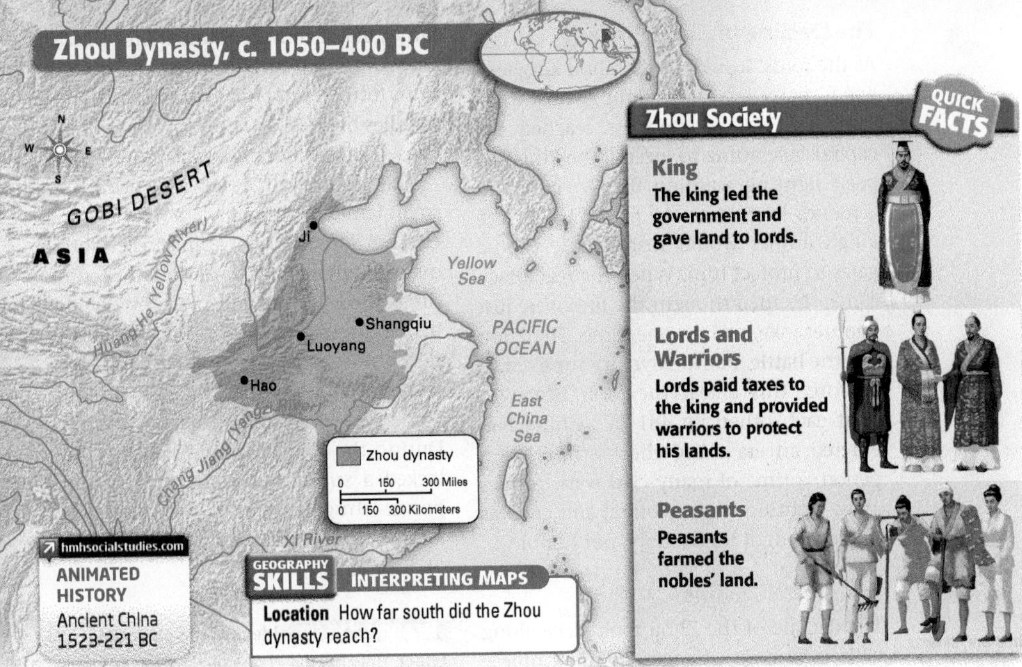

The Zhou Political System

The Zhou kings claimed to possess the mandate of heaven. According to this idea, heaven gave power to the king or leader, and no one ruled without heaven's permission. If a king was found to be bad, heaven would support another leader.

The Zhou came from an area to the west of the Shang kingdom. Early Zhou rulers used the mandate of heaven to justify their rebellion against the Shang. Later Zhou rulers expanded their territory to the northwest and the east. Zhou soldiers then moved south, eventually expanding their rule to the Chang Jiang.

The Zhou established a new political order. They granted land to others in return for loyalty, military support, and other services. The Zhou king was at the highest level. He granted plots of land to **lords**, or people of high rank. Lords paid taxes and provided soldiers to the king as needed. **Peasants**, or farmers with small farms, were at the bottom of the order. Each peasant family received a small plot of land and had to farm additional land for the noble. The system was described in the *Book of Songs*:

> "Everywhere under vast Heaven
> There is no land that is not the king's
> Within the borders of those lands
> There are none who are not the king's servants."
>
> –from the Zhou *Book of Songs*

The Zhou system brought order to China. Ruling through lords helped the Zhou control distant areas and helped ensure loyalty to the king. Over time, however, the political order broke down. Lords passed their power to their sons, who were less loyal to the king. Local rulers gained power. They began to reject the authority of the Zhou kings.

Direct Teach

Main Idea

1 The Zhou Dynasty

The Zhou dynasty expanded China but then declined.

Define What was the Zhou dynasty? *The longest-lasting Chinese dynasty, which began in the 1100s BC.*

Explain How did the Zhou use the mandate of heaven to justify their overthrow of the Shang? *possible answers—They claimed that heaven no longer gave the Shang permission to rule, because the Shang were bad rulers.*

Elaborate How did the new Zhou political order affect society? *It granted land to nobles, and required peasants to work the nobles' land.*

- Map Transparency: Zhou Dynasty, c. 1050–400 BC
- Quick Facts Transparency: Zhou Society

Other People, Other Places

Feudalism The political system established by the Zhou is sometimes described as feudalism. This system features an exchange of land in return for military and other services. Similar systems also developed in Japan in the 1100s and, most famously, in Europe during the Middle Ages. While each civilization practiced a slightly different system, the basic component, land for military service, was the same.

Critical Thinking: Comparing and Contrasting

Below Level

The Shang and Zhou Dynasties

1. Review with students the information from this section about the Zhou dynasty. Then have students re-read the portion of Section 1 that describes the Shang dynasty.
2. Have students work with a partner to create a graphic organizer comparing and contrasting the Shang and Zhou dynasties. Remind students to focus on such things as government, society, and territory.
3. Remind students to identify similarities as well as differences in their graphic organizers.
4. Ask volunteers to share their graphic organizers with the class.
   LS Verbal/Linguistic, Visual/Spatial

Alternative Assessment Handbook, Rubric 13: Graphic Organizers

Answers

Interpreting Maps *just south of the Chang Jiang*

Direct Teach

Main Idea

❶ The Zhou Dynasty

The Zhou dynasty expanded China but then declined.

Recall Why did the king's armies not rush to help him when invaders reached the capital in 771 BC? *They had been tricked by the king who was lighting the fires to entertain a friend, so they did not take the signal seriously.*

Describe What was the Warring States period? *a time marked by many civil wars and fights for territory among Chinese lords*

Evaluate Why do you think the decline of the Zhou weakened the Chinese family structure? *There was no strong government to stop power struggles within families.*

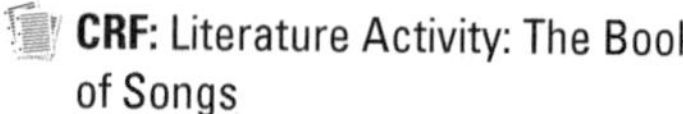
CRF: Literature Activity: The Book of Songs

Connect to Literature

A Guidebook for War *The Art of War* was probably written during the Warring States period. This well-known book offers philosophy, strategy, and logistics of war. It contains military theories such as, "Lure them in with the prospect of gain, take them by confusion," and "Though effective, appear to be ineffective." The book stresses the importance of accurate information, deception, surprise, and flexibility. *The Art of War* has influenced modern military leaders and even business strategists.

The Decline of Zhou Power

As the lords' loyalty to the Zhou king lessened, many refused to fight against invasions. In 771 BC invaders reached the capital. According to legend, the king had been lighting warning fires to entertain a friend. Each time the fires were lit, the king's armies would rush to the capital gates to protect him. When the real attack came, the men thought the fires were just another joke, and no one came. The Zhou lost the battle, but the dynasty survived.

After this defeat the lords began to fight each other. By 481 BC, China had entered an era called the Warring States period, a time of many civil wars. Armies grew. Fighting became brutal and cruel as soldiers fought for territory, not honor.

ACADEMIC VOCABULARY
structure the way something is set up or organized

Internal Problems

The decline of the Zhou took place along with important changes in the Chinese family <u>**structure**</u>. For many centuries the family had been the foundation of life in China. Large families of several generations formed powerful groups. When these families broke apart, they lost their power. Close relatives became rivals.

Bonds of loyalty even weakened within small families, especially among the upper classes. Sons plotted against each other over inheritances. A wealthy father sometimes tried to maintain peace by dividing his land among his sons. But this created new problems. Each son could build up his wealth and then challenge his brothers. Some sons even killed their own fathers. During the Warring States period, China lacked a strong government to stop the power struggles within the ruling-class families. Chinese society fell into a period of disorder.

READING CHECK **Identifying Cause and Effect** How did the Zhou's decline affect Chinese society?

The Warring States Period

During China's Warring States period, thousands of armies fought each other to gain territory. The armies used new weapons and battle techniques in the civil wars that lasted more than 200 years.

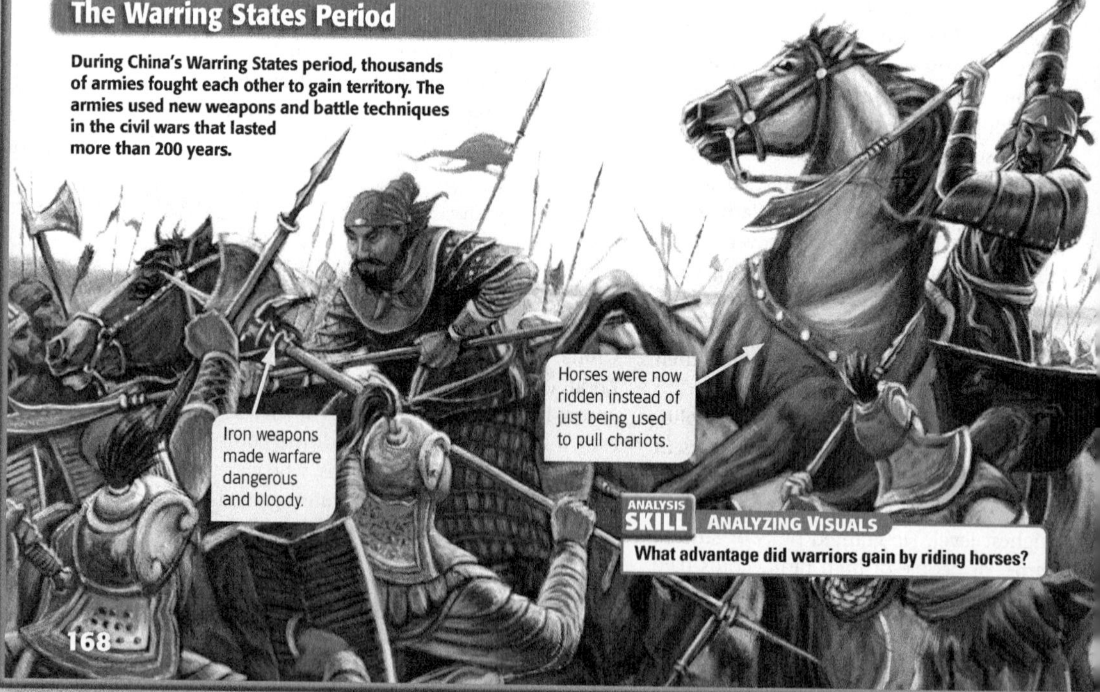

Iron weapons made warfare dangerous and bloody.
Horses were now ridden instead of just being used to pull chariots.

ANALYSIS SKILL **ANALYZING VISUALS**
What advantage did warriors gain by riding horses?

Differentiating Instruction

Struggling Readers **Below Level**

1. Review with students the period of the Warring States. Write the following main idea for students to see: *During the Warring States period, China entered a period of decline.* Help students understand what this statement means.
2. Ask students to write the main idea statement on their own paper. Then have each student re-read the information on the decline of the Zhou dynasty. Ask students to look for details that support the main idea above.
3. Have each student keep a list of the details they found to support the main idea statement. When students have finished, use their suggestions to create a master list for the class to see. **LS Verbal/Linguistic**

Alternative Assessment Handbook, Rubric 37: Writing Assignments

Answers

Reading Check *It weakened family structure and caused many civil wars among its citizens.*

Analyzing Visuals *speed, power, height, and maneuverability*

Confucius and Society

During the late Zhou period, thinkers came up with ideas about how to restore order to China. One such person, **Confucius**, became the most influential teacher in Chinese history. Confucius is a Western form of the Chinese title of "Master Kong" or "Kongfuzi."

Confucius felt that China was overrun with rude and dishonest people. Upset by the disorder and people's lack of decency, Confucius said that the Chinese needed to return to **ethics**, or moral values. The ideas of Confucius are known as **Confucianism**.

Confucius wanted China to return to ideas and practices from a time when people knew their proper roles in society. These are basic guidelines that Confucius thought would restore family order and social harmony:

- Fathers should display high moral values to inspire their families.
- Children should respect and obey their parents.
- All family members should be loyal to each other.

Confucius's ideas about government were similar to his ideas about family:

- Moral leadership, not laws, brought order to China.
- A king should lead by example, inspiring good behavior in all of his subjects.
- The lower classes would learn by following the example of their superiors. Confucius expressed this idea when he told kings:

> "Lead the people by means of government policies and regulate them through punishments, and they will be evasive and have no sense of shame. Lead them by means of virtue . . . and they will have a sense of shame and moreover have standards."
>
> –Confucius, from *The Analects*

BIOGRAPHY

Confucius

551–479 BC

Confucius, whose Chinese title is Kongfuzi, grew up in extreme poverty. Confucius was a dedicated student into his teenage years. Little is known about how he received his formal education, but he mastered many subjects, including music, mathematics, poetry, and history. He served in minor government positions, then he became a teacher. He never knew his teachings would transform Chinese life and thought.

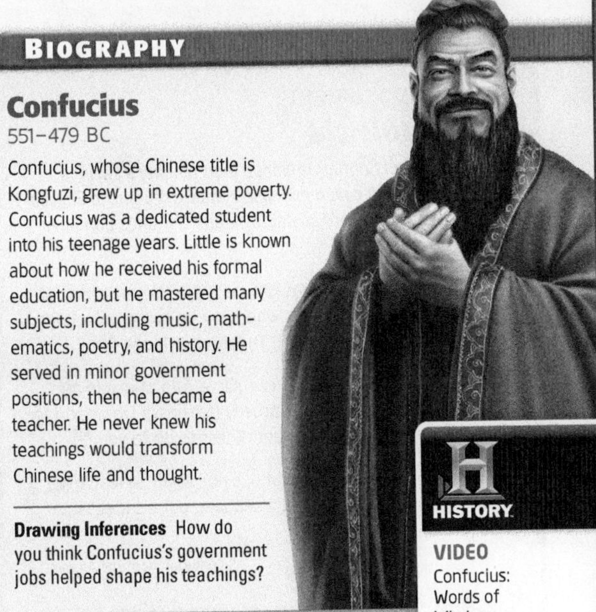

Drawing Inferences How do you think Confucius's government jobs helped shape his teachings?

HISTORY **VIDEO** Confucius: Words of Wisdom
hmhsocialstudies.com

As Confucius traveled to many different regions, he earned the reputation of a respected teacher. His ideas were passed down through his students and later compiled into a book called *The Analects*.

Because Confucianism focuses on morality, family, society, and government, people often think of it as a philosophy or way of thinking. But it is much more. Confucianism is a unique teaching that is both philosophical and religious. It has been a guiding force in human behavior and religious understanding in China.

Confucius believed that when people behaved well and acted morally, they were simply carrying out what heaven expected of them. Over the centuries Confucius's ideas about virtue, kindness, and learning became the dominant beliefs in China.

THE IMPACT TODAY Over time, Confucianism spread into Korea, Japan, and Vietnam. Many people in these countries still live by Confucian principles.

READING CHECK **Identifying Points of View** What did Confucius believe about good behavior?

Direct Teach

Main Idea

❷ Confucius and Society

Confucius offered ideas to bring order to Chinese society.

Explain Why did Confucius believe that China needed to return to ethics? *He was upset by disorder and a lack of decency in society.*

Summarize What was Confucius's view about how a family should be structured? *Fathers should set an example, children should obey parents, and family members should be loyal to each other.*

CRF: Biography Activity: Mencius

Biography

Mencius, Confucian Philosopher Next to Confucius, the second most important Confucian philosopher was Mencius. He argued that all people were basically good and could be perfected. He also believed that the job of government was to provide for the people—instead of the other way round. Like Confucius, Mencius emphasized the importance of ethics and education.

About the Illustration

This illustration of Confucius is an artist's conception based on available sources. However, historians are uncertain exactly what Confucius looked like.

Critical Thinking: Summarizing

Above Level

Research Required

Confucian Sayings

1. Review with students the beliefs and teachings of Confucius. Then have students examine the quotes on the next page from *The Analects*.
2. Have students use the library, Internet, or other resources to examine some of the sayings attributed to Confucius. Ask each student to select a short quote.
3. Have each student copy the quote onto his or her own paper. Ask students to put the quote in their own words.
4. Finally, have students create a plaque with his or her quote. Students can use cardboard or construction paper to display both the quote and their version of it. Students should add illustrations to the plaques. **LS Verbal/Linguistic**

Alternative Assessment Handbook, Rubric 28: Posters

Answers

Biography *He saw what condition his society was in and what was needed to fix society's problems.*

Reading Check *that when people behaved well they were simply carrying out what heaven expected of them*

• Direct Teach •

Main Idea

3 Daoism and Legalism

Daoism and Legalism also gained followers.

Define What is Daoism? *a philosophy that stresses living in harmony with the Dao, the guiding force of reality*

Identify Who was Laozi? *famous teacher credited with writing the basic text of Daoism*

Summarize What did Legalists believe society needed? *strict laws to keep people in line, punishments that fit the crimes, and holding citizens responsible for the crimes of others*

CRF: Primary Source Activity: The Teachings of Confucius and Laozi

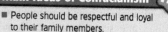

Quick Facts Transparency: Main Ideas of Confucianism

Connect to Art

Yin and Yang The Daoist idea of the balance of opposites often appears in Asian art. This principle is called yin-yang, or literally, the dark side and sunny side of a hill. The symbol of yin-yang is a circle with one dark side and one light side. Within each side is a small circle of the opposite color, which signifies that neither can exist without the other. Traditionally the dark side, yin, represents the feminine, moon, cold, and dark. The light side, or yang, represents the masculine, sun, heat, and light. Modern artists and designers have also embraced the yin-yang symbol.

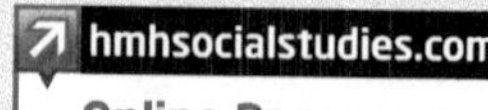

Online Resources
Activity: Dialogue

Primary Source

HISTORIC DOCUMENT

The Analects

The followers of Confucius placed their teacher's sayings together in a work called in Chinese the Lun Yü *and in English* The Analects. *The word* analects *means "writings that have been collected."*

"Yu, shall I teach you what knowledge is? When you know a thing, say that you know it; when you do not know a thing, admit that you do not know it. That is knowledge."

"Is there any one word that can serve as a principle for . . . life? Perhaps the word is reciprocity [fairness]: Do not do to others what you would not want others to do to you."

"I do not enlighten anyone who is not eager to learn, nor encourage anyone who is not anxious to put his ideas into words."

–Confucius, from *The Analects*

ANALYSIS SKILL ANALYZING PRIMARY SOURCES

What are some of the qualities that Confucius valued?

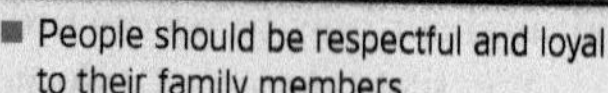

Main Ideas of Confucianism

- People should be respectful and loyal to their family members.
- Leaders should be kind and lead by example.
- Learning is a process that never ends.
- Heaven expects people to behave well and act morally.

Daoism and Legalism

Other beliefs besides Confucianism influenced China during the Zhou period. Two in particular attracted many followers.

Daoism

THE IMPACT TODAY

Like Confucianism, Daoism has long been practiced in such countries as Korea, Japan, and Vietnam.

Daoism (DOW-ih-zum) takes its name from *Dao*, meaning "the way." **Daoism** stressed living in harmony with the Dao, the guiding force of all reality. In Daoist teachings, the Dao gave birth to the universe and all things in it. Daoism developed in part as a reaction to Confucianism. Daoists didn't agree with the idea that active, involved leaders brought social harmony. Instead, they wanted the government to stay out of people's lives.

Daoists believed that people should avoid interfering with nature or each other. They should be like water and simply let things flow in a natural way. For Daoists, the ideal ruler was a wise man who was in harmony with the Dao. He would govern so effortlessly that his people would not even know they were being governed.

Daoists taught that the universe is a balance of opposites: female and male, light and dark, low and high. In each case, opposing forces should be in harmony.

While Confucianism focused its followers' attention on the human world, Daoists paid more attention to the natural world. Daoists regarded humans as just a part of nature, not better than any other thing. In time the Dao, as represented by nature, became so important to the Daoists that they worshipped it.

Laozi (LOWD-zuh) was the most famous Daoist teacher. He taught that people should not try to gain wealth, nor should they seek power. Laozi is credited with writing the basic text of Daoism, *The Way and Its Power*. Later writers created many legends about Laozi's achievements.

Legalism

Legalism, the belief that people were bad by nature and needed to be controlled, contrasted with both Confucianism and Daoism. Unlike the other two beliefs, Legalism was a political philosophy without religious concerns. Instead, it dealt only with government and social

Collaborative Learning

At Level

Understanding Chinese Philosophies

1. Review with the class the beliefs and teachings of Confucianism, Daoism, and Legalism.
2. Divide the class into small groups and assign each group one of the three belief systems. Have each group work together to create a guide for understanding their assigned belief system. Guides may be in the form of a brochure, a short paper, or a chart.
3. Each group's guide should explain the basic beliefs of their assigned philosophy, include information about the founder, if available, and present the main guidelines. Students should explain the ideas behind the philosophy in words that are easy to understand. Encourage students to make their guides visually appealing also.
4. Have each group present or display their guide for the class to see.
LS Verbal/Linguistic, Visual/Spatial

Alternative Assessment Handbook, Rubric 14: Group Activity

Answers

Analyzing Primary Sources *honesty, fairness, education*

control. Followers of Legalism disagreed with the moral preaching of Confucius. Legalists also rejected Daoism because it didn't stress respect for authority.

Legalists felt that society needed strict laws to keep people in line and that punishments should fit crimes. For example, they believed that citizens should be held responsible for each other's conduct. A guilty person's relatives and neighbors should also be punished. This way, everyone would obey the laws.

Unity and efficiency were also important to Legalists. They wanted appointed officials, not nobles, to run China. Legalists wanted the empire to continue to expand. Therefore, they urged the state to always be prepared for war.

Confucianism, Daoism, and Legalism competed for followers. All three beliefs became popular, but the Legalists were the first to put their ideas into practice throughout China.

READING CHECK **Contrasting** How did Daoism and Legalism differ in their theories about government?

BIOGRAPHY

Laozi

c. 500s or 400s BC

Scholars have found little reliable information about Laozi's life. Some believe that his book on Daoism was actually the work of several different authors. Most ancient sources of information about Laozi are myths. For example, one legend states that when Laozi was born, he was already an old man. In Chinese *Laozi* can mean "Old Baby." Over the years, many Daoists have worshipped Laozi as a supernatural being.

Drawing Inferences What do you think it meant to say Laozi was born "old"?

SUMMARY AND PREVIEW When the Zhou dynasty crumbled, political and social chaos erupted. In response, the new teachings of Confucianism, Daoism, and Legalism emerged. In the next section you will learn how the Qin dynasty applied the teachings of Legalism.

Section 2 Assessment

hmhsocialstudies.com ONLINE QUIZ

Reviewing Ideas, Terms, and People

1. a. **Identify** What is the mandate of heaven?
   b. **Explain** Describe the political order used by the Zhou kings to rule distant lands.
   c. **Elaborate** What happened when nobles began to reject the Zhou king's authority?
2. a. **Identify** Who was **Confucius**?
   b. **Analyze** Why did many of the teachings of Confucius focus on the family?
3. a. **Identify** Who was the most famous Daoist teacher?
   b. **Summarize** What were the main ideas of **Daoism**?
   c. **Elaborate** What might be some disadvantages of **Legalism**?

Critical Thinking

4. **Finding Main Ideas** Draw a chart like the one here. Use it and your notes on the Zhou dynasty to list two main ideas about each set of beliefs.

Confucianism	
Daoism	
Legalism	

Focus on Speaking

5. **Exploring the Importance of Historical Figures** Many important people in history are rulers or conquerors. People who think and teach, however, have also played major roles in history. How did thinkers and teachers shape China's history? Write some ideas in your notebook.

Direct Teach

Checking for Understanding

True or False Answer each statement *T* if it is true or *F* if it is false. If false, explain why.

1. Confucius taught that people should return to ethics. *T*
2. Daoists believed that people should pay more attention to the natural world. *T*
3. Daoists believe that people needed to be controlled by strict laws. *F; Legalists held this view.*

About the Illustration

This illustration of Laozi is an artist's conception based on available sources. However, historians are uncertain exactly what Laozi looked like.

Review & Assess

Close

Ask students how the legend in the Laozi biography feature may have originated.

Review

Online Quiz, Section 2

Assess

SE Section 2 Assessment
PASS: Section 2 Quiz
Alternative Assessment Handbook

Reteach/Classroom Intervention

Guided Reading Workbook, Section 2
Interactive Skills Tutor CD-ROM

Section 2 Assessment Answers

1. a. the idea that heaven gave kings the power to rule
   b. granted land to lords for loyalty, military support, and other services
   c. decreased loyalty, civil wars
2. a. a teacher and philosopher who wanted to restore family order and social harmony
   b. He believed that moral values needed to be taught by families.
3. a. Laozi
   b. Let things flow in a natural way; the universe is a balance of opposites; government should stay out of people's lives.
   c. possible answers—too much government power; innocent people punished
4. See information under *Confucius and Society* and *Daoism and Legalism* for possible answers.
5. Students should note the lasting influence of Confucius and other thinkers and teachers.

Answers

Biography *possible answer—he was always very wise*

Reading Check *Daoists believed government should stay out of people's lives; Legalists believed society needed strict laws.*

Preteach

Bellringer

If YOU were there . . . Use the **Daily Bellringer Transparency** to help students answer the question.

Daily Bellringer Transparency, Section 3

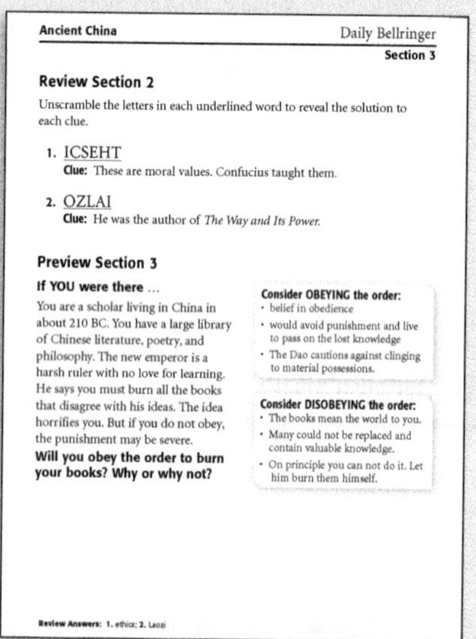

Ancient China — Daily Bellringer — **Section 3**

Review Section 2

Unscramble the letters in each underlined word to reveal the solution to each clue.

1. ICSEHT
   Clue: These are moral values. Confucius taught them.
2. OZLAI
   Clue: He was the author of *The Way and Its Power.*

Preview Section 3

If YOU were there ...

You are a scholar living in China in about 210 BC. You have a large library of Chinese literature, poetry, and philosophy. The new emperor is a harsh ruler with no love for learning. He says you must burn all the books that disagree with his ideas. The idea horrifies you. But if you do not obey, the punishment may be severe.

Will you obey the order to burn your books? Why or why not?

Consider OBEYING the order:
- belief in obedience
- would avoid punishment and live to pass on the lost knowledge
- The Dao cautions against clinging to material possessions.

Consider DISOBEYING the order:
- The books mean the world to you.
- Many could not be replaced and contain valuable knowledge.
- On principle you can not do it. Let him burn them himself.

Review Answers: 1. ethics; 2. Laozi

Building Vocabulary

Preteach or review the following terms:

mandate of heaven the idea that kings rule with the permission of heaven (p. 176)

standardized having made things similar (p. 174)

unified joined or combined (p. 176)

CRF: Vocabulary Builder Activity, Section 3

Taking Notes

Have students use the graphic organizer online to take notes on the section. This activity will prepare students for the Section Assessment, in which they will complete a graphic organizer that builds on the information using the Critical Thinking Skill: Evaluating.

SECTION 3

The Qin Dynasty

What You Will Learn...

Main Ideas

1. The first Qin emperor created a strong but strict government.
2. A unified China was created through Qin policies and achievements.

The Big Idea

The Qin dynasty unified China with a strong government and a system of standardization.

Key Terms and People

Shi Huangdi, *p. 172*
Great Wall, *p. 175*

hmhsocialstudies.com
TAKING NOTES

Use the graphic organizer online to take notes on the achievements and policies of Shi Huangdi. Note how he affected life in China.

If YOU were there...

You are a scholar living in China in about 210 BC. You have a large library of Chinese literature, poetry, and philosophy. The new emperor is a harsh ruler with no love for learning. He says you must burn all the books that disagree with his ideas. The idea horrifies you. But if you do not obey, the punishment may be severe.

Will you obey the order to burn your books? Why or why not?

BUILDING BACKGROUND Different dynasties held very different ideas about how to rule. As the Zhou period declined, putting new ideas into effect brought great changes.

The Qin Emperor's Strong Government

The Warring States period marked a time in China when several states battled each other for power. One state, the Qin (CHIN), built a strong army that defeated the armies of the rivaling states. Eventually, the Qin dynasty united the country under one government.

Shi Huangdi Takes the Throne

In 221 BC, the Qin king Ying Zheng succeeded in unifying China. He gave himself the title **Shi Huangdi** (SHEE hwahng-dee), which means "first emperor." Shi Huangdi followed Legalist political beliefs. He created a strong government with strict laws and harsh punishments.

Time Line

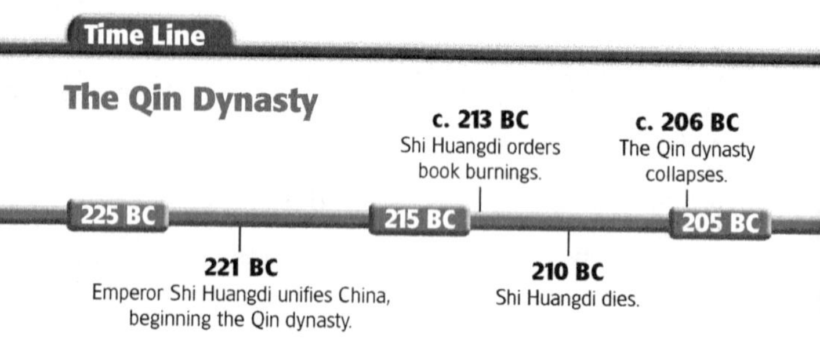
The Qin Dynasty
c. 213 BC
Shi Huangdi orders book burnings.
c. 206 BC
The Qin dynasty collapses.
225 BC
215 BC
205 BC
221 BC
Emperor Shi Huangdi unifies China, beginning the Qin dynasty.
210 BC
Shi Huangdi dies.

Teach the Big Idea

At Level

The Qin Dynasty

1. **Teach** Ask students the questions in the Main Idea boxes to teach this section.
2. **Apply** Have students copy the Qin dynasty time line on their own papers. Have students add two or three sentences with supporting details or additional information about the events listed. Have students add other additional events or accomplishments that occurred during the dynasty to their time lines. **LS Verbal/Linguistic, Visual/Spatial**
3. **Review** Have students exchange time lines and study the events and dates as a review.
4. **Practice/Homework** Have students illustrate their time lines by adding images that represent the events on the time line. **LS Visual/Spatial**

Alternative Assessment Handbook, Rubric 36: Time Lines

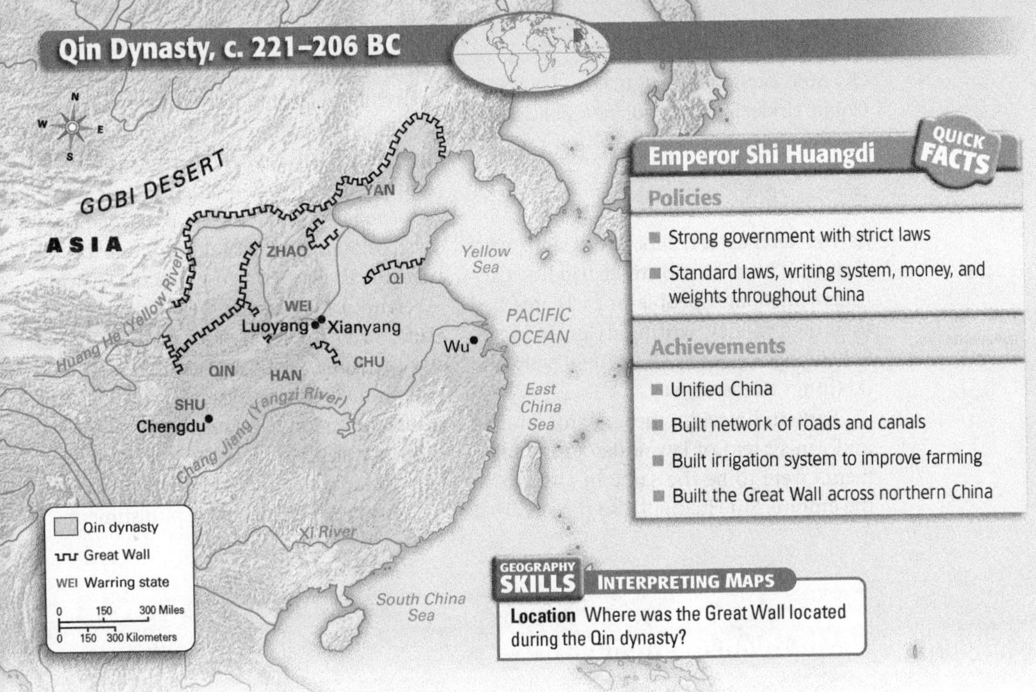

Shi Huangdi demanded that everyone follow his policies. He ordered the burning of all writings that did not agree with Legalism. The only other books that were saved dealt with farming, medicine, and predicting the future. Many scholars opposed the book burnings. The emperor responded to the opposition by burying 460 scholars alive.

Shi Huangdi also used his armies to expand the empire. First, they occupied the lands around both of China's major rivers. Then his soldiers turned north and advanced almost to the Gobi Desert. To the south, they invaded more lands and advanced as far as the Xi River.

Shi Huangdi ensured that there would not be any future revolts in his new territories. When his soldiers conquered a city, he had them destroy its walls and take all the weapons.

China under the Qin

Shi Huangdi changed China's old political system. He claimed all the power and did not share it with the lords. He even took land away from them and forced thousands of nobles to move with their families to the capital so he could keep an eye on them. He also forced thousands of commoners to work on government building projects. Workers faced years of hardship, danger, and often, death.

To control China, Shi Huangdi divided it into districts, each with its own governor. Districts were subdivided into counties that were governed by appointed officials. This organization helped the emperor enforce his tax system. It also helped the Qin enforce a strict chain of command.

READING CHECK **Summarizing** How did Shi Huangdi strengthen the government?

Direct Teach

Main Idea

1 The Qin Emperor's Strong Government

The first Qin emperor created a strong but strict government.

Recall How did Shi Huangdi prevent future revolts in his territory? *He had soldiers destroy city walls and take all the residents' weapons.*

Analyze How did Shi Huangdi change China's old political system? *He claimed all power and did not share any power with the lords.*

Predict If you were a scholar who lived in China under Shi Huangdi's rule, how might have you reacted if you heard about the book burnings? *Answers will vary, but students may reply that they would have hidden their books or fled to areas farther from the emperor's influence.*

Map Transparency: Qin Dynasty

Quick Facts Transparency: Emperor Shi Huangdi

Did you know . . .

After successfully unifying China and taking the title "first emperor," Shi Huangdi claimed that the Qin dynasty would survive for 10,000 generations. Instead, after his death, rival families defeated the Qin. The Qin dynasty had ruled all of China for fewer than 20 years.

Critical Thinking: Analyzing

At Level

Cost-Benefit Analysis

1. Review with students how Shi Huangdi united China and set up a strong government.
2. Write the following labels for students to see: *Actions, Benefits,* and *Cost.* Then discuss with students what specific actions Shi Huangdi took to unify and strengthen China. Have students examine the benefits of Shi Huangdi's policies versus the costs. List their replies for everyone to see. One example might be—action: began building projects, benefit: improved irrigation or transportation, cost: workers faced hardship, dangers, and death.
3. Ask students whether the benefits of Shi Huangdi's rule exceeded the costs. Encourage students to use the chart to help them make a determination. Then have each student write a one- to two-paragraph cost-benefit analysis of Shi Huangdi's rule.
4. Have volunteers share their analyses with the class. **LS Verbal/Linguistic**

Alternative Assessment Handbook, Rubric 37: Writing Assignments

Answers

Interpreting Maps *along the northwestern border*

Reading Check *He took all power, kept control of nobles, divided China into districts ruled by appointed officials, and organized a tax system.*

Direct Teach

Main Idea

2 A Unified China

A unified China was created through Qin policies and achievements.

Recall What steps did Shi Huangdi take to unify China? *He standardized laws, writing, and weights and measures, created a money system, and made trade easier.*

Draw Conclusions Why did Shi Huangdi standardize many elements of Chinese life? *possible answers—to ease trade, communication, and travel and to make the Chinese people feel more like one nation*

Evaluate Which of Shi Huangdi's achievements or policies do you think was most important? Why? *possible answers—building canals and roads, because they linked distant parts of China together; standardizing writing, because it gave the Chinese a common identity*

Info to Know

Shi Huangdi's Tomb In March 1974 farmers near the Chinese city of Xian were digging for a water well. What they uncovered was one of the most famous archaeological discoveries of the twentieth century. Measuring some 20 square miles, the tomb complex of Qin ruler Shi Huangdi is best known for the thousands of life-like terra-cotta soldiers that guard the tomb along with horses and chariots. While the inside of Shi Huangdi's actual tomb has yet to be excavated, historians believe it took some 700,000 workers over 36 years to complete.

A Unified China

Qin rule brought other major changes to China. Under Shi Huangdi, new policies and achievements united the Chinese people.

Qin Policies

Focus on Reading
How might you summarize the new Qin policies?

As you read earlier, mountains and rivers divided China into distinct regions. Customs varied, and people in each area had their own money, writing styles, and laws. Shi Huangdi wanted all Chinese people to do things the same way.

Early in his reign, the emperor set up a uniform system of law. Rules and punishments were to be the same in all parts of the empire. Shi Huangdi also standardized the written language. People everywhere were required to write using the same set of symbols. People from different regions could now communicate with each other in writing. This gave them a sense of shared culture and a common identity.

Next, the emperor set up a new money system. Standardized gold and copper coins became the currency used in all of China. Weights and measures were also standardized. Even the axle width of carts had to be the same. With all these changes and the unified writing system, trade between different regions became much easier. The Qin government strictly enforced these new standards. Any citizen who disobeyed the laws would face severe punishment.

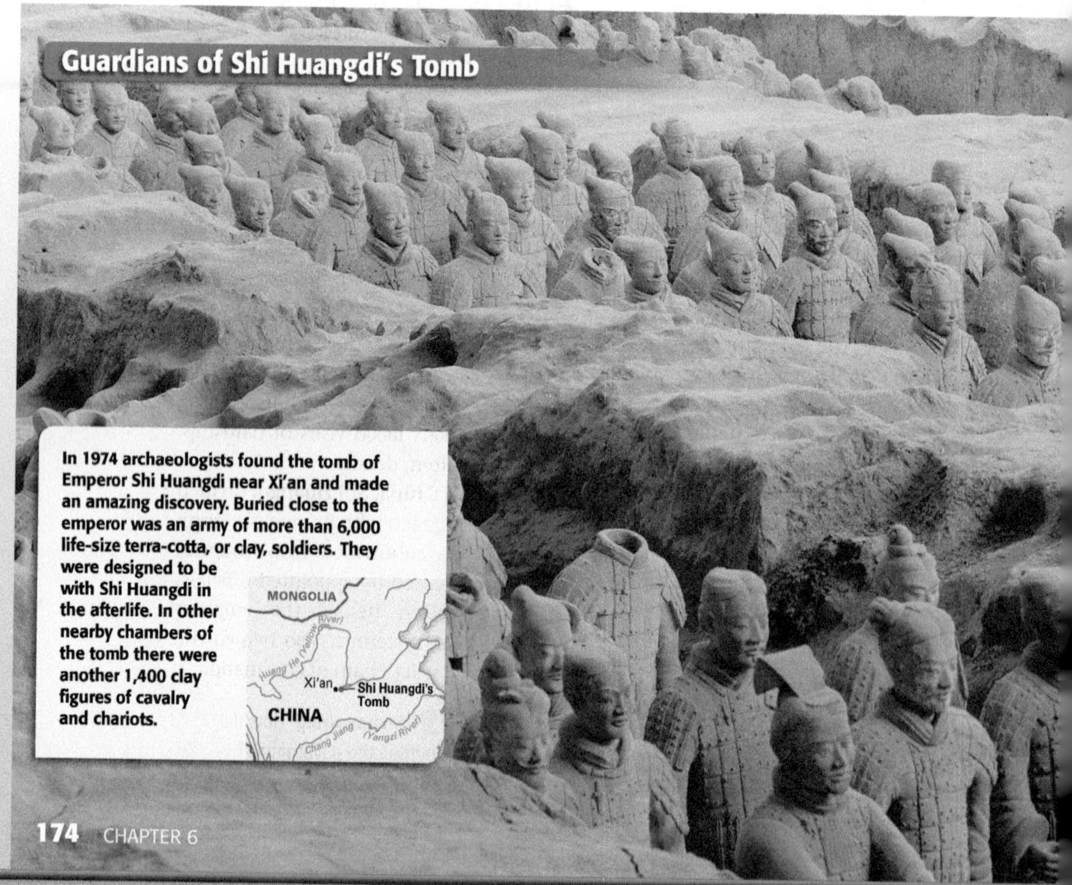

Guardians of Shi Huangdi's Tomb

In 1974 archaeologists found the tomb of Emperor Shi Huangdi near Xi'an and made an amazing discovery. Buried close to the emperor was an army of more than 6,000 life-size terra-cotta, or clay, soldiers. They were designed to be with Shi Huangdi in the afterlife. In other nearby chambers of the tomb there were another 1,400 clay figures of cavalry and chariots.

Collaborative Learning

Below Level

Terra-cotta Army Exhibit

Research Required

1. Discuss with students how Shi Huangdi's tomb was surrounded by an army of weapon-wielding terra-cotta soldiers, each with its own facial features and expression.
2. Organize the class into small groups. Have each group conduct research on the tomb using the library, Internet, or other resources. Ask each group to create a museum exhibit that provides information about the origins and history of the terra-cotta army and of Shi Huangdi's tomb. Encourage students to use images, illustrations, and written information to make an interesting exhibit. They might even want to make small figurines to represent the terra-cotta army.
3. Have each group display their museum exhibit on Shi Huangdi's tomb for the class to see. **LS Visual/Spatial, Verbal/Linguistic**

Alternative Assessment Handbook, Rubrics 14: Group Activity; and 29: Presentations

Qin Achievements

New, massive building projects also helped to unify the country. Under Shi Huangdi's rule, the Chinese built a network of roads that connected the capital to every part of the empire. These roads made travel easier for everyone. Each of these new roads was the same width, 50 paces wide. This design helped the army move quickly and easily to put down revolts in distant areas.

China's water system was also improved. Workers built canals to connect the country's rivers. Like the new roads, the canals improved transportation throughout the country. Using the new canals and rivers together made it easier and faster to ship goods from north to south. In addition, the Qin built an irrigation system to make more land good for farming. Parts of that system are still in use today.

Shi Huangdi also wanted to protect the country from invasion. Nomads from the north were fierce warriors, and they were a real threat to China. Hoping to stop them from invading, the emperor built the **Great Wall**, a barrier that linked earlier walls across China's northern frontier. The first section of the wall had been built in the 600s BC to keep invading groups out of China. The Qin connected earlier pieces of the wall to form a long, unbroken structure. Building the wall required years of labor from hundreds of thousands of workers. Many of them died building the wall.

The Great Wall is a major tourist attraction today.

HISTORY
VIDEO
The First Emperor of China
hmhsocialstudies.com

Each terra-cotta soldier was different, with its own facial features, hairstyle, and unique expression. Here, a computer model shows what a soldier might have looked like when it was created.

Direct Teach

Linking to Today

Chinese Currency One of Shi Huangdi's achievements was standardizing China's money. Today, the official currency in China is called the *renminbi*, which means "people's currency." The base unit of the currency is the *yuan*. Images used on different denominations of paper bills include Mao Zedong, the Chairman of the Chinese Communist Party from 1931 until 1976, and pictures of people who represent the various ethnic groups in China.

Did you know . . .

The standardized form of Chinese writing developed during the Qin dynasty is known as *xiaozhuan*, and was created by a government official named Li Si in the 200s BC. The script is no longer in use today, but can be seen occasionally in formal inscriptions.

MISCONCEPTION ALERT

The Great Wall from Space?
Students may have heard that the Great Wall of China is the only manmade object that can be seen from space or even from the moon. It's not true. Despite the fact that the Great Wall of China is thousands of miles long, it is only a few yards wide. Astronauts report that the Great Wall can indeed be seen from low orbit but so can many highways and airport runways.

Differentiating Instruction

Special Needs Learners — Below Level

1. Review with students the many achievements of the Qin dynasty. Be sure that students understand the importance of each achievement.
2. Ask each student to select one contribution made by the Qin. Have each student create a colorful poster that depicts the achievement.
3. Have each student write a few sentences that explain in his or her own words why the chosen achievement was important.
4. Ask volunteers to share their posters with the class. LS **Visual/Spatial, Verbal/Linguistic**

Alternative Assessment Handbook, Rubric 28: Posters

Direct Teach

Main Idea

2 A Unified China

A unified China was created through Qin policies and achievements.

Summarize What happened to China after the death of Shi Huangdi? *The government began to fall apart and the country fell into a civil war.*

Make Judgments Do you think China was better off because of Shi Huangdi? *Answers will vary but should address both his accomplishments and his harsh rule.*

Review & Assess

Close

Have students create a graphic organizer that includes the policies, achievements, and fall of the Qin dynasty under Shi Huangdi.

Review

Online Quiz, Section 3

Assess

SE Section 3 Assessment

PASS: Section 3 Quiz

Alternative Assessment Handbook

Reteach/Classroom Intervention

Guided Reading Workbook, Section 3

Interactive Skills Tutor CD-ROM

The Great Wall has been added to and rebuilt many times since Shi Huangdi ruled China.

The Fall of the Qin

Shi Huangdi's policies unified China. However, his policies also stirred resentment. Many peasants, scholars, and nobles hated his harsh ways.

Still, Shi Huangdi was powerful enough to hold the country together. When he died in 210 BC China was unified, but that didn't last. Within a few years, the government began to fall apart.

Rebel forces formed across the country. Each claimed to have received the mandate of heaven to replace the emperor. One of these groups attacked the Qin capital, and the new emperor surrendered. The palace was burned to the ground. Qin authority had disappeared. With no central government, the country fell into civil war.

READING CHECK **Recall** What massive building projects did Shi Huangdi order to unify China?

SUMMARY AND PREVIEW Qin emperor Shi Huangdi's policies and achievements unified China, but his harsh rule led to resentment. After his death, the dynasty fell apart. In the next section you will learn about the Han dynasty that came to power after the end of the Qin.

Section 3 Assessment

hmhsocialstudies.com ONLINE QUIZ

Reviewing Ideas, Terms, and People

1. a. **Identify** What does the title **Shi Huangdi** mean?
   b. **Explain** After unifying China, why did Shi Huangdi divide the country into military districts?
   c. **Rate** Which of the following acts do you think best showed how powerful Shi Huangdi was—burning books, forcing nobles to move, or forcing commoners to work on government projects? Explain your answer.
2. a. **Recall** Why was the **Great Wall** built?
   b. **Summarize** What actions did Shi Huangdi take to unify China and standardize things within the empire?
   c. **Evaluate** In your opinion, was Shi Huangdi a good ruler? Explain your answer.

Critical Thinking

3. **Evaluating** Using your notes and a diagram like this one, rank the effectiveness of the emperor's achievements and policies in unifying China.

Most important		Least important
1.	2.	3.

FOCUS ON SPEAKING

4. **Evaluating Contributions to History** When evaluating a person's contribution to history, it is important to consider both the person's good impact and bad impact. In what ways was Shi Huangdi great? What negative impact did he have on China? Write down your ideas.

Section 3 Assessment Answers

1. a. "first emperor"
   b. to make governing each area easier and more efficient and to collect taxes
   c. Answers will vary but should be supported by facts.
2. a. to stop invaders from the north
   b. He created a uniform system of laws; standardized written language, money, and weights and measures; built uniform roads.
   c. Answers will vary, but should be supported by facts from the text.
3. Road system—connected the capital to all parts of the empire, made travel easier; Canals—taking goods from north to south made easier and faster; Great Wall—kept out invaders
4. Possible responses might include that he unified all of China for the first time, but his policies caused resentment among many Chinese.

Answers

Reading Check *network of roads, improved water system including canals and irrigation, the Great Wall*

BIOGRAPHY

Emperor Shi Huangdi

If you were a powerful ruler, how would you protect yourself?

When did he live? c. 259–210 BC

Where did he live? Shi Huangdi built a new capital city at Xianyang, now called Xi'an (SHEE-AHN), in eastern China.

What did he do? Shi Huangdi didn't trust people. Several attempts were made on his life, and the emperor lived in fear of more attacks. He was constantly seeking new ways to protect himself and extend his life. By the time Shi Huangdi died, he didn't even trust his own advisors. Even in death, he surrounded himself with protectors: the famous terra-cotta army.

KEY EVENTS

- **246 BC** Shi Huangdi becomes emperor. Because he is still young, a high official rules in his name.
- **238 BC** He exiles the official, whom he suspects of plotting against him, and rules alone.
- **227 BC** An assassination attempt adds fuel to the emperor's paranoia.
- **221 BC** Shi Huangdi unites all of China under his rule.

Why is he important? Shi Huangdi was one of the most powerful rulers in Chinese history. The first ruler to unify all of China, he is also remembered for his building programs. He built roads and canals throughout China and expanded what would become the Great Wall.

Drawing Conclusions Why do you think Shi Huangdi feared for his life?

HISTORY VIDEO
Omens in Ancient China
hmhsocialstudies.com

This painting shows Shi Huangdi's servants burning books and attacking scholars.

177

Biography

Reading

Focus Question Have students briefly discuss the introductory question. Ask students how government leaders like the president are protected today. Ask students to name steps rulers in the past might have taken to ensure their personal safety. Ask students to keep these ideas in mind as they read the biography of Emperor Shi Huangdi.

Info to Know

The Quest for Immortality During the last 10 years of his life, Shi Huangdi traveled through China. One of the motivations for his travels was his interest in magic and a search for someone who could give him a potion that would allow him to live forever. With the exception of his travels, the emperor lived in relative isolation, and with good reason—at least three different times he was the subject of assassination attempts!

About the Illustration

This illustration of Shi Huangdi is an artist's conception based on available sources. However, historians are uncertain exactly what Shi Huangdi looked like.

Critical Thinking: Evaluating

Below Level

A Eulogy for Shi Huangdi

1. Review with students the contributions of Shi Huangdi. Then ask students what the pros and cons were of his rule over China.
2. Ask each student to imagine that he or she has been selected to give the eulogy for Shi Huangdi at his funeral. Point out that his family members, trusted friends, and advisors will be in attendance. Ask students to consider what they will say about the life of Shi Huangdi.
3. Then have each student write a one-page eulogy evaluating the life and achievements of the great Qin emperor.
4. Ask volunteers to deliver their eulogies to the class as if they were really speaking at the emperor's funeral. **LS Verbal/Linguistic**

Alternative Assessment Handbook, Rubric 37: Writing Assignments

Answers

Drawing Conclusions *He was known for strict laws and very harsh consequences for those who opposed him. Several attempts had already been made on his life.*

Preteach

Bellringer

If YOU were there . . . Use the **Daily Bellringer Transparency** to help students answer the question.

Daily Bellringer Transparency, Section 4

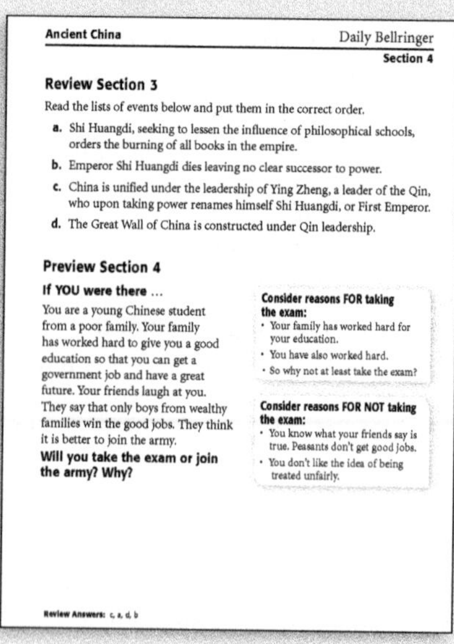

Ancient China — Daily Bellringer, Section 4

Review Section 3

Read the lists of events below and put them in the correct order.

a. Shi Huangdi, seeking to lessen the influence of philosophical schools, orders the burning of all books in the empire.

b. Emperor Shi Huangdi dies leaving no clear successor to power.

c. China is unified under the leadership of Ying Zheng, a leader of the Qin, who upon taking power renames himself Shi Huangdi, or First Emperor.

d. The Great Wall of China is constructed under Qin leadership.

Preview Section 4

If YOU were there ...

You are a young Chinese student from a poor family. Your family has worked hard to give you a good education so that you can get a government job and have a great future. Your friends laugh at you. They say that only boys from wealthy families win the good jobs. They think it is better to join the army.

Will you take the exam or join the army? Why?

Consider reasons FOR taking the exam:
- Your family has worked hard for your education.
- You have also worked hard.
- So why not at least take the exam?

Consider reasons FOR NOT taking the exam:
- You know what your friends say is true. Peasants don't get good jobs.
- You don't like the idea of being treated unfairly.

Review Answers: c, a, d, b

Academic Vocabulary

Review with students the high-use academic term in this section.

innovation a new idea, method, or device (p. 182)

Building Vocabulary

Preteach or review the following terms:

artisans a skilled craftsperson (p. 180)

influential having power to affect individuals or events (p. 179)

CRF: Vocabulary Builder Activity, Section 4

Taking Notes

Have students use the graphic organizer online to take notes on the section. This activity will prepare students for the Section Assessment, in which they will complete a graphic organizer that builds on the information using the Critical Thinking Skill: Analyzing.

SECTION 4

The Han Dynasty

What You Will Learn...

Main Ideas

1. Han dynasty government was based on the ideas of Confucius.
2. Family life was supported and strengthened in Han China.
3. The Han made many achievements in art, literature, and learning.

The Big Idea

The Han dynasty created a new form of government that valued family, art, and learning.

Key Terms

sundial, *p. 182*
seismograph, *p. 182*
acupuncture, *p. 183*

hmhsocialstudies.com
TAKING NOTES

Use the graphic organizer online to take notes on Han government, family life, and achievements.

If YOU were there...

You are a young Chinese student from a poor family. Your family has worked hard to give you a good education so that you can get a government job and have a great future. Your friends laugh at you. They say that only boys from wealthy families win the good jobs. They think it is better to join the army.

Will you take the exam or join the army? Why?

BUILDING BACKGROUND Though it was harsh, the rule of the first Qin emperor helped to unify northern China. With the building of the Great Wall, he strengthened defenses on the northern frontier. But his successor could not hold on to power. The Qin gave way to a remarkable new dynasty that would last for 400 years.

Han Dynasty Government

When the Qin dynasty collapsed in 207 BC, several different groups battled for power. After several years of fighting, an army led by Liu Bang (lee-oo bang) won control. Liu Bang became the first emperor of the Han dynasty. This Chinese dynasty lasted for more than 400 years.

The Rise of a New Dynasty

Liu Bang, a peasant, was able to become emperor in large part because of the Chinese belief in the mandate of heaven. He was the first common person to become emperor. He earned people's

Time Line

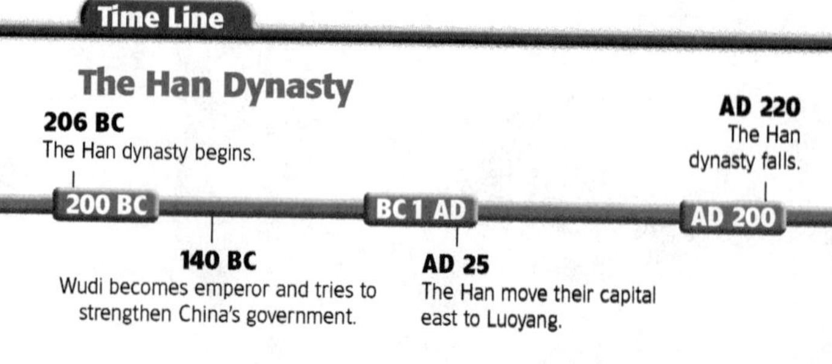
The Han Dynasty
206 BC
The Han dynasty begins.
AD 220
The Han dynasty falls.
200 BC
BC 1 AD
AD 200
140 BC
Wudi becomes emperor and tries to strengthen China's government.
AD 25
The Han move their capital east to Luoyang.

Teach the Big Idea

At Level

The Han Dynasty

1. **Teach** Ask students the questions in the Main Idea boxes to teach this section.
2. **Apply** Have students create an outline of the section. They should list all major heads and subheads that appear in this section. As students read, have them identify two or three supporting details within every head or subhead. Remind students to also include any key terms or people from the section. **LS Verbal/Linguistic**
3. **Review** As a review of the section, ask volunteers to share individual parts of their outlines and record the information for all to see. Have students add missing information and correct inaccurate information.
4. **Practice/Homework** Have each student use his or her outline to write five multiple-choice questions that cover important information from the section. **LS Verbal/Linguistic**

Alternative Assessment Handbook, Rubric 1: Acquiring Information

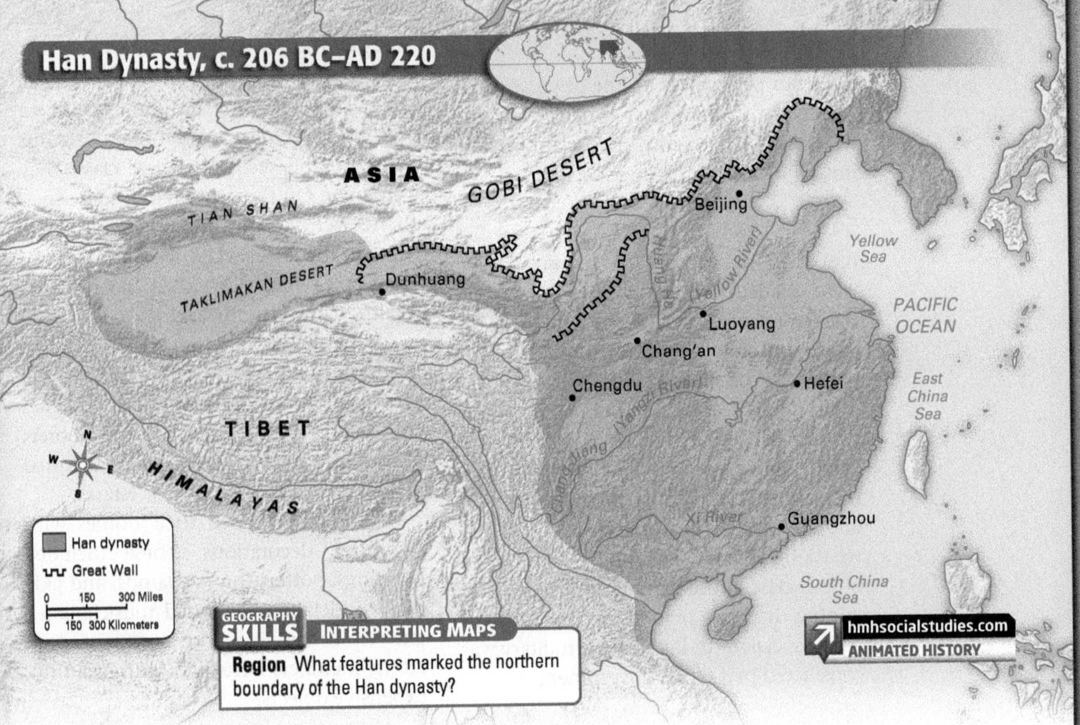

GEOGRAPHY SKILLS INTERPRETING MAPS

Region What features marked the northern boundary of the Han dynasty?

loyalty and trust. In addition, he was well liked by both soldiers and peasants, which helped him to maintain control.

Liu Bang's rule was different from the strict Legalism of the Qin. He wanted to free people from harsh government policies. He lowered taxes for farmers and made punishments less severe. He gave large blocks of land to his supporters.

In addition to setting new policies, Liu Bang changed the way government worked. He set up a government structure that built on the foundation begun by the Qin. He also relied on educated officials to help him rule.

Wudi Creates a New Government

In 140 BC Emperor Wudi (WOO-dee) took the throne. He wanted to create a stronger central government. To do that, he took land from the lords, raised taxes, and placed the supply of grain under the control of the government.

Under Wudi, Confucianism became China's official government philosophy. Government officials were expected to practice Confucianism. Wudi even began a university to teach Confucian ideas.

If a person passed an exam on Confucian teachings, he could get a good position in the government. However, not just anyone could take the test. The exams were only open to people who had been recommended for government service already. As a result, wealthy or influential families continued to control the government.

READING CHECK **Analyzing** How was the Han government based on the ideas of Confucius?

Direct Teach

Main Idea

1 Han Dynasty Government

Han dynasty government was based on the ideas of Confucius.

Summarize What changes did Liu Bang bring to China? *He freed people from harsh government policies, lowered taxes, made punishments less severe, gave blocks of land to his supporters, and used educated officials to help him rule.*

Analyze How did Wudi strengthen China's government? *He took lands from lords, raised taxes, placed the supply of grain under government control, made people take exams and get recommendations for government service.*

Elaborate Would you rather have lived under the rule of Liu Bang or Wudi? Why? *Answers will vary, but students should show an understanding of the policies of the emperor selected.*

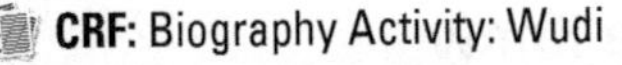
CRF: Biography Activity: Wudi

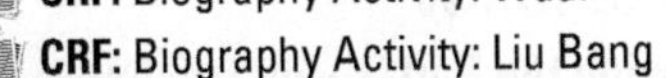
CRF: Biography Activity: Liu Bang

Map Transparency: Han Dynasty

Critical Thinking: Evaluating

At Level

Writing Resumés

1. Review with students the main beliefs of Confucianism from Section 2. Then discuss what qualities government officials during the Han dynasty possessed.
2. Tell students that they will be writing a resumé for an imaginary person seeking a job in the Han government. Have students provide details in the resumés regarding the person's education, family connections, and other qualifications.
3. Remind students to refer to the portion of the section that discusses the necessary qualification for obtaining a position in the Han government.
4. When students have finished, have them exchange resumés with another student. Then ask students to discuss whether or not they believe that resumé would earn a job in the Han government.

LS Verbal/Linguistic, Interpersonal

Alternative Assessment Handbook, Rubric 31: Resumés

Answers

Interpreting Maps *Tian Shan and the Gobi Desert*

Reading Check *Confucianism became government philosophy; government officials had to pass tests on Confucian teachings.*

Direct Teach

Main Idea

❷ Family Life

Family life was supported and strengthened in Han China.

Describe What were the social classes in Han China? *upper—emperor, royal court, scholars; second class—peasants; third class—artisans; lowest—merchants*

Analyze Why were wealthy merchants in the lowest class? *did not produce anything of their own, only bought and sold goods made by others*

Elaborate How were Han social classes different than most social divisions? *They were not based on wealth or power.*

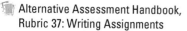

Activity A Day in the Life of . . . Have students write a description of a typical day in the life of a peasant in Han China.

Alternative Assessment Handbook, Rubric 37: Writing Assignments

Info to Know

Dressing the Part Even the clothes the ancient Chinese wore had social distinction. People in the upper classes, such as members of the emperor's court and high-ranking government officials, wore fine robes made of silk, a material that was both luxurious and expensive. The lower classes wore garments made of rough fabrics. Wearing silk was not just a matter of being able to afford the material; the supply of fabrics was regulated by the government. In later dynasties, some merchants who dealt in silk were even punished for wearing silk clothing.

Family Life

The Han period was a time of great social change in China. Class structure became more rigid. The family once again became important within Chinese society.

Social Classes

Based on the Confucian system, people were divided into four classes. The upper class was made up of the emperor, his court, and scholars who held government positions. The second class, the largest, was made up of the peasants. Next were artisans who produced items for daily life and some luxury goods. Merchants occupied the lowest class because they did not produce anything. They only bought and sold what others made. The military was not an official class in the Confucian system. Still, joining the army offered men a chance to rise in social status because the military was considered part of the government.

This Han artifact is an oil lamp held by a servant.

Lives of Rich and Poor

The classes only divided people into social rank. They did not indicate wealth or power. For instance, even though peasants made up the second highest class, they were poor. On the other hand, some merchants were wealthy and powerful despite being in the lowest class.

People's lifestyles varied according to wealth. The emperor and his court lived in a large palace. Less important officials lived in multilevel houses built around courtyards. Many of these wealthy families owned large estates and employed laborers to work the land. Some families even hired private armies to defend their estates.

The wealthy filled their homes with expensive decorations. These included paintings, pottery, bronze lamps, and jade figures. Rich families hired musicians for entertainment. Even the tombs of dead family members were filled with beautiful, expensive objects.

Most people in the Han dynasty, however, didn't live like the wealthy. Nearly 60 million people lived in China during the Han dynasty, and about 90 percent of them were peasants who lived in the countryside. Peasants put in long, tiring days working the land. Whether it was in the millet fields of the north or in the rice paddies of the south, the work was hard. In the winter, peasants were also forced to work on building projects for the government. Heavy taxes and bad weather forced many farmers to sell their land and work for rich landowners. By the last years of the Han dynasty, only a few farmers were independent.

Chinese peasants lived simple lives. They wore plain clothing made of fiber from a native plant. The main foods they ate were cooked grains like barley. Most peasants lived in small villages. Their small, wood-framed houses had walls made of mud or stamped earth.

Differentiating Instruction

Struggling Readers **Below Level**

1. Discuss with students the social structure under the Han dynasty. Ask students to identify the various social classes and what people were represented in each class.
2. Have students create a diagram or illustration that shows the social order of Han China. Ask students to include information that clearly shows the occupations of the people in each social class.
3. Then have students compare this social order to the social divisions that existed under the Zhou dynasty. Have students examine the differences between the two social orders. How did society change in China from the Zhou dynasty to the Han dynasty? Have each student write a short paragraph in which they explain the similarities and differences between the two.
4. Ask volunteers to share their illustrations and explanations with the class.

LS Visual/Spatial, Verbal/Linguistic

Alternative Assessment Handbook, Rubrics 3: Artwork; and 9: Comparing and Contrasting

The Importance of Family
Honoring one's family was an important duty in Han China. In this painting, people give thanks before their family shrine. Only the men participate. The women watch from inside the house.

How are these people giving thanks?

The Revival of the Family

Since Confucianism was the official government philosophy during Wudi's reign, Confucian teachings about the family were also honored. Children were taught from birth to respect their elders. Disobeying one's parents was a crime. Even emperors had a duty to respect their parents.

Confucius had taught that the father was the head of the family. Within the family, the father had absolute power. The Han taught that it was a woman's duty to obey her husband, and children had to obey their father.

Han officials believed that if the family was strong and people obeyed the father, then people would obey the emperor, too. Since the Han stressed strong family ties and respect for elders, some men even gained government jobs based on the respect they showed their parents.

Children were encouraged to serve their parents. They were also expected to honor dead parents with ceremonies and offerings. All family members were expected to care for family burial sites.

Chinese parents valued boys more highly than girls. This was because sons carried on the family line and took care of their parents when they were old. On the other hand, daughters became part of their husband's family. According to a Chinese proverb, "Raising daughters is like raising children for another family." Some women, however, still gained power. They could actually influence their sons' families. An older widow could even become the head of the family.

READING CHECK **Identifying Cause and Effect** Why did the family take on such importance during the Han dynasty?

Direct Teach

Main Idea

❷ Family Life

Family life was supported and strengthened in Han China.

Recall What were Confucius's ideas about family? *The father was the head of the family and had absolute power; wives and children had to obey their husbands and fathers.*

Explain Why were sons more highly valued that daughters? *Sons carried on the family line and took care of parents as they got older, while daughters went to live with their husbands' families.*

Activity **Flowcharts** Have students create a flowchart that shows the relationship and position of family members in Han China.

Info to Know

Respect for Family and Elders Teachings about respect for family and parents were taken very seriously in Han China. Confucius himself believed a dutiful child should not only respect his or her father while he was alive, but continue to do so after his death. Other Chinese philosophers even went so far as to describe evil-doers as people who, among other things, lied, disobeyed, or provoked their parents or did not take the spirits of their ancestors seriously.

Collaborative Learning

At Level

Documentary: Family Life in Han China

1. Review with students the Chinese attitudes toward family life and respect for parents. Ask students to discuss the behavior expected of fathers, sons, and women within a Chinese family in Han China. Ask students to identify behavior that would be acceptable and unacceptable.
2. Organize the class into small groups. Have each group prepare a script for a documentary film that focuses on family life in Han China. Remind students to present information about family duties and the roles of fathers, wives, and children. Students may wish to use the library, Internet, or other resources to find additional information on the topic.
3. Have each group videotape their documentary or perform it live for the class to see.
LS Visual/Spatial, Verbal/Linguistic, Interpersonal

Alternative Assessment Handbook, Rubrics 14: Group Activity; and 33: Skits and Reader's Theater

Answers

Illustration Caption *by bowing before their family shrine*

Reading Check *Han leaders promoted Confucianism, which emphasized strong family ties.*

Direct Teach

Main Idea

❸ Han Achievements

The Han made many achievements in art, literature, and learning.

Identify What were some of the cultural and scientific achievements of the Han? *artwork, poetry, history, paper, sundial, acupuncture, and the seismograph*

Contrast How did the *fu* style of poetry differ from the *shi* style? *Fu poetry combined prose and poetry in a long work of literature, while* shi *used short lines of verse that could be sung.*

Evaluate What do you think was the most important invention of the Han dynasty? Why? *possible answers—acupuncture because it improved medicine and is still used today; paper because it is part of our everyday lives.*

Connect to Science

Seismographs The Chinese seismograph pictured above was a very simple device. It showed when an earthquake occurred and the direction of the earthquake. Modern-day seismographs still serve the same function, but they also record the strength and duration of an earthquake. Scientists use several seismographs in different locations to pinpoint the epicenter of an earthquake. The scale used to measure the strength of an earthquake is known as the Richter scale and was developed by seismologists in 1935.

hmhsocialstudies.com

Online Resources
Activity: Chinese Art

Han Achievements

During the Han dynasty, the Chinese made many advances in art and learning. Some of these advances are shown here.

Science
This is a model of an ancient Chinese seismograph. When an earthquake struck, a lever inside caused a ball to drop from a dragon's mouth into a toad's mouth, indicating the direction from which the earthquake had come.

Han Achievements

Han rule was a time of great accomplishments. Art and literature thrived, and inventors developed many useful devices.

Art and Literature

The Chinese of the Han period produced many works of art. They became experts at figure painting—a style of painting that includes portraits of people. Portraits often showed religious figures and Confucian scholars. Han artists also painted realistic scenes from everyday life. Their creations covered the walls of palaces and tombs.

ACADEMIC VOCABULARY
innovation a new idea, method, or device

In literature, Han China is known for its poetry. Poets developed new styles of verse, including the *fu* style which was the most popular. *Fu* poets combined prose and poetry to create long works of literature. Another style, called *shi,* featured short lines of verse that could be sung. Han rulers hired poets known for the beauty of their verse.

Han writers also produced important works of history. One historian by the name of Sima Qian wrote a complete history of all the dynasties through the early Han. His format and style became the model for later historical writings.

Inventions and Advances

The Han Chinese invented one item that we use every day—paper. They made it by grinding plant fibers, such as mulberry bark and hemp, into a paste. Then they let it dry in sheets. Chinese scholars produced "books" by pasting several pieces of paper together into a long sheet. Then they rolled the sheet into a scroll.

The Han also made other innovations in science. These included the sundial and the seismograph. A **sundial** uses the position of shadows cast by the sun to tell the time of day. The sundial was an early type of clock. A **seismograph** is a device that measures the strength of an earthquake. Han emperors were very interested

Cross-Discipline Activity: Literature

Above Level

Fu and *Shi* Poems

Research Required

1. Review with the class the achievements in literature of the Han dynasty.
2. Organize the class into pairs. Have each pair use the library, Internet, or other sources to research *fu* and *shi* poems. Have each pair select one poem of either type. Tell students that they will create a scroll on which they will copy and illustrate their poems.
3. Check to make sure that students understand the meaning of the poems they selected. Remind students that Han paintings often depicted realistic scenes from everyday life.
4. Have volunteers from each group explain the Chinese poem they selected and then read their poems aloud.
5. Expand the activity by having students write their own *fu* or *shi* poems and illustrate them as well. **LS Visual/Spatial, Verbal/Linguistic**

Alternative Assessment Handbook, Rubrics 3: Artwork; and 26: Poems and Songs

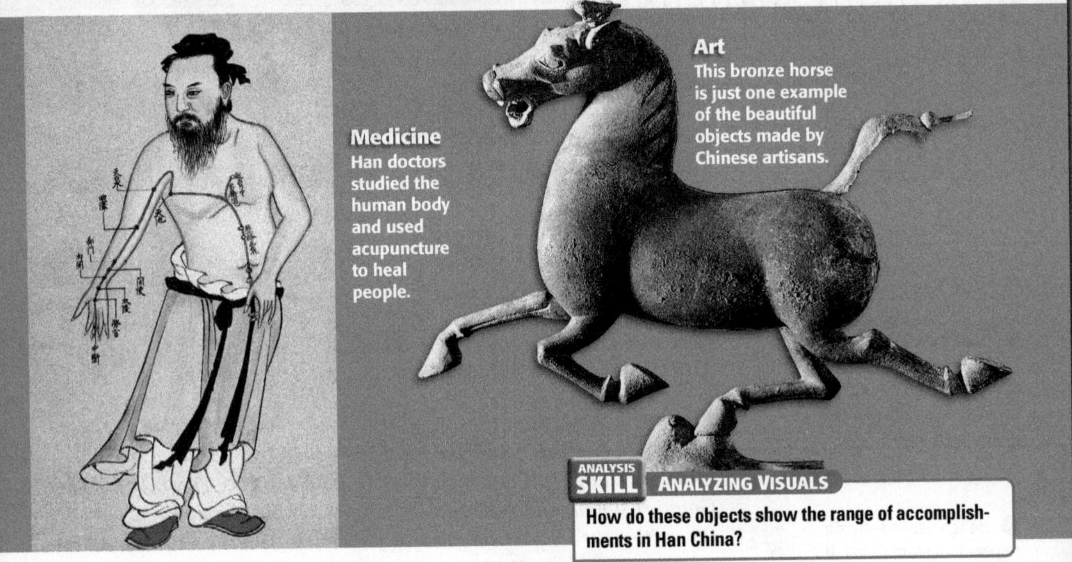

Medicine Han doctors studied the human body and used acupuncture to heal people.

Art This bronze horse is just one example of the beautiful objects made by Chinese artisans.

ANALYSIS SKILL ANALYZING VISUALS

How do these objects show the range of accomplishments in Han China?

in knowing about the movements of the earth. They believed that earthquakes were signs of future evil events.

Another Han innovation, acupuncture (AK-yoo-punk-cher), improved medicine. **Acupuncture** is the practice of inserting fine needles through the skin at specific points to cure disease or relieve pain. Many Han inventions in science and medicine are still used today.

READING CHECK **Categorizing** What advances did the Chinese make during the Han period?

SUMMARY AND PREVIEW Han rulers moved away from Legalism and based their government on Confucianism. This strengthened family bonds in Han China. In addition, art and learning thrived under Han rule. In the next section you will learn about China's contact beyond its borders.

Section 4 Assessment

hmhsocialstudies.com ONLINE QUIZ

Reviewing Ideas, Terms, and People

1. a. **Identify** Whose teachings were the foundation for government during the Han dynasty?
   b. **Summarize** How did Emperor Wudi create a strong central government?
   c. **Evaluate** Do you think that an exam system is the best way to make sure that people are fairly chosen for government jobs? Why or why not?
2. a. **Describe** What was the son's role in the family?
   b. **Contrast** How did living conditions for the wealthy differ from those of the peasants during the Han dynasty?
3. **Identify** What device did the Chinese invent to measure the strength of earthquakes?

Critical Thinking

4. **Analyzing** Use your notes to complete this diagram about how Confucianism influenced Han government and family.

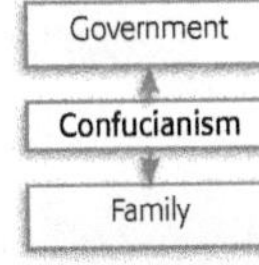

FOCUS ON SPEAKING

5. **Analyzing Impact on History** Sometimes a ruler has the biggest impact on history. Other times, ideas that develop within a society have a greater impact. Which had a greater impact on Han China? Why?

Direct Teach

Connect to Art

The Flying Horse The bronze horse shown was found in a Han dynasty tomb. It is poised with one hoof resting on a swallow, a type of bird. Although the horse is actually trotting, because three of its hooves are off the ground it appears to fly.

The beauty and power of horses made them popular subjects in Chinese art. This statue may portray a certain highly valued breed.

Review & Assess

Close

Point out that although the seismograph was mainly a scientific instrument, it is also a work of art.

Review

Online Quiz, Section 4

Assess

SE Section 4 Assessment
PASS: Section 4 Quiz
Alternative Assessment Handbook

Reteach/Classroom Intervention

Guided Reading Workbook, Section 4
Interactive Skills Tutor CD-ROM

Section 4 Assessment Answers

1. **a.** Confucius
   b. took lands from lords, raised taxes, controlled grain supply
   c. Answers will vary but should display familiarity with the exam system.
2. **a.** to obey his parents, carry on the family line, and take care of his parents
   b. wealthy—in large, richly furnished homes, had servants, wore luxurious clothing; peasants—simple houses, ate rice and grains, wore plain clothing, and worked hard
3. seismograph
4. Government—Officials practiced Confuciansim and had to pass an exam on Confucian teachings; some men gained government jobs based on respect for parents; Family—Children were taught to respect their parents and obey their father.
5. Answers will vary but should be supported by text-based facts.

Answers

Analyzing Visuals *They show advancements in art, science, and medicine.*

Reading Check *They invented paper, the seismograph, the sundial, and acupuncture.*

Literature in History

The Shiji

As You Read Have students keep a list of Bu Shi's qualities as they read the passage. After the students have read the passage, ask them to explain what type of person Bu Shi was. Why might a historian be interested in him?

Meet the Writer

Sima Qian Sima Qian was the son of Ssu-ma T'an, the grand historian of the Han court from 140–110 BC. The grand historian was responsible for keeping a daily record of state events and court ceremonies as well as astronomical observations. In his youth, Sima Qian traveled a great deal and even served in the entourage of the emperor. In 110 BC his father died, and Sima Qian was appointed to his father's office of grand historian. He spent many years working on *The Shiji*, fulfilling his father's dream of writing a history of China.

Info to Know

Offending the Emperor Before Sima Qian completed the *Shiji*, he deeply offended Emperor Wudi by defending a general who had fallen out of favor with the emperor. Sima Qian was arraigned for "defaming the Emperor," a crime punishable by death. Sima Qian's life was spared, however, either because the emperor thought he was too valuable or Sima Qian asked that he be allowed to finish his history of China. Later, the emperor lifted his punishment, and Sima Qian again rose in the ranks of the Han dynasty.

from The Shiji

by Sima Qian

Translated by Burton Watson

About the Reading *The* Shiji, *also called the* Records of the Grand Historian, *is a history that describes more than two thousand years of Chinese culture. The author, Sima Qian (soo-MAH chee-EN), held the title Grand Historian under the Han emperor Wudi. He spent 18 years of his life writing the* Shiji. *His hard work paid off, and his history was well received. In fact, the* Shiji *was so respected that it served as the model for every later official history of China. This passage describes a man named Bu Shi, who attracted the emperor's attention through his generosity and good deeds. Eventually, the emperor invited him to live in the imperial palace.*

AS YOU READ **Ask yourself why Sima Qian included Bu Shi in his history.**

Bu Shi was a native of Henan, where his family made a living by farming and animal raising. ❶ When his parents died, Bu Shi left home, handing over the house, the lands, and all the family wealth to his younger brother, who by this time was full grown. For his own share, he took only a hundred or so of the sheep they had been raising, which he led off into the mountains to pasture. In the course of ten years or so, Bu Shi's sheep had increased to over a thousand and he had bought his own house and fields. His younger brother in the meantime had failed completely in the management of the farm, but Bu Shi promptly handed over to him a share of his own wealth. This happened several times. Just at that time the Han was sending its generals at frequent intervals to attack the Xiongnu. ❷ Bu Shi journeyed to the capital and submitted a letter to the throne, offering to turn over half of his wealth to the district officials to help in the defense of the border. The emperor dispatched an envoy to ask if Bu Shi wanted a post in the government. ❸

"From the time I was a child," Bu Shi replied, "I have been an animal raiser. I have had no experience in government and would certainly not want such a position" . . .

GUIDED READING

WORD HELP

intervals periods of time
dispatched sent
envoy representative

❶ Henan (HUH-NAHN) is a region of eastern China. It is a productive agricultural region.

❷ The Xiongnu were a tribe of nomads. They lived in the north and often raided towns near China's border.

❸ ***Why do you think the emperor invites Bu Shi to work for the government?***

Differentiating Instruction

English-Language Learners **Below Level**

1. Review the passage with the class. Then organize students into small groups. Assign each group one paragraph of the story.
2. Have each group draw a cartoon or comic strip that illustrates their portion of the story, writing dialogue and identifying characters just as in an ordinary comic strip. Encourage students to distinguish between relevant and irrelevant information.
3. Have groups post their cartoons or comic strips around the classroom in order for all to see. **LS Visual/Spatial, Interpersonal**

Alternative Assessment Handbook, Rubric 27: Political Cartoons

Universal Access Resources

See p. 155c of the Chapter Planner for additional resources for differentiating instruction for universal access.

Answers

Guided Reading 3. *He showed his loyalty to the government by offering to give them half of his wealth.*

"If that is the case," said the envoy, "then what is your objective in making this offer?"

Bu Shi replied, "The Son of Heaven has sent out to punish the Xiongnu. 4 In my humble opinion, every worthy man should be willing to fight to the death to defend the borders, and every person with wealth ought to contribute to the expense . . ."

The emperor discussed the matter with the chancellor, but the latter said, "The proposal is simply not in accord with human nature! 5 Such eccentric people are of no use in guiding the populace, but only throw the laws into confusion. I beg Your Majesty not to accept his offer!"

For this reason the emperor put off answering Bu Shi for a long time, and finally after several years had passed, turned down the offer, whereupon Bu Shi went back to his fields and pastures . . .

The following year a number of poor people were transferred to other regions . . . At this point Bu Shi took two hundred thousand cash of his own and turned the sum over to the governor of Henan to assist the people who were emigrating to other regions . . . At this time the rich families were all scrambling to hide their wealth; only Bu Shi, unlike the others, had offered to contribute to the expenses of the government. 6 The emperor decided that Bu Shi was really a man of exceptional worth after all . . . Because of his simple, unspoiled ways and his deep loyalty, the emperor finally appointed him grand tutor to his son Liu Hong, the king of Qi.

In this painting from the 1600s, government officials deliver a letter.

GUIDED READING

WORD HELP

objective goal
chancellor high official
accord agreement
eccentric someone who acts strangely
populace people
tutor private teacher

4 The Chinese people believed that their emperor was the "Son of Heaven." They thought he received his power from heavenly ancestors.

5 The "latter" means the one mentioned last. In this case, the latter is the chancellor.

6 ***What is Bu Shi's attitude toward his wealth? How is it different from the attitude of the rich families?***

CONNECTING LITERATURE TO HISTORY

1. **Drawing Conclusions** Like many Chinese historians, Sima Qian wanted to use history to teach lessons. What lessons could the story of Bu Shi be used to teach?

2. **Analyzing** The Emperor Wudi based his government on the teachings of Confucius. What elements of Confucianism can you see in this story?

Literature in History

Teaching Tip

Ask students to point out the elements of Confucianism that are represented in the story of Bu Shi. Remind students that Confucianism is an ethical system that teaches moral values, respect for authority, and treating others as you would want to be treated.

Other People, Other Places

Writing History Sima Qian, the author of the *Shiji*, was the most influential historian of ancient China. His scholarly, authoritative approach to writing about the past served as an example for the historians who followed. In Europe, a similar role was played by the Greek historian Herodotus, who lived and wrote in the 400s BC. His major work, *The Histories,* was so influential that, centuries later, a Roman philosopher named Herodotus the "father of history."

Critical Thinking: Summarizing

At Level

The Story of Bu Shi

1. Read the passage from the *Shiji* aloud with the class, asking for volunteers to read different sections.
2. Then ask students to write a summary of the story of Bu Shi in their own words. Then have students write five multiple-choice questions about the story.
3. Have students work with a partner to quiz each other over the questions each wrote. Students may use their summaries if they cannot answer a question. Award students that answer each question correctly one point. At the end of the game, ask the pair with the most points to read its summary to the class.

LS Verbal/Linguistic

Alternative Assessment Handbook, Rubric 37: Writing Assignments

Answers

Guided Reading 6. *He believes wealth is to be shared and used his wealth to help the needy and the empire; the rich families wanted to keep their wealth to themselves.*

Connecting Literature to History 1. *possible answers—generosity, goodness towards others, treat others as you would like to be treated;* **2.** *Bu Shi feels it is his duty to help his government and others; the emperor rewards Bu Shi's loyalty and ethics.*

Preteach

Bellringer

If YOU were there . . . Use the **Daily Bellringer Transparency** to help students answer the question.

Daily Bellringer Transparency, Section 5

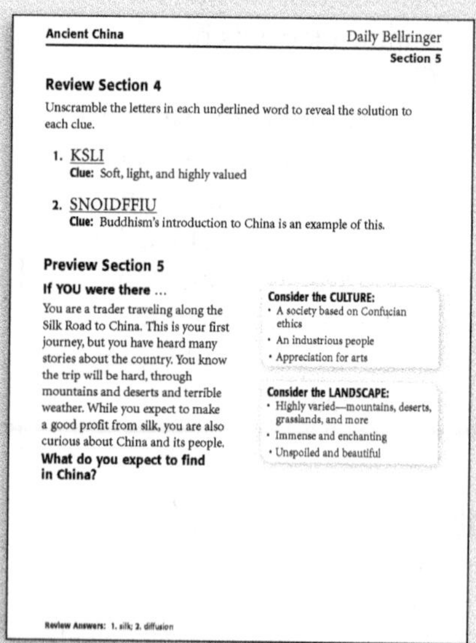

Ancient China Daily Bellringer

Section 5

Review Section 4

Unscramble the letters in each underlined word to reveal the solution to each clue.

1. KSLI
   Clue: Soft, light, and highly valued
2. SNOIDFFIU
   Clue: Buddhism's introduction to China is an example of this.

Preview Section 5

If YOU were there ...

You are a trader traveling along the Silk Road to China. This is your first journey, but you have heard many stories about the country. You know the trip will be hard, through mountains and deserts and terrible weather. While you expect to make a good profit from silk, you are also curious about China and its people.

What do you expect to find in China?

Consider the CULTURE:
- A society based on Confucian ethics
- An industrious people
- Appreciation for arts

Consider the LANDSCAPE:
- Highly varied—mountains, deserts, grasslands, and more
- Immense and enchanting
- Unspoiled and beautiful

Review Answers: 1. silk; 2. diffusion

Academic Vocabulary

Review with students the high-use academic term in this section.

procedure the way a task is accomplished (p. 187)

CRF: Vocabulary Builder Activity, Section 5

Taking Notes

Have students use the graphic organizer online to take notes on the section. This activity will prepare students for the Section Assessment, in which they will complete a graphic organizer that builds on the information using the Critical Thinking Skill: Categorizing.

SECTION 5

Han Contacts with Other Cultures

What You Will Learn...

Main Ideas

1. Farming and manufacturing grew during the Han dynasty.
2. Trade routes linked China with the Middle East and Rome.
3. Buddhism came to China from India and gained many fol lowers.

The Big Idea

Trade routes led to the exchange of new products and ideas among China, Rome, and other peoples.

Key Terms

silk, *p. 187*
Silk Road, *p. 187*
diffusion, *p. 189*

Use the graphic organizer online to take notes on Chinese products and trade routes and on the arrival of Buddhism in China.

If YOU were there...

You are a trader traveling along the Silk Road to China. This is your first journey, but you have heard many stories about the country. You know the trip will be hard, through mountains and deserts and terrible weather. While you expect to make a good profit from silk, you are also curious about China and its people.

What do you expect to find in China?

BUILDING BACKGROUND During the Han dynasty Chinese society returned its focus to Confucian ideas, and new inventions were developed. In addition, increased trade allowed other countries to learn about the rich culture of China.

Farming and Manufacturing

Many advances in manufacturing took place during the Han dynasty. As a result, productivity increased and the empire prospered. These changes paved the way for China to make contact with people of other cultures.

Silk Production

Teach the Big Idea

At Level

Han Contacts with Other Cultures

1. **Teach** Ask students the questions in the Main Idea boxes to teach this section.
2. **Apply** Have students create a chart with three columns labeled *Farming and Manufacturing, Trade Routes,* and *Buddhism Comes to China*. Have students fill in the chart with details about each topic. **LS Verbal/Linguistic**
3. **Review** As you review each of the Main Ideas, ask students to explain how each of these ideas relates to the others.
4. **Practice/Homework** Have each student create an advertisement for products a Chinese trader might try to sell to another country, including how the products will be sent to the buyer and how long it will take for the products to reach the buyer. **LS Visual/Spatial, Verbal/Linguistic**

Alternative Assessment Handbook, Rubrics 2: Advertisements; and 13: Graphic Organizers

By the Han period, the Chinese had become master ironworkers. They manufactured iron swords and armor that made the army more powerful.

Farmers also gained from advances in iron. The iron plow and the wheelbarrow, a single-wheeled cart, increased farm output. With a wheelbarrow a farmer could haul more than 300 pounds all by himself. With an iron plow, he could till more land and raise more food.

Another item that increased in production during the Han dynasty was **silk**, a soft, light, highly valued fabric. For centuries, Chinese women had known the complicated methods needed to raise silkworms, unwind the silk threads of their cocoons, and then prepare the threads for dyeing and weaving. The Chinese were determined to keep their procedure for making silk a secret. Revealing these secrets was punishable by death.

During the Han period, weavers used foot-powered looms to weave silk threads into beautiful fabric. Garments made from this silk were very expensive.

READING CHECK **Finding Main Ideas** How did advances in technology affect farming and silk production?

Trade Routes

Chinese goods, especially silk and fine pottery, were highly valued by people in other lands. During the Han period, the value of these goods to people outside China helped increase trade.

THE IMPACT TODAY

China still produces about 50 percent of the world's silk.

Expansion of Trade

Trade increased partly because Han armies conquered lands deep in Central Asia. Leaders there told the Han generals that people who lived still farther west wanted silk. At the same time, Emperor Wudi wanted strong, sturdy Central Asian horses for his army. China's leaders saw that they could make a profit by bringing silk to Central Asia and trading the cloth for the horses. The Central Asian peoples would then take the silk west and trade it for other products they wanted.

ACADEMIC VOCABULARY

procedure the way a task is accomplished

The Silk Road

Traders used a series of overland routes to take Chinese goods to distant buyers. The most famous trade route was known as the **Silk Road**. This 4,000-mile-long network of routes stretched westward from China across Asia's deserts and mountain ranges, through the Middle East, until it reached the Mediterranean Sea.

The technique for making silk was a well-kept secret in ancient China, as silk was a valuable trade good in distant lands. Workers made silk from the cocoons of silkworms, just as they do today.

Direct Teach

Main Idea

1 Farming and Manufacturing

Farming and manufacturing grew during the Han dynasty.

Recall What were two inventions that helped farmers become more productive during the Han dynasty? *iron plow and wheelbarrow*

Analyze How did the wheelbarrow aid farmers? *It allowed a single person to carry more than 300 pounds at a time.*

Elaborate Why do you think the Chinese were so determined to keep how they produced silk a secret? *Other countries would have been able to make the silk themselves if they knew the secret, thereby making the Chinese silk trade less valuable.*

CRF: Economic and History Activity: The Chinese Economy

Teaching Tip

Farming Techniques

The iron plow and the wheelbarrow may seem like very ordinary objects, but they are significant advances. Make sure all students understand how both of them work. Guide students in a discussion of basic farming techniques. Have students compare farming with and without a wheelbarrow or iron plow.

Differentiating Instruction

Advanced/Gifted and Talented

Above Level Research Required

1. Review with the class the advances in farming and manufacturing made in Han China. Ask students to explain how each advance helped the Chinese economy.
2. Have each student select one of the advances mentioned in the section—the iron plow, the wheelbarrow, or silk production. Have students conduct research on the item they selected. Students should identify how the advance aided the Chinese, how it worked, and how that item is used today, if at all.
3. Have each student write a short paper about the past and current uses of the advance they selected and read their papers to the class.

Alternative Assessment Handbook, Rubrics 30: Research; and 42: Writing to Inform

Answers

Reading Check *Technology yielded the wheelbarrow and the iron plow, which greatly increased productivity. Technology also yielded foot-powered looms, which increased silk production.*

Direct Teach

Main Idea

❷ Trade Routes

Trade routes linked China with the Middle East and Rome.

Recall For what items did the Chinese trade? *horses, gold, silver, and precious stones*

Summarize What were some of the difficulties traders on the Silk Road faced? *bandits trying to steal cargo and water; harsh weather such as blizzards, heat, and sandstorms*

Map Transparency: The Silk Road

Main Idea

❸ Buddhism Comes to China

Buddhism came to China from India and gained many followers.

Recall From what country did Buddhism come to China? *India*

Draw Conclusions How did the political environment in China lead to the acceptance of Buddhism? *As the government became less stable, hunger and violence became widespread. The Chinese embraced Buddhism because if offered relief from suffering.*

Did you know . . .

The Romans, who valued silk from China, called China *Serica*, which means "Land of Silk."

Chinese traders did not travel the entire Silk Road. Upon reaching Central Asia, they sold their goods to local traders who would take them the rest of the way.

Traveling the Silk Road was difficult. Hundreds of men and camels loaded down with valuable goods, including silks and jade, formed groups. They traveled the Silk Road together for protection. Armed guards were hired to protect traders from bandits who stole cargo and water, a precious necessity. Weather presented other dangers. Traders faced icy blizzards, desert heat, and blinding sandstorms.

Named after the most famous item transported along it, the Silk Road was worth its many risks. Silk was so popular in Rome, for example, that China grew wealthy from that trade relationship alone. Traders returned from Rome with silver, gold, precious stones, and horses.

READING CHECK **Summarizing** Why did Chinese trade expand under Han rule?

Buddhism Comes to China

When the Chinese people came into contact with other civilizations, they exchanged ideas along with trade goods. Among these ideas was a new religion. In the first century AD Buddhism spread from India to China along the Silk Road and other trade routes.

Arrival of a New Religion

Over time, the Han government became less stable. People ignored laws, and violence was common. As rebellions flared up, millions of peasants went hungry. Life became violent and uncertain. Many Chinese looked to Daoism or Confucianism to find out why they had to suffer so much, but they didn't find helpful answers.

Buddhism seemed to provide more hope than the traditional Chinese beliefs did. It offered rebirth and relief from suffering. This promise was a major reason the Chinese people embraced Buddhism.

hmhsocialstudies.com INTERACTIVE MAP

The Silk Road

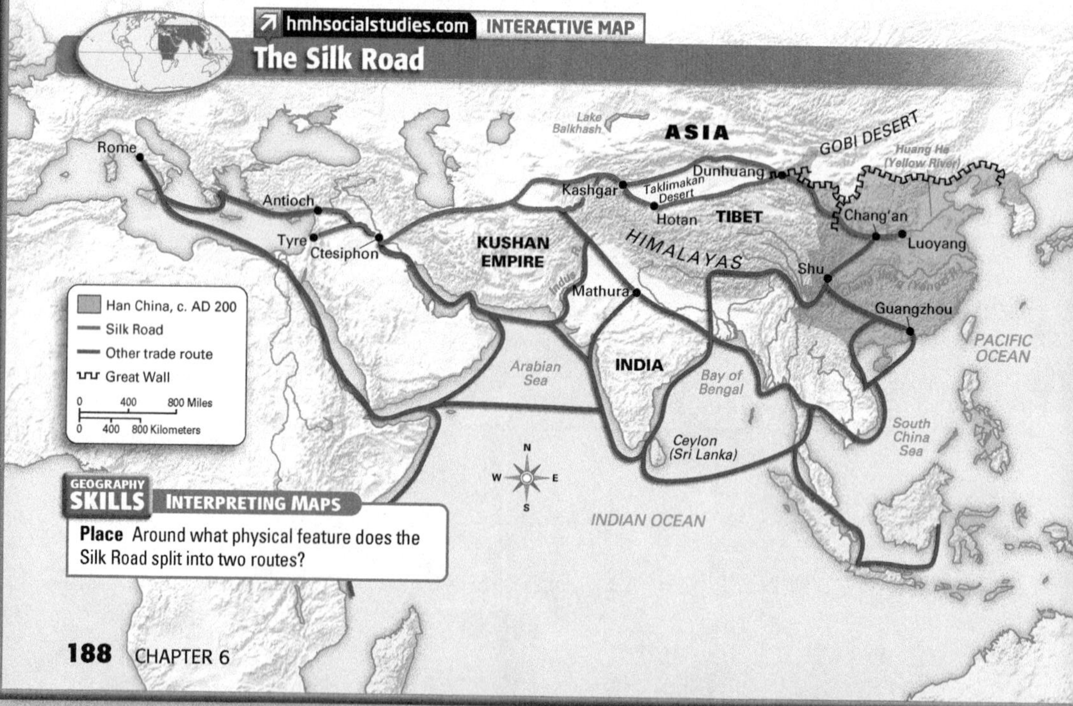

GEOGRAPHY SKILLS INTERPRETING MAPS

Place Around what physical feature does the Silk Road split into two routes?

Critical Thinking: Analyzing

Below Level

Re-creating the Silk Road

1. Review with students the map of the Silk Road. Ask students to identify the various regions that benefited from trade along the Silk Road.
2. Have students list the geographical features along the Silk Road.
3. Next, have each student write a letter to a new caravan guide who is going to travel the Silk Road for the first time. In their letters, students should explain the difficulties of the route, what problems lie ahead, where water can be found, and the length of the journey from Chang'an to Tyre. LS **Visual/Spatial, Verbal/Linguistic**

Alternative Assessment Handbook, Rubric 40: Writing to Describe

Answers

Interpreting Maps *the Taklimakan Desert*

Reading Check *Han conquests put the Chinese in contact with more distant peoples who wanted to trade for Chinese goods.*

Impact on China

At first, Indian Buddhists had trouble explaining their religion to the Chinese. Then they used ideas found in Daoism to help describe Buddhist beliefs. Many people grew curious about Buddhism.

Before long, Buddhism caught on in China with both the poor and the upper classes. By AD 200, Buddhist altars stood in the emperor's palace.

Buddhism's introduction to China is an example of **diffusion**, the spread of ideas from one culture to another. Elements of Chinese culture changed in response to the new faith. For example, scholars translated Buddhist texts into Chinese. Many Chinese became Buddhist monks and nuns. Artists carved towering statues of Buddha into mountain walls.

READING CHECK **Finding Main Ideas** How did Chinese people learn of Buddhism?

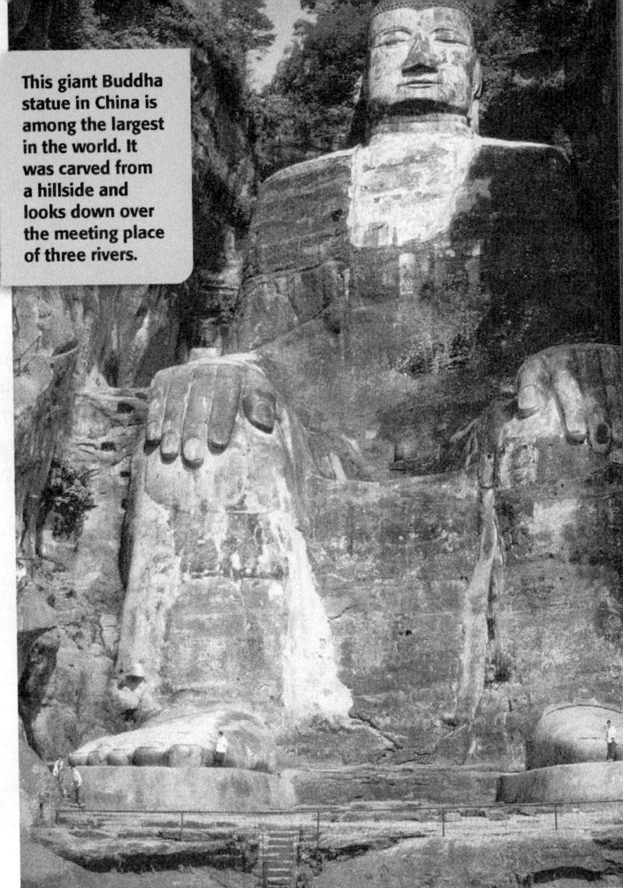

This giant Buddha statue in China is among the largest in the world. It was carved from a hillside and looks down over the meeting place of three rivers.

SUMMARY AND PREVIEW Under the Han, trade brought new goods and ideas, including Buddhism, to China. In the next chapter you'll read about the religion of another people—the Jews.

Section 5 Assessment

hmhsocialstudies.com ONLINE QUIZ

Reviewing Ideas, Terms, and People

1. a. **Describe** How did wheelbarrows help farmers?
   b. **Summarize** How was **silk** made in ancient China?
   c. **Elaborate** Why did the Chinese keep silk-making methods a secret?
2. a. **Identify** Where did the **Silk Road** begin and end?
   b. **Elaborate** What information would you use to support the argument that the silk trade must have been very valuable?
3. a. **Identify** What is **diffusion**?
   b. **Make Generalizations** What Buddhist beliefs appealed to millions of Chinese peasants?

Critical Thinking

4. **Categorizing** Copy the chart here. Use it and your notes on trade to identify goods and ideas that were exchanged along the Silk Road, both into and out of China.

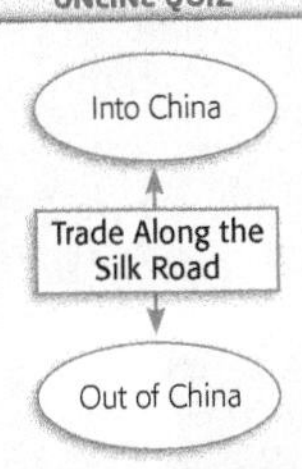

Focus on Speaking

5. **Evaluating the Importance of Events** Not all the important events in history are wars or invasions. What peaceful events in this section changed Chinese history? Write down some ideas.

Section 5 Assessment Answers

1. a. They allowed farmers to carry larger loads than before by themselves.
   b. Silkworm cocoons were unwound, the silk thread was prepared for dyeing and weaving, and then woven into fabric.
   c. so they could be the only people who knew how to make the valuable fabric
2. a. It began in central China and ended at the Mediterranean Sea.
   b. In exchange for silk, traders returned with gold, silver, horses, and precious stones.
3. a. the spread of ideas from one culture to another
   b. the promise that Buddhism offered rebirth and relief from suffering
4. Goods into China—gold, silver, precious stones, horses, and Buddhism; Goods out of China—precious goods, including silk and jade
5. technology, trade, and Buddhism

Direct Teach

Main Idea

3 Buddhism Comes to China

Buddhism came to China from India and gained many followers.

Summarizing How is Buddhism's spread into China an example of diffusion? *It represents the spread of one idea from one culture to another, and the resulting change in the culture.*

Review & Assess

Close

Challenge students to estimate the height of the statue shown on this page. They should use the human figures at the bottom of the photo as a guide. *The Buddha, called the Leshan Giant Buddha, is 233 feet (71 m) tall.*

Review

Online Quiz, Section 5

Assess

SE Section 5 Assessment
PASS: Section 5 Quiz
Alternative Assessment Handbook

Reteach/Classroom Intervention

Guided Reading Workbook, Section 5
Interactive Skills Tutor CD-ROM

Answers

Reading Check *Buddhism spread from India to China along the Silk Road and other trade routes.*

History and Geography

Activity **Remembering Successful Merchants** Have students select one of the merchants shown on these pages and write an obituary for him. Obituaries should include information on how the merchants benefited from Silk Road trade. Encourage students to use their imaginations to fill in other details of the merchants' lives, but to stay within historical possibility.

Teaching Tip

Movement Remind your students that movement is one of the five themes of geography. This theme deals not just with the migration of people, but also the movement of goods and ideas.

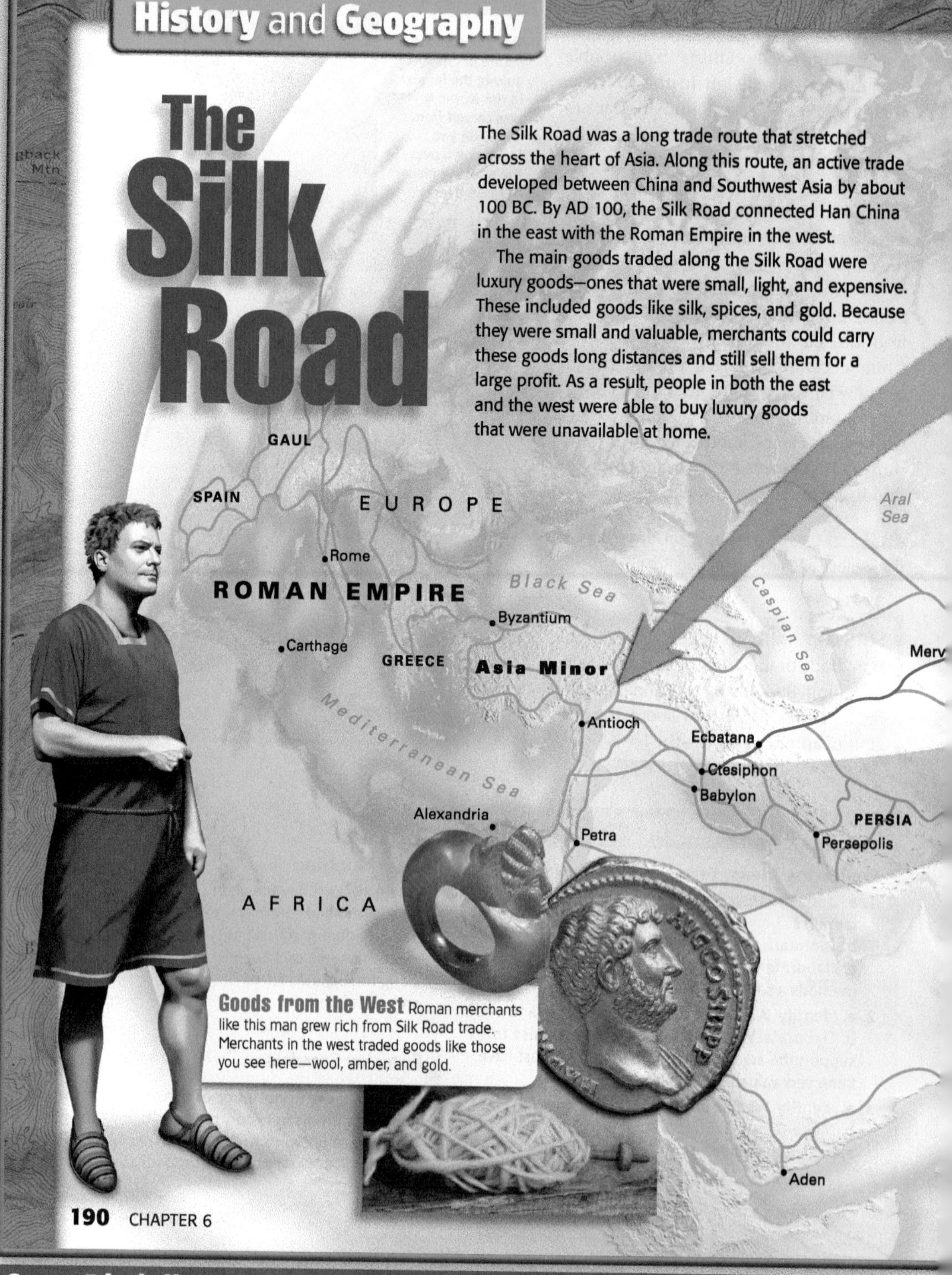

History and Geography
The Silk Road
The Silk Road was a long trade route that stretched across the heart of Asia. Along this route, an active trade developed between China and Southwest Asia by about 100 BC. By AD 100, the Silk Road connected Han China in the east with the Roman Empire in the west.
The main goods traded along the Silk Road were luxury goods—ones that were small, light, and expensive. These included goods like silk, spices, and gold. Because they were small and valuable, merchants could carry these goods long distances and still sell them for a large profit. As a result, people in both the east and the west were able to buy luxury goods that were unavailable at home.
GAUL
SPAIN
EUROPE
Rome
ROMAN EMPIRE
Black Sea
Caspian Sea
Aral Sea
Byzantium
Carthage
GREECE
Asia Minor
Merv
Mediterranean Sea
Antioch
Ecbatana
Ctesiphon
Babylon
Alexandria
Petra
PERSIA
Persepolis
AFRICA
Aden
Goods from the West Roman merchants like this man grew rich from Silk Road trade. Merchants in the west traded goods like those you see here—wool, amber, and gold.
190 CHAPTER 6

Cross-Discipline Activity: Economics

At Level

Long Road, High Price

1. Organize students into groups. Have students in each group decide if they want to represent a Roman or Chinese merchant and what items they want to trade on the Silk Road. They should also assign prices that manufacturers charge a trader for the merchandise.
2. Then have each group create a flowchart, showing where the merchandise is sold to the next trader and how much that trader pays for it. The goods may change hands several times as they make their way along the Silk Road, and each time the price is slightly higher.
3. Ask groups to report on the original and final prices of their merchandise. They should also calculate how much of the final price had been added along the way to the manufacturer's original price. Point out that every time the goods changed hands, a merchant made a profit.

LS Visual/Spatial, Logical/Mathematical

Alternative Assessment Handbook, Rubric 13: Graphic Organizers

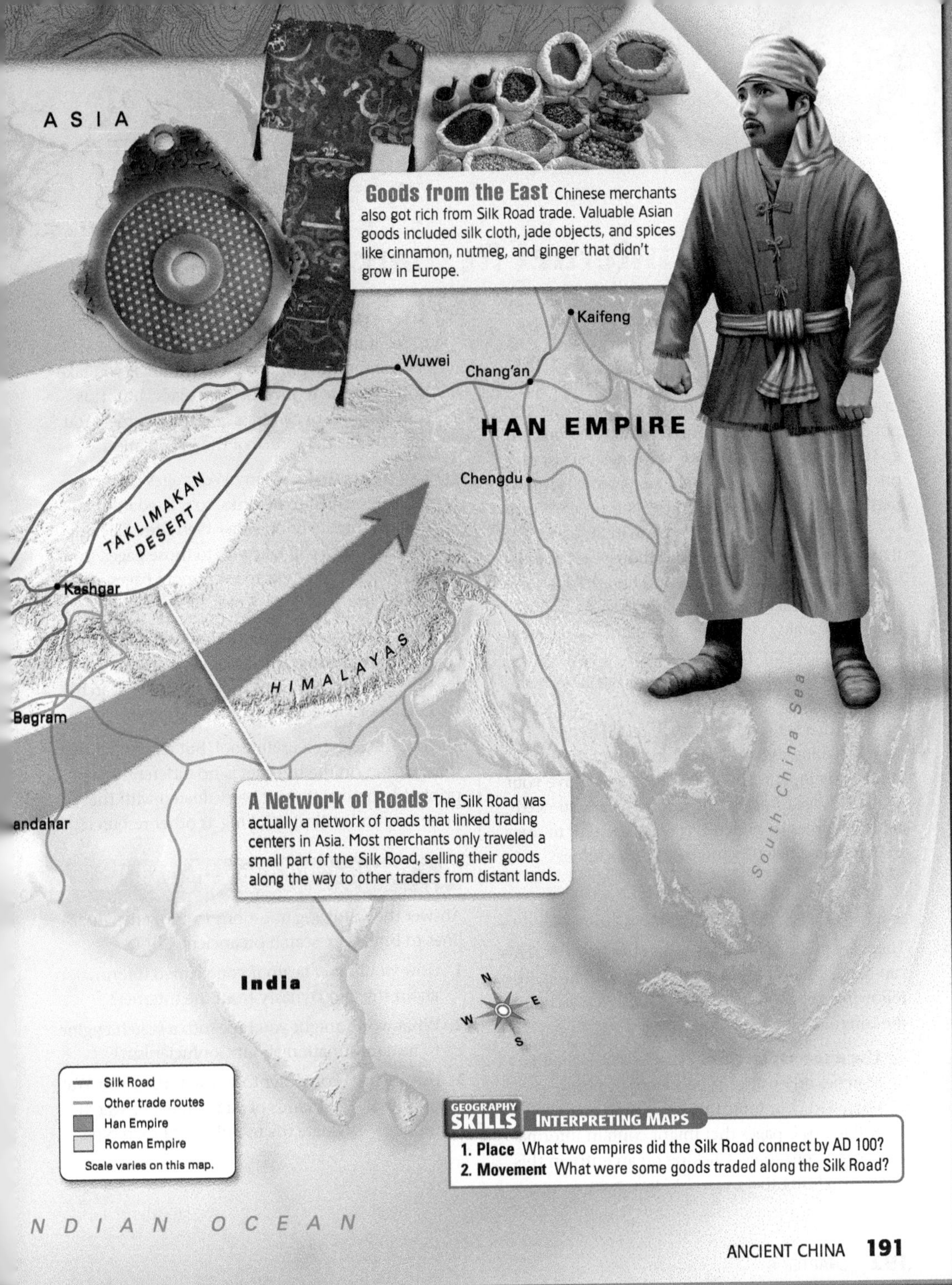
ASIA
Goods from the East Chinese merchants also got rich from Silk Road trade. Valuable Asian goods included silk cloth, jade objects, and spices like cinnamon, nutmeg, and ginger that didn't grow in Europe.
Kaifeng
Wuwei
Chang'an
HAN EMPIRE
Chengdu
TAKLIMAKAN DESERT
Kashgar
HIMALAYAS
Bagram
andahar
A Network of Roads The Silk Road was actually a network of roads that linked trading centers in Asia. Most merchants only traveled a small part of the Silk Road, selling their goods along the way to other traders from distant lands.
South China Sea
India
N
E
S
W
Silk Road
Other trade routes
Han Empire
Roman Empire
Scale varies on this map.
NDIAN OCEAN

GEOGRAPHY SKILLS INTERPRETING MAPS

1. **Place** What two empires did the Silk Road connect by AD 100?
2. **Movement** What were some goods traded along the Silk Road?

History and Geography

Info to Know

Traveling the Silk Road Today Fascination with the Silk Road has led to increased tourism. Since China opened its doors to foreign tourism, people have been able to travel along part of the Silk Road. Although travel in the harsh climate of western China is only for the hardy tourist, there are plenty of attractions, even in the deserts. Sites include ruined cities and caves full of Buddhist paintings. One city, Kashgar, has a market where tourists can get some idea of what trade along the old Silk Road was like long ago. At the market, people of many nationalities sell spices, wool, livestock, silver knives, and other items. Have students locate the city of Kashgar on the map on this page.

Connect to Science

From Worm to Wonderful Commercial silk is made by a single species of moth larvae. Each larva, or silkworm, lives on a diet of mulberry leaves before spinning a silk thread that wraps around and around to become a cocoon. This thread can be up to 3,000 feet long. To unwind the cocoon, the manufacturer must first find the end of the thread. Workers wash the silk and treat it with various chemicals to make different types of fabric.

Collaborative Learning

Below Level

Silk Road Collage

Prep Required

Materials: art supplies, butcher paper

1. Organize the class into four groups: Places, People, East to West Goods, and West to East Goods.
2. Have the students in the Places group create a large map that shows the roads themselves and important cities along the Silk Road. Have them draw or find pictures of physical features along the route.
3. Have students in the People group create or find images of the people who traveled the route, the animals that carried their cargo, and the trade caravans.
4. Students from each of the Goods groups should create or find images of goods that were traded along the route.
5. Next, have students create a collage of the Silk Road by placing images on the map created by the Places group. **LS Visual/Spatial**

Alternative Assessment Handbook, Rubric 8: Collages

Answers

Interpreting Maps: 1. *Han China and the Roman Empire;* **2.** *silk, jade objects, spices, wool, amber, gold*

Social Studies Skills

Conducting Internet Research

Activity Web Site for Using the Internet Explain to students that the Internet offers a wealth of information and sometimes misinformation on many topics. Have students review the Social Studies Skills lesson. Then organize students into small groups and have each group use the information to build a mock Web site explaining how to use the Internet. The page should be the home, or main, page for the site. Remind students to include links and other important features on their page. Students should also include a checklist that people can use to evaluate a Web site. **LS Interpersonal, Visual/Spatial**

Alternative Assessment Handbook, Rubrics 14: Group Activity; and 37: Writing Assignments

Interactive Skills Tutor CD-ROM, Lesson 4: Use a Variety of Sources to Gather Information

Social Studies Skills

Analysis | Critical Thinking | Economics | Study

Conducting Internet Research

Understand the Skill

The Internet is a huge network of computers that are linked together. You can connect to this network from a personal computer or from a computer at a public library or school. Once connected, you can go to places called Web sites. Web sites consist of one or more Web pages. Each page contains information that you can view on the computer screen.

Governments, businesses, individuals, and many different types of organizations such as universities, news organizations, and libraries have Web sites. Most library Web sites allow users to search their card catalog electronically. Many libraries also have databases on their Web sites. A database is a large collection of related information that is organized by topic.

The Internet can be a very good reference source. It allows you to gather information on almost any topic without ever having to leave your chair. However, finding the information you need can sometimes be difficult. Having the skill to use the Internet efficiently increases its usefulness.

Learn the Skill

There are millions of Web sites on the Internet. This can make it hard to locate specific information. The following steps will help you in doing research on the Internet.

1. **Use a search engine.** This is a Web site that searches other sites. Type a word or phrase related to your topic into the search engine. It will list Web pages that might contain information on your topic. Clicking on an entry in this list will bring that page to your screen.
2. **Study the Web page.** Read the information to see if it is useful. You can print the page on the computer's printer or take notes. If you take notes, be sure to include the page's URL. This is its location or "address" on the Internet. You need this as the source of the information.
3. **Use hyperlinks.** Many Web pages have connections, called hyperlinks, to related information on the site or on other Web sites. Clicking on these links will take you to those pages. You can follow their links to even more pages, collecting information as you go.
4. **Return to your results list.** If the information or hyperlinks on a Web page are not useful, return to the list of pages that your search engine produced and repeat the process.

The Internet is a useful tool. But remember that information on the Internet is no different than printed resources. It must be evaluated with the same care and critical thinking as other resources.

Practice and Apply the Skill

Answer the following questions to apply the guidelines to Internet research on ancient China.

1. How would you begin if you wanted information about the Qin Dynasty from the Internet?
2. What words might you type into a search engine to find information about Confucianism?
3. Use a school computer to research the Great Wall of China. What kinds of pages did your search produce? Evaluate the usefulness of each type.

Social Studies Skills Activity: Conducting Internet Research

Mock Internet Search

At Level | Prep Required

Materials: printouts of a Web search engine, Web search results, and Web sites for evaluation

1. Select one of the following topics or another topic from the chapter: *Laozi, terra-cotta warriors, Shi Huangdi,* or the *Silk Road.*
2. Before class, conduct an Internet search on the topic and print copies of the search engine you use, the search results, and two to three of the Web sites listed. Try to include at least one questionable Web site.
3. Display the printout of the search engine for students to see. Ask what terms they might enter to do a search on the topic you selected. Next, show students the printout of your search results. Have students discuss which of the listed sites look useful. Then show students the sites you printed. Help students to evaluate each site. **LS Visual/Spatial**

Alternative Assessment Handbook, Rubric 16: Judging Information

Answers

Practice and Apply the Skill

1. *possible answers—go to a search engine and type in "Qin Dynasty;" go to an online encyclopedia and look up Qin Dynasty;* **2.** *Confucius, Kongfuzi, Confucianism, Analects, Chinese philosophy;* **3.** *Students' results should exhibit an understanding of how to use a search engine and how to evaluate a Web page or site.*

Chapter Review

History's Impact
▶ **video series**
Review the video to answer the focus question:
How would you summarize the Confucian view of the family?

Visual Summary

Use the visual summary below to help you review the main ideas of the chapter.

QUICK FACTS

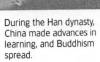

Chinese civilization began along the Huang He (Yellow River).

During the Zhou dynasty, armies fought for power, and the ideas of Confucius spread.

The Qin dynasty unified China with a strong government.

During the Han dynasty, China made advances in learning, and Buddhism spread.

Reviewing Vocabulary, Terms, and People

Match the "I" statement with the person or thing that might have made the statement. Not all of the choices will be used.

a. jade	**g.** Daoism
b. innovation	**h.** Shi Huangdi
c. lord	**i.** seismograph
d. oracle	**j.** wheelbarrow
e. peasant	**k.** Great Wall
f. Confucius	**l.** Legalism

1. "I stressed the importance of living in harmony with nature."
2. "I took a name that means 'first emperor.'"
3. "I stressed that people needed to be controlled with strict laws."
4. "I am a beautiful, hard gemstone that the Chinese made into many objects."
5. "I was built to keep invaders from attacking China."
6. "I can measure the strength of an earthquake."
7. "I am a person of high rank."
8. "I am a new idea, method, or device."
9. "I emphasized the importance of moral values and respect for the family."
10. "I am a farmer who tills a small plot of land."

Comprehension and Critical Thinking

SECTION 1 *(Pages 160–165)*

11. a. Identify In what region did the Shang dynasty develop?
b. Analyze How did China's geography contribute to the country's isolation?
c. Evaluate Considering the evidence, do you think the Xia dynasty was really China's first dynasty or a myth? Explain your answer.

Answers

Visual Summary

Review and Inquiry Have students write a short description of one of the drawings in the visual summary. Ask them to describe what is shown in the picture.

Quick Facts Transparency: Ancient China Visual Summary

Reviewing Vocabulary, Terms, and People

1. g
2. h
3. l
4. a
5. k
6. i
7. c
8. b
9. f
10. e

Comprehension and Critical Thinking

11. a. in the Huang He Valley of northern China
b. To the south and east, China was separated by water; to the north, by a vast desert; and to the west by tall mountain ranges.
c. possible answer—first dynasty, because there are many stories about it; a myth, because there is little to no direct evidence that the dynasty existed

Review and Assessment Resources

Review and Reinforce

SE Chapter Review
CRF: Chapter Review Activity
Quick Facts Transparency: Ancient China Visual Summary
Spanish Chapter Summaries Audio CD
Online Chapter Summaries in Six Languages
TOS Holt McDougal PuzzleView
Quiz Game CD-ROM

Assess

SE Standardized Test Practice
PASS: Chapter Test, Forms A and B
Alternative Assessment Handbook
TOS ExamView Assessment Suite, Chapter Test
Differentiated Instruction Modified Worksheets and Tests CD-ROM: Chapter Test
Online Assessment Program, in the Interactive Student Edition

Reteach/Intervene

Guided Reading Workbook
Differentiated Instruction Teacher Management System: Lesson Plans
Differentiated Instruction Modified Worksheets and Tests CD-ROM
Interactive Skills Tutor CD-ROM

hmhsocialstudies.com
Chapter Resources

Answers

12. a. Legalism

b. because Confucius said that the lower classes should learn by following the example of their superiors, which includes the emperor

c. Answers will vary, but students should be familiar with the concepts of both Daoism and Legalism.

13. a. Dissention from Shi Huangdi's policies helped stir up rebels after he died, and the government fell apart under the next two emperors.

b. to ensure they would not rise up and revolt against them

c. Answers will vary but should display familiarity with Shi Huangdi's rule.

14. a. The first group was the upper class, which included the emperor, his court, and government scholars. The second class was peasants.

b. to put only the people who were wealthy or influential and knew Confucianism into government

c. the seismograph and sundial

15. a. the Silk Road, the increased production of silk and the high demand for silk by other countries

b. wealthy people

c. The Chinese would no longer have dominated the silk trade.

Reviewing Themes

16. He was a harsh leader who inflicted many injustices on his people. Although he did many good things for China, his human rights practices were bad for the country.

17. Confucianism stressed moral values, loyalty among family members, good behavior by a king and his subjects, and carrying out what heaven expected of people.

Using the Internet

18. Go to hmhsocialstudies.com to access a rubric for this activity.

SECTION 2 *(Pages 166–171)*

12. a. Identify Which Chinese philosophy encouraged strict laws and severe punishments to keep order?

b. Analyze How would Confucianism benefit Chinese emperors?

c. Evaluate Would you be happier under a government influenced by Legalism or by Daoism? In which type of government would there be more order? Explain your answers.

SECTION 3 *(Pages 172–176)*

13. a. Describe What were the main reasons for the fall of the Qin dynasty?

b. Make Inferences Why did Shi Huangdi's armies destroy city walls and take weapons from people they conquered?

c. Evaluate Shi Huangdi was a powerful ruler. Was his rule good or bad for China? Why?

SECTION 4 *(Pages 178–183)*

14. a. Identify During the Han dynasty, who belonged to the first and second social groups?

b. Analyze What was the purpose of the exam system during Wudi's rule?

c. Elaborate What inventions show that the Chinese studied nature?

SECTION 5 *(Pages 186–189)*

15. a. Identify What factors led to the growth of trade during the Han dynasty?

b. Draw Conclusions Who do you think wore silk garments in China?

c. Predict What might have happened if the Chinese had told foreign visitors how to make silk?

Reviewing Themes

16. Politics Why might historians differ in their views of Shi Huangdi's success as a ruler?

17. Society and Culture How did Confucianism affect people's roles in their family, in government, and in society?

Using the Internet

18. Activity: Solving Problems Confucius was one of the most influential teachers in Chinese history. His ideas suggested ways to restore order in Chinese society. Using your online textbook, research Confucianism. Take note of the political and cultural problems Confucianism tried to address. Then investigate some of the current political and cultural problems in the United States. Could Confucianism solve problems in the United States? Prepare a persuasive argument to support your answer.

hmhsocialstudies.com

Reading Skills

19. Summarizing Historical Texts From the chapter, choose a subsection under a blue headline. For each paragraph within that subsection, write a sentence that summarizes the paragraph's main idea. Continue with the other subsections under the blue heading to create a study guide.

Social Studies Skills

20. Conducting Internet Research Find a topic in the chapter about which you would like to know more. Use the Internet to explore your topic. Compare the sources you find to determine which seem most complete and reliable. Write a short paragraph about your results.

Focus on Speaking

21. Giving Your Oral Presentation You have chosen a person or event and know why your choice was important to Chinese history. Now you must convince your classmates.

First, write a brief description of what the person did or what happened during the event. Then summarize why your person or event is important to Chinese history.

When you give your oral presentation, use vivid language to create pictures in your listeners' minds. Also, use a clear but lively tone of voice.

Reading Skills

19. Sentences will vary depending on the subsection selected, but should be concise summaries of the text ideas.

Social Studies Skills

20. Students should use sources from governmental, educational, and other reliable organizations.

Focus on Writing

21. Rubric Students' oral presentations should

- include a clear description of the person's or event's importance.
- compare the person or event to others in Chinese history.
- use vivid language.
- be delivered in a clear and lively voice.

CHAPTER 6

Standardized Test Practice

DIRECTIONS: Read each question, and write the letter of the best response.

1

> The connecting link between serving one's father and serving one's mother is love. The connecting link between serving one's father and serving one's prince is reverence [respect]. Thus the mother [brings forth] love, while the prince brings forth reverence. But to the father belong both—love and reverence . . . Likewise, to serve one's elders reverently paves the way for civic obedience.

The observation and advice in this passage *best* express the teachings of

A Buddhism.
B Confucianism.
C Daoism.
D Legalism.

2 Which feature of China's physical geography did *not* separate its early people from the rest of the world?

A the Gobi
B the Huang-He
C the Pacific Ocean
D the Tibetan Plateau

3 How did the Qin emperor Shi Huangdi unify and control China in the 200s BC?

A He created districts and counties that were governed by appointed officials.
B He gave land to China's nobles so that they would be loyal to him.
C He dissolved the army so that it could not be used against him by his enemies.
D He established the Silk Road to get goods from far away.

4 Which of the following developments in China is an example of diffusion?

A the growth of manufacturing and trade
B the building of the Great Wall
C the spread of Buddhism from India
D the use of inventions to improve farming

5 Which dynasty's rulers created a government based on the ideas of Confucius?

A the Shang dynasty
B the Zhou dynasty
C the Qin dynasty
D the Han dynasty

Connecting with Past Learnings

6 In your studies of ancient India, you learned about the Hindu belief in rebirth. Which belief system that influenced early China also emphasized rebirth?

A Buddhism
B Confucianism
C Daoism
D Legalism

7 What characteristic did early civilization in Mesopotamia share with early civilization in China?

A Both developed paper.
B Both were influenced by Buddhism.
C Both built ziggurats.
D Both first developed in river valleys.

Answers

Standardized Test Practice

1. B
Break Down the Question Students should recall that Confucianism stressed respect and obedience for family and for authority.

2. B
Break Down the Question Students should recall that the Huang He was a river in the heart of China, and would not have separated China from the rest of the world.

3. A
Break Down the Question This question requires students to recall factual information from Section 3.

4. C
Break Down the Question This question requires students to recall factual information from Section 5.

5. D
Break Down the Question Students should remember that the Han was the first dynasty to use Confucianism as a basis for government policy.

6. A
Break Down the Question This question requires students to recall factual information from Section 5.

7. D
Break Down the Question This question requires students to recall factual information from Chapter 3.

Intervention Resources

Reproducible

- Guided Reading Workbook
- Differentiated Instruction Teacher Management System: Lesson Plans

Technology

- Quick Facts Transparency: Ancient China Visual Summary
- Differentiated Instruction Modfied Worksheets and Tests CD-ROM
- Interactive Skills Tutor CD-ROM

Tips for Test Taking

I'm Done! Offer these test-taking tips to students: You aren't finished with your test until you check it. First, take a look at how much time you have left. Go back and review your answers for any careless mistakes you may have made. Be sure to erase any stray marks, review the hardest questions you answered, and turn the test in at the end of the time period. There is nothing to be gained from finishing first—or last either for that matter!

Multimedia Classroom

The **HISTORY™ Multimedia Classroom** is a set of exciting new social studies teaching tools featuring award-winning program content. These comprehensive lesson plans, correlated to individual state and national curriculum standards, are easy to use for both teachers and students.

Each lesson contains the following:
- Short video segments that bring history topics to life
- Maps and visual materials
- Discussion and review questions
- Easily printable primary source documents
- Classroom activities and Internet-based activity links

The Multimedia Classroom has been specially designed to be versatile and easily adaptable to existing courses, lesson plans, and syllabi. Every lesson is designed to offer maximum flexibility. Teachers can select entire plans or only the elements they need, allowing them to individually tailor each lesson. Each multimedia lesson is available in CD-ROM format and is accompanied by full-length award-winning programs on DVD from HISTORY™.

For more information or to purchase go to hmhsocialstudies.com

Because some of these lessons may contain video material of a sensitive nature, we recommend that teachers and parents review these materials in their entirety before screening them to students.

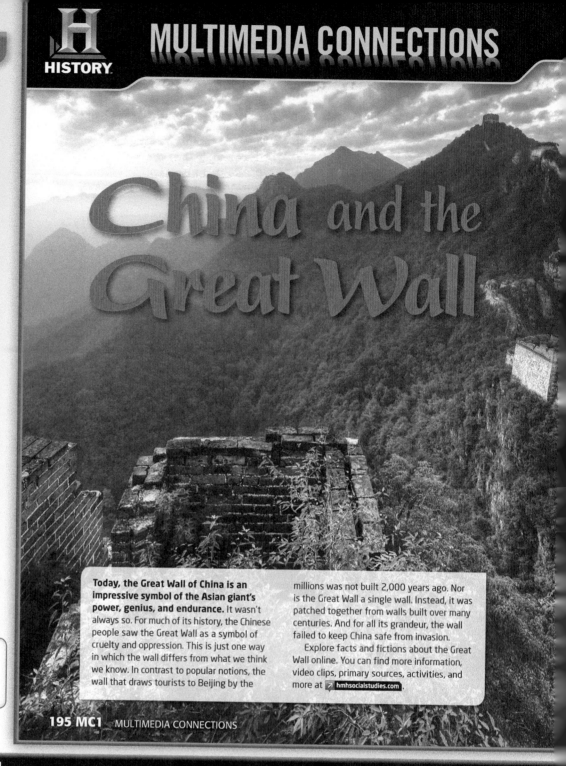

HISTORY

MULTIMEDIA CONNECTIONS

China and the Great Wall

Today, the Great Wall of China is an impressive symbol of the Asian giant's power, genius, and endurance. It wasn't always so. For much of its history, the Chinese people saw the Great Wall as a symbol of cruelty and oppression. This is just one way in which the wall differs from what we think we know. In contrast to popular notions, the wall that draws tourists to Beijing by the millions was not built 2,000 years ago. Nor is the Great Wall a single wall. Instead, it was patched together from walls built over many centuries. And for all its grandeur, the wall failed to keep China safe from invasion.

Explore facts and fictions about the Great Wall online. You can find more information, video clips, primary sources, activities, and more at hmhsocialstudies.com.

195 MC1 MULTIMEDIA CONNECTIONS

China and the Great Wall

Resources hmhsocialstudies.com

The following resources come with printable introductions, comprehension and critical thinking questions, transcripts, and vocabulary support.

Full Length DVD

Modern Marvels: Great Wall of China (50 mins)

Video Clips

- The Great Wall of China (2:30)
- Great Wall Facts and Fictions (3:24)
- A Land of Walls Within Walls (2:51)
- New Philosophies Emerge (1:33)
- The First Emperor of China (3:18)
- Constructing the Great Wall (3:52)
- The Human Costs of Building (3:19)
- China's Shortest Dynasty (3:59)
- A Mongol Empire in China (4:26)
- Ming Dynasty Wall Building (2:30)
- Guarding Against Invaders (3:18)
- Twentieth-Century China (4:06)

Primary Sources

- *The Analects* of Confucius
- A Legalist's View of Learning
- Memorial Stone Inscription
- Terra-cotta Tomb Soldiers
- Memoirs of an Italian Traveler
- The Gazetteer of Nanjing
- Hall of Supreme Harmony
- A Protest of the Opium Trade

CLICK THROUGH
INTER/ACTIVITIES
hmhsocialstudies.com

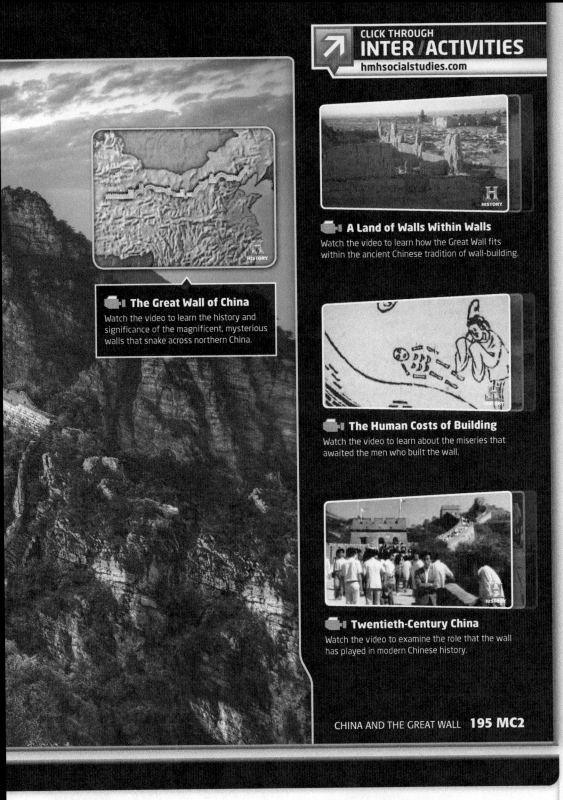

The Great Wall of China
Watch the video to learn the history and significance of the magnificent, mysterious walls that snake across northern China.

A Land of Walls Within Walls
Watch the video to learn how the Great Wall fits within the ancient Chinese tradition of wall-building.

The Human Costs of Building
Watch the video to learn about the miseries that awaited the men who built the wall.

Twentieth-Century China
Watch the video to examine the role that the wall has played in modern Chinese history.

Maps
- The Qin Empire
- The Han Empire

Activities
- Replicas of the Great Wall
- A Philosophical Debate
- Leaders Envision the Wall
- Silk Road Exchange
- Asia's Unparalleled Empire
- On the Road with Marco Polo
- Understanding Modern China

General Review Questions

General Discussion Questions

Web Links

Bibliography

Lesson Preview

The Great Wall of China

The Great Wall of China winds up to 4,000 miles across the Chinese landscape, from where the mountains meet the Yellow Sea to the eastern edge of the Gobi Desert. Yet the full history of this remarkable structure was long unknown in the West. Nor has the wall always been popular with the Chinese people, who at times have chipped away big chunks of it. Yet the wall endures and continues to capture our imaginations.

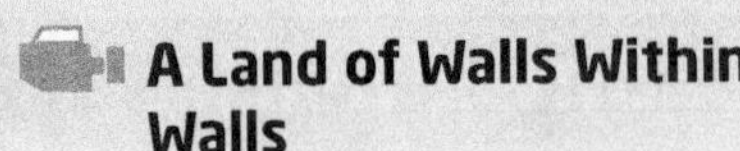

A Land of Walls Within Walls

Qin Shi Huangdi, China's first emperor, is credited with building the first version of the wall. But the idea of constructing an immense barrier across China's northern frontier developed from an ancient tradition. For centuries, the Chinese had built walls—around houses, temples, and huge tracts of land. In fact, during the Warring States period, warlords built some 2,800 miles of walls in frantic efforts to keep their enemies at bay.

The Human Costs of Building

Cold, heat, thirst, starvation, beatings by overseers—all were among the hardships that workers faced when they were sent north to build the wall. The laborers' sacrifices are highlighted in the story of the faithful Lady Meng, who traveled to the wall to find her husband, only to find him dead. Legend tells us that the corpses of men who died working on the wall were simply thrown in with the dirt and rocks that filled its center.

Twentieth-Century China

During the 20th century, the Great Wall's fortunes rose and fell just as the wall itself climbs up and down mountains. Early in the century, Western tourists were entranced with the wall's grandeur. The Chinese, however, were indifferent. During the Communist Revolution, the Great Wall was briefly a symbol of the people's struggle. Later, it became an emblem of imperial oppression. As China opened to the West, the Great Wall again became a positive image—both for Western visitors and the Chinese.

CHINA AND THE GREAT WALL 195 MC2

Preteach

Bellringer

Motivate Ask volunteers to name events that have happened recently in your school or town. For each event named, call on another volunteer to explain why that event occurred. Next, discuss as a class why it is important to know why events happen. Tell students that in this workshop they will write a paper explaining an event from ancient India or China.

Direct Teach

Considering Audience

Adjusting Readability Tell students that when they write something, they should consider whether their audience will understand it. One way to increase comprehension is to adjust readability. Explain that three main factors contribute to a text's readability: difficulty of vocabulary, sentence length, and paragraph length. Select a paragraph from the textbook and have students work as a class to rewrite it at a lower readability level. Help students simplify vocabulary, shorten sentences, and, if appropriate, break up the paragraph. Then have students practice the skill independently on a second paragraph. Remind students to make certain the new version makes sense, is grammatically and factually correct, and includes all the main points in the original.

Why Things Happen

Why do civilizations so often develop in river valleys? Why did early people migrate across continents? You learn about the forces that drive history when you ask why things happened. Then you can share what you learned by writing an expository essay, explaining why events turned out as they did.

Assignment

Write an expository essay explaining one of these topics:

- Why the Aryans developed the caste system
- Why Confucius is considered the most influential teacher in Chinese history

TIP Organizing Information

Essays that explain why should be written in a logical order. Consider using one of these:

- **Chronological order,** the order in which things happened
- **Order of importance,** the order of the least important reason to the most important, or vice versa.

1. Prewrite

Considering Topic and Audience

Choose one of the two topics in the assignment, and then start to think about your big idea. Your big-idea statement might start out like this:

- The Aryans developed the caste system to . . .
- Confucius is considered the most influential teacher in Chinese history because he . . .

Collecting and Organizing Information

You will need to collect information that answers the question *Why.* To begin, review the information in this unit of your textbook. You can find more information on your topic in the library or on the Internet.

You should not stop searching for information until you have at least two or three answers to the question *Why.* These answers will form the points to support your big idea. Then take another look at your big idea. You may need to revise it or add to it to reflect the information you have gathered.

2. Write

Here is a framework that can help you write your first draft.

A Writer's Framework

Introduction	Body	Conclusion
■ Start with an interesting fact or question. ■ Identify your big idea. ■ Include any important background information.	■ Include at least one paragraph for each point supporting your big idea. ■ Include facts and details to explain and illustrate each point. ■ Use chronological order or order of importance.	■ Summarize your main points. ■ Using different words, restate your big idea.

Differentiating Instruction

Struggling Readers Below Level

1. As students gather information, have them list any terms they do not understand.
2. Tell students to look up each of the terms in a thesaurus to find more familiar synonyms.
3. Then have students replace the difficult terms with the synonyms they found and reread the information. LS **Verbal/Linguistic**

Special Needs Learners Below Level

1. Have a group of three students role play. Have one student assume the role of a Chinese emperor. Have the other two students take on the roles of reporters for a fictional newspaper.
2. Have the student playing the emperor write a law on two pieces of paper and give them to the other two students. Each of these students should then ask the emperor questions to determine why he or she chose to issue this particular law. LS **Interpersonal, Kinesthetic**

3. Evaluate and Revise

Evaluating

Effective explanations require clear, straightforward language. Use the following questions to discover ways to improve your draft.

Evaluation Questions for an Expository Essay

- Does your essay begin with an interesting fact or question?
- Does the introduction identify your big idea?
- Have you developed at least one paragraph to explain each point?
- Is each point supported with facts and details?
- Have you organized your points clearly and logically?
- Did you explain any unusual words?
- Does the conclusion summarize your main points?
- Does the conclusion restate your big idea in different words?

Revising

Reread your draft. See whether each point is connected logically to the main idea and the other points you are making. If needed, add transitions—words and phrases that show how ideas fit together.

To connect points and information in time, use words like *after, before, first, later, soon, eventually, over time, as time passed,* and *then.* To show order of importance, use transitional words and phrases like *first, last, mainly, to begin with,* and *more important.*

4. Proofread and Publish

Proofreading

If you create a bulleted or numbered list, be sure to capitalize and punctuate the list correctly.

- **Capitalization:** It is always acceptable to capitalize the first word of each item in the list.
- **Punctuation:** (1) If the items are sentences, put a period at the end of each. (See the list in the tip above.) (2) If the items are not complete sentences, you usually do not need any end punctuation.

Publishing

Share your explanation with students from another class. After they read it, ask them to summarize your explanation. How well did they undertand the points you wanted to make?

Practice and Apply

Use the steps and strategies in this workshop to write your explanation.

TIP **Using Lists** To make an explanation easier to follow, look for information that can be presented in a list.

Sentence/Paragraph Form Confucius gave the Chinese people guidelines for behavior. He felt that fathers should display high moral values, and he thought it was important that women obey their husbands. Children were to be obedient and respectful.

List Form

Confucius gave the Chinese people guidelines for behavior:

- Fathers should display high moral values.
- Wives should obey their husbands.
- Children should obey and respect their parents.

Reteach

Using Graphics

Making a Flow Chart To help students having trouble understanding the relationships among events, make a flow chart illustrating the relationships. Use labeled arrows to explain the different relationships among the events. Then, for each arrow, have students write a few sentences explaining the relationship represented by that arrow.

Teaching Tip

Avoiding Passive Voice Tell students that they should not use passive voice when writing explanations. Have students exchange papers and circle any passive verbs. Then have students rewrite their papers to eliminate the passive verbs.

Practice & Apply

Rubric

Students' explanations of the chosen events should

- begin with a clear statement of the big idea.
- accurately and clearly explain why a specific event happened when it did.
- indicate an understanding of both direct and indirect causes for events.
- define key terms related to the chosen event.
- use a clear and logical organization.
- be written at a middle school level.
- include graphics as visual aids.
- end with a summary and a restatement of the big idea.
- use correct grammar, punctuation, spelling, and capitalization.

Advanced/Gifted and Talented

Above Level

1. Challenge advanced learners to incorporate excerpts from primary sources into their papers to support and enhance their explanations of ancient events.
2. Alternatively, have advanced students extend their papers by explaining the long-term effects of their chosen event and how it caused other events to occur. Encourage students to conduct outside research to expand upon the information covered in their papers. LS **Verbal/Linguistic**

Unit Preview

Introduce the Unit

Share the information in the chapter overviews with students.

Chapter 7 The Hebrew people appeared in Southwest Asia sometime between 2000 and 1500 BC. The Hebrews eventually established a kingdom called Israel. The lives of the Hebrews revolved around their religion, Judaism. In time, the Hebrews became known as Jews. Conquered by different groups, Jews dispersed around the world. Their shared beliefs and customs helped them maintain their religion and sense of identity, though.

Chapter 8 The geography of Greece shaped life there. Greece is a mountainous land surrounded by water. Travel across the mountains was difficult. As a result, Greeks turned to the sea for trade. They also developed independent city-states. The city-state became the foundation of Greek civilization. The ancient Greeks made lasting contributions. They created the first democracy as well as myths and works of literature that still influence life today.

Chapter 9 The powerful Greek city-states of Athens and Sparta were very different. They joined forces to defeat a Persian invasion, but later became enemies and went to war. The Spartans defeated the Athenians in 404 BC. Lack of unity among the city-states then helped Macedonia conquer Greece in the 300s BC. Macedonian Alexander the Great built a large empire across much of Europe, Asia, and Egypt. The ancient Greeks' lasting contributions include achievements in the arts, philosophy, and science.

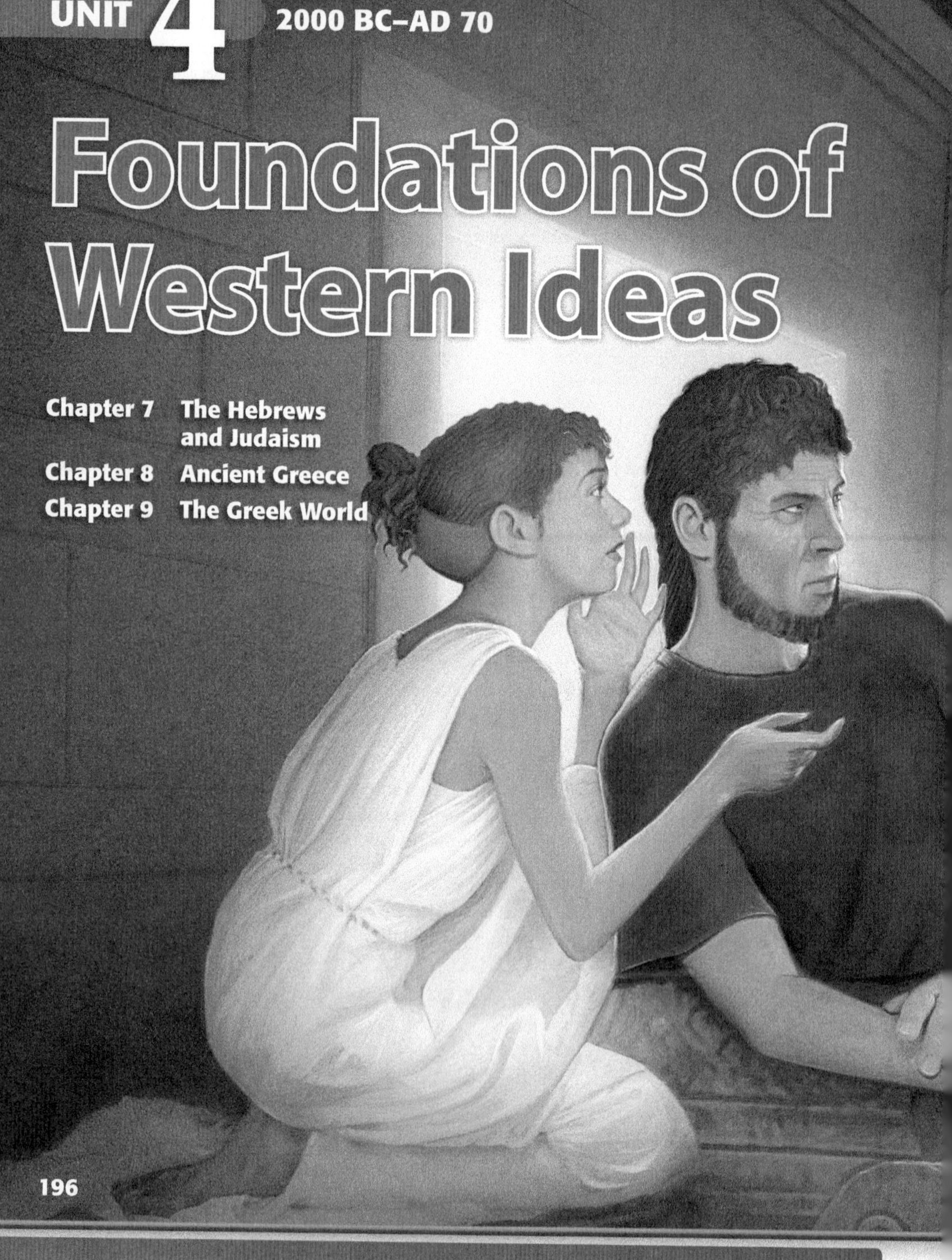

Unit Resources

Planning

- Differentiated Instruction Teacher Management System: Unit Instructional Benchmarking Guides
- TOS Calendar Planner
- Power Presentations with Media Gallery
- A Teacher's Guide to Religion in the Public Schools

Differentiating Instruction

- Differentiated Instruction Teacher Management System: Lesson Plans for Differentiated Instruction
- Differentiated Instruction Modified Worksheets and Tests CD-ROM

Enrichment

- **CRF 8:** Economics and History Activity: Imports and Exports: Sources of Wealth
- **CRF 9:** Economics and History Activity: The Importance of Trade
- **CRF 9:** Interdisciplinary Projects: Spartans Versus Athenians Debate; Contributions of Early Greeks
- Civic Participation Activities
- Primary Source Library CD-ROM

Assessment

- Progress Assessment System Solution: Unit Test
- TOS ExamView Assessment Suite: Unit Test
- Online Assessment Program, in the Interactive Student Edition
- Alternative Assessment Handbook

The **Differentiated Instruction Teacher Management System** provides a planning and instructional benchmarking guide for this unit.

What You Will Learn...

The foundations of Western civilization can be traced back more than 2,000 years to the eastern Mediterranean region. There, the ancient Hebrews and Greeks developed many of the ideas and traditions that have shaped the world today.

The Hebrews' religion, Judaism, was based on a belief in one God and basic ideas about right and wrong. The ancient Greeks created the world's first democracy. The Greeks also revolutionized science and mathematics and created some of the world's most famous art and literature.

In the next three chapters, you will learn how the Hebrews and Greeks helped shape the world you live in today.

Explore the Art

In this scene, the daughter of a Greek king warns her father not to trust a general who needs help in a war. What does this scene show about life in ancient Greece?

197

Democracy and Civic Education

At Level

Background Ancient Greece is the birthplace of democracy. Greek views about democracy have had a major impact on Western political thought.

1. Have students work in small groups to conduct research on democracy and U.S. representative democracy. Where do officials get their authority to make and enforce laws? In what ways is government in the United States by the people? What power do citizens have to influence lawmakers and the political process?
2. Have each group create a skit that explains what democracy is, the Greek origins of democracy, and the form of democracy that we have in the United States.
3. Groups should assign members specific tasks or roles to share the work and ensure that everyone participates.

LS Interpersonal, Kinesthetic

Alternative Assessment Handbook, Rubrics 14: Group Activity; 30: Research; and 33: Skits and Reader's Theater

Civic Participation Activities

Unit Preview

Connect to the Unit

Activity Landmarks of the Ancient World Ask students to identify some of the well known landmarks they have learned about so far (e.g., the Great Pyramid of Khufu or the Great Wall of China). Ask students if they have heard of the Seven Wonders of the Ancient World. Point out that this list included both the Great Pyramid of Khufu and the Hanging Gardens of Babylon. Explain that the Greeks, who students will learn about in this unit, built most of the other Seven Wonders of the Ancient World.

Tell students that they are going to create a large mural entitled "Landmarks of the Ancient World." Have students conduct research on the Seven Wonders of the Ancient World as well as on other landmarks of the civilizations they have studied so far and of the ones they will learn about in this unit. Have students draw or place images of these landmarks on a large piece of butcher paper. For each landmark, students should provide a caption giving the name, the location, and a brief description.

LS Interpersonal Visual/Spatial

Explore the Art

The scene at left shows young Gorgo offering advice to her father, the Spartan king Cleomenes. The general was trying to bribe her father to convince him to help. Gorgo told her father, "Go away, or the stranger will corrupt you." Cleomenes took her advice. Many years later, Gorgo married Leonidas, a king of Sparta.

About the Illustration

This illustration is an artist's conception based on available sources. However, historians are uncertain exactly what this scene looked like.

Answers

Explore the Art *shows clothing styles, architecture, and that there were kings and warfare*

Chapter 7 Planning Guide

The Hebrews and Judaism

<table>
<tr><th>Overview</th><th colspan="2">Instructional Resources</th></tr>
<tr><td>CHAPTER 7
Essential Question: How did the Hebrews defend themselves and maintain their beliefs?

Focus on the Essential Question Podcast</td><td>TOS Differentiated Instruction Teacher Management System:
• Instructional Benchmarking Guides
• Lesson Plans for Differentiated Instruction
Guided Reading Workbook
Chapter Resource File:
• Chapter Review Activity
• Focus on Writing Activity: A Web Site
• Social Studies Skills Activity: Identifying Short- and Long-Term Effects</td><td>TOS Calendar Planner
Power Presentations with Media Gallery
Differentiated Instruction Modified Worksheets and Tests CD-ROM
Primary Source Library CD-ROM for World History
Interactive Skills Tutor CD-ROM
Student Edition on Audio CD Program
HISTORY Video: Moses at Mount Sinai</td></tr>
<tr><td>Section 1:
The Early Hebrews
The Big Idea: Originally desert nomads, the Hebrews established a great kingdom called Israel.</td><td>TOS Differentiated Instruction Teacher Management System: Section 1 Lesson Plan
Guided Reading Workbook: Section 1
Chapter Resource File:
• Vocabulary Builder Activity, Section 1
• Biography Activity: Esther
• Biography Activity: Isaac and Ishmael
• Biography Activity: King Solomon</td><td>Daily Bellringer Transparency: Section 1
Map Transparency: Possible Routes of Abraham and Moses
Map Transparency: Kingdoms of Israel and Judah, c. 920 BC
Internet Activity: Connections to Today</td></tr>
<tr><td>Section 2:
Jewish Beliefs and Texts
The Big Idea: The central ideas and laws of Judaism are contained in sacred texts such as the Torah.</td><td>TOS Differentiated Instruction Teacher Management System: Section 2 Lesson Plan
Guided Reading Workbook: Section 2
Chapter Resource File:
• Vocabulary Builder Activity, Section 2
• Literature Activity: "The Creation Story," from the Torah
• Primary Source Activity: Mosaic Law and Punishments</td><td>Daily Bellringer Transparency: Section 2</td></tr>
<tr><td>Section 3:
Judaism over the Centuries
The Big Idea: Although many Jews were forced out of Israel by the Romans, shared beliefs and customs helped Jews maintain their religion.</td><td>TOS Differentiated Instruction Teacher Management System: Section 3 Lesson Plan
Guided Reading Workbook: Section 3
Chapter Resource File:
• Vocabulary Builder Activity, Section 3
• History and Geography Activity: Jewish Migration After AD 70</td><td>Daily Bellringer Transparency: Section 3
Map Transparency: Jewish Migration After AD 70
Internet Activity: Illustrated Guide to Jewish Holy Days
Animated History: Jewish Diaspora, AD 70–500</td></tr>
</table>

Chart Key:

SE Student Edition 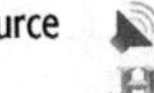 Presentation Resource  MP3 Audio

TOS Teacher One Stop  DVD/CD-ROM  HISTORY™

Printable Resource

Program Resources available on TOS and @ 

Review, Assessment, Intervention

 **Quick Facts Transparency:** The Hebrews and Judaism Visual Summary

 **Spanish Chapter Summaries Audio CD Program**

 **Quiz Game CD-ROM**

 **Progress Assessment Support System (PASS):** Chapter Test

 **Differentiated Instruction Modified Worksheets and Tests CD-ROM:** Modified Chapter Test

 TOS **ExamView® Assessment Suite (English/Spanish)**

 **Online Assessment Program,** in the Interactive Student Edition

 **PASS:** Section 1 Quiz

 **Online Quiz:** Section 1

 **Alternative Assessment Handbook**

 **PASS:** Section 2 Quiz

 **Online Quiz:** Section 2

 **Alternative Assessment Handbook**

 **PASS:** Section 3 Quiz

 **Online Quiz:** Section 3

 **Alternative Assessment Handbook**

Supporting Resources

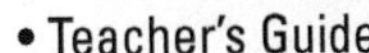

- Multimedia Classroom Global History Series
- Global History Teacher's Guide

Maps Globes Graphs Level F

- Student Workbook
- Teacher's Guide

Social Studies Trade Library Collections

- Premier Secondary World History Trade Collection
- Ancient World History Trade Collection

History's Impact

World History Video Program

- **The Impact of Judaism Throughout the World**

For more information or to purchase go to 

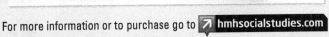

Power Presentations with Media Gallery

Power Presentations with Media Gallery are visual presentations of each chapter's main ideas. Presentations can be customized by including Quick Facts charts, images from the text, and video clips.

CHAPTER 7 PLANNING GUIDE

Differentiating Instruction

How do I address the needs of varied learners?

The Target Resource acts as your primary strategy for differentiated instruction.

ENGLISH-LANGUAGE LEARNERS & STRUGGLING READERS

Interactive Skills Tutor CD-ROM

The Interactive Skills Tutor CD-ROM contains lessons that provide additional practice for 20 different critical thinking skills.

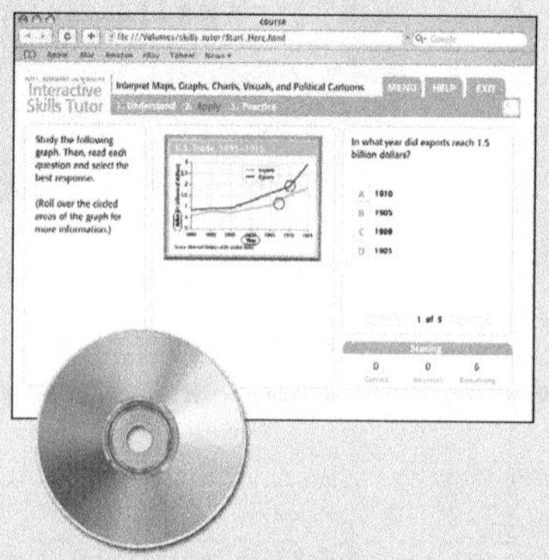

Additional Resources

Differentiated Instruction Teacher Management System: Lesson Plans for Differentiated Instruction

Chapter Resource File:

- Vocabulary Builder Activities
- Social Studies Skills Activity: Identifying Short- and Long-Term Effects

Quick Facts Transparencies: The Hebrews and Judaism Visual Summary

Student Edition on Audio CD Program

Spanish/English Guided Reading Workbook

SPECIAL NEEDS LEARNERS

Differentiated Instruction Modified Worksheets and Tests CD-ROM

- Vocabulary Flash Cards
- Vocabulary Builder Activities
- Chapter Review Activity
- Chapter Test

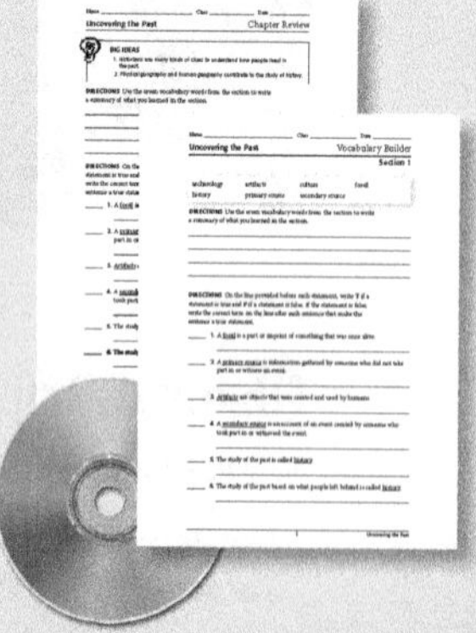

Additional Resources

Differentiated Instruction Teacher Management System: Lesson Plans for Differentiated Instruction

Guided Reading Workbook

Chapter Resource File: Social Studies Skills Activity: Identifying Short- and Long-Term Effects

Student Edition on Audio CD Program

Interactive Skills Tutor CD-ROM

ADVANCED/GIFTED-AND-TALENTED STUDENTS

Primary Source Library CD-ROM for World History

The Library contains longer versions of quotations in the text, extra sources, and images. Included are point-of-view articles, journals, diaries, historical fiction, and political documents.

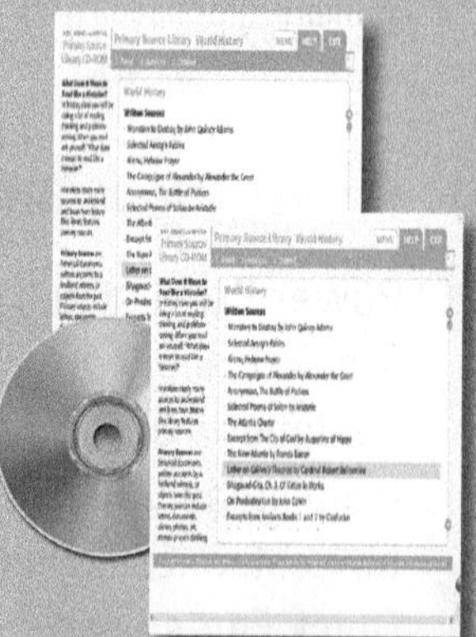

Additional Resources

Differentiated Instruction Teacher Management System: Lesson Plans for Differentiated Instruction

Chapter Resource File:

- Focus on Writing Activity: A Web Site
- Literature Activity: "The Creation Story," from the Torah

Document-Based Questions Activities

Differentiated Activities in the Teacher's Edition

- Vocabulary for the Ten Commandments, p. 204
- Word Mapping, p. 211

Teacher One Stop™

How can I manage the lesson plans and support materials for differentiated instruction?

With the Teacher One Stop, you can easily organize and print lesson plans, planning guides, and instructional materials for all learners. The Teacher One Stop includes the following materials to help you differentiate instruction:

- Interactive Teacher's Edition
- Calendar Planner and pacing guides
- Editable lesson plans
- All reproducible ancillaries in Adobe Acrobat (PDF) format
- ExamView Assessment Suite (English & Spanish)
- Transparency and video previews

Differentiated Activities in the Teacher's Edition

- Central Beliefs of Judaism Poster, p. 209
- Connecting to the Big Idea, p. 218

Interactive Student Edition

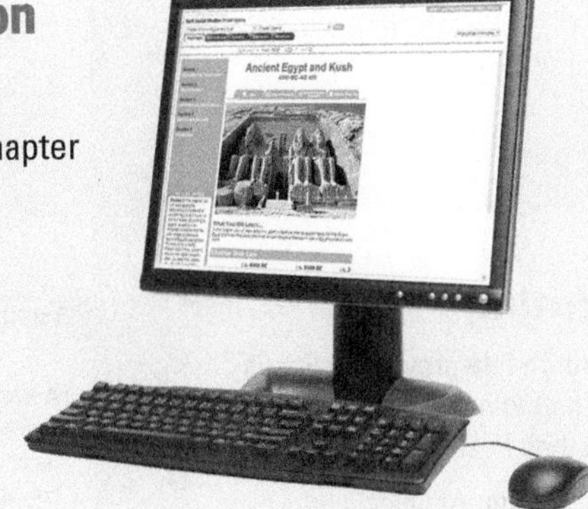

Complete online student edition with interactive multimedia support for chapter content assessment and reporting

- Interactive Maps and Notebook
- Graphic Organizers
- Standardized Test Prep
- Online Homework Practice and Research Activities
- Current Events
- Chapter-based Internet Activities
- Animated History Activities
- and more!

Differentiated Activities in the Teacher's Edition

- "Judaism over Time" Storyboards, p. 218

• Chapter Preview •

Essential Question

Introduce the Essential Question

- Point out that the Hebrews believed that they had a covenant with God. If they followed the laws of their faith, God would provide them a homeland.
- Explain that strong and wise leadership brought unity to the people of Israel and helped them overcome their enemies.
- Discuss the ways in which the Jews were able to maintain their faith during extended periods of exile.

CHAPTER 7 2000 BC–AD 70

The Hebrews and Judaism

Essential Question How did the Hebrews defend themselves and maintain their beliefs?

South Carolina Performance Standards

6-1.4 Explain the origins, fundamental beliefs, and spread of Eastern religions, including Hinduism (India), Judaism (Mesopotamia), Buddhism (India), and Confucianism and Taoism (China).

Literacy Skills for Social Studies

- Identify and explain the relationships among multiple causes and multiple effects.
- Select or design appropriate forms of social studies resources to organize and evaluate social studies information.

Partnership for the 21st Century Skills
Elaborate and refine ideas in order to improve and maximize creative efforts.

Focus on Writing

A Web Site Have you ever designed your own Web site? If not, here's your chance to create one. As you read this chapter, you'll gather information about Hebrew history, beliefs, values, and culture. Then you will write a description of how you would present this same information on a Web site.

In this photo, hundreds of people pray at the Western Wall, the holiest site in the world of Judaism. The wall was built around 19 BC.

Chapter Events	**c. 2000 BC** Abraham leaves Mesopotamia.
	2000 BC
World Events	**c. 1750 BC** Hammurabi issues his law code.

Focus on Writing

The **Chapter Resource File** provides a Focus on Writing worksheet to help students organize and describe their Web sites.

CRF: Focus on Writing Activity: A Web Site

Key to Differentiating Instruction

Below Level
Basic-level activities designed for all students encountering new material

At Level
Intermediate-level activities designed for average students

Above Level
Challenging activities designed for honors and gifted and talented students

Standard English Mastery
Activities designed to improve standard English usage

LS Learning Styles

Introduce the Chapter

At Level

Focus on the Hebrews and Israel

1. Write the following terms for students to see: *Hebrews, Israelites,* and *Jews.* Have students identify what the terms have in common. Help students understand that the terms all refer to the same people but at different times or locations.
2. Have students share anything they already know about the ancient Hebrews, such as the Bible stories of Noah and the Ark; of Abraham, Isaac, and Jacob; or of Moses and the Ten Commandments. Then identify for students the location of modern-day Israel on a political map of the Middle East.
3. Close by asking students why they think it is important to learn about ancient Hebrew history. Help students understand that the history of the Jews and other groups in the Middle East continues to shape the region today. **LS Verbal/Linguistic**

Chapter Preview

Explore the Picture

The Western Wall The Western Wall is all that is left of the Second Temple, the holiest site in ancient Israel. Today Jews come from around the world to pray at the Wall. One Jewish custom is to place small written prayers in the cracks between the Wall's stones.

Analyzing Visuals What can you learn about the religion of Judaism from the picture? *possible answers—that Judaism is an old religion, that holy sites and prayer are important parts of the religion, and that some followers of Judaism wear special articles of clothing*

HISTORY
Moses at Mount Sinai
hmhsocialstudies.com VIDEO

1200s BC Moses leads the Israelites out of Egypt during the Exodus.

586 BC The Jews are enslaved in Babylon.

AD 70 The Romans destroy the Second Temple in Jerusalem.

1475 BC — 950 BC — 425 BC — AD 100

c. 1240–1224 BC Ramses the Great rules Egypt.

c. 563 BC The Buddha is born in India.

27 BC Augustus becomes the first Roman emperor.

THE HEBREWS AND JUDAISM 199

Explore the Time Line

1. When did the Exodus occur? *c. 1200 BC*
2. Who destroyed the Second Temple in Jerusalem, and when? *the Romans; AD 70*
3. How long after the Jews were enslaved in Babylon was the Buddha born in India? *about 23 years*

Info to Know

The Second Temple After the Romans destroyed the Second Temple in AD 70, they deliberately did not clear away the ruins of the building. The Romans left the ruins in place as a symbol of the Roman Empire's power.

Reading Social Studies

Understanding Themes

The theme of this chapter is religion. Tell the students that in this chapter they will learn how the Hebrew people lived under a code of moral laws. Ask students to explain the purpose that laws serve in our society today. Then ask students how a government's laws might differ from moral or religious laws. Tell them that the teachings of Judaism have influenced Western cultures and some of their beliefs are reflected in our laws.

Facts, Opinions, and the Past

Focus on Reading Ask each student to write down two facts and two opinions about activities or clubs at their school or in the community. Collect the papers and share some of these facts and opinions with the class. Ask class members to decide if a particular sentence represents a fact or an opinion. Discuss how to test if a statement is factual by asking: Is there evidence available to prove or disprove this? Remind students that facts can be verified by using reliable sources.

Reading Social Studies

Economics | Geography | Politics | **Religion** | Society and Culture | Science and Technology

Focus on Themes In this chapter, you will read about the Hebrews and their descendents, the Israelites and Jews, and the religion called Judaism. You will learn about Jewish beliefs, texts such as the Torah and the Dead Sea Scrolls, and leaders such as Abraham and Moses. As you read, pay close attention to how people's beliefs affected where and how they lived. In the process, you will discover that the lives of the early Hebrews revolved around their **religious** beliefs and practices.

Facts and Opinions about the Past

Focus on Reading Why is it important to know the difference between a fact and an opinion? Separating facts from opinions about historical events helps you know what really happened.

Identifying Facts and Opinions Something is a **fact** if there is a way to prove it or disprove it. For example, research can prove or disprove the following statement: "The ancient Jews recorded their laws." But research can't prove the following statement because it is just an **opinion**, or someone's belief: "Everyone should read the records of the ancient Jews."

Use the process below to decide whether a statement is fact or opinion.

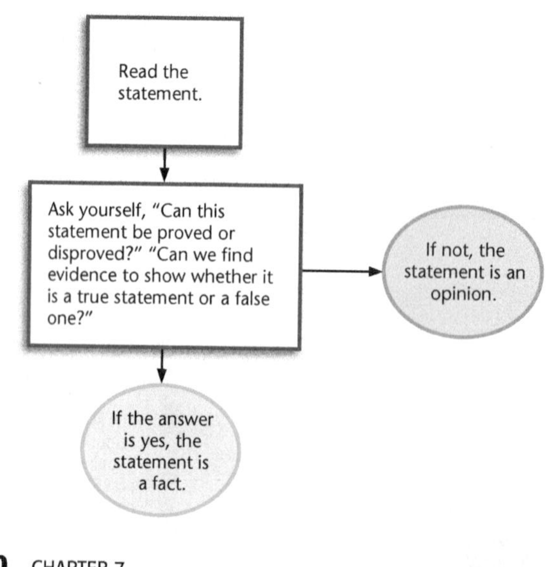

Read the statement.
Ask yourself, "Can this statement be proved or disproved?" "Can we find evidence to show whether it is a true statement or a false one?"
If not, the statement is an opinion.
If the answer is yes, the statement is a fact.

Reading and Skills Resources

Reading Support

- Guided Reading Workbook
- Student Edition on Audio CD
- Spanish Chapter Summaries Audio CD Program

Social Studies Skills Support

- Interactive Skills Tutor CD-ROM

Vocabulary Support

- **CRF:** Vocabulary Builder Activities
- **CRF:** Chapter Review Activity
- Differentiated Instruction Modified Worksheets and Tests CD-ROM:
  - Vocabulary Flash Cards
  - Vocabulary Builder Activity
  - Chapter Review Activity

TOS Holt McDougal PuzzleView

You Try It!

The following passage tells about boys who, years ago, found what came to be called the Dead Sea Scrolls. All the statements in this passage are facts. What makes them facts and not opinions?

Scrolls Reveal Past Beliefs

From Chapter 7, pages 212–213

Until 1947 no one knew about the Dead Sea Scrolls. In that year, young boys looking for a lost goat near the Dead Sea found a small cave. One of the boys went in to explore and found several old jars filled with moldy scrolls.

Scholars were very excited about the boy's find. Eager to find more scrolls, they began to search the desert. Over the next few decades, searchers found several more groups of scrolls.

Careful study revealed that most of the Dead Sea Scrolls were written between 100 BC and AD 50. The scrolls included prayers, commentaries, letters, and passages from the Hebrew Bible. These writings help historians learn about the lives of many Jews during this time.

Identify each of the following as a fact or an opinion and then explain your choice.

1. Boys discovered the Dead Sea Scrolls in 1947.
2. The discovery of the scrolls is one of the most important discoveries ever.
3. All religious leaders should study the Dead Sea Scrolls.
4. The Dead Sea Scrolls were written between 100 BC and AD 50.

Key Terms and People

Chapter 7

Section 1
Judaism *(p. 202)*
Abraham *(p. 202)*
Moses *(p. 203)*
Exodus *(p. 203)*
Ten Commandments *(p. 204)*
David *(p. 205)*
Solomon *(p. 205)*
Diaspora *(p. 206)*

Section 2
monotheism *(p. 208)*
Torah *(p. 210)*
synagogue *(p. 210)*
prophets *(p. 211)*
Talmud *(p. 212)*
Dead Sea Scrolls *(p. 212)*

Section 3
Zealots *(p. 214)*
rabbis *(p. 216)*
Passover *(p. 219)*
High Holy Days *(p. 219)*

Academic Vocabulary

Success in school is related to knowing academic vocabulary—the words that are frequently used in school assignments and discussions. In this chapter, you will learn the following academic word:

principles *(p. 210)*

As you read Chapter 7, look for clues that will help you determine which statements are facts.

Reading Social Studies

Key Terms and People

Read the terms and people to students. Then ask students to choose five terms with which they are unfamiliar. Have students define the terms they selected. Then have each student create a crossword puzzle using the definitions he or she wrote as clues. If time permits, have students exchange their puzzles with a partner and complete the other person's crossword. Then have students check their answers.

LS Verbal/Linguistic, Visual/Spatial

Focus on Reading

See the **Focus on Reading** questions in this chapter for more practice on this reading social studies skill.

Reading Social Studies Assessment

See the **Chapter Review** at the end of this chapter for student assessment questions related to this reading skill.

Teaching Tip

Help students who may have difficulty differentiating fact and opinion by instructing them to look for signal words. Oftentimes statements that are facts include phrases like *evidence shows* or gives specific facts or dates. Remind students that opinion statements use phrases like *in my view*, *people believe*, or *should.* Encourage students to circle or underline signal words to determine whether a statement is fact or opinion.

Answers

You Try It! 1. *fact; it is supported in the passage;* **2.** *opinion; that cannot be proved;* **3.** *opinion; there is no evidence to support this;* **4.** *fact; information in the passage supports this*

Preteach

Bellringer

If YOU were there . . . Use the **Daily Bellringer Transparency** to help students answer the question.

Daily Bellringer Transparency, Section 1

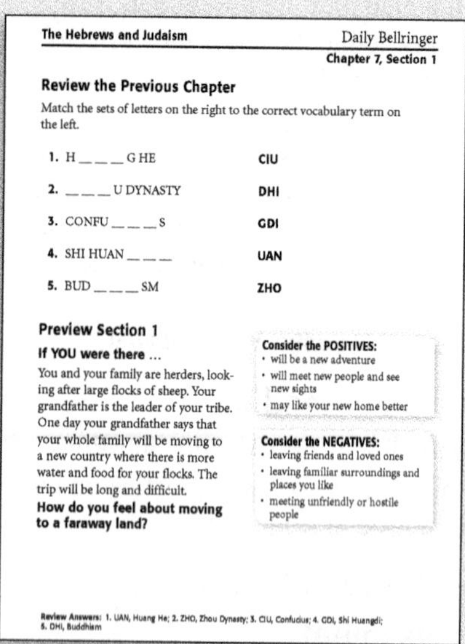

The Hebrews and Judaism — Daily Bellringer
Chapter 7, Section 1

Review the Previous Chapter

Match the sets of letters on the right to the correct vocabulary term on the left.

1. H___G HE	CIU
2. ___U DYNASTY	DHI
3. CONFU___S	GDI
4. SHI HUAN___	UAN
5. BUD___SM	ZHO

Preview Section 1

If YOU were there ...

You and your family are herders, looking after large flocks of sheep. Your grandfather is the leader of your tribe. One day your grandfather says that your whole family will be moving to a new country where there is more water and food for your flocks. The trip will be long and difficult.

How do you feel about moving to a faraway land?

Consider the POSITIVES:
- will be a new adventure
- will meet new people and see new sights
- may like your new home better

Consider the NEGATIVES:
- leaving friends and loved ones
- leaving familiar surroundings and places you like
- meeting unfriendly or hostile people

Review Answers: 1. UAN, Huang He; 2. ZHO, Zhou Dynasty; 3. CIU, Confucius; 4. GDI, Shi Huangdi; 5. DHI, Buddhism

Building Vocabulary

Preteach or review the following terms:

Hebrews a people who appeared in Southwest Asia sometime between 2000 and 1500 BC (p. 202)

Israelites descendants of Abraham through his grandson Jacob, also called Israel, who had settled in Canaan by the time of Moses (p. 203)

Jews inhabitants of the ancient kingdom of Judah (p. 206)

pharaoh ruler of Egypt (p. 203)

plagues disasters (p. 203)

CRF: Vocabulary Builder Activity, Section 1

Taking Notes

Have students use the graphic organizer online to take notes on the section. This activity will prepare students for the Section Assessment, in which they will complete a graphic organizer that builds on the information using the Critical Thinking Skill: Evaluating.

SECTION 1

The Early Hebrews

What You Will Learn...

Main Ideas

1. Abraham and Moses each led their people to Canaan and to a new religion.
2. Strong kings united the Israelites to fight off invaders.
3. Invaders conquered and ruled the Israelites after their kingdom broke apart.
4. Some women in Israelite society made great contributions to their history.

The Big Idea

Originally desert nomads, the Hebrews established a great kingdom called Israel.

Key Terms and People

Judaism, *p. 202*
Abraham, *p. 202*
Moses, *p. 203*
Exodus, *p. 203*
Ten Commandments, *p. 204*
David, *p. 205*
Solomon, *p. 205*
Diaspora, *p. 206*

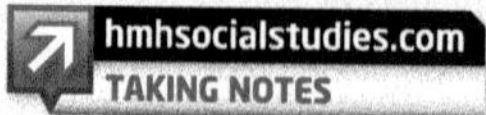

Use the graphic organizer online to take notes on the stages of Hebrew and later Jewish history from its beginnings in Canaan to Roman rule.

If YOU were there...

You and your family are herders, looking after large flocks of sheep. Your grandfather is the leader of your tribe. One day your grandfather says that your whole family will be moving to a new country where there is more water and food for your flocks. The trip will be long and difficult.

How do you feel about moving to a faraway land?

BUILDING BACKGROUND Like the family described above, the early Hebrews moved to new lands in ancient times. According to Jewish tradition, their history began when God told an early Hebrew leader to travel west to a new land.

Abraham and Moses Lead Their People

Sometime between 2000 and 1500 BC a new people appeared in Southwest Asia. They were the Hebrews (HEE-brooz), ancestors of the Israelites and Jews. The early Hebrews were simple herders, but they developed a culture that became a major influence on later civilizations.

Much of what is known about their early history comes from the work of archaeologists and from accounts written by Hebrew scribes. These accounts describe their early history and the laws of **Judaism** (JOO-dee-i-zuhm), their religion. In time these accounts became the Hebrew Bible. The Hebrew Bible is largely the same as the Old Testament of the Christian Bible.

The Beginnings in Canaan and Egypt

The Hebrew Bible traces the Hebrews back to a man named **Abraham**. One day, the Hebrew Bible says, God told Abraham to leave his home in Mesopotamia. He was to take his family on a long journey to the west. God promised to lead Abraham to a new land and make his descendants into a mighty nation.

Teach the Big Idea

At Level

The Early Hebrews

1. **Teach** Ask students the questions in the Main Idea boxes to teach this section.
2. **Apply** Have students write each of the blue heads in the section on a piece of paper. Tell students to leave space below each heading. Have students review the material under each heading and then write three to five main ideas under that heading on their papers. **LS Verbal/Linguistic**
3. **Review** To review the section, have volunteers share the main ideas that they wrote with the class. Then have students discuss the section's big idea.
4. **Practice/Homework** Have students write an imaginary interview with one of the key people in the section. The interviews should include at least five questions and answers. Provide students with sample questions. **LS Verbal/Linguistic**

Alternative Assessment Handbook, Rubric 37: Writing Assignments

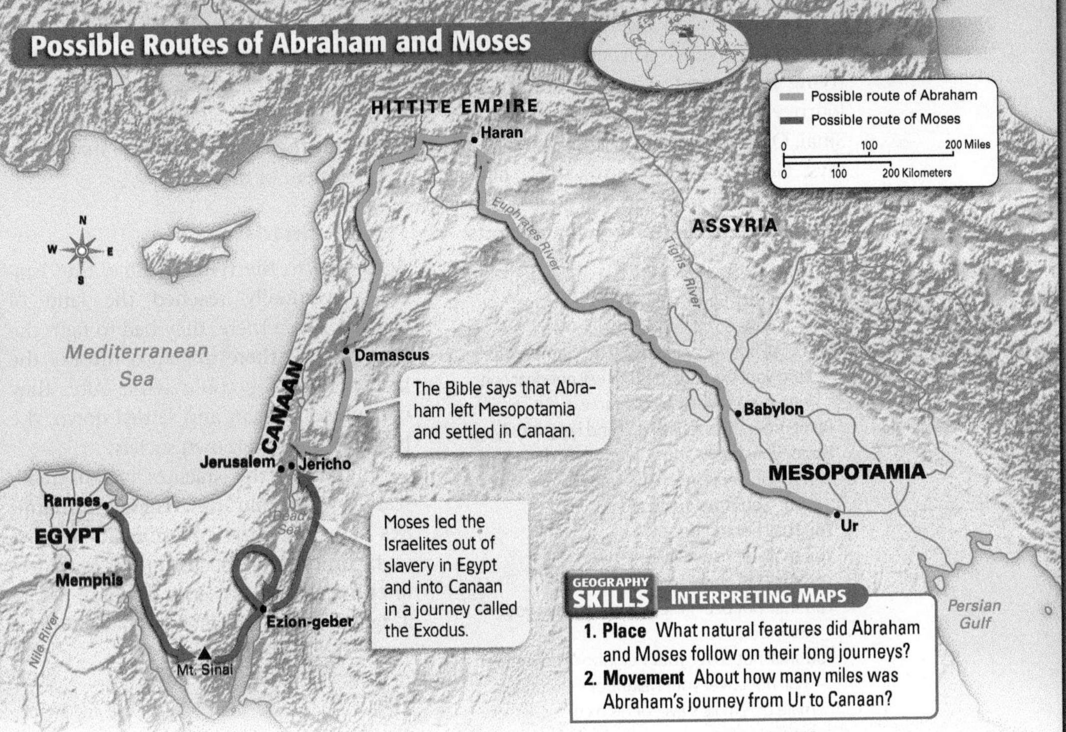

Abraham left Mesopotamia and settled in Canaan (KAY-nuhn), on the Mediterranean Sea. Some of his descendants, the Israelites, lived in Canaan for many years. Later, however, some Israelites moved to Egypt, perhaps because of famine in Canaan.

The Israelites lived well in Egypt, and their population grew. This growth worried Egypt's ruler, the pharaoh. He feared that the Israelites might soon become too powerful. To stop this from happening, the pharaoh made the Israelites slaves.

The Exodus

According to the Hebrew Bible, a leader named **Moses** appeared among the Israelites in Egypt. In the 1200s BC, God told Moses to lead the Israelites out of Egypt. Moses went to the pharaoh and demanded that the Israelites be freed. The pharaoh refused. Soon afterward a series of terrible plagues, or disasters, struck Egypt.

The plagues frightened the pharaoh so much that he agreed to free the Israelites. Overjoyed with the news of their release, Moses led his people out of Egypt in a journey called the **Exodus**. To the Israelites, the release from slavery proved that God was protecting and watching over them. They believed that they had been set free because God loved them.

The Exodus is a major event in Jewish history, but other people recognize its significance as well. Throughout history, for example, enslaved people have found hope in the story. Before the Civil War, American slaves sang about Moses to keep their hopes of freedom alive.

Direct Teach

Main Idea

1 Abraham and Moses Lead Their People

Abraham and Moses led their people to Canaan and to a new religion.

Identify According to the Bible, who was Abraham, and where did he move? *the man to whom the Bible traces the Hebrews; Canaan*

Sequence Briefly trace the events that led to the Exodus. *According to the Bible, in the 1200s BC, God told a leader named Moses to demand that the pharaoh free the Israelites enslaved in Egypt. After a series of plagues struck, the pharaoh agreed. Moses then led the Israelites out of Egypt in the Exodus.*

Map Transparency: Possible Routes of Abraham and Moses

Interpreting Maps

Possible Routes of Abraham and Moses

Activity Comparing Maps Display a current wall map of the region in the map at left. Have students determine the modern countries in which the following cities in the textbook map are located: Babylon, Haran, Jerusalem, and Ur. *(Babylon—Iraq; Haran—Turkey; Jerusalem—Israel; Ur—Iraq).*

LS Visual/Spatial

Map Transparency: Possible Routes of Abraham and Moses

Critical Thinking: Comparing and Contrasting

At Level

Abraham and Moses Venn Diagram

1. To help students compare and contrast the significance of Abraham and Moses in Jewish history and to the development of Judaism, draw the graphic organizer for students to see. Omit the blue, italicized answers.
2. Have students copy and complete the graphic organizer. Instruct students to refer to the part of the text titled "Abraham and Moses Lead Their People" to complete the activity. **LS Visual/Spatial**

Abraham
- lived in Mesopotamia
- *told by God to move to Canaan*
- *received God's promise that his descendants would become a mighty nation*

Both
- *significant person in Jewish history*
- *directed and spoken to by God*
- *led a major migration*

Moses
- lived in Egypt
- *told by God to gain freedom of Israelite slaves and lead them from Egypt*
- *received Ten Commandments from God on Mt. Sinai*

Answers

Interpreting Maps 1. *waterways, such as rivers and seas;* **2.** *about 1,200 miles*

Direct Teach

Main Idea

1 Abraham and Moses Lead Their People

Abraham and Moses led their people to Canaan and to a new religion.

Recall According to the Hebrew Bible, what code of moral laws did God give to Moses on Mt. Sinai? *the Ten Commandments*

Explain How did the Ten Commandments shape Israelite life? *The Israelites agreed to worship only God and to value human life, self-control, and justice.*

Draw Conclusions Why do you think Moses led the Israelites to Canaan? *possible answers—Canaan was where Abraham had settled.*

Activity Paraphrasing Have students use modern-day language to paraphrase the Ten Commandments.
LS Verbal/Linguistic

Reading Time Lines

Early Hebrew History

Activity Ask volunteers to use the entries and images in the time line to summarize the key events in the early history of the Hebrews. **LS Verbal/Linguistic**

For many years after their release, the Israelites traveled through the desert, trying to return to Canaan. During their journey they reached a mountain called Sinai. On that mountain, the Hebrew Bible says, God gave Moses two stone tablets. On the tablets was written a code of moral laws known as the **Ten Commandments**:

> "I the Lord am your God who brought you out of the land of Egypt, the house of bondage: You shall have no other gods besides Me. . . .
> You shall not swear falsely by the name of the Lord your God; for the Lord will not clear one who swears falsely by His name.
> Remember the sabbath day and keep it holy. . . .
> Honor your father and your mother, that you may long endure on the land that the Lord your God is assigning to you.
> You shall not murder.
> You shall not commit adultery.
> You shall not steal.
> You shall not bear false witness against your neighbor.
> You shall not covet your neighbor's house: you shall not covet your neighbor's wife, or his male or female slave, or his ox or his ass, or anything that is your neighbor's."
>
> —Exodus 20:2–14

As you can see, by accepting the Ten Commandments, the Israelites agreed to worship only God. They also agreed to value human life, self-control, and justice. Over time the commandments shaped the development of their society.

The Return to Canaan

According to the Hebrew Bible, the Israelites eventually reached the land of Canaan. Once there, they had to fight the people living there to gain control of the land before they could settle. After they conquered Canaan and settled down, the Israelites built their own society.

In Canaan, the Israelites lived in small, scattered communities. These communities had no central government. Instead, each community selected judges as leaders to enforce laws and settle disputes. Before long, though, a threat arose that called for a new kind of leadership.

READING CHECK Identifying Cause and Effect Why did Abraham leave Mesopotamia?

Time Line

Early Hebrew History

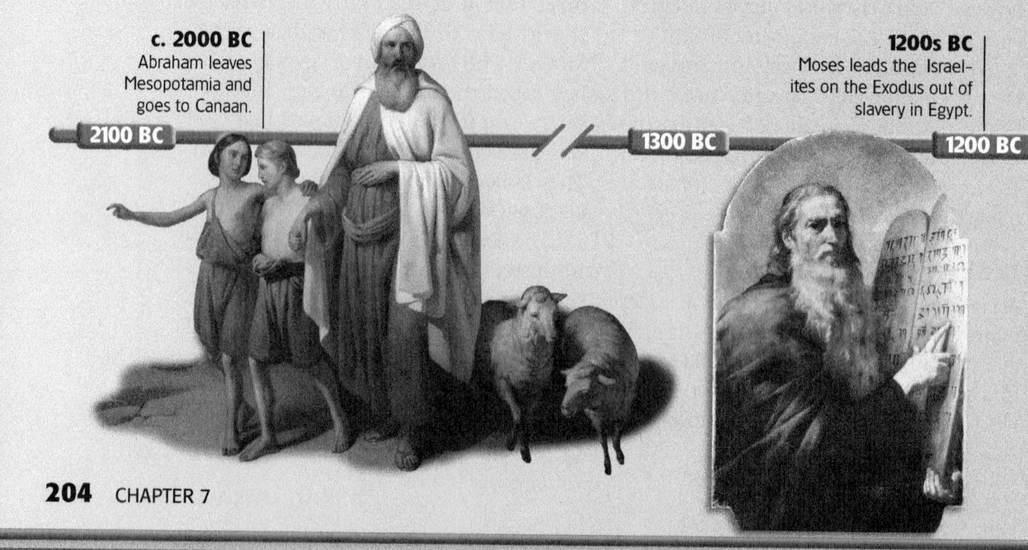
c. 2000 BC
Abraham leaves Mesopotamia and goes to Canaan.
2100 BC
1300 BC
1200s BC
Moses leads the Israelites on the Exodus out of slavery in Egypt.
1200 BC

Differentiating Instruction

English-Language Learners At Level

Vocabulary for the Ten Commandments

To help English learners with the vocabulary in and associated with the Ten Commandments, preteach the following terms:

- **adultery** sexual relations between a married person and someone to whom he or she is not married
- **envious** wanting what someone else has
- **holy** sacred; set apart; spiritually perfect
- **Sabbath** day of rest and prayer
- **tablet** thick, flat piece of stone for engraving
- **testify** give evidence; tell to a court of law
- **vain** without purpose or meaning
- **witness** onlooker; observer

LS Verbal/Linguistic

Universal Access Resources

See p. 197c of the Chapter Planner for additional resources for differentiating instruction for universal access.

Answers

Reading Check *According to the Bible, God told Abraham to leave and move to a new land—Canaan.*

Kings Unite the Israelites

The new threat to the Israelites came from the Philistines (FI-li-steenz), who lived along the Mediterranean coast. In the mid-1000s BC the Philistines invaded the Israelites' lands.

Frightened by these powerful invaders, the Israelites banded together under a single ruler who could lead them in battle. That ruler was a man named Saul, who became the first king of Israel. Saul had some success as a military commander, but he wasn't a strong king. He never won the total support of tribal and religious leaders. They often fought against his decisions.

King David

After Saul died, a man once declared an outlaw became king. That king's name was **David**. As a young man, David had been a shepherd. The Hebrew Bible tells how David slew the Philistine giant Goliath, which brought him to the attention of the king. David was admired for his military skills and as a poet; many of the Psalms are attributed to him. For many years, David lived in the desert, gathering support from local people. When Saul died, David used this support to become king.

Unlike Saul, David was well loved by the Israelites. He won the full support of Israel's tribal leaders. David defeated the Philistines and fought and won wars against many other peoples of Canaan. He established the capital of Israel in Jerusalem.

King Solomon

David's son **Solomon** (SAHL-uh-muhn) took the throne in about 965 BC. Like his father, Solomon was a strong king. He expanded the kingdom and made nearby kingdoms, including Egypt and Phoenicia, his allies. Trade with these allies made Israel very rich. With these riches, Solomon built a great temple to God in Jerusalem. This temple became the center of the Israelites' religious life and a symbol of their faith.

FOCUS ON READING Are the sentences in this paragraph facts or opinions? How can you tell?

READING CHECK **Finding Main Ideas** Why did the Israelites unite under a king?

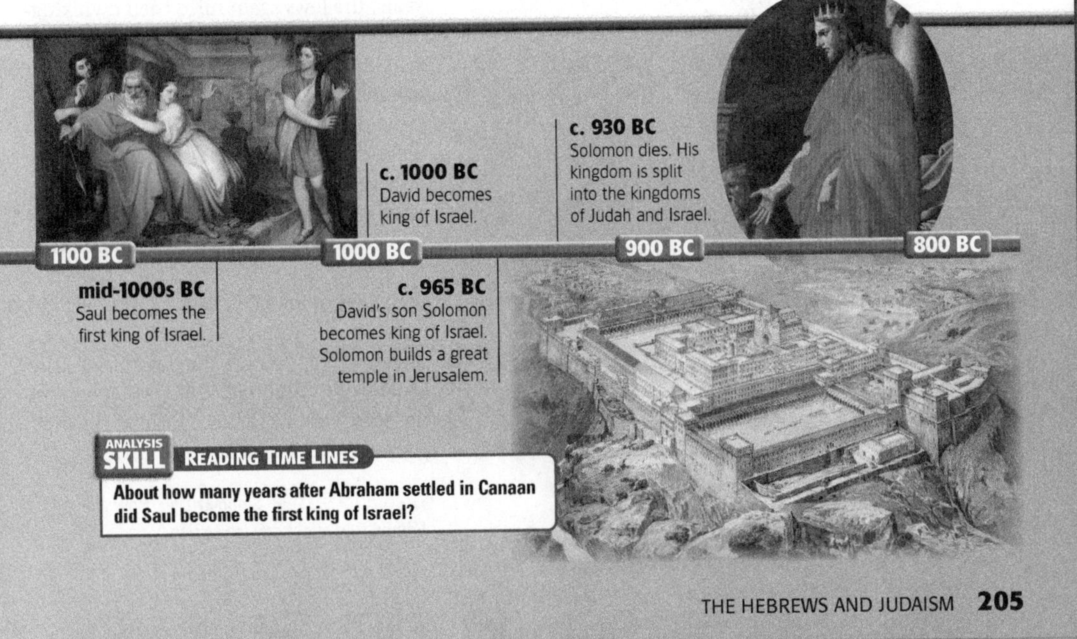

c. 1000 BC David becomes king of Israel.

c. 930 BC Solomon dies. His kingdom is split into the kingdoms of Judah and Israel.

mid-1000s BC Saul becomes the first king of Israel.

c. 965 BC David's son Solomon becomes king of Israel. Solomon builds a great temple in Jerusalem.

ANALYSIS SKILL **READING TIME LINES**

About how many years after Abraham settled in Canaan did Saul become the first king of Israel?

Direct Teach

Main Idea

❷ Kings Unite the Israelites

Strong kings united the Israelites to fight off invaders.

Recall How did the Israelites respond to the Philistine invasion? *chose a king to lead them in battle*

Explain Why is David significant in the history of Judaism? *first king of Israel to gain full support of tribal and religious leaders; established capital at Jerusalem*

Evaluate Who do you think was the greater king, David or Solomon? Why? *possible answers—David, because he was the first king to gain full support; well loved; Solomon, because he expanded kingdom and its wealth; built a temple to God*

CRF: Biography Activity: King Solomon

Info to Know

The Philistines The Philistines were a seafaring people. They arrived in Canaan in the 1100s BC and settled in the south along the Mediterranean coast. The Philistines had superior weapons to the Israelites and were a serious threat until David defeated them. The modern name *Palestine* comes from Greek and Latin words for the Philistines.

Critical Thinking: Summarizing

At Level

Three Kings of Israel Graphic Organizer

Materials: gold or yellow construction paper; colored markers or pens

1. Provide each student with a sheet of construction paper. Have each student draw three large crowns on the paper.
2. Tell students to label the crowns *Saul, David,* and *Solomon*. Students should leave enough room in each crown to write four to six lines of additional text.
3. In each crown, have students list the main characteristics and achievements of the named king.
4. Last, have students write a slogan or catch phrase that sums up the importance or significance of each king. **LS Verbal/Linguistic, Visual/Spatial**

Alternative Assessment Handbook, Rubric 13: Graphic Organizers

Answers

Focus on Reading *facts, because they can be verified*

Reading Time Lines *about 950 years*

Reading Check *The Israelites needed a single ruler to help them band together against the invading Philistines.*

Direct Teach

Main Idea

❸ Invaders Conquer and Rule

Invaders conquered and ruled the Jews after their kingdom broke apart.

Identify Causes What events led to the Diaspora? *Persians conquered the Chaldeans and let the Jews return to Jerusalem. But many Jews instead moved to other parts of the Persian Empire.*

Analyze Patterns Looking at Jewish history from Abraham to the Roman conquest in 63 BC, what patterns do you see? *patterns of migration, enslavement, and warfare/conquest*

Map Transparency: Kingdoms of Israel and Judah, c. 920 BC

hmhsocialstudies.com

Online Resources

Activity: Connections to Today

About the Illustration

The illustration of Naomi and Ruth on the facing page is an artist's conception based on available sources. However, historians are uncertain exactly what Naomi and Ruth looked like.

Invaders Conquer and Rule

After Solomon's death in about 930 BC, revolts broke out over who should be king. Within a year, conflict tore Israel apart. Israel split into two kingdoms called Israel and called Judah (JOO-duh). The people of Judah became known as Jews.

The two new kingdoms lasted for a few centuries. In the end, however, both were conquered. The Assyrians defeated Israel around 722 BC. As a result, the kingdom fell apart and most of its people scattered. Judah lasted longer, but before long it was defeated by the Chaldeans.

Kingdoms of Israel and Judah, c. 920 BC

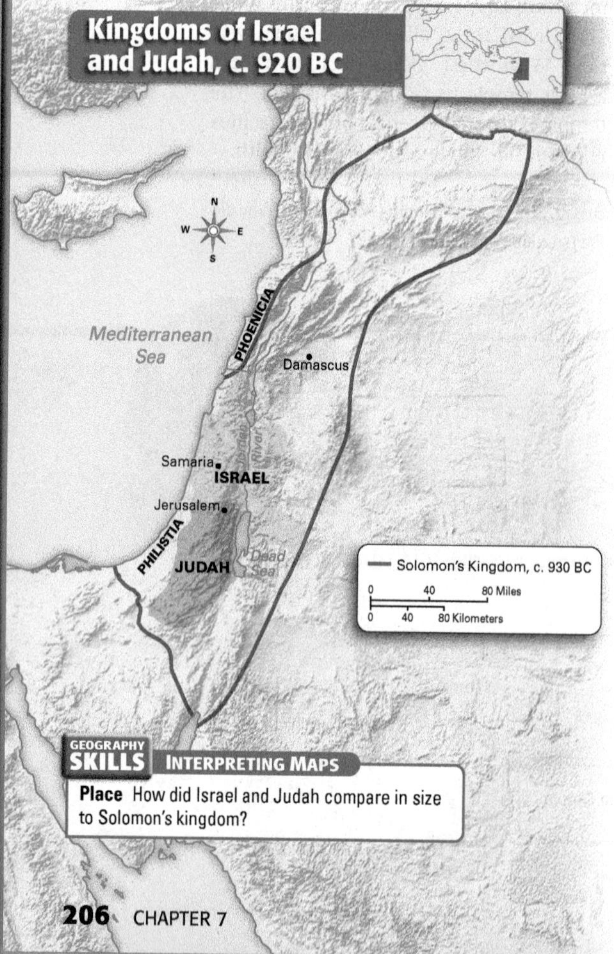

GEOGRAPHY SKILLS INTERPRETING MAPS

Place How did Israel and Judah compare in size to Solomon's kingdom?

The Dispersal of the Jews

The Chaldeans captured Jerusalem and destroyed Solomon's Temple in 586 BC. They marched thousands of Jews to their capital, Babylon, to work as slaves. The Jews called this enslavement the Babylonian Captivity. It lasted about 50 years.

In the 530s BC a people called the Persians conquered the Chaldeans and let the Jews return to Jerusalem. But many never took this opportunity to return home. Instead, they moved to other parts of the Persian Empire. Scholars call the dispersal of the Jews outside of Israel and Judah the **Diaspora** (dy-AS-pruh).

The rest of the Jews did return home to Jerusalem. There they rebuilt Solomon's Temple, which became known as the Second Temple. The Jews remained under Persian control until the 330s BC, when the Persians were conquered by invaders.

Independence and Conquest

Tired of foreign rule, a Jewish family called the Maccabees (MA-kuh-beez) led a successful revolt in the 160s BC. For about 100 years, the Jews again ruled their own kingdom. Their independence, however, didn't last. In 63 BC the Jews were conquered again, this time by the Romans.

Although Jewish leaders added to the Second Temple under Roman rule, life was difficult. Heavy taxes burdened the people. The Romans were brutal masters who had no respect for the Jewish religion and way of life.

Some rulers tried to force the Jews to worship the Roman Emperor. The Roman rulers even appointed the high priests, the leaders of the Temple. This was more than the Jews could bear. They called on their people to rebel against the Romans.

READING CHECK **Summarizing** How did Roman rule affect Jewish society?

Social Studies Skill Activity: Using Time Lines

At Level

Later Hebrew History Time Line

Materials: butcher paper or poster board

1. Have students examine the time line "Early Hebrew History" located on the previous two pages. Point out how the time line includes entries only for key events.
2. Have students work individually or in small groups to create a similar illustrated time line for the events in the material titled "Invaders Conquer and Rule."
3. When students are finished, ask volunteers to indicate some of the events they selected and to explain why they chose them.
4. Have students discuss which events they included were the most significant and why.

LS Visual/Spatial

SE Social Studies Skills: Interpreting Time Lines, p. 344

Alternative Assessment Handbook, Rubric 36: Time Lines

Answers

Interpreting Maps *Each was only a small part of Solomon's kingdom.*

Reading Check *Jewish society experienced many great advances, such as in religious education. However, the Jews were still unhappy with Roman rule.*

Women in Israelite Society

Israelite government and society were dominated by men, as were most ancient societies. Women had few rights. They had to obey their fathers and their husbands. A woman couldn't even choose her own husband. Instead, her husband was chosen by her father. A woman couldn't inherit property either, unless she had no brothers. If she did have a brother, all property went to him.

Some Israelite and Jewish women, however, made great contributions to their society. The Hebrew Bible describes them. Some were political and military leaders, such as Queen Esther and the judge Deborah. According to the Hebrew Bible, these women saved their people from their enemies. Other women, such as Miriam, the sister of Moses, were spiritual leaders.

Some women in the Hebrew Bible were seen as examples of how Israelite and Jewish women should behave. For example, Ruth, who left her people to care for her mother-in-law, was seen as a model of devotion to one's family. Ruth's story was told as an example of how people should treat their family members.

READING CHECK **Generalizing** What was life like for most Israelite women?

BIOGRAPHY

Ruth and Naomi

The story of Ruth and Naomi comes from the Book of Ruth, one of the books of the Hebrew Bible. According to this account, Ruth was not an Israelite, though her husband was. After he died, Ruth and her mother-in-law, Naomi, resettled in Israel. Inspired by Naomi's faith in God, Ruth joined Naomi's family and adopted her beliefs. She dedicated her life to supporting Naomi.

Drawing Inferences What lessons might the story of Ruth be used to teach?

SUMMARY AND PREVIEW The history of the Hebrews and their ancestors began some 3,500 to 4,000 years ago. The instructions that Jews believe God gave to the early Hebrews and Israelites shaped their religion, Judaism. In the next section, you will learn about the main teachings of Judaism.

Section 1 Assessment

hmhsocialstudies.com
ONLINE QUIZ

Reviewing Ideas, Terms, and People

1. a. **Identify** Who was **Abraham**?
   b. **Evaluate** Why was the **Exodus** a significant event in Israelite history?
2. **Summarize** How did **David** and **Solomon** strengthen the kingdom of Israel?
3. **Describe** What happened during the Babylonian Captivity?
4. a. **Describe** Who had more rights in Israelite society, men or women?
   b. **Make Inferences** How did Ruth and Naomi set an example for other Israelites?

Critical Thinking

5. **Evaluating** Review your notes on the chapter. In a chart like this one, note the contributions of the four most important people.

Key Figure	Contribution

FOCUS ON WRITING

6. **Taking Notes about Early Hebrew History** Make a list of events and people that played key roles in Hebrew and Israelite history. Look for ways to group your facts into features on your Web page.

Direct Teach

Main Idea

4 Women in Israelite Society

Some women in Israelite and Jewish society made great contributions to their history.

Identify Why is Ruth significant in Jewish history? *Her devotion to her mother-in-law served as a model for how to treat family.*

Summarize How could Israelite and Jewish women gain power in their society? *by becoming political, military, or spiritual leaders*

CRF: Biography Activity: Esther

Review & Assess

Close

Ask students to discuss what they think was the most important event in early Hebrew history. Remind students to provide reasons to support their point of view.

Review

Online Quiz, Section 1

Assess

SE Section 1 Assessment

PASS: Section 1 Quiz

Alternative Assessment Handbook

Reteach/Classroom Intervention

Guided Reading Workbook, Section 1

Interactive Skills Tutor CD-ROM

Section 1 Assessment Answers

1. a. The man to which the Hebrew Bible traces back Hebrew ancestry.
   b. Israelites believed it proved God loved and was protecting them.
2. They ruled with the full support of tribal leaders, conquered enemies, and added land.
3. The Chaldeans captured Jerusalem, destroyed Solomon's Temple, and enslaved many Jews.
4. a. men, because Israelite women had to obey their fathers and husbands
   b. Ruth's devotion to Naomi served as a model for how to treat family members.
5. Abraham—Hebrew ancestor; Moses—led Exodus; David—king; Solomon—king who built temple; Ruth—see 4.b.
6. people—see Answer 5 above; events—Abraham's move to Canaan; Exodus and Ten Commandments; kings and Solomon's Temple; split of kingdom; Babylonian Captivity and Diaspora; Roman conquest

Answers

Biography *lessons about how people should be devoted to family*

Reading Check *Most women had few rights and had to obey their fathers and husbands, but some Hebrew women made great contributions to their society.*

Direct Teach

Bellringer

If YOU were there . . . Use the **Daily Bellringer Transparency** to help students answer the question.

Daily Bellringer Transparency, Section 2

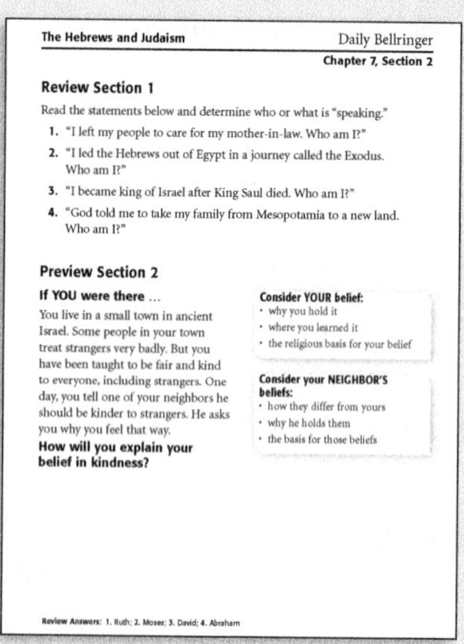

The Hebrews and Judaism — Daily Bellringer — **Chapter 7, Section 2**

Review Section 1

Read the statements below and determine who or what is "speaking."

1. "I left my people to care for my mother-in-law. Who am I?"
2. "I led the Hebrews out of Egypt in a journey called the Exodus. Who am I?"
3. "I became king of Israel after King Saul died. Who am I?"
4. "God told me to take my family from Mesopotamia to a new land. Who am I?"

Preview Section 2

If YOU were there ...

You live in a small town in ancient Israel. Some people in your town treat strangers very badly. But you have been taught to be fair and kind to everyone, including strangers. One day, you tell one of your neighbors he should be kinder to strangers. He asks you why you feel that way.

How will you explain your belief in kindness?

Consider YOUR belief:
- why you hold it
- where you learned it
- the religious basis for your belief

Consider your NEIGHBOR'S beliefs:
- how they differ from yours
- why he holds them
- the basis for those beliefs

Review Answers: 1. Ruth; 2. Moses; 3. David; 4. Abraham

Academic Vocabulary

Review with students the high-use academic term in this section.

principles basic beliefs, rules, or laws (p. 210)

CRF: Vocabulary Builder Activity, Section 2

Taking Notes

Have students use the graphic organizer online to take notes on the section. This activity will prepare students for the Section Assessment, in which they will complete a graphic organizer that builds on the information using the Critical Thinking Skill: Finding Main Ideas.

SECTION 2

Jewish Beliefs and Texts

What You Will Learn...

Main Ideas

1. Beliefs in God, education, justice, and obedience anchor Jewish society.
2. Jewish beliefs are listed in the Torah, the Hebrew Bible, and the Commentaries.
3. The Dead Sea Scrolls reveal many past Jewish beliefs.
4. The ideas of Judaism have helped shape later cultures.

The Big Idea

The central ideas and laws of Judaism are contained in sacred texts such as the Torah.

Key Terms

monotheism, *p. 208*
Torah, *p. 210*
synagogue, *p. 210*
prophets, *p. 211*
Talmud, *p. 212*
Dead Sea Scrolls, *p. 212*

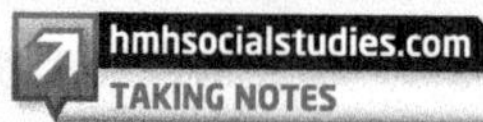

Use the graphic organizer online to record notes on Jewish beliefs and texts.

If YOU were there...

You live in a small town in ancient Israel. Some people in your town treat strangers very badly. But you have been taught to be fair and kind to everyone, including strangers. One day, you tell one of your neighbors he should be kinder to strangers. He asks you why you feel that way.

How will you explain your belief in kindness?

BUILDING BACKGROUND The idea that people should be fair and kind to everyone in the community is an important Jewish teaching. Sometimes, their teachings set the Jews apart from other people in society. But at the same time, their shared beliefs tie all Jews together as a religious community.

Jewish Beliefs Anchor Their Society

Religion is the foundation upon which the Jews base their whole society. In fact, much of Jewish culture is based directly on Jewish beliefs. The central beliefs of Judaism are beliefs in God, education, justice, and obedience.

Belief in One God

Most importantly, Jews believe in one God. The Hebrew name for God is YHWH, which is never pronounced by Jews, as it is considered too holy. The belief in only one God is called **monotheism**. Many people believe that Judaism was the world's first monotheistic religion. It is certainly the oldest such religion that is still widely practiced today.

In the ancient world where most people worshipped many gods, the Jews' worship of only God set them apart. This worship also shaped Jewish society. The Jews believed that God had guided their history through his relationships with Abraham, Moses, and other leaders.

208

Teach the Big Idea

At Level

Jewish Beliefs and Texts

1. **Teach** Ask students the questions in the Main Idea boxes to teach this section.
2. **Apply** Draw a four-column chart for students to see. Title the chart *Judaism* and label the columns *Central Beliefs, Sacred Texts, Dead Sea Scrolls,* and *Influence*. Have each student make a copy of the chart and complete it by listing the main ideas and events for each topic based on this section. **LS Verbal/Linguistic**
3. **Review** To review the section's main ideas, have students help you complete a master copy of the chart.
4. **Practice/Homework** For each topic in the chart, have students write one to three sentences summarizing the information in that column. **LS Verbal/Linguistic**

Alternative Assessment Handbook, Rubrics 7: Charts; and 37: Writing Assignments

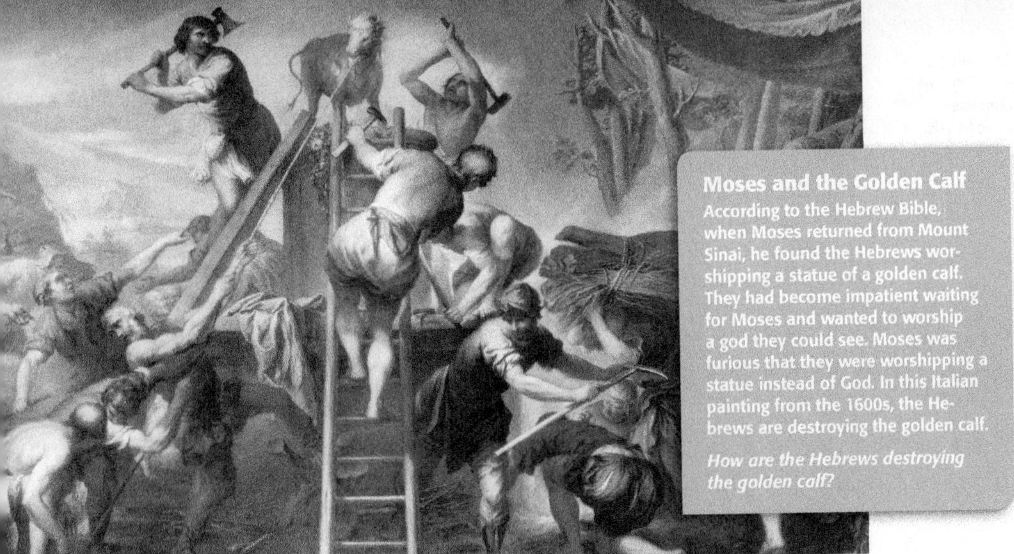

Moses and the Golden Calf
According to the Hebrew Bible, when Moses returned from Mount Sinai, he found the Hebrews worshipping a statue of a golden calf. They had become impatient waiting for Moses and wanted to worship a god they could see. Moses was furious that they were worshipping a statue instead of God. In this Italian painting from the 1600s, the Hebrews are destroying the golden calf.

How are the Hebrews destroying the golden calf?

Belief in Education

Another central element of Judaism is education and study. Teaching children the basics of Judaism has always been important in Jewish society. In ancient Jewish communities, older boys—but not girls—studied with professional teachers to learn their religion. Even today, education and study are central to Jewish life.

Justice and Righteousness

Also central to the Jews' religion are the ideas of justice and righteousness. To Jews, justice means kindness and fairness in dealing with other people. Everyone deserves justice, even strangers and criminals. Jews are expected to give aid to those who need it, including the poor, the sick, and orphans. Jews are also expected to be fair in business dealings.

Righteousness refers to doing what is proper. Jews are supposed to behave properly, even if others around them do not. For the Jews, righteous behavior is more important than formal ceremonies.

Observance of Religious and Moral Law

Observance of the law is closely related to justice and righteousness. Moral and religious laws have guided Jews through their history and continue to do so today. Jews believe that God gave them these laws to follow.

The most important Jewish laws are the Ten Commandments. The commandments, however, are only part of Jewish law. Jews believe that Moses recorded a whole system of laws that God had set down for them to obey. Named for Moses, this system is called Mosaic law.

Like the Ten Commandments, Mosaic laws guide many areas of Jews' daily lives. For example, Mosaic law governs how people pray and celebrate holidays. The laws forbid Jews to work on holidays or on the Sabbath, the seventh day of each week. The Sabbath is a day of rest because, in Jewish tradition, God created the world in six days and rested on the seventh. The Jewish Sabbath begins at sundown Friday and ends at nightfall Saturday, the seventh day of the week.

Direct Teach

Main Idea

❶ Jewish Beliefs Anchor Their Society

Beliefs in God, education, justice, and obedience anchor Jewish society.

Recall What is monotheism, and why did this belief set the ancient Hebrews apart? *a belief in only one God; most people in the ancient world worshipped many gods.*

Explain What is the Jewish view of justice and righteousness? *Justice means to treat all people kindly and fairly, and righteousness refers to doing what is proper.*

Draw Conclusions Why do you think that education and study are so important in Judaism? *Jews must learn about their religion and must learn to read and follow the laws.*

 **CRF:** Primary Source Activity: Mosaic Law and Punishments

Info to Know

Shabbat The Hebrew word for Sabbath is Shabbat. Shabbat begins at sunset on Friday evening and ends at nightfall on Saturday once three stars are visible in the sky.

Critical Thinking: Finding Main Ideas

Below Level

Central Beliefs of Judaism Poster

Materials: poster board, art supplies, markers

1. Have students identify and describe the four central beliefs of Judaism *(beliefs in God, education and study, justice and righteousness, and obedience and law)*. List the beliefs where students can see them.
2. Have each student create a poster identifying and describing the central beliefs of Judaism.
3. Encourage students to illustrate and decorate their posters. In addition, have each student write a paragraph summarizing how the central beliefs of Judaism shape Jewish life.
4. Display students' posters in the classroom. **LS Visual/Spatial**

Alternative Assessment Handbook, Rubric 28: Posters

Answers

Moses and the Golden Calf *They are using axes and sledgehammers to break the calf apart while preparing a fire to melt the pieces.*

Direct Teach

Main Idea

❷ Texts List Jewish Beliefs

Jewish beliefs are listed in the Torah, the Hebrew Bible, and the Commentaries.

Define What is the Torah? *most sacred text of Judaism; five books of laws as well as a history of the Jews until the death of Moses*

Recall What are the three parts of the Hebrew Bible? *Torah; eight books of messages of prophets; 11 books of poetry, songs, stories, lessons, and history*

Draw Conclusions Why do Jews consider the Torah the most sacred text of Judaism? *because the Torah contains the laws that Jews believe God set down for them to follow, and because it affirms their participation in the continuity of the Jewish people from ancient times to the present.*

CRF: Literature Activity: The Creation Story, from the Torah

Info to Know

Torah Scrolls The Torah is also known as the Chumash or the Five Books of Moses. Torah scrolls are made from kosher animal parchment. The text of the scriptures are then handwritten on the scroll. When not being read, Torah scrolls are covered with fabric and stored in a special cabinet called an ark.

ACADEMIC VOCABULARY
principles basic beliefs, rules, or laws

Among the Mosaic laws are rules about the foods that Jews can eat and rules that must be followed in preparing them. For example, the laws state that Jews cannot eat pork or shellfish, which are thought to be unclean. Other laws say that meat has to be killed and prepared in a way that makes it acceptable for Jews to eat. Today foods that have been so prepared are called kosher (KOH-shuhr), or fit.

In many Jewish communities today, people still strictly follow Mosaic law. They are called Orthodox Jews. Other Jews choose not to follow many of the ancient laws. They are known as Reform Jews. A third group, the Conservative Jews, falls between the other two groups. These are the three largest groups of Jews in the world today.

READING CHECK **Generalizing** What are the most important beliefs of Judaism?

Texts List Jewish Beliefs

The laws and **principles** of Judaism are described in several sacred texts, or writings. Among the main texts are the Torah, the Hebrew Bible, and the Commentaries.

The Torah

The ancient Jews recorded most of their laws in five books. Together these books are called the **Torah**, the most sacred text of Judaism. In addition to laws, the Torah includes a history of the Jews until the death of Moses.

Readings from the Torah are central to Jewish religious services today. Nearly every **synagogue** (SI-nuh-gawg), or Jewish house of worship, has at least one Torah. Out of respect for the Torah, readers do not touch it. They use special pointers to mark their places in the text.

Hebrew Texts

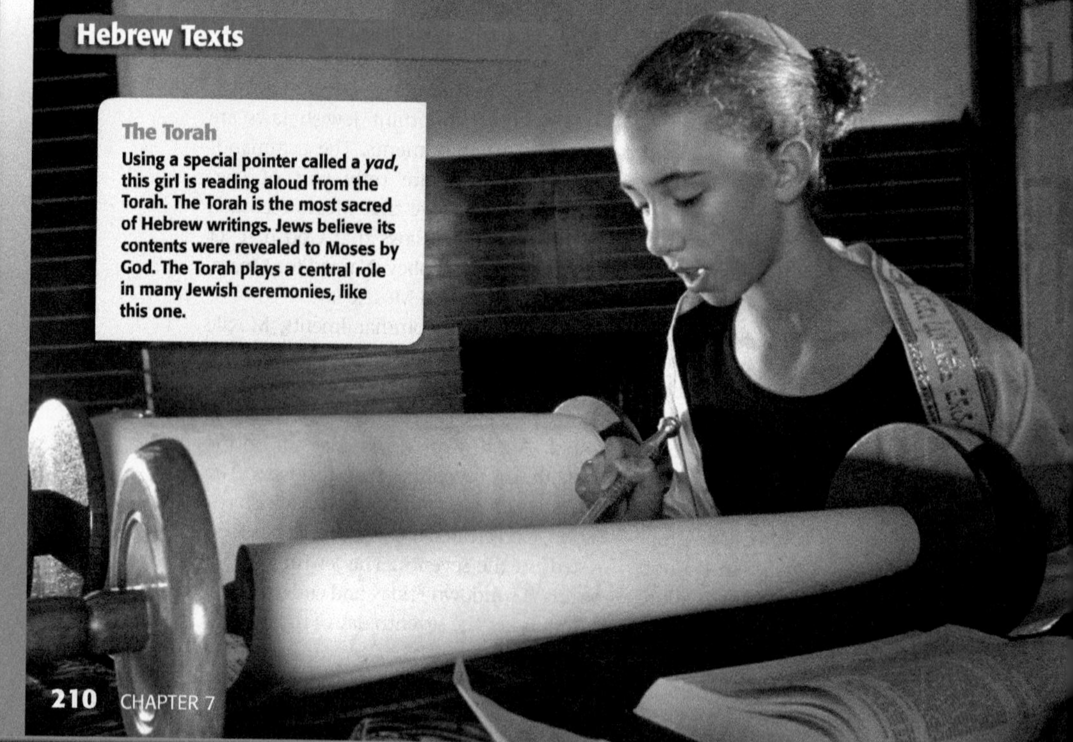

The Torah
Using a special pointer called a *yad*, this girl is reading aloud from the Torah. The Torah is the most sacred of Hebrew writings. Jews believe its contents were revealed to Moses by God. The Torah plays a central role in many Jewish ceremonies, like this one.

Collaborative Learning

At Level
Prep Required

Jewish Sacred Texts Scrolls

Materials: butcher paper, wooden rods, art supplies

1. Have students identify and describe the main sacred texts of Judaism *(the Torah, Hebrew Bible, and Commentaries).*
2. Organize students into small groups. Give each group a strip of butcher paper and two wooden rods. Students will use the materials to create scrolls.
3. Have each group create a scroll describing the sacred texts of Judaism. Encourage students to illustrate and decorate their scrolls. If time allows, have students conduct research to include additional information.
4. Display the scrolls around the classroom.
LS Interpersonal, Kinesthetic

Alternative Assessment Handbook, Rubrics 3: Artwork; and 14: Group Activity

Answers

Reading Check *beliefs in one God, education and study, justice and righteousness, and obedience and law*

The Hebrew Bible

The Torah is the first of three parts of a group of writings called the Hebrew Bible, or Tanakh (tah-NAHK). The second part is made up of eight books that describe the messages of Jewish prophets. **Prophets** are people who are said to receive messages from God to be taught to others.

The final part of the Hebrew Bible is 11 books of poetry, songs, stories, lessons, and history. For example, the Book of Daniel tells about a prophet named Daniel, who lived during the Babylonian Captivity. According to the book, Daniel angered the king who held the Jews as slaves. As punishment, the king had Daniel thrown into a den of lions. The story tells that Daniel's faith in God kept the lions from killing him, and he was released. Jews tell this story to show the power of faith.

Also in the final part of the Hebrew Bible are the Proverbs, short expressions of Jewish wisdom. Many of these sayings are attributed to Israelite leaders, especially King Solomon. For example, Solomon is supposed to have said, "A good name is to be chosen rather than great riches." In other words, it is better to be seen as a good person than to be rich and not respected.

The third part of the Hebrew Bible also includes the Book of Psalms. Psalms are poems or songs of praise to God. Many of these are attributed to King David. One of the most famous psalms is the Twenty-third Psalm. It includes lines often read today during times of difficulty:

> "The Lord is my shepherd; I lack nothing.
> He makes me lie down in green pastures;
> He leads me to water in places of repose;
> He renews my life;
> He guides me in right paths as befits His name."
>
> —Psalms 23:1–3

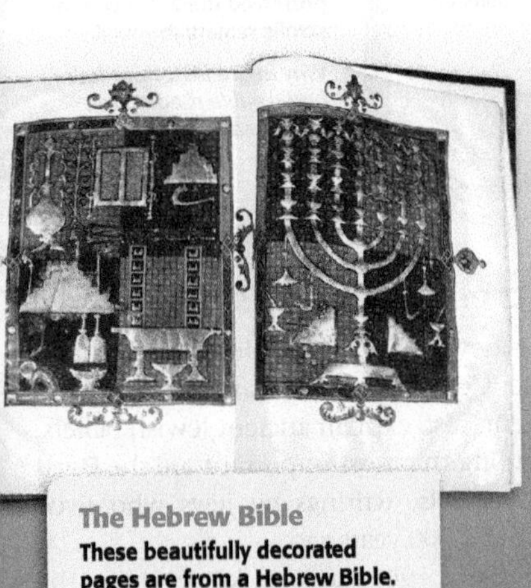

The Hebrew Bible

These beautifully decorated pages are from a Hebrew Bible. The Hebrew Bible, sometimes called the Tanakh, includes the Torah and other ancient writings.

The Commentaries

The Talmud is a collection of commentaries and discussions about the Torah and the Hebrew Bible. The Talmud is a rich source of information for discussion and debate. Rabbis and religious scholars like these young men study the Talmud to learn about Jewish history and laws.

ANALYSIS SKILL ANALYZING VISUALS

How does the Torah look different from the Hebrew Bible and the commentaries?

Direct Teach

Info to Know

The Tanach Jews refer to the Hebrew Bible as Tanakh. This term is an acronym made from the letters of the three parts of the Hebrew Bible—Torah, Nevi'im (Prophets), and Ketuvim (Writings).

Did you know . . .

The Torah has a total of 613 commandments. According to Jewish tradition, the pomegranate fruit has 613 seeds. Pomegranates, which are common in the region of Israel, are one of the traditional foods eaten during the Jewish New Year, called Rosh Hashanah.

Analyzing Visuals

Hebrew Texts

Yarmulke The small round hats the two men are wearing in the photo at left are called yarmulke, or kippah (key-pah) in Hebrew. Ancient Jews covered their heads when praying to show respect for God. Over time, the yarmulke became the customary choice of head covering for Jews.

Activity **Jewish Symbols** Have students conduct research on other symbols or items connected with Judaism or Israel, such as the menorah or the Star of David. Have students orally present their findings to the class.

LS Verbal/Linguistic

Alternative Assessment Handbook, Rubric 24: Oral Presentations

Differentiating Instruction

English-Language Learners

At Level

Word Mapping Have students work in mixed-ability pairs to create word maps for the following terms: *Commentaries, justice, monotheism, prophets, proverbs, principles, righteousness, Sabbath, synagogue, Talmud, Tanakh,* and *Torah.* Each word map should provide the term's definition, a sentence using the term, and one to three related words or ideas. A sample word map is shown here.

LS Verbal/Linguistic, Visual/Spatial

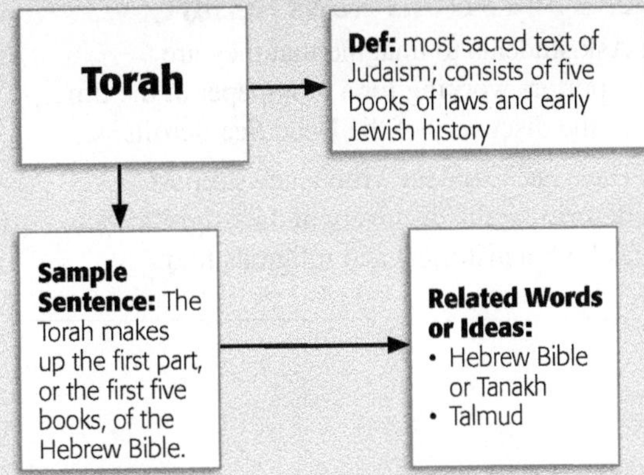

Torah
Def: most sacred text of Judaism; consists of five books of laws and early Jewish history
Sample Sentence: The Torah makes up the first part, or the first five books, of the Hebrew Bible.
Related Words or Ideas:
• Hebrew Bible or Tanakh
• Talmud

Answers

Analyzing Visuals *The Torah is a large scroll, whereas both the Hebrew Bible and the Commentaries are in bound book form.*

Direct Teach

Main Idea

3 Scrolls Reveal Past Beliefs

The Dead Sea Scrolls reveal many past Jewish beliefs.

Recall What are the Dead Sea Scrolls, and when were they first discovered? *writings by Jewish scholars who lived about 2,000 years ago; in 1947*

Analyze How have the Dead Sea Scrolls affected Judaism? *They have provided Jewish scholars with additional insights into the teachings of Judaism and into Jewish history.*

Analyzing Visuals

The Dead Sea Scrolls

Based on the image of the cave at right, what challenges might scholars have faced in searching for additional scrolls? *possible answers—having to work in small or dark caves; difficulties bringing scientific equipment into the caves*

Linking to Today

The Shrine of the Book A popular tourist attraction in Israel today is the Shrine of the Book, where visitors can see fragments of the Dead Sea Scrolls. Built specifically to house the scrolls, the building resembles one of the clay jars in which the scrolls were found. The Shrine of the Book is part of the Israel Museum in Jerusalem.

Answers

The Dead Sea Scrolls *difficulty in understanding the language or script; missing text; fragile remains*

Reading Check *Torah, Hebrew Bible, and Commentaries*

The Dead Sea Scrolls

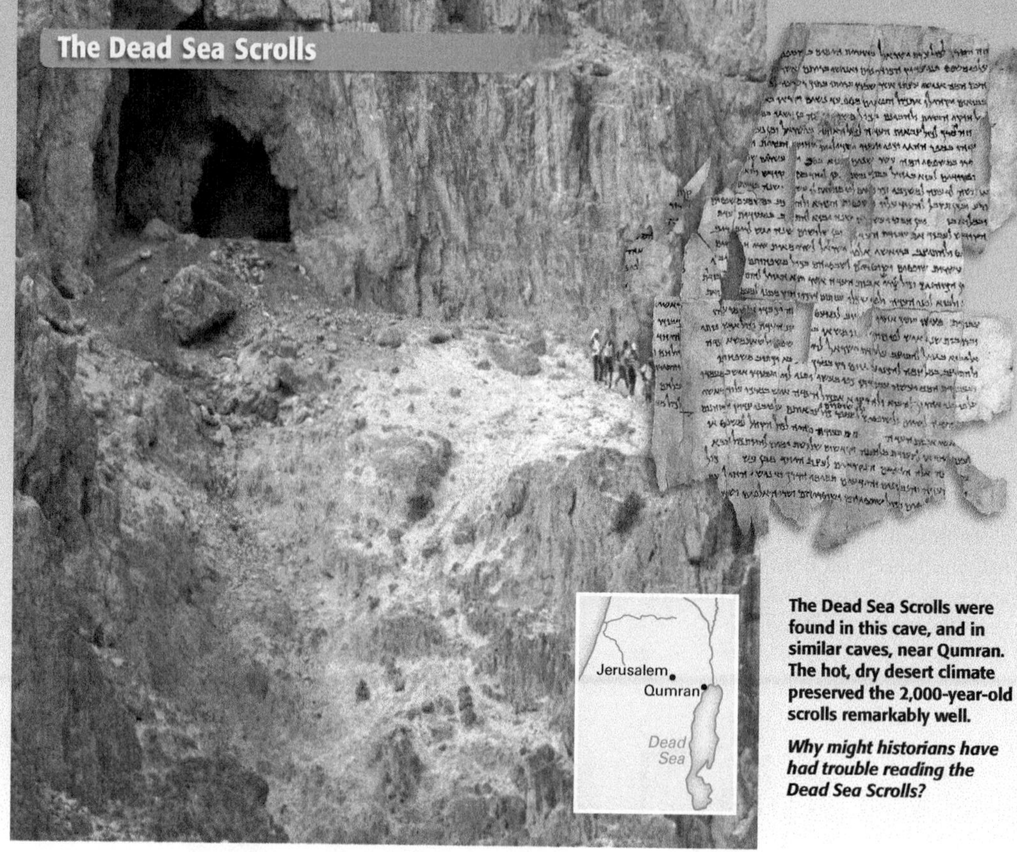

The Dead Sea Scrolls were found in this cave, and in similar caves, near Qumran. The hot, dry desert climate preserved the 2,000-year-old scrolls remarkably well.

Why might historians have had trouble reading the Dead Sea Scrolls?

Commentaries

For centuries scholars have studied the Torah and Jewish laws. Because some laws are hard to understand, the scholars write commentaries to explain them.

Many such commentaries are found in the **Talmud** (TAHL-moohd), a set of commentaries and lessons for everyday life. The writings of the Talmud were produced between AD 200 and 600. Many Jews consider them second only to the Hebrew Bible in their significance to Judaism.

READING CHECK **Analyzing** What texts do Jews consider sacred?

Scrolls Reveal Past Beliefs

Besides the Torah, the Hebrew Bible, and the Commentaries, many other documents also explain ancient Jewish beliefs. Among the most important are the **Dead Sea Scrolls**, writings by Jews who lived about 2,000 years ago.

Until 1947 no one knew about the Dead Sea Scrolls. In that year, young boys looking for a lost goat near the Dead Sea found a small cave. One of the boys went in to explore and found several old jars filled with moldy scrolls.

Scholars were very excited about the boy's find. Eager to find more scrolls, they

Critical Thinking: Evaluating Information

At Level

Dead Sea Scrolls News Report

1. Ask students to imagine that they are reporters working for a newspaper at the time of the discovery of the Dead Sea Scrolls.
2. Have each student write a news report describing the discovery and its significance as both a historical and religious find.
3. Remind students to address the journalistic questions "who, what, when, where, why, and how" in their reports. Have volunteers read their reports aloud. **LS Verbal/Linguistic**

Alternative Assessment Handbook, Rubric 42: Writing to Inform

began to search the desert. Over the next few decades, searchers found several more groups of scrolls.

Careful study revealed that most of the Dead Sea Scrolls were written between 100 BC and AD 50. The scrolls included prayers, commentaries, letters, and passages from the Hebrew Bible. These writings help historians learn about the lives of many Jews during this time.

READING CHECK **Finding Main Ideas** What did the Dead Sea Scrolls contain?

Judaism and Later Cultures

For centuries, Jewish ideas have greatly influenced other cultures, especially those in Europe and the Americas. Historians call European and American cultures the Western world to distinguish them from the Asian cultures to the east of Europe.

Because Jews lived all over the Western world, people of many cultures learned of Jewish ideas. In addition, these ideas helped shape the largest religion of Western society today, Christianity. Jesus, whose teachings are the basis of Christianity, was Jewish, and many of his teachings reflected Jewish ideas. These ideas were carried forward into Western civilization by both Jews and Christians. Judaism also influenced the development of another major religion, Islam. The first people to adopt Islam believed that they, like the Hebrews, were descendants of Abraham.

How are Jewish ideas reflected in our society? Many people still look to the Ten Commandments as a guide to how they should live. For example, people are expected to honor their parents, families, and neighbors and not to lie or cheat. Although these ideas were not unique to Judaism, it was through the Jews that they entered Western culture.

Not all of the ideas adopted from Jewish teachings come from the Ten Commandments. Other Jewish ideas can also be seen in how people live today. For example, many people do not work on weekends in honor of the Sabbath. In addition, people give money or items to charities to help the poor and needy. This concept of charity is based largely on Jewish teachings.

READING CHECK **Summarizing** How have Jewish ideas helped shape modern laws?

SUMMARY AND PREVIEW Judaism is based on the belief in and obedience to God as described in the Torah and other sacred texts. In the next section you will learn how religion helped unify Jews even when they were forced out of Jerusalem.

Section 2 Assessment

Reviewing Ideas, Terms, and People

1. a. **Define** What is **monotheism**?
   b. **Explain** What is the Jewish view of justice and righteousness?
2. a. **Identify** What are the main sacred texts of Judaism?
   b. **Predict** Why do you think the commentaries are so significant to many Jews?
3. **Recall** Why do historians study the Dead Sea Scrolls?
4. **Describe** How are Hebrew teachings reflected in Western society today?

Critical Thinking

5. **Finding Main Ideas** Using the information in your notes, identify four basic beliefs of Judaism and explain them in a diagram like the one shown here.

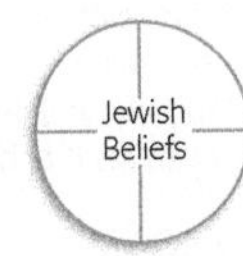

FOCUS ON WRITING

6. **Thinking about Basic Values and Teachings** While the information in Section 1 was mostly historical, this section has different kinds of topics. As you write down this information for your Web site, what links do you see between these topics and items already on the list you started in Section 1?

Direct Teach

Main Idea

❹ Judaism and Later Cultures

The ideas of Judaism have helped shape later cultures.

Recall What two major religions have been influenced by Judaism? *Christianity and Islam*

Elaborate How have Jewish views of justice influenced our court system? *possible answer—Everyone has a right to an attorney and to justice in a court of law.*

Review & Assess

Close

Have students discuss how shared beliefs tie all Jews together as a religious community. Encourage students to provide examples using information from the section.

Review

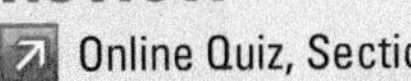
Online Quiz, Section 2

Assess

SE Section 2 Assessment

PASS: Section 2 Quiz

Alternative Assessment Handbook

Reteach/Classroom Intervention

Guided Reading Workbook, Section 2

Interactive Skills Tutor CD-ROM

Section 2 Assessment Answers

1. a. the belief in only one God
   b. Justice means to treat all people kindly and fairly, and righteousness refers to doing what is proper.
2. a. Torah, Hebrew Bible, and commentaries
   b. possible answer—because many of them were written by scholars long ago, and they help explain the Torah and Jewish teachings
3. to learn about the lives of Jews at the time the scrolls were written
4. Jewish teachings have helped shape modern Western society's laws and rules of behavior.
5. beliefs in one God, education and study, righteousness and justice, and obedience and law
6. possible links—central belief in monotheism and Abraham's worship of one God; education and Yohanan ben Zaccai; synagogues and the Temple

Answers

Reading Check (left) *prayers, commentaries, letters, and passages from the Hebrew Bible.*

Reading Check (right) *some modern laws are based on the laws set forth in the Ten Commandments and in other Jewish teachings.*

Preteach

Bellringer

If YOU were there . . . Use the **Daily Bellringer Transparency** to help students answer the question.

Daily Bellringer Transparency, Section 3

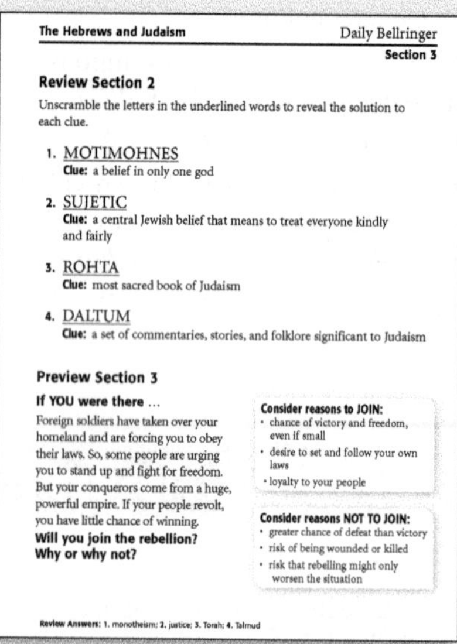

The Hebrews and Judaism — Daily Bellringer **Section 3**

Review Section 2

Unscramble the letters in the underlined words to reveal the solution to each clue.

1. MOTIMOHNES
   Clue: a belief in only one god
2. SUJETIC
   Clue: a central Jewish belief that means to treat everyone kindly and fairly
3. ROHTA
   Clue: most sacred book of Judaism
4. DALTUM
   Clue: a set of commentaries, stories, and folklore significant to Judaism

Preview Section 3

If YOU were there ...

Foreign soldiers have taken over your homeland and are forcing you to obey their laws. So, some people are urging you to stand up and fight for freedom. But your conquerors come from a huge, powerful empire. If your people revolt, you have little chance of winning.

Will you join the rebellion? Why or why not?

Consider reasons to JOIN:
- chance of victory and freedom, even if small
- desire to set and follow your own laws
- loyalty to your people

Consider reasons NOT TO JOIN:
- greater chance of defeat than victory
- risk of being wounded or killed
- risk that rebelling might only worsen the situation

Review Answers: 1. monotheism; 2. justice; 3. Torah; 4. Talmud

Building Vocabulary

Preteach or review the following term:

synagogue Jewish house of worship (p. 216)

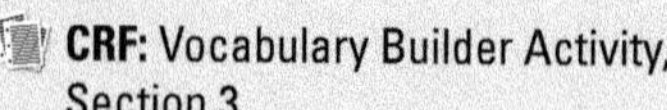

CRF: Vocabulary Builder Activity, Section 3

Taking Notes

Have students use the graphic organizer online to take notes on the section. This activity will prepare students for the Section Assessment, in which they will complete a graphic organizer that builds on the information using the Critical Thinking Skill: Evaluating.

SECTION 3

Judaism over the Centuries

What You Will Learn...

Main Ideas

1. Revolt, defeat, and migration led to great changes in Jewish culture.
2. Because Jews settled in different parts of the world, two cultural traditions formed.
3. Jewish traditions and holy days celebrate their history and religion.

The Big Idea

Although many Jews were forced out of Israel by the Romans, shared beliefs and customs helped Jews maintain their religion.

Key Terms

Zealots, *p. 214*
rabbis, *p. 216*
Passover, *p. 219*
High Holy Days, *p. 219*

hmhsocialstudies.com
TAKING NOTES

Use the graphic organizer online to take notes on events that threatened the survival of Jewish society, and notes on beliefs and customs that helped strengthen it.

If YOU were there...

Foreign soldiers have taken over your homeland and are forcing you to obey their laws. So, some people are urging you to stand up and fight for freedom. But your conquerors come from a huge, powerful empire. If your people revolt, you have little chance of winning.

Will you join the rebellion? Why or why not?

BUILDING BACKGROUND By about AD 60, many Jews in Jerusalem had to decide whether they would join a rebellion against their foreign conquerors. For a little over a century, Jerusalem had been ruled by Rome. The Romans had a strong army, but their disrespect for Jewish traditions angered many Jews.

Revolt, Defeat, and Migration

The teachings of Judaism helped unite the ancient Jews. After the conquest of Israel by the Romans, many events threatened to tear Jewish society apart.

One threat to Jewish society was foreign rule. By the beginning of the first century AD, many Jews in Jerusalem had grown tired of foreign rule. If they could regain their independence, these Jews thought they could re-create the kingdom of Israel.

Revolt against Rome

The most rebellious of these Jews were a group called the **Zealots** (ZE-luhts). This group didn't think that Jews should answer to anyone but God. As a result, they refused to obey Roman officials. The Zealots urged their fellow Jews to rise up against the Romans. Tensions between Jews and Romans increased. Finally, in AD 66, the Jews revolted. Led by the Zealots, they fought fiercely.

Teach the Big Idea

At Level

Judaism over the Centuries

1. **Teach** Ask students the questions in the Main Idea boxes to teach this section.
2. **Apply** Have each student, working either individually or in pairs, write five main-idea or summary statements for each main part of this section. **LS Verbal/Linguistic**
3. **Review** Have volunteers share their statements with the class to review the section's main ideas.
4. **Practice/Homework** Have each student use the information in this section to write one to three paragraphs expanding upon the section's big idea statement. **LS Verbal/Linguistic**

Alternative Assessment Handbook, Rubric 37: Writing Assignments

In the end, the Jews' revolt against the Romans was not successful. The revolt lasted four years and caused terrible damage. By the time the fighting ended, Jerusalem lay in ruins. The war had wrecked buildings and cost many lives. Even more devastating to the Jews was the fact that the Romans burned the Second Temple during the last days of fighting in AD 70:

> "As the flames went upward, the Jews made a great clamor [shout], such as so mighty an affliction [ordeal] required, and ran together to prevent it; and now they spared not their lives any longer, nor suffered any thing to restrain their force, since that holy house was perishing."
>
> –Flavius Josephus, *The Wars of the Jews*

After the Temple was destroyed, most Jews lost their will to fight and surrendered. But a few refused to give up their fight. That small group of about 1,000 Zealots locked themselves in a mountain fortress called Masada (muh-SAH-duh).

Intent on smashing the revolt, the Romans sent 15,000 soldiers to capture these Zealots. However, Masada was hard to reach. The Romans had to build a huge ramp of earth and stones to get to it. For two years, the Zealots refused to surrender, as the ramp grew. Finally, as the Romans broke through Masada's walls, the Zealots took their own lives. They refused to become Roman slaves.

THE IMPACT TODAY

The western retaining wall of the Second Temple survived the fire and still stands. Thousands of Jews each year visit the wall.

History Close-up

Destruction of the Second Temple

Frustrated by a century of Roman rule, many Jews rose up in armed rebellion. Led by the Zealots, they fought furiously for four years. But the experienced Roman army crushed the revolt. The Romans even destroyed the Jews' holiest site, the Second Temple in Jerusalem.

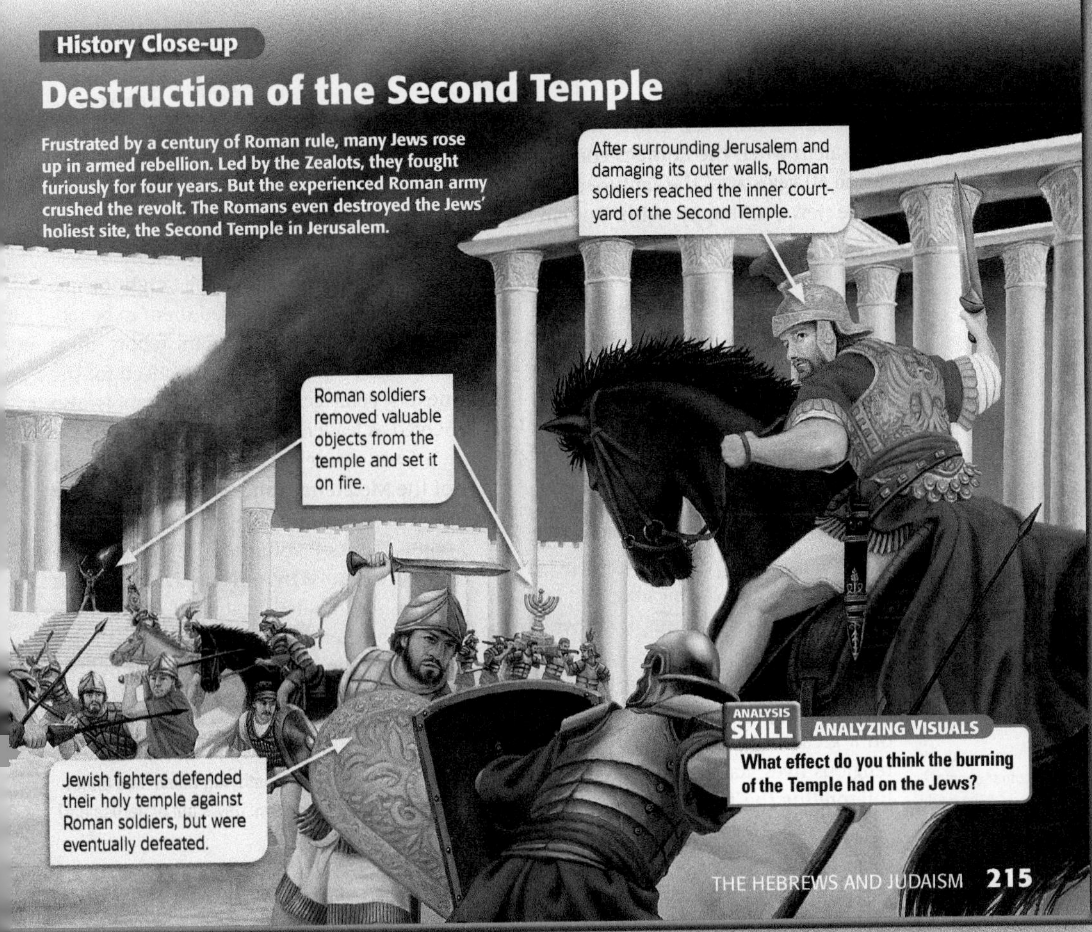

After surrounding Jerusalem and damaging its outer walls, Roman soldiers reached the inner courtyard of the Second Temple.
Roman soldiers removed valuable objects from the temple and set it on fire.
Jewish fighters defended their holy temple against Roman soldiers, but were eventually defeated.

ANALYSIS SKILL ANALYZING VISUALS

What effect do you think the burning of the Temple had on the Jews?

Direct Teach

Main Idea

1 Revolt, Defeat, and Migration

Revolt, defeat, and migration led to great changes in Jewish culture.

Identify Who were the Zealots? *A group of Jews who refused to obey Roman officials and led their fellow Jews in a revolt.*

Recall Why did the Jews revolt against the Romans? *The Jews were tired of foreign rule and wanted to recreate the kingdom of Israel; Zealots also believed Jews should not answer to anyone but God.*

Make Inferences Why was the Roman destruction of the Second Temple so devastating to the Jews? *The Temple was the center of Jewish religious life and the holiest Jewish site.*

Linking to Today

Masada The fortress of Masada has become a symbol to modern Jews of their survival as a people and a religious group. Today, Israeli soldiers go to Masada and take the oath, "Masada shall not fall again." The mountain fortress is the second most popular site for Jewish tourists in Israel after the city of Jerusalem.

History Close-up

Destruction of the Second Temple

Analyzing Visuals What valuable items did the Jews lose as part of the destruction of the Second Temple? *sacred Temple objects*

Critical Thinking: Summarizing and Sequencing

At Level

Jewish Revolt News Flashes

1. Ask students to imagine that television was available in AD 70 and that they are reporters working for the Roman News Network.
2. Have each student write a series of short news flashes covering the main events in the Jewish revolt against Rome.
3. Remind students to address the journalistic questions "who, what, when, where, why, and how" and to be objective in their reporting. In addition, encourage students to make their news flashes exciting while keeping them historically accurate.
4. Model the activity for students by writing one news flash as an example.
5. Have volunteers deliver their news flashes to the class in the correct order. Then have students summarize the results of the revolt. **LS Verbal/Linguistic**

Alternative Assessment Handbook, Rubric 42: Writing to Inform

Answers

History Close-up *greatly upset the Jews because the Temple was their holiest site and the center of Jewish religious life*

Direct Teach

Main Idea

1 Revolt, Defeat, and Migration

Revolt, defeat, and migration led to great changes in Jewish culture.

Recall How did the nature of Judaism change after the loss of the Second Temple? *Local synagogues became more important in Jewish life, and leaders called rabbis began serving as religious teachers.*

Identify Who was Yohanan ben Zaccai? *a Jewish rabbi who established a school at Yavneh to train rabbis*

Make Inferences Jews have returned to Jerusalem throughout history. Why do you think this is so? *possible answer—because Jerusalem is the most holy place in the world to Jews and is the site of the Western Wall of the Jews' biblical Temple.*

CRF: History and Geography Activity: Jewish Migration After AD 70

Map Transparency: Jewish Migration after AD 70

Answers

Reading Check *as punishment for Jewish revolts against Roman rule*

Results of the Revolt

With the capture of Masada in AD 73, the Jewish revolt was over. As punishment for the Jews' rebellion, the Romans killed much of Jerusalem's population. They took many of the surviving Jews to Rome as slaves. The Romans dissolved the Jewish power structure and took over the city.

Besides those taken as slaves, thousands of Jews left Jerusalem after the destruction of the Second Temple. With the Temple destroyed, they didn't want to live in Jerusalem anymore. Many moved to Jewish communities in other parts of the Roman Empire. One common destination was Alexandria in Egypt, which had a large Jewish community. The populations of these Jewish communities grew after the Romans destroyed Jerusalem.

A Second Revolt

Some Jews, however, chose not to leave Jerusalem when the Romans conquered it. Some 60 years after the capture of Masada, these Jews, unhappy with Roman rule, began another revolt. Once again, however, the Roman army defeated the Jews. After this rebellion in the 130s the Romans banned all Jews from the city of Jerusalem. Roman officials declared that any Jew caught in or near the city would be killed. As a result, Jewish migration throughout the Mediterranean region increased.

Migration and Discrimination

For Jews not living in Jerusalem, the nature of Judaism changed. Because the Jews no longer had a single temple at which to worship, local synagogues became more important. At the same time, leaders called **rabbis** (RAB-yz), or religious teachers, took on a greater role in guiding Jews in their religious lives. Rabbis were responsible for interpreting the Torah and teaching.

THE IMPACT TODAY The United States today has a larger Jewish population than any other country in the world.

The Sephardim are descended from Jews who migrated to Spain and Portugal during the Diaspora, or dispersal, of the Jews. This Sephardic rabbi is working on part of a Torah scroll.

ATLANTIC OCEAN

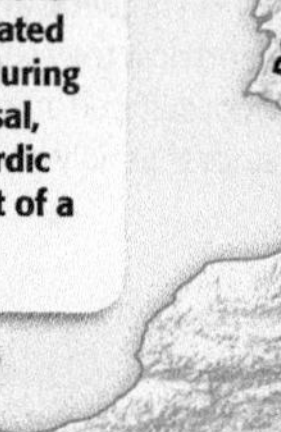

AFRICA

This change was largely due to the actions of Yohanan ben Zaccai, a rabbi who founded a school at Yavneh, near Jerusalem. In this school, he taught people about Judaism and trained them to be rabbis. Influenced by Yohanan, rabbis' ideas shaped how Judaism was practiced for the next several centuries. Many rabbis also served as leaders of Jewish communities.

Over many centuries, Jews moved out of the Mediterranean region to other parts of the world. In many cases this movement was not voluntary. The Jews were forced to move by other religious groups who discriminated against them or were unfair to them. Jews were forced to leave their cities and find new places to live. As a result, some Jews settled in Asia, Russia, and much later, the United States.

READING CHECK **Identifying Cause and Effect** Why did the Romans force Jews out of Jerusalem?

Social Studies Skill Activity: Understanding Short- and Long-Term Effects

At Level

Charting Short- and Long-Term Effects

1. To help students identify short and long-term effects of the Jewish revolt against the Romans, draw the chart here for students to see. Omit the blue, italicized answers.
2. Have students copy the chart and use the section to complete it.

SE Social Studies Skills: Understanding Short- and Long-Term Effects, p. 220

CRF: Social Studies Skills Activity: Understanding Short- and Long-Term Effects

Jewish Revolt Against Rome, AD 66–70

Short-Term Effects	Long-Term Effects
• *loss of many lives, particulary Jews* • *destruction of Jerusalem, Second Temple* • *Roman enslavement of many surviving Jews* • *end of Jewish power structure in Jerusalem* • *migration of many Jews throughout Roman Empire*	• *second unsuccessful revolt against Rome* • *ban of Jews from Jerusalem* • *scattering of Jews throughout world* • *changes in nature of Judaism (synagogues, rabbis)* • *discrimination against Jews*

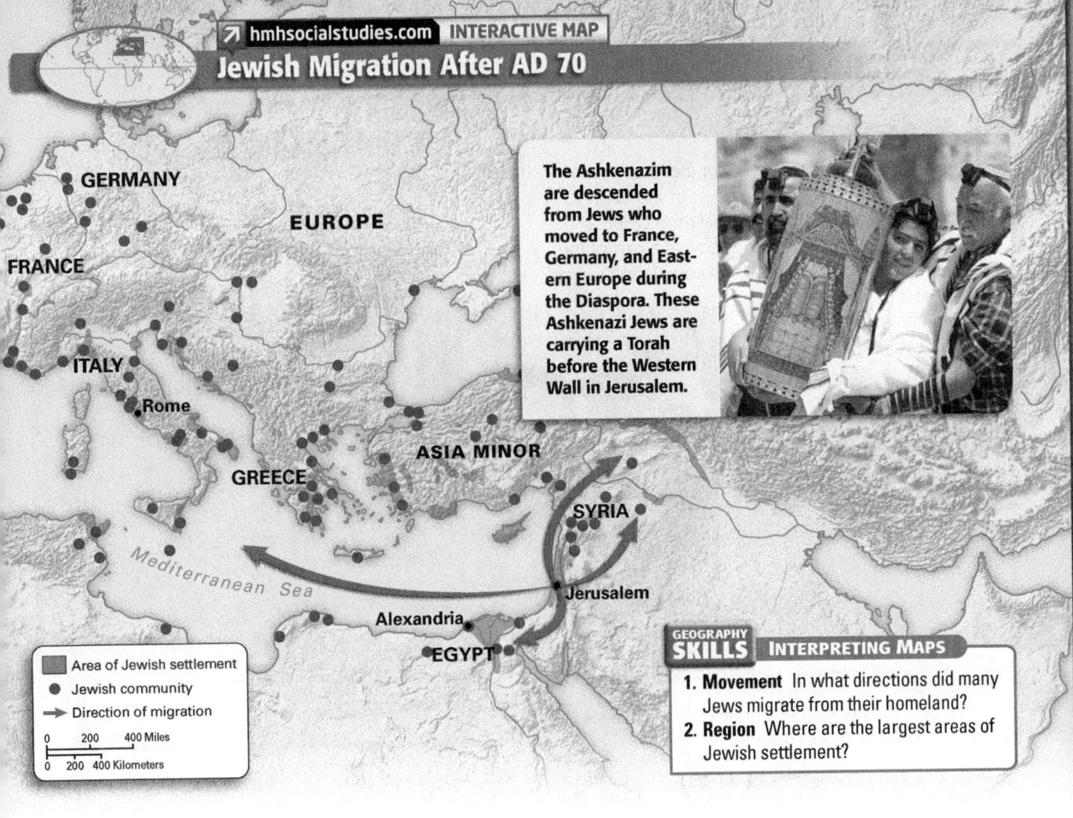

The Ashkenazim are descended from Jews who moved to France, Germany, and Eastern Europe during the Diaspora. These Ashkenazi Jews are carrying a Torah before the Western Wall in Jerusalem.

GEOGRAPHY SKILLS INTERPRETING MAPS

1. **Movement** In what directions did many Jews migrate from their homeland?
2. **Region** Where are the largest areas of Jewish settlement?

Two Cultural Traditions

As you read earlier, the dispersal of Jews around the world is called the Diaspora. It began after the Babylonian Captivity in the 500s BC. After that time, Jewish communities developed all around the world.

Jews everywhere shared the basic beliefs of Judaism. For example, all Jews still believed in God and tried to obey his laws as set forth in the sacred texts. But communities in various parts of the world had different customs. As a result, the Jewish communities in different parts of the world began to develop their own languages, rituals, and cultures. These differences led to the creation of two main cultural traditions, both of which still exist today.

The Jews in Eastern Europe

One of the two traditions, the Ashkenazim (ahsh-kuh-NAH-zuhm), is made up of descendants of Jews who moved to France, Germany, and eastern Europe during the Diaspora. For the most part, these Jews had communities separate from their non-Jewish neighbors. Therefore, they developed their own customs that were unlike those of their neighbors. As an example, they developed their own language, Yiddish. Yiddish is similar to German but is written in the Hebrew alphabet.

The Jews in Spain and Portugal

Another Jewish cultural tradition developed during the Diaspora in what are now Spain and Portugal in Western Europe.

hmhsocialstudies.com
ANIMATED HISTORY
Jewish Diaspora, AD 70-500

THE IMPACT TODAY
Some Yiddish words have entered the English language. For example, *schlep* means "to carry."

Direct Teach

Main Idea

❷ Two Cultural Traditions

Because Jews settled in different parts of the world, two cultural traditions formed.

Recall What language did each Jewish cultural tradition develop? *Ashkenazim—Yiddish; Sephardim—Ladino*

Contrast How do the Ashkenazim and Sephardim differ? *Ashkenazim—settled in France, Germany, and eastern Europe; lived apart from non-Jews and developed a unique culture; spoke Yiddish; Sephardim—settled in Spain and Portugal; mixed with and borrowed from surrounding cultures; spoke Ladino*

Interpreting Maps

Jewish Migration After AD 70

Location Along what body of water were most Jewish communities located? *the Mediterranean Sea*

Map Transparency: Jewish Migration after AD 70

Info to Know

Yiddish in America Many Yiddish words and expressions have gained common usage in the United States. Share the following with students.

chutzpah	guts; nerve
cockamamie	crazy
futz	to fiddle around
mazel tov	congratulations
mensch	nice gentleman
nosh	to snack
oy	sigh
schlemiel	fool
schmoozing	talking about nothing

Collaborative Learning

At Level

Jewish Populations Map and Chart

Research Required

1. Have students conduct research on Jewish populations and communities throughout the world today.
2. Organize students into small groups for the project and assign each group a continent or specific part of the world to research.
3. Have each group create a map and chart to present its findings. Remind the groups to include a title, legend, compass rose, and scale on their maps.
4. Have each group present its work to the class. Have students compare and contrast Jewish populations in the world today to those in the map on this page.
LS Interpersonal, Visual/Spatial

Alternative Assessment Handbook, Rubrics 7: Charts; 20: Map Creation; and 30: Research

Answers

Interpreting Maps **1.** *north, west, and southwest;* **2.** *Spain; France; Germany; Italy; Greece; Asia Minor; Syria; and Alexandria, Egypt*

Direct Teach

Main Idea

❸ Traditions and Holy Days

Jewish traditions and holy days celebrate their history and religion.

Define What is Hanukkah? *a Jewish holy day remembering an event where enough oil for one day lasted for eight*

Identify What is the most sacred Jewish holy day, and what event does it mark? *Yom Kippur—the day Jews ask God to forgive their sins*

Summarize How do Jewish traditions and holy days unite Jews? *help connect Jews to their long history and help create a strong unifying Jewish identity and culture*

Linking to Today

A Passover Meal

Origins of Passover The name "Passover" refers back to an event right before the Exodus. The Hebrew Bible says that in the last plague on Egypt, God came and killed all the firstborn males. But God "passed over" the Israelites' firstborn. This event led the pharaoh to free the Israelites.

LINKING TO TODAY

A Passover Meal

Passover honors the Exodus, one of the most important events in Jewish history. In honor of this event from their past, Jews share a special meal called a seder. Each item in the seder symbolizes a part of the Exodus. For example, bitter herbs represent the Israelites' bitter years of slavery in Egypt. Before eating the meal, everyone reads prayers from a book called the Haggadah (huh-GAH-duh). It tells the story of the Exodus and reminds everyone present of the Jews' history. The small picture shows a seder in a copy of a Haggadah from the 1300s.

ANALYSIS SKILL **ANALYZING INFORMATION**

How does the Passover seder reflect the importance of the Exodus in Jewish history?

The descendants of the Jews there are called the Sephardim (suh-FAHR-duhm). They also have a language of their own—Ladino. It is a mix of Spanish, Hebrew, and Arabic. Unlike the Ashkenazim, the Sephardim mixed with the region's non-Jewish residents. As a result, Sephardic religious and cultural practices borrowed elements from other cultures. Known for their writings and their philosophies, the Sephardim produced a golden age of Jewish culture in the AD 1000s and 1100s. During this period, for example, Jewish poets wrote beautiful works in Hebrew and other languages. Jewish scholars also made great advances in mathematics, astronomy, medicine, and philosophy.

READING CHECK **Summarizing** What were the two main Jewish cultural traditions?

Traditions and Holy Days

Jewish culture is one of the oldest in the world. Because their roots go back so far, many Jews feel a strong connection with the past. They also feel that understanding their history will help them better follow Jewish teachings. Their traditions and holy days help them understand and celebrate their history.

Hanukkah

One Jewish tradition is celebrated by Hanukkah, which falls in December. It honors the rededication of the Second Temple during the revolt of the Maccabees.

The Maccabees wanted to celebrate a great victory that had convinced their non-Jewish rulers to let them keep their

Differentiating Instruction

Struggling Readers — Below Level

Connecting to the Big Idea Students may have difficulty with the section's transition from a chronological to a topical narrative. Explain the connection between the sequence of events at the start of the section and the Jewish cultural traditions discussed next. Last, explain how shared Jewish beliefs and traditions have helped unite Jews and maintain Judaism.

LS Verbal/Linguistic

Advanced/Gifted and Talented — Above Level

"Judaism over Time" Storyboards Organize students into small groups. Have each group create a storyboard for a documentary discussing how Judaism has survived and how Jews have maintained a sense of identity and community in spite of the Diaspora.

LS Interpersonal, Verbal/Linguistic

Alternative Assessment Handbook, Rubrics 1: Acquiring Information; and 14: Group Activity.

Answers

Linking to Today *Each item and event in the Passover seder tells the story of or symbolizes a part of the Exodus in Jewish history.*

Reading Check *Ashkenazim, Sephardim*

religion. According to legend, though, the Maccabees didn't have enough lamp oil to perform the rededication ceremony. Miraculously, the oil they had—enough to burn for only one day—burned for eight full days.

Today Jews celebrate this event by lighting candles in a special candleholder called a menorah (muh-NOHR-uh). Its eight branches represent the eight days through which the oil burned. Many Jews also exchange gifts on each of the eight nights.

Passover

More important than Hanukkah to Jews, Passover is celebrated in March or April. **Passover** is a time for Jews to remember the Exodus, the journey of the Israelites out of slavery in Egypt.

According to Jewish tradition, the Israelites left Egypt so quickly that bakers didn't have time to let their bread rise. Therefore, during Passover Jews eat only matzo, a flat, unrisen bread. They also celebrate the holy day with ceremonies and a ritual meal called a seder (SAY-duhr). During the seder, participants recall and reflect upon the events of the Exodus.

High Holy Days

Ceremonies and rituals are also part of the **High Holy Days**, the two most sacred of all Jewish holy days. They take place each year in September or October. The first two days of the celebration, Rosh Hashanah (rahsh uh-SHAH-nuh), celebrate the beginning of a new year in the Jewish calendar.

On Yom Kippur (yohm ki-POOHR), which falls soon afterward, Jews ask God to forgive their sins. Jews consider Yom Kippur to be the holiest day of the entire year. Because it is so holy, Jews don't eat or drink anything for the entire day. Many of the ceremonies they perform for Yom Kippur date back to the days of the Second Temple. These ceremonies help many Jews feel more connected to their long past, to the days of Abraham and Moses.

READING CHECK **Finding Main Ideas** What name is given to the two most important Jewish holy days?

SUMMARY AND PREVIEW The Jewish culture is one of the oldest in the world. Over the course of their long history, the Jews' religion and customs have helped them maintain a sense of identity and community. This sense has helped the Jewish people endure many hardships. In the next chapter you will learn about another people who made major contributions to Western culture. These were the Greeks.

Section 3 Assessment

hmhsocialstudies.com ONLINE QUIZ

Reviewing Ideas, Terms, and People

1. a. **Recall** Who won the battle at Masada?
   b. **Evaluate** How did the defeat by the Romans affect Jewish history?
2. a. **Identify** What language developed in the Jewish communities of eastern Europe?
   b. **Contrast** How did communities of Ashkenazim differ from communities of Sephardim?
3. **Identify** What event does **Passover** celebrate?

Critical Thinking

4. **Evaluating** Review your notes. Then use a graphic organizer like the one shown to describe the belief or custom that you think may have had the biggest role in strengthening Jewish society.

Major Belief or Custom

FOCUS ON WRITING

5. **Organizing Your Information** Add notes about what you've just read to the notes you have already collected. Now that you have all your information, organize it into categories that will be windows, links, and other features on your Web page.

Review & Assess

Info to Know

High Holy Days Jews call the period from Rosh Hashanah to Yom Kippur the Days of Awe. During this time, Jews ask God and others for forgiveness of their sins over the past year. Jews believe that on Rosh Hashanah, God writes in books the names of who will have a good or bad year and who will live or die in the coming year. But the books are not sealed until Yom Kippur. So prayer, good deeds, and asking for forgiveness during the Days of Awe can change what is written.

hmhsocialstudies.com
Online Resources
Activity: Illustrated Guide to Jewish Holy Days

Close

Have students identify three to five details for each section main idea, listed at the start of the section.

Review

Online Quiz, Section 3

Assess

SE Section 3 Assessment
PASS: Section 3 Quiz
Alternative Assessment Handbook

Reteach/Classroom Intervention

Guided Reading Workbook, Section 3
Interactive Skills Tutor CD-ROM

Section 3 Assessment Answers

1. a. the Romans
   b. The Jews slowly scattered throughout the world, and two Jewish cultural traditions developed in Europe.
2. a. Yiddish
   b. Ashkenazim—lived apart from non-Jews and developed a unique culture; spoke Yiddish; Sephardim—mixed with and borrowed from surrounding cultures; spoke Ladino
3. the Exodus
4. Answers will vary but should reflect understanding of Jewish beliefs and customs.
5. Students should add notes that relate to each of the section's main ideas—revolt, defeat, and migration; two cultural traditions; and traditions and holy days.

Answers

Reading Check *High Holy Days*

Social Studies Skills

Identifying Short- and Long-Term Effects

Activity **Analyzing Effects** Identify a topic or concern that students care about—for example, a local issue, a specific environmental issue, or a current international conflict. Write the issue for students to see and below it create a two-column chart. Label the columns *Short-Term Effects* and *Long-Term Effects*. Have the class brainstorm short-term effects first. List them in the appropriate column. If students need help, list a few examples to get them started. Then help students to consider and list possible long-term effects of the event. Then ask the class to summarize the difference between short- and long-term effects. **LS Visual/Spatial**

Alternative Assessment Handbook, Rubric 7: Charts

Interactive Skills Tutor CD-ROM, Lesson 7: Identify Cause and Effect

Social Studies Skills

Analysis | Critical Thinking | Economics | Study

Identifying Short- and Long-Term Effects

Understand the Skill

Many events of the past are the result of other events that took place earlier. When something occurs as the result of things that happened earlier, it is an effect of those things.

Some events take place soon after the things that cause them. These events are short-term effects. Long-term effects can occur decades or even hundreds of years after the events that caused them. Recognizing cause-and-effect relationships will help you to better understand the connections between historical events.

Learn the Skill

As you learned in Chapter 5, "clue words" can reveal cause-and-effect connections between events. Often, however, no such words are present. Therefore, you should always be looking for what happened as a result of an action or event.

Short-term effects are usually fairly easy to identify. They are often closely linked to the event that caused them. Take this sentence, for example:

"After Solomon's death around 930 BC, revolts broke out over who should be king."

It is clear from this information that a short-term effect of Solomon's death was political unrest.

Now, consider this other passage:

"Some Israelites . . . moved to Egypt . . . The Israelites lived well in Egypt and their population grew. But this growing population worried Egypt's ruler, the pharaoh. He feared that the Israelites would soon become too powerful. To prevent this from happening, the pharaoh made the Israelites slaves."

Look carefully at the information in the passage. No clue words exist. However, it shows that one effect of the Israelites' move to Egypt was the growth of their population. It takes time for a population to increase, so this was a long-term effect of the Israelites' move.

Recognizing long-term effects is not always easy, however, because they often occur well after the event that caused them. Therefore, the long-term effects of those events may not be discussed at the time. This is why you should always ask yourself why an event might have happened as you study it.

For example, many of our modern laws are based on the Ten Commandments of the ancient Israelites. Religion is a major force in history that makes things happen. Other such forces include economics, science and technology, geography, and the meeting of peoples with different cultures. Ask yourself if one of these forces is a part of the event you are studying. If so, the event may have long-term effects.

Practice and Apply the Skill

Review the information in Chapter 7 and answer the following questions.

1. What were the short-term effects of King Solomon's rule of the Israelites? What long-term benefit resulted from his rule?
2. What was the short-term effect of the destruction of the temple at Jerusalem in AD 70? What effect has that event had on the world today?

Answers

Practice and Apply the Skill

1. *short-term effects—expansion of the kingdom of Israel, growth of the kingdom's trade and wealth, construction of a temple to God; long-term benefit—The temple became the center of the Israelites' religious life and a symbol of their faith.* **2.** *short-term effect—Romans killed much of Jerusalem's population and took many of the surviving Jews to Rome as slaves; long-term effects—spread of Jewish people and development of Jewish communities around the world*

Social Studies Skills Activity: Identifying Short- and Long-Term Effects

Effects of the Exodus Flowchart

At Level

1. Write the following for students to see: *The Egyptian pharaoh agrees to free the Israelites.* Pair students and have each pair create a large flowchart showing the short- and long-term effects of this event. Suggest that students use different colors to distinguish between short- and long-term effects.
2. Model the activity by listing the first short-term effect—*Moses led the Israelites out of Egypt in a journey called the Exodus.* Students should include long-term effects of events such as the Ten Commandments. Circulate as students work to help them structure their flowcharts.
3. Then have students use their work to help you create a master flowchart.
LS Interpersonal, Visual/Spatial

Alternative Assessment Handbook, Rubrics 6: Cause and Effect; and 13: Graphic Organizers

CHAPTER 7

Chapter Review

History's Impact
▶ **video series**
Review the video to answer the focus question:
What is the Jewish Diaspora, and how has it affected Jews around the world?

Visual Summary

Use the visual summary below to help you review the main ideas of the chapter.

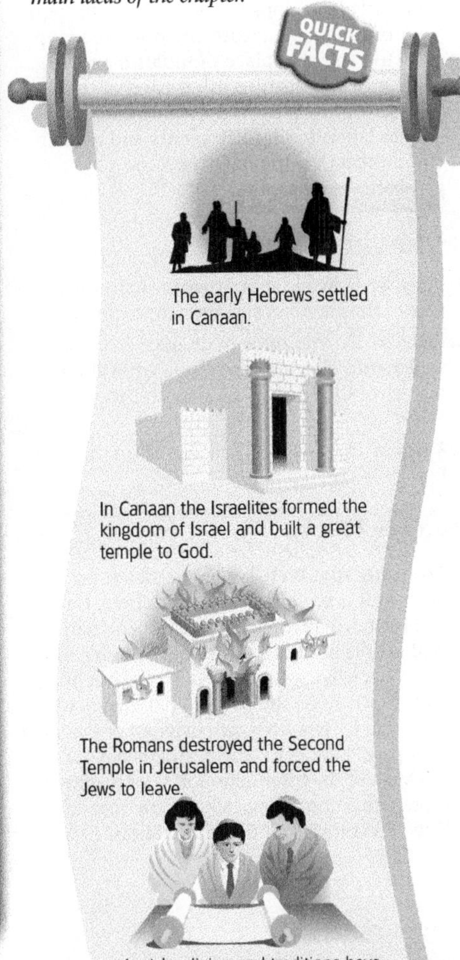

The early Hebrews settled in Canaan.

In Canaan the Israelites formed the kingdom of Israel and built a great temple to God.

The Romans destroyed the Second Temple in Jerusalem and forced the Jews to leave.

Jewish religion and traditions have united the Jews over the centuries.

Reviewing Vocabulary, Terms, and People

For each group of terms below, write a sentence that shows how the terms in the group are related.

1. Abraham
   Judaism
2. Moses
   Exodus
3. David
   Solomon
4. Torah
   Talmud
5. Passover
   High Holy Days
6. Moses
   Ten Commandments
7. Passover
   Exodus
8. monotheism
   Judaism
9. synagogues
   rabbis
10. principles
    Torah

Comprehension and Critical Thinking

SECTION 1 *(Pages 202–207)*

11. a. **Describe** How did Abraham and Moses shape the history of the Hebrews and Israelites?
    b. **Compare and Contrast** What did Saul, David, and Solomon have in common? How did they differ?
    c. **Evaluate** Of Esther, Deborah, Miriam, and Ruth, which do you think provided the best example of how people should treat their families? Explain your answer.

SECTION 2 *(Pages 208–213)*

12. a. **Identify** What are the basic beliefs of Judaism?
    b. **Analyze** What do the various sacred Jewish texts contain?
    c. **Elaborate** How are Jewish ideas observed in modern Western society?

Answers

Visual Summary

Review and Inquiry Use the visual summary to help students recall and discuss the chapter's main points.

Quick Facts Transparency: The Hebrews and Judaism Visual Summary

Reviewing Vocabulary, Terms, and People

1. Abraham is considered the ancestor of the Hebrews, whose religion is Judaism.
2. Moses led the Israelites out of slavery in Egypt in the Exodus.
3. Solomon was David's son.
4. The Torah and Talmud are among the sacred texts of Judaism.
5. Passover and the High Holy Days, which includes Rosh Hashanah and Yom Kippur, are important Jewish celebrations.
6. The Hebrew Bible says that God gave Moses the Ten Commandments, a code of moral laws written on two stone tablets, on Mt. Sinai.
7. The Jewish festival Passover commemorates the freeing of the Israelites from slavery and their journey out of Egypt in the Exodus.
8. Judaism was the first religion to follow monotheism, the belief in only one God, that is still widely practiced today.
9. At synagogues, Jewish teachers called rabbis interpret the Torah and guide other Jews in Judaism.
10. The Torah describes the laws and principles of Judaism.

Comprehension and Critical Thinking

11. a. Abraham—led his family to Canaan and became father of the Hebrew people; Moses—led Israelites out of Egypt, where the Israelite people had been enslaved, and received Ten Commandments for the Israelite people.
    b. all kings of Israel; Saul—military commander, not a strong king, not loved by all the Hebrews; David—military leader, strong king, well loved by the Israelite people;

Review and Assessment Resources

Review and Reinforce

SE Chapter Review

CRF: Chapter Review Activity

Quick Facts Transparency: The Hebrews and Judaism Visual Summary

Spanish Chapter Summaries Audio CD Program

Online Chapter Summaries in Six Languages

TOS Holt McDougal PuzzleView

Quiz Game CD-ROM

Assess

SE Standardized Test Practice

PASS: Chapter Test, Forms A and B

Alternative Assessment Handbook

TOS ExamView Assessment Suite

Differentiated Instruction Modified Worksheets and Tests CD-ROM: Chapter Test

Online Assessment Program, in the Interactive Student Edition

Answers

Solomon—expanded the kingdom with trade and allies, strong king, built the great temple

c. Ruth, because she dedicated her life to supporting her mother-in-law

12. a. monotheism, education, justice and righteousness, obedience and law

b. Torah—laws, history of the Hebrews until the death of Moses; second and third parts of the Hebrew Bible—messages of Hebrew prophets and poetry songs, stories, lessons, history, Proverbs, Psalms; Talmud—commentaries, stories, folklore; Dead Sea Scrolls—prayers, commentaries, letters, passages from Hebrew Bible

c. possible answer—in the shaping of Christianity and the Ten Commandments as a guide for how to live

13. a. The Jews, led by the Zealots, revolted against Roman rule.

b. the Diaspora

c. Answers will vary but should acknowledge the importance of traditions in Judaism and their survival over many centuries.

Reading Skills

14. fact

15. opinion

16. opinion

17. fact

18. fact

Social Studies Skills

19. the Exodus—short-term: left Egypt, received Ten Commandments, wandered through desert, settled in Canaan; long-term: provided Jews with a significant and culturally binding historical event, which they remember during Passover; the Babylonian Captivity—short-term: Jews enslaved in Babylon for 50 years; long-term: After their release, many Jews did not return and thus began what is called the Diaspora; the expulsion of the Jews from Jerusalem—short-term: Jews slowly dispersed throughout Mediterranean region and rest of world; long-term: changed nature of Judaism, led to creation of two Jewish cultural traditions

SECTION 3 *(Pages 214–219)*

13. a. Describe What happened as a result of tensions between the Romans and the Jews?

b. Analyze What led to the creation of the two main Jewish cultural traditions?

c. Predict In the future, what role do you think holy days and other traditions will play in Judaism? Explain your answer.

Reading Skills 

Identifying Facts and Opinions *Identify each of the following statements as a fact or an opinion.*

14. Much of what we know about Hebrew history comes from the work of archaeologists.

15. Archaeologists should spend more time studying Hebrew history.

16. The Exodus is one of the most fascinating events in world history.

17. Until 1947, scholars did not know about the Dead Sea Scrolls.

18. Hanukkah is a Jewish holy day that takes place every December.

Social Studies Skills 

19. Identifying Short- and Long-Term Effects *Identify both the short-term and long-term effects of each of the following events.*

	Short-Term Effects	Long-Term Effects
the Exodus		
the Babylonian Captivity		
the expulsion of the Jews from Jerusalem		

Using the Internet 

20. Activity: Interpreting Maps Migration and conflict were key factors shaping Jewish history and culture. The Exodus, the Babylonian Captivity, and the revolts against Rome forced Israelites and later Jews to adapt their culture and settle in regions outside Israel. Through your online book, create an annotated map showing the birthplace of Judaism and the Jews' movements into other parts of the world. Your map should include a legend as well as labels to identify events and explain their impact on the Jewish people.

hmhsocialstudies.com

Reviewing Themes

21. Religion How did monotheism shape the history of the Hebrews and their descendents?

22. Religion Do you agree or disagree with this statement: "The history of Judaism is also the history of the Hebrew and Jewish people." Why?

23. Religion How does Mosaic law affect the daily lives of Jewish people?

Focus on Writing 

24. Designing Your Web Site Look back at your notes and how you've organized them. Have you included all important facts and details? Will people be able to find information easily?

What will appear in menus or as hot links, and elsewhere on the page? What images will you include? Draw a rough diagram or sketch of your page. Be sure to label the parts of your page.

Most of the information in your textbook is presented chronologically, by the year or era. How did you present the information?

Using the Internet

20. Go to hmhsocialstudies.com to access a rubric for this activity.

Reviewing Themes

21. Monotheism shaped the Hebrews' religion, culture, and history, guiding Hebrew patriarchs and leaders and bringing the Hebrews into conflict with others.

22. possible answers—agree, because Judaism has shaped Jewish history and helped the Jews maintain an identity throughout their history; disagree, because Jewish history includes more than just the history of their religion

23. Mosaic law governs how Jews pray and celebrate, when Jews should work and worship, and what Jews may eat, among other activities.

Focus on Writing

24. Rubric Students' Web sites should:

- have a title and clear labels.
- describe what appears on the home page, menus, and hot links.
- include descriptions of images.
- respect the beliefs and traditions of Judaism.

CRF: Focus on Writing: A Web Site

CHAPTER 7

Standardized Test Practice

DIRECTIONS: Read each question, and write the letter of the best response.

1 Use the map to answer the following question.

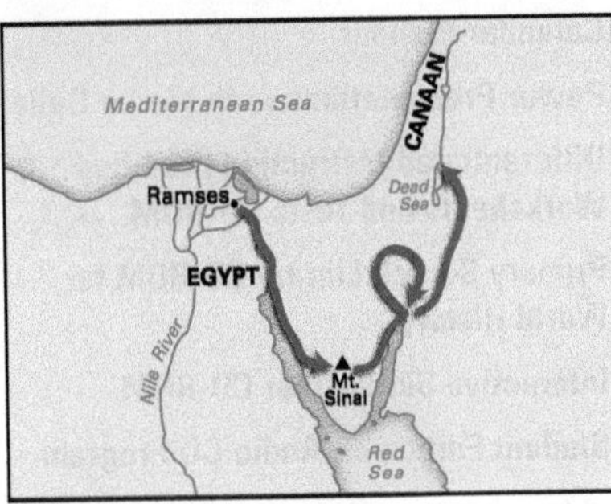

The map above illustrates

A the Babylonian Captivity.
B the Exodus.
C Abraham's migration to Canaan.
D the capture of Jerusalem by the Romans.

2 The Jews believe that the Ten Commandments were given by God to

A Moses.
B Abraham.
C King David.
D King Solomon.

3 The ancient Jews probably were the first people to

A conduct religious ceremonies.
B have a code of laws.
C practice monotheism.
D hold religious beliefs.

4 The basic teachings and laws that guide the Jewish people are found in the

A Talmud.
B Torah.
C Book of the Dead.
D Dead Sea Scrolls.

5 Which group was *most* responsible for the migration of Jews out of Jerusalem to other parts of the Mediterranean region?

A the Israelites
B the Philistines
C the Egyptians
D the Romans

Connecting with Past Learnings

6 Moses issued a set of laws for the Hebrew people to follow. What other ancient leader is famous for issuing a code of laws?

A Gilgamesh
B Tutankhamen
C Asoka
D Hammurabi

7 Jewish teachings required people to honor and respect their parents. This was an idea also common in China. In his writings, who else encouraged people to respect their parents?

A Chandragupta Maurya
B Shi Huangdi
C Confucius
D Abraham

Answers

Standardized Test Practice

1. B
Break Down the Question Remind students to look at the full routes when reading a map showing movement. Students who answered *C* may have read the map too quickly.

2. A
Break Down the Question This question requires students to recall factual information.

3. C
Break Down the Question Help students see that answers *A, B,* and *D* refer to practices common to many ancient religions.

4. B
Break Down the Question Students may confuse the Talmud and the Torah. You might suggest a memory aid to help students distinguish between the two sacred texts.

5. D
Break Down the Question Remind students that italicized words in test questions often significantly affect the question's meaning.

6. D
Break Down the Question This question connects to information in the chapter on Mesopotamia and the Fertile Crescent.

7. C
Break Down the Question This question connects to information in the chapter on China.

Intervention Resources

Reproducible

- Guided Reading Workbook
- Differentiated Instruction Teacher Management System: Lesson Plans

Technology

- Quick Facts Transparency: The Hebrews and Judaism Visual Summary
- Differentiated Instruction Modified Worksheets and Tests CD-ROM
- Interactive Skills Tutor CD-ROM

Tips for Test Taking

Read and Re-read If students are taking a reading comprehension test, they should read the selection, master all the questions, and then re-read the selection. The answers will probably pop out the second time around. Students should remember that the test isn't trying to trick them; it's trying to test their knowledge and their ability to think clearly.

Chapter 8 Planning Guide

Ancient Greece

Overview	Instructional Resources	
CHAPTER 8 **Essential Question:** What factors shaped government in Greece? **Focus on the Essential Question Podcast**	**TOS Differentiated Instruction Teacher Management System:** • Instructional Benchmarking Guides • Lesson Plans for Differentiated Instruction **Guided Reading Workbook** **Chapter Resource File:** • Chapter Review Activity • Focus on Writing Activity: A Myth • Social Studies Skills Activity: Analyzing Costs and Benefits **Multimedia Connections:** Ancient Greece	**TOS Calendar Planner** **Power Presentations with Media Gallery** **Differentiated Instruction Modified Worksheets and Tests CD-ROM** **Primary Source Library CD-ROM for World History** **Interactive Skills Tutor CD-ROM** **Student Edition on Audio CD Program** **Video:** Origins of Western Culture
Section 1: **Geography and the Early Greeks** **The Big Idea:** Greece's geography and its nearness to the sea strongly influenced the development of trade and the growth of city-states.	**TOS Differentiated Instruction Teacher Management System:** Section 1 Lesson Plan **Guided Reading Workbook:** Section 1 **Chapter Resource File:** • Vocabulary Builder Activity, Section 1 • History and Geography Activity: Greek City-States and Colonization	**Daily Bellringer Transparency:** Section 1 **Map Transparency:** Greece: Physical **Map Transparency:** Minoan and Mycenaean Civilizations **Map Transparency:** Greek City-States and Colonies, c. 600 BC **Internet Activity:** Minoans Museum Exhibit **Animated History:** Greek Trade, 500 BC
Section 2: **Government in Athens** **The Big Idea:** The people of Athens tried many different forms of government before creating a democracy.	**TOS Differentiated Instruction Teacher Management System:** Section 2 Lesson Plan **Guided Reading Workbook:** Section 2 **Chapter Resource File:** • Vocabulary Builder Activity, Section 2 • Biography Activity: Aspasia • Biography Activity: Pericles • Primary Source Activity: Aristotle's Athenian Constitution	**Daily Bellringer Transparency:** Section 2 **Quick Facts Transparency:** Government in Athens **Quick Facts Transparency:** Democracy Then and Now
Section 3: **Greek Mythology and Literature** **The Big Idea:** The ancient Greeks created great myths and works of literature that influence the way we speak and write today.	**TOS Differentiated Instruction Teacher Management System:** Section 3 Lesson Plan **Guided Reading Workbook:** Section 3 **Chapter Resource File:** • Vocabulary Builder Activity, Section 3 • Biography Activity: Sappho • Literature Activity: "Midas," from *Bulfinch's Mythology* • Primary Source Activity: Sappho's Poetry	**Daily Bellringer Transparency:** Section 3 **Internet Activity:** First Olympic Games Trading Cards **Video:** The Panathenaia

Chart Key:

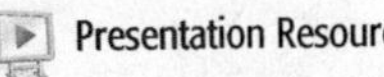

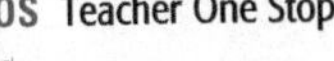

SE Student Edition | Presentation Resource | MP3 Audio
TOS Teacher One Stop | DVD/CD-ROM | HISTORY™
Printable Resource

Program Resources available on TOS and @ hmhsocialstudies.com

Review, Assessment, Intervention

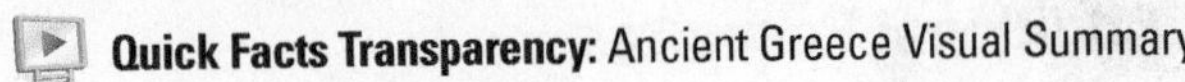

Quick Facts Transparency: Ancient Greece Visual Summary

Spanish Chapter Summaries Audio CD Program

Quiz Game CD-ROM

Progress Assessment Support System (PASS): Chapter Test

Differentiated Instruction Modified Worksheets and Tests CD-ROM: Modified Chapter Test

TOS **ExamView® Assessment Suite (English/Spanish)**

Online Assessment Program, in the Interactive Student Edition

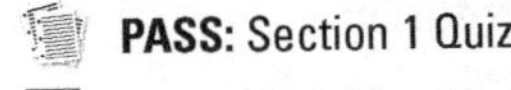

PASS: Section 1 Quiz

Online Quiz: Section 1

Alternative Assessment Handbook

PASS: Section 2 Quiz

Online Quiz: Section 2

Alternative Assessment Handbook

PASS: Section 3 Quiz

Online Quiz: Section 3

Alternative Assessment Handbook

Supporting Resources

- Multimedia Classroom Global History Series
- Global History Teacher's Guide

Maps Globes Graphs Level F

- Student Workbook
- Teacher's Guide

Social Studies Trade Library Collections

- Premier Secondary World History Trade Collection
- Ancient World History Trade Collection

History's Impact

World History Video Program

- **Democracy**

For more information or to purchase go to hmhsocialstudies.com

Power Presentations with Media Gallery

Power Presentations with Media Gallery are visual presentations of each chapter's main ideas. Presentations can be customized by including Quick Facts charts, images from the text, and video clips.

Differentiating Instruction

How do I address the needs of varied learners?

The Target Resource acts as your primary strategy for differentiated instruction.

ENGLISH-LANGUAGE LEARNERS & STRUGGLING READERS

Interactive Skills Tutor CD-ROM

The Interactive Skills Tutor CD-ROM contains lessons that provide additional practice for 20 different critical thinking skills.

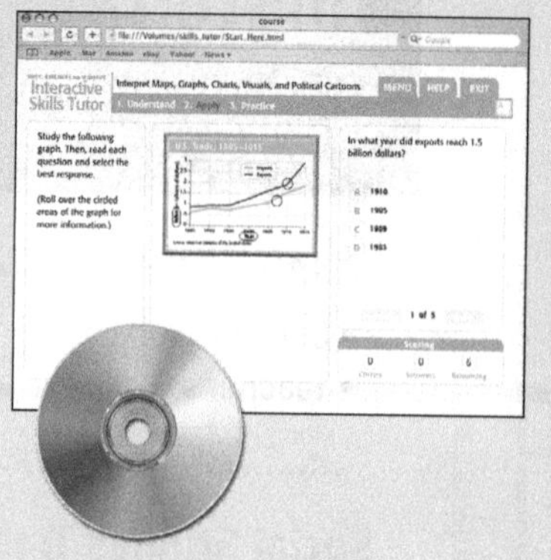

Additional Resources

Differentiated Instruction Teacher Management System: Lesson Plans for Differentiated Instruction

Chapter Resource File:
- Vocabulary Builder Activities
- Social Studies Skills Activity: Analyzing Costs and Benefits

Quick Facts Transparencies:
- Government in Athens
- Democracy Then and Now
- Ancient Greece Visual Summary

Student Edition on Audio CD Program

Interactive Skills Tutor CD-ROM

Spanish/English Guided Reading Workbook

SPECIAL NEEDS LEARNERS

Differentiated Instruction Modified Worksheets and Tests CD-ROM

- Vocabulary Flash Cards
- Vocabulary Builder Activities
- Chapter Review Activity
- Chapter Test

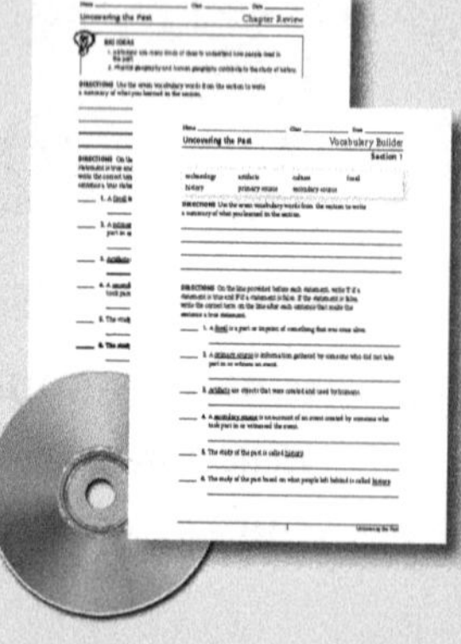

Additional Resources

Differentiated Instruction Teacher Management System: Lesson Plans for Differentiated Instruction

Guided Reading Workbook

Chapter Resource File: Social Studies Skills Activity: Analyzing Costs and Benefits

Student Edition on Audio CD Program

Interactive Skills Tutor CD-ROM

ADVANCED/GIFTED-AND-TALENTED STUDENTS

Primary Source Library CD-ROM for World History

The Library contains longer versions of quotations in the text, extra sources, and images. Included are point-of-view articles, journals, diaries, historical fiction, and political documents.

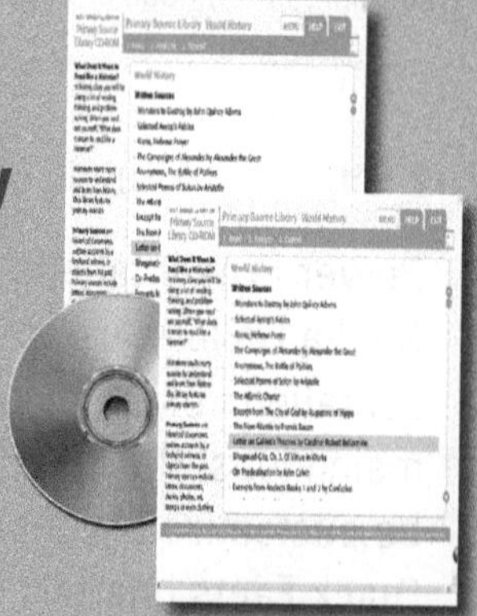

Additional Resources

Differentiated Instruction Teacher Management System: Lesson Plans for Differentiated Instruction

Chapter Resource File:
- Focus on Writing Activity: A Myth
- Literature Activity: "Midas," from *Bulfinch's Mythology*

Document-Based Questions Activities

Differentiated Activities in the Teacher's Edition

- Defining Key Terms, p. 237
- Illustrating a Story, p. 246

Teacher One Stop™

How can I manage the lesson plans and support materials for differentiated instruction?

With the Teacher One Stop, you can easily organize and print lesson plans, planning guides, and instructional materials for all learners. The Teacher One Stop includes the following materials to help you differentiate instruction:

- Interactive Teacher's Edition
- Calendar Planner and pacing guides
- Editable lesson plans
- All reproducible ancillaries in Adobe Acrobat (PDF) format
- ExamView Assessment Suite (English & Spanish)
- Transparency and video previews

Differentiated Activities in the Teacher's Edition

- Identifying the Effects of Geography, p. 229
- Evaluating the Athenian Assembly, p. 238

Interactive Student Edition

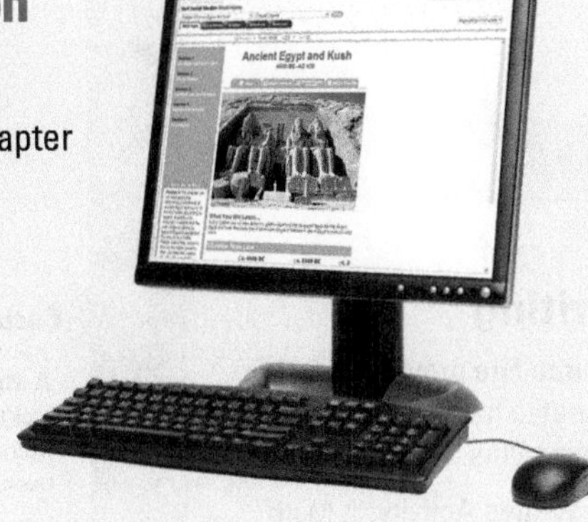

Complete online student edition with interactive multimedia support for chapter content assessment and reporting

- Interactive Maps and Notebook
- Graphic Organizers
- Standardized Test Prep
- Online Homework Practice and Research Activities
- Current Events
- Chapter-based Internet Activities
- Animated History Activities
- and more!

Differentiated Activities in the Teacher's Edition

- Writing Reviews of Stories, p. 247
- Comparing with Similes, p. 250

• Chapter Preview •

Essential Question

Introduce the Essential Question

- Point out that Greece was covered by mountains.
- Explain that the rugged terrain made land travel difficult.
- Discuss how the landscape might lead to many smaller communities instead of one large country.

CHAPTER 8 2000–500 BC

Ancient Greece

Essential Question What factors shaped government in Greece?

South Carolina Performance Standards

6-2.1 Describe the development of ancient Greek culture (the Hellenic period), including the concept of citizenship and the early forms of democracy in Athens; **6-2.2** Analyze the role of Alexander the Great (Hellenistic period), Socrates, Plato, Archimedes, Aristotle, and others in the creation and spread of Greek governance, literature, philosophy, the arts, math, and science; **6-2.6** Compare the polytheistic belief systems of the Greeks and the Romans with the origins, foundational beliefs, and spread of Christianity.

Literacy Skills for Social Studies

- Interpret Earth's physical and human systems by using maps, mental maps, geographic models, and other social studies resources.
- Compare the locations of places, the conditions at places, and the connections between places.
- Explain how political, social, and economic institutions are similar or different across time and/or throughout the world.

FOCUS ON WRITING

A Myth Like most people, the Greeks enjoyed good stories. But they also took their stories seriously. They used stories called myths to explain everything from the creation of the world to details of everyday life. Reading this chapter will provide you with ideas you can use to create your own myth.

CHAPTER EVENTS **c. 2000 BC** The Minoan civilization prospers in Crete.

2000 BC

WORLD EVENTS **c. 2000 BC** The main part of Stonehenge is built in England.

Focus on Writing

The **Chapter Resource File** provides a Focus on Writing worksheet to help students organize and create their myths.

CRF: Focus on Writing Activity: A Myth

Introduce the Chapter

At Level

Focus on Greek Contributions

1. Discuss with students what they already know about ancient Greece. Ask students if they can name any contributions of the Greeks to our modern world. Write students' ideas for the class to see.
2. Give the students several categories to consider if they are having difficulty thinking of ideas. Categories could include government, literature, sports, and culture. Students may require hints to develop ideas for the list. Students may come up with ideas such as the Olympics, democracy, or Greek mythology.
3. Review with students the list of ideas they developed. Help students to see which ideas are correct and which are incorrect.
4. Have students draw an illustration for one of the contributions from the list. Ask for volunteers to share their illustrations with the class. LS **Verbal/Linguistic, Visual/Spatial**

Key to Differentiating Instruction

Below Level
Basic-level activities designed for all students encountering new material

At Level
Intermediate-level activities designed for average students

Above Level
Challenging activities designed for honors and gifted and talented students

Standard English Mastery
Activities designed to improve standard English usage

LS **Learning Styles**

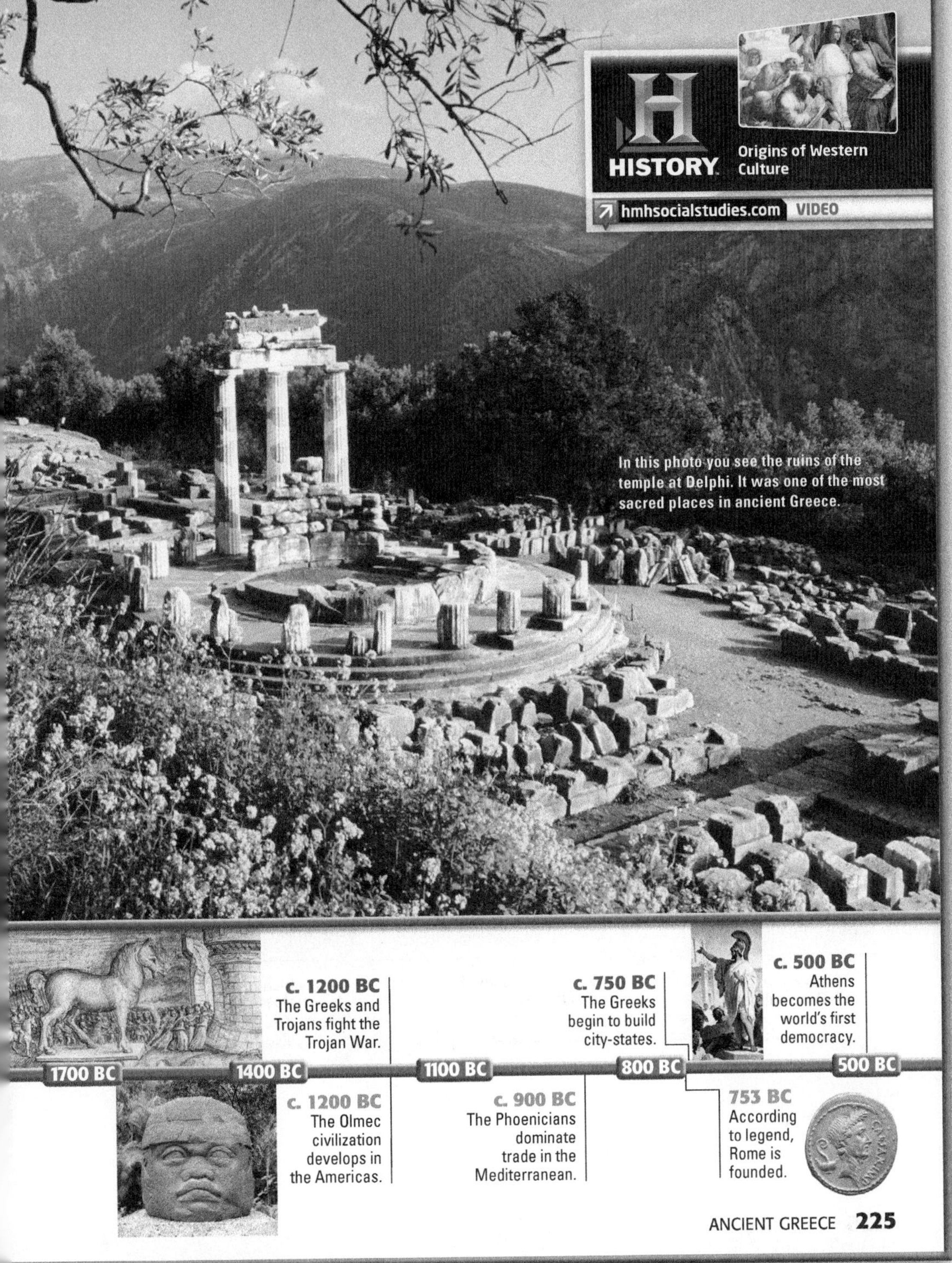

In this photo you see the ruins of the temple at Delphi. It was one of the most sacred places in ancient Greece.

c. 1200 BC The Greeks and Trojans fight the Trojan War.

c. 750 BC The Greeks begin to build city-states.

c. 500 BC Athens becomes the world's first democracy.

1700 BC | 1400 BC | 1100 BC | 800 BC | 500 BC

c. 1200 BC The Olmec civilization develops in the Americas.

c. 900 BC The Phoenicians dominate trade in the Mediterranean.

753 BC According to legend, Rome is founded.

ANCIENT GREECE 225

Chapter Preview

Explore the Picture

The Temple at Delphi The Tholos temple at the sanctuary of Athena Pronaia near Delphi was built around 380 BC. The Greeks believed that the oracle of Delphi could foresee the future.

Analyzing Visuals What can you tell about the geography of Greece by looking at this photo? *possible answers—It is very mountainous; Greek cities were built in the mountains; there is considerable vegetation.*

hmhsocialstudies.com Teacher Resources

Explore the Time Line

1. What was happening in the Americas at about the time of the Trojan War? *The Olmec civilization was developing.*
2. In about what year did Athens create the world's first democracy? *c. 500 BC*

Info to Know

Minoan Civilization The image of the dolphins in the time line was one of many frescoes, or wall paintings, discovered in the ruins of the Minoan palace at Knossos on the island of Crete.

Reading Social Studies

Understanding Themes

Introduce the two main themes in this chapter—geography and politics. Remind students that where people live influences their history. Ask students to suggest ways in which people are affected by where they live. What effects does geography have on trade and culture? Tell students that the geography of Greece led to the establishment of small political units known as city-states. These city-states practiced many different types of government. Tell students that ancient Greeks developed the first democracy. Help students understand the importance of democratic government.

Greek Word Origins

Focus on Reading Review the chart on this page with students. Ask students to examine the Greek roots in the third column. Ask students how they might find out if a word comes from a Greek root. Remind students that word origins are given in dictionary entries. Have students work in pairs to find at least three words that use each of the roots in the chart. Examples for *–graphy* might include *cartography*, *biography*, and *bibliography*. Encourage students to share their lists with the class.

Reading Social Studies

Economics | **Geography** | **Politics** | Religion | Society and Culture | Science and Technology

Focus on Themes In this chapter, you will read about the civilizations of ancient Greece. Whether reading about the Minoans and Mycenaeans or the Spartans and Athenians, you will see that where the people lived affected how they lived. You will also read how the government of these ancient people changed over the years. By the end of this chapter, you will have learned a great deal about the **geography** and the **politics** of the ancient Greeks.

Greek Word Origins

Focus on Reading Sometimes when you read an unusual word, you can figure out what it means by using the other words around it. Other times you might need to consult a dictionary. But sometimes, if you know what the word's root parts mean, you can figure out its meaning. The chart below shows you several English words that have Greek roots.

In this chapter you'll find...	which means...	and comes from the Greek root
1. geography, *p. 228* (jee-AH-gruh-fee)	the study of the earth's surface	*ge-*, which means "earth" *-graphy*, which means "writing about"
2. acropolis, *p. 232* (uh-KRAH-puh-luhs)	fortress of a Greek city up on a high hill	*acr-*, which means "top" *polis*, which means "city"
3. democracy, *p. 236* (di-MAH-kruh-see)	a form of government in which people hold power	*dem-*, which means "people" *-cracy*, which means "power"
4. tyrant, *p. 237* (TY-ruhnt)	a ruler [in modern times, a harsh ruler]	*tyrannos*, which means "master"
5. oligarchy, *p. 237* (AH-luh-gahr-kee)	rule by a few people	*olig-*, which means "few" *-archy*, which means "rule"
6. mythology, *p. 243* (mi-THAH-luh-jee)	a body of stories about gods and heroes	*mythos*, which means "stories about gods or heroes" *-ology*, which means "study of"

Reading and Skills Resources

Reading Support

- Guided Reading Workbook
- Student Edition on Audio CD
- Spanish Chapter Summaries Audio CD Program

Social Studies Skills Support

- Interactive Skills Tutor CD-ROM

Vocabulary Support

- **CRF:** Vocabulary Builder Activities
- **CRF:** Chapter Review Activity
- Differentiated Instruction Modified Worksheets and Tests CD-ROM:
  - Vocabulary Flash Cards
  - Vocabulary Builder Activity
  - Chapter Review Activity

TOS Holt McDougal PuzzleView

You Try It!

Study each of the words below. Use the chart on the opposite page to find a Greek root or roots for each of them. How do the words' roots relate to their definitions?

Word	Definition
1. geology	a science that deals with the study of the makeup of the earth
2. police	the people who keep order in a city
3. Tyrannosaurus	one of the largest and fiercest dinosaurs
4. architect	the person in charge of designing buildings
5. acrophobia	the fear of heights
6. monarchy	rule by a single person
7. politics	the art or science of governing a city, state, or nation
8. demographer	a scientist who studies the growth of populations

Think about it.

1. How can studying Greek origins help you understand English?
2. Use the chart of roots on the previous page to answer this question. Where do you think a demagogue gets his or her power: the support of the people or a written constitution? Justify your answer.
3. Do you know words in other languages that help you understand English?

Key Terms and People

Chapter 8

Section 1
polis *(p. 232)*
classical *(p. 232)*
acropolis *(p. 232)*

Section 2
democracy *(p. 236)*
aristocrats *(p. 237)*
oligarchy *(p. 237)*
citizens *(p. 237)*
tyrant *(p. 237)*
Pericles *(p. 240)*

Section 3
mythology *(p. 243)*
Homer *(p. 246)*
Sappho *(p. 247)*
Aesop *(p. 247)*
fables *(p. 247)*

Academic Vocabulary

Success in school is related to knowing academic vocabulary—the words that are frequently used in school assignments and discussions. In this chapter, you will learn the following academic word:

influence *(p. 230)*

As you read Chapter 8, pay close attention to the highlighted words. Many of those words are Greek or come from Greek roots. Refer to the chart on the opposite page to help you understand what those words mean.

Reading Social Studies

Key Terms and People

Introduce this chapter's key terms and people by reading the list aloud so that students will know how to pronounce each term or name. Then organize the students into pairs and assign each pair a person or term from the list. Have each pair identify the importance of the person or term. Then have each group draw a picture that represents the significance of that term or person. Have students present their term, description, and illustration to the class. Encourage students to take notes on the presentations.
LS Verbal/Linguistic, Visual/Spatial

Focus on Reading

See the **Focus on Reading** questions in this chapter for more practice on this reading social studies skill.

Reading Social Studies Assessment

See the **Chapter Review** at the end of this chapter for student assessment questions related to this reading skill.

Teaching Tip

Have students create a chart that lists roots from commonly used words, as well as their meaning. Remind students to look in a dictionary for word origins. Some possible roots might be *aud-*, hear; *philo-*, loving; *anthro-*, man, and *med-*, middle. Then have students list words in which those roots are used.

Answers

You Try It! 1. *By learning the meaning of Greek root words, we can guess the meaning of some English words that have these roots.* **2.** *The root–*dem *means people, so a demagogue gets his or her power from the support of the people.* **3.** *possible answer—Words with Latin roots might help students who understand Spanish, French, Italian, or Portuguese understand many English words.*

Preteach

Bellringer

If YOU were there . . . Use the **Daily Bellringer Transparency** to help students answer the question.

Daily Bellringer Transparency, Section 1

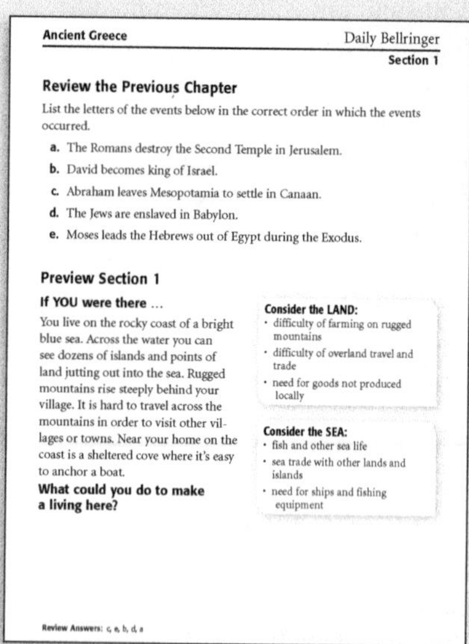

Ancient Greece — Daily Bellringer **Section 1**

Review the Previous Chapter

List the letters of the events below in the correct order in which the events occurred.

a. The Romans destroy the Second Temple in Jerusalem.
b. David becomes king of Israel.
c. Abraham leaves Mesopotamia to settle in Canaan.
d. The Jews are enslaved in Babylon.
e. Moses leads the Hebrews out of Egypt during the Exodus.

Preview Section 1

If YOU were there ...

You live on the rocky coast of a bright blue sea. Across the water you can see dozens of islands and points of land jutting out into the sea. Rugged mountains rise steeply behind your village. It is hard to travel across the mountains in order to visit other villages or towns. Near your home on the coast is a sheltered cove where it's easy to anchor a boat.

What could you do to make a living here?

Consider the LAND:
- difficulty of farming on rugged mountains
- difficulty of overland travel and trade
- need for goods not produced locally

Consider the SEA:
- fish and other sea life
- sea trade with other lands and islands
- need for ships and fishing equipment

Review Answers: c, e, b, d, a

Academic Vocabulary

Review with students the high-use academic term in this section.

influence change, or have an effect on (p. 230)

CRF: Vocabulary Builder Activity, Section 1

Taking Notes

Have students use the graphic organizer online to take notes on the section. This activity will prepare students for the Section Assessment, in which they will complete a graphic organizer that builds on the information using the Critical Thinking Skill: Summarizing.

SECTION 1

Geography and the Early Greeks

What You Will Learn...

Main Ideas

1. Geography helped shape early Greek civilization.
2. Trading cultures developed in the Minoan and Mycenaean civilizations.
3. The Greeks created city-states for protection and security.

The Big Idea

Greece's geography and its nearness to the sea strongly influenced the development of trade and the growth of city-states.

Key Terms

polis, *p. 232*
classical, *p. 232*
acropolis, *p. 232*

Use the graphic organizer online to take notes on how Greece's geography affected the development of trade and city-states.

If YOU were there...

You live on the rocky coast of a bright blue sea. Across the water you can see dozens of islands and points of land jutting out into the sea. Rugged mountains rise steeply behind your village. It is hard to travel across the mountains in order to visit other villages or towns. Near your home on the coast is a sheltered cove where it's easy to anchor a boat.

What could you do to make a living here?

BUILDING BACKGROUND The paragraph you just read could be describing many parts of Greece, a peninsula in southern Europe. Greece's mountain ranges run right up to the coast in many places, making travel and farming difficult. Although it does not seem like the easiest place in the world to live, Greece was home to some of the ancient world's greatest civilizations.

Greece is a land of rugged mountains, rocky coastlines, and beautiful islands. The trees you see are olive trees. Olives were grown by the early Greeks for food and oil.

Teach the Big Idea

At Level

Geography and the Early Greeks

1. **Teach** Ask students the questions in the Main Idea boxes to teach this section.
2. **Apply** Re-create the geography of Greece in your classroom by moving desks to create physical boundaries. Place students into "city-state" groups. Make city-states large, small, isolated, etc. Ask groups to list resources available to their city-states and to solve any issues of scarcity. Ask students to identify the benefits and drawbacks of their cities. **LS Kinesthetic**
3. **Review** As you review the section, have students relate their city-states to those of ancient Greece.
4. **Practice/Homework** Have students write an essay that describes how geography affected the development of city-states. **LS Verbal/Linguistic**

Alternative Assessment Handbook, Rubrics 11: Discussions; and 42: Writing to Inform

Geography Shapes Greek Civilization

The Greeks lived on rocky, mountainous lands surrounded by water. The mainland of Greece is a peninsula, an area of land that is surrounded on three sides by water. But the Greek peninsula is very irregular. It's one big peninsula made up of a series of smaller peninsulas. The land and sea intertwine like your hand and fingers in a bowl of water. In addition, there are many islands. Look at the map of Greece and notice the rugged coastline.

In your mind, picture those peninsulas and islands dominated by mountains that run almost to the sea. Just a few small valleys and coastal plains provide flat land for farming and villages. Now you have an image of Greece, a land where one of the world's greatest civilizations developed.

Mountains and Settlements

Because mountains cover much of Greece, there are few flat areas for farmland. People settled in those flat areas along the coast and in river valleys. They lived in villages and towns separated by mountains and seas.

Travel across the mountains and seas was difficult, so communities were isolated from one another. As a result, the people created their own governments and ways of life. Even though they spoke the same language, Greek communities saw themselves as separate countries.

Seas and Ships

Since travel inland across the rugged mountains was so difficult, the early Greeks turned to the seas. On the south was the huge Mediterranean Sea, to the west was the Ionian (eye-OH-nee-uhn) Sea, and to the east was the Aegean (ee-JEE-uhn) Sea.

Greece: Physical

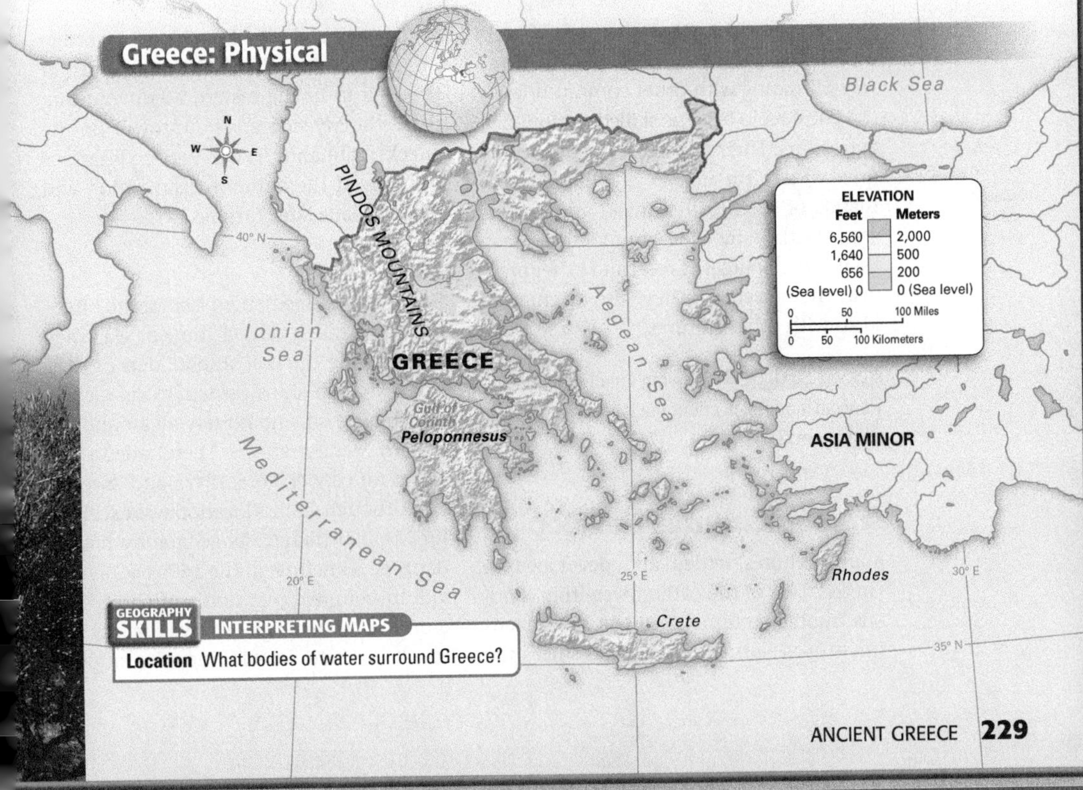

GEOGRAPHY SKILLS INTERPRETING MAPS

Location What bodies of water surround Greece?

Direct Teach

Main Idea

1 Geography Shapes Greek Civilization

Geography helped shape early Greek civilization.

Identify On what geographic feature is Greece located? *a peninsula*

Draw Conclusions Why was travel difficult in Greece? *Mountains and seas were difficult to cross.*

Activity Travel Advertisements Have students create posters attracting travelers to ancient Greece. Advertisements should highlight the elements of Greek geography. **LS Verbal/Linguistic**

Alternative Assessment Handbook, Rubric 2: Advertisements

Map Transparency: Greece: Physical

Interpreting Maps

Greece: Physical

Review with students the map of Greece. Ask the following questions:

Place What is the name of the large peninsula in southern Greece? *Peloponnesus*

Region How is the geography of Greece different from that of other civilizations? *It is on a peninsula and is made up of many small islands.*

Differentiating Instruction

Special Needs Learners — Below Level

1. Review with the class the main features of the geography of Greece.
2. To help students identify the ways in which the Greeks were affected by their geography, draw the graphic organizer for students to see. Omit the blue, italicized answers.
3. Have students copy the graphic organizer and complete it by identifying ways in which mountains and seas affected the ancient Greeks. **LS Visual/Spatial**

Mountains	Seas
Effect on Greeks	**Effect on Greeks**
little farmland	*source of food*
villages and towns separated from each other	*means of trade*
travel difficult	*transportation*
little contact between towns	*helped exchange ideas with other cultures*

Answers

Interpreting Maps *Ionian, Mediterranean, and Aegean seas*

Direct Teach

Main Idea

❷ Trading Cultures Develop

Trading cultures developed in the Minoan and Mycenaean civilizations.

Recall Where was the Minoan civilization located? *on the island of Crete*

Compare How was the decline of the Minoans and Mycenaeans similar? *They both experienced natural disasters.*

Make Inferences Why did the Mycenaeans put such importance on building powerful fortresses? *Answers will vary, but students should indicate that they were used for protection.*

Early Trading Cultures

The Minotaur Greek legend tells of a horrifying half-man, half-bull creature known as the Minotaur that lived in a maze beneath the palace of Knossos.

hmhsocialstudies.com

Online Resources
Activity: Minoans Museum Exhibit

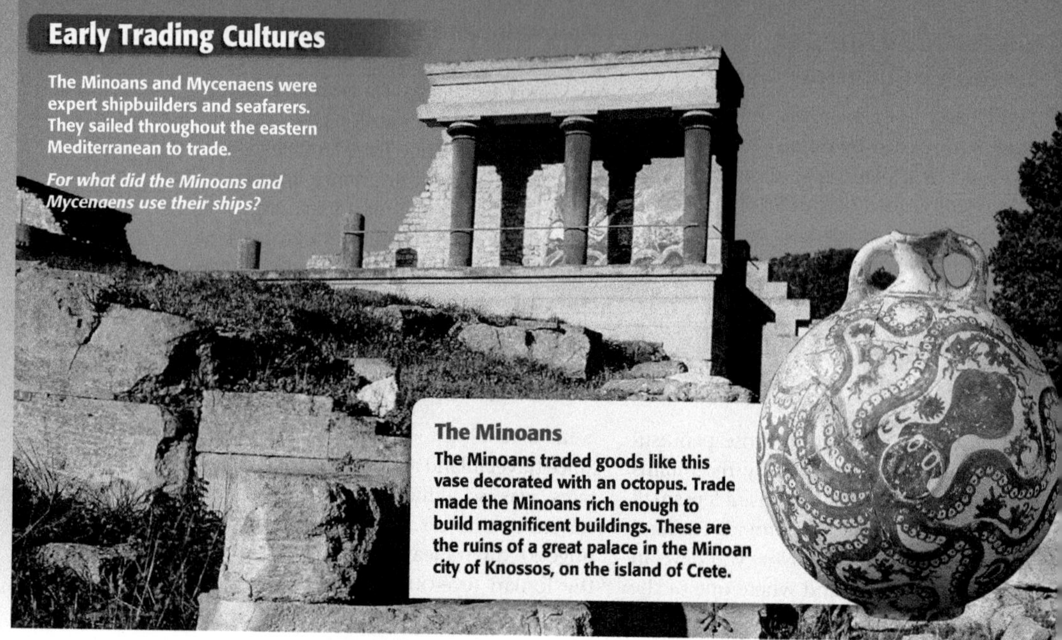

Early Trading Cultures

The Minoans and Mycenaens were expert shipbuilders and seafarers. They sailed throughout the eastern Mediterranean to trade.

For what did the Minoans and Mycenaens use their ships?

The Minoans

The Minoans traded goods like this vase decorated with an octopus. Trade made the Minoans rich enough to build magnificent buildings. These are the ruins of a great palace in the Minoan city of Knossos, on the island of Crete.

It's not surprising that the early Greeks used the sea as a source for food and as a way of trading with other communities.

The Greeks became skilled shipbuilders and sailors. Their ships sailed to Asia Minor (present-day Turkey), to Egypt, and to the islands of the Mediterranean and Aegean seas. As they traveled around these seas, they found sources of food and other products they needed. They also exchanged ideas with other cultures.

ACADEMIC VOCABULARY
influence change, or have an effect on

READING CHECK **Drawing Conclusions** How did mountains affect the location of Greek settlements?

Trading Cultures Develop

Many cultures settled and developed in Greece. Two of the earliest were the Minoans (muh-NOH-uhnz) and the Mycenaens (my-suh-NEE-uhns). By 2000 BC the Minoans had built an advanced society on the island of Crete. Crete lay south of the Aegean in the eastern Mediterranean. Later, the Mycenaeans built towns on the Greek mainland. These two civilizations **influenced** the entire Aegean region and helped shape later cultures in Greece.

The Minoans

Because they lived on an island, the Minoans spent much of their time at sea. They were among the best shipbuilders of their time. Minoan ships carried goods such as wood, olive oil, and pottery all around the eastern Mediterranean. They traded these goods for copper, gold, silver, and jewels.

Although Crete's location was excellent for Minoan traders, its geography had its dangers. Sometime in the 1600s BC a huge volcano erupted just north of Crete. This eruption created a giant wave that flooded much of Crete. In addition, the eruption

Social Studies Skill Activity: Using Time Lines

Below Level

Time Line of the Trading Cultures

1. Discuss with students the early trading cultures of the Minoans and Mycenaeans and key events in the history of each society.
2. Next, write the following events on the board for students to copy. Omit dates in italics.
   - Minoan civilization declines *(mid-1400s BC)*
   - Minoans establish society on Crete *(2000 BC)*
   - Invaders enter Greece *(1200s BC)*
   - Volcanic eruption floods Crete *(1600s BC)*
3. Have each student create a time line that includes entries and years(s) for the events listed in the correct chronological order in which each occurred. **LS Visual/Spatial**

Alternative Assessment Handbook, Rubric 36: Time Lines

Interactive Skills Tutor CD-ROM

Answers

Early Trading Cultures *to trade in the Mediterranean*

Reading Check *Villages and towns were separated by mountains.*

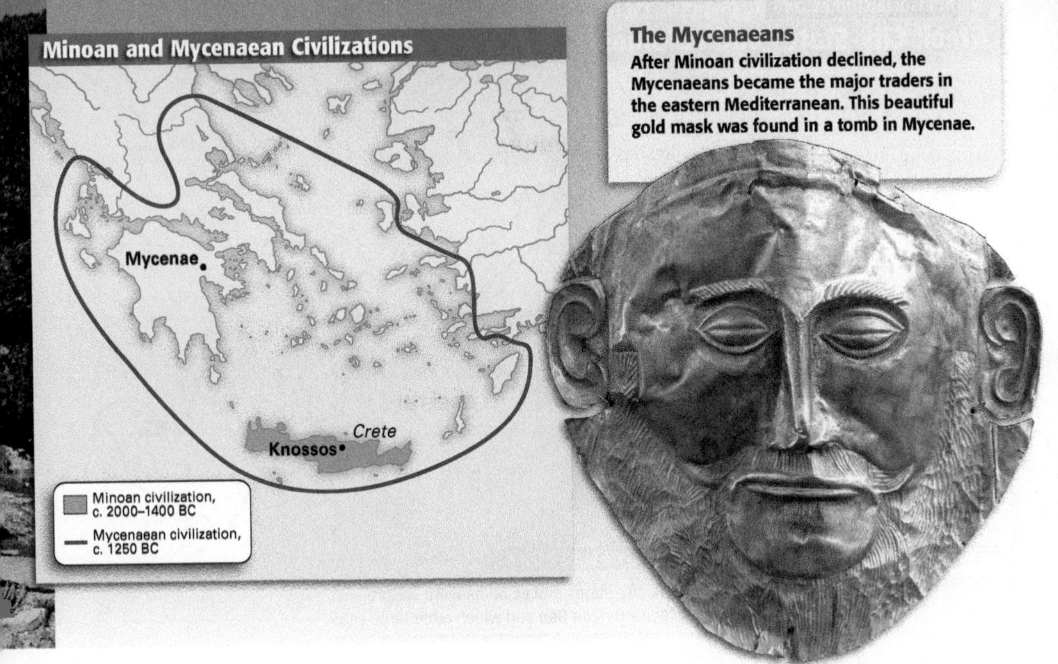

The Mycenaeans
After Minoan civilization declined, the Mycenaeans became the major traders in the eastern Mediterranean. This beautiful gold mask was found in a tomb in Mycenae.

threw up huge clouds of ash, ruining crops and burying cities. This eruption may have led to the end of Minoan civilization.

The Mycenaeans

Although they lived in what is now Greece and influenced Greek society, historians don't consider the Minoans to be Greek. This is because the Minoans didn't speak the Greek language. The first people to speak Greek, and therefore the first to be considered Greek, were the Mycenaeans.

While the Minoans were sailing the Mediterranean, the Mycenaeans were building fortresses all over the Greek mainland. The largest and most powerful fortress was Mycenae (my-SEE-nee), after which the Mycenaeans were named.

By the mid-1400s, Minoan society had declined. That decline allowed the Mycenaeans to take over Crete and become the major traders in the eastern Mediterranean. They set up colonies in northern Greece and Italy from which they shipped goods to markets around the Mediterranean and Black seas.

The Mycenaeans didn't think trade had to be conducted peacefully. They often attacked other kingdoms. Some historians think the Mycenaeans attacked the city of Troy, possibly starting the legendary Trojan War, which is featured in many works of literature.

Mycenaean society began to fall apart in the 1200s BC when invaders from Europe swept into Greece. At the same time, earthquakes destroyed many cities. As Mycenaean civilization crumbled, Greece slid into a period of warfare and disorder, a period called the Dark Age.

READING CHECK **Finding Main Ideas**
To what regions did Minoan and Mycenaean traders travel?

Direct Teach

Interpreting Maps

Minoan and Mycenaean Civilizations

Review with students the map of the Minoan and Mycenaean civilizations. Ask the following questions:

Location Where is Knossos located? *on the island of Crete*

Movement In what direction would the Mycenaeans have had to travel to reach the Minoan civilization? *southeast*

Human/Environment Interaction How might the Minoans' location provide them with protection? *They were surrounded by water and would not be easy to invade.*

Map Transparency: Minoan and Mycenaean Civilizations

Did you know . . .

The Trojan War was believed to be only a legend until the ruins of the city of Troy were discovered in the late 1800s.

Cross-Discipline Activity: Arts and the Humanities

At Level

Minoan Frescoes

Materials: butcher paper, art supplies

1. Have students examine the photo of the palace at Knossos. Point out the mural behind the columns. Explain that these murals are called frescoes.
2. Explain to students that frescoes are a type of painting in which artists paint onto a wall while the wall's plaster is still wet. This technique allows frescoes to survive for very long periods of time.
3. Tell students that Minoan frescoes generally depicted everyday life such as sports, trade, and animals.
4. Organize students into small groups. Have them decide what images of their daily life they would include in a class fresco. Then have students create a fresco on butcher paper. **LS Visual/Spatial**

Alternative Assessment Handbook, Rubric 3: Artwork

Answers

Reading Check *Minoans—eastern Mediterranean; Mycenaeans—Mediterranean and Black seas*

Direct Teach

Interpreting Maps

Greek City-States and Colonies, c. 600 BC

Activity **Creating a Map** Using an outline map of the Mediterranean, have students label the major Greek colonies and trade routes. Then have students use a current world atlas to identify the modern-day countries where the Greeks had influence.
LS Visual/Spatial

Alternative Assessment Handbook: Rubric 20: Map Creation

Main Idea

3 Greeks Create City-States

The Greeks created city-states for protection and security.

Define What is a classical age? *a time marked by great achievements*

Summarize Why did Greeks decide to establish colonies? *They wanted to trade, learn more about their neighbors, and deal with their growing population.*

Draw Conclusions How did city walls and acropolises benefit Greek city-states? *They protected the city-states from attack.*

CRF: History and Geography Activity: Greek City-States and Colonization

Map Transparency: Greek City-States and Colonies, c. 600 BC

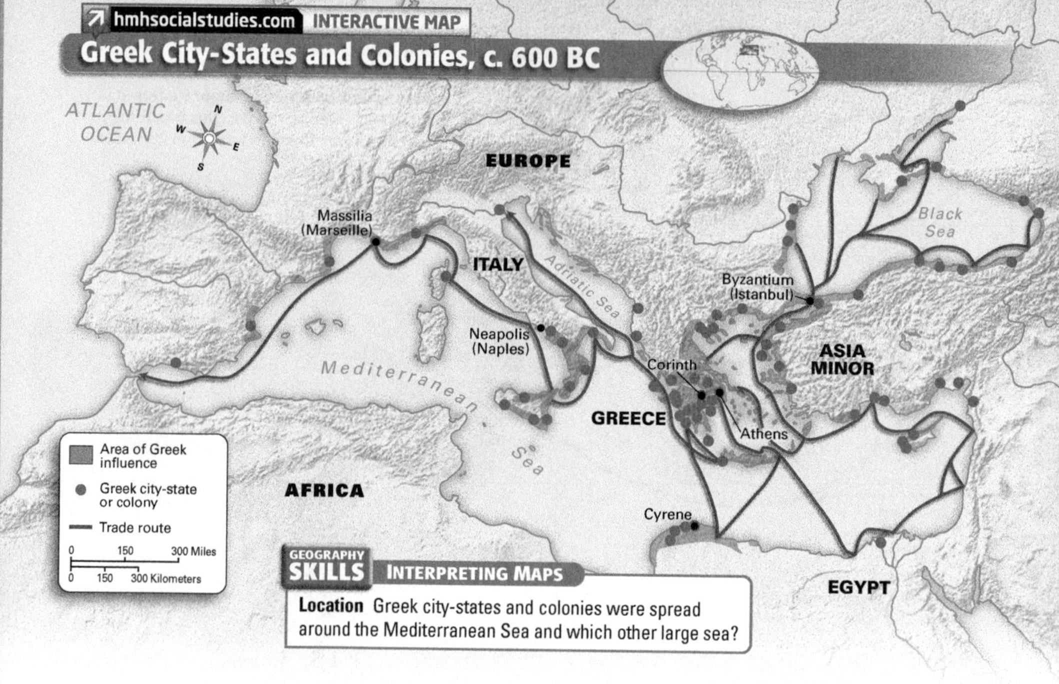

GEOGRAPHY SKILLS **INTERPRETING MAPS**

Location Greek city-states and colonies were spread around the Mediterranean Sea and which other large sea?

Greeks Create City-States

The Greeks of the Dark Age left no written records. All that we know about the period comes from archaeological findings.

About 300 years after the Mycenaean civilization crumbled, the Greeks started to join together in small groups for protection and stability. Over time, these groups set up independent city-states. The Greek word for a city-state is **polis** (PAH-luhs). The creation of city-states marks the beginning of what is known as Greece's classical age. A **classical** age is one that is marked by great achievements.

THE IMPACT TODAY Historians also call the classical age in Greece the Hellenic Period. The word *Hellenic* means "Greek."

Life in a City-State

A Greek city was usually built around a strong fortress. This fortress often stood on top of a high hill called the **acropolis** (uh-KRAH-puh-luhs). The town around the acropolis was surrounded by walls for added protection.

Not everyone who lived in the city-state actually lived inside the city walls. Farmers, for example, usually lived near their fields outside the walls. In times of war, however, women, children, and elderly people all gathered inside the city walls for protection. As a result, they remained safe while the men of the polis formed an army to fight off its enemies.

Life in the city often focused on the marketplace, or agora (A-guh-ruh) in Greek. Farmers brought their crops to the market to trade for goods made by craftsmen in the town. Because it was a large open space, the market also served as a meeting place. People held both political and religious assemblies in the market. It often contained shops as well.

The city-state became the foundation of Greek civilization. Besides providing security for its people, the city gave them an identity. People thought of themselves

Critical Thinking: Identifying Points of View

At Level

Letter Supporting Colonization

1. Discuss with students the reasons many Greeks had for establishing colonies in the Mediterranean.
2. Next, have students identify some of the ways in which the Greeks benefited from having colonies. Remind students to consider economic benefits as well as others.
3. Ask students to imagine that they live in a Greek city-state that does not have colonies. Have each student write a letter to the leaders of their city-state encouraging them to establish colonies in the region.
4. Student letters should be persuasive and should point out the benefits of creating colonies, based on the reasons provided in the section. **LS Verbal/Linguistic**

Alternative Assessment Handbook: Rubric 43: Writing to Persuade

Answers

Interpreting Maps *the Black Sea*

Focus on Reading Polis *means city-state, so one can infer that it is some type of city.*

as residents of a city, not as Greeks. Because the city-state was so central to their lives, the Greeks expected people to participate in its affairs, especially in its economy and its government.

City-States and Colonization

Life in Greece eventually became more settled. People no longer had to fear raiders swooping down on their cities. As a result, they were free to think about things other than defense. Some Greeks began to dream of becoming rich through trade. Others became curious about neighboring lands around the Mediterranean Sea. Some also worried about how to deal with Greece's growing population. Despite their different reasons, all these people eventually reached the same idea: the Greeks should establish colonies.

Before long, groups from city-states around Greece began to set up colonies in distant lands. After they were set up, Greek colonies became independent. In other words, each colony became a new polis. In fact, some cities that began as colonies began to create colonies of their own. Eventually Greek colonies spread all around the Mediterranean and Black seas. Many big cities around the Mediterranean today began as Greek colonies. Among them are Istanbul (is-tahn-BOOL) in Turkey, Marseille (mahr-SAY) in France, and Naples in Italy.

Patterns of Trade

Although the colonies were independent, they often traded with city-states on the mainland. The colonies sent metals such as copper and iron back to mainland Greece. In return, the Greek city-states sent wine, olive oil, and other products.

Trade made the city-states much richer. Because of their locations, some city-states became great trading centers. By 550 BC the Greeks had become the greatest traders in the whole Aegean region. Greek ships sailed to Egypt and cities around the Black Sea.

hmhsocialstudies.com
ANIMATED HISTORY
Greek Trade, 500 BC

READING CHECK **Analyzing** Why did the Greeks develop city-states?

SUMMARY AND PREVIEW In this section you learned about the creation of city-states and how they affected Greek society. In the next section you will read about how the government of one city-state changed as people became more interested in how they were ruled.

Section 1 Assessment

hmhsocialstudies.com ONLINE QUIZ

Reviewing Ideas, Terms, and People

1. a. **Identify** What kinds of landforms are found in Greece?
   b. **Interpret** How did the sea help shape early Greek society?
   c. **Predict** How might the difficulty of mountain travel have been a benefit to the Greeks?
2. a. **Recall** What was the first major civilization to develop in Greece?
   b. **Compare** How were the Minoans and Mycenaeans similar?
3. a. **Define** What is a **polis**?
   b. **Elaborate** Why do you think the Greeks built their cities around a high **acropolis**?

Critical Thinking

4. **Summarizing** Using your notes, write one descriptive sentence about Greece's geography and one about city-states. Then write a sentence summarizing the influence of geography on city-states.

Geography → City-States → Summary

FOCUS ON WRITING

5. **Thinking About Geographical Features as Characters** Have you ever thought about physical features as having personalities? For example, you might describe a strong, blustery wind as angry. Think about the physical features of Greece you read about in this section. What kinds of personalities might they have? Write your ideas down in your notebook.

• Review & Assess •

Close

Have students briefly explain in writing how Greek geography affected the early civilizations of ancient Greece and the development of city-states.

Review

Online Quiz, Section 1

Assess

SE Section 1 Assessment

PASS: Section 1 Quiz

Alternative Assessment Handbook

Reteach/Classroom Intervention

Guided Reading Workbook, Section 1

Interactive Skills Tutor CD-ROM

Section 1 Assessment Answers

1. a. mountains, valleys, and coastal plains
   b. It provided jobs in shipbuilding and a means of trading with other communities.
   c. Mountains would provide a form of protection, keeping others from easily attacking.
2. a. the Minoan civilization
   b. They both traded with other societies, both influenced Greek culture, and both used the sea for travel.
3. a. Greek word for city-state
   b. Answers will vary, but students should indicate an understanding that acropolises served to protect the city-state.
4. functions of polis—provided protection; centers for trade; gave people an identity as members of the city-state
5. possible answers—Calm seas might be friendly and inviting; towering mountains might be heartless and cruel.

Answers

Reading Check *to band together for protection and stability*

History and Geography

Activity **A Bad Day in Crete** Lead a discussion about how the eruption would have affected the buildings and people of Knossos. Then have students work in groups to create storyboards depicting scenes from a movie about the Thera eruption. Or, have students create posters advertising the movie.
LS Visual/Spatial

Info to Know

From Reality to Legend The Minoan civilization may have inspired stories about Atlantis, a legendary island kingdom that supposedly disappeared beneath waves caused by earthquakes. The Greek philosopher Plato wrote about Atlantis. He may have gotten the story from ancient Egyptian records that report the Thera eruption.

History and Geography

Natural Disaster!

Nature is a powerful force. Throughout history, great natural disasters have affected civilizations. One natural disaster was so devastating that it may have contributed to the destruction of the entire Minoan civilization.

In the 1600s BC a volcano on the Greek island of Thera erupted. The colossal explosion was one of the largest in history. It was so powerful that people could see and hear it from hundreds of miles away. In a moment of nature's fury, the history of the Mediterranean world was changed forever.

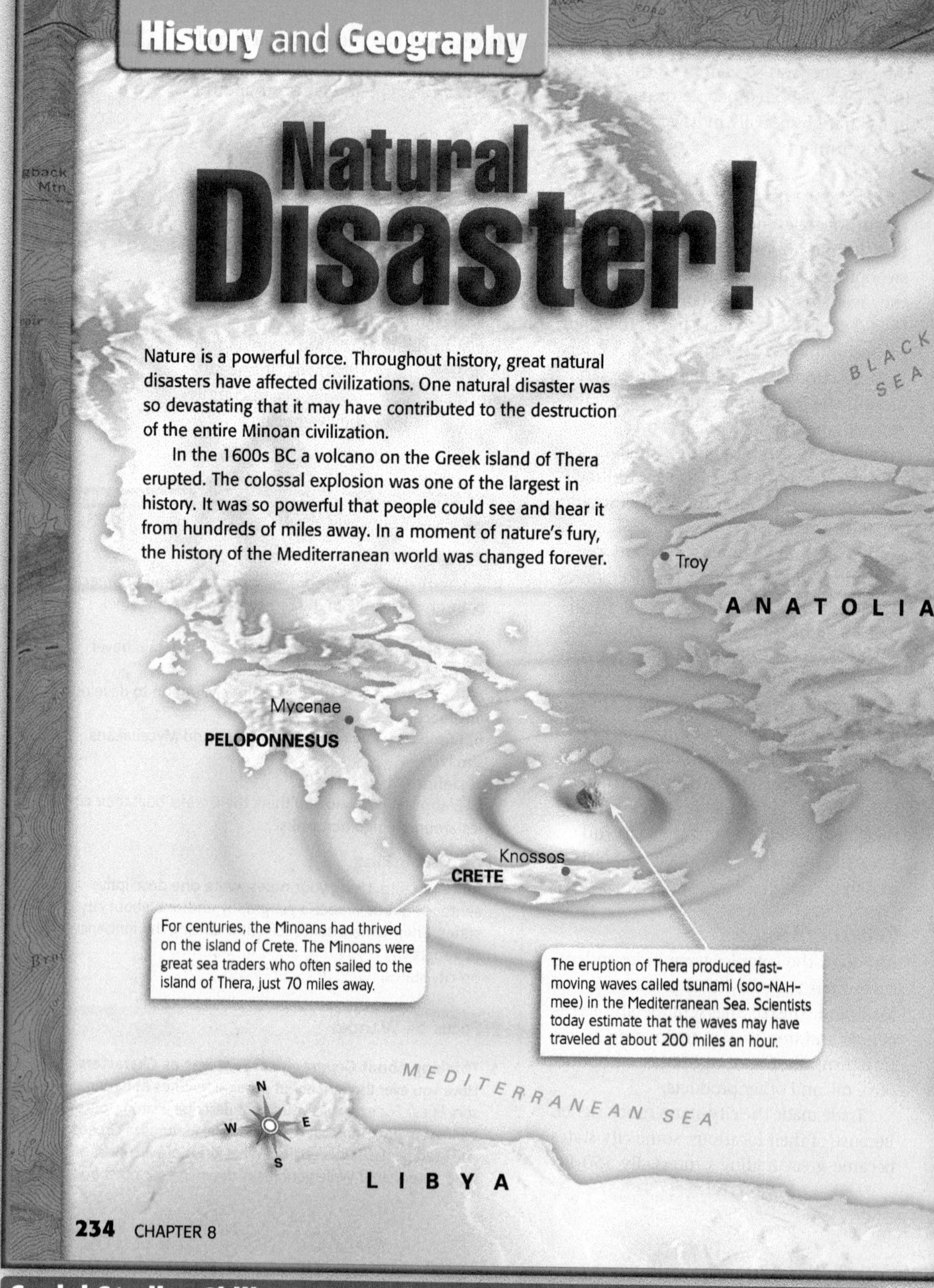

For centuries, the Minoans had thrived on the island of Crete. The Minoans were great sea traders who often sailed to the island of Thera, just 70 miles away.

The eruption of Thera produced fast-moving waves called tsunami (soo-NAH-mee) in the Mediterranean Sea. Scientists today estimate that the waves may have traveled at about 200 miles an hour.

Social Studies Skills: Recognizing the Role of Chance in History

Changing History

Above Level

1. Ask students to skim the remainder of this chapter and the next one. Then ask students to consider these questions. How would the history of the Mediterranean world have proceeded if the Thera volcano had not erupted violently, but instead the lava had flowed slowly into the sea? How may the eruption have affected Greek history? Point out that immediate effects of physical events can have a ripple effect that extends over centuries.
2. Have each student create a booklet in which he or she rewrites key heads and subheads for the rest of this chapter and the next one, basing the rewrites on the assumption that the Thera volcano was not violent.
3. Extend the activity by discussing how even today things could be very different if history had changed that day on Thera.
LS Interpersonal, Verbal/Linguistic

Alternative Assessment Handbook, Rubric 11: Discussions

Three Stages of
Disaster
Stage 1
Warning Signs Following a series of earthquakes, the volcano begins to shoot ash into the sky. People flee the island in fear.
Stage 2
Explosion Ash and rock are flung into the air and sweep down the volcano's sides, destroying everything in their path. Cracks through the island rock begin to form from the powerful explosions.
Stage 3
Collapse The volcano collapses and falls into the sea, creating massive waves. The powerful waves slam into Crete, flooding coastal areas.
Aleppo
CYPRUS
Jericho
EGYPT

The ancient island of Thera is known as Santorini today. The huge gap on the island's western side and the water in the middle are evidence of the explosion more than 3,500 years ago.

The explosion produced a massive cloud of ash that smothered crops, cities, and people. For years afterward, the ash dimmed the sunlight, making it difficult for farmers to grow their crops.

GEOGRAPHY SKILLS INTERPRETING MAPS

1. **Location** What direction did the ash cloud travel after the island's eruption?
2. **Human-Environment Interaction** How might the effects of the ash cloud have influenced Minoan civilization?

History and Geography

Connect to Science

Stealthy Killer Waves Tsunamis like those that hit Crete in the 1600s BC may be mere ripples way out at sea. A severe earthquake in the middle of the ocean may send out waves more than 100 miles apart. These waves race across the ocean at speeds of up to 450 miles per hour. The tops of the waves are very low, however, so people on board a ship would probably not notice such a wave as it raced by. The trouble comes when the waves near the shore. As the water gets shallower, the waves slow down and grow taller. When they finally crash onto the shore, tsunamis can be 100 feet high.

On December 26, 2004, an underwater earthquake caused tsunamis to hit the coasts of Sri Lanka, Indonesia, India, Thailand, Somalia, and several other countries. The devastation was terrible. A month after the waves struck, the death toll had climbed to more than 212,000. Millions more people were homeless.

MISCONCEPTION ALERT

Name that Wave! Tsunamis are often mistakenly called tidal waves. An alternate and accurate name for a tsunami is seismic sea wave. Tsunamis are not related to tidal action in any way, so the term *tidal wave* is incorrect.

Critical Thinking: Comparing and Contrasting

At Level

Natural Disasters and History

Research Required

1. Organize the class into groups. Have each group conduct research on a different major natural disaster. Possibilities may include the eruption of Krakatoa (Indonesia, 1883), the New Madrid earthquakes (North America, 1811), the Tunguska Event (Russia, 1908), or the flood of the Huang He (China, 1887).
2. Ask students to concentrate their research on the short- and long-term effects the disaster had on areas both near and far away.
3. Then have students compare the assigned disaster's effects with the impact that the Thera eruption had on Minoan civilization. Challenge students to compare specific factors, such as the number of people in the area that were affected, communication capabilities, and so on.
4. Ask each group to report to the class in the form of a newscast.

LS Interpersonal, Kinesthetic

Alternative Assessment Handbook, Rubric 9: Comparing and Contrasting

Answers

Interpreting Maps: 1. *northeast* **2.** *possible answers—caused immediate death and destruction and long-term decline of Minoan civilization due to damage to ships, harbors, and farmland*

Preteach

Bellringer

If YOU were there . . . Use the **Daily Bellringer Transparency** to help students answer the question.

Daily Bellringer Transparency, Section 2

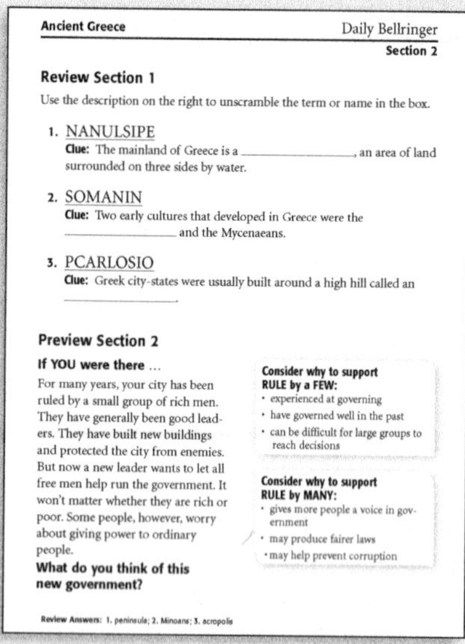

Ancient Greece — Daily Bellringer — **Section 2**

Review Section 1

Use the description on the right to unscramble the term or name in the box.

1. NANULSIPE
   Clue: The mainland of Greece is a ________, an area of land surrounded on three sides by water.
2. SOMANIN
   Clue: Two early cultures that developed in Greece were the ________ and the Mycenaeans.
3. PCARLOSIO
   Clue: Greek city-states were usually built around a high hill called an ________.

Preview Section 2

If YOU were there ...

For many years, your city has been ruled by a small group of rich men. They have generally been good leaders. They have built new buildings and protected the city from enemies. But now a new leader wants to let all free men help run the government. It won't matter whether they are rich or poor. Some people, however, worry about giving power to ordinary people.

What do you think of this new government?

Consider why to support RULE by a FEW:
- experienced at governing
- have governed well in the past
- can be difficult for large groups to reach decisions

Consider why to support RULE by MANY:
- gives more people a voice in government
- may produce fairer laws
- may help prevent corruption

Review Answers: 1. peninsula; 2. Minoans; 3. acropolis

Building Vocabulary

Preteach or review the following term:

prosperity the state of being successful (p. 237)

CRF: Vocabulary Builder Activity, Section 2

Taking Notes

Have students use the graphic organizer online to take notes on the section. This activity will prepare students for the Section Assessment, in which they will complete a graphic organizer that builds on the information using the Critical Thinking Skill: Finding Main Ideas.

SECTION 2

Government in Athens

What You Will Learn...

Main Ideas

1. Aristocrats and tyrants ruled early Athens.
2. Athens created the world's first democracy.
3. Ancient democracy was different than modern democracy.

The Big Idea

The people of Athens tried many different forms of government before creating a democracy.

Key Terms and People

democracy, *p. 236*
aristocrats, *p. 237*
oligarchy, *p. 237*
citizens, *p. 237*
tyrant, *p. 237*
Pericles, *p. 240*

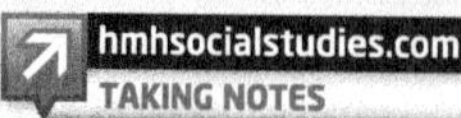

Use the graphic organizer online to take notes on the various types of government the people of Athens tried.

If YOU were there...

For many years, your city has been ruled by a small group of rich men. They have generally been good leaders. They have built new buildings and protected the city from enemies. But now a new leader wants to let all free men help run the government. It won't matter whether they are rich or poor. Some people, however, worry about giving power to ordinary people.

What do you think of this new government?

BUILDING BACKGROUND The decision to change a city's government was not unusual in Greece. Many cities tried several forms of government before people were satisfied. To see how these changes came about, we can look at one city whose government changed many times—Athens.

Aristocrats and Tyrants Rule

Greece is the birthplace of **democracy**, a type of government in which people rule themselves. The word democracy comes from Greek words meaning "rule of the people." But Greek city-states didn't start as democracies, and not all became democratic.

Government in Athens QUICK FACTS

Oligarchy

Early Athens was governed by a small group of powerful aristocrats. This type of government is called an oligarchy. Oligarchy means "rule by a few."

Teach the Big Idea

At Level

Government in Athens

1. **Teach** Ask students the questions in the Main Idea boxes to teach this section.
2. **Apply** Write the main ideas from the section for students to see, and discuss each concept with the class. Organize the students into small groups and assign each group one or more main ideas. Ask each group to create a one-to-two minute skit for its main ideas. Ask for groups to volunteer to perform their skits for the class. **LS Interpersonal, Kinesthetic**
3. **Review** After each group performs, review with the class the major concepts from each skit that pertain to the main ideas.
4. **Practice/Homework** Have students select their favorite performance and write a review of the skit, making sure to include the main points that were addressed in the presentation. **LS Verbal/Linguistic**

Alternative Assessment Handbook, Rubrics 33: Skits and Reader's Theater; and 41: Writing to Express

Rule by a Few People

Even Athens, the city where democracy was born, began with a different kind of government. In early Athens, kings ruled the city-state. Later, a group of rich landowners, or **aristocrats** (uh-RIS-tuh-krats), took power. A government in which only a few people have power is called an **oligarchy** (AH-luh-gar-kee).

The aristocrats dominated Athenian society. As the richest men in town, they ran the city's economy. They also served as its generals and judges. Common people had little say in the government.

In the 600s BC a group of rebels tried to overthrow the aristocrats. They failed. Possibly as a result of their attempt, however, a man named Draco (DRAY-koh) created a new set of laws for Athens. These laws were very harsh. For example, Draco's laws made minor crimes such as loitering punishable by death.

The people of Athens thought Draco's laws were too strict. In the 590s BC a man named Solon (SOH-luhn) created a set of laws that were much less harsh and gave more rights to nonaristocrats. Under Solon's laws, all free men living in Athens became **citizens**, people who had the right to participate in government. But his efforts were not enough for the Athenians. They were ready to end the rule of the aristocracy.

The Rise of the Tyrants

Because the Athenians weren't pleased with the rule of the aristocrats, they wanted a new government. In 546 BC a noble named Peisistratus (py-SIS-truht-uhs) overthrew the oligarchy. He became the ruler of Athens. Peisistratus was called a **tyrant**, which meant a leader who held power through the use of force.

Today the word *tyrant* means a ruler who is harsh, but the word had a different meaning in ancient Greece. Athenian tyrants were usually good leaders. Tyrants were able to stay in power because they had strong armies and because the people supported them.

Peisistratus brought peace and prosperity to the city. He began new policies meant to unify the city. He created new festivals and built temples and monuments. During his rule, many improvements were made in Athens.

After Peisistratus died, his son took over as tyrant. Many aristocrats, however, were unhappy because their power was gone. Some of these aristocrats convinced a rival city-state to attack Athens. As a result of this invasion, the tyrants lost power and, for a short time, aristocrats returned to power in Athens.

READING CHECK **Finding Main Ideas** What was a tyrant in ancient Greece?

FOCUS ON READING
How do Greek roots give you clues to the meaning of *oligarchy*?

THE IMPACT TODAY
Today very harsh laws or rules are called "draconian" after Draco.

Tyranny
Peisistratus overthrew the oligarchy in 546 BC, and Athens became a tyranny. Tyranny means "rule by a tyrant"—a strong leader who has power.

Democracy
Around 500 BC Athens became a democracy. Democracy means "rule by the people." For the first time in history, a government was based on the votes of its free citizens.

Direct Teach

Main Idea

1 Aristocrats and Tyrants Rule

Aristocrats and tyrants ruled early Athens.

Describe What were Greek tyrants like? *They were good leaders with strong armies and who had the support of the people.*

Explain Why was Athens considered at one point an oligarchy? *because it was ruled by a few nobles*

Draw Conclusions Why did many Athenians support the rule of tyrants? *possible answers—They improved life in Athens and removed aristocrats from power.*

Activity **Slogans for Rulers**
Have each student select one of the rulers mentioned on this page. Ask students to create a poster that contains a slogan for that ruler.
LS Verbal/Linguistic

Alternative Assessment Handbook: Rubric 34: Slogans and Banners

Quick Facts Transparency: Government in Athens

QUICK FACTS **Government in Athens**

How does each illustration reflect a different style of government? *oligarchy—men are wealthy aristocrats; tyranny—leader has military power; democracy—people are participating in political debate*

Quick Facts Transparency: Government in Athens

Differentiating Instruction

English-Language Learners **At Level**

1. Review with students the key terms from this section: democracy, aristocrats, oligarchy, citizens, and tyrant.
2. Draw a tic-tac-toe diagram (nine-square grid) for students to see. Divide the students into two groups: X's and O's.
3. Determine which group will go first. Then select one student in that group to answer a question. Given one of the vocabulary words, students are to define the term and use it in a sentence. Upon answering correctly, that group puts their mark in the square of their choosing. The first group to get three in a row wins. **LS Interpersonal, Verbal/Linguistic**

Alternative Assessment Handbook, Rubric 11: Discussions

CRF: Vocabulary Builder Activity, Section 2

Answers

Focus on Reading Oli- *means a few and* -garchy *means to rule, so oligarchy means rule by a few.*

Reading Check *In Greece, a good leader who held power through the use of force and who had the people's support.*

Direct Teach

Main Idea

2 Athens Creates Democracy

Athens created the world's first democracy.

Recall Who was the father of democracy in Athens? *Cleisthenes*

Analyze Why were slaves sent to round up citizens? *because more citizens were needed to vote on a law*

Explain Why was a smaller council of officials necessary? *It was easier to make decisions about which laws the assembly should vote on.*

Activity Democracy Political Cartoon Have each student create an original political cartoon that deals with an element of the democratic process in Athens. Ask for volunteers to share their completed cartoons with the class. **LS Visual/Spatial**

- Alternative Assessment Handbook: Rubric 27: Political Cartoons
- **CRF:** Primary Source Activity: Aristotle's Athenian Constitution

Info to Know

Cleisthenes In order to break the power of the aristocrats, Cleisthenes re-organized all Athenians into 10 new tribes. The tribes were an important part of local politics, and many had local assemblies similar to the Athenian assembly.

History Close-up

Democracy in Action

Ancient Athens was the birthplace of democracy—the system of government in which the people rule themselves. Democracy was perhaps the greatest achievement of ancient Athens. In time, it became the Greeks' greatest gift to the world.

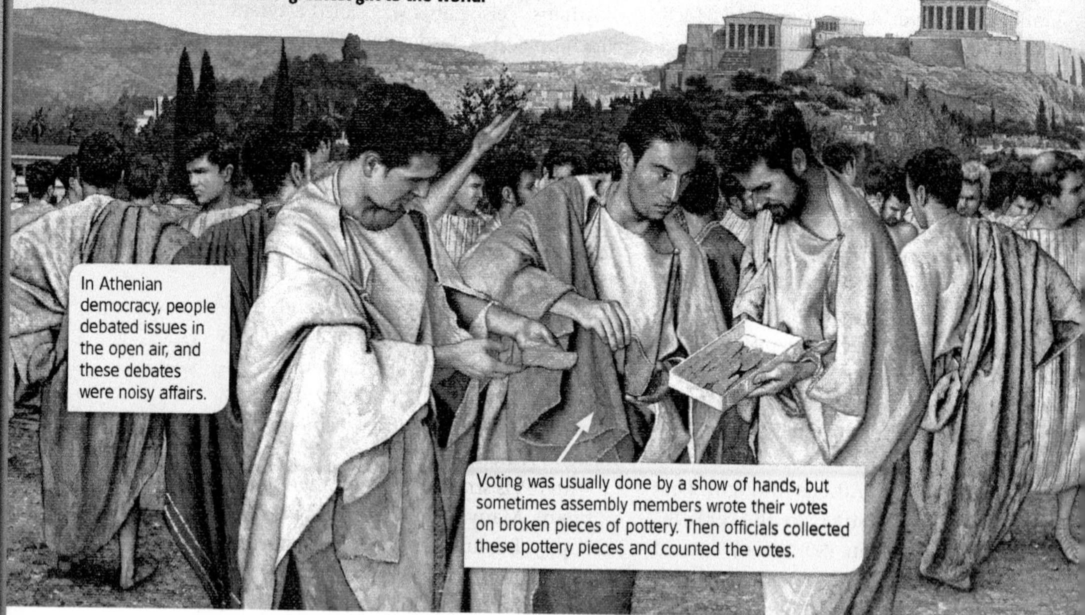

Only free male citizens of Athens were members of the assembly with the right to vote. Women, slaves, and foreigners could not participate.

In Athenian democracy, people debated issues in the open air, and these debates were noisy affairs.

Voting was usually done by a show of hands, but sometimes assembly members wrote their votes on broken pieces of pottery. Then officials collected these pottery pieces and counted the votes.

Athens Creates Democracy

Around 500 BC a new leader named Cleisthenes (KLYS-thuh-neez) gained power in Athens. Although he was a member of one of the most powerful families in Athens, Cleisthenes didn't want aristocrats to run the government. He thought they already had too much influence. By calling on the support of the people, Cleisthenes was able to overthrow the aristocracy once and for all. In its place, he established a completely new form of government.

Under Cleisthenes' leadership, Athens developed the world's first democracy. For this reason, he is sometimes called the father of democracy.

Democracy under Cleisthenes

Under Cleisthenes, all citizens in Athens had the right to participate in the assembly, or gathering of citizens, that created the city's laws. The assembly met outdoors on a hillside so that everyone could attend the meetings. During meetings, people stood before the crowd and gave speeches on political issues. Every citizen had the right to speak his opinion. In fact, the Athenians encouraged people to speak. They loved to hear speeches and debates. After the speeches were over, the assembly voted. Voting was usually done by a show of hands, but sometimes the Athenians used secret ballots.

Critical Thinking: Evaluating Information

Below Level

Evaluating the Athenian Assembly

1. Review with students the creation of democracy in Athens as well as the description of the Athenian assembly.
2. Draw the graphic organizer for students to see. Omit the blue, italicized answers. Ask students to identify the benefits and drawbacks of democracy in Athens.
3. Have students evaluate whether democracy in Athens was good or bad. **LS Visual/Spatial**

Athenian Democracy	
Benefits	**Drawbacks**
• *All citizens have a say in government.*	• *Women, slaves, and foreigners have no say.*
• *All citizens can express opinions.*	• *Sometimes forced to attend assembly.*
• *Power of nobles is limited.*	• *Difficult to make decisions with so many people.*

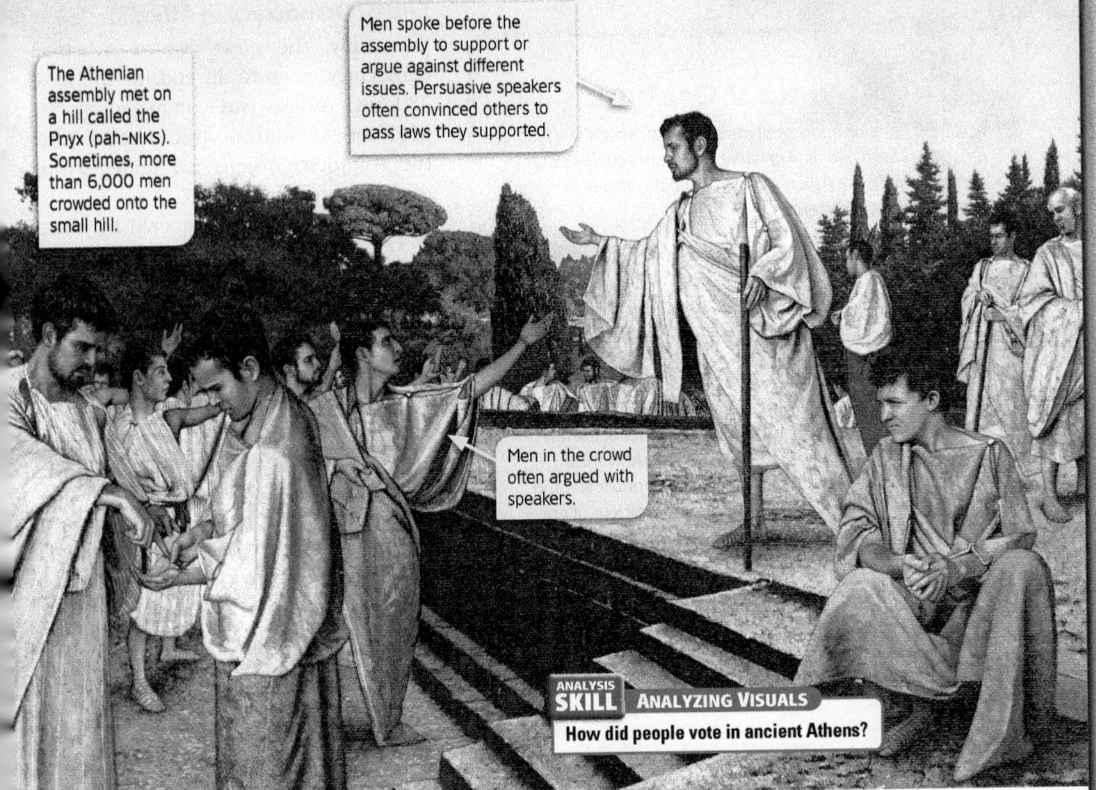

The Athenian assembly met on a hill called the Pnyx (pah-NIKS). Sometimes, more than 6,000 men crowded onto the small hill.
Men spoke before the assembly to support or argue against different issues. Persuasive speakers often convinced others to pass laws they supported.
Men in the crowd often argued with speakers.
ANALYSIS SKILL ANALYZING VISUALS
How did people vote in ancient Athens?

The number of people who voted in the assembly changed from day to day. For major decisions, however, the assembly needed about 6,000 people to vote. But it wasn't always easy to gather that many people together in one place.

According to one Greek writer, the government sent slaves to the market to round up more citizens if necessary. In one of the writer's plays, slaves walked through the market holding a long rope between them. The rope was covered in red dye and would mark the clothing of anyone it touched. Any citizen with red dye on his clothing had to go to the assembly meeting or pay a large fine.

Because the assembly was so large, it was sometimes difficult to make decisions. The Athenians therefore selected citizens to be city officials and to serve on a smaller council. These officials decided which laws the assembly should discuss. This helped the government run more smoothly.

Changes in Athenian Democracy

As time passed, citizens gained more powers. For example, they served on juries to decide court cases. Juries had anywhere from 200 to 6,000 people, although juries of about 500 people were much more common. Most juries had an odd number of members to prevent ties.

THE IMPACT TODAY

Like the ancient Greeks, we use juries to decide court cases. But our modern juries have only 12 people.

Direct Teach

History Close-up

Democracy in Action

Review with students the illustration of the assembly of Athens. Ask the following questions:

Recall How did voting take place in the assembly? *by a show of hands or a secret ballot*

Make Inferences Why did the assembly meet outdoors? *so that as many as 6,000 citizens could meet together*

Did you know . . .

The assembly would vote once a year to ostracize, or exile, citizens of Athens. If enough citizens voted in favor of ostracism, citizens would gather to cast a vote for the person they wanted to see exiled from Athens. The citizen receiving the most votes would be forced to leave the city for up to 10 years.

Answers

Analyzing Visuals *usually by a show of hands; sometimes by secret ballot*

Collaborative Learning

Above Level

Greek Assembly Simulation

1. Review with the class the way in which the Athenian assembly functioned. The council decided what laws to present to the assembly. The assembly debated the laws, then voted on them.
2. Organize the class into groups of four to five students. Have each group select members to serve as recorder, council member, and citizens.
3. Ask the students to generate ideas for laws that could be proposed for their school, city, or nation. Write the list of ideas for students to see. Then ask the council members from each group to meet briefly to decide on what law they will propose to the assembly. Write the law to be debated for everyone to see.
4. Ask each student group to briefly debate the law that has been proposed. Encourage students to see both sides of the issue. The recorder from each group should keep track of the arguments made for and against the law.
5. Call the groups together and have the assembly hold a vote on the law. All students will cast their vote for or against the law.
6. Announce the results of the vote to the class. Ask students to reflect on the process of the assembly. **LS Interpersonal, Verbal/Linguistic**

Alternative Assessment Handbook, Rubrics 10: Debates; and 14: Group Activity

Direct Teach

Primary Source

Pericles' Funeral Oration

Interpret What does Pericles mean when he says that Athens serves as an example to its neighbors? *The government of Athens is so great that it is copied by other city-states.*

 **CRF:** Biography Activity: Pericles

Main Idea

3 Ancient Democracy Differs from Modern Democracy

Ancient democracy was different than modern democracy.

Define What is a direct democracy? *a democracy in which each person has a direct vote*

Summarize How does a representative democracy work? *Citizens elect officials to represent them in the government and to make laws.*

Draw Conclusions Why didn't the United States establish a direct democracy? *There are too many people to make voting directly on every law practical.*

CRF: Biography Activity: Aspasia

CRF: Biography Activity: Pericles

Quick Facts Transparency: Democracy Then and Now

Primary Source

SPEECH

Pericles' Funeral Oration

In 430 BC Pericles addressed the people of Athens at a funeral for soldiers who had died in battle. In his speech, Pericles tried to comfort the Athenians by reminding them of the greatness of their government.

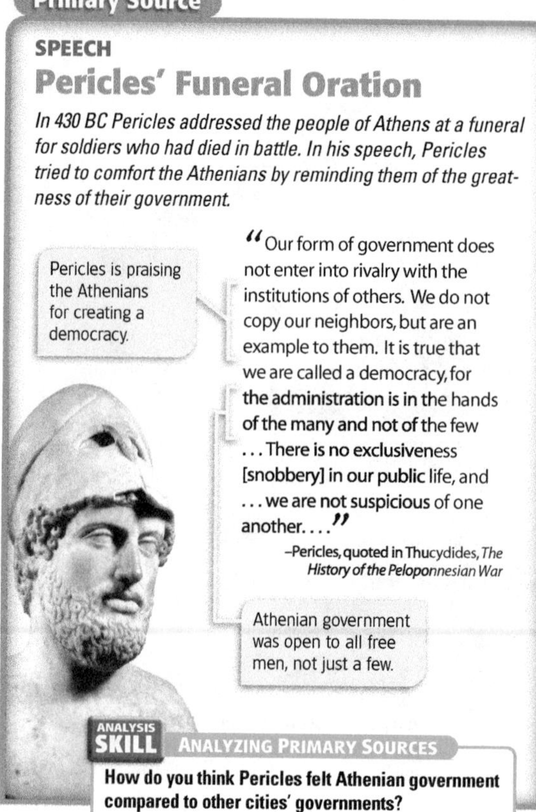

"Our form of government does not enter into rivalry with the institutions of others. We do not copy our neighbors, but are an example to them. It is true that we are called a democracy, for the administration is in the hands of the many and not of the few . . . There is no exclusiveness [snobbery] in our public life, and . . . we are not suspicious of one another. . . ."

–Pericles, quoted in Thucydides, *The History of the Peloponnesian War*

Pericles is praising the Athenians for creating a democracy.

Athenian government was open to all free men, not just a few.

ANALYSIS SKILL ANALYZING PRIMARY SOURCES

How do you think Pericles felt Athenian government compared to other cities' governments?

Athens remained a democracy for about 170 years. It reached its height under a brilliant elected leader named **Pericles** (PER-uh-kleez). He led the government from about 460 BC until his death in 429 BC.

Pericles encouraged the Athenians to take pride in their city. He believed that participating in government was just as important as defending Athens in war. To encourage people to participate in government, Pericles began to pay people who served in public offices or on juries. Pericles also encouraged the people of Athens to introduce democracy into other parts of Greece.

End of Democracy in Athens

Eventually, the great age of Athenian democracy came to an end. In the mid-330s BC Athens was conquered by the Macedonians from north of Greece. After the conquest, Athens fell under strong Macedonian influence.

Even after being conquered by Macedonia, Athens kept its democratic government. But it was a democracy with very limited powers. The Macedonian king ruled his country like a dictator, a ruler who held all the power. No one could make any decisions without his approval.

In Athens, the assembly still met to make laws, but it had to be careful not to upset the king. The Athenians didn't dare make any drastic changes to their laws without the king's consent. They weren't happy with this situation, but they feared the king's powerful army. Before long, though, the Athenians lost even this limited democracy. In the 320s BC a new king took over Greece and ended Athenian democracy forever.

READING CHECK **Summarizing** How were citizens involved in the government of Athens?

Ancient Democracy Differs from Modern Democracy

Like ancient Athens, the United States has a democratic government in which the people hold power. But our modern democracy is very different from the ancient Athenians' democracy.

Direct Democracy

All citizens in Athens could participate directly in the government. We call this form of government a direct democracy. It is called direct democracy because each person's decision directly affects the outcome of a vote. In Athens, citizens gathered

Critical Thinking: Sequencing

Below Level

Illustrated Time Line

1. Review with students the different governments that existed in ancient Athens.
2. Ask students to make a list of the different governments and the order in which each existed. Then ask students to identify the approximate dates of each government.
3. Finally, have students create an illustrated time line of the different governments of Athens. Time lines should list each government, explain the form of the government, and include an illustration that reflects that style of government (time line answers: *oligarchy—600s BC, tyranny—546 to 500 BC, democracy—500 to 330 BC, monarchy—330 BC*) LS **Visual/Spatial**

Alternative Assessment Handbook, Rubrics 3: Artwork; and 36: Time Lines

Answers

Analyzing Primary Sources *that the government of Athens was better than that of other cities*

Reading Check *They participated in the assembly, on juries, and held public offices.*

together to discuss issues and vote on them. Each person's vote counted, and the majority ruled.

The United States is too large for direct democracy to work for the whole country. For example, it would be impossible for all citizens to gather in one place for a debate. Instead, the founders of the United States set up another kind of democracy.

Representative Democracy

The democracy created by the founders of the United States is a representative democracy, or republic. In this system, the citizens elect officials to represent them in the government. These elected officials then meet to make the country's laws and to enforce them. For example, Americans elect senators and representatives to Congress, the body that makes the country's laws. Americans don't vote on each law that Congress passes but trust their chosen representatives to vote for them.

READING CHECK **Contrasting** How are direct democracy and representative democracy different?

Democracy Then and Now

In Athenian Direct Democracy...	In American Representative Democracy...
■ All citizens met as a group to debate and vote directly on every issue.	■ Citizens elect representatives to debate and vote on issues for them.
■ There was no separation of powers. Citizens created laws, enforced laws, and acted as judges.	■ There is a separation of powers. Citizens elect some people to create laws, others to enforce laws, and others to be judges.
■ Only free male citizens could vote. Women and slaves could not vote.	■ Men and women who are citizens have the right to vote.

SUMMARY AND PREVIEW In this section, you learned about the development and decline of democracy in Athens. You also learned how Athenian democracy influenced the government of the United States. In the next section, you will learn about the beliefs and culture of the ancient Greeks and how they affect our culture and literature today.

Section 2 Assessment

hmhsocialstudies.com ONLINE QUIZ

Reviewing Ideas, Terms, and People

1. a. **Define** What are **aristocrats**?
   b. **Contrast** How were **oligarchy** and **tyranny** different?
2. a. **Describe** Describe the **democracy** created by Cleisthenes.
   b. **Analyze** How did **Pericles** change Athenian democracy?
3. a. **Identify** What type of democracy did Athens have?
   b. **Develop** In what situations would a representative democracy work better than a direct democracy?

Critical Thinking

4. **Finding Main Ideas** Draw a chart like the one shown. Using your notes, identify who held power in each type of government. Then write a sentence explaining what role common people had in each government.

Oligarchy	Tyranny	Democracy

Focus on Writing

5. **Connecting Personalities and Governments** Think back to the personalities you assigned to natural features in Section 1. What if people with these same personalities were working to create a government? What kind would they create? Would they rule as tyrants or build a democracy? Write your thoughts in your notebook.

Direct Teach

Democracy Then and Now

Review the differences between Athenian and American democracy. Ask the following question: How does the role of a citizen in American democracy differ from that in Athenian democracy? *American—vote to elect officials; Athenian—vote on laws, enforce laws, act as judges*

Quick Facts Transparency: Democracy Then and Now

Review & Assess

Close

Have students discuss the various governments of ancient Athens and the benefits and drawbacks of each.

Review

Online Quiz, Section 2

Assess

SE Section 2 Assessment

PASS: Section 2 Quiz

Alternative Assessment Handbook

Reteach/Classroom Intervention

Guided Reading Workbook, Section 2

Interactive Skills Tutor CD-ROM

Section 2 Assessment Answers

1. a. rich landowners
   b. oligarchy—rule by a few wealthy aristocrats; tyranny—rule by one powerful leader
2. a. All citizens could participate in assembly, vote on laws, and debate issues
   b. encouraged people to participate in government and paid public officials
3. a. direct democracy
   b. when there are many citizens
4. oligarchy—aristocrats ruled; tyranny—powerful leader ruled; democracy—all citizens ruled; possible sentence—Common people had no role in government under oligarchy and tyranny but were very active in democracy.
5. possible answers—Cruel individuals might create a harsh government, whereas friendly people might tend to create a democratic government.

Answers

Reading Check *direct democracy—each citizen participates directly in government; representative democracy—elected officials represent citizens in government and make and vote on laws*

Preteach

Bellringer

If YOU were there . . . Use the **Daily Bellringer Transparency** to help students answer the question.

Daily Bellringer Transparency, Section 3

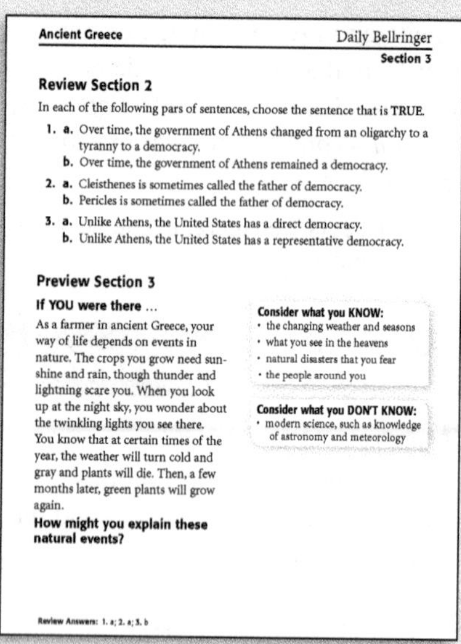

Ancient Greece Daily Bellringer

Section 3

Review Section 2

In each of the following pars of sentences, choose the sentence that is TRUE.

1. a. Over time, the government of Athens changed from an oligarchy to a tyranny to a democracy.
   b. Over time, the government of Athens remained a democracy.
2. a. Cleisthenes is sometimes called the father of democracy.
   b. Pericles is sometimes called the father of democracy.
3. a. Unlike Athens, the United States has a direct democracy.
   b. Unlike Athens, the United States has a representative democracy.

Preview Section 3

If YOU were there ...

As a farmer in ancient Greece, your way of life depends on events in nature. The crops you grow need sunshine and rain, though thunder and lightning scare you. When you look up at the night sky, you wonder about the twinkling lights you see there. You know that at certain times of the year, the weather will turn cold and gray and plants will die. Then, a few months later, green plants will grow again.

How might you explain these natural events?

Consider what you KNOW:
- the changing weather and seasons
- what you see in the heavens
- natural disasters that you fear
- the people around you

Consider what you DON'T KNOW:
- modern science, such as knowledge of astronomy and meteorology

Review Answers: 1. a; 2. a; 3. b

Building Vocabulary

Preteach or review the following term:

oracle a person through whom the gods were believed to speak (p. 244)

CRF: Vocabulary Builder Activity, Section 3

Taking Notes

Have students use the graphic organizer online to take notes on the section. This activity will prepare students for the Section Assessment, in which they will complete a graphic organizer that builds on the information using the Critical Thinking Skill: Analyzing.

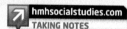

SECTION 3

Greek Mythology and Literature

What You Will Learn...

Main Ideas

1. The Greeks created myths to explain the world.
2. Ancient Greek literature provides some of the world's greatest poems and stories.
3. Greek literature lives on and influences our world even today.

The Big Idea

The ancient Greeks created great myths and works of literature that influence the way we speak and write today.

Key Terms and People

mythology, *p. 243*
Homer, *p. 246*
Sappho, *p. 247*
Aesop, *p. 247*
fables, *p. 247*

hmhsocialstudies.com
TAKING NOTES

Use the graphic organizer online to record characteristics of Greek myths and literature.

If YOU were there...

As a farmer in ancient Greece, your way of life depends on events in nature. The crops you grow need sunshine and rain, though thunder and lightning scare you. When you look up at the night sky, you wonder about the twinkling lights you see there. You know that at certain times of the year, the weather will turn cold and gray and plants will die. Then, a few months later, green plants will grow again.

How might you explain these natural events?

BUILDING BACKGROUND The Greeks lived in a time long before the development of science. To them, natural events like thunderstorms and changing seasons were mysterious. Today we can explain what causes these events. But to the Greeks, they seemed like the work of powerful gods.

Teach the Big Idea

At Level

Greek Mythology and Literature

1. **Teach** Ask students the questions in the Main Idea boxes to teach this section.
2. **Apply** Organize the class into small groups of three to four students. Assign each group a main idea from this section. Each group will create a poster that uses illustrations to cover the main terms and concepts for its main idea. Groups will present and explain their posters to the class. **LS Visual/Spatial**
3. **Review** As each group presents its poster to the class, review the main idea and concepts with the class.
4. **Practice/Homework** Instruct students to write a letter to a friend in which they summarize all the main ideas from this section that were presented in the group posters. **LS Verbal/Linguistic**

Alternative Assessment Handbook, Rubrics 25: Personal Letters; and 28: Posters

Myths Explain the World

The ancient Greeks believed in many gods. These gods were at the center of Greek **mythology**—a body of stories about gods and heroes that try to explain how the world works. Each story, or myth, explained natural or historical events.

Greek Gods

People today have scientific explanations for events like thunder, earthquakes, and volcanic eruptions. The ancient Greeks did not. They believed their gods caused these events to happen, and they created myths to explain the gods' actions.

Among the most important Greek gods were the ones in the picture below:

- Zeus, king of the gods
- Hera, queen of the gods
- Poseidon, god of the sea
- Hades, god of the underworld
- Demeter, goddess of agriculture
- Hestia, goddess of the hearth
- Athena, goddess of wisdom
- Apollo, god of the sun
- Artemis, goddess of the moon
- Ares, god of war
- Aphrodite, goddess of love
- Hephaestus, god of metalworking
- Dionysus, god of celebration
- Hermes, the messenger god

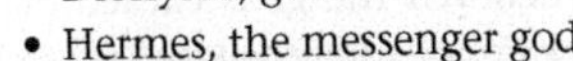

HISTORY
VIDEO
The Panathenaia
hmhsocialstudies.com

Olympian Gods

ANALYSIS SKILL **ANALYZING VISUALS**

What can you see that indicates the Olympian gods have superhuman powers?

Direct Teach

Main Idea

1 Myths Explain the World

The Greeks created myths to explain the world.

Recall What was the purpose of telling myths? *to explain natural or historical events, to explain how the world works*

Explain What was often the explanation for natural events such as earthquakes? *The gods had caused the events.*

Analyzing Visuals

Olympian Gods

Review with students the illustration of the Olympian gods. As you review the various Greek gods described in the text above the illustration, ask students to identify in the illustration what indicates the powers or responsibilities of each god. For example, Demeter, the goddess of agriculture, is holding a bundle of wheat.

Critical Thinking: Making Generalizations

Above Level

Research Required

Biographies of the Gods

1. Review with students the important Greek gods and their powers or responsibilities.
2. Allow students to select one of the Greek gods listed on this page. Students should then research some of the myths relating to that particular god. Good sources are Bulfinch's *Mythology* and Edith Hamilton's *Mythology*.
3. Students will write a brief biography of that god. The biography should explain the god's relationship to the other gods, summarize major myths related to that god, and explain the importance of that god to the Greeks.
4. Ask for volunteers to share their biographies with the class. LS **Verbal/Linguistic**

Alternative Assessment Handbook, Rubrics 4: Biographies, and 30: Research

Answers

Analyzing Visuals *possible answers—Poseidon is riding a dolphin; Zeus is holding a lightning bolt.*

Direct Teach

Main Idea

1 Myths Explain the World

The Greeks created myths to explain the world.

Summarize What were some events that the Greeks believed their gods were responsible for? *volcanic eruptions and the seasons*

Explain What role did heroes play in Greek myths? *They were featured in adventure stories where they often had special abilities and faced terrible monsters.*

Identify Who are some of the Greek heroes that are featured in myths? *Theseus, Jason, Hercules*

Info to Know

The Labyrinth The Minotaur lived in the Labyrinth, a large chamber with many twisting passageways. Before entering the Labyrinth, Theseus was given a ball of string, which he tied to the door and used to find his way back out of the mazelike chamber after he killed the Minotaur.

Gods and Mythology

The Greeks saw the work of the gods in events all around them. For example, the Greeks lived in an area where volcanic eruptions were common. To explain these eruptions, they told stories about the god Hephaestus (hi-FES-tuhs), who lived underground. The fire and lava that poured out of volcanoes, the Greeks said, came from the huge fires of the god's forge. At this forge he created weapons and armor for the other gods.

The Greeks did not think the gods spent all their time creating disasters, though. They also believed the gods caused daily events. For example, they believed the goddess of agriculture, Demeter (di-MEE-tuhr), created the seasons. According to Greek myth, Demeter had a daughter who was kidnapped by another god. The desperate goddess begged the god to let her daughter go, and eventually he agreed to let her return to her mother for six months every year. During the winter, Demeter is separated from her daughter and misses her. In her grief, she doesn't let plants grow. When her daughter comes home, the goddess is happy, and summer comes to Greece. To the Greeks, this story explained why winter came every year.

To keep the gods happy, the Greeks built great temples to honor them all around Greece. In return, however, they expected the gods to give them help when they needed it. For example, many Greeks in need of advice traveled to Delphi, a city in central Greece. There they spoke to the oracle, a female priest of Apollo to whom they thought the god gave answers. The oracle at Delphi was so respected that Greek leaders sometimes asked her for advice about how to rule their cities.

Theseus the Hero
According to legend, Athens had to send 14 people to Crete every year to be eaten by the Minotaur, a terrible monster. But Theseus, a hero from Athens, traveled to Crete and killed the Minotaur, freeing the people of Athens from this burden.

244

Collaborative Learning

At Level

Mythology Newspaper

Research Required

1. Organize the class into groups of four to five students. Assign each group several different Greek gods or heroes to research.
2. Students will work together to create a newspaper that reports on the activities of the gods and legendary heroes they have been assigned.
3. Groups should write a news article for each god or hero they have been assigned. Remind students to focus on the "who, what, when, where, and why" of a specific event.
4. Encourage students to create illustrations to coordinate with their news articles and to develop creative and interesting headlines.
5. Ask for groups to volunteer to share their newspapers with the class.

LS **Interpersonal, Verbal/Linguistic, Visual/Spatial**

Alternative Assessment Handbook, Rubrics 14: Group Activity; and 23: Newspapers

LINKING TO TODAY

Let the Games Begin!

One way the ancient Greeks honored their gods was by holding sporting contests like the one shown on the vase. The largest took place every four years at Olympia, a city in southern Greece. Held in honor of Zeus, this event was called the Olympic Games. Athletes competed in footraces, chariot races, boxing, wrestling, and throwing events. Only men could compete. The Greeks held these games every four years for more than 1,000 years, until the AD 320s.

In modern times, people began to hold the Olympics again. The first modern Olympics took place in Athens in 1896. Since then, athletes from many nations have assembled in cities around the world to compete. Today the Olympics include 28 sports, and both men and women participate. They are still held every four years. In 2004 the Olympic Games once again returned to their birthplace, Greece.

ANALYSIS SKILL ANALYZING INFORMATION

How do you think the modern Olympics are similar to the ancient Games? How do you think they are different?

Heroes and Mythology

Not all Greek myths were about gods. Many told about the adventures of great heroes. Some of these heroes were real people, while others were not. The Greeks loved to tell the stories of heroes who had special abilities and faced terrible monsters. The people of each city had their favorite hero, usually someone from there.

The people of Athens, for example, told stories about the hero Theseus. According to legend, he traveled to Crete and killed the Minotaur, a terrible monster that was half human and half bull. People from northern Greece told myths about Jason and how he sailed across the seas in search of a great treasure, fighting enemies the whole way.

Perhaps the most famous of all Greek heroes was a man called Hercules. The myths explain how Hercules fought many monsters and performed nearly impossible tasks. For example, he fought and killed the hydra, a huge snake with nine heads and poisonous fangs. Every time Hercules cut off one of the monster's heads, two more heads grew in its place. In the end, Hercules had to burn the hydra's neck each time he cut off a head to keep a new head from growing. People from all parts of Greece enjoyed stories about Hercules and his great deeds.

READING CHECK **Finding Main Ideas** How did the Greeks use myths to explain the world around them?

Direct Teach

Linking to Today

Let the Games Begin!

Review with students the feature on the Olympic Games. Ask the following questions:

Recall What was the purpose of the ancient Olympic Games? *to honor the gods*

Drawing Conclusions Why is it important that the 2004 Olympic Games took place in Athens? *Greece was the birthplace of the Olympics.*

Activity **Olympic Artwork** Have students select an Olympic event and create an illustration for it similar to the one on the vase pictured in the feature. **LS Visual/Spatial**

Alternative Assessment Handbook, Rubric 3: Artwork

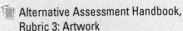

hmhsocialstudies.com

Online Resources
Activity: First Olympic Games Trading Cards

Cross-Discipline Activity: English-Language Arts

Above Level

Olympic Poetry

1. Review again the Linking to Today feature, "Let the Games Begin!", on this page.
2. Explain to students that in ancient times, Greek poets would often attend the Olympic Games and write poems in praise of the Olympic athletes. These poems were very popular among the Greeks.
3. Discuss with students the elements of a poem, such as vivid imagery, rhyme, and rhythm.
4. Have students select an athletic event from the modern Olympics with which they are familiar. Students will create an original poem that celebrates an imaginary competitor in that event. Their poems should attempt to "paint a picture" of the athlete and the event. Ask volunteers to share their poems with the class. **LS Intrapersonal, Verbal/Linguistic**

Alternative Assessment Handbook, Rubric 26: Poems and Songs

Answers

Analyzing Information *similar—take place every four years; include footraces, boxing, wrestling; different—Only men competed in ancient times, while men and women compete today; today there are many more sports than in ancient times.*

Reading Check *to explain natural events like volcanic eruptions*

Direct Teach

Main Idea

2 Ancient Greek Literature

Ancient Greek literature provides some of the world's greatest poems and stories.

Explain What purposes did Homer's *Iliad* and *Odyssey* serve for the Greeks? *were used for entertainment and as part of their lessons*

Analyze How have recent writers been influenced by the poems of Homer? *have copied his writing style and borrowed stories from his poems*

Activity Epic Poem Advertisement Have students read the descriptions of the *Iliad* and the *Odyssey* on this page. Ask students to select one of the epic poems and create an advertisement encouraging others to read or buy that poem. LS **Visual/Spatial, Verbal/Linguistic**

Alternative Assessment Handbook, Rubric 2: Advertisements

Ancient Greek Literature

Because the Greeks loved myths and stories, it is no surprise that they created great works of literature. Early Greek writers produced long epic poems, romantic poetry, and some of the world's most famous stories.

Homer and Epic Poetry

Among the earliest Greek writings are two great epic poems, the *Iliad* and the *Odyssey*, by a poet named **Homer**. Like most epics, both poems describe the deeds of great heroes. The heroes in Homer's poems fought in the Trojan War. In this war, the Mycenaean Greeks fought the Trojans, people of the city called Troy.

The *Iliad* tells the story of the last years of the Trojan War. It focuses on the deeds of the Greeks, especially Achilles (uh-KIL-eez), the greatest of all Greek warriors. It describes in great detail the battles between the Greeks and their Trojan enemies.

The *Odyssey* describes the challenges that the Greek hero Odysseus (oh-DI-see-uhs) faced on his way home from the war. For 10 years after the war ends, Odysseus tries to get home, but many obstacles stand in his way. He has to fight his way past terrible monsters, powerful magicians, and even angry gods.

Both the *Iliad* and the *Odyssey* are great tales of adventure. But to the Greeks Homer's poems were much more than just entertainment. They were central to the ancient Greek education system. People memorized long passages of the poems as part of their lessons. They admired Homer's poems and the heroes described in them as symbols of Greece's great history.

Homer's poems influenced later writers. They copied his writing styles and borrowed some of the stories and ideas he wrote about in his works. Homer's poems are considered some of the greatest literary works ever produced.

BIOGRAPHY

Homer
800s–700s BC

Historians know nothing about Homer, the greatest poet of the ancient world. Some don't think such a person ever lived. The ancient Greeks believed he had, though, and seven different cities claimed to be his birthplace. According to ancient legend, Homer was blind and recited the *Iliad* and the *Odyssey* aloud. It wasn't until much later that the poems were written down.

Making Predictions Why might scholars not be sure that Homer existed?

In Homer's *Odyssey*, the half woman and half bird Sirens sang sweet songs that made passing sailors forget everything and crash their ships. To get past the Sirens, Odysseus plugged his crew's ears with wax and had himself tied to his ship's mast.

Answers

Biography *possible answers—There are no records of his life; his poems were never written down.*

Differentiating Instruction

English-Language Learners
Prep Required | Below Level

1. Discuss with students the characteristics of Greek literature and fables. Remind the class that literature often told exciting stories about adventures of Greek heroes, whereas fables attempt to teach the reader some type of lesson.
2. Next, share with students a short story from Greek literature or a fable. Use one discussed in the text above or find your own. Tell the class the entire story or fable.
3. Divide the class into small groups of mixed-ability levels. Instruct each group to draw a series of illustrations that tell the entire story. Each student should participate in illustrating the story or fable.
4. Select one of the illustrated stories and share it with the class. Ask the entire class to develop the text of the story. Write down student suggestions for everyone to see. When the story is complete, ask the students to copy the text of the story on their own paper. Ask for a volunteer to read the story aloud. LS **Verbal/Linguistic, Visual/Spatial**

Alternative Assessment Handbook, Rubrics 3: Artwork; and 14: Group Activity

Lyric Poetry

Other poets wrote poems that were often set to music. During a performance, the poet played a stringed instrument called a lyre while reading a poem. These poets were called lyric poets after their instrument, the lyre. Today, the words of songs are called lyrics after these ancient Greek poets.

Most poets in Greece were men, but the most famous lyric poet was a woman named **Sappho** (SAF-oh). Her poems were beautiful and emotional. Most of her poems were about love and relationships with her friends and family.

Fables

Other Greeks told stories to teach people important lessons. **Aesop** (EE-sahp), for example, is famous for his fables. **Fables** are short stories that teach the reader lessons about life or give advice on how to live.

In most of Aesop's fables, animals are the main characters. The animals talk and act like humans. One of Aesop's most famous stories is the tale of the ants and the grasshopper:

BIOGRAPHY

Aesop
before 400 BC

Historians don't know for sure if a man named Aesop ever really lived, but many ancient legends are told about him. According to one story, Aesop was a slave in the 500s BC. Another story says he was an adviser to a king. Some historians think that the fables credited to Aesop were actually written by many different people and collected together under a single name.

Drawing Inferences Why might the Greeks have wanted to list a single author for the fables?

"The ants were spending a fine winter's day drying grain collected in the summertime. A Grasshopper, perishing [dying] with famine [hunger], passed by and earnestly [eagerly] begged for a little food. The Ants inquired [asked] of him, "Why did you not treasure up food during the summer?" He replied, "I had not leisure enough. I passed the days in singing." They then said in derision: "If you were foolish enough to sing all the summer, you must dance supperless to bed in the winter."

–Aesop, from "The Ants and the Grasshopper"

The lesson in this fable is that people shouldn't waste time instead of working. Those who do, Aesop says, will be sorry.

Another popular fable by Aesop, "The Tortoise and the Hare," teaches that it is better to work slowly and carefully than to hurry and make mistakes. "The Boy Who Cried Wolf" warns readers not to play pranks on others. Since we still read these fables, you may be familiar with them.

READING CHECK **Summarizing** Why did the Greeks tell fables?

Direct Teach

Main Idea

2 Ancient Greek Literature

Ancient Greek literature provides some of the world's greatest poems and stories.

Recall What types of stories are credited to Aesop? *fables*

Make Inferences Why do you think most of Aesop's main characters are animals rather than humans? *possible answers—They are more interesting; they are more humorous.*

CRF: Biography Activity: Sappho

CRF: Primary Source Activity: Sappho's Poetry

Linking to Today

Fables Today Some fables by Aesop are so famous that they have given us expressions that we still use today. When someone "cries wolf," they are warning of danger that is not really there. The expression "a wolf in sheep's clothing" is from another fable by Aesop. It means a person who appears harmless but is really not.

About the Illustration

The illustrations of Homer and Aesop are an artist's conception based on available sources. However, historians are uncertain exactly what Homer and Aesop looked like.

Differentiating Instruction

Advanced/Gifted and Talented Above Level

1. Locate an excerpt from either the *Iliad* or the *Odyssey*. The story of the Trojan horse or the story of Odysseus and the Cyclops would work well.
2. Ask students to read the excerpt and write a review of the story. Reviews should give a brief summary of the story and a reaction to the story itself. Did the student enjoy the story? Why or why not? Would they recommend it to a friend? What might they change about the story? Why?
3. Ask students to share their reviews with the class. LS **Verbal/Linguistic**

Alternative Assessment Handbook, Rubric 37: Writing Assignments

Answers

Biography *possible answers—to make them more popular with readers; it would be easier to list just one author.*

Reading Check *to give advice about life or to teach a lesson*

• Direct Teach •

Main Idea

❸ Greek Literature Lives

Greek literature lives in and influences our world even today.

Recall Give two examples of terms in our language that have been influenced by Greek stories. *possible answers—odyssey, titanic, Europe, Atlas Mountains, Aegean Sea*

Identify What are some modern references to Greek mythology? *using mythical figures as team mascots or business symbols; borrowing from myths in modern movies and books*

Make Inferences Why have many modern writers and moviemakers borrowed from Greek stories and myths? *possible answers—The stories are interesting; they are heroic examples to live up to.*

CRF: Literature Activity: Midas

Greek Literature Lives

The works of ancient Greek writers such as Homer, Sappho, and Aesop are still alive and popular today. In fact, Greek literature has influenced modern language, literature, and art. Did you know that some of the words you use and some of the stories you hear come from ancient Greece?

Language

Probably the most obvious way we see the influence of the Greeks is in our language. Many English words and expressions come from Greek mythology. For example, we call a long journey an "odyssey" after Odysseus, the wandering hero of Homer's poem. Something very large and powerful is called "titanic." This word comes from the Titans, a group of large and powerful gods in Greek myth.

Many places around the world today are also named after figures from Greek myths. For example, Athens is named for Athena, the goddess of wisdom. Africa's Atlas Mountains were named after a giant from Greek mythology who held up the sky. The name of the Aegean Sea comes from Aegeus, a legendary Greek king. Europe itself was named after a figure from Greek myth, the princess Europa. Even places in space bear names from mythology. For example, Jupiter's moon Io was named after a goddess's daughter.

Literature and the Arts

Greek myths have inspired artists for centuries. Great painters and sculptors have used gods and heroes as the subjects of their works. Writers have retold ancient stories, sometimes set in modern times. Moviemakers have also borrowed stories from ancient myths. Hercules, for example, has been the subject of dozens of films. These films range from early classics to a Walt Disney cartoon.

Mythological references are also common in today's popular culture. Many sports teams have adopted the names of powerful figures from myths, like Titans or

Greek Influence on Language

In Greek Literature and Mythology...	Today...
Achilles was a great warrior who was killed when an arrow struck his heel.	An "Achilles heel" is a person's weak spot.
Hercules was the strongest man on earth who completed 12 almost impossible tasks.	When a person has a really hard job to do it is called a "Herculean" task.
A fox wanted to eat some grapes but he couldn't reach the branch they were on, so he said, "Those grapes are probably sour anyway."	When people pretend they don't want something after they find out they can't have it, they are said to have "sour grapes."
King Midas was granted one wish by the god Dionysus, so he wished that everything he touched turned to gold.	A person who seems to get rich easily is said to have a "Midas touch."
Tantalus was punished for offending the gods. He had to stand up to his chin in water and he was always thirsty, but if he tried to drink the water it went away.	Something is "tantalizing" if you want it but it's just out of your reach.

Cross Discipline Activity: English–Language Arts

Above Level

Identifying Greek Word Origins

1. Review the chart "Greek Influence on Language" with the class. Ask the class if they can think of any other examples of Greek stories that are used in our modern language.
2. Divide the class into small groups of three to four students. Write the list of words at right for students to see. Omit answers in italics.
3. Ask the students to look up the following list of words in a dictionary. Students should determine the modern-day meaning of the word as well as the origin of the word in Greek mythology.
   - **hypnosis** *modern: a state that resembles sleep; origins: Hypnos, the Greek god of sleep*
   - **Pandora's box** *modern: a source of troubles; origins: a box sent by the gods which, when opened, set loose a swarm of troubles*
   - **echo** *modern: a repetition of sound; origins: a nymph who suffered from unreturned love until nothing remained but her voice*
   - **Trojan horse** *modern: a seemingly harmless computer program that destroys data files; origins: the large wooden horse filled with soldiers that helped the Greeks destroy Troy*

LS Verbal/Linguistic

Greek Names Today

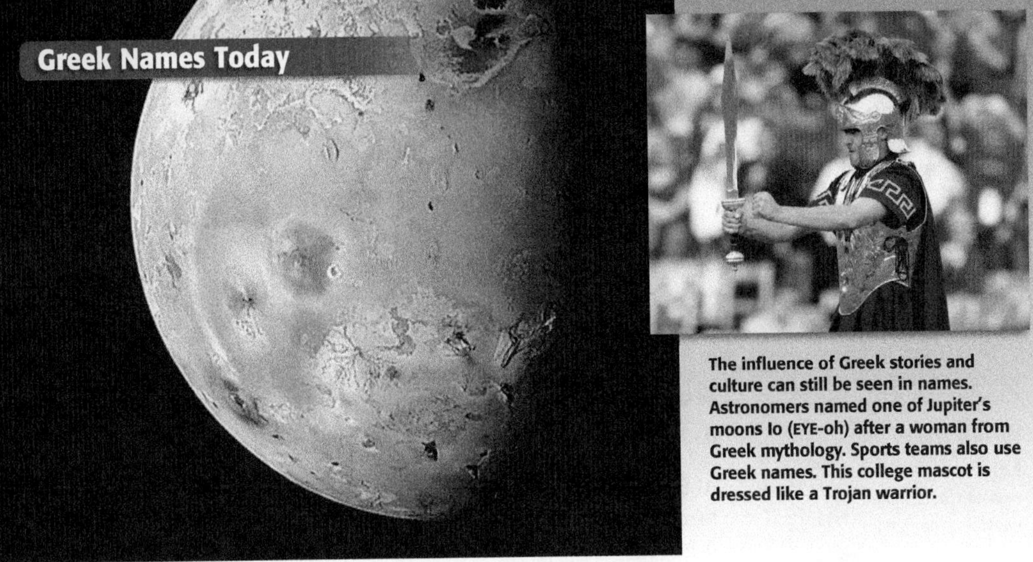

The influence of Greek stories and culture can still be seen in names. Astronomers named one of Jupiter's moons Io (EYE-oh) after a woman from Greek mythology. Sports teams also use Greek names. This college mascot is dressed like a Trojan warrior.

Trojans. Businesses frequently use images or symbols from mythology in their advertising. Although people no longer believe in the Greek gods, mythological ideas can still be seen all around us.

READING CHECK **Finding Main Ideas**

How did Greek myths influence later language and art?

SUMMARY AND PREVIEW The myths, stories, and poems of ancient Greece have shaped how people today speak, read, and write. Like democracy, these myths, stories, and poems are part of ancient Greece's gift to the world. In the next chapter you will learn more about life and culture in ancient Greece.

Section 3 Assessment

hmhsocialstudies.com ONLINE QUIZ

Reviewing Ideas, Terms, and People

1. a. **Define** What is **mythology**?
   b. **Summarize** Why did the ancient Greeks create myths?
2. a. **Identify** What are **Homer**'s most famous works?
   b. **Contrast** How are **fables** different from myths?
3. a. **Recall** In what areas have Greek myths influenced our culture?
   b. **Analyze** Why do you think mythological references are popular with sports teams and businesses today?
   c. **Evaluate** Why do you think Greek literature has been so influential throughout history?

Critical Thinking

4. **Analyzing** Using your notes and a chart like this, explain the influence of myths and literature on the world today.

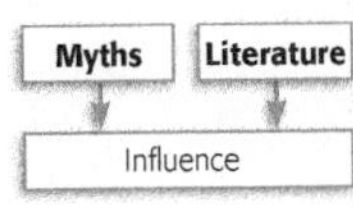

Focus on Writing

5. **Putting Your Ideas Together** Look at your notes from the previous sections. Think about the personalities you gave physical features and government leaders. Now imagine that those personalities belonged to gods. What stories might be told about these gods? Write down some ideas.

Direct Teach

Did you know . . .

Another element of Greek mythology used in our modern world is the story of the lost city of Atlantis. Famous Greek philosopher Plato tells us that the island of Atlantis was located in the Atlantic Ocean and was "larger than Libya and Asia combined."

Review & Assess

Close

Have students work in pairs to write a brief summary of this section.

Review

Online Quiz, Section 3

Assess

SE Section 3 Assessment

PASS: Section 3 Quiz

Alternative Assessment Handbook

Reteach/Classroom Intervention

Guided Reading Workbook, Section 3

Interactive Skills Tutor CD-ROM

Section 3 Assessment Answers

1. a. stories about gods and heroes that try to explain how the world works
   b. to explain the gods' actions and how the world works
2. a. the *Iliad* and the *Odyssey*
   b. fables—teach some lesson to the reader; myths—are meant to entertain or explain
3. a. language, literature, moviemaking, art, team mascots
   b. Answers will vary, but students should indicate an understanding that myths are still very popular and exciting.
   c. Answers will vary, but students should show an understanding that the stories told are timeless and interesting.
4. epic poetry—describe deeds of heroes, tales of adventure; lyric poetry—set to music, emotional; fables—teach a lesson, animals as characters
5. possible answers—The friendly gods would help humans, while the cold god would cause many problems for humans.

Answers

Reading Check *They contributed many stories, words, and symbols that we use today.*

Literature in History

The *Iliad*

As You Read Ask the students to think about what characteristics they associate with a hero. Make a list of several ideas for students to see. Ask students how they might use imagery to describe some of the traits listed.

Info to Know

Greek Heroes Greek literature often centers around a hero who has special talents and is tested on a quest or adventure. Greek heroes are faced with many challenges and sometimes receive assistance from the gods.

Meet the Writer

Homer While not much is certain about the life of Homer, most historians believe that his poems were not written down until many years after he created them. In fact, the *Iliad* and the *Odyssey* were likely meant to be spoken aloud as entertainment.

Literature in History

The Epic Poetry of Homer

from the *Iliad*

as translated by Robert Fitzgerald

About the Reading *The* Iliad *describes one part of a ten-year war between the Greeks and the city of Troy. As the poem opens, the Greek hero Achilles (uh-KIL-eez) has left the battle to wait for help from the gods. When he learns that his best friend Patroclus is dead, however, Achilles springs back into action. In this passage, the angry Achilles sprints across the plain toward Troy—and Hector, the Trojan warrior who has killed his friend.*

AS YOU READ Look for words and actions that tell you Achilles is a hero.

Then toward the town with might and main
he ran magnificent, like a racing chariot horse
that holds its form at full stretch on the plain. ❶
So light-footed Achilles held the pace.
And aging Priam was the first to see him
sparkling on the plain, bright as that star
in autumn rising, whose unclouded rays
shine out amid a throng of stars at dusk—
the one they call Orion's dog, most brilliant... ❷
So pure and bright
the bronze gear blazed upon him as he ran.
The old man gave a cry. ❸ With both his hands
thrown up on high he struck his head, then
shouted, groaning, appealing to his dear son.
Unmoved, Lord Hector stood in the gateway,
resolute to fight Achilles.
                    Stretching out his hands,
old Priam said, imploring him:
                    "No, Hector!
... don't try to hold your ground against this man,
or soon you'll meet the shock of doom..."

The painting on this vase shows people fighting in the Trojan War.

GUIDED READING

WORD HELP

main strength
resolute determined
imploring begging

❶ ***To what is Achilles being compared?***

❷ Priam, Hector's father, knows that the gods have protected and strengthened Achilles.

❸ Achilles' armor was made by the god of metalworking. ***Why might the very sight of this armor make Priam afraid?***

Differentiating Instruction

Advanced/Gifted and Talented — Above Level

Point out to students that the comparison of Achilles to a "racing chariot horse" is a simile—a comparison of two seemingly unalike things. Using the characteristics of heroes that the class generated earlier, ask each student to choose one of those characteristics and a hero, real or imagined, who embodies that characteristic. Have students create a simile that compares that hero to another object. Ask each student to explain his or her simile in writing. **LS Verbal/Linguistic**

English-Language Learners — At Level

Organize the class into small groups of two to three students of mixed-ability levels. Write the following list of terms for students to see, omitting answers in italics. Ask students to determine the meaning of the words or phrases.

- "with might and main he ran"—*he ran with great strength*
- "light-footed Achilles"—*quick and light on his feet*
- "Orion's dog"—*Sirius, the dog star*

LS Verbal/Linguistic

Answers

Guided Reading 1. *a racing chariot horse.* **3.** *possible answer—He was intimidated by the sight of Achilles' brilliant armor.*

from the *Odyssey*

About the Reading *The* Odyssey *takes place after the Trojan War has ended. It describes the adventures of another hero, Odysseus (oh-*DIS*-ee-uhs), as he makes his way home to his kingdom of Ithaca. His voyage is full of obstacles—including the two sea monsters described in this passage. The idea for these monsters probably came from an actual strait in the Mediterranean Sea, where a jagged cliff rose on one side and dangerous whirlpools churned on the other.*

AS YOU READ **Try to picture the action in your mind.**

And all this time,
in travail, sobbing, gaining on the current,
we rowed into the strait—Scylla to port
and on our starboard beam Charybdis, dire
gorge of the salt sea tide. ❶ By heaven! when she
vomited, all the sea was like a cauldron
seething over intense fire, when the mixture
suddenly heaves and rises.
The shot spume
soared to the landside heights, and fell like rain.
But when she swallowed the sea water down
we saw the funnel of the maelstrom, heard
the rock bellowing all around, and dark
sand raged on the bottom far below. ❷
My men all blanched against the gloom, our eyes
were fixed upon that yawning mouth in fear
of being devoured.
Then Scylla made her strike,
whisking six of my best men from the ship.
I happened to glance aft at ship and oarsmen
and caught sight of their arms and legs, dangling
high overhead. Voices came down to me
in anguish, calling my name for the last time . . . ❸
We rowed on.
The Rocks were now behind; Charybdis, too,
and Scylla dropped astern.

GUIDED READING

WORD HELP

travail pain
dire gorge terrible throat
spume foam or froth
maelstrom whirlpool
blanched grew pale
anguish great suffering

❶ Odysseus is the speaker. He is referring to himself and his crew.

Why might the crew be sobbing?

❷ Three times a day, the monster Charybdis (cuh-RIB-duhs) takes in water and then spits it out.

❸ Like many Greek monsters, Scylla (SIL-uh) is part human and part animal. She has the body of a woman, six heads with snake-like necks, and twelve feet.

CONNECTING LITERATURE TO HISTORY

1. **Comparing** Many Greek myths were about heroes who had special abilities. What heroic abilities or traits do Achilles, Hector, and Odysseus share?
2. **Analyzing** The Greeks used myths to explain the natural world. How does the *Odyssey* passage illustrate this?

Literature in History

The *Odyssey*

As You Read Ask students to think about the dangers that heroes typically encounter. Create a list of dangerous situations or monsters that heroes might face. Inform students that in the *Odyssey*, Odysseus faced several monsters. In this passage Odysseus and his men are at sea and must pass between two monsters—Scylla, a six-headed monster who lived on a rock, and Charybdis, a deadly whirlpool.

Info to Know

Between Scylla and Charybdis Homer's epic poems have given our modern language many expressions. The phrase "between Scylla and Charybdis" means that someone is caught between two dangerous or difficult alternatives.

Critical Thinking: Summarizing

At Level

Epic Poem Collage

Materials: glue, old magazines, paper

1. Review with the class the two excerpts from the *Iliad* and the *Odyssey*. Discuss the characteristics of the heroes depicted in each story.
2. Ask each student to choose one of the two excerpts for which to create a summary. Students will create a collage that summarizes the story and the characteristics of the hero in each story. Ask students to write a brief caption for each image used in their collage. The caption should explain how the image relates to the story.
3. Ask volunteers to share their collages with the class. LS **Visual/Spatial, Verbal/Linguistic**

Alternative Assessment Handbook, Rubric 8: Collages

Answers

Guided Reading 1. *out of fear of dying and because of the pain from rowing through such a rough sea*

Connecting Literature to History
1. *They are all brave warriors.* **2.** *The passage uses sea monsters to explain a dangerous strait in the Mediterranean.*

Social Studies Skills

Analyzing Costs and Benefits

Activity Cost-Benefit Analysis in the News Find a newspaper article about a current event in which students might be interested (an election, trial, arrest, environmental concern, and so on). The event and the article's coverage of it should provide students with enough information to determine costs and benefits. Provide each student with a photocopy of the article. Create a costs-benefits chart for students to see. Model the activity by listing one cost and one benefit. Then have students complete the chart independently. Review students' answers as a class. Encourage discussion of any effects that some students see as benefits and other students see as costs.

LS Logical/Mathematical, Visual/Spatial

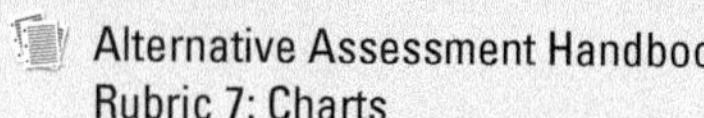

Alternative Assessment Handbook, Rubric 7: Charts

Social Studies Skills

Analysis | Critical Thinking | **Economics** | Study

Analyzing Costs and Benefits

Understand the Skill

Everything you do has both costs and benefits connected to it. *Benefits* are what you gain from something. *Costs* are what you give up to obtain benefits. For example, if you buy a video game, the benefits of your action include the game itself and the enjoyment of playing it. The most obvious cost is what you pay for the game. However, there are also costs that do not involve money. One of these costs is the time you spend playing the game. This is a cost because you give up something else, such as doing your homework or watching a TV show, when you choose to play the game.

The ability to analyze costs and benefits is a valuable life skill as well as a useful tool in the study of history. Weighing an action's benefits against its costs can help you decide whether or not to take it.

Learn the Skill

Analyzing the costs and benefits of historical events will help you to better understand and evaluate them. Follow these guidelines to do a cost-benefit analysis of an action or decision in history.

1. First determine what the action or decision was trying to accomplish. This step is needed in order to determine which of its effects were benefits and which were costs.
2. Then look for the positive or successful results of the action or decision. These are its benefits.
3. Consider the negative or unsuccessful effects of the action or decision. Also think about what positive things would have happened if it had *not* occurred. All these things are its costs.
4. Making a chart of the costs and benefits can be useful. By comparing the list of benefits to the list of costs you can better understand the action or decision and evaluate it.

For example, you learned in Chapter 8 that because of Greece's geography, the early Greeks settled near the sea. A cost-benefit analysis of their dependence on the sea might produce a chart like this one.

Benefits	Costs
Sea was a source of some food. Didn't have to depend on Greece's poor soil for food. Became great shipbuilders and sailors Became great traders and grew rich from trade Settled colonies throughout the region	Would have paid more attention to agriculture than they did. Had to rely on trade with other peoples for some food and other necessities.

Based on this chart, one might conclude that the Greeks' choice of where to settle was a good one.

Practice and Apply the Skill

In 546 BC a noble named Peisistratus overthrew the oligarchy and ruled Athens as a tyrant. Use information from the chapter and the guidelines above to do a cost-benefit analysis of this action. Then write a paragraph explaining whether or not it was good for the people of Athens.

Social Studies Skills Activity: Analyzing Costs and Benefits

Democracy Costs-and-Benefits Chart

At Level

1. Write the terms *Direct Democracy* and *Representative Democracy* for students to see. Briefly review the meaning of each term.
2. Divide the class. Have the students in one half of the class create costs-and-benefits charts for direct democracy in Athens. Have the students in the other half of the class create costs-and-benefits charts for representative democracy in the United States.
3. Have volunteers share their answers as you complete master charts for the class to see. Then have students compare the two charts to evaluate whether direct democracy or representative democracy is the better system.

LS Logical/Mathematical, Visual/Spatial

Alternative Assessment Handbook, Rubric 7: Charts

Answers

Practice and Apply the Skill

benefits—brought peace and prosperity to Athens; began new policies to unify the city, created new festivals, built temples and monuments, oversaw many improvements during his rule; costs—ruled by force; took power from aristocrats, who became unhappy and eventually convinced a rival city-state to attack Athens. Students' paragraphs will vary, but most students will probably say that the rule of Peisistratus was good for the people of Athens.

CHAPTER 8

Chapter Review

History's Impact

▶ **video series**

Review the video to answer the focus question:

How was ancient Greek democracy different from democracy in the United States today?

Visual Summary

Use the visual summary below to help you review the main ideas of the chapter.

QUICK FACTS

The early Greeks developed trading cultures and independent city-states.

Athens had the world's first direct democracy.

The stories of Greek literature and mythology have influenced language and culture today.

Reviewing Vocabulary, Terms, and People

Unscramble each group of letters below to spell a term that matches the given definition.

1. **olpsi**—a Greek city-state
2. **iciznets**—people who have the right to participate in government
3. **ntaryt**—a person who rules alone, usually through military force
4. **comdeyacr**—rule by the people
5. **bleafs**—stories that teach lessons
6. **tsrarciotas**—rich landowners
7. **coiglhary**—rule by a few people
8. **siclalacs**—referring to a period of great achievements

Comprehension and Critical Thinking

SECTION 1 *(Pages 228–233)*

9. a. Describe How did geography affect the development of the Greek city-states?

b. Compare and Contrast What did the Minoans and Mycenaeans have in common? How were the two civilizations different?

c. Elaborate How did the concept of the polis affect the growth of Greek colonies?

SECTION 2 *(Pages 236–241)*

10. a. Identify What roles did Draco, Solon, and Peisistratus play in the history of Greek government?

b. Contrast The Greeks tried many forms of government before they created a democracy. How did these various forms of government differ?

c. Evaluate Do you agree or disagree with this statement: "Representative democracy works better than direct democracy in large countries." Defend your answer.

Answers

Visual Summary

Review and Inquiry Use the visual summary to review the chapter's main ideas. Have students discuss the significance of each image shown.

Quick Facts Transparency: Ancient Greece Visual Summary

Reviewing Vocabulary, Terms, and People

1. polis
2. citizens
3. tyrant
4. democracy
5. fables
6. aristocrats
7. oligarchy
8. classical

Comprehension and Critical Thinking

9. a. Mountains divided the cities, so the city-states developed independently, and each one saw itself as a different state.

b. in common—traded around Mediterranean, ended partly because of volcanic activity; different—Minoans: lived on Crete, did not speak Greek; Mycenaeans—lived on Greek mainland, built fortresses, spoke Greek, more warlike, established colonies, conquered by invaders from Europe

c. The polis made people feel safe, so they were free to focus on activities like colonization and trade.

10. a. Draco—created strict laws to prevent a government overthrow;

Review and Assessment Resources

Review and Reinforce

- SE Chapter Review
- **CRF:** Chapter Review Activity
- Quick Facts Transparency: Ancient Greece Visual Summary
- Spanish Chapter Summaries Audio CD Program
- Online Chapter Summaries in Six Languages
- TOS Holt McDougal PuzzleView
- Quiz Game CD-ROM

Assess

- SE Standardized Test Practice
- PASS: Chapter Test, Forms A and B
- Alternative Assessment Handbook
- TOS ExamView Assessment Suite, Chapter Test
- Differentiated Instruction Modified Worksheets and Tests CD-ROM: Chapter Test
- Online Assessment Program, in the Interactive Student Edition

Reteach/Intervene

- Guided Reading Workbook
- Differentiated Instruction Teacher Management System: Lesson Plans
- Differentiated Instruction Modified Worksheets and Tests CD-ROM
- Interactive Skills Tutor CD-ROM

hmhsocialstudies.com
Chapter Resources

Answers

Solon—created new laws not as strict as Draco's, gave rights to nonaristocrats; Peisistratus—tyrant who unified Athens and made improvements

b. oligarchy—only a few people have power; tyrant—an individual held power through the use of force; democracy—all citizens had right to participate

c. Answers will vary, but students should conclude that direct democracy is hard to achieve in large countries.

11. a. Zeus, Hera, Poseidon, Hades, Demeter, Hestia, Athena, Apollo, Artemis, Ares, Aphrodite, Hephaestus, Dionysus, Hermes; Theseus, Jason, Hercules, Achilles, Odysseus

b. possible answers—adventures, war, heroes, winning despite obstacles, history

c. possible answer—yes, because the English language has many Greek roots and Greek literature appeals to people of many places and times

Reading Skills

12. b

13. a

14. very small

Using the Internet

15. Go to hmhsocialstudies.com to access a rubric for this activity.

Social Studies Skills

16. possible answers—Costs: difficult to make decisions, not everyone represented; Benefits: more rights for all citizens, more pride in Athens, citizens gained power; Sentences will vary but should be supported.

SECTION 3 *(Pages 242–249)*

11. a. Recall Who were some of the main gods of Greek mythology? Who were some of the main heroes?

b. Analyze What are some of the topics that appear in ancient Greek literature, such as the *Iliad* and the *Odyssey*?

c. Predict Do you think the language and literature of ancient Greece will play roles in Western civilization in years to come? Why or why not?

Reading Skills 

Greek Word Origins *Look at the list of Greek words and their meanings below. Then answer the questions that follow.*

archos (ruler)	*monos* (single)
bios (life)	*oligos* (few)
geo (earth)	*pente* (five)
micros (small)	*treis* (three)

12. Which of the following words means rule by a single person?

a. oligarchy **c.** pentarchy
b. monarchy **d.** triarchy

13. Which of the following words means the study of life?

a. biology **c.** archaeology
b. geology **d.** pentology

14. Is something that is *microscopic* very small or very large?

Using the Internet 

15. Activity: Comparing Greek Governments Greek government had many forms: tyranny, oligarchy, direct democracy, and monarchy. Use your online book to research Greek government, and then create a three-dimensional model, a drawing, or a diagram to illustrate what a person's life under each type of government might have looked like. Include information about the type of government you are representing.

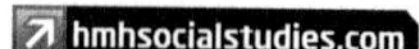

Social Studies Skills 

16. Analyzing Costs and Benefits Under Cleisthenes' leadership, Athens developed the world's first democracy. Create a chart comparing costs and benefits of this event. Then write a sentence explaining whether or not it was good for the people of Athens.

Cleisthenes' Leadership

Costs	Benefits

Reviewing Themes

17. Geography How do you think Greek society would have been different if Greece were a landlocked country?

18. Geography How did Crete's physical geography both help and hurt the development of Minoan civilization?

19. Politics Why was citizenship so important in Athens?

Focus on Writing

20. Writing Your Myth First, decide if your main character is going to be a god or if it will be a human who interacts with the gods. Think about the situations and decisions that your character will face, and how he or she will react to them.

Now it's time to write your myth down. Write a paragraph of seven to eight sentences about your character. You may want to include terrible monsters or heroes with great powers. Don't forget that a myth is supposed to explain something about the world.

Reviewing Themes

17. possible answer—The Greek people would have been more unified and would not have developed city-states; they would not have traded by sea or founded colonies.

18. helped—allowed it to trade around the Mediterranean; hurt—may have been destroyed by volcano and wave

19. People who were not citizens could not take part in the government.

Focus on Writing

20. Rubric Students' myths should:

- feature a main character.
- describe that character's actions and personality.
- have a beginning, middle, and end.
- explain something about the world.
- use exact verbs.

CRF: Focus on Writing: A Myth

CHAPTER 8

Standardized Test Practice

DIRECTIONS: Read each question, and write the letter of the best response.

1

> . . . that multitude of gleaming helms and bossed shields issued from the ships, with plated cuirasses [armor] and ashwood spears. Reflected glintings flashed to heaven, as the plain in all directions shone with glare of bronze and shook with trampling feet of men. Among them Prince Achilles armed. One heard his teeth grind hard together, and his eyes blazed out like licking fire, for unbearable pain had fixed upon his heart. Raging at Trojans, he buckled on the arms Hephaestus forged.

The content of this passage suggests that it was written by

A Homer.
B Zeus.
C Apollo.
D Cleisthenes.

2 What type of ancient Greek literature would *most* likely describe the deeds of a great hero?

A fable
B epic poem
C lyric poem
D oration

3 Which was the main cause for the independence of city-states in ancient Greece?

A the Greeks' location on the sea
B the threat of warlike neighbors to the north
C the geography of mountainous peninsulas
D the spread of Minoan culture

4 Athens was ruled by a single person under the type of government known as

A direct democracy.
B representative democracy.
C oligarchy.
D tyranny.

5 The citizens' assembly in ancient Athens was an example of

A trial by jury.
B rule by aristocrats.
C direct democracy.
D representative democracy.

Connecting with Past Learnings

6 Recently you learned about Hebrew history and beliefs. The ancient Hebrew and Greek civilizations shared all of the following characteristics *except*

A great written works.
B democratic governments.
C strong political leaders.
D influence on later civilizations.

7 You know that early towns in India were controlled by small groups of priests. Like ancient Greek government, this early Indian government was an example of

A oligarchy.
B tyranny.
C monarchy.
D democracy.

Answers

Standardized Test Practice

1. A
Break Down the Question Students can eliminate Zeus and Apollo, as they are Greek gods. Students can eliminate Cleisthenes, since he was a politician.

2. B
Break Down the Question Students can eliminate a fable, since the passage does not feature animals. They can eliminate lyric poem and oration, as the passage clearly does not represent those styles.

3. C
Break Down the Question Refer students who miss this question to Section 1.

4. D
Break Down the Question Students can eliminate choices *A, B,* and *C* because they involve rule by multiple persons.

5. C
Break Down the Question Direct democracy features input directly from citizens through the assembly.

6. B
Break Down the Question This question connects to information covered in a previous chapter.

7. A
Break Down the Question This question connects to information covered in a previous chapter.

Intervention Resources

Reproducible

- Guided Reading Workbook
- Differentiated Instruction Teacher Management System: Lesson Plans

Technology

- Quick Facts Transparency: Ancient Greece Visual Summary
- Differentiated Instruction Modified Worksheets and Tests CD-ROM
- Interactive Skills Tutor CD-ROM

Tips for Test Taking

Anticipate the Answers Give students this important tip: Before you read the answer choices, answer the question yourself. Then, read the choices. If the answer you gave is among the choices listed, it is probably correct!

Multimedia Classroom

The **HISTORY™ Multimedia Classroom** is a set of exciting new social studies teaching tools featuring award-winning program content. These comprehensive lesson plans, correlated to individual state and national curriculum standards, are easy to use for both teachers and students.

Each lesson contains the following:

- Short video segments that bring history topics to life
- Maps and visual materials
- Discussion and review questions
- Easily printable primary source documents
- Classroom activities and Internet-based activity links

The Multimedia Classroom has been specially designed to be versatile and easily adaptable to existing courses, lesson plans, and syllabi. Every lesson is designed to offer maximum flexibility. Teachers can select entire plans or only the elements they need, allowing them to individually tailor each lesson. Each multimedia lesson is available in CD-ROM format and is accompanied by full-length award-winning programs on DVD from HISTORY™.

For more information or to purchase go to hmhsocialstudies.com

Because some of these lessons may contain video material of a sensitive nature, we recommend that teachers and parents review these materials in their entirety before screening them to students.

HISTORY

MULTIMEDIA CONNECTIONS

ANCIENT GREECE

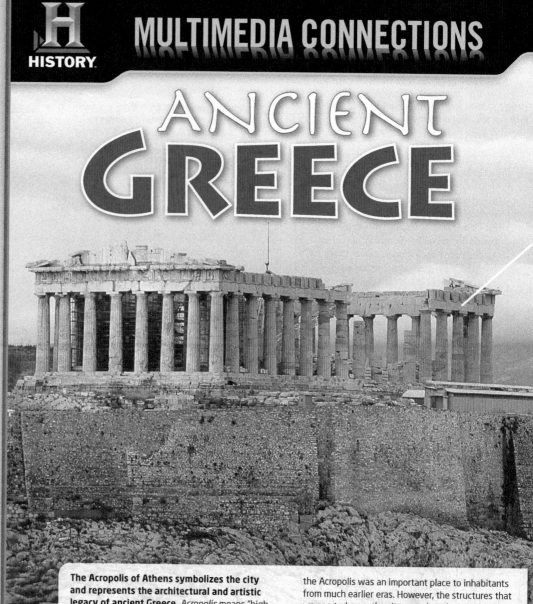

The Acropolis of Athens symbolizes the city and represents the architectural and artistic legacy of ancient Greece. *Acropolis* means "highest city" in Greek, and there are many such sites in Greece. Historically, an acropolis provided shelter and defense against a city's enemies. The Acropolis of Athens—the best known of them all—contained temples, monuments, and artwork dedicated to the Greek gods. Archaeological evidence indicates that the Acropolis was an important place to inhabitants from much earlier eras. However, the structures that we see today on the site were largely conceived by the statesman Pericles during the Golden Age of Athens in the 5th century B.C.

Explore the Acropolis of ancient Greece and learn about the legacy of Greek civilization. You can find a wealth of information, video clips, primary sources, activities, and more at hmhsocialstudies.com.

255 MC1 MULTIMEDIA CONNECTIONS

Ancient Greece

Resources 

The following resources come with printable introductions, comprehension and critical thinking questions, transcripts, and vocabulary support.

Full Length DVD

Ancient Greece (45 minutes)

Video Clips

- Athens' Spiritual Citadel (1:43)
- Athena as Divine Guardian (1:47)
- At War with the Persians (1:56)
- Pericles and the Golden Age (3:37)
- The Panathenaia Festival (3:52)
- Origins of Western Culture (4:29)
- Dionysus and Greek Theater (1:57)
- The Death of a Philosopher (1:13)
- Bringing Down the Parthenon (4:10)
- Elgin's Contested Collection (1:43)
- Mysteries and Discoveries (5:11)

Primary Sources

- *Oedipus Rex*
- *The Republic*
- *The Histories*
- The Porch of the Caryatids
- A Panathenaic Amphora
- Greek Fables
- A Greek Funeral Stele

CLICK THROUGH
INTER/ACTIVITIES
hmhsocialstudies.com

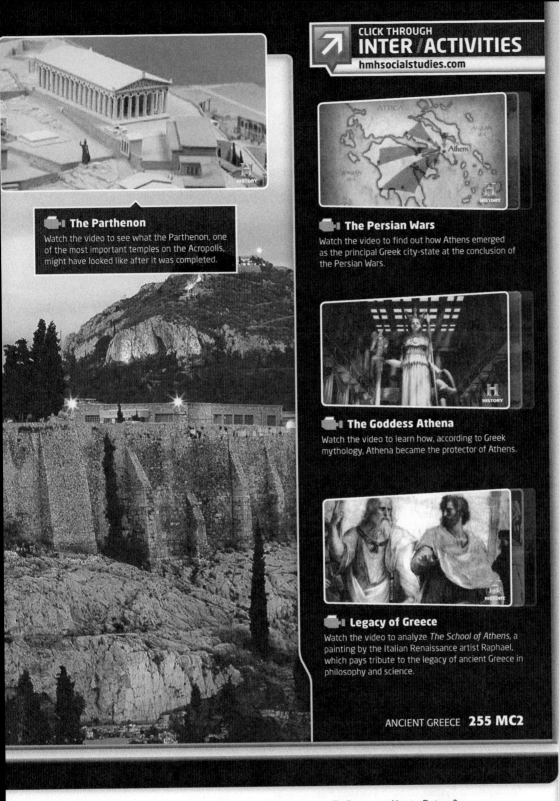

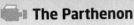

The Parthenon
Watch the video to see what the Parthenon, one of the most important temples on the Acropolis, might have looked like after it was completed.

The Persian Wars
Watch the video to find out how Athens emerged as the principal Greek city-state at the conclusion of the Persian Wars.

The Goddess Athena
Watch the video to learn how, according to Greek mythology, Athena became the protector of Athens.

Legacy of Greece
Watch the video to analyze *The School of Athens*, a painting by the Italian Renaissance artist Raphael, which pays tribute to the legacy of ancient Greece in philosophy and science.

ANCIENT GREECE **255 MC2**

Maps
- Greco-Persian Wars
- The Athenian Acropolis

Activities
- Women of Ancient Greece
- Greek Games and Festivals
- Quotable Greek Philosophers
- Taking to the Greek Stage
- A New Trial for Socrates
- To Return or Not to Return?
- Things to See in Athens

General Review Questions

General Discussion Questions

Web Links

Bibliography

Lesson Preview

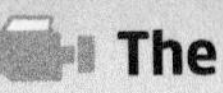

The Parthenon

No other building on the Acropolis was as magnificent as the Parthenon. Begun by Pericles in 447 B.C., the Parthenon took about 15 years to build. When finished, the marble temple was more than 225 feet long and 100 feet wide. However, the Parthenon was impressive for the elegant proportion of its columns, not for its size. Visitors did not enter the temple; they could only view it from outside. As they walked around the Parthenon, visitors admired the colorful sculptures that rose in the frieze above its columns until they finally glimpsed the huge gold and ivory statue of Athena standing within.

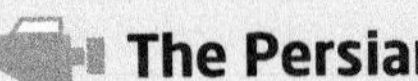

The Persian Wars

From about 490 to 479 B.C., the Greek city-states fought the vast and powerful Persian Empire. Surprisingly, Greece defeated the Persians at their first major battle at Marathon, a town that lay not far from Athens. According to legend, an Athenian messenger ran from Marathon to Athens after the battle to announce the Greeks' victory. He completed the 26-mile run but died from exhaustion after he delivered the message. This legend inspired the modern marathon race.

The Goddess Athena

According to Greek mythology, Athena, the goddess of wisdom, and Poseidon, the god of the sea, competed for a city in Greece by presenting it with valuable gifts. Poseidon gave the city a spring, but the people had little use for its salty water. Athena planted an olive tree, which would provide the city with food, oil, and wood. The goddess won and named her city Athens.

Legacy of Greece

Raphael's *The School of Athens* depicts the great philosophers of ancient Greece. Its central figures are Plato on the left—portrayed as Leonardo da Vinci—and his student, Aristotle, on the right. Raphael portrayed himself in a less significant area of the painting, peering out from among a group of scholars.

Chapter 9 Planning Guide

The Greek World

Overview	Instructional Resources	
CHAPTER 9 **Essential Question:** What advances did the Greeks make that still influence the world today? **Focus on the Essential Question Podcast**	TOS **Differentiated Instruction Teacher Management System:** • Instructional Benchmarking Guides • Lesson Plans for Differentiated Instruction **Guided Reading Workbook** **Chapter Resource File:** • Chapter Review • Focus on Writing: A Poem • Social Studies Skills: Interpreting Charts and Tables	TOS **Calendar Planner** **Differentiated Instruction Modified Worksheets and Tests CD-ROM** **Interactive Skills Tutor CD-ROM** **Student Edition on Audio CD Program for World History** **The World's Music Audio Program** **Video:** Peter on the Parthenon
Section 1: **Greece and Persia** **The Big Idea:** Over time the Persians came to rule a great empire which eventually brought them into conflict with the Greeks.	TOS **Differentiated Instruction Teacher Management System:** Section 1 Lesson Plan **Guided Reading Workbook:** Section 1 **Chapter Resource File:** • Vocabulary Builder, Section 1 • Biography: Leonidas	**Daily Bellringer Transparency:** Section 1 **Map Transparency:** The Persian Empire **Map Transparency:** The Persian Wars **Video:** The Battle of Marathon **Animated History:** The Persian Wars, 490-479 BC
Section 2: **Sparta and Athens** **The Big Idea:** The two most powerful city-states in Greece, Sparta and Athens, had very different cultures and became bitter enemies in the 400s BC.	TOS **Differentiated Instruction Teacher Management System:** Section 2 Lesson Plan **Guided Reading Workbook:** Section 2 **Chapter Resource File:** • Vocabulary Builder, Section 2 • Economics and History: The Importance of Trade	**Daily Bellringer Transparency:** Section 2 **Quick Facts Transparency:** Life in Sparta **Quick Facts Transparency:** Life in Athens **Map Transparency:** The Peloponnesian War, c. 431–404 BC **Internet Activity:** Sparta vs. Athens
Section 3: **Alexander the Great** **The Big Idea:** Alexander the Great built a huge empire and helped spread Greek culture into Egypt and Asia.	TOS **Differentiated Instruction Teacher Management System:** Section 3 Lesson Plan **Guided Reading Workbook:** Section 3 **Chapter Resource File:** • Vocabulary Builder, Section 3 • History and Geography: Alexander's Empire • Primary Source: "Alexander" from Plutarch's *Lives*	**Daily Bellringer Transparency:** Section 3 **Map Transparency:** Alexander the Great's Empire, c. 323 BC **Animated History:** The Empire of Alexander, 323 BC
Section 4: **Greek Achievements** **The Big Idea:** Ancient Greeks made lasting contributions in the arts, philosophy, and science.	TOS **Differentiated Instruction Teacher Management System:** Section 4 Lesson Plan **Guided Reading Workbook:** Section 4 **Chapter Resource File:** • Vocabulary Builder Activity, Section 4 • Biography Activities: Hipparchia; Hypatia; Thucydides • Primary Source Activity: Greek Lyric Poetry	**Daily Bellringer Transparency:** Section 4 **Internet Activity:** Art of Greece's Golden Age **Video:** The Death of a Philosopher

Chart Key:

SE Student Edition
 Presentation Resource
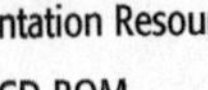 MP3 Audio
TOS Teacher One Stop
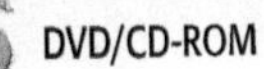 DVD/CD-ROM
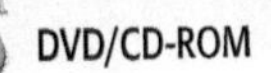 HISTORY™
 Printable Resource

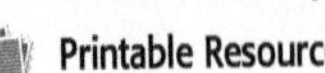
Program Resources available on TOS and @ hmhsocialstudies.com

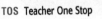

Review, Assessment, Intervention

 **Quick Facts Transparency:** The Greek World Visual Summary

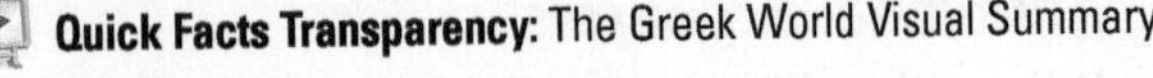 **Spanish Chapter Summaries Audio CD Program**

 **Quiz Game CD-ROM**

 **Progress Assessment Support System (PASS):** Chapter Test

 **Differentiated Instruction Modified Worksheets and Tests CD-ROM:** Modified Chapter Test

TOS **ExamView® Assessment Suite (English/Spanish)**

 **Online Assessment Program,** in the Interactive Student Edition

 **PASS:** Section 1 Quiz

 **Online Quiz:** Section 1

 **Alternative Assessment Handbook**

 **PASS:** Section 2 Quiz

Online Quiz: Section 2

Alternative Assessment Handbook

 **PASS:** Section 3 Quiz

 **Online Quiz:** Section 3

 **Alternative Assessment Handbook**

 **PASS:** Section 4 Quiz

 **Online Quiz:** Section 4

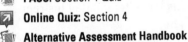

 **Alternative Assessment Handbook**

Supporting Resources

- Multimedia Classroom Global History Series
- Global History Teacher's Guide

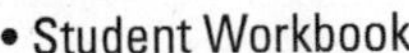

Maps Globes Graphs Level F

- Student Workbook
- Teacher's Guide

Social Studies Trade Library Collections

- Premier Secondary World History Trade Collection
- Ancient World History Trade Collection

History's Impact

World History Video Program

- **The Greek Scholars**

For more information or to purchase go to hmhsocialstudies.com

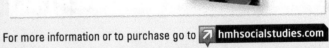

Power Presentations with Media Gallery

Power Presentations with Media Gallery are visual presentations of each chapter's main ideas. Presentations can be customized by including Quick Facts charts, images from the text, and video clips.

Differentiating Instruction

How do I address the needs of varied learners?

The Target Resource acts as your primary strategy for differentiated instruction.

ENGLISH-LANGUAGE LEARNERS & STRUGGLING READERS

Interactive Skills Tutor CD-ROM

The Interactive Skills Tutor CD-ROM contains lessons that provide additional practice for 20 different critical thinking skills.

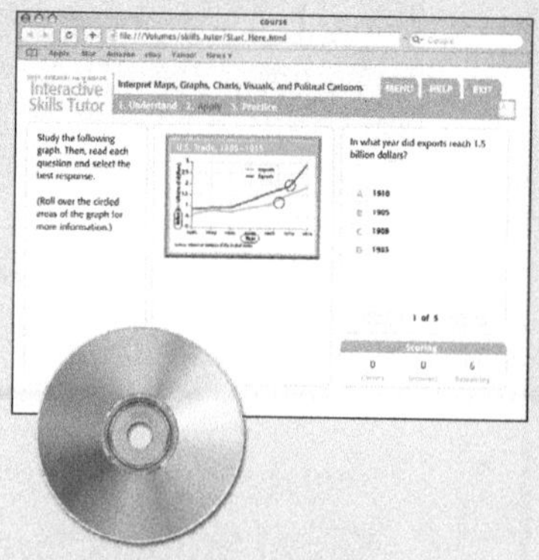

Additional Resources

Differentiated Instruction Teacher Management System: Lesson Plans for Differentiated Instruction

Resource File:
- Vocabulary Builder Activities
- Social Studies Skills Activity: Interpreting Charts and Tables

Quick Facts Transparencies:
- Life in Sparta
- Life in Athens
- The Greek World Visual Summary

Student Edition on Audio CD Program

Spanish/English Guided Reading Workbook

SPECIAL NEEDS LEARNERS

Differentiated Instruction Modified Worksheets and Tests CD-ROM

- Vocabulary Flash Cards
- Vocabulary Builder Activities
- Chapter Review Activity
- Chapter Test

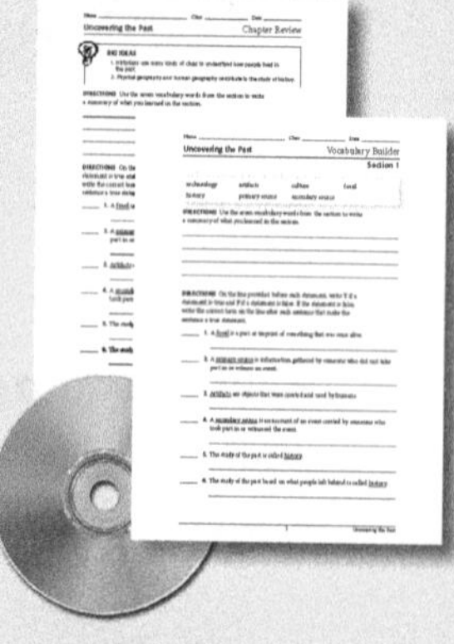

Additional Resources

Differentiated Instruction Teacher Management System: Lesson Plans for Differentiated Instruction

Guided Reading Workbook

Chapter Resource File: Social Studies Skills Activity: Interpreting Charts and Tables

Student Edition on Audio CD Program

Interactive Skills Tutor CD-ROM

ADVANCED/GIFTED-AND-TALENTED STUDENTS

Primary Source Library CD-ROM for World History

The Library contains longer versions of quotations in the text, extra sources, and images. Included are point-of-view articles, journals, diaries, historical fiction, and political documents.

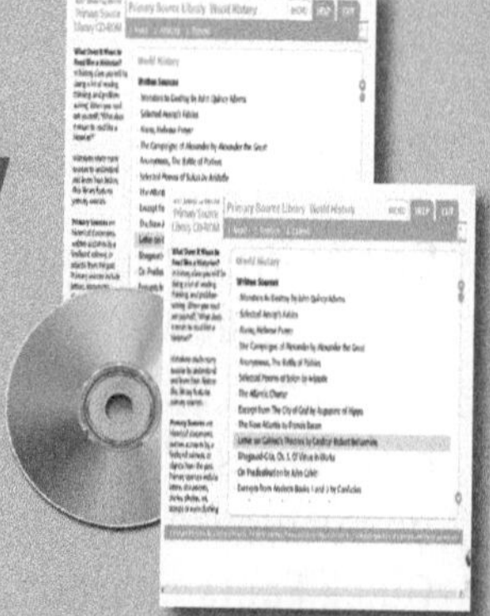

Additional Resources

Differentiated Instruction Teacher Management System: Lesson Plans for Differentiated Instruction

Chapter Resource File:
- Focus on Writing Activity: A Poem
- Literature Activity: *Oedipus the King*, by Sophocles

Document-Based Questions Activities

Differentiated Activities in the Teacher's Edition

- Creating a Mural, p. 264

Teacher One Stop™

How can I manage the lesson plans and support materials for differentiated instruction?

With the Teacher One Stop, you can easily organize and print lesson plans, planning guides, and instructional materials for all learners. The Teacher One Stop includes the following materials to help you differentiate instruction:

- Interactive Teacher's Edition
- Calendar Planner and pacing guides
- Editable lesson plans
- All reproducible ancillaries in Adobe Acrobat (PDF) format
- ExamView Assessment Suite (English & Spanish)
- Transparency and video previews

Differentiated Activities in the Teacher's Edition

- Creating a Poster, p. 268

Interactive Student Edition

Complete online student edition with interactive multimedia support for chapter content assessment and reporting

- Interactive Maps and Notebook
- Graphic Organizers
- Standardized Test Prep
- Online Homework Practice and Research Activities
- Current Events
- Chapter-based Internet Activities
- Animated History Activities
- and more!

Differentiated Activities in the Teacher's Edition

- Modeling Architectural Style, p. 278

Chapter Preview

Essential Question

Introduce the Essential Question

- Explain that classical Greece, the period Chapter 9 covers, is part of the larger era known as ancient Greece.
- Point out that the classical period lasted only about 150 years, from the end of the Persian Wars in 479 BC to the death of Alexander the Great in 323 BC.
- Explain that the period is called classic because Greek civilization reached its peak at this time.

CHAPTER 9 550–30 BC

The Greek World

Essential Question What advances did the Greeks make that still influence the world today?

South Carolina Performance Standards

6-2.1 Describe the development of ancient Greek culture (the Hellenic period), including the concept of citizenship and the early forms of democracy in Athens;
6-2.2 Analyze the role of Alexander the Great (Hellenistic period), Socrates, Plato, Archimedes, Aristotle, and others in the creation and spread of Greek governance, literature, philosophy, the arts, math, and science.

Literacy Skills for Social Studies

- Evaluate multiple points of view or biases and attribute the perspectives to the influences of individual experiences, societal values, and cultural traditions.
- Compare the locations of places, the conditions at places, and the connections between places.

Partnership for the 21st Century Skills
Create a thesis support by research to convince an audience of its validity.

Focus on Writing

A Poem Ancient Greek poets often wrote poems in praise of great leaders, victorious military commanders, star athletes, and other famous people. As you read this chapter, you will learn about the accomplishments of Greek and Persian kings, generals, writers, thinkers, and scientists. As you read, you'll choose the one person you most admire and write a five-line poem praising that person.

Chapter Events
c. 550 BC Cyrus the Great founds the Persian Empire.

550 BC

World Events
c. 551 BC Confucius is born in China.

Focus on Writing

The **Chapter Resource File** provides a Focus on Writing worksheet to help students organize and write their poem.

CRF: Focus on Writing, A Poem

Key to Differentiating Instruction

Below Level
Basic-level activities designed for all students encountering new material

At Level
Intermediate-level activities designed for average students

Above Level
Challenging activities designed for honors and gifted and talented students

Standard English Mastery
Activities designed to improve standard English usage

LS Learning Styles

Introduce the Chapter

At Level

Building on Knowledge of Ancient Greece

1. Ask students to list some things they already know about ancient Greece based on their study of the previous chapter. List the responses for the class to see.
2. Have students help you organize their responses into categories, such as government, economy, culture, religion, and so on. In addition, have students identify any categories for which they have not provided any information.
3. Then ask students to create charts organized by the categories they identified and enter the information listed.
4. As students study the chapter, have them add to their charts by listing additional information that they learn in appropriate categories. **LS Verbal/Linguistic, Visual/Spatial**

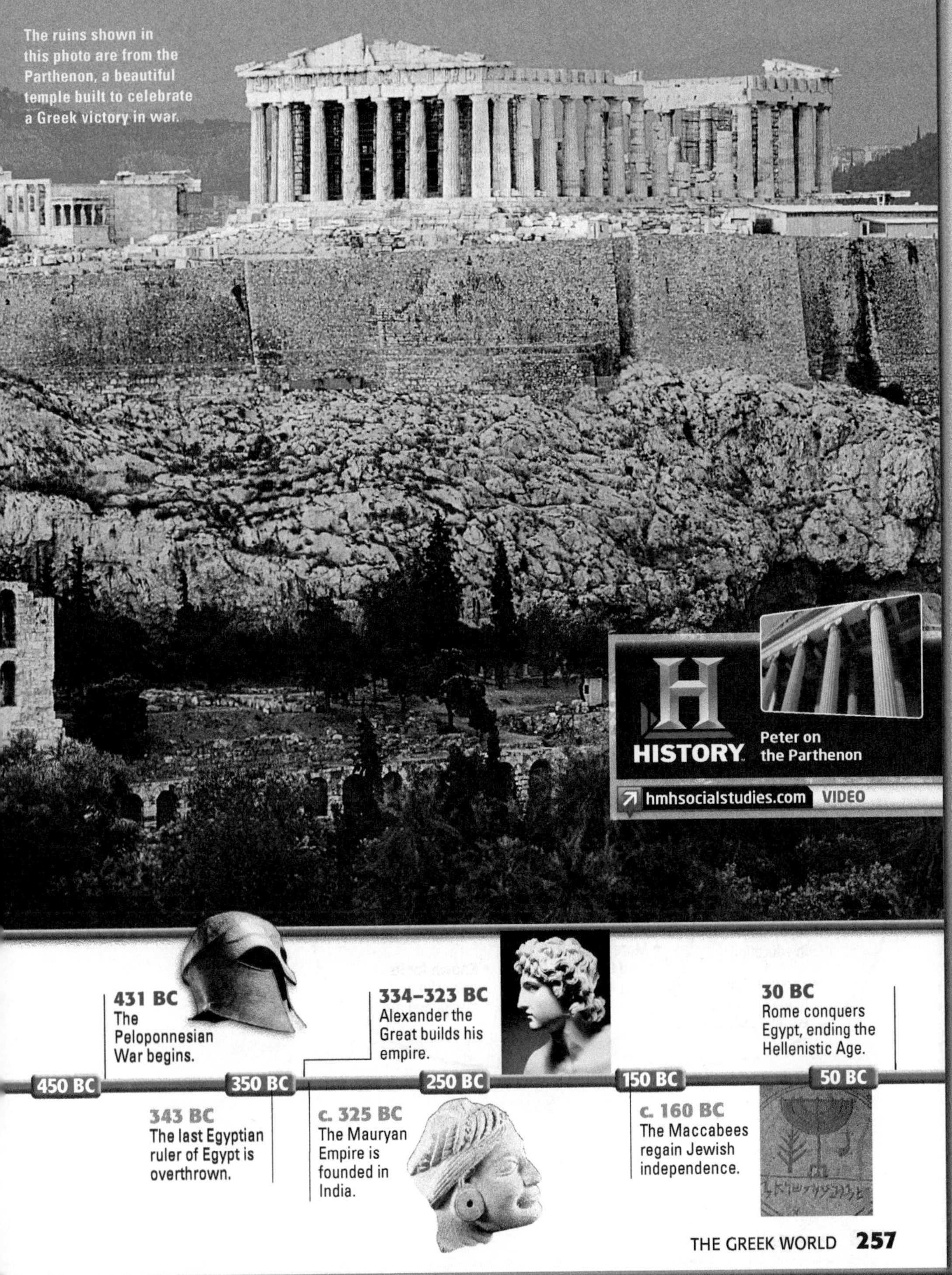
The ruins shown in this photo are from the Parthenon, a beautiful temple built to celebrate a Greek victory in war.

431 BC The Peloponnesian War begins.

334–323 BC Alexander the Great builds his empire.

30 BC Rome conquers Egypt, ending the Hellenistic Age.

343 BC The last Egyptian ruler of Egypt is overthrown.

c. 325 BC The Mauryan Empire is founded in India.

c. 160 BC The Maccabees regain Jewish independence.

THE GREEK WORLD 257

• Chapter Preview •

Explore the Picture

The Parthenon in Athens The most famous building in ancient Athens—and one of the most famous buildings in the world—is the Parthenon. After the Athenians defeated the Persians nearly 2,500 years ago, the people of Athens built the temple to thank the goddess Athena, the protector of Athens, for the victory.

Analyzing Visuals Based on the photo, how does the Parthenon illustrate the lasting influence of ancient Greece? *possible answers—It still stands; care has been taken to protect the structure, which now sits surrounded by modern buildings.*

hmhsocialstudies.com
Teacher Resources

Explore the Time Line

1. At about the time Alexander the Great was building his empire, where was another empire being founded? What was this empire called? *India; the Mauryan Empire*
2. In what year did the Hellenistic Age end? *30 BC*

Info to Know

The Acropolis The Parthenon was built on the Acropolis in Athens. *Acropolis* is a Greek term meaning "upper city" and refers to the highest point in the city. From a military point of view, why do you think Athenians (and people in many other cities) built sacred buildings on an acropolis? *possible answer—It is easier to defend a hilltop against invaders, so sacred buildings can be protected better if they are on an acropolis.*

Reading Social Studies

Understanding Themes

Introduce the key themes of this chapter by writing the labels *Politics* and *Society and Culture* for students to see. Ask students to use what they learned about Greece in the previous chapter to help them make predictions about this chapter. How might the political systems of Greece change? What might be some characteristics of Greece's society and culture during the next phase in their history? Ask students to identify some political and social contributions that the Greeks have made to our world.

Comparing and Contrasting Historical Facts

Focus on Reading Ask students to select two items to compare and contrast—for example, hockey and basketball. Then draw a large Venn diagram for students to see. Ask students to think of similarities and differences between the two items. Add students' suggestions to the Venn diagram. When the class is finished, have students use the diagram to write a paragraph or two in which they compare and contrast these items. Ask students to use signal words to indicate similarities and differences.

Reading Social Studies

Economics | Geography | **Politics** | Religion | **Society and Culture** | Science and Technology

Focus on Themes In this chapter, you will learn about Persia's attempt to take over Greece. You will also read about two great Greek cities, Sparta and Athens, and how they both worked to protect Greece from this invader. Finally, you will discover how, even though another invader conquered Greece, Greek influence continued to spread. Without a doubt, you need to understand the **politics** of the time in order to understand the Greek world and its **society and culture**.

Comparing and Contrasting Historical Facts

Focus on Reading Comparing and contrasting are good ways to learn. That's one reason historians use comparison and contrast to explain people and events in history.

Understanding Comparison and Contrast To **compare** is to look for likenesses, or similarities. To **contrast** is to look for differences. Sometimes writers point out similarities and differences. Other times you have to look for them yourself. You can use a diagram like this one to keep track of similarities and differences as you read.

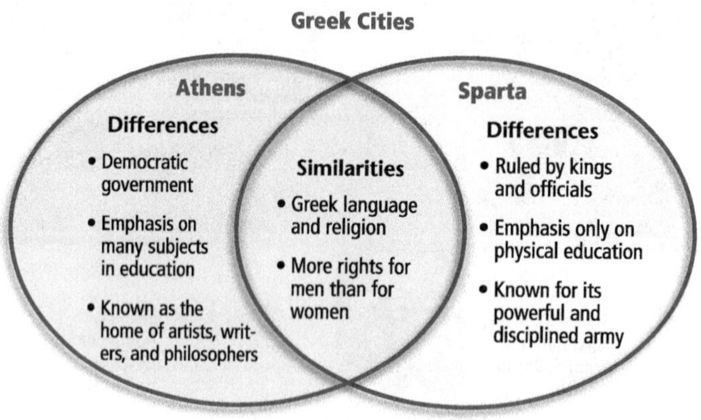

Greek Cities

Athens — Differences
- Democratic government
- Emphasis on many subjects in education
- Known as the home of artists, writers, and philosophers

Similarities
- Greek language and religion
- More rights for men than for women

Sparta — Differences
- Ruled by kings and officials
- Emphasis only on physical education
- Known for its powerful and disciplined army

Clues for Comparison-Contrast

Writers sometimes signal comparisons or contrasts with words like these:

Comparison—*similarly, like, in the same way, too*

Contrast—*however, unlike, but, while, although, in contrast*

Reading and Skills Resources

Reading Support

- Guided Reading Workbook
- Student Edition on Audio CD
- Spanish Chapter Summaries Audio CD Program

Social Studies Skills Support

- Interactive Skills Tutor CD-ROM

Vocabulary Support

- **CRF:** Vocabulary Builder
- **CRF:** Chapter Review
- Differentiated Instruction Modified Worksheets and Tests CD-ROM:
  - Vocabulary Flash Cards
  - Vocabulary Builder Activity
  - Chapter Review Activity

TOS Holt McDougal PuzzleView

You Try It!

The following passage is from the chapter you are getting ready to read. As you read the passage, look for word clues about similarities and differences.

Boys and Men in Athens

From a young age, Athenian boys from rich families worked to improve both their bodies and their minds. Like Spartan boys, Athenian boys had to learn to run, jump, and fight. But this training was not as harsh or as long as the training in Sparta.

Unlike Spartan men, Athenian men didn't have to devote their whole lives to the army. All men in Athens joined the army, but only for two years. They helped defend the city between the ages of 18 and 20. Older men only had to serve in the army in times of war.

After you read the passage, answer the following questions.

1. What does the word *like* (line 3 of the passage) compare or contrast?
2. Which boys had harsher training, Athenian boys or Spartan boys? What comparison or contrast signal word helped you answer this question?
3. What other comparison or contrast words do you find in the passage? How do these words or phrases help you understand the passage?
4. How are the similarities and differences organized in the passage—alternating back and forth between topics (ABAB) or first one topic and then the next (AABB)?

Key Terms and People

Chapter 9

Section 1
Cyrus the Great *(p. 261)*
cavalry *(p. 262)*
Darius I *(p. 262)*
Persian Wars *(p. 263)*
Xerxes I *(p. 264)*

Section 2
alliance *(p. 270)*
Peloponnesian War *(p. 271)*

Section 3
Philip II *(p. 272)*
phalanx *(p. 273)*
Alexander the Great *(p. 274)*
Hellenistic *(p. 275)*

Section 4
Socrates *(p. 281)*
Plato *(p. 281)*
Aristotle *(p. 281)*
reason *(p. 281)*
Euclid *(p. 282)*
Hippocrates *(p. 282)*

Academic Vocabulary

Success in school is related to knowing academic vocabulary—the words that are frequently used in school assignments and discussions. In this chapter, you will learn the following academic word:

strategy *(p. 262)*

As you read Chapter 9, think about the organization of the ideas. Look for comparison and contrast signal words.

Reading Social Studies

Key Terms and People

Organize the class into small groups. Preteach the key terms and people for this chapter by instructing the groups to write each of the terms and people as a list. Then have groups look up each term in the chapter. For people or events, have students write a date next to each entry. For example, *Cyrus the Great, 550 B.C.* Then have each group construct a time line, adding the significance of the person or event near each entry. Have students write the terms that may not go on the time line on the other side of the paper. Display the time lines for the class to see.
LS Verbal/Linguistic, Visual/Spatial

Focus on Reading

See the **Focus on Reading** questions in this chapter for more practice on this reading social studies skill.

Reading Social Studies Assessment

See the **Chapter Review** at the end of this chapter for student assessment questions related to this reading skill.

Teaching Tip

Help students identify comparison and contrast by discussing different ways in which text is organized. Point out to students that sometimes writers will compare and contrast by alternating back and forth between topics. For example, hockey is a game played on ice, while basketball is often played on a wood court. Then tell students that at other times, writers will concentrate on one topic at a time. For example, the writer might describe basketball in one paragraph, and hockey in a separate paragraph. Have students practice comparing and contrasting two items using both styles of organization.

Answers

You Try It! 1. *It compares Athenian boys to Spartan boys.* **2.** *Spartan boys;* but; **3.** unlike; also; *by indicating comparison and contrast;* **4.** *Athenian men—improved minds and bodies, training not harsh or long, did not devote lives to army, served in army for two years, learned to read, write, count, sing; similarities—learned to run, jump and fight, served in army; Spartan men —received long, harsh training, devoted their lives to the army, did not learn to read, write or count*

Preteach

Bellringer

If YOU were there . . . Use the **Daily Bellringer Transparency** to help students answer the question.

Daily Bellringer Transparency, Section 1

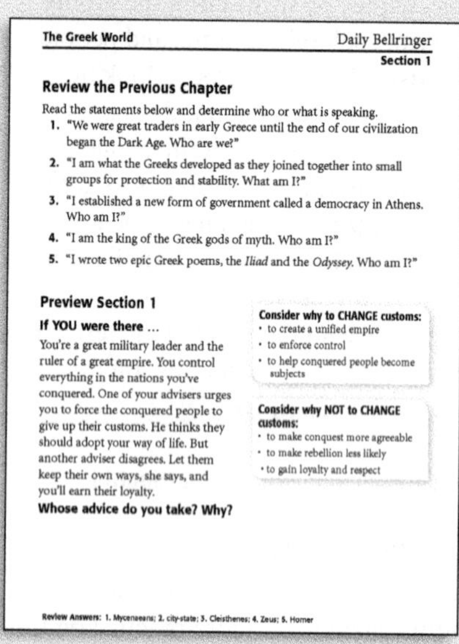

The Greek World — Daily Bellringer — Section 1

Review the Previous Chapter

Read the statements below and determine who or what is speaking.

1. "We were great traders in early Greece until the end of our civilization began the Dark Age. Who are we?"
2. "I am what the Greeks developed as they joined together into small groups for protection and stability. What am I?"
3. "I established a new form of government called a democracy in Athens. Who am I?"
4. "I am the king of the Greek gods of myth. Who am I?"
5. "I wrote two epic Greek poems, the *Iliad* and the *Odyssey*. Who am I?"

Preview Section 1

If YOU were there ...

You're a great military leader and the ruler of a great empire. You control everything in the nations you've conquered. One of your advisers urges you to force the conquered people to give up their customs. He thinks they should adopt your way of life. But another adviser disagrees. Let them keep their own ways, she says, and you'll earn their loyalty.

Whose advice do you take? Why?

Consider why to CHANGE customs:
- to create a unified empire
- to enforce control
- to help conquered people become subjects

Consider why NOT to CHANGE customs:
- to make conquest more agreeable
- to make rebellion less likely
- to gain loyalty and respect

Review Answers: 1. Mycenaeans; 2. city-state; 3. Cleisthenes; 4. Zeus; 5. Homer

Academic Vocabulary

Review with students the high-use academic term in this section.

strategy plan for fighting a battle or war (p. 262)

Building Vocabulary

Preteach or review the following term:

satraps Persian provincial governors with very wide powers (p. 262)

CRF: Vocabulary Builder, Section 1

Taking Notes

Have students use the graphic organizer online to take notes on the section. This activity will prepare students for the Section Assessment, in which they will complete a graphic organizer that builds on the information using the Critical Thinking Skill: Categorizing.

SECTION 1

Greece and Persia

What You Will Learn...

Main Ideas

1. Persia became an empire under Cyrus the Great.
2. The Persian Empire grew stronger under Darius I.
3. The Persians fought Greece twice in the Persian Wars.

The Big Idea

Over time the Persians came to rule a great empire which eventually brought them into conflict with the Greeks.

Key Terms and People

Cyrus the Great, *p. 261*
cavalry, *p. 262*
Darius I, *p. 262*
Persian Wars, *p. 263*
Xerxes I, *p. 264*

Use the graphic organizer online to take notes on Persia and its conflicts with Greece.

If YOU were there...

You're a great military leader and the ruler of a great empire. You control everything in the nations you've conquered. One of your advisers urges you to force conquered people to give up their customs. He thinks they should adopt your way of life. But another adviser disagrees. Let them keep their own ways, she says, and you'll earn their loyalty.

Whose advice do you take? Why?

BUILDING BACKGROUND Among the rulers who faced decisions like the one described above were the rulers of the Persian Empire. Created in 550 BC, the empire grew quickly. Within about 30 years, the Persians had conquered many peoples, and Persian rulers had to decide how these people would be treated.

Persia Becomes an Empire

While the Athenians were taking the first steps toward creating a democracy, a new power was rising in the East. This power, the Persian Empire, would one day attack Greece. But early in their history, the Persians were an unorganized nomadic people. It took the skills of leaders like Cyrus the Great and Darius I to change that situation. Under these leaders, the Persians created a huge empire, one of the mightiest of the ancient world.

Cyrus the Great

Early in their history, the Persians often fought other peoples of Southwest Asia. Sometimes they lost. In fact, they lost a fight to a people called the Medes (MEEDZ) and were ruled by them for about 150 years. In 550 BC, however, Cyrus II (SY-ruhs) led a Persian revolt against the Medes. His revolt was successful. Cyrus won independence for Persia and conquered the Medes. His victory marked the beginning of the Persian Empire.

Teach the Big Idea

At Level

Greece and Persia

1. **Teach** Ask students the questions in the Main Idea boxes to teach this section.
2. **Apply** Help students list the main people, events, and issues in the section. Write the list for students to see. Then ask students to imagine that they are creating a newspaper story. Have each student write one or two sentences summarizing the information about each of the section's main people, events, and issues. Model the activity for students by doing the first summary as a class. LS **Verbal/Linguistic**
3. **Review** As you review the section, select students to read their summaries to the class.
4. **Practice/Homework** Have each student use his or her summary to write a one-page newspaper article about the Persian Empire. LS **Verbal/Linguistic**

Alternative Assessment Handbook, Rubrics 23: Newspapers; and 42: Writing to Inform

hmhsocialstudies.com INTERACTIVE MAP

The Persian Empire

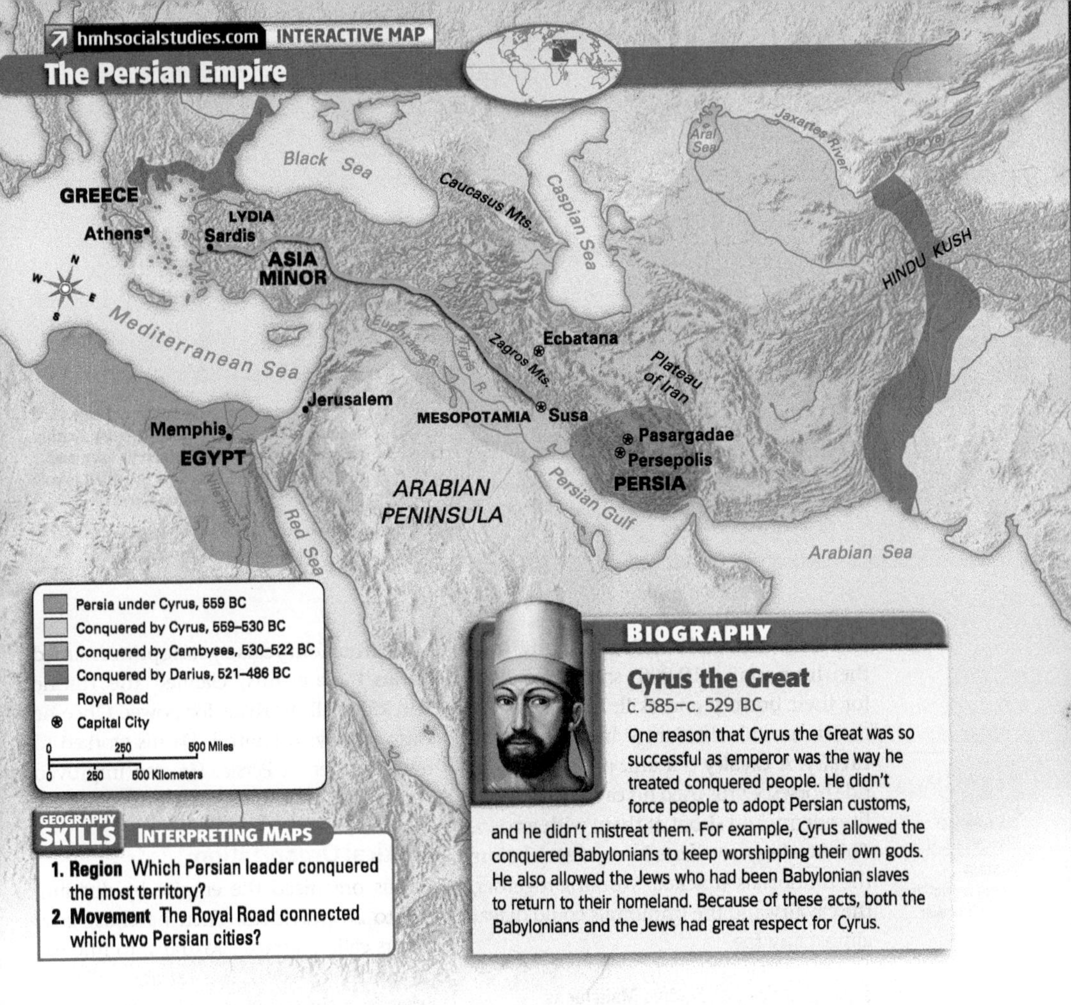

GEOGRAPHY SKILLS **INTERPRETING MAPS**

1. **Region** Which Persian leader conquered the most territory?
2. **Movement** The Royal Road connected which two Persian cities?

BIOGRAPHY

Cyrus the Great
c. 585–c. 529 BC

One reason that Cyrus the Great was so successful as emperor was the way he treated conquered people. He didn't force people to adopt Persian customs, and he didn't mistreat them. For example, Cyrus allowed the conquered Babylonians to keep worshipping their own gods. He also allowed the Jews who had been Babylonian slaves to return to their homeland. Because of these acts, both the Babylonians and the Jews had great respect for Cyrus.

As you can see on the map, Cyrus conquered much of Southwest Asia, including nearly all of Asia Minor, during his rule. Included in this region were several Greek cities that Cyrus took over. He then marched south to conquer Mesopotamia.

Cyrus also added land to the east. He led his army into central Asia to the Jaxartes River, which we now call the Syr Darya. When he died around 529 BC, Cyrus ruled the largest empire the world had ever seen.

Cyrus let the people he conquered keep their own customs. He hoped this would make them less likely to rebel. He was right. Few people rebelled against Cyrus, and his empire remained strong. Because of his great successes, historians call him **Cyrus the Great**.

The Persian Army

Cyrus was successful in his conquests because his army was strong. It was strong because it was well organized and loyal.

Direct Teach

Interpreting Maps

The Persian Empire

Location Approximately how many miles did Cyrus's Persian Empire stretch from west to east? How many kilometers? *approximately 2,500 miles or 4,000 km* LS **Logical/Mathematical**

Map Transparency: The Persian Empire

Main Idea

1 Persia Becomes an Empire

Persia became an empire under Cyrus the Great.

Identify Why do historians call King Cyrus of Persia "Great"? *Cyrus is called "Great" because of his military successes and because of the way he treated conquered peoples.*

Draw Inferences Why was Cyrus able to create and rule the largest empire the world had ever seen? *Cyrus was successful militarily because he led a strong army and politically because he did not disrupt people's daily lives or force them to adopt new customs, so people were less likely to rebel.*

Activity **Rules for Rulers** Have each student create a guide for new conquerors. The guide should list five rules that the student thinks a conquering ruler should follow to minimize the possibility that the conquered people will rebel. LS **Verbal/Linguistic**

Alternative Assessment Handbook, Rubric 37: Writing Assignments

Cross-Discipline Activity: Government

Above Level

Research Required

The Cyrus Cylinder

1. Have students research Cyrus the Great and the Cyrus Cylinder, which is in the British Museum. (The Cyrus Cylinder is a clay cylinder inscribed by Cyrus reciting his conquest of Babylon and promising reforms that will improve the lives of his subjects.)
2. Ask students to describe the reforms that Cyrus promised in his declaration on the cylinder. Students can write a short report or make a poster or pamphlet to describe their findings.
3. Have students explain how Cyrus the Great and the Cyrus Cylinder are related to human rights documents of today, such as the Declaration of Independence.
4. **Extend** Have students research the tradition among Mesopotamian kings to begin their reigns by declaring reforms. LS **Verbal/Linguistic**

Alternative Assessment Handbook, Rubrics 3: Artwork; and 42: Writing to Inform

Answers

Interpreting Map **1.** *Cyrus the Great;* **2.** *Sardis and Susa*

Direct Teach

Main Idea

❷ The Persian Empire Grows Stronger

The Persian Empire grew stronger under Darius I.

Recall How did Darius I organize the Persian Empire politically? *by dividing it into 20 provinces and appointing a satrap to rule each one in his place*

Evaluate What is your opinion about Darius's use of satraps and his system of roads and messengers as ways to govern his empire? *Students' opinions should reflect an understanding of how the combination of political subdivisions, governors, and roads enabled Darius to manage his vast empire.*

Checking for Understanding

True or False Answer each statement *T* if it is true or *F* if it is false. If false, explain why.

1. The Immortals were a group of 10,000 soldiers mounted on horses. *F; Cavalry are horse-mounted soldiers.*
2. Darius I, Cyrus's son, claimed the throne and killed all his rivals for power. *F; Darius was a young prince not related to Cyrus.*

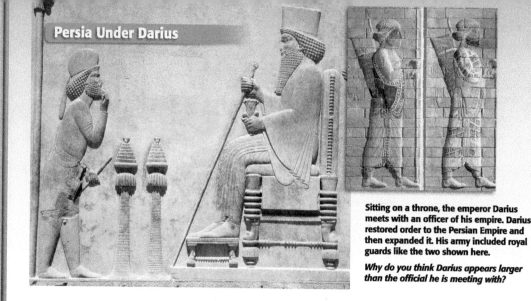

Persia Under Darius

Sitting on a throne, the emperor Darius meets with an officer of his empire. Darius restored order to the Persian Empire and then expanded it. His army included royal guards like the two shown here.

Why do you think Darius appears larger than the official he is meeting with?

At the heart of the Persian army were the Immortals, 10,000 soldiers chosen for their bravery and skill. In addition to the Immortals, the army had a powerful cavalry. A **cavalry** is a unit of soldiers who ride horses. Cyrus used his cavalry to charge the enemy and shoot at them with arrows. This strategy weakened the enemy before the Immortals attacked. Working together, the cavalry and the Immortals could defeat almost any foe.

ACADEMIC VOCABULARY
strategy a plan for fighting a battle or war

READING CHECK **Finding Main Ideas** Who created the Persian Empire?

The Persian Empire Grows Stronger

Cyrus's son Cambyses continued to expand the Persian Empire after Cyrus died. For example, he conquered Egypt and added it to the empire. Soon afterward, though, a rebellion broke out in Persia. During this rebellion, Cambyses died. His death left Persia without a clear leader.

Within four years a young prince named **Darius I** (da-RY-uhs) claimed the throne and killed all his rivals for power. Once he was securely in control, Darius worked to restore order in Persia. He also improved Persian society and expanded the empire.

Political Organization

Darius organized the empire by dividing it into 20 provinces. Then he chose governors called satraps (SAY-traps) to rule the provinces for him. The satraps collected taxes for Darius, served as judges, and put down rebellions within their territories. Satraps had great power within their provinces, but Darius remained the empire's real ruler. His officials visited each province to make sure the satraps were loyal to Darius. He called himself king of kings to remind other rulers of his power.

Persian Society

After Darius restored order to the empire, he made many improvements to Persian society. For example, he built many roads.

Critical Thinking: Making Decisions

At Level

Ruling an Empire

Research Required

1. Ask students to imagine that they are the ruler of the Persian Empire. They have to govern their vast empire and, at the same time, maintain peace and order.
2. Brainstorm with students a list of strategies for holding their empire together and maintaining peace. **LS Verbal/Linguistic**
3. Have each student select one strategy from the list and write an explanation about how he or she would use it to rule the empire.
4. Have students conduct research on King Darius and his use of satraps. Then have each student compare his or her strategy with Darius's use of satraps and make a decision about which strategy would be best. Students should indicate and explain their decision in writing.
LS Verbal/Linguistic, Logical/Mathematical

Alternative Assessment Handbook, Rubrics 30: Research; and 37: Writing Assignments

Answers

Persia Under Darius *because Darius is the king, and the king is more important and more powerful than any official. The respective size of the images is meant to convey their relative power and importance.*

Reading Check *Cyrus the Great*

Darius had roads built to connect various parts of the empire. Messengers used these roads to travel quickly throughout Persia. One road, called the Royal Road, was more than 1,700 miles long. Even Persia's enemies admired these roads and the Persian messenger system. For example, one Greek historian wrote:

> "Nothing mortal travels so fast as these Persian messengers . . . these men will not be hindered from accomplishing at their best speed the distance which they have to go, either by snow, or rain, or heat, or by the darkness of night."
>
> –Herodotus, from *History of the Persian Wars*

Darius also built a new capital for the empire. It was called Persepolis. Darius wanted his capital to reflect the glory of his empire, so he filled the city with beautiful works of art. For example, 3,000 carvings like the ones on the previous page line the city's walls. Statues throughout the city glittered with gold, silver, and precious jewels.

During Darius's rule a new religion arose in the Persian Empire as well. This religion, which was called Zoroastrianism (zawr-uh-WAS-tree-uh-nih-zuhm), taught that there were two forces fighting for control of the universe. One force was good, and the other was evil. Its priests urged people to help the side of good in its struggle. This religion remained popular in Persia for many centuries.

Persian Expansion

Like Cyrus, Darius wanted the Persian Empire to grow. In the east, he conquered the entire Indus Valley. He also tried to expand the empire westward into Europe. However, before Darius could move very far into Europe, he had to deal with a revolt in the empire.

READING CHECK **Summarizing** How did Darius I change Persia's political organization?

The Persians Fight Greece

In 499 BC several Greek cities in Asia Minor rebelled against Persian rule. To help their fellow Greeks, a few city-states in mainland Greece sent soldiers to join the fight against the Persians.

The Persians put down the revolt, but Darius was still angry with the Greeks. Although the cities that had rebelled were in Asia, Darius was enraged that other Greeks had given them aid. He swore to get revenge on the Greeks.

The Battle of Marathon

Nine years after the Greek cities rebelled, Darius invaded Greece. He and his army sailed to the plains of Marathon near Athens. This invasion began a series of wars between Persia and Greece that historians call the **Persian Wars**.

The Athenian army had only about 11,000 soldiers, while the Persians had about 15,000. However, the Greeks won the battle because they had better weapons and clever leaders.

The Persian Wars
This Greek vase shows a Persian soldier (at left) and a Greek soldier in a fight to the death. During the Persian Wars, the Greeks fiercely defended their homeland against massive invasions by the Persians.

With what kinds of weapons are the two soldiers fighting?

Direct Teach

Main Idea

3 The Persians Fight Greece

The Persians fought Greece twice in the Persian Wars.

Recall Why did Darius swear to get revenge on the Greeks? *Darius was enraged that some mainland Greek city-states had aided Greek cities in Asia Minor that had rebelled against Persia.*

Identify What was the name of the place near Athens where the Persian Wars began? *the plains of Marathon*

CRF: Biography, Leonidas

Linking to Today

The Postal Service Some historians think that the first postal system was created under Cyrus the Great. Cyrus's postal system inspired Herodotus to write of the messengers that they "are stayed neither by snow nor rain nor heat nor darkness from accomplishing their appointed course with all speed."

Collaborative Learning

At Level

Changes in the Persian Empire

Research Required

1. Discuss with students the growth and strengthening of the Persian Empire under Darius I. Make sure that students understand how Darius built upon what Cyrus had begun.
2. Organize the class into groups of three. Assign each group (or let each group select) one of the following topics, related to the reign of Darius: Political Organization, Persian Society, or Persian Expansion.
3. Have each group use the Internet or the library to conduct research on King Darius and changes in the Persian Empire related to their topic.
4. **Extend** Reorganize the groups so that each new group has at least one member from each of the previous groups. Have each new group prepare a brief presentation on all three topics.

LS Verbal/Linguistic

Alternative Assessment Handbook, Rubrics 1: Acquiring Information; and 29: Presentations

Answers

The Persian Wars *bows and arrows and spears*

Reading Check *Darius organized the empire into 20 provinces, then appointed a governor (satrap) for each province. The satraps had considerable authority to collect taxes, act as judges, and exercise military power in Darius's name.*

Direct Teach

Main Idea

3 The Persians Fight Greece

The Persians fought Greece twice in the Persian Wars.

Identify What were the names of the three battles in Persia's second invasion of Greece? *Thermopylae, Salamis, and Plataea*

Predict After Athens and Sparta joined to defeat Persia, do you think they remained allies? *possible answer— became enemies because each one wanted to be the most influential city-state*

Map Transparency: The Persian War

Linking to Today

Marathons Although athletes today run marathon races inspired by the legend of the messenger's feat, some historians question whether the legend is true.

Activity Have students conduct research on the legend and write a summary of their findings. Remind students to include their own assessment of the validity of the legend and the latest research. **LS Verbal/Linguistic**

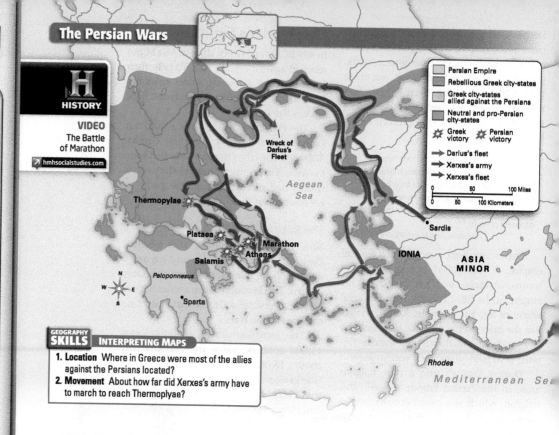

Answers

Interpreting Maps **1.** *near Sparta and Athens* **2.** *about 700 miles*

Reading Check (p. 265) *Darius and Xerxes wanted to invade Greece because parts of Greece were rebelling against the Persian Empire and were trying to break away from Persian rule.*

The Persian Wars

HISTORY VIDEO The Battle of Marathon
hmhsocialstudies.com

Persian Empire
Rebellious Greek city-states
Greek city-states allied against the Persians
Neutral and pro-Persian city-states
Greek victory
Persian victory
Darius's fleet
Xerxes's army
Xerxes's fleet
0 50 100 Miles
0 50 100 Kilometers

Wreck of Darius's Fleet
Aegean Sea
Thermopylae
Plataea
Marathon
Athens
Salamis
Peloponnesus
Sparta
Sardis
IONIA
ASIA MINOR
Rhodes
Mediterranean Sea

GEOGRAPHY SKILLS INTERPRETING MAPS

1. **Location** Where in Greece were most of the allies against the Persians located?
2. **Movement** About how far did Xerxes's army have to march to reach Thermoplyae?

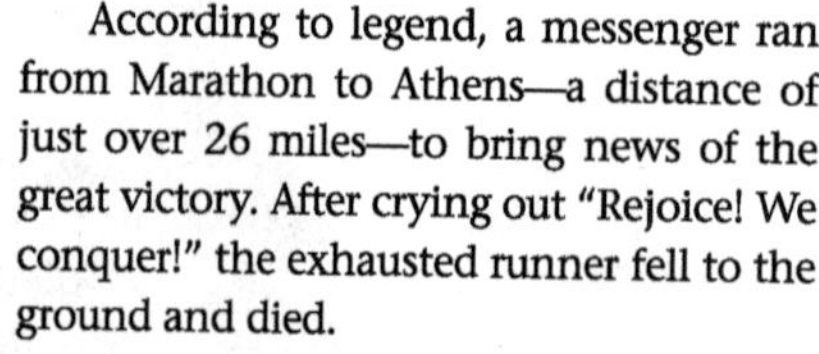

THE IMPACT TODAY

Athletes today re-create the Greek messenger's run in 26-mile races called marathons.

According to legend, a messenger ran from Marathon to Athens—a distance of just over 26 miles—to bring news of the great victory. After crying out "Rejoice! We conquer!" the exhausted runner fell to the ground and died.

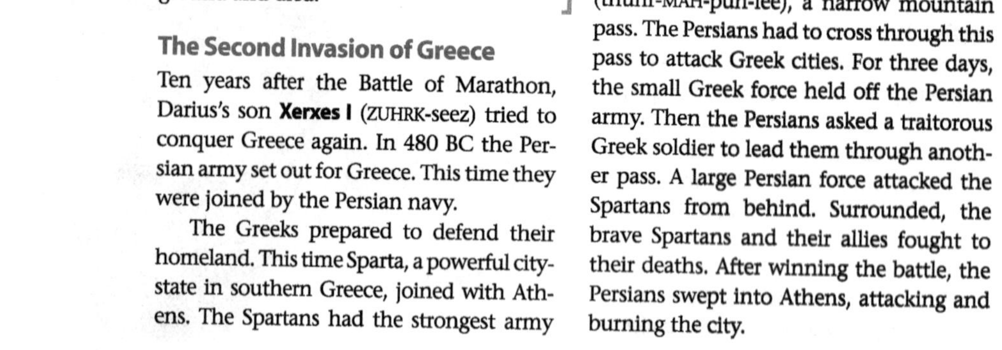

The Second Invasion of Greece

Ten years after the Battle of Marathon, Darius's son **Xerxes I** (ZUHRK-seez) tried to conquer Greece again. In 480 BC the Persian army set out for Greece. This time they were joined by the Persian navy.

The Greeks prepared to defend their homeland. This time Sparta, a powerful city-state in southern Greece, joined with Athens. The Spartans had the strongest army in Greece, so they went to fight the Persian army. Meanwhile, the Athenians sent their powerful navy to attack the Persian navy.

To slow the Persian army, the Spartans sent about 1,400 soldiers to Thermopylae (thuhr-MAH-puh-lee), a narrow mountain pass. The Persians had to cross through this pass to attack Greek cities. For three days, the small Greek force held off the Persian army. Then the Persians asked a traitorous Greek soldier to lead them through another pass. A large Persian force attacked the Spartans from behind. Surrounded, the brave Spartans and their allies fought to their deaths. After winning the battle, the Persians swept into Athens, attacking and burning the city.

Differentiating Instruction

English-Language Learners

At Level | Research Required

Materials: butcher paper; art supplies

1. Discuss with students Persia's two invasions of Greece. Make sure that students understand that the two invasions were at different times and under different rulers.
2. Organize the class into three groups. Assign the first group the battle at Marathon, the second group the battle at Thermopylae, and the third group the battle at Salamis.
3. Have each group conduct research to find out more about its assigned battle.
4. Have each group create a mural depicting its battle. The mural should illustrate the location of the battle, the size and relative positions of each force, and military movements during the battle. **LS Visual/Spatial**

Alternative Assessment Handbook, Rubric 3: Artwork

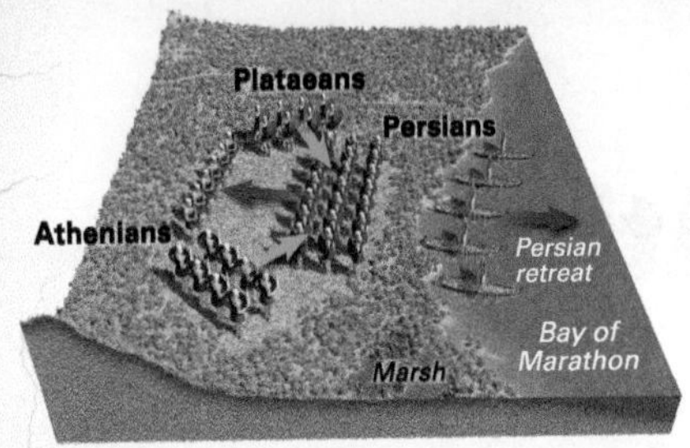

Marathon

At Marathon, the Greeks defeated a larger Persian force by luring the Persians into the middle of their forces. The Athenians then surrounded and defeated the Persians.

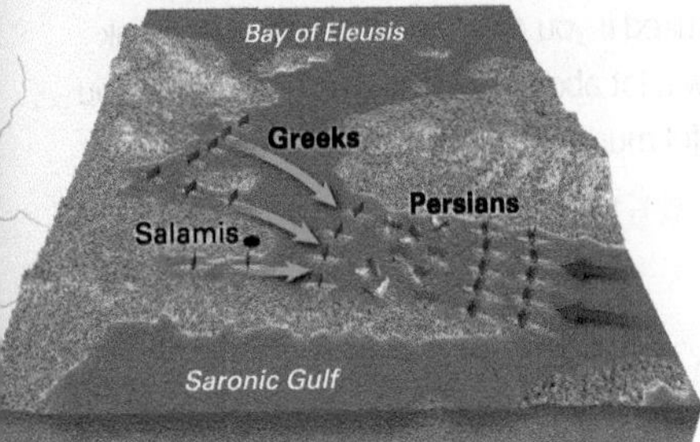

Salamis

At Salamis, the Greeks destroyed the Persian navy by attacking in a narrow strait where the Persian ships could not maneuver well.

Although the Persians won the battle in the pass, the Greeks quickly regained the upper hand. A few days after Athens was burned, the Athenians defeated the Persian navy through a clever plan. They led the larger Persian navy into the narrow straits of Salamis (SAH-luh-muhs). The Persians had so many ships that they couldn't steer well in the narrow strait. As a result, the smaller Athenian boats easily sank many Persian ships. Those ships that were not destroyed soon returned home.

Soon after the Battle of Salamis, an army of soldiers from all over Greece beat the Persians at Plataea (pluh-TEE-uh). This battle ended the Persian Wars. Defeated, the Persians left Greece.

For the Persians, this defeat was humiliating, but it was not a major blow. Their empire remained strong for more than a century after the war. For the Greeks, though, the defeat of the Persians was a triumph. They had saved their homeland.

hmhsocialstudies.com
ANIMATED HISTORY
The Persian Wars, 490–479 BC

READING CHECK **Analyzing** Why did Darius and Xerxes want to conquer Greece?

SUMMARY AND PREVIEW Athens and Sparta fought together against Persia. Their friendship didn't last long, though. In the next section, you will learn what happened when they became enemies.

Section 1 Assessment

hmhsocialstudies.com ONLINE QUIZ

Reviewing Ideas, Terms, and People

1. a. **Describe** Describe the empire of **Cyrus the Great**.
   b. **Make Generalizations** Why did peoples conquered by Cyrus the Great seldom rebel?
2. a. **Identify** How did **Darius I** change Persia's political organization?
   b. **Make Generalizations** How did Persia's roads help improve the empire's organization?
3. a. **Explain** Why did Persia want to invade Greece?
   b. **Predict** How might the **Persian Wars** have ended if the Spartans had not slowed the Persians at Thermopylae?

Critical Thinking

4. **Categorizing** Review your notes on major events. Using a chart like the one below, list the battles you have identified in the first column. In the other columns identify who fought, who won, and what happened as a result of each battle.

Battle	Armies	Winner	Result

FOCUS ON WRITING

5. **Taking Notes on Persian Leaders** Draw a table with three columns. In the first column, write the names of each leader mentioned in this section. In the second column, list each person's military accomplishments. In the third column, list any other accomplishments.

• Review & Assess •

Close

Ask students to discuss why, after the Greeks defeated the Persians, the city-states of Sparta and Athens might have become rivals.

Review

Online Quiz, Section 1

Assess

SE Section 1 Assessment
PASS: Section 1 Quiz
Alternative Assessment Handbook

Reteach/Classroom Intervention

Guided Reading Workbook, Section 1
Interactive Skills Tutor CD-ROM

Section 1 Assessment Answers

1. a. almost all of Southwest and Central Asia, Mesopotamia, and several Greek cities
   b. He allowed them to keep their customs.
2. a. by dividing it into 20 provinces, each with a satrap to rule for Darius
   b. allowed the king to send orders to and receive information from all parts of his empire relatively rapidly
3. a. because many Greek city-states were rebelling against the Persian Empire
   b. possible answer—The Greek army would have had less time to prepare and they might have been defeated.
4. Battle of Marathon—armies: Greeks and Persians; winner: Greeks; result: Persians withdrew (marked start of Persian Wars) [Students' charts should also include the Battles of Thermopylae, Salamis, and Plataea.]
5. Students' tables should include Cyrus the Great, Darius I, and Xerxes I and the accomplishments of each.

Preteach

Bellringer

If YOU were there . . . Use the **Daily Bellringer Transparency** to help students answer the question.

Daily Bellringer Transparency, Section 2

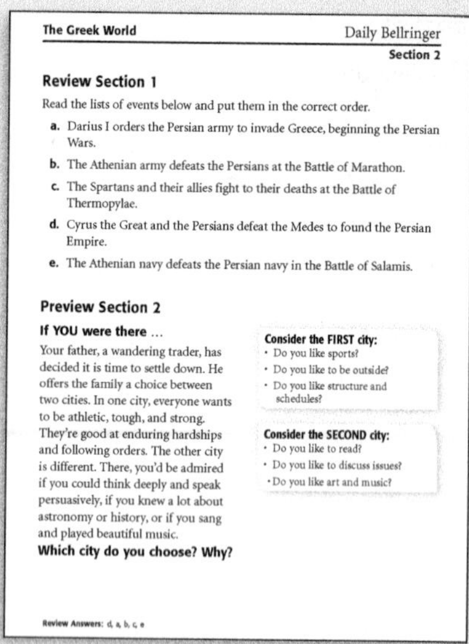
The Greek World — Daily Bellringer, Section 2

Review Section 1

Read the lists of events below and put them in the correct order.

a. Darius I orders the Persian army to invade Greece, beginning the Persian Wars.
b. The Athenian army defeats the Persians at the Battle of Marathon.
c. The Spartans and their allies fight to their deaths at the Battle of Thermopylae.
d. Cyrus the Great and the Persians defeat the Medes to found the Persian Empire.
e. The Athenian navy defeats the Persian navy in the Battle of Salamis.

Preview Section 2

If YOU were there ...

Your father, a wandering trader, has decided it is time to settle down. He offers the family a choice between two cities. In one city, everyone wants to be athletic, tough, and strong. They're good at enduring hardships and following orders. The other city is different. There, you'd be admired if you could think deeply and speak persuasively, if you knew a lot about astronomy or history, or if you sang and played beautiful music.

Which city do you choose? Why?

Consider the FIRST city:
- Do you like sports?
- Do you like to be outside?
- Do you like structure and schedules?

Consider the SECOND city:
- Do you like to read?
- Do you like to discuss issues?
- Do you like art and music?

Review Answers: d, a, b, c, e

Building Vocabulary

Preteach or review the following term:

league a collection of people, groups, or countries that combine for mutual protection or cooperation (p. 270)

CRF: Vocabulary Builder, Section 2

Taking Notes

Have students use the graphic organizer online to take notes on the section. This activity will prepare students for the Section Assessment, in which they will complete a graphic organizer that builds on the information using the Critical Thinking Skill: Comparing and Contrasting.

SECTION 2

Sparta and Athens

What You Will Learn...

Main Ideas

1. The Spartans built a military society to provide security and protection.
2. The Athenians admired the mind and the arts in addition to physical abilities.
3. Sparta and Athens fought over who should have power and influence in Greece.

The Big Idea

The two most powerful city-states in Greece, Sparta and Athens, had very different cultures and became bitter enemies in the 400s BC.

Key Terms

alliance, *p. 270*
Peloponnesian War, *p. 271*

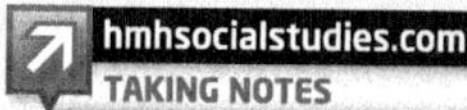

Use the graphic organizer online to take notes on Athens and Sparta.

If YOU were there...

Your father, a wandering trader, has decided it is time to settle down. He offers the family a choice between two cities. In one city, everyone wants to be athletic, tough, and strong. They're good at enduring hardships and following orders. The other city is different. There, you'd be admired if you could think deeply and speak persuasively, if you knew a lot about astronomy or history, or if you sang and played beautiful music.

Which city do you choose? Why?

BUILDING BACKGROUND Two of the greatest city-states in Greece were Sparta and Athens. Sparta, like the first city mentioned above, had a culture that valued physical strength and military might. The Athenian culture placed more value on the mind. However, both city-states had military strength, and they both played important roles in the defense of ancient Greece.

Spartans Build a Military Society

Spartan society was dominated by the military. According to Spartan tradition, their social system was created between 900 and 600 BC by a man named Lycurgus (ly-KUHR-guhs) after a slave revolt. To keep such a revolt from happening again, he increased the military's role in society. The Spartans believed that military power was the way to provide security and protection for their city. Daily life in Sparta reflected this belief.

Boys and Men in Sparta

Daily life in Sparta was dominated by the army. Even the lives of children reflected this domination. When a boy was born, government officials came to look at him. If he was not healthy, the baby was taken outside of the city and left to die. Healthy boys were trained from an early age to be soldiers.

Teach the Big Idea

At Level

Sparta and Athens

1. **Teach** Ask students the questions in the Main Idea boxes to teach this section.
2. **Apply** As students read this section, have them make an outline of the section using the blue heads (such as "Spartans Build a Military Society") as main ideas and the red heads (such as "Boys and Men in Sparta") as supporting ideas. Have students fill in their outlines. **LS Verbal/Linguistic**
3. **Review** Ask volunteers to share their outlines with the class. Ask the class to suggest additional information they might add to the outline.
4. **Practice/Homework** Have each student use his or her outline to write a brief, two-paragraph summary comparing and contrasting life in Athens and Sparta. **LS Verbal/Linguistic**

Alternative Assessment Handbook, Rubric 9: Comparing and Contrasting

As part of their training, boys ran, jumped, swam, and threw javelins to increase their strength. They also learned to endure the hardships they would face as soldiers. For example, boys weren't given shoes or heavy clothes, even in winter. They also weren't given much food. Boys were allowed to steal food if they could, but if they were caught, they were whipped. At least one boy chose to die rather than admit to his theft:

> "One youth, having stolen a fox and hidden it under his coat, allowed it to tear out his very bowels [organs] with its claws and teeth and died rather than betray his theft."
>
> –Plutarch, from *Life of Lycurgus*

To this boy—and to most Spartan soldiers—courage and strength were more important than one's own safety.

Soldiers between the ages of 20 and 30 lived in army barracks and only occasionally visited their families. Spartan men stayed in the army until they turned 60.

The Spartans believed that the most important qualities of good soldiers were self-discipline and obedience. To reinforce self-discipline they required soldiers to live tough lives free from comforts. For example, the Spartans didn't have luxuries like soft furniture and expensive food. They thought such comforts made people weak. Even the Spartans' enemies admired their discipline and obedience.

Girls and Women in Sparta

Because Spartan men were often away at war, Spartan women had more rights than other Greek women. Some women owned land in Sparta and ran their households when their husbands were gone. Unlike women in other Greek cities, Spartan women didn't spend time spinning cloth or weaving. They thought of those tasks as the jobs of slaves, unsuitable for the wives and mothers of soldiers.

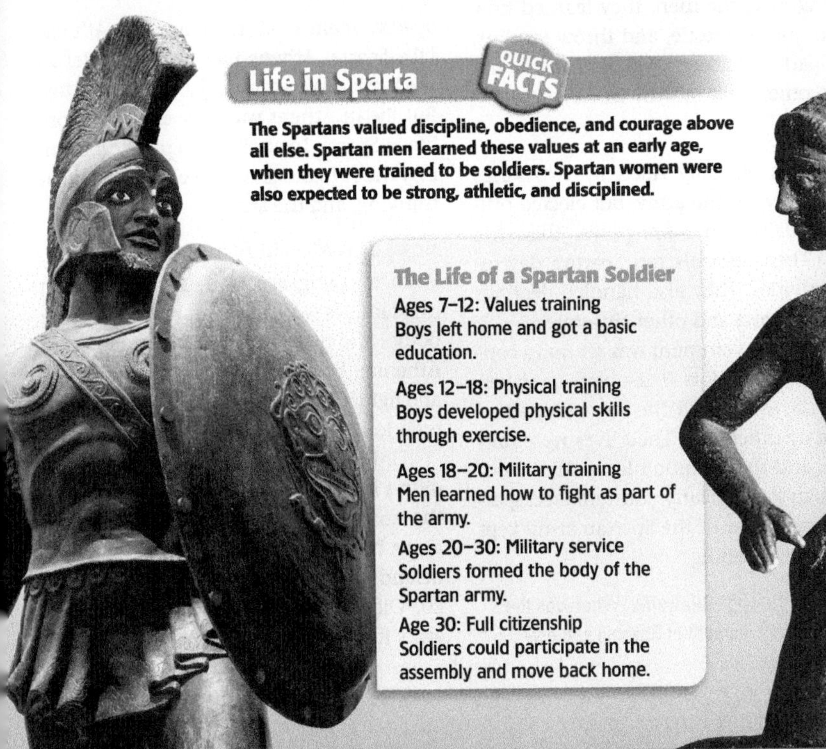

Life in Sparta — QUICK FACTS

The Spartans valued discipline, obedience, and courage above all else. Spartan men learned these values at an early age, when they were trained to be soldiers. Spartan women were also expected to be strong, athletic, and disciplined.

The Life of a Spartan Soldier

Ages 7–12: Values training
Boys left home and got a basic education.

Ages 12–18: Physical training
Boys developed physical skills through exercise.

Ages 18–20: Military training
Men learned how to fight as part of the army.

Ages 20–30: Military service
Soldiers formed the body of the Spartan army.

Age 30: Full citizenship
Soldiers could participate in the assembly and move back home.

267

Direct Teach

Main Idea

1 Spartans Build a Military Society

The Spartans built a military society to provide security and protection.

Identify According to legend, who was responsible for the beginnings of the Spartan social system? *Lycurgus, sometime between 900 and 600 BC*

Recall What two qualities did the Spartans think were most important in a good soldier? *self-discipline and obedience*

Analyze In a society organized such as Sparta was, why might women have more rights and responsibilities than in a society organized as Athens was? *While the boys and young men in Sparta were away from home serving as soldiers, women filled the roles, such as property owners and heads of households, that men filled in other societies.*

Quick Facts Transparency: Life in Sparta

Did you know. . .

Although some modern historians think that Lycurgus was a real person, many other historians think that Lycurgus existed only in legend.

hmhsocialstudies.com
Online Resources
Activity: Sparta vs. Athens

Critical Thinking: Evaluating Information

At Level

Sparta Builds a Military Society

1. Ask students to describe, in their own words, the structure and organization of Spartan society.
2. Ask students to give their opinion about the following statement: *Sparta's model of a military society is a model that countries should follow today.* Remind students to give reasons for their opinions and to support their opinions with facts. **LS Verbal/Linguistic**
3. **Extend** Have students who hold opposing viewpoints debate the issue. Afterward, have the class vote on which side made the better arguments.

Alternative Assessment Handbook, Rubrics 10: Debates; and 11: Discussions

Direct Teach

Main Idea

1 Spartans Build a Military Society

The Spartans built a military society to provide security and protection.

Recall How many kings officially ruled Sparta? *two*

Draw Conclusions Why did Spartan elected officials have more power than the kings? *Elected officials ran Sparta's day-to-day activities and handled Sparta's dealings with other city-states.*

Linking to Today

Women of Greece Women of Sparta and Athens had different rights. Because Greece is no longer divided into city-states, all Greek women now have the same rights. They have gained some of those rights, however, just in recent decades. In the 1980s the power of Greek fathers over their daughters was limited. At the same time, women received more freedom to divorce. Women can serve in the military and are active in the government.

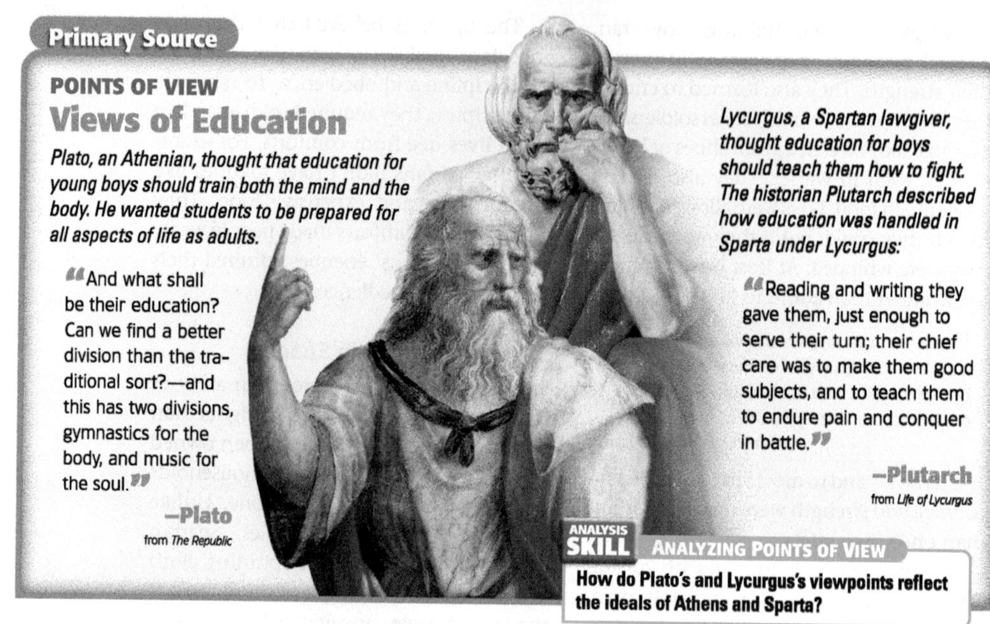

Primary Source

POINTS OF VIEW

Views of Education

Plato, an Athenian, thought that education for young boys should train both the mind and the body. He wanted students to be prepared for all aspects of life as adults.

"And what shall be their education? Can we find a better division than the traditional sort?—and this has two divisions, gymnastics for the body, and music for the soul."

—Plato
from *The Republic*

Lycurgus, a Spartan lawgiver, thought education for boys should teach them how to fight. The historian Plutarch described how education was handled in Sparta under Lycurgus:

"Reading and writing they gave them, just enough to serve their turn; their chief care was to make them good subjects, and to teach them to endure pain and conquer in battle."

—Plutarch
from *Life of Lycurgus*

ANALYSIS SKILL **ANALYZING POINTS OF VIEW**

How do Plato's and Lycurgus's viewpoints reflect the ideals of Athens and Sparta?

Spartan women also received physical training. Like the men, they learned how to run, jump, wrestle, and throw javelins. The Spartans believed this training would help women bear healthy children.

Government

Sparta was officially ruled by two kings who jointly led the army. But elected officials actually had more power than the kings. These officials ran Sparta's day-to-day activities. They also handled dealings between Sparta and other city-states.

Focus on Reading
How can the words ***like*** and ***unlike*** help you compare and contrast Athens and Sparta?

Sparta's government was set up to control the city's helots (HEL-uhts), or slaves. These slaves grew all the city's crops and did many other jobs. Their lives were miserable, and they couldn't leave their land. Although slaves greatly outnumbered Spartan citizens, fear of the Spartan army kept them from rebelling.

READING CHECK **Analyzing** What was the most important element of Spartan society?

Athenians Admire the Mind

Sparta's main rival in Greece was Athens. Like Sparta, Athens had been a leader in the Persian Wars and had a powerful army. But life in Athens was very different from life in Sparta. In addition to physical training, the Athenians valued education, clear thinking, and the arts.

Boys and Men in Athens

From a young age, Athenian boys from rich families worked to improve both their bodies and their minds. Like Spartan boys, Athenian boys had to learn to run, jump, and fight. But this training was not as harsh or as long as the training in Sparta.

Unlike Spartan men, Athenian men didn't have to devote their whole lives to the army. All men in Athens joined the army, but for only two years. They helped defend the city between the ages of 18 and 20. Older men only had to serve in the army in times of war.

Answers

Analyzing Points of View *Lycurgus's viewpoint stresses that most of a boy's education should be focused on how to fight and endure pain and how to conquer in battle. This viewpoint is the basis for Sparta's military society. Plato's viewpoint is that both a boy's mind and his body should be trained and educated. This viewpoint reflects the value that Athens placed on both the mind and the body.*

Focus on Reading Like *is used to show how two things are similar;* unlike *is used to show how two things are different. As you read, these words will give you clues about the similarities and differences between Sparta and Athens.*

Reading Check *the military*

Differentiating Instruction

Special Needs Learners Below Level

1. Organize the class into four groups.
2. Have each group create a mural or posters that depict the lives of men and women in Sparta and Athens. LS **Visual/Spatial**
3. Ask each group to present its mural or posters to the rest of the class.
4. Have students, using the images on the mural or posters, discuss which parts of both Spartan and Athenian society they like or don't like. LS **Verbal/Linguistic**
5. **Extend** Refer students back to the carving of Darius meeting with an officer in the previous section. Ask students if any of their images are larger than others. If so, ask if they can explain why.

Alternative Assessment Handbook, Rubrics 3: Artwork; and 28: Posters

In addition to their physical training, Athenian students, unlike the Spartans, also learned other skills. They learned to read, write, and count as well as sing and play musical instruments. Boys also learned about Greek history and legend. For example, they studied the *Iliad*, the *Odyssey*, and other works of Greek literature.

Boys from very rich families often continued their education with private tutors. These tutors taught their students about philosophy, geometry, astronomy, and other subjects. They also taught the boys how to be good public speakers. This training prepared boys for participation in the Athenian assembly.

Very few boys had the opportunity to receive this much education, however. Boys from poor families usually didn't get any education, although most of them could read and write at least a little. Most of the boys from poor families became farmers and grew food for the city's richer citizens. A few went to work with craftspeople to learn other trades.

Girls and Women in Athens

While many boys in Athens received good educations, girls didn't. In fact, girls received almost no education. Athenian men didn't think girls needed to be educated. A few girls were taught how to read and write at home by private tutors. However, most girls only learned household tasks like weaving and sewing.

Despite Athens's reputation for freedom and democracy, women there had fewer rights than women in many other city-states. Athenian women could not

- serve in any part of the city's government, including the assembly and juries,
- leave their homes, except on special occasions,
- buy anything or own property, or
- disobey their husbands or fathers.

In fact, women in Athens had almost no rights at all.

READING CHECK **Identifying Cause and Effect** Why did girls in Athens receive little education?

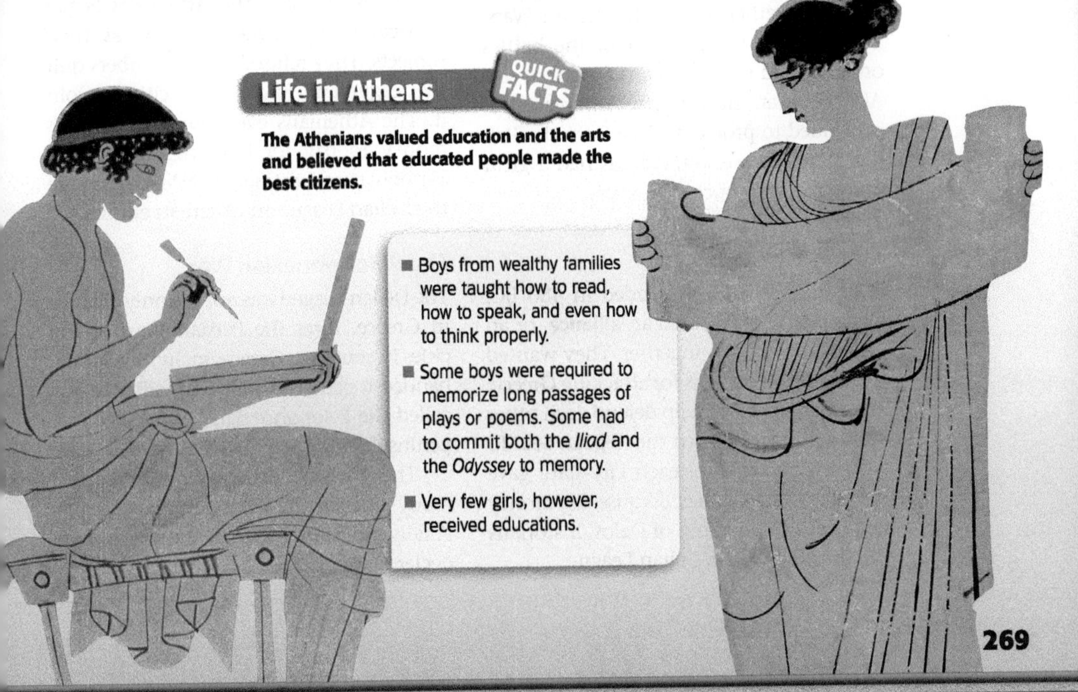

The Athenians valued education and the arts and believed that educated people made the best citizens.

- Boys from wealthy families were taught how to read, how to speak, and even how to think properly.
- Some boys were required to memorize long passages of plays or poems. Some had to commit both the *Iliad* and the *Odyssey* to memory.
- Very few girls, however, received educations.

Critical Thinking: Comparing and Constrasting

At Level

Understanding Charts and Tables

Materials: butcher paper, markers

1. Organize the class into small groups.
2. Have each group make a table comparing and contrasting education in ancient Athens with education today. The table should have two main heads (*Education in Ancient Athens* and *Education Today*), and each of those main heads should have two subheads, (*Education for Boys* and *Education for Girls*).
3. Have students complete the table.
4. Have each group present its table to the rest of the class. Have the class discuss similarities and differences between education in ancient Athens and education today. Ask students which education system they would rather have and why. **LS Logical/Mathematical**

Alternative Assessment Handbook, Rubric 9: Comparing and Contrasting

Direct Teach

Main Idea

2 Athenians Admire the Mind

The Athenians admired the mind and the arts in addition to physical abilities.

Recall What were Athenian girls taught? *to weave and sew, care for the home*

Contrast What was the basic difference between life in Sparta and life in Athens? *Sparta—focused on and organized around the military, so all training and education supported the military; Athens—thought that the mind and the body should be trained, so education, clear thinking, and the arts were valued*

Evaluate Considering only Athens and Sparta, in which city-state would you rather have lived? *possible answer—I would rather have lived in Sparta because I could have owned property, taken care of my house, and been defended by the strong army.*

CRF: Interdisciplinary Project: Spartans vs Athenians Debate

CRF: Economics and History, The Importance of Trade

Quick Facts Transparency: Life in Athens

Biography

Anaxagoras of Clazomenae (500–428 BC) Anaxagoras was a Greek philosopher who believed that the sun is a white-hot stone and that the moon is made of material similar to Earth and reflects light from the sun.

Answers

Reading Check *because men didn't think women needed education*

Direct Teach

Main Idea

3 Sparta and Athens Fight

Sparta and Athens fought over who should have power and influence in Greece.

Define In your own words, define the term alliance. *an agreement between parties to work together or to help each other, especially for defense or trade*

Summarize What happened to the Delian League? *Athens increased its influence over the other city-states in the league, began to treat other members unfairly, and used the league's money to benefit Athens. The league became an Athenian empire.*

Map Transparency: The Peloponnesian War, c. 431–404 BC

Interpreting Maps

The Peloponnesian War, c. 431–404 BC

Activity Ask students to imagine that they are generals for either Athens or Greece. Have students analyze the map to see who might have the military advantage in a possible Peloponnesian War. Students should consider the location of Athens and Sparta, the location of their allies, the distance their military would have to travel to fight a battle, and any other things that you as a general might worry about. Who has the advantage? *possible answer—Sparta and its allies, because they control more territory than Athens and its allies; Sparta and its allies can attack Athens from two directions.*

Map Transparency: Peloponnesian War, c. 431–404 BC.

Answers

Interpreting Maps

1. *Athens* 2. *about 550 miles*

hmhsocialstudies.com INTERACTIVE MAP

The Peloponnesian War, c. 431–404 BC

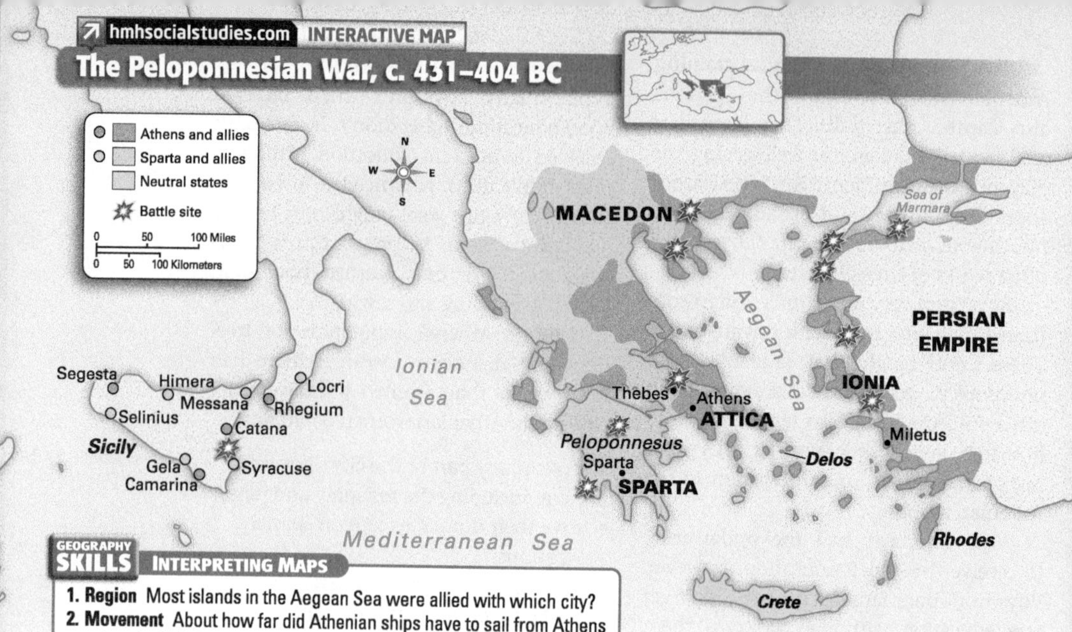

GEOGRAPHY SKILLS INTERPRETING MAPS

1. **Region** Most islands in the Aegean Sea were allied with which city?
2. **Movement** About how far did Athenian ships have to sail from Athens to invade Sicily?

Sparta and Athens Fight

As you learned earlier, Sparta and Athens worked together to win the Persian Wars. The Spartans fought most of the battles on land, and the Athenians fought at sea. After the war, the powerful Athenian fleet continued to protect Greece from the Persian navy. As a result, Athens had a great influence over much of Greece.

Athenian Power

After the Persian Wars ended in 480 BC, many city-states formed an **alliance**, or an agreement to work together. They wanted to punish the Persians for attacking Greece. They also agreed to help defend each other and to protect trade in the Aegean Sea. To pay for this defense, each city-state gave money to the alliance. Because the money was kept on the island of Delos, historians call the alliance the Delian League.

With its navy protecting the islands, Athens was the strongest member of the league. As a result, the Athenians began to treat other league members as their subjects. They refused to let members quit the league and forced more cities to join it. The Athenians even used the league's money to pay for buildings in Athens. Without even fighting, the Athenians made the Delian League an Athenian empire.

The Peloponnesian War

The Delian League was not the only alliance in Greece. After the Persian Wars, many cities in southern Greece, including Sparta, banded together as well. This alliance was called the Peloponnesian League after the peninsula on which the cities were located.

The growth of Athenian power worried many cities in the Peloponnesian League. Finally, to stop Athens's growth, Sparta declared war.

Critical Thinking: Evaluating Information

Above Level

The Peloponnesian War

Research Required

Materials: butcher paper; art supplies

1. Organize the class into small groups. Assign each group either Sparta's attack on Athens in 431 BC, Athens's attack on Sicily in 415 BC, or Sparta's attack on Athens (and Athens's surrender) in 405–404 BC.
2. Have each group conduct research on its assigned battle. Then ask each group to create a large map or a mural showing the details of its battle and the strategy and tactics used by both sides.
3. Have members of each group prepare a brief presentation explaining its battle to the class.
4. Have the class discuss each battle and evaluate the strategy and tactics used by each side. **LS Logical/Mathematical, Visual Spatial**

Alternative Assessment Handbook, Rubrics 1: Acquiring Information; 3: Artwork; and 16: Judging Information

This declaration of war began the **Peloponnesian War**, a war between Athens and Sparta that threatened to tear all of Greece apart. In 431 BC the Spartan army marched north to Athens. They surrounded the city, waiting for the Athenians to come out and fight. But the Athenians stayed in the city, hoping that the Spartans would leave. Instead, the Spartans began to burn the crops in the fields around Athens. They hoped that Athens would run out of food and be forced to surrender.

The Spartans were in for a surprise. The Athenian navy escorted merchant ships to Athens, bringing plenty of food to the city. The navy also attacked Sparta's allies, forcing the Spartans to send troops to defend other Greek cities. At the same time, though, disease swept through Athens, killing thousands. For 10 years neither side could gain an advantage over the other. Eventually, they agreed to a truce. Athens kept its empire, and the Spartans went home.

A few years later, in 415 BC, Athens tried again to expand its empire. It sent its army and navy to conquer the island of Sicily. This effort failed. The entire Athenian army was defeated by Sicilian allies of Sparta and taken prisoner. Even worse, these Sicilians also destroyed most of the Athenian navy.

Taking advantage of Athens's weakness, Sparta attacked Athens, and the war started up once more. Although the Athenians fought bravely, the Spartans won. They cut off the supply of food to Athens completely. In 404 BC, the people of Athens, starving and surrounded, surrendered. The Peloponnesian War was over, and Sparta was in control.

Fighting Among the City-States

With the defeat of Athens, Sparta became the most powerful city-state in Greece. For about 30 years, the Spartans controlled nearly all of Greece, until other city-states started to resent them. This resentment led to a period of war. Control of Greece shifted from city-state to city-state. The fighting went on for many years, which weakened Greece and left it open to attack from outside.

READING CHECK **Identifying Cause and Effect** What happened to Greece after the Peloponnesian War?

SUMMARY AND PREVIEW In this section you read about conflicts among city-states for control of Greece. In the next section, you will learn what happened when all of Greece was conquered by a foreign power.

Section 2 Assessment

Reviewing Ideas, Terms, and People

1. a. **Recall** How long did Spartan men stay in the army?
   b. **Summarize** How did the army affect life in Sparta?
2. a. **Identify** What skills did rich Athenian boys learn in school?
   b. **Elaborate** How might the government of Athens have influenced the growth of its educational system?
3. a. **Identify** Which city-state won the Peloponnesian War?
   b. **Explain** Why did many city-states form an **alliance** against Athens?

Critical Thinking

4. **Comparing and Contrasting** Look through your notes on Athens and Sparta to find similarities and differences between the two city-states. Use a graphic organizer like the one on the right to organize the information.

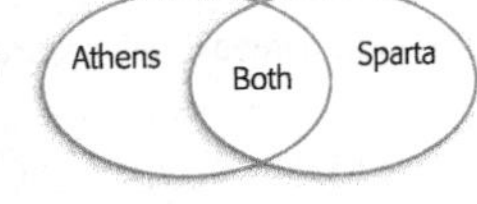

FOCUS ON WRITING

5. **Analyzing Greek Accomplishments** Think about the characteristics you would expect to be admired in Sparta and Athens. Write down some of these characteristics in your notebook. How do they relate to the Persian leaders you listed before?

• Review & Assess •

Close

Have students discuss why Spartan society depended so heavily on slaves whereas Athenian society did not. Ask students, "Why might the dependence on slaves be a weakness in the society in Sparta?"

Review

Online Quiz, Section 2

Assess

SE Section 2 Assessment

PASS: Section 2 Quiz

Alternative Assessment Handbook

Reteach/Classroom Intervention

Guided Reading Workbook, Section 2

Interactive Skills Tutor CD-ROM

Section 2 Assessment Answers

1. a. 40 years
   b. Boys trained for military service from age 18 to 20, and men served in the army from age 20 to 60. Spartan women had more rights than other Greek women.
2. a. reading, writing, counting, singing, playing a musical instrument, history, and thinking
   b. It didn't emphasize the military, and it encouraged the arts and sciences.
3. a. Sparta
   b. because Athens treated them like subjects
4. Sparta—military: main element in society; education: limited to basics; women: had rights, owned land, trained physically; Athens—military: limited service; education: wealthy boys given education; women: few rights and not educated
5. Students may compare and contrast characteristics, such as the emphasis on military training or on education.

Answers

Reading Check *Sparta became the most powerful city-state in Greece.*

Preteach

Bellringer

If YOU were there . . . Use the **Daily Bellringer Transparency** to help students answer the question.

Daily Bellringer Transparency, Section 3

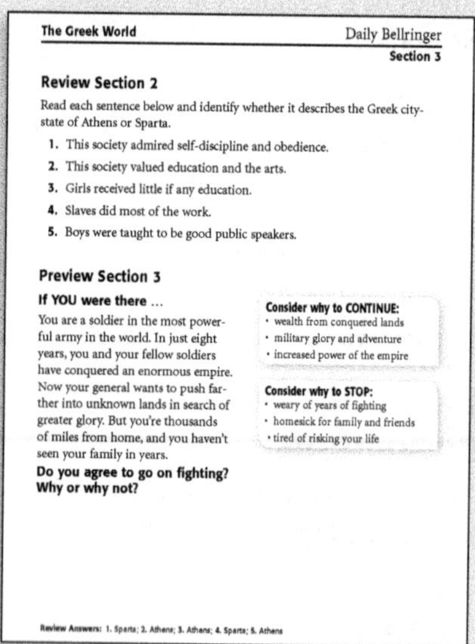

The Greek World — Daily Bellringer, Section 3

Review Section 2

Read each sentence below and identify whether it describes the Greek city-state of Athens or Sparta.

1. This society admired self-discipline and obedience.
2. This society valued education and the arts.
3. Girls received little if any education.
4. Slaves did most of the work.
5. Boys were taught to be good public speakers.

Preview Section 3

If YOU were there ...

You are a soldier in the most powerful army in the world. In just eight years, you and your fellow soldiers have conquered an enormous empire. Now your general wants to push farther into unknown lands in search of greater glory. But you're thousands of miles from home, and you haven't seen your family in years.

Do you agree to go on fighting? Why or why not?

Consider why to CONTINUE:
- wealth from conquered lands
- military glory and adventure
- increased power of the empire

Consider why to STOP:
- weary of years of fighting
- homesick for family and friends
- tired of risking your life

Review Answers: 1. Sparta; 2. Athens; 3. Athens; 4. Sparta; 5. Athens

Vocabulary Builder

Preteach or review the following term:

Hellenic an adjective meaning "Greek"; applied to the cultures of Greek-speaking societies (p. 275)

opponent someone who takes the opposite side in a contest or fight (p. 273)

CRF: Vocabulary Builder, Section 3

Taking Notes

Have students use the graphic organizer online to take notes on the section. This activity will prepare students for the Section Assessment, in which they will complete a graphic organizer that builds on the information using the Critical Thinking Skill: Generalizing.

SECTION 3

Alexander the Great

What You Will Learn...

Main Ideas

1. Macedonia conquered Greece in the 300s BC.
2. Alexander the Great built an empire that united much of Europe, Asia, and Egypt.
3. The Hellenistic kingdoms formed from Alexander's empire blended Greek and other cultures.

The Big Idea

Alexander the Great built a huge empire and helped spread Greek culture into Egypt and Asia.

Key Terms and People

Philip II, *p. 272*
phalanx, *p. 273*
Alexander the Great, *p. 274*
Hellenistic, *p. 275*

Use the graphic organizer online to take notes on Alexander the Great and how he spread Greek culture.

If YOU were there...

You are a soldier in the most powerful army in the world. In just eight years, you and your fellow soldiers have conquered an enormous empire. Now your general wants to push farther into unknown lands in search of greater glory. But you're thousands of miles from home, and you haven't seen your family in years.

Do you agree to go on fighting? Why or why not?

BUILDING BACKGROUND The world's most powerful army in the 300s BC was from Macedonia, a kingdom just north of Greece. The Greeks had long dismissed the Macedonians as unimportant. They thought of the Macedonians as barbarians because they lived in small villages and spoke a strange form of the Greek language. But the Greeks underestimated the Macedonians, barbarians or not.

Macedonia Conquers Greece

In 359 BC **Philip II** became king of Macedonia. Philip spent the first year of his rule fighting off invaders who wanted to take over his kingdom. Once he defeated the invaders, he was ready to launch invasions of his own.

Philip's main target was Greece. The leaders of Athens, knowing they were the target of Philip's powerful army, called for all Greeks to join together. Few people responded.

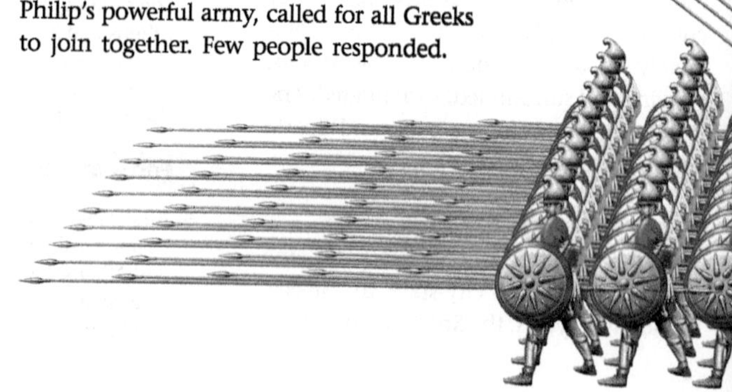

Teach the Big Idea

At Level

Alexander the Great

1. **Teach** Ask students the questions in the Main Idea boxes to teach this section.
2. **Apply** Organize the class into four groups. Assign each group one of the following: *Macedonia conquers Greece, Alexander builds an empire, Alexander spreads Greek culture, and Alexander's empire after his death.* Have the groups prepare posters about their topics. Have each group present its findings and discuss them. **LS Visual/Spatial**
3. **Review** Have the class review Alexander's goals and whether he was successful in attaining them.
4. **Practice/Homework** Have students write a short speech either supporting or opposing Alexander the Great from the point of view of a Greek citizen or a citizen of another conquered area. **LS Verbal/Linguistic**

Alternative Assessment Handbook, Rubrics 28: Posters; and 43: Writing to Persuade

As a result, the armies of Athens and its chief ally Thebes were easily defeated by the Macedonians. Having witnessed this defeat, the rest of the Greeks agreed to make Philip their leader.

Philip's Military Strength

Philip defeated the Greeks because he was a brilliant military leader. He borrowed and improved many of the strategies Greek armies used in battle. For example, Philip's soldiers, like the Greeks, fought as a phalanx (FAY-langks). A **phalanx** was a group of warriors who stood close together in a square. Each soldier held a spear pointed outward to fight off enemies. As soldiers in the front lines were killed, others stepped up from behind to fill their spots.

Philip improved upon the Greeks' idea. He gave his soldiers spears that were much longer than those of his opponents. This allowed his army to attack effectively in any battle. Philip also sent cavalry and archers into battle to support the phalanx.

After conquering Greece, Philip turned his attention to Persia. He planned to march east and conquer the Persian Empire, but he never made it. He was murdered in 336 BC while celebrating his daughter's wedding. When Philip died, his throne—and his plans—passed to his son, Alexander.

READING CHECK **Summarizing** How was Philip II able to conquer Greece?

Alexander Builds an Empire

When Philip died, the people in the Greek city of Thebes rebelled. They thought that the Macedonians would not have a leader strong enough to keep the kingdom together. They were wrong.

Controlling the Greeks

Although he was only 20 years old, Philip's son Alexander was as strong a leader as his father had been. He immediately went south to end the revolt in Thebes.

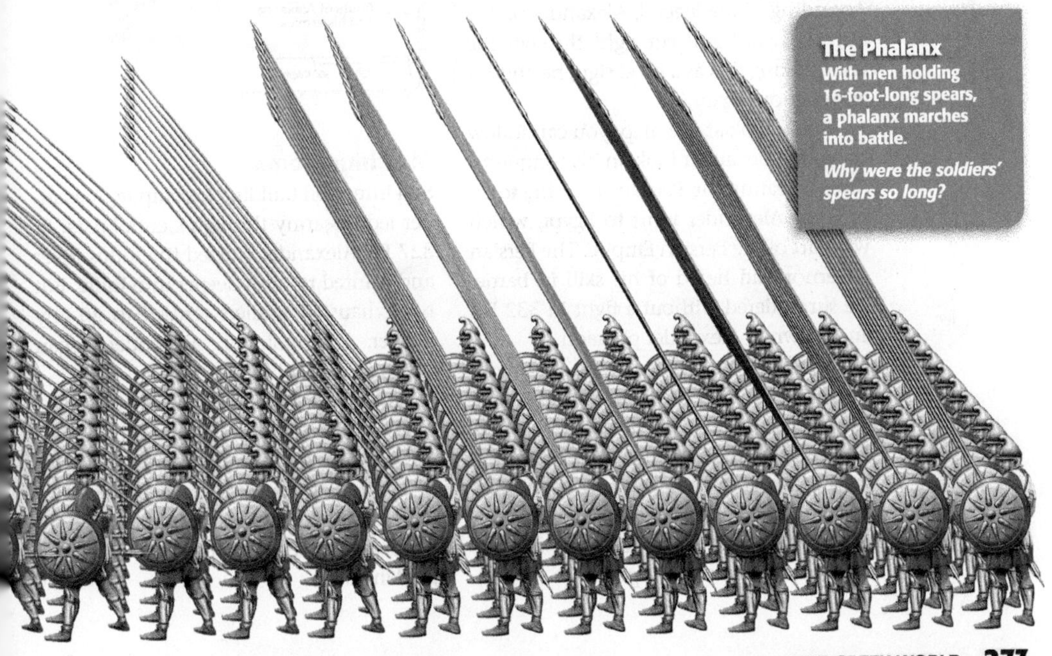

The Phalanx
With men holding 16-foot-long spears, a phalanx marches into battle.

Why were the soldiers' spears so long?

Direct Teach

Main Idea

1 Macedonia Conquers Greece

Macedonia conquered Greece in the 300s BC.

Define In your own words, define the term phalanx. *a military formation of foot soldiers holding long spears and standing close together in the shape of a square*

Recall Philip wanted to conquer the Persian Empire. Was he successful? Why or why not? *unsuccessful, because he was murdered*

Draw Conclusions After Athens and Thebes were defeated by Philip, why did the rest of Greece agree to make Philip their leader? *Greece had been in turmoil for more than 30 years when Philip became king. Athens and Thebes were powerful city-states, and Philip beat them easily. Most Greeks probably realized that life would be more peaceful and stable under Philip's rule than under conditions of war and unrest.*

Collaborative Learning

At Level

Evaluating Alexander's Leadership

1. Organize students into small groups.
2. Have each group brainstorm a list of qualities or characteristics that make someone a great leader.
3. From the group lists, create a master list of qualities of great leaders and write the list for the class to see.
4. Ask students to discuss which of the listed qualities Alexander possessed. If students disagree, hold a brief debate and have the class vote on whether it thinks Alexander had the quality or not. LS **Verbal/Linguistic**

Alternative Assessment Handbook, Rubric 11: Discussions

Answers

The Phalanx *Longer spears enabled Philip's army to attack first in any battle.*

Reading Check *Philip was able to defeat Greece because few Greeks responded to Athens's call for all Greeks to join together to fight. As a result, the armies of Athens and their chief ally were easily defeated.*

Direct Teach

Main Idea

2 Alexander Builds an Empire

Alexander the Great built an empire that united much of Europe, Asia, and Egypt.

Explain Why is Alexander called "the Great"? *because he took over his father's throne at 20 and then built one of the largest empires the world has ever seen*

Summarize Using the information on this page and in the map of Alexander's empire, summarize Alexander's efforts to conquer the world. *Between 336 and 323 BC, Alexander conquered Greece, Egypt, the Persian Empire, and parts of central Asia and India. He didn't conquer the whole world, but he did create a vast empire.*

CRF: Primary Source, "Alexander" from Plutarch's *Lives*

Info to Know

Bucephalus Alexander had a favorite horse named Bucephalus. According to Plutarch, Alexander was 12 years old when he won the horse. No one could tame the animal, but Alexander wanted to try. He promised to pay for the horse if he failed. Alexander succeeded by turning the horse toward the sun so it couldn't see its own shadow, which was frightening it. Alexander named his prize Bucephalus. He loved the animal so much that when Bucephalus died, Alexander named a city—Bucephala—after the animal.

Within a year, Alexander had destroyed Thebes and enslaved the Theban people. He used Thebes as an example to other Greeks of what would happen if they turned against him. Then, confident that the Greeks would not rebel again, he set out to build an empire.

Alexander's efforts to build an empire made him one of the greatest conquerors in history. These efforts earned him the name **Alexander the Great.**

Building a New Empire

Like his father, Alexander was a brilliant commander. In 334 BC he attacked the Persians, whose army was much larger than his own. But Alexander's troops were well trained and ready for battle. They defeated the Persians time after time.

According to legend, Alexander visited a town called Gordium in Asia Minor while he was fighting the Persians. There he heard an ancient tale about a knot tied by an ancient king. The tale said that whoever untied the knot would rule all of Asia. According to the legend, Alexander pulled out his sword and cut right through the knot. Taking this as a good sign, he and his army set out again.

THE IMPACT TODAY We still use the phrase "cutting the Gordian knot" to mean solving a difficult problem easily.

If you look at the map, you can follow the route Alexander took on his conquests. After defeating the Persians near the town of Issus, Alexander went to Egypt, which was part of the Persian Empire. The Persian governor had heard of his skill in battle. He surrendered without a fight in 332 BC and crowned Alexander pharaoh.

After a short stay in Egypt, Alexander set out again. Near the town of Gaugamela (gaw-guh-MEE-luh), he defeated the Persian army for the last time. After the battle, the Persian king fled. The king soon died, killed by one of his nobles. With the king's death, Alexander became the ruler of what had been the Persian Empire.

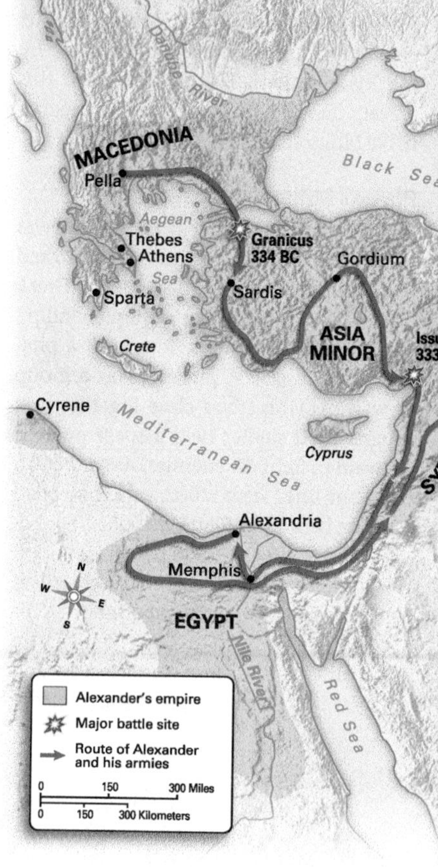

Marching Home

Still intent on building his empire, Alexander led his army through Central Asia. In 327 BC Alexander crossed the Indus River and wanted to push deeper into India. But his exhausted soldiers refused to go any farther. Disappointed, Alexander began the long march home.

Alexander left India in 325 BC, but he never made it back to Greece. In 323 BC, on his way back, Alexander visited the city of Babylon and got sick. He died a few days later at age 33. After he died, Alexander's body was taken to Egypt and buried in a golden coffin.

Cross-Discipline Activity: English–Language Arts

Above Level

Creating a Philippic

Prep Required | Research Required

1. Discuss with students the Greek belief in using language effectively and persuasively.
2. Have students use the Internet or the library to find information about the orator Demosthenes and his *philippics* (bitter verbal attacks on or denunciations of someone).
3. Read portions of Demosthenes' speeches against Philip. Discuss with students the way Demosthenes used words against Philip in his speeches.
4. Organize the class into small groups. Have each group prepare a philippic against Alexander from the viewpoint of a soldier in the army, a Greek citizen, or a citizen of another country. Ask for volunteers to share their philippics. **LS Verbal/Linguistic**

Alternative Assessment Handbook, Rubrics 1: Acquiring Information; and 14: Group Activity

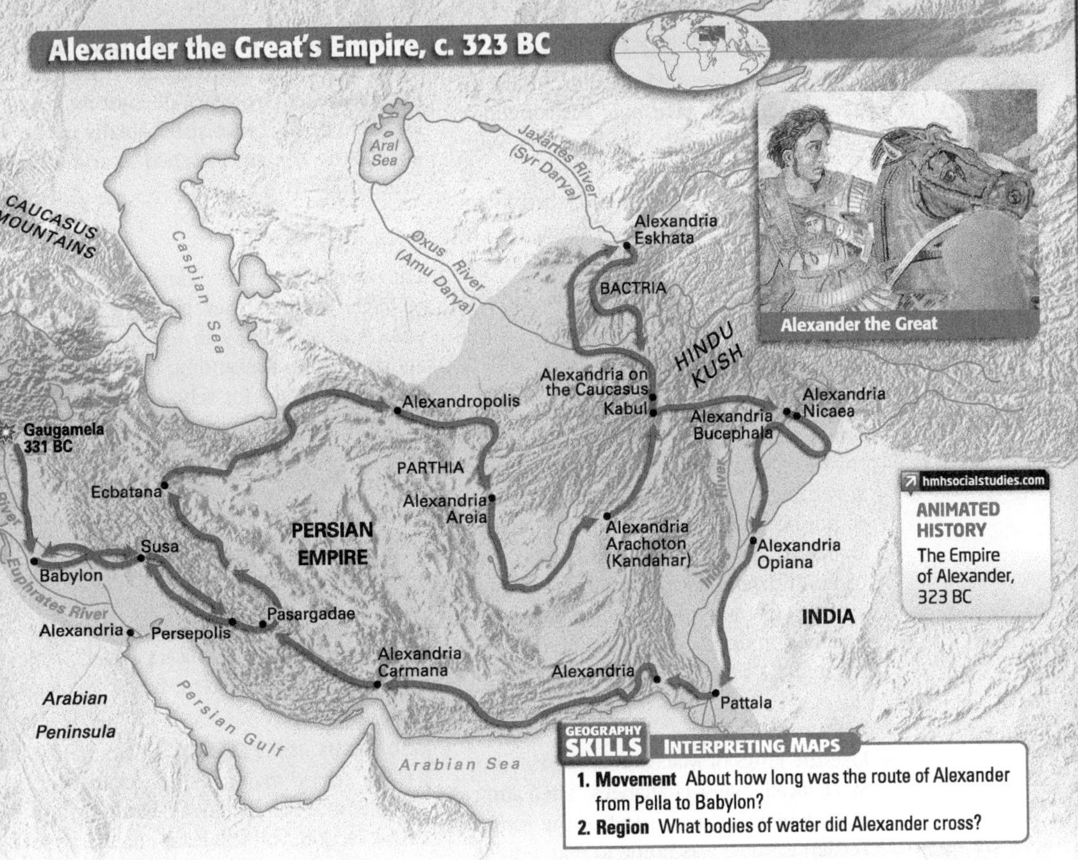

GEOGRAPHY SKILLS INTERPRETING MAPS

1. **Movement** About how long was the route of Alexander from Pella to Babylon?
2. **Region** What bodies of water did Alexander cross?

Spreading Greek Culture

Alexander's empire was the largest the world had ever seen. An admirer of Greek culture, he worked to spread Greek influence throughout his empire by founding cities in the lands he conquered.

Alexander modeled his new cities after the cities of Greece. He named many of them Alexandria, after himself. He built temples and theaters like those in Greece. He then encouraged Greek settlers to move to the new cities. These settlers spoke Greek, which became common throughout the empire. In time, Greek art, literature, and science spread into surrounding lands.

Even as he supported the spread of Greek culture, however, Alexander encouraged conquered people to keep their own customs and traditions. As a result, a new blended culture developed in Alexander's empire. It combined elements of Persian, Egyptian, Syrian, and other cultures with Greek ideas. Because this new culture was not completely Greek, or Hellenic, historians call it **Hellenistic**, or Greek-like. It wasn't purely Greek, but it was heavily influenced by Greek ideas.

READING CHECK **Sequencing** What steps did Alexander take to create his empire?

Direct Teach

Main Idea

2 Alexander Builds an Empire

Alexander the Great built an empire that united much of Europe, Asia, and Egypt.

Explain How did Alexander help spread Greek culture throughout his empire? *built new cities modeled on Greek cities, built theaters and temples like those in Greece, and encouraged Greek settlers to move to these new cities*

Analyze Why did Alexander model new cities after the cities of Greece? *possible answer—Alexander admired Greek culture; wanted the cities to resemble Greek cities.*

Map Transparency: Alexander the Great's Empire, c. 323 BC

CRF: History and Geography, Alexander's Empire

Linking to Today

The Library of Alexandria In 2004, archaeologists announced they had found the site of the Library of Alexandria. The city of Alexandria, founded by Alexander to be the capital of his empire, became a major seat of learning in ancient times. The library, which ancient historians say held as many as 400,000 scrolls, was destroyed in a fire around 20 BC.

Critical Thinking: Sequencing

At Level

Alexander the Great Time Line

Materials: butcher paper, markers, art supplies

1. Organize the class into four or five groups.
2. Have each group make an illustrated time line showing the major events in Alexander's life, including his birth and death. Dates for each event should be clearly shown.
3. Have groups decorate and illustrate their time lines. When necessary, groups should also write a brief explanation for an event.
4. Have each group share its time line with the class and describe its illustrations and text notes. LS **Visual/Spatial**
5. **Extend** Ask students to extend their time line to include Philip at one end and Alexander's empire after Alexander's death at the other end.

Alternative Assessment Handbook, Rubric 36: Time Lines

Answers

Interpreting Maps 1. *about 3,300 miles* **2.** *the Aegean Sea, Nile, Tigris, and Euphrates rivers*

Reading Check *Alexander destroyed Thebes, attacked the Persian Empire in Asia Minor, went to Egypt and was crowned pharaoh, and defeated the Persian army for the final time. As he traveled, he built new cities modeled after Greek cities and encouraged Greek settlers to move.*

Direct Teach

Main Idea

3 Hellenistic Kingdoms

The Hellenistic kingdoms formed from Alexander's empire blended Greek and other cultures.

Describe What happened to Alexander's empire after his death? *Three generals divided the empire among themselves. Within 300 years, all of Alexander's empire had been conquered by Rome.*

Evaluate Do you think Alexander was successful as a conqueror? Should he be called "Great"? *possible answer—Alexander was a good conqueror. He built a big empire, and he spread Greek culture everywhere he went. His empire broke up soon after his death, so I'm not sure he was "Great."*

Review & Assess

Close

Ask students to discuss whether blended cultures, such as the Hellenistic cultures, are weaker or stronger than cultures with one source.

Review

Online Quiz, Section 3

Assess

SE Section 3 Assessment

PASS: Section 3 Quiz

Alternative Assessment Handbook

Reteach/Classroom Intervention

Guided Reading Workbook, Section 3

Interactive Skills Tutor CD-ROM

Answers

Reading Check *When Alexander died without an obvious heir, his generals divided the empire.*

Hellenistic Kingdoms

When Alexander died, he didn't have an obvious heir to take over his kingdom, and no one knew who was in power. With no clear direction, Alexander's generals fought for power. In the end, three powerful generals divided the empire among themselves. One became king of Macedonia and Greece, one ruled Syria, and the third claimed Egypt.

Hellenistic Macedonia

As you might expect, the kingdom of Macedonia and Greece was the most Greek of the three. However, it also had the weakest government. The Macedonian kings had to put down many revolts by the Greeks. Damaged by the revolts, Macedonia couldn't defend itself. Armies from Rome, a rising power from the Italian Peninsula, marched in and conquered Macedonia in the mid-100s BC.

Hellenistic Syria

Like the kings of Macedonia, the rulers of Syria faced many challenges. Their kingdom, which included most of the former Persian Empire, was home to many different peoples with many different customs.

Unhappy with Hellenistic rule, many of these people rebelled against their leaders. Weakened by years of fighting, the kingdom slowly broke apart. Finally in the 60s BC the Romans marched in and took over Syria.

Hellenistic Egypt

The rulers of Egypt encouraged the growth of Greek culture. They built the ancient world's largest library in the city of Alexandria. Also in Alexandria, they built the Museum, a place for scholars and artists to meet. Through their efforts, Alexandria became a great center of culture and learning. In the end, the Egyptian kingdom lasted longer than the other Hellenistic kingdoms. However, in 30 BC it too was conquered by Rome.

READING CHECK **Analyzing** Why were three kingdoms created from Alexander's empire?

SUMMARY AND PREVIEW Alexander the Great caused major political changes in Greece and the Hellenistic world. In the next section, you will learn about artistic and scientific advances that affected the lives of people in the same areas.

Section 3 Assessment

hmhsocialstudies.com ONLINE QUIZ

Reviewing Ideas, Terms, and People

1. **Identify** What king conquered Greece in the 300s BC?
2. a. **Describe** What territories did **Alexander the Great** conquer?
   b. **Interpret** Why did Alexander destroy Thebes?
   c. **Elaborate** Why do you think Alexander named so many cities after himself?
3. a. **Recall** What three kingdoms were created out of Alexander's empire after his death?
   b. **Explain** Why were these kingdoms called **Hellenistic**?

Critical Thinking

4. **Generalizing** Review your notes on Alexander. Then, write one sentence explaining why he is an important historical figure.

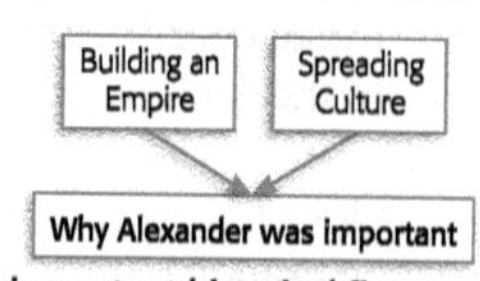

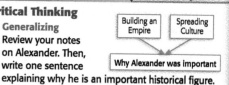

FOCUS ON WRITING

5. **Evaluating Alexander** Add Alexander the Great to the table you created earlier. Remember that although Alexander was a military man, not all of his accomplishments were in battle.

Section 3 Assessment Answers

1. Philip II of Macedonia
2. a. Asia Minor, Egypt, and the Persian Empire
   b. because they rebelled; to make them an example for other Greeks so they would not turn against him
   c. to demonstrate his control and power
3. a. Macedonia, Syria, and Egypt
   b. because they were Greek-like
4. successful military leader (conquered Greece and Egypt); conquered the Persian Empire; built new cities; spread Greek culture, and built temples and theatres
5. Alexander—conquered the Persian Empire; spread Greek culture; built cities, temples, theatres

Greek Achievements

If YOU were there...

Everyone in Athens has been talking about a philosopher and teacher named Socrates, so you decide to go and see him for yourself. You find him sitting under a tree, surrounded by his students. "Teach me about life," you say. But instead of answering, he asks you, "What is life?" You struggle to reply. He asks another question, and another. If he's such a great teacher, you wonder, shouldn't he have all the answers? Instead, all he seems to have are questions.

What do you think of Socrates?

BUILDING BACKGROUND Socrates was only one of the brilliant philosophers who lived in Athens in the 400s BC. The city was also home to some of the world's greatest artists and writers. In fact, all over Greece men and women made great advances in the arts and sciences. Their work inspired people for centuries.

The Arts

Among the most notable achievements of the ancient Greeks were those they made in the arts. These arts included sculpture, painting, architecture, and writings.

Statues and Paintings

The ancient Greeks were master artists. Their paintings and statues have been admired for hundreds of years. Examples of these works are still displayed in museums around the world.

Greek sculpture is admired for its realism, natural look, and details.

SECTION 4

What You Will Learn...

Main Ideas

1. The Greeks made great contributions to the arts.
2. The teachings of Socrates, Plato, and Aristotle are the basis of modern philosophy.
3. In science, the Greeks made key discoveries in math, medicine, and engineering.

The Big Idea

Ancient Greeks made lasting contributions in the arts, philosophy, and science.

Key Terms and People

Socrates, *p. 281*
Plato, *p. 281*
Aristotle, *p. 281*
reason, *p. 281*
Euclid, *p. 282*
Hippocrates, *p. 282*

Use the graphic organizer online to take notes on Greek achievements in the arts, philosophy, and science.

Teach the Big Idea

At Level

Greek Achievements

1. **Teach** Ask students the questions in the Main Idea boxes to teach this section.
2. **Apply** Organize the class into eight groups. Assign each group one of the following: *Greek statues and painting, Greek architecture, Greek drama, Greek history, Greek philosophy, Greek mathematics, Greek engineering,* and *Greek medicine.* Have each group prepare a presentation on its topic that shows how contributions by the ancient Greeks still affect our ideas and practices.
3. Have each group make its presentation. **LS Verbal/Linguistic**
4. **Review** Discuss with the class how the contributions made by the ancient Greeks have shaped life today.
5. **Practice/Homework** Have students write a paragraph describing Greek contributions to our world and why they are important. **LS Verbal/Linguistic**

Alternative Assessment Handbook, Rubrics 11: Discussions; and 29: Presentations

Preteach

Bellringer

If YOU were there . . . Use the **Daily Bellringer Transparency** to help students answer the question.

Daily Bellringer Transparency, Section 4

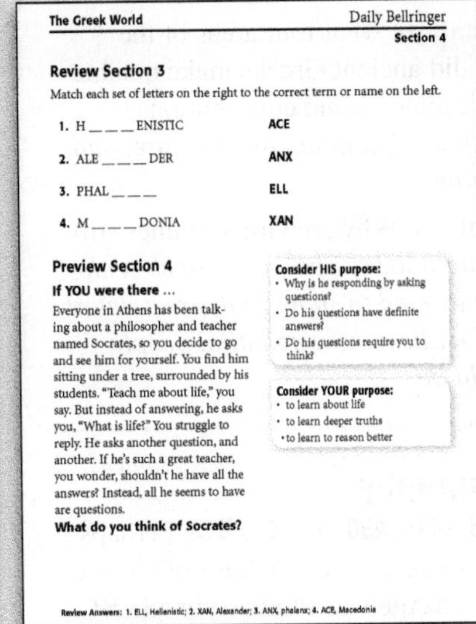

The Greek World — Daily Bellringer — Section 4

Review Section 3

Match each set of letters on the right to the correct term or name on the left.

1. H _ _ _ ENISTIC	**ACE**
2. ALE _ _ _ DER	**ANX**
3. PHAL _ _ _	**ELL**
4. M _ _ _ DONIA	**XAN**

Preview Section 4

If YOU were there ...

Everyone in Athens has been talking about a philosopher and teacher named Socrates, so you decide to go and see him for yourself. You find him sitting under a tree, surrounded by his students. "Teach me about life," you say. But instead of answering, he asks you, "What is life?" You struggle to reply. He asks another question, and another. If he's such a great teacher, you wonder, shouldn't he have all the answers? Instead, all he seems to have are questions.

What do you think of Socrates?

Consider HIS purpose:
- Why is he responding by asking questions?
- Do his questions have definite answers?
- Do his questions require you to think?

Consider YOUR purpose:
- to learn about life
- to learn deeper truths
- to learn to reason better

Review Answers: 1. ELL, Hellenistic; 2. XAN, Alexander; 3. ANX, phalanx; 4. ACE, Macedonia

Vocabulary Builder

Preteach or review the following term:

philosopher a person who studies the meaning of life, problems of right and wrong, how we know things, and other related areas (p. 280)

CRF: Vocabulary Builder, Section 4

Taking Notes

Have students use the graphic organizer online to take notes on the section. This activity will prepare students for the Section Assessment, in which they will complete a graphic organizer that builds on the information using the Critical Thinking Skill: Summarizing.

Direct Teach

Main Idea

1 The Arts

The Greeks made great contributions to the arts.

Recall In what four areas of the arts did ancient Greeks make notable achievements and contributions? *sculpture, painting, architecture, and writing*

Explain Why are Greek statues still admired today? *because Greek sculptors wanted to show, with great detail and realism, how beautiful people could be*

Biography

Phidias (c. 490 to c. 430 BC) Perhaps the greatest Greek sculptor of Greece's Golden Age was Phidias. In 433 BC, Phidias created the gold and ivory statue of Zeus for the temple of Zeus at Olympia. This huge statue stood about 40 feet (12 m) tall. The statue of Zeus was considered one of the Seven Wonders of the World. Phidias also created a similar gold and ivory statue of the goddess Athena for the Parthenon in Athens.

hmhsocialstudies.com
Online Resources
Activity: Art of Greece's Golden Age

Greek statues are so admired because the sculptors who made them tried to make them look perfect. They wanted their statues to show how beautiful people could be. To improve their art, these sculptors carefully studied the human body, especially how it looked when it was moving. Then, using what they had learned, they carved stone and marble statues. As a result, many Greek statues look as though they could come to life at any moment.

Greek painting is also admired for its realism and detail. For example, Greek artists painted detailed scenes on vases, pots, and other vessels. These vessels often show scenes from myths or athletic competitions. Many of the scenes were created using only two colors, black and red. Sometimes artists used black glaze to paint scenes on red vases. Other artists covered whole vases with glaze and then scraped parts away to let the red background show through.

Greek Architecture

If you went to Greece today, you would see the ruins of many ancient buildings. Old columns still hold up parts of broken roofs, and ancient carvings decorate fallen walls. These remains give us an idea of the beauty of ancient Greek buildings.

History Close-up

The Parthenon

The Parthenon was a beautiful temple to the goddess Athena, whom the people of Athens considered their protector. The temple, which stood on the Athenian acropolis, was built by Pericles and is still one of the most famous buildings in the world.

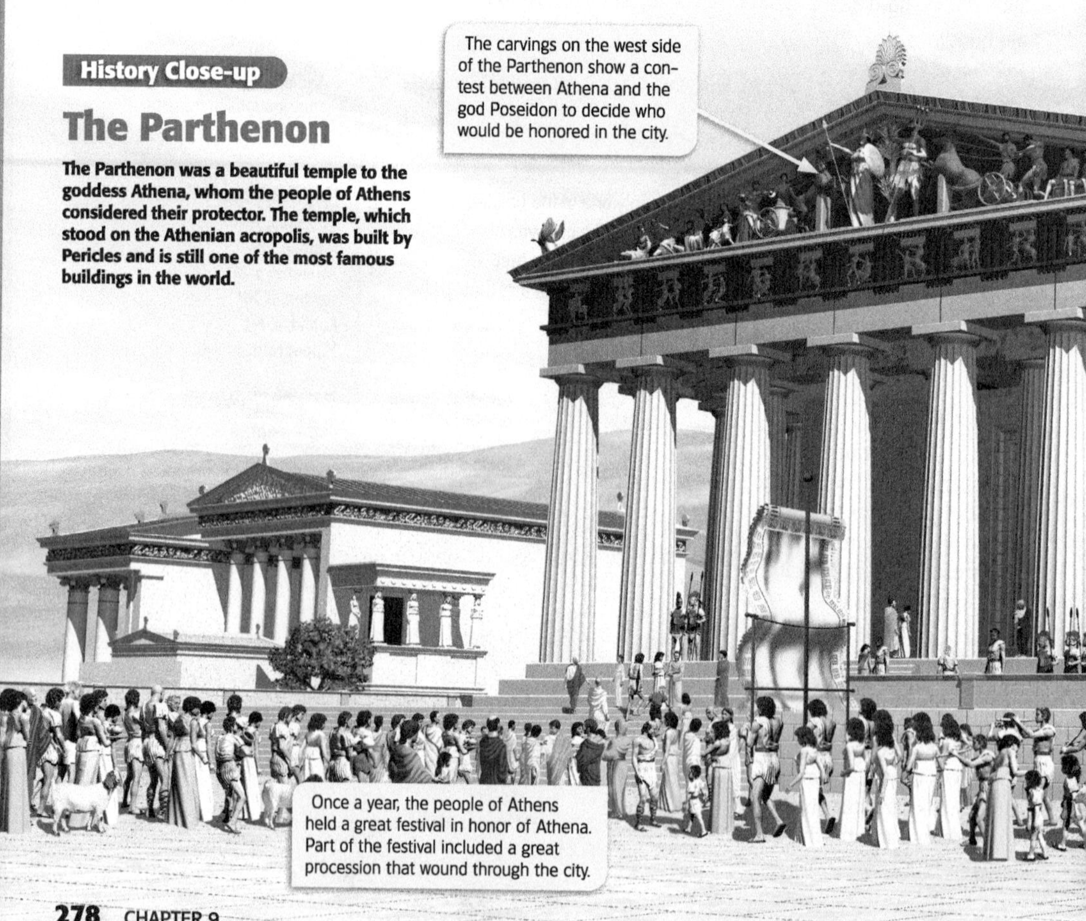

The carvings on the west side of the Parthenon show a contest between Athena and the god Poseidon to decide who would be honored in the city.

Once a year, the people of Athens held a great festival in honor of Athena. Part of the festival included a great procession that wound through the city.

Differentiating Instruction

Advanced/Gifted and Talented

Above Level | Research Required

1. Organize students into groups of three or four.
2. Assign each group one of the following architectural styles to research: Doric, Ionic, or Corinthian.
3. Have each group research its architectural style. Each group should prepare an illustrated report giving the history and design principles of the style. Reports should be two to three pages long. LS **Verbal/Linguistic**
4. Discuss with the class the similarities and differences of the architectural styles. Ask students which style they prefer and why.
5. Have each group make a model of a column or building that demonstrates the principles of its architectural style. LS **Kinesthetic**

Alternative Assessment Handbook, Rubrics 1: Acquiring Information; and 3: Artwork

The Greeks took great care in designing their buildings, especially their temples. Rows of tall columns surrounded the temples, making the temples look stately and inspiring. Greek designers were very careful when they measured these columns. They knew that columns standing in a long row often looked as though they curved in the middle. To prevent this optical illusion, they made their columns bulge slightly in the middle. As a result, Greek columns look perfectly straight.

Ancient Greek designers took such care because they wanted their buildings to reflect the greatness of their cities. The most impressive of all ancient Greek buildings was the Parthenon (PAHR-thuh-nahn) in Athens, pictured below. This temple to Athena was built in the 400s BC on the Athenian acropolis. It was designed to be magnificent not only outside, but inside as well. As you can see, the interior was decorated with carvings and columns.

New Forms of Writing

Sculpture, painting, and architecture were not the only Greek art forms. The Greeks also excelled at writing. In fact, Greek writers created many new writing forms, including drama and history.

Inside the Parthenon was a magnificent statue of Athena by the sculptor Phidias, whom many people considered the greatest sculptor in all of Greece.
The Parthenon's 46 columns are a type called Doric columns. These simple columns have no decoration at the top.
ANALYSIS SKILL ANALYZING VISUALS
Why do you think people are bringing animals and goods with them to the temple?

Direct Teach

Main Idea

1 The Arts

The Greeks made great contributions to the arts.

Recall Why did the people of Athens build the Parthenon? *to honor the goddess Athena, whom the people of Athens considered their protector*

Analyze In your opinion, why is the Parthenon considered the most impressive of all ancient Greek buildings? *possible answer—The Parthenon sits on a hilltop above Athens; it was a very large building magnificently decorated inside and out, with a huge statue of Athena inside.*

Biography

Pericles (495–429 BC) During its Golden Age, Athens was ruled by Pericles, the best orator in a city of great orators. Pericles built the Parthenon, other temples around Athens, the Propylaea (the large gateway or arch at the entrance to the Acropolis), and the long walls to the port city of Piraeus (connecting Athens to its port). While Pericles was building the Parthenon, Socrates and Plato were teaching, and Aeschylus, Sophocles, and Euripides were writing plays.

Cross-Discipline Activity: Drama

Above Level

Research Required

Plays: A New Form of Writing

1. Have students use the Internet or library to conduct research on the use of masks in ancient Greek drama. As students do their research, ask them to create a time line of the development of ancient Greek drama from about 625 BC to about 300 BC.
2. Ask students to make a poster showing one or more Greek masks or to make a model of a Greek mask to show to the class. Students should explain what their masks represented, why the masks were important in the play, and whether masks are used the same way in drama today.
   LS Verbal/Linguistic, Visual/Spatial
3. **Extend** Have students conduct research on the use of a chorus and the addition of a second and third actor in Greek plays. Students should compare and contrast the results of their research with modern plays.
   LS Verbal/Linguistic

Alternative Assessment Handbook, Rubrics 3: Artwork; 30: Research; and 36: Time Lines

Answers

Analyzing Visuals *Students may answer to trade or for sacrifices to the gods.*

Direct Teach

Main Idea

1 The Arts

The Greeks made great contributions to the arts.

Identify What were two of the many new forms of writing created by the Greeks? *drama and history*

Analyze How has Thucydides shaped the modern study of history? *His impartial history of the Peloponnesian War influenced later historians to cover history impartially as well.*

- **CRF:** Biography, Thucydides
- **CRF:** Literature, *Oedipus the King*, by Sophocles
- **CRF:** Primary Source, Greek Lyric Poetry

Biography

Herodotus (c. 484–c. 432 BC) The ancient Greek researcher and storyteller Herodotus is often considered the first historian. His work *The Histories* is not strictly a history text, though. Herodotus wrote about people, places, legends, battles, and heroes—whatever interested him.

Answers

Analyzing Primary Sources *"Be quiet then, and have patience."*

Reading Check *The Greeks created sculptures, paintings, and buildings, and wrote drama and history.*

The Greeks created drama, or plays, as part of their religious ceremonies. Actors and singers performed scenes in honor of the gods and heroes. These plays became a popular form of entertainment, especially in Athens.

ACADEMIC VOCABULARY
neutral unbiased, not favoring either side in a conflict

In the 400s BC Athenian writers created many of the greatest plays of the ancient world. Some writers produced tragedies, which described the hardships faced by Greek heroes. Among the best tragedy writers were Aeschylus (ES-kuh-luhs) and Sophocles (SAHF-uh-kleez). For example, Sophocles wrote about a Greek hero who mistakenly killed his own father. Other Greek dramatists focused on comedies, which made fun of people and ideas. One famous comedy writer was Aristophanes (ar-uh-STAHF-uh-neez). He used his comedy to make serious points about war, courts of law, and famous people.

The Greeks were also among the first people to write about history. They were interested in the lessons history could teach. One of the greatest of the Greek historians was Thucydides (thoo-SID-uh-deez). His history of the Peloponnesian War was based in part on his experiences as an Athenian soldier. Even though he was from Athens, Thucydides tried to be **neutral** in his writing. He studied the war and tried to figure out what had caused it. He may have hoped the Greeks could learn from their mistakes and avoid similar wars in the future. Many later historians modeled their works after his.

READING CHECK **Summarizing** What were some forms of art found in ancient Greece?

Philosophy

The ancient Greeks worshipped gods and goddesses whose actions explained many of the mysteries of the world. But by around 500 BC a few people had begun to think about other explanations. We call these people philosophers. They believed in the power of the human mind to think, explain, and understand life.

Primary Source

BOOK

The Death of Socrates

In 399 BC Socrates was arrested and charged with corrupting the young people of Athens and ignoring religious traditions. He was sentenced to die by drinking poison. Socrates spent his last hours surrounded by his students. One of them, Plato, later described the event in detail.

Socrates himself does not protest against his sentence but willingly drinks the poison.

The students and friends who have visited Socrates, including the narrator, are much less calm than he is.

"Then raising the cup to his lips, quite readily and cheerfully he drank off the poison. And hitherto most of us had been able to control our sorrow; but now when we saw him drinking . . . my own tears were flowing fast; so that I covered my face and wept . . . Socrates alone retained his calmness: What is this strange outcry? he said . . . I have been told that a man should die in peace. Be quiet then, and have patience."

–Plato, from *Phaedo*

ANALYSIS SKILL ANALYZING PRIMARY SOURCES

How does Socrates tell his students to act when they see him drink the poison?

Critical Thinking: Analyzing Information

Above Level

The Socratic Method

1. Ask students, "What is courage?" or "What is beauty?" (You could also ask what is truth, or honor.) Have students brainstorm answers to your question.
2. Engage the class in a Socratic dialogue. Give the students questions, not answers. Follow answers with more questions. Choose questions that move the discussion along. The table lists some kinds of Socratic questions. Copy the questions for students to see.
3. At the end of the exercise, have students write a brief, one-paragraph response to the original question. Students should indicate if their response is different after the discussion and the reason(s) why they have changed their point of view. **LS Verbal/Linguistic**

Alternative Assessment Handbook, Rubric 11: Discussions

Type of Question	Examples
Clarification	What do you mean by . . .? Could you give me an example?
Probe Assumptions	What are you assuming? Is that always the case? Why do you think the assumption holds here?
Probe Reasons and Evidence	Why do you say that? What other information do we need? Is there good evidence for believing that? Is there reason to doubt that evidence?
Viewpoints or Perspectives	How would other groups/types of people respond? Why? Can anyone see this another way? What would someone who disagrees say? How are his and her ideas alike/different?

Socrates

Among the greatest of these thinkers was a man named **Socrates** (SAHK-ruh-teez). He believed that people must never stop looking for knowledge.

Socrates was a teacher as well as a thinker. Today we call his type of teaching the Socratic method. Socrates taught by asking questions. His questions were about human qualities such as love and courage. He would ask, "What is courage?" When people answered, he challenged their answers with more questions.

Socrates wanted to make people think and question their own beliefs. But he made people angry, even frightened. They accused him of questioning the authority of the gods. For these reasons, he was arrested and condemned to death. His friends and students watched him calmly accept his death. He took the poison he was given, drank it, and died.

BIOGRAPHY

Euclid

c. 300 BC

Euclid is considered one of the world's greatest mathematicians. He lived and taught in Alexandria, Egypt, a great center of learning. Euclid wrote about the relationship between mathematics and other fields, including astronomy and music. But it is for geometry that he is best known. In fact, his works were so influential that the branch of geometry we study in school—the study of flat shapes and lines—is called Euclidean geometry.

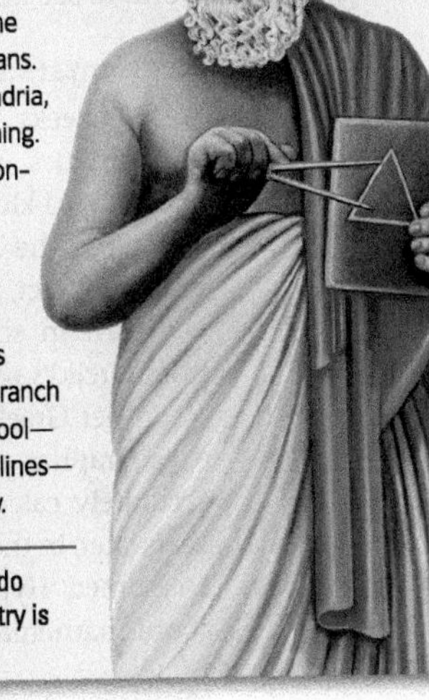

Drawing Conclusions Why do you think a branch of geometry is named after Euclid?

Plato

Plato (PLAYT-oh) was a student of Socrates. Like Socrates, he was a teacher as well as a philosopher. Plato created a school, the Academy, to which students, philosophers, and scientists could come to discuss ideas.

Although Plato spent much of his time running the Academy, he also wrote many works. The most famous of these works was called *The Republic*. It describes Plato's idea of an ideal society. This society would be based on justice and fairness to everyone. To ensure this fairness, Plato argued, society should be run by philosophers. He thought that only they could understand what was best for everyone.

Aristotle

Perhaps the greatest Greek thinker was **Aristotle** (ar-uh-STAH-tuhl), Plato's student. He taught that people should live lives of moderation, or balance. For example, people should not be greedy, but neither should they give away everything they own. Instead, people should find a balance between these two extremes.

Aristotle believed that moderation was based on **reason**, or clear and ordered thinking. He thought that people should use reason to govern their lives. In other words, people should think about their actions and how they will affect others.

Aristotle also made great advances in the field of logic, the process of making inferences. He argued that you could use facts you knew to figure out new facts. For example, if you know that Socrates lives in Athens and that Athens is in Greece, you can conclude that Socrates lives in Greece. Aristotle's ideas about logic helped inspire many later Greek scientists.

READING CHECK **Generalizing** What did ancient Greek philosophers like Socrates, Plato, and Aristotle want to find out?

Direct Teach

Main Idea

2 Philosophy

The teachings of Socrates, Plato, and Aristotle are the basis of modern philosophy.

Identify Who were Socrates, Plato, and Aristotle? *the three philosophers from ancient Greece who used reason to examine the mysteries of the world and to study and explain life*

Recall Why did people become angry with Socrates? *He wanted people to examine and question their beliefs about human qualities such as love and courage, and some people thought that this questioned the authority of the gods.*

Evaluate In your opinion, do you think that Aristotle's idea that people should live lives of moderation is a good way to live? Why or why not? *possible answer—It is a good idea. I think that if everyone lived that way and thought about how their actions would affect other people, there might be less crime and there might be more peace in the world.*

CRF: Biography, Hipparchia; Hypatia

Biography

Euclid Euclid is usually remembered for his contributions to geometry, but he also wrote about a wide variety of mathematical ideas—lowest common denominators, prime numbers, integers, proportions, and others. His major work was titled *The Elements*.

About the Illustration

This illustration of Euclid is an artist's conception based on available sources. However, historians are uncertain exactly what Euclid looked like.

Critical Thinking: Finding Main Ideas

At Level

Greek Philosophers

1. Have students work in pairs to review the information on this page about Socrates, Plato, and Aristotle.
2. Ask each pair to write a short paragraph expressing the main idea of each man's philosophy. Then have students compare and contrast the main ideas of the three philosophers. **LS Verbal/Linguistic**
3. Discuss with students what they have written. Ask them if they have an opinion about any of these philosophers. Have a class discussion about the different opinions.
4. **Extend** Ask students what issues, such as justice or fairness, they would explore using the Socratic method.

Alternative Assessment Handbook, Rubrics 9: Comparing and Contrasting; and 11: Discussions

Answers

Biography *because he was a great mathematician who influenced the development of geometry*

Reading Check *how the human mind works, how individuals live and make decisions about behavior*

Direct Teach

Main Idea

3 Science

In science, Greeks made key discoveries in math, medicine, and engineering.

Explain What did Hippocrates contribute to medicine? *studied diseases to try to figure out how to cure them; gave rules for doctors' behavior.*

Recall Who invented the water screw? *Archimedes*

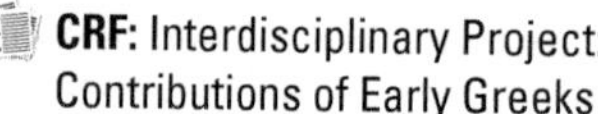

CRF: Interdisciplinary Project: Contributions of Early Greeks

Review & Assess

Close

Ask students to discuss Aristotle's ideas about reason and moderation.

Review

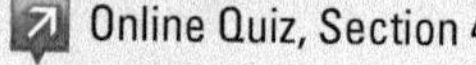

Online Quiz, Section 4

Assess

SE Section 4 Assessment

PASS: Section 4 Quiz

Alternative Assessment Handbook

Reteach/Classroom Intervention

Guided Reading Workbook, Section 4

Interactive Skills Tutor CD-ROM

Science

Aristotle's works inspired many Greek scientists. They began to look closely at the world to see how it worked.

THE IMPACT TODAY

Many doctors recite the Hippocratic Oath, a pledge to behave ethically, when they finish medical school.

Mathematics

Some Greeks spent their lives studying mathematics. One of these people was **Euclid** (YOO-kluhd). He was interested in geometry, the study of lines, angles, and shapes. In fact, many of the geometry rules we learn in school today come straight from Euclid's writings.

Other Greek mathematicians included a geographer who used mathematics to accurately calculate the size of the earth. Years later, in the AD 300s and 400s, a woman named Hypatia (hy-PAY-shuh) taught about mathematics and astronomy.

Medicine and Engineering

Not all Greek scientists studied numbers. Some studied other areas of science, such as medicine and engineering.

Greek doctors studied the human body to understand how it worked. In trying to cure diseases and keep people healthy, Greek doctors made many discoveries.

The greatest Greek doctor was **Hippocrates** (hip-AHK-ruh-teez). He wanted to figure out what caused diseases so he could better treat them. Hippocrates is better known today, though, for his ideas about how doctors should behave.

Greek engineers also made great discoveries. Some devices they invented are still used today. For example, farmers in many countries still use water screws to bring water to their fields. This device, which brings water from a lower level to a higher one, was invented by a Greek scientist named Archimedes (ahr-kuh-MEED-eez) in the 200s BC. Greek inventors could be playful as well as serious. For example, one inventor created mechanical toys like birds, puppets, and coin-operated machines.

READING CHECK **Summarizing** What advances did Greek scientists make in medicine?

SUMMARY AND PREVIEW Through their art, philosophy, and science, the Greeks have greatly influenced Western civilization. In the next chapter, you will learn about another group that has helped shape the Western world—the Romans.

Section 4 Assessment

hmhsocialstudies.com ONLINE QUIZ

Reviewing Ideas, Terms, and People

1. a. **Identify** What two types of drama did the Greeks invent?
   b. **Explain** Why did Greek columns bulge in the middle?
   c. **Elaborate** How did studying the human body help Greek artists make their statues look real?
2. **Describe** How did **Socrates** teach? What is this method of teaching called?
3. a. **Identify** In what fields did **Hippocrates** and **Euclid** make their greatest achievements?
   b. **Make Inferences** Why do some people call Greece the birthplace of the Western world?

Critical Thinking

4. **Summarizing** Add a box to the bottom of your note-taking chart. Use it to summarize Greek contributions in the arts, philosophy, and science.

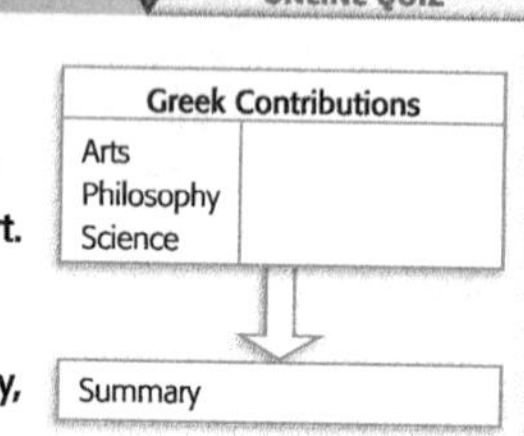

Focus on Writing

5. **Taking Notes about Artists and Thinkers** Add the artists and thinkers from this section to your chart. Because these people were not military leaders, all of your notes will go in the third column of your chart.

Section 4 Assessment Answers

1. a. comedies and tragedies
   b. to counter an optical illusion that made straight columns look curved
   c. Sculptors were able to capture movement and create a realistic body carefully, especially while it was moving.
2. by asking questions; the Socratic method
3. a. Hippocrates—medicine; Euclid—mathematics
   b. Many of the philosophies, dramas, and scientific ideas upon which our society is based come from ancient Greece.
4. possible answers: Thucydides—wrote history; Socrates—created Socratic method, challenged existing ideas; Plato—founded Academy, proposed a model for a perfect society; Aristotle—taught people to live in moderation, stressed importance of reason; Euclid—created rules of geometry; Hypatia—wrote about mathematics and astronomy
5. See the answer to item 4.

Answers

Reading Check *studied human body to see how it worked; causes and treatments of diseases*

BIOGRAPHY

Greek Philosophers—Socrates, Plato, and Aristotle

What would the world be like if no one believed in the importance of knowledge and truth?

When did they live? the 400s and 300s BC

Where did they live? Athens

What did they do? They thought. Socrates, Plato, and Aristotle thought about the world and searched for knowledge, wisdom, and truth. Between them they created the Socratic method of learning, the first political science book, and a method of scientific reasoning.

Why are they important? In most of the ancient world, strong fighters won all the glory. But in Athens, great thinkers and wise men were honored. People listened to them and followed their advice. Even today, people admire the ideas of Socrates, Plato, and Aristotle. Their teachings are at the root of modern philosophy and science.

Making Inferences Do you think these philosophers would have been as influential if they had lived in a different city? Why or why not?

KEY FACTS

How did Socrates, Plato, and Aristotle influence history?

- **Socrates** taught Plato.
- **Plato** taught Aristotle.
- **Aristotle** taught Alexander the Great, who helped spread Greek ideas through much of the world.

This drawing shows how one artist imagined Plato (left), Aristotle (center), and Socrates (right) to look.

HISTORY

VIDEO
The Death of a Philosopher

hmhsocialstudies.com

283

Critical Thinking: Analyzing Information

At Level

Analyzing the Ideas of the Philosophers

1. Organize the class into three groups and have each group conduct research on—and represent—the ideas of either Socrates, Plato, or Aristotle.
2. Have students in each group decide how they will present their findings. For example, a group may decide to elect one person to speak for the philosopher, or a group may decide that all members will represent the philosopher.
3. Ask each group about its assigned philosopher's views on topics such as government, truth, education, or how the world works. Ask each group if its philosopher held a special view about any topic. LS **Verbal/Linguistic**
4. **Extend** Have students discuss the similarities and differences between each of the philosophers. Have each group create a Venn diagram that compares and contrasts their beliefs. LS **Verbal/Linguistic**

Alternative Assessment Handbook, Rubrics 4: Biographies; and 24: Oral Presentations

Biography

Reading Focus Question

Write the expressions *Ignorance is bliss and Knowledge is power* for students to see. Have students discuss each expression and consider how the Greek philosophers would have felt about them.

Info to Know

Socrates (469–399 BC) Socrates never wrote any philosophical works. Instead, Socrates explored his ideas by holding conversations with almost anyone. Through these conversations, or dialogues, Socrates sought to answer questions such as "What is justice?" and "What is knowledge?" Socrates asked similar questions about piety, truth, courage, art, and love.

Plato (427–347 BC) Plato was a student of Socrates. After Socrates' death, Plato left Athens and traveled to Egypt, Italy, and Sicily. Eventually, Plato returned to Athens and founded his Academy, where he taught philosophy. Many of Plato's writings are in the form of dialogues, a style he learned from Socrates. Plato's best-known work is *The Republic*, a dialogue on the nature of justice. It is often considered the first book about political science.

Aristotle (384–322 BC) At the age of 18, Aristotle went to Athens to study at Plato's Academy. In 343 BC, Aristotle was asked to be the tutor of a young man named Alexander—who later came to be known as Alexander the Great. Aristotle wrote about a wide variety of topics, including logic, politics and ethics, meteorology, learning, anthropology, poetry, and theology.

About the Illustration *This illustration of Socrates, Plato, and Aristotle is an artist's conception based on available sources. However, historians are uncertain exactly what the philosophers looked like.*

Answers

Making Inferences *No, because Athens placed a higher value on knowledge, truth, and trying to understand life than other city-states did. Athens honored philosophers more than other places did.*

Social Studies Skills

Interpreting Charts and Tables

Activity Guided Practice with Charts Photocopy a number of charts from this book as well as other books. If the charts include captions, cover them up. Then display each of the charts in turn for students to see. Have students identify the type of each chart and its purpose. Then select one of the charts and have each student write a caption for the chart. **LS Visual/Spatial**

Alternative Assessment Handbook, Rubric 7: Charts

Interactive Skills Tutor CD-ROM, Lesson 6: Interpret Maps, Graphs, Charts, Visuals, and Political Cartoons

Answers

Practice and Apply the Skill

1. *organizational chart; to show the relationships among the different parts of Sparta's government;* **2.** *The Assembly elected the ephors;* **3.** *The Council of Elders served for life and proposed actions; Assembly members voted on the Council's proposals but could not propose actions of their own.* **4.** *kings*

Social Studies Skills

Analysis | Critical Thinking | Economics | **Study**

Interpreting Charts and Tables

Understand the Skill

Charts present information visually to make it easier to understand. Different kinds of charts have different purposes. *Organizational charts* can show relationships among the parts of something. *Flowcharts* show steps in a process or cause-and-effect relationships. *Classification charts* group information so it can be easily compared. *Tables* are a type of classification chart that organize information into rows and columns for easy comparison. The ability to interpret charts helps you to analyze information and understand relationships.

Learn the Skill

Use these basic steps to interpret a chart:

1. Identify the type of chart and read its title in order to understand its purpose and subject.
2. Note the parts of the chart. Read the headings of rows and columns to determine the categories and types of information. Note any other labels that accompany the information presented in the chart. Look for any lines that connect its parts. What do they tell you?
3. Study the chart's details. Look for relationships in the information it presents. If it is a classification chart, analyze and compare all content in the rows and columns. In flowcharts and organizational charts, read all labels and other information. Follow and analyze directional arrows or lines.

Sparta's Government, c. 450 BC

Ephors
- Five adult male citizens
- Elected to one-year terms
- Presided over Assembly and Council
- Ran Sparta's daily affairs

Kings
- Two hereditary rulers
- Commanded armies
- Served as high priests
- Served as judges in minor cases

Assembly
- All male citizens age 30 and above
- Passed or rejected proposals made by Council
- Could not propose actions on its own
- Elected ephors

Council of Elders
- 28 male citizens over age 60
- Elected for life by citizens
- Proposed actions to Assembly
- Served as judges in important cases

Practice and Apply the Skill

Apply the strategies given to interpret the chart above and answer the following questions.

1. What type of chart is this and what is its purpose?
2. In what ways were the ephors and the Assembly connected?
3. How did the roles of the Assembly and the Council of Elders differ?
4. What position in Spartan government had no direct relationship with the Assembly?

Social Studies Skills Activity: Interpreting Charts and Tables

Persia or Alexander the Great Charts

At Level

1. Assign students either the Persian Empire or Alexander the Great. Have each student create a chart of his or her own choosing to show information related to the assigned topic. For example, students might create a classification chart giving information about the key battles of the Persian Wars or a flow chart showing the events in the growth of Alexander the Great's empire.
2. Have volunteers display their charts. Have other students identify the type and purpose of each chart. **LS Visual/Spatial**
3. **Extend** Have students select a chart from the textbook that they find interesting. Instruct students to create a five-question quiz that must be answered by looking at the chart. Then have students exchange quizzes and charts, complete the quizzes they receive, and return the quizzes for grading. **LS Interpersonal, Visual/Spatial**

Alternative Assessment Handbook, Rubric 7: Charts

CHAPTER 9

Chapter Review

History's Impact

▶ **video series**

Review the video to answer the focus question:

How have ancient Greek theories influenced American civilization?

Visual Summary

Use the visual summary below to help you review the main ideas of the chapter.

Sparta and Athens fought together to defeat Persia in the Persian Wars.

Spartan culture centered on the military, while Athenian culture emphasized government and the arts.

Alexander the Great built a huge empire and spread Greek culture.

The ancient Greeks made lasting contributions to architecture, philosophy, science, and many other fields.

Reviewing Vocabulary, Terms, and People

Choose one word from each word pair to correctly complete each sentence below.

1. A ruler named _________ created the Persian Empire. **(Cyrus the Great/Xerxes I)**
2. A _________ was a group of soldiers that stood in a square to fight. **(cavalry/phalanx)**
3. _________ built the largest empire the world had ever seen. **(Alexander the Great/Aristotle)**
4. The _________ War(s) pitted two city-states against each other. **(Persian/Peloponnesian)**
5. The philosopher _________ taught people by asking them questions. **(Darius/Socrates)**
6. The greatest medical scholar of ancient Greece was _________. **(Philip II/Hippocrates)**
7. Aristotle taught the importance of _________ in his writings. **(reason/alliance)**
8. _________ was a great mathematician. **(Plato/Euclid)**

Comprehension and Critical Thinking

SECTION 1 *(Pages 260–265)*

9. **a. Identify** Who were Cyrus the Great, Darius I, and Xerxes I?
   b. Analyze How did the Greeks use strategy to defeat a larger fighting force?
   c. Elaborate What were some factors that led to the success of the Persian Empire?

SECTION 2 *(Pages 266–271)*

10. **a. Describe** What was life like for Spartan women? for Athenian women?
    b. Compare and Contrast How was the education of Spartan boys different from the education of Athenian boys? What did the education of both groups have in common?
    c. Evaluate Do you agree or disagree with this statement: "The Athenians brought the Peloponnesian War on themselves." Defend your argument.

Answers

Visual Summary

Review and Inquiry Use the visual summary to discuss the chapter's main points.

Quick Facts Transparency: The Greek World Visual Summary

Reviewing Vocabulary, Terms, and People

1. Cyrus the Great
2. phalanx
3. Alexander the Great
4. Peloponnesian
5. Socrates
6. Hippocrates
7. reason
8. Euclid

Comprehension and Critical Thinking

9. **a.** Persian kings
   b. The Greeks led the larger Persian navy into the narrow straits of Salamis, in which the Persian navy could not fit. As a result, the smaller Athenian boats easily sank many Persian ships.
   c. a strong army, efficient political organization under Darius I, good roads
10. **a.** Sparta—Women had rights and responsibilities. They ran households when men were gone, received physical training and competed in sporting events. Athens—Women received no education, could not serve in the government, own property, or even leave their homes.

Review and Assessment Resources

Review and Reinforce

SE Chapter Review

CRF: Chapter Review Activity

Quick Facts Transparency: The Greek World Visual Summary

Spanish Chapter Summaries Audio CD Program

Online Chapter Summaries in Six Languages

TOS Holt McDougal PuzzleView

Quiz Game CD-ROM

Assess

SE StandardizedTest Practice

PASS: Chapter Test, Forms A and B

Alternative Assessment Handbook

TOS ExamView Test Generator, Chapter Test

Differentiated Instruction Modified Worksheets and Tests CD-ROM: Chapter Test

Online Assessment Program (in the Premier Online Edition)

Reteach/Intervene

Guided Reading Workbook

Differentiated Instruction Teacher Management System: Lesson Plans

Differentiated Instruction Modified Worksheets and Tests CD-ROM

Interactive Skills Tutor CD-ROM

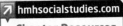

hmhsocialstudies.com

Chapter Resources

Answers

b. Sparta—trained from an early age to be soldiers and then stayed in the army until they were 60 years old; Athens—only served in the army from ages 18 to 20, learned to read, write and play instruments; in common—had athletic and military training

c. Answers will vary, but students should understand the effect of Athens' treatment of other city-states in the Delian League.

11. a. gave the soldiers longer spears and sent cavalry and archers into battle to support the phalanx

b. They kept some of their own customs and combined others with Greek ideas to create a new culture—Hellenistic.

c. possible answer—Greek rule might have spread throughout India and the rest of Asia, heavily influencing the people there.

12. a. a temple on the acropolis of Athens; Athena

b. All were teachers and philosophers.

c. possible answer—because they still relate to the daily lives of many people

Reviewing Themes

13. The Persians felt humiliated because they had been defeated by a smaller force. The Greeks felt proud for successfully defending their homeland against a larger military force.

14. The kings who led the government also led the army.

15. Women in Sparta had more rights. They could own land, run a household, and get an education. Women in Athens could do none of those things.

Using the Internet

16. Go to hmhsocialstudies.com to access a rubric for this activity.

Social Studies Skills

17. Charts will vary but should reflect chapter content.

SECTION 3 *(Pages 272–276)*

11. a. Describe How did Philip II improve the phalanx?

b. Analyze How did the cultures that Alexander conquered change after his death?

c. Predict How might history have been different if Alexander had not died so young?

SECTION 4 *(Pages 277–282)*

12. a. Identify What is the Parthenon? For which goddess was it built?

b. Compare What did Socrates, Plato, and Aristotle have in common?

c. Evaluate Why do you think Greek accomplishments in the arts and sciences are still admired today?

Reviewing Themes

13. Politics Why did the Persians and the Greeks react differently to the end of the Persian Wars?

14. Politics How were the government and the army related in Sparta?

15. Society and Culture How were the roles of women different in Athens and Sparta?

Using the Internet 

16. Activity: Writing a Dialogue While rulers such as Alexander and Cyrus fought to gain land, thinkers like Socrates may have questioned their methods. Through your online book, write a dialogue between Socrates and a student on whether it was right to invade another country. Socrates should ask at least 10 questions to his student.

hmhsocialstudies.com

Social Studies Skills 

17. Interpreting Charts and Tables Create a chart in your notebook that identifies key Greek achievements in architecture, art, writing, philosophy, and science. Complete the chart with details from this chapter.

Reading Skills 

18. Comparing and Contrasting Historical Facts Complete the chart below to compare and contrast two powerful leaders you studied in this chapter, Cyrus the Great and Alexander the Great.

Compare	List two characteristics that Cyrus and Alexander shared.
	a. ________
	b. ________

Contrast	How did Cyrus's and Alexander's backgrounds differ?	
	Cyrus c. ________	Alexander d. ________
	What happened to their empires after they died?	
	Cyrus e. ________	Alexander f. ________

Focus on Writing

19. Writing Your Poem Look back over your notes from this chapter. Ask yourself which of the accomplishments you noted are the most significant. Do you admire people for their ideas? their might? their leadership? their brilliance?

Choose one person whose accomplishments you admire. Look back through the chapter for more details about the person's accomplishments. Then write a poem in praise of your chosen figure. Your poem should be five lines long. The first line should identify the subject of the poem. The next three lines should note his or her accomplishments, and the last line should sum up why he or she is respected.

Reading Skills

18. possible answers—
(a) Both had powerful, well-organized armies and created great empires. (b) Both conquered Mesopotamia and Egypt.
(c) Cyrus was a Persian who led a revolt to take power. (d) Alexander was a Macedonian who inherited his throne from his father.
(e) Cyrus passed his empire on to his son.
(f) Alexander's empire fell apart because he had no clear heir.

Focus on Writing

19. Rubric Students' poems should:

- introduce a person that the student admires.
- describe this person's accomplishments.
- contain a summary of why he or she is respected.
- offer precise language to bring the subject to life.

RF: Focus on Writing, A Poem

CHAPTER 9

Standardized Test Practice

DIRECTIONS: Read each question and write the letter of the best response.

1

> The freedom which we enjoy in our government extends also to our ordinary life . . . Further, we provide plenty of means for the mind to refresh itself from business. We celebrate games and sacrifices all the year round . . . Where our rivals from their very cradles by a painful discipline seek after manliness . . . we live exactly as we please and yet are just as ready to encounter every legitimate danger.

The information in this passage suggests that the person who wrote it probably lived in

A Athens.
B Persia.
C Sparta.
D Troy.

2 The Athenians' main rivals were from

A Sparta.
B Rome.
C Macedonia.
D Persia.

3 Which people were the chief enemies of the Greeks in the 400s BC?

A the Romans
B the Persians
C the Egyptians
D the Macedonians

4 All of the following were Greek philosophers *except*

A Aristotle.
B Plato.
C Socrates.
D Zoroaster.

5 Hellenistic culture developed as a result of the activities of which person?

A Darius I
B Philip II
C Cyrus the Great
D Alexander the Great

Connecting with Past Learnings

6 Cyrus the Great and Alexander the Great both built huge empires. What other leader that you have studied in this course also created an empire?

A Moses
B Shi Huangdi
C Confucius
D Hatshepsut

7 In this chapter you have read about many great philosophers and thinkers. Which of the following people you have studied was *not* a philosopher or thinker?

A Socrates
B Ramses the Great
C Confucius
D Siddhartha Gautama

Answers

Standardized Test Practice

1. A
Break Down the Question Have students who miss the question review the comparisons between Sparta and Athens in Section 2.

2. A
Break Down the Question Point out to students who miss the question that Sparta also fought Persia alongside the Athenians.

3. B
Break Down the Question This question requires students to recall factual information from Section 1.

4. D
Break Down the Question Point out that Zoroaster was a Persian.

5. D
Break Down the Question This question requires students to recall factual information. Students who miss this question should review Section 3.

6. B
Break Down the Question This item connects to information covered in a previous chapter in this textbook.

7. B
Break Down the Question This item connects to information covered in a previous chapter in this textbook.

Intervention Resources

Reproducible

- Guided Reading Workbook
- Differentiated Instruction Teacher Management System: Lesson Plans

Technology

- Quick Facts Transparency: The Greek World Visual Summary
- Differentiated Instruction Modified Worksheets and Tests CD-ROM
- Interactive Skills Tutor CD-ROM

Tips for Test Taking

How Much Do I Write? Point out to students that if a writing question contains any of the following terms, they will need to write several sentences for a complete answer: *describe*, *justify*, *why*, *explain*, or *elaborate*. These are not the only words, however, that may indicate several sentences are required.

Preteach

Bellringer

Motivate Ask students to think about topics related to the ancient Hebrews or Greeks that interested them. What topics would students like to know more about? What questions do students have about these topics? Write the questions for students to see. Then tell students that in this workshop they will answer a similar question by conducting research and writing an informative report.

Direct Teach

Finding Historical Information

Ask an Expert Another source students might consult is an expert on their topic. Students might arrange an interview with an expert or attend a presentation that he or she is giving. If students plan to interview a person, they should write out several questions in advance and leave space after each question for taking notes. If students wish to record an interview, remind them to ask the person's permission in advance.

Taking Notes

Keep It Relevant Tell students that when they are not sure whether to take notes on a piece of information, they should ask themselves, "Does this information help answer my research question?" If the answer is yes, they should include the information in their notes. If the answer is no, they should not.

A Social Studies Report

Assignment
Collect information and write an informative report on a topic related to the Hebrews or the ancient Greeks.

The purpose of a social studies report is to share information. Often, this information comes from research. You begin your research by asking questions about a subject.

TIP Narrowing a Topic
Broad: Sparta
Less Broad: Women and Girls in Sparta
Focus Question: What was life like for women and girls in Sparta?

1. Prewrite

Choosing a Subject

You could ask many questions about the unit you have just studied.

- Why was Ruth an important person in the history of the Jewish religion?
- What was the role of mythology in the lives of the ancient Greeks?
- What were the most important accomplishments of Alexander the Great?

Jot down some topics that interested you. Then, brainstorm a list of questions about one or more of these topics. Make sure your questions are narrow and focused. Choose the question that seems most interesting.

Finding Historical Information

Use at least three sources besides your textbook to find information on your topic. Good sources include

- books, maps, magazines, newspapers
- television programs, movies, videos
- Internet sites, CD-ROMs, DVDs

Keep track of your sources of information by writing them in a notebook or on cards. Give each source a number as shown below.

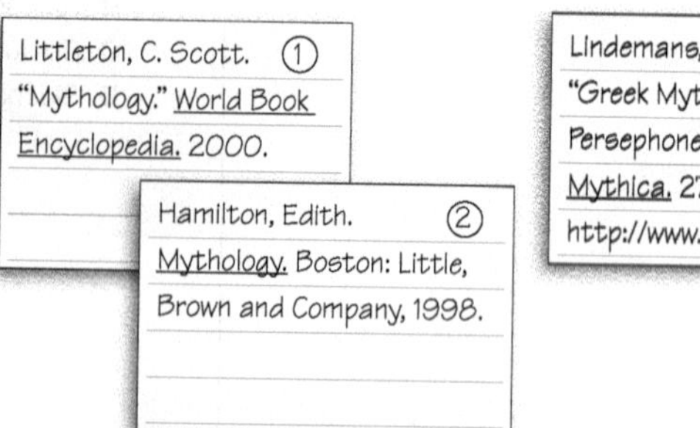

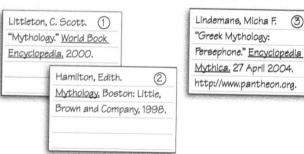

Differentiating Instruction

Struggling Readers Below Level

1. When doing research, students need to learn to evaluate each source quickly to determine its usefulness. As guided practice, write the list of fictional sources at right for students to see. Have students identify which of the sources they think would be most helpful for an informative report on Alexander the Great.
2. Have students use the following scale to rate each source: 4 = extremely useful; 3 = useful; 2 = might be useful; 1 = not useful.

- *The Life of Alexander the Great* (book)
- *Heroes of the Peloponnesian War* (book)
- "Alexander's Army" (historical journal article)
- "Accounts of the Conquests of Alexander the Great" (university Web site)
- "Alexander is My Hero" (personal Web site)

LS **Verbal/Linguistic**

Taking Notes

Take notes on important facts and details from your sources. Historical writing needs to be accurate. Carefully record all names, dates, and other information from sources. Copy any direct quotation word for word and enclose the words in quotation marks. Along with each note, include the number of its source and its page number.

Stating the Big Idea of Your Report

You can easily turn your original question into the big idea for your report. If your question changes a bit as you do your research, rewrite it before turning it into a statement. The big idea of a report is often, but not always, stated in the first paragraph.

TIP Statement or Question Your big idea statement can be a statement of the point you want to make in your paper.

> The ancient Greeks used mythology to explain nature.

It can also be a question, similar to your original research question.

> How did the ancient Greeks use mythology to explain their lives?

Organizing Your Ideas and Information

Sort your notes into topics and subtopics. Put them in an order that is logical, that will make sense to your reader. We often use one of these ways to organize information:

- placing events and details in the order they happened
- grouping causes with their effects
- grouping information by category, usually in the order of least to most important

Here is a partial outline for a paper on Greek mythology.

> Big Idea: The ancient Greeks told myths to explain the world.
> I. Purpose of mythology in ancient Greece
> A. Greeks' questions about the world around them
> B. Greeks' use of myths for answers
> II. Myths about everyday events in the Greeks' lives
> A. The myth of Hestia, goddess of the home
> B. The myth of Hephaestus, god of crafts and fire
> III. Myths about the natural world of the Greeks
> A. The myth of Apollo, god of the sun
> B. The myth of Persephone, goddess of the seasons

TIP Making the Most of Your Outline If you write each of your topics and subtopics as a complete sentence, you can use those sentences to create your first draft.

2. Write

It is good to write a first draft fairly quickly, but it's also helpful to organize it as you go. Use the following framework as a guide.

A Writer's Framework

Introduction
- Start with a quotation or interesting historical detail.
- State the big idea of your report.
- Provide any historical background readers need in order to understand your big idea.

Body
- Present your information under at least three main ideas.
- Write at least one paragraph for each of these main ideas.
- Add supporting details, facts, or examples to each paragraph.

Conclusion
- Restate your main idea, using slightly different words.
- Close with a general comment about your topic or tell how the historical information in your report relates to later historical events.

Direct Teach

Writing Introductions

First Things Last Tell students that they will probably be able to write a stronger introduction after they have drafted the body of the paper. Have students begin by writing their thesis statement. They should then start a new paragraph to begin the body of the report. After they have drafted the body, have students reread the report and then write the introduction. Have students ask themselves the following questions before they write the introduction:

- How can I grab my readers' attention?
- How can I set the scene for what I am about to discuss in the rest of my report?
- How can I make my readers want to read more?

Writing the Body

The Right Fit Explain to students that if they are having trouble making their reports flow, they may need to reconsider the kind of organization they chose. Tell students to scan their papers for transitions and other words that determine the logical relationship of the information. For example, words such as *because, therefore,* and *so* indicate a cause-and-effect relationship. Words such as *first, next, then,* and *after* indicate a chronological relationship. Words such as *primarily, main,* and *major* indicate a relationship based on importance. Students should make sure they are using the organization that best matches what they are trying to say. If not, students should create a new outline with a different organization and then use the outline to revise their drafts.

Advanced/Gifted and Talented — Above Level

1. Challenge students to choose a research topic about which there is some disagreement or controversy. Students should then address in their reports the complexity of their topics, the reasons for controversy, and the discrepancies in the available information.
2. Check students' topics to make sure you approve before students begin their research. **LS Verbal/Linguistic**

Special Needs Learners — Below Level

1. Assign all special education students one topic.
2. Have an aide take the students as a group to the library to assist with research. The aide should instruct students in the use of card catalogs, computer catalogs, and library media centers.
3. The aide should then help the students select and find sources. **LS Verbal/Linguistic**

Direct Teach

Studying a Model

Identify Organization Lead a class discussion to identify the type of organization used in the model research paper. Write the three types of organization for students to see. Have students consider each type of organization in turn.

- **Chronological order:** Point out that the body paragraphs make no mention of which types of myths came first or last, which indicates that the report is not organized chronologically.
- **Comparison-contrast:** Point out that while the report describes several types of myths, the writer does not directly compare or contrast their characteristics.
- **Listing:** Students should conclude that the model is organized by categories, with similar details grouped together.

Then discuss categories the writer has used *(myths about daily life, myths about the natural world, creation myths).*

Technology Tip

Using Technology to Provide Visual Aids Students may want to include maps, charts, diagrams, or illustrations in their papers. Explain that many word-processing programs include drawing tools or provide ways to import graphics from other computer programs. Encourage students who want to include visual aids to find out more about the graphic tools available.

Studying a Model

Here is a model of a social studies report. Study it to see how one student developed a social studies paper. The first and the concluding paragraphs are shown in full. The paragraphs in the body of the paper are summarized.

INTRODUCTORY PARAGRAPH

Attention grabber

Statement of Big Idea

The ancient Greeks faced many mysteries in their lives. How and why did people fall in love? What made rain fall and crops grow? What are the planets and stars, and where did they come from? Through the myths they told about their heroes, gods, and goddesses, the Greeks answered these questions. They used mythology to explain all things, from everyday events to forces of nature to the creation of the universe.

Body Paragraphs

The first body paragraph opens with a statement about how the Greeks used myths to explain their daily lives. Then two examples of those kinds of myths are given. The student summarizes myths about Aphrodite, goddess of love, and Hephaestus, god of crafts and fire.

In the next paragraph, the student shows how the Greeks used myths to explain the natural world. The example of such a story is Persephone and her relationship to the seasons.

The last paragraph in the body contains the student's final point, which is about creation myths. The two examples given for these myths are stories about Helios, god of the sun, and Artemis, goddess of the moon.

CONCLUDING PARAGRAPH

First two sentences restate the thesis

Last three sentences make a general comment about the topic, Greek myths.

The Greeks had a huge number of myths. They needed that many to explain all of the things that they did and saw. Besides explaining things, myths also gave the Greeks a feeling of power. By praying and sacrificing to the gods, they believed they could affect the world around them. All people want to have some control over their lives, and their mythology gave the Greeks that feeling of control.

Notice that each paragraph is organized in the same way as the entire paper. Each paragraph expresses a main idea and includes information to support that main idea. One big difference is that not every paragraph requires a conclusion. Only the last paragraph needs to end with a concluding statement.

Cross-Discipline Activity: Math-Science

At Level

Research Guided Practice

1. Have students research a significant figure in ancient Greek science or math. Encourage students to select figures who are credited with a practical application of science or math rather than abstract theories. Examples include:
   - Archimedes, who invented a method for drawing water upward
   - Eratosthenes, who calculated the circumference of the Earth
   - Hero of Alexandria, who invented an early steam engine
   - Thales, who used geometry to calculate the height of Egypt's pyramids
2. Ask each student to draw a diagram that illustrates their chosen subject's achievements. Remind students to clearly label all parts of their diagrams.
3. Discuss how the inventions and processes shown in the diagrams might still be used by scientists and engineers today. LS **Logical/Mathematical, Visual/Spatial**

3. Evaluate and Revise

It is important to evaluate your first draft before you begin to revise it. Follow the steps below to evaluate and revise your draft.

Evaluating and Revising an Informative Report

1. Does the introduction grab the readers' interest and state the big idea of your report?
2. Does the body of your report have at least three paragraphs that develop your big idea? Is the main idea in each paragraph clearly stated?
3. Have you included enough information to support each of your main ideas? Are all facts, details, and examples accurate? Are all of them clearly related to the main ideas they support?
4. Is the report clearly organized? Does it use chronological order, order of importance, or cause and effect?
5. Does the conclusion restate the big idea of your report? Does it end with a general comment about your topic?
6. Have you included at least three sources in your bibliography? Have you included all the sources you used and not any you did not use?

4. Proofread and Publish

Proofreading

To correct your report before sharing it, check the following:

- the spelling and capitalization of all proper names for specific people, places, things, and events
- punctuation marks around any direct quotation
- punctuation and capitalization in your bibliography

Publishing

Choose one or more of these ideas to share your report.

- Create a map to accompany your report. Use a specific color to highlight places and routes that are important in your report.
- File a copy of your report in your school's library for other students' reference. Include illustrations to go with the report.
- If your school has a Web site, you might post your report there. See if you can link to other sources on your topic.

TIP Bibliography

- Underline the titles of all books, television programs, and Web sites.
- Use quotation marks around titles of articles and stories.

Practice and Apply

Use the steps and strategies outlined in this workshop to research and write an informative report.

Reteach

Proofreading

Shift into Reverse

Standard English Mastery Tell students that one reason it is difficult for people to proofread their own work is that they are too familiar with it. Since they know what they meant to say, it can be difficult for them to realize when their words do not convey their ideas. One way to counteract this familiarity is to proofread backwards. First, have students start at the end of the paper and look at each word in reverse order to make sure every word is used and spelled correctly. Then have students start at the end of the paper and read each sentence in reverse order to make sure every sentence is grammatically correct and written in standard English.

Practice & Apply

Integrating Facts, Details, and Examples

Go with the Flow Some students may become bogged down in details. Direct these students to write a first draft without worrying about including specific facts, details, or examples. Next, instruct students to put a letter next to each fact, detail, or example in their notes. Then have students write each letter next to the paragraph in their drafts where they want to insert the information.

Rubric

Students' reports should

- start with an interesting quote or historical detail.
- provide a clear thesis statement.
- present at least three main points about the chosen topic.
- provide at least one paragraph for each main point.
- provide supporting details, facts, and examples for each main point.
- end with a summary and a general comment about the topic.
- use correct grammar, punctuation, spelling, and capitalization.

Collaborative Learning

At Level

Peer Editing

Standard English Mastery

1. Divide students into groups of four.
2. One student will pretend to be an author submitting his or her work to a scholarly journal. The other three students will pretend to be the editorial board of the journal. The first board member will examine the report to see if it meets the journal's standards for grammar, usage, and mechanics. The second board member will determine whether the report is coherent and interesting enough to publish. The third board member will decide whether the report meets professional standards for factual accuracy based on the provided documentation and Bibliography or Works Cited.
3. The report will be "accepted" only if all board members agree that it meets the journal's standards. Have students trade roles until all four reports have been reviewed.

LS Interpersonal, Verbal/Linguistic

Unit Preview

Introduce the Unit

Share the information in the chapter overviews with students.

Chapter 10 Rome's location and climate helped it to become a major world power. In 509 BC, Roman nobles overthrew the monarchy and established a new form of government, called a republic. Rome's representative government and sophisticated system of laws established many legal traditions we have today. In its later years, the Roman Republic expanded through warfare and trade, while facing growing challenges at home.

Chapter 11 The Roman Empire began when the Senate gave Octavian a new name—Augustus, which means "revered one." The empire spread Roman law and technology across the Mediterranean Sea. Its achievements in science, engineering, architecture, and culture influenced later civilizations. Christianity arose in the 1st century and spread throughout the eastern Mediterranean under the Roman Empire. It was eventually adopted by the empire as its official religion. Internal weaknesses and Germanic invasions caused the collapse of the western empire in the late 400s. The eastern empire, centered in Constantinople, continued as the Byzantine Empire.

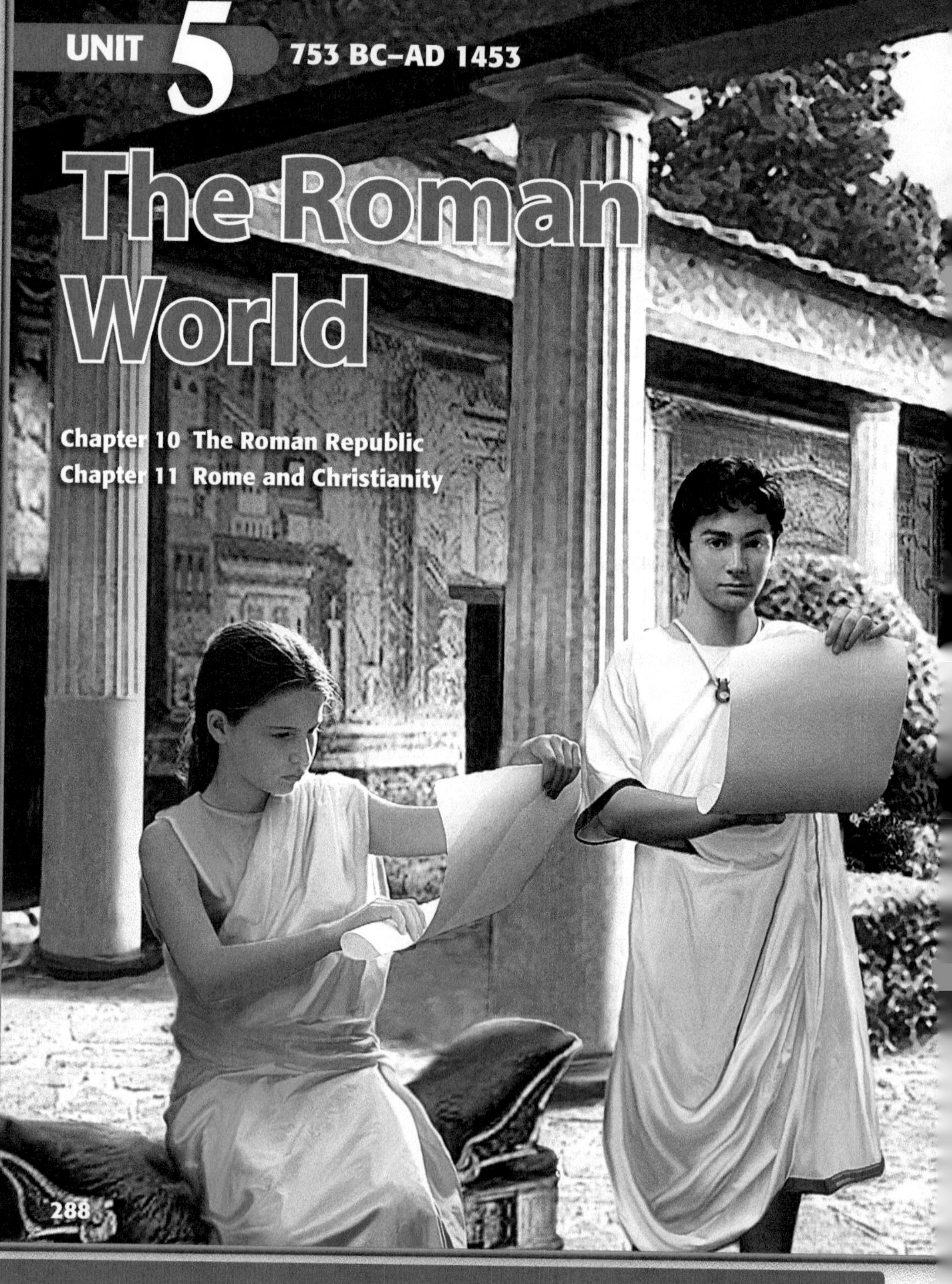

Unit Resources

Planning

- Differentiated Instruction Teacher Management System: Unit Instructional Benchmarking Guides
- TOS Calendar Planner
- Power Presentations with Media Gallery
- A Teacher's Guide to Religion in the Public Schools

Differentiating Instruction

- Differentiated Instruction Teacher Management System: Lesson Plans for Differentiated Instruction
- Differentiated Instruction Modified Worksheets and Tests CD-ROM

Enrichment

- **CRF 10:** Interdisciplinary Project: The Roman Republic: Unemployment
- **CRF 11:** Economics and History Activities: The Romans and Money; Slavery in Ancient Rome; and Inflation and the Fall of the Roman Empire
- **CRF 11:** Interdisciplinary Projects: The Roman Republic: Response Rally; and The Fall of Rome
- Civic Participation Activities
- Primary Source Library CD-ROM

Assessment

- Progress Assessment System Solution: Unit Test
- TOS ExamView Assessment Suite: Unit Test
- Online Assessment Program, in the Interactive Student Edition
- Alternative Assessment Handbook

The **Differentiated Instruction Teacher Management System** provides a planning and instructional benchmarking guide for this unit.

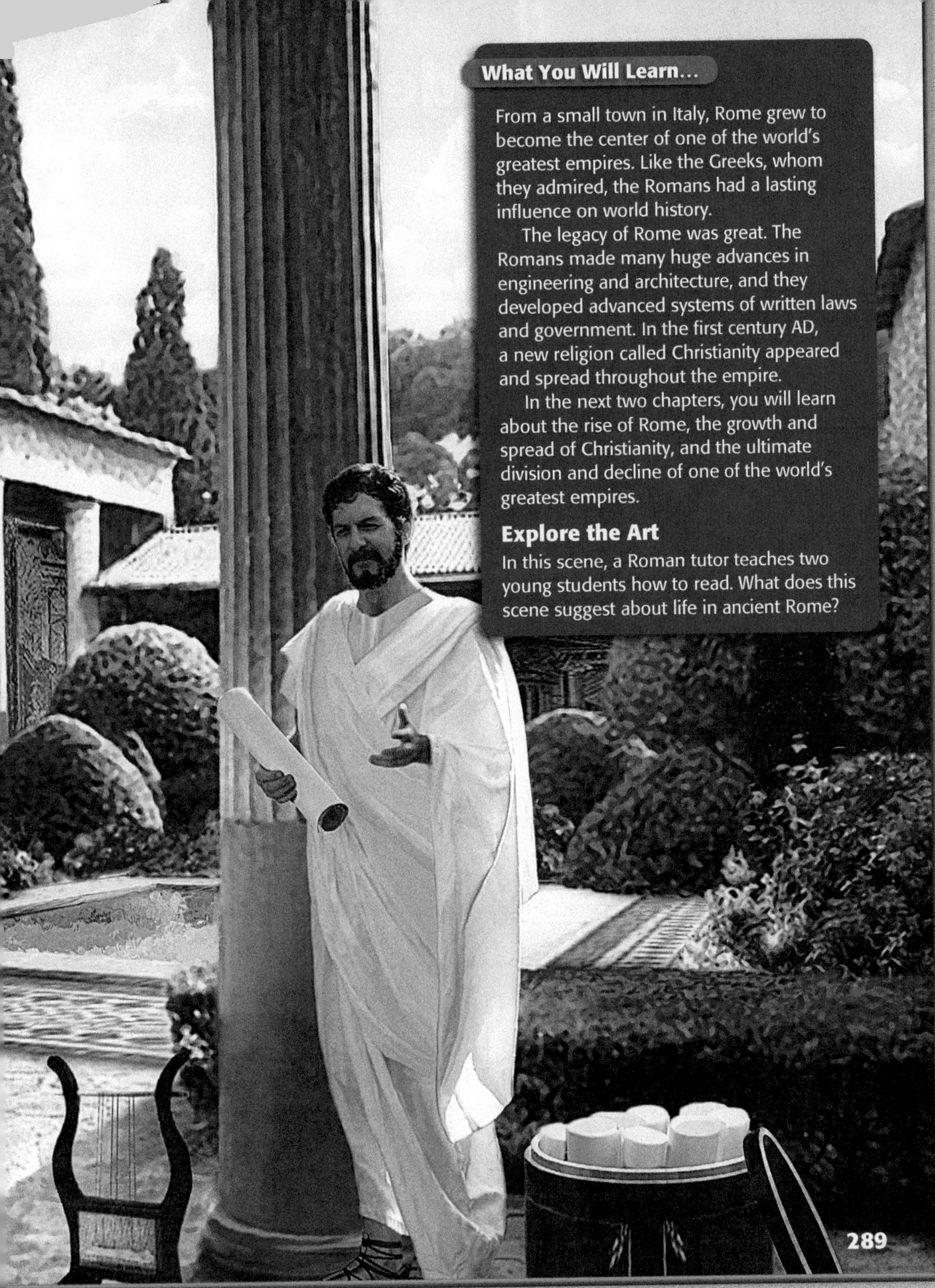

What You Will Learn...

From a small town in Italy, Rome grew to become the center of one of the world's greatest empires. Like the Greeks, whom they admired, the Romans had a lasting influence on world history.

The legacy of Rome was great. The Romans made many huge advances in engineering and architecture, and they developed advanced systems of written laws and government. In the first century AD, a new religion called Christianity appeared and spread throughout the empire.

In the next two chapters, you will learn about the rise of Rome, the growth and spread of Christianity, and the ultimate division and decline of one of the world's greatest empires.

Explore the Art

In this scene, a Roman tutor teaches two young students how to read. What does this scene suggest about life in ancient Rome?

289

Unit Preview

Connect to the Unit

Activity Roman Classroom Ask students: What is the first thing that comes to mind when you think of the Roman world? Tell them that gladiators and togas only make up a small part of Roman history. Rearrange the classroom so that it resembles the layout of the Roman Empire based on maps in the chapter "Rome and Christiantity." Organize the class into small groups and instruct those groups to stand around the room in the relative positions of Roman colonies in AD 100. Locations can include Asia Minor, Carthage, Britain, Gaul, Greece, Jerusalem, and Spain. Stand in the middle of the room in the position of Rome and tell the students that you are the emperor. Discuss with students the challenges an emperor and other officials might face in such a vast empire. **LS Interpersonal, Kinesthetic**

Explore the Art

Rome was full of sophisticated and beautiful art and architecture. Artists and engineers were respected individuals in Roman society. The Roman world was remarkable for valuing literacy, culture, and a society based on law.

About the Illustration

This illustration is an artist's conception based on available sources. However, historians are uncertain exactly what this scene looked like.

Democracy and Civic Education

At Level

Responsibility: Contributing to the Community

Research Required

Background Explain that the Roman Republic relied on the active participation of the people. Romans participated in their government out of a sense of civic duty, or duty to their city.

1. Discuss with students why it is important in a republic to have a citizenry that actively participates in the political process.
2. Organize students into small groups and have each group conduct research on the responsibilities of citizens and the ways in which they could participate in the political process in ancient democratic Athens, the Roman Republic, and the United States.
3. Have each group use its research to create a triptych, with one panel for each main topic.
4. Conclude by having students discuss their responsibilities as U.S. citizens and how they can participate in the political process now.

LS Interpersonal, Verbal/Linguistic

Alternative Assessment Handbook, Rubrics 14: Group Activity; 29: Presentations

Civic Participation Activities

Answers

Explore the Art *People were educated, had a writing system, wrote on scrolls, and wore togas and sandals. The image also shows styles of art and architecture, such as the courtyard, columns, and pond.*

Chapter 10 Planning Guide

The Roman Republic

Overview	Instructional Resources	
CHAPTER 10 **Essential Question:** How did Rome become the dominant power in the Mediterranean region? **Focus on the Essential Question Podcast**	TOS **Differentiated Instruction Teacher Management System:** • Instructional Benchmarking Guides • Lesson Plans for Differentiated Instruction **Guided Reading Workbook** **Chapter Resource File:** • Chapter Review Activity • Focus on Speaking Activity: A Legend • Social Studies Skills Activity: Interpreting Culture Maps	TOS **Calendar Planner** **Power Presentations with Media Gallery** **Differentiated Instruction Modified Worksheets and Tests CD-ROM** **Primary Source Library CD-ROM for World History** **Interactive Skills Tutor CD-ROM** **Student Edition on Audio CD Program** **The World's Music Audio Program** **Video:** The Roman Republic is Born
Section 1: **Geography and the Rise of Rome** **The Big Idea:** Rome's location and government helped it become a major power in the ancient world.	TOS **Differentiated Instruction Teacher Management System:** Section 1 Lesson Plan **Guided Reading Workbook:** Section 1 **Chapter Resource File:** • Vocabulary Builder Activity, Section 1 • Literature Activity: "Romulus and Remus," retold by Robert Hull	**Daily Bellringer Transparency:** Section 1 **Map Transparency:** Italy: Physical **Map Transparency:** Italy, 500 BC **Quick Facts Transparency:** Legendary Founding of Rome **Quick Facts Transparency:** Roman Society **Internet Activity:** *Aeneid* Adaptation **Animated History:** Seven Hills of Rome
Section 2: **Government and Society** **The Big Idea:** Rome's tripartite government and written laws helped create a stable society.	TOS **Differentiated Instruction Teacher Management System:** Section 2 Lesson Plan **Guided Reading Workbook:** Section 2 **Chapter Resource File:** • Vocabulary Builder Activity, Section 2	**Daily Bellringer Transparency:** Section 2 **Quick Facts Transparency:** Government of the Roman Republic **Internet Activity:** Government Comparisons **Video:** The Glory of Rome's Forum
Section 3: **The Late Republic** **The Big Idea:** The later period of the Roman Republic was marked by wars of expansion and political crises.	TOS **Differentiated Instruction Teacher Management System:** Section 3 Lesson Plan **Guided Reading Workbook:** Section 3 **Chapter Resource File:** • Vocabulary Builder Activity, Section 3 • Biography Activities: Cornelia, Scipio • History and Geography Activity: The Punic Wars • Primary Source Activity: "The Story of Spartacus," by Plutarch	**Daily Bellringer Transparency:** Section 3 **Map Transparency:** The Roman Republic, 509–270 BC **Map Transparency:** The Roman Republic, 270–100 BC **Video:** Carthage: Defeat at Zama

Chart Key:

SE Student Edition 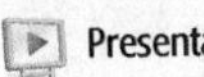 Presentation Resource  MP3 Audio

TOS Teacher One Stop DVD/CD-ROM  HISTORY™

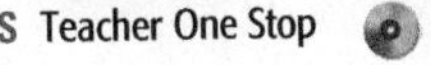

Printable Resource

Program Resources available on TOS and @ hmhsocialstudies.com

Review, Assessment, Intervention

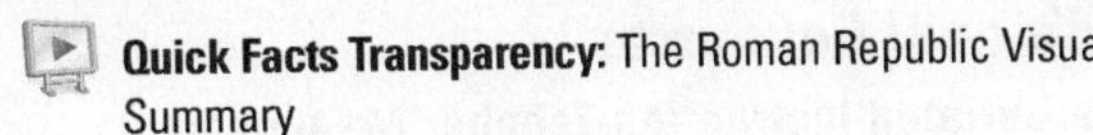

- **Quick Facts Transparency:** The Roman Republic Visual Summary

- **Spanish Chapter Summaries Audio CD Program**
- **Quiz Game CD-ROM**
- **Progress Assessment Support System (PASS):** Chapter Test
- **Differentiated Instruction Modified Worksheets and Tests CD-ROM:** Modified Chapter Test
- TOS **ExamView® Assessment Suite (English/Spanish)**

- **Online Assessment Program**, in the Interactive Student Edition

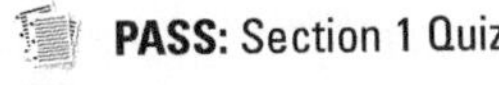

- **PASS:** Section 1 Quiz

- **Online Quiz:** Section 1

- **Alternative Assessment Handbook**

- **PASS:** Section 2 Quiz
- **Online Quiz:** Section 2
- **Alternative Assessment Handbook**

- **PASS:** Section 3 Quiz
- **Online Quiz:** Section 3
- **Alternative Assessment Handbook**

Supporting Resources

- Multimedia Classroom Global History Series
- Global History Teacher's Guide

Maps Globes Graphs Level F

- Student Workbook
- Teacher's Guide

Social Studies Trade Library Collections

- Premier Secondary World History Trade Collection
- Ancient World History Trade Collection

History's Impact

World History Video Program

- **Roman Government and American Government**

For more information or to purchase go to hmhsocialstudies.com

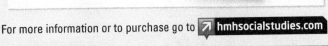

Power Presentations with Media Gallery

Power Presentations with Media Gallery are visual presentations of each chapter's main ideas. Presentations can be customized by including Quick Facts charts, images from the text, and video clips.

Differentiating Instruction

How do I address the needs of varied learners?

The Target Resource acts as your primary strategy for differentiated instruction.

ENGLISH-LANGUAGE LEARNERS & STRUGGLING READERS

Interactive Skills Tutor CD-ROM

The Interactive Skills Tutor CD-ROM contains lessons that provide additional practice for 20 different critical thinking skills.

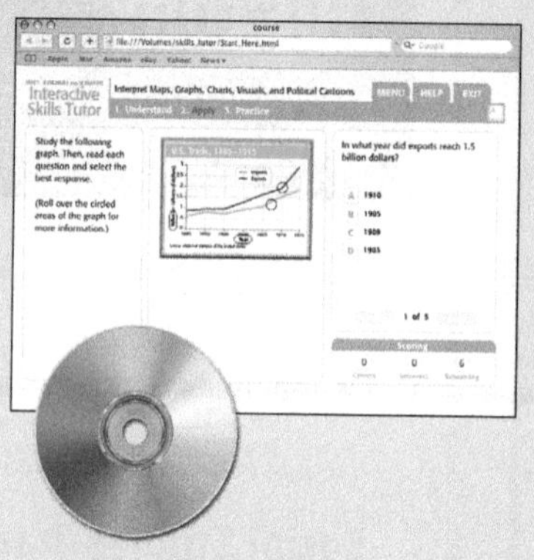

Additional Resources

Differentiated Instruction Teacher Management System: Lesson Plans for Differentiated Instruction

Chapter Resource File:

- Vocabulary Builder Activities
- Social Studies Skills Activity: Interpreting Culture Maps

Quick Facts Transparencies: The Roman Republic Visual Summary

Student Edition on Audio CD Program

Spanish/English Guided Reading Workbook

SPECIAL NEEDS LEARNERS

Differentiated Instruction Modified Worksheets and Tests CD-ROM

- Vocabulary Flash Cards
- Vocabulary Builder Activities
- Chapter Review Activity
- Chapter Test

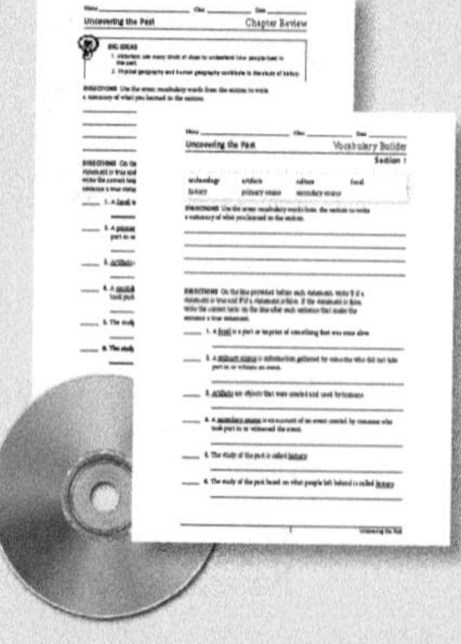

Additional Resources

Differentiated Instruction Teacher Management System: Lesson Plans for Differentiated Instruction

Guided Reading Workbook

Chapter Resource File: Social Studies Skills Activity: Interpreting Culture Maps

Student Edition on Audio CD Program

Interactive Skills Tutor CD-ROM

ADVANCED/GIFTED-AND-TALENTED STUDENTS

Primary Source Library CD-ROM for World History

The Library contains longer versions of quotations in the text, extra sources, and images. Included are point-of-view articles, journals, diaries, historical fiction, and political documents.

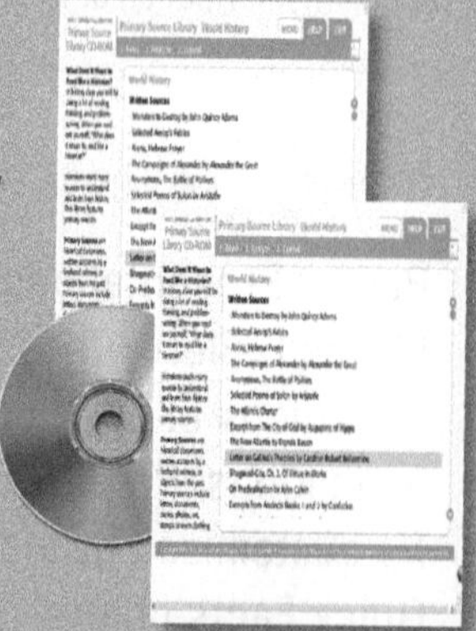

Additional Resources

Differentiated Instruction Teacher Management System: Lesson Plans for Differentiated Instruction

Chapter Resource File:

- Focus on Speaking Activity: A Legend
- Literature Activity: "Romulus and Remus," retold by Robert Hull

Document-Based Questions Activities

Differentiated Activities in the Teacher's Edition

- Creating Collages of the Italian Landscape, p. 295
- Your Elected Officials Graphic Organizer, p. 303

Teacher One Stop™

How can I manage the lesson plans and support materials for differentiated instruction?

With the Teacher One Stop, you can easily organize and print lesson plans, planning guides, and instructional materials for all learners. The Teacher One Stop includes the following materials to help you differentiate instruction:

- **Interactive Teacher's Edition**
- **Calendar Planner and pacing guides**
- **Editable lesson plans**
- **All reproducible ancillaries in Adobe Acrobat (PDF) format**
- **ExamView Assessment Suite (English & Spanish)**
- **Transparency and video previews**

Differentiated Activities in the Teacher's Edition

- Main Ideas on Rome's Beginnings, p. 296
- Roman Forum Video Game, p. 306

Interactive Student Edition

Complete online student edition with interactive multimedia support for chapter content assessment and reporting

- Interactive Maps and Notebook
- Graphic Organizers
- Standardized Test Prep
- Online Homework Practice and Research Activities
- Current Events
- Chapter-based Internet Activities
- Animated History Activities
- and more!

Differentiated Activities in the Teacher's Edition

- Etruscan Civilization, p. 297
- Writing Latinus' Journal Entry, p. 300

• Chapter Preview •

Essential Question

Introduce the Essential Question

- Remind students of other powerful civilizations about which they have read.
- Point out on the map Rome's favorable location near the center of the Mediterranean Sea.
- Explain that Roman civilization reached its height shortly after AD 100, by which time it had been in existence for more than 800 years.

CHAPTER 10 753–27 BC

The Roman Republic

Essential Question How did Rome become the dominant power in the Mediterranean region?

South Carolina Performance Standards

6-2.3 Describe the development of Roman civilization, including language, government, architecture, and engineering; 6-2.4 Describe the expansion and transition of the Roman government from monarchy to republic to empire, including the roles of Julius Caesar and Augustus Caesar (Octavius).

Literacy Skills for Social Studies

- Interpret Earth's physical and human systems by using maps, mental maps, geographic models, and other social studies resources.
- Compare the locations of places, the conditions at places, and the connections between places.
- Elaborate and refine ideas in order to improve and maximize creative efforts.

Focus on Speaking

A Legend The ancient Romans created many legends about their early history. They told of heroes and kings who performed great deeds to build and rule their city. As you read this chapter, look for people or events that could be the subjects of legends. When you finish studying this chapter, you will create and present a legend about one of the people or events that you have studied.

CHAPTER EVENTS

753 BC According to legend, Rome is founded.

800 BC

WORLD EVENTS

c. 700 BC The Assyrians conquer Israel.

Focus on Speaking

The **Chapter Resource File** provides a Focus on Speaking worksheet to help students create and present their legends.

CRF: Focus on Speaking Activity: A Legend

Key to Differentiating Instruction

Below Level
Basic-level activities designed for all students encountering new material

At Level
Intermediate-level activities designed for average students

Above Level
Challenging activities designed for honors and gifted and talented students

Standard English Mastery
Activities designed to improve standard English usage

LS Learning Styles

Introduce the Chapter

At Level

Focus on the Impact of the Roman Republic

1. Ask students to imagine that they are establishing a new country. What form of government would they choose? Would a government run by a single person or by an elected group be better? Ask for a show of hands for each type. Call on volunteers to defend their choices.
2. Explain to students that the Romans also struggled with the question about which type of government is best. During the period of the Republic the Romans had a government that involved several people. In fact, elements of the Republic's government can be seen in the U.S. government today.
3. Have students name different parts of the U.S. government. *possible answers—Congress, House of Representatives, Senate, court system, executive branch*
4. Point out that all these elements connect to parts of the government in the Roman Republic. **LS Verbal/Linguistic**

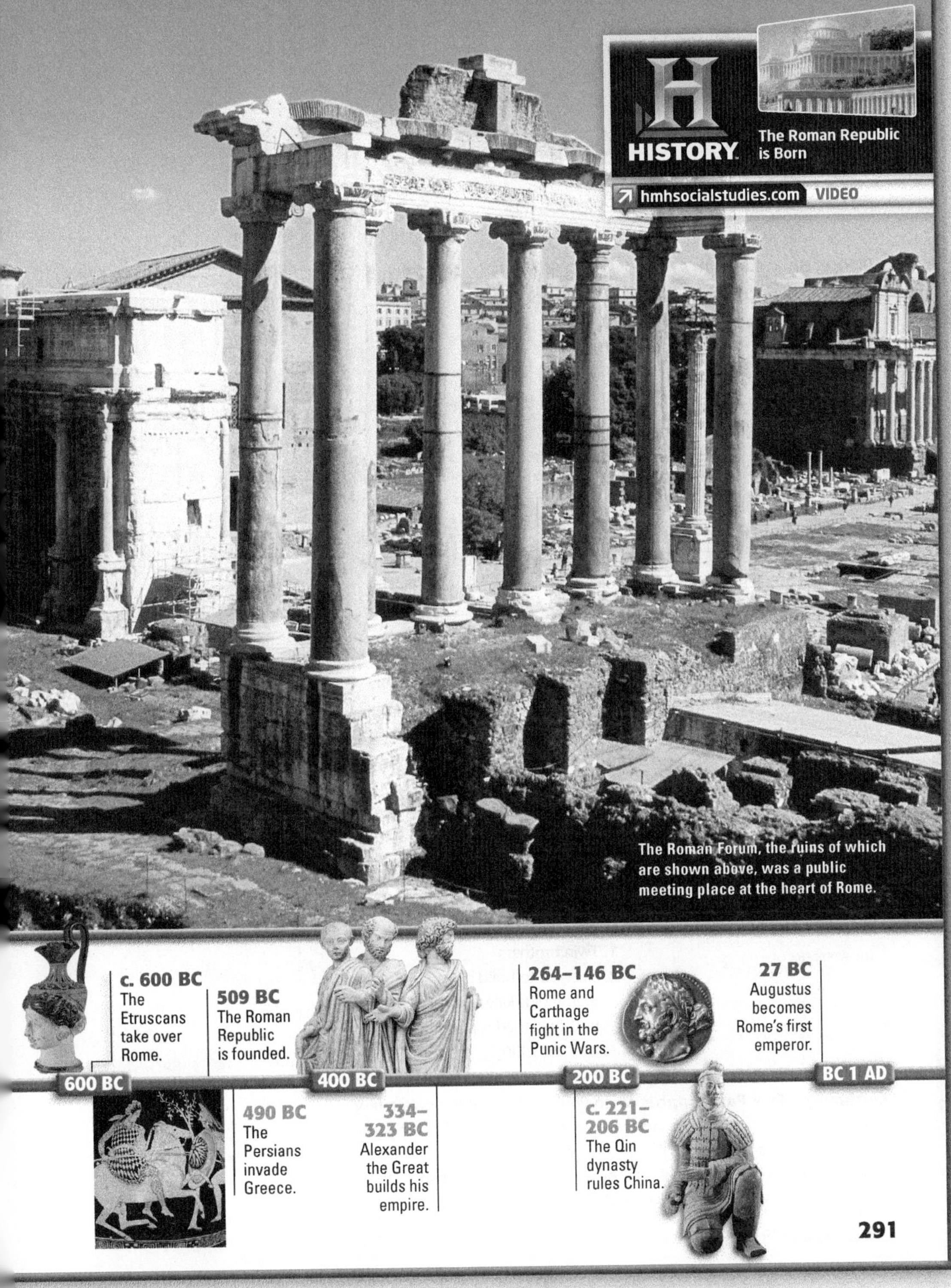
HISTORY
The Roman Republic is Born
hmhsocialstudies.com VIDEO
c. 600 BC
The Etruscans take over Rome.
509 BC
The Roman Republic is founded.
264–146 BC
Rome and Carthage fight in the Punic Wars.
27 BC
Augustus becomes Rome's first emperor.
600 BC
400 BC
200 BC
BC 1 AD
490 BC
The Persians invade Greece.
334–323 BC
Alexander the Great builds his empire.
c. 221–206 BC
The Qin dynasty rules China.
291

The Roman Forum, the ruins of which are shown above, was a public meeting place at the heart of Rome.

• Chapter Preview •

Explore the Picture

From Marshy to Majestic Point out that just beyond the edges of the picture are two of Rome's famous hills—the Palatine and the Capitoline. Other hills enclose the space on the other sides. Because the land on which the Forum was built lay between these hills, water collected there. Rome's first sewer, the Cloaca Maxima, was built on the site to drain the marshy land.

Analyzing Visuals Ask why the building in the background on the left page is intact, while those in the foreground are in ruins. *It was built hundreds of years after the foreground structures.* Then ask why the Roman buildings are in ruins. *possible answers—damaged by earthquakes, wars, intentional destruction by enemies, or gradual destruction by people taking stones for building material*

hmhsocialstudies.com
Teacher Resources

Explore the Time Line

1. When was the Roman Republic founded? *509 BC*
2. When did a series of wars between Rome and Carthage begin? *264 BC*
3. What did the Persians do in 490 BC? *invaded Greece*
4. What dynasty ruled China during the same time period as the Punic Wars? *Qin dynasty*
5. How long may one infer that the Etruscans ruled Rome? *about 91 years*

Info to Know

The Temple of Saturn The large eight-columned ruin in the foreground is the Temple of Saturn, an ancient Roman god of harvests. A temple to Saturn was first built on the site in about 498 BC. These ruins, however, date from the third temple built there in about 42 BC.

Reading Social Studies

Understanding Themes

Introduce the key themes of this chapter—geography and politics—by asking students to find Rome on a map of the world. Point out to students that while Rome today is a city in Italy, the Roman Republic spread throughout Italy and the Mediterranean. Ask students to draw conclusions about the geography of this area. Then have students make predictions about the role the government of Rome might have played during the years of the Republic.

Outlining and History

Focus on Reading Have each student bring in a newspaper article on a topic that interests him or her. Have students work in pairs to create an outline of the story covered in their articles following the format shown here. When their outline is complete, have each pair use scissors to cut the major topics, supporting ideas, and details of their outline into separate strips of paper. Have students cut off the outline numbers and letters. Then have students exchange their outlines with another pair. Ask them to use the article to put the outlines back together in correct form.

Reading Social Studies

Economics | **Geography** | **Politics** | Religion | Society and Culture | Science and Technology

Focus on Themes In this chapter, you will read about the Roman Republic, about how Rome's location and **geography** helped it become a major power in the ancient world. You will also read about the city's **politics** and discover how its three-pronged government affected all of society. Finally, you will read about the wars the Roman Republic fought as it expanded its boundaries. You will see how this growth led to problems that were difficult to solve.

Outlining and History

Focus on Reading How can you make sense of all the facts and ideas in a chapter? One way is to take notes in the form of an outline.

Outlining a Chapter Here is an example of a partial outline for Section 1 of this chapter. Compare the outline to the information on pages 294–297. Notice how the writer looked at the heads in the chapter to determine the main and supporting ideas.

The writer picked up the first heading in the chapter (page 294) as the first main idea. She identified it with Roman numeral I.

Section 1, Geography and the Rise of Rome

I. The Geography of Italy
- **A.** Physical features—many types of features
  - **1.** Mountain ranges
  - **2.** Hills
  - **3.** Rivers
- **B.** Climate—warm summers, mild winters

II. Rome's Legendary Origins
- **A.** Aeneas
  - **1.** Trojan hero
  - **2.** Sailed to Italy and became ruler
- **B.** Romulus and Remus
  - **1.** Twin brothers
  - **2.** Decided to build city
    - **a.** Romulus killed Remus
    - **b.** City named for Romulus
- **C.** Rome's Early Kings

The writer saw two smaller heads under the bigger head on pages 294–295 and listed them as A and B.

The writer identified two facts that supported II.A (the head on page 296). She listed them as numbers 1 and 2.

The writer decided it was important to note some individual facts under B.2. That's why she added a and b.

Outlining a Few Paragraphs When you need to outline only a few paragraphs, you can use the same outline form. Just look for the main idea of each paragraph and give each one a Roman numeral. Supporting ideas within the paragraph can be listed with A, B, and so forth. You can use Arabic numbers for specific details and facts.

Reading and Skills Resources

Reading Support

- Guided Reading Workbook
- Student Edition on Audio CD
- Spanish Chapter Summaries Audio CD Program

Social Studies Skills Support

- Interactive Skills Tutor CD-ROM

Vocabulary Support

- **CRF:** Vocabulary Builder Activities
- **CRF:** Chapter Review Activity
- Differentiated Instruction Modified Worksheets and Tests CD-ROM:
  - Vocabulary Flash Cards
  - Vocabulary Builder Activity
  - Chapter Review Activity

TOS Holt McDougal PuzzleView

You Try It!

Read the following passage from this chapter. Then fill in the blanks to complete the outline below.

Growth of Territory

From Chapter 10, page 308

Roman territory grew mainly in response to outside threats. In about 387 BC a people called the Gauls attacked Rome and took over the city. The Romans had to give the Gauls a huge amount of gold to leave the city.

Inspired by the Gauls' victory, many of Rome's neighboring cities also decided to attack. With some difficulty, the Romans fought off these attacks. As Rome's attackers were defeated, the Romans took over their lands. As you can see on the map, the Romans soon controlled all of the Italian Peninsula except far northern Italy.

One reason for the Roman success was the organization of the army. Soldiers were organized in legions . . . This organization allowed the army to be very flexible.

Complete this outline based on the passage you just read.

I. Roman territory grew in response to outside threats.

A. Gauls attacked Rome in 387 BC.

1. Took over the city
2. ____________________

B. The Gauls' victory inspired other people to attack Rome.

1. ____________________
2. Romans took lands of defeated foes.
3. ____________________

II. ____________________

A. Soldiers were organized in legions.

B. ____________________

Key Terms and People

Chapter 10

Section 1

Aeneas *(p. 296)*
Romulus and Remus *(p. 297)*
republic *(p. 298)*
dictators *(p. 298)*
Cincinnatus *(p. 298)*
plebeians *(p. 299)*
patricians *(p. 299)*

Section 2

magistrates *(p. 303)*
consuls *(p. 303)*
Roman Senate *(p. 303)*
veto *(p. 304)*
Latin *(p. 304)*
checks and balances *(p. 305)*
Forum *(p. 305)*

Section 3

legions *(p. 309)*
Punic Wars *(p. 309)*
Hannibal *(p. 310)*
Gaius Marius *(p. 312)*
Lucius Cornelius Sulla *(p. 313)*
Spartacus *(p. 313)*

Academic Vocabulary

Success in school is related to knowing academic vocabulary—the words that are frequently used in school assignments and discussions. In this chapter, you will learn the following academic words:

primary *(p. 303)*
purpose *(p. 312)*

As you read Chapter 10, identify the main ideas you would use in an outline of this chapter.

Reading Social Studies

Key Terms and People

Preteach the key terms and people for this chapter by hosting a vocabulary game for students. Write the terms and people for students to see. Then organize the class into teams. Read aloud definitions or descriptions, and have teams take turns guessing which term identifies the description you gave. If one team guesses incorrectly, allow the next team an opportunity to guess the answer. Assign points for each correct answer. You might want to have students keep a list of correct descriptions for each term.

LS Interpersonal, Verbal/Linguistic

Focus on Reading

See the **Focus on Reading** questions in this chapter for more practice on this reading social studies skill.

Reading Social Studies Assessment

See the **Chapter Review** at the end of this chapter for student assessment questions related to this reading skill.

Teaching Tip

Some students may not be familiar with outlining. Explain to the class that outlines use main ideas to break down information in a way that is easy to understand and simple to write. Point out to students that major topics from a passage are usually noted as Roman numerals (I, II, III). Under each big idea are supporting ideas, noted as capital letters (A, B, C). Supporting details for each idea are identified with Arabic numerals (1, 2, 3). Lastly, information that supports those ideas can be noted by lowercase letters (a, b, c).

Answers

You Try It! I. A. 2. *Romans gave Gauls gold to leave the city.* **I. B. 1.** *Romans fought off attacks.* **I. B. 3.** *Romans gained control of most land except for northern Italy.* **II.** *Romans gained success due to an organized army.* **II. B.** *Organization allowed the army to be flexible.*

Preteach

Bellringer

If YOU were there . . . Use the **Daily Bellringer Transparency** to help students answer the question.

Daily Bellringer Transparency, Section 1

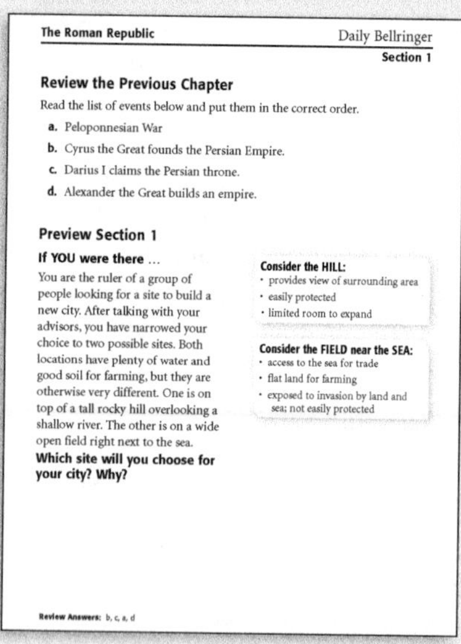

The Roman Republic — Daily Bellringer, **Section 1**

Review the Previous Chapter

Read the list of events below and put them in the correct order.

a. Peloponnesian War
b. Cyrus the Great founds the Persian Empire.
c. Darius I claims the Persian throne.
d. Alexander the Great builds an empire.

Preview Section 1

If YOU were there ...

You are the ruler of a group of people looking for a site to build a new city. After talking with your advisors, you have narrowed your choice to two possible sites. Both locations have plenty of water and good soil for farming, but they are otherwise very different. One is on top of a tall rocky hill overlooking a shallow river. The other is on a wide open field right next to the sea.

Which site will you choose for your city? Why?

Consider the HILL:
- provides view of surrounding area
- easily protected
- limited room to expand

Consider the FIELD near the SEA:
- access to the sea for trade
- flat land for farming
- exposed to invasion by land and sea; not easily protected

Review Answers: b, c, a, d

Building Vocabulary

Preteach or review the following terms:

legendary mythical or imaginary (p. 296)

territories regions (p. 294)

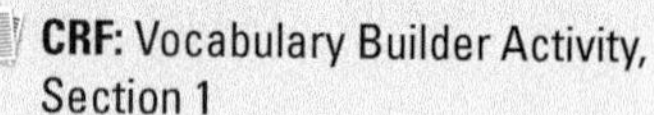

CRF: Vocabulary Builder Activity, Section 1

Taking Notes

Have students use the graphic organizer online to take notes on the section. This activity will prepare students for the Section Assessment, in which they will complete a graphic organizer that builds on the information using the Critical Thinking Skill: Categorizing.

SECTION 1

Geography and the Rise of Rome

What You Will Learn...

Main Ideas

1. The geography of Italy made land travel difficult but helped the Romans prosper.
2. Ancient historians were very interested in Rome's legendary history.
3. Once a monarchy, the Romans created a republic.

The Big Idea

Rome's location and government helped it become a major power in the ancient world.

Key Terms and People

Aeneas, *p. 296*
Romulus and Remus, *p. 297*
republic, *p. 298*
dictators, *p. 298*
Cincinnatus, *p. 298*
plebeians, *p. 299*
patricians, *p. 299*

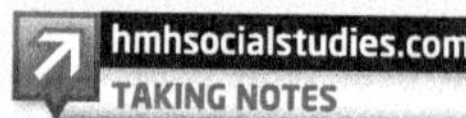

hmhsocialstudies.com TAKING NOTES

Use the graphic organizer online to take notes on Italy's geography and the rise of Rome.

If YOU were there...

You are the ruler of a group of people looking for a site to build a new city. After talking with your advisors, you have narrowed your choice to two possible sites. Both locations have plenty of water and good soil for farming, but they are otherwise very different. One is on top of a tall rocky hill overlooking a shallow river. The other is on a wide open field right next to the sea.

Which site will you choose for your city? Why?

BUILDING BACKGROUND From a small town on the Tiber River, Rome grew into a mighty power. Rome's geography—its central location and good climate—were important factors in its success and growth. The city's rise as a military power began when the Romans went to war and conquered neighboring Italian tribes.

The Geography of Italy

Rome eventually became the center of one of the greatest civilizations of the ancient world. In fact, the people of Rome conquered many of the territories you have studied in this book, including Greece, Egypt, and Asia Minor.

Italy, where Rome was built, is a peninsula in southern Europe. If you look at the map, you can see that Italy looks like a high-heeled boot sticking out into the Mediterranean Sea.

Physical Features

Look at the map again to find Italy's two major mountain ranges. In the north are the Alps, Europe's highest mountains. Another range, the Apennines (A-puh-nynz), runs the length of the Italian Peninsula. This rugged land made it hard for ancient people to cross from one side of the peninsula to the other. In addition, some of Italy's mountains, such as Mount Vesuvius, are volcanic. Their eruptions could devastate Roman towns.

Teach the Big Idea

At Level

Geography and the Rise of Rome

1. **Teach** Ask students the questions in the Main Idea boxes to teach this section.
2. **Apply** Have students write down the dates—or estimated dates—in this section. Have students work in pairs to create time lines for the history of Rome from its creation to the later years of the Republic. **LS Visual/Spatial**
3. **Review** As you review the section's main ideas, have students check to see if their time lines are accurate. Call on volunteers to supply details about the events that appear on their time lines.
4. **Practice/Homework** Have each student write a paragraph titled *How Geography May Have Affected the Development and History of the Roman Republic.*

Alternative Assessment Handbook, Rubric 36: Time Lines

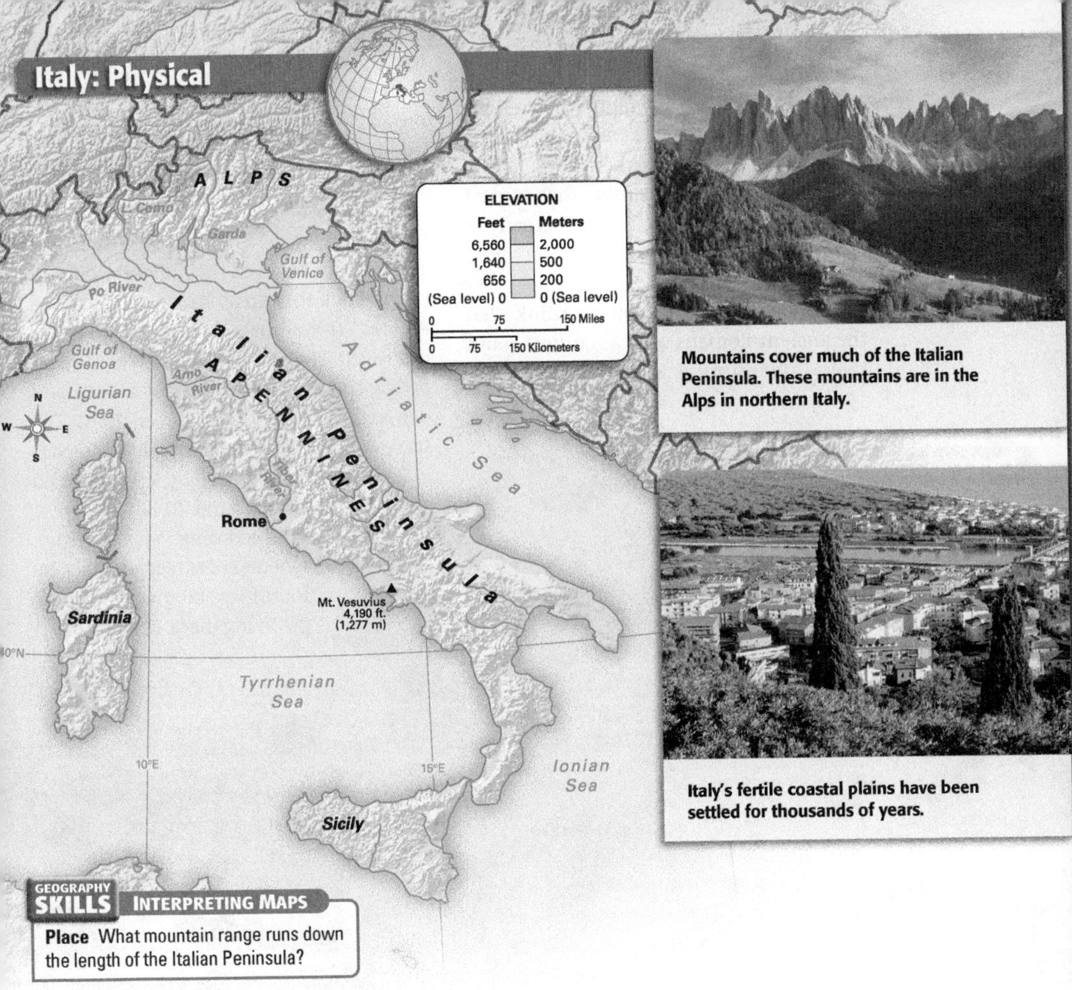

Mountains cover much of the Italian Peninsula. These mountains are in the Alps in northern Italy.

Italy's fertile coastal plains have been settled for thousands of years.

GEOGRAPHY SKILLS INTERPRETING MAPS

Place What mountain range runs down the length of the Italian Peninsula?

Not much of Italy is flat. Most of the land that isn't mountainous is covered with hills. Throughout history, people have built cities on these hills for defense. As a result, many of the ancient cities of Italy—including Rome—sat atop hills. Rome was built on seven hills.

Several rivers flow out of Italy's mountains. Because these rivers were a source of fresh water, people also built their cities near them. For example, Rome lies on the Tiber (TY-buhr) River.

Climate

Most of Italy, including the area around Rome, has warm, dry summers and mild, rainy winters. This climate is similar to that of southern California. Italy's mild climate allows people to grow a wide variety of crops. Grains, citrus fruits, grapes, and olives all grow well there. A plentiful food supply was one key factor in Rome's early growth.

hmhsocialstudies.com
ANIMATED HISTORY
Seven Hills of Rome

READING CHECK **Drawing Conclusions** How did Rome's location affect its early history?

Direct Teach

Main Idea

1 The Geography of Italy

The geography of Italy made land travel difficult but helped the Romans prosper.

Identify What mountain ranges are in Italy, and where are they located? *the Alps in the north, the Apennines along the length of the Italian Peninsula*

Explain Why could Romans grow a wide variety of crops? *good climate for growing many crops*

Elaborate How did Romans take advantage of Italy's physical geography? *They used hills for defense and captured the fresh water flowing down from mountains.*

Map Transparency: Italy: Physical

Connect to Geography

A Dangerous Neighbor Mount Etna on Sicily's east coast is the highest volcano in Europe and has erupted more than 100 times since 1500 BC. Perhaps the most violent eruption occurred in 1669, when the volcano threw out almost a billion cubic yards of lava. The most serious recent eruption was in 1993. Still, the area surrounding Mt. Etna has been densely populated for centuries and is still so today. Ask students why they think this is so. *possible answers—rich agricultural area because volcanic soil is very fertile, danger lessened by advances in early warnings systems*

Differentiating Instruction

English-Language Learners **Below Level**

Materials: poster board, geography and travel magazines and brochures, art supplies

1. Provide students with geography magazines, travel magazines, and travel brochures. Have students use these sources to create collages of the Italian landscape. Images should focus on the natural landscape rather than on buildings.
2. Remind students that Italy has varying landscapes, including coastal and mountain areas, and to include as many different views of the Italian landscape as possible. Students could also draw pictures to fill in gaps.
3. Have students title their collages in large letters and write captions or tag lines for all the images.
4. Then have each student write three sentences to describe the Italian landscape as shown in the collages.
5. Display the collages. **LS Visual/Spatial**

Alternative Assessment Handbook, Rubric 8: Collages

Answers

Interpreting Maps *Apennines*

Reading Check *It determined where Romans settled and what food they could grow.*

Direct Teach

Main Idea

❷ Rome's Legendary Origins

Ancient historians were very interested in Rome's legendary history.

Recall What epic poem tells the story of Aeneas? Who was its author? *the Aeneid; Virgil*

Explain What was remarkable about the childhood of the legendary Romulus and Remus? *The twins were thrown into a river in a basket, rescued and raised by a wolf, and adopted by a shepherd.*

Develop How might a legendary beginning make a country or empire more stable? *possible answer—Belief in the legend could reduce the danger of people trying to destroy the coun try from within, because they would believe the country was very special.*

CRF: Literature Activity: Romulus and Remus

Quick Facts Transparency: Legendary Founding of Rome

Other People, Other Places

Another Legendary Beginning Other peoples, too, have created legends about the founding of their countries or empires. For example, Japanese tradition says that a god and goddess came down from heaven to create the Japanese islands. Legend also claims that Japan's royal family is descended directly from Amaterasu, the sun goddess of the Shinto religion.

hmhsocialstudies.com

Online Resources
Activity: The *Aeneid* in Your Own Words

Rome's Legendary Origins

Rome's early history is wrapped in mystery. No written records exist, and we have little evidence of the city's earliest days. All we have found are ancient ruins that suggest people lived in the area of Rome as early as the 800s BC. However, we know very little about how they lived.

Would it surprise you to think that the ancient Romans were as curious about their early history as we are today? Rome's leaders wanted their city to have a glorious past that would make the Roman people proud. Imagining that glorious past, they told legends, or stories, about great heroes and kings who built the city.

Aeneas

The Romans believed their history could be traced back to a great Trojan hero named **Aeneas** (i-NEE-uhs). When the Greeks destroyed Troy in the Trojan War, Aeneas fled with his followers. After a long and dangerous journey, he reached Italy. The story of this trip is told in the *Aeneid* (i-NEE-id), an epic poem written by a poet named Virgil (VUHR-juhl) around 20 BC.

According to the story, when Aeneas reached Italy, he found several groups of people living there. He formed an

Legendary Founding of Rome QUICK FACTS

Roman historians traced their city's history back to legendary figures such as Aeneas, Romulus, and Remus.

Aeneas
According to the *Aeneid*, Aeneas carried his father from the burning city of Troy and then searched for a new home for the Trojans. After traveling around the Mediterranean, Aeneas finally settled in Italy.

296

Critical Thinking: Finding Main Ideas

Below Level

Main Ideas on Rome's Beginnings

1. Organize the class into small groups. Call on one student in each group to read the text under *Rome's Legendary Origins* quietly to his or her group, while the other members read silently.
2. Then ask another group member to tell the main idea of the passage. Students should discuss among themselves if the main idea described was correct.
3. Instruct students to take turns reading and naming the main idea in the remaining subheads on these two pages.
4. As a class, review the main ideas for the entire subsection.

LS Verbal/Linguistic, Auditory/Musical

alliance with one of these groups, a people called the Latins. Together they fought the other people of Italy. After defeating these opponents, Aeneas married the daughter of the Latin king. Aeneas, his son, and their descendants became prominent rulers in Italy.

Romulus and Remus

Among the descendants of Aeneas were the founders of Rome. According to Roman legends, these founders were twin brothers named **Romulus** (RAHM-yuh-luhs) and **Remus** (REE-muhs). In the story, these boys led exciting lives. When they were babies, they were put in a basket and thrown into the Tiber River. They didn't drown, though, because a wolf rescued them. The wolf cared for the boys for many years. Eventually, a shepherd found the boys and adopted them.

After they grew up, Romulus and Remus decided to build a city to mark the spot where the wolf had rescued them. While they were planning the city, Remus mocked one of his brother's ideas. In a fit of anger, Romulus killed Remus. He then built the city and named it Rome after himself.

Rome's Early Kings

According to ancient historians, Romulus was the first king of Rome, taking the throne in 753 BC. Modern historians believe that Rome could have been founded within 50 years before or after that date.

Roman records list seven kings who ruled the city. Not all of them were Roman. Rome's last three kings were Etruscans (i-TRUHS-kuhnz), members of a people who lived north of Rome. The Etruscans, who had been influenced by Greek colonies in Italy, lived in Italy before Rome was founded.

The Etruscan kings made great contributions to Roman society. They built huge temples and Rome's first sewer. Many historians think that the Romans learned their alphabet and numbers from the Etruscans.

The last Roman king was said to have been a cruel man who had many people killed, including his own advisors. Finally, a group of nobles rose up against him. According to tradition, he was overthrown in 509 BC. The nobles, who no longer wanted kings, created a new government.

READING CHECK **Drawing Conclusions** Why did early Romans want to get rid of the monarchy?

Romulus and Remus
The Romans believed that the twins Romulus and Remus were descendants of Aeneas. In Roman legend, Romulus and Remus were rescued and raised by a wolf. Romulus later killed Remus and built the city of Rome.

Direct Teach

Connect to Arts and the Humanities

Romulus and Remus Several sculptures of Romulus and Remus can be seen in Italy today. Probably the most famous features an Etruscan sculpture of the wolf, with statues of the infant twins that were added about a thousand years later.

Info to Know

King Tarquin of Rome King Tarquinius Priscus was the fifth king of Rome and the first of Etruscan birth. After moving to Rome, he became the guardian of the current king's children. When the king died, Tarquin convinced the people that he should be king instead of the underage children. As king, he built Rome's first sewer, which drained the area that became the Forum. He also built a massive temple to the god Jupiter and held the first games in what became the Circus Maximus.

Checking for Understanding

True or False Answer each statement *T* if it is true or *F* if it is false. If false, explain why.

1. According to legend, Remus named the city of Rome after his brother Romulus. *F; Romulus named the city after himself.*
2. Roman records show that Rome's last three kings were not Romans, but Etruscans. *T*
3. The Roman Republic is said to have been founded by Rome's last king, who was known for his visionary leadership and kindness. *F; The last Roman king was said to have been cruel, and a group of nobles rose up against him to create a new government.*

Collaborative Learning

Above Level

Etruscan Civilization

Background: Tell students that historians know less about the Etruscans than about some other ancient peoples because scholars have not been able to decipher Etruscan writing. However, many Etruscan archaeological sites have been explored, and examples of Etruscan painting, sculpture, and jewelry have been found.

1. Organize students into groups and have them compile a portfolio of Etruscan artifacts. Direct students to library or Internet resources for those images. Many museums display them online. Instruct groups to label the artifacts with basic information.
2. Then lead a class discussion about what we may conclude about the Etruscans by examining their art and how those conclusions may change if Etruscan writing is ever deciphered. **LS Interpersonal, Visual/Spatial**

Alternative Assessment Handbook, Rubric 1: Acquiring Information

Answers

Reading Check *The last Roman king was said to have been cruel.*

Direct Teach

Main Idea

3 The Early Republic

Once a monarchy, the Romans created a republic.

Identify What was the Roman office of dictator? *a ruler with almost absolute power who was in power for only six months*

Explain How is a republic different from a monarchy? *A monarchy is ruled by a king or queen; a republic is governed by elected leaders.*

Make Generalizations What were the first 50 years like for the Roman Republic? *It faced wars and won most of them, but the Romans lost many lives and much property.*

Activity Cincinnatus Writes a Letter Have students imagine they are Cincinnatus after he has returned to his farm. Ask students to write letters to the editor of a Roman newspaper in the voice of Cincinnatus explaining why he wanted to give up his position as dictator. Explain to students that a letter to the editor is often used by people to voice their opinion about a particular issue or current event.

LS Verbal/Linguistic

Map Transparency: Italy, 500 BC

Quick Facts Transparency: Roman Society

The Early Republic

The government of the United States today is a republic.

The government the Romans created in 509 BC was a republic. In a **republic**, people elect leaders to govern them. Each year the Romans elected officials to rule the city. These officials had many powers but only stayed in power for one year. This system was supposed to keep any one person from becoming too powerful in the government.

But Rome was not a democracy. The city's elected officials nearly all came from a small group of wealthy and powerful men. These wealthy and powerful Romans held all the power, and other people had little to no say in how the republic was run.

Challenges from Outside

Shortly after the Romans created the republic, they found themselves at war. For about 50 years the Romans were at war with other peoples of the region. For the most part the Romans won these wars. But they lost several battles, and the wars destroyed many lives and much property.

During particularly difficult wars, the Romans chose **dictators**—rulers with almost absolute power—to lead the city. To keep them from abusing their power, dictators could only stay in power for six months. When that time was over, the dictator gave up his power.

One of Rome's famous dictators was **Cincinnatus** (sin-suh-NAT-uhs), who gained power in 458 BC. Although he was a farmer, the Romans chose him to defend the city against a powerful enemy that had defeated a large Roman army.

Cincinnatus quickly defeated the city's enemies. Immediately, he resigned as dictator and returned to his farm, long before his six-month term had run out.

The victory by Cincinnatus did not end Rome's troubles. Rome continued to fight its neighbors on and off for many years.

Italy, 500 BC

Romans
Etruscans
Greeks
Carthaginians
0 30 60 Miles
0 30 60 Kilometers
Ligurian Sea
Adriatic Sea
Rome
Tyrrhenian Sea
Mediterranean Sea
Ionian Sea
Carthage

GEOGRAPHY SKILLS INTERPRETING MAPS

Location What group lived mostly north of Rome?

BIOGRAPHY

Cincinnatus

c. 519 BC–?

Cincinnatus is the most famous dictator from the early Roman Republic. Because he wasn't eager to hold on to his power, the Romans considered Cincinnatus an ideal leader. They admired his abilities and his loyalty to the republic. The early citizens of the United States admired the same qualities in their leaders. In fact, some people called George Washington the "American Cincinnatus" when he refused to run for a third term as president. The people of the state of Ohio also honored Cincinnatus by naming one of their major cities, Cincinnati, after him.

298

Critical Thinking: Comparing

At Level

Challenges to the Republic

1. Copy the graphic organizer for students to see, omitting the italicized answers. Instruct students to copy and complete the graphic organizer.
2. Students should describe the internal and external challenges the Roman Republic faced during its early years.
3. Lead a discussion about which challenges might have been the greater threat to the republic. **LS Visual/Spatial**

Challenges to the Republic	
Challenges from the Outside	Challenges from the Inside
many wars with other peoples of the region	*plebeians calling for change in the government and forming their own council*

Answers

Interpreting Maps *Etruscans*

Challenges within Rome

Enemy armies weren't the only challenge facing Rome. Within the city, Roman society was divided into two groups. Many of Rome's **plebeians** (pli-BEE-uhnz), or common people, were calling for changes in the government. They wanted more of a say in how the city was run.

Rome was run by powerful nobles called **patricians** (puh-TRI-shuhnz). Only patricians could be elected to office, so they held all political power.

The plebeians were peasants, craftspeople, traders, and other workers. Some of these plebeians, especially traders, were as rich as patricians. Even though the plebeians outnumbered the patricians, they couldn't take part in the government.

In 494 BC the plebeians formed a council and elected their own officials, an act that frightened many patricians. They feared that Rome would fall apart if the two groups couldn't cooperate. The patricians decided that it was time to change the government.

READING CHECK **Contrasting** How were patricians and plebeians different?

Roman Society — QUICK FACTS

Patricians	Plebeians
Wealthy, powerful citizens	Common people
Nobles	Peasants, craftspeople, traders, other workers
Small minority of the population	Majority of the population
Once controlled all aspects of government	Gained right to participate in government
After 218 BC, not allowed to participate in trade or commerce	Only Romans who could be traders, so many became wealthy

SUMMARY AND PREVIEW In this section you read about the location and founding of Rome, its early rule by kings, and the creation of the city's republican government. In the next section you'll learn more about that government, its strengths and weaknesses, how it worked, and how it changed over time.

Section 1 Assessment

hmhsocialstudies.com ONLINE QUIZ

Reviewing Ideas, Terms, and People

1. a. **Describe** Where is Italy located?
   b. **Explain** How did mountains affect life in Italy?
   c. **Predict** How do you think Rome's location on the Mediterranean affected its history as it began to grow into a world power?
2. a. **Identify** What brothers supposedly founded the city of Rome?
   b. **Summarize** What role did **Aeneas** play in the founding of Rome?
3. a. **Describe** What type of government did the Romans create in 509 BC?
   b. **Contrast** How were **patricians** and **plebeians** different?

Critical Thinking

4. **Categorizing** As you review your notes, separate the legends from the historical events in Rome's founding and growth. Then use a diagram like the one below to list the key legendary events.

FOCUS ON SPEAKING

5. **Gathering Background Ideas** In this section you read about several legends the Romans told about their own history. Look back at the text to get some ideas about what you might include in your own legend. Write some ideas in your notebook.

Direct Teach

Teaching Tip

Review with students the creation of Rome's government. Ask them to think about how well the government might have functioned over time. This question may help prepare students for the next section.

Review & Assess

Close

Have students review how the Roman Republic was established.

Review

Online Quiz, Section 1

Assess

SE Section 1 Assessment

PASS: Section 1 Quiz

Alternative Assessment Handbook

Reteach/Classroom Intervention

Guided Reading Workbook, Section 1

Interactive Skills Tutor CD-ROM

Section 1 Assessment Answers

1. a. southern Europe, extending into the Mediterranean Sea
   b. They made inland travel difficult and dictated where people lived.
   c. Its location in the middle of the Mediterranean region made it easy for Rome to control surrounding areas.
2. a. Romulus and Remus
   b. He formed an alliance with the Latins, fought other people of Italy, and started a line of prominent rulers in Italy.
3. a. a republic
   b. Patricians were nobles who could be elected to office; plebeians were peasants, craftspeople, traders, and other workers who at first were not able to be in government.
4. Aeneas arrives in Italy; Aeneas becomes a ruler in Italy; Romulus and Remus are saved by a wolf and raised by a shepherd; Romulus builds a city and names it Rome.
5. Ideas should be creative and may include a description of the local geography.

Answers

Reading Check *Patricians were nobles who could be elected to office; plebeians were peasants, craftspeople, traders, and other workers who at first were not able to be in government.*

Literature in History

The Aeneid

As You Read As students read the passage, have them record the goals and desires of Ilioneus and his men and those of Latinus, the king of the Latins. Point out that sometimes people don't reveal their true goals or desires. Ask students to consider if Ilioneus and Latinus seem to be expressing their true feelings in the passage.

Meet the Writer

Virgil Publius Vergilius Maro, later known as Virgil, grew up on a farm in northern Italy. Life on the farm provided much material for the writer's early poetry. Virgil was reportedly encouraged by Augustus to write about the glory of Rome. He spent much of the rest of his life composing the *Aeneid*.

Virgil's poems were so respected and loved that the Romans used them in schools as textbooks. The Romans loved Virgil not just because he was an excellent writer, but also because he fulfilled the role of a national poet. Virgil's popularity has endured for centuries.

Did you know . . .

Notice that Aeneas was supposedly the son of Venus. In many stories from ancient Greece and Rome, heroes are said to be the sons of a human being and a god or goddess. Having such a marvelous parent gave a hero extra strength, wisdom, or talents. In these stories, the supernatural parent could also provide extra protection.

Answers

Guided Reading *Ilioneus addresses the king with respect and honesty; because he needs to ask a favor of him.*

from the Aeneid

by Virgil

Translated by Robert Fitzgerald

About the Reading *Virgil wrote the* Aeneid *to record the glorious story of Rome's founding and to celebrate the Rome of his day. At the center of the poem stands the hero Aeneas, survivor of the Trojan War and son of the goddess Venus. After wandering for seven years, Aeneas finally reaches southern Italy—then known as Ausonia. Here, Aeneas's friend Ilioneus leads a group of representatives to visit a nearby Latin settlement.*

AS YOU READ **Try to identify each group's goals and desires.**

Latinus
Called the Teucrians before him, saying
Tranquilly as they entered:
"Sons of Dardanus—
You see, we know your city and your nation,
As all had heard you laid a westward course—
Tell me your purpose. ❶ What design or need
Has brought you through the dark blue sea so far
To our Ausonian coast? Either astray
Or driven by rough weather, such as sailors
Often endure at sea, you've broached the river,
Moored ship there. Now do not turn away
From hospitality here. Know that our Latins
Come of Saturn's race, that we are just—
Not by constraint or laws, but by our choice
And habit of our ancient god . . ."
Latinus then fell silent, and in turn
Ilioneus began:
"Your majesty,
Most noble son of Faunus, no rough seas
Or black gale swept us to your coast, no star
Or clouded seamark put us off our course. ❷

Aeneas, from an Italian painting of the 1700s

GUIDED READING

WORD HELP

tranquilly calmly
astray off course
broached crossed
moored anchored
constraint force
gale storm

❶ Both "Teucrians" and "sons of Dardanus" are ways of referring to Trojans.

❷ Ilioneus says that the Trojans are not lost. A seamark is similar to a landmark, a feature sailors use to find their way.

How does Ilioneus address the king? Why do you think he does so?

Differentiating Instruction

Advanced/Gifted and Talented — Above Level

Have students imagine they are Latinus a few hours after he has met Ilioneus. Ask students to write journal entries as Latinus about the meeting. Encourage students to reread the poem closely for tone and meaning to help them make inferences about Latinus' mood. Call on volunteers to read their diary entries aloud.
LS Verbal/Linguistic

Alternative Assessment Handbook, Rubric 15: Journals

Struggling Readers — Below Level

Organize the class into small groups. Assign each group a few lines from the passage. Have groups determine which words in their assigned lines are essential subjects and verbs, and which are adjectives and adverbs. Have students read the lines in their basic forms and then add the modifiers back in. Point out that a passage's tone and meaning are often expressed with adjectives and adverbs. **LS Verbal/Linguistic**

Alternative Assessment Handbook, Rubric 14: Group Activity

We journey to your city by design
And general consent, driven as we are
From realms in other days greatest by far
The Sun looked down on, passing on his way
From heaven's far eastern height. ❸ Our line's from Jove,
In his paternity the sons of Dardanus
Exult, and highest progeny of Jove
Include our king himself—Trojan Aeneas,
Who sent us to your threshold . . . ❹
So long on the vast waters, now we ask
A modest settlement of the gods of home,
A strip of coast that will bring harm to no one,
Air and water, open and free to all . . .
Our quest was for your country. Dardanus
Had birth here, and Apollo calls us back,
Directing us by solemn oracles
To Tuscan Tiber . . . ❺ Here besides
Aeneus gives you from his richer years
These modest gifts, relics caught up and saved
From burning Troy . . ."
Latinus heard
Ilioneus out, his countenance averted,
Sitting immobile, all attention, eyes
Downcast but turning here and there. The embroidered
Purple and the scepter of King Priam
Moved him less in his own kingliness
Than long thoughts on the marriage of his daughter,
As he turned over in his inmost mind
Old Faunus' prophecy.
"This is the man,"
he thought, "foretold as coming from abroad
To be my son-in-law, by fate appointed,
Called to reign here with equal authority—
The man whose heirs will be brilliant in valor
And win the mastery of the world." ❻

GUIDED READING

WORD HELP

progeny offspring
threshold door
oracle person who gives advice
averted turned away
immobile unmoving

❸ Ilioneus explains that the Trojans have come to Italy "by design"—both on purpose and with help from the gods.

❹ Aeneas and Dardanus, the founder of Troy, were both believed to be descendants of Jove, the king of the gods.

❺ The Romans believed that Troy's founder Dardanus was born in Italy.

What does Ilioneus ask the king to give the Trojans?

❻ Virgil included this vision of Rome's great future to point out the city's greatness to his readers.

CONNECTING LITERATURE TO HISTORY

1. **Analyzing** Rome's leaders wanted their city to have a glorious past that would make the Roman people proud. What details in this passage would make Roman readers proud of their past?
2. **Drawing Conclusions** When Aeneas reached Italy, he formed an alliance with the Latins. Think about how Virgil portrays the Latins in this passage. What words or phrases would you use to describe them? Why might such people make good allies?

Direct Teach

Did you know . . .

People have written many epic poems throughout history. Although these poems are not histories, they can give us clues about the societies that produced them. They can also tell us how people viewed their own past. Other epic poems and the lands where the events are set include the *Iliad* and the *Odyssey* (ancient Greece), the *Epic of Gilgamesh* (Mesopotamia), the *Mahabharata* and the *Ramayana* (India), *Beowulf* (Denmark and Sweden), the *Chanson de Roland (Song of Roland,* medieval France), *El Cantar de Mio Cid (Song of the Cid,* medieval Spain), and the *Heike Monogatari (Tale of the Heike,* Japan).

Activity Researching Epic Poems Have students conduct research on an epic poem from another culture. Direct students to library or Internet resources to discover an epic poem and to explore its cultural significance. Tell students that some epic poems served as religious texts, while others were primarily for entertainment. Have each student write a one-page report on the epic poem he or she has chosen. Optional: Have students create epic poems of their own based on the culture and time in which they live. LS **Verbal/Linguistic**

Alternative Assessment Handbook, Rubrics 30: Research; and 37: Writing Assignments

Cross-Discipline Activity: English/Language Arts

At Level

Understanding Poetry

1. Work with the English teacher, English textbooks, or dictionaries to define and describe such terms as meter, diction, rhythm, and syntax. Write definitions for the class to see. Tell students that a poet is constantly using these elements to create an effective poem.
2. Once students understand these terms, ask them to find examples of each element of poetry in the excerpt from the *Aeneid.*
3. Then have students write two lines for each term. The two lines should demonstrate an understanding of the term. For example, the two lines should have different rhythm or different diction.
4. Tell students that it might help them if they read the lines aloud. Ask for volunteers to read their lines and demonstrate one of the key terms. LS **Verbal/Linguistic**

Alternative Assessment Handbook, Rubric 26: Poems and Songs

Answers

Guided Reading *a piece of land on the coast where the Trojans can settle*

Connecting Literature to History
1. *the heroic trip of Aeneas and his men, the family history of Aeneas and Ilioneus, the story of heroic people working together to found Rome;* **2.** *possible answers—noble, respectful, welcoming, kind, generous; because they would treat an ally as an equal*

Preteach

Bellringer

If YOU were there . . . Use the **Daily Bellringer Transparency** to help students answer the question.

Daily Bellringer Transparency, Section 2

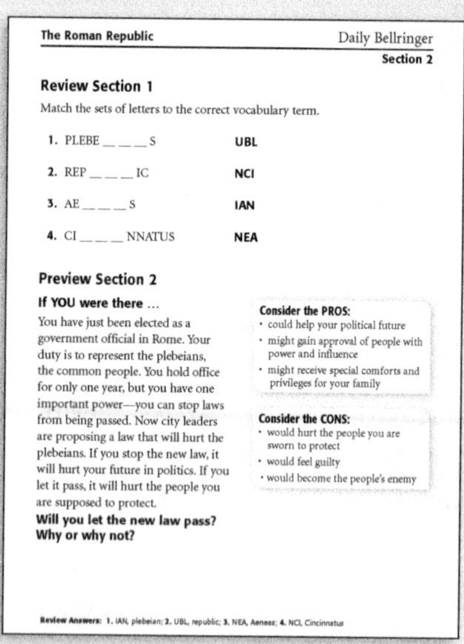

The Roman Republic — Daily Bellringer — **Section 2**

Review Section 1

Match the sets of letters to the correct vocabulary term.

1. PLEBE ___ S — **UBL**
2. REP ___ IC — **NCI**
3. AE ___ S — **IAN**
4. CI ___ NNATUS — **NEA**

Preview Section 2

If YOU were there ...

You have just been elected as a government official in Rome. Your duty is to represent the plebeians, the common people. You hold office for only one year, but you have one important power—you can stop laws from being passed. Now city leaders are proposing a law that will hurt the plebeians. If you stop the new law, it will hurt your future in politics. If you let it pass, it will hurt the people you are supposed to protect.

Will you let the new law pass? Why or why not?

Consider the PROS:
- could help your political future
- might gain approval of people with power and influence
- might receive special comforts and privileges for your family

Consider the CONS:
- would hurt the people you are sworn to protect
- would feel guilty
- would become the people's enemy

Review Answers: **1.** IAN, plebeian; **2.** UBL, republic; **3.** NEA, Aeneas; **4.** NCI, Cincinnatus

Academic Vocabulary

Review with students the high-use academic term in this section.

primary main, most important (p. 303)

CRF: Vocabulary Builder Activity, Section 2

Taking Notes

Have students use the graphic organizer online to take notes on the section. This activity will prepare students for the Section Assessment, in which they will complete a graphic organizer that builds on the information using the Critical Thinking Skill: Analyzing.

SECTION 2

Government and Society

What You Will Learn...

Main Ideas

1. Roman government was made up of three parts that worked together to run the city.
2. Written laws helped keep order in Rome.
3. The Roman Forum was the heart of Roman society.

The Big Idea

Rome's tripartite government and written laws helped create a stable society.

Key Terms

magistrates, *p. 303*
consuls, *p. 303*
Roman Senate, *p. 303*
veto, *p. 304*
Latin, *p. 304*
checks and balances, *p. 305*
Forum, *p. 305*

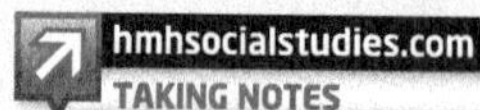

hmhsocialstudies.com
TAKING NOTES

Use the graphic organizer online to take notes about how government, written laws, and the Forum contributed to the development of Roman society.

If YOU were there...

You have just been elected as a government official in Rome. Your duty is to represent the plebeians, the common people. You hold office for only one year, but you have one important power—you can stop laws from being passed. Now city leaders are proposing a law that will hurt the plebeians. If you stop the new law, it will hurt your future in politics. If you let it pass, it will hurt the people you are supposed to protect.

Will you let the new law pass? Why or why not?

BUILDING BACKGROUND Government in Rome was often a balancing act. Like the politician above, leaders had to make compromises and risk the anger of other officials to keep the people happy. To keep anyone from gaining too much power, the Roman government divided power among many different officials.

Roman Government

When the plebeians complained about Rome's government in the 400s BC, the city's leaders knew they had to do something. If the people stayed unhappy, they might rise up and overthrow the whole government.

To calm the angry plebeians, the patricians made some changes to Rome's government. For example, they created new offices that could only be held by plebeians. The people who held these offices protected the plebeians' rights and interests. Gradually, the distinctions between patricians and plebeians began to disappear, but that took a very long time.

As a result of the changes the patricians made, Rome developed a tripartite (try-PAHR-tyt) government, or a government with three parts. Each part had its own responsibilities and duties. To fulfill its duties, each part of the government had its own powers, rights, and privileges.

Teach the Big Idea

At Level

Government and Society

1. **Teach** Ask students the questions in the Main Idea boxes to teach this section.
2. **Apply** Have students skim over the section and the Quick Facts information. Then have students pick out the names of key offices, assemblies, and other concepts. Write the names and terms for students to see, but not as a list; space them out randomly across the page to form the basis of an idea web. **LS Verbal/Linguistic**
3. **Review** As you review the section's main ideas, call on volunteers to add arrows or other symbols to the display of terms to indicate how they were related to each other. Students should also add labels to describe the connections among terms.
4. **Practice/Homework** Have students copy the idea webs and add more connections and/or details.

Alternative Assessment Handbook, Rubric 13: Graphic Organizers

Magistrates

The first part of Rome's government was made up of elected officials, or **magistrates** (MA-juh-strayts). The two most powerful magistrates in Rome were called **consuls** (KAHN-suhlz). The consuls were elected each year to run the city and lead the army. There were two consuls so that no one person would be too powerful.

Below the consuls were other magistrates. Rome had many different types of magistrates. Each was elected for one year and had his own duties and powers. Some were judges. Others managed Rome's finances or organized games and festivals.

Senate

The second part of Rome's government was the Senate. The **Roman Senate** was a council of wealthy and powerful Romans that advised the city's leaders. It was originally created to advise Rome's kings. After the kings were gone, the Senate continued to meet to advise consuls.

Unlike magistrates, senators—members of the Senate—held office for life. By the time the republic was created, the Senate had 300 members. At first most senators were patricians, but as time passed many wealthy plebeians became senators as well. Because magistrates became senators after completing their terms in office, most didn't want to anger the Senate and risk their future jobs.

As time passed the Senate became more powerful. It gained influence over magistrates and took control of the city's finances. By 200 BC the Senate had great influence in Rome's government.

FOCUS ON READING
If you were outlining the discussion on this page, what headings would you use?

Assemblies and Tribunes

The third part of Rome's government, the part that protected the common people, had two branches. The first branch was made up of assemblies. Both patricians and plebeians took part in these assemblies. Their **primary** job was to elect the magistrates who ran the city of Rome.

ACADEMIC VOCABULARY
primary main, most important

Government of the Roman Republic QUICK FACTS

Magistrates	Senate	Assemblies and Tribunes
■ Consuls led the government and army, judged court cases ■ Served for one year ■ Had power over all citizens, including other officials	■ Advised the consuls ■ Served for life ■ Gained control of financial affairs	■ Represented the common people, approved or rejected laws, declared war, elected magistrates ■ Roman citizens could take part in assemblies all their adult lives, tribunes served for one year ■ Could veto the decisions of consuls and other magistrates

Direct Teach

Main Idea

1 Roman Government

Roman government was made up of three parts that worked together to run the city.

Define What was a consul? *the most powerful magistrate in Rome*

Explain Why was the Senate so powerful? *because senators held office for life and because magistrates didn't want to anger the Senate*

Draw Conclusions Why were the assemblies and tribunes a necessary part of the government? *They protected the rights of plebeians and had the power to veto actions by other government officials.*

Quick Facts Transparency: Government of the Roman Republic

hmhsocialstudies.com
Online Resources
Activity: Government Comparisons

Other People, Other Places

The Qin Dynasty At about the same time that the Romans were developing a republic, a Chinese dynasty was forming a very different sort of government. Emperor Shi Huangdi, the founder of the Qin dynasty, held complete power over the Chinese people. He ruled by very strict laws and made the peasants pay heavy taxes. To prevent criticism and free thought, he ordered all books burned except for those on practical subjects, such as medicine.

Differentiating Instruction

Struggling Readers **Below Level**

1. Copy the graphic organizer for students to see, omitting the blue, italicized answers. Have students copy it.
2. Remind students that the Roman government had three levels. Tell them the U.S. government also has levels, such as federal, state, and local.
3. Have students use phone books and the Internet to find the names of their government officials at these levels. LS **Visual/Spatial**

Alternate Assessment Handbook, Rubric 1: Acquiring Information

Your Elected Officials

Federal	State	Local
President, Senator, Congressperson	*Governor, State Senator, State Representative*	*Mayor, City Council Member, Sheriff*

Answers

Focus on Reading *Magistrates, Senate, Assemblies and Tribunes*

Direct Teach

Main Idea

1 Roman Government

Roman government was made up of three parts that worked together to run the city.

Identify What was the veto? Which branch of the Roman government had this authority? *to stop or prohibit actions of other government officials; tribunes*

Explain How did the government keep tribunes from becoming too powerful? *They were limited to serving for only one year.*

Draw Conclusions How was civic duty demonstrated in Rome? *People participated in government by attending meetings and voting; the wealthy felt it was their duty to serve.*

 **CRF:** Interdisciplinary Project: The Romans: Response Rally

Connect to Government

Checks and Balances An elaborate system of checks and balances is written into the U.S. Constitution. This ensures that no one branch obtains too much power. For example, the president has the authority to veto bills from Congress. Only Congress has the authority to declare war, not the president. The Supreme Court has the authority to interpret laws passed by Congress. Every branch of government has some form of check over the other two branches.

Answers

Analyzing Information *possible answers—because it was a government run by many people, not just a few; because it worked well for the Roman Republic*

LINKING TO TODAY

Do as the Romans Do

The government of the Roman Republic was one of its greatest strengths. When the founders of the United States sat down to plan our government, they copied many elements of the Roman system. Like the Romans, we elect our leaders. Our government also has three branches—the president, Congress, and the federal court system. The powers of these branches are set forth in our Constitution, just like the Roman officials' powers were. Our government also has a system of checks and balances to prevent any one branch from becoming too strong. For example, Congress can refuse to give the president money to pay for programs. Like the Romans, Americans have a civic duty to participate in the government to help keep it as strong as it can be.

ANALYSIS SKILL **ANALYZING INFORMATION**

Why do you think the founders of the United States borrowed ideas from Roman government?

THE IMPACT TODAY

Like tribunes, the president of the United States has the power to veto actions by other government officials.

The second branch was made up of a group of elected officials called tribunes. Elected by the plebeians, tribunes had the ability to **veto** (VEE-toh), or prohibit, actions by other officials. Veto means "I forbid" in **Latin**, the Romans' language. This veto power made tribunes very powerful in Rome's government. To keep them from abusing their power, each tribune remained in office only one year.

Civic Duty

Rome's government would not have worked without the participation of the people. People participated in the government because they felt it was their civic duty, or their duty to the city. That civic duty included doing what they could to make sure the city prospered. For example, they were expected to attend assembly meetings and to vote in elections. Voting in Rome was a complicated process, and not everyone was allowed to do it. Those who could, however, were expected to take part in all elections.

Wealthy and powerful citizens also felt it was their duty to hold public office to help run the city. In return for their time and commitment, these citizens were respected and admired by other Romans.

Checks and Balances

In addition to limiting terms of office, the Romans put other restrictions on their leaders' power. They did this by giving government officials the ability to restrict the powers of other officials. For example, one consul could block the actions of the other.

Critical Thinking: Comparing

At Level

Civic Duty, Then and Now

1. Discuss with students what they have learned about civic duty in the Roman Republic. Tell them that, just as our government is similar to the Romans' form of government, Americans have similar civic duties.
2. Have students write a brief essay comparing the civic duty of American citizens to the civic duty of a Roman citizen. Tell them to include specific examples of how an American can fulfill his or her civic duty. Encourage students to consider and discuss in their papers how citizens who are not yet old enough to vote can still perform such duties.
3. Ask for volunteers to read their essays to the class. LS **Verbal/Linguistic**

Alternative Assessment Handbook, Rubric 42: Writing to Inform

Laws proposed by the Senate had to be approved by magistrates and ratified by assemblies. We call these methods to balance power **checks and balances.** Checks and balances keep any one part of a government from becoming stronger or more influential than the others.

Checks and balances made Rome's government very complicated. Sometimes quarrels arose when officials had different ideas or opinions. When officials worked together, however, Rome's government was strong and efficient, as one Roman historian noted:

> "In unison [together] they are a match for any and all emergencies, the result being that it is impossible to find a constitution that is better constructed. For whenever some common external danger should come upon them and should compel [force] them to band together in counsel [thought] and in action, the power of their state becomes so great that nothing that is required is neglected [ignored]."
>
> –Polybius, from *The Constitution of the Roman Republic*

READING CHECK **Finding Main Ideas** What were the three parts of the Roman government?

Written Laws Keep Order

Rome's officials were responsible for making the city's laws and making sure that people followed them. At first these laws weren't written down. The only people who knew all the laws were the patricians who had made them.

Many people were unhappy with this situation. They did not want to be punished for breaking laws they didn't even know existed. As a result, they began to call for Rome's laws to be written down and made accessible to everybody.

Rome's first written law code was produced in 450 BC on 12 bronze tables, or tablets. These tables were displayed in the **Forum**, Rome's public meeting place. Because of how it was displayed, this code was called the Law of the Twelve Tables.

Over time, Rome's leaders passed many new laws. Throughout their history, though the Romans looked to the Law of the Twelve Tables as a symbol of Roman law and of their rights as Roman citizens.

READING CHECK **Drawing Inferences** Why did many people want a written law code?

Primary Source

HISTORIC DOCUMENT

Law of the Twelve Tables

The Law of the Twelve Tables governed many parts of Roman life. Some laws were written to protect the rights of all Romans. Others only protected the patricians. The laws listed here should give you an idea of the kinds of laws the tables included.

A Roman who did not appear before a government official when called or did not pay his debts could be arrested.

[from Table I] If anyone summons a man before the magistrate, he must go. If the man summoned does not go, let the one summoning him call the bystanders to witness and then take him by force.

[from Table III] One who has confessed a debt, or against whom judgment has been pronounced, shall have thirty days to pay it. After that forcible seizure of his person is allowed . . . unless he pays the amount of the judgment.

Women—even as adults—were legally considered to be children.

[from Table V] Females should remain in guardianship even when they have attained their majority.

No one in Rome could be executed without a trial.

[from Table IX] Putting to death of any man, whosoever he might be, unconvicted is forbidden.

–Law of the Twelve Tables, translated in *The Library of Original Sources* edited by Oliver J. Thatcher

ANALYSIS SKILL ANALYZING PRIMARY SOURCES

How are these laws similar to and different from our laws today?

Direct Teach

Main Idea

❷ Written Laws Keep Order

Written laws helped keep order in Rome.

Identify How were the first Roman laws written down? *They were carved into 12 bronze tablets.*

Explain Why did the Romans display the Law of the Twelve Tables in a public place? *so they would be accessible to everyone*

Make Inferences Despite the laws' changing over time, how did the Law of the Twelve Tables remain important? *It continued to be a symbol of how Roman society was governed by laws.*

Primary Source

Reading Like a Historian

Law of the Twelve Tables Help students practice reading the document like historians. Ask:

- In which of the quoted Tables does the government show mercy toward persons accused of crimes?
- How do the Tables emphasize that social status should play no role in whether or not someone is executed without a trial?

Critical Thinking: Comparing and Contrasting

At Level

Connecting with Past Learnings

Prep Required

1. Locate, print, and duplicate copies of the complete Code of Hammurabi and the Law of the Twelve Tables. Both documents are readily available from online sources.
2. Organize the class into pairs. Give a copy of each document to each pair. While one member of a pair skims the Code, the other should skim the Twelve Tables.
3. Ask each pair to discuss the documents, compare and contrast them, and make a list of ways in which the documents are similar and different.
4. Lead a class discussion based on pairs' findings. **LS Interpersonal**

Alternative Assessment Handbook, Rubric 9: Comparing and Contrasting

Answers

Analyzing Primary Sources *possible answers—similar to: if summoned, a person has to go to court; a person cannot be executed without a trial; different from: now persons cannot be jailed for debt, women have more rights*

Reading Check (left) *magistrates, Senate, assemblies and tribunes*

Reading Check (right) *They did not want to be accused of breaking laws they didn't know existed.*

Direct Teach

Main Idea

3 The Roman Forum

The Roman Forum was the heart of Roman society.

Recall Where was the Law of the Twelve Tables kept? *the Forum*

Identify What kind of buildings were in the Forum, and what else drew people there? *important government buildings and temples; shops, fights, public ceremonies*

Predict How do you think an Italian farmer who had never before been to the city of Rome would feel when he first stepped into the Roman Forum? *possible answers—impressed, proud that he was part of so grand a republic*

Linking to Today

The Basilica Aemilia The building shown to the right of the Senate House, the Basilica Aemilia, was a gathering place for moneylenders and moneychangers. Built in 179 BC, the building was larger than a football field. Today, visitors to the site can still see small round greenish spots on the ruin's pavement stones. These spots may be all that is left of copper coins that melted when fire destroyed the basilica in AD 410. Ask students why the Forum was a good place for moneychangers to do business. *possible answers—because people gathered there from all over the republic, and they may have had different kinds of money*

History Close-up

The Roman Forum

The Forum was the center of life in ancient Rome. The city's most important temples and government buildings were located there, and Romans met there to talk about the issues of the day. The word *forum* means "public place."

HISTORY
The Glory of Rome's Forum
hmhsocialstudies.com
The Temple of Jupiter stood atop the Capitoline Hill, overlooking the Forum.
Important government records were stored in the Tabularium.
Roman citizens often wore togas, loose-fitting garments wrapped around the body. Togas were symbols of Roman citizenship.
Public officials often addressed people from this platform.

ANALYSIS SKILL **ANALYZING VISUALS**

What can you see in this illustration that indicates the Forum was an important place?

The Roman Forum

The Roman Forum, the place where the Law of the Twelve Tables was kept, was the heart of the city of Rome. It was the site of important government buildings and temples. Government and religion were only part of what made the Forum so important, though. It was also a popular meeting place for Roman citizens. People met there to shop, chat, and gossip.

Collaborative Learning

Below Level

Roman Forum Video Game

Standard English Mastery

1. Organize the class into small groups. Ask students to imagine that they work for a video game company that wants to create a new game called *Roman Forum.*
2. Have students work together to plan some characters and events for their game. For example, they may include government officials and shopkeepers, amazing spectacles, and fiery speeches.
3. Then have students use standard English to write five sentences describing the game's characters and events. Each sentence should have at least 10 words.
4. Call on a volunteer from each group to read the group's sentences. As a class, discuss any necessary corrections to the sentences to align them with standard English usage.

LS Interpersonal, Verbal/Linguistic

Answers

Analyzing Visuals *possible answers—The buildings are large and impressive, and the square is well maintained; the square is full of citizens.*

The Forum lay in the center of Rome, between two major hills. On one side was the Palatine (PA-luh-tyn) Hill, where Rome's richest people lived. Across the forum was the Capitoline (KA-pet-uhl-yn) Hill, where Rome's grandest temples stood. Because of this location, city leaders could often be found in or near the forum, mingling with the common people. These leaders used the Forum as a speaking area, delivering speeches to the crowds.

But the Forum also had attractions for people not interested in speeches. Various shops lined the open square, and fights between gladiators were sometimes held there. Public ceremonies were commonly held in the Forum as well. As a result, the forum was usually packed with people.

READING CHECK **Generalizing** How was the Forum the heart of Roman society?

SUMMARY AND PREVIEW In this section you read about the basic structure of Roman government. In the next section you'll see how that government changed as Rome's territory grew and its influence expanded.

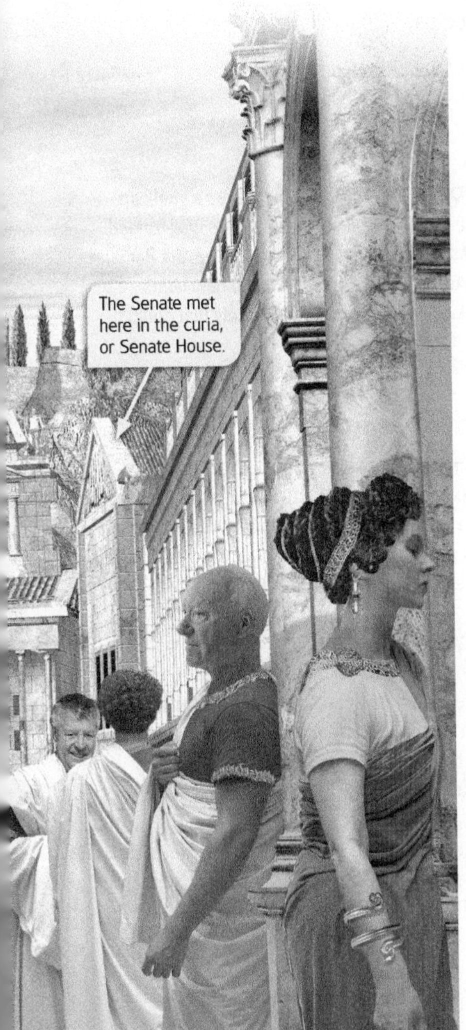

The Senate met here in the curia, or Senate House.

Section 2 Assessment

hmhsocialstudies.com ONLINE QUIZ

Reviewing Ideas, Terms, and People

1. a. **Identify** Who were the **consuls**?
   b. **Explain** Why did the Romans create a system of **checks and balances**?
   c. **Elaborate** How do you think the **Roman Senate** gained power?
2. a. **Recall** What was Rome's first written law code called?
   b. **Draw Conclusions** Why did Romans want their laws written down?
3. a. **Describe** What kinds of activities took place in the Roman **Forum**?

Critical Thinking

4. **Analyzing** Review your notes on Roman government. Use this diagram to note information about the powers of the parts of Rome's government.

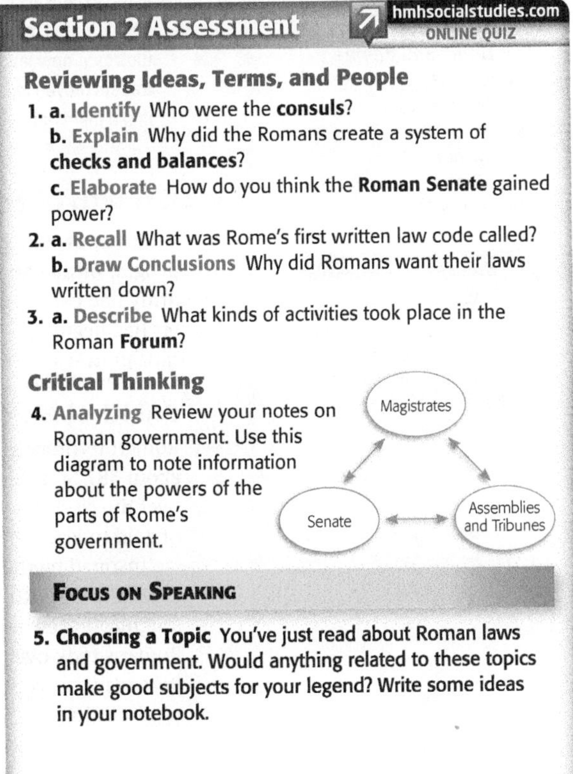

Focus on Speaking

5. **Choosing a Topic** You've just read about Roman laws and government. Would anything related to these topics make good subjects for your legend? Write some ideas in your notebook.

Direct Teach

Linking to Today

The Roman Forum Over time, 50 feet of debris accumulated on the site of the Roman Forum. People built new buildings on top of the rubble. Since the late 1800s, that debris has been cleared to the level that was ground level during the time of Julius Caesar. Despite the fact that all of the ancient buildings are in ruins, the Forum is a very impressive and popular tourist destination.

Review & Assess

Close

Ask students if they think they would approve of the government of the Roman Republic if they lived in it.

Review

Online Quiz, Section 2

Assess

SE Section 2 Assessment
PASS: Section 2 Quiz
Alternative Assessment Handbook

Reteach/Classroom Intervention

Guided Reading Workbook, Section 2
Interactive Skills Tutor CD-ROM

Section 2 Assessment Answers

1. a. two leaders elected to run the city of Rome
   b. to prevent any one person from gaining too much power
   c. Possible answer—They controlled Rome's finances, which gave them power over magistrates who needed money to do their jobs.
2. a. Law of the Twelve Tables
   b. so people wouldn't be accused of breaking laws they didn't know existed
3. religious ceremonies, speeches, social gatherings, shopping, gladiatorial combat
4. Magistrates: elected officials who were judges, managed finances or organized games and festivals; Senate: advised city leaders and later took control of the city finances; Assemblies and Tribunes: assemblies—patricians and plebeians who elected city leaders; tribunes—elected officials who could veto actions of other government officials
5. Ideas should include details about how rulers came into power.

Answers

Reading Check *It was the location of important government buildings and temples. It was also a popular meeting place for citizens.*

Preteach

Bellringer

If YOU were there . . . Use the **Daily Bellringer Transparency** to help students answer the question.

Daily Bellringer Transparency, Section 3

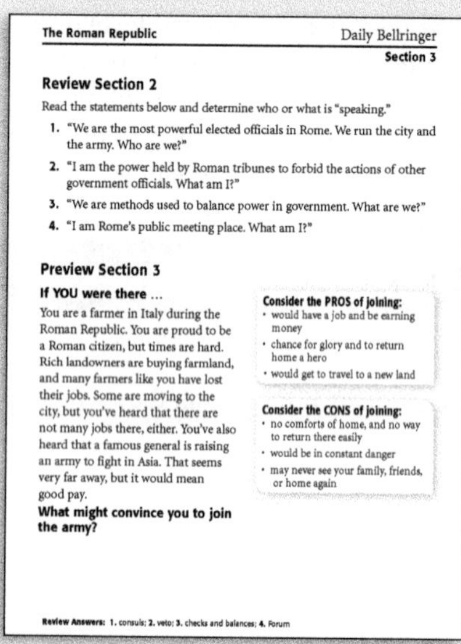

The Roman Republic Daily Bellringer **Section 3**

Review Section 2

Read the statements below and determine who or what is "speaking."

1. "We are the most powerful elected officials in Rome. We run the city and the army. Who are we?"
2. "I am the power held by Roman tribunes to forbid the actions of other government officials. What am I?"
3. "We are methods used to balance power in government. What are we?"
4. "I am Rome's public meeting place. What am I?"

Preview Section 3

If YOU were there ...

You are a farmer in Italy during the Roman Republic. You are proud to be a Roman citizen, but times are hard. Rich landowners are buying farmland, and many farmers like you have lost their jobs. Some are moving to the city, but you've heard that there are not many jobs there, either. You've also heard that a famous general is raising an army to fight in Asia. That seems very far away, but it would mean good pay.

What might convince you to join the army?

Consider the PROS of joining:
- would have a job and be earning money
- chance for glory and to return home a hero
- would get to travel to a new land

Consider the CONS of joining:
- no comforts of home, and no way to return there easily
- would be in constant danger
- may never see your family, friends, or home again

Review Answers: **1.** consuls; **2.** veto; **3.** checks and balances; **4.** Forum

Academic Vocabulary

Review with students the high-use academic term in this section.

purpose: the reason something is done (p. 312)

 **CRF:** Vocabulary Builder Activity, Section 3

Taking Notes

Have students use the graphic organizer online to take notes on the section. This activity will prepare students for the Section Assessment, in which they will complete a graphic organizer that builds on the information using the Critical Thinking Skill: Summarizing.

SECTION 3

The Late Republic

What You Will Learn...

Main Ideas

1. The late republic period saw the growth of territory and trade.
2. Through wars, Rome grew beyond Italy.
3. Several crises struck the republic in its later years.

The Big Idea

The later period of the Roman Republic was marked by wars of expansion and political crises.

Key Terms and People

legions, *p. 309*
Punic Wars, *p. 309*
Hannibal, *p. 310*
Gaius Marius, *p. 312*
Lucius Cornelius Sulla, *p. 313*
Spartacus, *p. 313*

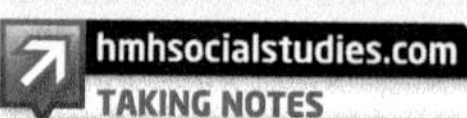

Use the graphic organizer online to take notes on Rome's expansion and on crises in the later years of the Republic.

If YOU were there...

You are a farmer in Italy during the Roman Republic. You are proud to be a Roman citizen, but times are hard. Rich landowners are buying farmland, and many farmers like you have lost their jobs. Some are moving to the city, but you've heard that there are not many jobs there, either. You've also heard that a famous general is raising an army to fight in Asia. That seems very far away, but it would mean good pay.

What might convince you to join the army?

BUILDING BACKGROUND The Roman army played a vital part in the expansion of the republic. Roman soldiers were well trained and defeated many of the city's enemies. As they did so, the Romans took over new lands. As the army conquered these new lands, traders moved in, seeking new products and markets that could make them rich.

Growth of Territory and Trade

After about 400 BC the Roman Republic grew quickly, both geographically and economically. Within 200 years the Roman army had conquered nearly all of Italy. Meanwhile Roman traders had begun to ship goods back and forth around the Mediterranean in search of new products and wealth.

Growth of Territory

Roman territory grew mainly in response to outside threats. In about 387 BC a people called the Gauls attacked Rome and took over the city. The Romans had to give the Gauls a huge amount of gold to leave the city.

Inspired by the Gauls' victory, many of Rome's neighboring cities also decided to attack. With some difficulty, the Romans fought off these attacks. As Rome's attackers were defeated, the Romans took over their lands. As you can see on the map, the Romans soon controlled all of the Italian Peninsula except far northern Italy.

Teach the Big Idea

At Level

The Late Republic

1. **Teach** Ask students the questions in the Main Idea boxes to teach this section.
2. **Apply** Have students study the sequencing of this section's events by creating a flowchart that traces the growth of and changes within the late republic. Flowcharts should consist of boxes connected by arrows. The first box should be labeled *Gauls attack Rome.* From there, have students trace the events as the republic faced various crises. **LS Visual/Spatial**
3. **Review** As you review the section's main ideas, have students fill in their flowcharts.
4. **Practice/Homework** Have students add relevant facts to the boxes. **LS Visual/Spatial**

Alternative Assessment Handbook, Rubric 7: Charts

One reason for the Roman success was the organization of the army. Soldiers were organized in **legions** (LEE-juhnz), or groups of up to 6,000 soldiers. Each legion was divided into centuries, or groups of 100 soldiers. This organization allowed the army to be very flexible. It could fight as a large group or as several small ones. This flexibility allowed the Romans to defeat most enemies.

Farming and Trade

Before Rome conquered Italy, most Romans were farmers. As the republic grew, many people left their farms for Rome. In place of these small farms, wealthy Romans built large farms in the countryside. These farms were worked by slaves who grew one or two crops. The owners of the farms didn't usually live on them. Instead, they stayed in Rome or other cities and let others run the farms for them.

Roman trade also expanded as the republic grew. Rome's farmers couldn't grow enough food to support the city's increasing population, so merchants brought food from other parts of the Mediterranean. These merchants also brought metal goods and slaves to Rome. To pay for these goods, the Romans made coins out of copper, silver, and other metals. Roman coins began to appear in markets all around the Mediterranean.

READING CHECK **Identifying Cause and Effect** Why did the Romans conquer their neighbors?

Rome Grows Beyond Italy

As Rome's power grew other countries came to see the Romans as a threat to their own power and declared war on them. In the end the Romans defeated their opponents, and Rome gained territory throughout the Mediterranean.

The Roman Republic, 509–270 BC

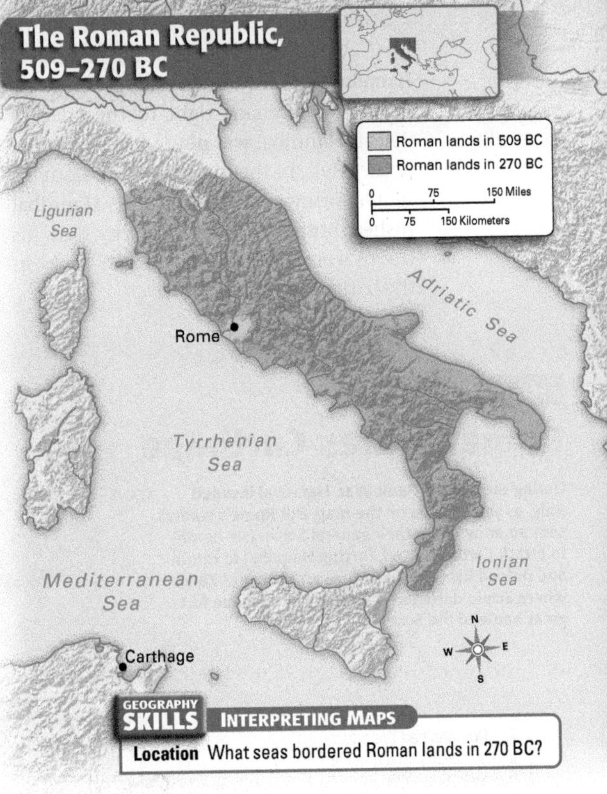

GEOGRAPHY SKILLS **INTERPRETING MAPS**

Location What seas bordered Roman lands in 270 BC?

The Punic Wars

The fiercest of the wars Rome fought were the **Punic** (PYOO-nik) **Wars**, a series of wars against Carthage, a city in northern Africa. The word *Punic* means "Phoenician" in Latin. As you learned earlier in this book, the Phoenicians were an ancient civilization that had built the city of Carthage.

Rome and Carthage went to war three times between 264 and 146 BC. The wars began when Carthage sent its armies to Sicily, an island just southwest of Italy. In response, the Romans also sent an army to the island. Before long, war broke out between them. After almost 20 years of fighting, the Romans forced their enemies out and took control of Sicily.

Direct Teach

Main Idea

1 Growth of Territory and Trade

The late republic period saw the growth of territory and trade.

Identify In the Roman army what was a legion? a century? *a group of 6,000 soldiers; a group of 100 soldiers*

Explain What happened to the tradition of the small farm in Italy? *Many farmers went to Rome, leaving their land to be bought by wealthy Romans who created large farms worked by slaves.*

Draw Conclusions How did the growth of the city of Rome affect trade? *Rome had grown so much that local farmers couldn't grow enough food to support the city. Merchants brought in food from other parts of the Mediterranean, along with metal goods and slaves.*

CRF: Economics and History: Rome and Money

Map Transparency: The Roman Republic, 509–270 BC

Did you know . . .

Roman coins display various images and words, such as the word *Roma,* the Latin spelling of Rome. Some coins commemorate a victory in battle. These coins were called *victoriates.* When economic times were bad, the crisis was reflected in the coins. Coins made then would contain less of the precious metal. As a result, these coins weighed less than those made during prosperous periods.

Differentiating Instruction

English-Language Learners **Below Level**

1. Have students design a coin for the late Roman Republic. Coins may commemorate a trend, such as the expansion of trade, or a person.
2. Coins that commemorate a person should bear a drawing to represent that person on one side of the coin. Students should use other images of Romans in this chapter for guidance. Then for the other side, students should draw something that celebrates that person, such as a victory in battle or a noble cause for which the person fought.
3. Ask for volunteers to explain their designs to the class.
4. Display the coin designs around the classroom. **LS Visual/Spatial**

Alternative Assessment Handbook, Rubric 3: Artwork

Answers

Interpreting Maps *Adriatic Sea, Ionian Sea, Tyrrhenian Sea, Ligurian Sea*

Reading Check *because many of their neighbors had been attacking them*

Direct Teach

Main Idea

❷ Rome Grows Beyond Italy

Through wars, Rome grew beyond Italy.

Identify Who did Rome fight in the Punic Wars? *Carthage*

Recall Who was the Carthaginian general who almost defeated Rome? *Hannibal*

Predict How might history have turned out differently if a bad storm at sea had delayed the Romans' crossing to northern Africa? *possible answer—Hannibal might have had time to capture Rome itself, ending the Roman Republic and eliminating Roman power in the region.*

Activity **Letters from Spies**

Have students write excerpts from mock correspondence between Roman or Carthaginian spies and the generals to whom they reported about the progress of the Punic Wars.

CRF: Biography Activity: Scipio

CRF: History and Geography Activity: The Punic Wars

Info to Know

Battle of Zama Scipio had about the same number of troops as Hannibal, but his cavalry was stronger. Despite Hannibal's well-organized defense outside of Carthage, Scipio's troops crushed Hannibal's army. About 20,000 of the Carthaginian soldiers were killed. The city of Carthage quickly accepted Scipio's terms for surrender.

In 218 BC Carthage tried to attack Rome itself. An army led by the brilliant general **Hannibal** set out for Rome. Although he forced the Romans right to the edge of defeat, Hannibal was never able to capture Rome itself. In the meantime, the Romans sent an army to attack Carthage. Hannibal rushed home to defend his city, but his troops were defeated at Zama (ZAY-muh) in the battle illustrated below.

By the 140s BC many senators had grown alarmed that Carthage was growing powerful again. They convinced Rome's consuls to declare war on Carthage, and once again the Romans sent an army to Africa and destroyed Carthage. After this victory, the Romans burned the city, killed most of its people, and sold the rest of the people into slavery. They also took control of northern Africa.

History Close-up

Rome Battles Carthage

During the Second Punic War, Hannibal invaded Italy, as you can see on the map. But Rome's leaders sent an army under their general Scipio (SIP-ee-oh) to attack Carthage itself, forcing Hannibal to return and defend his city. The two generals met at Zama, where Scipio defeated Hannibal's army in the last great battle of the Second Punic War.

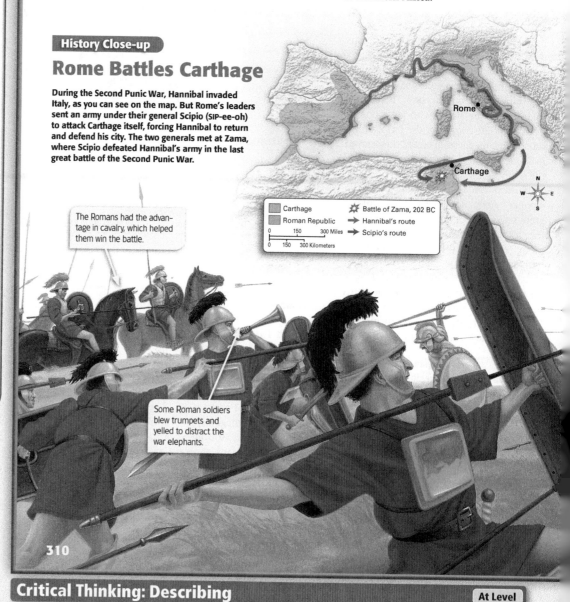

Scipio's route

The Romans had the advantage in cavalry, which helped them win the battle.

Critical Thinking: Describing

At Level

Making News

1. Tell students that a newsreel was a short film that discussed current events. Tell them that newsreels were often shown before movies in the 1930s and 1940s, often to give news about events that led up to World War II and about the war itself.
2. Have students write the text for a newsreel announcing the defeat of Hannibal at the Battle of Zama. Tell students newsreels were often sensational and dramatic, and they should include similar language.
3. Ask volunteers to read the texts aloud, using dramatic voices. **LS Verbal/Linguistic**

Alternative Assessment Handbook, Rubric 42: Writing to Inform

Later Expansion

During the Punic Wars, Rome took control of Sicily, Corsica, Spain, and North Africa. As a result, Rome controlled most of the western Mediterranean region.

In the years that followed, Roman legions marched north and east as well. In the 120s Rome conquered the southern part of Gaul. By that time, Rome had also conquered Greece and parts of Asia.

Although the Romans took over Greece, they were greatly changed by the experience. We would normally expect the victor to change the conquered country. Instead, the Romans adopted ideas about literature, art, philosophy, religion, and education from the Greeks.

READING CHECK **Summarizing** How did the Romans gain territory?

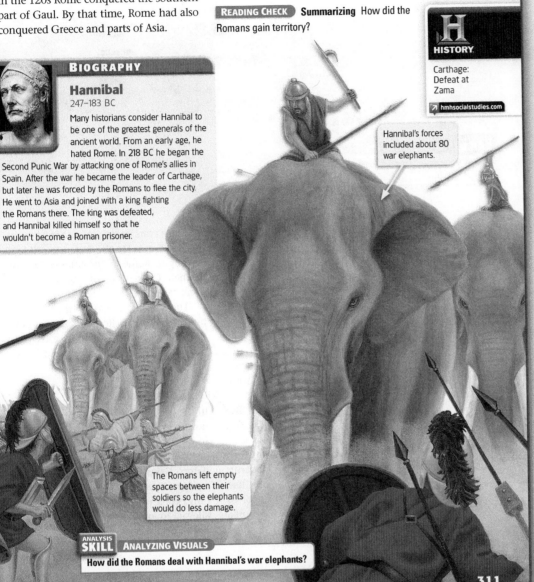

HISTORY. Carthage: Defeat at Zama

hmhsocialstudies.com

BIOGRAPHY

Hannibal

247–183 BC

Many historians consider Hannibal to be one of the greatest generals of the ancient world. From an early age, he hated Rome. In 218 BC he began the Second Punic War by attacking one of Rome's allies in Spain. After the war he became the leader of Carthage, but later he was forced by the Romans to flee the city. He went to Asia and joined with a king fighting the Romans there. The king was defeated, and Hannibal killed himself so that he wouldn't become a Roman prisoner.

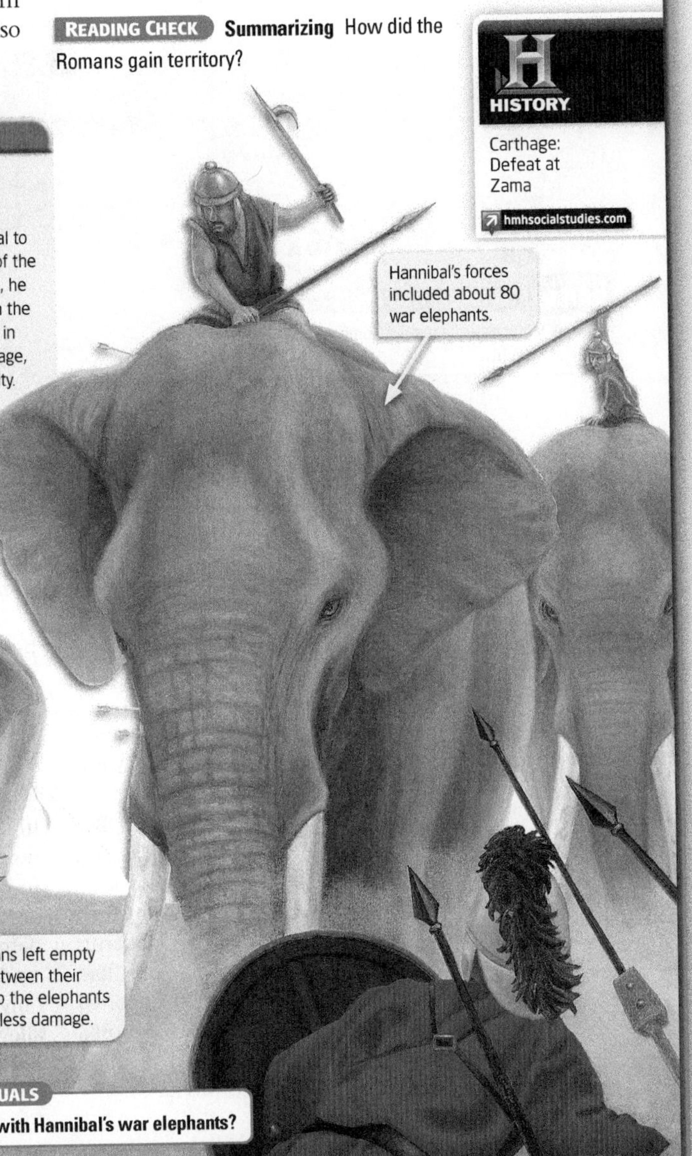

Hannibal's forces included about 80 war elephants.
The Romans left empty spaces between their soldiers so the elephants would do less damage.

ANALYSIS SKILL **ANALYZING VISUALS**

How did the Romans deal with Hannibal's war elephants?

311

Direct Teach

Did you know . . .

While fighting in Italy, Hannibal found his route blocked by a Roman army. To get past the Romans, Hannibal used a clever tactic. He sent a very odd force out under cover of night—2,000 oxen with lighted torches tied to their horns. The Romans thought they were under attack and moved from their position, clearing the way for Hannibal to march through.

Activity **Hannibal's Journal** Have students imagine they are Hannibal at the time he is about to defeat Rome. Ask them to imagine how he felt when he heard the Romans were attacking Carthage. Instruct students to write a journal entry in the voice of Hannibal expressing his feelings about events that led up to the Battle of Zama. Ask for volunteers to read their entries aloud. **LS Verbal/Linguistic**

Collaborative Learning

At Level

Mapping the Elephants' March

Research Required

Background Hannibal attempted an amazing feat by leading his army, including more than 30 elephants, overland from Spain to Italy. However, all but one of the elephants died along the way.

1. Organize students into small groups to conduct research on Hannibal's trip.
2. Direct students to library or Internet resources where they can find maps of Hannibal's route through Spain and France, through the Alps, and into Italy.
3. Have each group create a map of the Mediterranean that shows Hannibal's route.
4. Tell students to add location names and illustrations to the map. **LS Interpersonal, Visual/Spatial**

Alternative Assessment Handbook, Rubrics 14: Group Activity; and 20: Map Creation

Answers

Analyzing Visuals *spread out so they would suffer fewer loses; blew trumpets and yelled to distract elephants*

Reading Check *They took control of areas during the Punic Wars. From there, they spread north and east, conquering Gaul, Greece, and parts of Asia.*

Direct Teach

Main Idea

❸ Crises Strike the Republic

Several crises struck the republic in its later years.

Describe How did Tiberius and Gaius Gracchus try to help poor Romans? *They tried to create farms for poor Romans and to sell food cheaply to poor citizens.*

Explain Why was violence more common after the Gracchus brothers than before? *People saw that violence could be used as a political weapon.*

Find the Main Idea Why might it be a problem if a nation's army is more loyal to leaders than to the government? *The army could become a political tool, and individuals could take control of the government if they had the army on their side.*

CRF: Biography Activity: Cornelia

Map Transparency: The Roman Republic, 270–100 BC

Biography

Gaius Gracchus (153–121 BC) In today's political language, Gaius Gracchus would be called a grassroots reformer. He tried to harness the many votes of poor citizens in passing his reforms. These agricultural reforms were similar to the ones for which his brother had been killed. Unfortunately for Gaius, his actions were also unpopular with many senators. He never saw his reforms put into place.

Answers

Interpreting Maps *most of Spain, southern Gaul, northern Italy, islands in the Mediterranean (including Sicily, Corsica, and Sardinia), part of northern Africa, Greece, Macedonia, and Asia Minor*

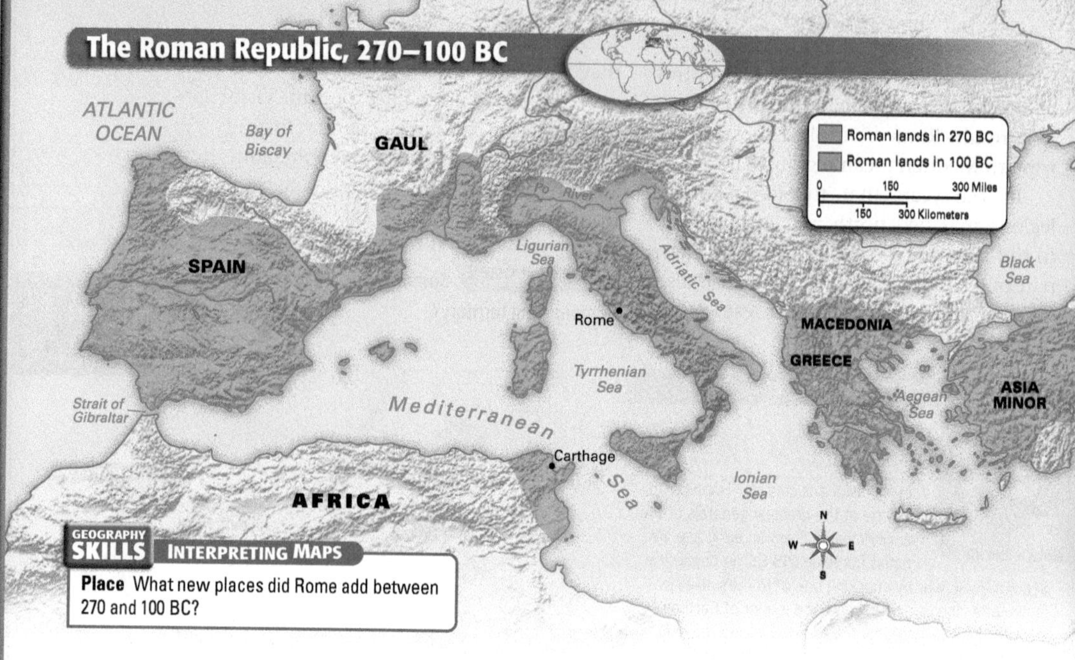

GEOGRAPHY SKILLS INTERPRETING MAPS

Place What new places did Rome add between 270 and 100 BC?

Crises Strike the Republic

As the Romans' territory grew, problems arose in the republic. Rich citizens were getting richer, and many leaders feared that violence would erupt between rich and poor.

Tiberius and Gaius Gracchus

Among the first leaders to address Rome's problems were brothers named Tiberius (ty-BIR-ee-uhs) and Gaius Gracchus (GY-uhs GRAK-uhs). Both served as tribunes.

Tiberius, who took office in 133 BC, wanted to create farms for poor Romans. The **purpose** of these farms was to keep the poor citizens happy and prevent rebellions. Tiberius wanted to create his farms on public land that wealthy citizens had illegally taken over. The public supported this idea, but the wealthy citizens opposed it. Conflict over the idea led to riots in the city, during which Tiberius was killed.

ACADEMIC VOCABULARY
purpose the reason something is done

A few years later Gaius also tried to create new farms. He also began to sell food cheaply to Rome's poor citizens. Like his brother, Gaius angered many powerful Romans and was killed for his ideas.

The violent deaths of the Gracchus brothers changed Roman politics. From that time on people saw violence as a political weapon. They often attacked leaders with whom they disagreed.

Marius and Sulla

In the late 100s BC another social change nearly led to the end of the republic. In 107 BC the Roman army desperately needed more troops. In response, a consul named **Gaius Marius** (MER-ee-uhs) encouraged poor people to join the army. Before, only people who owned property had been allowed to join. As a result of this change, thousands of poor and unemployed citizens joined Rome's army.

Cross-Discipline Activity: Arts and the Humanities

Below Level

Honoring Heroes

1. Have each student design a memorial honoring the Gracchus brothers. Tell students that memorials can take many forms, such as walls, buildings, plaques, or statues.
2. Remind students to remember the causes for which the Gracchus brothers fought, including help for the poor and agricultural reform. The memorials should reflect these causes.
3. Have students sketch their designs from two different angles.
4. Call on volunteers to discuss their designs. Display memorial designs in the classroom.

LS Intrapersonal, Visual/Spatial

Alternative Assessment Handbook, Rubric 3: Artwork

Because Marius was a good general, his troops were more loyal to him than they were to Rome. The army's support gave Marius great political power. Following his example, other ambitious politicians also sought their armies' support.

One such politician, **Lucius Cornelius Sulla** (LOO-shuhs kawr-NEEL-yuhs SUHL-uh), became consul in 88 BC. Sulla soon came into conflict with Marius, a conflict that led to a civil war in Rome. A civil war is a war between citizens of the same country. In the end Sulla defeated Marius. He later named himself dictator and used his power to punish his enemies.

BIOGRAPHY

Lucius Cornelius Sulla

138–78 BC

Although the two eventually became enemies, Sulla learned much of what he knew about military affairs from Gaius Marius. He had been an assistant to Marius before he became consul. Sulla changed Rome's government forever when he became dictator, but he actually had many traditional ideas. For example, he believed the Senate should be the main ruling group in Rome, and he increased its power during his rule.

Analyzing Information Do you think Sulla was a traditional Roman leader? Why or why not?

Spartacus

Not long after Sulla died, another crisis arose to challenge Rome's leaders. Thousands of slaves led by a former gladiator, **Spartacus** (SPAHR-tuh-kuhs), rose up and demanded freedom.

Spartacus and his followers defeated an army sent to stop them and took over much of southern Italy. Eventually, though, Spartacus was killed in battle. Without his leadership, the revolt fell apart. Victorious, the Romans executed 6,000 rebellious slaves as an example to others who thought about rebelling. The rebellion was over, but the republic's problems were not.

READING CHECK **Predicting** How do you think Marius and Sulla influenced later leaders?

SUMMARY AND PREVIEW You have read about crises that arose in the late Roman Republic. These crises eventually led to changes in Roman society, as you will see in the next chapter.

Section 3 Assessment

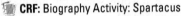

hmhsocialstudies.com ONLINE QUIZ

Reviewing Ideas, Terms, and People

1. a. **Define** What was a Roman **legion**?
   b. **Explain** Why did the Romans decide to conquer all of Italy?
   c. **Elaborate** How did the growth of territory help increase Roman trade?
2. a. **Recall** Who fought in the **Punic Wars**?
   b. **Summarize** What led to the beginning of the Punic Wars?
   c. **Elaborate** Why do you think the Romans borrowed many ideas from Greek culture?
3. a. **Identify** Who was **Spartacus**?
   b. **Explain** How did the deaths of the Gracchus brothers change Roman politics?

Critical Thinking

4. **Summarizing** Draw a diagram like the one here. Use your notes on crises Rome faced to list three crises during the later period of the republic. Then list two facts about each crisis.

FOCUS ON SPEAKING

5. **Selecting Characters** In this section you learned about many major figures in Roman history. Choose one of them to be the subject of your legend. Now look back at your notes. How will you make the subject of your legend interesting for your listeners?

Direct Teach

Main Idea

3 Crises Strike the Republic

Several crises struck the republic in its later years.

Analyze How did Sulla turn what he had learned from Marius against him? *possible answer—used his army's loyalty in a civil war against Marius*

Evaluate Why may some Romans have considered Spartacus a hero, while others considered him an enemy of Rome? *Romans' reactions would vary, depending on their own wealth, poverty, freedom, or lack of freedom.*

CRF: Biography Activity: Spartacus

CRF: Primary Source: *The Story of Spartacus,* by Plutarch

Review & Assess

Close

Have students list the steps that led to a more violent Roman Republic.

Review

Online Quiz, Section 3

Assess

SE Section 3 Assessment

PASS: Section 3 Quiz

Alternative Assessment Handbook

Reteach/Classroom Intervention

Guided Reading Workbook, Section 3

Interactive Skills Tutor CD-ROM

Section 3 Assessment Answers

1. a. a group of up to 6,000 soldiers
   b. because other groups continually attacked them
   c. Because local farmers couldn't grow enough food to support the city of Rome, merchants brought in food from elsewhere, along with metals and slaves.
2. a. Rome and Carthage
   b. Carthage sent armies into Sicily.
   c. possible answer—They admired Greek culture.
3. a. a former gladiator who led a slave revolt
   b. After their deaths, people began to see violence as a political tool.
4. possible answers—Crises: Punic Wars, conflicts between the Gracchus brothers and powerful Romans, change in the army under Marius, civil war between Marius and Sulla, slave revolt under Spartacus; Supporting facts will vary but should be consistent with text.
5. possible answers—descriptive words, detailed battle scenes, colorful setting

Answers

Analyzing Information *possible answers—yes, because he maintained the role of the Senate; no, because he took control of the military himself and, at times, acted as a dictator*

Reading Check *They proved that the army could be used as a tool to take control of the republic.*

Social Studies Skills

Interpreting Culture Maps

Activity Culture Map Scavenger Hunt Have students go on a culture map scavenger hunt. Give students a set amount of time to find three examples of culture maps in their textbooks. Have students mark the pages of each map. Award the first student to find three maps a prize of some kind. Have the winning student identify the pages on which the maps are located. Then guide students in interpreting each of the three maps. Conclude by having each student write a few sentences describing in his or her own words what a culture map is.
LS Visual/Spatial

Alternative Assessment Handbook, Rubric 21: Map Reading

Interactive Skills Tutor CD-ROM, Lesson 6: Interpret Maps, Graphs, Charts, Visuals, and Political Cartoons

Social Studies Skills

Analysis | Critical Thinking | Economics | Study

Interpreting Culture Maps

Understand the Skill

A culture map is a special type of political map. As you know, physical maps show natural features, such as mountains and rivers. Political maps show the human features of an area, such as boundaries, cities, and roads. The human features shown on a culture map are cultural ones, such as the languages spoken or religions practiced in an area. Historians often use culture maps in their work. Therefore, being able to interpret them is important for understanding history.

Learn the Skill

Follow these guidelines to interpret a culture map.

1. Use map basics. Read the title to identify the subject. Note the labels, legend, and scale. Pay extra attention to special symbols for cultural features. Be sure you understand what these symbols represent.
2. Study the map as a whole. Note the location of the cultural symbols and features. Ask yourself how they relate to the rest of the map.
3. Connect the information on the map to any written information about the subject in the text.

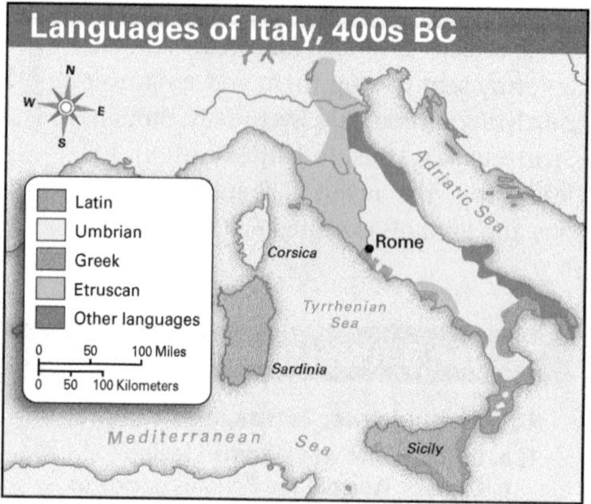

Practice and Apply the Skill

Apply the guidelines to the map on this page and answer the following questions.

1. What makes this map a culture map?
2. What language was most widely spoken on the Italian Peninsula? What other language was widely spoken?
3. Where was Greek spoken? Why did the people there talk in Greek?
4. What language did the Romans speak?

Social Studies Skills Activity: Interpreting Culture Maps

At Level

Comparing and Contrasting Maps

Display the map transparencies "Italy: Physical" and "Italy, 500 BC." Both maps are in Section 1 of this chapter. Have students compare and contrast the two maps. Then ask the following questions:

- How are the two maps similar? *They both show the region of the Italian Peninsula.*
- How are the two maps different? *One is a physical map showing elevations; one is a political map showing culture regions.*
- Based on the maps, how did the topography of Italy affect settlement there? *The culture map shows less settlement in the highly mountainous regions, such as the Apennines.*
- What groups lived on the Italian Peninsula in 500 BC? *Etruscans, Greeks, Romans*

LS Visual/Spatial

Alternative Assessment Handbook, Rubric 21: Map Reading

Map Transparencies: Italy: Physical; Italy, 500 BC

Answers

Practice and Apply the Skill
1. *It shows where different languages were spoken in Italy in the 400s BC.* **2.** *Umbrian, Etruscan;* **3.** *along parts of the coast on the Italian Peninsula; because the Greeks had founded colonies and traded there*

CHAPTER 10 Chapter Review

History's Impact
▶ **video series**
Review the video to answer the focus question:
What were some similarities between the Roman Republic and American democracy?

Visual Summary

Use the visual summary below to help you review the main ideas of the chapter.

QUICK FACTS

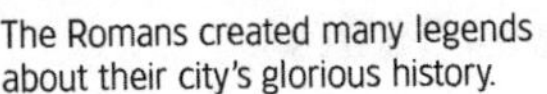

The Romans created many legends about their city's glorious history.

The early Romans set up a type of government called a republic.

The Roman Republic conquered lands in Italy and around the Mediterranean.

Reviewing Vocabulary, Terms, and People

Match each numbered definition with the correct lettered vocabulary term.

a. republic
b. plebeians
c. Spartacus
d. legions
e. Aeneas
f. consuls
g. Forum
h. dictator
i. veto
j. Roman Senate
k. patricians
l. primary

1. Rome's public meeting place
2. groups of about 6,000 soldiers
3. the legendary Trojan founder of Rome
4. main, most important
5. a government in which people elect leaders
6. a council that advised Rome's leaders
7. a leader with absolute power for six months
8. the common people of Rome
9. the two most powerful officials in Rome
10. leader of a slave rebellion
11. prohibit
12. noble, powerful Romans

Comprehension and Critical Thinking

SECTION 1 *(Pages 294–299)*

13. a. Describe What are two legends that describe Rome's founding? How are the two legends connected?

b. Compare and Contrast What roles did the plebeians and the patricians take in the early Roman government? In what other ways were the two groups different?

c. Predict How do you think Italy's geography and Rome's location would affect the spread of Rome's influence?

Answers

Visual Summary

Review and Inquiry Use the visual summary to review the chapter's main ideas. Call on students to provide as many key concepts related to the three images as they can.

Quick Facts Transparency: The Roman Republic Visual Summary

Reviewing Vocabulary, Terms, and People

1. g
2. d
3. e
4. l
5. a
6. j
7. h
8. b
9. f
10. c
11. i
12. k

Comprehension and Critical Thinking

13. a. the legend of Aeneas and his search for a home that ends in Italy; the legend of Romulus and Remus and their desire to build a city to mark the spot where a wolf had rescued and cared for them; Romulus and Remus believed to have been descendants of Aeneas

b. plebeians—couldn't take part in government; patricians—could be elected to office, so they held all political power; Plebeians were the majority and were common people;

Review & Assessment Resources

Review and Reinforce

SE Chapter Review
CRF: Chapter Review Activity
Quick Facts Transparency: The Roman Republic Visual Summary
Spanish Chapter Summaries Audio CD Program
Online Chapter Summaries in Six Languages
TOS Holt McDougal PuzzleView
Quiz Game CD-ROM

Assess

SE Standardized Test Practice
PASS: Chapter Test, Forms A and B
Alternative Assessment Handbook
TOS ExamView Assessment Suite, Chapter Test
Differentiated Instruction Modified Worksheets and Tests CD-ROM: Chapter Test
Online Assessment Program, in the Interactive Student Edition

Reteach/Intervene

Guided Reading Workbook
Differentiated Instruction Teacher Management System: Lesson Plans
Differentiated Instruction Modified Worksheets and Tests CD-ROM
Interactive Skills Tutor CD-ROM

Chapter Resources

Answers

Patricians were the minority, and were wealthy, powerful citizens.

c. possible answer—Italy had a mild climate, so people there could raise plenty of food. Its location in the middle of the Mediterranean would allow the people of Italy to spread control in all directions. Rome's inland location protected it somewhat from invasion by sea.

14. a. magistrates, the senate, assemblies and tribunes

b. Checks and balances keep one part of the government from being stronger than others; written laws protect people from being punished for breaking laws they did not know existed.

c. possible answers—shopping malls, courthouse squares, college campuses, recreation/activity centers, downtown plazas

15. a. Hannibal—invaded Italy, fought Rome; Sulla—started a conflict with Marius, which incited a civil war in Rome; Spartacus—incited a slave riot

b. occupations—fewer small farmers; economics—expanded trade; society—increased violence, civil war

c. Both were commercial powers in the central Mediterranean region, and both wanted to expand.

Reviewing Themes

16. to keep them from becoming too powerful

17. Italy was in the center of the Mediterranean, which meant that the Romans did not have to travel too far to face any opponents.

Using the Internet

18. Go to hmhsocialstudies.com to access a rubric for this activity.

Reading Skills

19. Outlines will vary, but the main heads should coincide with red heads in text.

Social Studies Skills

20. Etruscans

21. Greeks, because the areas they settled were far from Greece and on the coast; and Carthaginians, because areas they settled are across the sea from Carthage

22. Their territories lie next to each other.

Focus on Speaking

23. Rubric Students' legends should:

- include at least one major figure from Roman history.
- introduce characters, a setting, and an event in the first paragraph.
- tell about an event from history.
- include a conflict that is resolved in the final paragraph.

CRF: Focus on Writing: A Legend

SECTION 2 *(Pages 302–307)*

14. a. Describe What were the three parts of Rome's government?

b. Analyze How do checks and balances protect the rights of the people? How do written laws do the same thing?

c. Elaborate What are some places in modern society that serve purposes similar to those of the Roman Forum?

SECTION 3 *(Pages 308–313)*

15. a. Identify What difficulties did Hannibal, Lucius Cornelius Sulla, and Spartacus cause for Rome?

b. Analyze How did Roman occupations, economics, and society change during the Late Republic?

c. Evaluate Some historians say that Rome and Carthage were destined to fight each other. Why do you think they say this?

Reviewing Themes

16. Politics Why did Roman magistrates only hold office for one year?

17. Geography How do you think Rome's location helped the Romans in their quest to conquer the entire Mediterranean region?

Using the Internet

18. Activity: Explaining Roman Society A key reason the Roman Republic fell was because the Roman people gave up on it. The army, once Rome's protector, let itself be turned against the Roman people. The Senate gave up on debate and compromise when it turned to political violence. Use your online textbook to research the fall of the Roman Republic and create an exhibit for a local history museum. Make sure your exhibit contains information about key figures in the Roman military and government. Use words and pictures to explain the political, religious, and social structures that made Rome an empire and what caused its eventual downfall.

hmhsocialstudies.com

Reading Skills

19. Outlining and History Look back at the discussion "Crises Strike the Republic" in the last section of this chapter. Prepare an outline that will help clarify the people, events, and ideas of this discussion. Before you prepare your outline, decide what your major headings will be. Then choose the details that will appear below each heading. Remember that most outlines follow this basic format:

I. Main Idea
  A. Supporting Idea
  B. Supporting Idea
    1. Detail
    2. Detail
II. Main Idea
  A. Supporting Idea

Social Studies Skills

Interpreting Culture Maps *Look at the culture map on page 314. Then answer the following questions.*

20. What was the main language spoken in Italy during the 400s BC?

21. Which language do you think was spoken by the fewest people? Why do you think this?

Focus on Speaking

22. Presenting Your Legend Now that you've chosen the subject for your legend, it's time to write and present it. As you write your legend, focus on exciting details that will bring the subject to life in your listeners' minds. Once you've finished writing, share your legend with the class. Try to make your legend exciting as you present it. Remember to alter the tone and volume of your voice to convey the appropriate mood.

CHAPTER 10 Standardized Test Practice

DIRECTIONS: Read each question, and write the letter of the best response.

1 Use the map to answer the following question.

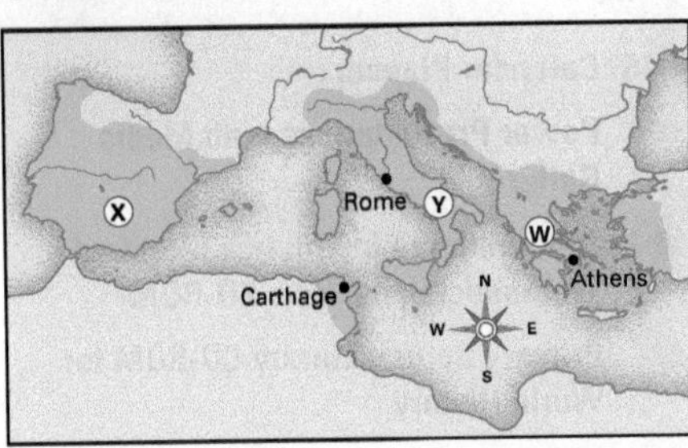

The order in which Rome expanded its control in the Mediterranean region is shown by which of the following sequences of letters?

A Y–W–X
B X–W–Y
C Y–X–W
D W–X–Y

2 Which was the *least* important reason for the growth of Rome's power and influence in the Mediterranean region?

A religion
B trade
C military organization
D wars and conquests

3 According to Roman legend, the city of Rome was founded by

A Latin peoples who moved to Italy from ancient Egypt.
B two men named Romulus and Remus who were raised by a wolf.
C the gods of Greece, who were looking for a new home.
D a Greek warrior named Achilles who had fled from the destruction of Troy.

4 Roman nobles were called

A patricians.
B plebeians.
C tribunes.
D magistrates.

5 Which of the following characteristics did *not* apply to Roman government?

A system of checks and balances
B sense of civic duty
C written code of laws
D equality of all people

Connecting with Past Learnings

6 You learned earlier in this course about other ancient peoples who, like the Romans, founded their civilizations along rivers. These peoples include all of the following *except* the

A Chinese.
B Egyptians.
C Sumerians.
D Hebrews.

7 Virgil's *Aeneid* is similar to what other piece of ancient literature that you've learned about in this course?

A the *Shiji*
B the *Book of the Dead*
C *The Odyssey*
D the *Bhagavad Gita*

Answers

Standardized Test Practice

1. C
Break Down the Question This question requires students to recall that Rome took control of Spain during the Punic Wars and then took over Greece.

2. A
Break Down the Question Remind students who miss the question that they have not yet studied Roman religion.

3. B
Break Down the Question Although each of the answers includes an element that is correct—for example, "who had fled from the destruction of Troy"—in only one answer are both parts of the phrase correct.

4. A
Break Down the Question This question requires students to recall factual information. Refer students who miss it to *Challenges within Rome* in Section 1.

5. D
Break Down the Question This question requires students to recall what the differences were between the classes in Roman society.

6. D
Break Down the Question This question requires students to recall information covered in previous chapters in this textbook.

7. C
Break Down the Question This question requires students to recall information in the chapters on the ancient Greeks in this textbook.

Intervention Resources

Reproducible

- Guided Reading Workbook
- Differentiated Instruction Teacher Management System: Lesson Plans

Technology

- Quick Facts Transparency: The Roman Republic Visual Summary
- Differentiated Instruction Modified Worksheets and Tests CD-ROM
- Interactive Skills Tutor CD-ROM

Tips for Test Taking

Rely on 50/50 Ask students if they have ever said "I have no clue" while taking a test. That is the time to make an educated guess. They should read every choice carefully. Give students these pointers:

- Watch out for distracters—choices that may be true, but are too broad, too narrow, or not relevant to the question.
- Eliminate the least likely choice. Eliminate the next, until you find the best one.
- If two choices seem equally correct, look to see if "All of the above" is an option.

Chapter 11 Planning Guide

Rome and Christianity

Overview	Instructional Resources	
CHAPTER 11 **Essential Question:** Why did the Roman Empire fall, and what is its legacy? **Focus on the Essential Question Podcast**	TOS **Differentiated Instruction Teacher Management System:** • Instructional Benchmarking Guides • Lesson Plans for Differentiated Instruction  **Guided Reading Workbook** **Chapter Resource File:** • Chapter Review Activity • Focus on Writing Activity: Note Cards for a Screenplay • Social Studies Skills Activity: Interpreting Time Lines	TOS **Calendar Planner** **Power Presentations with Media Gallery** **Differentiated Instruction Modified Worksheets and Tests CD-ROM** **Primary Source Library CD-ROM for World History** **Interactive Skills Tutor CD-ROM** **Student Edition on Audio CD Program** **Video:** The Rise of Roman Cities **Multimedia Connections:** Rome: Engineering an Empire
Section 1: **From Republic to Empire** **The Big Idea:** After changing from a republic to an empire, Rome grew politically and economically, and developed a culture that influenced later civilizations.	TOS **Differentiated Instruction Teacher Management System:** Section 1 Lesson Plan  **Guided Reading Workbook:** Section 1 **Chapter Resource File:** • Vocabulary Builder Activity, Section 1 • Biography Activities: Cicero, Marc Antony • Primary Source Activity: from *The Amores* by Ovid	**Daily Bellringer Transparency:** Section 1 **Map Transparency:** Expansion of Rome, 100 BC–AD 117 **Internet Activity:** Campaign Poster **Animated History:** Expansion of Rome **Animated History:** Roman Aqueducts **Video:** The Glory of the Colosseum **Video:** Ancient Rome: Mobile Security
Section 2: **The Roman Empire and Religion** **The Big Idea:** People in the Roman Empire practiced many religions before Christianity, based on the teachings of Jesus of Nazareth, spread and became Rome's official religion.	TOS **Differentiated Instruction Teacher Management System:** Section 2 Lesson Plan **Guided Reading Workbook:** Section 2  **Chapter Resource File:** • Vocabulary Builder Activity, Section 2 • Biography Activity: Saint Peter • History and Geography Activity: Spread of Christianity	**Daily Bellringer Transparency:** Section 2 **Map Transparency:** The Spread of Christianity, AD 300–AD 400  **Internet Activity:** Art Inspired by Jesus
Section 3: **The End of the Empire** **The Big Idea:** Problems from both inside and outside caused the Roman Empire to split into a western half, which collapsed, and an eastern half that prospered for hundreds of years.	TOS **Differentiated Instruction Teacher Management System:** Section 3 Lesson Plan  **Guided Reading Workbook:** Section 3  **Chapter Resource File:** • Vocabulary Builder Activity, Section 3 • Economics and History Activity: Inflation and the Fall of the Roman Empire • History and Geography Activity: Constantinople • Primary Source Activity: Byzantine Mosaic Panels, St. Vitale Church, Ravenna, Italy	 **Daily Bellringer Transparency:** Section 3 **Map Transparency:** Invasions of the Roman Empire, 340–500  **Internet Activity:** Barbarian Invasions **Animated History:** The Division of the Roman Empire, AD 395

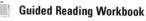

Chart Key:

SE Student Edition 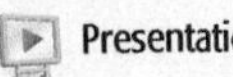 Presentation Resource  MP3 Audio HISTORY™

TOS Teacher One Stop DVD/CD-ROM

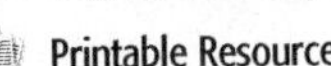 Printable Resource

Program Resources available on TOS and @ 

Review, Assessment, Intervention

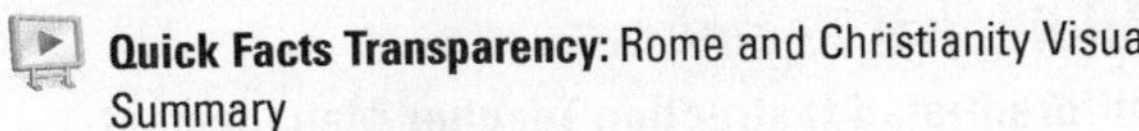

- **Quick Facts Transparency:** Rome and Christianity Visual Summary
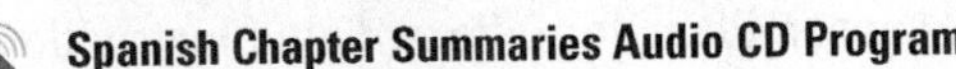
- **Spanish Chapter Summaries Audio CD Program**
- **Quiz Game CD-ROM**
- **Progress Assessment Support System (PASS):** Chapter Test
- **Differentiated Instruction Modified Worksheets and Tests CD-ROM:** Modified Chapter Test
- TOS **ExamView® Assessment Suite (English/Spanish)**
- **Online Assessment Program,** in the Interactive Student Edition

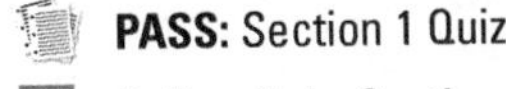

- **PASS:** Section 1 Quiz
- **Online Quiz:** Section 1
- **Alternative Assessment Handbook**

- **PASS:** Section 2 Quiz
- **Online Quiz:** Section 2
- **Alternative Assessment Handbook**

- **PASS:** Section 3 Quiz
- **Online Quiz:** Section 3
- **Alternative Assessment Handbook**

Supporting Resources

- Multimedia Classroom Global History Series
- Global History Teacher's Guide

Maps Globes Graphs Level F

- Student Workbook
- Teacher's Guide

Social Studies Trade Library Collections

- Premier Secondary World History Trade Collection
- Ancient World History Trade Collection

History's Impact

World History Video Program

- **Ancient Rome and the World Today**

For more information or to purchase go to hmhsocialstudies.com

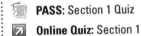

Power Presentations with Media Gallery

Power Presentations with Media Gallery are visual presentations of each chapter's main ideas. Presentations can be customized by including Quick Facts charts, images from the text, and video clips.

Differentiating Instruction

How do I address the needs of varied learners?

The Target Resource acts as your primary strategy for differentiated instruction.

ENGLISH-LANGUAGE LEARNERS & STRUGGLING READERS

Interactive Skills Tutor CD-ROM

The interactive Skills tutor CD-ROM contains lessons that provide additional practice for 20 different critical thinking skills.

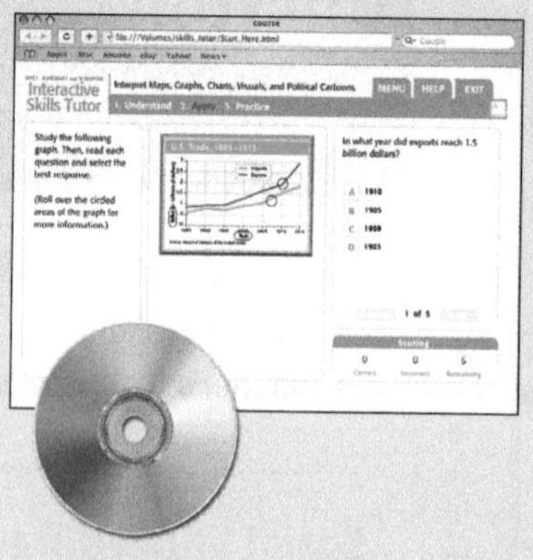

Additional Resources

Differentiated Instruction Teacher Management System: Lesson Plans for Differentiated Instruction

Chapter Resource File:

- Vocabulary Builder Activities
- Social Studies Skills Activity: Interpreting Time Lines

Quick Facts Transparencies: Rome and Christianity Visual Summary

Student Edition on Audio CD Program

Spanish/English Guided Reading Workbook

SPECIAL NEEDS LEARNERS

Differentiated Instruction Modified Worksheets and Tests CD-ROM

- Vocabulary Flash Cards
- Vocabulary Builder Activities
- Chapter Review Activity
- Chapter Test

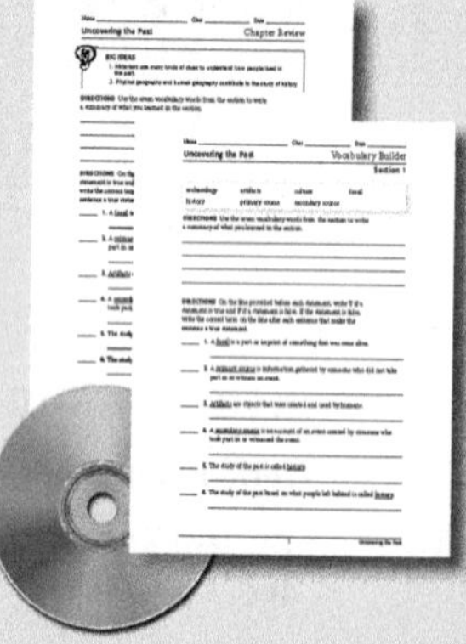

Additional Resources

Differentiated Instruction Teacher Management System: Lesson Plans for Differentiated Instruction

Guided Reading Workbook

Chapter Resource File: Social Studies Skills Activity: Interpreting Time Lines

Student Edition on Audio CD Program

Interactive Skills Tutor CD-ROM

ADVANCED/GIFTED-AND-TALENTED STUDENTS

Primary Source Library CD-ROM for World History

The Library contains longer versions of quotations in the text, extra sources, and images. Included are point-of-view articles, journals, diaries, historical fiction, and political documents.

Additional Resources

Differentiated Instruction Teacher Management System: Lesson Plans for Differentiated Instruction

Chapter Resource File:

- Focus on Writing Activity: Note Cards for a Screenplay
- Literature Activity: The Parable of the Prodigal Son

Document-Based Questions Activities

Differentiated Activities in the Teacher's Edition

- Qualities of Julius Caesar, p. 323
- Comparing Maps, p. 330
- Using Graphic Organizers, p. 334

Teacher One Stop™

How can I manage the lesson plans and support materials for differentiated instruction?

With the Teacher One Stop, you can easily organize and print lesson plans, planning guides, and instructional materials for all learners. The Teacher One Stop includes the following materials to help you differentiate instruction:

- Interactive Teacher's Edition
- Calendar Planner and pacing guides
- Editable lesson plans
- All reproducible ancillaries in Adobe Acrobat (PDF) format
- ExamView Assessment Suite (English & Spanish)
- Transparency and video previews

Differentiated Activities in the Teacher's Edition

- Building Models, p. 326
- Sequencing Events, p. 341
- Causes of Rome's Collapse, p. 342

Interactive Student Edition

Complete online student edition with interactive multimedia support for chapter content assessment and reporting

- Interactive Maps and Notebook
- Graphic Organizers
- Standardized Test Prep
- Online Homework Practice and Research Activities
- Current Events
- Chapter-based Internet Activities
- Animated History Activities
- and more!

Differentiated Activities in the Teacher's Edition

- Evaluating Web Sites, p. 321
- Calculating Distances, p. 330
- Writing Parables, p. 335

• Chapter Preview •

Essential Question

Introduce the Essential Question

- Point out that nomadic peoples often attack settlements to gain the goods that civilizations produce.
- Economic, military, political, and social problems all contributed to the empire's decline.
- The Eastern Roman Empire survived after the Western Empire had fallen.
- The Roman Empire had a profound influence on the cultures of Europe, the United States, and other parts of the world.

CHAPTER 11 50 BC–AD 1453

Rome and Christianity

Essential Question Why did the Roman Empire fall, and what is its legacy?

South Carolina Performance Standards

6-2.3 Describe the development of Roman civilization, including language, government, architecture, and engineering; **6-2.4** Describe the expansion and transition of the Roman government from monarchy to republic to empire, including the roles of Julius Caesar and Augustus Caesar (Octavius); **6-2.5** Explain the decline and collapse of the Roman Empire and the impact of the Byzantine Empire, including the Justinian Code and the preservation of ancient Greek and Roman learning, architecture, and government; **6-2.6** Compare the polytheistic belief systems of the Greeks and the Romans with the origins, foundational beliefs, and spread of Christianity.

Literacy Skills for Social Studies

- Interpret parallel time lines from different times and cultures.
- Explain how political, social, and economic institutions are similar or different across time and/or throughout the world.

Focus on Writing

Note Cards for a Screenplay Imagine that you are a research assistant for a movie studio that is planning to make a movie about the Roman Empire. Your job is to find out about the important people, places, and events in the history of the empire and to report this information to a group of writers who will create a screenplay. As you read this chapter, look for descriptions of the people, places, and events of the Roman world from the 70s BC to the end of the Eastern Roman Empire.

CHAPTER EVENTS

44 BC Julius Caesar is assassinated.

27 BC Augustus becomes Rome's first emperor.

25 BC

WORLD EVENTS

Focus on Writing

The **Chapter Resource File** provides a Focus on Writing worksheet to help students prepare their description note cards for a screenplay.

CRF: Focus on Writing Activity: Note Cards for a Screenplay

Introduce the Chapter

At Level

Focus on Rome and Christianity

1. Create a two-column chart titled *Rome and Christianity* for students to see with these heads: *From textbooks* and *From other sources.* Ask students to tell the impressions they have of the Roman Empire and the spread of Christianity from schoolwork for the first column and from TV shows, movies, video games, comic books, cartoons, and similar sources for the second column.
2. Ask students which impressions they feel are probably accurate and which are false or exaggerations. Point out that some of the facts of the Roman Empire's history are so amazing that they may seem to be exaggerations but are not.
3. Have students copy the completed chart. Encourage students to refer to the chart as they study the chapter to check which impressions are factual. **LS Verbal/Linguistic**

Key to Differentiating Instruction

Below Level
Basic-level activities designed for all students encountering new material

At Level
Intermediate-level activities designed for average students

Above Level
Challenging activities designed for honors and gifted and talented students

Standard English Mastery
Activities designed to improve standard English usage

LS Learning Styles

HISTORY
The Rise of Roman Cities
hmhsocialstudies.com VIDEO
c. AD 30 Jesus is crucified.
AD 312 Emperor Constantine ends the persecution of Christians.
AD 476 The last Roman emperor in the West is overthrown.
AD 1453 The Byzantine Empire ends.
BC 1 AD
250
500
1450
c. AD 65 Buddhism is introduced to China.
AD 250 The Maya Classic Age begins in Mexico.
AD 570 Muhammad is born in Mecca.
ROME AND CHRISTIANITY 319
This photo shows the Colosseum, an impressive example of ancient Roman architecture that still influences the design of stadiums around the world.

Chapter Preview

Explore the Picture

The Colosseum While the Colosseum's original decoration has been stripped away, the massive scale of the structure remains. The Colosseum's outside dimensions are 620 feet by 513 feet. In length it is about twice the size of a football field! Some 50,000 spectators could sit in the stands.

Analyzing Visuals The wall on the left side of the picture is taller than that on the right. What can you conclude about the original structure? *The wall on the right was an inner wall. The outer wall of that section, which would have continued from the diagonal walls, no longer stands.*

hmhsocialstudies.com
Teacher Resources

Explore the Time Line

1. Who was Rome's first emperor, and when did he come to power? *Augustus; 27 BC*
2. When did Emperor Constantine end the persecution of Christians? *AD 312*
3. When and where did the Maya Classic Age begin? *AD 250 in Mexico*
4. How many years separated the overthrow of the last Roman emperor in the West and the end of the Byzantine Empire? *977 years*

Info to Know

Naval Battles in the Colosseum? Roman writers tell that the Colosseum was sometimes flooded with water so that ships could fight mock naval battles there. However, for years scholars have argued over whether such a feat was possible. Recently, some archaeologists and computer experts said that the Colosseum could indeed have been flooded to a depth of five feet. Filling the arena floor would have required 4 million gallons of water. Research and discussions on this topic will probably continue.

Reading Social Studies

Understanding Themes

This chapter on the Roman Empire and Christianity focuses on geography in terms of the expansion of the Roman Empire. The other theme is science and technology, which was crucial to the development of Rome's far-flung provinces. Ask students to imagine what it would be like to be the subjects of an empire whose capital and emperor were hundreds, if not thousands, of miles away. This was the way of life for many people in the Roman Empire. However, people in distant lands were still connected to Rome through advances in science and technology, including roads and aqueducts.

Evaluating Web-Based Information

Focus on Reading Organize the class into small groups. Have students in each group discuss how they use the Internet and sites that they find useful for conducting research. Ask groups to list what they find most valuable about those sites (quality of information, layout, ease of use, etc.). Remind students that not all sites contain verifiable information. Ask students to list how they determine the quality of information when they are using the Internet. Have each group report its opinions to the class. Discuss the most important qualities of a Web site.

Tell students that much of the information they read or hear on any given day may be biased, whether it is on Web sites, television, or radio, or in newspapers, magazines, or books. Remind students that asking some of the questions listed in this feature will help them evaluate not just Web sites but all sources of information. Remind them that by asking questions and thinking critically, they can avoid getting fooled by incorrect information. They can also become responsible, informed citizens.

Reading Social Studies

Economics | Geography | Politics | Religion | Society and Culture | Science and Technology

Focus on Themes This chapter describes the development of Rome as it grew from a republic into a strong and vast empire. First, you will learn about the **geographic** expansion of the empire. You will read about powerful leaders such as Julius Caesar, Marc Antony, and Augustus. Finally, you will learn about how the people of the Roman Empire lived and worked. You will read about their many contributions to literature, language, law, and **science and technology.**

Online Research

Focus on Reading Finding information on the World Wide Web can be easy. Just enter a word or two into a search engine and you will instantly find dozens—if not hundreds—of sites full of information.

Evaluating Web Sites However, looking through all those sites can be overwhelming. In addition, not all Web sites have good or accurate information. How do you know which sites are the ones you want? You have to evaluate, or judge, the sites. You can use an evaluation form like the one below to evaluate a Web site.

Evaluating Web-Based Resources

Name of site: ____________ Topic of site ____________
URL: ____________ Date of access: ____________

Scroll through the site then answer the questions below.

I. Evaluating the author of the site
- **A.** Who is the author? What are his or her qualifications?
- **B.** Is there a way to contact the author?

II. Evaluating the content of the site
- **A.** Is the site's topic related to the topic you are studying?
- **B.** Is there enough information at this site to help you?
- **C.** Is there too much information for you to read or understand?
- **D.** Does the site include pictures or illustrations to help you understand the information?
- **E.** Does the site discuss more than one point of view about the topic?
- **F.** Does the site express the author's opinions rather than facts?
- **G.** Does the site provide references for any of its information, including quotes?
- **H.** Are there links to other sites that have valuable information?

III. Evaluating the overall design and quality
- **A.** Is the site easy to navigate or to find information on?
- **B.** When was the site last updated?

IV. My overall impression
- **A.** I think this site has good information that will help me with my research. ________
- **B.** I think this site either is too hard or too easy or has information I can't verify. ________

Reading and Skills Resources

Reading Support
- Guided Reading Workbook
- Student Edition on Audio CD
- Spanish Chapter Summaries Audio CD Program

Social Studies Skills Support
- Interactive Skills Tutor CD-ROM

Vocabulary Support
- **CRF:** Vocabulary Builder Activities
- **CRF:** Chapter Review Activity
- Differentiated Instruction Modified Worksheets and Tests CD-ROM:
  - Vocabulary Flash Cards
  - Vocabulary Builder Activity
  - Chapter Review Activity

TOS Holt McDougal PuzzleView

You Try It!

The information below is an example of a student's evaluation of a fictional Web site on Julius Caesar. Review the student's answers to the questions on the previous page and then answer the questions at the bottom of the page.

Web Site Evaluation

I. Evaluating the author

A. Author is listed as Klee O. Patra. She has read many books about Julius Caesar.

B. No information is listed for contacting the author.

II. Evaluating content of the site

A. Yes. It is about Julius Caesar.

B. There appears to be a great deal of information about Julius Caesar.

C. No, it looks easy to understand.

D. There are pictures, but most are from movies. There are no maps or historical images.

E. No.

F. Yes, it is all about how she loves Caesar.

G. I can't find any references.

H. There are two links, but they are both dead.

III. Evaluating overall design and quality

A. No. It takes a long time to find any specific information. Also, the layout of the page is confusing.

B. It was last updated in July 1998.

Study the evaluation then answer the following questions.

1. What do you know about the author of this site? Based on the evaluation information, do you think she is qualified to write about Caesar?
2. Does the content of the site seem valuable and reliable? Why?
3. The site has not been updated for many years, but that may not be a major problem for a site about Julius Caesar. Why? When might recent updates be more important?
4. Overall, would you say this site would be helpful? Why or why not?

Key Terms and People

Chapter 11

Section 1
Cicero *(p. 322)*
Julius Caesar *(p. 323)*
Pompey *(p. 323)*
Augustus *(p. 324)*
currency *(p. 326)*
Pax Romana *(p. 326)*
aqueduct *(p. 327)*
Romance languages *(p. 328)*
civil law *(p. 328)*

Section 2
Christianity *(p. 334)*
Jesus of Nazareth *(p. 334)*
Bible *(p. 335)*
crucifixion *(p. 336)*
Resurrection *(p. 336)*
disciples *(p. 336)*
Paul *(p. 337)*
Constantine *(p. 338)*

Section 3
Diocletian *(p. 340)*
Attila *(p. 341)*
corruption *(p. 342)*
Justinian *(p. 342)*
Theodora *(p. 343)*
Byzantine Empire *(p. 343)*

Academic Vocabulary

Success in school is related to knowing academic vocabulary—the words that are frequently used in school assignments and discussions. In this chapter, you will learn the following academic word:

efficient *(p. 342)*

As you read Chapter 11, think about what topics would be interesting to research on the Web. If you do some research on the Web, remember to evaluate the site and its contents.

Reading Social Studies

Key Terms and People

Introduce the key terms and people from this chapter by briefly reviewing each term and person with the class. Instruct students to look in the chapter for more information on each term or person. Then have students write a statement for each term or person that provides a description of the item, and then ask, "Who am I?" For example, "I am a structure that carries water from mountains into the city. Who am I?" *aqueduct* Collect the statements from students and read some statements aloud to the class. **LS Verbal/Linguistic**

Focus on Reading

See the **Focus on Reading** questions in this chapter for more practice on reading social studies skills.

Reading Social Studies Assessment

See the **Chapter Review** at the end of this chapter for student assessment questions related to this reading skill.

Differentiating Instruction

Advanced/Gifted and Talented — Above Level

1. Before beginning this activity, select five Web sites that you would most like students to evaluate.
2. Divide students into groups of four. Instruct students that they are to each play a particular role within their groups. Each group should have one of the following experts: Content, Credibility, Bias/Purpose, and Usability/Design.
3. Ask students to develop a checklist of specific criteria in their area of expertise and to use this checklist to evaluate the five sites. Have them rank the sites 1–5 (best-worst).
4. Have students share their findings on a large chart and lead a discussion about their observations. **LS Verbal/Linguistic**

Answers

You Try It! 1. *just that she has read many books about Julius Caesar; she might not be a reliable source or have validated her information.* **2.** *no, because it seems to just be a personal Web site on a topic the author finds interesting, but for which she does not provide sources* **3.** *Because Julius Caesar has been dead a long time, information about him has not changed. Recent topics or topics about which new information is being added require updated information.* **4.** *not very helpful; the information cannot be verified; lack of historical information; biased*

Preteach

Bellringer

If YOU were there . . . Use the **Daily Bellringer Transparency** to help students answer the question.

Daily Bellringer Transparency, Section 1

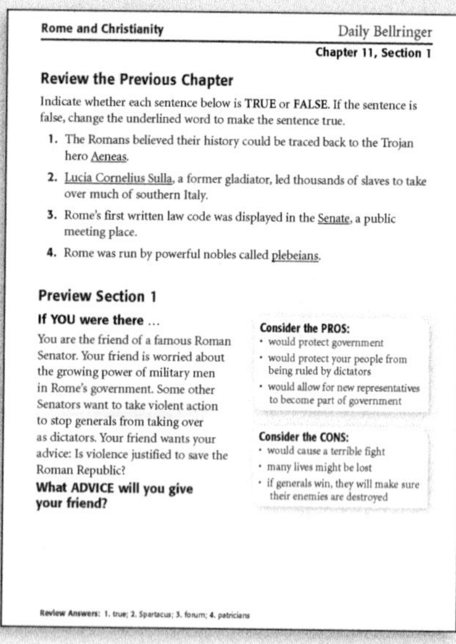

Rome and Christianity Daily Bellringer
Chapter 11, Section 1

Review the Previous Chapter

Indicate whether each sentence below is **TRUE** or **FALSE**. If the sentence is false, change the underlined word to make the sentence true.

1. The Romans believed their history could be traced back to the Trojan hero Aeneas.
2. Lucia Cornelius Sulla, a former gladiator, led thousands of slaves to take over much of southern Italy.
3. Rome's first written law code was displayed in the Senate, a public meeting place.
4. Rome was run by powerful nobles called plebeians.

Preview Section 1

If YOU were there ...

You are the friend of a famous Roman Senator. Your friend is worried about the growing power of military men in Rome's government. Some other Senators want to take violent action to stop generals from taking over as dictators. Your friend wants your advice: Is violence justified to save the Roman Republic?

What ADVICE will you give your friend?

Consider the PROS:
- would protect government
- would protect your people from being ruled by dictators
- would allow for new representatives to become part of government

Consider the CONS:
- would cause a terrible fight
- many lives might be lost
- if generals win, they will make sure their enemies are destroyed

Review Answers: 1. true; 2. Spartacus; 3. forum; 4. patricians

Building Vocabulary

Preteach or review the following terms:

conquest land gotten by military force (p. 323)

alliance connection formed for a common purpose (p. 323)

confrontation face-to-face conflict (p. 323)

boundary border (p. 323)

assassination murder of a politically important person (p. 324)

avenge take revenge for (p. 324)

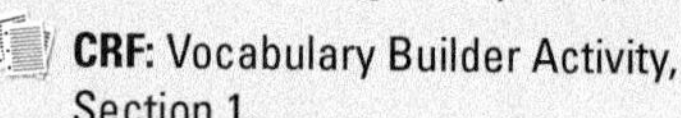

CRF: Vocabulary Builder Activity, Section 1

Taking Notes

Have students use the graphic organizer online to take notes on the section. This activity will prepare students for the Section Assessment, in which they will complete a graphic organizer that builds on the information using the Critical Thinking Skill: Analyzing.

SECTION 1

From Republic to Empire

What You Will Learn...

Main Ideas

1. Disorder in the Roman Republic created an opportunity for Julius Caesar to gain power.
2. The Republic ended when Augustus became Rome's first emperor.
3. The Roman Empire grew to control the entire Mediterranean world.
4. The Romans accomplished great things in science, engineering, architecture, art, literature, and law.

The Big Idea

After changing from a republic to an empire, Rome grew politically and economically, and developed a culture that influenced later civilizations.

Key Terms and People

Cicero, *p. 322*
Julius Caesar, *p. 323*
Pompey, *p. 323*
Marc Antony, *p. 324*
Augustus, *p. 324*
Pax Romana, *p. 326*
aqueduct, *p. 327*
Romance languages, *p. 328*
civil law, *p. 328*

hmhsocialstudies.com
TAKING NOTES

Use the graphic organizer online to take notes on Rome's change from a republic to an empire and the accomplishments of the empire.

If YOU were there...

You are a friend of a famous Roman Senator. Your friend is worried about the growing power of military men in Rome's government. Some other Senators want to take violent action to stop generals from taking over as dictators. Your friend wants your advice: Is violence justified to save the Roman Republic?

What advice will you give your friend?

BUILDING BACKGROUND By the first century BC, the government of the Roman Republic was in trouble. Politicians looked for ways to solve the problems. Philosophers offered ideas, too. In the end, however, the Republic could not survive the great changes that were taking place in Rome.

Disorder in the Republic

Rome in the 70s BC was a dangerous place. Politicians and generals went to war to increase their power even as political order broke down in Rome. There were politically inspired riots to restore the power of the tribunes. All the while, more and more people from throughout the republic flooded into the city, further adding to the confusion.

Calls for Change

Some Romans tried to stop the chaos in Rome's government. One such person was **Cicero** (SIS-uh-roh), a philosopher and gifted orator, or public speaker. In his speeches, Cicero called on upperclass Romans to work together to make Rome a better place. One way to do this, he argued, was to limit the power of generals. Cicero wanted the Romans to give more support to the Senate and to restore checks and balances on government.

But the government did not change. Many Romans didn't agree with Cicero. Others were too busy to listen. Meanwhile, several

Teach the Big Idea

At Level

From Republic to Empire

1. **Teach** Ask students the questions in the Main Idea boxes to teach this section.
2. **Apply** Draw a chart with two columns for students to see. Label the columns *Julius Caesar* and *Octavian (Augustus)*. Have each student copy the chart and enter five or more facts about each man. **LS Visual/Spatial**
3. **Review** Have volunteers share the information they listed. Write the facts on the chart. Then add columns titled *Before* and *After* to the left and right of the chart. Call on volunteers to add information on the events that led to Julius Caesar's rise and on the events that followed Augustus' rise to power. Add the information to the *Before* and *After* columns in the chart.
4. **Practice/Homework** Have each student write a paragraph contending which man had the greater influence on Rome. **LS Verbal/Linguistic**

Alternative Assessment Handbook, Rubrics 7: Charts; and 40: Writing to Describe

generals were working to take over the government. The most powerful of these generals was **Julius Caesar** (JOOL-yuhs SEE-zuhr).

Caesar's Rise to Power

Caesar was a great general. Romans admired him for his bravery and skill in battle. His soldiers respected him for treating them well. Between 58 BC and 50 BC Caesar conquered nearly all of Gaul—an area that is today the country of France. He wrote about this conquest in great detail. In this description of one battle, notice how he refers to himself as Caesar:

> "Caesar, having divided his forces . . . and having hastily [quickly] constructed some bridges, enters their country in three divisions, burns their houses and villages, and gets possession of a large number of cattle and men."
>
> —Julius Caesar, *The Gallic Wars*

Caesar's military successes made him a key figure in Roman politics. In addition to being a strong leader, Caesar was an excellent speaker. He won many supporters with his speeches in the forum.

Caesar also had powerful friends. Before he went to Gaul, he made an alliance with two of Rome's most influential men, **Pompey** (PAHM-pea) and Crassus (KRAS-uhs). Together the three ruled Rome.

Challenges to Caesar

The partnership lasted about 10 years. But after his conquests in Gaul, Caesar was so popular that even his friends were jealous of him. In 50 BC Pompey's allies in the Senate ordered Caesar to give up command of his armies. They wanted Pompey to control Rome alone.

Caesar refused. Instead he led his troops back toward Rome for a confrontation. Once his men crossed the Rubicon River, the boundary between Gaul and Italy, Caesar knew that there was no turning back.

People now use the phrase "crossing the Rubicon" when they do something that can't be undone.

Julius Caesar conquered Gaul and added it to the empire. This painting from the late 1800s shows a Gallic leader surrendering to Caesar by dropping his weapons at Caesar's feet.

323

Direct Teach

Main Idea

1 Disorder in the Republic

Disorder in the Roman Republic created an opportunity for Julius Caesar to gain power.

Identify Who was Cicero? *a philosopher and orator who wanted to make Rome a better place*

Describe What problems plagued Rome in the 70s BC? *wars, breakdown of political order, riots, overcrowding*

Evaluate How might Cicero have been more successful in his efforts to improve Rome? *possible answer—appeal more to people's self-interest*

Identify What position did Caesar first hold in the government? *general*

Finding Main Ideas Why did Caesar cross the Rubicon with his army? *Caesar wanted to force a confrontation with Pompey, so he entered Rome with his army to fight.*

 **CRF:** Biography Activity: Cicero

Biography

Julius Caesar (c. 100 BC–44 BC) Julius Caesar was an effective leader partly because he was so energetic. Even before he had completed his conquest of Gaul, he had written seven books, called *The Gallic Wars,* about his experiences in the provinces. Caesar was also physically vigorous. He was known for traveling quickly on horseback over long distances, and once saved himself from drowning.

Critical Thinking: Organizing Information

Below Level

Qualities of Julius Caesar

1. Have students think of specific qualities an effective leader should possess.
2. Discuss those qualities and write a list for students to see.
3. Draw the graphic organizer at right for the class to see. Have each student copy the organizer and fill in each empty box with details of why that quality was useful to Julius Caesar as a leader. **LS Visual/Spatial**

Leadership Qualities of Julius Caesar		
military leader	good speaker	alliance builder

Direct Teach

Main Idea

❷ The End of the Republic

The Republic ended when Augustus became Rome's first emperor.

Recall What did Caesar do to Pompey? *pursued him for a year until Pompey was defeated in Greece*

Make Generalizations Why was Caesar killed? *Romans, especially Senators, feared that Caesar was trying to make himself king.*

Identify How did most Romans feel about the death of Caesar? *angry*

Recall What happened to Caesar's killers after the assassination? *Marc Antony and Octavian defeated them, and the leaders killed themselves.*

Drawing Conclusions Why did Octavian turn against Marc Antony? *Antony divorced his wife, who was Octavian's sister, in order to marry Cleopatra. Octavian saw this as an insult to his sister and to himself.*

CRF: Biography Activity: Marc Antony

hmhsocialstudies.com

Online Resources
Activity: Campaign Poster

War was certain since Roman law said no general could enter Italy with his army.

Pompey and his allies fled Italy. They didn't think they had enough troops to defeat Caesar. But Caesar's army chased Pompey's forces for a year. They finally defeated Pompey in Greece in 48 BC. Pompey was killed by orders of an Egyptian king.

After Caesar returned to Rome in 45 BC, he made himself dictator for life. Although Caesar worked to improve Roman society, many people resented the way he gained power. They were also concerned that Caesar wanted to become king of Rome.

The Senators were especially angry with Caesar. He had reduced their powers, and they feared his growing strength. On March 15—a date known as the Ides of March—in 44 BC a group of Senators attacked Caesar in the Senate and stabbed him to death.

READING CHECK **Sequencing** How did Caesar gain power in Rome?

The End of the Republic

After Caesar's assassination,two great leaders emerged to take control of Roman politics. One was Caesar's former assistant, **Marc Antony**. The other was Caesar's adopted son Octavian (ahk-TAY-vee-uhn), later called **Augustus** (aw-GUHS-tuhs).

Antony and Octavian

One priority for Antony and Octavian was punishing the men who killed Caesar. The murderers had thought they would become heroes. Instead they were forced to flee for their lives. Rome was shocked by Caesar's murder. Many people loved Caesar, and riots broke out after his death. In order to end the chaos that followed Caesar's assassination, the Senate had to act quickly to restore order.

At Caesar's funeral, Antony delivered a famous speech that turned even more Romans against the killers. Shortly afterward, he and Octavian set out with an army to try to avenge Caesar's death.

Their army caught up to the killers near Philippi (FI-luh-py) in northern Greece. In 42 BC Antony and Octavian soundly defeated their opponents. After the battle, the last of Caesar's murderers killed themselves.

Octavian Becomes Emperor

After the Battle of Philippi, Octavian returned to Italy. Antony went east to fight Rome's enemies. In 40 BC Antony married Octavian's sister, Octavia. Eight years later, however, he divorced her to marry Cleopatra, the queen of Egypt. Octavian saw this divorce as an insult to his sister and to himself.

Antony's behavior led to civil war in Rome. In 31 BC Octavian sent a fleet to attack Antony. Antony sailed out to meet it, and the two forces met just west of Greece in the Battle of Actium (AK-shee-uhm). Antony's fleet was defeated, but he escaped back to Egypt with Cleopatra. There the two committed suicide so they wouldn't be taken prisoner by Octavian.

Octavian then became Rome's sole ruler. Over the next few years he gained nearly limitless power. He took the title *princeps* (PRIN-seps), or first citizen.

In 27 BC Octavian announced that he was giving up his power to the Senate, but, in reality, he kept all his power. The Senate gave him a new name—Augustus, which means "revered one." Modern historians consider the naming of Augustus to mark the end of the Roman Republic and the beginning of the Roman Empire.

READING CHECK **Summarizing** How did the Roman Republic become an empire?

Cross-Discipline Activity: Literature

At Level

Reader's Theater

Materials: copies of scenes from Shakespeare's *Julius Caesar*

1. Organize the class into small groups and give each group a scene from *Julius Caesar* to read. Tell students that they will read scenes from a historical play.
2. Have each group practice its scene by having each member take turns reading different characters' lines.
3. Call on groups to read their scenes to the class. Encourage students to act out the scenes as much as possible and to read with expression.
4. Discuss each scene and help students interpret the meaning of Shakespeare's language.
LS Interpersonal, Verbal/Linguistic

Alternative Assessment Handbook, Rubric 33: Skits and Reader's Theater

Answers

Reading Check (left) *Caesar defeated Pompey in Greece, then returned to Rome and made himself the dictator.*

Reading Check (right) *After Marc Antony's death, the Senate gave Octavian nearly limitless powers and named him Augustus, meaning "revered one."*

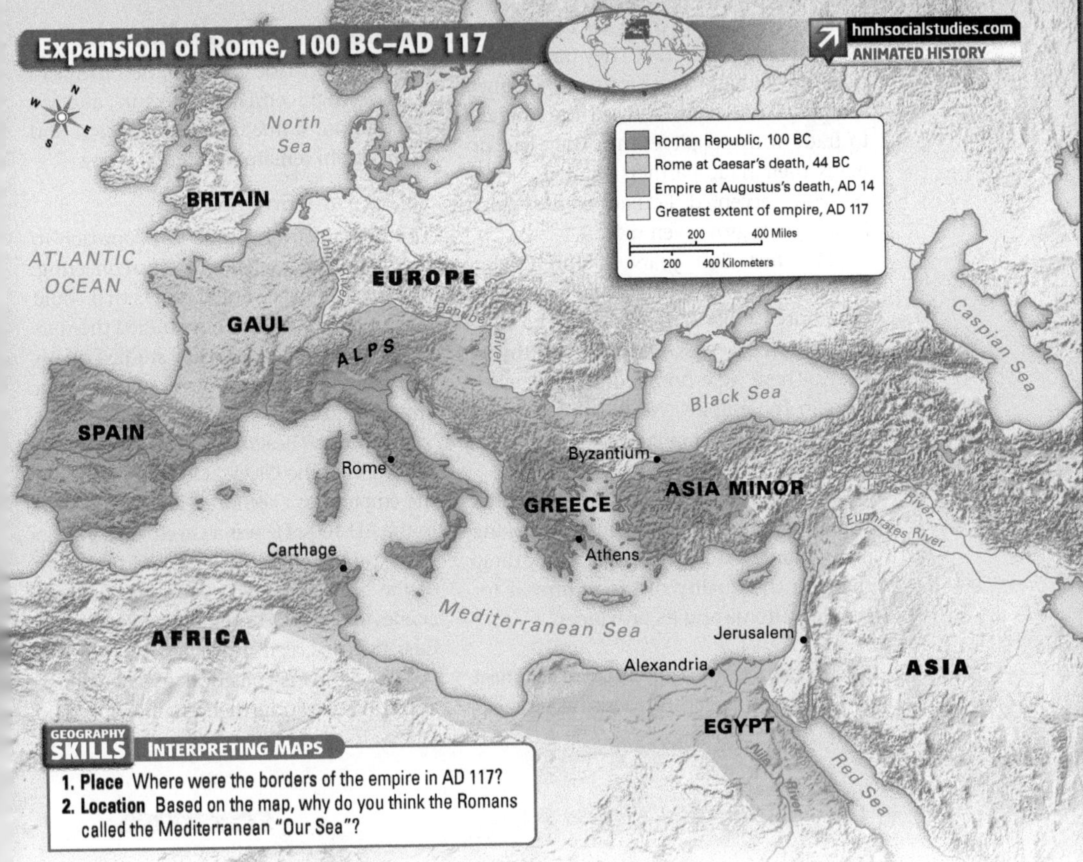

GEOGRAPHY SKILLS INTERPRETING MAPS

1. **Place** Where were the borders of the empire in AD 117?
2. **Location** Based on the map, why do you think the Romans called the Mediterranean "Our Sea"?

Rome's Growing Empire

When Rome became an empire, it already controlled most of the Mediterranean world. Augustus and the emperors who followed him further expanded the empire. Some emperors conquered territories to control hostile neighbors. Other Roman leaders wanted to gain control of gold, farmland, and other resources.

By the early AD 100s the Romans had taken over Gaul and much of central Europe. Under the emperor Claudius, the Romans conquered most of the island of Britain. Rome also controlled Asia Minor, Mesopotamia, and the eastern coast of the Mediterranean. All of the north African coast belonged to Rome as well.

The Roman conquests promoted trade. People in Rome needed raw materials that were lacking in Italy. Many of the materials, though, could be found in Rome's provinces, the outlying areas that the Romans controlled. Traders brought metals, cloth, and food from the provinces to the city. They also brought more exotic goods, like spices and silk from Asia and animals from Africa. In return, the Romans sent goods made by artisans to the provinces. These goods included jewelry, glass, and clothing.

Direct Teach

Main Idea

❸ Rome's Growing Empire

The Roman Empire grew to control the entire Mediterranean world.

Identify What kinds of economic resources did Romans want? *gold, farmland, and other valuable resources*

Recall What areas did the Romans take over by the early 100s? *Gaul, central Europe*

Map Transparency: Expansion of Rome, 100 BC–AD 117

Differentiating Instruction

A Vast Empire **At Level**

1. Ask students to imagine that they were residents of the Roman Republic in about 200 BC who fell into a magical sleep. They awaken 200 years later and find themselves citizens of the Roman Empire. Have each student write a paragraph that starts with "When I awoke after my long sleep, I was amazed to find that . . ." LS **Verbal/Linguistic**
2. Call on volunteers to read their paragraphs. If any major events or characteristics of the empire were not covered, discuss those as a class.
3. Have each student write a second paragraph in which they describe the change they like or dislike the most. LS **Verbal/Linguistic**

Alternative Assessment Handbook, Rubric 37: Writing Assignments

Answers

Interpreting Maps 1. *roughly—northern Britain, Rhine River, Danube River, north shore of the Black Sea, eastern Asia Minor, Mesopotamia, eastern coast of the Mediterranean Sea, North Africa* **2.** *because it was surrounded by Roman territory*

Direct Teach

Main Idea

4 Rome's Accomplishments

The Romans accomplished great things in science, engineering, architecture, art, literature, and law.

Make Inferences Why do you think a Roman sailor would be glad that Rome controlled the entire Mediterranean Sea? *possible answer—because there would be few pirates and many friendly ports*

Identify What is an example of an important medical discovery during the Roman Empire? *Galen's description of the valves of the heart and the differences between arteries and veins*

Linking to Today

The Segovia Aqueduct Residents of Segovia, Spain, still benefit from Roman engineering. In about AD 100, Romans built a huge aqueduct there that required some 24,000 stone blocks. One section of the aqueduct, shown in the photo at right, still stands. The part that is above ground stands 30 feet high in most places. Where the ground level dips very low, the aqueduct is 93.5 feet tall. The aqueduct continues to carry water to Segovia.

Connect to the Arts and Humanities

Neoclassical Style Tell students they can see elements of Roman architecture in some modern-day buildings. Today, when architects design a building with features such as columns, domes, or prominent arches, the building is said to be in the neoclassical style. Artists and architects use the word *classical* to describe Greek and Roman styles. When modern architects imitate that style, it is called *neoclassical.* The prefix *neo-* means "new."

To pay for their trade goods, Romans used currency, or money. They traded coins made of gold and silver for the items they wanted. These coins allowed the Romans to trade with people even if they had no items their trade partners wanted. Nearly everyone accepted Roman coins, which helped trade grow even more.

The first 200 years of the Roman Empire was a time of general peace and prosperity. Stable government and a well-run army helped Rome grow wealthy in safety. There were no major wars or rebellions in the empire. We call this peaceful period the **Pax Romana**, or Roman peace. It lasted until the AD 180s.

During the Pax Romana, the empire's population grew. Trade increased, making many Romans wealthy. As a result of these changes, the quality of life improved for people in Rome and its provinces.

READING CHECK **Identifying Cause and Effect** How did Rome's territorial expansion affect trade?

Rome's Accomplishments

The Romans made lasting achievements in science, engineering, architecture, and art. In addition, Rome's literary tradition and legal system remain influential today.

Science and Engineering

The Romans took a practical approach to their study of science and engineering. Roman scientists wanted results that could benefit their society. They studied the stars to produce a calendar. They studied plants and animals to learn how to obtain better crops and meat.

To improve health, Roman doctors studied the works of the Greeks. One great doctor in the empire was Galen (GAY-luhn), who lived in the AD 100s. He was a Greek surgeon who studied the body. Galen described the valves of the heart and noted differences between arteries and veins. For centuries doctors based their ideas on Galen's teachings.

The Romans' practical use of science also can be seen in their engineering. The

The Roman Arch

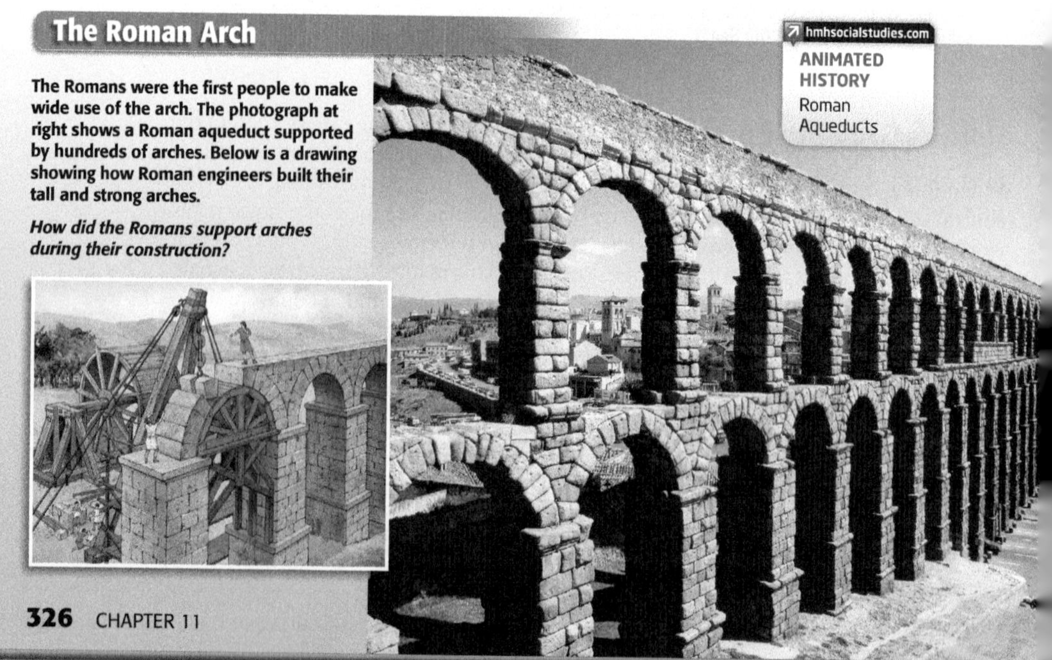

The Romans were the first people to make wide use of the arch. The photograph at right shows a Roman aqueduct supported by hundreds of arches. Below is a drawing showing how Roman engineers built their tall and strong arches.

How did the Romans support arches during their construction?

Differentiating Instruction

Special Needs Learners — Below Level

Materials: blocks or small boxes of various sizes and shapes, including half-circles; large gumdrops; toothpicks

1. Organize the class into small groups. Provide each group with the listed materials.
2. Use blocks or boxes to demonstrate how the Romans built forms for their arches, referring to the drawing on this page. Help students build similar structures.
3. Then point out that the gumdrops have a narrow end and a wide end, like the stone blocks that made the arches. Help students build arches from the gumdrops, resting the arches on the block forms and holding them together with toothpicks.
4. Students should be able to remove the forms when finished and the gumdrop arches should remain intact. **LS Interpersonal, Kinesthetic**

Alternative Assessment Handbook, Rubric 14: Group Activity

Answers

Reading Check *With expansion, the population grew, increasing trade.*

The Roman Arch *with a wooden form that supported the weight of the arch*

Romans were great builders. They developed new materials to help their structures last. For example, the Romans made cement by mixing a mineral called lime with volcanic rock and ash. The resulting material dried to be very hard and watertight.

More important than the materials they used, though, were the designs the Romans had for their structures. They built their roads in layers. Each layer was made of a different material. This layered construction made the road highly durable. Many Roman roads have not worn down even after centuries of traffic.

The Romans also created lasting structures by using arches. Because of its rounded shape, an arch can support much more weight than other shapes can. This strength has allowed many arched Roman bridges to last until the present.

The Romans also used arches in their aqueducts (A-kwuh-duhkts). An **aqueduct** is a raised channel used to carry water from mountains into cities. Because they crossed deep valleys, Roman aqueducts needed to be strong. Many still stand today.

Roman builders also learned how to combine arches to create vaults. A vault is a set of arches that supports the roof of a building. The Romans used vaults to create huge, open areas within buildings.

Architecture and Art

The Romans weren't interested only in practicality. They also admired beauty. This appreciation can be seen in the new designs of architecture and art that they created.

Roman architecture also copied some older Greek designs. For example, the Romans used columns to make their public buildings look impressive. The Romans also copied the Greeks by covering many of their buildings with marble.

Their engineering techniques allowed the Romans to make new architectural advances. The vault, for example, let them build huge structures, much larger than anything the Greeks could build. One such structure was the Colosseum in Rome—a huge building constructed for gladiator fights. Many other Roman structures are topped with domes.

Roman artists were known for their beautiful mosaics, paintings, and statues. Mosaics and paintings were used to decorate Roman buildings. Most Roman paintings were frescoes. A fresco is a type of painting done on plaster. Many Roman painters were particularly skilled at creating portraits, or pictures of people. Roman sculptors were also very talented. They studied what the Greeks had done and tried to re-create this brilliance in their own statues.

Literature and Language

Rich in art and architecture, Rome was also home to many of the greatest authors in the ancient world. One such author was Virgil, who wrote a great epic about the founding of Rome, the *Aeneid* (ih-NEE-uhd). Another was Ovid (AHV-uhd), who wrote poems about Roman mythology.

Quick Facts: Roman Accomplishments

Government	Architecture
Importance of written laws	Large and strong buildings
Equal treatment for all citizens	Columns and open spaces
Rights and duties of citizens	

Engineering	Art
Excellent, durable roads	Realistic statues
Strong bridges	Lifelike portraits
Aqueducts to move water	
Building designs that inspired later societies	

Philosophy
Focused on improving people's lives
Stoic philosophy emphasizing people's civic duty

HISTORY
The Glory of the Colosseum
hmhsocialstudies.com

Focus on Reading
What key words would you use to search for Web information on a subject discussed in this paragraph?

Direct Teach

Main Idea

4 Rome's Accomplishments

The Romans accomplished great things in science, engineering, architecture, art, literature, and law.

Explain Why was cement such a useful material? *It was very hard and watertight when it dried.*

Identify What architectural features did the Romans copy from the Greeks? *columns, covering buildings with marble*

Draw Conclusions How were the Romans able to increase the size of their buildings? *by combining arches to create vaults*

Recall What are four types of art at which the Romans excelled? *possible answers—mosaics, paintings, frescoes, portraits, sculpture*

CRF: Primary Source Activity: From *The Amores* by the Roman Poet Ovid

hmhsocialstudies.com
Online Resources
Activity: Roman Model

Checking for Understanding

True or False Answer each statement *T* if it is true or *F* if it is false. If false, explain why.

1. The Romans studied the world just to know more about it. *F; The Romans wanted results that could benefit their society.*
2. Many Roman structures have lasted because of the use of strong materials and designs, such as cement and arches. *T*
3. Romans preferred to keep the design of their buildings simple with little art. *F; Many Roman homes and businesses had elaborate mosaics and frescoes.*

Critical Thinking: Describing

At Level

Local Architecture

Prep Required

1. Ask students to list examples of Roman architecture, such as courthouses or other government buildings, in or near your community. Roman influence is apparent in details such as columns, arches, and domes.
2. If your community lacks such buildings, provide books on American architecture to familiarize students with the style.
3. Have each student write a short description of how the community buildings or buildings in the books have been influenced by Roman architecture. **LS Verbal/Linguistic, Visual/Spatial**

Alternative Assessment Handbook, Rubric 40: Writing to Describe

Direct Teach

Teaching Tip

Refer students to Chapter 9 in this book titled "The Greek World" to review information on Alexander the Great and his conquests in the Mediterranean world.

Review & Assess

Close

Ask students how both Caesar and Octavian undermined, or took the power away from, the Roman Senate.

Review

Online Quiz Section 1

Assess

SE Section 1 Assessment

PASS: Section 1 Quiz

Alternative Assessment Handbook

Reteach/Classroom Intervention

Guided Reading Workbook, Section 1

Interactive Skills Tutor CD-ROM

Answers

Reading Check *Latin evolved into the Romance languages and influenced other languages as well.*

In addition, Roman writers produced histories, speeches, and dramas that are still studied and enjoyed today.

Virgil, Ovid, and other poets wrote in Latin, the language of government and law. People throughout the Roman world wrote, conducted business, and kept records in Latin. In the eastern half of the empire, Greek was just as important.

Latin later developed into many different languages. These languages are called **Romance languages**. They include Italian, French, Spanish, Portuguese, and Romanian.

Latin also influenced other languages. Many non-Romance languages, including English, contain Latin words. Words like *et cetera, circus,* and *veto* were all originally Latin terms. Latin words are also common in scientific terms and mottoes.

Law

Rome's greatest influence may have been in the field of law. Roman law was enforced across much of Europe. Even after the empire fell, Roman laws continued to exist in the kingdoms that followed.

Over time, Roman law inspired a system called civil law. **Civil law** is a legal system based on a written code of laws, like the one created by the Romans.

Most countries in Europe today have civil law traditions. In the 1500s and 1600s, colonists from some of these countries carried civil law around the world. As a result, many countries in Africa, Asia, and the Americas developed law codes as well.

READING CHECK **Finding the Main Idea** How did Roman literature and language influence later societies?

SUMMARY AND PREVIEW Augustus made the Roman Republic into an empire. The empire grew during its first 200 years, and the Romans made many lasting contributions to the world. In the next section, you will learn about an influential development that changed life in Rome—Christianity.

Section 1 Assessment

hmhsocialstudies.com ONLINE QUIZ

Reviewing Ideas, Terms, and People

1. a. **Recall** To whom did **Cicero** want to give power?
   b. **Making Inferences** Why did many Senators consider **Julius Caesar** a threat?
   c. **Evaluate** What role did the military play in Caesar's rise to power?
2. a. **Identify** Who took over Rome after Caesar's death?
   b. **Summarize** How did Octavian take power from **Marc Antony**?
   c. **Evaluate** Why is it significant that Octavian did not take the title of dictator?
3. a. **Identify** What areas of the world did the Romans take over?
   b. **Elaborate** Why did trade increase during the **Pax Romana**?
4. a. **Recall** What type of law is based on the Roman law code?
   b. **Draw Conclusions** Latin is no longer spoken. Why do you think people still study it?

Critical Thinking

5. **Analyzing** Review your notes on Rome's accomplishments. Describe how the effects of one Roman accomplishment in each of the fields below is being felt today.

Engineering	
Language	
Law	
Literature	

Focus on Writing

6. **Taking Notes for a Screenplay** In your notebook, create a three-columned chart labeled "Characters," "Setting," and "Plot." Under the columns, write notes about the people and events from this section that you think would make good material for a movie.

Section 1 Assessment Answers

1. a. the Senate
   b. The Senators thought he was trying to make himself king. They did not want a king.
   c. Soldiers respected Caesar; his military successes made him a key political figure; Caesar's armies defeated Pompey.
2. a. Octavian and Marc Antony
   b. Octavian defeated him in battle.
   c. His title of princeps made him seem he was not keeping all the power.
3. a. parts of Europe, Africa, and Asia
   b. There was peace, a stable government, and an accepted currency.
4. a. civil law
   b. Many languages contain Latin and Latin-influenced words. Latin is used in science.
5. possible answers—Engineering: the strong Roman arch is used in architecture; Language: today's Romance languages are influenced by Latin; Law: civil law traditions in use today originated in Roman law; Literature: the works of Roman authors and poets are still read today.
6. Charts will vary, but students should include major details from the section.

BIOGRAPHY

Augustus

What would you do if you had great power?

When did he live? 63 BC–AD 14

Where did he live? Rome

What did he do? As the leader of Rome, Augustus made many improvements in the city. He created a fire department and a police force to protect the city's people. He built new aqueducts and repaired old ones to increase Rome's water supply. Augustus also worked on improving and expanding Rome's road network.

Why is he important? As Rome's first emperor, Augustus is one of the most significant figures in Roman history. Almost singlehandedly, he changed the nature of Roman government forever. But Augustus is also known for the great monuments he had built around Rome. He built a new forum that held statues, monuments, and a great temple to the god Mars. In writing about his life, Augustus declared, "I found Rome a city of brick and left it a city of marble."

Identifying Points of View Why do you think many Romans greatly admired Augustus?

KEY EVENTS

- **45 BC** Julius Caesar adopts Octavian as his son and heir.
- **44 BC** Octavian moves to Rome when Caesar dies.
- **42 BC** Octavian and Antony defeat Brutus.
- **31 BC** Octavian defeats Antony.
- **27 BC** Octavian takes the name Augustus and becomes emperor of Rome.

Augustus was responsible for the construction of many impressive buildings in Rome.

Critical Thinking: Analyzing Information

At Level

Augustus the Candidate

1. Ask students to imagine that, in contrast to what was really the situation, Augustus had to be elected to a second term as emperor.
2. Ask students to further imagine that they are workers in Augustus's political campaign.

2. Have students write slogans and design bumper stickers and banners for Augustus's campaign. Call on volunteers to read, display, and explain their slogans or banners. **LS Verbal/Linguistic**

Alternative Assessment Handbook, Rubric 34: Slogans and Banners

Biography

Reading Focus Question

Ask students to think about what they would do if they ruled their households as absolute leaders. What rules would they change? What improvements would they make? Would they declare any special holidays? How would they keep family members happy so that they would not rebel?

Did you know . . .

When you are the ruler of the largest empire in the world, your name shows up in many places. For example, Augustus had a month named after him. (Ask students which month.) August was originally called Sextilis, but was renamed for Augustus in 8 BC.

Connect to Economics

Activity Designing a Coin for Augustus Augustus had his own name printed on coins. Some of the coins contained symbols that glorified the emperor. For example, he could add the name *Caesar* to Augustus to remind everyone that the popular Julius Caesar was his great uncle and adoptive father.

Have students design coins to commemorate the life or achievements of Augustus. Display the coins in the classroom. **LS Visual/Spatial**

Alternative Assessment Handbook, Rubric 3: Artwork

Analyzing Visuals

Roman Architecture Have students look at the drawing of the Roman Forum. Ask students to describe the features of Roman architecture shown. *arches, columns* Ask them to name a building in this country that has one of these features. *possible answers—the White House (columns); the Lincoln Memorial (columns, rectangular shape)*

Answers

Biography *He made many improvements to Rome.*

History and Geography

Ask students to imagine that they are road builders in the Roman Empire. What geographical, political, or logistical challenges and dangers might they face as they build roads through newly conquered provinces? Lead a class discussion about these challenges.

Info to Know

The Appian Way Of all the roads leading to Rome, the most famous is the *Via Appia Antica,* or Old Appian Way. Begun in 312 BC, the Appian Way was the first Roman road built. It eventually stretched more than 350 miles (563 km.) from Rome to Brindisi, a seaport in southern Italy on the Adriatic Sea. The road served as the main highway to Greece and points east. Large monuments and tombs lined the first few miles of the road as it left Rome. The solid construction of the road has passed the test of time, and the Appian Way remains. The initial stretch of the road from Rome is now protected and is a popular tourist attraction.

The Postal Service One of the most important uses of the Roman road system was the *cursus publicus,* or postal service. Although average citizens were not allowed to use the postal service, it provided the Roman government with an important means of sending information and instructions across the empire.

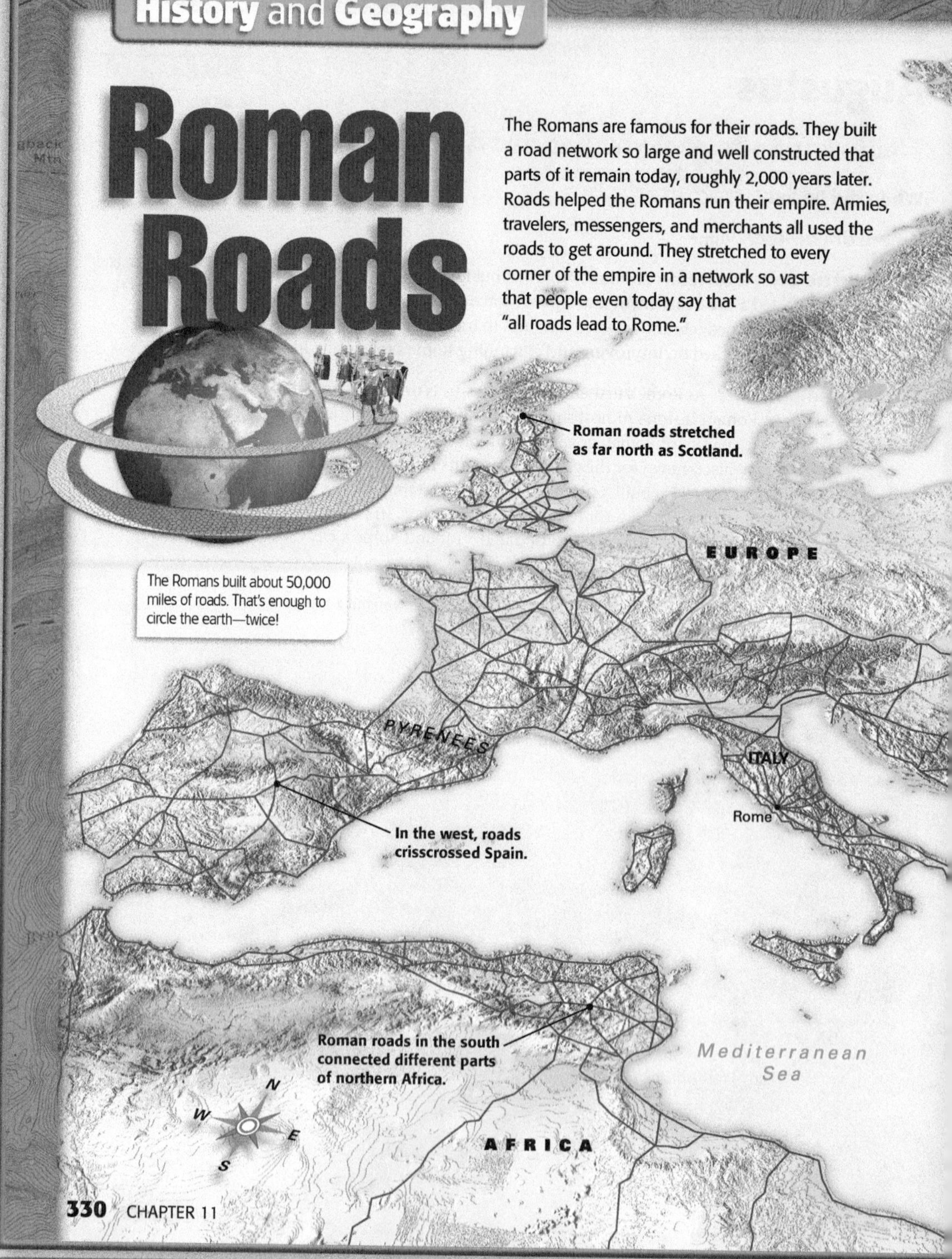
History and Geography
Roman Roads
The Romans are famous for their roads. They built a road network so large and well constructed that parts of it remain today, roughly 2,000 years later. Roads helped the Romans run their empire. Armies, travelers, messengers, and merchants all used the roads to get around. They stretched to every corner of the empire in a network so vast that people even today say that "all roads lead to Rome."
Roman roads stretched as far north as Scotland.
EUROPE
The Romans built about 50,000 miles of roads. That's enough to circle the earth—twice!
PYRENEES
ITALY
Rome
In the west, roads crisscrossed Spain.
Roman roads in the south connected different parts of northern Africa.
Mediterranean Sea
AFRICA
N
W
E
S
330 CHAPTER 11

Differentiating Instruction

Struggling Readers

Below Level

Comparing Maps To help students understand the full extent of the Roman road network, have students compare the map on this page with the map on p. 325 and with a current world map. Have students identify the regions through which the Roman roads passed during the Roman Empire and some of the countries located in those areas today. **LS Visual/Spatial**

Alternative Assessment Handbook, Rubric 21: Map Reading

Advanced/Gifted and Talented

Above Level

Calculating Distances Organize the class into small groups. Assign each group a present-day country that was once partially or completely within the Roman Empire. Have each group use modern maps of the Mediterranean area to calculate about how many miles of roads the Romans built within its assigned country.
LS Logical/Mathematical

Alternative Assessment Handbook, Rubrics 14: Group Activity; and 21: Map Reading

Paving stones
Drainage ditch
Curbstones
Sand, clay, and gravel
Stone chips
Gravel concrete
Roman roads were built to last. They were constructed of layers of sand, concrete, rock, and stone. Drainage ditches let water drain off, preventing water damage.
The roads were built by and for the military. The main purpose of the roads was to allow Rome's armies to travel quickly throughout the empire.
VIDEO
Ancient Rome: Mobile Security
HISTORY
hmhsocialstudies.com
In the east, Roman roads stretched into Southwest Asia.
The Romans built tall "milestones" along their roads to mark distances. Just like modern highway signs, the markers told travelers how far it was to the next town.

GEOGRAPHY SKILLS **INTERPRETING MAPS**

1. **Movement** Why did the Romans build their roads?
2. **Location** How does the map show that "all roads lead to Rome"?

History and Geography

Info to Know

Travel Along Roman Roads The most common vehicle on Roman roads was the two-wheeled chariot pulled by either two or four horses. Four-wheeled versions provided transportation for passengers. Goods were hauled in carts pulled by 8 to 10 horses. Average speeds along Roman roads ranged from 15 to 75 miles per day.

Did you know . . .

The thickness of a completed Roman road was from three to six feet.

Connect to Science and Technology

The First Roads The first roads were animal paths that were improved by early people. Records refer to such paths being used as roads around Jericho in about 6000 BC. The earliest known constructed roads date to about 4000 BC. Roads from this period have been found in Ur, in what is now Iraq, and in Glastonbury, England.

Social Studies Skills: Creating and Interpreting Maps

At Level

Roman Road Maps

Prep Required

Materials: color markers; photocopies of the map on p. 330

1. Provide each student with a photocopy of the map and color markers.
2. Have students use the maps in this chapter to add the following to the map: major Roman cities; borders of the Roman Empire at its peak.
3. Then have students refer to their maps as you lead a discussion about transportation in the Roman Empire. **LS Visual/Spatial**

Alternative Assessment Handbook, Rubric 21: Map Reading

Answers

Interpreting Maps 1. *to allow Rome's armies to travel quickly throughout the empire* **2.** *All roads are connected to a road that goes to Rome.*

Preteach

Bellringer

If YOU were there . . . Use the **Daily Bellringer Transparency** to help students answer the question.

Daily Bellringer Transparency, Section 2

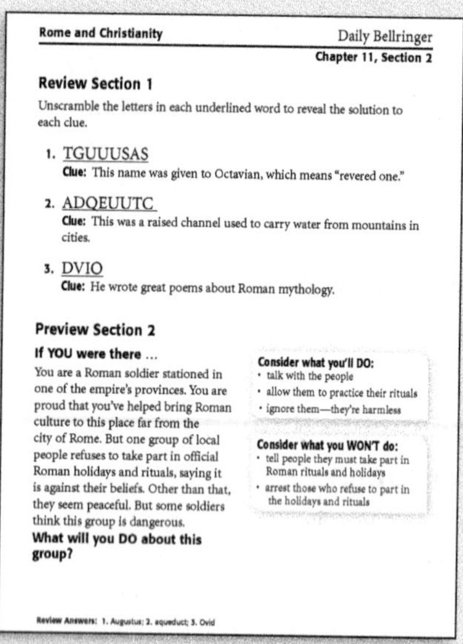

Rome and Christianity — Daily Bellringer
Chapter 11, Section 2

Review Section 1

Unscramble the letters in each underlined word to reveal the solution to each clue.

1. TGUUUSAS
   Clue: This name was given to Octavian, which means "revered one."
2. ADQEUUTC
   Clue: This was a raised channel used to carry water from mountains in cities.
3. DVIO
   Clue: He wrote great poems about Roman mythology.

Preview Section 2

If YOU were there ...

You are a Roman soldier stationed in one of the empire's provinces. You are proud that you've helped bring Roman culture to this place far from the city of Rome. But one group of local people refuses to take part in official Roman holidays and rituals, saying it is against their beliefs. Other than that, they seem peaceful. But some soldiers think this group is dangerous.

What will you DO about this group?

Consider what you'll DO:
- talk with the people
- allow them to practice their rituals
- ignore them—they're harmless

Consider what you WON'T do:
- tell people they must take part in Roman rituals and holidays
- arrest those who refuse to part in the holidays and rituals

Review Answers: 1. Augustus; 2. aqueduct; 3. Ovid

Building Vocabulary

Preteach or review the following terms:

Olympian gods the gods of ancient Greece, who lived on Mount Olympus (p. 332)

prophecy predictions of things to come (p. 334)

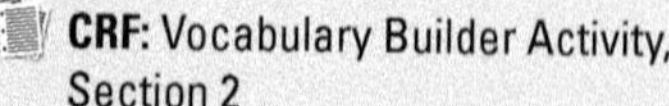

CRF: Vocabulary Builder Activity, Section 2

Taking Notes

Have students use the graphic organizer online to take notes on the section. This activity will prepare students for the Section Assessment, in which they will complete a graphic organizer that builds on the information using the Critical Thinking Skill: Summarizing.

SECTION 2

What You Will Learn...

Main Ideas

1. Despite its general religious tolerance, Rome came into conflict with the Jews.
2. A new religion, Christianity, grew out of Judaism.
3. Many considered Jesus of Nazareth to be the Messiah.
4. Christianity grew in popularity and eventually became the official religion of Rome.

The Big Idea

People in the Roman Empire practiced many religions before Christianity, based on the teachings of Jesus of Nazareth, spread and became Rome's official religion.

Key Terms and People

Christianity, *p. 334*
Jesus of Nazareth, *p. 334*
Messiah, *p. 334*
crucifixion, *p. 336*
Resurrection, *p. 336*
Apostles, *p. 337*
Paul of Tarsus, *p. 337*
Constantine, *p. 338*

hmhsocialstudies.com
TAKING NOTES

Use the graphic organizer online to take notes on the religious practices in Rome, Jesus's teachings, and the early history of Christianity.

The Roman Empire and Religion

If YOU were there...

You are a Roman soldier stationed in one of the empire's provinces. You are proud that you've helped bring Roman culture to this place far from the city of Rome. But one group of local people refuses to take part in official Roman holidays and rituals, saying it is against their religious beliefs. Other than that, they seem peaceful. Even so, some soldiers think this group is dangerous.

What will you do about this group?

BUILDING BACKGROUND As the Roman Empire expanded, it came to include many people who spoke many different languages and followed many different religions. While Roman officials were generally tolerant of local religions and cultures, they did not allow anything—like the religion noted above—that might threaten their authority.

Religious Tolerance and Conflict

The Romans were a very religious people. They held many festivals in honor of their gods. However, they did not insist on imposing their beliefs on others.

Freedom of Worship

When the Romans conquered people, they generally allowed them to keep their own religious beliefs and customs. Sometimes these beliefs also spread to the Romans who lived nearby. As time passed, the Romans built temples to these adopted gods, and people worshipped them throughout the empire.

For example, many Romans worshipped the Olympian gods of Greece. When the Romans conquered Greece, they learned about Greek mythology. Before long, the Greek gods became

Teach the Big Idea

At Level

The Roman Empire and Religion

1. **Teach** Ask students the questions in the Main Idea boxes to teach this section.
2. **Apply** Have students construct an illustrated time line that depicts the history presented in this section. Where dates do not appear in the text, have students write out the sequenced events on the time line. Ask students to include a simple illustration or symbol to signify each event on the time line. **LS Visual/Spatial**
3. **Review** As you review the section's main ideas, have students discuss why conflict existed between Jews, Romans, and Christians.
4. **Practice/Homework** Have students share their time lines, filling in anything they missed. Tell them to use this time line when reviewing the chapter later. **LS Visual/Spatial, Interpersonal**

Alternative Assessment Handbook, Rubric 36: Time Lines

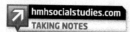

the main gods of Rome as well, although they were known by different names. In the same way, many Romans also adopted gods and beliefs from the Egyptians, Gauls, and Persians.

In their religious lives, the Romans were very practical. They were not sure which gods did or did not exist. To avoid offending any gods, the Romans prayed to a wide variety of gods and goddesses.

The only time the Romans banned a religion was when the rulers of Rome considered it a political problem. In these cases, government officials took steps to prevent problems. Sometimes they placed restrictions on when and where members of a religion could meet. Judaism was one religion that some Roman leaders came to consider a political problem.

Clashes with the Jews

Unlike the Romans, the Jews did not worship many gods. They believed that their God was the only god. Some Romans thought the Jews insulted Rome's gods by not praying to them.

Still, the Romans did not attempt to ban Judaism in the empire. They allowed the Jews to keep their religion and practice it as they pleased. The Jews, however, created political conflict by rebelling against Roman rule. Judea, the territory in which most Jews lived, had been conquered by Rome in 63 BC. Since then, many Jews had resented Roman rule. They did not want to answer to outsiders. As a result, the Jews rebelled against the Romans in AD 66–70. There were other disturbances as well, but each time the Jews were defeated.

The Romans built many temples to honor their many gods. Temples built to honor all the gods were called pantheons, and the most famous of these is the Pantheon in Rome, first built in the 20s BC. Its huge dome awes visitors even today.

333

Direct Teach

Main Idea

1 Religious Tolerance and Conflict

Despite its general religious tolerance, Rome came into conflict with the Jews.

Identify What kind of religion did Romans practice? *They worshipped many gods and held many festivals to honor them.*

Recall From what peoples did Romans adopt some gods? *Greeks, Egyptians, Gauls, and Persians*

Analyze How did the Romans deal with other religions? *They generally permitted other religions and often adopted gods and beliefs from other religions; only when a religious group caused a problem did Rome restrict them.*

Recall When did Rome conquer Judea? *63 BC*

Did you know . . .

As the Romans adopted elements of Greek religion, they renamed the gods and goddesses to give them Latin names. For instance, Athena, the goddess of wisdom, became Minerva, and Ares, the god of war, became Mars. The Romans adopted gods from civilizations other than Greece as well. From Egypt they adopted the goddess of motherhood, Isis, and from Persia, the god of soldiers, Mithras.

Critical Thinking: Supporting a Point of View

At Level

Research Required

Writing a Speech

1. Remind students that Romans often adopted gods or goddesses from the people with whom they came in contact.
2. Have each student select a god or goddess that was worshipped in Rome but originated in a different civilization. Examples include Isis, Cybele, Mithras, Osiris, and many of the Greek gods and goddesses.
3. Have students use the library, Internet, or other resources to research information regarding the god or goddess they selected.
4. Have each student imagine that he or she is a speechwriter for a provincial official. Each student should write a speech for the official expressing why that god or goddess should be included in a Roman pantheon. Remind students to back their argument with specific facts from their research.
5. Ask volunteers to share their speeches with the class. LS **Verbal/Linguistic**

Alternative Assessment Handbook, Rubric 43: Writing to Persuade

Direct Teach

Main Idea

❶ Religious Tolerance and Conflict

Despite its general religious tolerance, Rome came into conflict with the Jews.

Contrast How was Hadrian's policy different from previous Roman policies? *Hadrian banned the practice of some Jewish rituals and eventually destroyed Jerusalem.*

Analyze Although the Romans did not ban Judaism, why did the Jews continue to rebel? *They wanted to be ruled only by Jews and did not want to worship Roman gods and violate their religious beliefs.*

Main Idea

❷ A New Religion

A new religion, Christianity, grew out of Judaism.

Identify On what religion were the teachings of Christianity based? *Judaism*

Summarize Why did many Jews believe the Messiah would soon appear? *Prophets had been announcing the coming arrival of the Messiah.*

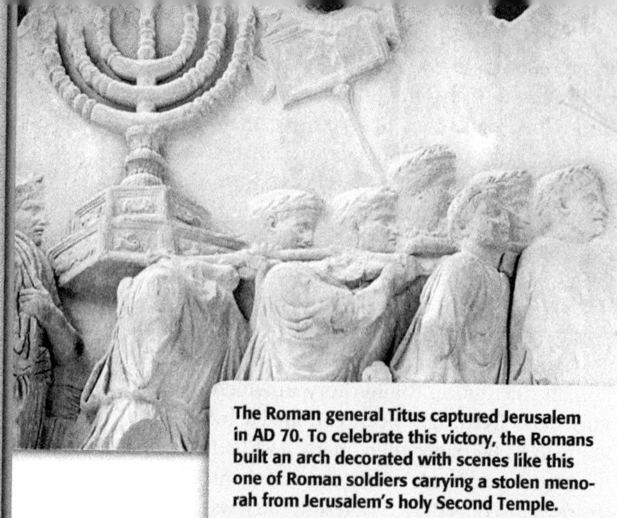

The Roman general Titus captured Jerusalem in AD 70. To celebrate this victory, the Romans built an arch decorated with scenes like this one of Roman soldiers carrying a stolen menorah from Jerusalem's holy Second Temple.

By the early 100s the Romans had become more hostile toward the Jews. Treated harshly and taxed heavily, the Jews grew increasingly bitter. Matters worsened when the emperor Hadrian banned the practice of certain Jewish rituals. He thought this ban would end the Jewish people's desire for independence and cause them to give up Judaism.

Instead Hadrian's actions made the Jews even more upset. Once again they rebelled. This time, Hadrian decided to end the rebellions once and for all.

The Roman army crushed the Jewish revolt and destroyed Jerusalem in 135. Soon after, they forced the remaining Jews to leave the city. Then the Romans built a new city on the ruins of Jerusalem and brought settlers from other parts of the empire to live there. Jews were forbidden to enter this new city more than once a year. Driven out of their ancient city, many Jews moved into other parts of the Roman world.

READING CHECK **Drawing Conclusions** Why did the Romans consider Judaism a threat?

A New Religion

At the beginning of the first century AD, what would become a new religion appeared in Judea. Called **Christianity**, this religion was based on the life and teachings of **Jesus of Nazareth**. Christianity was rooted in the ideas and traditions of Judaism, but it developed as a separate faith.

At the time that Jesus was born, around the end of the first century BC, there were several groups of Jews in Judea. The largest of these groups was stricter than the others in its religious practices. Its members were particularly careful about obeying the laws of Moses, whom you read about in Chapter 7. Jews believe that Moses gave them a set of laws to follow.

In keeping with their observance of the laws, Jews led structured lives. For example, they performed daily rituals and avoided eating certain foods.

Many Jews followed the laws closely because Jewish prophets had said a new leader would appear among them. Many thought this leader was more likely to appear if they were strict in their religious behavior.

According to the prophecy, the Jews' new leader would be a descendant of King David. When he came, he would restore the greatness of King David's ancient kingdom, Israel. The prophets called this leader the **Messiah** (muh-SY-uh), which means "God's anointed one" in Hebrew. In other words, the Jews believed that God would choose the Messiah that would lead them.

When the Romans took over Judea in 63 BC, many Jews believed that the Messiah would soon appear. Jewish prophets wandered through Judea, announcing that the Messiah was coming. Many Jews anxiously awaited his arrival.

READING CHECK **Summarizing** Why were Jews waiting for the Messiah to arrive?

Differentiating Instruction

Struggling Readers Below Level

1. To help students understand the reasons why Jews rebelled against the Roman Empire and what the results of that rebellion were, draw the graphic organizer here for students to see. Omit the blue, italicized answers.
2. Have students copy and complete the graphic organizer. Then review the answers as a class. LS **Visual/Spatial**

Causes	Event	Effects
• *Romans conquer Judea.* • *Jews oppose Roman rule.* • *Differing religious views*	**Jews rebel against Rome.**	• *Hadrian bans certain Jewish rituals.* • *Revolts are crushed.* • *Jerusalem is destroyed.* • *Jews forced to leave Jerusalem.*

Answers

Reading Check (left) *because Jews continued to rebel and demand independence*

Reading Check (right) *For hundreds of years, Jewish prophets had said a Messiah, or new leader, would appear to restore the greatness of Israel.*

Jesus of Nazareth

Jesus of Nazareth, the man many people believe was the Jewish Messiah, lived at the very beginning of the first century AD. Although Jesus was one of the most influential figures in all of world history, we know relatively little about his life. Most of what we know is contained in the Bible, the holy book of the religion of Christianity.

The Christian Bible is made up of two parts. The first part, the Old Testament, is largely the same as the Hebrew Bible. It tells the history and ideas of the Hebrew and Jewish people. The second part, the New Testament, is sacred to Christians. The New Testament contains accounts of the life and teachings of Jesus and the early history of Christianity. The New Testament also contains letters written by some followers of Jesus.

The Birth of Jesus

According to the New Testament, Jesus was born in a town called Bethlehem (BETH-li-hem). In our dating system, the birth of Jesus marks the shift from BC to AD. Jesus's mother, Mary, was married to a carpenter named Joseph. But Christians believe God, not Joseph, was Jesus's father.

As a young man, Jesus lived in the town of Nazareth and probably studied with Joseph to become a carpenter. Like most young Jewish men of the time, he also studied the laws and teachings of Judaism. By the time he was about 30, Jesus had begun to travel and teach about religion. Stories of his teachings and actions make up the beginning of the Bible's New Testament. According to the Bible, Jesus created excitement wherever he went.

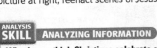

LINKING TO TODAY

Christian Holidays

For centuries, Christians have honored key events in Jesus's life. Some of these events inspired holidays that Christians celebrate today.

The most sacred holiday for Christians is Easter, which is celebrated each spring. Easter is a celebration of the Resurrection, Jesus's rising from the dead. Christians usually celebrate Easter by attending church services. Many people also celebrate by dyeing eggs because eggs are seen as a symbol of new life.

Another major Christian holiday is Christmas. It honors Jesus's birth and is celebrated every December 25. Although no one knows on what date Jesus was actually born, Christians have placed Christmas in December since the 200s. Today, people celebrate with church services and the exchange of gifts. Some, like people in the picture at right, reenact scenes of Jesus's birth.

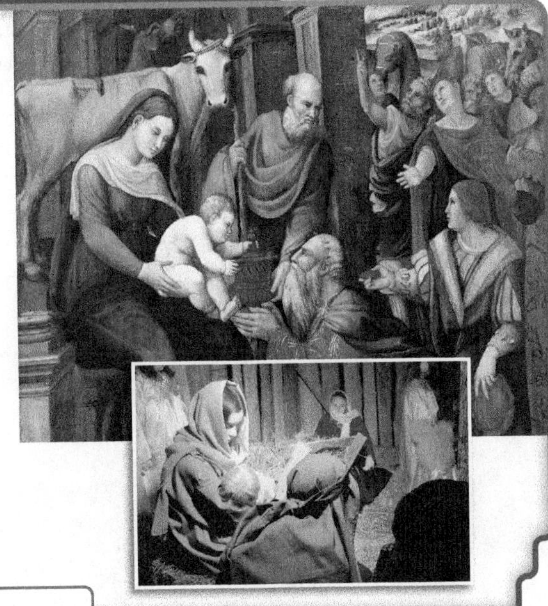

ANALYSIS SKILL **ANALYZING INFORMATION**

Why do you think Christians celebrate events in Jesus's life?

Direct Teach

Main Idea

③ Jesus of Nazareth

Many considered Jesus of Nazareth to be the Messiah.

Identify Where is the story of Jesus recorded? *in the New Testament of the Bible*

Linking to Today

Christian Holidays Some people celebrate Christmas with a Christmas tree. But why? In the 700s, the monk Saint Boniface said that the triangular shape of an evergreen tree resembled a triangle, a symbol of the Trinity—the Father, the Son, and the Holy Ghost. Several hundred years later, evergreen trees were set up inside homes during Christmas. A thousand years later, millions of people still set up and decorate a Christmas tree as part of their celebration of the birth of Jesus.

Info to Know

BC and AD A Roman monk and mathematician first introduced the terms BC and AD about the year 525 AD. BC refers to the years before the birth of Christ. AD, which is Latin for "in the year of our Lord," is used to denote the years after the birth of Christ. While Christian in origin, the BC and AD labels are widely used throughout the world. In recent years, however, the terms BCE, or Before the Common Era, and CE, Common Era, have gained popularity with some people.

hmhsocialstudies.com

Online Resources
Activity: Art Inspired by Jesus

Differentiating Instruction

Advanced/Gifted and Talented **Above Level**

1. Remind students that Jesus often attracted large crowds of followers who gathered to hear his teachings. Discuss with the class how Jesus often taught his followers by telling parables that linked his message to events in everyday life with which the people might be familiar. His famous parables include "The Parable of the Prodigal Son" and "The Parable of the Tares [Weeds] and the Wheat."
2. Encourage students to read a parable, such as the "Parable of the Good Samaritan," to become familiar with the style and the way in which a moral lesson is delivered.
3. Have students write a parable or short story that teaches a lesson. If they have difficulty thinking of a moral, suggest "be nice to your neighbor," or "don't be greedy," or "always be prepared."
4. Ask volunteers to share their parable with the class. LS **Verbal/Linguistic**

Alternative Assessment Handbook, Rubric 37: Writing Assignments

Answers

Analyzing Information *possible answer—A celebration of his life is a celebration of his beliefs and teachings.*

Direct Teach

Main Idea

❸ Jesus of Nazareth

Many considered Jesus of Nazareth to be the Messiah.

Make Inferences Why was Jesus arrested and executed? *He was a threat to the authority of political and religious leaders in Judea.*

Draw Conclusions Why do Christians consider the Resurrection important? *It was proof to many that Jesus was the Messiah.*

Explain How did Jesus spread his message? *He traveled from village to village, speaking to the Jewish people.*

Compare What two teachings of Jesus were rooted in Jewish traditions? *love for God and love for others*

Analyze Why did different denominations of Christianity develop over time? *because different people interpreted the teachings of Jesus in different ways*

CRF: Biography Activity: Saint Peter

Crucifixion and Resurrection

As a teacher, Jesus attracted many followers. As he traveled the Judean countryside, he greatly influenced many who listened to his message. But at the same time, his teachings challenged the authority of political and religious leaders. According to the Bible, Roman leaders arrested Jesus while he was in Jerusalem in or around AD 30.

THE IMPACT TODAY
Because Jesus was crucified, the cross is an important symbol of Christianity today.

Shortly after his arrest, Jesus was executed. He was killed by **crucifixion** (kroo-suh-FIK-shuhn), a type of execution in which a person was nailed to a cross. In fact, the word crucifixion comes from the Latin word for "cross." After Jesus died, his followers buried him.

According to Christian beliefs, Jesus rose from the dead on the third day after he was crucified. Christians refer to Jesus's rise from the dead as the **Resurrection** (re-suh-REK-shuhn). After the Resurrection, several groups of Jesus's disciples (di-SY-puhls), or followers, claimed to see him.

Early Christians believe that the Resurrection was a sign that Jesus was the Messiah and the Son of God. Some people began to call him Jesus Christ, from the Greek word for Messiah, *Christos*. It is from this word that the words *Christian* and *Christianity* later developed.

The Teachings of Jesus

Jesus had traveled from village to village spreading his message to the Jewish people. Much of Jesus's message was rooted in older Jewish traditions. For example, he emphasized two rules that were also taught in the Torah: love God, and love other people.

Jesus expected his followers to love all people, not just friends or family. He encouraged his followers to be generous to the poor and the sick. He told people that they should even love their enemies. The way people treated others, Jesus said, showed how much they loved God.

Another important theme in Jesus's teachings was salvation, or the rescue of people from sin. Jesus taught that people who were saved from sin would enter the kingdom of God when they died. Many of Jesus's teachings dealt with how people could reach the kingdom. Jesus warned that people who loved money or goods more than they loved God would not be saved.

Over the many centuries since Jesus lived, people have interpreted his teachings in different ways. As a result, many different denominations of Christians have developed. A denomination is a group of people who hold the same religous beliefs. Still, despite their differences, Christians around

The Last Supper

This famous painting by Italian artist Leonardo da Vinci shows the Last Supper—the final meal that Jesus and his Apostles shared before Jesus was arrested.

Critical Thinking: Drawing Inferences

Below Level

Writing Interview Questions

1. Review with the class the teachings of Jesus and his followers. Write the main rules and teachings for students to see. Ask students to infer what people's reactions might have been to the teachings of Jesus. Why might people have become followers of Jesus based on his message?
2. Ask students to imagine that they are newspaper reporters covering an event where Jesus is speaking to a large crowd. Have students create 10 interview questions a reporter might ask a person in the crowd who has just heard Jesus or one of his followers speak.
3. Remind students to keep their interview questions objective. Questions could cover such topics as the roots of Jesus's message, key ideas and beliefs of his teachings, Jesus's parables, or reactions to his message.
4. Ask volunteers to share their questions with the class. **LS Verbal/Linguistic**

Alternative Assessment Handbook, Rubric 37: Writing Assignments

Primary Source

LETTER

Paul's Letter to the Romans

In the late AD 50s Paul traveled to Corinth, a city in Greece. While there, he wrote a letter to the people of Rome. In this letter he told the Romans that he planned to come to their city to deliver God's message. In the meantime, he told them, they should learn to live together peacefully.

"Let love be genuine; hate what is evil, hold fast to what is good; love one another with mutual affection; outdo one another in showing honor. Do not lag in zeal, be ardent [strong] in spirit, serve the Lord. Rejoice in hope, be patient in suffering, persevere in prayer. Contribute to the needs of the saints; extend hospitality to strangers.

Bless those who persecute you; bless and do not curse them. Rejoice with those who rejoice, weep with those who weep. Live in harmony with one another; do not be haughty, but associate with the lowly; do not claim to be wiser than you are. Do not repay anyone evil for evil, but take thought for what is noble in the sight of all. If it is possible, so far as it depends on you, live peaceably with all."

–Romans 12:9–18 NRSV

ANALYSIS SKILL ANALYZING PRIMARY SOURCES

How did Paul's letter express Jesus's teachings?

the world share some basic beliefs about Jesus and his importance.

The Spread of Jesus's Teachings

The **Apostles** (uh-PAHS-uhls) were 12 disciples whom Jesus chose to receive special training. After the Resurrection, the Apostles traveled widely telling about Jesus and his teachings. Some of Jesus's disciples wrote accounts of his life and teachings. These accounts are called the Gospels. Four Gospels are found in the New Testament of the Bible. They were written by men known as Matthew, Mark, Luke, and John. Historians and religious scholars depend on the Gospels for information about Jesus's life.

Probably the most important figure in the spread of Christianity after Jesus's death was named **Paul of Tarsus**. Paul traveled throughout the Roman world spreading Christian teachings. In his letters he wrote about the Resurrection and about salvation. Paul also told Christians that they didn't have to obey all Jewish laws and rituals. These ideas helped the Christian Church break away from Judaism.

READING CHECK **Summarizing** What do Christians believe happened after Jesus died?

The Growth of Christianity

The first Christians spread Jesus's teachings only among Jews. But Paul and other Christians introduced Christianity to non-Jews as well. As a result, Christianity began to spread rapidly. Within a hundred years after Jesus's death, thousands of Christians lived in the Roman Empire.

However, Christians trying to spread their beliefs faced challenges from local officials. Some officials even arrested and killed Christians who refused to worship Rome's gods. A few Roman emperors feared that Christians would cause unrest, so they banned Christianity. This began a period of persecution (puhr-si-KYOO-shuhn) against Christians. Persecution is the punishment of a group because of its beliefs.

Direct Teach

Primary Source

Reading Like a Historian

Paul's Letter to the Romans Help students practice reading the document like historians. Ask:

- What was Paul's purpose in writing this letter to the Romans?
- Why might Paul's message appeal to the Romans?

Main Idea

4 The Growth of Christianity

Christianity grew in popularity and eventually became the official religion of Rome.

Recall Who were the Apostles? *12 close followers of Jesus who spread his teachings after the Resurrection*

Evaluate Why were the Gospels important? *They provide information about Jesus's life.*

Make Inferences Why was it important for the Christian Church to break away from Judaism? *possible answer—because Jesus was believed to be the Messiah and his teachings differed from Jewish law*

Identify Who was persecuted? *The Christians were persecuted, or punished, for their religious beliefs.*

Predict Why might persecution have made Christianity stronger? *possible answer—It created unity among Christians.*

CRF: History and Geography Activity: Spread of Christianity

Map Transparency: The Spread of Christianity, AD 300–AD 400

Collaborative Learning

At Level

Research Required

Writing a Travelogue

1. Review with students the contributions of Paul of Tarsus. Remind students that Paul is best known for his efforts to spread Christianity.
2. Organize students into small groups. Have each group use the library, Internet, or other resources to find information about the areas in which Paul traveled on his four journeys. What cities did he visit? How did he travel from place to place?
3. Next, explain to students that a travelogue is a description of a person's travels. Have each group create a travelogue that describes where and how Paul traveled on each of his journeys. Encourage students to create illustrations and maps to enhance their travelogues.
4. Ask groups to share their travelogues with the class. LS **Verbal/Linguistic, Visual/Spatial**

Alternative Assessment Handbook, Rubric 42: Writing to Inform

Answers

Reading Check *After three days he rose from the dead, and this was a sign that Jesus was the Messiah.*

Analyzing Primary Sources *It tells the reader to love one's neighbor and to live peaceably with all.*

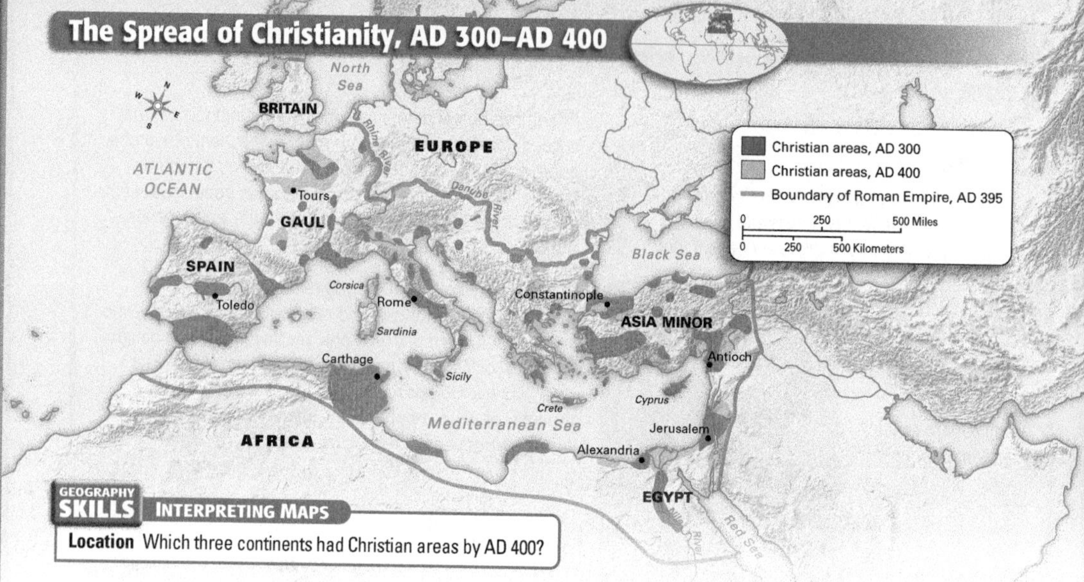

GEOGRAPHY SKILLS INTERPRETING MAPS

Location Which three continents had Christian areas by AD 400?

Review & Assess

Close

Ask students to summarize why the Roman policy of religious tolerance did not work in the case of the Jews. Summarize the teachings of Christianity.

Review

Online Quiz, Section 2

Assess

SE Section 2 Assessment

PASS: Section 2 Quiz

Alternative Assessment Handbook

Reteach/Classroom Intervention

Guided Reading Workbook, Section 2

Interactive Skills Tutor CD-ROM

Christians began to meet in secret but continued to spread their faith. In the early 300s, the emperor **Constantine** (KAHN-stuhn-teen) became a Christian. He removed the bans on the religion. A later emperor made Christianity Rome's official religion.

READING CHECK **Identifying Cause and Effect** How did Paul's ideas help to spread Christianity?

SUMMARY AND PREVIEW Although usually tolerant, Roman authorities persecuted Jews and Christians in the empire. However, both Judaism and Christianity survived. In fact, Christianity eventually became the empire's official religion. Next, you will read about the fall of Rome.

Section 2 Assessment

hmhsocialstudies.com ONLINE QUIZ

Reviewing Ideas, Terms, and People

1. a. **Recall** Why did Roman leaders ban some religions?
   b. **Explain** What was one religion that Roman leaders considered a problem? Why?
2. a. **Describe** What traditions were practiced by the Jews of Judea?
   b. **Explain** Describe Jewish beliefs about the **Messiah**.
3. a. **Identify** From where does most of the information about **Jesus of Nazareth** come?
   b. **Analyze** How did the teachings of **Paul of Tarsus** change Christianity's relationship to Judaism?
4. a. **Summarize** What challenges did early Christians face in practicing and spreading their religion?
   b. **Elaborate** How did **Constantine** affect Christianity?

Critical Thinking

5. **Summarizing** Using your notes and a chart like the one below, identify the main teachings of Christianity. Then describe its spread and how Rome's policy toward it changed over time.

Christian Teachings	Spread	Changes in Rome's Policy

Focus on Writing

6. **Adding Details** Write down some notes and add details to your columns about what life might have been like for Jews and Christians in this period.

Section 2 Assessment Answers

1. a. Roman leaders saw these religions as political threats.
   b. Judaism; Jews rebelled against Roman rule.
2. a. the worship of one God; following the laws of Moses
   b. leader who restores the kingdom of Israel
3. a. the Gospels; the New Testament; the Bible
   b. He spread Christianity through the Roman Empire, explained Jesus's teachings, and separated Christianity from Judaism.
4. a. were persecuted, had to meet in secret.
   b. Constantine became a Christian and removed the bans on the religion.
5. Christian teachings—love God, love others, salvation, Jesus was the Messiah; Spread—Apostles spread Jesus's teachings; Rome's policy—first persecuted and banned, then Constantine removed bans, became official religion
6. Jews—persecuted by the Romans, taxed heavily, Jerusalem destroyed, forced to move; Christians—first persecuted, later accepted

Answers

Reading Check *Paul spread Jesus's teachings throughout the Roman Empire and further developed the religion, separating it from Judaism.*

Interpreting Maps *Africa, Europe, and Asia*

The End of the Empire

SECTION 3

If YOU were there...

You are a former Roman soldier who has settled on lands in Gaul. In the last few months, groups of foreigners have been raiding local towns and burning farms. The commander of the local army post is an old friend, but he says he is short of loyal soldiers. Many troops have been called back to Rome. You don't know when the next raid will come.

How will you defend your lands?

BUILDING BACKGROUND Though the Roman Empire remained large and powerful, it faced serious threats from both outside and inside. Beyond the borders of the empire, many different groups of people were on the move. They threatened the peace in the provinces—and eventually attacked the heart of the empire itself.

Problems in the Empire

At its height the Roman Empire included all the land around the Mediterranean Sea. In the early AD 100s, the empire stretched from Britain south to Egypt, and from the Atlantic Ocean all the way to the Syrian Desert.

But the empire did not stay that large for long. By the end of the 200s, emperors had given up some of the land the Roman army had conquered. These emperors feared that the empire had become too large to defend or govern efficiently. As later rulers discovered, these emperors were right.

External and Internal Threats

Even as emperors were giving up territory, new threats to the empire were appearing. Tribes of fierce Germanic warriors attacked Rome's northern borders. At the same time, Persian armies invaded in the east. The Romans defended themselves from these invasions for 200 years, but only at great cost.

What You Will Learn...

Main Ideas

1. Many problems threatened the Roman Empire, leading one emperor to divide it in half.
2. Rome declined as a result of invasions and political and economic problems.
3. In the eastern empire, people created a new society and religious traditions that were very different from those in the west.

The Big Idea

Problems from both inside and outside caused the Roman Empire to split into a western half, which collapsed, and an eastern half that prospered for hundreds of years.

Key Terms and People

Diocletian, *p. 340*
Attila, *p. 341*
corruption, *p. 342*
Justinian, *p. 342*
Theodora, *p. 343*
Byzantine Empire, *p. 343*

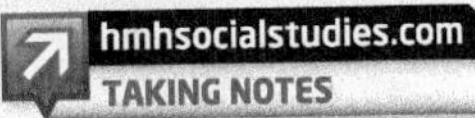

Use the graphic organizer online to take notes on the Western Roman Empire and the Eastern Roman Empire.

Preteach

Bellringer

If YOU were there . . . Use the **Daily Bellringer Transparency** to help students answer the question.

Daily Bellringer Transparency, Section 3

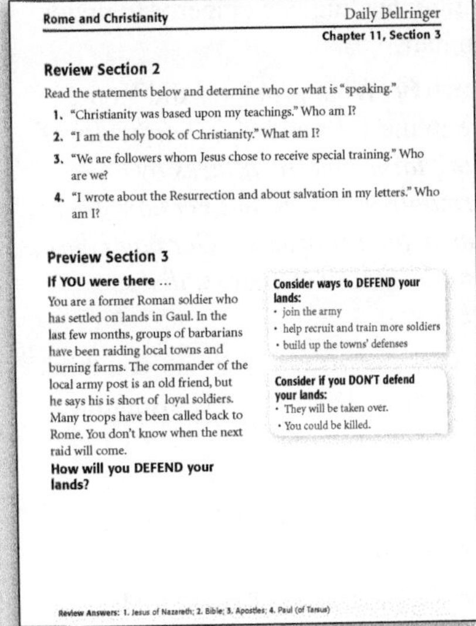

Rome and Christianity — Daily Bellringer, Chapter 11, Section 3

Review Section 2

Read the statements below and determine who or what is "speaking."

1. "Christianity was based upon my teachings." Who am I?
2. "I am the holy book of Christianity." What am I?
3. "We are followers whom Jesus chose to receive special training." Who are we?
4. "I wrote about the Resurrection and about salvation in my letters." Who am I?

Preview Section 3

If YOU were there ...

You are a former Roman soldier who has settled on lands in Gaul. In the last few months, groups of barbarians have been raiding local towns and burning farms. The commander of the local army post is an old friend, but he says his is short of loyal soldiers. Many troops have been called back to Rome. You don't know when the next raid will come.

How will you DEFEND your lands?

Consider ways to DEFEND your lands:
- join the army
- help recruit and train more soldiers
- build up the towns' defenses

Consider if you DON'T defend your lands:
- They will be taken over.
- You could be killed.

Review Answers: 1. Jesus of Nazareth; 2. Bible; 3. Apostles; 4. Paul (of Tarsus)

Academic Vocabulary

Review with students the high-use academic term in this section.

efficient productive not wasteful (p. 342)

CRF: Vocabulary Builder Activity, Section 3

Taking Notes

Have students use the graphic organizer online to take notes on the section. This activity will prepare students for the Section Assessment, in which they will complete a graphic organizer that builds on the information using the Critical Thinking Skill: Drawing Conclusions.

Teach the Big Idea

At Level

The End of the Empire

1. **Teach** Ask students the questions in the Main Idea boxes to teach this section.
2. **Apply** Write the labels *Internal Problems, External Problems,* and *Invasions* for students to see. Have each student create a three-column chart on his or her own paper that uses the labels as column headings. Then have each student identify problems mentioned in the section and determine under which category each problem falls. **LS Visual/Spatial**
3. **Review** Have students discuss the problems they identified on their charts and agree upon a class list of problems that led to the fall of Rome.
4. **Practice/Homework** Have each student write a short paragraph identifying the problem the student feels played the largest role in the fall of the western Roman Empire. Students should provide reasons to support their choices. **LS Verbal/Linguistic**

Direct Teach

Main Idea

1 Problems in the Empire

Many problems threatened the Roman Empire, leading one emperor to divide it in half.

Identify What problems did Rome face in the 100s and 200s? *difficulty of ruling large empire, attacks by Germanic warriors and Persian armies, food shortages, German communities ignore emperors, disease, high taxes*

Make Inferences Why do you think power moved east when Constantine moved the empire's capital? *possible answers—The power went with the emperor; power was in the capital, which had moved.*

Activity Division Debate Have students conduct a debate between supporters of Diocletian, who want the empire to remain divided, and supporters of Constantine, who want to reunite the empire. Remind students to think about the pros and cons of each position.

LS Verbal/Linguistic

Alternative Assessment Handbook, Rubric 10: Debates

Map Transparency: Invasions of the Roman Empire, 340–500

Did you know . . .

Emperor Diocletian tried to strengthen the empire in other ways as well. In 301 he issued an imperial edict that fixed the price for over 1,000 items to protect buyers from unfair price increases by merchants. Violators could be punished by death!

hmhsocialstudies.com
ANIMATED HISTORY
The Division of the Roman Empire, AD 395

The Romans struggled with problems within the empire as well. The raids against Rome made people near the border nervous. In time, these people abandoned their land. To grow enough food, the Romans invited Germanic farmers to grow crops on Roman lands. These farmers often came from the same tribes that threatened Rome's borders. Over time, whole German communities had moved into the empire. They chose their own leaders and largely ignored the emperors. This caused problems for the Romans.

THE IMPACT TODAY
Constantinople is now called Istanbul, and is a major urban center.

Other internal problems also threatened Rome's survival. Disease swept through the empire, killing many people. The government was also forced to increase taxes to pay for the defense of the empire. Desperate, the Romans looked for a strong emperor. They found one in Diocletian.

Division of the Empire

Diocletian (dy-uh-KLEE-shuhn) became emperor in the late 200s. Convinced that the empire was too big for one person to rule, Diocletian ruled the eastern half and named a co-emperor to rule the west.

Not long after Diocletian left power, the emperor Constantine (KAHN-stuhn-teen) reunited the empire for a short time. He also moved the capital to the east, into what is now Turkey. He built a grand new capital city there. It was called Constantinople (kahn-stant-uhn-OH-puhl), which means "the city of Constantine." Although the empire was still called the Roman Empire, Rome was no longer the real center of power. Power had moved to the east.

READING CHECK **Identifying Cause and Effect** Why did Diocletian divide the Roman Empire?

hmhsocialstudies.com INTERACTIVE MAP

Invasions of the Roman Empire, 340–500

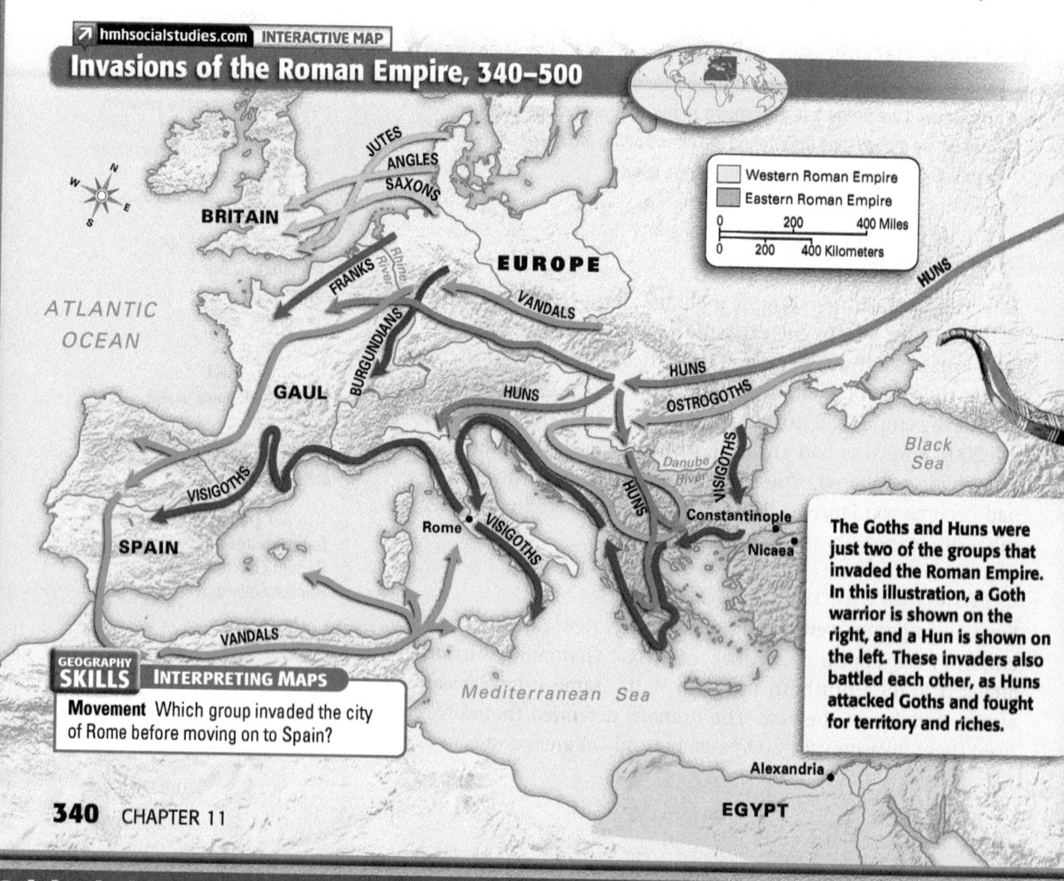

The Goths and Huns were just two of the groups that invaded the Roman Empire. In this illustration, a Goth warrior is shown on the right, and a Hun is shown on the left. These invaders also battled each other, as Huns attacked Goths and fought for territory and riches.

GEOGRAPHY SKILLS **INTERPRETING MAPS**

Movement Which group invaded the city of Rome before moving on to Spain?

Critical Thinking: Drawing Conclusions

At Level

Studying Invasion Routes

1. Review with students the invasions that troubled the Roman Empire in 340–500.
2. Have students examine the map. Then have students create a chart in which they list the groups of invaders and identify what parts of the Roman Empire each invaded.
3. Ask: Which invaders would have needed ships to reach their target? *Saxon, Angles, Jutes, Vandals;* Which parts of the empire had the least problems with invaders? *Asia Minor, Syria, and Egypt;* Why do you think the Huns did not invade Asia Minor? *possible answer—Mountains might have prevented easy access into Asia Minor.*
4. After analyzing the map, ask each student to select one of the groups of invaders. Have students write a series of short journal entries as if he or she was a member of the invading tribe. Have students describe what part of the Roman Empire they were located in and what sights they might have seen there. Have volunteers share their journal entries with the class.

Answers

Interpreting Maps *Visigoths*

Reading Check *He was convinced the empire was too big for one person to govern.*

The Decline of Rome

As you have read, foreign tribes had settled along the Roman Empire's northern border in the 200s. A century later, these bands of fighters began raiding deep into the heart of the empire.

Early Invasions

The source of these raids was a group of people called the Huns, fierce warriors from Central Asia. The Huns first invaded southeastern Europe and then launched raids on nearby kingdoms. Among the Huns' victims were several groups of people called the Goths, made up of the Visigoths and Ostrogoths. Unable to defeat the Huns, the Goths fled into Roman territory.

Rome's leaders feared that the Goths would destroy Roman land and property. They fought to keep the Goths out of Roman territory. The eastern armies were largely successful. They forced the Goths to move farther west. As a result, however, the western armies were defeated by the Goths. After their victory, large numbers of Goths moved into the Roman Empire.

The Romans fought desperately to keep the Goths from Rome. They even paid the Goths not to attack. In 408, however, the Romans stopped making payments. The Visigoths marched into Rome and sacked, or destroyed, the city in 410. This devastated the Romans. No one had attacked their city in nearly 800 years. Many Romans began to fear for the future of their empire.

The Fall of the Western Empire

The Gothic victory inspired other groups of foreign warriors to invade the western half of the empire. The Vandals, Angles, Saxons, Jutes, and Franks all launched attacks. Meanwhile, the Huns, under a fearsome leader named **Attila** (AT-uhl-uh), raided Roman territory in the east.

THE IMPACT TODAY

We still use the word *vandal* today to describe someone who destroys property.

Rome needed strong leaders to survive these attacks, but the emperors were weak. Military leaders took power away from the emperors and, by the 450s, ruled Rome.

Conflict among these military leaders gave the invaders an opening. In 476 one of the foreign generals overthrew the last emperor in Rome and named himself king of Italy. Many historians consider this event the end of the Western Roman Empire.

Factors in Rome's Fall

There were several causes of Rome's decline. One was the vast size of the empire. Communication among various parts of the empire was difficult, especially during times of conflict. The Roman world simply became too big to govern effectively.

Direct Teach

Main Idea

❷ The Decline of Rome

Rome declined as a result of invasions and political and economic problems.

Recall How did the Romans deal with Goth invaders? *They sent armies against the invaders and even paid some invaders not to attack.*

Sequence What sequence of events led to the sack of Rome in 410? *The Huns pushed the Goths into Roman territory; the Goths defeated western Roman armies; Goths were paid to withhold their attacks on Rome; when payments from Rome stopped, the Goths destroyed Rome.*

Identify What factors weakened Roman government? *The empire was too large to govern efficiently; corrupt officials ignored needs of citizens.*

Linking to Today

The Vandals Among the threats posed by the many groups that troubled Rome, one of the most serious came from the Vandals. A Germanic tribe from Northern Europe, the Vandals attacked Gaul, Spain, and North Africa before setting their sights on the heart of the western empire. In 455 they launched an attack on Rome. Today's use of the word *vandal* comes from the damage and destruction Vandal raids caused in the Roman Empire.

hmhsocialstudies.com

Online Resources
Activity: Barbarian Invasions

Differentiating Instruction

Special Needs Learners **Below Level**

1. To help students understand the events leading up to the decline of Rome, write the following list of events in random order for students to see. *Huns invade southeastern Europe; Huns launch raids on Goths; Goths flee to Roman territory; Romans try to fight off Goths; Rome is sacked in 410.*
2. Organize students into mixed-ability-level pairs. Have each pair work together to place the events in their proper sequence. Remind students to work together.
3. Once students have properly sequenced the events, have each group use a blank outline map of Europe to depict the events on their list. **LS Logical/Mathematical, Visual/Spatial**

Alternative Assessment Handbook, Rubrics 14: Group Activity; and 20: Map Creation

Direct Teach

Main Idea

3 A New Eastern Empire

In the eastern empire, people created a new society and religious traditions that were very different from those in the west.

Identify Cause and Effect What were the effects of wealthy citizens leaving Rome? *Rome's population decreased, taxes and prices soared, schools closed, and wealthy citizens set up estates in the countryside with their own private armies, which weakened the emperors.*

Elaborate Which factor do you think played the biggest part in the downfall of Rome? Why? *Answers will vary, but students should indicate a rationale for their choice.*

Recall What were Justinian's passions as emperor? *reuniting the old Roman Empire, organizing Roman law, and the church*

Identify Who was Theodora, and what role did she play in the Byzantine Empire? *She was the wife of Emperor Justinian; she helped him rule effectively.*

CRF: Primary Source Activity: Byzantine Mosaic Panels, St. Vitale Church, Ravenna, Italy

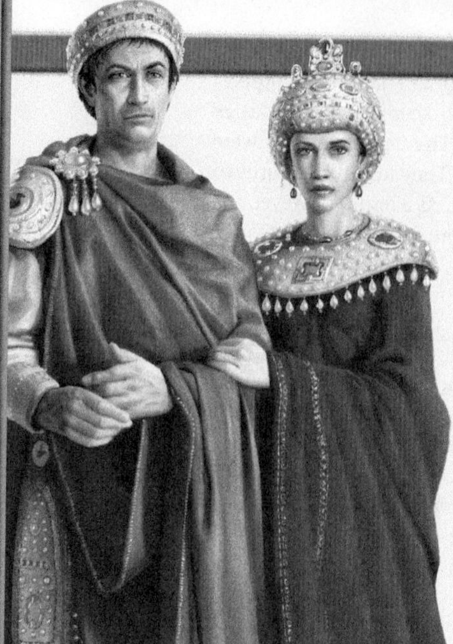

BIOGRAPHY

Justinian and Theodora

483–565; c. 500–548

Justinian I was the emperor of the Byzantine Empire from AD 527 to AD 565. As emperor, Justinian reconquered parts of the fallen western empire and simplified Roman laws. He also ordered the building of many beautiful public structures and churches, including the Church of Hagia Sophia.

He married Theodora in about AD 522. Together they worked to restore the power, beauty, and strength of a vast empire. While Justinian was waging military campaigns, Theodora helped create laws to aid women and children and to end government corruption.

Evaluating Which of Justinian and Theodora's accomplishments do you find most impressive? Why?

Political crises also contributed to the decline. By the 400s **corruption**, the decay of people's values, had become widespread in Roman government. Corrupt officials used threats and bribery to achieve their goals, often ignoring the needs of Roman citizens. As a result, Rome's government was no longer **efficient**.

ACADEMIC VOCABULARY
efficient (i-FI-shuhnt) productive and not wasteful

Many wealthy citizens fled to their country estates and created their own armies for protection. Some, however, used these armies to overthrow emperors and take power for themselves. For those people who remained in the cities, life became more difficult. Rome's population decreased, and schools closed. Taxes and prices soared, leaving more Romans poor. By the late 400s Rome was a changed city, and the empire slowly collapsed around it.

READING CHECK **Analyzing Information** Why did Rome fall to invaders in the 400s?

A New Eastern Empire

Despite the fall of Rome, the eastern empire grew in wealth and power. Its people created a new society that was different from the society in the west.

Justinian

The eastern emperors dreamed of retaking Rome. For **Justinian** (juh-STIN-ee-uhn), an emperor who ruled from 527 to 565, reuniting the old Roman Empire was a passion. His armies conquered Italy and much land around the Mediterranean.

Justinian's other passions were the law and the church. He ordered officials to remove any out-of-date or unchristian laws. He then organized all the laws into a new legal system called Justinian's Code. By simplifying Roman law, this code helped guarantee fair treatment for all.

Despite his successes, Justinian made many enemies. In 532 an uprising

Critical Thinking: Identifying Cause and Effect

Below Level

Causes of Rome's Collapse

1. Discuss with students the factors involved in the decline of the western Roman Empire.
2. To help students understand the cause and effect of factors that led to the fall of Rome, draw the chart for students to see. Omit the blue, italicized answers.
3. Have students copy and complete the chart. Then review the answers as a class.
LS Verbal/Linguistic, Visual/Spatial

Alternative Assessment Handbook, Rubric 7: Charts

Causes	Events	Effects
weak emperors; growing power of military	**Military Leaders take Power**	*leaders fight among themselves; Rome falls*
corrupt government ignores citizens	**Wealthy Citizens Flee Rome**	*taxes and prices rise; rich create private armies*

Answers

Evaluating *possible answers—reuniting the Roman Empire, because it brought order to the West; simplifying Roman law, because it promoted fairness for all people*

Reading Check *because the emperors were weak and military leaders were busy fighting among themselves, which allowed a foreign general to overthrow the last emperor in Rome and name himself king of Italy*

The Church of Hagia Sophia
Hagia Sophia rises high above Istanbul, Turkey, the city once called Constantinople. Built by Justinian, the church with its many domes is the best example of a new style of architecture that developed in the Byzantine Empire.

threatened to drive him from Constantinople. However, his smart and powerful wife **Theodora** (thee-uh-DOHR-uh) convinced him to stay and fight. Taking her advice, Justinian crushed the riots and ruled effectively for the rest of his reign.

After Justinian's death, the eastern empire began to decline. Invaders took over all the land Justinian had gained. The empire continued to shrink for the next several hundred years. In 1453 the Ottoman Turks captured Constantinople, bringing an end to the Eastern Roman Empire.

Byzantine Society

The society of the eastern empire was distinct from that of the west. Scholars studied both Greek and Roman works, and many people spoke Greek rather than Latin. Historians call the society of the Eastern Roman Empire the **Byzantine** (BI -zuhn-teen) **Empire**, after Byzantium, the Greek town Constantinople had replaced.

The importance of Christianity in the eastern empire is reflected in the Byzantines' beautiful works of art and magnificent churches. As time passed, people began to interpret and practice Christianity differently in the east and the west. Eventually these differences led to a split within the Christian Church. In the 1000s Christians in the east formed the Orthodox Church. As a result, eastern and western Europe were divided by religion.

THE IMPACT TODAY
The Orthodox faith is still the main religion in Russia, Greece, and other parts of eastern Europe.

READING CHECK **Drawing Conclusions** Why did Justinian reorganize Roman law?

SUMMARY AND PREVIEW After the fall of Rome, Roman power shifted east. The Orthodox Church became a major force in the Byzantine Empire. Next, you will learn about members of another religious group—the Muslims.

Section 3 Assessment

hmhsocialstudies.com ONLINE QUIZ

Reviewing Ideas, Terms, and People

1. a. **Recall** To where did Constantine move Rome's capital?
   b. **Explain** What effect did Roman farmers' fear of raids have on the empire?
2. a. **Identify** Who was **Attila**?
   b. **Analyze** Why did the Goths move into the Roman Empire?
3. a. **Summarize** What were two of **Justinian's** major accomplishments?
   b. **Contrast** Name two ways that the **Byzantine Empire** was different from the Western Roman Empire.

Critical Thinking

4. **Drawing Conclusions** Draw a word web like the one shown. In each of the outer circles, list a factor that helped lead to the fall of the Western Roman Empire. You may make more circles if needed.

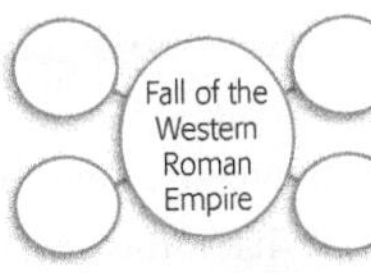

Focus on Writing

5. **Adding the Final Details** Add the key events, persons, and places that were covered in this section to the list you have been making. Once your list is complete, review it to get an idea of what to include in your screenplay.

Direct Teach

Main Idea

3 A New Eastern Empire

In the eastern empire, people created a new society and religious traditions that were very different from those in the west.

Draw Conclusions Why did the empire decline after the rule of the emperor Justinian? *invaders took over land, Ottoman Turks captured Constantinople, non-Roman cultural influences took hold in the east*

Recall In what ways did the eastern empire change from the western empire? *People began to speak Greek rather than Latin and interpret and practice Christianity differently.*

Analyze What caused the complete division of eastern and western Europe? *Two societies developed with different languages and cultures. The division was complete when the Christian Church divided.*

Review & Assess

Close

Briefly review the ways in which outside and inside problems contributed to the fall of the western Roman Empire.

Review

Online Quiz, Section 3

Assess

SE Section 3 Assessment
PASS: Section 3 Quiz
Alternative Assessment Handbook

Reteach/Classroom Intervention

Guided Reading Workbook, Section 3
Interactive Skills Tutor CD-ROM

Section 3 Assessment Answers

1. **a.** to the east in what is now Turkey; he called it Constantinople
   b. The people along the border abandoned their land. Germanic farmers were invited to farm the land; in turn they ignored Roman emperors.
2. **a.** leader of the Huns who invaded the Roman Empire
   b. They were driven into Rome by armies of Huns from Central Asia.
3. **a.** possible answers—He reconquered parts of the former Roman Empire; he simplified Roman law; he put down a rebellion.
   b. People in the Byzantine Empire spoke Greek, not Latin, and practiced and interpreted Christianity differently from the West.
4. possible answers—foreign invasions; corruption in the government; closing of schools; rising taxes and prices; size of the empire
5. possible responses—400s: Rome falls; 527–565: Justinian rules; 1453: Ottoman Turks capture Constantinople; 1000s: Christian Church splits

Answers

Reading Check *to help guarantee fair treatment for all*

Social Studies Skills

Interpreting Time Lines

Activity Life Events Time Lines
Ask two volunteers to identify at least five important events in their lives since they were born. Make a time line that shows the events for one student on one side and the events for the other student on the other side. Then ask students questions that prompt them to compare and contrast the events in the two students' lives. To extend the activity, have students find important world events that happened at about the same time as one of the student's personal events. Have volunteers add these world events to the time line. LS **Visual/Spatial**

Alternative Assessment Handbook, Rubric 36: Time Lines

Interactive Skills Tutor CD-ROM, Lesson 3: Interpret and Create a Time Line and Sequence Events

Social Studies Skills

Analysis | Critical Thinking | Economics | Study

Interpreting Time Lines

Understand the Skill

A time line is a visual summary of important events that occurred during a period of history. It displays the events in the order in which they happened. It also shows how long after one event another event took place. In this way time lines allow you to see at a glance what happened and when. You can better see relationships between events and remember important dates when they are displayed on a timeline.

Learn the Skill

Some time lines cover huge spans of time—sometimes even many centuries. Other time lines, such as the one on this page, cover much shorter periods of time.

Time lines can be arranged either vertically or horizontally. This time line is vertical. Its dates are read from top to bottom. Horizontal time lines are read from left to right.

Follow these steps to interpret a time line.

1. Read the time line's title. Note the range of years covered and the intervals of time into which it is divided.
2. Study the order of events on the time line. Note the length of time between events.
3. Note relationships. Ask yourself how an event relates to others on the time line. Look for cause-and-effect relationships and long-term developments.

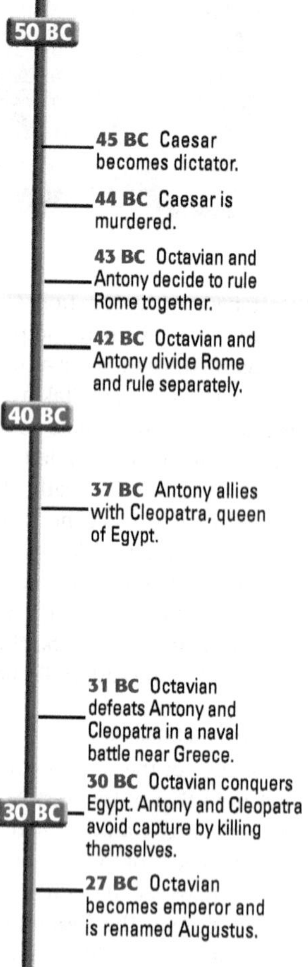

AUGUSTUS BECOMES EMPEROR
50 BC
45 BC Caesar becomes dictator.
44 BC Caesar is murdered.
43 BC Octavian and Antony decide to rule Rome together.
42 BC Octavian and Antony divide Rome and rule separately.
40 BC
37 BC Antony allies with Cleopatra, queen of Egypt.
31 BC Octavian defeats Antony and Cleopatra in a naval battle near Greece.
30 BC Octavian conquers Egypt. Antony and Cleopatra avoid capture by killing themselves.
30 BC
27 BC Octavian becomes emperor and is renamed Augustus.
23 BC Augustus becomes ruler for life.

Practice and Apply the Skill

Interpret the time line to answer the following questions.

1. What is the subject of this time line? What years does it cover?
2. How long did Octavian and Antony rule after dividing Rome?
3. How long after dividing the empire did Antony ally with Cleopatra?
4. What steps did Octavian take to end his alliance with Antony and become emperor? When did he take them? How long did it take?

Social Studies Skills Activity

At Level

Roman Empire Time Line

Materials: art supplies, chart paper, color markers

1. Have students work as a class to create a large time line on chart paper of the events covered in this chapter.
2. Organize students into groups and assign each group a specific part of the time line to complete. Start by having students copy the events from the time line at the beginning of the chapter. Tell students to leave out the other world events or suggest that they keep the chapter events and other world events separate, as on the chapter time line.
3. Have group members complete the time line by adding events from the chapter. Each group should also add photos, images, drawings, and quotes to illustrate the time line. LS **Interpersonal, Visual/Spatial**

Alternative Assessment Handbook, Rubric 36: Time Lines

Answers

Practice and Apply the Skill
1. *events leading to Augustus becoming emperor; 45 BC–23 BC* **2.** *one year* **3.** *five years* **4.** *31 BC: Octavian defeated Antony and Cleopatra in a naval battle; 30 BC: Octavian conquered Egypt; 27 BC: Octavian became emperor. It took four years for Octavian to end his alliance with Antony and become emperor.*

CHAPTER 11

Chapter Review

History's Impact

▶ **video series**
Review the video to answer the focus question:
What are two ways in which Roman achievements have influenced American culture?

Visual Summary

Use the visual summary below to help you review the main ideas of the chapter.

QUICK FACTS

An architectural wonder, the Colosseum in Rome was the site of many types of public entertainment.

The New Testament of the Bible tells the story of Jesus of Nazareth and his disciples.

The Hagia Sophia, the enormous church built during Justinian's reign, served as the spiritual center of the Byzantine Empire.

Reviewing Vocabulary, Terms, and People

1. The orator and philosopher who called on Romans to work together was
   - **a.** Constantine.
   - **b.** Caesar.
   - **c.** Augustus.
   - **d.** Cicero.
2. Latin developed into
   - **a.** Byzantium.
   - **b.** Romance languages.
   - **c.** satire.
   - **d.** Latvian.
3. Another word for God's anointed one is
   - **a.** disciple.
   - **b.** Judea.
   - **c.** Messiah.
   - **d.** Apostle.
4. The Eastern Roman Empire is also called the
   - **a.** Lost Empire.
   - **b.** Byzantine Empire.
   - **c.** Constantinople Empire.
   - **d.** Ottoman Empire.
5. Rome's 200-year period of peace was the
   - **a.** Resurrection.
   - **b.** Pax Romana.
   - **c.** crucifixion.
   - **d.** Age of Theodora.

Comprehension and Critical Thinking

SECTION 1 *(pages 322–328)*

6. **a. Describe** What action did Cicero recommend? How were the goals of Julius Caesar, Pompey, and Crassus different from Cicero's?

   b. Analyze What were the most important events in the life of Julius Caesar? What event best qualifies as a turning point in Caesar's life? Defend your choice.

   c. Elaborate How did personal relationships—between Marc Antony and Octavian, and between Marc Antony and Cleopatra—affect the history of the Roman Empire?

SECTION 2 *(pages 332–338)*

7. **a. Describe** How did the Romans' attitude about religion differ from that of the Jews?

   b. Compare What were the crucifixion and the Resurrection? What did early Christians believe that the Resurrection showed?

Answers

Visual Summary

Review and Inquiry Have students use the visual summary to discuss contributions of the Roman Empire, the growth and spread of Christianity in Rome, and characteristics of the Byzantine Empire.

Quick Facts Transparency: Rome and Christianity Visual Summary

Reviewing Vocabulary, Terms and People

1. d
2. b
3. c
4. b
5. b

Comprehension and Critical Thinking

6. **a.** to limit the power of generals and give more support to the Roman Senate; wanted to take more power for themselves rather than give it to the Senate

   b. possible answers—conquered Gaul; made Pompey and Crassus his allies; refused to give up command of his armies; crossed the Rubicon River into Italy with his army; made himself dictator. Turning points and defenses will vary, but students should display familiarity with events listed. Students should understand the importance of the Rubicon crossing.

Review and Assessment Resources

Review and Reinforce

- SE Chapter Review
- **CRF:** Chapter Review Activity
- Quick Facts Transparency: Rome and Christianity Visual Summary
- Spanish Chapter Summaries Audio CD Program
- Online Chapter Summaries in Six Languages
- TOS Holt McDougal PuzzleView

Assess

- SE Standardized Test Practice
- PASS: Chapter Test
- Alternative Assessment Handbook
- TOS ExamView Assessment Suite, Chapter Test
- Differentiated Instruction Modified Material CD-ROM: Chapter Test
- Online Assessment Program, in the Interactive Student Edition

Reteach/Intervene

- Guided Reading Workbook
- Differentiated Instruction Teacher Management System: Lesson Plans
- Differentiated Instruction Modified Worksheets and Tests CD-ROM
- Interactive Skills Tutor CD-ROM

hmhsocialstudies.com
Chapter Resources

Answers

c. Marc Antony and Octavian—became allies to defeat Julius Caesar's killers, but became enemies; Marc Antony and Cleopatra—fell in love and became allies, making Octavian angry; all these relationships led to Octavian's rise.

7. a. The Romans honored many gods but did not impose their religion on others. Jews believed in one god and rebelled against Roman rule.

b. the death of Jesus and his rise from the dead; that Jesus is the Messiah

c. because he helped spread Christian teachings

8. a. Huns—warriors from Central Asia who raided the Roman Empire; Goths—groups who fled the Huns into into Roman territory; Visigoths—Gothic group that destroyed Rome in 410

b. in common—both were Roman emperors; different—Diocletian wanted the empire divided and Constantine wanted it united.

c. Byzantine emperor and empress; together they saved the emperor's throne and helped restore the power, beauty, and strength of the Roman Empire.

Reviewing Themes

9. possible answer—Roman roads and navigable waterways made travel and the spread of Christianity possible.

10. Answers will vary but should display knowledge of Roman achievements.

11. Christians worshipped only one God. Unlike early Romans, they believed Jesus was the Messiah sent by God to save people.

Using the Internet

12. Go to hmhsocialstudies.com to access a rubric for this activity.

Reading Skills

13. the author, the content, and the overall design and quality; any three questions from p. 320 would be acceptable responses

Social Studies Skills

14. Possible answers—Cicero tries to limit power of generals; Cicero calls on Romans to restore Senate's power. Entry should appear before the 44 BC entry.

Focus on Writing

15. Rubric Students' note cards should:

- accurately describe a person, place, or event from the Roman Empire.
- include interesting details to engage potential viewers' interest.
- explain their reasons for selecting the subject they did.
- all pertain to one topic.

Alternative Assessment Handbook, Rubric 37: Writing Assignments

---

c. Evaluate Why is Paul of Tarsus considered one of the most important people in the history of Christianity?

SECTION 3 *(pages 339–343)*

8. a. Identify Who were the Huns? Who were the Goths? Who were the Visigoths?

b. Compare and Contrast What did Diocletian and Constantine have in common? How did their actions differ?

c. Elaborate Who were Justinian and Theodora, and what did they accomplish?

Reviewing Themes

9. Geography How did the geography of the Roman Empire affect the spread of Christianity?

10. Science and Technology What do you feel was Rome's greatest scientific or technological advance? Why?

11. Religion How was Christianity different from the polytheistic religion common in early Rome?

Using the Internet 

12. Activity Use your online textbook to conduct research on Roman law, especially Justinian's Code. Then create a chart that summarizes the ways in which Justinian's Code influences modern issues such as the rights and responsibilities of individuals.

Reading Skills 

13. Online Research Imagine you are evaluating a Web site about ancient Roman architecture. What are some important elements you might look for to determine whether the site will be helpful and accurate? Write three questions you could use to evaluate the site's value.

Social Studies Skills

14. Interpreting Time Lines Look at the time line on page 344. Then, using information you will find in the first section of this chapter, add an entry about Cicero to the time line. Be sure you put it in the correct place.

Focus on Writing 

15. Creating Your Note Cards Now that you've taken notes about the people, places, and events of Rome during this time period, you're ready to prepare note cards. Choose the most interesting details from your chart to include on your cards. On each card write a one-to-two sentence description of a person, place, or event that you think should be featured in this screenplay. Then write another sentence that tells why you think the person, place, or event should be featured. Prepare six cards that you could give to a screenwriter to use to develop the script.

Look back at the information in Chapter 6 and create a time line of events in Han dynasty China. Compare your China time line to the one on page 344. What can you learn by analyzing the two time lines side by side?

CHAPTER 11

Standardized Test Practice

DIRECTIONS: Read each question and write the letter of the best response. Use the time line below to answer question 1.

1

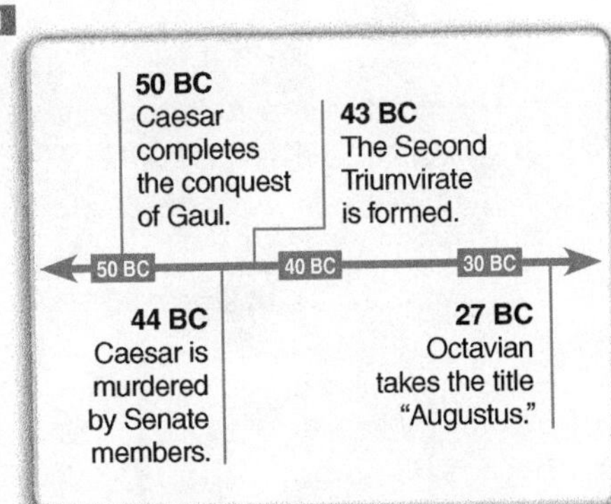
50 BC
Caesar completes the conquest of Gaul.
43 BC
The Second Triumvirate is formed.
50 BC
40 BC
30 BC
44 BC
Caesar is murdered by Senate members.
27 BC
Octavian takes the title "Augustus."

Most historians mark the end of the Roman Republic and the beginning of the Roman Empire as taking place in the year

A 50 BC.
B 44 BC.
C 43 BC.
D 27 BC.

2 **Which Roman leader seized power from the Senate and became the dictator of the entire Roman Republic?**

A Julius Caesar
B Hadrian
C Brutus
D Marc Antony

3 **Rome's contributions to the world include all of the following *except***

A techniques used to build strong bridges and other structures.
B the building of pyramids.
C the idea of civil law.
D the use of Latin, which led to the development of the Romance languages.

4 **Who was most responsible for spreading the Christian faith immediately after the death of Jesus?**

A Octavian
B Diocletian
C Paul of Tarsus
D Theodora of Constantinople

5 **In AD 410 the city of Rome was destroyed for the first time in 800 years by the army of a foreign people called the**

A Vandals.
B Visigoths.
C Huns.
D Franks.

Connecting with Past Learnings

6 **Constantine united the entire Roman Empire and introduced a new religion into the Roman government. Which leader that you learned about in an earlier chapter is known for his similar accomplishments?**

A Asoka
B Hammurabi
C Alexander
D Piankhi

7 **Earlier in this course, you learned that the Persians threatened Greek civilization for a time. All the following peoples played a similar role in Roman history *except***

A the Byzantines.
B the Goths.
C the Vandals.
D the Huns.

Answers

Standardized Test Practice

1. D
Break Down the Question: Remind students who missed the question that Octavian became the first emperor of Rome, and an emperor rules an empire.

2. A
Break Down the Question This question requires students to recall factual information. If students missed the question, review the identities of the men with students.

3. B
Break Down the Question This question requires students to recall that, although the Romans had many achievements, building pyramids was not among them.

4. C
Break Down the Question This question requires students to recall factual information from Section 2. If students missed the question, review the identities of the people with students.

5. B
Break Down the Question This question requires students to recall factual information from Section 3.

6. A
Break Down the Question This question requires students to recall information from Chapter 5.

7. A
Break Down the Question Point out to students that the word *except* indicates that they should identify which people did *not* threaten the Romans.

Tips for Test Taking

Master the Question Have you ever said, "I knew the answer, but I thought the question asked something else"? Be very sure that you **know what a question is asking.** Read the question at least twice before reading the answer choices. Approach it as you would a mystery story or a riddle. Look for clues. Watch especially for words like *not* and *except*—they tell you to look for the choice that is false or different from the other choices or opposite in some way.

Intervention Resources

Reproducible

- Guided Reading Workbook
- Differentiating Instruction Teacher Management System: Lesson Plans

Technology

- Quick Facts Transparency: Rome and Christianity Visual Summary
- Modified Material for Struggling Students CD-ROM
- Interactive Skills Tutor CD-ROM

Multimedia Classroom

The **HISTORY™ Multimedia Classroom** is a set of exciting new social studies teaching tools featuring award-winning program content. These comprehensive lesson plans, correlated to individual state and national curriculum standards, are easy to use for both teachers and students.

Each lesson contains the following:
- Short video segments that bring history topics to life
- Maps and visual materials
- Discussion and review questions
- Easily printable primary source documents
- Classroom activities and Internet-based activity links

The Multimedia Classroom has been specially designed to be versatile and easily adaptable to existing courses, lesson plans, and syllabi. Every lesson is designed to offer maximum flexibility. Teachers can select entire plans or only the elements they need, allowing them to individually tailor each lesson. Each multimedia lesson is available in CD-ROM format and is accompanied by full-length award-winning programs on DVD from HISTORY™.

For more information or to purchase go to hmhsocialstudies.com

Because some of these lessons may contain video material of a sensitive nature, we recommend that teachers and parents review these materials in their entirety before screening them to students.

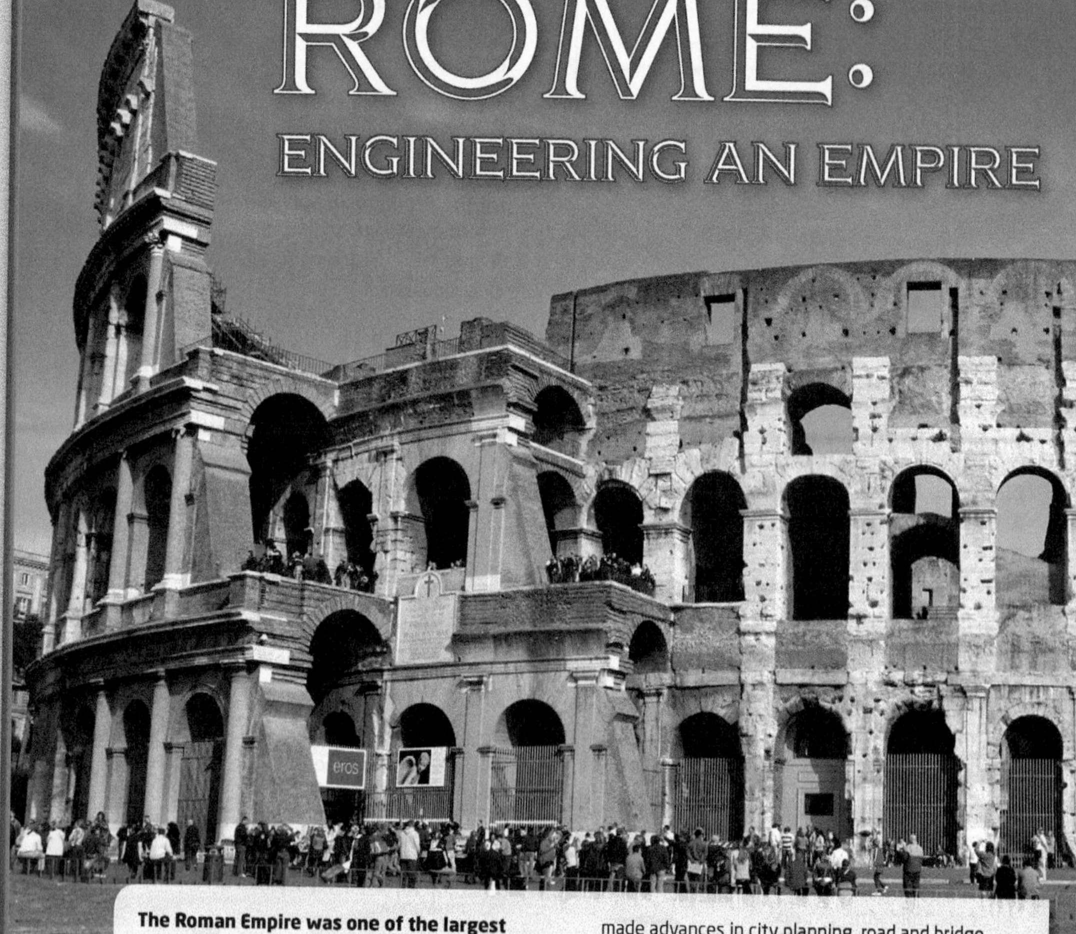

The Roman Empire was one of the largest and most powerful empires in ancient history. With its strong military, the Roman Empire expanded to dominate the entire Mediterranean region, including much of western Europe and northern Africa. Keys to this expansion were the engineering and construction innovations made by Roman engineers. As the empire grew and prospered, Roman engineers made advances in city planning, road and bridge design, water and sewage systems, and many other areas.

Explore some of the incredible monuments and engineering achievements of the Roman Empire online. You can find a wealth of information, video clips, primary sources, activities, and more at hmhsocialstudies.com.

347 MC1 MULTIMEDIA CONNECTIONS

Rome: Engineering an Empire

Resources 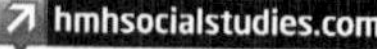

The following resources come with printable introductions, comprehension and critical thinking questions, transcripts, and vocabulary support.

Full Length DVD

Rome: Engineering an Empire (1 hr 40 mins)

Video Clips

- The Roman Republic Is Born (3:32)
- Crossing the Rhine River (3:19)
- Caesar Builds an Empire (2:15)
- The Rise of Roman Cities (1:48)
- Bringing Water to Romans (1:27)
- Arches, Angles, Innovations (2:07)
- The Glory of the Colosseum (4:52)
- The Glory of Rome's Forum (4:20)
- Defending Rome's Borders (3:35)
- Hadrian and the Pantheon (2:20)
- Caracalla's Public Baths (4:39)
- The Roman Empire Falls (2:50)

Primary Sources

- Caesar's *Battle for Gaul*
- *On Duties*
- *The Aeneid*
- Pliny on Entertainment
- Augustus of Prima Porta
- A Fresco from Pompeii
- A Roman Imperial Coin

CLICK THROUGH
INTER/ACTIVITIES
hmhsocialstudies.com

The Glory of the Colosseum

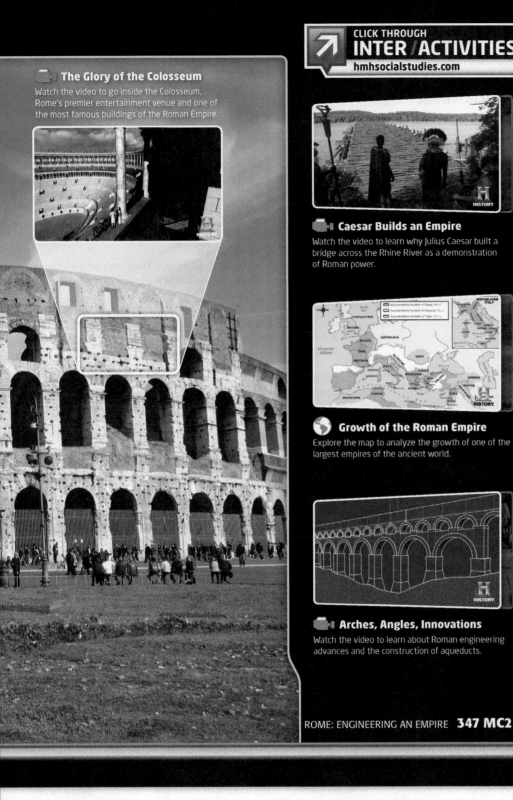

Watch the video to go inside the Colosseum, Rome's premier entertainment venue and one of the most famous buildings of the Roman Empire.

Caesar Builds an Empire

Watch the video to learn why Julius Caesar built a bridge across the Rhine River as a demonstration of Roman power.

Growth of the Roman Empire

Explore the map to analyze the growth of one of the largest empires of the ancient world.

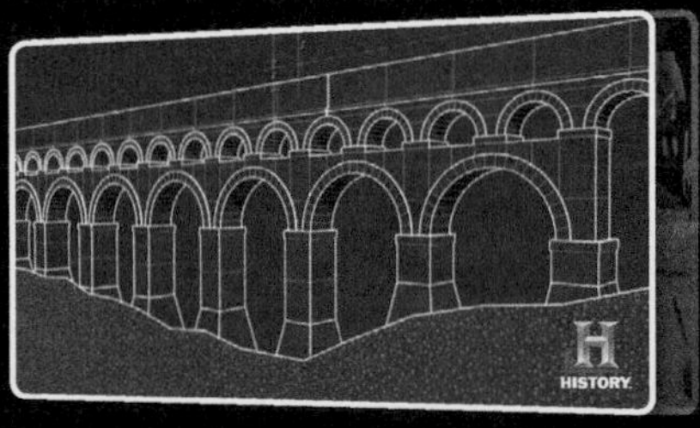

Arches, Angles, Innovations

Watch the video to learn about Roman engineering advances and the construction of aqueducts.

Maps

- Growth of the Roman Empire
- Migration within the Empire

Activities

- Julius Caesar
- Images of Roman Women
- The Rome that Slaves Built
- Rebuilding Rome
- Tracing the Empire's History
- Reenacting Rome's Past

General Review Questions

General Discussion Questions

Web Links

Bibliography

Lesson Preview

The Glory of the Colosseum

The Flavian Amphitheater, known today as the Colosseum, was an engineering marvel when it was completed around A.D. 80. The Colosseum stood 160 feet high and held more than 50,000 spectators. A state of the art facility, it hosted gladiatorial battles, exotic animal contests, mock naval battles, and more, as Roman society developed a new public culture of mass entertainment.

Caesar Builds an Empire

Before he became emperor, Julius Caesar had proven himself as one of the greatest generals of the ancient world. In 55 B.C., Caesar traveled from Gaul to Germany with the goal of conquering the Germanic tribes there. Upon reaching the Rhine River, Caesar ordered his engineers to build a bridge across it so he could march into Germany with his army rather than cross the river by boat. The Romans' rapid and successful construction of the bridge was so intimidating to the Germans that German forces refused to engage the Romans in combat, and Caesar marched across the Rhine unopposed.

Growth of the Roman Empire

After the establishment of the Roman Empire in 44 B.C., Rome grew to dominate the Mediterranean basin. Roman armies pushed the empire's borders farther into North Africa, Europe, and Southwest Asia, bringing more and more area under the government's control. This expansion also brought increased trade and economic and urban development.

Arches, Angles, Innovations

It took centuries to construct Rome's aqueducts. Two major aqueducts, the Aqua Claudia and the Aqua Anio Novus, brought millions of gallons of water into the city each day, providing a source of clean water for all of Rome's citizens. Roman aqueducts relied chiefly on one particular type of architectural form—the arch.

Preteach

Bellringer

Motivate Ask students to review the chapters in this unit to identify problems faced by the people of ancient Rome. Have them write down three or four problems that they might be interested in analyzing. Tell students that in this workshop they will explore the solutions the Romans used to address these problems and write papers to evaluate those solutions.

Direct Teach

Choosing a Subject

Choosing a Variety of Sources
Tell students that they may wish to choose several possible topics when researching a new subject. This makes it easier to locate an interesting problem about which to write. Tell students not to be tempted to choose the very first topic they see and not to get too caught up in research. Students should limit themselves to fifteen minutes to a half hour in order to save time to complete the project. Lastly, have students check to see if their selection will allow them to answer the questions under the heading *Finding a Solution and Proof* on this page.

Assignment

Write about a problem the Romans faced and what their solution was or what you think would be a better solution.

Historical Problem and Solution

History is the story of how individuals have solved political, economic, and social problems. Learning to write an effective problem-solution paper will be useful in school and in many other situations.

1. Prewrite

Identifying a Problem

Think of a problem the Romans faced. Look at the problem closely. What caused it? What were its effects? Here is an example.
Problem: The Gauls overran Rome.
Solution A: Pay the Gauls a huge ransom to leave Rome. [caused other cities to attack in the hope of getting similar ransoms]
Solution B: Attack other cities. [caused other cities to stop attacking Rome; let Rome gain power and wealth]

Finding a Solution and Proof

Compare the Roman solution to the problem to one they didn't try. Choose either the Roman solution or your own solution to write about. Your explanation should answer these questions.

- How does the solution address the cause of the problem?
- How does the solution fix the effects of the problem?

Use historical evidence to support what you say about the problem:

- facts, examples, or quotations
- comparisons with similar problems your readers know about

2. Write

This framework can help you clearly explain the problem and its solution.

A Writer's Framework

Introduction	Body	Conclusion
■ Tell your reader what problem the Romans faced. ■ Explain the causes and effects of the problem. ■ State your purpose in presenting this problem and its solution.	■ Explain the solution. ■ Connect the solution directly to the problem. ■ Give supporting historical evidence and details that show how the solution deals with the problem.	■ Summarize the problem and the solution. ■ Discuss how well the solution deals with the problem.

Differentiating Instruction

Advanced/Gifted and Talented

Above Level

1. Challenge students to locate primary sources from ancient writers supporting or refuting the solutions examined in their papers. Remind students that they can find primary sources online, in reference books, and in other library sources.
2. Have students incorporate quotes from their primary sources in the body of their paper. **LS Verbal/Linguistic**

English-Language Learners

Below Level
Standard English Mastery

1. Encourage students to identify their problems and solutions in simple statements like those presented under the heading *Identifying a Problem* above. Encourage students to rephrase each of the statements in their own words to be sure they understand its meaning.
2. Write some sample sentences for students to imitate as they compose each section of their papers. **LS Verbal/Linguistic**

3. Evaluate and Revise

Evaluating

Now you'll want to evaluate your draft to see where you can improve your paper. Try using the following questions to decide what to revise.

Evaluation Questions for a Historical Problem and Solution

- Does your introduction state the problem clearly and describe it fully?
- Does the introduction give causes and effects of the problem?
- Do you clearly explain how the solution relates to the problem?
- Do you give supporting historical evidence showing how the solution deals with the problem?
- Do you conclude by summarizing the problem and the solution?

TIP Problem-Solution Clue Words. It's not enough simply to tell your reader what the problem and solution are. You need to show how they are related. Here is a list of words and phrases that will help you do so.

as a result	therefore
consequently	this led to
nevertheless	thus

Revising

Revise your draft to make what you say clear and convincing. You may need to

- Add historical facts, examples, quotations and other evidence to give your readers all the information they need to understand the problem and solution
- Reorganize paragraphs to present information in a clear, logical order
- Insert words like *thus, therefore,* and *as a result* to show how causes link to effects and how the solution deals with the problem

4. Proofread and Publish

Proofreading

To improve your paper before sharing it, check the following:

- spelling of all names, places, and other historical information, especially Latin words, because they can be tricky
- punctuation around linking words such as *so, thus,* and *in addition* that you use to connect causes with effects and solutions with problems

Publishing

Choose one or more of these ideas to share your report.

- Create a poster that Roman leaders might put up to announce how they will solve the problem.
- Hold a debate between teams of classmates who have chosen similar problems but different solutions. Have the rest of the class vote on whose solutions are best.

TIP Seeing Your Paper as Others See It. To you, your paper makes perfect sense. To others, it may not. Whenever possible, ask someone else to read your paper. Others can see flaws and errors that you never will see. Listen closely to questions and suggestions. Do your best to see the other person's point before defending what you have written.

Practice and Apply

Use the steps and strategies outlined in this workshop to write a problem-solution paper.

Reteach

Evaluating

Thinking It Through Point out to students that the solutions they analyze in their papers must be viable and realistic. For example, students should not suggest that the Romans could have evacuated the entire city of Rome as the Gauls approached, because such a prospect would have been logistically impossible. Likewise, students should not suggest that the Romans could have bombed the Gallic army, because such technology did not exist at that point in history. Encourage students to discuss their solutions with you or their fellow classmates if they have questions about their viability.

Teaching Tip

Avoiding Fragments

In casual conversation, bits and pieces of language make sense because they are surrounded by gestures and other clues. This leads many students to use fragments of sentences in their writing. One very effective way for students to check for fragments in their writing is to read the entire paper backwards. The idea is to read one whole sentence at a time, but last sentence first. If each sentence makes sense by itself, it carries the entire meaning and is complete. If it does not, it is probably missing a subject or a verb.

Special Needs Learners Below Level

1. Instruct students to cover the Writer's Framework boxes on the previous page so that only the Introduction box is showing.
2. Have students compose a one-sentence response to each bulleted point in the Introduction instructions.
3. Tell students to indent each sentence so that it is the first sentence of three paragraphs. Now have students uncover the Body and Conclusion boxes.

Standard English Mastery

4. Have students write statements to address the points in these boxes and write their introduction, body, and concluding paragraphs.
5. A classroom aide or fellow student may help record students' ideas if necessary. **LS Verbal/Linguistic, Visual/Spatial**

Practice & Apply

Rubric

Students' analyses should

- identify a problem faced by the Romans and a possible solution to that problem.
- explain how this solution addresses the cause of the problem and resolves it.
- use historical evidence to support the writer's conclusions.
- use correct grammar, punctuation, spelling, and capitalization.

Unit Preview

Introduce the Unit

Share the information in the chapter overviews with students.

Chapter 12 The harsh environment of Arabia, which is mostly desert, was the birthplace of the religion of Islam. Muhammad, a merchant from Mecca, became a prophet. His teachings, which had similarities to Judaism and Christianity, formed the basis of Islam. Although rejected at first, Islam soon spread through Arabia. Sacred texts called the Qur'an and the Sunnah guide Muslims in their religion, daily life, and laws. Islam continued to spread through both military conquests and trade. In time, three large Islamic empires formed—the Ottoman, Safavid, and Mughal. Muslim scholars and artists made important contributions to science, art, and literature.

Chapter 13 West Africa has varied environments and valuable resources. The Niger River flows through rain forests, savannah, and desert in this varied region and provides a source of water, food, and transportation. The resources of West Africa enabled the region's population to establish villages, where people lived in extended family groups. Iron technology and trade contributed to the growth of West African societies. As these societies grew, the empires of Ghana, Mali, and Songhai in turn dominated the region. These empires grew rich and powerful by controlling trade across the Sahara Desert. Throughout these empires, West African culture was passed down through oral history, accounts written by visitors, and the arts.

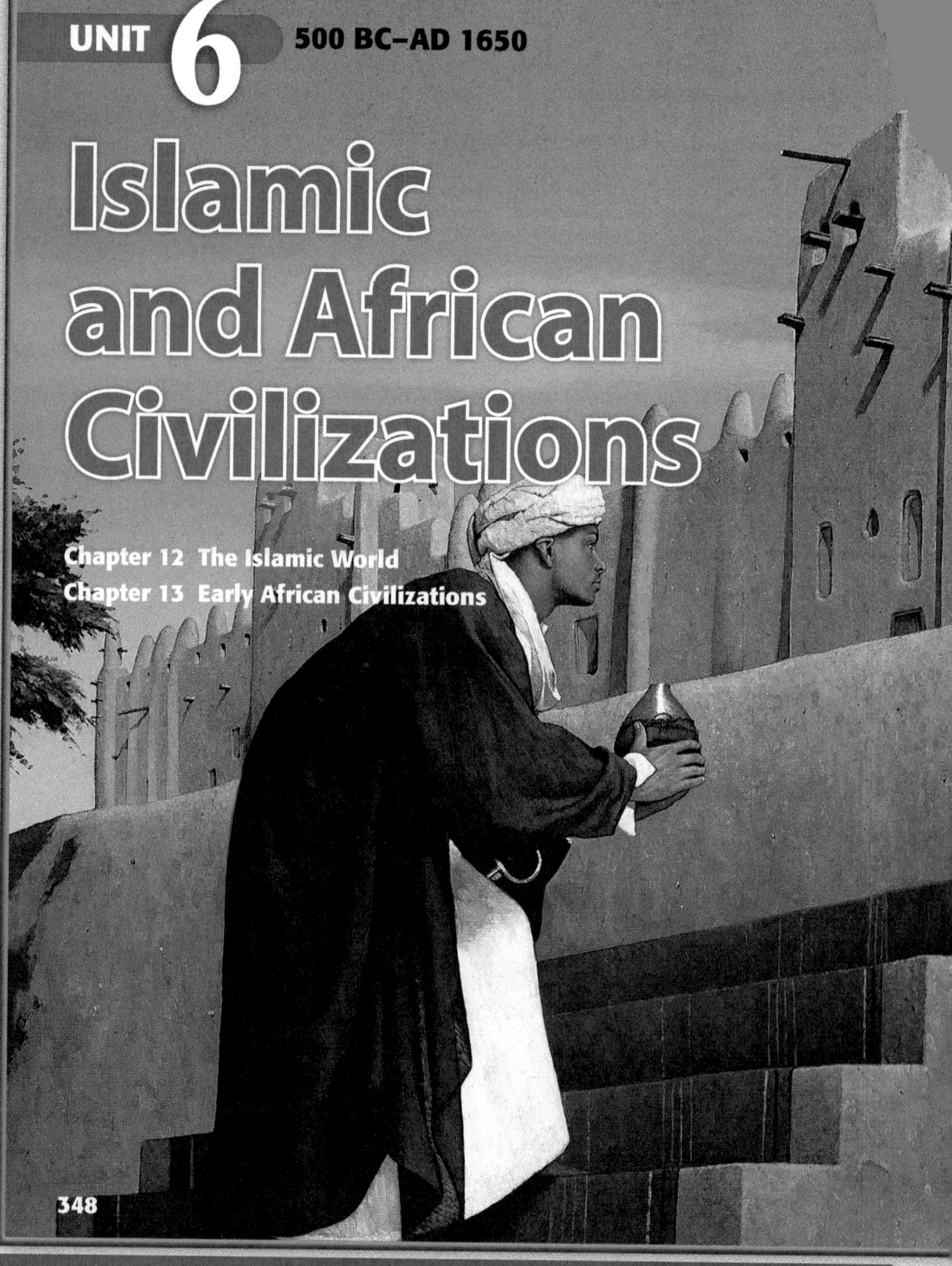

Unit Resources

Planning

- Differentiated Instruction Teacher Management System: Unit Instructional Benchmarking Guides
- TOS Calendar Planner
- Power Presentations with Media Gallery
- A Teacher's Guide to Religion in the Public Schools

Differentiating Instruction

- Differentiated Instruction Teacher Management System: Lesson Plans for Differentiated Instruction
- Differentiated Instruction Modified Worksheets and Tests CD-ROM

Enrichment

- **CRF 12:** Economics and History Activity: Muslim Trade: An Empire Builder
- **CRF 12:** Interdisciplinary Project: The Islamic World's Legacy
- **CRF 13:** Economics and History Activity: Specialization of Labor
- **CRF 13:** Interdisciplinary Project: West Africa: Tales, Fables, and Stories
- Civic Participation Activities
- Primary Source Library CD-ROM

Assessment

- Progress Assessment System Solution: Unit Test
- TOS ExamView Assessment Suite: Unit Test
- Online Assessment Program, in the Interactive Student Edition
- Alternative Assessment Handbook

The **Differentiated Instruction Teacher Management System** provides a planning and instructional benchmarking guide for this unit.

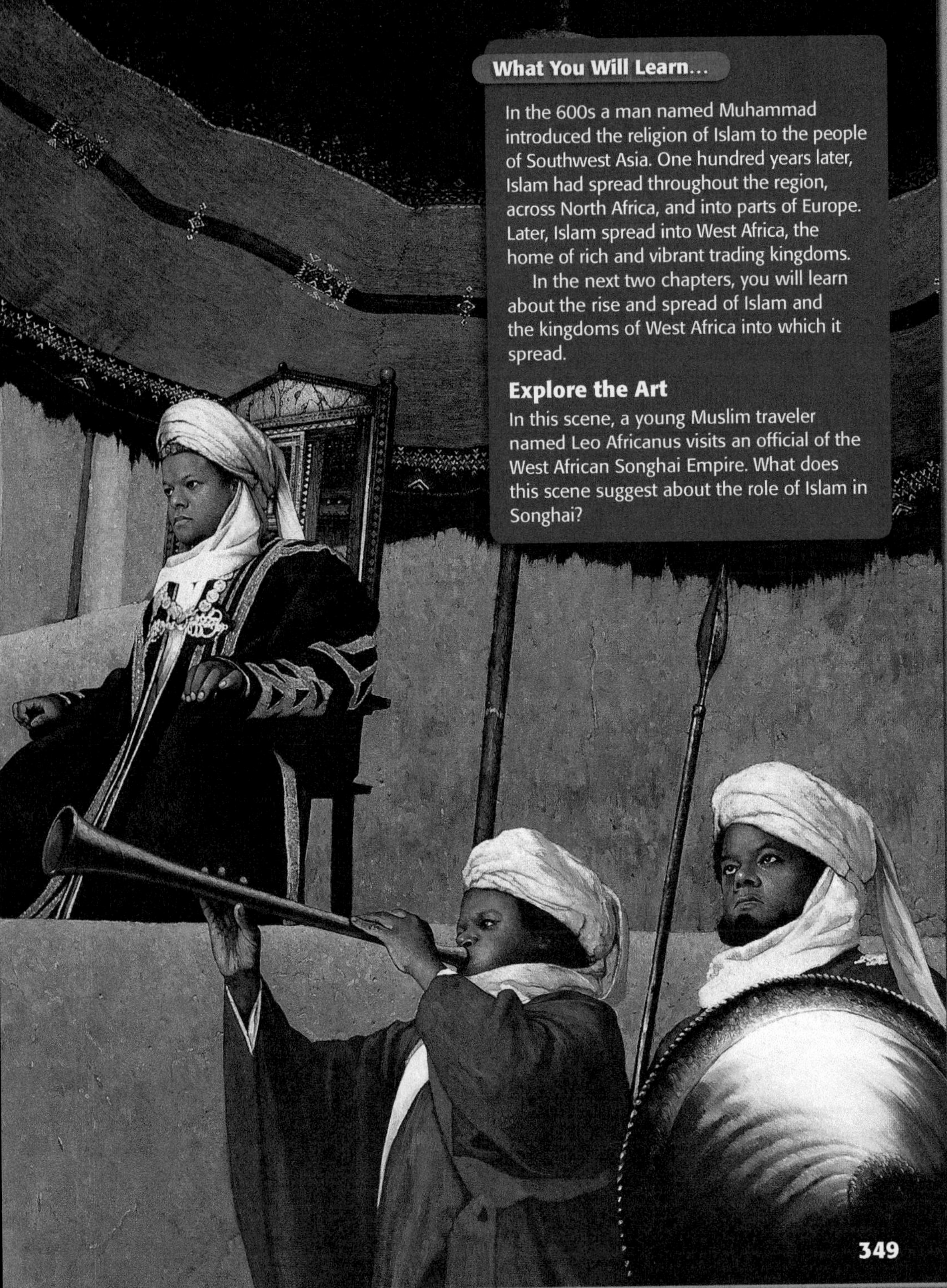

What You Will Learn...

In the 600s a man named Muhammad introduced the religion of Islam to the people of Southwest Asia. One hundred years later, Islam had spread throughout the region, across North Africa, and into parts of Europe. Later, Islam spread into West Africa, the home of rich and vibrant trading kingdoms.

In the next two chapters, you will learn about the rise and spread of Islam and the kingdoms of West Africa into which it spread.

Explore the Art

In this scene, a young Muslim traveler named Leo Africanus visits an official of the West African Songhai Empire. What does this scene suggest about the role of Islam in Songhai?

349

Unit Preview

Connect to the Unit

Activity **Building a Mosque** Ask students if they can identify some major world religions *(e.g., Buddhism, Christianity, Confucianism, Hinduism, Islam, and Judaism).*

Next, ask students how many of these religions are represented in their local community. Can students identify the different buildings of worship for each of these religions? Remind students that they should respect other's religious beliefs and differences.

During the course of the unit, have students work in small groups to build models of Muslim mosques. Students should conduct research on mosques and might select a famous mosque for their model. Each group should divide the tasks up among members to ensure that everyone participates in the project.

LS Interpersonal, Kinesthetic

Explore the Art

The city of Timbuktu is located about 8 miles north of the Niger River along the southern edge of the Sahara Desert. During the Songhai Empire, Timbuktu flourished. A great city of learning, it contained universities, schools, libraries, and mosques and drew people from across West Africa. The city also served as an important trading center. Over time, Timbuktu declined. Today, it is reached mainly by boat or camel. The city has been named a World Heritage site.

About the Illustration

This illustration is an artist's conception based on available sources. However, historians are uncertain exactly what this scene looked like.

Democracy and Civic Education

At Level

Responsibility: Contributing to the Community

Research Required

Background Explain that in early West African villages, each person—from the very young to the very old—had specific duties to perform. All the people had to do their part and work together to help the village thrive. So to, all U.S. citizens should do their part to support their local communities.

1. Lead a discussion about the ways in which students can support their local community, such as through volunteering or community service, participating in local politics, or staying informed about local issues.
2. Have students work in small groups to create brochures that explain why citizens should support their communities and ways in which they can do so. For example, students might list area volunteer and community-service opportunities for students.

LS Interpersonal, Verbal/Linguistic

Alternative Assessment Handbook, Rubrics 14: Group Activity; and 37: Writing Assignments

Civic Participation Activities

Answers

Explore the Art *possible answers—It was the official religion, it depended on trade, official visits were important.*

Chapter 12 Planning Guide

The Islamic World

Overview	Instructional Resources	
CHAPTER 12 **Essential Question:** How were Muslim leaders able to spread Islam and create an empire? **Focus on the Essential Question Podcast**	TOS **Differentiated Instruction Teacher Management System:** • Instructional Benchmarking Guides • Lesson Plans for Differentiated Instruction **Guided Reading Workbook** **Chapter Resource File:** • Chapter Review Activity • Focus on Writing Activity: A Web Site • Social Studies Skills Activity: Determining the Context of Statements	TOS **Calendar Planner** **Power Presentations with Media Gallery** **Differentiated Instruction Modified Worksheets and Tests CD-ROM** **Interactive Skills Tutor CD-ROM** **Student Edition on Audio CD Program** **The World's Music Audio Program** **Video:** The Taj Mahal
Section 1: **The Roots of Islam** **The Big Idea:** In the harsh desert climate of Arabia, Muhammad, a merchant from Mecca, introduced a major world religion called Islam.	TOS **Differentiated Instruction Teacher Management System:** Section 1 Lesson Plan **Guided Reading Workbook:** Section 1 **Chapter Resource File:** • Vocabulary Builder Activity, Section 1 • History and Geography Activity: Arabia, AD 750 • Biography Activity: Khadijah • Primary Source Activity: Reading from the *Koran*	**Daily Bellringer Transparency:** Section 1 **Map Transparency:** Arabia, AD 570 **Internet Activity:** Life of Muhammad Time Line **Animated History:** Trade Routes, AD 570 **Animated History:** Muslim Army: Spread of Islam, AD 661
Section 2: **Islamic Beliefs and Practices** **The Big Idea:** Sacred texts called the Qur'an and the Sunnah guide Muslims in their religion, daily life, and laws.	TOS **Differentiated Instruction Teacher Management System:** Section 2 Lesson Plan **Guided Reading Workbook:** Section 2 **Chapter Resource File:** • Vocabulary Builder Activity, Section 2	**Daily Bellringer Transparency:** Section 2 **Quick Facts Transparency:** The Five Pillars of Islam **Quick Facts Transparency:** Sources of Islamic Beliefs **Internet Activity:** Islamic Beliefs and Practices Presentation
Section 3: **Islamic Empires** **The Big Idea:** After the early spread of Islam, three large Islamic empires formed—the Ottoman, Safavid, and Mughal.	TOS **Differentiated Instruction Teacher Management System:** Section 3 Lesson Plan **Guided Reading Workbook:** Section 3 **Chapter Resource File:** • Vocabulary Builder Activity, Section 3 • Biography Activity: Akbar • Economics and History Activity: Muslim Trade: Spreading Islam	**Daily Bellringer Transparency:** Section 3 **Map Transparency:** The Ottoman Empire **Map Transparency:** The Safavid Empire **Map Transparency:** The Mughal Empire **Internet Activity:** Córdoba Brochure **Animated History:** Muslim World, AD 1200
Section 4: **Cultural Achievements** **The Big Idea:** Muslim scholars and artists made important contributions to science, art, and literature.	TOS **Differentiated Instruction Teacher Management System:** Section 4 Lesson Plan **Guided Reading Workbook:** Section 4 **Chapter Resource File:** • Vocabulary Builder Activity, Section 4	**Daily Bellringer Transparency:** Section 4 **Internet Activity:** Islamic Calligraphy

Chart Key:

SE Student Edition  Presentation Resource  MP3 Audio
TOS Teacher One Stop  DVD/CD-ROM  HISTORY™
Printable Resource

Program Resources available on TOS and @ hmhsocialstudies.com

Review, Assessment, Intervention

- **Quick Facts Transparency:** The Islamic World Visual Summary
- **Spanish Chapter Summaries Audio CD Program**
- **Quiz Game CD-ROM**
- **Progress Assessment Support System (PASS):** Chapter Test
- **Differentiated Instruction Modified Worksheets and Tests CD-ROM:** Modified Chapter Test
- TOS **ExamView® Assessment Suite (English/Spanish)**
- **Online Assessment Program,** in the Interactive Student Edition

- **PASS:** Section 1 Quiz
- **Online Quiz:** Section 1
- **Alternative Assessment Handbook**

- **PASS:** Section 2 Quiz
- **Online Quiz:** Section 2
- **Alternative Assessment Handbook**

- **PASS:** Section 3 Quiz
- **Online Quiz:** Section 3
- **Alternative Assessment Handbook**

- **PASS:** Section 4 Quiz
- **Online Quiz:** Section 4
- **Alternative Assessment Handbook**

Supporting Resources

- Multimedia Classroom Global History Series
- Global History Teacher's Guide

Maps Globes Graphs Level F

- Student Workbook
- Teacher's Guide

Social Studies Trade Library Collections

- Premier Secondary World History Trade Collection

History's Impact

World History Video Program

- **Islamic Traditions and the World Today**

For more information or to purchase go to  hmhsocialstudies.com

Power Presentations with Media Gallery

Power Presentations with Media Gallery are visual presentations of each chapter's main ideas. Presentations can be customized by including Quick Facts charts, images from the text, and video clips.

Differentiating Instruction

How do I address the needs of varied learners?

The Target Resource acts as your primary strategy for differentiated instruction.

ENGLISH-LANGUAGE LEARNERS & STRUGGLING READERS

Interactive Skills Tutor CD-ROM

The Interactive Skills Tutor CD-ROM contains lessons that provide additional practice for 20 different critical thinking skills.

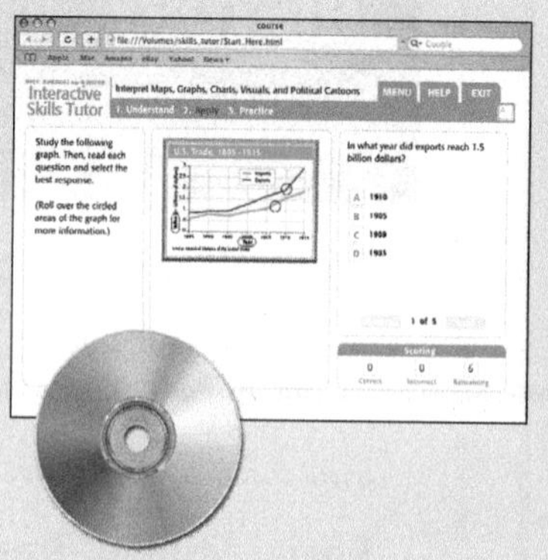

Additional Resources

Differentiated Instruction Teacher Management System: Lesson Plans for Differentiated Instruction

Chapter Resource File:
- Vocabulary Builder Activities
- Social Studies Skills Activity: Determining the Context of Statements

Quick Facts Transparencies:
- The Five Pillars of Islam
- Sources of Islamic Beliefs
- The Islamic World Visual Summary

Student Edition on Audio CD Program

Spanish/English Guided Reading Workbook

SPECIAL NEEDS LEARNERS

Differentiated Instruction Modified Worksheets and Tests CD-ROM

- Vocabulary Flash Cards
- Vocabulary Builder Activities
- Chapter Review Activity
- Chapter Test

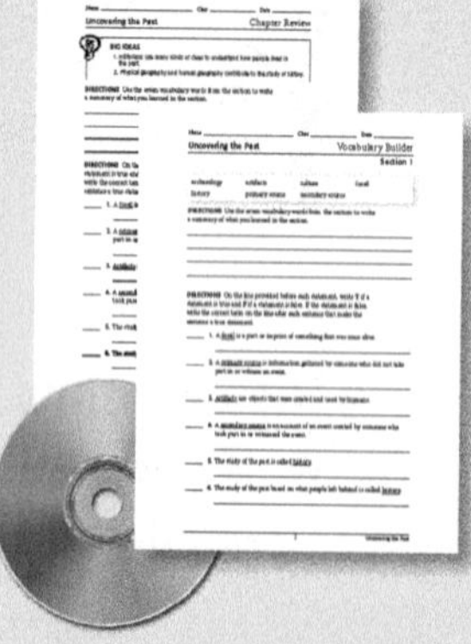

Additional Resources

Differentiated Instruction Teacher Management System: Lesson Plans for Differentiated Instruction

Guided Reading Workbook

Chapter Resource File: Social Studies Skills Activity: Determining the Context of Statements

Student Edition on Audio CD Program

Interactive Skills Tutor CD-ROM

ADVANCED/GIFTED-AND-TALENTED STUDENTS

Primary Source Library CD-ROM for World History

The Library contains longer versions of quotations in the text, extra sources, and images. Included are point-of-view articles, journals, diaries, historical fiction, and political documents.

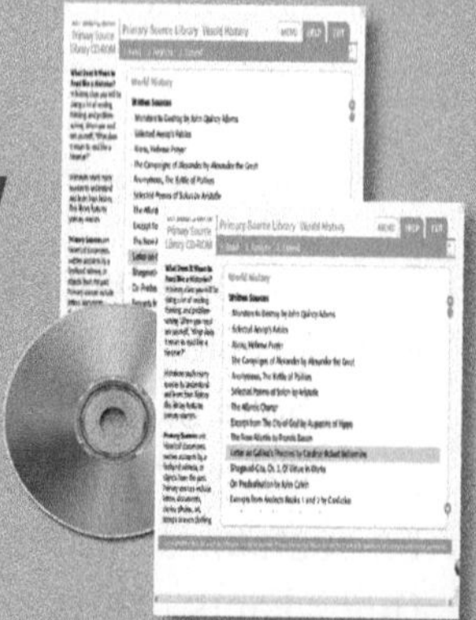

Additional Resources

Differentiated Instruction Teacher Management System: Lesson Plans for Differentiated Instruction

Chapter Resource File:
- Focus on Writing Activity: A Web Site

Document-Based Questions Activities

Differentiated Activities in the Teacher's Edition

- The Five Pillars of Islam Book Jacket, p. 360
- Using Graphic Organizers, p. 366

Teacher One Stop™

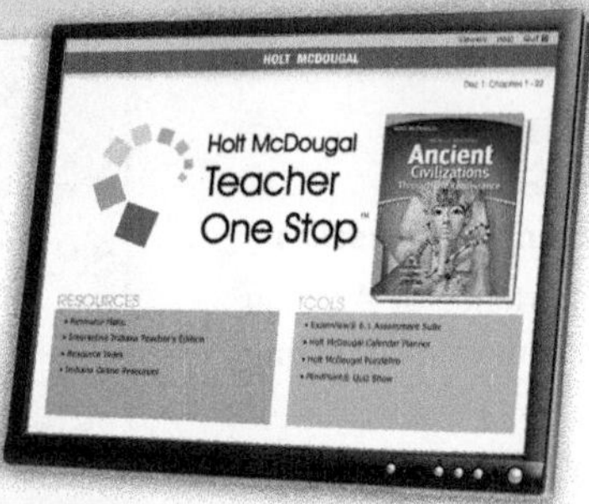

How can I manage the lesson plans and support materials for differentiated instruction?

With the Teacher One Stop, you can easily organize and print lesson plans, planning guides, and instructional materials for all learners. The Teacher One Stop includes the following materials to help you differentiate instruction:

- **Interactive Teacher's Edition**
- **Calendar Planner and pacing guides**
- **Editable lesson plans**
- **All reproducible ancillaries in Adobe Acrobat (PDF) format**
- **ExamView Assessment Suite (English & Spanish)**
- **Transparency and video previews**

Differentiated Activities in the Teacher's Edition

- Categorizing the Major Beliefs of Islam, p. 359
- Muslim Achievements: "New and Improved" Ads, p. 369

Interactive Student Edition

Complete online student edition with interactive multimedia support for chapter content assessment and reporting

- Interactive Maps and Notebook
- Graphic Organizers
- Standardized Test Prep
- Online Homework Practice and Research Activities
- Current Events
- Chapter-based Internet Activities
- Animated History Activities
- and more!

Differentiated Activities in the Teacher's Edition

- Comparing Christianity, Judaism, and Islam, p. 356
- Exploring Muslim Architecture, p. 363
- Making Predictions about the Ottoman Empire, p. 365

Chapter Preview

Essential Question

Introduce the Essential Question

- Discuss the importance of Arabian peninsula trade routes in spreading religion.
- Describe the role of Muhammad in spreading Islam to others.
- Point out that military victories by Muslim armies and Muslim policies toward conquered peoples played important roles in the expansion of the empire.
- Discuss significant advances in science and the arts made by those living in Muslim lands.

CHAPTER 12 550–1650

The Islamic World

Essential Question How were Muslim leaders able to spread Islam and create an empire?

South Carolina Performance Standards

6-3.4 Explain the origin and fundamental beliefs of Islam and the geographic and economic aspects of its expansion.

Literacy Skills for Social Studies

- Evaluate multiple points of view or biases and attribute the perspectives to the influences of individual experiences, societal values, and cultural traditions.
- Interpret Earth's physical and human systems by using maps, mental maps, geographic models, and other social studies resources.
- Compare the locations of places, the conditions at places, and the connections between places.
- Explain why trade occurs and how historical patterns of trade have contributed to global interdependence.

Partnership for the 21st Century Skills
Elaborate and refine ideas in order to improve and maximize creative efforts.

Focus on Writing

A Web Site for Children Design a Web site to tell children about the life of the prophet Muhammad, the religion of Islam, and the history and culture of the Muslim people. You'll design five pages: a home page and four links—Who Was Muhammad? What Is Islam? The Islamic Empires, and Islamic Cultural Achievements. As you read, think about what information will be interesting to your audience.

Chapter Events

c. 550 Trade routes cross Arabia.

c. 570 Muhammad is born in Mecca.

550 | 600

World Events

618 The Tang dynasty begins in China.

Focus on Writing

The **Chapter Resource File** provides a Focus on Writing worksheet to help students design their Web sites.

CRF: Focus on Writing Activity: A Web Site

Key to Differentiating Instruction

Below Level
Basic-level activities designed for all students encountering new material

At Level
Intermediate-level activities designed for average students

Above Level
Challenging activities designed for honors and gifted and talented students

Standard English Mastery
Activities designed to improve standard English usage

LS Learning Styles

Introduce the Chapter

At Level

Impressions of the Islamic World

1. Ask students to examine the Asia: Political map in the Atlas and to locate Mecca (Saudi Arabia). Have students identify the country that Mecca is located in and the nearby bodies of water.
2. Tell students that Mecca is the place where one of the world's major religions began—Islam. Explain that people who follow Islam are called Muslims. Ask students if they can identify some largely Muslim countries, such as Pakistan, Iraq, and Saudi Arabia.
3. Ask students to write down words or phrases they associate with the word "Islam." Then have them skim the chapter and make a list predicting what they will learn about. Have students circle what is new or unfamiliar in the second list. **LS Verbal/Linguistic**

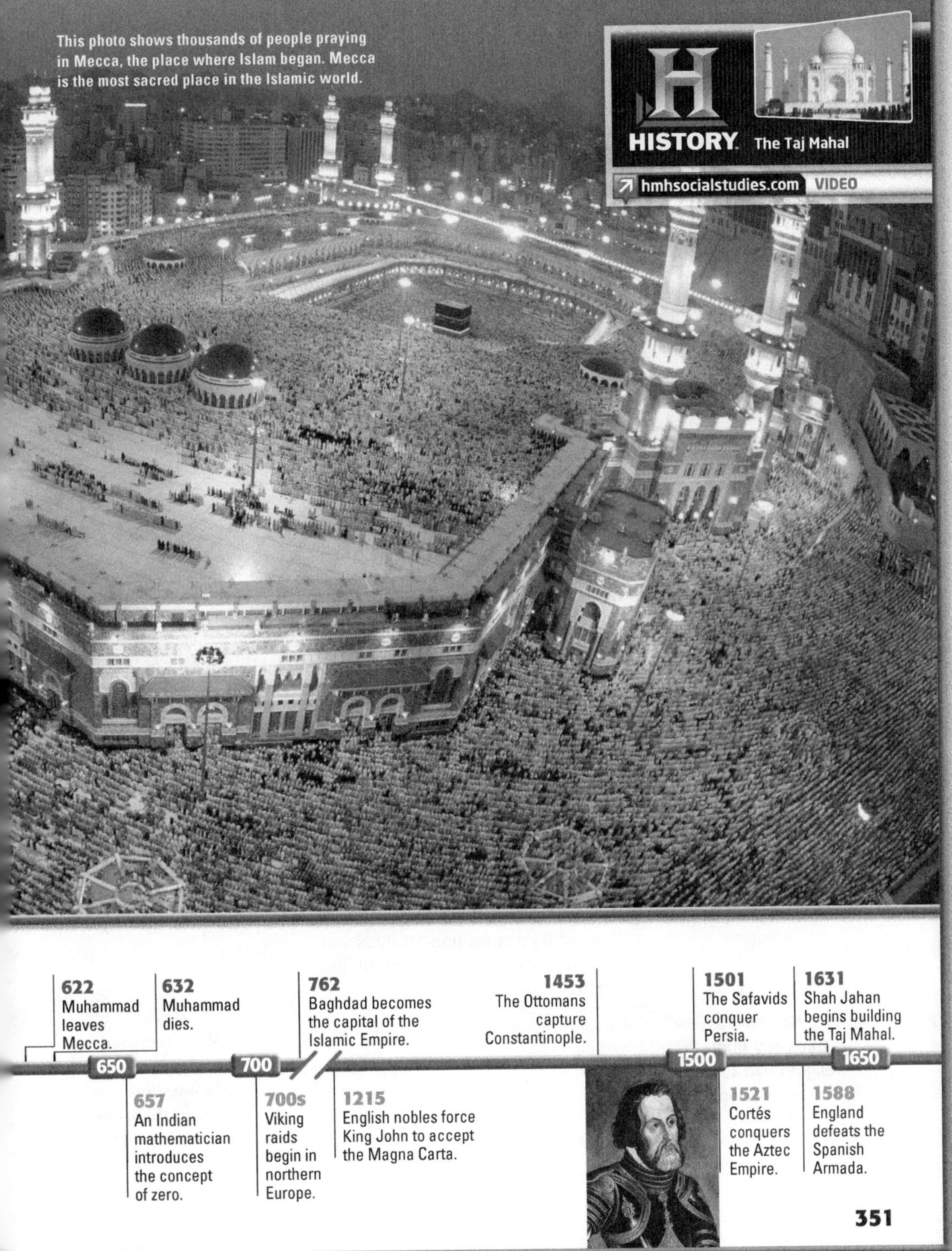
This photo shows thousands of people praying in Mecca, the place where Islam began. Mecca is the most sacred place in the Islamic world.
HISTORY. The Taj Mahal
hmhsocialstudies.com VIDEO
622 Muhammad leaves Mecca.
632 Muhammad dies.
762 Baghdad becomes the capital of the Islamic Empire.
1453 The Ottomans capture Constantinople.
1501 The Safavids conquer Persia.
1631 Shah Jahan begins building the Taj Mahal.
650
700
1500
1650
657 An Indian mathematician introduces the concept of zero.
700s Viking raids begin in northern Europe.
1215 English nobles force King John to accept the Magna Carta.
1521 Cortés conquers the Aztec Empire.
1588 England defeats the Spanish Armada.
351

• Chapter Preview •

Explore the Picture

The Kaaba This picture shows Islam's most holy place, the Kaaba, the shrine in Mecca that Muslims are required to visit at least once in their lifetimes, according to the fifth pillar of Islam. Tell students the Kaaba is the cube-shaped structure pictured in the middle of the mosque. Worshippers circle the Kaaba seven times in a counterclockwise direction in an act called the tawaf. They then walk between two sacred hills seven times. Completing these two acts completes the umrah, or basic hajj, but some pilgrims elect to travel to Medina and visit the Mosque of the Prophet where Muhammad and Abu Bakr are entombed.

Analyzing Visuals What do the thousands of people in the picture appear to be focused around? *the cube-shaped structure in the shallow depression near the center of the picture*

hmhsocialstudies.com
Teacher Resources

Info to Know

Beyond the Time Line Tell students that the Ottoman conquest of Constantinople in 1453 is regarded as one of the most significant events in world history. The city was named in AD 330 after the great Roman emperor Constantine I. Constantine I officially declared the city the capital of the Roman Empire. Constantine XI was defeated by Mehmed II and died in the final defense of Constantinople. The capture of the city by the Ottomans signaled the end of the Eastern Roman Empire (also called the Byzantine Empire). By conquering the city, the Ottomans gained control of lucrative trading routes in the region.

Explore the Time Line

1. How old was Muhammad when he died? *about 62 years old*
2. What was happening worldwide in the sixteenth century? *Great upheavals of established powers: specifically, the Safavids conquered Persia, Cortés (from Spain) conquered the Aztec Empire in the Western Hemisphere, and later in the century, England defeated the massive Spanish Armada.*

Reading Social Studies

Understanding Themes

One theme of this chapter is politics. Discuss with students how politics might have been a factor in the expansion of Muslim rule. Have them think about how politics may have affected the spread and acceptance of Islam. Then, tell students that the Muslim empires were responsible for many advances in science and technology.

Using Questions to Analyze Texts

Focus on Reading Ask students to select a paragraph or two from this chapter. Have students read the paragraphs they selected and create a graphic organizer like the one on this page. Have students write the main heading in the box in the middle, and then answer the six questions on the side. When students have finished, have them exchange papers with a partner. Ask students to read their partner's graphic organizer. Ask: Does information seem to be missing? Do the answers to the questions provide you with a good grasp of the subject?

Reading Social Studies

Economics | **Geography** | Politics | **Religion** | Society and Culture | Science and Technology

Focus on Themes In this chapter, you will learn about the origins and **geographic** spread of one of the world's great **religions**, Islam. You will read about the founder, Muhammad, and how he united much of Arabia under Muslim rule. You will also learn about great conquests and powerful Muslim rulers. Finally, you will read about the outstanding achievements of Islamic scientists, artists, and scholars.

Questioning

Focus on Reading Asking yourself questions is a good way to be sure that you understand what you are reading. You should always ask yourself who the most important people are, when and where they lived, and what they did.

Analytical Questions Questions can also help you make sense of what happened in the past. Asking questions about how and why things happened will help you better understand historical events.

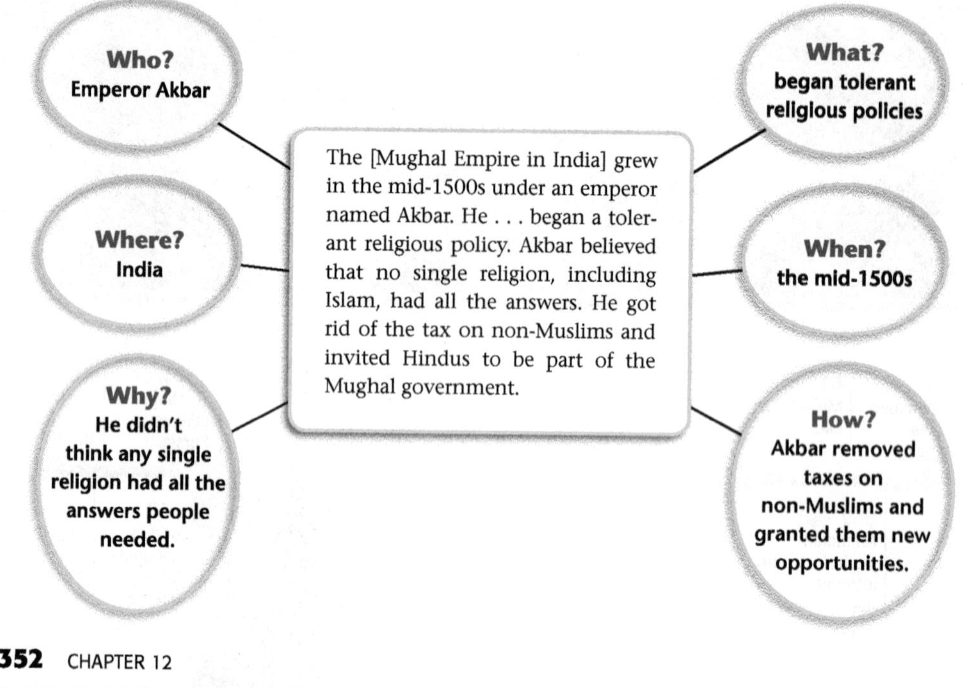

Who? Emperor Akbar
Where? India
Why? He didn't think any single religion had all the answers people needed.
The [Mughal Empire in India] grew in the mid-1500s under an emperor named Akbar. He . . . began a tolerant religious policy. Akbar believed that no single religion, including Islam, had all the answers. He got rid of the tax on non-Muslims and invited Hindus to be part of the Mughal government.
What? began tolerant religious policies
When? the mid-1500s
How? Akbar removed taxes on non-Muslims and granted them new opportunities.

Reading and Skills Resources

Reading Support

- Guided Reading Workbook
- Student Edition on Audio CD
- Spanish Chapter Summaries Audio CD Program

Social Studies Skills Support

- Interactive Skills Tutor CD-ROM

Vocabulary Support

- **CRF:** Vocabulary Builder Activities
- **CRF:** Chapter Review Activity
- Differentiated Instruction Modified Worksheets and Tests CD-ROM:
  - Vocabulary Flash Cards
  - Vocabulary Builder Activity
  - Chapter Review Activity

TOS Holt McDougal PuzzleView

You Try It!

Read the following passage and then answer the questions.

Geography

During the mid-1100s, a Muslim geographer named al-Idrisi collected information from Arab travelers. He was writing a geography book and wanted it to be very accurate. When al-Idrisi had a question about where a mountain, river, or coastline was, he sent trained geographers to figure out its exact location. Using the information the geographers brought back, al-Idrisi made some important discoveries. For example, he proved that land did not go all the way around the Indian Ocean as many people thought.

Answer these questions based on the passage you just read.

1. Who is this passage about?
2. What is he known for doing?
3. When did he live?
4. Why did he do what he did?
5. How did he accomplish his task?
6. How can knowing this information help you understand the past?

As you read Chapter 12, ask questions to help you understand what you are reading.

Key Terms and People

Chapter 12

Section 1
oasis *(p. 354)*
caravan *(p. 355)*
Muhammad *(p. 356)*
Islam *(p. 356)*
Muslim *(p. 356)*
Qur'an *(p. 356)*
pilgrimage *(p. 356)*
mosque *(p. 357)*

Section 2
jihad *(p. 359)*
Sunnah *(p. 359)*
Five Pillars of Islam *(p. 360)*

Section 3
Abu Bakr *(p. 362)*
caliph *(p. 362)*
tolerance *(p. 364)*
Janissaries *(p. 364)*
Mehmed II *(p. 364)*
Suleyman I *(p. 364)*
Shia *(p. 365)*
Sunni *(p. 365)*

Section 4
Ibn Battutah *(p. 369)*
Sufism *(p. 369)*
Omar Khayyám *(p. 371)*
patrons *(p. 371)*
minaret *(p. 371)*
calligraphy *(p. 371)*

Academic Vocabulary

Success in school is related to knowing academic vocabulary—the words that are frequently used in school assignments and discussions. In this chapter, you will learn the following academic words:

influence *(p. 356)*
development *(p. 364)*

Reading Social Studies

Key Terms and People

Preteach the key terms and people from this chapter to the class. Then have each student write a sentence for each key term. Remind students to use each term correctly. Have students rewrite their sentences, leaving blanks where the key term or person belongs. Have students exchange papers with a partner and complete the fill-in-the-blank activity. **LS Verbal/Linguistic**

Focus on Reading

See the **Focus on Reading** questions in this chapter for more practice on reading social studies skills.

Reading Social Studies Assessment

See the **Chapter Review** at the end of this chapter for student assessment questions related to this reading skill.

Teaching Tip

One way to help students use questions to understand texts is to have students take notes on a reading assignment. Ask students to read a section from the chapter and apply these six questions to the section. First have students write the main headings and subheadings on their paper. Under each subheading, have students write the questions and then answer each question. When students have finished, ask them to exchange papers. Ask students whether they have the same questions and answers. If not, have them determine why they are different.

Answers

You Try It! 1. Muslim geographer al-Idrisi; **2.** writing a very accurate geography book; **3.** in the mid-1100s; **4.** He wanted to provide people with accurate information about geography. **5.** He sent trained geographers to determine the exact location of places. **6.** It helps us understand that, almost 1,000 years ago, Muslims had a very accurate knowledge of geography.

Preteach

Bellringer

If YOU were there . . . Use the **Daily Bellringer Transparency** to help students answer the question.

Daily Bellringer Transparency, Section 1

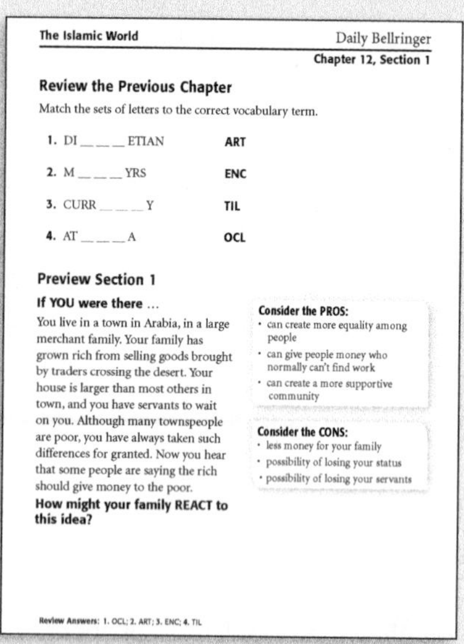

The Islamic World — Daily Bellringer

Chapter 12, Section 1

Review the Previous Chapter

Match the sets of letters to the correct vocabulary term.

1. DI ___ ___ ___ ETIAN — **ART**
2. M ___ ___ ___ YRS — **ENC**
3. CURR ___ ___ ___ Y — **TIL**
4. AT ___ ___ ___ A — **OCL**

Preview Section 1

If YOU were there ...

You live in a town in Arabia, in a large merchant family. Your family has grown rich from selling goods brought by traders crossing the desert. Your house is larger than most others in town, and you have servants to wait on you. Although many townspeople are poor, you have always taken such differences for granted. Now you hear that some people are saying the rich should give money to the poor.

How might your family REACT to this idea?

Consider the PROS:
- can create more equality among people
- can give people money who normally can't find work
- can create a more supportive community

Consider the CONS:
- less money for your family
- possibility of losing your status
- possibility of losing your servants

Review Answers: 1. OCL; 2. ART; 3. ENC; 4. TIL

Academic Vocabulary

Review with students the high-use academic term in this section.

influence change, or have an effect on (p. 356)

CRF: Vocabulary Builder Activity, Section 1

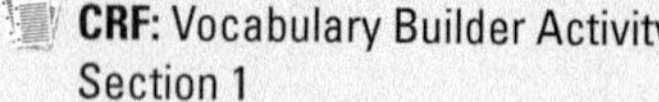

Taking Notes

Have students use the graphic organizer online to take notes on the section. This activity will prepare students for the Section Assessment, in which they will complete a graphic organizer that builds on the information using the Critical Thinking Skill: Sequencing.

SECTION 1

The Roots of Islam

What You Will Learn...

Main Ideas

1. Arabia is mostly a desert land, where two ways of life, nomadic and sedentary, developed.
2. A new religion called Islam, founded by Muhammad, spread throughout Arabia in the 600s.

The Big Idea

In the harsh desert climate of Arabia, Muhammad, a merchant from Mecca, introduced a major world religion called Islam.

Key Terms

oasis, *p. 354*
caravan, *p. 355*
Muhammad, *p. 356*
Islam, *p. 356*
Muslim, *p. 356*
Qur'an, *p. 356*
pilgrimage, *p. 356*
mosque, *p. 357*

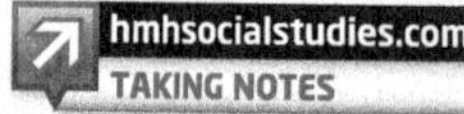

hmhsocialstudies.com
TAKING NOTES

Use the graphic organizer online to take notes on key places, people, and events in the origins of Islam.

If YOU were there...

You live in a town in Arabia, in a large merchant family. Your family has grown rich from selling goods brought by traders crossing the desert. Your house is larger than most others in town, and you have servants to wait on you. Although many townspeople are poor, you have always taken such differences for granted. Now you hear that some people are saying the rich should give money to the poor.

How might your family react to this idea?

BUILDING BACKGROUND For thousands of years, traders have crossed the deserts of Arabia to bring goods to market. Scorching temperatures and lack of water have made the journey difficult. But Arabia not only developed into a thriving trade center, it also became the birthplace of a new religion that challenged old ideas.

Life in a Desert Land

The Arabian Peninsula, or Arabia, is located in the southwest corner of Asia. It lies near the intersection of Africa, Europe, and Asia. For thousands of years Arabia's location, physical features, and climate have shaped life in the region.

Physical Features and Climate

Arabia lies in a region with hot and dry air. With a blazing sun and clear skies, summer temperatures in the interior reach 100°F daily. This climate has created a band of deserts across Arabia and northern Africa. Sand dunes, or hills of sand shaped by the wind, can rise to 800 feet high and stretch for hundreds of miles!

Arabia's deserts have a very limited amount of water. What water there is exists mainly in scattered oases. An **oasis** is a wet, fertile area in a desert. Oases have long been key stops along Arabia's overland trade routes.

Two Ways of Life

To live in Arabia's difficult desert environment, people developed two main ways of life. Nomads lived in tents and raised herds of sheep, goats, and camels. The animals provided milk,

Teach the Big Idea

At Level

The Roots of Islam

1. **Teach** Ask students the questions in the Main Idea boxes to teach this section.
2. **Apply** Have students write each of the red titles in the section on a piece of paper. Ask students to review the material under each title. Have students write one sentence that expresses the main idea of the information under each title. **LS Verbal/Linguistic**
3. **Review** Have students share the main idea statements they created for each heading. Ask students to list supporting details for each main idea. Have students add the details below their main ideas.
4. **Practice/Homework** Ask students to imagine they are nomads, craftspeople, or traders. Have each student write a letter describing that lifestyle to a friend. **LS Verbal/Linguistic**

Alternative Assessment Handbook, Rubric 25: Personal Letters

meat, wool, and leather. The camels also carried heavy loads. Nomads traveled with their herds across the desert in search of food and water for their animals.

Among the nomads, water and grazing land belonged to tribes. Membership in a tribe, a group of related people, offered protection from desert dangers.

While nomads moved around the desert, other Arabs lived a sedentary, or settled, life. These people made their homes in oases where they could farm. These settlements, particularly the ones along trade routes, became towns. Merchants and craftspeople lived there and worked with people in the caravan trade. A **caravan** is a group of traders that travel together.

Towns became centers of trade. Many had a market or bazaar. There, nomads traded animal products and desert herbs for goods such as cooking supplies and clothing. Merchants sold spices, gold, leather, and other goods brought by the caravans.

READING CHECK **Categorizing** What two ways of life were common in Arabia?

hmhsocialstudies.com
ANIMATED HISTORY
Trade Routes, AD 570

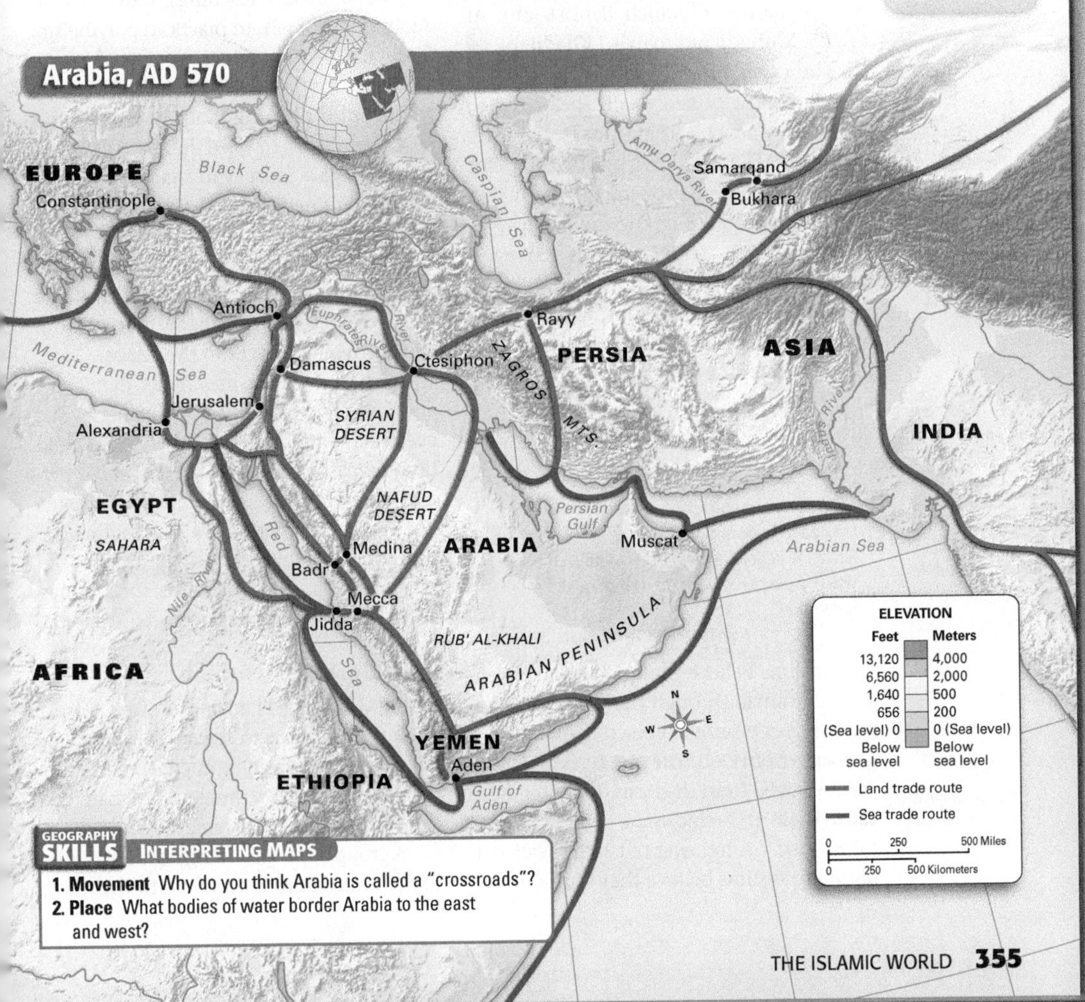

GEOGRAPHY SKILLS **INTERPRETING MAPS**

1. **Movement** Why do you think Arabia is called a "crossroads"?
2. **Place** What bodies of water border Arabia to the east and west?

Direct Teach

Main Idea

1 Life in a Desert Land

Arabia is mostly a desert land, where two ways of life, nomadic and sedentary, developed.

Define What is a caravan? *a group of traders that travel together*

Draw Conclusions How did townspeople and nomads rely on each other? *Townspeople obtained desert herbs and animal products from nomads; nomads obtained cooking supplies and clothing from townspeople.*

Activity **Collage** Have each student create a collage that depicts the two main features of Arabia's geography—the desert and the oases.
LS Visual/Spatial

Map Transparency: Arabia, AD 570

Interpreting Maps

Arabia, AD 570

Activity **Creating a Map** Prepare outline maps of Arabia for the class. Have students indicate the major trade routes that passed through Arabia around 570. Ask students to label the civilizations the Arabs traded with along each route as well as what items were traded. **LS Verbal/Linguistic, Visual/Spatial**

MISCONCEPTION ALERT

Arabia Many people think that modern-day Arabia consists of only one country, Saudi Arabia. Actually, there are seven modern-day nations on the Arabian Peninsula: Bahrain, Kuwait, Oman, Qatar, Saudi Arabia, the United Arab Emirates, and Yemen.

Critical Thinking: Making Generalizations

At Level

A Day in the Life

1. Review with the class the two main lifestyles found in Arabia—sedentary and nomadic.
2. Explain to students that they will write a one-page description of a typical day in the life of an ancient Arab. Have students select one of the two lifestyles of early Arabia and brainstorm a list of tasks that a member of that lifestyle might have to accomplish on a typical day.
3. Students should write their "day in the life" in the form of a descriptive paper. Their papers should describe events from morning to night and should paint a picture of what a typical day might have been like for someone of that particular lifestyle.
4. Ask volunteers to share their descriptions with the class. **LS Verbal/Linguistic**
5. **Extend** Organize a class debate on which lifestyle is preferable to young people. **LS Verbal/Linguistic**

Alternative Assessment Handbook, Rubrics 10: Debates; and 40: Writing to Describe

Answers

Reading Check *nomadic and sedentary*

Interpreting Maps **1.** *It is near the intersection of three continents and trade routes pass through the region.* **2.** *east—Persian Gulf, Arabian Sea; west—Red Sea*

Direct Teach

Main Idea

2 A New Religion

A new religion called Islam, founded by the prophet Muhammad, spread throughout Arabia in the 600s.

Recall In what business was Muhammad involved? *caravan trade*

Explain What is the difference between the terms *Islam* and *Muslim*? *Islam is a religion, while a Muslim is a follower of that religion.*

Draw Conclusions Why did Muhammad not tell people right away that an angel had spoken to him? *He may have been afraid that no one would believe him or that his message would make people angry.*

CRF: Biography Activity: Khadijah

CRF: Primary Source Activity: Reading from the Koran

Info to Know

The Qur'an Muhammad continued to receive messages for the rest of his life. These revelations make up Islam's Qur'an, or Koran. While Muhammad himself did not write down the messages, it is likely that he dictated them to others. The Qur'an was collected and organized about 644, about 12 years after Muhammad's death.

A New Religion

In early times, Arabs worshipped many gods. That changed, however, when a man named **Muhammad** brought a new religion to Arabia. Historians know little about Muhammad. What they do know comes from religious writings.

Muhammad, Prophet of Islam

FOCUS ON READING
Write a question you could use to analyze the text in this paragraph. Then answer it.

Muhammad was born into an important family in the city of Mecca around 570. As a child, he traveled with his uncle's caravans. Once he was grown, he managed a caravan business owned by a wealthy woman named Khadijah (ka-DEE-jah). At age 25, Muhammad married Khadijah.

The caravan trade made Mecca a rich city. But most of the wealth belonged to just a few people. Traditionally, wealthy people in Mecca had helped the poor. But as Muhammad was growing up, many rich merchants began to ignore the needy.

Concerned about these changes, Muhammad often went to the hills to pray and meditate. One day, when he was about 40 years old, he went to meditate in a cave. According to religious writings, an angel spoke to Muhammad, telling him to "Recite! Recite!" Muhammad asked what he should recite. The angel answered:

> "Recite in the name of your Lord who created, created man from clots of blood!
> Recite! Your Lord is the Most Bountiful One,
> Who by the pen taught man what he did not know."
>
> —From *The Koran*, translated by N. J. Dawood

ACADEMIC VOCABULARY
influence change, or have an effect on

Muslims believe that God had spoken to Muhammad through the angel and had made him a prophet, a person who tells of messages from God. The messages Muhammad received form the basis of the religion called **Islam**. In Arabic, *Islam* means "to submit to God." A follower of Islam is called a **Muslim**. Muslims believe that Muhammad continued receiving messages from God for the rest of his life. These messages were collected in the **Qur'an** (kuh-RAN), the holy book of Islam.

Muhammad's Teachings

In 613 Muhammad began to talk about his messages. He taught that there was only one God, Allah, which means "the God" in Arabic. Islam is monotheistic, a religion based on the belief in one God, like Judaism and Christianity. Although people of all three religions believe in one God, their beliefs about God are not the same.

Muhammad's teachings were new to Arabs, most of whom practiced polytheism. They had many shrines, or special places where they worshipped their gods. A very important shrine, the Kaaba (KAH-bah), was in Mecca. People traveled there every year on a **pilgrimage**, a journey to a sacred place.

Muhammad's teachings upset many Arabs. First, they didn't like being told to stop worshipping their gods. Second, Muhammad's new religion seemed like a threat to people who made money from the yearly pilgrimages to the Kaaba.

Mecca's wealthy merchants didn't like another of Muhammad's teachings: that everyone who believed in Allah would become part of a community in which rich and poor would be equal. Rich merchants also disliked Muhammad's idea that people should give money to help the poor. The merchants wanted to keep all of their money and remain more powerful than the poor.

Islam Spreads in Arabia

At first Muhammad had few followers. Slowly, more people began to listen to his ideas. As Islam began to influence people, Mecca's rulers became worried. They threatened Muhammad and even planned to kill him.

A group of people living north of Mecca invited Muhammad to move to their city.

Differentiating Instruction

Advanced/Gifted and Talented

Above Level | Research Required

1. Review with students the similarities among Christianity, Judaism, and Islam.
2. Have students conduct research in a library, on the Internet, or in other resources to find more similarities among these three major religions.
3. Have students create a graphic organizer that shows the similarities that exist among the three religions. Ask students to be creative in the design of their graphic organizers and to respect the beliefs and practices of each religion.
4. Ask volunteers to share their comparisons with the class. Write the similarities for the entire class to see.

LS Verbal/Linguistic, Visual/Spatial

Alternative Assessment Handbook, Rubric 13: Graphic Organizers

Time Line

Beginnings of Islam

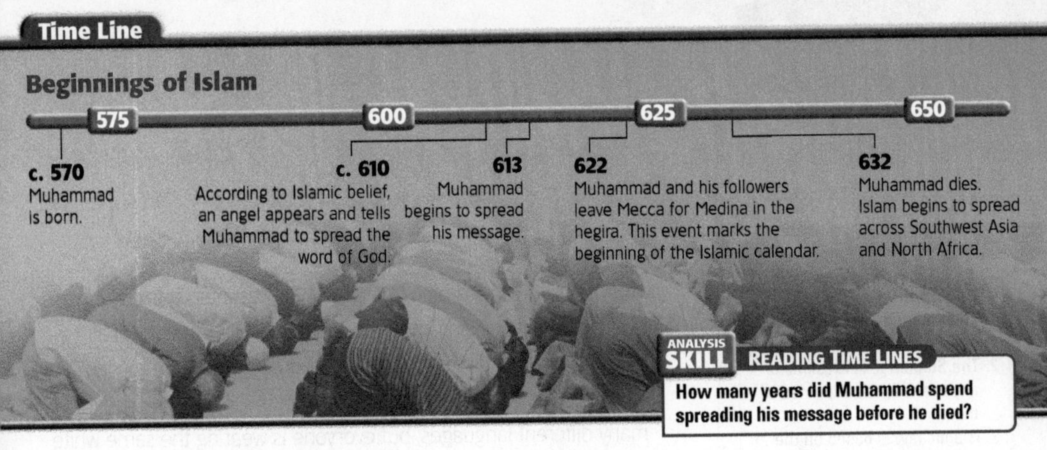

575
600
625
650
c. 570
Muhammad is born.
c. 610
According to Islamic belief, an angel appears and tells Muhammad to spread the word of God.
613
Muhammad begins to spread his message.
622
Muhammad and his followers leave Mecca for Medina in the hegira. This event marks the beginning of the Islamic calendar.
632
Muhammad dies. Islam begins to spread across Southwest Asia and North Africa.

ANALYSIS SKILL READING TIME LINES

How many years did Muhammad spend spreading his message before he died?

So in 622 Muhammad and many followers went to Medina (muh-DEE-nuh). *Medina* means "the Prophet's city" in Arabic. Muhammad's departure from Mecca is known as the hegira (hi-JY-ruh), or journey.

Muhammad became a spiritual and political leader in Medina. His house became the first **mosque** (mahsk), or building for Muslim prayer.

As the Muslim community in Medina grew stronger, other Arab tribes began to accept Islam. But conflict with the Meccans increased. In 630, after several years of fighting, the people of Mecca gave in. They accepted Islam as their religion.

Soon most of the Arabian tribes accepted Muhammad as their spiritual and political leader and became Muslims. Muhammad died in 632, but the religion he taught would soon spread far beyond Arabia.

READING CHECK **Summarizing** How did Islam spread in Arabia?

SUMMARY AND PREVIEW The geography of Arabia encouraged trade and influenced the development of nomadic and sedentary lifestyles. In the early 600s Muhammad introduced a new religion to Arabia. Many people in Arabia became Muslims. In the next section, you will learn more about the main Islamic teachings and beliefs.

hmhsocialstudies.com
ANIMATED HISTORY
Muslim Army: Spread of Islam, AD 661

Section 1 Assessment

hmhsocialstudies.com ONLINE QUIZ

Reviewing Ideas, Terms, and People

1. a. **Define** What is an **oasis**?
   b. **Make Generalizations** Why did towns often develop near oases?
   c. **Predict** Do you think life would have been better for nomads or townspeople in early Arabia? Explain your answer.
2. a. **Identify** What is a key Islamic belief about God?
   b. **Explain** According to Islamic belief, how did **Muhammad** get the ideas that started **Islam**?
   c. **Evaluate** In what ways was Muhammad's time in Medina important to the growth of Islam?

Critical Thinking

3. **Sequencing** Draw a time line like the one below. Using your notes on Muhammad, identify the key dates in his life.

FOCUS ON WRITING

4. **Writing about Muhammad** Review your notes to answer the question, "Who was Muhammad?" It may help to think of Muhammad's life in three parts: "Early Life," "Muhammad Becomes a Prophet," and "Muhammad's Teachings."

Direct Teach

Main Idea

2 A New Religion

A new religion called Islam, founded by the prophet Muhammad, spread throughout Arabia in the 600s.

Recall What was the hegira? *Muhammad's departure from Mecca to Medina*

Compare What is one major belief that is the same in Judaism, Christianity, and Islam? *monotheism, or belief in one God*

Reading Time Lines

Activity Illustrated Time Line Ask students to examine the time line titled "Beginnings of Islam." Have each student create an illustrated version of the time line with one illustration for each entry. **LS Visual/Spatial**

Review & Assess

Close

Have students work in pairs to write one-paragraph summaries of the geography of Arabia. Then have students discuss the origins of Islam as well as early reactions to Muhammad and his teachings.

Review

Online Quiz, Section 1

Assess

SE Section 1 Assessment
PASS: Section 1 Quiz
Alternative Assessment Handbook

Reteach/Classroom Intervention

Guided Reading Workbook, Section 1
Interactive Skills Tutor CD-ROM

Section 1 Assessment Answers

1. a. a wet, fertile area in a desert
   b. access to water; could farm there
   c. Answers will vary, but students should show an understanding that sedentary lifestyles were safer and more convenient, while nomads led more adventurous lifestyles.
2. a. There is only one God.
   b. received a message from God from an angel while he was meditating in a cave
   c. It was easier for Muhammad to convert people in a safer environment like Medina. People there accepted his ideas and he gained enough support to eventually spread his message to Mecca and beyond.
3. **Sequencing** c. 570, Muhammad is born; c. 610, he hears the voice of an angel in a cave; 613, he begins spreading his message; 622, he leaves Mecca for Medina; 632, he dies.
4. Notes will vary but should reflect an understanding of section content.

Answers

Analysis Skills Reading Time Lines *19 years (from 613 to 632)*

Reading Check *It spread with Muhammad's move to Medina and became popular with Arab tribes.*

Preteach

Bellringer

If YOU were there . . . Use the **Daily Bellringer Transparency** to help students answer the question.

Daily Bellringer Transparency, Section 2

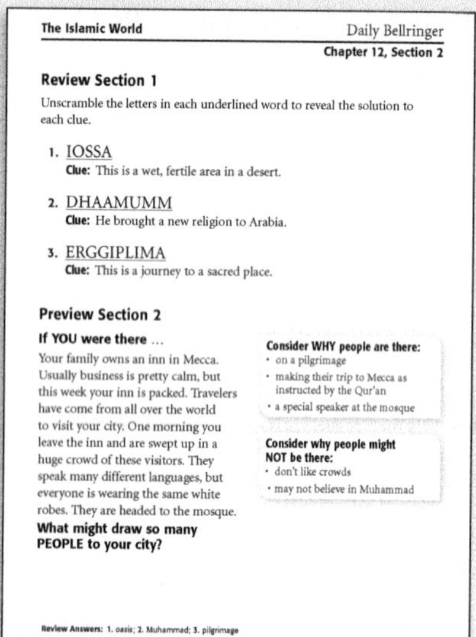

The Islamic World — Daily Bellringer — Chapter 12, Section 2

Review Section 1

Unscramble the letters in each underlined word to reveal the solution to each clue.

1. IOSSA
   Clue: This is a wet, fertile area in a desert.
2. DHAAMUMM
   Clue: He brought a new religion to Arabia.
3. ERGGIPLIMA
   Clue: This is a journey to a sacred place.

Preview Section 2

If YOU were there ...

Your family owns an inn in Mecca. Usually business is pretty calm, but this week your inn is packed. Travelers have come from all over the world to visit your city. One morning you leave the inn and are swept up in a huge crowd of these visitors. They speak many different languages, but everyone is wearing the same white robes. They are headed to the mosque.

What might draw so many PEOPLE to your city?

Consider WHY people are there:
- on a pilgrimage
- making their trip to Mecca as instructed by the Qur'an
- a special speaker at the mosque

Consider why people might NOT be there:
- don't like crowds
- may not believe in Muhammad

Review Answers: 1. oasis; 2. Muhammad; 3. pilgrimage

Building Vocabulary

Preteach or review the following terms:

charity gift to help people in need (p. 360)
convert change beliefs (p. 359)
fast go without food and drink (p. 360)
guidance advice, directions (p. 359)
paradise heaven (p. 358)

CRF: Vocabulary Builder Activity, Section 2

Taking Notes

Have students use the graphic organizer online to take notes on the section. This activity will prepare students for the Section Assessment, in which they will complete a graphic organizer that builds on the information using the Critical Thinking Skill: Categorizing.

SECTION 2

Islamic Beliefs and Practices

What You Will Learn...

Main Ideas

1. The Qur'an guides Muslims' lives.
2. The Sunnah tells Muslims of important duties expected of them.
3. Islamic law is based on the Qur'an and the Sunnah.

The Big Idea

Sacred texts called the Qur'an and the Sunnah guide Muslims in their religion, daily life, and laws.

Key Terms

jihad, *p. 359*
Sunnah, *p. 359*
Five Pillars of Islam, *p. 360*

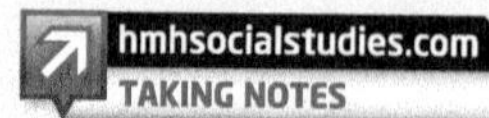

Use the graphic organizer online to take notes on the most important beliefs and practices of Islam.

If YOU were there...

Your family owns an inn in Mecca. Usually business is pretty calm, but this week your inn is packed. Travelers have come from all over the world to visit your city. One morning you leave the inn and are swept up in a huge crowd of these visitors. They speak many different languages, but everyone is wearing the same white robes. They are headed to the mosque.

What might draw so many people to your city?

BUILDING BACKGROUND One basic Islamic belief is that everyone who can must make a trip to Mecca sometime during his or her lifetime. More Islamic teachings can be found in Islam's holy books—the Qur'an and the Sunnah.

The Qur'an

During Muhammad's life, his followers memorized his messages and his words and deeds. After Muhammad's death, they collected his teachings and wrote them down to form the book known as the Qur'an. Muslims believe the Qur'an to be the exact word of God as it was told to Muhammad.

Beliefs

The central teaching in the Qur'an is that there is only one God—Allah—and that Muhammad is his prophet. The Qur'an says people must obey Allah's commands. Muslims learned of these commands from Muhammad.

Islam teaches that the world had a definite beginning and will end one day. Muhammad said that on the final day God will judge all people. Those who have obeyed his orders will be granted life in paradise. According to the Qur'an, paradise is a beautiful garden full of fine food and drink. People who have not obeyed God, however, will suffer.

Teach the Big Idea

At Level

Islamic Beliefs and Practices

Materials: poster board, art supplies

1. **Teach** Ask students the questions in the Main Idea boxes to teach this section.
2. **Apply** Have each student create a poster that lists the important beliefs, guidelines, and practices of Islam. Students should decorate their posters to look like an official set of rules. Remind students to include the Five Pillars of Islam and guidelines for behavior.
   LS Verbal/Linguistic, Visual/Spatial
3. **Review** Ask each student to write two questions that cover guidelines or practices from his or her poster. Go around the room and have students ask one another their questions. Discuss the answers with the class.
4. **Practice/Homework** Have students write a short paragraph to explain the importance of the Qur'an, the Sunnah, and Shariah.
   LS Verbal/Linguistic

Alternative Assessment Handbook, Rubric 28: Posters; and 42: Writing to Inform

Studying the Qur'an
The Qur'an plays a central role in the lives of many Muslims. Children study and memorize verses from the Qur'an at home, at Islamic schools, and in mosques. Muslims who memorize the entire book are respected as "Keepers" of the Qur'an.

Where do you think these children are studying the Qur'an?

Guidelines for Behavior

Like holy books of other religions, the Qur'an describes acts of worship, guidelines for moral behavior, and rules for social life. Muslims look to the Qur'an for guidance in their daily lives. For example, the Qur'an describes how to prepare for worship. Muslims must wash themselves before praying so they will be pure before Allah. The Qur'an also tells Muslims what they should not eat or drink. Muslims are not allowed to eat pork or drink alcohol.

In addition to guidelines for individual behavior, the Qur'an describes relations among people. Many of these ideas changed Arabian society. For example, before Muhammad's time many Arabs owned slaves. Although slavery didn't disappear among Muslims, the Qur'an encourages Muslims to free slaves. Also, women in Arabia had few rights. The Qur'an describes rights of women, including rights to own property, earn money, and get an education. However, most Muslim women still have fewer rights than men.

Another important subject in the Qur'an has to do with **jihad** (ji-HAHD), which means "to make an effort, or to struggle." Jihad refers to the inner struggle people go through in their effort to obey God and behave according to Islamic ways. Jihad can also mean the struggle to defend the Muslim community, or, historically, to convert people to Islam. The word has also been translated as "holy war."

READING CHECK **Analyzing** Why is the Qur'an important to Muslims?

The Sunnah

The Qur'an is not the only source of Islamic teachings. Muslims also study the hadith (huh-DEETH), the written record of Muhammad's words and actions. This record is the basis for the Sunnah. The **Sunnah** (SOOH-nuh) refers to the way Muhammad lived, which provides a model for the duties and the way of life expected of Muslims. The Sunnah guides Muslims' behavior.

Direct Teach

Main Idea

1 The Qur'an

The Qur'an guides Muslims' lives.

Explain What does the Qur'an say about slavery? *It encourages Muslims to free their slaves.*

Summarize What are the different meanings of the term *jihad*? *inner struggle to obey God; struggle to defend Muslim community; haps also been translated as "holy war"*

Did you know...

The Sunnah consists of a collection of hadith, or reports about Muhammad's deeds and sayings. The hadith were originally memorized by Muhammad's followers and were written down approximately 200 years following his death. Many Muslims accept six collections of hadith known as the Six Books.

Answers

Studying the Qur'an *possible answers—at a religious school or a mosque*

Reading Check *because Muslims believe it is the exact word of God as told to Muhammad*

Differentiating Instruction for Universal Access

Special Needs Learners Below Level

1. Discuss with students the different guidelines described in the Qur'an. Remind students that the Qur'an covers the major beliefs of Islam, guidelines for worship, moral behavior, and social life. Explain to students the differences between these categories.
2. Write the blue, italicized statements in the graphic organizer in a random order for students to see. Then draw a copy of the graphic organizer for students to see. Omit the blue, italicized answers.
3. Have students copy the graphic organizer and complete it by listing each statement in the correct category.
4. Review the answers with the class. If necessary, explain to students why statements belong in a particular category.
LS Verbal/Linguistic

Alternative Assessment Handbook, Rubric 13: Graphic Organizer

The Qur'an	
Beliefs	• *There is only one God.* • *God will judge all people.* • *The good will live in paradise.* • *The bad will suffer.*
Rules for Worship	• *Don't eat pork or drink alcohol.* • *Do ritual washing before praying.*
Rules for Society	• *Slaves should be freed.* • *Women have the right to own property, earn money, and receive an education.*

Direct Teach

Main Idea

❷ The Sunnah

The Sunnah tells Muslims of important duties expected of them.

Define What is the Sunnah? *It is the record of the way Muhammad lived; it serves as a model for the expected duties and way of life of Muslims.*

Identify List the Five Pillars of Islam. *statement of faith, daily prayer, yearly donation to charity, fasting during Ramadan, pilgrimage to Mecca*

Draw Conclusions How does the Sunnah affect the daily lives of Muslims? *It sets forth the Five Pillars of Islam and forms the basis of rules regarding business, government, and personal relations.*

Quick Facts Transparency: The Five Pillars of Islam

hmhsocialstudies.com

Online Resources
Activity: Islamic Beliefs and Practices Presentation

Info to Know

Ramadan Muslims mark the end of Ramadan with a three-day celebration known as the *'Eid ul-Fitr*, or the Festival of Fast-Breaking. Muslims celebrate with services at the mosque, gatherings with family and friends, and carnivals. Gifts for children and special sweets are often handed out during this holiday.

The Five Pillars of Islam
QUICK FACTS
Saying "There is no god but God, and Muhammad is his prophet"
Praying five times a day
Giving to the poor and needy
Fasting during the holy month of Ramadan
Traveling to Mecca at least once on a hajj

ANALYSIS SKILL **ANALYZING VISUALS**

Which of the five pillars shows how Muslims are supposed to treat other people?

The Five Pillars of Islam

The first duties of a Muslim are known as the **Five Pillars of Islam**, which are five acts of worship required of all Muslims. The first pillar is a statement of faith. At least once in their lives, Muslims must state their faith by saying, "There is no god but God, and Muhammad is his prophet." Muslims say this when they accept Islam. They also say it in their daily prayers.

The second pillar of Islam is daily prayer. Muslims must pray five times a day: before sunrise, at midday, in late afternoon, right after sunset, and before going to bed. At each of these times, a call goes out from a mosque, inviting Muslims to come pray. Muslims try to pray together at a mosque. They believe prayer is proof that someone has accepted Allah.

The third pillar of Islam is a yearly donation to charity. Muslims must pay part of their wealth to a religious official. This money is used to help the poor, build mosques, or pay debts. Helping and caring for others is important in Islam.

The fourth pillar is fasting—going without food and drink. Muslims fast daily during the holy month of Ramadan (RAH-muh-dahn). The Qur'an says Allah began his revelations to Muhammad in this month. During Ramadan, most Muslims will not eat or drink anything between dawn and sunset. Muslims believe fasting is a way to show that God is more important than one's own body. Fasting also reminds Muslims of people in the world who struggle to get enough food.

The fifth pillar of Islam is the hajj (HAJ), a pilgrimage to Mecca. All Muslims must travel to Mecca at least once in their lives if they can. The Kaaba, in Mecca, is Islam's most sacred place.

The Sunnah and Daily Life

In addition to the five pillars, the Sunnah has other examples of Muhammad's actions and teachings. These form the basis for rules about how to treat others. According to Muhammad's example, people should treat guests with generosity.

Critical Thinking: Summarizing

At Level

The Five Pillars of Islam Book Jacket

1. Explain to students what a book jacket looks like and its purpose. You might want to provide a sample book jacket.
2. Point out to students that book jackets include a picture or illustration and the title on the front cover; a brief summary of the book's contents on the inside flaps; the title, author, and publisher on the spine; and comments about the book on the back cover.
3. Have students prepare a book jacket for a book titled The Five Pillars of Islam. Draw a sample layout of the elements of a book jacket for students to follow.
4. Ask volunteers to share their finished book jackets with the class.
   LS Verbal/Linguistic, Visual/Spatial

Alternative Assessment Handbook, Rubrics 3: Artwork; and 37: Writing Assignments

Answers

Analyzing Visuals *the third pillar, giving to the poor and needy*

In addition to describing personal relations, the Sunnah provides guidelines for relations in business and government. For example, one Sunnah rule says that it is bad to owe someone money. Another rule says that people should obey their leaders.

READING CHECK **Generalizing** What do Muslims learn from the Sunnah?

Sources of Islamic Beliefs QUICK FACTS

Qur'an	Sunnah	Shariah
Holy book that contains the messages Muhammad claimed to receive from God	Muhammad's example for the duties and way of life expected of Muslims	Islamic law, based on interpretations of the Qur'an and Sunnah

Islamic Law

The Qur'an and the Sunnah are important guides for how Muslims should live. They also form the basis of Islamic law, or Shariah (shuh-REE-uh). Shariah is a system based on Islamic sources and human reason that judges the rightness of actions an individual or community might take. These actions fall on a scale ranging from required to accepted to disapproved to forbidden. Islamic law makes no distinction between religious beliefs and daily life, so Islam affects all aspects of Muslims' lives.

Shariah sets rewards for good behavior and punishments for crimes. It also describes limits of authority. It was the basis for law in Muslim countries until modern times. Most Muslim countries today blend Islamic law with legal systems like those in the United States or western Europe.

Islamic law is not found in one book. Instead, it is a set of opinions and writings that have changed over the centuries. Different ideas about Islamic law are found in different Muslim regions.

READING CHECK **Finding Main Ideas** What is the purpose of Islamic law?

SUMMARY AND PREVIEW The Qur'an, the Sunnah, and Shariah teach Muslims how to live their lives. In the next chapter, you will learn more about Muslim culture and the spread of Islam from Arabia to other lands.

Section 2 Assessment

hmhsocialstudies.com ONLINE QUIZ

Reviewing Ideas, Terms, and People

1. a. **Recall** What is the central teaching of the Qur'an?
   b. **Explain** How does the Qur'an guide Muslims' daily lives?
2. a. **Recall** What are the **Five Pillars of Islam**?
   b. **Make Generalizations** Why do Muslims fast during Ramadan?
3. a. **Identify** What is Islamic law called?
   b. **Make Inferences** How is Islamic law different from law in the United States?
   c. **Elaborate** What is a possible reason that opinions and writings about Islamic law have changed over the centuries?

Critical Thinking

4. **Categorizing** Draw a chart like the one to the right. Use it to list three teachings from the Qur'an and three teachings from the Sunnah.

Qur'an	Sunnah

FOCUS ON WRITING

5. **Describing Islam** Answer the following questions to help you write a paragraph describing Islam. What is the central teaching of the Qur'an? What are Islam's Five Pillars? What is the function of the Sunnah?

Direct Teach

Main Idea

3 Islamic Law

Islamic law is based on the Qur'an and the Sunnah.

Define What is Shariah? *system of Islamic law that judges the rightness of actions*

Draw Conclusions What role does Shariah play in modern Islam? *It makes up a portion of their legal system.*

Quick Facts Transparency: Sources of Islamic Beliefs

Review & Assess

Close

Review the three sources of Islamic beliefs with students.

Review

Online Quiz, Section 2

Assess

SE Section 2 Assessment

PASS: Section 2 Quiz

Alternative Assessment Handbook

Reteach/Classroom Intervention

Guided Reading Workbook, Section 2

Interactive Skills Tutor CD-ROM

Section 2 Assessment Answers

1. **a.** There is only one God, and Muhammad is his prophet.
   b. It lists rules God gave for good behavior.
2. **a.** statement of faith, daily prayer, donation to charity, fasting, hajj
   b. reminder that God is more important than their body; reminder of people in the world who struggle to get enough food
3. **a.** Shariah
   b. It governs religious beliefs and practices. It makes no distinction between religion and daily life; in the United States there is a separation of church and state.
   c. possible answers—As some countries have incorporated Western legal systems, opinions may have changed.
4. Possible answers: Qur'an—wash before praying, don't eat pork or drink alcohol, free slaves, women have some rights, jihad; Sunnah—Five Pillars of Islam, shouldn't owe someone money, obey leaders
5. Answers will vary but should include: there is one God, Allah, and Muhammad is his prophet; Muslims honor God by praying five times a day and fasting; the Sunnah functions as a model for how Muslims should live.

Answers

Reading Check (left) *Five Pillars of Islam; how to treat others; to treat guests with generosity; guidelines for relations in business and government*

Reading Check (right) *limits authority and sets rewards and punishments for behavior*

Preteach

Bellringer

If YOU were there . . . Use the **Daily Bellringer Transparency** to help students answer the question.

Daily Bellringer Transparency, Section 3

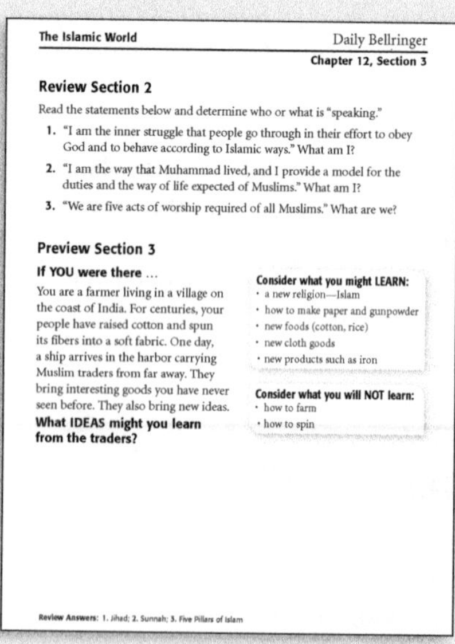

The Islamic World — Daily Bellringer

Chapter 12, Section 3

Review Section 2

Read the statements below and determine who or what is "speaking."

1. "I am the inner struggle that people go through in their effort to obey God and to behave according to Islamic ways." What am I?
2. "I am the way that Muhammad lived, and I provide a model for the duties and the way of life expected of Muslims." What am I?
3. "We are five acts of worship required of all Muslims." What are we?

Preview Section 3

If YOU were there ...

You are a farmer living in a village on the coast of India. For centuries, your people have raised cotton and spun its fibers into a soft fabric. One day, a ship arrives in the harbor carrying Muslim traders from far away. They bring interesting goods you have never seen before. They also bring new ideas.

What IDEAS might you learn from the traders?

Consider what you might LEARN:
- a new religion—Islam
- how to make paper and gunpowder
- new foods (cotton, rice)
- new cloth goods
- new products such as iron

Consider what you will NOT learn:
- how to farm
- how to spin

Review Answers: 1. Jihad; 2. Sunnah; 3. Five Pillars of Islam

Academic Vocabulary

Review with students the high-use academic term in this section.

development the process of growing or improving (p. 364)

CRF: Vocabulary Builder Activity, Section 3

Taking Notes

Have students use the graphic organizer online to take notes on the section. This activity will prepare students for the Section Assessment, in which they will complete a graphic organizer that builds on the information using the Critical Thinking Skill: Comparing and Contrasting.

SECTION 3

Islamic Empires

What You Will Learn...

Main Ideas

1. Muslim armies conquered many lands into which Islam slowly spread.
2. Trade helped Islam spread into new areas.
3. Three Muslim empires ruled large areas of Asia and Africa and parts of Europe from the 1400s to the 1800s.

The Big Idea

After the early spread of Islam, three large Islamic empires formed—the Ottoman, Safavid, and Mughal.

Key Terms and People

Abu Bakr, *p. 362*
caliph, *p. 362*
tolerance, *p. 364*
Janissaries, *p. 364*
Mehmed II, *p. 364*
Suleyman I, *p. 364*
Shia, *p. 365*
Sunni, *p. 365*

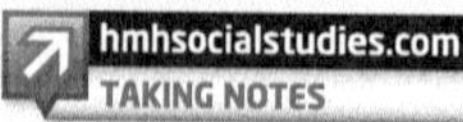

Use the graphic organizer online to take notes on the spread of Islam and the three Islamic empires that were created after Muhammad's death.

If YOU were there...

You are a farmer living in a village on the coast of India. For centuries, your people have raised cotton and spun its fibers into a soft fabric. One day, a ship arrives in the harbor carrying Muslim traders from far away. They bring interesting goods you have never seen before. They also bring new ideas.

What ideas might you learn from the traders?

BUILDING BACKGROUND You know that for years traders traveled through Arabia to markets far away. Along the way, they picked up new goods and ideas, and they introduced these to the people they met. Some of the new ideas the traders spread were Islamic ideas.

Muslim Armies Conquer Many Lands

After Muhammad's death his followers quickly chose **Abu Bakr** (UH-boo BAK-uhr), one of Muhammad's first converts, to be the next leader of Islam. He was the first **caliph** (KAY-luhf), a title that Muslims use for the highest leader of Islam. In Arabic, the word *caliph* means "successor." As Muhammad's successors, the caliphs had to follow the prophet's example. This meant ruling according to the Qur'an. Unlike Muhammad, however, early caliphs were not religious leaders.

Beginnings of an Empire

Abu Bakr directed a series of battles to unite Arabia. By his death in 634, he had made Arabia into a unified Muslim state. With Arabia united, Muslim leaders turned their attention elsewhere. Their armies, strong after their battles in Arabia, won many stunning victories. They defeated the Persian and Byzantine empires, which were weak from many years of fighting.

When the Muslims conquered lands, they set certain rules for non-Muslims living there. For example, some non-Muslims could not build new places of worship or dress like Muslims. However, Christians and Jews could continue to practice their own religion. They were not forced to convert to Islam.

Teach the Big Idea

At Level

Islamic Empires

1. **Teach** Ask students the questions in the Main Idea boxes to teach this section.
2. **Apply** Help students identify cause and effect in the spread of Islam after Muhammad's death. Have students list major events in the history of Islam's expansion. Write the list for students to see. Then have students identify different causes and effects of these events.
   LS Verbal/Linguistic
3. **Review** As you review the section's main ideas, have students share the causes and effects that they identified.
4. **Practice/Homework** Have each student create a flowchart that illustrates some of the developments in the early spread of Islam. Development should be connected with arrows. *Flowcharts may include military conquest, moving the capital, increased trade, new cities, spread of ideas through trade, and blending of cultures.*
   LS Visual/Spatial

Alternative Assessment Handbook, Rubrics 7: Charts

Growth of the Empire

Many early caliphs came from the Umayyad (oom-EYE-yuhd) family. The Umayyads moved the capital to Damascus, in Muslim-conquered Syria, and continued to expand the empire. They took over lands in Central Asia and in northern India. The Umayyads also gained control of trade in the eastern Mediterranean and conquered parts of North Africa.

The Berbers, the native people of North Africa, resisted Muslim rule at first. After years of fighting, however, many Berbers converted to Islam.

In 711 a combined Arab and Berber army invaded Spain and quickly conquered it. Next the army moved into what is now France, but it was stopped by a Christian army near the city of Tours (TOOR). Despite this defeat, Muslims called Moors ruled parts of Spain for the next 700 years.

A new Islamic dynasty, the Abbasids (uh-BAS-idz), came to power in 749. They reorganized the government to make it easier to rule such a large region.

READING CHECK **Analyzing** What role did armies play in spreading Islam?

Trade Helps Islam Spread

Islam gradually spread through areas the Muslims conquered. Trade also helped spread Islam. Along with their goods, Arab merchants took Islamic beliefs to India, Africa, and Southeast Asia. Though Indian kingdoms remained Hindu, coastal trading cities soon had large Muslim communities. In Africa, societies often had both African and Muslim customs. Many African leaders converted to Islam. Between 1200 and 1600, Muslim traders carried Islam east to what are now Malaysia and Indonesia.

Trade also brought new products to Muslim lands. For example, Arabs learned from the Chinese how to make paper and use gunpowder. New crops such as cotton, rice, and oranges arrived from India, China, and Southeast Asia.

Many Muslim merchants traveled to African market towns too. They wanted African products such as ivory, cloves, and slaves. In return they offered fine white pottery called porcelain from China, cloth goods from India, and iron from Southwest Asia and Europe. Arab traders grew wealthy from trade between regions.

ANIMATED HISTORY
Muslim World, AD 1200

THE IMPACT TODAY
Indonesia now has the largest Muslim population in the world.

The City of Córdoba

By the early 900s, Córdoba, Spain, was one of the wealthiest cities in Europe and a center of Islamic learning. Rich examples of Islamic architecture can still be seen in the city.

Direct Teach

Main Idea

1 Muslim Armies Conquer Many Lands

Muslim armies conquered many lands into which Islam slowly spread.

Identify What region did the Muslims first unify, and what caliph led this unification? *Arabia; Abu Bakr*

Analyze Why do you think the Umayyad caliphs moved the capital from Medina to Damascus? (You may want to direct students to the map on p. 365 and help them locate Medina and Damascus.) *possible answers—more central location within growing empire; better position from which to spread Muslim rule; near the Mediterranean Sea with better access to trade*

CRF: History and Geography Activity: Arabia, AD 750

Main Idea

2 Trade Helps Islam Spread

Trade helped Islam spread into new areas.

Recall What feature of Arabia gave Muslim merchants easy access to many parts of the world? *location at the crossroads between Asia, Africa, and Europe*

Summarize What did Arab Muslims gain through trade? *new products, crops, and technologies; wealth*

CRF: Economics and History Activity: Muslim Trade: Spreading Islam

Differentiating Instruction

Advanced/Gifted and Talented

Above Level **Research Required**

1. Tell students that evidence of Islam's growth in southern Europe and northern Africa can be seen in Muslim architecture that remains in the region.
2. Ask students to research "Muslim architecture" and look for large, color photographs or images.
3. Invite students to create artistic renderings of what they find. They can draw sketches or blueprints of side and aerial views, or make models using arts and crafts. Display students' creations in the classroom.
LS Visual/Spatial

Answers

Reading Check *As Muslim armies conquered new lands, Islam slowly spread into the conquered regions.*

Direct Teach

Info to Know . . .

Baghdad The city of Baghdad was one of the largest cities in the world in the 800s. More than 300,000 residents lived in Baghdad and enjoyed its markets, zoos, and horse races. Baghdad also had many public buildings. These buildings included hospitals, libraries, and public baths. The House of Wisdom, an institution of learning, was a gathering place for scholars whose work contributed much to civilization.

Main Idea

❸ Three Muslim Empires

Three Muslim empires controlled much of Europe, Asia, and Africa from the 1400s to the 1800s.

Identify What city became the Ottoman capital? *Constantinople, renamed Istanbul*

Describe How was Mehmed II able to conquer Constantinople? *fierce warriors, huge cannons, gunpowder*

Analyze How did the conquest of Constantinople help the Ottoman Empire expand? *Its location made expanding into Europe much easier.*

CRF: Primary Source Activity: Jewelled Canteen from Istanbul

Map Transparency: The Ottoman Empire

Connect to Geography

Constantinople (Istanbul)

Constantinople's position between eastern Europe and Asia at the point that connects the Black Sea with the Mediterranean Sea has made it useful as both a barrier and bridge. It was an important center for religion, culture, and power for centuries.

A Mix of Cultures

As Islam spread through trade and warfare, Arabs came into contact with people who had different beliefs and lifestyles than they did. Muslims generally practiced religious **tolerance**, or acceptance, with regard to people they conquered. The Muslims did not ban all other religions in their lands. Because they shared some beliefs with Muslims, Christians and Jews in particular kept many of their rights. They did, however, have to pay a special tax. Members of both faiths were also forbidden from converting anyone to their religion.

Many people conquered by the Arabs converted to Islam. These people often adopted other parts of Arabic culture, including the Arabic language. The Arabs, in turn, adopted some customs from the people they conquered. This cultural blending changed Islam from a mostly Arab religion into a religion of many cultures. But the Arabic language and shared religion helped unify the different groups of the Islamic world.

The Growth of Cities

The growing cities of the Muslim world reflected the blending of cultures. Trade had brought people together and created wealth, which supported great cultural **development** in Muslim cities.

ACADEMIC VOCABULARY
development the process of growing or improving

Baghdad, in what is now Iraq, became the capital of the Islamic Empire in 762. Trade and farming made Baghdad one of the world's richest cities. Caliphs at Baghdad supported science and the arts. The city was a center of culture and learning.

Córdoba (KAWR-doh-bah), in Spain, became another showplace of Muslim civilization. By the early 900s Córdoba was the largest and most advanced city in Europe.

READING CHECK **Finding the Main Idea** How did trade affect the spread of Islam?

Three Muslim Empires

The great era of Arab Muslim expansion lasted until the 1100s. Afterward, three non-Arab Muslim groups built large, powerful empires that ruled large areas in Asia and Africa and parts of Europe.

The Ottoman Empire

In the mid-1200s Muslim Turkish warriors known as Ottomans began to take territory from the Christian Byzantine Empire. They eventually ruled land from eastern Europe to North Africa and Arabia.

The key to the empire's expansion was the Ottoman army. The Ottomans trained Christian boys from conquered towns to be soldiers. These slave soldiers, called **Janissaries**, converted to Islam and became fierce warriors. The Ottomans also benefitted from their use of new gunpowder weapons.

In 1453 Ottomans led by **Mehmed II** used huge cannons to conquer Constantinople. With the city's capture, Mehmed defeated the Byzantine Empire. He became known as "the Conqueror." Mehmed made Constantinople, which the Ottomans called Istanbul, his new capital. He also turned the Byzantines' great church, Hagia Sophia, into a mosque.

A later sultan, or Ottoman ruler, continued Mehmed's conquests. He expanded the empire to the east through the rest of Anatolia, another name for Asia Minor. His armies also conquered Syria and Egypt. The holy cities of Mecca and Medina then accepted Ottoman rule.

The Ottoman Empire reached its height under **Suleyman I** (soo-lay-MAHN), "the Magnificent." During his rule from 1520 to 1566, the Ottomans took control of the eastern Mediterranean and pushed farther into Europe, areas they would control until the early 1800s.

Critical Thinking: Comparing and Contrasting

At Level

Explaining Trading Goods and Ideas

1. Discuss with students how ideas and cultures can be shared just as material goods can be shared.
2. Ask students to think about what "cultural blending" means. Have students list some items they use or have come into contact with that are from other cultures. Food, music, and holidays are examples most students may be familiar with. For non-native students, ask them what American customs they have adopted or come to enjoy. (Use your discretion; not all students will be comfortable with this activity.)
3. Have students share, compare, and contrast their lists. Then relate the activity to the blending of Arabic and other cultures as Islam spread.
4. Close by guiding students in a discussion of how their lives are richer as a result of the mixing of cultures. **LS Interpersonal**

Alternative Assessment Handbook, Rubric 11: Discussions

Answers

Reading Check *As Arab merchants traveled, they shared their Muslim faith with the people they met.*

The Ottoman Empire

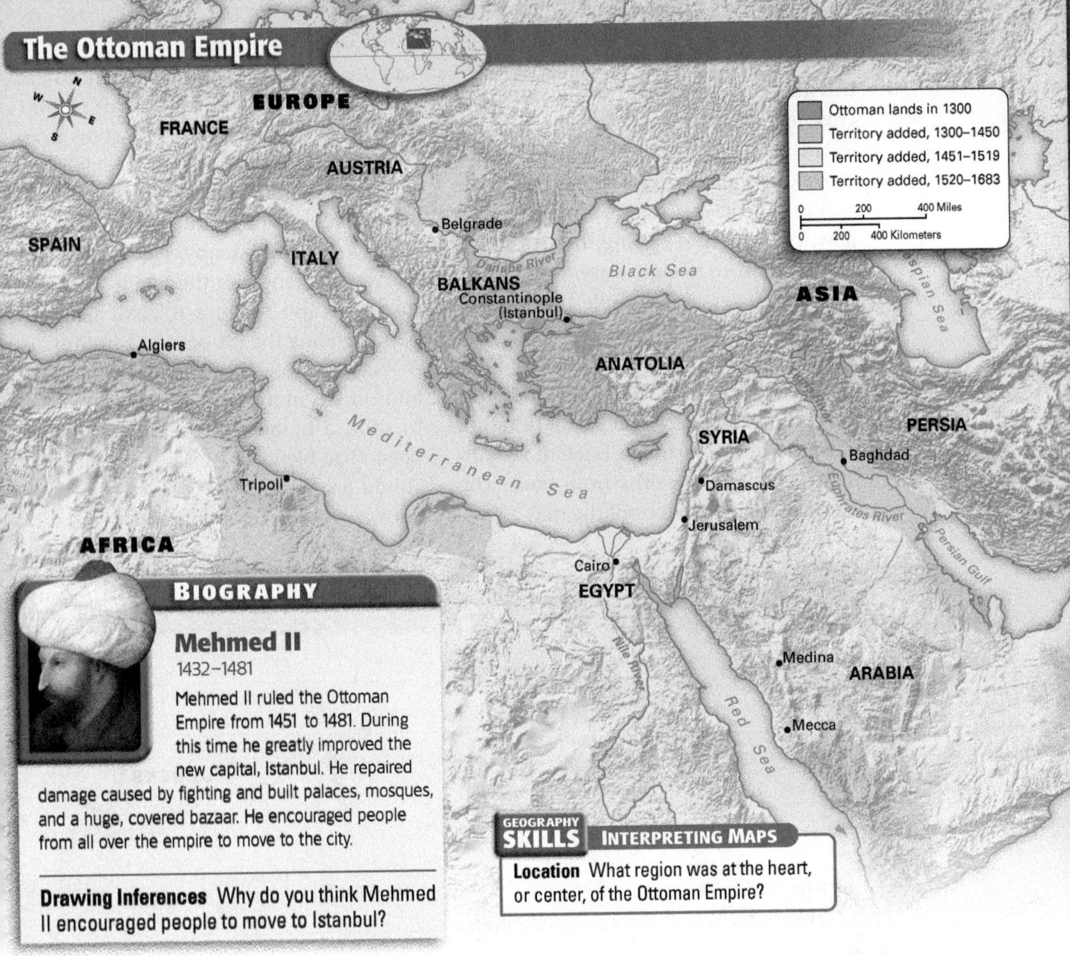

BIOGRAPHY

Mehmed II
1432–1481

Mehmed II ruled the Ottoman Empire from 1451 to 1481. During this time he greatly improved the new capital, Istanbul. He repaired damage caused by fighting and built palaces, mosques, and a huge, covered bazaar. He encouraged people from all over the empire to move to the city.

Drawing Inferences Why do you think Mehmed II encouraged people to move to Istanbul?

GEOGRAPHY SKILLS INTERPRETING MAPS

Location What region was at the heart, or center, of the Ottoman Empire?

The Safavid Empire

As the Ottoman Empire reached its height, a group of Persian Muslims known as the Safavids (sah-FAH-vuhds) was gaining power to the east, in the area of present-day Iran. Before long, the Safavids came into conflict with the Ottomans and other Muslims.

The conflict arose from an old disagreement among Muslims about who should be caliph. In the mid-600s, Islam split into two groups. The two groups were the Shia (SHEE-ah) and the Sunni (SOO-nee). The **Shia** were Muslims who thought that only Muhammad's descendants could become caliphs. The **Sunni** didn't think caliphs had to be related to Muhammad. The Ottomans were Sunnis and the Safavid leaders were Shia.

THE IMPACT TODAY
Most Muslims today belong to the Sunni branch of Islam.

The Safavid Empire began in 1501 when the Safavid leader Esma'il (is-mah-EEL) conquered Persia. He took the ancient Persian title of shah, or king.

Esma'il made Shiism—the beliefs of the Shia—the official religion of the empire. But he wanted to spread Shiism farther.

Direct Teach

Main Idea

❸ Three Muslim Empires

Three Muslim empires controlled much of Europe, Asia, and Africa from the 1400s to the 1800s.

Identify What two cultural traditions did the Safavid Empire blend? *Persian and Muslim*

Define How do the Sunnis and Shia differ? *The Shia thought that only Muhammad's descendants could be caliph. The Sunni did not think caliphs had to be related to Muhammad.*

Did you know . . .

Tell students that the two major branches of Islam—Sunni and Shia—are found throughout the world today. The Sunni form the majority of the world's Muslims. Countries with large populations of Shia include Iran, Iraq, and Yemen. Shia populations are also found in East Africa, India, Lebanon, Pakistan, and Syria.

Differentiating Instruction

Above Level

Advanced/Gifted and Talented

1. Have students study the map on this page. Point out that the Ottoman conquest of Constantinople is one of the key events in world history.
2. Organize the class into small groups. Have the members of each group discuss the conquest and predict how it might have affected the region, the people living in the city, and the Ottoman Empire.
3. If students have difficulty, suggest that they consider the importance of trade routes, and the city's central location. Students should also consider the differences between Byzantine and Ottoman rule and cultures.
4. Ask for volunteers from each group to share some of their predictions with the class.
LS Verbal/Linguistic

Answers

Drawing Inferences *to establish a Muslim population to support him in the conquered capital*

Interpreting Maps *Anatolia and Balkans*

Direct Teach

Linking to Today

Iran Much of what was the Safavid Empire is now part of the nation of Iran. Today more than 69 million people live in Iran. Some 89 percent are Shia Muslims. In addition, Shia religious leaders have run Iran's government since 1979.

Main Idea

❸ Three Muslim Empires

Three Muslim empires controlled much of Europe, Asia, and Africa from the 1400s to the 1800s.

Identify Where did the Mughals come from? *Central Asia*

Explain How did Akbar's policies help to unify the Mughal Empire? *His policy of tolerance helped unite the empire and make it peaceful.*

Finding Main Ideas How did peace and unity in the Mughal Empire lead to a rich culture? *Various groups, such as Muslims and Hindus, lived together and over time elements of Persian, Islamic, and Hindu cultures blended.*

CRF: Biography: Akbar

CRF: Biography: Mumtaz

Map Transparency: The Safavid Empire

He tried to gain more Muslim lands and convert more Muslims to Shiism. He battled the Uzbek people, but he suffered a crushing defeat by the Ottomans in 1514.

In 1588 the greatest Safavid leader, 'Abbas, became shah. He strengthened the military and gave his soldiers modern gunpowder weapons. Copying the Ottomans, 'Abbas trained foreign slave boys to be soldiers. Under 'Abbas's rule the Safavids defeated the Uzbeks and took back land that had been lost to the Ottomans.

The Safavids blended Persian and Muslim cultural traditions. They built beautiful mosques in their capital, Esfahan (es-fah-HAHN), and grew wealthy from trade. The Safavid Empire lasted until the mid-1700s.

The Mughal Empire

East of the Safavid Empire, in northern India, lay the Mughal (MOO-guhl) Empire. The Mughals were Turkish Muslims from Central Asia. Their empire was established in 1526 by Babur (BAH-boohr).

In the mid-1500s an emperor named Akbar conquered many new lands and worked to strengthen the Mughal government. He also began a tolerant religious policy, ending the tax on non-Muslims.

Akbar's tolerance allowed Muslims and Hindus in the empire to live in peace. In time, a unique Mughal culture developed that blended Persian, Islamic, and Hindu elements. The Mughals became known for their monumental works of

hmhsocialstudies.com INTERACTIVE MAP

The Safavid Empire

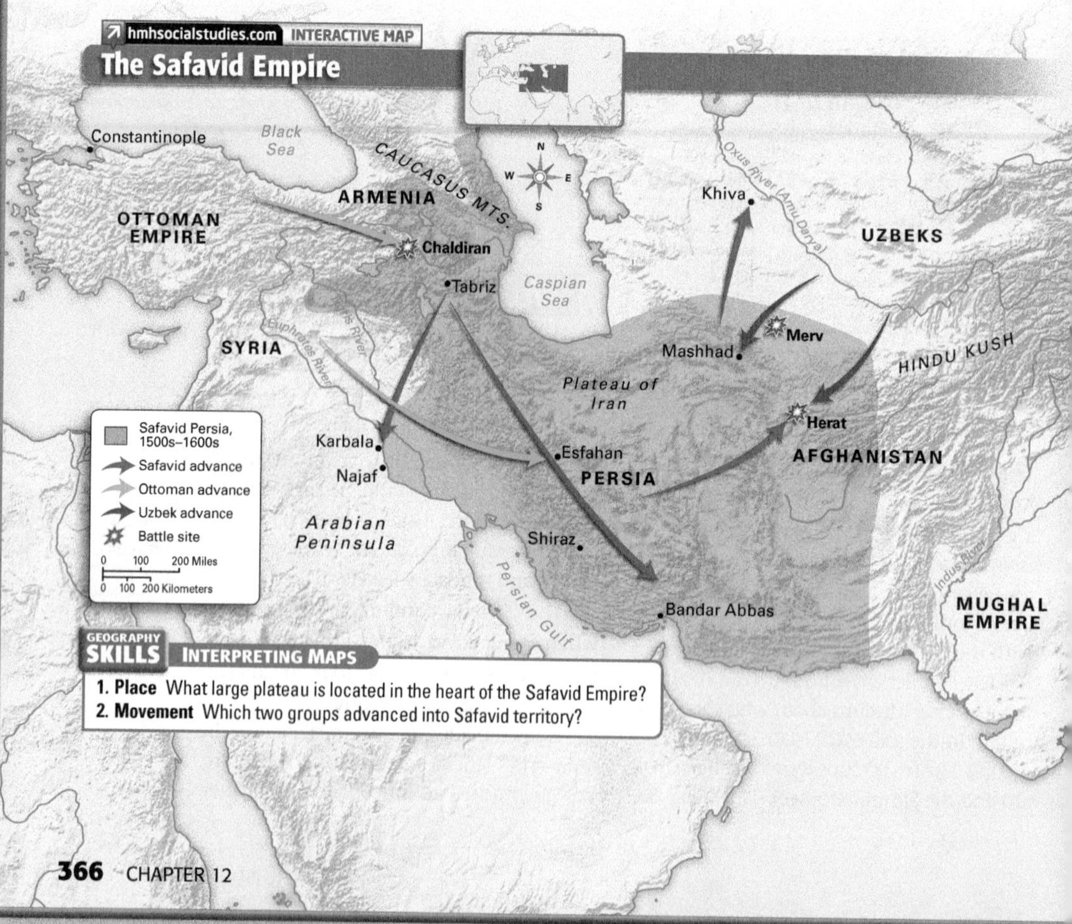

GEOGRAPHY SKILLS INTERPRETING MAPS

1. **Place** What large plateau is located in the heart of the Safavid Empire?
2. **Movement** Which two groups advanced into Safavid territory?

Differentiating Instruction

English-Language Learners **Below Level**

1. To help students understand the richness of Safavid culture, draw the graphic organizer here for students to see.
2. Have students copy the graphic organizer. As you discuss the accomplishments of Safavid culture, have students fill in the circles of the graphic organizer. *Circles should mention strengthening of military, conquest of Uzbeks, regaining of land lost to Ottomans, building of mosques, and trade.* **LS Visual/Spatial**

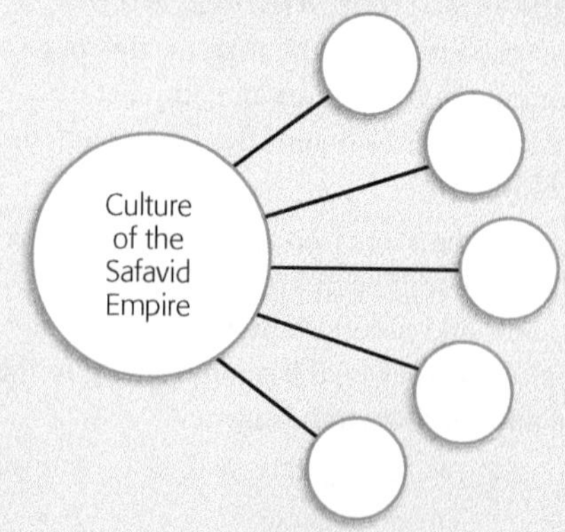

Answers

Interpreting Maps **1.** *Plateau of Iran* **2.** *Ottomans and Uzbeks*

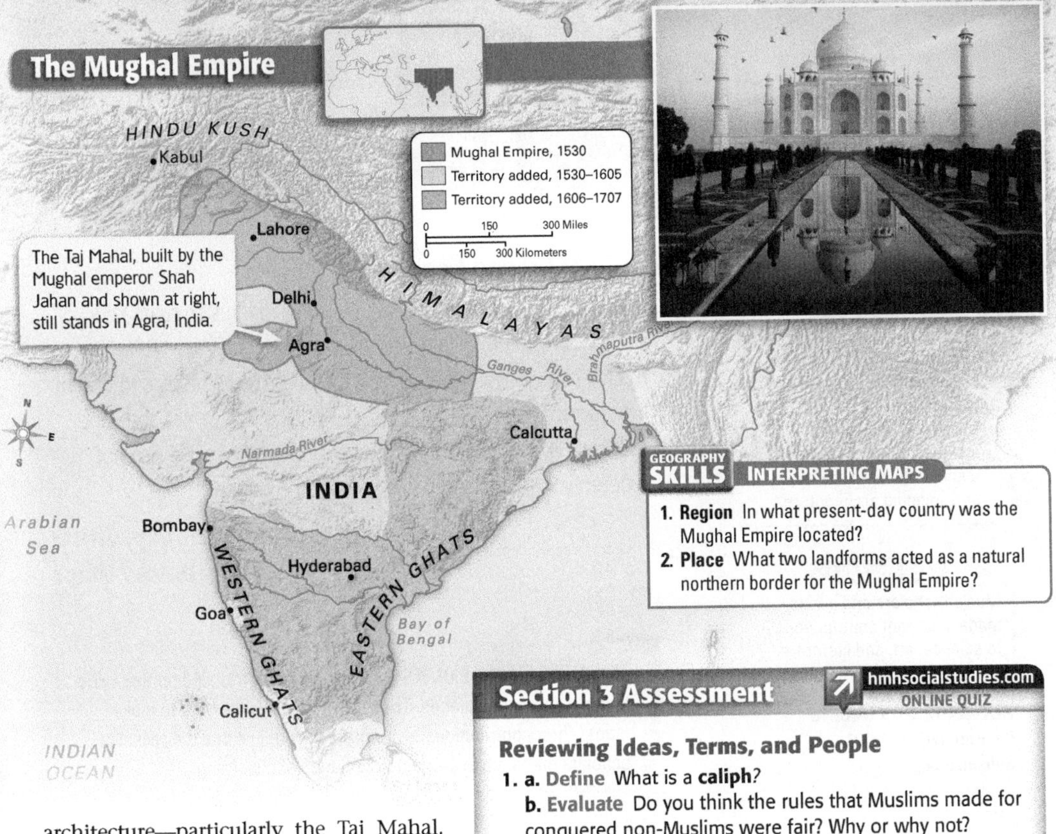

The Taj Mahal, built by the Mughal emperor Shah Jahan and shown at right, still stands in Agra, India.

GEOGRAPHY SKILLS **INTERPRETING MAPS**

1. **Region** In what present-day country was the Mughal Empire located?
2. **Place** What two landforms acted as a natural northern border for the Mughal Empire?

architecture—particularly the Taj Mahal, a tomb built in the 1600s by emperor Shah Jahan.

In the late 1600s, an emperor reversed Akbar's tolerant policies. He destroyed many Hindu temples, and violent revolts broke out. The Mughal Empire soon fell apart.

READING CHECK **Analyzing** How did the Ottomans gain land for their empire?

SUMMARY AND PREVIEW Islam spread beyond Arabia through warfare and trade. The Ottomans, Safavids, and Mughals built great empires and continued the spread of Islam. In Section 4, you will learn about the cultural achievements of the Islamic world.

Section 3 Assessment

hmhsocialstudies.com ONLINE QUIZ

Reviewing Ideas, Terms, and People

1. a. **Define** What is a **caliph**?
   b. **Evaluate** Do you think the rules that Muslims made for conquered non-Muslims were fair? Why or why not?
2. a. **Identify** Name three places Islam spread to through trade.
   b. **Explain** How did trade help spread Islam?
3. a. **Recall** Who were the **Janissaries**?
   b. **Contrast** How did Sunni and Shia beliefs about caliphs differ?

Critical Thinking

4. **Comparing and Contrasting** Draw a chart like the one below. Use your notes to compare and contrast characteristics of the Ottoman, Safavid, and Mughal empires.

	Ottomans	Safavids	Mughals
Leaders			
Location			
Religious policy			

FOCUS ON WRITING

5. **Writing about Islamic Empires** Review this section and write a paragraph about the three powerful Islamic empires that began to form in the 1200s.

Info to Know

Building the Taj Mahal Shah Jahan brought workers and materials from all over India and Central Asia to build the Taj Mahal. Construction required more than 20,000 workers and over 20 years to complete.

MISCONCEPTION ALERT

Many people think the Taj Mahal is a palace. Point out that the amazing structure was built as a tomb for Shah Jahan's wife, Mumtaz Mahal.

Other People, Other Places

Spain's American Empire During the 1500s, other empires were developing around the world. For example, during this time Spain was building an empire in North and South America. This empire brought Spain great wealth and power.

Map Transparency: The Mughal Empire

Review & Assess

Close

Briefly review the ways in which Islam spread throughout the Ottoman, Safavid, and Mughal empires. Point out that by the end of the 1600s, Islam was the dominant religion in the region.

Review

Online Quiz, Section 3

Assess

SE Section 3 Assessment
PASS: Section 3 Quiz
Alternative Assessment Handbook

Reteach/Classroom Intervention

Guided Reading Workbook, Section 3
Interactive Skills Tutor CD-ROM

Section 3 Assessment Answers

1. a. Muslim title for highest leader of Islam
   b. possible answers: fair—because they allowed conquered people to practice their religion; unfair—because conquered people didn't have the same rights
2. a. possible answers—Africa, India, Southeast Asia
   b. As they traveled, Muslim merchants shared their beliefs with other people.
3. a. Christian boys the Ottomans captured, converted to Islam, and used as slave troops
   b. Sunnis didn't think caliphs had to be related to Muhammad. The Shia thought caliphs had to be members of Muhammad's family.
4. Ottoman: leaders—Mehmed II, Suleyman I; location—Anatolia (Turkey) and eastern Europe; religious policy—tolerant; Safavid: leaders—Esma'il, 'Abbas; location—Persia; religious policy—Shia; Mughal: leaders—Babur, Akbar; location—India; religious policy—tolerant, then strict
5. Student answers will vary but should include information such as that in number 4 above.

Answers

Reading Check *The Ottomans trained Christian boys from conquered towns to be fierce soldiers and take territory from the Byzantine Empire; they used new gunpowder weapons and huge cannons.*

Interpreting Maps 1. *India;* 2. *Himalayas and Hindu Kush*

Preteach

Bellringer

If YOU were there . . . Use the **Daily Bellringer Transparency** to help students answer the question.

Daily Bellringer Transparency, Section 4

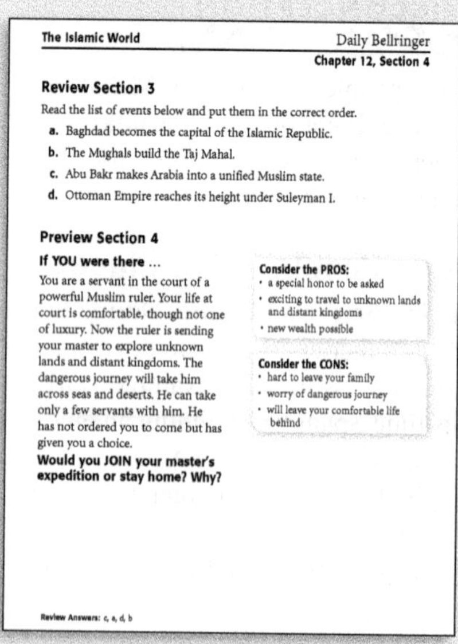

The Islamic World — Daily Bellringer — **Chapter 12, Section 4**

Review Section 3

Read the list of events below and put them in the correct order.

a. Baghdad becomes the capital of the Islamic Republic.
b. The Mughals build the Taj Mahal.
c. Abu Bakr makes Arabia into a unified Muslim state.
d. Ottoman Empire reaches its height under Suleyman I.

Preview Section 4

If YOU were there ...

You are a servant in the court of a powerful Muslim ruler. Your life at court is comfortable, though not one of luxury. Now the ruler is sending your master to explore unknown lands and distant kingdoms. The dangerous journey will take him across seas and deserts. He can take only a few servants with him. He has not ordered you to come but has given you a choice.

Would you JOIN your master's expedition or stay home? Why?

Consider the PROS:
- a special honor to be asked
- exciting to travel to unknown lands and distant kingdoms
- new wealth possible

Consider the CONS:
- hard to leave your family
- worry of dangerous journey
- will leave your comfortable life behind

Review Answers: c, a, d, b

Building Vocabulary

Preteach or review the following words:

accurate correct (p. 369)
pharmacy knowledge of making medicines; drugstore (p. 369)
rational logical (p. 369)
unique one-of-a-kind (p. 371)

CRF: Vocabulary Builder Activity, Section 4

Taking Notes

Have students use the graphic organizer online to take notes on the section. This activity will prepare students for the Section Assessment, in which they will complete a graphic organizer that builds on the information using the Critical Thinking Skill: Analyzing.

SECTION 4

Cultural Achievements

What You Will Learn...

Main Ideas

1. Muslim scholars made lasting contributions to the fields of science and philosophy.
2. In literature and the arts, Muslim achievements included beautiful poetry, memorable short stories, and splendid architecture.

The Big Idea

Muslim scholars and artists made important contributions to science, art, and literature.

Key Terms and People

Ibn Battutah, *p. 369*
Sufism, *p. 369*
Omar Khayyám, *p. 371*
patrons, *p. 371*
minaret, *p. 371*
calligraphy, *p. 371*

hmhsocialstudies.com
TAKING NOTES

Use the graphic organizer online to take notes on the achievements and advances the Muslims made in various fields.

If YOU were there...

You are a servant in the court of a powerful Muslim ruler. Your life at court is comfortable, though not one of luxury. Now the ruler is sending your master to explore unknown lands and distant kingdoms. The dangerous journey will take him across seas and deserts. He can take only a few servants with him. He has not ordered you to come but has given you a choice.

Would you join your master's expedition or stay home? Why?

BUILDING BACKGROUND Muslim explorers traveled far and wide to learn about new places. They used what they learned to make maps. Their contributions to geography were just one way Muslim scholars made advancements in science and learning.

Science and Philosophy

The empires of the Islamic world contributed to the achievements of Islamic culture. Muslim scholars made advances in astronomy, geography, math, and science. Scholars at Baghdad and Córdoba translated many ancient writings on these subjects into Arabic. Having a common language helped scholars throughout the

Islamic Achievements

Astronomy
Muslim scientists used astrolabes like this one to figure out their location, direction, and even the time of day. Although the Greeks invented the astrolabe, Muslims scholars greatly improved it.

368

Teach the Big Idea

At Level

Cultural Achievements

1. **Teach** Ask students the questions in the Main Idea boxes to teach this section.
2. **Apply** Organize the students into small groups. Assign each group a Muslim figure or achievement discussed in the section, such as Ibn Battutah or Omar Khayyám. Each group is to take notes on its assigned scholar or achievement. Have representatives share information about their group's scholar or achievement. Compile a class list. **LS Interpersonal, Verbal/Linguistic**
3. **Review** As you review the section have students discuss the class list of scholars and achievements. Ask students to evaluate the list and select the scholar and the achievement they think are most significant.
4. **Practice/Homework** Have each student create illustrations related to a scholar or achievement he or she thinks is most significant. Illustrations might include art, maps, and inventions. **LS Visual/Spatial**

Alternative Assessment Handbook, Rubrics 3: Artwork; and 14: Group Activity

Islamic world share what they learned with each other.

Astronomy

Many Muslim cities had observatories where people could study the sun, moon, and stars. This study of astronomy helped scientists to better understand time and clockmaking. Muslim scientists also improved the astrolabe, which the Greeks had invented to chart the position of the stars. Arab scholars used the astrolabe to figure out their location on Earth.

Geography

Studying astronomy also helped Muslims explore the world. As people learned to use the stars to calculate time and location, merchants and explorers began to travel widely. The explorer **Ibn Battutah** traveled to Africa, India, China, and Spain in the 1320s. To help travelers, Muslim geographers made more accurate maps than were available before, and developed better ways of calculating distances.

Math

Muslim scholars also made advances in mathematics. In the 800s they combined the Indian number system, including the use of zero, with the Greek science of mathematics. A Muslim mathematician used these ideas to write two important books. One laid the foundation for modern algebra. The other explained the new number system. When his works reached Europe, Europeans called the new numbers "Arabic" numerals.

THE IMPACT TODAY

We still call the numerals 0, 1, 2, 3, 4, 5, 6, 7, 8, and 9 Arabic or Hindu-Arabic numerals.

Medicine

Muslims may have made their greatest advances in medicine. They combined Greek and Indian knowledge with discoveries of their own. Muslim doctors started the first pharmacy school to teach people how to make medicine. A doctor in Baghdad discovered how to treat smallpox. Another doctor, known in the West as Avicenna (av-uh-SEN-uh), wrote a medical encyclopedia. It was used throughout Europe until the 1600s and is one of the most famous books in the history of medicine.

Philosophy

Many Muslim doctors and scientists studied the ancient Greek philosophy of rational thought. Others focused on spiritual issues, leading to a movement called **Sufism** (SOO-fi-zuhm). People who practice Sufism are Sufis (SOO-feez). Sufis believe they can find God's love by having a personal relationship with God. Sufism has attracted many followers to Islam.

READING CHECK **Drawing Conclusions** How did Muslims influence the fields of science and medicine?

Math
Muslim mathematicians combined Indian and Greek ideas with their own to dramatically increase human knowledge of mathematics. The fact that we call our numbers today "Arabic numerals" is a reminder of this contribution.

$2x + 4$

Medicine
Muslim doctors made medicines from plants and used them to treat pain and illnesses. Muslim doctors developed better ways to prevent, diagnose, and treat many diseases.

Critical Thinking: Finding Main Ideas

At Level

Muslim Achievements: "New and Improved" Ads

Materials: art supplies

1. Ask students to imagine that they work in public relations work for a patron of Muslim scholars and that their job is to promote the scholars' contributions to math or science.
2. Have each student create a "New and Improved" print advertisement promoting one of the Muslim advances in math or science in this section. Tell students to focus on how the advance helps people or improves their lives.
3. Encourage students to use catchy phrases and to incorporate visuals or graphics into their ads.
4. Have volunteers share their ads with the class. Have students vote on the best advertisement.

LS Verbal/Linguistic

Alternative Assessment Handbook, Rubric 2: Advertisements

Direct Teach

Main Idea

1 Science and Philosophy

Muslim scholars made lasting contributions to the fields of science and philosophy.

Recall What was one benefit of Muslim advances in astronomy? *possible answers—increased exploration; improved understanding of time and clockmaking*

Define In your own words, define Sufism. *a movement within Islam that stressed a personal relationship with God*

Evaluating What do you think was the most important advance that Muslim scholars made in math or science? Why? *Answers will vary, but students should select one of the advances mentioned and provide reasons to support their choice.*

hmhsocialstudies.com
Online Resources
Activity: Islamic Calligraphy

Connect to Science

Muslim Hospitals Among the most significant of Muslim medical advances is the idea of the hospital. Although treatment facilities existed in other cultures and in earlier times, Muslim hospitals provided a much wider range of functions. They served as treatment and recovery facilities as well as a home for the elderly, disabled, and mentally ill. Most Muslim hospitals treated both Muslims and non-Muslims, rich and poor alike.

Answers

Reading Check *possible answers—improved astrolabe and maps, laid foundation for algebra; wrote medical encyclopedia, pioneered pharmaceutical schooling, found treatment for smallpox*

Direct Teach

History-Close Up

The Blue Mosque

The Blue Mosque was built to rival Hagia Sophia, which stands nearby. The Mosque can hold some 10,000 worshippers at a time. The large dome soars 140 feet above the ground, and four pillars, each about 16 feet in diameter, support the roof.

According to one legend, the Blue Mosque's six minarets were a mistake. The story goes that the sultan had asked for minarets of gold, which is *altin* in Turkish. But the architect thought the sultan had said *alti,* which means "six." So he built six minarets, and the sultan decided he liked the results.

Did you know . . .

Most Muslim prayer rugs also have an image of a mihrab at one end. The prayer rug must be placed on the floor so that this mihrab, or arch-shaped design, points toward Mecca.

Activity **Mosques in Your Community** If your community or area has any mosques, suggest that students visit and tour one. Tell students who plan to tour a mosque to call ahead so that they do not visit during the five daily prayer times. Or, ask volunteers who attend a mosque to describe the building to the class. LS **Visual/Spatial**

History Close-up

The Blue Mosque

The Blue Mosque in Istanbul was built in the early 1600s for an Ottoman sultan. It upset many people at the time it was built because they thought its six minarets—instead of the usual four—were an attempt to make it as great as the mosque in Mecca.

Domes are a common feature of Islamic architecture. Huge columns support the center of this dome, and more than 250 windows let light into the mosque.

The mosque gets its name from its beautiful blue Iznik tiles.

The most sacred part of a mosque is the mihrab, the niche that points the way to Mecca. This man is praying facing the mihrab.

Tall towers called minarets are a common feature of many mosques.

ANALYSIS SKILL ANALYZING VISUALS

Why do you think the decoration of the Blue Mosque is so elaborate?

Cross-Discipline Activity: Arts and the Humanities

At Level

Mosque Web Site

Research Required

1. Have students study this page closely. Ask students what interests them most about the Blue Mosque. Have students share and discuss their answers.
2. Then organize students into small groups and have each group conduct research on mosques.
3. Have each group use its findings to create a design for a Web site about mosques. The Web site should include information about the architectural and religious features of mosques and identify some of the famous mosques that exist today. Tell students that their Web site design should include a home, or main, page as well as links to supporting pages on specific topics.

LS **Interpersonal, Verbal/Linguistic**

Alternative Assessment Handbook, Rubric 30: Research; and 42: Writing to Inform

Answers

Analyzing Visuals *possible answers—The patrons wanted the mosque to be impressive as a sign of their wealth and status; the elaborate decorations are a way for Muslims to glorify God and their religion.*

Literature and the Arts

Literature, especially poetry, was popular in the Muslim world. Much poetry was influenced by Sufism. Sufi poets often wrote about their loyalty to God. One of the most famous Sufi poets was **Omar Khayyám** (OH-mahr ky-AHM).

Muslims also enjoyed reading short stories. One famous collection of short stories is *The Thousand and One Nights*. It includes tales about legendary characters such as Sinbad, Aladdin, and Ali Baba.

Architecture was one of the most important Muslim art forms. Rich Muslim rulers became great **patrons**, or sponsors, of architecture. They used their wealth to have beautiful mosques built to honor God and inspire religious followers. The main part of a mosque is a huge hall where people pray. Many mosques also have a large dome and a **minaret**, or narrow tower from where Muslims are called to prayer.

Muslim architects also built palaces, marketplaces, and libraries. Many of these buildings have complicated domes and arches, colored bricks, and decorated tiles.

You may notice, though, that most Muslim art does not show any people or animals. Muslims think only God can create humans and animals or their images. As a result, Muslim art is instead full of complex patterns. Muslim artists also turned to **calligraphy**, or decorative writing. They made sayings from the Qur'an into works of art and used them to decorate mosques and other buildings.

Muslim art and literature combined Islamic influences with the regional traditions of the places Muslims conquered. This mix of Islam with cultures from Asia, Africa, and Europe gave literature and the arts a unique style and character.

READING CHECK **Generalizing** Most mosques include which two architectural elements?

SUMMARY AND PREVIEW Islamic culture produced great achievements in science, philosophy, literature, architecture, and art. In the next chapter, you'll learn about an area that was greatly influenced by Muslim ideas—West Africa.

Section 4 Assessment

hmhsocialstudies.com ONLINE QUIZ

Reviewing Ideas, Terms, and People

1. a. **Identify** Who traveled to India, Africa, China, and Spain and contributed his knowledge to the study of geography?
   b. **Explain** How did Muslim scholars help preserve learning from the ancient world?
   c. **Rank** In your opinion, what was the most important Muslim scientific achievement? Why?
2. a. **Describe** What function do **minarets** serve in mosques?
   b. **Explain** How did Muslim artists create art without showing humans or animals?

Critical Thinking

3. **Analyzing** Using your notes, complete a chart like the one at right. For each category in the first column, list one important achievement or advance the Muslims made.

Category	Achievement or Advance
Astronomy	
Geography	
Math	
Medicine	
Philosophy	

FOCUS ON WRITING

4. **Describing Muslim Accomplishments** Review the answers you provided for the graphic organizer above and the information under the Literature and the Arts heading on this page. Then organize what you have learned into a paragraph that describes the cultural achievements of the Muslim world.

Direct Teach

Main Idea

❷ Literature and the Arts

In literature and the arts, Muslim achievements included beautiful poetry, memorable short stories, and splendid architecture.

Identify What forms of literature were most often read by Muslims? *poems and short stories*

Recall What Muslim collection of short stories is still popular today, and who are some of the well-known characters in these stories? *The Thousand and One Nights; Sinbad the Sailor, Aladdin, and Ali Baba*

Make Generalizations What are some characteristic features of mosques? *huge halls for prayer, large domes, minarets*

 **CRF:** Primary Source Activity: Jahangir Presenting a Book to a Sufi

Review & Assess

Close

Ask students how their lives might be different now because of the achievements of the Islamic empires. Have students consider all the various Islamic achievements, from mathematics to literature.

Review

Online Quiz, Section 4

Assess

SE Section 4 Assessment

PASS: Section 4 Quiz

Alternative Assessment Handbook

Reteach/Classroom Intervention

Guided Reading Workbook, Section 4

Interactive Skills Tutor CD-ROM

Section 3 Assessment Answers

1. a. Ibn Battutah
   b. They translated works from the ancient world into Arabic so they could study them and share their knowledge.
   c. possible answers—better maps, algebra, medical advances
2. a. provide a place from which calls to prayer were made
   b. used patterns; turned calligraphy into an art form
3. astronomy—refined astrolabe to help figure out location; geography—mapped much of the world; math—invented algebra; medicine—discovered cures, established public hospitals and a pharmacy school, produced a medical encyclopedia; philosophy—developed Sufism
4. Students' writings should include the contributions and advances listed in the previous answer and the names of the Muslim scholars mentioned in the section.

Answers

Reading Check *minarets and domes*

Social Studies Skills

Understanding Historical Context

Activity **The Need for Context** Show the Primary Source below for students to read. Ask students to identify parts that might be interpreted incorrectly if taken out of context. (*"with great speed" and "to a thousand dinars" is information that might not mean the same if judged by today's standards.*) Explain that speed and value of money are examples of information that must be considered in the context of the time to be interpreted correctly.
LS Verbal/Linguistic

Primary Source In *The Travels,* Ibn Battutah talks about crossing the desert from Syria to Medina: "From Tabuk the caravan travels with great speed night and day, for fear of this desert. Halfway through is the valley of al-Ukhaydir. . . . One year the pilgrims suffered terribly here from the samoom-wind; the water-supplies dried up and the price of a single drink rose to a thousand dinars, but both seller and buyer perished. Their story is written on a rock in the valley."

Interactive Skills Tutor CD-ROM, Lesson 18: Identify Point of View and Frame of Reference

Social Studies Skills

Analysis | Critical Thinking | Economics | Study

Understanding Historical Context

Understand the Skill

A *context* is the circumstances under which something happens. *Historical context* includes values, beliefs, conditions, and practices that were common in the past. At times, some of these were quite different than what they are today. To truly understand a historical statement or event, you have to take its context into account. It is not right to judge what people in history did or said based on present-day values alone. To be fair, you must also consider the historical context of the statement or event.

Learn the Skill

To better understand something a historical figure said or wrote, use the following guidelines to understand the context of the statement.

1. Identify the speaker or writer, the date, and the topic and main idea of the statement.
2. Determine the speaker's or writer's attitude and point of view about the topic.
3. Review what you know about beliefs, conditions, or practices related to the topic that were common at the time. Find out more about those times if you need to.
4. Decide how the statement reflects the values, attitudes, and practices of people living at that time. Then determine how the statement reflects values, attitudes, and practices of today.

Applying these guidelines will give you a better understanding of a clash between Muslim and European armies in 1191. The following account of this clash was written by Baha' ad-Din, an advisor to the Muslim leader Saladin. He witnessed the battle.

> "The [king of the] Franks [the Muslim term for all Europeans] . . . ordered all the Musulman [Muslim] prisoners . . . to be brought before him. They numbered more than three thousand and were all bound with ropes. The Franks then flung themselves upon them all at once and massacred them with sword and lance in cold blood."
>
> –Baha' ad-Din, from *The Crusade of Richard I,* by John Gillingham

By modern standards this event seems barbaric. But such massacres were not uncommon in those times. Plus, the description is from one side's point of view. This context should be considered when making judgments about the event.

Practice and Apply the Skill

Baha' ad-Din also described the battle itself. Read the following passage. Then answer the questions.

> "The center of the Muslim ranks was broken, drums and flags fell to the ground . . . Although there were almost 7,000 . . . killed that day God gave the Muslims victory over their enemies. He [Saladin] stood firm until . . . the Muslims were exhausted, and then he agreed to a truce at the enemy's request."
>
> –Baha' ad-Din, from *Arab Historians of the Crusades,* translated by E. J. Costello

1. What happened to Saladin's army? Why do you think the writer calls the battle a Muslim victory?
2. History records this battle as a European victory. Plus, this account is part of a larger statement written in praise of Saladin. Does this additional context change your understanding and answer to the first question? Explain how or why not.

Social Studies Skills Activity: Understanding Historical Context

Historical Context Analysis Chart

1. To extend the "Practice and Apply the Skill" activity, create a chart with four rows for students to see.
2. Have students help you complete the chart by providing responses for each of the four steps listed under "Learn the Skill" for the first quotation by Baha' ad-Din.
3. Then have students discuss how Baha' ad-Din's statement might be misinterpreted if viewed by today's values and standards.
LS Verbal/Linguistic, Visual/Spatial

Alternative Assessment Handbook, Rubrics 7: Charts; and 11: Discussions

Answers

Practice and Apply the Skill **1.** *Its ranks were broken, some 7,000 soldiers were killed, and the army agreed to a truce. Students may state that the author considered the battle a Muslim victory because the Europeans, not the Muslims, asked for the truce, and the Muslims did not retreat.* **2.** *Answers will vary, but the additional context should alter students' interpretation of the passage because reasons for the claim of a Muslim victory can now be seen in light of the author's desire to praise Saladin.*

CHAPTER 12

Chapter Review

History's Impact
▶ **video series**
Review the video to answer the focus question:
What is Mecca, and why do millions of Muslims go there every year?

Visual Summary

Use the visual summary below to help you review the main ideas of the chapter.

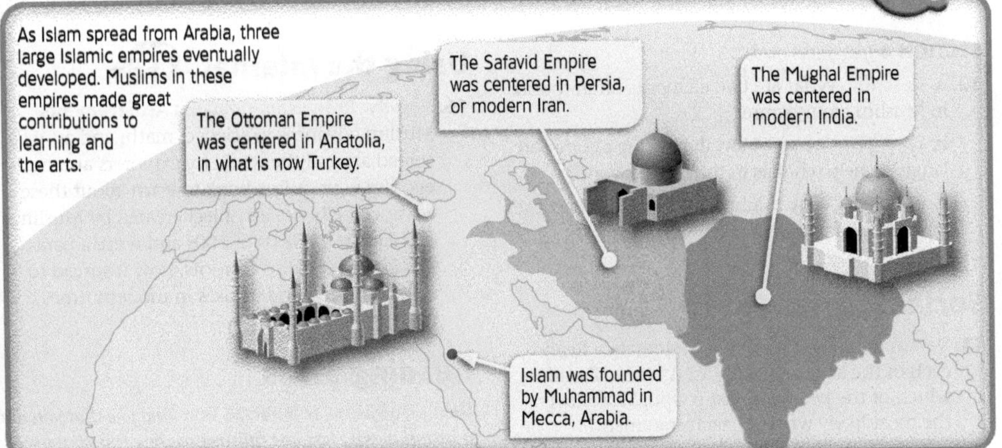

QUICK FACTS
As Islam spread from Arabia, three large Islamic empires eventually developed. Muslims in these empires made great contributions to learning and the arts.
The Ottoman Empire was centered in Anatolia, in what is now Turkey.
The Safavid Empire was centered in Persia, or modern Iran.
The Mughal Empire was centered in modern India.
Islam was founded by Muhammad in Mecca, Arabia.

Reviewing Vocabulary, Terms, and People

For each statement below, write T if it is true and F if it is false. If the statement is false, write the correct term that would make the sentence a true statement.

1. Muslims gather to pray at a **jihad**.
2. Traders often traveled in **caravans** to take their goods to markets.
3. An **Islam** is a person who submits to God and follows the teachings of Muhammad.
4. According to Islamic belief, God's messages to Muhammad during his lifetime make up the **Sunnah**.
5. A **caliph** is a journey to a sacred place.
6. A **minaret** is a tower from where Muslims are called to prayer.
7. **Janissaries** converted to Islam and became fierce warriors in the Ottoman army.
8. The **Sunni** believed that only a descendant of Muhammad could become the highest leader of Islam.

Comprehension and Critical Thinking

SECTION 1 *(pages 354–357)*

9. a. **Recall** What two ways of life developed in Arabia's desert environment?
   b. **Analyze** Why did Muhammad have a hard time getting people in Mecca to accept his teachings?
   c. **Evaluate** What are some possible benefits to a nomadic lifestyle, and what are some possible benefits to a sedentary lifestyle?

SECTION 2 *(pages 358–361)*

10. a. **Define** What is the hajj?
    b. **Contrast** Both the Qur'an and the Sunnah guide Muslims' behavior. Apart from discussing different topics, how do these two differ?
    c. **Predict** Which of the Five Pillars of Islam do you think would be the most difficult to perform? Why?

Answers

Visual Summary

Review and Inquiry Have students use the visual summary to review main events, belief systems, and achievements of the Islamic World and the time of Muhammad to the late 1660s.

Quick Facts Transparency: The Islamic World Visual Summary

Reviewing Terms, and People

1. F, mosque
2. T
3. F, A Muslim
4. F, Qur'an
5. F, pilgrimage (hajj)
6. T
7. T
8. F, Shia

Comprehension and Critical Thinking

9. a. nomadic and sedentary
   b. His teachings conflicted with the desires of people in power and called on people to make sacrifices by fasting and giving charity to the poor.
   c. possible answers: nomadic lifestyle—freedom, no "real" job; sedentary lifestyle—could grow food, more people with whom to interact
10. a. the journey Muslims must make to Mecca if they can
    b. Sunnah—record of Muhammad's actions; Qur'an—the word of God, God's messages to Muhammad
    c. possible answer—the hajj, because it involves travel and expense

Review and Assessment Resources

Review and Reinforce

- SE Chapter Review
- **CRF:** Chapter Review Activity
- Quick Facts Transparency: The Islamic World Visual Summary
- Spanish Chapter Summaries Audio CD
- Online Chapter Summaries in Six Languages
- TOS Holt McDougal PuzzleView

Assess

- SE Standardized Test Practice
- PASS: Chapter Test
- Alternative Assessment Handbook
- TOS ExamView Assessment Suite, Chapter Test
- Differentiating Instruction Modified Material CD-ROM: Chapter Test
- Online Assessment Program, in the Interactive Student Edition

Reteach/Intervene

- Guided Reading Workbook
- Differentiating Instruction Teacher Management System: Lesson Plans
- Differentiating Instruction Modified Material for Struggling Students CD-ROM
- Interactive Skills Tutor CD-ROM

hmhsocialstudies.com
Chapter Resources

Answers

11. a. Bakr was the first caliph and he won battles to make Arabia a unified Muslim state.
b. because of a conflict concerning how to decide who should become caliph.
c. Answers will vary, but students should provide a logical answer supported with information in the text.

12. a. possible answer—domes and decorative tiles
b. It allowed scholors separated by great distances to have a shared method of communication
c. possible answer—to preserve his legacy

Social Studies Skills

13.
1. b
2. f
3. d
4. c
5. a
6. e

Reviewing Themes

14. They had to travel to find enough food and water for their herds.

15. Answers will vary, but students should provide logical answers and support them with information in the text.

Using the Internet

16. Go to hmhsocialstudies.com to access a rubric for this activity.

Reading Skills

17. possible answer—What was the total area of the Ottoman Empire at its prime?
18. possible answer—What Muslim mathematician laid the foundation for algebra?
19. possible answer—How has culture in Baghdad changed from ancient to modern times?

SECTION 3 *(pages 362–367)*

11. a. Identify Who was Abu Bakr and why is he important in the history of Islam?
b. Analyze Why did the Safavids come into conflict with the Ottomans?
c. Evaluate In your opinion, was conquest or trade more effective in spreading Islam? Why?

SECTION 4 *(pages 368–371)*

12. a. Describe What are two elements often found in Muslim architecture?
b. Draw Conclusions How did having a common language help scholars in the Islamic world?
c. Elaborate Why might a ruler want to become a patron of a mosque?

Social Studies Skills 

13. Determining the Context of Statements Read each of the statements in List A below. Decide which of the people in List B would have been the most likely writer of each statement.

List A

1. "I have conquered Constantinople."
2. "I want to build a new palace, the finest ever built in India."
3. "I want to conquer more Muslim lands and convert the people within them to Shiism."
4. "I hope my medical encyclopedia helps others to use what I have learned about treating diseases."
5. "I have decided to accept the invitation to move north to Medina."
6. "Being chosen as the first caliph is a high honor for me."

List B

a. Muhammad
b. Mehmed II
c. Avicenna
d. Esma'il
e. Abu Bakr
f. a Mughal emperor

Reviewing Themes

14. Geography How did the geography of the Arabian desert influence the lives of nomads?

15. Religion Take a position, agreeing or disagreeing with this statement: "Muslim leaders were tolerant of those they conquered." Defend your answer.

Using the Internet 

16. Activity: Researching Muslim Achievements Muslim advances in science, math, and art were spread around the world by explorers and traders. Use your online book to learn about these advances. Choose an object created by Muslim scholars in the 600s or 700s and write a paragraph that explains its roots, how it spread to other cultures, and its uses in modern times.

hmhsocialstudies.com

Reading Skills

Using Questions to Analyze Text *Imagine that you are a historian who has just finished reading this chapter and you want to learn more about the Islamic world. For each of the topics listed below, write one question for which you could attempt to find an answer in your research. For example, for the topic Islamic law, you might ask, "What Muslim countries today have a legal system that blends Shariah with Western law?*

17. growth of the Ottoman Empire
18. Muslim achievements in math
19. culture and learning in Baghdad

Focus on Writing 

20. Creating Your Web Site Look back over your notes from this chapter. Then, design a home page and the four links titled "Who Was Muhammad?" "What Is Islam?" "The Islamic Empires," and "Islamic Cultural Achievements." Write four or five sentences for each link on your Web site. You may design the pages either online or on a large sheet of paper.

Remember that your audience is children, so you should keep your text simple. Use plenty of vivid language and bright colors to keep your audience interested in your topic.

Focus on Writing

20. Rubric Students' web sites should:

- contain accurate and unbiased information about Islam and the Islamic world.
- be written at an appropriate level for young readers.
- include relevant illustrations or suggestions for illustrations that contribute to the site's utility.
- be designed in a visually interesting and engaging style.

Alternative Assessment Handbook, Rubric 22: Multimedia Presentations

CHAPTER 12

Standardized Test Practice

DIRECTIONS: ***Read each question and write the letter of the best response.***

> "The office of Imam was set up in order to replace the office of Prophet in the defense of the faith and the government of the world. . . . One group says it derives from reason, since it is the nature of reasonable men to submit to a leader who will prevent them from injuring one another and who will settle quarrels and disputes. . . . Another group says that the obligation derives from Holy Law and not from reason, since the Imam deals with matters of Holy Law. . . ."
>
> —Abu al-Hasan al-Mawardi (972–1058)

1 From the passage, it can be concluded that Imams in early Islam were

A religious leaders.
B government leaders.
C both religious and government leaders.
D neither religious nor government leaders.

2 Which of the following responsibilities of Muslims is not one of the Five Pillars of Islam?

A jihad
B frequent prayer
C hajj
D giving to the poor

3 The teachings of Muhammad are found mainly in the Qur'an and the

A Commentaries.
B Sunnah.
C Analects.
D Torah.

4 Which area of the world was least influenced by Muslim conquest and trade between the AD 600s and 1600s?

A North Africa
B South America
C Southwest Asia
D Southeast Asia

5 Muslim scholars are credited with developing

A geometry.
B algebra.
C calculus.
D physics.

Connecting with Past Learnings

6 Muslims believe that Muhammad revealed Allah's teaching to the world. Which of the following leaders that you learned about earlier did not reveal a religion's teachings to his people?

A Moses
B Hammurabi
C Buddha
D Jesus

7 You have learned that Muslim architects were known for their use of the dome. Which culture that you studied earlier also used many domes?

A the Chinese
B the Egyptians
C the Greeks
D the Romans

Answers

Standardized Test Practice

1. C
Break Down the Question Point out to students that option C directly relates to the third line in the passage, which states that the office of Imam was to defend "the faith and the government."

2. A
Break Down the Question Point out to students that the word "not" means they should eliminate answers that are among the Five Pillars, listed in Section 2.

3. B
Break Down the Question This question requires students to recall factual information from Section 2.

4. B
Break Down the Question Point out to students that the word "least" indicates they should select an area that was not influenced as much as the others.

5. B
Break Down the Question Refer students who missed the question to the Math segment in Section 4.

6. B
Break Down the Question Students should remember that Hammurabi issued a famous code of laws in Mesopotamia.

7. D
Break Down the Question This question requires students to recall information from a previous chapter.

Intervention Resources

Reproducible

- Guided Reading Workbook
- Differentiating Instruction Teacher Management System: Lesson Plans

Technology

- Quick Facts Transparency: The Spread of Islam Visual Summary
- Differentiating Instruction Modified Worksheets and Tests CD-ROM
- Interactive Skills Tutor CD-ROM

Tips for Test Taking

Go for the Grammar Point out to students that questions and answers should make grammatical sense. When answering a matching question, the word and the matching definition will probably be the same part of speech. Definitions may be phrases, of course. So, for example, one would match a noun such as *sultan* with a noun phrase, such as *ruler of the Ottoman Empire*.

Chapter 13 Planning Guide

Early African Civilizations

Overview	Instructional Resources	
CHAPTER 13 **Essential Question:** What factors shaped early African civilizations? **Focus on the Essential Question Podcast**	**TOS Differentiated Instruction Teacher Management System:** • Instructional Benchmarking Guides • Lesson Plans for Differentiated Instruction **Guided Reading Workbook** **Chapter Resource File:** • Chapter Review Activity • Focus on Writing Activity: A Journal Entry • Social Studies Skills Activity: Interpreting Political Maps: Expansion of Empires	**TOS Calendar Planner** **Differentiated Instruction Modified Worksheets and Tests CD-ROM** **Student Edition on Audio CD Program** **The World's Music Audio Program**
Section 1: **Geography and Early Africa** **The Big Idea:** Geography, resources, culture, and trade influenced the growth of societies in West Africa.	**TOS Differentiated Instruction Teacher Management System:** Section 1 Lesson Plan **Guided Reading Workbook:** Section 1 **Chapter Resource File:** • Vocabulary Builder Activity, Section 1 • History and Geography Activity: The Geography of Africa	**Daily Bellringer Transparency:** Section 1 **Map Transparency:** Africa: Physical **Quick Facts Transparency:** Village Society **Internet Activity:** Congo Basin Ecosystems **Internet Activity:** African Ancestry **Animated History:** Vegetation Regions of Africa
Section 2: **The Empire of Ghana** **The Big Idea:** The rulers of Ghana built an empire by controlling the salt and gold trade.	**TOS Differentiated Instruction Teacher Management System:** Section 2 Lesson Plan **Guided Reading Workbook:** Section 2 **Chapter Resource File:** • Vocabulary Builder Activity, Section 2	**Daily Bellringer Transparency:** Section 2 **Map Transparency:** Ghana Empire, c. 1050 **Internet Activity:** Trading Groups
Section 3: **Later Empires** **The Big Idea:** Between 1000 and 1500 three great kingdoms—Mali, Songhai, and Great Zimbabwe—developed in Africa.	**TOS Differentiated Instruction Teacher Management System:** Section 3 Lesson Plan **Guided Reading Workbook:** Section 3 **Chapter Resource File:** • Vocabulary Builder Activity, Section 3 • Biography Activity: Sundiata • Primary Source Activity: Two Descriptions of Emperors of Mali	**Daily Bellringer Transparency:** Section 3 **Map Transparency:** Mali and Songhai **Quick Facts Transparency:** West African Empires **Internet Activity:** Askia Time Line **Animated History:** West African Trading Empires, 800s–1500s
Section 4: **Historical and Artistic Traditions** **The Big Idea:** Although the people of West Africa did not have a written language, their culture has been passed down through oral history, writings by other people, and the arts.	**TOS Differentiated Instruction Teacher Management System:** Section 4 Lesson Plan **Guided Reading Workbook:** Section 4 **Chapter Resource File:** • Vocabulary Builder Activity, Section 4	**Daily Bellringer Transparency:** Section 4 **Animated History:** Modern Griots

Chart Key:

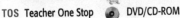

SE Student Edition  Presentation Resource  MP3 Audio
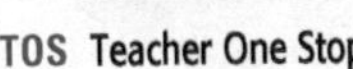
TOS Teacher One Stop 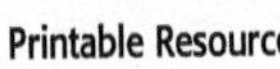 DVD/CD-ROM  HISTORY™
Printable Resource

Program Resources available on TOS and @ hmhsocialstudies.com

Review, Assessment, Intervention

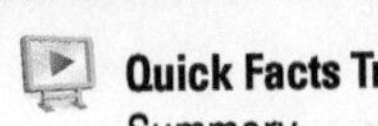

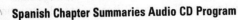

- **Quick Facts Transparency:** Early African Civilizations Visual Summary
- 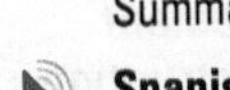 **Spanish Chapter Summaries Audio CD Program**
- 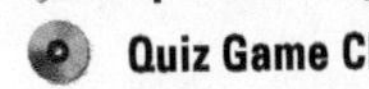 **Quiz Game CD-ROM**
- 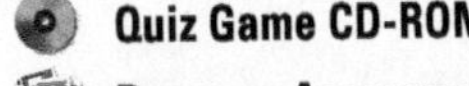 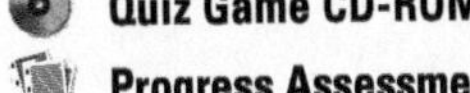 **Progress Assessment Support System (PASS):** Chapter Test
-  **Differentiated Instruction Modified Worksheets and Tests CD-ROM:** Modified Chapter Test
- TOS **ExamView® Assessment Suite (English/Spanish)**
-  **Online Assessment Program,** in the Interactive Student Edition

---

-  **PASS:** Section 1 Quiz
-  **Online Quiz:** Section 1
-  **Alternative Assessment Handbook**

-  **PASS:** Section 2 Quiz
-  **Online Quiz:** Section 2
-  **Alternative Assessment Handbook**

-  **PASS:** Section 3 Quiz
-  **Online Quiz:** Section 3
-  **Alternative Assessment Handbook**

-  **PASS:** Section 4 Quiz
-  **Online Quiz:** Section 4
-  **Alternative Assessment Handbook**

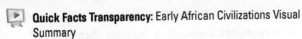

Supporting Resources

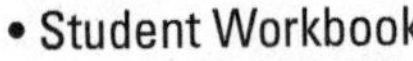
- Multimedia Classroom Global History Series
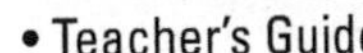
- Global History Teacher's Guide

Maps Globes Graphs Level F

- Student Workbook
- Teacher's Guide

Social Studies Trade Library Collections

- Premier Secondary World History Trade Collection

History's Impact

World History Video Program

- **Early African Civilizations and Africa Today**

For more information or to purchase go to hmhsocialstudies.com

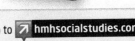

Power Presentations with Media Gallery

Power Presentations with Media Gallery are visual presentations of each chapter's main ideas. Presentations can be customized by including Quick Facts charts, images from the text, and video clips.

Differentiating Instruction

How do I address the needs of varied learners?

The Target Resource acts as your primary strategy for differentiated instruction.

ENGLISH-LANGUAGE LEARNERS & STRUGGLING READERS

Interactive Skills Tutor CD-ROM

The Interactive Skills Tutor CD-ROM contains lessons that provide additional practice for 20 different critical thinking skills.

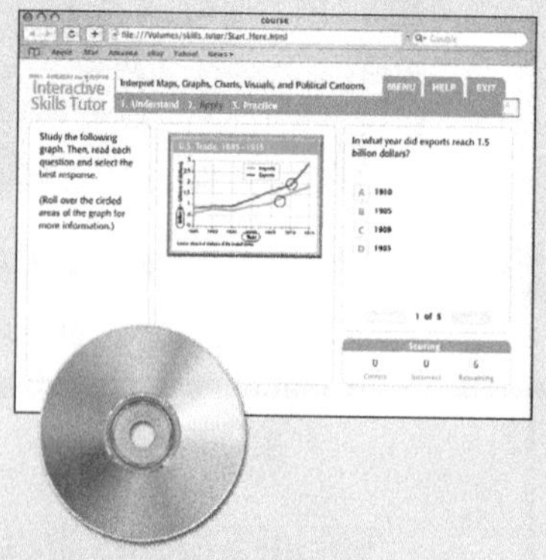

Additional Resources

Differentiated Instruction Teacher Management System: Lesson Plans for Differentiated Instruction

Chapter Resource File:

- Vocabulary Builder Activities
- Social Studies Skills Activity: Interpreting Political Maps: Expansion of Empires

Quick Facts Transparencies:

- Village Society
- West African Empires
- Early African Civilizations Visual Summary

Student Edition on Audio CD Program

Spanish/English Guided Reading Workbook

SPECIAL NEEDS LEARNERS

Differentiated Instruction Modified Worksheets and Tests CD-ROM

- Vocabulary Flash Cards
- Vocabulary Builder Activities
- Chapter Review Activity
- Chapter Test

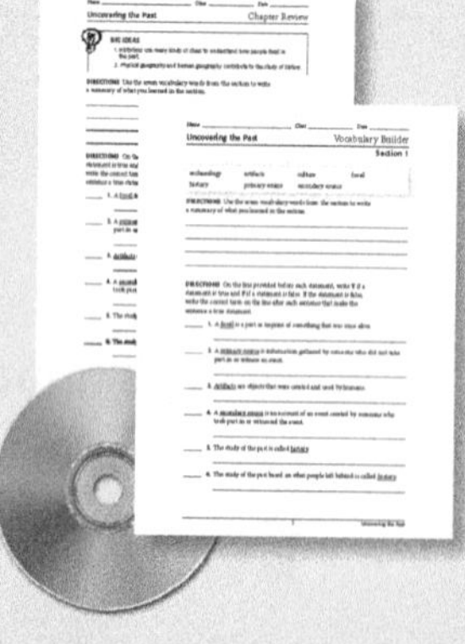

Additional Resources

Differentiated Instruction Teacher Management System: Lesson Plans for Differentiated Instruction

Guided Reading Workbook

Chapter Resource File: Social Studies Skills Activity: Interpreting Political Maps: Expansion of Empires

Student Edition on Audio CD Program

Interactive Skills Tutor CD-ROM

ADVANCED/GIFTED-AND-TALENTED STUDENTS

Primary Source Library CD-ROM for World History

The Library contains longer versions of quotations in the text, extra sources, and images. Included are point-of-view articles, journals, diaries, historical fiction, and political documents.

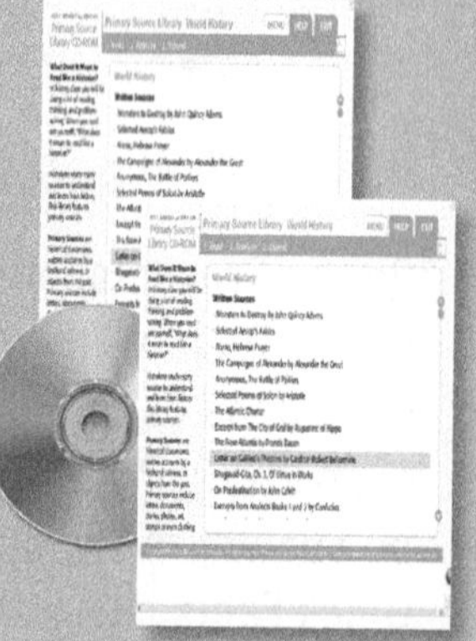

Additional Resources

Differentiated Instruction Teacher Management System: Lesson Plans for Differentiated Instruction

Chapter Resource File:

- Focus on Writing Activity: A Journal Entry

Document-Based Questions Activities

Differentiated Activities in the Teacher's Edition

- Using Graphic Organizers, p. 393
- Writing and Performing Oral Histories, p. 397

Teacher One Stop™

How can I manage the lesson plans and support materials for differentiated instruction?

With the Teacher One Stop, you can easily organize and print lesson plans, planning guides, and instructional materials for all learners. The Teacher One Stop includes the following materials to help you differentiate instruction:

- Interactive Teacher's Edition
- Calendar Planner and pacing guides
- Editable lesson plans
- All reproducible ancillaries in Adobe Acrobat (PDF) format
- ExamView Assessment Suite (English & Spanish)
- Transparency and video previews

Differentiated Activities in the Teacher's Edition

- Loading a Caravan, p. 385
- Ghana's Illustrated Time Line, p. 388

Interactive Student Edition

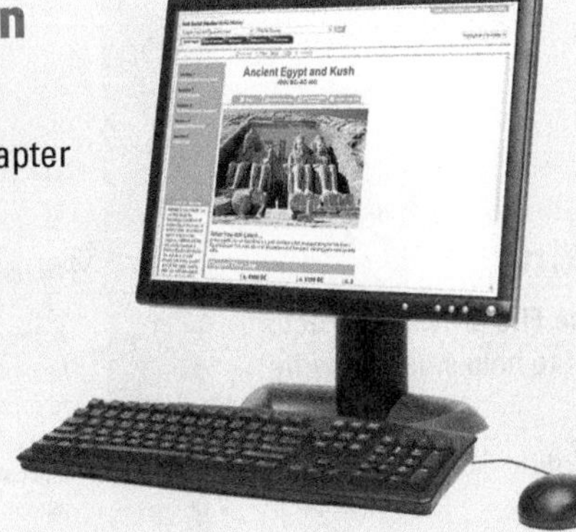

Complete online student edition with interactive multimedia support for chapter content assessment and reporting

- Interactive Maps and Notebook
- Graphic Organizers
- Standardized Test Prep
- Online Homework Practice and Research Activities
- Current Events
- Chapter-based Internet Activities
- Animated History Activities
- and more!

Differentiated Activities in the Teacher's Edition

- Writing and Performing a West African Conversation, p. 382
- Long-Distance Trade Then and Now, p. 384

• Chapter Preview •

Essential Question

Introduce the Essential Question

- Discuss the role of Africa's physical geography in shaping the development of its early civilizations.
- Summarize how the location of the empires of Ghana, Mali, and Songhai affected their growth.
- Explore how trade influenced the civilizations of central and eastern Africa, such as Great Zimbabwe.

CHAPTER 13 500 BC–AD 1600

Early African Civilizations

Essential Question What factors shaped early African civilizations?

South Carolina Performance Standards

6-4.1 Compare the major contributions of the African civilizations of Ghana, Mali, and Songhai, including the impact of Islam on the cultures of these kingdoms; **6-4.2** Describe the influence of geography on trade in the African kingdoms, including the salt and gold trades.

Literacy Skills for Social Studies

- Interpret Earth's physical and human systems by using maps, mental maps, geographic models, and other social studies resources.
- Compare the locations of places, the conditions at places, and the connections between places.
- Explain how the endowment and development of productive resources affects economic decisions and global interactions.
- Explain why trade occurs and how historical patterns of trade have contributed to global interdependence.

Focus on Writing

A Journal Entry Many people feel that recording their lives in journals helps them to understand their own experiences. Writing a journal entry from someone else's point of view can help you to understand what that person's life is like. In this chapter, you will read about the land, people, and culture of early Africa. Then you will imagine a character and write a journal entry from his or her point of view.

Chapter Events

c. 500 BC West Africans begin using iron and making clay sculptures.

500 BC

World Events

c. 480 BC Greece defeats Persia in the Persian Wars.

376 CHAPTER 13

Focus on Writing

The **Chapter Resource File** provides a Focus on Writing worksheet to help students write their journal entries.

- **CRF:** Focus on Writing Activity: Writing a Journal Entry

Key to Differentiating Instruction

Below Level

Basic-level activities designed for all students encountering new material

At Level

Intermediate-level activities designed for average students

Above Level

Challenging activities designed for honors and gifted and talented students

Standard English Mastery

Activities designed to improve standard English usage

LS Learning Styles

Introduce the Chapter

At Level

Early African Civilizations

1. Ask students what life might have been like in West Africa more than 1,000 years ago. Remind them that the region is hot and dry most of the year. Then ask why gold and salt would become important trade items in a hot, dry climate. *possible answer—Salt and gold aren't affected by weather; people need to replace salt in their bodies.*
2. Explain to students that they are going to learn about the early West African empires. Discuss with students that they will learn about three different empires and the various economic and geographic factors that affected them all.
3. Have students take notes on all three empires using maps and timelines in this chapter. **LS Visual/Spatial**

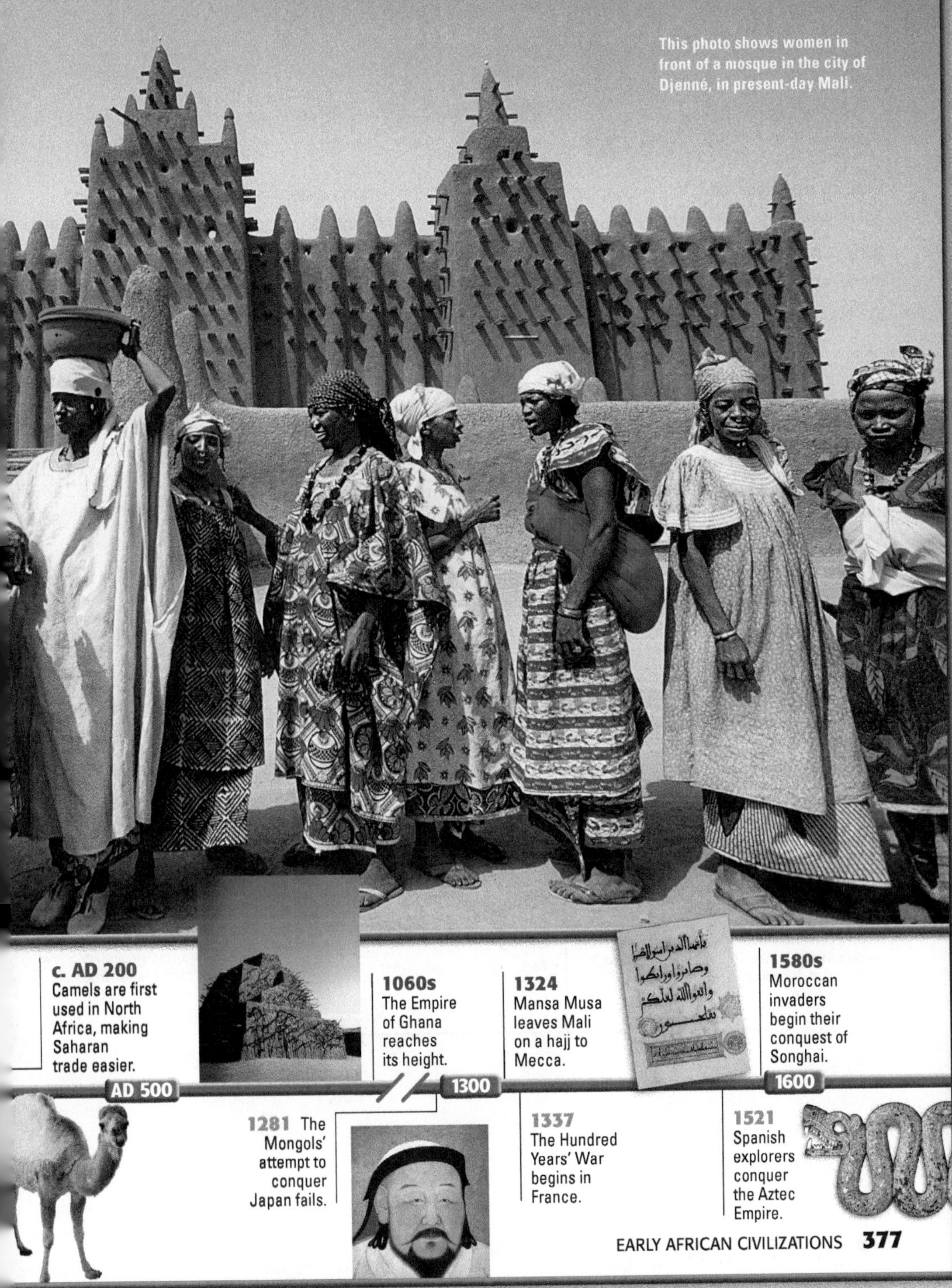
c. AD 200
Camels are first used in North Africa, making Saharan trade easier.
AD 500
1281 The Mongols' attempt to conquer Japan fails.
1060s
The Empire of Ghana reaches its height.
1300
1324
Mansa Musa leaves Mali on a hajj to Mecca.
1337
The Hundred Years' War begins in France.
1580s
Moroccan invaders begin their conquest of Songhai.
1600
1521
Spanish explorers conquer the Aztec Empire.
EARLY AFRICAN CIVILIZATIONS 377

This photo shows women in front of a mosque in the city of Djenné, in present-day Mali.

• Chapter Preview •

Explore the Picture

Djenné Mosque The building in the background of this photo is the famous Djenné Mosque. Built in 1906, the mosque is typical of mud-building styles of West Africa. In fact, it is the largest mud structure in the world. The building was constructed of mud bricks held together with mud-based mortar. Annual rains have been known to deteriorate portions of the mud structure, making frequent repair work necessary.

Analyzing Visuals Most towns in Mali have market day once a week, and it is a gathering place for the entire region. Usually the market is held near the mosque. Why do you think the market was located so close to the mosque? *possible answers—The mosque was a center of the community, much like the market; they are the oldest locations in the city, and therefore close together.*

hmhsocialstudies.com
Teacher Resources

Explore the Time Line

1. Which cultures were fighting wars while the Nok were making clay sculptures? *Greeks and Persians*
2. What animals helped make trade across the Sahara easier, and when were they first used? *camels; c. AD 200*
3. In what year did Mansa Musa make his famous hajj? *1324*
4. When did Morocco begin its conquest of Songhai? *in the 1580s*
5. What event began in Europe shortly after Mansa Musa's pilgrimage to Mecca? *the Hundred Years' War*

Info to Know

French West Africa If you were traveling through West Africa today, you might be surprised to hear the French language. Around 1900, the French colonized the region and created French West Africa. French became the official language and was used for all official purposes until around 1960 when most West African nations achieved independence. Today, French is still very common. However, dozens of other languages are still spoken throughout the large region. One of the languages is even called Songhai, the name of one of the empires you will learn about in this chapter.

Social Studies Skills

Understanding Themes

Introduce students to two key themes in this chapter—geography and technology. Tell students that the geography of West Africa affected the technology used there. Ask students to share what they know about the geography of West Africa. Then ask students to make inferences about how the geography might affect the technology that the people developed. Possible responses might include that the many rivers in West Africa provided a means of transportation, allowing those civilizations to share technology and ideas with other people. Write students' suggestions for the class to see.

Organization of Facts and Information

Focus on Reading Assign students to work in pairs. Provide each pair of students with a newspaper article from the news, business, or feature section. Ask each pair to read through the article and find one or more examples of each of the three patterns of organization. Have students use a three-column chart like the one on this page to analyze the article. Have them identify pattern and clue words and to use the graphic organizers in column three to map relationships among the facts and details. When students have finished, have one student from each pair read a portion of the article aloud and report on the pattern of organization. Ask other students if they agree or disagree with the analysis.

Reading Social Studies

Economics | **Geography** | Politics | Religion | Society and Culture | Science and Technology

Focus on Themes In this chapter, you will read about West Africa—its physical **geography** and early cultures. You will see West Africa is a land of many resources and varied features. One feature, the Niger River, has been particularly important in the region's history, providing water, food, and transportation for people. In addition, salt and iron deposits can be found in the region. Such resources were the basis for a **technology** that allowed people to create strong tools and weapons.

Organization of Facts and Information

Focus on Reading How are books organized in the library? How are the groceries organized in the store? Clear organization helps us find the product we need, and it also helps us find facts and information.

Understanding Structural Patterns Writers use structural patterns to organize information in sentences or paragraphs. What's a structural pattern? It's simply a way of organizing information. Learning to recognize those patterns will make it easier for you to read and understand social studies texts.

Patterns of Organization

Pattern	Clue Words	Graphic Organizer
Cause-effect shows how one thing leads to another	as a result, because, therefore, this led to	Cause → Effect; Cause → Effect; Cause → Effect
Chronological Order shows the sequence of events or actions.	after, before, first, then, not long after, finally	First → Next → Next → Last
Listing presents information in categories such as size, location, or importance.	also, most important, for example, in fact	Category • Fact • Fact • Fact • Fact

To use text structure to improve your understanding, follow these steps:

1. Look for the main idea of the passage you are reading.
2. Then look for clues that signal a specific pattern.
3. Look for other important ideas and think about how the ideas connect. Is there any obvious pattern?
4. Use a graphic organizer to map the relationships among the facts and details.

Reading and Skills Resources

Reading Support

- Guided Reading Workbook
- Student Edition on Audio CD
- Spanish Chapter Summaries Audio CD Program

Social Studies Skills Support

- Interactive Skills Tutor CD-ROM

Vocabulary Support

- **CRF:** Vocabulary Builder Activities
- **CRF:** Chapter Review Activity
- Differentiated Instruction Modified Worksheets and Tests CD-ROM:
  - Vocabulary Flash Cards
  - Vocabulary Builder Activity
  - Chapter Review Activity
- TOS Holt McDougal PuzzleView

You Try It!

The following passages are from the chapter you are about to read. As you read each set of sentences, ask yourself what structural pattern the writer used to organize the information.

Recognizing Structural Patterns

A. "As the people of West Africa became more productive, villages had more than they needed to survive. West Africans began to trade the area's resources with buyers who lived thousands of miles away." (p. 383)

B. "When Sundiata was a boy, a harsh ruler conquered Mali. But as an adult, Sundiata built up an army and won back his country's independence. He then conquered nearby kingdoms, including Ghana, in the 1230s . . . After Sundiata conquered Ghana, he took over the salt and gold trades. He also worked to improve agriculture in Mali." (p. 390)

C. "Four different regions make up the area surrounding the Niger River . . . The northern band is the southern part of the Sahara . . . The next band is the Sahel (sah-HEL), a strip of land with little rainfall that divides the desert from wetter areas . . . Farther south is savannah, or open grassland . . . The fourth band, near the equator, gets heavy rain." (p. 382)

After you read the passages, answer the questions below:

1. What structural pattern did the writer use to organize the information in passage A? How can you tell?
2. What structural pattern did the writer use to organize the information in passage B? How can you tell?
3. What structural pattern did the writer use to organize the information in passage C? How can you tell?

Key Terms and People

Chapter 13

Section 1
rifts *(p. 380)*
sub-Saharan Africa *(p. 380)*
Sahel *(p. 382)*
savannah *(p. 382)*
rain forests *(p. 382)*
extended family *(p. 382)*
animism *(p. 383)*

Section 2
silent barter *(p. 386)*
Tunka Manin *(p. 388)*

Section 3
Sundiata *(p. 390)*
Mansa Musa *(p. 391)*
Sunni Ali *(p. 392)*
Askia the Great *(p. 393)*

Section 4
oral history *(p. 396)*
griots *(p. 396)*
proverbs *(p. 397)*
kente *(p. 399)*

Academic Vocabulary

Success in school is related to knowing academic vocabulary—the words that are frequently used in school assignments and discussions. In this chapter, you will learn the following academic word:

process *(p. 397)*

As you read Chapter 13, think about the organization of the ideas. Look for signal words and ask yourself why the author has arranged the text in this way.

Social Studies Skills

Key Terms and People

Preview the key terms and names of people with students and have them find each term or name within the chapter. Organize the class into pairs. Assign each pair one key term or person. Have them note the structural pattern of the paragraph or paragraphs where they find the term or name. Is it cause-effect, chronological order, listing, or another pattern? After 5 minutes, have each pair report on their term or name by having them tell about it and the structural pattern of the surrounding text.

LS Interpersonal, Verbal/Linguistic

Focus on Reading

See the **Focus on Reading** questions in this chapter for more practice on reading social studies skills.

Reading Social Studies Assessment

See the **Chapter Review** at the end of this chapter for student assessment questions related to this reading skill.

Teaching Tip

Remind students to look for organization of ideas whenever they read nonfiction material. Suggest that they use the chart on p. 378 as a study aid to help them identify patterns of organization for this and other chapters in this book. Tell students that finding the structural organization will help them become more active readers, better note-takers, and better able to remember the facts and information they are studying.

Answers

You Try It! 1. *cause-effect; Productivity caused the villages to have more than they needed. The effect of a surplus was the development of trade with buyers who lived far away.* **2.** *chronological order; The ideas are told in time order of what happened first, Sundiata as a boy, through what happened last, Sundiata took over salt and gold trades and improved agriculture.* **3.** *listing; the information is a list of the four regions that surround the Niger River.*

Preteach

Bellringer

If YOU were there . . . Use the **Daily Bellringer Transparency** to help students answer the question.

Daily Bellringer Transparency, Section 1

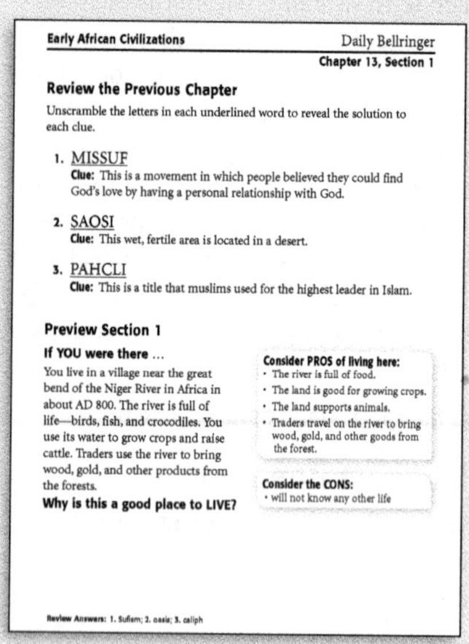

Early African Civilizations | Daily Bellringer
Chapter 13, Section 1

Review the Previous Chapter

Unscramble the letters in each underlined word to reveal the solution to each clue.

1. MISSUF
   Clue: This is a movement in which people believed they could find God's love by having a personal relationship with God.
2. SAOSI
   Clue: This wet, fertile area is located in a desert.
3. PAHCLI
   Clue: This is a title that muslims used for the highest leader in Islam.

Preview Section 1

If YOU were there ...

You live in a village near the great bend of the Niger River in Africa in about AD 800. The river is full of life—birds, fish, and crocodiles. You use its water to grow crops and raise cattle. Traders use the river to bring wood, gold, and other products from the forests.

Why is this a good place to LIVE?

Consider PROS of living here:
- The river is full of food.
- The land is good for growing crops.
- The land supports animals.
- Traders travel on the river to bring wood, gold, and other goods from the forest.

Consider the CONS:
- will not know any other life

Review Answers: 1. Sufism; 2. oasis; 3. caliph

Building Vocabulary

Preteach or review the following terms:

bonds ties, close connections (p. 382)

elders respected older people (p. 382)

plentiful present in large numbers (p. 380)

terrain physical features of the land (p. 380)

CRF: Vocabulary Builder Activity, Section 1

Taking Notes

Have students use the graphic organizer online to take notes on the section. This activity will prepare students for the Section Assessment, in which they will complete a graphic organizer that builds on the information using the Critical Thinking Skill: Drawing Conclusions.

SECTION 1

Geography and Early Africa

What You Will Learn...

Main Ideas

1. Landforms, climate, and resources affected the history of West Africa.
2. The way of life of early peoples in West Africa was shaped by family ties, religion, iron technology, and trade.

The Big Idea

Geography, resources, culture, and trade influenced the growth of societies in West Africa.

Key Terms and People

rifts, *p. 380*
sub-Saharan Africa, *p. 380*
Sahel, *p. 382*
savannah, *p. 382*
rain forests, *p. 382*
extended family, *p. 382*
animism, *p. 383*

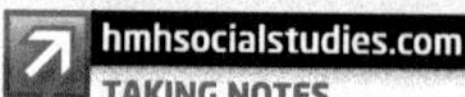

Use the graphic organizer online to record information about the geography and traditional ways of life in Africa.

If YOU were there...

You live in a village near the great bend of the Niger River in Africa in about AD 800. The river is full of life—birds, fish, crocodiles. You use its water to grow crops and raise cattle. Traders use the river to bring wood, gold, and other products from the forests.

Why is this a good place to live?

BUILDING BACKGROUND The continent of Africa is so large that it includes many varied kinds of terrain, from barren deserts to thick rain forests. Each region has a different climate and provides different resources for the people who live there. In West Africa rivers provide water to grow crops in drier areas. The land is also a rich source of minerals, especially gold and iron. These two resources played a large role in the development of West African cultures.

Landforms, Climate, and Resources

Africa is the earth's second largest continent. An immense desert, the Sahara, stretches across most of North Africa. Along the northwestern edge of the Sahara lie the Atlas Mountains. At the opposite edge of the continent, in the southeast, the Drakensberg Mountains rise. In eastern Africa, mountains extend alongside great rifts. These **rifts** are long, deep valleys formed by the movement of the earth's crust. From all these mountains the land dips into plateaus and wide, low plains. The plains of **sub-Saharan Africa**, or Africa south of the Sahara, are crossed by mighty rivers. These rivers include the Congo, the Zambezi, and the Niger.

Regions of West Africa

As a source of water, food, and transportation, the Niger River allowed many people to live in West Africa. Along the Niger's middle section is a low-lying area of lakes and marshes. Many animals find food and shelter there. Fish are also plentiful.

380

Teach the Big Idea

At Level

Geography and Early Africa

1. **Teach** Ask students the questions in the Main Idea boxes to teach this section.
2. **Apply** Refer students to the map of Africa on p. 381. Have students use their own paper to draw basic maps of Africa and add major physical features, including the Niger River. Students should also draw symbols and illustrations on their maps to depict such features as resources, climate regions, and vegetation. **LS Visual/Spatial**
3. **Review** As you review the section's main ideas, have students discuss how West Africa's geography has affected the people who lived there.
4. **Practice/Homework** Have students further illustrate their maps. Instruct students to include a key that explains the various symbols they have used. **LS Visual/Spatial**

Alternative Assessment Handbook, Rubric 20: Map Creation

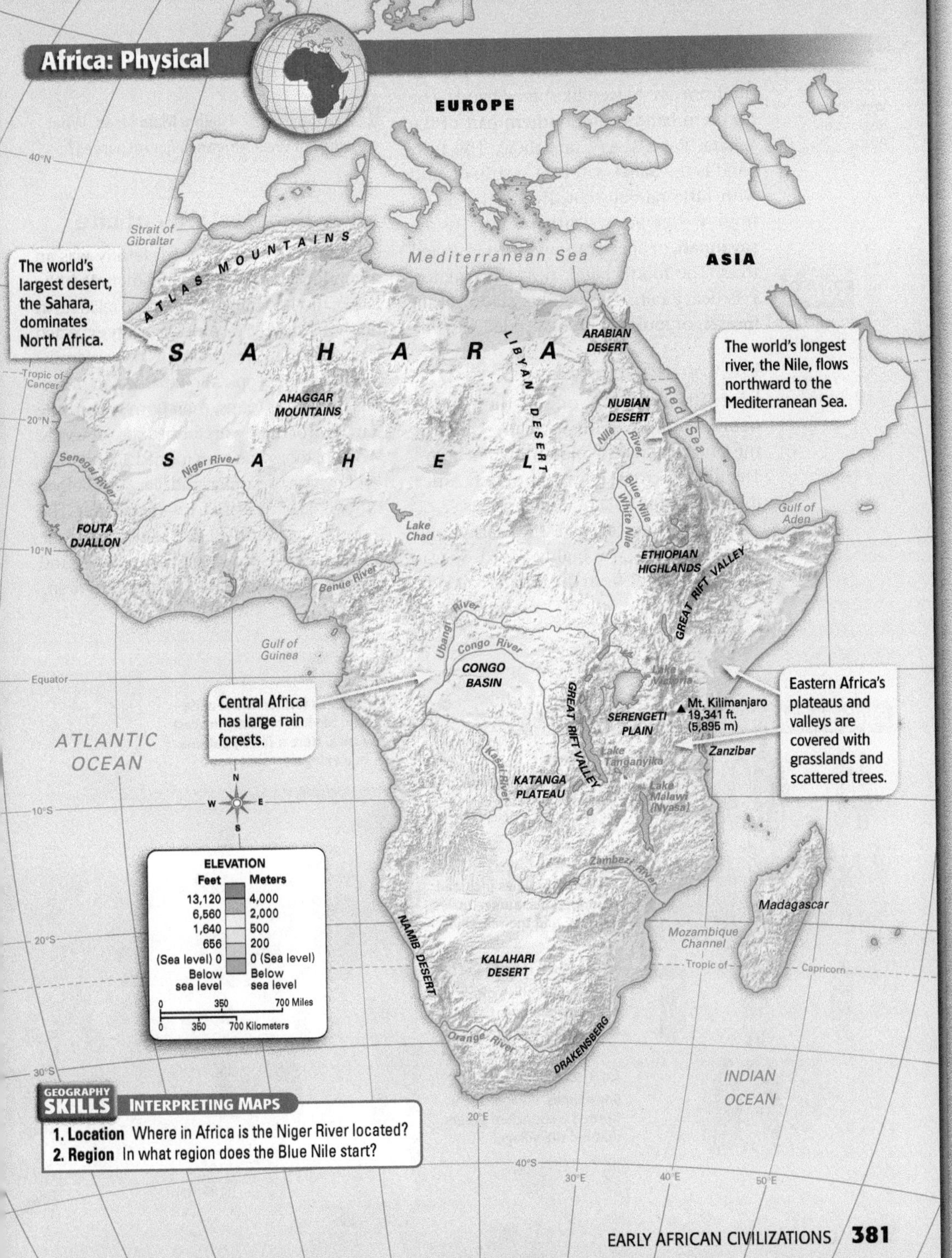

GEOGRAPHY SKILLS INTERPRETING MAPS

1. **Location** Where in Africa is the Niger River located?
2. **Region** In what region does the Blue Nile start?

Direct Teach

Main Idea

1 Landforms, Climate, and Resources

Landforms, climate, and resources affected the history of West Africa.

Define What does *sub-Saharan Africa* mean? *Africa south of the Sahara*

Summarize What did the Niger River provide people living in the region? *water, food, and transportation*

Predict What impact might the vast Sahara have on the people of this continent? *possible answer—The Sahara might act as a trade and travel barrier between the sub-Saharan people and people in the north.*

CRF: History and Geography Activity: The Geography of Africa

Map Transparency: Africa: Physical

Interpreting Maps

Africa: Physical

Have students name the main rivers, mountain ranges, and deserts of Africa. Lead a discussion about the regions in which people may live mainly by farming and the ones in which they would need to follow other occupations. Then ask where in Africa transportation may be relatively easy and why.

hmhsocialstudies.com

Online Resources
Activity: Congo Basin Ecosystem

Cross-Discipline Activity: Geography

At Level

The Niger River

1. Have students review the "Africa: Physical" map. Discuss how geographical features affect the course of the Niger River in western Africa. For example, the river starts in the mountainous area called Fouta Djallon and flows toward a lowland area.
2. Instruct students to use the atlas in the back of this book to list the present-day countries through which the Niger River passes.
3. Have students write a brief description, either in essay or journal form, of what a trip from the headwaters of the Niger River to its outlet into the Gulf of Guinea in the Atlantic Ocean would be like. Challenge students to draw logical conclusions about the climates and vegetation through which they would travel.
4. Ask for volunteers to share their descriptions.

LS Verbal/Linguistic, Visual/Spatial

Alternative Assessment Handbook, Rubrics 21: Map Reading; and 40: Writing to Describe

Answers

Interpreting Maps **1.** *West Africa;* **2.** *Ethiopian Highlands*

Direct Teach

Main Idea

❶ Landforms, Climate, and Resources

Landforms, climate, and resources affected the history of West Africa.

Draw Conclusions Why might more people live in the savannah than in the Sahel? *Because the savannah has more vegetation, it can support more people than the drier Sahel.*

Predict How might the different climates in West Africa affect settlement patterns and the growth of towns? *possible answer—People would be more likely to settle and cities would be more likely to develop in the more hospitable regions, such as the savannah.*

Recall What crops were harvested in West Africa? *dates, kola nuts, grains*

Explain Why was salt important to West Africans? *It kept food from spoiling and was essential to their diets.*

Quick Facts Transparency: Village Society

Connect to Science

Elephants of West Africa Dry regions of West Africa are home to some unexpected wildlife. For example, a type of elephant lives in the Sahel. These animals move from one water hole to the next, traveling an average of 6 miles a day. When some water holes dry up, the elephants may have to walk almost 50 miles in a day to reach water. The elephants' remarkable sense of hearing helps them survive in the harsh climate. They may be able to hear rainfall from miles away.

hmhsocialstudies.com
ANIMATED HISTORY
Vegetation Regions of Africa

Four different regions make up the area surrounding the Niger River. The regions run from east to west like broad bands. The northern band is the southern part of the Sahara. Rain is very rare there. The next band is the **Sahel** (sah-HEL), a strip of land with little rainfall that divides the desert from wetter areas. Farther south is the **savannah**, or open grassland with scattered trees. The fourth band, near the equator, gets heavy rain. This band is made of **rain forests**, or moist, densely wooded areas.

THE IMPACT TODAY
Human activities like logging and farming are rapidly destroying Africa's rain forests.

West Africa's Resources

West Africa's land is one of the region's many resources. With its many climates, the land can produce many different crops. Traditional crops grown in West Africa included dates, kola nuts, and grains.

Other resources were minerals. Gold, from the forests, was highly prized. So was salt, which came from the Sahara. Salt kept food from spoiling, and people needed it in their diet to survive Africa's hot climate.

READING CHECK **Finding Main Ideas** What are some of West Africa's major resources?

Early Peoples' Way of Life

A typical early West African family was an **extended family**. It usually included the father, mother, children, and close relatives in one household. West African society expected each person to be loyal to his or her family. In some areas people also became part of age-sets. In these groups, men born within the same two or three years formed special bonds. Women, too, sometimes formed age-sets.

Loyalty to family and age-sets helped the people of a village to work together. The men hunted, farmed, and raised livestock. Women farmed, collected firewood, ground grain, carried water, and cared for children.

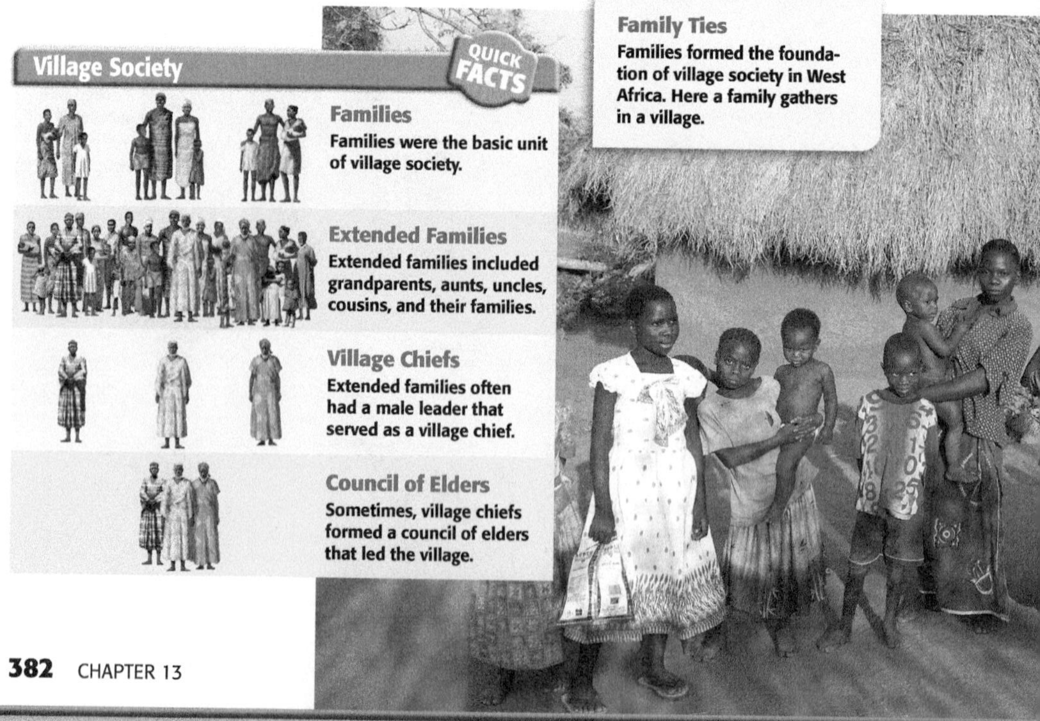

Village Society
QUICK FACTS
Families
Families were the basic unit of village society.
Extended Families
Extended families included grandparents, aunts, uncles, cousins, and their families.
Village Chiefs
Extended families often had a male leader that served as a village chief.
Council of Elders
Sometimes, village chiefs formed a council of elders that led the village.

Family Ties
Families formed the foundation of village society in West Africa. Here a family gathers in a village.

Differentiating Instruction

Advanced/Gifted and Talented **Above Level**

1. Organize the class into groups of about five. Ask students to imagine that each group is an early West African family similar to the one shown in the photo on this page.
2. Have each group write a conversation that the family might have over dinner or at another gathering. Encourage students to include as many of the subsections topics as possible. For example, family members may discuss the foods being served, experiences with livestock, or participation in age-sets.
3. Have groups perform their conversations for the class. Students should use gestures and lively voices, just as they would in a true family conversation. Make certain that each member of each group participates.

LS Interpersonal, Verbal/Linguistic

Answer

Reading Check *land; minerals, such as gold and salt*

Religion was another central feature of village life. Many West Africans believed that their ancestors' spirits stayed nearby. To honor these spirits, families marked places as sacred by putting specially carved statues there. They also offered food to their ancestors. Another common West African belief was **animism**—the belief that bodies of water, animals, trees, and other natural objects have spirits.

As time passed, the people of West Africa developed advanced cultures. Changes in technology helped early communities grow. Around 500 BC West Africans found that they could heat certain kinds of rock to get a hard metal. This was iron. Stronger than other metals, iron was good for making tools and weapons. Iron tools allowed farmers to clear land faster and to grow food more easily than they could with earlier tools.

As the people of West Africa became more productive, villages had more than they needed to survive. West Africans began to trade the area's resources with buyers who lived thousands of miles away.

West Africa's gold and salt mines became a source of great wealth. Traders used camels to cross the Sahara. They took gold, salt, cloth, slaves, and other items to North Africa and the Islamic world.

READING CHECK **Analyzing** How did religion in West Africa reflect the importance of family?

SUMMARY AND PREVIEW Physical geography affected culture and trade in West Africa. When West Africans developed iron technology, communities grew. Trade, especially in gold and salt, expanded. Next, you will read about a West African empire based on this trade—Ghana.

Section 1 Assessment

Reviewing Ideas, Terms, and People

1. a. **Recall** Where in Africa are the **rifts** located?
   b. **Explain** How were two of West Africa's valuable mineral resources related to local physical geography.
2. a. **Identify** What are two groups to which a person in early West Africa may have owed loyalty?
   b. **Analyze** How did the use of iron change farming?

Critical Thinking

3. **Drawing Conclusions** Draw a diagram like the one shown. Based on your notes, write a statement in the center circle of the diagram about how Africa's geography has shaped life there.

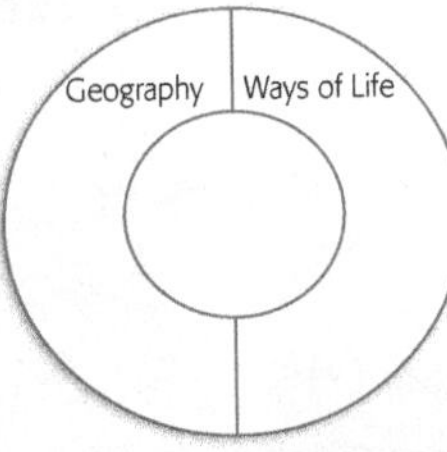

Focus on Writing

4. **Reviewing Notes on Early West Africa** Review your notes on the geography and early peoples of West Africa. Consider what your character saw every day. What challenges did the environment present? What role did family, religion, and technology play in your character's way of life?

Direct Teach

Main Idea

❷ Early People's Way of Life

The way of life of early peoples in West Africa was shaped by family ties, religion, iron technology, and trade.

Identify Who made up an extended family? *father, mother, children, close relatives*

Analyze What role did animism play in West African culture? *Animism was a belief system that was connected to religion, which was a central feature of village life.*

Elaborate Why were extended families and age-sets important in early West African cultures? *Work could be divided among members, and the groups helped each other.*

Quick Facts Transparency: Village Society

Review & Assess

Close

Have students describe how life in West Africa changed after about 500 BC.

Review

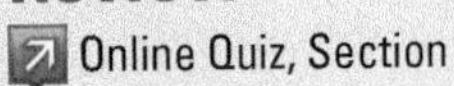

Assess

SE Section 1 Assessment

PASS: Section 1 Quiz

Alternative Assessment Handbook

Reteach/Classroom Intervention

Guided Reading Workbook, Section 1

Interactive Skills Tutor CD-ROM

Section 1 Assessment Answers

1. a. eastern Africa
   b. Salt came from the Sahara, and gold came from the forests.
2. a. extended family and age-sets
   b. Iron tools made farming easier; they helped farmers clear land and grow crops.
3. possible answer—The grasslands of the savannah provide the people with good hunting and farming.
4. Notes might include the following: daily environment—river, Sahel, savannah, farms, animals; challenges—possible droughts in hot, dry regions and heavy rain in rain forests; family—loyalty to family and age-sets; religion—sacred ancestor spirits; technology—use of iron made farming easier.

Answer

Reading Check *Many West Africans believed that the spirits of their ancestors stayed nearby.*

History and Geography

Activity **A Saharan Mural** Discuss with students items that were traded across the Sahara. Then have students work together to draw a mural of a Saharan caravan on a long piece of butcher paper. Suggest that students include camels and different trade items discussed in this feature. Display the mural in the classroom. **LS Visual/Spatial**

Alternative Assessment Handbook: Rubric 3: Artwork

Did you know . . .

Although conditions are harsh, people do live in the Sahara. A people called the Tuareg live in or near the desert and roam the southern Sahara from the south of Algeria into Libya, Niger, and Mali. The Tuareg wear blue robes that reduce harmful UVB radiation from the sun. Their dark clothing and the veils that protect their faces earned the Tuareg the nicknames "Blue Men" and "Veiled Men of the Sahara."

Teaching Tip

Comparing Distances
To help students understand the distances involved in Saharan trade, refer them to the physical and political maps of Africa in the atlas at the back of this book. Challenge students to correspond features on those maps to features on the "Crossing the Sahara" map (pp. 384-385) and to use the scale in the atlas to calculate sample distances on this map.

History and Geography

Crossing the Sahara

Crossing the Sahara has never been easy. Bigger than the entire continent of Australia, the Sahara is one of the hottest, driest, and most barren places on earth. Yet for centuries, people have crossed the Sahara's gravel-covered plains and vast seas of sand. Long ago, West Africans crossed the desert regularly to carry on a rich trade.

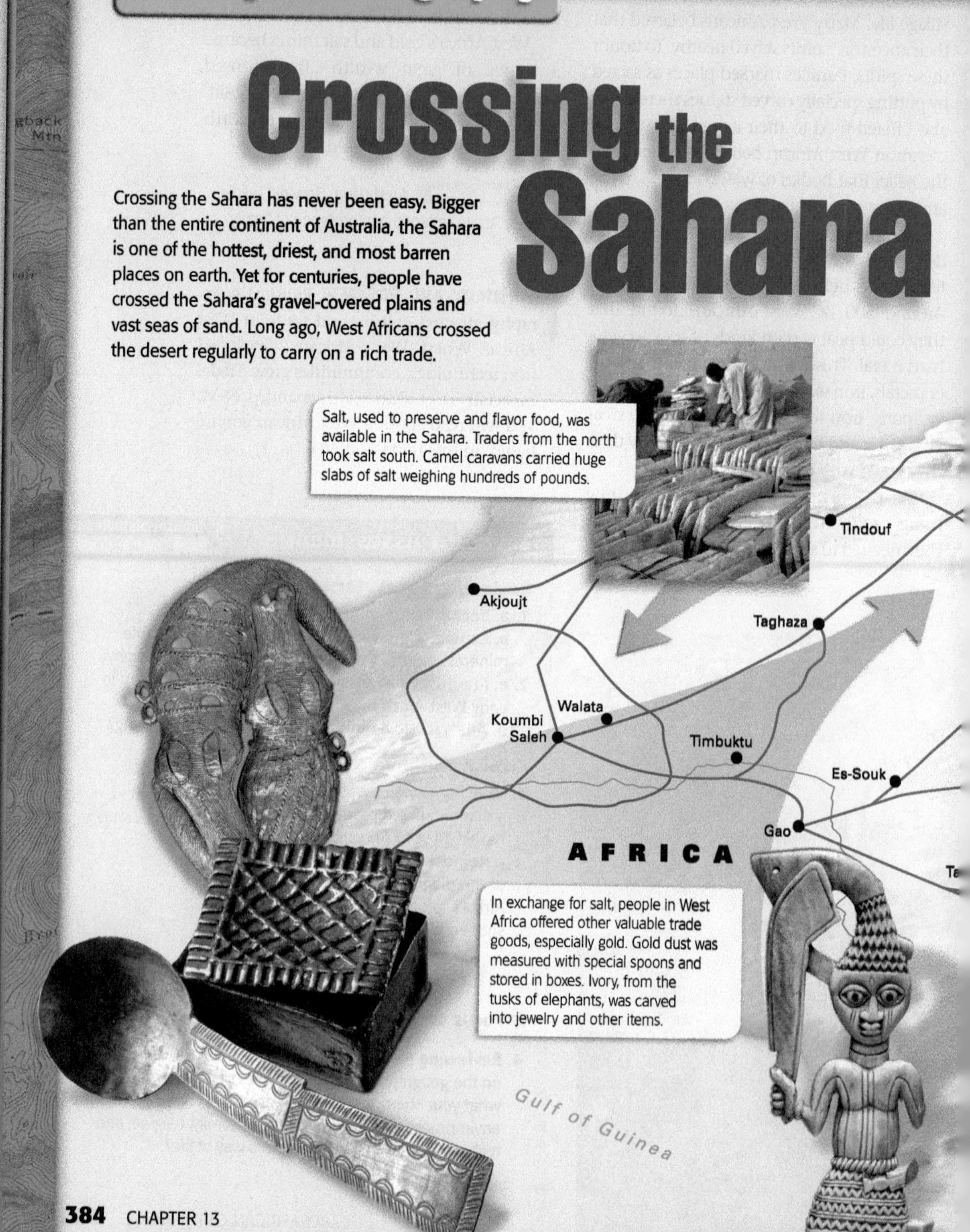

Salt, used to preserve and flavor food, was available in the Sahara. Traders from the north took salt south. Camel caravans carried huge slabs of salt weighing hundreds of pounds.

In exchange for salt, people in West Africa offered other valuable trade goods, especially gold. Gold dust was measured with special spoons and stored in boxes. Ivory, from the tusks of elephants, was carved into jewelry and other items.

Critical Thinking: Comparing

Above Level

Long-Distance Trade Then and Now

Materials: business sections of newspapers or magazines

1. To help students compare the ancient Saharan trade with international trade today, first distribute the business pages from newspapers or magazines. The print material does not have to be current or local.
2. Call on students to make generalizations about what they read in the newspapers or magazines about long-distance trade. *possible topics—security concerns, differences in resources among countries, high costs of transport*
3. Then lead a discussion about how these same topics also concerned traders in the Sahara. Challenge students to make direct comparisons.
LS Verbal/Linguistic, Logical/Mathematical

Alternative Assessment Handbook, Rubric 11: Discussions

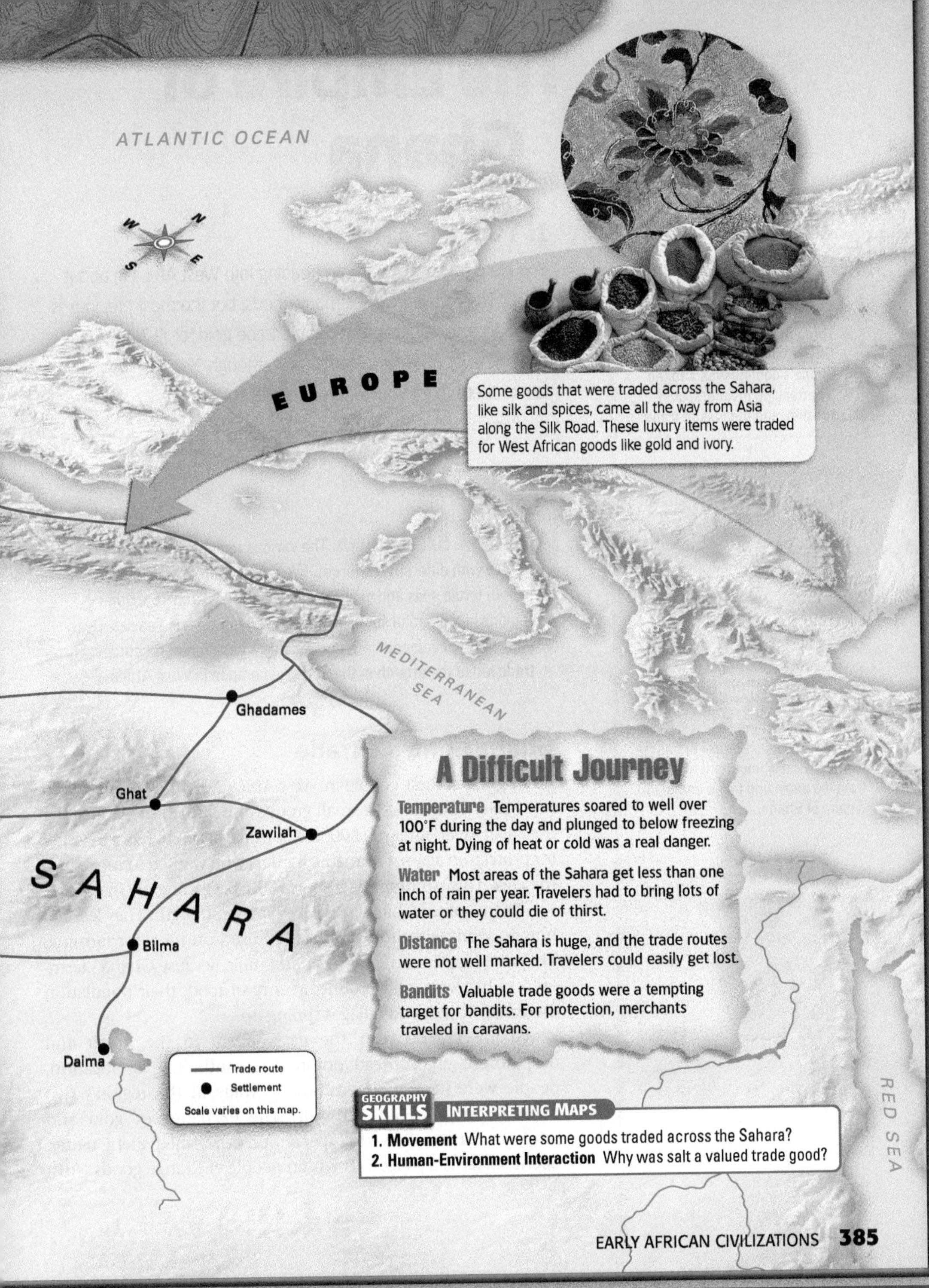

Some goods that were traded across the Sahara, like silk and spices, came all the way from Asia along the Silk Road. These luxury items were traded for West African goods like gold and ivory.

A Difficult Journey

Temperature Temperatures soared to well over 100°F during the day and plunged to below freezing at night. Dying of heat or cold was a real danger.

Water Most areas of the Sahara get less than one inch of rain per year. Travelers had to bring lots of water or they could die of thirst.

Distance The Sahara is huge, and the trade routes were not well marked. Travelers could easily get lost.

Bandits Valuable trade goods were a tempting target for bandits. For protection, merchants traveled in caravans.

GEOGRAPHY SKILLS INTERPRETING MAPS

1. **Movement** What were some goods traded across the Sahara?
2. **Human-Environment Interaction** Why was salt a valued trade good?

History and Geography

Activity A Desert Travelogue A travelogue is an illustrated account of a journey. There is a long history of travelogues for both entertainment and education. Have students imagine they have traveled with a caravan across the Sahara. Instruct them to write and illustrate a descriptive one-page travelogue about the experience. Tell them to include details that they have learned in this feature, "Crossing the Sahara."
LS Verbal/Linguistic

Alternative Assessment Handbook, Rubric 40: Writing to Describe

Connect to Science

Desert Plant Survival The Rose of Jericho is plant that grows in the Sahara. How does it survive and reproduce in the harsh desert climate? It sheds its leaves during its last few hours before it dies. Then the bare stem and branches dry up and become a lightweight ball that is easily tumbled along by the wind. As the dead Rose of Jericho rolls, it scatters its seeds, which will remain dormant until a desert rainfall. Then the seeds will quickly sprout to begin the next generation of the Rose of Jericho.

Collaborative Learning

At Level

Loading a Caravan

1. Discuss with students the necessities and limitations of loading a caravan. Ask students to suggest items travelers would need as they traveled in a caravan. Write a list of these items for students to see.
2. Remind students that travelers would not only be carrying food and water, but they would also need protection from the daytime heat and nighttime cold of a desert climate. Students should consider the type of clothing needed and the kinds of food that could be transported in a caravan.
3. Have students copy the list. Instruct them to write a sentence for each listed item that explains why the item is necessary.
LS Verbal/Linguistic

Alternative Assessment Handbook, Rubric 38: Writing to Classify

Answers

Interpreting Maps 1. *gold, salt, ivory, silk, spices* **2.** *Salt was used to preserve and flavor food.*

Preteach

Bellringer

If YOU were there . . . Use the **Daily Bellringer Transparency** to help students answer the question.

Daily Bellringer Transparency, Section 2

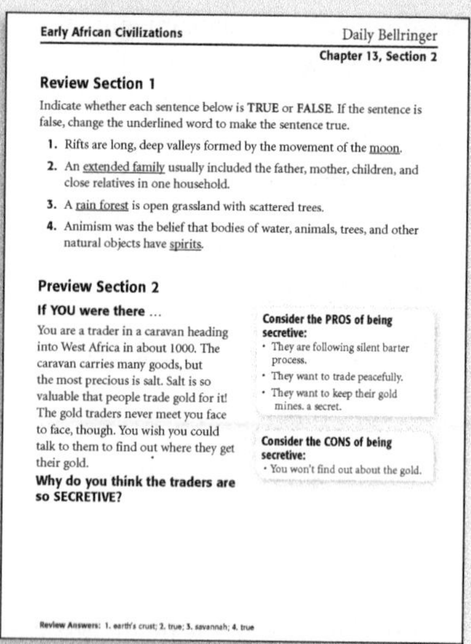

Early African Civilizations Daily Bellringer

Chapter 13, Section 2

Review Section 1

Indicate whether each sentence below is **TRUE** or **FALSE**. If the sentence is false, change the underlined word to make the sentence true.

1. Rifts are long, deep valleys formed by the movement of the moon.
2. An extended family usually included the father, mother, children, and close relatives in one household.
3. A rain forest is open grassland with scattered trees.
4. Animism was the belief that bodies of water, animals, trees, and other natural objects have spirits.

Preview Section 2

If YOU were there ...

You are a trader in a caravan heading into West Africa in about 1000. The caravan carries many goods, but the most precious is salt. Salt is so valuable that people trade gold for it! The gold traders never meet you face to face, though. You wish you could talk to them to find out where they get their gold.

Why do you think the traders are so SECRETIVE?

Consider the PROS of being secretive:
- They are following silent barter process.
- They want to trade peacefully.
- They want to keep their gold mines. a secret.

Consider the CONS of being secretive:
- You won't find out about the gold.

Review Answers: 1. earth's crust; 2. true; 3. savannah; 4. true

Academic Vocabulary

Review with students the high-use academic term in this section.

process a series of steps by which a task is accomplished (p. 386)

CRF: Vocabulary Builder Activity: Section 2

Taking Notes

Have students use the graphic organizer online to take notes on the section. This activity will prepare students for the Section Assessment, in which they will complete a graphic organizer that builds on the information using the Critical Thinking Skill: Categorizing.

SECTION 2

The Empire of Ghana

What You Will Learn...

Main Ideas

1. Ghana controlled trade and became wealthy.
2. Through its control of trade, Ghana built an empire.
3. Ghana's decline was caused by attacking invaders, overgrazing, and the loss of trade.

The Big Idea

The rulers of Ghana built an empire by controlling the salt and gold trade.

Key Terms and People

silent barter, *p. 386*
Tunka Manin, *p. 388*

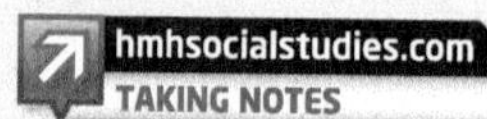

Use the graphic organizer online to make a list of important events from the beginning to the end of the empire of Ghana.

If YOU were there...

You are a trader in a caravan heading into West Africa in about 1000. The caravan carries many goods, but the most precious is salt. Salt is so valuable that people trade gold for it! The gold traders never meet you face to face, though. You wish you could talk to them to find out where they get their gold.

Why do you think the traders are so secretive?

BUILDING BACKGROUND The various regions of Africa provided people with different resources. West Africa, for example, was rich in both fertile soils and minerals, especially gold and iron. Other regions had plentiful supplies of other resources, such as salt. Over time, trade developed between regions with different resources. This trade led to the growth of the first great empire in West Africa.

Ghana Controls Trade

Among the earliest people in West Africa were the Soninke (soh-NING-kee). They lived in small groups and farmed the land along the Niger River. After AD 300, the Soninke began to band together for protection against nomadic herders who wanted to move into the area. This banding together was the beginning of Ghana.

The people of Ghana gradually grew in strength. They learned how to work with iron and how to use iron tools for farming. They also herded cattle for meat and milk. Because Ghana's farmers and herders could produce plenty of food, their population increased. Towns and villages sprang up.

Ghana lay between the vast Sahara to the north and deep forests that spread out to the south. In this location, people were in a good position to trade in the region's two main resources—gold and salt. The exchange of gold and salt sometimes followed a specific process called silent barter. **Silent barter** is a process in which people exchange goods with-

Teach the Big Idea

At Level

The Empire of Ghana

1. **Teach** Ask students the questions in the Main Idea boxes to teach this section.
2. **Apply** Have students write each of the blue headings in the section on a piece of paper. Tell students to leave space between each heading. Have students use the main ideas from this page and identify which one corresponds with each blue heading. Then have students review the material under each heading and write three to five specific details that support the main idea. LS **Verbal/Linguistic**
3. **Review** To review the section, have volunteers share their supporting details with the class. Then have the class discuss the section's big idea.
4. **Practice/Homework** Have students write a one-paragraph summary of this section that uses the supporting details they have identified. LS **Verbal/Linguistic**

Alternative Assessment Handbook, Rubric 42: Writing to Inform

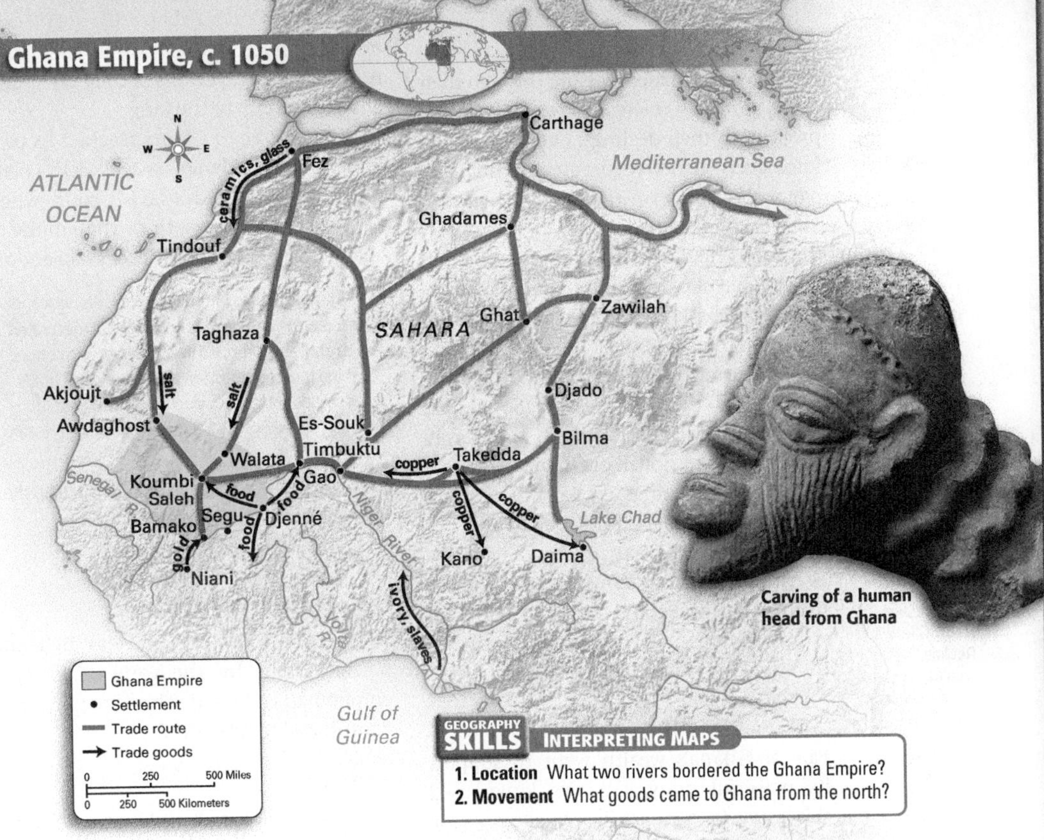

Carving of a human head from Ghana

GEOGRAPHY SKILLS INTERPRETING MAPS

1. **Location** What two rivers bordered the Ghana Empire?
2. **Movement** What goods came to Ghana from the north?

out contacting each other directly. In Ghana salt traders left slabs of salt on a riverbank. In exchange, gold miners left what they thought was a fair amount of gold. The method made sure that trade was done peacefully. It also kept the location of the gold mines secret.

As trade in gold and salt increased, Ghana's rulers gained power. They built armies equipped with iron weapons that were superior to the weapons of nearby peoples. Over time, Ghana took over control of trade from the North African merchants. Then, additional goods were added to the mix of items traded. Wheat came from the north. Sheep, cattle, and honey came from the south. Local products, such as leather and cloth, were also traded. Before long, this extensive trade made Ghana very prosperous indeed.

READING CHECK **Generalizing** How did trade help Ghana develop?

Ghana Builds an Empire

By 800 Ghana was firmly in control of West Africa's trade routes. Nearly all trade between northern and southern Africa passed through Ghana. Ghana's army kept the trade routes safe. Trade increased, and so did Ghana's wealth.

Cross-Discipline Activity: Geography

Above Level

Creating a Web Page

1. Have students study the map on this page. Guide students in a discussion of where various resources, such as salt and gold, are located on the map. Ask students to describe the geography of the region around Ghana.
2. Then ask students to imagine a Web site that would give information about the ancient empire of Ghana. Tell students that their assignment is to plan a Web page about the effect of Ghana's geography on the economy of Ghana.
3. Suggest that students make a sketch on paper of images and text they could include on their Web page. Encourage students to be creative and use drawings and symbols for their sites. To help students get started, show them examples of interesting, informative, and visually appealing Web sites.
4. Ask volunteers to show and explain their Web page plans to the class. Encourage the students to ask questions about the information or construction of the Web page.

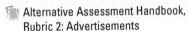

Direct Teach

Main Idea

1 Ghana Controls Trade

Ghana controlled trade and became wealthy.

Recall Where was the ancient empire of Ghana located? *in West Africa between the Niger and Senegal Rivers; between the Sahara Desert to the north and the forests of the south*

Explain How did early Soninke farmers create a strong state? *They banded together against nomadic herders, grew in strength, used iron tools to produce more food, and formed villages and towns.*

Summarize What was the silent barter of gold and salt? *the process in which people trade without any direct contact; in Ghana it provided for peaceful exchange of salt for gold and kept the location of gold mines secret.*

Activity **Trade Advertisements** Have students look closely at the map on this page. Ask students to identify the trade goods exchanged in Africa. Then have students create an advertisement for one of the trade goods. **LS Visual/Spatial**

- Alternative Assessment Handbook, Rubric 2: Advertisements
- Map Transparency: Ghana Empire, c. 1050

Did you know . . .

The Iron Age took a long time to catch on. Iron was being used in the Middle East by 1000 BC. By around 500 BC, the use of iron had spread throughout most of Europe. When people in Ghana began using it several hundred years later, they learned how effective it could be. The use of iron tools allowed farmers to grow much more food than before. Soldiers also appreciated their new iron weapons, which made the soldiers far superior to their neighbors without iron.

Answers

Interpreting Maps **1.** *Senegal and Niger;* **2.** *salt, ceramics, and glass*

Reading Check: *As trade in gold and salt increased, Ghana's rulers gained power, aiding the growth of their military, which in turn helped them take over others' trade.*

Direct Teach

Main Idea

❷ Ghana Builds an Empire

Through its control of trade, Ghana built an empire.

Recall How did Ghana's rulers raise money? *Traders had to pay taxes when they entered and exited Ghana; the people of Ghana had to pay taxes; and the army conquered neighboring tribes, who paid tribute.*

Analyze How did Ghana's rulers acquire huge amounts of gold? *from taxes and banning others from owning gold*

Evaluate Do you think trade was safer when Ghana controlled it? *possible answers: yes—The army protected all traders from bandits; no—Traders had to carry more money to pay taxes and might have been attacked more often.*

Activity Living under Tunka Manin Ask students to imagine that they live in a village in Ghana that Tunka Manin has just visited. Have students write a journal entry in the voice of a villager, describing what it was like to talk to the king. Entries should include details about the king and his visit to the village.
LS Verbal/Linguistic, Intrapersonal

Alternative Assessment Handbook, Rubric 15: Journals

hmhsocialstudies.com
Online Resources
Activity: Trading Groups

Taxes and Gold

With so many traders passing through their lands, Ghana's rulers looked for ways to profit from their dealings. One way was to force every trader who entered Ghana to pay a special tax on the goods he carried. Then each trader had to pay another tax on the goods he took with him when he left. The people of Ghana also had to pay taxes. In addition, Ghana forced small neighboring tribes to pay tribute.

THE IMPACT TODAY

Along with wealth, traders brought Islam to West Africa, where it remains a major religion today. Muslims occupied a special district in Ghana's capital, but they had little influence in politics or culture. The king and his advisers kept their traditional beliefs.

Ghana's gold mines brought even more income into the royal treasury. Some gold was carried by traders to lands as far away as England. But not all of Ghana's gold was traded. Ghana's kings also kept huge stores of the precious metal for themselves.

The rulers of Ghana banned everyone else in Ghana from owning gold nuggets. Common people could only own gold dust, which they used as money. This ensured that the king was richer than his subjects.

FOCUS ON READING

In the section titled "Ghana's Decline," what type of structural pattern is used? How do you know?

Expansion of the Empire

Part of Ghana's wealth went to support its powerful army. Ghana's kings used this army to conquer many neighboring areas. To keep order in their large empire, Ghana's kings allowed conquered rulers to retain much of their power. These local rulers acted as governors of their territories, answering only to the king.

The empire of Ghana reached its peak under **Tunka Manin** (TOOHN-kah MAH-nin). This king had a lavish court where he displayed the wealth of the empire. A Spanish writer noted the court's splendor.

> "The king adorns himself . . . round his neck and his forearms, and he puts on a high cap decorated with gold and wrapped in a turban of fine cotton. Behind the king stand ten pages [servants] holding shields and swords decorated with gold."
>
> —al-Bakri, from *The Book of Routes and Kingdoms*

READING CHECK **Summarizing** How did the rulers of Ghana control trade?

BIOGRAPHY

Tunka Manin

Ruled around 1068

All we know about Tunka Manin comes from the writings of a Muslim geographer who wrote about Ghana. From his writings, we know that Tunka Manin was the nephew of the previous king, a man named Basi. Kingship and property in Ghana did not pass from father to son, but from uncle to nephew. Only the king's sister's son could inherit the throne. Once he did become king, Tunka Manin surrounded himself with finery and many luxuries.

Contrasting How was inheritance in Ghana different from inheritance in other societies you have studied?

Ghana's Decline

In the mid-1000s, Ghana was rich and powerful, but by the early 1200s, the empire had collapsed. Three major factors contributed to its end.

Invasion

The first factor that hurt Ghana was invasion. A group of North African Muslims called the Almoravids (al-moh-RAH-vidz) attacked Ghana in the 1060s. After 14 years of fighting, the Almoravids defeated the people of Ghana. The Almoravids didn't control Ghana for long, but they weakened the empire. They cut off many trade routes and formed new trading partnerships with Muslim leaders. Without this trade, Ghana could not support its empire.

Overgrazing

A second factor in Ghana's decline also involved the Almoravids. These invaders brought herds of animals with them. These animals ate all the grass in many pastures, leaving the soil exposed to hot desert winds.

Critical Thinking: Sequencing

At Level

Ghana's Illustrated Time Line

1. Review with the class the events that led to the decline of the empire of Ghana. Then tell students that they will create an illustrated time line of the rise and fall of Ghana.
2. Have each student make a list of four to five important events during the history of the empire of Ghana. Next to each event, have students indicate why the event was significant or what impact it had on the people of Ghana.
3. Have each student create an illustrated time line using the events he or she developed. Remind students to place the events in the order in which they occurred, and to have a picture that illustrates the importance of the event.
4. Ask students to post their time lines for the class to see. **LS Verbal/Linguistic, Visual/Spatial**

Alternative Assessment Handbook, Rubric 36: Time Lines

Answers

Biography *Inheritance was handed down to the king's sister's son, rather than to the king's son.*

Reading Check *They taxed traders coming and leaving Ghana ,and they used their armies to protect trade routes.*

Focus on Reading *listing categories; it lists a "first factor," "second factor," and so on.*

Overgrazing

Too many animals grazing in one area can lead to problems, such as the loss of farmland that occurred in West Africa.

1 Animals are allowed to graze in areas with lots of grass.

2 With too many animals grazing, however, the grass disappears, leaving the soil below exposed to the wind.

3 The wind blows the soil away, turning what was once grassland into desert.

These winds blew away the soil, leaving it worthless for farming or herding. Many farmers had to leave in search of new homes.

Internal Rebellion

A third factor also helped bring about the decline of Ghana's empire. In about 1200 the people of a country that Ghana had conquered rose up in rebellion. Within a few years these rebels had taken over the entire empire of Ghana.

Once in control, however, the rebels found that they could not keep order. Weakened, Ghana was attacked and defeated by one of its neighbors. The empire fell apart.

READING CHECK **Identifying Cause and Effect** Why did Ghana decline in the AD 1000s?

SUMMARY AND PREVIEW The empire of Ghana in West Africa grew rich and powerful through its control of trade routes and its gold production. The empire lasted from about 800 to 1200. In the next section, you will learn about two empires that arose after Ghana—Mali and Songhai.

Section 2 Assessment

hmhsocialstudies.com ONLINE QUIZ

Reviewing Ideas, Terms, and People

1. a. **Identify** What were the two major resources traded in Ghana?
   b. **Explain** How did the **silent barter** system work?
2. a. **Identify** Who was **Tunka Manin**?
   b. **Generalize** What did Ghana's kings do with the money they raised from taxes and gold mining?
   c. **Elaborate** Why did the rulers of Ghana not want everyone to have gold?
3. a. **Recall** What group invaded Ghana in the late 1000s?
   b. **Analyze** How did overgrazing help cause the fall of Ghana?

Critical Thinking

4. **Categorizing** Look through the events you listed in your notes. Decide which contributed to Ghana's rise and which led to its fall. Organize the events in a diagram like this one.

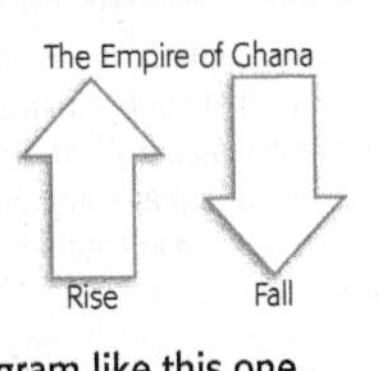

Focus on Writing

5. **Reviewing Notes on Ghana** Review this section and your notes on the rise and fall of Ghana's trading empire. Keep in mind how your character's life may have been impacted by Ghana's history.

Section 2 Assessment Answers

1. a. gold and salt
   b. Traders exchanged goods without contacting each other directly, and business was peacefully conducted.
2. a. a king of Ghana
   b. The rulers built a powerful army.
   c. to ensure the king was richer than his subjects
3. a. the Almoravids
   b. Overgrazing left the soil exposed to hot desert winds, making it worthless for farmers.
4. Rise—location, silent barter, trade from the north and south, and control of trade routes; Fall—invasion, overgrazing, and internal rebellion
5. Student notes will vary but should reflect knowledge of the causes of Ghana's rise and fall and the impact on individual lives.

Direct Teach

Main Idea

3 Ghana's Decline

Ghana's decline was caused by attacking invaders, overgrazing, and the loss of trade.

Recall What group attacked Ghana in the 1060s, and what effect did the attack have? *Almoravids greatly weakened Ghana's trade empire.*

Draw Conclusions What was the significance of overgrazing? *The Almoravids overgrazed the lands in Ghana, leaving the soil worthless for farming or herding. This greatly hurt Ghana's economy and society and caused many farmers to leave.*

Make Judgments Why do you think people rebelled in about 1200? *possible answer—They were angry that they had been conquered by Ghana.*

Review & Assess

Close

Ask students to imagine what life was like in Ghana at the height of its empire about 800. Discuss the peace and prosperity of the empire. Ask students to imagine what life was like around 1200, when the empire began to fall apart.

Review

Online Quiz Section 2

Assess

SE Section 2 Assessment

PASS: Section 2 Quiz

Alternative Assessment Handbook

Reteach/Classroom Intervention

Guided Reading Workbook, Section 2

Interactive Skills Tutor CD-ROM

Answer

Reading Check *invasion, overgrazing, and internal rebellion*

Preteach

Bellringer

If YOU were there . . . Use the **Daily Bellringer Transparency** to help students answer the question.

Daily Bellringer Transparency, Section 3

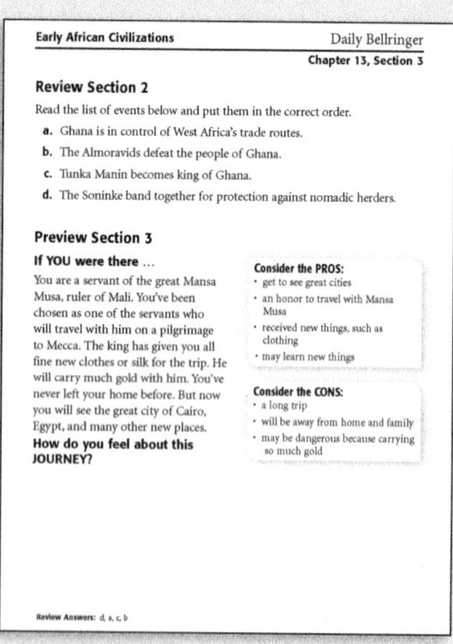

Early African Civilizations Daily Bellringer

Chapter 13, Section 3

Review Section 2

Read the list of events below and put them in the correct order.

- **a.** Ghana is in control of West Africa's trade routes.
- **b.** The Almoravids defeat the people of Ghana.
- **c.** Tunka Manin becomes king of Ghana.
- **d.** The Soninke band together for protection against nomadic herders.

Preview Section 3

If YOU were there ...

You are a servant of the great Mansa Musa, ruler of Mali. You've been chosen as one of the servants who will travel with him on a pilgrimage to Mecca. The king has given you all fine new clothes or silk for the trip. He will carry much gold with him. You've never left your home before. But now you will see the great city of Cairo, Egypt, and many other new places.

How do you feel about this JOURNEY?

Consider the PROS:
- get to see great cities
- an honor to travel with Mansa Musa
- received new things, such as clothing
- may learn new things

Consider the CONS:
- a long trip
- will be away from home and family
- may be dangerous because carrying so much gold

Review Answers: d, a, c, b

Building Vocabulary

Preteach or review the following terms:

fibers threads (p. 390)

fortress fort, stronghold (p. 394)

harmony peace, getting along together (p. 393)

harsh severe (p. 390)

pilgrimage travel to a holy place (p. 391)

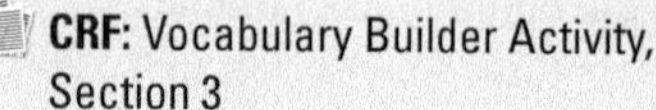

CRF: Vocabulary Builder Activity, Section 3

Taking Notes

Have students use the graphic organizer online to take notes on the section. This activity will prepare students for the Section Assessment, in which they will complete a graphic organizer that builds on the information using the Critical Thinking Skill: Finding Main Ideas.

SECTION 3

Later Empires

What You Will Learn...

Main Ideas

1. The empire of Mali reached its height under the ruler Mansa Musa, but the empire fell to invaders in the 1400s.
2. The Songhai built a new Islamic empire in West Africa, conquering many of the lands that were once part of Mali.
3. Great Zimbabwe was a powerful state that developed in southern Africa.

The Big Idea

Between 1000 and 1500, three great kingdoms—Mali, Songhai, and Great Zimbabwe—developed in Africa.

Key People

Sundiata, *p. 390*
Mansa Musa, *p. 391*
Sunni Ali, *p. 392*
Askia the Great, *p. 393*

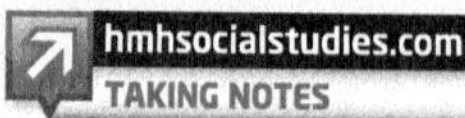

Use the graphic organizer online to take notes about life in the cultures that developed in West Africa—Mali and Songhai—and the one that developed in southern Africa—Great Zimbabwe.

If YOU were there...

You are a servant of the great Mansa Musa, ruler of Mali. You've been chosen as one of the servants who will travel with him on a pilgrimage to Mecca. The king has given you all fine new clothes of silk for the trip. He will carry much gold with him. You've never left your home before. But now you will see the great city of Cairo, Egypt, and many other new places.

How do you feel about going on this journey?

BUILDING BACKGROUND Mansa Musa was one of Africa's greatest rulers, and his empire, Mali, was one of the largest in African history. Rising from the ruins of Ghana, Mali took over the trade routes of West Africa and grew into a powerful state.

Mali

Like Ghana, Mali (MAH-lee) lay along the upper Niger River. This area's fertile soil helped Mali grow. Mali's location on the Niger also allowed its people to control trade on the river. As a result, the empire grew rich and powerful. According to legend, Mali's rise to power began under a ruler named **Sundiata** (soohn-JAHT-ah).

Sundiata Makes Mali an Empire

When Sundiata was a boy, a harsh ruler conquered Mali. But as an adult, Sundiata built up an army and won back his country's independence. He then conquered nearby kingdoms, including Ghana, in the 1230s.

After Sundiata conquered Ghana, he took over the salt and gold trades. He also worked to improve agriculture in Mali. Sundiata had new farmlands cleared for beans, onions, rice, and other crops. Sundiata even introduced a new crop—cotton. From the cotton fibers people made clothing that was comfortable in the warm climate. They also sold cotton to other people.

To keep order in his prosperous kingdom, Sundiata took power away from local leaders. Each of these local leaders had the title *mansa* (MAHN-sah), a title Sundiata now took

Teach the Big Idea

At Level

Later Empires

1. **Teach** Ask students the questions in the Main Idea boxes to teach this section.
2. **Apply** Review with students the history of Mali and Songhai, including the rule of Sundiata, Mansa Musa, and Askia the Great, and the decline of the empires. Have students work with a partner to create a children's book that briefly outlines the history of Mali or of Songhai and provides illustrations to support the story. Encourage students to create an outline for their story before they begin to write. Remind students to include important events and people in their history. **LS Visual/Spatial, Verbal/Linguistic**
3. **Review** Have students exchange and read each other's children's books as a review of the information from the section.
4. **Practice/Homework** Have each student write a book review of another group's book. **LS Verbal/Linguistic**

Alternative Assessment Handbook, Rubrics 3: Artwork; and 42: Writing to Inform

Mali and Songhai

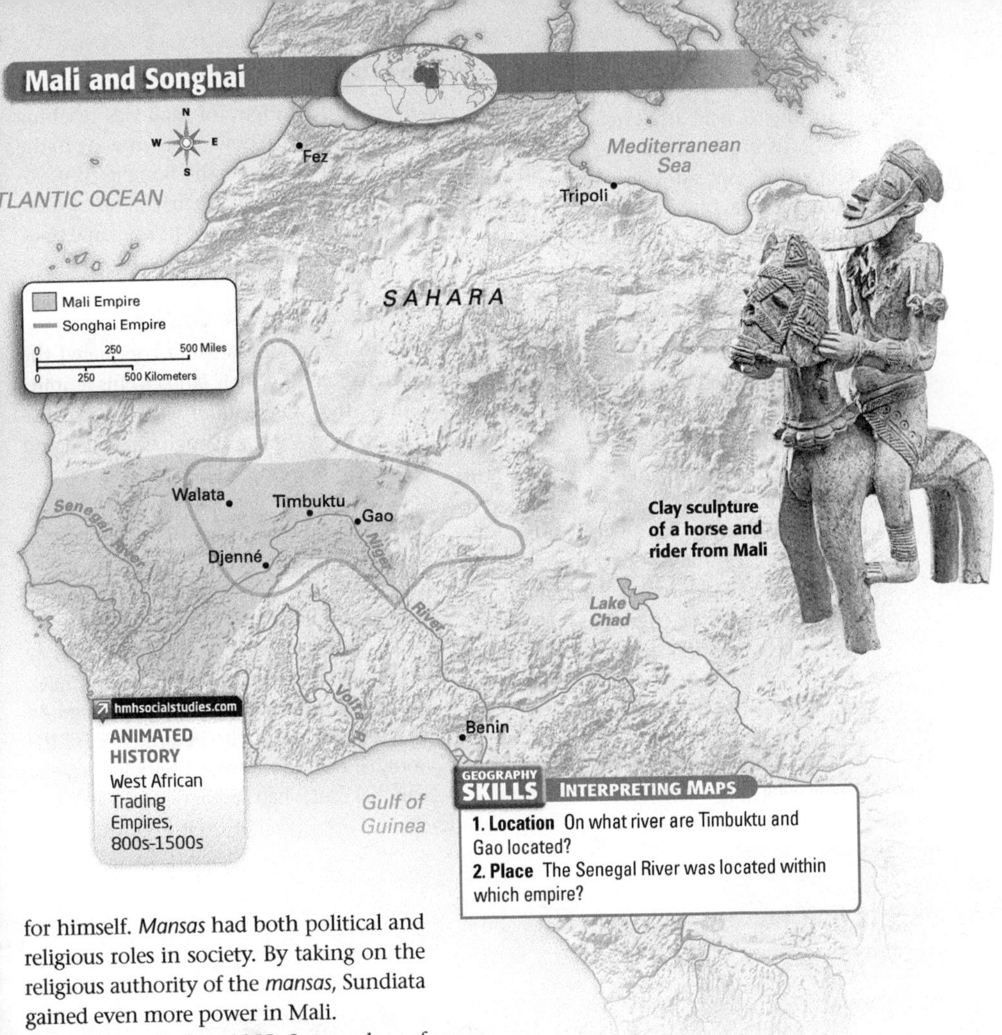

Clay sculpture of a horse and rider from Mali

GEOGRAPHY SKILLS INTERPRETING MAPS

1. **Location** On what river are Timbuktu and Gao located?
2. **Place** The Senegal River was located within which empire?

for himself. *Mansas* had both political and religious roles in society. By taking on the religious authority of the *mansas*, Sundiata gained even more power in Mali.

Sundiata died in 1255. Later rulers of Mali took the title of *mansa*. Unlike Sundiata, most of these rulers were Muslims.

Mansa Musa

Mali's most famous ruler was a Muslim named **Mansa Musa** (MAHN-sah moo-SAH). Under his skillful leadership, Mali reached the height of its wealth, power, and fame in the 1300s. Because of Mansa Musa's influence, Islam spread through a large part of West Africa, gaining many new believers.

Mansa Musa ruled Mali for about 25 years, from 1312 to 1337. During that time, Mali added many important trade cities to its empire, including Timbuktu (tim-buhk-TOO).

Religion was very important to Mansa Musa. In 1324 he left Mali on a pilgrimage to Mecca. Through his journey, Mansa Musa introduced his empire to the Islamic world. He spread Mali's fame far and wide.

Mansa Musa also supported education. He sent many scholars to study in Morocco.

Direct Teach

Main Idea

❶ Mali

The empire of Mali reached its height under the ruler Mansa Musa, but the empire fell to invaders in the 1400s.

Identify After conquering nearby kingdoms, on what did Sundiata focus? *improving agriculture and taking over the salt and gold trade*

Explain How did Sundiata consolidate political and religious power? *by taking power away from local leaders; by taking on the religious authority of local mansas*

Make Inferences Why do you think it was important for the ruler of Mali to take away power from local leaders? *Taking power from local leaders meant they could not rise up against the ruler.*

CRF: Primary Source Activity: Reading from *The Sundiata*

CRF: Biography Activity: Sundiata

Map Transparency: Mali and Songhai

Biography

Sundiata (c. 1210—c.1255) Born Mari Diata, Sundiata was the son of the king of the small kingdom of Kangaba. When his father's kingdom was overtaken by King Sumanguru of the Soso Empire, Mari Diata was forced to live in exile. Eventually, however, he returned to defeat Sumanguru in the Battle of Kirina. After the battle, he took the name Sundiata, which means the "lion prince," and went on to establish one of the greatest empires in African history.

Critical Thinking: Comparing and Contrasting

At Level

The Empires of West Africa

Materials: map pencils or markers, blank outline map of Africa

1. Review with students the locations of the Ghana, Mali, and Songhai Empires.
2. Using the maps of Ghana (p. 387), and Mali and Songhai (p. 391), have students indicate the area of all three West African empires on a blank outline map of Africa. Remind students to use a different color or pattern for each empire and to label each empire and the approximate time period represented by the map.
3. Ask students to make a graphic organizer to compare and contrast the three empires. Discuss with the class the similarities and differences between the empires in terms of size, location, and time periods of the empires. **LS Visual/Spatial, Verbal/Linguistic**

Alternative Assessment Handbook, Rubrics 11: Discussions; and 20: Map Creation

Answers

Interpreting Maps 1. *Niger River;* **2.** *Mali*

These scholars later set up schools in Mali. Mansa Musa stressed the importance of learning to read the Arabic language so that Muslims in his empire could read the Qur'an. To spread Islam in West Africa, Mansa Musa hired Muslim architects to build mosques throughout his empire.

Some of the mosques built by Mansa Musa can still be seen in West Africa today.

The Fall of Mali

When Mansa Musa died, his son Maghan (MAH-gan) took the throne. Maghan was a weak ruler. When raiders from the southeast poured into Mali, he couldn't stop them. The raiders set fire to Timbuktu's great schools and mosques. Mali never fully recovered from this terrible blow. The empire continued to weaken and decline.

In 1431 the Tuareg (TWAH-reg), nomads from the Sahara, seized Timbuktu. The people living at the edges of Mali's empire broke away. By 1500 nearly all of the lands the empire had once ruled were lost. Only a small area of Mali remained.

READING CHECK **Sequencing** What steps did Sundiata take to turn Mali into an empire?

Songhai

Even as the Empire of Mali was reaching its height, a rival power was growing in the area. That rival was the Songhai (SAHNG-hy) kingdom. From their capital at Gao, the Songhai participated in the same trade that had made Ghana and Mali so rich.

The Building of an Empire

In the 1300s Mansa Musa conquered the Songhai, adding their lands to his empire. But as the Mali Empire weakened in the 1400s, the people of Songhai rebelled and regained their freedom.

The Songhai leaders were Muslims. So too were many of the North African Berbers who traded in West Africa. Because of this shared religion, the Berbers were willing to trade with the Songhai, who grew richer.

As the Songhai gained in wealth, they expanded their territory and built an empire. Songhai's expansion was led by **Sunni Ali** (SOOH-nee ah-LEE), who became ruler of the Songhai in 1464. Before he took over, the Songhai state had been disorganized and

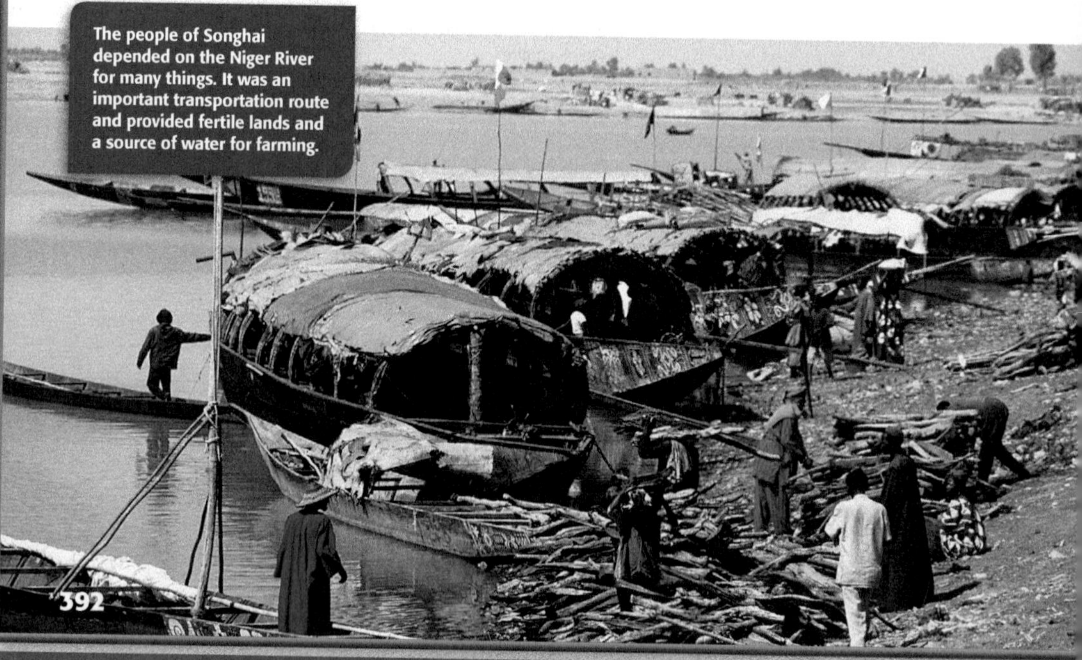

The people of Songhai depended on the Niger River for many things. It was an important transportation route and provided fertile lands and a source of water for farming.

Direct Teach

Main Idea

1 Mali

The empire of Mali reached its height under the ruler Mansa Musa, but the empire fell to invaders in the 1400s.

Identify To what religion did Mansa Musa belong? *Islam*

Recall To where did Mansa Musa travel in 1324? *He made a pilgrimage to Mecca.*

Making Inferences How did Mansa Musa spread his religion throughout Mali? How do you think this affected the people of Mali? *He sent scholars to study in Morocco who later established schools to teach the Qur'an, stressed the teaching and learning of the Arabic language, and hired Muslims to build mosques in Mali. Mali's people likely became more knowledgeable about the Qur'an and Arabic.*

Recall What are two reasons for the decline of Mali? *weak leaders, problems with invaders, parts of the empire broke away*

Activity **Journal Writing** Ask students to imagine that they lived in Mali during the time of Mansa Musa's rule. Instruct them to use facts from the section to write a journal entry recording changes in Mali.
LS Verbal/Linguistic

- Alternative Assessment Handbook, Rubric 15: Journals
- **CRF:** Primary Source Activity: Two Descriptions of Emperors of Mali

Critical Thinking: Categorizing

At Level

The Rule of Mansa Musa

1. Review the description of Mansa Musa's reign.
2. To help students understand the influence of Mansa Musa, copy the graphic organizer for students. Omit the blue, answers.
3. Have students copy and complete the graphic organizer. Review the answers with the class.
4. Discuss with students why they feel Mansa Musa was significant. Then have each student create a report card in which they evaluate the rule of Mansa Musa. Cards should list contributions of Mansa Musa, a grade for each, and why was assigned that grade.

LS Verbal/Linguistic, Visual/Spatial

Trade	Religion	Education
• *captured important trade city of Timbuktu*	• *encouraged study of Islam* • *built mosques* • *encouraged study of Arabic for the study of the Qur'an*	• *built schools* • *sent scholars to study in Morocco, who later set up schools*

Answers

Reading Check *Sundiata built a powerful army, conquered many neighboring kingdoms, took control of gold and salt trade routes, took power away from local chiefs, and took the authority of a mansa.*

poorly run. As ruler, Sunni Ali worked to unify, strengthen, and enlarge his empire. Much of the land that he added to Songhai had been part of Mali.

As king, Sunni Ali encouraged everyone in his empire to work together. To build religious harmony, he participated in both Muslim and local religions. As a result, he brought stability to Songhai.

Askia the Great

Sunni Ali died in 1492. He was followed as king by his son Sunni Baru, who was not a Muslim. The Songhai people feared that if Sunni Baru didn't support Islam, they would lose their trade with Muslim lands. They rebelled against the king.

The leader of that rebellion was a general named Muhammad Ture (moo-HAH-muhd too-RAY). After overthrowing Sunni Baru, Muhammad Ture chose the title *askia,* a title of high military rank. Eventually, he became known as **Askia the Great.**

Askia supported education and learning. Under his rule, Timbuktu flourished, drawing thousands to its universities, schools, libraries, and mosques. The city was especially known for the University of Sankore (san-KOH-rah). People arrived there from North Africa and other places to study math, science, medicine, grammar, and law. Djenné was another city that became a center of learning.

Most of Songhai's traders were Muslim, and as they gained influence in the empire so did Islam. Askia, himself a devout Muslim, encouraged the growth of Islamic influence. He made many laws similar to those in other Muslim nations.

To help maintain order, Askia set up five provinces within Songhai. He removed local leaders and appointed new governors who were loyal to him. Askia also created a professional army and specialized departments to oversee specific tasks.

BIOGRAPHY

Askia the Great
c. 1443–1538

Askia the Great became the ruler of Songhai when he was nearly 50 years old. He ruled Songhai for about 35 years. During his reign the cities of Songhai gained power over the countryside.

When he was in his 80s, Askia went blind. His son Musa forced him to leave the throne. Askia was sent to live on an island. He lived there for nine years until another of his sons brought him back to the capital, where he died. His tomb is still one of the most honored places in all of West Africa.

Drawing Inferences Why do you think Askia the Great's tomb is still considered an honored place?

Songhai Falls to Morocco

A northern rival of Songhai, Morocco, wanted to gain control of Songhai's salt mines. So the Moroccan army set out for the heart of Songhai in 1591. Moroccan soldiers carried advanced weapons, including the terrible arquebus (AHR-kwih-buhs). The arquebus was an early form of a gun.

The swords, spears, and bows used by Songhai's warriors were no match for the Moroccans' guns and cannons. The invaders destroyed Timbuktu and Gao.

Changes in trade patterns completed Songhai's fall. Overland trade declined as port cities on the Atlantic coast became more important. Africans south of Songhai and European merchants both preferred trading at Atlantic ports to dealing with Muslim traders. Slowly, the period of great West African empires came to an end.

READING CHECK **Evaluating** What do you think was Askia's greatest accomplishment?

Direct Teach

Main Idea

❷ Songhai

The Songhai built a new Islamic empire in West Africa, conquering many of the lands that were once part of Mali.

Draw Conclusions Was the leader of the Songhai, Sunni Ali, a strong or weak leader? Why? *He led the Songhai expansion, which showed him to be a strong leader.*

Recall How did Askia the Great improve Timbuktu? *He supported education and learning, drew thousands to schools, libraries, and mosques.*

Making Inferences How might Askia's beliefs have helped him as a ruler? *Residents of his empire supported him because he was a Muslim; he would have had more peaceful relations with Songhai's Muslim neighbors.*

CRF: Biography Activity: Sunni Ali

Info to Know

The Fall of Songhai Even before attacks by Moroccan armies, the Songhai Empire had begun to decline. A civil war in the 1580s weakened the empire, and Songhai control of trade routes had diminished. In fact, Songhai gold supplies had declined as a great deal of gold was used to trade with Europeans who had arrived on the coast of West Africa in the late 1400s.

hmhsocialstudies.com
Online Resources
Activity: Askia Timeline

Differentiating Instruction

Struggling Readers At Level

1. To help students understand the contributions of Askia the Great and the significance of his rule, draw the graphic organizer for students to see. Omit the blue, italicized answers. Explain each category to the students. Ask students for an example for each category.
2. Have students fill in the graphic organizer by providing details about Askia the Great's accomplishments in each category. Point out to students where details on each category can be found in the textbook.
3. When students have completed the graphic organizer, review the answers with the class.

LS Visual/Spatial

Accomplishments of Askia the Great

Government	Religion	Education
• *set up five provinces* • *appointed governors loyal to him* • *created departments to oversee tasks*	• *encouraged Islamic influence*	• *drew thousands to schools and universities* • *encouraged study of math, medicine, science, grammar, law*

Answers

Biography *because his rule was marked by many achievements*

Reading Check *possible answer—his support of education, because it increased learning throughout the Songhai Empire*

Direct Teach

Main Idea

3 Great Zimbabwe

Great Zimbabwe was a powerful state that developed in southern Africa.

Identify Where was Great Zimbabwe? When and why did it begin? *southern Africa; began in late 1000s as a trading and herding center*

Summarize What led to the fall and the decline of Great Zimbabwe? *It was a trading center, which made the leaders wealthy and powerful; when gold trade declined, Great Zimbabwe was weakened.*

Review & Assess

Close

Have students create a time line of the key events in the history of the empires of Mali, Songhai, and Zimbabwe.

Review

Online Quiz, Section 3

Assess

SE Section 3 Assessment

PASS: Section 3 Quiz

Alternative Assessment Handbook

Reteach/Classroom Intervention

Guided Reading Workbook, Section 3

Interactive Skills Tutor CD-ROM

Time Line QUICK FACTS

West African Empires

- **1060s** The Empire of Ghana reaches its height.
- **c. 1200** Ghana falls.
- **c. 1235** The Empire of Mali begins.
- **1400s** Songhai begins to attack Mali.
- **c. 1500** Mali falls.
- **1590s** Songhai falls to Moroccan invaders.

1000 | 1200 | 1400 | 1600

ANALYSIS SKILL **READING TIME LINES**

About how many years after the fall of Ghana did Mali fall?

Great Zimbabwe

Strong kingdoms also arose in other parts of Africa. Great Zimbabwe, for example, was a powerful kingdom in southern Africa. Great Zimbabwe was founded in the late 1000s as a small trading and herding center. Gold mining increased in the area in the 1100s. Farming expanded and the kingdom's population grew. In time, Great Zimbabwe became the center of a large trading network.

THE IMPACT TODAY

The stone fortress remains a major cultural monument in the modern nation of Zimbabwe.

Trade made Great Zimbabwe's rulers wealthy and powerful. They built a huge stone-walled fortress to protect their capital. In the 1400s the gold trade declined. Deprived of its main source of wealth, Great Zimbabwe weakened. By 1500 it was no longer a political and trading center.

READING CHECK **Comparing** How was Great Zimbabwe similar to the empires of West Africa?

SUMMARY AND PREVIEW Sundiata and Mansa Musa helped Mali become a large empire famous for its wealth and centers of learning. Songhai similarly thrived under leaders such as Askia the Great. In the next section, you will read more about the major West African cultures.

Section 3 Assessment

hmhsocialstudies.com ONLINE QUIZ

Reviewing Ideas, Terms, and People

1. a. **Identify** Who was **Sundiata**?
   b. **Explain** What major river was important to the people of Mali? Why?
   c. **Elaborate** What effects did the rule of **Mansa Musa** have on Mali and West Africa?
2. a. **Identify** Who led the expansion of Songhai in the 1400s?
   b. **Explain** How did **Askia the Great's** support of education affect Timbuktu?
3. a. **Recall** What made Great Zimbabwe's rulers wealthy and powerful?
   b. **Analyze** What led to the decline of Great Zimbabwe?

Critical Thinking

4. **Finding Main Ideas** Use your notes to help you list three major accomplishments of Sundiata and Askia.

Sundiata	Askia

Focus on Writing

5. **Comparing and Contrasting** Review this section and your notes on the empires of Mali and Songhai. Consider how your character's life may have been shaped by the empire in which he or she lived. What were the differences between the empires? How were they the same? How did specific leaders affect the development of the lands they ruled?

Section 3 Assessment Answers

1. **a.** ruler of the empire of Mali
   b. Niger; its fertile soil helped Mali grow; people could control trade along the river.
   c. He spread Islam and supported education.
2. **a.** Sunni Ali
   b. Timbuktu flourished, with universities, schools, libraries, and mosques.
3. **a.** gold mining and being a trading center
   b. Gold trade declined in 1400s, taking away Zimbabwe's main source of wealth.
4. Sundiata—won back Mali's independence; conquered Ghana and took over salt and gold trades; improved agriculture in Mali; Askia—supported education and learning; encouraged growth of Islamic influence; set up five provinces in Songhai
5. possible answers: differences—Mali fell in the 1400s and Songhai fell in the late 1500s, Songhai took over Mali lands; similarities—made wealthy by trade, spread Islamic influence; specific rulers—Mali reached its height under Mansa Musa; Songhai had its greatest development under Askia the Great.

Answers

Reading Time Lines *300 years*

Reading Check *Zimbabwe was also a trading center with powerful leaders; like Songhai and Ghana, when trade weakened, the empire also weakened.*

BIOGRAPHY

Mansa Musa

How could one man's travels become a major historic event?

When did he live? the late 1200s and early 1300s

Where did he live? Mali

What did he do? Mansa Musa, the ruler of Mali, was one of the Muslim kings of West Africa. He became a major figure in African and world history largely because of a pilgrimage he made to the city of Mecca.

Why is he important? Mansa Musa's spectacular journey attracted the attention of the Muslim world and of Europe. For the first time, other people's eyes turned to West Africa. During his travels, Mansa Musa gave out huge amounts of gold. His spending made people eager to find the source of such wealth. Within 200 years, European explorers would arrive on the shores of western Africa.

Identifying Points of View How do you think Mansa Musa changed people's views of West Africa?

KEY FACTS

According to chroniclers of the time, Mansa Musa was accompanied on his journey to Mecca by some 60,000 people. Of those people

- **12,000** were servants to attend to the king.
- **500** were servants to attend to his wife.
- **14,000** more were slaves wearing rich fabrics such as silk.
- **500** carried staffs heavily decorated with gold. Historians have estimated that the gold Mansa Musa gave away on his trip would be worth more than $100 million today.

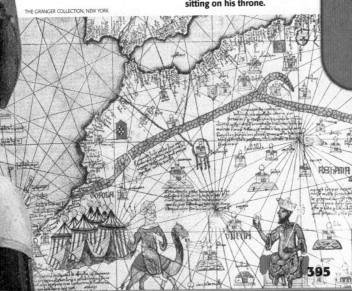

THE GRANGER COLLECTION, NEW YORK

This Spanish map from the 1300s shows Mansa Musa sitting on his throne.

395

Biography

Reading Focus Question

Have students think about historical figures and how their travels have affected history. Have students consider what possible effects might result from the travels of one person.

Info to Know

Mansa Musa's Journey On his famous pilgrimage to Mecca, Mansa Musa passed through several kingdoms in North Africa. From his capital of Niani, on the Upper Niger River, Mansa Musa and his entourage of thousands traveled north to Walata, to Tuat in modern-day Algeria, then to Cairo, Egypt. From Egypt, Mansa Musa traveled to Mecca in Arabia.

Linking to Today

The Hajj, a pilgrimage or journey, is still an important ritual for Muslims today. Every year, millions of Muslims travel to Mecca for the annual hajj. During the pilgrimage, which lasts six days, pilgrims perform special rites, including circling the Kaaba, a sacred shrine, seven times. Making the hajj is one of five duties expected of every Muslim who is physically and financially able.

About the Illustration

The illustration on this page is from a fourteenth century map by Spanish mapmaker, Abraham Cresques. Mansa Musa is depicted at the left sitting in a throne and holding a gold scepter. This illustration of Mansa Musa is an artist's conception based on available sources. However, historians are uncertain exactly what Mansa Musa looked like.

Critical Thinking: Summarizing

At Level

Writing a Eulogy

1. Review with students the biography of Mansa Musa. Tell students that they will write a eulogy that could have been read at Mansa Musa's funeral. A eulogy is a speech given to honor someone who has died.
2. Ask students to include details found in this section in the eulogy. Encourage students to include one or two short accounts of interesting events from the life of Mansa Musa. Remind students to consider the purpose of the eulogy and their audience when choosing what to write about Mansa Musa.
3. Ask for volunteers to deliver their eulogies to the class. Discuss with students the important contributions or accomplishments of Mansa Musa. LS **Verbal/Linguistic**

Alternative Assessment Handbook, Rubric 41: Writing to Express

Answers

Identifying Points of View *possible answers—Mansa Musa spread new knowledge that West Africa had great wealth. This caused European and African interest in West Africa, which brought new trade and even more wealth for Mali.*

Preteach

Bellringer

If YOU were there . . . Use the **Daily Bellringer Transparency** to help students answer the question.

Daily Bellringer Transparency, Section 4

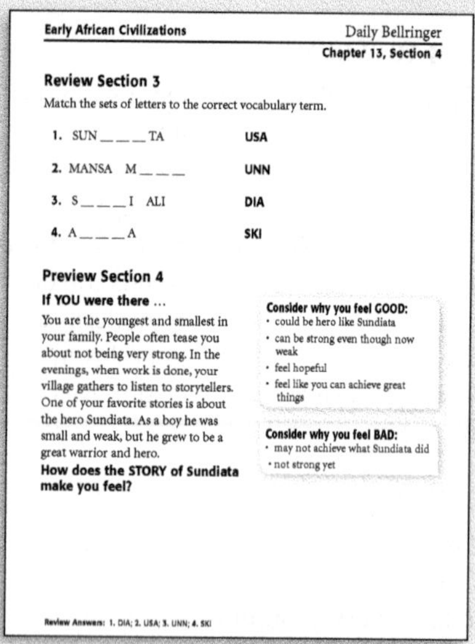

Early African Civilizations — Daily Bellringer

Chapter 13, Section 4

Review Section 3

Match the sets of letters to the correct vocabulary term.

1. SUN _ _ _ TA	USA
2. MANSA M _ _ _	UNN
3. S _ _ _ I ALI	DIA
4. A _ _ _ A	SKI

Preview Section 4

If YOU were there ...

You are the youngest and smallest in your family. People often tease you about not being very strong. In the evenings, when work is done, your village gathers to listen to storytellers. One of your favorite stories is about the hero Sundiata. As a boy he was small and weak, but he grew to be a great warrior and hero.

How does the STORY of Sundiata make you feel?

Consider why you feel GOOD:
- could be hero like Sundiata
- can be strong even though now weak
- feel hopeful
- feel like you can achieve great things

Consider why you feel BAD:
- may not achieve what Sundiata did
- not strong yet

Review Answers: 1. DIA; 2. USA; 3. UNN; 4. SKI

Building Vocabulary

Preteach or review the following term:

distorted twisted in meaning (p. 397)

CRF: Vocabulary Builder Activity, Section 4

Taking Notes

Have students use the graphic organizer online to take notes on the section. This activity will prepare students for the Section Assessment, in which they will complete a graphic organizer that builds on the information using the Critical Thinking Skill: Summarizing.

SECTION 4

Historical and Artistic Traditions

What You Will Learn...

Main Ideas

1. West Africans have preserved their history through storytelling and the written accounts of visitors.
2. Through art, music, and dance, West Africans have expressed their creativity and kept alive their cultural traditions.

The Big Idea

Although the people of West Africa did not have a written language, their culture has been passed down through oral history, writings by other people, and the arts.

Key Terms

oral history, *p. 396*
griots, *p. 396*
proverbs, *p. 397*
kente, *p. 399*

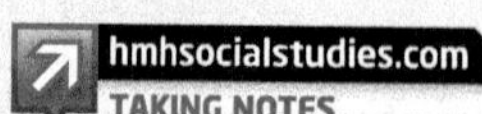

Use the graphic organizer online to take notes on West African historical and artistic traditions.

If YOU were there...

You are the youngest and smallest in your family. People often tease you about not being very strong. In the evenings, when work is done, your village gathers to listen to storytellers. One of your favorite stories is about the hero Sundiata. As a boy he was small and weak, but he grew to be a great warrior and hero.

How does the story of Sundiata make you feel?

BUILDING BACKGROUND Although trading empires rose and fell in West Africa, many traditions continued through the centuries. In every town and village, storytellers passed on the people's histories, legends, and wise sayings. These were at the heart of West Africa's arts and cultural traditions.

Preserving History

Writing was never very common in West Africa. In fact, none of the major early civilizations of West Africa developed a written language. Arabic was the only written language they used. The lack of a native written language does not mean that the people of West Africa didn't know their history, though. They passed along information through oral histories. An **oral history** is a spoken record of past events. The task of remembering and telling West Africa's history was entrusted to storytellers.

The Griots

The storytellers of early West Africa were called **griots** (GREE-ohz). They were highly respected in their communities because the people of West Africa were very interested in the deeds of their ancestors. Griots helped keep this history alive for each new generation.

Teach the Big Idea

At Level

Historical and Artistic Traditions

1. **Teach** Ask students the questions in the Main Idea boxes to teach this section.
2. **Apply** Have students create a two-column chart, labeling the columns *Historical Traditions* and *Artistic Traditions.* In one column, have students list how we have learned about West Africa's past. In the other column, have students identify art forms from West Africa. Then ask: What problems might result from keeping history only in oral form? *Facts might be forgotten or distorted.* What West African artistic traditions influence our world? *styles of music like jazz, blues, and rock; sculpture; and traditional dances.*
   LS Verbal/Linguistic
3. **Review** Have students exchange charts and discuss the answers to the questions.
4. **Practice/Homework** Have students create a collage that depicts the historical and artistic traditions of West Africa.
   LS Visual/Spatial

Alternative Assessment Handbook, Rubrics 8: Collages; and 13: Graphic Organizers

The griots' stories were both entertaining and informative. They told of important past events and of the accomplishments of distant ancestors. For example, some stories explained the rise and fall of the West African empires. Other stories described the actions of powerful kings and warriors. Some griots made their stories more lively by acting out the events like scenes in a play.

In addition to stories, the griots recited **proverbs**, or short sayings of wisdom or truth. They used proverbs to teach lessons to the people. For example, one West African proverb warns, "Talking doesn't fill the basket in the farm." This proverb reminds people that they must work to accomplish things. It is not enough for people just to talk about what they want to do.

In order to tell their stories and proverbs, the griots memorized hundreds of names and events. Through this memorization **process** the griots passed on West African history from generation to generation. However, some griots confused names and events in their heads. When this happened, the facts of some historical events became distorted. Still, the griots' stories tell us a great deal about life in the West African empires.

hmhsocialstudies.com
ANIMATED HISTORY
Modern Griots

West African Epics

Some of the griot poems are epics—long poems about kingdoms and heroes. Many of these epic poems are collected in the *Dausi* (DAW-zee) and the *Sundiata*.

The *Dausi* tells the history of Ghana. Intertwined with historical events, though, are myths and legends. One story is about a seven-headed snake god named Bida. This god promised that Ghana would prosper if the people sacrificed a young woman to him every year. One year a mighty warrior killed Bida. As the god died, he cursed Ghana. The griots say that this curse caused the empire of Ghana to fall.

The *Sundiata* is about Mali's great ruler. According to the epic, when Sundiata was still a boy, a conqueror captured Mali and killed Sundiata's father and 11 brothers.

ACADEMIC VOCABULARY
process a series of steps by which a task is accomplished

Oral Traditions
West African storytellers called griots had the job of remembering and passing on their people's history. Here, people gather to perform traditional dances and to listen to the stories of a griot.

397

Direct Teach

Main Idea

1 Preserving History

West Africans have preserved their history through storytelling and the written accounts of visitors.

Recall What are proverbs, and what are they intended to do? *short sayings of wisdom or truth; to teach a lesson or provide a warning*

Identify Name two West African epic poems and the subject of each. Dausi—*the history of Ghana; tells the story of the killing of the god, Bida, and of the decline of Ghana;* Sundiata—*tells the story of Mali's first great ruler; how Sundiata overthrew the ruler and became king*

Make Judgments Why do you think griots were so valued in West African society? *because their stories were both informative and entertaining*

Activity Epic Poem Illustrations Ask students to select a scene from one of the epic poems discussed in this section. Then have each student create an illustration that depicts that scene. **LS Visual/Spatial**

Linking to Today

Griots of Mali Griots are alive and active in Mali today. They still sing and tell stories in villages across the country. In fact, some wealthy nobles in modern Mali even employ their own personal griot to remind them of their family's past. Several griots have achieved international fame. Singers such as Salif Keita and Ali Farke Toure continue the griot tradition by touring the world and selling recordings of their music.

Differentiating Instruction

English-Language Learners **At Level**

1. Review with the class the use of oral histories in West Africa.
2. Organize the class into small groups of mixed-ability levels. Instruct group members to create oral histories that describe a story they know well. Each group should have a different story. To help students think of stories, suggest well-known stories like the first Thanksgiving, Christopher Columbus's voyage to the Americas, or an event from a recent unit of study.
3. Group members should discuss details of the story. Remind students that oral histories often try to teach a lesson. Encourage students to memorize their oral history and to try to use language that will entertain their listeners.
4. Have each group perform its oral history for the rest of the class. Encourage students to set their oral history to music, if they wish. **LS Auditory/Musical, Interpersonal**

Alternative Assessment Handbook, Rubrics 14: Group Activity; and 24: Oral Presentations

Direct Teach

Main Idea

1 Preserving History

West Africans have preserved their history through storytelling and the written accounts of visitors.

Explain How do we know the history of early West Africa if the people of West Africa left no written histories? *from oral histories and the writings of travelers and scholars from Muslim lands*

Identify What is included in Ibn Battutah's account of his journey to West Africa? *details of the political and cultural lives of West Africans*

CRF: Biography Activity, Leo Africanus

Linking to Today

Western pop music has influenced African music over the past several decades. Pop music, in particular, has become a part of modern African life. African musicians borrow ideas freely from Western music while adding their own unique sounds. The result of this blending process is called Afro-pop. This vibrant music, which one can hear everywhere in African cities, now influences Western pop artists in return.

LINKING TO TODAY

Music from Mali to Memphis

Did you know that the music you listen to today may have begun with the griots? From the 1600s to the 1800s, many people from West Africa were brought to America as slaves. In America, these slaves continued to sing the way they had in Africa. They also continued to play traditional instruments such as the *kora* played by Senegalese musician Soriba Kouyaté (right), the son of a griot. Over time, this music developed into a style called the blues, made popular by such artists as B.B. King (left). In turn, the blues shaped other styles of music, including jazz and rock. So, the next time you hear a Memphis blues track or a cool jazz tune, listen for its ancient African roots!

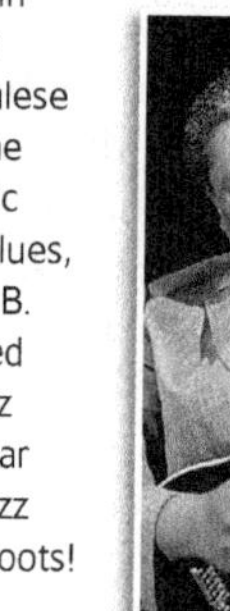

ANALYSIS SKILL ANALYZING INFORMATION

How did West African music affect modern American music?

He didn't kill Sundiata, however, because the boy was sick and didn't seem like a threat. But Sundiata grew up to be an expert warrior. Eventually he overthrew the conqueror and became king.

Visitors' Written Accounts

In addition to the oral histories told about West Africa, visitors wrote about the region. In fact, much of what we know about early West Africa comes from the writings of travelers and scholars from Muslim lands such as Spain and Arabia.

Ibn Battutah was the most famous Muslim visitor to write about West Africa. From 1353 to 1354 he traveled through the region. Ibn Battutah's account of this journey describes the political and cultural lives of West Africans in great detail.

READING CHECK **Drawing Conclusions** Why were oral traditions important in West Africa?

Art, Music, and Dance

Like most peoples, West Africans valued the arts. They expressed themselves creatively through sculpture, mask-making, cloth-making, music, and dance.

Sculpture

Of all the visual art forms, the sculpture of West Africa is probably the best known. West Africans made ornate statues and carvings out of wood, brass, clay, ivory, stone, and other materials.

Most statues from West Africa are of people—often the sculptor's ancestors. Usually these statues were made for religious rituals, to ask for the ancestors' blessings. Sculptors made other statues as gifts for the gods. These sculptures were kept in holy places. They were never meant to be seen by people.

Because their statues were used in religious rituals, many African artists were

Social Studies Skill: Analyzing Visuals

At Level

Art Appreciation

Research Required

1. Review with the class the importance of art to West African life. Ask students to recall the various artistic traditions of West Africa.
2. Ask students to think about pieces of art they may have seen in pictures or museums and what they may reveal about the artist's culture or heritage. To help students understand, show them a painting or sculpture with which they may be familiar.
3. Have students use the library, Internet, or other resources to research different types of African art. Have students select two images to analyze. Ask students to note any background information that gives clues about the artist's society, culture, or heritage.
4. Have students write a brief analysis for each image they select. They should explain how each artwork reflects the culture in which it was created. **LS Verbal/Linguistic, Visual/Spatial**

Answers

Analyzing Information *Over time, the musical traditions of Africans brought to the Americas by enslaved people have developed into new, modern styles.*

Reading Check *They were the only forms of recording or remembering West African history.*

deeply respected. People thought artists had been blessed by the gods.

Long after the decline of Ghana, Mali, and Songhai, West African art is still admired. Museums around the world display African art. In addition, African sculpture inspired some European artists of the 1900s, including Henri Matisse and Pablo Picasso.

Masks and Clothing

In addition to statues, the artists of West Africa carved elaborate masks. Made of wood, these masks bore the faces of animals such as hyenas, lions, monkeys, and antelopes. Artists often painted the masks after carving them. People wore the masks during rituals as they danced around fires. The way firelight reflected off the masks made them look fierce and lifelike.

Many African societies were famous for the cloth they wove. The most famous of these cloths is called kente (ken-TAY). **Kente** is a hand-woven, brightly colored fabric. The cloth was woven in narrow strips that were then sewn together. Kings and queens in West Africa wore garments made of kente for special occasions.

Music and Dance

In many West African societies, music and dance were as important as the visual arts. Singing, drumming, and dancing were great entertainment, but they also helped people honor their history and mark special occasions. For example, music was played when a ruler entered a room.

Dance has long been a central part of African society. Many West African cultures used dance to celebrate specific events or ceremonies. For example, they may have performed one dance for weddings and another for funerals. In some parts of West Africa, people still perform dances similar to those performed hundreds of years ago.

READING CHECK **Summarizing** Summarize how traditions were preserved in West Africa.

SUMMARY AND PREVIEW The societies of West Africa did not have written languages, but they preserved their histories and cultures through storytelling and the arts. You will next read about another place where traditions are important—China.

Section 4 Assessment

hmhsocialstudies.com ONLINE QUIZ

Reviewing Ideas, Terms, and People

1. a. **Define** What is **oral history**?
   b. **Make Generalizations** Why were **griots** and their stories important in West African society?
   c. **Evaluate** Why may an oral history provide different information than a written account of the same event?
2. a. **Identify** What were two forms of visual art popular in West Africa?
   b. **Make Inferences** Why do you think that the sculptures made as gifts for the gods were not meant to be seen by people?
   c. **Elaborate** What role did music and dance play in West African society?

Critical Thinking

3. **Summarizing** Use a chart like this one and your notes to summarize the importance of each tradition in West Africa.

Tradition	Importance
Storytelling	
Epics	
Sculpture	

Focus on Writing

4. **Reviewing West African Traditions** Review this section and your notes on the oral and written history of Western Africa and the art, music, and dance of the region. Think about how the griots, visitors from distant lands, or the arts may have affected your character.

Section 4 Assessment Answers

1. a. a spoken record of past events
   b. The griots helped keep history alive for each new generation.
   c. possible answer—because people sometimes confuse and embellish facts
2. a. sculpture, masks, cloth
   b. possible answer—Statues were personalized and holy gifts to the gods.
   c. Music and dance were used to honor and celebrate people and events.
3. griots—helped preserve history and traditions through oral history; epics—*Dausi* tells the history of Ghana and *Sundiata* tells the story of Mali's first great ruler; sculpture—has lasted through the ages and has influenced contemporary artists
4. Students' notes will vary, but should reflect knowledge of Western African oral and written history, art, music, and dance.

Direct Teach

Main Idea

2 Art, Music, and Dance

Through art, music, and dance, West Africans have expressed their creativity and kept alive their cultural traditions.

Identify What is the best known visual art form of West Africa? *sculpture*

Recall How were masks used in West African culture? *Dancers wore the masks during rituals.*

Analyze Why were singing and dancing so important in West Africa? *Besides being forms of entertainment, they were creative expressions and they helped people honor their history and most special occasions.*

Review & Assess

Close

Have students discuss the elements of historical and artistic traditions that have had a lasting effect on West Africa. Ask students to identify elements that still exist today.

Review

Online Quiz, Section 4

Assess

SE Section 4 Assessment

PASS: Section 4 Quiz

Alternative Assessment Handbook

Reteach/Classroom Intervention

Guided Reading Workbook, Section 4

Interactive Skills Tutor CD-ROM

Answers

Reading Check *through the arts, such as sculpture, the making of masks and cloth, music, and dance*

Social Studies Skills

Interpreting Political Maps

Activity **Comparing Maps** Display a modern political map of West Africa for students to see. A political map of the region is available in the Atlas in the back of the textbook. Have students compare the map to the one shown on this page. Then ask students to identify the modern countries that are located in the regions of Mali and Songhai at the different stages in their empire's growth. **LS Visual/Spatial**

- Alternative Assessment Handbook, Rubric 21: Map Reading
- Interactive Skills Tutor CD-ROM Lesson 6: Interpret Maps, Graphs, Charts, Visuals, and Political Cartoons

Social Studies Skills

Analysis | Critical Thinking | Economics | Study

Interpreting Political Maps

Understand the Skill

Many types of maps are useful in the study of history. *Physical maps* show natural features on Earth's surface. *Political maps* show human cultural features such as cities, states, and countries. Modern political maps show the present-day borders of states and countries. Historical political maps show what cultural features were in the past.

Some historical political maps show how boundaries and features changed over time. Being able to interpret such maps makes the growth and disintegration of countries and empires easier to visualize and understand.

Learn the Skill

Use these guidelines to interpret maps that show political change.

1. Read the title to find out what the map is about.
2. Read the legend. The map's title may state the time period covered by the map. However, in this type of map, information about dates is often found in the legend.
3. Study the legend carefully to be sure you understand what each color or symbol means. Pay special attention to colors or symbols that might indicate changes in borders, signs of the growth or loss of a country's territory.
4. Study the map itself. Compare the colors and symbols in the legend to those on the map. Note any labels, especially those that may show political change. Look for other indications of political changes on the map.

Practice and Apply the Skill

Interpret the map below to answer the following questions about the Mali and Songhai Empires.

1. Which empire was older? Which empire expanded the most?
2. Was Songhai ever part of the Mali Empire? Explain how the map provides this information.
3. Who controlled the city of Gao in the year 1100? in 1325? in 1515?
4. By what date do you know for sure that the Mali Empire had disintegrated? How do you know?

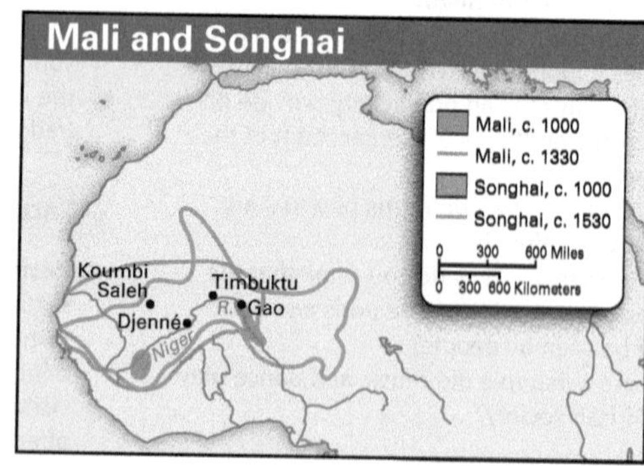

Social Studies: Interpreting Political Maps

Map of Ghana, Mali, and Songhai

At Level

Materials: outline maps of West Africa, color pencils or markers

1. Have students examine the map in Section 2 (p. 387) titled "Ghana Empire, c. 1050." A transparency of this map is also available.
2. Provide each student with an outline map of West Africa. Have each student make a map that shows the information in the map titled "Mali and Songhai" (p. 391) plus the region of the Ghana Empire, c. 1050.
3. Tell students to show each empire in a different color, as in the map on this page. In addition, remind students to include a map title, legend, and compass rose.
4. When students have completed their maps, have them discuss how adding Ghana helps them compare and contrast the locations and growth of the three West African empires. **LS Visual/Spatial**

- Alternative Assessment Handbook, Rubrics 20: Map Creation; and 21: Map Reading

Answers

Practice and Apply the Skill
1. *According to the map, both empires began about the same time; Songhai expanded the most.* **2.** *Yes, the borders of Mali in c. 1330 include the area indicated as Songhai at that time.* **3.** *Songhai; Mali, Songhai;* **4.** *by c. 1530, because at that time the borders of Songhai included much of what had been Mali*

CHAPTER 13 Chapter Review

History's Impact
▶ video series
Review the video to answer the focus question:
How did the salt trade influence the rise of Timbuktu?

Visual Summary

Use the visual summary below to help you review the main ideas of the chapter.

QUICK FACTS
The Ghana Empire developed in West Africa and controlled the trade of salt and gold.
Mali's kings built an empire and spread Islam in West Africa.
The Songhai Empire continued to spread Islam.
The history of West Africa has been preserved through story telling, visitors' accounts, art, music, and dance.

Reviewing Vocabulary, Terms, and People

Choose the letter of the answer that best completes each statement below.

1. An area near the equator that has many trees and heavy rainfall may be called a
a. tropical area. **c.** savannah.
b. rain forest. **d.** woodland.

2. The belief that natural objects have spirits is called
a. animism. **c.** animalism.
b. vegetism. **d.** naturalism.

3. Between the Sahara and the savannah lies the
a. rain forest. **c.** Zambezi.
b. inland delta. **d.** Sahel.

4. Mali's rise to power began under a ruler named
a. Tunka Manin. **c.** Ibn Battutah.
b. Sunni Ali. **d.** Sundiata.

5. A spoken record of the past is
a. a Soninke. **c.** a Gao.
b. an oral history. **d.** an age-set proverb.

6. A West African storyteller is
a. an Almoravid. **c.** an arquebus.
b. a griot. **d.** a rift.

7. The Muslim leader of Mali who supported education, spread Islam, and made a famous pilgrimage to Mecca was
a. Sunni Baru. **c.** Mansa Musa.
b. Askia the Great. **d.** Muhammad Ture.

8. A brightly colored fabric woven in many African societies is a
a. kente. **c.** Timbuktu.
b. mansa. **d.** Tuareg.

Answers

Visual Summary

Review and Inquiry Have students use the visual summary to explain the history of the three large empires of early West Africa and how we know about this history.

Quick Facts Transparency: Early African Civilizations Visual Summary

Reviewing Terms and People

1. b
2. a
3. d
4. d
5. b
6. b
7. c
8. a

Comprehension and Critical Thinking

9. a. Niger River
b. because people needed it to survive and to preserve food
c. possible answer—West African families would benefit by working together in farming, hunting, and everyday activities. Extended families would also be able to pass on knowledge, culture, and religious practices.

10. a. Gold from the south and salt from the Sahara in the north.
b. possible answers—because the traders might mine the gold for themselves; Ghana would lose its position of power and control.

Review and Assessment Resources

Review and Reinforce

- SE Chapter Review
- **CRF:** Chapter Review Activity
- Quick Facts Transparency: Early African Civilizations Visual Summary
- Spanish Chapter Summary Audio CD
- Online Chapter Summaries in Six Languages
- TOS Holt McDougal PuzzleView

Assess

- SE Chapter Standardized Test Practice
- PASS: Chapter Test
- Alternative Assessment Handbook
- TOS ExamView Assessment Suite, Chapter Test
- Differentiating Instruction Modified Material CD-ROM: Chapter Test
- Online Assessment Program, in the Interactive Student Edition

Reteach/Intervene

- Guided Reading Workbook
- Differentiating Instruction Teacher Management System: Lesson Plans for Differentiating Instruction
- Differentiating Instruction Modified Material CD-ROM
- Interactive Skills Tutor CD-ROM

hmhsocialstudies.com
Chapter Resources

Answers

c. possible answers: people of Ghana—they rebelled in about 1200, taking over, but also weakening Ghana, then invaders took over; outsiders—invaders called Almoravids attacked and weakened Ghana and overgrazed their lands.

11. a. Arabic became a major language; many mosques were built; schools were built to teach Muslims to read the Qur'an.

b. similar—Both were great rulers of Mali; both increased the wealth of the country. different—Mansa Musa was Muslim and he stressed Islam and the importance of learning; his death began the decline of the Mali empire. Sundiata was not Muslim; his rule marked the beginning of Mali's power.

c. warriors—The warriors or professional army kept the peace; traders—They helped keep the nation's economy strong.

12. a. history and the deeds of people's ancestors

b. Visitors, such as Ibn Battutah, give details in their writings about political and cultural lives of West Africans; unlike oral histories, writings are not open to changes over time.

c. possible answer—music and dance, which helped people celebrate their history and were central to many religious celebrations

Reviewing Themes

13. Religion did not play a major role in Ghana's society. Islam was present, but Muslims had limited influence. In Mali and Songhai, Islam was more influential. Many rulers were Muslim, and their religion shaped culture in their empires.

14. Iron technology improved farming, hunting, and fighting.

Reading Skills

15. cause-effect; Memorizing stories resulted in stories being passed on to future generations. Confusion caused some facts in the stories to become distorted.

Using the Internet

16. Go to hmhsocialstudies.com to access a rubric for this activity.

Social Studies Skills

17. Songhai

Focus on Writing

18. Rubric Students' journals should:

- be written from the perspective of an early African character.
- accurately reflect life in the time and place appropriate to their chosen characters.
- include vivid detail.
- employ proper spelling, grammar, and usage.

Alternative Assessment Handbook, Rubric 15: Journals

Comprehension and Critical Thinking

SECTION 1 *(pages 380–383)*

9. a. Identify Along what river did great civilizations develop in early West Africa?

b. Draw Conclusions Today salt is not nearly as valuable as gold. Why do you think salt was so important in West Africa?

c. Predict How might West Africans have benefited from living in extended families?

SECTION 2 *(pages 386–389)*

10. a. Identify What were the two major trade goods that made Ghana rich? Where did each come from?

b. Make Inferences Why did merchants in Ghana not want other traders to know where their gold came from?

c. Evaluate Who do you think was more responsible for the collapse of Ghana, the people of Ghana or outsiders? Why?

SECTION 3 *(pages 390–394)*

11. a. Describe How did Islam influence society in Mali?

b. Compare and Contrast How were Sundiata and Mansa Musa similar? How were they different?

c. Evaluate Which group do you think played a more important role in Songhai society, warriors or traders?

SECTION 4 *(pages 396–399)*

12. a. Recall What different types of information did griots pass on to their listeners?

b. Analyze Why are the writings of visitors to West Africa so important to our understanding of the region?

c. Evaluate Which of the various arts of West Africa do you think is most important? Why?

Reviewing Themes

13. Religion Compare the roles played by religion, specifically Islam, in the empires of Ghana, Mali, and Songhai.

14. Technology How did the development of iron technology affect life in West Africa?

Reading Skills 

15. Organization of Facts and Information *Read the paragraph below. What form of organization does the paragraph use? How can you tell?*

> In order to tell their stories and proverbs, the griots memorized hundreds of names and events. Through this memorization process the griots passed on West African history from generation to generation. However, some griots confused names and events in their heads. When this happened, the facts of some historical events became distorted. Still, the griots' stories tell us a great deal about life in the West African empires. *(p. 397)*

Using the Internet 

16. Activity: Writing a Proverb Does the early bird get the worm? If you go outside at sunrise to check, you missed the fact that this is a proverb that means "The one that gets there first can earn something good." Griots created many proverbs that expressed wisdom or truth. Through your online book, use the Internet resources to write three proverbs that might have been said by griots during the time of the great West African empires. Make sure your proverbs are written from the point of view of a West African person living during those centuries.

hmhsocialstudies.com

Social Studies Skills

Interpreting Maps *Look at the map on page 400. Then answer the following question.*

17. Which empire extended farther eastward?

Focus on Writing

18. Writing Your Journal Entry Review your notes and choose an imaginary character. You might choose, for example, a Berber caravan leader, someone who trades goods with a nearby village, or a griot. Then match that person with a place. Finally, write 5–6 sentences as your journal entry. Include details on what the character sees, feels, and does on a typical day.

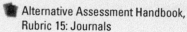

CHAPTER 13 Standardized Test Practice

DIRECTIONS: Read each question and write the letter of the best response.

> Well placed for the caravan trade, it was badly situated to defend itself from the Tuareg raiders of the Sahara. These restless nomads were repeatedly hammering at the gates of Timbuktu, and often enough they burst them open with disastrous results for the inhabitants. Life here was never quite safe enough to recommend it as the centre [center] of a big state.
>
> —Basil Davidson, from *A History of West Africa*

1 In this quote, the author is discussing why Timbuktu was

A a good place for universities.
B not a good place for a capital city.
C a good location for trade.
D not a good location for the center of the Tuareg state.

2 In the second sentence of the passage above, what does the phrase *hammering at the gates of Timbuktu* mean?

A driving nails into Timbuktu's gates
B knocking on the door to get into the city
C trying to get into and conquer the city
D making noise to anger the inhabitants

3 The region in Africa of open grasslands and scattered trees is the

A griot.
B Sahara.
C savannah.
D Sahel.

4 How were social groups defined in traditional West African cultures?

A by family and age-set
B by religion and family
C by age-set, family, and religion
D by extended family only

5 The two rulers who were most responsible for spreading Islam in West Africa were

A Sunni Ali and Mansa Musa.
B Sundiata and Sunni Ali.
C Ibn Battutah and Tunka Manin.
D Mansa Musa and Askia the Great.

Connecting with Past Learnings

6 You learned earlier about civilizations that developed along the Tigris and Euphrates rivers in what is now Iraq, and along the Huang He in ancient China. Such developments can be compared to changes along which river in West Africa?

A the Niger
B the Congo
C the Nile
D the Zambezi

7 Like Ghana, which East African kingdom that you learned about earlier grew rich from trade but eventually collapsed due to factors that included overgrazing and invasion?

A Sumer
B Kush
C Babylon
D Mohenjo Daro

Answers

Standardized Test Practice

1. B
Break Down the Question: Point out to students that the last sentence of the quote contains the answer.

2. C
Break Down the Question: Explain to students that the nomads were attacking the city gates.

3. C
Break Down the Question For students who missed the question, review the four climate and vegetation bands of West Africa in Section 1.

4. A
Break Down the Question For students who missed the question, point out that, although religion was important to village life, it did not define loyalties as family and age-sets did.

5. D
Break Down the Question: This question requires students to recall factual information from Section 3.

6. A
Break Down the Question This question requires students to recall information taught in Chapters 3 and 6. Some students may have selected the Nile, but point out that the question stipulates West Africa.

7. B
Break Down the Question: This question requires students to recall information taught in Chapter 4.

Intervention Resources

Reproducible

- Guided Reading Workbook
- Differentiating Instruction Teacher Management System: Differentiating Instruction Lesson Plans

Technology

- Quick Facts Transparency: Early African Civilizations Visual Summary
- Modified Material for Struggling Students CD-ROM
- Interactive Skills Tutor CD-ROM

Tips for Test Taking

Look All Around If the test item asks for vocabulary knowledge, look at the surrounding sentences, or context, to see which definition fits. To identify the best definition of an underlined word as it is used in the **context,** consider the surrounding words and phrases.

Preteach

Bellringer

Motivate Ask students to tell you about a book they have read or a movie they have seen recently. Once students have finished, point out that they did not tell you every detail about the book or movie. Instead, they summarized it, telling you only the most important or relevant details. Point out that summarizing is an important skill for historians, who do not want to overwhelm their readers with every detail about a period or topic. Tell students that in this workshop, they will write summaries of historical lessons.

Direct Teach

Choosing Details

Getting to the Good Parts Tell students that, in writing a summary, it is neither necessary nor desirable to include every detail of the original lesson. Instead, a writer should judge which details he or she believes to be most important to understanding the topic being discussed. The point of the summary is to help the reader remember what was discussed, and too many details can make a reader lose the point.

A Summary of a History Lesson

Assignment
Write a summary of one section in a chapter you read in Unit 6, "Islamic and African Civilizations."

After you read something, do you have trouble recalling what it was about? Many people do. Writing a summary briefly restating the main ideas and details of something you have read can help you remember it.

TIP How Long Is a Summary?
Here are some guidelines you can use to plan how much to write in a summary. If you are summarizing

- only a few paragraphs, your summary should be about one third as long as the original.
- longer selections such as an article or textbook chapter, write one sentence for each paragraph or heading in the original.

1. Prewrite

Reading to Understand

The first thing you need to do is to read the section at least twice.

- **Read** it straight through the first time to see what it is about.
- **Reread** it as many times as necessary to be sure you understand the main topic of the whole section.

Identifying the Main Idea

Next, identify the main idea in each paragraph or for each heading in the chapter. Look back at the facts, examples, quotations, and other information in each of them. Ask yourself, *What is the main idea that they all support, or refer to?* State this idea in your own words.

Noting Details

Note the information that directly and best supports each main idea. Often, several details and examples are given to support a single idea. Choose only those that are most important and provide the strongest support.

2. Write

As you write your summary, refer to the framework below to help you keep on track.

A Writer's Framework

Introduction
- Give the section number and title.
- State the main topic of the section.
- Introduce the first main heading in the section and begin your summary by identifying the main idea and supporting information under it.

Body
- Give the main idea, along with its most significant supporting details, for each heading in the section.
- Use words and phrases that show connections between ideas.
- Use your own words as much as you can, and limit quotations in number and length.

Conclusion
- Restate the main idea of the section.
- Comment on maps, charts, other visual content, or other features that were especially important or useful.

Differentiating Instruction

Special Needs Learners

Below Level **Standard English Mastery**

1. Assign one topic to an entire group of special needs learners. Have a classroom aide assist the students with their summarizing.
2. Provide students with printed copies of the lesson to highlight as they read. Have them cut out only the parts they will use, arrange the ideas in order, and tape them to another piece of paper. Students may use their organized notes as they write their articles.
LS **Visual/Spatial**

Struggling Readers

Below Level **Standard English Mastery**

1. Tell students that creating an outline can help them organize the material they wish to summarize. The main topics they include in their outline will become the main idea statements in their written summaries. Likewise, creating an outline can help determine which details are most important and therefore most necessary to include in the summary.
2. To help students save time, organize struggling readers into pairs so they can divide the reading tasks. LS **Verbal/Linguistic, Interpersonal**

3. Evaluate and Revise

Now you need to evaluate your summary to make sure that it is complete and accurate. The following questions can help you decide what to change.

Evaluation Questions for a Summary

- Does your introduction identify the number and title of the section and its main topic?
- Do you identify the main idea of the section?
- Do you include supporting details for each heading or paragraph in the section?
- Do you connect ideas and information by using words that show how they are related?
- Have you written the summary in your own words and limited the number and length of your quotations?
- Does your conclusion state the underlying meaning, or main idea, of the section?

TIP **Finding Main Ideas in a History Chapter** Boldfaced headings in textbooks usually tell what subject is discussed under those headings. The first and last sentences of paragraphs under headings can also be a quick guide to what is said about a subject.

4. Proofread and Publish

Proofreading

Be sure to enclose all quotations in quotation marks and to place other marks of punctuation correctly before or after closing quotation marks.

- **Commas** and **periods** go **inside** closing quotation marks.
- **Semicolons** and **dashes** go **outside** closing quotation marks.
- **Question marks** and **exclamation points** go **inside** closing quotation marks **when they are part of the quotation** and **outside when they are not**.

TIP **Using Special Historical Features** Don't forget to look at maps, charts, timelines, pictures, historical documents, and even study questions and assignments. They often contain important ideas and information.

Publishing

Team up with classmates who have written summaries on different sections of the same chapter you have. Review each other's summaries. Make sure the summaries include all the main ideas and most significant details in each section.

Collect all the summaries to create a chapter study guide for your team. If possible, make copies for everyone on the team. You may also want to make extra copies so that you can trade study guides with teams who worked on other chapters.

Practice and Apply

Use the steps and strategies outlined in this workshop to write a summary of one section of a chapter in this unit.

Reteach

Publishing

Creating a Classroom Summary

By assigning students a variety of topics from your lesson to summarize, you can create a classroom summary of the entire lesson to help students with their studies. Combine students' summaries into a single document that all students can print and review before a test or class discussion.

Teaching Tip

Sample Summaries

Ask local newspaper publishers if they donate newspaper subscriptions to schools or you can bring in your own Sunday paper on Mondays. Have students read articles to appreciate how reporters summarize local, national, and world events in relatively small passages of text. Ask students if they have specific interests, such as sports or the arts. Have these students read the sections that cover those areas.

Practice & Apply

Rubric

Students' summaries should

- include all major ideas from the lesson.
- exclude unnecessary detail.
- capture the intent and essence of the lesson as it was originally presented.
- use correct grammar, punctuation, spelling, and capitalization.

Advanced/Gifted and Talented

Above Level

1. Have students conduct research to learn more about a topic related to the contents of this chapter. Possible topics include Muslim expansion in Europe or Southeast Asia, the Bantu migrations in southern and central Africa, or the kingdoms of Shona and Kongo in East Africa. Tell students that they will summarize what they learn about these topics to create lessons for the rest of the class.
2. Have students write summaries of their research. Review these summaries for content and accuracy. Then have students present their summaries to the class as part of a daily lesson. Encourage students to use visual aids such as images and multimedia slides to help in their presentations. **LS Verbal/Linguistic**

Unit Preview

Introduce the Unit

Share the information in the chapter overviews with students.

Chapter 14 China's reunification helped establish it as a world power. The Tang and Song dynasties oversaw great cultural sophistication and the development of a complex system of government. The Mongol Ascendancy and Ming Dynasty pushed the borders of China as far as they would ever reach.

Chapter 15 Japanese life, based on family loyalty and various forms of Buddhism, culminated in a golden age of art and literature in the 900s. A complex military society developed in Japan that was notable for its social structure and warrior code of the samurai.

Chapter 16 In Mesoamerica, the Maya developed an advanced culture by AD 200. Maya civilization was characterized by great cities and trade, and impressive achievements in art, science, math, and writing. In what is now central Mexico, the Aztecs built a great empire through warfare and trade. The Aztecs' magnificent capital, Tenochtitlán, was built on an island and was one of the grandest cities in the world at the time. In South America, the Incas built a huge empire centered in the Andes Mountains. The Inca developed irrigation and terracing techniques as well as a large road system. Maya civilization declined for reasons which are not known, but the Aztecs and the Incas were both conquered by Spanish forces in the early 1500s.

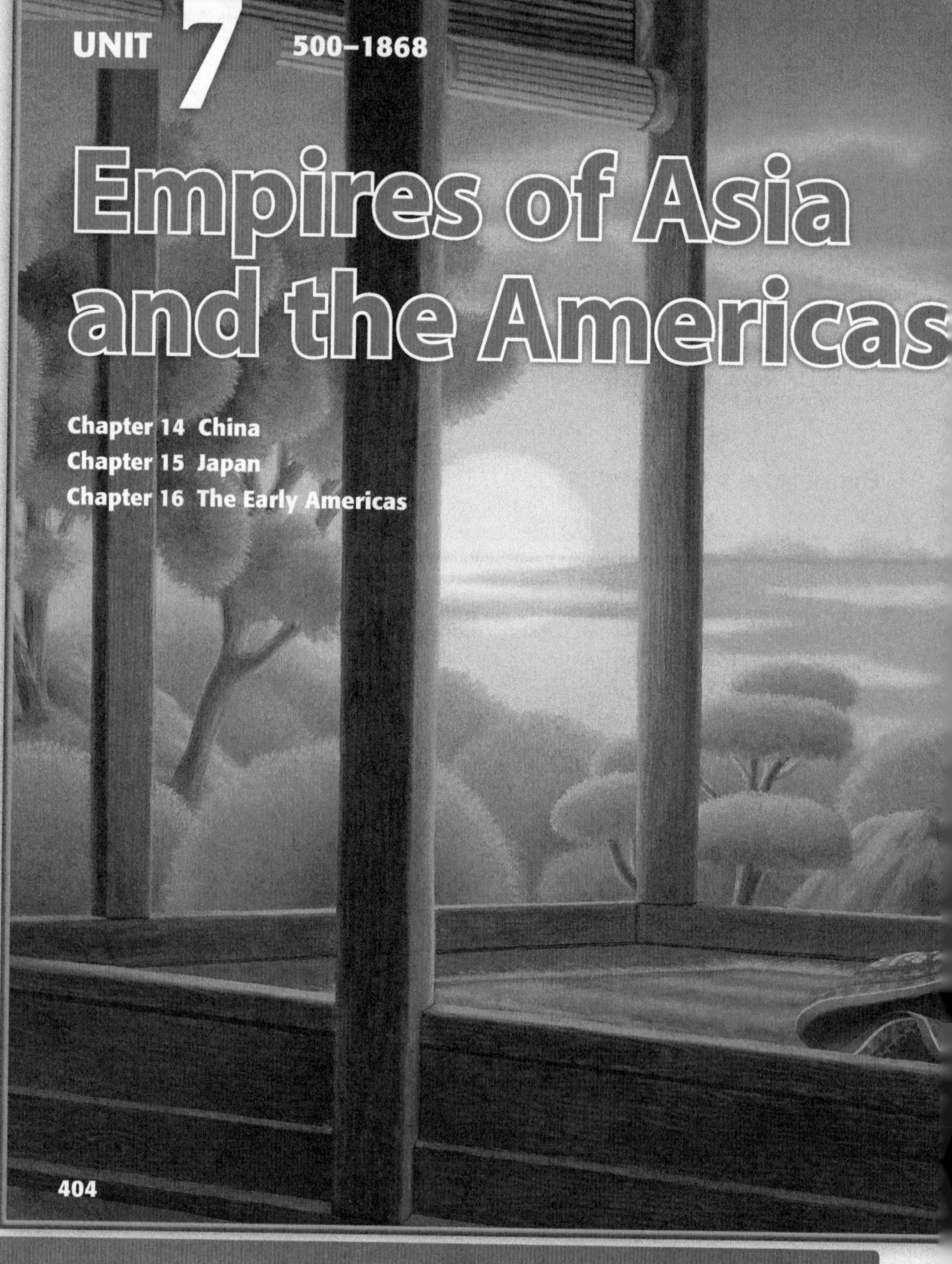

Unit Resources

Planning

- Differentiated Instruction Teacher Management System: Unit Instructional Benchmarking Guides
- TOS Calendar Planner
- Power Presentations with Media Gallery
- A Teacher's Guide to Religion in the Public Schools

Differentiating Instruction

- Differentiated Instruction Teacher Management System: Lesson Plans for Differentiated Instruction
- Differentiated Instruction Modified Worksheets and Tests CD-ROM

Enrichment

- **CRF 14:** Economics and History: The Origins of Paper Money
- **CRF 15:** Interdisciplinary Projects: China and Japan: Art Exhibition
- **CRF 16:** Economics and History: The Inca Economy
- **CRF 16:** Interdisciplinary Projects: Postcards from Mesoamerica; and The Maya: Web It
- Civic Participation Activities
- Primary Source Library CD-ROM

Assessment

- Progress Assessment System Solution: Unit Test
- TOS ExamView Assessment Suite: Unit Test
- Online Assessment Program, in the Interactive Student Edition
- Alternative Assessment Handbook

The **Differentiated Instruction Teacher Management System** provides a planning and instructional benchmarking guide for this unit.

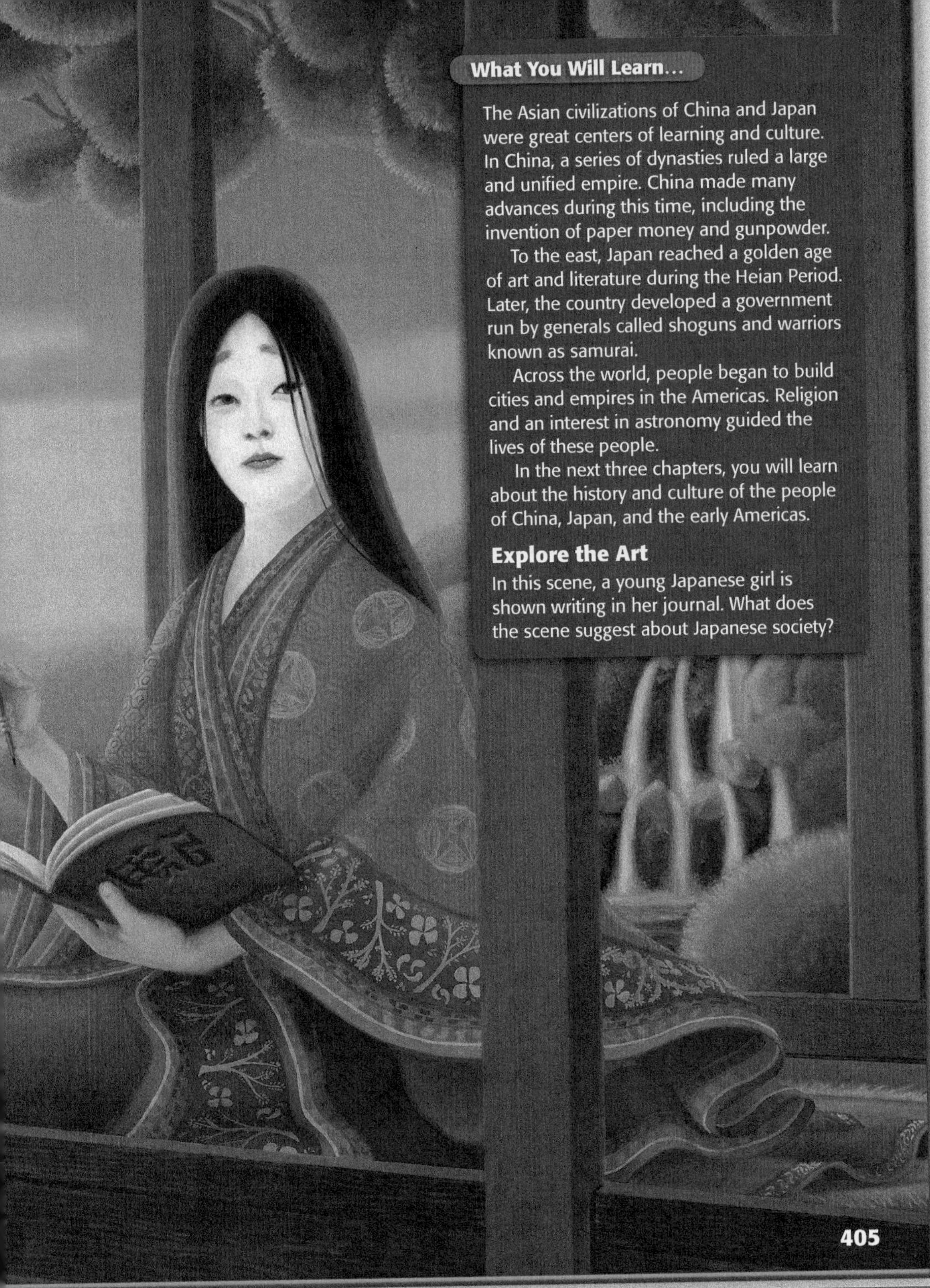

What You Will Learn...

The Asian civilizations of China and Japan were great centers of learning and culture. In China, a series of dynasties ruled a large and unified empire. China made many advances during this time, including the invention of paper money and gunpowder.

To the east, Japan reached a golden age of art and literature during the Heian Period. Later, the country developed a government run by generals called shoguns and warriors known as samurai.

Across the world, people began to build cities and empires in the Americas. Religion and an interest in astronomy guided the lives of these people.

In the next three chapters, you will learn about the history and culture of the people of China, Japan, and the early Americas.

Explore the Art

In this scene, a young Japanese girl is shown writing in her journal. What does the scene suggest about Japanese society?

405

Unit Preview

Connect to the Unit

Activity Comparing China and Japan Draw a Venn diagram for students to see and label the circles China and Japan. Challenge students to identify aspects of each modern culture. Explain to students that the cultures of ancient China and Japan have shaped both regions. At the end of the unit, have students review their answers in the Venn diagram. Then have them complete a second Venn diagram that compares and contrasts the periods of China and Japan covered in the unit. **LS Visual/Spatial**

Explore the Art

Asian art and writing of this period reflected many of the values of China and Japan. Many of these values can be seen in the Japanese painting at left. Ask: What are prominent elements of this painting? What do the foreground and the background have in common? What do you think the artist wants to express in this work? *possible answers—nature, beauty, harmony; order, harmony, peace; writing or learning, culture, and peace and harmony*

About the Illustration

This illustration is an artist's conception based on available sources. However, historians are uncertain exactly what this scene looked like.

Democracy and Civic Education

At Level

Responsibility: Recycling

Research Required

Background The Chinese invented paper in about 105. One of the greatest of all Chinese inventions, it gave them a cheap and easy way of keeping records and made printing possible. Today, we still rely on paper, and most people use it every day for many purposes. At the same time, the large amounts of paper we deal with contribute to the rising landfill problem.

1. Have students work either as a class or in small group to develop a recycling program for their school or, if one already exists, for another organization that does not have one.
2. Students should conduct research on the types of items that can be recycled, how they need to be contained and separated, what options are available for pickup of recycled materials, and the cost of various options.
3. Students should create a report presenting their plan. **LS Interpersonal, Verbal/Linguistic**

Alternative Assessment Handbook, Rubrics 14: Group Activity; 29: Presentations

Civic Participation Activities

Answers

Explore the Art *possible answer—Writing was important, and women knew how to write.*

Chapter 14 Planning Guide

China

Overview	Instructional Resources	
CHAPTER 14 **Essential Question:** How did China change after the fall of the Han dynasty? **Focus on the Essential Question Podcast**	TOS **Differentiated Instruction Teacher Management System:** • Instructional Benchmarking Guides • Lesson Plans for Differentiated Instruction **Guided Reading Workbook** **Chapter Resource File:** • Chapter Review Activity • Focus on Writing Activity: A Magazine Article • Social Studies Skills Activity: Analyzing Benefits and Costs	TOS **Calendar Planner** **Power Presentations with Media Gallery** **Differentiated Instruction Modified Worksheets and Tests CD-ROM** **Interactive Skills Tutor CD-ROM** **Student Edition on Audio CD Program** **The World's Music Audio Program** **Video:** Ming Dynasty Wall Building
Section 1: **China Reunifies** **The Big Idea:** The Period of Disunion was followed by reunification by rulers of the Sui, Tang, and Song dynasties.	TOS **Differentiated Instruction Teacher Management System:** Section 1 Lesson Plan **Guided Reading Workbook:** Section 1 **Chapter Resource File:** • Vocabulary Builder Activity, Section 1	**Daily Bellringer Transparency:** Section 1 **Map Transparency:** Chinese Dynasties, 589–1279 **Map Transparency:** Spread of Buddhism **Animated History:** Spread of Buddhism
Section 2: **Tang and Song Achievements** **The Big Idea:** The Tang and Song dynasties were periods of economic, cultural, and technological accomplishments.	TOS **Differentiated Instruction Teacher Management System:** Section 2 Lesson Plan **Guided Reading Workbook:** Section 2 **Chapter Resource File:** • Vocabulary Builder Activity, Section 2 • Economics and History Activity: The Origins of Paper Money	**Daily Bellringer Transparency:** Section 2 **Quick Facts Transparency:** Chinese Inventions
Section 3: **Confucianism and Government** **The Big Idea:** Confucian thought influenced the Song government.	TOS **Differentiated Instruction Teacher Management System:** Section 3 Lesson Plan **Guided Reading Workbook:** Section 3 **Chapter Resource File:** • Vocabulary Builder Activity, Section 3	**Daily Bellringer Transparency:** Section 3 **Internet Activity:** Confucianism
Section 4: **The Yuan and Ming Dynasties** **The Big Idea:** The Chinese were ruled by foreigners during the Yuan dynasty, but they threw off Mongol rule and prospered during the Ming dynasty.	TOS **Differentiated Instruction Teacher Management System:** Section 4 Lesson Plan **Guided Reading Workbook:** Section 4 **Chapter Resource File:** • Vocabulary Builder Activity, Section 4 • Biography Activity: Genghis Khan • History and Geography Activity: The Mongol Empire • Primary Source Activity: A Mongol Oath to Genghis Khan	**Daily Bellringer Transparency:** Section 4 **Map Transparency:** Mongol Empire, 1294 **Internet Activity:** Marco Polo **Animated History:** The Voyages of Zheng He **Animated History:** The Forbidden City **Animated History:** The Great Wall of China **Video:** Genghis Khan: Terror and Conquest

Chart Key:

SE Student Edition

Presentation Resource

MP3 Audio
TOS Teacher One Stop
DVD/CD-ROM
HISTORY™
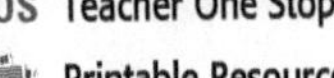
Printable Resource

Program Resources available on TOS and @ 

Review, Assessment, Intervention

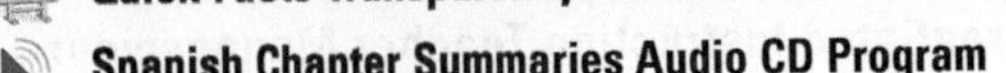

- **Quick Facts Transparency:** China Visual Summary
- **Spanish Chapter Summaries Audio CD Program**
- **Quiz Game CD-ROM**
- **Progress Assessment Support System (PASS):** Chapter Test
- **Differentiated Instruction Modified Worksheets and Tests CD-ROM:** Modified Chapter Test
- TOS **ExamView® Assessment Suite (English/Spanish)**
- **Online Assessment Program,** in the Interactive Student Edition

---

- **PASS:** Section 1 Quiz
- **Online Quiz:** Section 1
- **Alternative Assessment Handbook**

- **PASS:** Section 2 Quiz
- **Online Quiz:** Section 2
- **Alternative Assessment Handbook**

- **PASS:** Section 3 Quiz
- **Online Quiz:** Section 3
- **Alternative Assessment Handbook**

- **PASS:** Section 4 Quiz
- **Online Quiz:** Section 4
- **Alternative Assessment Handbook**

Supporting Resources

- Multimedia Classroom Global History Series
- Global History Teacher's Guide

Maps Globes Graphs Level F

- Student Workbook
- Teacher's Guide

Social Studies Trade Library Collections

- Premier Secondary World History Trade Collection
- Pacific Rim Trade Collection

History's Impact

World History Video Program

- **Chinese Achievements and World History**

For more information or to purchase go to 

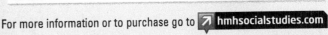

Power Presentations with Media Gallery

Power Presentations with Media Gallery are visual presentations of each chapter's main ideas. Presentations can be customized by including Quick Facts charts, images from the text, and video clips.

Differentiating Instruction

How do I address the needs of varied learners?

The Target Resource acts as your primary strategy for differentiated instruction.

ENGLISH-LANGUAGE LEARNERS & STRUGGLING READERS

Interactive Skills Tutor CD-ROM

The interactive Skills tutor CD-ROM contains lessons that provide additional practice for 20 different critical thinking skills.

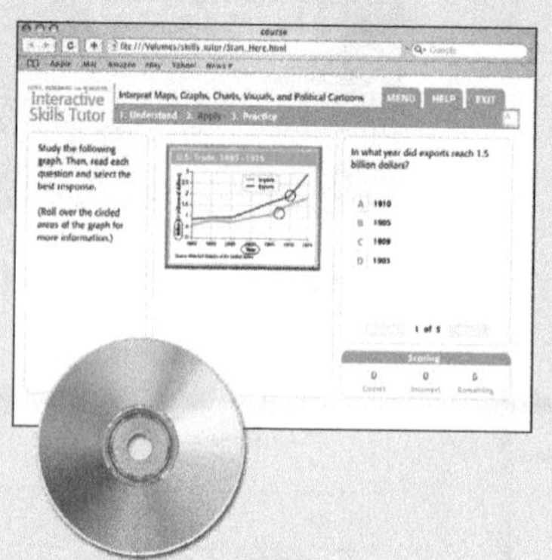

Additional Resources

Differentiated Instruction Teacher Management System: Lesson Plans for Differentiated Instruction

Teacher Management System: Lesson Plans for Differentiated Instruction

Chapter Resource File:

- Vocabulary Builder Activities
- Social Studies Skills Activity: Analyzing Benefits and Costs

Quick Facts Transparencies:

- Chinese Inventions
- China Visual Summary

Student Edition on Audio CD Program

Spanish/English Guided Reading Workbook

SPECIAL NEEDS LEARNERS

Differentiated Instruction Modified Worksheets and Tests CD-ROM

- Vocabulary Flash Cards
- Vocabulary Builder Activities
- Chapter Review Activity
- Chapter Test

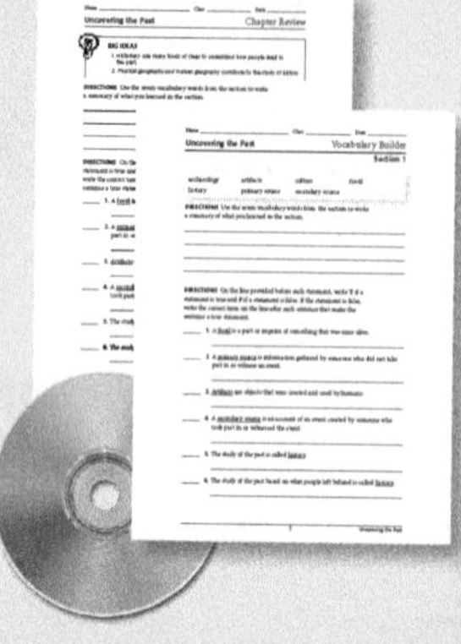

Additional Resources

Differentiated Instruction Teacher Management System: Lesson Plans for Differentiated Instruction

Guided Reading Workbook

Chapter Resource File: Social Studies Skills Activity: Analyzing Benefits and Costs

Student Edition on Audio CD Program

Interactive Skills Tutor CD-ROM

ADVANCED/GIFTED-AND-TALENTED STUDENTS

Primary Source Library CD-ROM for World History

The Library contains longer versions of quotations in the text, extra sources, and images. Included are point-of-view articles, journals, diaries, historical fiction, and political documents.

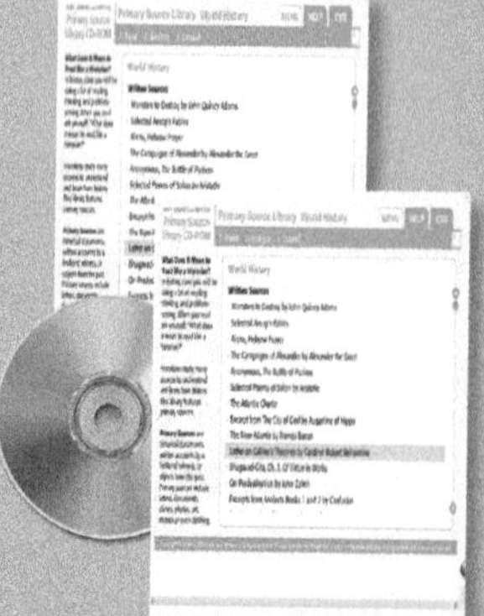

Additional Resources

Differentiated Instruction Teacher Management System: Lesson Plans for Differentiated Instruction

Chapter Resource File:

- Focus on Writing Activity: A Magazine Article
- Literature Activity: Poems from the Tang and Song Dynasties

Document-Based Questions Activities

Differentiated Activities in the Teacher's Edition

- Buddhism Time Line, p. 412
- Illustrating Terms, p. 422

Teacher One Stop™

How can I manage the lesson plans and support materials for differentiated instruction?

With the Teacher One Stop, you can easily organize and print lesson plans, planning guides, and instructional materials for all learners. The Teacher One Stop includes the following materials to help you differentiate instruction:

- Interactive Teacher's Edition
- Calendar Planner and pacing guides
- Editable lesson plans
- All reproducible ancillaries in Adobe Acrobat (PDF) format
- ExamView Assessment Suite (English & Spanish)
- Transparency and video previews

Differentiated Activities in the Teacher's Edition

- Writing a Captain's Log, p. 416
- Summarizing Information, p. 422

Interactive Student Edition

Complete online student edition with interactive multimedia support for chapter content assessment and reporting

- Interactive Maps and Notebook
- Graphic Organizers
- Standardized Test Prep
- Online Homework Practice and Research Activities
- Current Events
- Chapter-based Internet Activities
- Animated History Activities
- and more!

Differentiated Activities in the Teacher's Edition

- Imperial Report Cards, p. 411
- Writing Poems, p. 417

• Chapter Preview •

Essential Question

Introduce the Essential Question

- Point out that after the Han Dynasty fell, China had many years of unrest.
- Explain that eventually the Chinese regained control of the land and experienced a period of brilliant achievements.
- Point out that control of China changed hands several times before the rule of dynasties finally ended.

Focus on Writing

The **Chapter Resource File** provides a Focus on Writing work sheet to help students organize and write their magazine articles.

CRF: Focus on Writing Activity: A Magazine Article

Key to Differentiating Instruction

Below Level

Basic-level activities designed for all students encountering new material

At Level

Intermediate-level activities designed for average students

Above Level

Challenging activities designed for honors and gifted and talented students

Standard English Mastery

Activities designed to improve standard English usage

LS Learning Styles

CHAPTER 14 589–1644

China

Essential Question How did China change after the fall of the Han dynasty?

South Carolina Performance Standards

6-1.4 Explain the origins, fundamental beliefs, and spread of Eastern religions, including Hinduism (India), Judaism (Mesopotamia), Buddhism (India), and Confucianism and Taoism (China); **6-3.1** Summarize the major contributions of the Chinese civilization from the Qin dynasty through the Ming dynasty, including the golden age of art and literature, the invention of gunpowder and woodblock printing, and the rise of trade via the Silk Road.

Literacy Skills for Social Studies

- Explain change and continuity over time and across cultures.
- Identify and explain the relationships among multiple causes and multiple effects.
- Interpret Earth's physical and human systems by using maps, mental maps, geographic models, and other social studies resources.
- Examine the costs and benefits of economic choices made by a particular society and explain how those choices affect overall economic well-being.

Partnership for the 21st Century Skills

Articulate his or her own thoughts and ideas and those of others objectively through speaking and writing.

Focus on Writing

A Magazine Article In this chapter you will read about a great period in the history of China. You will learn about many important accomplishments made during this period, and then you will write a magazine article about them. The purpose of the article will be to explain Chinese contributions to world society.

Chapter Events

589 China is reunified under the Sui dynasty.

600

World Events

613 Muhammad begins teaching the basic beliefs of Islam.

Introduce the Chapter

At Level

Chinese Inventions

1. Write the list of the following items for students to see: *paper, fireworks, compass, paper money, gunpowder.* Ask students to discuss the importance of each item and how each has affected our world.
2. Point out to students that the Chinese developed each of these items, all of which are still used today. Discuss with students why they think that one civilization was responsible for these important developments. What might have led to such technological accomplishments?
3. Explain to students that in this chapter they will be learning about the Chinese dynasties of the Sui, Tang, Song, Yuan, and Ming. Point out that these were important dynasties in the history of China. **LS Verbal/Linguistic**

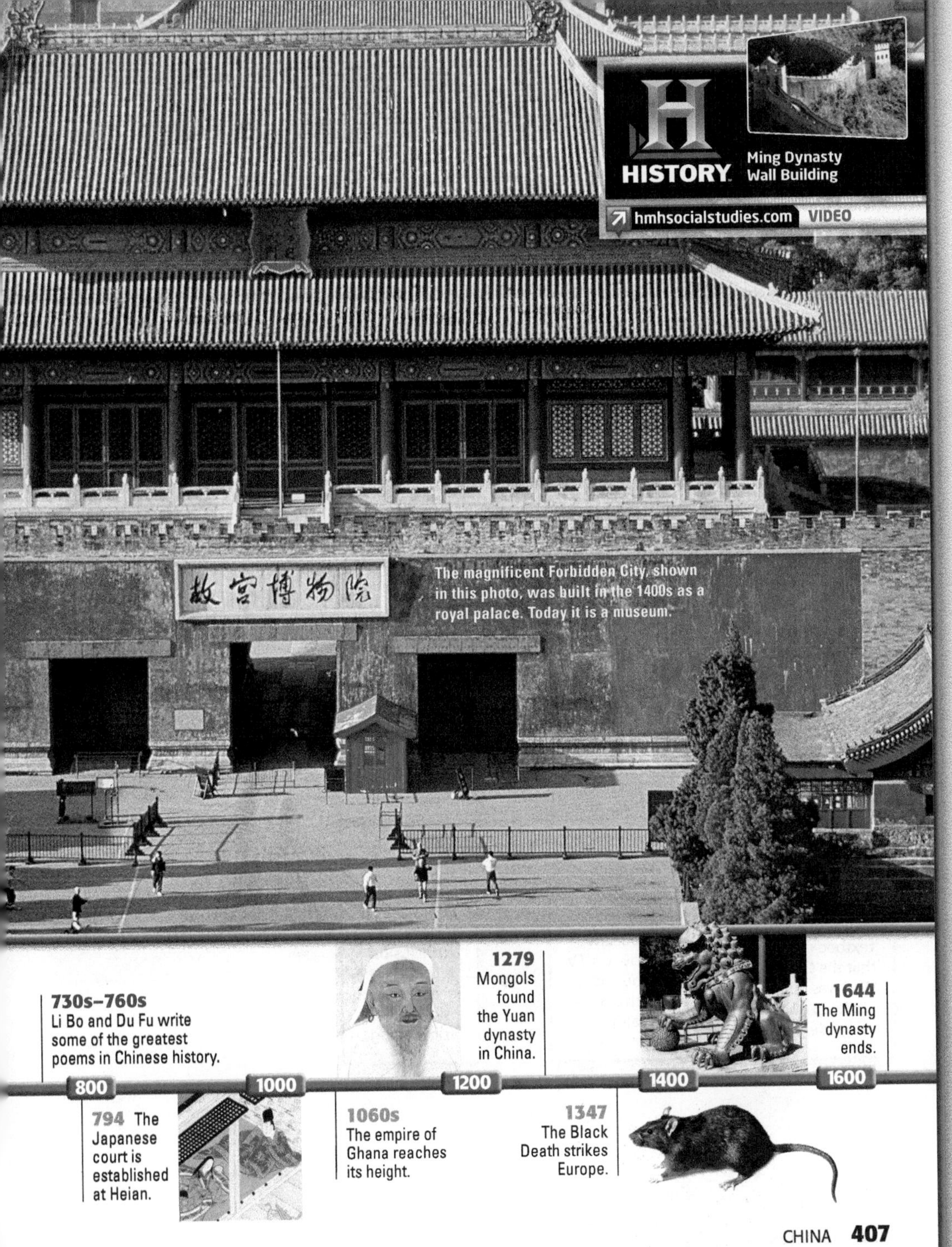
HISTORY
Ming Dynasty Wall Building
hmhsocialstudies.com VIDEO
故宫博物院
730s–760s Li Bo and Du Fu write some of the greatest poems in Chinese history.
1279 Mongols found the Yuan dynasty in China.
1644 The Ming dynasty ends.
800
1000
1200
1400
1600
794 The Japanese court is established at Heian.
1060s The empire of Ghana reaches its height.
1347 The Black Death strikes Europe.
CHINA 407
The magnificent Forbidden City, shown in this photo, was built in the 1400s as a royal palace. Today it is a museum.

• Chapter Preview •

Explore the Picture

The Forbidden City This photo shows China's famous Forbidden City. Not an actual city, this huge compound is the site of the imperial palaces of China's emperors from the 1400s until the early 1900s. Located in the city of Beijing, the Forbidden City is surrounded by 35-foot-high walls and was off-limits to anyone but members of the royal household. Since 1925, the Forbidden City has served as China's Palace Museum.

Analyzing Visuals What does the photograph of the Forbidden City indicate about how royalty were treated? *The huge structure indicates that royalty were treated well and were isolated from commoners.*

hmhsocialstudies.com
Teacher Resources

Explore the Time Line

1. Which dynasty unified China in 589? *Sui dynasty*
2. When was the Yuan Dynasty founded, and by whom? *1279; Mongols*
3. How many years passed from the beginning of the Yuan dynasty to the end of the Ming dynasty? *365 years*
4. What was happening elsewhere in the world at the time of the Sui dynasty's reunification of China? *Muhammad began teaching Islam.*

Did you know . . .

Statues of lions, such as the one shown above, were once a common feature of Chinese architecture. Made of stone or bronze, statues of lions were used to flank gates or buildings. Oftentimes two lion statues, one male and one female, were used to guard the entrance to homes of the wealthy or powerful. According to legend, these lions were capable of warding off evil spirits or danger.

Reading Social Studies

Understanding Themes

Introduce the themes of this chapter to the class by asking students to consider what they already know about Chinese history. Then write the labels *Economics* and *Science and Technology* for students to see. Ask the class to use their knowledge about China to make predictions about economics and science and technology. Students may require some hints. Tell them that China led seven trade expeditions into Africa, the Middle East, and Southeast Asia. Ask students how those voyages might have affected economics. Then ask students what science and technology the Chinese would have needed to make those voyages.

Drawing Conclusions about the Past

Focus on Reading Write the following for the class to see: *A nutritious breakfast is a healthy way to start the day* and *Getting plenty of sleep is important for mental and physical health.* Have students copy these sentences and instruct them to combine each fact with one or two observations from their own life. Then, from the information they have written, ask students to draw conclusions. Ask for volunteers to share their conclusions with the class. A possible conclusion might be: proper nutrition and rest are important to good health.

Reading Social Studies

Economics | Geography | Politics | Religion | Society and Culture | Science and Technology

Focus on Themes This chapter will explore the history of China from the late 500s until the 1600s. As you read, you will discover that many different dynasties ruled the country during that period, leading to great political changes. Some of those dynasties supported trade, leading to great **economic** growth and stability. Others favored isolation, limiting Chinese contact with the rest of the world. You will also learn that this period saw huge leaps forward in **science and technology**.

Drawing Conclusions about the Past

Focus on Reading You have no doubt heard the phrase, "Put two and two together." When people say that, they don't mean "two + two = four." They mean, "Put the information together."

Using Background Knowledge to Draw Conclusions A **conclusion** is a judgment you make by combining information. You put information from what you are reading together with what you already know, your background knowledge.

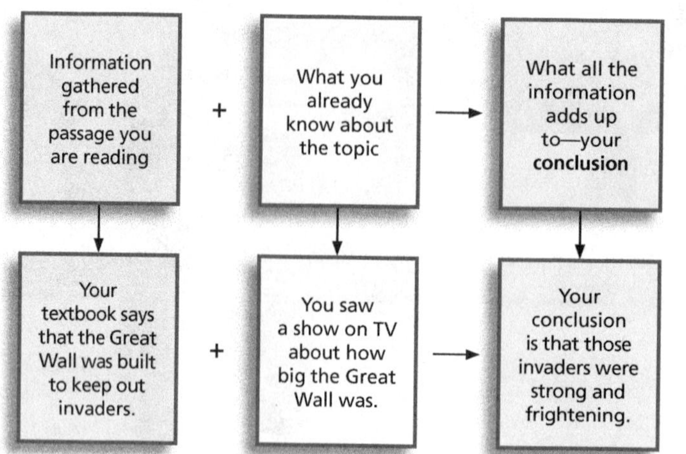

Steps for Drawing Conclusions

1. Read the passage, looking for information the author gives you about the topic.
2. Think about what you already know about the topic. Consider things you've studied, books you've read, or movies you've seen.
3. Put your background knowledge together with what the passage says.

Reading and Skills Resources

Reading Support

- Guided Reading Workbook
- Student Edition on Audio CD
- Spanish Chapter Summaries Audio CD Program

Social Studies Skills Support

- Interactive Skills Tutor CD-ROM

Vocabulary Support

- **CRF:** Vocabulary Builder Activities
- **CRF:** Chapter Review Activity
- Differentiated Instruction Modified Worksheets and Tests CD-ROM:
  - Vocabulary Flash Cards
  - Vocabulary Builder Activity
  - Chapter Review Activity
- TOS Holt McDougal PuzzleView

You Try It!

The following passage is from the chapter you are getting ready to read. As you read the passage, look for facts about China.

Advances in Agriculture

From Chapter 14, p. 414

Chinese civilization had always been based on agriculture. Over thousands of years, the Chinese had become expert farmers. In the north farmers grew wheat, barley, and other grains. In the warmer and wetter south they grew rice.

During the Song dynasty, though, Chinese farming reached new heights. The improvement was largely due to new irrigation techniques. For example, some farmers dug underground wells. A new irrigation device, the dragon backbone pump, allowed one person to do the work of several. With this light and portable pump, a farmer could scoop up water and pour it into an irrigation canal. Using these new techniques, farmers created elaborate irrigation systems.

After you have finished the passage, answer the questions below, drawing conclusions about what you have read.

1. Think back on what you've learned about irrigation systems in other societies. What do you think irrigation was like in China before the Song dynasty?
2. What effect do you think this improved irrigation had on Chinese society? Why do you think this?
3. Based on this passage, what kinds of conditions do you think rice needs to grow? How does this compare to the conditions wheat needs?
4. Which crop was most likely grown near the Great Wall—wheat or rice? Why do you think so?

Key Terms and People

Chapter 14

Section 1
Period of Disunion *(p. 410)*
Grand Canal *(p. 411)*
Empress Wu *(p. 412)*

Section 2
porcelain *(p. 417)*
woodblock printing *(p. 418)*
gunpowder *(p. 418)*
compass *(p. 418)*

Section 3
bureaucracy *(p. 422)*
civil service *(p. 422)*
scholar-official *(p. 422)*

Section 4
Genghis Khan *(p. 424)*
Kublai Khan *(p. 425)*
Zheng He *(p. 427)*
isolationism *(p. 430)*

Academic Vocabulary

Success in school is related to knowing academic vocabulary—the words that are frequently used in school assignments and discussions. In this chapter, you will learn the following academic words:

function *(p. 421)*
incentive *(p. 422)*
consequences *(p. 430)*

As you read Chapter 14, think about what you already know about China and draw conclusions to fill gaps in what you are reading.

Reading Social Studies

Key Terms and People

Challenge students to create a matching game using the key terms and people from this chapter. Organize the class into pairs then assign each pair a term or person from the list. Have each group write a description or definition for their term on one index card and the word or name on a separate index card. Collect all the index cards and place them in a basket. Have each student draw a card from the basket. Then have students try to find the person whose word or name matches the description on their card. Challenge the students even more by not allowing any talking while they match terms and descriptions!
LS Interpersonal, Verbal/Linguistic

Focus on Reading

See the **Focus on Reading** questions in this chapter for more practice on this reading social studies skill.

Reading Social Studies Assessment

See the **Chapter Review** at the end of this chapter for student assessment questions related to this reading skill.

Teaching Tip

Sometimes students will have to draw conclusions to fill in small gaps in the text. Authors don't provide every detail about their subject. They assume readers can draw conclusions to fill in some minor details. Remind students to look at the labels of questions carefully. When they see a label that says *Draw Conclusions,* students should use facts from the text and their own knowledge to draw a logical conclusion. Help students practice this skill by asking them questions that require them to draw on their own knowledge.

Answers

You Try It! 1. *They may have carried water or dug canals to move water from rivers to fields.* **2.** *it may have led to more crops, which in turn led to population growth; irrigation makes it possible to have higher crop yields, more crops allow people to live longer, healthier lives, thus leading to population growth.* **3.** *warm, wet conditions; wheat needs cooler, drier climates;* **4.** *wheat; because the Great Wall is in the north.*

Preteach

Bellringer

If YOU were there . . . Use the **Daily Bellringer Transparency** to help students answer the question.

Daily Bellringer Transparency, Section 1

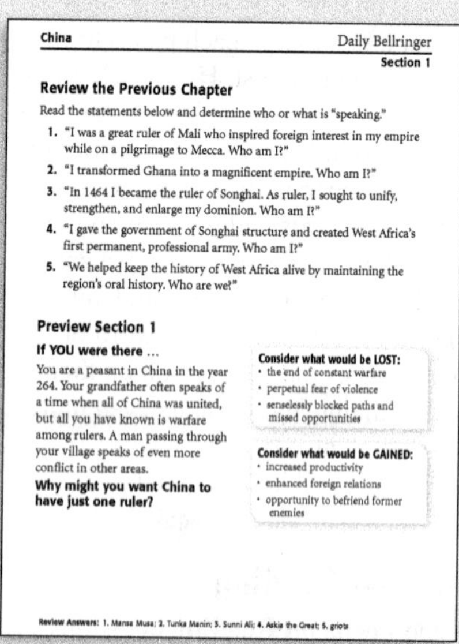

China — Daily Bellringer — Section 1

Review the Previous Chapter

Read the statements below and determine who or what is "speaking."

1. "I was a great ruler of Mali who inspired foreign interest in my empire while on a pilgrimage to Mecca. Who am I?"
2. "I transformed Ghana into a magnificent empire. Who am I?"
3. "In 1464 I became the ruler of Songhai. As ruler, I sought to unify, strengthen, and enlarge my dominion. Who am I?"
4. "I gave the government of Songhai structure and created West Africa's first permanent, professional army. Who am I?"
5. "We helped keep the history of West Africa alive by maintaining the region's oral history. Who are we?"

Preview Section 1

If YOU were there ...

You are a peasant in China in the year 264. Your grandfather often speaks of a time when all of China was united, but all you have known is warfare among rulers. A man passing through your village speaks of even more conflict in other areas.

Why might you want China to have just one ruler?

Consider what would be LOST:
- the end of constant warfare
- perpetual fear of violence
- senselessly blocked paths and missed opportunities

Consider what would be GAINED:
- increased productivity
- enhanced foreign relations
- opportunity to befriend former enemies

Review Answers: 1. Mansa Musa; 2. Tunka Manin; 3. Sunni Ali; 4. Askia the Great; 5. griots

Building Vocabulary

Preteach or review the following terms:

golden age a period of wealth or great achievement (p. 411)

reform to change for the better (p. 411)

CRF: Vocabulary Builder Activity, Section 1

Taking Notes

Have students use the graphic organizer online to take notes on the section. This activity will prepare students for the Section Assessment, in which they will complete a graphic organizer that builds on the information using the Critical Thinking Skill: Sequencing.

SECTION 1

China Reunifies

What You Will Learn...

Main Ideas

1. The Period of Disunion was a time of war and disorder that followed the end of the Han dynasty.
2. China was reunified under the Sui, Tang, and Song dynasties.
3. The Age of Buddhism saw major religious changes in China.

The Big Idea

The Period of Disunion was followed by reunification by rulers of the Sui, Tang, and Song dynasties.

Key Terms and People

Period of Disunion, *p. 410*
Grand Canal, *p. 411*
Empress Wu, *p. 412*

hmhsocialstudies.com
TAKING NOTES

Use the graphic organizer online to take notes about important dates and events in China during the dynasties following the Period of Disunion.

If YOU were there...

You are a peasant in China in the year 264. Your grandfather often speaks of a time when all of China was united, but all you have known is warfare among rulers. A man passing through your village speaks of even more conflict in other areas.

Why might you want China to have just one ruler?

BUILDING BACKGROUND Most of China's history is divided into dynasties. The first dynasties ruled China for centuries. But when the Han dynasty collapsed in 220, China plunged into disorder.

The Period of Disunion

When the Han dynasty collapsed, China split into several rival kingdoms, each ruled by military leaders. Historians sometimes call the time of disorder that followed the collapse of the Han the **Period of Disunion**. It lasted from 220 to 589.

Although war was common during the Period of Disunion, peaceful developments also took place at the same time. During this period, nomadic peoples settled in northern China. Some Chinese people adopted the nomads' culture, while the invaders adopted some Chinese practices. For example, one former nomadic ruler ordered his people to adopt Chinese names, speak Chinese, and dress like the Chinese. Thus, the culture of the invaders and traditional Chinese mixed.

A similar cultural blending took place in southern China. Many northern Chinese, unwilling to live under the rule of the nomadic invaders, fled to southern China. There, northern Chinese culture mixed with the more southern cultures.

As a result of this mixing, Chinese culture changed. New types of art and music developed. New foods and clothing styles became popular. The new culture spread over a wider geographic area than ever before, and more people became Chinese.

READING CHECK **Finding Main Ideas** How did Chinese culture change during the Period of Disunion?

Teach the Big Idea

At Level

China Reunifies

1. **Teach** Ask students the questions in the Main Idea boxes to teach this section.
2. **Apply** After students have reviewed the section, have each student write two questions for each main idea. Have students write their questions on note cards, one question per card. Ask students to write the answer and the number of the main idea on the back of the card. **LS Verbal/Linguistic**
3. **Review** As a review, conduct a game show by dividing the class into teams and using the students' note cards to ask each team questions. Assign points to the questions based on difficulty. You might reward the winning team with a prize.
4. **Practice/Homework** Have students use the section headings and the questions and answers on their note cards to create outlines of the section. **LS Verbal/Linguistic**

Alternative Assessment Handbook, Rubric 37: Writing Assignments

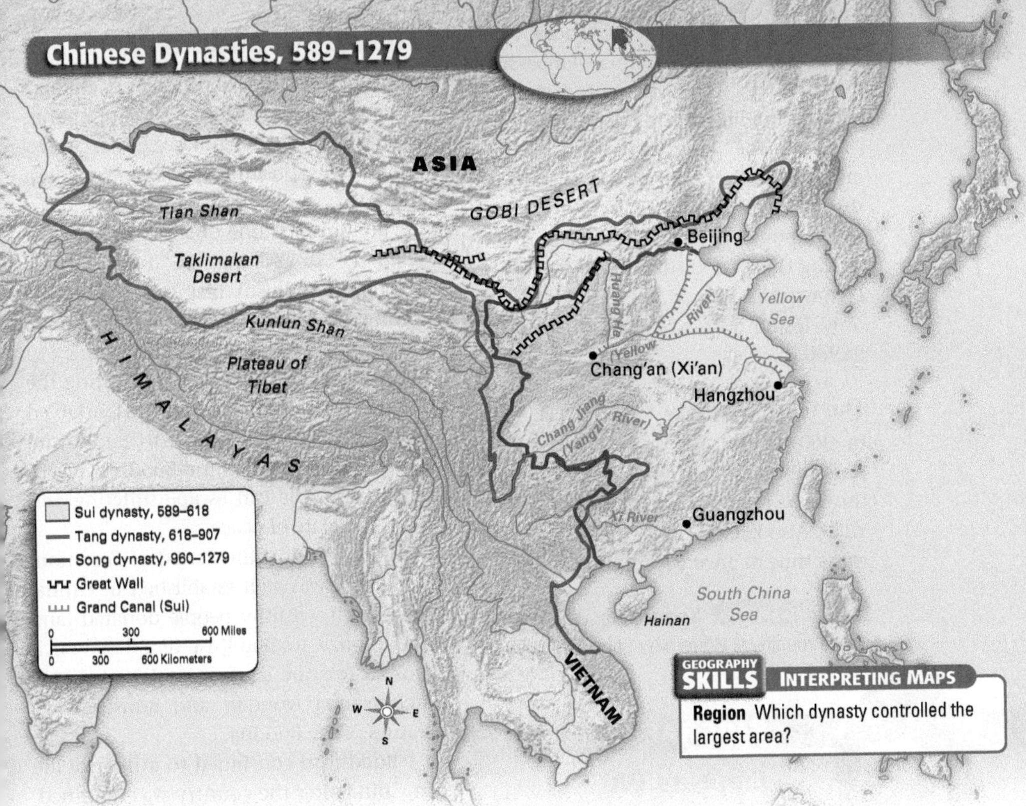

GEOGRAPHY SKILLS INTERPRETING MAPS

Region Which dynasty controlled the largest area?

The Sui, Tang, and Song

Finally, after centuries of political confusion and cultural change, China was reunified. For about 700 years, it remained unified under a series of powerful dynasties.

The Sui Dynasty

The man who finally ended the Period of Disunion was a northern ruler named Yang Jian (YANG jee-EN). In 589, he conquered the south, unified China, and created the Sui (SWAY) dynasty.

The Sui dynasty didn't last long, only from 589 to 618. During that time, though, its leaders restored order to China and began the **Grand Canal,** a canal linking northern and southern China.

The Tang Dynasty

A new dynasty arose in China in 618 when a former Sui official overthrew the old government. This dynasty, the Tang, would rule for nearly 300 years. As you can see on the map, China grew under the Tang dynasty to include much of eastern Asia, as well as large parts of Central Asia.

Historians view the Tang dynasty as a golden age of Chinese civilization. One of its greatest rulers was Taizong (TY-tzoong). He conquered many lands, reformed the military, and created law codes. Another brilliant Tang ruler was Xuanzong (SHOO-AN-tzoong). During his reign, culture flourished. Many of China's finest poets wrote while Xuanzong ruled.

Direct Teach

Main Idea

1 The Period of Disunion

The Period of Disunion was a time of war and disorder that followed the end of the Han dynasty.

Explain What happened to China following the collapse of the Han dynasty? *The empire split into rival kingdoms ruled by military leaders during the Period of Disunion.*

Recall Why did some people move from northern China to southern China? *to escape nomadic invaders*

Main Idea

2 The Sui, Tang, and Song

China was reunified under the Sui, Tang, and Song dynasties.

Recall How long did the Tang dynasty last? *nearly 300 years*

Sequence Place the Chinese dynasties in the order in which they ruled. *Sui, Tang, Song*

Identify Who was Empress Wu? *The only woman to rule China, she ruled after her sickly husband died.*

Activity **Tang Scrapbook** Have students create a scrapbook page that illustrates the accomplishments of the Tang dynasty. LS **Visual/Spatial**

Alternative Assessment Handbook, Rubric 32: Scrapbooks

Map Transparency: Chinese Dynasties, 589–1279

Critical Thinking: Evaluating Informatiion

Above Level

Research Required

Imperial Report Cards

1. Organize the class into pairs. Then assign each pair one of the three dynasties, Sui, Tang, or Song.
2. Have students use the library, Internet, or other resources to find the names of different emperors from their assigned dynasties. Have each student select a different emperor and conduct research on that person.
3. Have each pair create report cards for the emperors they selected. Students' report cards should list the categories on which the grade is based, such as leadership, accomplishments, and government. In addition, students should provide each emperor with an overall grade.
4. Encourage students to share their report cards with the class. LS **Verbal/Linguistic**

Alternative Assessment Handbook, Rubric 16: Judging Information

Answers

Interpreting Maps *Tang*

Reading Check (p.410) *New types of art, music, food, and clothing styles developed as a result of the mixing of cultures.*

Direct Teach

Main Idea

3 The Age of Buddhism

The Age of Buddhism saw major religious changes in China.

Recall When did Buddhism develop into a major religion in China? *during the Period of Disunion*

Explain What influence did Buddhism have in China? *It influenced architecture, art, and literature, and even spread to Japan, Korea, and other Asian lands.*

Draw Conclusions Why might the Tang emperor have wanted to end the age of Buddhism? *possible answers—He felt threatened by its power, did not agree with its teachings.*

Map Transparency: Spread of Buddhism

Info to Know

Empress Wu and Buddhism Empress Wu gained much of her support through her dedication to Buddhism. In addition to promoting Buddhism, Empress Wu gave large donations to have Buddhist temples built around China. One impressive Buddhist site is the Longmen Grottoes in China's Henan Province. This series of caves features the well-known statue called the Grand Vairocana Buddha, which was carved out of a cave wall. The statue, standing over 56 feet high, is believed to have been modeled after the face of Empress Wu.

About the Illustration

This illustration of Empress Wu is an artist's conception based on available sources. However, historians are uncertain exactly what Empress Wu looked like.

The Tang dynasty also included the only woman to rule China—**Empress Wu**. Her methods were sometimes vicious, but she was intelligent and talented.

After the Tang dynasty fell, China entered another brief period of chaos and disorder, with separate kingdoms competing for power. In fact, China was so divided during this period that it is known as Five Dynasties and Ten Kingdoms. The disorder only lasted 53 years, though, from 907 to 960.

The Song Dynasty

In 960, China was again reunified, this time by the Song dynasty. Like the Tang, the Song ruled for about 300 years, until 1279. Also like the Tang, the Song dynasty was a time of great accomplishments.

READING CHECK **Sequencing** When was China reunified? When was China not unified?

BIOGRAPHY

Empress Wu

625–705

Married to a sickly emperor, Empress Wu became the virtual ruler of China in 655. After her husband died, Wu decided her sons were not worthy of ruling. She kept power for herself, and ruled with an iron fist. Those who threatened her power risked death. Unlike many earlier rulers, she chose advisors based on their abilities rather than their ranks. Although she was not well liked, Wu was respected for bringing stability and prosperity to China.

Drawing Conclusions Why do you think Empress Wu was never very popular?

412

The Age of Buddhism

While China was experiencing changes in its government, another major change was taking place in Chinese culture. A new religion was spreading quickly throughout the vast land.

Buddhism is one of the world's major religions, originating in India around 500 BC. Buddhism first came to China during the Han dynasty. But for some time, there were few Buddhists in China.

Buddhism's status changed during the Period of Disunion. During this troubled time, many people turned to Buddhism. They took comfort in the Buddhist teaching that people can escape suffering and achieve a state of peace.

By the end of the Period of Disunion, Buddhism was well established in China. As a result, wealthy people donated land and money to Buddhist temples, which arose across the land. Some temples were architectural wonders and housed huge statues of the Buddha.

Buddhism continued to influence life in China after the country was reunified. In fact, during the Sui and Tang dynasties, Buddhism continued to grow and spread. Chinese missionaries, people who travel to spread their religion, introduced Buddhism to Japan, Korea, and other Asian lands.

Buddhism influenced many aspects of Chinese culture, including art, literature, and architecture. In fact, so important was Buddhism in China that the period from about 400 to about 845 can be called the Age of Buddhism.

This golden age of Buddhism came to an end when a Tang emperor launched a campaign against the religion. He burned many Buddhist texts, took lands from Buddhist temples, destroyed many temples, and turned others into schools.

Critical Thinking: Sequencing

At Level

Buddhism Time Line

Standard English Mastery | Research Required

1. Review with students the information on the Age of Buddhism in China. Ask students what the significance of Buddhism was in China.
2. Have students use the library, Internet, or other resources to conduct research on the history of Buddhism in China. Ask students to compile a list of 10 important events relating to Buddhism in China. Have students identify the dates of the events, if possible.
3. Have each student create a time line that shows the important events from his or her list. When dates of events are not available, ask students to put the events in the order in which they occurred. Then have students write short captions that describe the significance of the events.
4. Display the time lines around the classroom. **LS Verbal/Linguistic, Visual/Spatial**

Alternative Assessment Handbook, Rubrics 30: Research; and 36: Time Lines

Answers

Biography *She ruled with an iron fist.*

Reading Check *reunified in 589 by Sui dynasty; not unified from 907–960 during Five Dynasties and Ten Kingdoms*

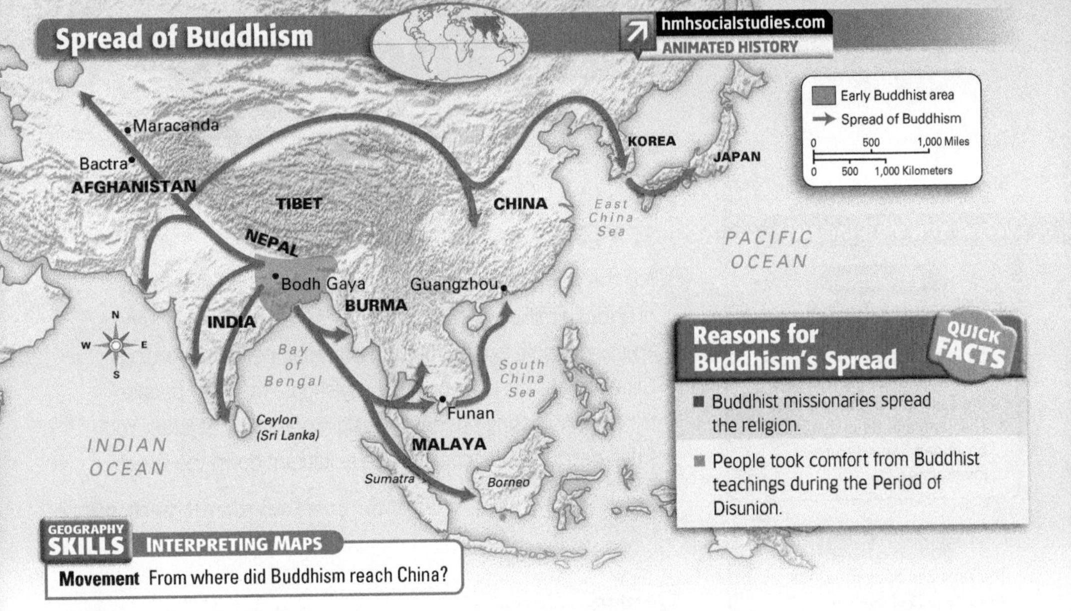

Reasons for Buddhism's Spread QUICK FACTS

- Buddhist missionaries spread the religion.
- People took comfort from Buddhist teachings during the Period of Disunion.

GEOGRAPHY SKILLS INTERPRETING MAPS

Movement From where did Buddhism reach China?

The emperor's actions weakened the influence of Buddhism in China, but they did not destroy it completely. Buddhism continued to play a key role in Chinese society for centuries. As it had during the early Tang period, it continued to shape Chinese art and literature. But even as it influenced life in China, Buddhism changed. People began to blend elements of Buddhism with elements of other philosophies, especially Confucianism and Daoism, to create a new way of thinking.

READING CHECK **Identifying Cause and Effect** Why did Buddhism spread more easily during the Period of Disunion?

SUMMARY AND PREVIEW From the disorder that followed the fall of the Han dynasty, new dynasties arose to restore order in China. You will read about their many advances in the next section.

Section 1 Assessment

hmhsocialstudies.com ONLINE QUIZ

Reviewing Ideas, Terms, and People

1. a. **Define** What was the **Period of Disunion**?
   b. **Explain** How did Chinese culture change during the Period of Disunion?
2. a. **Identify** Who was **Empress Wu**? What did she do?
   b. **Evaluate** How do you think the reunification of China affected the common people?
3. a. **Identify** When was the Age of Buddhism in China?
   b. **Explain** Why did people turn to Buddhism during the Period of Disunion?
   c. **Elaborate** How did Buddhism influence Chinese culture?

Critical Thinking

4. **Sequencing** Draw a time line like this one. Using your notes on important events, place the main events and their dates on the time line.

FOCUS ON WRITING

5. **Getting an Overview** In this section you read an overview of three major dynasties and the contributions of Buddhism. Make a note of any ideas or contributions that you might want to include in your article.

Direct Teach

Teaching Tip

Cultural Diffusion

Remind students of the concept of cultural diffusion—the spread of an idea or philosophy from one culture or society to another. Ask students why the spread of Buddhism is considered an example of cultural diffusion.

Review & Assess

Close

Have students describe the cycles of peace and disunion in China. Ask them to identify the important dynasties that ruled at this time.

Review

Online Quiz, Section 1

Assess

SE Section 1 Assessment
PASS: Section 1 Quiz
Alternative Assessment Handbook

Reteach/Classroom Intervention

Guided Reading Workbook, Section 1
Interactive Skills Tutor CD-ROM

Section 1 Assessment Answers

1. **a.** a period when China was split into several competing kingdoms, ruled by military leaders
   b. Northern and southern Chinese cultures mixed to develop new art, music, food, and clothing styles.
2. **a.** the only woman to ever rule China; she brought stability and prosperity to China.
   b. possible answer—The common people felt more at peace throughout the land without having to fear so many wars.
3. **a.** about 400 to about 845
   b. People took comfort in the Buddhist teaching that people can escape suffering and achieve a state of peace.
   c. It influenced many aspects including art, literature, and architecture.
4. Period of Disunion, 220–589; Age of Buddhism, about 400–845; Sui dynasty, 589–618; Tang dynasty, 618–907; Five Dynasties and Ten Kingdoms, 907–960; Song dynasty, 960–1279
5. possible answers: Tang dynasty—golden age of Chinese civilization; Buddhism—influenced culture

Answers

Interpreting Maps *from Nepal to Afghanistan to China*

Reading Check *People took comfort in the Buddhist teaching that people can escape suffering and achieve a state of peace.*

Preteach

Bellringer

If YOU were there . . . Use the **Daily Bellringer Transparency** to help students answer the question.

Daily Bellringer Transparency, Section 2

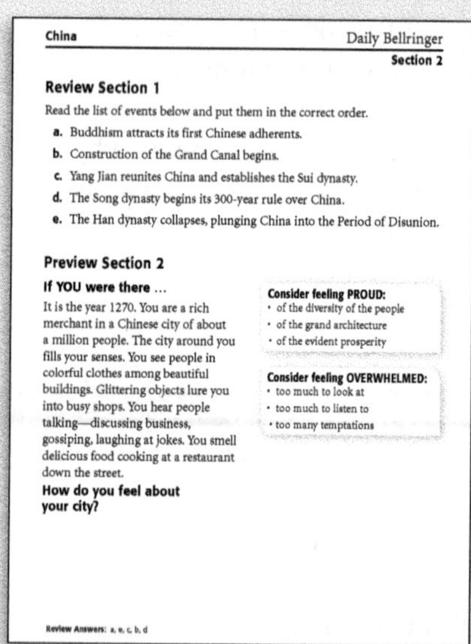
China — Daily Bellringer — Section 2

Review Section 1

Read the list of events below and put them in the correct order.

a. Buddhism attracts its first Chinese adherents.
b. Construction of the Grand Canal begins.
c. Yang Jian reunites China and establishes the Sui dynasty.
d. The Song dynasty begins its 300-year rule over China.
e. The Han dynasty collapses, plunging China into the Period of Disunion.

Preview Section 2

If YOU were there ...

It is the year 1270. You are a rich merchant in a Chinese city of about a million people. The city around you fills your senses. You see people in colorful clothes among beautiful buildings. Glittering objects lure you into busy shops. You hear people talking—discussing business, gossiping, laughing at jokes. You smell delicious food cooking at a restaurant down the street.

How do you feel about your city?

Consider feeling PROUD:
- of the diversity of the people
- of the grand architecture
- of the evident prosperity

Consider feeling OVERWHELMED:
- too much to look at
- too much to listen to
- too many temptations

Review Answers: a, e, c, b, d

Building Vocabulary

Preteach or review the following terms:

irrigation supplying dry land with water artificially (p. 414)

maritime of or relating to the sea (p. 417)

revolutionized changed completely (p. 418)

CRF: Vocabulary Builder Activity, Section 2

Taking Notes

Have students use the graphic organizer online to take notes on the section. This activity will prepare students for the Section Assessment, in which they will complete a graphic organizer that builds on the information using the Critical Thinking Skill: Categorizing.

SECTION 2

Tang and Song Achievements

What You Will Learn...

Main Ideas

1. Advances in agriculture led to increased trade and population growth.
2. Cities and trade grew during the Tang and Song dynasties.
3. The Tang and Song dynasties produced fine arts and inventions.

The Big Idea

The Tang and Song dynasties were periods of economic, cultural, and technological accomplishments.

Key Terms

porcelain, *p. 417*
woodblock printing, *p. 418*
gunpowder, *p. 418*
compass, *p. 418*

Use the graphic organizer online to take notes about accomplishments of the Tang and Song dynasties.

If YOU were there...

It is the year 1270. You are a rich merchant in a Chinese city of about a million people. The city around you fills your senses. You see people in colorful clothes among beautiful buildings. Glittering objects lure you into busy shops. You hear people talking—discussing business, gossiping, laughing at jokes. You smell delicious food cooking at a restaurant down the street.

How do you feel about your city?

BUILDING BACKGROUND The Tang and Song dynasties were periods of great wealth and progress. Changes in farming formed the basis for other advances in Chinese civilization.

Advances in Agriculture

Chinese civilization had always been based on agriculture. Over thousands of years, the Chinese had become expert farmers. In the north farmers grew wheat, barley, and other grains. In the warmer and wetter south they grew rice.

During the Song dynasty, though, Chinese farming reached new heights. The improvement was largely due to new irrigation techniques. For example, some farmers dug underground wells. A new irrigation device, the dragon backbone pump, allowed one person to do the work of several. With this light and portable pump, a farmer could scoop up water and pour it into an irrigation canal. Using these new techniques, farmers created elaborate irrigation systems.

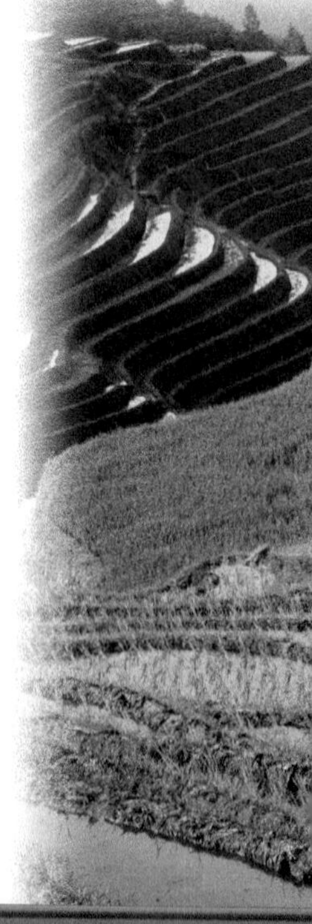

Teach the Big Idea

At Level

Tang and Song Achievements

1. **Teach** Ask students the questions in the Main Idea boxes to teach this section.
2. **Apply** Have students write a series of cause-and-effect statements as they read the section. The statements can be simple phrases connected by an arrow. *Possible statements: increased agricultural production—population growth; increased trade—cities grow; cities grow—art flourishes; printing innovations—literature flourishes.* **LS Verbal/Linguistic**
3. **Review** As you review the section's main ideas, call on students to read aloud their cause-and-effect statements.
4. **Practice/Homework** Have students use the Quick Facts chart in this section to identify important Chinese inventions from this period. Then have students create a collage that illustrates modern uses of these inventions. **LS Visual/Spatial**

Alternative Assessment Handbook, Rubrics 6: Cause and Effect; and 8: Collages

Under the Song, the amount of land under cultivation increased. Lands along the Chang Jiang that had been wild now became farmland. Farms also became more productive, thanks to the discovery of a new type of fast-ripening rice. Because it grew and ripened quickly, this rice enabled farmers to grow two or even three crops in the time it used to take to grow just one.

Chinese farmers also learned to grow new crops, such as cotton, efficiently. Workers processed cotton fiber to make clothes and other goods. The production of tea, which had been grown in China for centuries, also increased.

Agricultural surpluses helped pay taxes to the government. Merchants also traded food crops. As a result, food was abundant not just in the countryside but also in the cities. Because food was plentiful, China's population grew quickly. During the Tang dynasty, the population had been about 60 million. During the Song dynasty, the farmers of China fed a country of nearly 100 million people. At the time, China was the largest country in the world.

THE IMPACT TODAY

China is still the world's most populous country. More than 1.3 billion people live there today.

READING CHECK **Identifying Cause and Effect** How did agricultural advances affect population growth?

Growing Rice

Rice has long been a vital crop in southern China, where the warm, wet climate is perfect for rice growing.

At harvest time, farmers remove rice kernels from the rest of the plant.
Sometimes farmers build terraces to create level land for rice farming.
Rice seedlings are planted in flooded fields.
415

Direct Teach

Main Idea

❶ Advances in Agriculture

Advances in agriculture led to increased trade and population growth.

Identify What crops were grown in China? *wheat, barley, rice, other grains, cotton, and tea*

Explain What new developments aided food production, and how did they improve it? *The dragon backbone pump helped irrigate crops; fast-ripening rice allowed farmers to grow more than one crop in the time it took to grow just one.*

Draw Conclusions How were agricultural surpluses related to the growth of cities? *The extra food grown in the country could feed more people in cities, which grew.*

Connect to Science

Three Gorges Dam China is still controlling its water supply. Recently, the Chinese government built a large and controversial dam across the Chang Jiang. How large? The dam, measuring almost 600 feet in height, is the world's largest dam—and the largest electricity generating plant of any type. It created a lake about 400 miles long, and provided as much hydroelectric power as 15 power plants. How controversial? Many critics were outraged by the dam's construction because it forced more than 1.2 million people to relocate, flooded several environmental and archeological treasures under water, and cost 30 billion dollars. Despite the controversy, construction on the dam was completed in 2008.

Critical Thinking: Predicting

At Level

Writing a Letter to the Emperor

1. Review with students the advances the Chinese made in agriculture during this time period. Ask students to discuss the results of agricultural production. What effect did improvements in farming have on China? Help students understand why farming surpluses occurred, and how these farming surpluses led to population growth.
2. Ask each student to make a list of the possible results of China's increase in population during the Song dynasty. Students might want to categorize the results into positive and negative results.
3. Have each student write a letter to the emperor or a high-ranking government official to inform him or her of the predictions they have made about China's population growth. Ask students to make suggestions for how the empire might plan for each result.
4. Ask volunteers to share their letters with the class. **LS Verbal/Linguistic**

Alternative Assessment Handbook, Rubrics 5: Business Letters; and 37: Writing Assignments

Answers

Reading Check *Due to agricultural advances, food became abundant, which led to population growth.*

Direct Teach

Main Idea

2 Cities and Trade

Cities and trade grew during the Tang and Song dynasties.

Identify What was the largest city in the world at this time, and what was it's population? *Chang'an; more than one million*

Analyze How were Chinese trade cities unique? *They were a mix of people from many cultures and religions and were quite large in population.*

Drawing Conclusions How did the Grand Canal play a role in trade? *It connected major cities and allowed a large amount of goods and crops to be transported from agricultural areas to the cities.*

Info to Know

Chinese Cities China had the largest cities in the world during the Tang and Song dynasties. One of the most remarkable of these cities was the Song capital of Hangzhou. The city had a wide variety of diversions, including bookstores, pet shops, restaurants, teahouses, popular entertainment, and boating. The city also tried to take care of its citizens through a state hospital, orphanages, and homes for the elderly.

Activity Grand Canal Map Have students use a blank outline map of China to locate the route of the Grand Canal. Then have students list trade goods from different regions of China that traveled along the Grand Canal. **LS Visual/Spatial**

Alternative Assessment Handbook, Rubric 20: Map Creation

Cities and Trade

Throughout the Tang and Song dynasties, much of the food grown on China's farms flowed into the growing cities and towns. China's cities were crowded, busy places. Shopkeepers, government officials, doctors, artisans, entertainers, religious leaders, and artists made them lively places as well.

City Life

FOCUS ON READING What can you conclude about the link between the Grand Canal and the growth of cities?

China's capital and largest city of the Tang dynasty was Chang'an (chahng-AHN), a huge, bustling trade center. With a population of more than a million, it was by far the largest city in the world at the time.

Chang'an, like other trading cities, had a mix of people from many cultures—China, Korea, Persia, Arabia, and Europe. It was also known as a religious and philosophical center, not just for Buddhists and Daoists but for Asian Christians as well.

Cities continued to grow under the Song. Several cities, including the Song capital, Kaifeng (KY-fuhng), had about a million people. A dozen more cities had populations of close to half a million.

Trade in China and Beyond

Trade grew along with Chinese cities. This trade, combined with China's agricultural base, made China richer than ever before.

Much trade took place within China itself. Traders used the country's rivers to ship goods on barges and ships.

The Grand Canal, a series of waterways that linked major cities, carried a huge amount of trade goods, especially farm products. Construction on the canal had begun during the Sui dynasty. During the Tang dynasty, it was improved and expanded. The Grand Canal allowed the Chinese to move goods and crops from distant agricultural areas into cities.

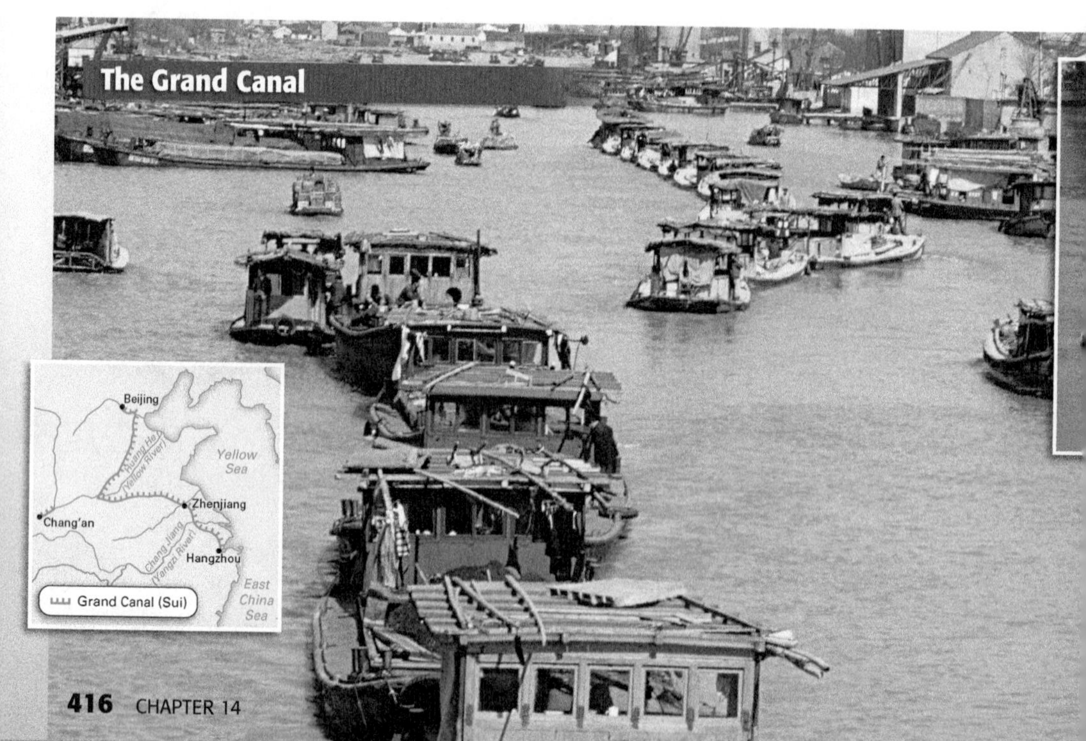

Differentiating Instruction

Struggling Readers — Below Level

1. Ask students to imagine that they are captains of barges on the Grand Canal during the Song dynasty. The barge is set to travel from the countryside to the city and back again.
2. Instruct each student to write a captain's log with three entries. The first entry should include a list of items on board the ship as it is headed to the city. The second entry should be a description of the city and its inhabitants. The third entry should be a list of items on board being taken back to the countryside. Remind students to include details that can be found in this section.
3. When students have finished, guide the class in a discussion of trade within China, such as agricultural goods exchanged for city-made, manufactured goods. Ask students to share their logs with the class. **LS Verbal/Linguistic**

Alternative Assessment Handbook, Rubric 40: Writing to Describe

Answers

Focus on Reading *Trade on the canal probably led to the growth of the size and economy of cities located along the canal.*

The Chinese also carried on trade with other lands and peoples. During the Tang dynasty, most foreign trade was over land routes leading west to India and Southwest Asia, though Chinese traders also went to Korea and Japan in the east. The Chinese exported many goods, including tea, rice, spices, and jade. However, one export was especially important—silk. So valuable was silk that the Chinese tried to keep the method of making it secret. In exchange for their exports, the Chinese imported different foods and plants, wool, glass, gold, and silver.

During the Song dynasty, maritime trade, or sea trade, became more important. China opened its Pacific ports to foreign traders. The sea-trade routes connected China to many other countries. During this time, the Chinese also developed another valuable product—a thin, beautiful type of pottery called **porcelain**.

China's Grand Canal is the world's longest human-made waterway. It was built largely to transport rice and other foods from the south to feed China's cities and armies in the north. Barges like the ones at left crowd the Grand Canal, which is still an important transportation link in China. Some people even live on the canal in small houseboats like the one above.

All of this trade helped create a strong economy. As a result, merchants became important members of Chinese society during the Song dynasty. Also as a result of the growth of trade and wealth, the Song invented the world's first system of paper money in the 900s.

READING CHECK **Summarizing** How far did China's trade routes extend?

Arts and Inventions

While China grew rich economically, its cultural riches also increased. In literature, art, and science, China made huge advances.

Artists and Poets

The artists and writers of the Tang dynasty were some of China's greatest. Wu Daozi (DOW-tzee) painted murals that celebrated Buddhism and nature. Li Bo and Du Fu wrote poems that readers still enjoy for their beauty. This poem by Li Bo expresses the homesickness that one feels late at night:

> "Before my bed
> there is bright moonlight
> So that it seems
> like frost on the ground:
> Lifting my head
> I watch the bright moon,
> Lowering my head
> I dream that I'm home."
>
> –Li Bo, *Quiet Night Thoughts*

THE IMPACT TODAY Porcelain became so popular in the West that it became known as chinaware, or just china.

Also noted for its literature, the Song period produced Li Qingzhao (ching-ZHOW), perhaps China's greatest female poet. She once said that the purpose of her poetry was to capture a single moment in time.

Artists of both the Tang and Song dynasties made exquisite objects in clay. Tang figurines of horses clearly show the animals' strength. Song artists made porcelain items covered in a pale green glaze called celadon (SEL-uh-duhn).

Direct Teach

Main Idea

2 Cities and Trade

Cities and trade grew during the Tang and Song dynasties.

Identify What were some of China's exports? *tea, rice, spices, jade, silk, and porcelain*

Identify Cause and Effect What result did China's trade with other lands have on Chinese society? *It led to the rise of merchants in Chinese society.*

Evaluate How important do you think trade was in China? Why? *possible answer—very important; it brought great wealth to China from foreign lands and united different regions of the empire.*

Did you know . . .

In addition to the barges pictured on this page, another means of transportation in China was the junk, a ship with large sails. Originally, the square sails were made of bamboo mats sewn together. As cotton became more common in China, the sails were redesigned to feature cotton cloth stretched between bamboo strips. Junks of differing sizes were built to carry trade goods on China's rivers and seas.

Cross-Discipline Activity: Literature

Above Level

Writing a Poem

1. Tell the class that students of poetry often write imitations, or poems that copy the style of a certain poet. This helps them understand the structure and style of different poems.
2. Read Li Bo's poem aloud to the class. Make sure all students understand the words and the message of the poem.
3. Instruct students to write an imitation of the poem. The topic can be anything students want, but the style should imitate Li Bo's poem. Students should use colorful imagery to capture a moment in time. Students having difficulty might want to create an illustration of Li Bo's poem.
4. Ask for volunteers to read their poems to the class. **LS Verbal/Linguistic**

Alternative Assessment Handbook, Rubric 26: Poems and Songs

Answers

Reading Check *as far as India and Southwest Asia, into Korea and Japan*

Direct Teach

Main Idea

3 Arts and Inventions

The Tang and Song dynasties produced fine arts and inventions.

Identify What types of art and literature were popular during this period? *murals, poetry, and porcelain figurines*

Recall How was gunpowder first used? *in fireworks*

Make Generalizations How was the magnetic compass significant to world history? *It allowed explorers all over the world to travel long distances and to discover parts of the world they previously did not know existed.*

- **CRF:** Literature Activity: Poems from the Tang and Song Dynasties
- **CRF:** Economics and History Activity: The Origins of Paper Money
- Quick Facts Transparency: Chinese Inventions

Info to Know

Woodblock Printing Chinese woodblock printing began during the Tang dynasty. Originally the method was used to print designs on cloth, but later was applied to writing Buddhist texts and other information. Chinese printers would write the text on a thin sheet of paper, which they then pasted face down to a wood block. The text was carved out in the wood, creating an image that could be inked and stamped onto paper and reused many times. Not only text was copied in this way, but illustrations as well.

Chinese Inventions

Paper
Invented during the Han dynasty around 105, paper was one of the greatest of all Chinese inventions. It gave the Chinese a cheap and easy way of keeping records and made printing possible.

Porcelain
Porcelain was first made during the Tang dynasty, but it wasn't perfected for many centuries. Chinese artists were famous for their work with this fragile material.

Woodblock printing
The Chinese invented printing during the Tang dynasty, centuries before it was known in Europe. Printers could copy drawings or texts quickly, much faster than they could be copied by hand.

Gunpowder
Invented during the late Tang or early Song dynasty, gunpowder was used to make fireworks and signals. The Chinese did not generally use it as a weapon.

Movable type
Inventors of the Song dynasty created movable type, which made printing much faster. Carved letters could be rearranged and reused to print many different messages.

Magnetic compass
Invented no later than the Han period, the compass was greatly improved by the Tang. The new compass allowed sailors and merchants to travel vast distances.

Paper money
The world's first paper money was invented by the Song. Lighter and easier to handle than coins, paper money helped the Chinese manage their growing wealth.

Important Inventions

The Tang and Song dynasties produced some of the most remarkable—and most important—inventions in human history. Some of these inventions influenced events around the world.

According to legend, a man named Cai Lun invented paper in the year 105 during the Han dynasty. A later Tang invention built on Cai Lun's achievement—**woodblock printing,** a form of printing in which an entire page is carved into a block of wood. The printer applies ink to the block and presses paper against the block to create a printed page. The world's first known printed book was printed in this way in China in 868.

Another invention of the Tang dynasty was gunpowder. **Gunpowder** is a mixture of powders used in guns and explosives. It was originally used only in fireworks, but it was later used to make small bombs and rockets. Eventually, gunpowder was used to make explosives, firearms, and cannons. Gunpowder dramatically altered how wars were fought and, in doing so, changed the course of human history.

One of the most useful achievements of Tang China was the perfection of the magnetic **compass.** This instrument, which uses the earth's magnetic field to show direction, revolutionized travel. A compass made it possible to find direction more accurately than ever before. The perfection of the compass had far-reaching effects. Explorers the world over used the compass to travel vast distances. The navigators of trading ships and warships also came to rely on the compass. Thus, the compass has been a key factor in some of the most important sailing voyages in history.

The Song dynasty also produced many important inventions. Under the Song, the Chinese invented movable type. Movable type is a set of letters or characters that are

Cross-Discipline Activity: Science

At Level

Chinese Technology Exhibits

Research Required

1. Review with students the various technological innovations of the Chinese during the Tang and Song period. Make a list for students to see.
2. Organize students into pairs or small groups. Have each pair or group select one Chinese innovation to research. Tell students that they will create an exhibit for a science fair that presents one piece of Chinese technology from this period.
3. Have each group use the library, Internet, or other resources to research information about the technology they have chosen. Student exhibits should explain how each device or process works, what it was used for, and what it looked like.
4. Have each group present its exhibit to the class or conduct a class science fair for everyone to see.

LS Interpersonal, Verbal/Linguistic

Alternative Assessment Handbook, Rubrics 29: Presentations; and 30: Research

LINKING TO TODAY

The Paper Trail

The dollar bill in your pocket may be crisp and new, but paper money has been around a long time. Paper money was printed for the first time in China in the AD 900s and was in use for about 700 years, through the Ming dynasty, when the bill shown here was printed. However, so much money was printed that it lost value. The Chinese stopped using paper money for centuries. Its use caught on in Europe, though, and eventually became common. Most countries now issue paper money.

ANALYZING INFORMATION

What are some advantages of paper money?

used to print books. Unlike the blocks used in block printing, movable type can be rearranged and reused to create new lines of text and different pages.

The Song dynasty also introduced the concept of paper money. People were used to buying goods and services with bulky coins made of metals such as bronze, gold, and silver. Paper money was far lighter and easier to use. As trade increased and many people in China grew rich, paper money became more popular.

READING CHECK **Finding Main Ideas** What were some important inventions of the Tang and Song dynasties?

SUMMARY AND PREVIEW The Tang and Song dynasties were periods of great advancement. Many great artists and writers lived during these periods. Tang and Song inventions also had dramatic effects on world history. In the next section you will learn about the government of the Song dynasty.

Section 2 Assessment

Reviewing Ideas, Terms, and People

1. a. **Recall** What advances in farming occurred during the Song dynasty?
   b. **Explain** How did agricultural advancements affect China's population?
2. a. **Describe** What were the capital cities of Tang and Song China like?
   b. **Draw Conclusions** How did geography affect trade in China?
3. a. **Identify** Who was Li Bo?
   b. **Draw Conclusions** How may the inventions of paper money and **woodblock printing** have been linked?
   c. **Rank** Which Tang or Song invention do you think was most important? Defend your answer.

Critical Thinking

4. **Categorizing** Copy the chart at right. Use it to organize your notes on the Tang and Song into categories.

	Tang dynasty	Song dynasty
Agriculture		
Cities		
Trade		
Art		
Inventions		

FOCUS ON WRITING

5. **Identifying Achievements** You have just read about the achievements of the Tang and Song dynasties. Make a list of those you might include in your article.

Direct Teach

Checking for Understanding

1. Advances in agriculture during the Tang and Song dynasties led to
   a. *population growth.*
   b. development of paper money.
   c. the decline of Buddhism.
   d. a period of disunion.
2. What did the invention of gunpowder lead to?
   a. long-distance sailing voyages
   b. population growth
   c. *firearms and fireworks*
   d. printed books
3. During which dynasty did many innovations take place?
   a. Yuan
   b. Ming
   c. Sui
   d. *Tang*

Review & Assess

Close

Ask students how life changed in China's countryside and cities during the Tang and Song dynasties.

Review

Online Quiz, Section 2

Assess

SE Section 2 Assessment

PASS: Section 2 Quiz

Alternative Assessment Handbook

Reteach/Classroom Intervention

Guided Reading Workbook, Section 2

Interactive Skills Tutor CD-ROM

Section 2 Assessment Answers

1. a. dragon backbone pump, cultivation of cotton, fast-ripening rice
   b. The population grew.
2. a. bustling trade centers, with a mix of cultures and religions and large populations
   b. Rivers and canals were used to connect major cities and deliver trade goods.
3. a. a poet during the Tang dynasty
   b. Woodblock printing allowed identical printings, so paper money could be produced.
   c. Answers will vary, but students should demonstrate an understanding of the invention and its impact on Chinese society.
4. Agriculture—Tang: new methods invented, Song: cultivated land increased, farmed cotton, rice, used more irrigation; Cities—Tang: huge trade centers; Song: many cities with population of half a million; Trade—Tang: trade along the Grand Canal expanded; Song: sea trade important; Art—Tang: writers and artists celebrated Buddhism and nature; Song: Li Qingzhao was a famous female poet; Inventions—Tang: woodblock printing, gunpowder, compass; Song: movable type, paper money
5. Answers will vary but might include poetry, porcelain, or other achievements from previous answer.

Answers

Analyzing Information *It is easier to carry than coins.*

Reading Check *paper, porcelain, woodblock printing, gunpowder, movable type, magnetic compass, paper money*

Preteach

Bellringer

If YOU were there . . . Use the **Daily Bellringer Transparency** to help students answer the question.

Daily Bellringer Transparency, Section 3

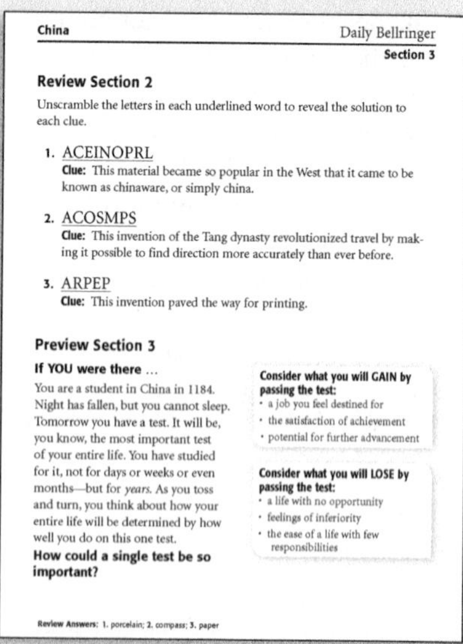

China Daily Bellringer
Section 3

Review Section 2

Unscramble the letters in each underlined word to reveal the solution to each clue.

1. ACEINOPRL
   Clue: This material became so popular in the West that it came to be known as chinaware, or simply china.
2. ACOSMPS
   Clue: This invention of the Tang dynasty revolutionized travel by making it possible to find direction more accurately than ever before.
3. ARPEP
   Clue: This invention paved the way for printing.

Preview Section 3

If YOU were there ...

You are a student in China in 1184. Night has fallen, but you cannot sleep. Tomorrow you have a test. It will be, you know, the most important test of your entire life. You have studied for it, not for days or weeks or even months—but for *years.* As you toss and turn, you think about how your entire life will be determined by how well you do on this one test.

How could a single test be so important?

Consider what you will GAIN by passing the test:
- a job you feel destined for
- the satisfaction of achievement
- potential for further advancement

Consider what you will LOSE by passing the test:
- a life with no opportunity
- feelings of inferiority
- the ease of a life with few responsibilities

Review Answers: 1. porcelain; 2. compass; 3. paper

Academic Vocabulary

Review with students the high-use academic terms in this section.

function work or perform (p.421)

incentive something that leads people to follow a certain course of action (p.422)

CRF: Vocabulary Builder Activity, Section 3

Taking Notes

Have students use the graphic organizer online to take notes on the section. This activity will prepare students for the Section Assessment, in which they will complete a graphic organizer that builds on the information using the Critical Thinking Skill: Sequencing.

SECTION 3

Confucianism and Government

What You Will Learn...

Main Ideas

1. Confucianism underwent changes and influenced Chinese government.
2. Scholar-officials ran China's government during the Song dynasty.

The Big Idea

Confucian thought influenced the Song government.

Key Terms

bureaucracy, *p. 422*
civil service, *p. 422*
scholar-official, *p. 422*

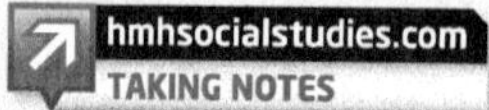

Use the graphic organizer online to take notes on Confucianism and the Song government.

If YOU were there...

You are a student in China in 1184. Night has fallen, but you cannot sleep. Tomorrow you have a test. You know it will be the most important test of your entire life. You have studied for it, not for days or weeks or even months—but for *years.* As you toss and turn, you think about how your entire life will be determined by how well you do on this one test.

How could a single test be so important?

BUILDING BACKGROUND The Song dynasty ruled China from 960 to 1279. This was a time of improvements in agriculture, growing cities, extensive trade, and the development of art and inventions. It was also a time of major changes in Chinese government.

Teach the Big Idea

At Level

Confucianism and Government

1. **Teach** Ask students the questions in the Main Idea boxes to teach this section.
2. **Apply** Have students work in pairs to create a concept web using the term *Confucianism* as their central concept. Remind students that concept webs are used to show relationships between ideas, events, or objects. Ask students to show the relationship of Confucianism to such ideas as government, society, ethics, and any others they can support.
   LS **Verbal/Linguistic, Visual/Spatial**
3. **Review** As you review the section's main ideas, have students write down specific ways in which China was influenced by Confucianism.
4. **Practice/Homework** Have each student use the concept web he or she created to write a one-page summary of the importance of Confucianism in Song China.
   LS **Verbal/Linguistic**

Alternative Assessment Handbook, Rubrics 13: Graphic Organizers; and 37: Writing Assignments

Confucianism

The dominant philosophy in China, Confucianism is based on the teachings of Confucius. He lived more than 1,500 years before the Song dynasty. His ideas, though, had a dramatic effect on the Song system of government.

Confucian Ideas

Confucius's teachings focused on ethics, or proper behavior, for individuals and governments. He said that people should conduct their lives according to two basic principles. These principles were *ren*, or concern for others, and *li*, or appropriate behavior. Confucius argued that society would **function** best if everyone followed *ren* and *li*.

Confucius thought that everyone had a proper role to play in society. Order was maintained when people knew their place and behaved appropriately. For example, Confucius said that young people should obey their elders and that subjects should obey their rulers.

The Influence of Confucianism

After his death, Confucius's ideas were spread by his followers, but they were not widely accepted. In fact, the Qin dynasty officially suppressed Confucian ideas and teachings. By the time of the Han dynasty, Confucianism had again come into favor, and Confucianism became the official state philosophy.

During the Period of Disunion, which followed the Han dynasty, Confucianism was overshadowed by Buddhism as the major tradition in China. As you recall, many Chinese people turned to Buddhism for comfort during these troubled times. In doing so, they largely turned away from Confucian ideas and outlooks.

Later, during the Sui and early Tang dynasties, Buddhism was very influential. Unlike Confucianism, which stressed ethical behavior, Buddhism stressed a more spiritual outlook that promised escape from suffering. As Buddhism became more popular in China, Confucianism lost some of its influence.

ACADEMIC VOCABULARY
function work or perform

In addition to ethics, Confucianism stressed the importance of education. This painting, created during the Song period, shows earlier Confucian scholars during the Period of Disunion sorting scrolls containing classic Confucian texts.

Direct Teach

Main Idea

1 Confucianism

Confucianism underwent changes and influenced Chinese government.

Recall What was the focus of the teachings of Confucius? *ethics, or proper behavior, for individuals and governments*

Explain Why did Confucianism decline in popularity during the Period of Disunion? *People turned to Buddhism for comfort in the troubled times of the Period of Disunion.*

Make Generalizations Why do you think the Song and later governments emphasized Neo-Confucianism? *possible answer—The emphasis on proper behavior would encourage people to obey their government; They saw problems in the government they hoped to eliminate by emphasizing Neo-Confucianism.*

Biography

Confucius (551–479 BC) According to tradition Confucius, or Master Kong, served in minor government positions until he became a teacher. As a teacher, Confucius traveled throughout China teaching his ethical philosophy to many students. Today, Confucius is considered one of the most influential teachers in the world. In fact, his birthday is an official holiday in Taiwan, where September 28 is celebrated as Teacher's Day.

Online Resources
Activity: Confucianism

Cross-Discipline Activity: Civics

At Level

Responsibility and Law-Making

1. Discuss with the class the teachings of Confucianism. Remind students that two important principles are *ren*, or concern for others, and *li*, or appropriate behavior. Ask students why these beliefs might have appealed to Song officials who eventually made Confucian ideas formal government teachings.
2. Ask students to think of examples of behaviors that illustrate the concepts of *ren* and *li*. Discuss with the class how living by these principles might benefit society.
3. Then have the class work together to create a list of laws that reflect the principles of *ren* and *li*. Encourage everyone to contribute to the list. Post the list for students to see. Ask students how they might feel about living according to the laws they created.

LS Interpersonal, Verbal/Linguistic

Alternative Assessment Handbook, Rubric 11: Discussions

Direct Teach

Main Idea

② Scholar-Officials

Scholar-officials ran China's government during the Song dynasty.

Recall How did people join the bureaucracy? *by passing a civil service examination*

Explain What benefits did scholar-officials have? *They held an elite position in society, earned respect, and received reduced penalties for breaking the law.*

Make Inferences Why did the civil service examination system help bring stability to the Song government? *It ensured that government officials were intelligent and talented, which made the government better and more stable.*

Info to Know

Civil Service Exams China's civil service examination system was very difficult. Even though students would spend years studying for an exam, passing rates were very low. In 1093, only 1 out of every 10 students passed the highest level of examination, known as the *jinshi.* Not all government positions, however, were based on performance on a civil service exam. In fact, only some 30 percent of Song officials were selected through examination.

Civil Service Exams

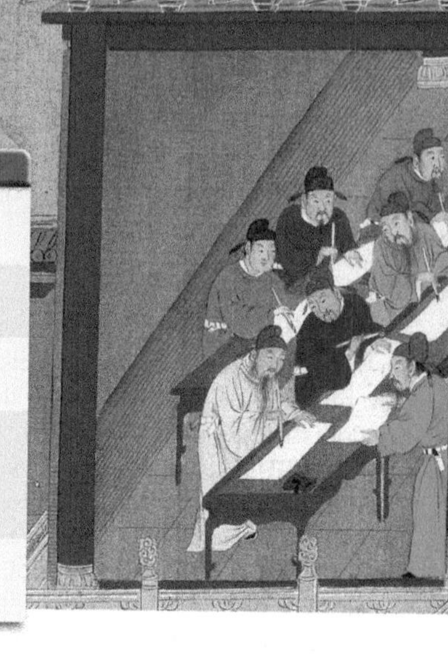

This painting from the 1600s shows civil servants writing essays for China's emperor. Difficult exams were designed to make sure that government officials were chosen by ability—not by wealth or family connections.

Difficult Exams

- Students had to memorize entire Confucian texts.
- To pass the most difficult tests, students might study for more than 20 years!
- Some exams lasted up to 72 hours, and students were locked in private rooms while taking them.
- Some dishonest students cheated by copying Confucius's works on the inside of their clothes, paying bribes to the test graders, or paying someone else to take the test for them.
- To prevent cheating, exam halls were often locked and guarded.

Neo-Confucianism

Late in the Tang dynasty, many Chinese historians and scholars again became interested in the teachings of Confucius. Their interest was sparked by their desire to improve Chinese government and society.

During and after the Song dynasty, a new philosophy called Neo-Confucianism developed. The term *neo* means "new." Based on Confucianism, Neo-Confucianism was similar to the older philosophy in that it taught proper behavior. However, it also emphasized spiritual matters. For example, Neo-Confucian scholars discussed such issues as what made human beings do bad things even if their basic nature was good.

Neo-Confucianism became much more influential under the Song. Later its influence grew even more. In fact, the ideas of Neo-Confucianism became official government teachings after the Song dynasty.

ACADEMIC VOCABULARY
incentive something that leads people to follow a certain course of action

READING CHECK **Contrasting** How did Neo-Confucianism differ from Confucianism?

Scholar-Officials

The Song dynasty took another major step that affected China for centuries. They improved the system by which people went to work for the government. These workers formed a large **bureaucracy,** or a body of unelected government officials. They joined the bureaucracy by passing civil service examinations. **Civil service** means service as a government official.

To become a civil servant, a person had to pass a series of written examinations. The examinations tested students' grasp of Confucianism and related ideas.

Because the tests were so difficult, students spent years preparing for them. Only a very small fraction of the people who took the tests would reach the top level and be appointed to a position in the government. However, candidates for the civil service examinations had a strong <u>incentive</u> for studying hard. Passing the tests meant life as a **scholar-official**—an educated member of the government.

Differentiating Instruction

Struggling Readers — Below Level

1. Review with students the information about scholar-officials in China under the Song. Help students understand the key terms *bureaucracy, civil service,* and *scholar-official.*
2. Have students write a short summary of the information about the Song scholar-officials. Remind students to be sure to explain how people became scholar-officials and what responsibilities they had. LS **Verbal/Linguistic**

English-Language Learners — Below Level

1. Write the terms *bureaucracy, civil service, incentive,* and *scholar-official* for students to see.
2. Organize students into mixed-ability pairs. Have each pair define each term. Check to make sure that all students understand the meaning of each term. Then have each pair create an illustration that represents the meaning of each term.
LS **Visual/Spatial, Verbal/Linguistic**

Answers

Reading Check *Neo-Confucianism emphasized both spiritual matters and proper behavior, whereas Confucianism focused on ethical behavior.*

Scholar-Officials

First rising to prominence under the Song, scholar-officials remained important in China for centuries. These scholar-officials, for example, lived during the Qing dynasty, which ruled from the mid-1600s to the early 1900s. Their typical responsibilities might include running government offices; maintaining roads, irrigation systems, and other public works; updating and maintaining official records; or collecting taxes.

Scholar-officials were elite members of society. They performed many important jobs in the government and were widely admired for their knowledge and ethics. Their benefits included considerable respect and reduced penalties for breaking the law. Many also became wealthy from gifts given by people seeking their aid.

The civil service examination system helped ensure that talented, intelligent people became scholar-officials. The civil service system was a major factor in the stability of the Song government.

READING CHECK **Analyzing** How did the Song dynasty change China's government?

SUMMARY AND PREVIEW During the Song period, Confucian ideas helped shape China's government. In the next section, you will read about the two dynasties that followed the Song—the Yuan and the Ming.

Section 3 Assessment

hmhsocialstudies.com ONLINE QUIZ

Reviewing Ideas, Terms, and People

1. a. **Identify** What two principles did Confucius believe people should follow?
   b. **Explain** What was Neo-Confucianism?
   c. **Elaborate** Why do you think Neo-Confucianism appealed to many people?
2. a. **Define** What was a **scholar-official**?
   b. **Explain** Why would people want to become scholar-officials?
   c. **Evaluate** Do you think **civil service** examinations were a good way to choose government officials? Why or why not?

Critical Thinking

3. **Sequencing** Review your notes to see how Confucianism led to Neo-Confucianism and Neo-Confucianism led to government bureaucracy. Use a graphic organizer like the one here.

FOCUS ON WRITING

4. **Gathering Ideas about Confucianism and Government** In this section you read about Confucianism and new ideas about government. What did you learn that you could add to your list of achievements?

Direct Teach

Linking to Today

China's Government Today China has one of the last remaining Communist governments in the world. Political power in China is centralized much more than in the United States, with most decisions coming from high-level national officials rather than from state or local officials. However, China still has a bureaucracy. Over 10 million officials are employed by the Chinese government to keep the country running.

Review & Assess

Close

Have students discuss how Confucian philosophy affected multiple aspects of Chinese life during the Song dynasty.

Review

Online Quiz, Section 3

Assess

SE Section 3 Assessment
PASS: Section 3 Quiz
Alternative Assessment Handbook

Reteach/Classroom Intervention

Guided Reading Workbook, Section 3
Interactive Skills Tutor CD-ROM

Section 3 Assessment Answers

1. **a.** *ren*, concern for others, and *li*, appropriate behavior
   b. the Song dynasty's new version of Confucianism that blended proper behavior and spiritual matters
   c. It included spiritual matters and ethics.
2. **a.** an educated member of the government who had passed a test about the knowledge of Confucianism and related ideas
   b. considerable respect, reduced penalties for breaking the law, many became wealthy
   c. Student answers will vary, but students should be familiar with the idea of civil service examinations.
3. Confucianism—official philosophy of the Han dynasty; Neo-Confucianism—combined Confucianism with spiritual ideas; Government bureaucracy—public officials were tested on the ideas of Confucianism
4. Possible responses might include the renewal of Confucian ideas mixed with spiritual matters, and scholar-officials added stability to the Song government.

Answers

Reading Check *It improved the bureaucracy, which created stability in government.*

Preteach

Bellringer

If YOU were there . . . Use the **Daily Bellringer Transparency** to help students answer the question.

Daily Bellringer Transparency, Section 4

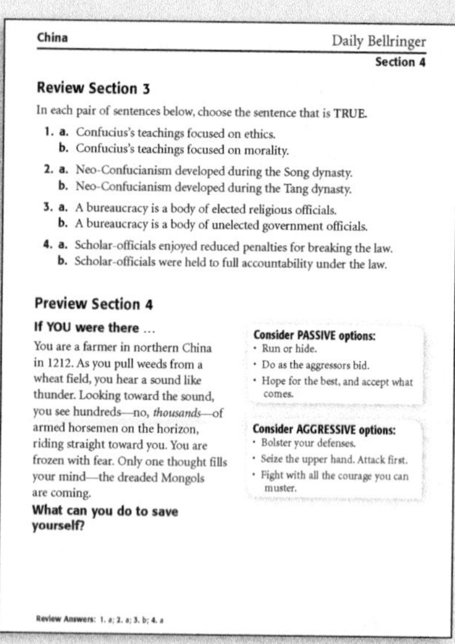
China | Daily Bellringer
Section 4

Review Section 3

In each pair of sentences below, choose the sentence that is TRUE.

1. a. Confucius's teachings focused on ethics.
   b. Confucius's teachings focused on morality.
2. a. Neo-Confucianism developed during the Song dynasty.
   b. Neo-Confucianism developed during the Tang dynasty.
3. a. A bureaucracy is a body of elected religious officials.
   b. A bureaucracy is a body of unelected government officials.
4. a. Scholar-officials enjoyed reduced penalties for breaking the law.
   b. Scholar-officials were held to full accountability under the law.

Preview Section 4

If YOU were there ...

You are a farmer in northern China in 1212. As you pull weeds from a wheat field, you hear a sound like thunder. Looking toward the sound, you see hundreds—no, *thousands*—of armed horsemen on the horizon, riding straight toward you. You are frozen with fear. Only one thought fills your mind—the dreaded Mongols are coming.

What can you do to save yourself?

Consider PASSIVE options:
- Run or hide.
- Do as the aggressors bid.
- Hope for the best, and accept what comes.

Consider AGGRESSIVE options:
- Bolster your defenses.
- Seize the upper hand. Attack first.
- Fight with all the courage you can muster.

Review Answers: 1. a; 2. a; 3. b; 4. a

Academic Vocabulary

Review with students the high-use academic term in this section.

consequences effects of a particular event or events (p.430)

Building Vocabulary

Preteach or review the following terms:

chronicler one who records events (p. 425)

public-works projects government-led construction plans paid for with public funds (p. 426)

Taking Notes

Have students use the graphic organizer online to take notes on the section. This activity will prepare students for the Section Assessment, in which they will complete a graphic organizer that builds on the information using the Critical Thinking Skill: Comparing and Contrasting.

SECTION 4

The Yuan and Ming Dynasties

What You Will Learn...

Main Ideas

1. The Mongol Empire included China, and the Mongols ruled China as the Yuan dynasty.
2. The Ming dynasty was a time of stability and prosperity.
3. China under the Ming saw great changes in its government and relations with other countries.

The Big Idea

The Chinese were ruled by foreigners during the Yuan dynasty, but they threw off Mongol rule and prospered during the Ming dynasty.

Key Terms and People

Genghis Khan, *p. 424*
Kublai Khan, *p. 425*
Zheng He, *p. 427*
isolationism, *p. 430*

Use the graphic organizer online to take notes about the Yuan and Ming dynasties.

If YOU were there...

You are a farmer in northern China in 1212. As you pull weeds from a wheat field, you hear a sound like thunder. Looking toward the sound, you see hundreds—no, *thousands*—of armed horsemen on the horizon, riding straight toward you. You are frozen with fear. Only one thought fills your mind—the dreaded Mongols are coming.

What can you do to save yourself?

BUILDING BACKGROUND Throughout its history, northern China had been attacked over and over by nomadic peoples. During the Song dynasty these attacks became more frequent and threatening.

The Mongol Empire

Among the nomadic peoples who attacked the Chinese were the Mongols. For centuries, the Mongols had lived as separate tribes in the vast plains north of China. Then in 1206, a powerful leader, or khan, united them. His name was Temüjin. When he became leader, though, he was given a new title: "Universal Ruler," or **Genghis Khan** (JENG-guhs KAHN).

The Mongol Conquest

Genghis Khan organized the Mongols into a powerful army and led them on bloody expeditions of conquest. The brutality of the Mongol attacks terrorized people throughout much of Asia and Eastern Europe. Genghis Khan and his army killed all of the men, women, and children in countless cities and villages. Within 20 years, he ruled a large part of Asia.

Genghis Khan then turned his attention to China. He first led his armies into northern China in 1211. They fought their way south, wrecking whole towns and ruining farmland. By the time of Genghis Khan's death in 1227, all of northern China was under Mongol control.

Teach the Big Idea

At Level

The Yuan and Ming Dynasties

1. **Teach** Ask students the questions in the Main Idea boxes to teach this section.
2. **Apply** Have each student create a graphic organizer of his or her own design to compare and contrast the Yuan and Ming dynasties of China. Remind students to indicate both similarities and differences between the two dynasties.
   Verbal/Linguistic
3. **Review** Have students write a short summary of the rule of both the Yuan and Ming dynasties.
4. **Practice/Homework** Have students write a 10-question quiz using facts from this section. On the back of the paper, students should write the answers to the questions. Have students keep their quizzes and remind them that the quiz will be a useful tool to review later. **Verbal/Linguistic**

Alternative Assessment Handbook, Rubric 13: Graphic Organizers

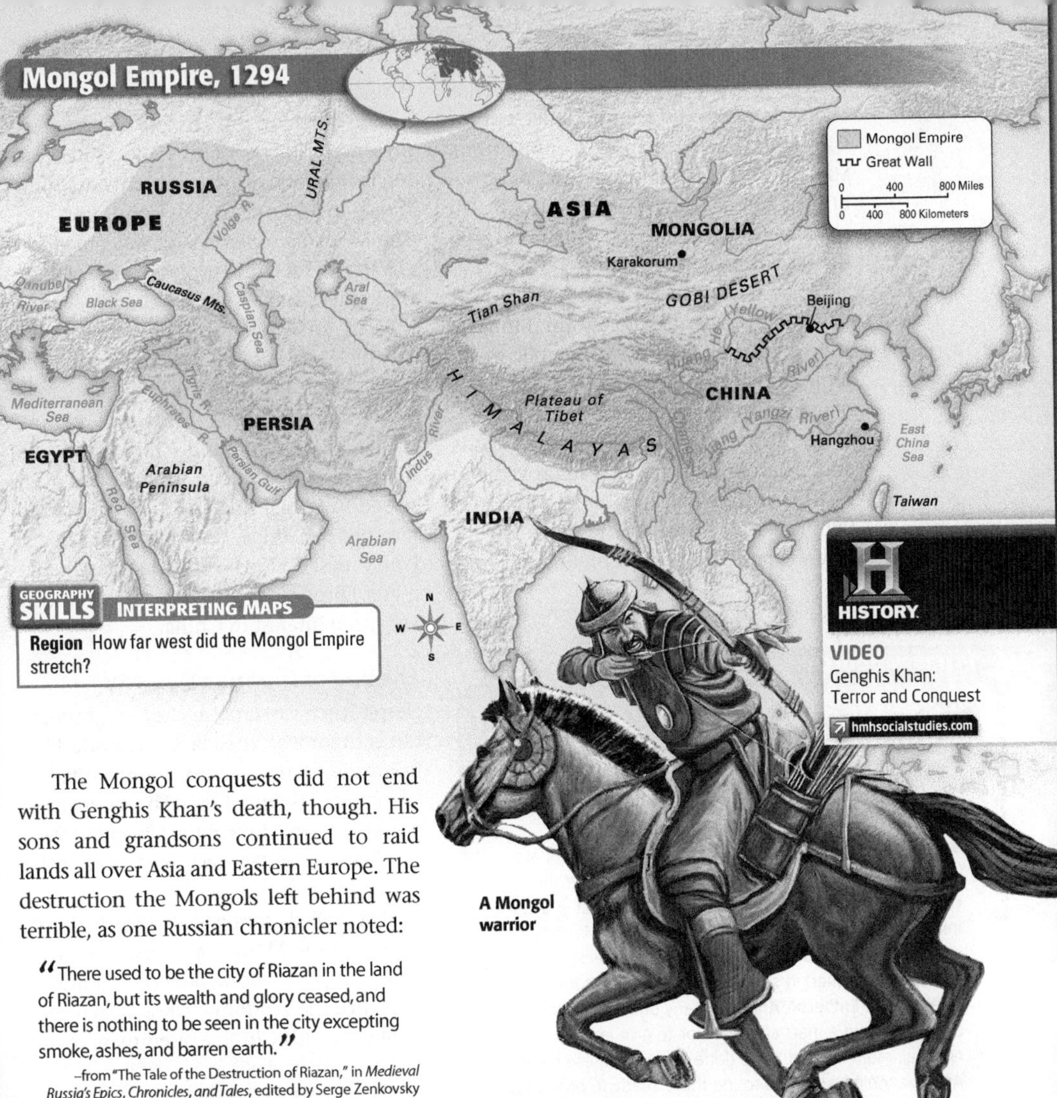

GEOGRAPHY SKILLS INTERPRETING MAPS

Region How far west did the Mongol Empire stretch?

HISTORY

VIDEO
Genghis Khan: Terror and Conquest
hmhsocialstudies.com

A Mongol warrior

The Mongol conquests did not end with Genghis Khan's death, though. His sons and grandsons continued to raid lands all over Asia and Eastern Europe. The destruction the Mongols left behind was terrible, as one Russian chronicler noted:

> "There used to be the city of Riazan in the land of Riazan, but its wealth and glory ceased, and there is nothing to be seen in the city excepting smoke, ashes, and barren earth."
>
> –from "The Tale of the Destruction of Riazan," in *Medieval Russia's Epics, Chronicles, and Tales*, edited by Serge Zenkovsky

In 1260 Genghis Khan's grandson **Kublai Khan** (KOO-bluh KAHN) became ruler of the Mongol Empire. He completed the conquest of China and in 1279 declared himself emperor of China. This began the Yuan dynasty, a period that some people also call the Mongol Ascendancy. For the first time in its long history, foreigners ruled all of China.

Life in Yuan China

Kublai Khan and the Mongol rulers he led belonged to a different ethnic group than the Chinese did. They spoke a different language, worshipped different gods, wore different clothing, and had different customs. The Chinese resented being ruled by these foreigners, whom they saw as rude and uncivilized.

Direct Teach

Main Idea

❶ The Mongol Empire

The Mongol Empire included China, and the Mongols ruled China as the Yuan dynasty.

Identify From where did the Mongols originate? *the plains north of China*

Analyze Why was the period of the Yuan dynasty a significant time in China's history? *It was the first time all of China was ruled by foreigners.*

Summarize How were the Mongol rulers different than the Chinese? *They spoke a different language, dressed differently, worshipped different gods, and had different customs.*

- **CRF:** Biography: Genghis Khan
- **CRF:** History and Geography Activity: The Mongol Empire
- **CRF:** Primary Source: A Mongol Oath to Genghis Khan
- Map Transparency: Mongol Empire, 1294

Did you know . . .

By 1240, Mongol armies had conquered much of southern Russia and Hungary, and had advanced as far west as Vienna, in modern-day Austria. Mongol armies of the Golden Horde were ready to launch an attack on western Europe, when their leaders were called to attend an election for a new great khan. In a sense, the death of Genghis Khan's son, Ogödei, saved Europe from Mongol invasion.

Differentiating Instruction

Advanced/Gifted and Talented **Above Level**

1. Review with students the information about the Mongol conquests. Ask students what important elements helped the Mongols conquer such a large empire. Make a list of ideas for students to see. Possible responses might include the Mongol army, Genghis Khan, fear of the Mongols, and technology.
2. Organize students into small groups. Have each group select one element from the list. Then have groups conduct research on the topics they selected.
3. Have each group create a presentation for the class that explains how the topic the group researched aided the Mongols in their conquests. Encourage students to use visual aids to enhance their presentations.
   LS Verbal/Linguistic, Visual/Spatial

Alternative Assessment Handbook, Rubrics 29: Presentations; and 30: Research

Answers

Interpreting Maps *to the Danube River in Eastern Europe*

Direct Teach

Main Idea

❶ The Mongol Empire

The Mongol Empire included China, and the Mongols ruled China as the Yuan dynasty.

Make Predictions What effect might Marco Polo's description of life in China have on European traders? *possible answer—They might want to go to China to trade.*

Analyze What led to the downfall of the Yuan dynasty? *failed campaigns against Japan, expensive public-works projects that weakened the economy, Chinese resentment, all of which led to rebellions*

CRF: Biography: Sorghaghtani Beki

CRF: Biography: Khutulun

Info to Know

Mongol Trade Historians believe that it was during the Yuan dynasty that many Chinese ideas and inventions were first introduced to foreigners. Gunpowder and the compass were among the ideas introduced from China to other civilizations during the Mongol Ascendancy.

Primary Source

Reading Like a Historian

A Chinese City Help students practice reading the document like historians. Ask:

- What features of Hangzhou is the author describing?
- What features do you think the author has omitted?

However, Kublai Khan did not force the Chinese to accept Mongol ways of life. Some Mongols even adopted aspects of the Chinese culture, such as Confucianism. Still, the Mongols made sure to keep control of the Chinese. They prohibited Confucian scholars from gaining too much power in the government, for example. The Mongols also placed heavy taxes on the Chinese.

Much of the tax money the Mongols collected went to pay for vast public-works projects. These projects required the labor of many Chinese people. The Yuan extended the Grand Canal and built new roads and palaces. Workers also improved the roads that were part of China's postal system. In addition, the Yuan emperors built a new capital, Dadu, near modern Beijing.

Mongol soldiers were sent throughout China to keep the peace as well as to keep a close watch on the Chinese. The soldiers' presence kept overland trade routes safe for merchants. Sea trade between China, India, and Southeast Asia continued, too. The Mongol emperors also welcomed foreign traders at Chinese ports. Some of these traders received special privileges.

Part of what we know about life in the Yuan dynasty comes from one such trader, an Italian merchant named Marco Polo. Between 1271 and 1295 he traveled in and around China. Polo was highly respected by the Mongols and even served in Kublai Khan's court. When Polo returned to Europe, he wrote of his travels. Polo's descriptions of China fascinated many Europeans. His book sparked much European interest in China.

Primary Source

BOOK

A Chinese City

In this passage Marco Polo describes his visit to Hangzhou (HAHNG-JOH), a city in southeastern China.

"Inside the city there is a Lake . . . and all round it are erected [built] beautiful palaces and mansions, of the richest and most exquisite [finest] structure that you can imagine . . . In the middle of the Lake are two Islands, on each of which stands a rich, beautiful and spacious edifice [building], furnished in such style as to seem fit for the palace of an Emperor. And when any one of the citizens desired to hold a marriage feast, or to give any other entertainment, it used to be done at one of these palaces. And everything would be found there ready to order, such as silver plate, trenchers [platters], and dishes, napkins and table-cloths, and whatever else was needful. The King made this provision for the gratification [enjoyment] of his people, and the place was open to every one who desired to give an entertainment."

–Marco Polo, from *Description of the World*

ANALYSIS SKILL **ANALYZING PRIMARY SOURCES**

From this description, what impression might Europeans have of Hangzhou?

The End of the Yuan Dynasty

Despite their vast empire, the Mongols were not content with their lands. They decided to invade Japan. A Mongol army sailed to Japan in 1274 and 1281. The campaigns, however, were disastrous. Violent storms and fierce defenders destroyed most of the Mongol force.

The failed campaigns against Japan weakened the Mongol military. The huge, expensive public-works projects had already weakened the economy. These weaknesses, combined with Chinese resentment, made China ripe for rebellion.

In the 1300s many Chinese groups rebelled against the Yuan dynasty. In 1368 a former monk named Zhu Yuanzhang (JOO yoo-ahn-JAHNG) took charge of a rebel army. He led this army in a final victory over the Mongols. China was once again ruled by the Chinese.

READING CHECK **Finding Main Ideas** How did the Mongols come to rule China?

Critical Thinking: Supporting a Point of View

Above Level

An Editorial for a New Dynasty

1. Ask students to imagine that they are Zhu Yuanzhang immediately after his defeat of the Mongols. He has arrived in the capital city and intends to start a new dynasty.
2. Have students write a front-page editorial from Zhu Yuanzhang to be published in the largest newspaper in China. The editorial should explain why he felt it was necessary to replace the Mongols and should give an account of the problems the Mongols had brought to China.
3. Remind students to include both facts and opinions in their editorial and to try to persuade the Chinese people to support their new ruler.
4. Ask for volunteers to read their editorials to the class. **LS Verbal/Linguistic**

Alternative Assessment Handbook, Rubric 43: Writing to Persuade

Answers

Analyzing Primary Sources *that it is a beautiful and very wealthy city*

Reading Check *Kublai Khan conquered all of China after his grandfather, Genghis Khan, began the conquest.*

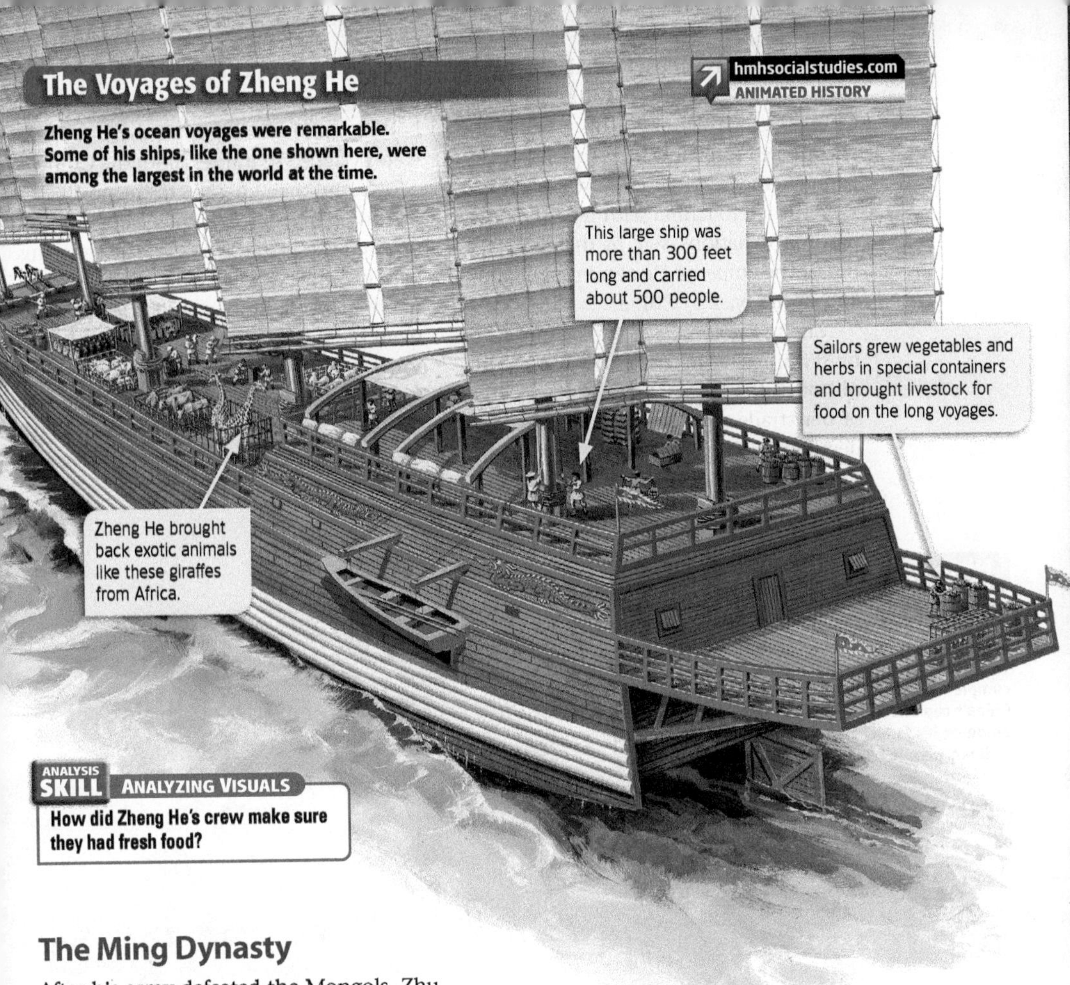
The Voyages of Zheng He
Zheng He's ocean voyages were remarkable. Some of his ships, like the one shown here, were among the largest in the world at the time.
hmhsocialstudies.com
ANIMATED HISTORY
This large ship was more than 300 feet long and carried about 500 people.
Sailors grew vegetables and herbs in special containers and brought livestock for food on the long voyages.
Zheng He brought back exotic animals like these giraffes from Africa.

ANALYSIS SKILL ANALYZING VISUALS

How did Zheng He's crew make sure they had fresh food?

The Ming Dynasty

After his army defeated the Mongols, Zhu Yuanzhang became emperor of China. The Ming dynasty that he founded ruled China from 1368 to 1644—nearly 300 years. Ming China proved to be one of the most stable and prosperous times in Chinese history. The Ming expanded China's fame overseas and sponsored incredible building projects across China.

Great Sea Voyages

During the Ming dynasty, the Chinese improved their ships and their sailing skills. The greatest sailor of the period was **Zheng He** (juhng HUH). Between 1405 and 1433, he led seven grand voyages to places around Asia. Zheng He's fleets were huge. One included more than 60 ships and 25,000 sailors. Some of the ships were gigantic too, perhaps more than 300 feet long. That is longer than a football field!

In the course of his voyages Zheng He sailed his fleet throughout the Indian Ocean. He sailed as far west as the Persian Gulf and the easternmost coast of Africa.

Direct Teach

Main Idea

❷ The Ming Dynasty

The Ming dynasty was a time of stability and prosperity.

Recall How long did the Ming dynasty last? *nearly 300 years*

Explain Where did the expeditions of Zheng He travel? *throughout the Indian Ocean and as far west as the Persian Gulf and the easternmost coast of Africa*

Make Generalizations Why do you think it was significant that the Chinese had such a capable fleet of ships? *possible answer—It proved that Chinese technology was advanced and that the country was sophisticated enough to support such projects.*

CRF: Biography: Admiral Zheng He

Other People, Other Places

East Versus West Almost 60 years after the voyages of Chinese admiral Zheng He ended, Christopher Columbus set off on his famous voyage. While Columbus's expedition to the Americas might be better known, the voyages of Zheng He are, perhaps, more impressive. With about 27,000 crew members and dozens of ships, the Chinese expeditions made Columbus's three-ship, 90-member crew look tiny in comparison.

hmhsocialstudies.com
Online Resources
Activity: Marco Polo

Critical Thinking: Generalizing

At Level

Zheng He's Expeditions

1. Ask students to imagine that they are traveling along the coast of East Africa and have come across the ruins of a small village. Inside they find a personal journal written about 600 years ago in the native language.
2. Scholars believe the text, which describes Zheng He's ships, proves that Chinese sailors visited the area in the year 1410.
3. As the translators, have students re-create the first two pages of this journal. Students should try to use vivid language to describe the first sighting of the ships, the animals that were on board, and the sailors' dress and behavior. Encourage students to illustrate their pages. **LS Verbal/Linguistic, Visual/Spatial**

Alternative Assessment Handbook, Rubrics 3: Artwork; and 15; Journals

Answers

Analyzing Visuals *Sailors grew vegetables and herbs and brought livestock on board the ship.*

Direct Teach

Main Idea

❷ The Ming Dynasty

The Ming dynasty was a time of stability and prosperity.

Recall How did the Forbidden City gets its name? *Common people were forbidden from entering the city.*

Explain Why is the Forbidden City called "a city within a city"? *It was a huge complex of almost 1,000 buildings located within the capital city.*

Elaborate Why do you think the Ming rulers were interested in building projects? *possible answers—to glorify their empire, to impress their people, to instill fear in their neighbors*

Info to Know

The Forbidden City The Forbidden City was used for almost 500 years as the imperial residence of China's rulers. It was built between 1406 and 1420 by Emperor Yung-lo of the Ming dynasty. In 1912, when the imperial government was overthrown, the last Chinese emperor, P'u-i (pu-YEE), was allowed to continue living in the Forbidden City. After his departure in 1924, the Forbidden City was made into a national museum.

Everywhere his ships landed, Zheng He presented leaders with beautiful gifts from China. He boasted about his country and encouraged foreign leaders to send gifts to China's emperor. From one voyage, Zheng He returned to China with representatives of some 30 nations, sent by their leaders to honor the emperor. He also brought goods and stories back to China.

Zheng He's voyages rank among the most impressive in the history of seafaring. Although they did not lead to the creation of new trade routes or the exploration of new lands, they served as a clear sign of China's power.

Great Building Projects

The Ming were also known for their grand building projects. Many of these projects were designed to impress both the Chinese people and their enemies to the north.

In Beijing, for example, Ming emperors built the Forbidden City. This amazing palace complex included hundreds of imperial residences, temples, and other government buildings. Within the buildings were some 9,000 rooms. The name "Forbidden City" came from the fact that the common people were not even allowed to enter the complex. For centuries, this city within a city was a symbol of China's glory.

History Close-up

The Forbidden City

The Forbidden City is not actually a city. It's a huge complex of almost 1,000 buildings in the heart of China's capital. The Forbidden City was built for the emperor, his family, his court, and his servants, and ordinary people were forbidden from entering.

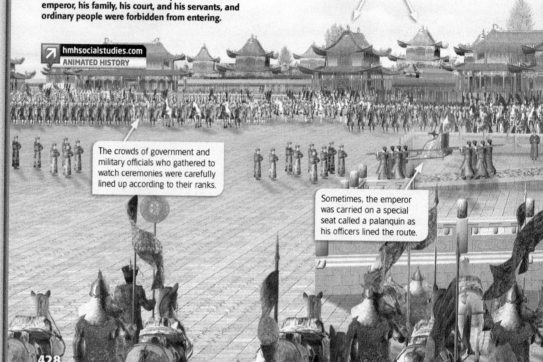

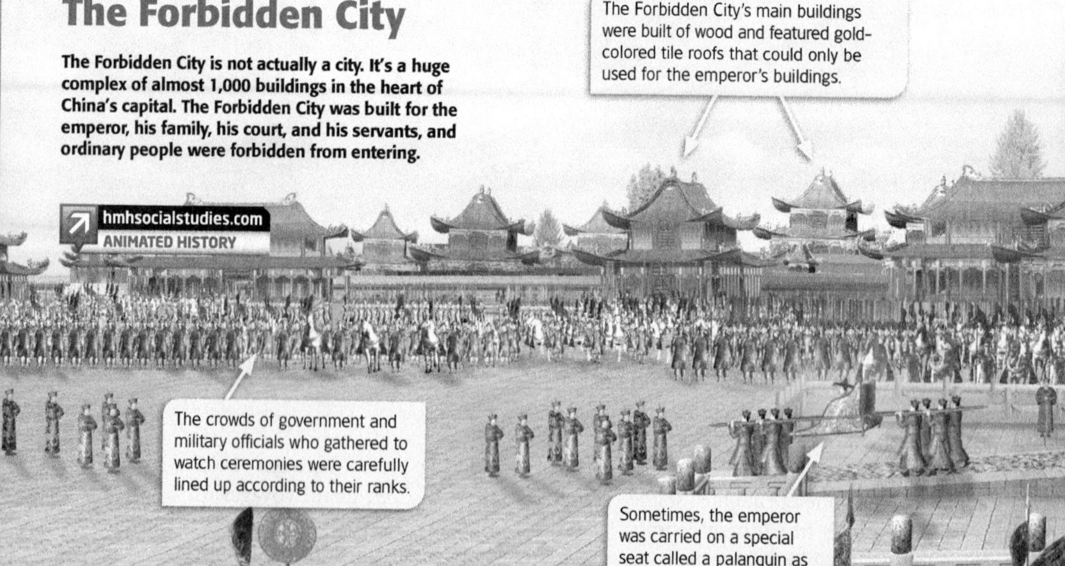

hmhsocialstudies.com
ANIMATED HISTORY
The Forbidden City's main buildings were built of wood and featured gold-colored tile roofs that could only be used for the emperor's buildings.
The crowds of government and military officials who gathered to watch ceremonies were carefully lined up according to their ranks.
Sometimes, the emperor was carried on a special seat called a palanquin as his officers lined the route.
428

Cross-Discipline Activity: English–Language Arts

At Level

Description of the Forbidden City

1. Ask students to imagine that they are military or government officials who have been invited to enter the Forbidden City in order to pay tribute to the emperor. They will gather there with thousands of other officials, but it is still an immense honor.
2. Because they have never been allowed into the Forbidden City, they are very impressed by its size, beautiful buildings, and beautiful decorations.
3. When they return home, what will they tell their friends and family? Tell students to write a one-page dialogue of their conversation after the event in which they describe what they saw, including details about the emperor and the architecture of the palace. Students should also include how they might have felt when in the Forbidden City.

LS Verbal/Linguistic

Alternative Assessment Handbook, Rubric 40: Writing to Describe

Ming rulers also directed the restoration of the famous Great Wall of China. Large numbers of soldiers and peasants worked to rebuild collapsed portions of walls, connect existing walls, and build new ones. The result was a construction feat unmatched in history. The wall was more than 2,000 miles long. It would reach from San Diego to New York! The wall was about 25 feet high and, at the top, 12 feet wide. Protected by the wall—and the soldiers who stood guard along it—the Chinese people felt safe from invasions by the northern tribes.

READING CHECK **Generalizing** In what ways did the Ming dynasty strengthen China?

China Under the Ming

During the Ming dynasty, Chinese society began to change. This change was largely due to the efforts of the Ming emperors. Having expelled the Mongols, the Ming emperors worked to eliminate all foreign influences from Chinese society. As a result, China's government and relations with other countries changed dramatically.

hmhsocialstudies.com
ANIMATED HISTORY
The Great Wall of China

The Hall of Supreme Harmony is the largest building in the Forbidden City. Grand celebrations for important holidays, like the emperor's birthday and the New Year, were held there.

ANALYSIS SKILL **ANALYZING VISUALS**

How did the Forbidden City show the power and importance of the emperor?

429

Direct Teach

Main Idea

3 China Under the Ming

China under the Ming saw great changes in its government and relations with other countries.

Explain How were the Ming emperors more powerful than Tang and Song rulers? *They abolished the offices of powerful officials, took a larger role in running the government, and punished anyone who challenged their authority.*

Describe What was the job of a Chinese censor? *to investigate and report on local officials and local institutions*

Draw Conclusions Why do you think the Ming dynasty turned to isolationism? *possible answer—The period of Mongol rule made the Ming suspicious of foreigners.*

Activity **Letters to the Emperor** Have students write a formal letter to the Ming emperor supporting or opposing the policy of isolationism.
LS Verbal/Linguistic

Alternative Assessment Handbook, Rubric 5: Business Letters

CRF: Primary Source: Good Behavior in 1600s China: Meritorious Deeds at No Cost

Cross-Discipline Activity: Math

At Level

A Forbidden and Very Large City

1. Tell students that the Forbidden City covers approximately 178 acres. Then tell students that one acre equals 43,560 square feet.
2. Have students compute how many square feet there are in the Forbidden City. *(178 acres × 43,560 sq. ft. per acre = 7,997,680 sq. ft.)*
3. Have students measure the length and width of the classroom. Then have students compute how many of their classrooms could fit inside the Forbidden City. *(First, compute the size of your classroom by multiplying the length of the room times its width. Then divide that area into the area of the City. For example, 20 feet × 30 feet = 600 sq. ft. per classroom; 7,997,680 sq. ft / 600 sq. ft. per classroom = 12,922.8 classrooms)* **LS Logical/Mathematical**

Alternative Assessment Handbook, Rubric 35: Solving Problems

Answers

Analyzing Visuals *possible answer—elaborate buildings, large size*

Reading Check *by promoting China across the world, great building projects*

Direct Teach

Teaching Tip

Isolationism Some students may not understand how China's policy of isolationism led to a decline. Ask volunteers to describe how it would feel if, for one week, they had to stay at home, could not watch television, go to the movies, read a magazine or newspaper, or talk to anyone on the phone. The result is that they would not know what their friends or anyone else outside of their homes were doing. This is an example of isolationism. China did not know about advances in the Western world, and China's power and glory faded.

Review & Assess

Close

Ask students to list the similarities and differences between the Yuan and Ming dynasties.

Review

Online Quiz, Section 4

Assess

SE Section 4 Assessment

PASS: Section 4 Quiz

Alternative Assessment Handbook

Reteach/Classroom Intervention

Guided Reading Workbook, Section 4

Interactive Skills Tutor CD-ROM

Answers

Reading Check *Over time, China was technologically outpaced by the world and as a result was weakened and controlled by other countries.*

Government

When the Ming took over China, they adopted many government programs that had been created by the Tang and the Song. However, the Ming emperors were much more powerful than the Tang and Song emperors had been. They abolished the offices of some powerful officials and took a larger role in running the government themselves. These emperors fiercely protected their power, and they punished anyone whom they saw as challenging their authority.

ACADEMIC VOCABULARY
consequences effects of a particular event or events

Despite their personal power, though, the Ming did not disband the civil service system. Because he personally oversaw the entire government, the emperor needed officials to keep his affairs organized.

The Ming also used examinations to appoint censors. These officials were sent throughout China to investigate the behavior of local leaders and to judge the quality of schools and other institutions. Censors had existed for many years in China, but under the Ming emperors their power and influence grew.

Relations with Other Countries

In the 1430s a new Ming emperor made Zheng He return to China and dismantle his fleet. At the same time, he banned foreign trade. China entered a period of isolationism. **Isolationism** is a policy of avoiding contact with other countries.

In the end, this isolationism had great consequences for China. In 1644 the Ming dynasty was overthrown. By the late 1800s the Western world had made huge leaps in technological progress. Westerners were then able to gain influence in Chinese affairs. Partly due to its isolation and lack of progress, China was too weak to stop them.

READING CHECK **Identifying Cause and Effect** How did isolationism affect China?

SUMMARY AND PREVIEW Under the Yuan and Ming dynasties, Chinese society changed. Eventually, the Ming began a policy of isolationism. In the next chapter you will read about Japan, another country that was isolated at times.

Section 4 Assessment

hmhsocialstudies.com ONLINE QUIZ

Reviewing Ideas, Terms, and People

1. a. Identify Who was **Genghis Khan**?
   b. Explain How did the Mongols gain control of China?
   c. Evaluate Judge this statement: "The Mongols should never have tried to invade Japan."
2. a. Identify Who was **Zheng He**, and what did he do?
   b. Analyze What impression do you think the Forbidden City had on the residents of Beijing?
   c. Develop How may the Great Wall have both helped and hurt China?
3. a. Define What is **isolationism**?
   b. Explain How did the Ming change China?
   c. Develop How might a policy of isolationism have both advantages and disadvantages?

Critical Thinking

4. Comparing and Contrasting Draw a diagram like this one. Use your notes to see how the Yuan and Ming dynasties were alike and different.

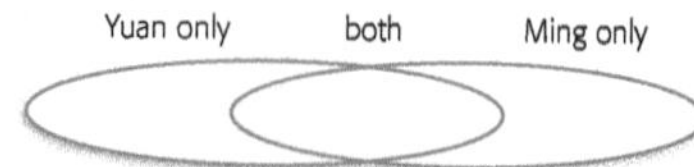

Focus on Writing

5. **Identifying Achievements of the Later Dynasties** Make a list of the achievements of the Yuan and Ming dynasties. Then look back over all your notes and rate the achievements or inventions. Which three do you think are the most important?

Section 4 Assessment Answers

1. a. leader of the Mongols who conquered a large part of Asia
   b. by attacking and terrorizing Chinese towns
   c. possible answer—Statement is valid; attack on Japan contributed to the Yuan dynasty's failure.
2. a. the greatest sailor of the Ming dynasty; led voyages of exploration to Asia and Africa
   b. possible answers—that the emperor was divine; emphasized power of the emperor
   c. The Great Wall protected the Chinese, but it was costly to build.
3. a. removing, or isolating, a country from contact with other countries
   b. building projects, instituted isolationism.
   c. advantages—protection, safety; disadvantages—lack of trade, development
4. Yuan—foreign rule, Mongol and Chinese customs, trade by sea; Both—great building projects; Ming—Chinese rule, stable dynasty, great sea voyages, isolationism
5. Possible responses might include the Forbidden City, restoration of the Great Wall, and voyages of exploration.

BIOGRAPHY

Kublai Khan

How did a Mongol nomad settle down to rule a vast empire?

When did he live? 1215–1294

Where did he live? Kublai came from Mongolia but spent much of his life in China. His capital, Dadu, was near the modern city of Beijing.

What did he do? Kublai Khan completed the conquest of China that Genghis Khan had begun. He ruled China as the emperor of the Yuan dynasty.

Why is he important? The lands Kublai Khan ruled made up one of the largest empires in world history. It stretched from the Pacific Ocean to Eastern Europe. As China's ruler, Kublai Khan welcomed foreign visitors, including the Italian merchant Marco Polo and the Arab historian Ibn Battutah. The stories these two men told helped create interest in China and its products among Westerners.

Generalizing How did Kublai Khan's actions help change people's views of China?

KEY FACTS

- Unified all of China under his rule
- Established peace, during which China's population grew
- Extended the Grand Canal so that food could be shipped from the Huang He (Yellow River) to his capital near modern Beijing
- Linked China to India and Persia with better roads
- Increased contact with the West

This painting from the 1200s shows Kublai Khan hunting on horseback.

431

Cross Discipline Activity: English–Language Arts

At Level

Writing an Introduction

1. Tell students that when a notable person is scheduled to give a speech, it is common for someone to introduce him or her. These short introductory speeches always include the person's accomplishments and present the person in a favorable light.
2. Have each student write an introduction that someone might have written and then read to introduce Kublai Khan to a group of foreigners. Make sure students include details about Kublai Khan found in this section.
3. Ask for volunteers to read their introductions to the class. LS **Verbal/Linguistic**

Alternative Assessment Handbook, Rubric 37: Writing Assignments

Biography

Reading Focus Question

Review with students how nomads live and contrast that style of life with city dwellers or farmers. Ask students if they believe it would be difficult to stay in the same place if for generations their family had moved from one location to another. Discuss students' views.

Info to Know

Kublai Khan: A Kinder, Gentler Khan While he could be violent, Kublai Khan was different from his grandfather, Genghis Khan. He urged his generals to be humane in their conquests. He was concerned with running an effective government and encouraging religious tolerance. Among the religions in Kublai Khan's China were Tibetan Lamaism, Islam, Buddhism, Confucianism, and Daoism.

Kublai Khan: A Challenged Emperor Despite his efforts, Kublai Khan was never able to build a strong empire in China. While the economy often looked healthy, much of the economic gain went only to the wealthy. The civil service system had crumbled, and censors were no longer working across China. Kublai Khan had a difficult time controlling all of his officials. Economic conditions for most Chinese worsened during this period.

About the Illustration

This illustration of Kublai Khan is an artist's conception based on available sources. However, historians are uncertain exactly what Kublai Khan looked like.

Answers

Generalizing *He made internal improvements in China and welcomed foreign visitors to serve and write about the empire.*

Social Studies Skills

Using Mental Maps

Activity Real-Life Examples Ask students to think about the mental maps they use in their daily lives. Point out the example in the skills lesson text about mental maps of our neighborhoods. Have each student sketch the floor plan of your school from memory. Direct students to locate and label important places, including classrooms that they visit each day. Also have students identify the fastest or easiest routes between these classrooms.

Discuss the difficulties one can face in navigating an area when one has no mental maps of that area, such as after moving to a new town or visiting a city on vacation.

LS **Intrapersonal, Visual/Spatial**

Alternative Assessment Handbook, Rubric 20: Map Creation

Social Studies Skills

Analysis | Critical Thinking | Economics | Study

Using Mental Maps

Define the Skill

Think about the town in which you live. What part of town is your favorite place to relax with friends? Where would you most like to live? What is the best route to take to get from your home to your school?

The image you have of your town in your mind is called a mental map. A mental map represents the mental image you have of an area. You will not find a mental map in a textbook or atlas. Instead, all people have their own mental maps that live in their heads. These maps reflect our personal knowledge of places, such as the locations of landmarks or physical features. They also reflect our perceptions of places: which places are fun, which are dangerous, and so on.

You use mental maps every day. You probably have a mental map of the layout of your home and one of your community. You know where friends' homes, schools, businesses, and the like are located. You use mental maps to plan routes to those places.

Learn the Skill

Mental maps can also be useful in the study of world history. Keeping an image in your head of where places are located can help you understand and interpret historical events. Below are a few tips for using mental maps in your studies.

1. **Consider what you know about a place and its location.** For example, you know that China is located in East Asia. You are also probably familiar with some of its major physical and cultural features, such as the Huang He and the Great Wall.
2. **Don't worry about too much detail.** Your mental map does not have to be a perfect representation of an area. The mental map is a rough image that will help you see patterns.
3. **Visualize relationships between places.** When you read about contact between places in history, consult your mental map to think about where they are in relation to each other. For example, Buddhism was brought to China from India, which is southwest of China.
4. **Sketch maps as necessary.** If you have trouble envisioning a location or region in your head, draw a rough sketch. A sketch can sometimes help you make sense of what you are having trouble seeing in your mind. You may wish to check your sketch against a printed map to be sure it is accurate.

Practice the Skill

Without consulting the maps in this chapter, compose a mental map of China and its surroundings. Use the mental map to answer the questions below. If you find that you cannot answer the questions, you may need to study the printed maps again.

1. What are the main bodies of water in China?
2. In which region of China was the Tang capital of Chang'an?
3. When the Mongols sent an army to invade Japan in 1274, in which direction did they have to travel?

Social Studies Skills Activity: Using Mental Maps

Critical Thinking

At Level

1. Have each student review the material in Section 4 about the Ming dynasty and its building projects in Beijing.
2. Remind students that a person's opinions, attitudes, and experiences will shape his or her mental maps of an area. As an example, ask students how a car driver's mental map of the roads in your town might differ from a bicyclist's. *(Sample answer—The car driver will more likely be aware of the locations of freeways and gas stations.)*
3. Discuss how each of the following people's mental maps of Beijing would have differed under the Ming: a servant who never left the Forbidden City, a merchant, and a farmer who lived just outside the city. *(Possible answers—The servant and farmer would know little of the city. The merchant would have the most developed maps.)*
4. Have each student write a diary entry reflecting one resident's knowledge of the city. LS **Visual/Spatial**

Alternative Assessment Handbook, Rubric 15: Journals

Answers

Practice and Apply the Skill

1. *Huang He, Chang Jiang, East China Sea, South China Sea, Grand Canal;* **2.** *northeast China;* **3.** *southeast*

CHAPTER 14 Chapter Review

History's Impact
▶ video series
Review the video to answer the focus question:
What do you think are some consequences of living in an isolated society?

Visual Summary

Use the visual summary below to help you review the main ideas of the chapter.

QUICK FACTS

China was reunified, and Buddhism spread during the Sui and Tang dynasties.

Farming and trade grew under the Tang and Song dynasties.

Confucian thought influenced Chinese government and education.

The powerful Yuan and Ming dynasties strengthened China, and expanded trade, but then China became isolated.

Reviewing Vocabulary, Terms, and People

Match the words or names with their definitions or descriptions.

a. Kublai Khan
b. movable type
c. scholar-official
d. Empress Wu
e. bureaucracy
f. Zheng He
g. compass
h. porcelain
i. Genghis Khan
j. isolationism
k. incentive
l. gunpowder

1. ruthless but effective Tang dynasty ruler
2. a set of letters or characters that can be moved to create different lines of text
3. leader who united the Mongols and began invasion of China
4. body of unelected government officials
5. thin, beautiful pottery
6. a device that indicates direction
7. policy of avoiding contact with other countries
8. founder of the Yuan dynasty
9. a mixture of powders used in explosives
10. commanded huge fleets of ships
11. educated government worker
12. something that leads people to follow a certain course of action

Comprehension and Critical Thinking

SECTION 1 *(Pages 410–413)*

13. a. Identify What period did China enter after the Han dynasty collapsed? What dynasty brought an end to this period?

b. Analyze Why is the Tang dynasty considered a golden age of Chinese civilization?

c. Predict How might Chinese culture have been different in the Tang and Song dynasties if Buddhism had not been introduced to China?

Answers

Visual Summary

Review and Inquiry Have students use the visual summary to write a paragraph summarizing the important events depicted in the illustration.

Quick Facts Transparency: China Visual Summary

Reviewing Vocabulary, Terms and People

1. d
2. b
3. i
4. e
5. h
6. g
7. j
8. a
9. l
10. f
11. c
12. k

Comprehension and Critical Thinking

13. a. the period of disunion; the Sui dynasty

b. possible answer—because many laws, reforms, poems, and other cultural achievements during the dynasty led to the growth and prosperity of China.

c. Buddhism would not have become a major religion in China, and missionaries would not have spread Buddhism to other Asian lands. Also, much of the art and architecture might not exist because Buddhism inspired so much of it.

Review and Assessment Resources

Review and Reinforce

SE Chapter Review
CRF: Chapter Review Activity
Quick Facts Transparency: China Visual Summary
Spanish Chapter Summaries Audio CD Program
Online Chapter Summaries in Six Languages
TOS Holt McDougal PuzzleView
Quiz Game CD-ROM

Assess

SE Standardized Test Practice
PASS: Chapter Test
Alternative Assessment Handbook
TOS ExamView Assessment Suite, Chapter Test
Differentiated Instruction Modified Worksheets and Tests CD-ROM: Chapter Test
Online Assessment Program, in the Interactive Student Edition

Reteach/Intervene

Guided Reading Workbook
Differentiated Instruction Teacher Management System: Lesson Plans
Differentiated Instruction Modified Worksheets and Tests CD-ROM
Interactive Skills Tutor CD-ROM

Chapter Resources

SECTION 2 *(Pages 414–419)*

14. a. Describe What did Wu Daozi, Li Bo, Du Fu, and Li Qingzhao contribute to Chinese culture?

b. Analyze What led to the growth of cities in China? What were China's cities like during the Tang and Song dynasties?

c. Evaluate Which Chinese invention has had a greater effect on world history—the magnetic compass or gunpowder? Why do you think so?

SECTION 3 *(Pages 420–423)*

15. a. Define What is Confucianism? How did it change during and after the Song dynasty?

b. Make Inferences Why do you think the civil service examination system was created?

c. Elaborate Why were China's civil service examinations so difficult?

SECTION 4 *(Pages 424–430)*

16. a. Describe How did the Mongols create their huge empire? What areas were included in it?

b. Draw Conclusions How did Marco Polo and Zheng He help shape ideas about China?

c. Elaborate Why do you think the Ming emperors spent so much time and money rebuilding and enlarging the Great Wall?

Using the Internet

17. Activity: Creating a Mural The Tang and Song periods saw many agricultural, technological, and commercial developments. New irrigation techniques, movable type, and gunpowder were a few of them. Use your online textbook to learn more about such developments. Imagine that a city official has hired you to create a mural showing all of the great things the Chinese developed during the Tang and Song dynasties. Create a large mural that depicts as many advances as possible.

hmhsocialstudies.com

Reviewing Themes

18. Science and Technology How did Chinese inventions alter the course of world history?

19. Economics How did the strong agricultural and trading economy of Tang and Song China affect the country?

Reading Skills

20. Drawing Conclusions about the Past Read the statements about the Ming dynasty below. For each conclusion that follows, decide whether the statements provide sufficent evidence to justify the conclusion.

The Ming ruled China from 1368 to 1644.

Zhu Yuanzhang was a Ming emperor.

The Great Wall was rebuilt by the Ming.

a. The Great Wall is located in China.

b. Zhu Yuanzhang was a good emperor.

c. Zhu Yuanzhang ruled some time between 1368 and 1644.

d. Zhu Yuanzhang rebuilt the Great Wall.

Social Studies Skills

Using Mental Maps Using only your mental map of China and not consulting the maps in this chapter, answer the questions below.

21. In what direction did the Mongols travel to get from their homeland in modern Mongolia to China?

22. The Mongol Empire extended west into Europe. Besides China, what regions were included in the empire?

Focus on Writing

23. Writing a Magazine Article Now that you have identified three achievements or inventions you want to write about, begin your article. Open with a sentence that states your main idea. Include three or four sentences about each achievement or invention you have chosen. These sentences should describe the achievement or invention and explain why it was so important. End your article with a sentence or two summarizing China's importance to the world.

Answers

14. a. Wu Daozi painted murals that celebrated Buddhism and nature; Li Bo and Du Fu wrote many beautiful poems that are still enjoyed; Li Qingzhao is perhaps China's greatest female poet.

b. The growth of agriculture, increased food production, and trade led to the growth of cities. Most were large, prosperous, and had people from many cultures.

c. possible answers—the compass because it helped sailors find their way; gunpowder because it changed warfare forever

15. a. a set of two basic principles that would allow society to function in an orderly manner, created by Confucius; became Neo-Confucianism, which emphasized spiritual matters

b. possible answer—to ensure that only the most qualified officials ran the government and to improve government efficiency

c. The scholar-official was a very elite member of society, so they had to prove that they were worthy of the position. The exams filtered out people who may not have been suited for the position.

16. a. conquests by Genghis Khan's and Kublai Khan; most of China, Mongolia, Persia, parts of northern Arabia, eastern Europe, and western Russia

b. Both Marco Polo and Zheng He helped expose the beauty and wonder of China to a world that had never heard of China and helped spur demands for Chinese goods.

c. to protect China from northern invaders, like the Mongols; so that outsiders never ruled them again

Using the Internet

17. Go to hmhsocialstudies.com to access a rubric for this activity.

Reviewing Themes

18. Paper and movable type helped people spread new ideas long distances. The compass allowed explorers to travel far in greater safety. Gunpowder changed how wars were fought, making warfare much more destructive.

19. The strong economy allowed some people to concentrate their talents and skills on the arts and inventions, instead of working constantly just to survive.

Reading Skills

20. a. yes

b. no

c. yes

d. no

Social Studies Skills

21. south and southeast

22. Persia, Central Asia, Russia

Focus on Writing

23. Rubric Students' magazine articles should:

- include the main idea in an introduction.
- describe three major accomplishments and explain their importance.
- conclude with a summary.
- use proper capitalization, spelling, punctuation, and grammar.

CRF: Focus on Writing: A Magazine Article

CHAPTER 14

Standardized Test Practice

DIRECTIONS: Read each question, and write the letter of the best response.

1

This object displays Chinese expertise at working with

A woodblocks.
B gunpowder.
C cotton fibers.
D porcelain.

2 Trade and other contact with peoples far from China stopped under which dynasty?

A Ming
B Yuan
C Song
D Sui

3 Which of the following was *not* a way that Confucianism influenced China?

A emphasis on family and family values
B expansion of manufacturing and trade
C emphasis on service to society
D well-educated government officials

4 What was a major cause for the spread of Buddhism to China and other parts of Asia?

A the teachings of Kublai Khan
B the writings of Confucius
C the travels of Buddhist missionaries
D the support of Empress Wu

5 All of the following flourished during *both* the Tang and the Song dynasties, *except*

A art and culture.
B sea voyages of exploration.
C science and technology.
D trade.

Connecting with Past Learnings

6 Earlier you learned about the deeds of emperor Shi Huangdi. He had laborers work on a structure that Ming rulers improved. What was that structure?

A the Great Wall
B the Great Tomb
C the Forbidden City
D the Temple of Buddha

7 Earlier you learned that the ancient Egyptians increased food production by digging irrigation canals to water their fields. Under which dynasty did the Chinese develop new irrigation techniques to increase their production of food?

A Han
B Ming
C Song
D Sui

Answers

Standardized Test Practice

1. D
Break Down the Question Students should recall the vase in the Quick Facts information on Chinese inventions.

2. A
Break Down the Question This question requires students to recall factual information from Section 4.

3. B
Break Down the Question Point out to students that the word *not* in the question indicates that they should select the statement that is *not* true.

4. C
Break Down the Question Point out to students that Buddhism arrived in China and spread from there thanks to Buddhist missionaries.

5. B
Break Down the Question Point out to students that sea voyages of exploration occurred during the Ming dynasty.

6. A
Break Down the Question This question requires students to recall factual information from Chapter 6.

7. C
Break Down the Question This question requires students to recall factual information from Section 2.

Intervention Resources

Reproducible

- Guided Reading Workbook
- Differentiated Instruction Teacher Management System: Lesson Plans

Technology

- Quick Facts Transparency: China Visual Summary
- Differentiated Instruction Modified Worksheets and Tests CD-ROM
- Interactive Skills Tutor CD-ROM

Tips for Test Taking

I'm Stuck! Provide these tips to students: If you come across a question that stumps you, don't get frustrated. First master the question to make sure you understand what is being asked. Then work through strategies you have previously learned. If you are still stuck, circle the question and go on to others. Come back to the problem question later. What if you still have no idea? Practice the 50/50 strategy and then take your best educated guess.

Chapter 15 Planning Guide

Japan

Overview	Instructional Resources	
CHAPTER 15 **Essential Question:** How did the Japanese blend borrowed customs and native traditions into a unique culture? **Focus on the Essential Question Podcast**	TOS **Differentiated Instruction Teacher Management System:** • Instructional Benchmarking Guides • Lesson Plans for Differentiated Instruction  **Guided Reading Workbook**  **Chapter Resource File:** • Chapter Review Activity • Focus on Writing Activity: Writing a Travel Brochure • Social Studies Skills Activity: Solving Problems	TOS **Calendar Planner**  **Power Presentations with Media Gallery** **Differentiated Instruction Modified Worksheets and Tests CD-ROM** **Primary Source Library CD-ROM for World History** **Interactive Skills Tutor CD-ROM** **Student Edition on Audio CD Program** **The World's Music Audio Program** **Video:** Rise of the Samurai Class **Multimedia Connections:** Japan and the Samurai Warrior
Section 1: **Geography and Early Japan** **The Big Idea:** Japan's early societies were both isolated from and influenced by China and Korea.	TOS **Differentiated Instruction Teacher Management System:** Section 1 Lesson Plan **Guided Reading Workbook:** Section 1  **Chapter Resource File:** • Vocabulary Builder Activity, Section 1 • Biography Activity: Empress Suiko	**Daily Bellringer Transparency:** Section 1 **Map Transparency:** Japan: Physical **Quick Facts Transparency:** Influences from China and Korea
Section 2: **Art and Culture in Heian** **The Big Idea:** Japanese culture experienced a golden age during the Heian period of the 800s to the 1100s.	TOS **Differentiated Instruction Teacher Management System:** Section 2 Lesson Plan 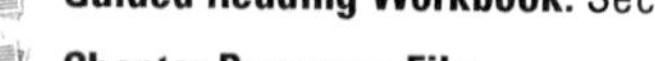 **Guided Reading Workbook:** Section 2 **Chapter Resource File:** • Vocabulary Builder Activity, Section 2 • Biography Activity: Sei Shonagon • Interdisciplinary Project: China and Japan Art Exhibition • Literature Activity: Japanese Poetry: Tanka and Haiku • Primary Source Activity: Eisai's Prescription: Drink Tea and Prolong Life	**Daily Bellringer Transparency:** Section 2 **Internet Activity:** Art of Japan
Section 3: **Growth of a Military Society** **The Big Idea:** Japan developed a military society led by generals called shoguns.	TOS **Differentiated Instruction Teacher Management System:** Section 3 Lesson Plan **Guided Reading Workbook:** Section 3 **Chapter Resource File:** • Vocabulary Builder Activity, Section 3 • Biography Activity: Tokugawa Ieyasu • History and Geography Activity: The Winds that Saved Japan • Primary Source Activity: The Mongol Invasion Scrolls	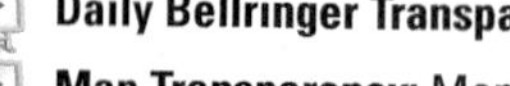 **Daily Bellringer Transparency:** Section 3 **Map Transparency:** Mongol Invasions of Japan  **Quick Facts Transparency:** Samurai Society **Internet Activity:** Japan's Samurai **Animated History:** Samurai Society **Video:** Samurai in the Modern World

Chart Key:

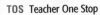

SE Student Edition   Presentation Resource  MP3 Audio

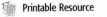

TOS Teacher One Stop 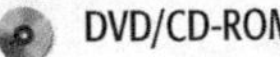 DVD/CD-ROM 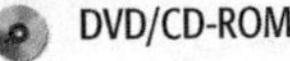 HISTORY™

Printable Resource

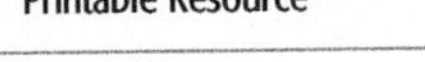 Program Resources available on TOS and @  hmhsocialstudies.com

Review, Assessment, Intervention

- **Quick Facts Transparency:** Japan Visual Summary

- **Spanish Chapter Summaries Audio CD Program**
- **Quiz Game CD-ROM**

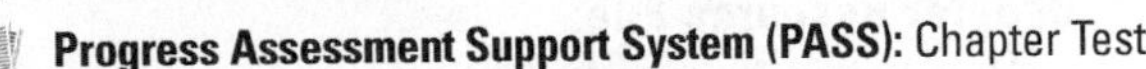
- **Progress Assessment Support System (PASS):** Chapter Test
- **Differentiated Instruction Modified Worksheets and Tests CD-ROM:** Modified Chapter Test
- TOS **ExamView® Assessment Suite (English/Spanish)**
- **Online Assessment Program,** in the Interactive Student Edition

---

 **PASS:** Section 1 Quiz

 **Online Quiz:** Section 1

 **Alternative Assessment Handbook**

 **PASS:** Section 2 Quiz

 **Online Quiz:** Section 2

 **Alternative Assessment Handbook**

 **PASS:** Section 3 Quiz

 **Online Quiz:** Section 3

 **Alternative Assessment Handbook**

Supporting Resources

- Multimedia Classroom Global History Series
- Global History Teacher's Guide

Maps Globes Graphs Level F

- Student Workbook
- Teacher's Guide

Social Studies Trade Library Collections

- Premier Secondary World History Trade Collection
- Pacific Rim Trade Collection

History's Impact

World History Video Program

- **The Samurai Tradition and Japan Today**

For more information or to purchase go to  hmhsocialstudies.com

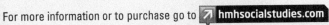

Power Presentations with Media Gallery

Power Presentations with Media Gallery are visual presentations of each chapter's main ideas. Presentations can be customized by including Quick Facts charts, images from the text, and video clips.

Differentiating Instruction

How do I address the needs of varied learners?
The Target Resource acts as your primary strategy for differentiated instruction.

ENGLISH-LANGUAGE LEARNERS & STRUGGLING READERS

Interactive Skills Tutor CD-ROM

The Interactive Skills Tutor CD-ROM contains lessons that provide additional practice for 20 different critical thinking skills.

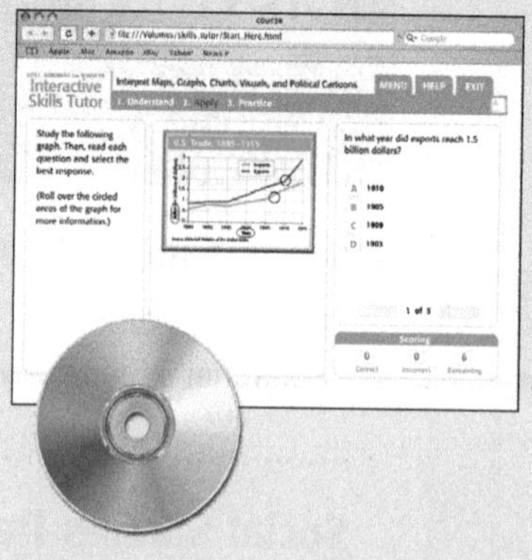

Additional Resources

Differentiated Instruction Teacher Management System: Lesson Plans for Differentiated Instruction

Chapter Resource File:
- Vocabulary Builder Activities
- Social Studies Skills Activity: Solving Problems

Quick Facts Transparencies:
- Influences from China and Korea
- Samurai Society
- Japan Visual Summary

Student Edition on Audio CD Program

Spanish/English Guided Reading Workbook

SPECIAL NEEDS LEARNERS

Differentiated Instruction Modified Worksheets and Tests CD-ROM

- Vocabulary Flash Cards
- Vocabulary Builder Activities
- Chapter Review Activity
- Chapter Test

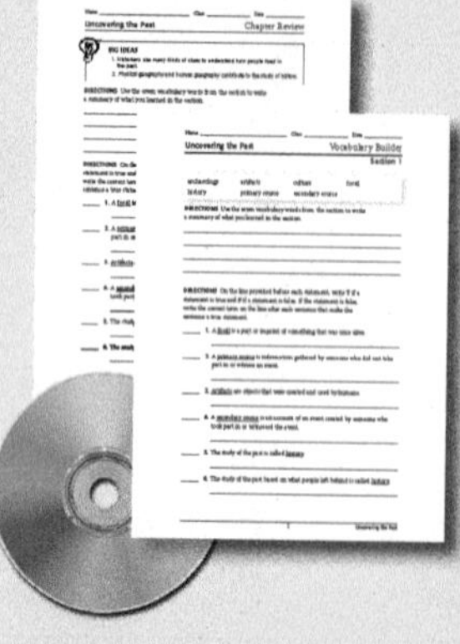

Additional Resources

Differentiated Instruction Teacher Management System: Lesson Plans for Differentiated Instruction

Guided Reading Workbook

Chapter Resource File: Social Studies Skills Activity: Solving Problems

Student Edition on Audio CD Program

Interactive Skills Tutor CD-ROM

ADVANCED/GIFTED-AND-TALENTED STUDENTS

Primary Source Library CD-ROM for World History

The Library contains longer versions of quotations in the text, extra sources, and images. Included are point-of-view articles, journals, diaries, historical fiction, and political documents.

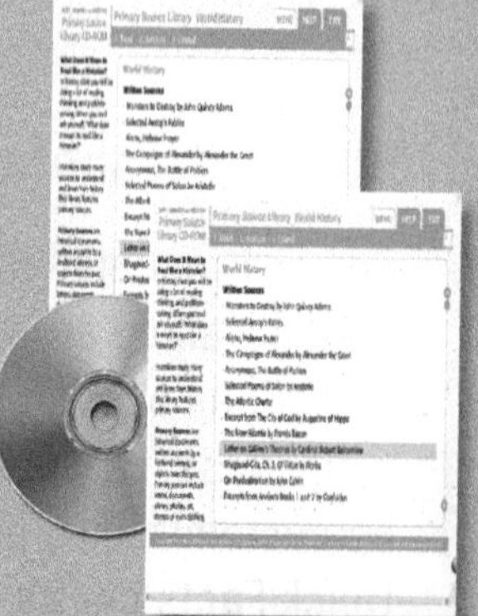

Additional Resources

Differentiated Instruction Teacher Management System: Lesson Plans for Differentiated Instruction

Chapter Resource File:
- Focus on Writing Activity: Writing a Travel Brochure
- Literature Activity: Japanese Poetry: Tanka and Haiku

Document-Based Questions Activities

Differentiated Activities in the Teacher's Edition

- Labeling Maps, p. 441
- Heian Culture Graphic Organizer, p. 448
- Building Vocabulary Through Games, p. 455

Differentiated Activities in the Teacher's Edition

- Annotated Time Line, p. 442
- Analyzing Characters, p. 452

Differentiated Activities in the Teacher's Edition

- Researching Heian Art Forms, p. 449
- Writing a *Tanka* Poem, p. 451

Teacher One Stop™

How can I manage the lesson plans and support materials for differentiated instruction?

With the Teacher One Stop, you can easily organize and print lesson plans, planning guides, and instructional materials for all learners. The Teacher One Stop includes the following materials to help you differentiate instruction:

- **Interactive Teacher's Edition**
- **Calendar Planner and pacing guides**
- **Editable lesson plans**
- **All reproducible ancillaries in Adobe Acrobat (PDF) format**
- **ExamView Assessment Suite (English & Spanish)**
- **Transparency and video previews**

Interactive Student Edition

Complete online student edition with interactive multimedia support for chapter content assessment and reporting

- Interactive Maps and Notebook
- Graphic Organizers
- Standardized Test Prep
- Online Homework Practice and Research Activities
- Current Events
- Chapter-based Internet Activities
- Animated History Activities
- and more!

DIFFERENTIATED INSTRUCTION PLANNING GUIDE

• Chapter Preview •

Essential Question

Introduce the Essential Question

- Point out that Japan's island nature and isolation from the mainland helped it develop a distinct culture.
- Explain that the exchange of visitors with China and Korea led to great cultural changes in Japan.
- Point out that Chinese influences such as language and religion were major factors in the development of Japan.

CHAPTER 15 550–1868

Japan

Essential Question How did the Japanese blend borrowed customs and native traditions into a unique culture?

South Carolina Performance Standards

6-3.2 Summarize the major contributions of the Japanese civilization, including the Japanese feudal system, the Shinto traditions, and works of art and literature.

Literacy Skills for Social Studies

- Interpret Earth's physical and human systems by using maps, mental maps, geographic models, and other social studies resources.
- Compare the locations of places, the conditions at places, and the connections between places.
- Explain how political, social, and economic institutions are similar or different across time and/or throughout the world.

Partnership for the 21st Century Skills

Cite specific textual evidence to support the analysis of primary and secondary sources.

Focus on Writing

A Travel Brochure You've been hired to create a travel brochure called "Japan's Rich History." Your brochure will describe tourist attractions in Japan that show the country's fascinating past. As you read this chapter, think about how you might encourage people to visit Japan.

Chapter Events

c. 550 Buddhism is introduced into Japan from China.

550

World Events

632–651 Arab armies conquer Southwest Asia.

436 CHAPTER 15

Focus on Writing

The **Chapter Resource File** provides a Focus on Writing worksheet to help students organize and create their travel brochures.

CRF: Focus on Writing Activity: Writing a Travel Brochure

Key to Differentiating Instruction

Below Level

Basic-level activities designed for all students encountering new material

At Level

Intermediate-level activities designed for average students

Above Level

Challenging activities designed for honors and gifted and talented students

Standard English Mastery

Activities designed to improve standard English usage

LS Learning Styles

Introduce the Chapter

At Level

Focus on Japan

1. Discuss with students what they already know about Japan. Ask students to name contributions of the Japanese to our modern world. Write students' ideas for the class to see.
2. Give the students several categories to consider if they are having difficulty thinking of ideas. Categories could include technology, history, the automobile industry, and culture. Students may require hints to develop ideas for the list.
3. Review with students the list of ideas they developed. Help students to see which ideas are correct and which are incorrect.
4. Have students draw an illustration for one of the contributions from the list. Ask for volunteers to share their illustrations with the class. **LS Verbal/Linguistic, Visual/Spatial**

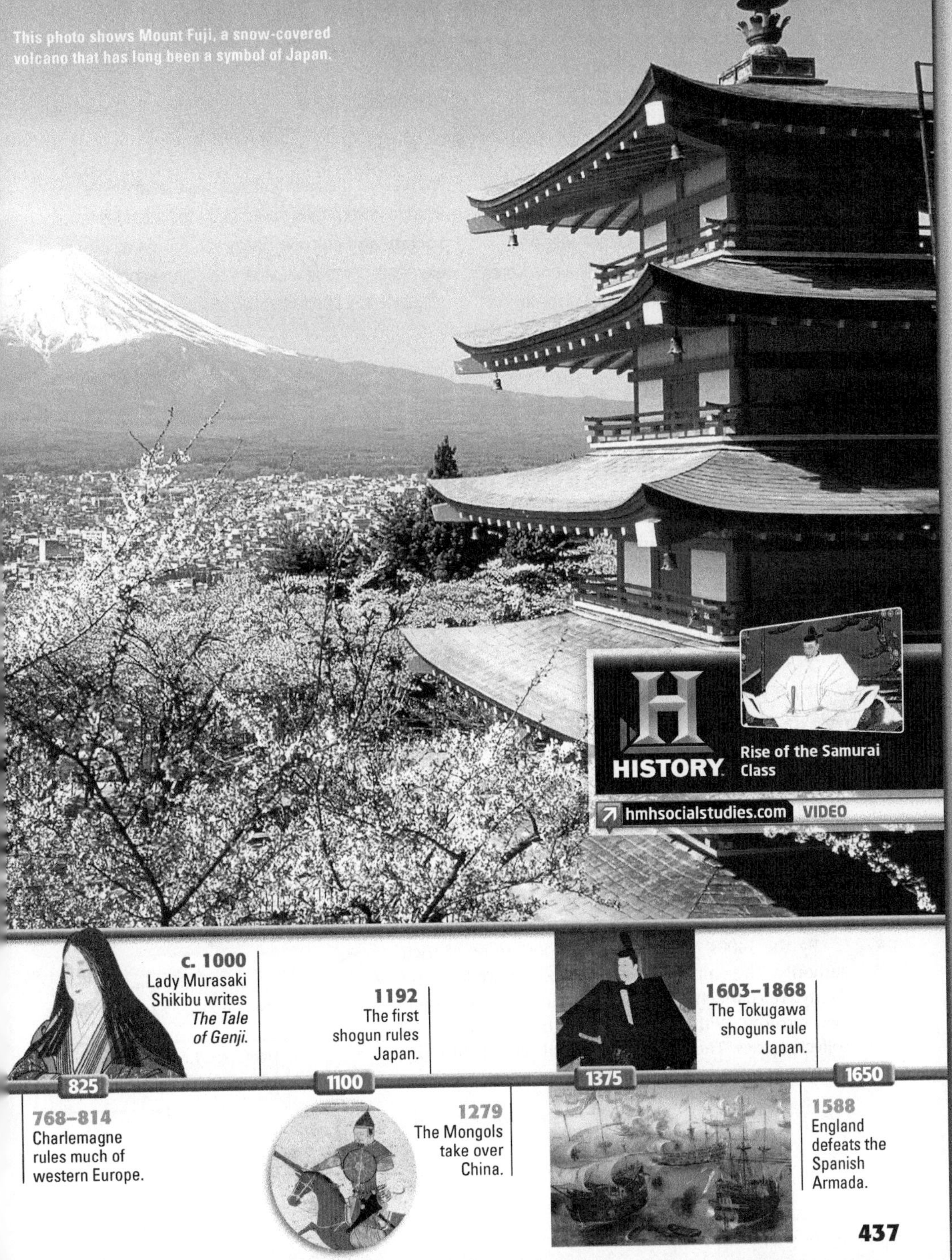

HISTORY
Rise of the Samurai Class
hmhsocialstudies.com VIDEO
c. 1000 Lady Murasaki Shikibu writes *The Tale of Genji.*
1192 The first shogun rules Japan.
1603–1868 The Tokugawa shoguns rule Japan.
825
1100
1375
1650
768–814 Charlemagne rules much of western Europe.
1279 The Mongols take over China.
1588 England defeats the Spanish Armada.
437

This photo shows Mount Fuji, a snow-covered volcano that has long been a symbol of Japan.

Chapter Preview

Explore the Picture

Mount Fuji Mount Fuji, located about 55 miles west of Tokyo, is Japan's highest mountain. Many Japanese consider the volcanic mountain a sacred symbol of the country. Although a volcano, Mount Fuji has not erupted since 1707. Every summer thousands of Japanese climb the mountain to visit a shrine located near the peak.

Analyzing Visuals What can you tell from the photo about the geography of Japan? *possible answers—It is very mountainous, it has temperature extremes between the different climates.*

hmhsocialstudies.com
Teacher Resources

Explore the Time Line

1. What world event occurred almost 90 years after the first shogun took power in Japan? *The Mongols took over China.*
2. In what year did England defeat the Spanish Armada? *1588*

Info to Know

Buddhist Temples Prince Shotuku helped initiate the spread of Buddhism and the construction of several impressive Buddhist temples throughout Japan during his reign. These temples are still considered symbols of Japan's culture today. The stone sculpture depicted in the time line is one of many images of Buddha that can be seen in Japan today.

Reading Social Studies

Understanding Themes

Ask students to share what they know about Japanese culture. Have students consider things like clothing, foods, and customs. Point out to students that in this chapter they will learn about the history of Japanese culture and society. Then ask students to predict which political systems the Japanese used. Ask students if they think the Japanese used an existing system, like monarchy, or developed a new one. Help students understand that at times Japanese politics played a large role in their social structure.

Main Ideas and Their Support

Focus on Reading Explain to students that writers are more effective when they provide credible statements that explain or prove their points. To illustrate this to students, ask each student to write a short paragraph explaining what they know about their school. Ask students to evaluate their paragraphs. Ask them what is missing that could make their writing more effective. Help students to see that by adding anecdotes, facts and statistics, quotes, and examples, their paragraph could be made more interesting and informative.

Reading Social Studies

Economics | Geography | **Politics** | Religion | **Society and Culture** | Science and Technology

Focus on Themes As you read this chapter, you will step into the world of early Japan. You will learn about the first Japanese people and their religion, Shinto, and about how the people of China and Korea began to influence the development of Japanese culture. As you read about the history of Japan, you will learn about the **political** systems the Japanese used to govern their nation and their attitudes toward **society and culture**. Finally, you will learn how social elements of medieval Japanese culture continue to affect life in Japan to this day.

Main Ideas and Their Support

Focus on Reading You know that if you take the legs out from under a table it will fall flat on the floor. In just the same way, a main idea will fall flat without details to support it.

Understanding a Writer's Support for Ideas A writer can support main ideas with several kinds of details. These details might be facts, statistics, eyewitness accounts, brief stories, examples, definitions, or comments from experts on the subject.

Notice the types of details the writer uses to support the main idea in the passage below.

After the Mongol invasion, new problems arose for the shogun. The emperor, tired of having no say in the government, began to fight the shogun for control of the country. At the same time daimyo, the nobles who owned much of Japan's land, fought to break free of the shogun's control. During these struggles for power, small wars broke out all over Japan.

By the 1400s, the shoguns had lost most of their authority. The emperor was still largely powerless, and daimyo ruled much of Japan. Each daimyo controlled his own territory. Within that territory, he made laws and collected taxes. There was no powerful central authority of any sort to impose order in Japan.

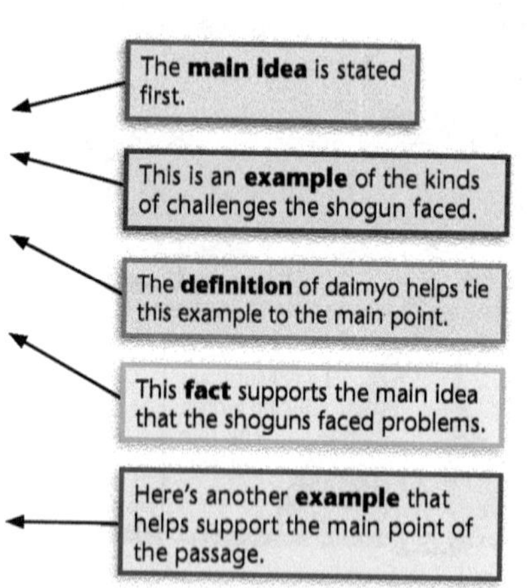

The **main idea** is stated first.
This is an **example** of the kinds of challenges the shogun faced.
The **definition** of daimyo helps tie this example to the main point.
This **fact** supports the main idea that the shoguns faced problems.
Here's another **example** that helps support the main point of the passage.

Reading and Skills Resources

Reading Support

- Guided Reading Workbook
- Student Edition on Audio CD
- Spanish Chapter Summaries Audio CD Program

Social Studies Skills Support

- Interactive Skills Tutor CD-ROM

Vocabulary Support

- **CRF:** Vocabulary Builder Activities
- **CRF:** Chapter Review Activity
- Differentiated Instruction Modified Worksheets and Tests CD-ROM:
  - Vocabulary Flash Cards
  - Vocabulary Builder Activity
  - Chapter Review Activity

TOS Holt McDougal PuzzleView

You Try It!

The following passage is from the chapter you are about to read. As you read it, look for the writer's main idea and supporting details.

Samurai

From Chapter 15, p. 455

The word *samurai* comes from the Japanese word for servant. Every samurai, from the weakest soldier to the most powerful warrior, was supposed to serve his lord. Because all lords in Japan were supposed to serve the emperor, all samurai were required to be loyal to him.

An army of samurai was expensive to support. Few lords could afford to buy armor and weapons for their warriors. As a result, lords paid their samurai with land and food.

After you read the passage, answer the following questions.

1. Which sentence best states the main idea of the passage?
   a. Samurai, which comes from the word servant, were supposed to serve their lords.
   b. Samurai were paid with land and food.
   c. Few lords could afford to buy armor and weapons for their warriors.
2. Which of the following is not a detail that supports the main idea of the passage?
   a. An army of samurai was expensive to support.
   b. Every samurai was supposed to serve his lord.
   c. In Japan at this time, there were more than 10,000 samurai.
3. Which of the following methods of supporting a main idea does the author use in this passage?
   a. statistics
   b. eyewitness account
   c. facts

Key Terms and People

Chapter 15

Section 1
clans *(p. 440)*
Shinto *(p. 440)*
Prince Shotoku *(p. 442)*
regent *(p. 442)*

Section 2
court *(p. 444)*
Lady Murasaki Shikibu *(p. 445)*
Zen *(p. 448)*

Section 3
daimyo *(p. 454)*
samurai *(p. 454)*
figurehead *(p. 455)*
shogun *(p. 455)*

Academic Vocabulary

Success in school is related to knowing academic vocabulary—the words that are frequently used in school assignments and discussions. In this chapter, you will learn the following academic words:

structure *(p. 439)*
values *(p. 457)*

As you read Chapter 15, look for the types of details that the writer uses to support the main ideas.

Reading Social Studies

Key Terms and People

Preteach these words by instructing students to create a Tri-Fold FoldNote. Ask students to label each column with the title of the sections in the chapter. As you read each word or name to the class, have students repeat it after you to practice pronouncing each term or name. Then have students write the terms and names in the correct column of the Tri-Fold. Discuss any terms or individuals that the students do not recognize. Encourage students to use the Tri-Fold to define or describe the terms and people as they read the chapter.
LS Verbal/Linguistic, Visual/Spatial

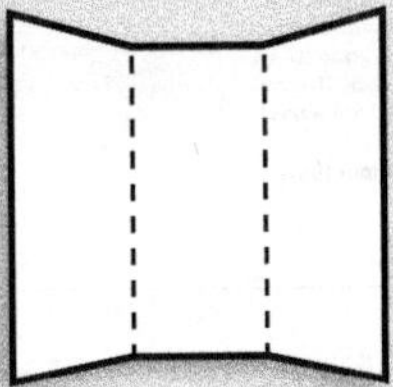

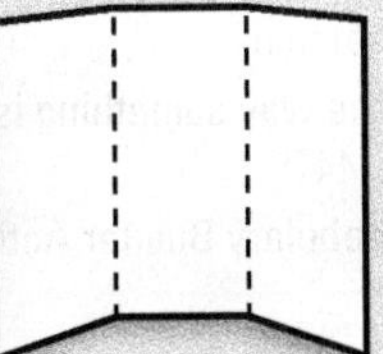

Focus on Reading

See the **Focus on Reading** questions in this chapter for more practice on this reading social studies skill.

Reading Social Studies Assessment

See the **Chapter Review** at the end of this chapter for student assessment questions related to this reading skill.

Teaching Tip

Point out to students that they should be on the lookout for stereotype and bias whenever they read a text or document. Looking for stereotype and bias are two important parts of being a critical reader. Bring in political cartoons, primary source documents, and editorials for students to examine for stereotype and bias. Ask students questions about each item to help them identify stereotype and bias.

Answers

You Try It! 1. *Yes, the author is biased in favor of the upper class.* **2.** *that common people are disrespectful of nobles, who are better than commoners;* **3.** *They are disrespectful, impatient, and have no regard for others.* **4.** *They might feel angry and resent being looked down upon.*

Preteach

Bellringer

If YOU were there . . . Use the **Daily Bellringer Transparency** to help students answer the question.

Daily Bellringer Transparency, Section 1

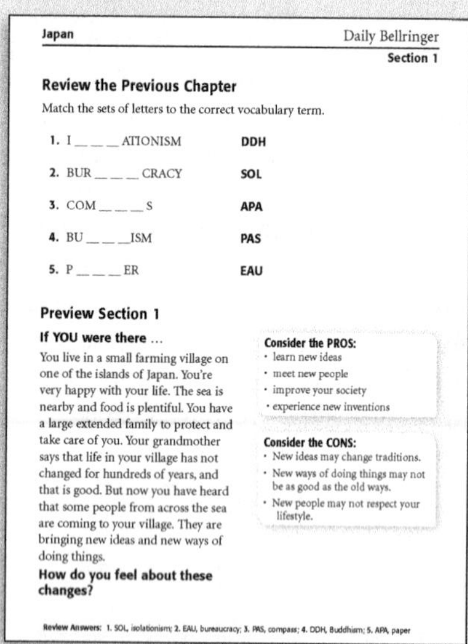

Japan — Daily Bellringer — Section 1

Review the Previous Chapter

Match the sets of letters to the correct vocabulary term.

1. I ___ ATIONISM — **DDH**
2. BUR ___ CRACY — **SOL**
3. COM ___ S — **APA**
4. BU ___ ISM — **PAS**
5. P ___ ER — **EAU**

Preview Section 1

If YOU were there ...

You live in a small farming village on one of the islands of Japan. You're very happy with your life. The sea is nearby and food is plentiful. You have a large extended family to protect and take care of you. Your grandmother says that life in your village has not changed for hundreds of years, and that is good. But now you have heard that some people from across the sea are coming to your village. They are bringing new ideas and new ways of doing things.

How do you feel about these changes?

Consider the PROS:
- learn new ideas
- meet new people
- improve your society
- experience new inventions

Consider the CONS:
- New ideas may change traditions.
- New ways of doing things may not be as good as the old ways.
- New people may not respect your lifestyle.

Review Answers: 1. SOL, isolationism; 2. EAU, bureaucracy; 3. PAS, compass; 4. DDH, Buddhism; 5. APA, paper

Academic Vocabulary

Review with students the high-use academic term in this section.

structure the way something is set up or organized (p. 441)

CRF: Vocabulary Builder Activity, Section 1

Taking Notes

Have students use the graphic organizer online to take notes on the section. This activity will prepare students for the Section Assessment, in which they will complete a graphic organizer that builds on the information using the Critical Thinking Skill: Categorizing.

SECTION 1

Geography and Early Japan

What You Will Learn...

Main Ideas

1. Geography shaped life in Japan.
2. Early Japanese society was organized in clans, which came to be ruled by an emperor.
3. Japan learned about language, society, and government from China and Korea.

The Big Idea

Japan's early societies were both isolated from and influenced by China and Korea.

Key Terms and People

clans, *p. 442*
Shinto, *p. 442*
Prince Shotoku, *p. 444*
regent, *p. 444*

Use the graphic organizer online to take notes on how geography, early peoples, and neighboring countries affected the Japanese people's way of life, government, and religion.

If YOU were there...

You live in a small farming village on one of the islands of Japan. You're very happy with your life. The sea is nearby and food is plentiful. You have a large, extended family to protect and take care of you. Your grandmother says that life in your village has not changed for hundreds of years, and that is good. But now you have heard that some people from across the sea are coming to your village. They are bringing new ideas and new ways of doing things.

How do you feel about these changes?

BUILDING BACKGROUND Japan is a large group of islands located east of the Asian mainland. Life in Japan has always been influenced by many factors. The islands' geography and location shaped how people lived there, and as you read above, visitors from other lands also affected Japanese society.

Geography Shapes Life in Japan

The islands of Japan are really just the tops of undersea mountains and volcanoes, sticking up out of the ocean. Those mountains, as you can see on the map, cover nearly all of Japan. Only about 20 percent of the land is flat. Because it is difficult to live and farm on mountain slopes, most Japanese people have always lived in those flat areas, the coastal plains.

In addition to the mountains and the lack of flat land, the nearness of the sea shaped the lives of Japanese people. Their homes were never far from the sea. Naturally, they turned to the sea for food. They learned to prepare all kinds of seafood, from eel to shark to octopus to seaweed. As a result, seafood has been a key part of the Japanese diet for thousands of years.

The islands' location affected the Japanese people in another way as well. Because they lived on islands, the Japanese were separated from the other people of Asia. This separation allowed

Teach the Big Idea

At Level

Geography and Early Japan

1. **Teach** Ask students the questions in the Main Idea boxes to teach this section.
2. **Apply** Have students create an outline of the section using the subheads as main points. Help students identify at least two main ideas for each subhead in the section. **LS Verbal/Linguistic**
3. **Review** As a class, review student outlines. Have students identify the elements in their outlines that they feel are most important or most interesting.
4. **Practice/Homework** Select one of the points students thought was important in the review. Ask students to decide if they think that point was important or not. Have students write a journal entry in which they explain why they agree or disagree with the importance of the point. Students should be able to give at least two persuasive reasons to support their position. **LS Logical/Mathematical, Verbal/Linguistic**

Alternative Assessment Handbook, Rubric 43: Writing to Persuade

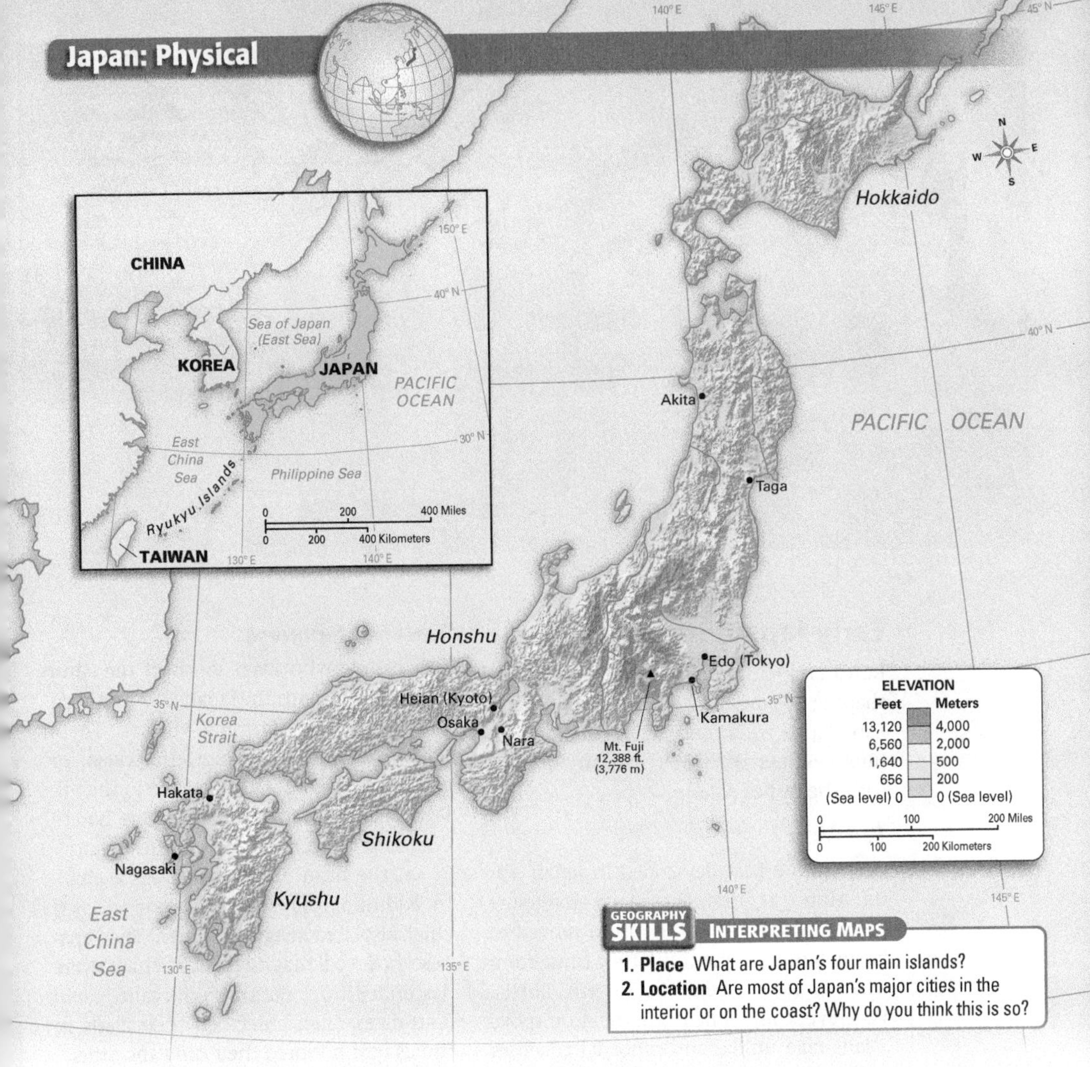

GEOGRAPHY SKILLS INTERPRETING MAPS

1. **Place** What are Japan's four main islands?
2. **Location** Are most of Japan's major cities in the interior or on the coast? Why do you think this is so?

the Japanese to develop their own culture. For example, they created a religion and a social **structure** very different from those in other parts of Asia. This separation has always been an important part of Japanese society.

Japan isn't totally isolated, however. Look at the inset map above to find Korea and China. As you can see, neither country is very far from the Japanese islands. Korea is only about 100 miles away from Japan. China is about 400 miles away. Those short distances allowed the older Korean and Chinese cultures to influence the new culture of Japan.

ACADEMIC VOCABULARY
structure the way something is set up or organized

READING CHECK **Summarizing** What is Japan's geography like?

Direct Teach

Main Idea

1 Geography Shapes Life in Japan

Geography shaped life in Japan.

Recall About what percentage of Japan is located on flat land? *about 20 percent*

Analyze Why have the Japanese turned to the sea for food? *Their homes and farms are very close to the sea, and there is little flat land.*

Evaluate Why did Japan develop a very different culture from those in other parts of Asia? *It was separated physically from the rest of Asia.*

Map Transparency: Japan: Physical

Interpreting Maps

Japan: Physical

Review the map with students. Ask the following questions:

Place How does the elevation of central Japan differ from that along the coast? *It is higher and more mountainous.*

Location About how far is Heian (Kyoto) from Mount Fuji? *less than 200 miles*

Map Transparency: Japan: Physical

Did you know . . .

Mount Fuji, Japan's tallest mountain, is an active volcano, but it has not erupted since 1707.

Differentiating Instruction

Struggling Readers **Below Level**

1. Give students blank outline maps of Japan. Have students identify the bodies of water that surround Japan. Use a large map or transparency to show students the Pacific Ocean, the Sea of Japan, and the East China Sea. Ask students to label their outline maps with the appropriate names.
2. Help students identify and label the four major islands of Japan *(Hokkaido, Honshu, Kyushu,* and *Shikoku).* Then help students place Mount Fuji on their outline maps.
3. Help students locate Tokyo and label it on their maps. Explain that this city is Japan's current capital and one of the largest cities in the world. Lastly, help students locate Kyoto. Explain that it was originally called Heian and was Japan's capital from 794 to 1868.
4. Have students keep their maps for reference as they study the rest of the chapter.

Map Transparency, Japan: Physical

Answers

Interpreting Maps 1. *Hokkaido, Honshu, Shikoku, and Kyushu;* **2.** *on the coast; possible answer—that is where the land is flattest*

Reading Check *isolated group of islands; tops of undersea volcanoes; about 20 percent of the land is flat, coastal plains*

Direct Teach

Main Idea

❷ Early Japanese Society

Early Japanese society was organized in clans, which came to be ruled by an emperor.

Explain How were the Ainu different from other people of Japan? *They looked different and spoke a different language.*

Make Inferences Why were the clan chiefs held in such high respect? *possible answers—they were leaders of the villages; they were descended from* kami; *they had important religious duties.*

Draw Conclusions Why did many Japanese accept control by the Yamato clan? *They believed the Yamato were descended from the sun goddess.*

Info to Know

Changing Attitudes towards the Ainu In the late 1800s the government hoped to assimilate the Ainu into Japanese culture. As a result, Ainu traditions and language were replaced by Japanese traditions. In fact, the Ainu language almost disappeared entirely. However attitudes towards this minority group have changed over time. In 1997 the Japanese government passed a law that officially recognizes the Ainu people and promotes Ainu culture.

Linking to Today

A Shinto Shrine Visitors to Shinto shrines in modern-day Japan often write wishes on small boards of wood, known as *ema,* in the hope that their wishes will come true.

Activity **Creating *Ema*** Have students create their own *ema* by writing a wish on a sheet of paper. Hang the *ema* around the room.

Answers

A Shinto Shrine *trees and plants*

A Shinto Shrine

Visitors to a Shinto shrine gather near a gate called a torii (TOR-ee). The torii marks the boundary of a shrine or other sacred Shinto site. Over time, the torii has become a symbol of Shinto, Japan's ancient religion.

What elements of nature can you see in this painting?

Early Japanese Society

Korea and China did play a major part in shaping Japanese society, but not at first. Early Japan was home to two different cultures, neither of which had any contact with the rest of Asia.

The Ainu

One culture that developed in Japan was the Ainu (EYE-noo). Historians aren't sure exactly when or how the Ainu moved to Japan. Some people think they came from what is now Siberia in eastern Russia. Wherever they came from, the Ainu spoke a language unlike any other language in eastern Asia. They also looked different from the other people of Japan.

Over time, the Ainu began to fight with other people for land. They lost most of these fights, and so they lost their land as well. Eventually the Ainu were driven back onto a single island, Hokkaido. Over time the Ainu culture almost disappeared. Many people gave up the Ainu language and adopted new customs.

THE IMPACT TODAY

Few Ainu remain in Japan today, and most of them live on Hokkaido.

The First Japanese

The people who lived south of the Ainu eventually became the Japanese. They lived mostly in small farming villages. These villages were ruled by powerful **clans**, or extended families. Other people in the village, including farmers and workers, had to obey and respect members of these clans.

At the head of each clan was a chief. In addition to his political power, each chief also had religious duties. The Japanese believed that their clan chiefs were descended from nature spirits called *kami* (KAH-mee). Clan chiefs led their clans in rituals that honored their *kami* ancestors.

Over time, these rituals became a central part of the traditional religion of Japan, **Shinto**. According to Shinto teachings, everything in nature—the sun, the moon, trees, waterfalls, and animals—has *kami*. Shintoists believe that some *kami* help people live and keep them from harm. They build shrines to *kami* and perform ceremonies in which they ask the *kami* to bless them.

Critical Thinking: Sequencing

Below Level

Annotated Time Line

1. Write the events at right for students to see. Scramble the order of events and ask students to place the events in a time line in their proper order.
2. After students have completed their time lines, discuss the events with the class. Have students annotate their time lines by noting why each event was important.
LS Visual/Spatial, Verbal/Linguistic

Ainu culture develops → Ainu driven back to Hokkaido → Japanese clans control villages → Yamato clan gains control of Honshu → Japanese visit China and Korea to study culture

Alternative Assessment Handbook, Rubric 36: Time Lines

The First Emperors

The clans of early Japan weren't all equal. Some clans were larger and more powerful than others. In time a few of these powerful clans built up armies and set out to conquer their neighbors.

One clan that gained power in this way lived in the Yamato region, the western part of Japan's largest island, Honshu. In addition to military might, the Yamato rulers claimed to have a glorious family history. They believed they were descended from the most powerful of all *kami*, the goddess of the sun.

By the 500s the Yamato rulers had extended their control over much of Honshu. Although they didn't control the whole country, the leaders of the Yamato clan began to call themselves the emperors of all Japan.

READING CHECK **Sequencing** How did emperors take power in Japan?

Japan Learns from China and Korea

Early Japanese society received very little influence from cultures on the Asian mainland. Occasionally, officials from China, Korea, or other parts of Asia visited Japan. For the most part, however, these visits didn't have a great impact on the Japanese way of life.

By the mid-500s, though, some Japanese leaders thought that Japan could learn a great deal from other cultures. In particular, they wanted to learn more about the cultures of China and Korea.

To learn what they wanted to know, the rulers of Japan decided to send representatives to China and Korea to gather information about their cultures. They also invited people from China and Korea to move to Japan. The emperors hoped that these people could teach the Japanese new ways of working and thinking.

Influences from China and Korea

QUICK FACTS

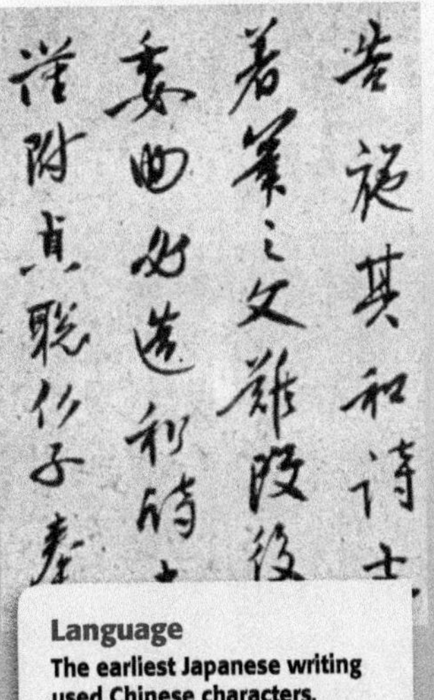

Language
The earliest Japanese writing used Chinese characters.

THE GRANGER COLLECTION, NEW YORK

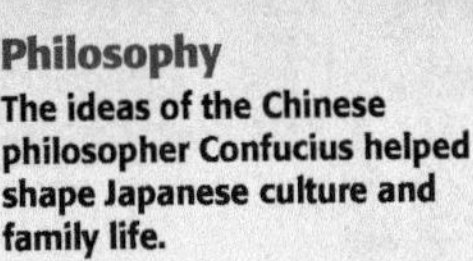

Philosophy
The ideas of the Chinese philosopher Confucius helped shape Japanese culture and family life.

Religion
Buddhism came to Japan from Korea.

Direct Teach

Main Idea

3 Japan Learns from China and Korea

Japan learned about language, society, and government from China and Korea.

Analyze Why did Japanese leaders send representatives to China and Korea in the mid-500s? *to learn about their cultures*

Recall What were the main influences that China and Korea had on Japan? *language, philosophy, and religion*

Quick Facts Transparency: Influences from China and Korea

Info to Know

The Japanese Emperor According to legend, the first Japanese emperor, Jimmu Tenno, was the direct descendant of Amaterasu, the sun goddess. All Japanese emperors trace their line back to the first emperor. The current emperor, Akihito, is the 125th emperor of Japan.

Collaborative Learning

At Level

Cultural-Borrowing Collage

1. Discuss with students the meaning of the term *cultural borrowing*. Ask students to explain in their own words what *borrowing* means and how one culture can borrow customs from another. Point out to students that one area of human geography deals with *cultural diffusion*—how ideas, customs, and beliefs spread.
2. Remind students that Japan borrowed and adapted many elements of Chinese and Korean culture. Point out that many things in our modern culture have been borrowed from other cultures. Have students work in small groups to list all the items that they can think of that come from other cultures. Food, music, and clothing are examples of cultural exchange with which students will be familiar.
3. Have each group create a collage that depicts various elements from the group's list. Ask groups to share their lists and collages with the class. **LS Interpersonal, Visual/Spatial**

Alternative Assessment Handbook, Rubrics 8: Collages; and 11: Discussions

Answers

Reading Check *by building up armies and conquering neighbors; by claiming to be descended from the sun goddess*

Direct Teach

Main Idea

3 Japan Learns from China and Korea

Japan learned about language, society, and government from China and Korea.

Analyze Why was Prince Shotoku important? *He admired the culture of China and sent scholars there to study and learn everything they could about it.*

Evaluate What influences from China and Korea do you think were most important for Japan? *possible answers—written language; Confucianism; Buddhism*

Activity **Résumés** Ask students to review the information about Prince Shotoku and write a résumé that highlights his qualifications for ruler.

Alternative Assessment Handbook, Rubric 31: Résumés

CRF: Biography Activity: Empress Suiko

Changes in Language

One of the first things the Japanese learned from China and Korea was language. The early Japanese didn't have a written language. Therefore, many learned to write in Chinese. They continued to speak in Japanese, however, which is very different from Chinese. It wasn't until about 200 years later that people devised a way of writing in Japanese. They used Chinese characters to represent the sounds used in Japanese.

As Japan's contact with China increased, some Japanese people—especially rich and well-educated people—began to write in the Chinese language. Japanese writers used Chinese for their poems and stories. One of the first histories of Japan, written in the 700s, is in Chinese. For many years Chinese was even the official language of Japan's government.

Changes in Religion and Philosophy

One of the people most influential in bringing Chinese ideas to Japan was **Prince Shotoku** (shoh-toh-koo). He served from 593 to 621 as regent (REE-juhnt) for his aunt, the empress. A **regent** is a person who rules a country for someone who is unable to rule alone.

All his life, Prince Shotoku admired Chinese culture. As regent, Shotoku saw a chance for Japan to adopt more Chinese ideas. He sent scholars to China to learn all they could about Chinese society.

The ideas these scholars brought back changed Japanese society. For example, they taught the Japanese about Confucianism.

BIOGRAPHY

Prince Shotoku
573–621

Prince Shotoku was one of Japan's greatest leaders. He helped rule Japan when he was only 20 years old. For many centuries, people have admired him. Legends have developed about his wisdom. According to one early biography, Shotoku was able to talk as soon as he was born and never made a wrong decision.

Prince Shotoku's Japan

Under Prince Shotoku, Buddhism spread across Japan. Shotoku ordered beautiful Buddhist temples to be built, such as the one below in Nara, Japan. The spread of Buddhism changed many areas of Japanese culture during Prince Shotoku's time.

Social Studies Skills Activity: Solving Problems

At Level

Choosing a Written Language

1. Have students review the text above titled "Changes in Language."
2. Ask students to imagine that they have been asked by the emperor to come up with a way of keeping written records. Have students come up with as many different ways as possible of addressing this problem. Write students' suggestions for everyone to see.
3. Ask students to list arguments for and against each of the methods suggested. Lead students in a discussion of the relative merits of each method. Remind students to think about the practicality of each suggestion.
4. Conclude by having students summarize their suggestions and vote for the solution they think works best. How does it compare with the way the Japanese actually solved their problem?

LS Logical/Mathematical, Verbal/Linguistic

Alternative Assessment Handbook, Rubric 35: Solving Problems

Among other things, Confucianism outlined how families should behave. Confucius taught that fathers should rule their families. He believed that wives should obey their husbands, children should obey their parents, and younger brothers should obey older brothers. Families in China lived according to these rules. As Confucian ideas spread through Japan, the Japanese began to live by them as well.

More important than these social changes, though, were the vast religious changes Shotoku made in Japan. He was a Buddhist, and he wanted to spread Buddhism throughout his country. Buddhism wasn't new to Japan. Korean visitors had introduced the religion to Japan about 50 years earlier. But it was not very popular. Most people preferred to keep their traditional religion, Shinto.

Shotoku worked to change people's minds about Buddhism. He built a grand Buddhist temple that still stands today. He also wrote commentaries on Buddhist teachings. Largely because of his efforts, Buddhism became very popular, especially among Japanese nobles.

Statue of the Buddha in Horyuji

Changes in Government

Shotoku also wanted to change Japan's government to be more like China's. He especially wanted Japan's emperors to have more power, like China's emperors did.

Afraid that they would lose power to the emperor, many clan leaders opposed Shotoku's government plans. As a result, Japan's emperors gained little power.

READING CHECK **Categorizing** What aspects of Chinese society did Shotoku bring to Japan?

SUMMARY AND PREVIEW In this section, you learned how early Japan grew and developed. Next you'll see how Japan's emperors encouraged nobles to create great works of art and literature.

Section 1 Assessment

hmhsocialstudies.com ONLINE QUIZ

Reviewing Ideas, Terms, and People

1. a. **Recall** What types of landforms cover most of Japan?
   b. **Explain** How did Japan's location both separate it from and tie it to China and Korea?
2. a. **Define** What is **Shinto**?
   b. **Sequence** How did the Yamato rulers gain power?
3. a. **Explain** How did **Prince Shotoku** help spread Buddhism in Japan?
   b. **Rate** What do you think was the most important idea the Japanese borrowed from China or Korea? Why?

Critical Thinking

4. **Categorizing** Draw a diagram like this one. Using your notes on Japan's culture, list ideas that developed within Japan in the circle and ideas that the Japanese borrowed from other people in the arrow.

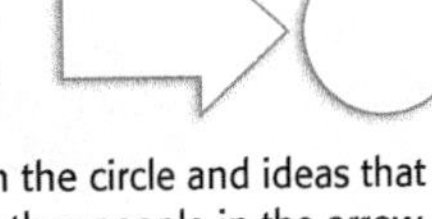

Focus on Writing

5. **Taking Notes on Early Japan** Think about the section you have just read. Which details from this section might be appealing to tourists? Write down some thoughts in your notebook. Plan to include them in a section of your travel brochure called "Fun Facts."

Direct Teach

Linking to Today

Japanese Writing Systems Today the Japanese language has three writing systems. Kanji uses characters borrowed from the Chinese. Most kanji characters can be read in two ways: either in native Japanese or using the original Chinese pronunciation.

The other writing systems use characters that represent Japanese syllables. One form, hiragana, is often used along with kanji. The other form, katakana, is used mainly to write words borrowed from English, French, and other Western languages.

Review & Assess

Close

Guide students in a review of Japan's geography, including the effects of its proximity to China and Korea.

Review

Online Quiz, Section 1

Assess

SE Section 1 Assessment

PASS: Section 1 Quiz

Alternative Assessment Handbook

Reteach/Classroom Intervention

Guided Reading Workbook, Section 1

Interactive Skills Tutor CD-ROM

Section 1 Assessment Answers

1. a. mountains
   b. Japan is far enough from China and Korea that Japan could create its own culture, but close enough to borrow ideas from China and Korea.
2. a. a traditional religion based on nature that began in Japan
   b. They built up armies and conquered their neighbors until they ruled much of Honshu.
3. a. built temples and wrote interpretations of Buddhist teachings
   b. possible answers—Confucianism, because it outlined the way families should behave; Buddhism, because it became so popular
4. arrow—language, Buddhism, Confucian ideas, government ideas; circle—Shinto, clan system
5. possible answers—Japan's dramatic geography, such as Mount Fuji; Buddhist temples, for example, the statue of Buddha in Horyuji

Answers

Reading Check *Confucian ideas, Buddhism, government*

Preteach

Bellringer

If YOU were there . . . Use the **Daily Bellringer Transparency** to help students answer the question.

Daily Bellringer Transparency, Section 2

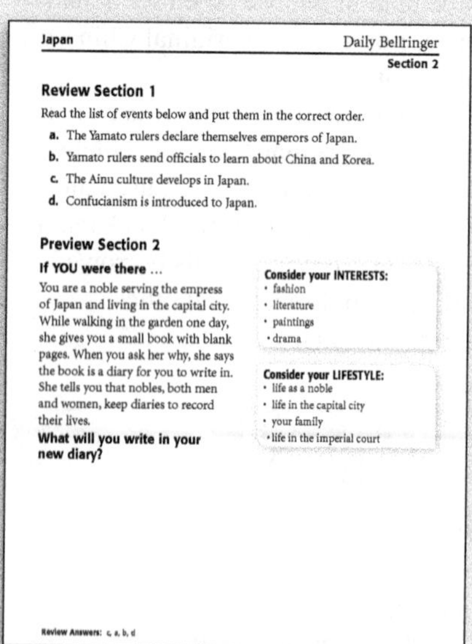

Japan Daily Bellringer

Section 2

Review Section 1

Read the list of events below and put them in the correct order.

- **a.** The Yamato rulers declare themselves emperors of Japan.
- **b.** Yamato rulers send officials to learn about China and Korea.
- **c.** The Ainu culture develops in Japan.
- **d.** Confucianism is introduced to Japan.

Preview Section 2

If YOU were there …

You are a noble serving the empress of Japan and living in the capital city. While walking in the garden one day, she gives you a small book with blank pages. When you ask her why, she says the book is a diary for you to write in. She tells you that nobles, both men and women, keep diaries to record their lives.

What will you write in your new diary?

Consider your INTERESTS:
- fashion
- literature
- paintings
- drama

Consider your LIFESTYLE:
- life as a noble
- life in the capital city
- your family
- life in the imperial court

Review Answers: c, a, b, d

Building Vocabulary

Preteach or review the following terms:

novel a lengthy fictional tale (p. 447)

privilege a benefit or advantage (p. 446)

CRF: Vocabulary Builder Activity, Section 2

Taking Notes

Have students use the graphic organizer online to take notes on the section. This activity will prepare students for the Section Assessment, in which they will complete a graphic organizer that builds on the information using the Critical Thinking Skill: Categorizing.

SECTION 2

Art and Culture in Heian

What You Will Learn…

Main Ideas

1. Japanese nobles created great art in their court at Heian.
2. Buddhism changed in Japan during the Heian period.

The Big Idea

Japanese culture experienced a golden age during the Heian period of the 800s to the 1100s.

Key Terms and People

court, *p. 446*
Lady Murasaki Shikibu, *p. 447*
Zen, *p. 450*

Use the graphic organizer online to take notes on the changes in Japanese art and religion in the golden age of the Heian period.

If YOU were there...

You are a noble, serving the empress of Japan and living in the capital city. While walking in the garden one day, she gives you a small book with blank pages. When you ask her why, she says the book is a diary for you to write in. She tells you that nobles, both men and women, keep diaries to record their lives.

What will you write in your new diary?

BUILDING BACKGROUND In 794 the emperor and empress of Japan moved to Heian (HAY-ahn), a city now called Kyoto. Many nobles, like the one you just read about, followed their rulers to the new city. These nobles loved art and beauty, and they tried to make their new home a beautiful place.

Japanese Nobles Create Great Art

The nobles who followed Japan's emperor to Heian wanted to win his favor by living close to him. In Heian, these nobles created an imperial **court**, a group of nobles who live near and serve or advise a ruler.

Members of the noble court had little to do with the common people of Heian. They lived apart from poorer citizens and seldom left the city. These nobles enjoyed their lives of ease and privilege. In fact, their lives were so easy and so removed from the rest of Japan that many nobles called themselves "dwellers among the clouds."

The nobles of this court loved beauty and elegance. Because of this love, many nobles were great supporters of the arts. As a result, the court at Heian became a great center of culture and learning. In fact, the period between 794 and 1185 was a golden age of the arts in Japan.

Heian (Kyoto)

Teach the Big Idea

At Level

Art and Culture in Heian

Prep Required

1. **Teach** Ask students the questions in the Main Idea boxes to teach this section.
2. **Apply** Have students work with a partner to create a scrapbook that presents the accomplishments of art and culture in Heian Japan. Each scrapbook should contain pages that cover the following topics: art, architecture, literature, and religion. Remind students to provide illustrations and captions for each topic and to define any vocabulary terms. LS **Visual/Spatial**
3. **Review** As a review of the section, have students exchange scrapbooks with other pairs.
4. **Practice/Homework** Have students write a paragraph that describes what the same cultural elements are like in modern-day Japan. LS **Verbal/Linguistic**

Alternative Assessment Handbook, Rubrics 32: Scrapbooks; and 42: Writing to Inform

Primary Source

JOURNAL ENTRY

The Pillow Book

Sei Shonagon (SAY shoh-nah-gohn), author of The Pillow Book*, served Japan's empress from 991 to 1000.* The Pillow Book *was her journal. In it she wrote poems and thoughts about nature as well as descriptions of daily events. Here she describes the first time she met the empress.*

"When I first entered her Majesty's service I felt indescribably shy, and was indeed constantly on the verge of tears. When I came on duty the first evening, the Empress was sitting with only a three-foot screen in front of her, and so nervous was I that when she passed me some picture or book to look at, I was hardly capable of putting out my hand to take it. While she was talking about what she wanted me to see—telling me what it was or who had made it—I was all the time wondering whether my hair was in order."

–Sei Shonagon, from *The Pillow Book*

An actress playing Sei Shonagon in the 1800s

ANALYSIS SKILL ANALYZING PRIMARY SOURCES

How did Sei Shonagon feel when she met the empress?

Fashion

The nobles' love of beauty began with their own appearances. They had magnificent wardrobes full of silk robes and gold jewelry. Nobles loved elaborate outfits. For example, women wore long gowns made of 12 layers of colored silk cleverly cut and folded to show off many layers at once.

To complete their outfits, nobles often carried delicate decorative fans. These fans were painted with flowers, trees, and birds. Many nobles also attached flowers and long silk cords to their fans.

Literature

In addition to how they looked, Japanese nobles took great care with how they spoke and wrote. Writing was very popular among the nobles, especially among the women. Many women wrote diaries and journals about their lives at court. In their diaries, these women carefully chose their words to make their writing beautiful.

Unlike men, who usually wrote in Chinese, noble women wrote in the Japanese language. As a result, many of the greatest works of early Japanese literature were written by women.

One of the greatest writers in early Japanese history was **Lady Murasaki Shikibu** (moohr-ah-sahk-ee shee-kee-boo). Around 1000, she wrote *The Tale of Genji*. Many historians consider this book to be the world's first full-length novel. Many readers also consider it one of the best.

The Tale of Genji is the story of a prince named Genji and his long quest for love. During his search he meets women from many different social classes.

Many people consider *The Tale of Genji* one of Japan's greatest novels. The characters it describes are very colorful and seem real. In addition, Lady Murasaki's writing is clear and simple but graceful at the same time. She describes court life in Japan with great detail.

Direct Teach

Main Idea

1 Japanese Nobles Create Great Art

Japanese nobles created great art in their court at Heian.

Define What is an imperial court? *a group of nobles who serve and advise the ruler*

Analyze Why did Heian become a center of culture? *Nobles there loved beauty and elegance, so they were great supporters of the arts.*

Explain What was the main reason that most early Japanese literature was written by women? *Men usually wrote in Chinese, but women wrote in Japanese.*

CRF: Biography Activity: Sei Shonagon

Primary Source

The Pillow Book

Activity Writing a Journal Entry Ask students to imagine that they have been assigned to serve a powerful ruler. Have students write a journal entry in which they describe their feelings upon first meeting the ruler.

LS Intrapersonal, Verbal/Linguistic

Alternative Assessment Handbook, Rubric 15: Journals

Critical Thinking: Summarizing

At Level

The Tale of Genji Book Jacket

Materials: sample book jacket, art supplies

1. Have students read the description of *The Tale of Genji* on this page and in the Literature in History feature later in this chapter.
2. Explain to students what a book jacket looks like and what purpose it serves. Provide an actual book jacket for students to see.
3. Point out to students that book jackets include an illustration and the title on the front cover; a brief summary of the book's contents on the inside flaps; the title, author, and publisher on the spine; and comments and quotes about the book's importance on the back cover.
4. Have each student prepare a book jacket for *The Tale of Genji.* Draw a sample layout of a book jacket for students to follow.
5. Ask volunteers to share their finished book jackets with the class.

LS Verbal/Linguistic, Visual/Spatial

Alternative Assessment Handbook, Rubrics 3: Artwork; and 37: Writing Assignments

Answers

Analyzing Primary Sources *shy and nervous*

Direct Teach

Main Idea

1 Japanese Nobles Create Great Art

Japanese nobles created great art in their court at Heian.

Summarize What were Japanese poems usually like? *short and very structured, usually about love or nature*

Explain Why was calligraphy considered an important art form in Heian? *because people wanted poems to look as beautiful as they sounded*

Define What is Noh? *a kind of play that combines music, speaking, and dance*

- **CRF:** Literature Activity: Japanese Poetry: Tanka and Haiku
- **CRF:** Interdisciplinary Project: China and Japan Art Exhibition
- **CRF:** Primary Source Activity: Eisai's Prescription: Drink Tea and Prolong Life

Connect to Literature

In the Heian period the most popular form of poetry was the *tanka,* a poem with 31 syllables. *Tanka* are written to mark an event of some sort. Men and women in the imperial court were expected to be able to compose beautiful *tanka* poetry. The poem on this page is an example of a *tanka.*

Activity **Writing *Tanka*** Have students select an event or occasion and write a *tanka* to describe it. Remind students that tanka often are five lines long with a syllable count of 5 - 7 - 5 - 7 - 7.

- **CRF:** Literature Activity, Japanese Poetry
- Alternative Assessment Handbook, Rubric 26: Poems and Songs

Most early Japanese prose was written by women, but both men and women wrote poetry. Nobles loved to read and write poems. Some nobles held parties at which they took turns writing poetry and reading their poems aloud to each other.

Poems from this time usually had only five lines. They followed a specific structure that outlined how many syllables each line could include. Most were about love or nature, but some described everyday events. Here is an example of a nature poem about the end of winter:

> "The breezes of spring
> Are blowing the ripples astray
> Along the water—
> Today they will surely melt
> The sheet of ice on the pond."
>
> –Kino Tomonori, from the *Gosenshu*

Visual Art

Besides literature, Japan's nobles also loved the visual arts. The most popular art forms of the period were paintings, calligraphy, and architecture.

In their paintings, the nobles of Heian liked bright, bold colors. They also liked paintings that illustrated stories. In fact, many of the greatest paintings from this period illustrate scenes from literature, such as *The Tale of Genji.* Other paintings show scenes from nature or from court life. Many artists painted on doors and furniture rather than on paper.

Another popular form of art in Heian was calligraphy, or decorative writing. Calligraphers spent hours carefully copying poems. They wanted the poems to look as beautiful as they sounded.

The Arts in Heian

Heian was Japan's capital for many centuries. The wealthy nobles who lived there were great supporters of the arts. With their support, literature, painting, calligraphy, and other arts flourished in Heian.

A favorite theme in Japanese painting was *The Tale of Genji.* In this illustration of a scene from the novel, Genji's son is reading a letter as his wife approaches.

Differentiating Instruction

Struggling Readers **Below Level**

1. Review with students the various forms of culture that interested the nobles of Heian.
2. Draw the graphic organizer for students to see. Omit the blue, italicized answers.
3. Have students copy the graphic organizer and identify specific examples of Japanese culture for each category.
4. Review the answers with students.
   LS Verbal/Linguistic

Heian Culture	
Fashion	*robes, gowns, jewelry, fans*
Literature	*diaries, journals, novels, poetry*
Visual Arts	*paintings, calligraphy*
Architecture	*temples, gardens*
Performing Arts	*juggling, acrobatics, Noh, music*
Religion	*Pure Land and Zen Buddhism*

Architecture

The nobles of Heian worked to make their city beautiful. They greatly admired Chinese architecture and modeled Heian after the Chinese capital, Chang'an. They copied Chinese building styles, especially in the many temples they built. These styles featured buildings with wooden frames that curved slightly upward at the ends. The wooden frames were often left unpainted to look more natural. Thatched roofs also added to the natural feel.

For other buildings, the nobles liked simple, airy designs. Most buildings were made of wood with tiled roofs and large, open spaces inside. To add to the beauty of these buildings, the nobles surrounded them with elegant gardens and ponds. Similar gardens are still popular in Japan.

Performing Arts

The performing arts were also popular in Japan during the Heian period. The roots of later Japanese drama can be traced back to this time. People often gathered to watch performances by musicians, jugglers, and acrobats. These performances were wild and fun. Especially popular were the plays in which actors skillfully mimicked other people.

In later centuries, these types of performances developed into a more serious form of drama called Noh. Created in the 1300s, Noh plays combine music, speaking, and dance. These plays often tell about great heroes or figures from Japan's past.

THE IMPACT TODAY Noh plays are still popular in Japan today.

READING CHECK **Categorizing** What forms of art were popular in the Heian period?

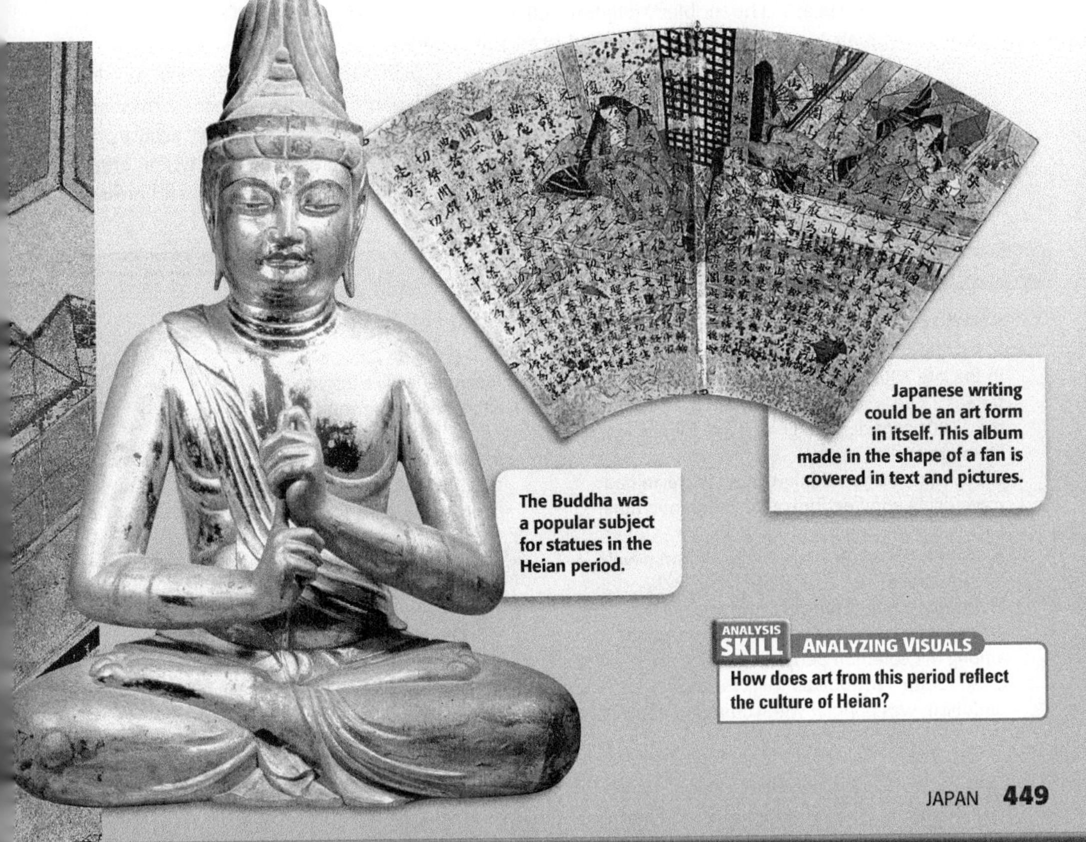

Japanese writing could be an art form in itself. This album made in the shape of a fan is covered in text and pictures.

The Buddha was a popular subject for statues in the Heian period.

ANALYSIS SKILL **ANALYZING VISUALS**

How does art from this period reflect the culture of Heian?

Direct Teach

Info to Know

Japanese Architecture The introduction of Buddhism to Japan also brought new ideas about architecture. Korean visitors were probably the first to introduce Chinese architectural styles to Japan. One well-known type of Japanese building is a pagoda. Pagodas are multiple-storied buildings that were built as monuments near Buddhist temples.

Connect to the Arts and the Humanities

Noh drama is one of the world's oldest forms of theater. Noh plays were usually performed only for nobles. The plays themselves feature one or two actors who use masks and dance movements to tell a story. Noh masks are intended to show the emotions of the character. There are traditionally five types of Noh plays—plays about gods, plays about warriors, plays about women, plays about supernatural creatures, and realistic plays.

hmhsocialstudies.com
Online Resources
Activity: Art of Japan

Differentiating Instruction

Advanced/Gifted and Talented — Above Level — Research Required

1. Review with students the different art forms that were popular among nobles in Heian. Ask students to select one form of art that appeals to them.
2. Have students use the library, the Internet, or other resources to research the art form they selected. Have students identify the following elements about the art form: origins, characteristics, and modern-day influences.
3. When students have completed their research, have them create a multimedia presentation that summarizes the information they discovered. Have students include visuals and sound to enhance their presentations.
4. Ask volunteers to share their presentations with the class. **LS Verbal/Linguistic, Visual/Spatial**

Alternative Assessment Handbook, Rubrics 30: Research; and 22: Multimedia Presentations

Answers

Analyzing Visuals *It shows how important art and culture were at the time.*

Reading Check *literature, visual art, architecture, fashion, and performing arts*

Direct Teach

Main Idea

2 Buddhism Changes

Buddhism changed in Japan during the Heian period.

Recall What forms of Buddhism developed in Japan? *Zen, Pure Land*

Contrast How do the beliefs of Zen Buddhists differ from those of other Buddhists? *Zen Buddhists believe in self-discipline and meditation rather than in faith and good behavior.*

Review & Assess

Close

Have students write a short summary of the cultural and religious changes that occurred in Heian.

Review

Online Quiz, Section 2

Assess

SE Section 2 Assessment

PASS: Section 2 Quiz

Alternative Assessment Handbook

Reteach/Classroom Intervention

Guided Reading Workbook, Section 2

Interactive Skills Tutor CD-ROM

Many Zen gardens like this one include raked gravel shaped to look like water and small boulders arranged like mountains.

Buddhism Changes

Religion became something of an art form in Heian. The nobles' religion reflected their love of elaborate rituals. Most of the common people in Japan, though equally religious, didn't have the time or money for these ceremonies. As a result, different forms of Buddhism developed in Japan.

One new form of Buddhism was very popular with Japan's common people. It was called Pure Land Buddhism and didn't require any special rituals. Instead, Pure Land Buddhists chanted the Buddha's name over and over to achieve an enlightened state.

In the 1100s another popular new form of Buddhism called **Zen** arrived from China. Zen Buddhists believed that neither faith nor good behavior led to wisdom. Instead, people seeking wisdom should practice self-discipline and meditation, or quiet thinking. These ideas appealed to many Japanese, especially warriors. As these warriors gained more influence in Japan, so did Zen Buddhism.

READING CHECK **Finding Main Ideas** How did Buddhism change in Japan?

SUMMARY AND PREVIEW At Heian, Japan's emperors presided over an elegant court. In the next section, you'll learn what happened when emperors and the court lost power and prestige.

Section 2 Assessment

hmhsocialstudies.com ONLINE QUIZ

Reviewing Ideas, Terms, and People

1. a. **Recall** Where did Japan's **court** move in the late 700s?
   b. **Make Generalizations** Why are the 800s to the 1100s considered a golden age for Japanese literature and art?
   c. **Evaluate** Do you think women in Heian had more rights and freedoms than women in other societies? Why or why not?
2. a. **Identify** What new form of Buddhism developed in Japan?
   b. **Compare and Contrast** How was religion among Japan's nobles different from religion among the common people?
   c. **Elaborate** Why do you think Pure Land Buddhism was popular with common people?

Critical Thinking

3. **Categorizing** Draw a Japanese fan like the one shown here. Use your notes about the arts to list two contributions that the Japanese made in each category shown here.

Visual Art | Fashion | Literature | Architecture | Performing Arts

Focus on Writing

4. **Writing about Japanese Art** Japan's nobles left a legacy of beautiful art that today's visitors can still enjoy. Choose two art forms described in this section and take notes for your brochure. What kinds of pictures could you use to illustrate your text?

Section 2 Assessment Answers

1. a. Heian
   b. Nobles supported the arts and made great advances in literature, painting, calligraphy, and drama.
   c. Answers will vary, but students should indicate that women were able to take part in and write about court society.
2. a. Pure Land and Zen Buddhism
   b. Nobles enjoyed rituals and ceremonies, whereas the common people did not have time or money for that.
   c. possible answers—They liked the teachings of Buddhism; it was simple and lacked elaborate rituals.
3. possible fan: architecture—natural style, elegant gardens and ponds; visual art—paintings, calligraphy; fashion—silk robes, gold jewelry; literature—diaries, novels; performing arts—Noh, musicians
4. possible answers—Noh plays combined music, speaking, and dance; poetry was often about love or nature; illustrations could be an actor in a play and a poem.

Answers

Reading Check *It became more of an art form for nobles, commoners developed Pure Land Buddhism, and Zen Buddhism appealed to warriors.*

BIOGRAPHY

Lady Murasaki Shikibu

How would you describe the people you observe in life every day?

When did she live? around 1000

Where did she live? Heian

What did she do? Lady Murasaki was a noble and a servant to the Empress Akiko. While in the empress's service, she wrote lively observations of court life in her diaries. She also wrote the novel *The Tale of Genji.*

Why is she important? *The Tale of Genji* is one of the world's oldest novels, and—some would argue—one of the best. Besides entertaining readers for hundreds of years, *The Tale of Genji* describes the daily lives, customs, and attitudes of Japanese nobles of the time.

Drawing Conclusions What qualified Lady Murasaki to comment on upper-class life in Japan?

KEY IDEAS

Observations of Lady Murasaki Shikibu

"Lady Dainagon is very small and refined . . . Her hair is three inches longer than her height."

"Lady Senji is also a little person, and haughty . . . She puts us to shame, her carriage is so noble."

"Lady Koshosho, all noble and charming. She is like a weeping-willow tree at budding time. Her style is very elegant and we all envy her her manners."

–from The Diary of Lady Murasaki Shikibu, in *Anthology of Japanese Literature*, edited by Donald Keene

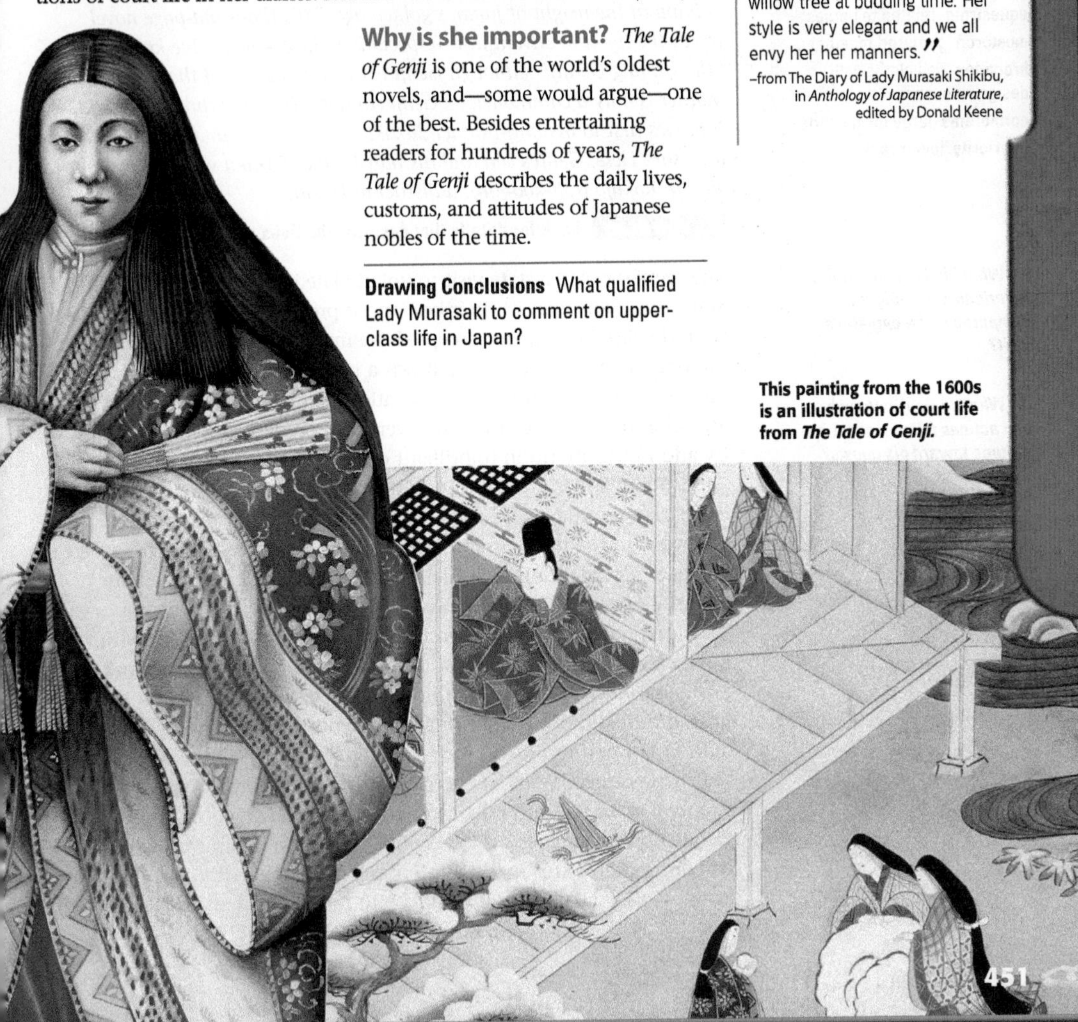

This painting from the 1600s is an illustration of court life from *The Tale of Genji.*

451

Cross-Discipline Activity: Arts and the Humanities

Above Level

Writing a *Tanka* Poem

Materials: samples of Japanese *tanka* poetry (available in *Holt Literature and Language Arts, Sixth Edition*)

Background: During the Heian period, Japanese nobles wrote poems called *tanka*, meaning "short songs." These poems are brief and lyrical. Each *tanka* expresses a private emotion or thought. The traditional *tanka* consists of five lines with a syllable count of 5 - 7 - 5 - 7 - 7.

1. Provide examples of *tanka* for students to see. Explain that they will be creating *tankas* of their own.
2. Ask students to consider Lady Murasaki Shikibu as a subject. Have them think about words they would use to describe her.
3. Have students list their words and then use them to write a *tanka*. Ask volunteers to read their *tanka* to the class. LS **Verbal/Linguistic**

Alternative Assessment Handbook, Rubric 39: Writing to Create

Biography

Reading Focus Question

Have students briefly discuss the introductory question. Ask students to choose one or two anonymous people and think about how they would describe them in a few sentences. Have volunteers share their descriptions. Tell students to keep the focus question in mind as they read the biography. When students have completed the reading, have them discuss how Lady Murasaki Shikibu described the people around her.

Analyzing Visuals

Drawing Inferences Ask students to analyze the illustration depicting court life from *The Tale of Genji.* Ask them what conclusions they can draw about Japanese court life during the Heian period from the picture. Tell students to look for clues in the image, such as the clothing, hairstyles, and objects.

Did you know . . .

When Lady Murasaki Shikibu was a child, her mother died, so she was raised by her father.

About the Illustration

This illustration of Lady Murasaki Shikibu is an artist's conception based on available sources. However, historians are uncertain exactly what Lady Murasaki looked like.

Answers

Drawing Conclusions *Her position as a noble and as a servant to Empress Akiko enabled her to observe and comment upon court and upper-class life in Japan.*

Literature in History

The Tale of Genji

As You Read As students read the excerpt, have them list words, phrases, and details that describe the lives of Japanese nobles. For example, the mention of equestrian grounds gives clues about the activities nobles enjoyed, and the descriptions of the music and dancing give clues about the nobles' taste in entertainment.

CRF: Literature Activity: Japanese Poetry: Tanka and Haiku

Literary Focus

Characterization Remind students that authors use clues to help readers get to know characters in their stories. Some clues for students to look for to learn more about a character are the person's appearance, actions, statements, thoughts and feelings, and reactions to others.

Activity **Making Inferences about Genji's Character** Ask students to use clues from the story to draw conclusions about Genji's character. Have students identify clues and explain what they reveal about Genji. **LS Verbal/Linguistic**

from The Tale of Genji

by Lady Murasaki Shikibu

translated by Edward G. Seidensticker

About the Reading The Tale of Genji *was written by Lady Murasaki Shikibu at the height of Japan's golden age. This thousand-page novel traces the life and adventures—especially in love—of a noble known as "the shining Genji." Although Genji is the favorite son of the emperor, his mother is only a commoner, so Genji cannot inherit the throne. Instead, it passes first to his half-brother Suzaku (soo-zah-koo) and then to Genji's own son. Here, Genji's son and his half-brother Suzaku visit Genji's mansion in Rokujo (roh-koo-joh), a district of Heian.*

AS YOU READ **Look for details that describe the lives of Japanese nobles.**

The emperor paid a state visit to Rokujo late in the Tenth Month. ❶ Since the colors were at their best and it promised to be a grand occasion, the Suzaku emperor accepted the invitation of his brother, the present emperor, to join him. It was a most extraordinary event, the talk of the whole court. The preparations, which occupied the full attention of everyone at Rokujo, were unprecedented in their complexity and in the attention to brilliant detail.

Arriving late in the morning, the royal party went first to the equestrian grounds, where the inner guards were mustered for mounted review in the finery usually reserved for the iris festival. There were brocades spread along the galleries and arched bridges and awnings over the open places when, in early afternoon, the party moved to the southeast quarter. The royal cormorants had been turned out with the Rokujo cormorants on the east lake, where there was a handsome take of small fish. Genji hoped that he was not being a fussy and overzealous host, but he did not want a single moment of the royal progress to be dull. ❷ The autumn leaves were splendid, especially in Akikonomu's southwest garden. Walls had been taken down and gates opened, and not so much as an autumn mist was permitted to obstruct the royal view. Genji showed his guests to seats on a higher level than his own. The emperor ordered this mark of inferiority dispensed with, and thought again what a satisfaction it would be to honor Genji as his father.

GUIDED READING

WORD HELP

unprecedented having no equal
equestrian related to horses
mustered gathered together
brocades rich cloths with designs woven into them
cormorants large diving birds
inferiority lower rank

❶ ***What kind of modern-day American event might be compared to the emperor's visit?***

❷ ***What do Genji's thoughts and actions tell you about his attitude toward his guests?***

Differentiating Instruction

Struggling Learners **Below Level**

1. To help students better understand characterization, ask them to think of a character from a popular movie, television show, or comic book. Have students list the character's appearance, actions, and speech. Then ask students how other characters' actions reveal what this character is like.
2. Ask volunteers to identify the characters they selected and some of the things they listed about them. See if students can agree on a label for each character.
3. Then have students apply the same approach to the character of Genji in the story. If students had to come up with a label on a T-shirt to describe Genji, what would it be? Encourage class discussion. **LS Verbal/Linguistic**

Alternative Assessment Handbook, Rubric 11: Discussions

Answers

Guided Reading **1.** *a visit by the U.S. president or by an important foreign dignitary;* **2.** *possible answer—His fussiness, nervousness, and attention to detail show the respect in which he holds his guests, how honored he is by their visit, and that he wants to make their visit as exciting as possible.*

The lieutenants of the inner guards advanced from the east and knelt to the left and right of the stairs before the royal seats, one presenting the take from the pond and the other a brace of fowl taken by the royal falcons in the northern hills. To no Chujo received the royal command to prepare and serve these delicacies. ❸ An equally interesting repast had been laid out for the princes and high courtiers. The court musicians took their places in late afternoon . . . The concert was quiet and unpretentious and there were court pages to dance for the royal guests. It was as always the excursion to the Suzaku Palace so many years before that people remembered. One of To no Chujo's sons, a boy of ten or so, danced "Our Gracious Monarch" most elegantly. The emperor took off a robe and laid it over his shoulders, and To no Chujo himself descended into the garden for ritual thanks . . .

A portrait of Lady Murasaki Shikibu, author of *The Tale of Genji*

The evening breeze had scattered leaves of various tints to make the ground a brocade as rich and delicate as the brocades along the galleries. The dancers were young boys from the best families, prettily dressed in coronets and the usual grayblues and roses, with crimsons and lavenders showing at their sleeves. They danced very briefly and withdrew under the autumn trees, and the guests regretted the approach of sunset. The formal concert, brief and unassuming, was followed by impromptu music in the halls above, instruments having been brought from the palace collection. As it grew livelier a koto was brought for each of the emperors and a third for Genji. ❹ . . . It was cause for general rejoicing that the two houses should be so close.

GUIDED READING

WORD HELP

brace pair
repast meal
unpretentious simple; modest
coronets small crowns

❸ To no Chujo is Genji's best friend. During the Heian period, food preparation was considered an art, and chefs were highly honored for their skill.

❹ A koto is a stringed instrument sometimes called a Japanese harp.

CONNECTING LITERATURE TO HISTORY

1. **Summarizing** The nobles of the court at Heian loved beauty and elegance. Because of this love, many nobles were great supporters of the arts. Based on this passage, what specific arts did Japanese nobles enjoy?
2. **Generalizing** The nobles enjoyed their lives of ease and privilege. What details suggest that Japanese nobles lived lives of luxury?
3. **Evaluating** After reading this passage, what is your overall impression of Japanese court life?

Literature in History

Meet the Writer

Lady Murasaki Shikibu (c. 978–c. 1014) Contrary to the customs of the time, Lady Murasaki's father gave her an education similar to what male children of the day received. As a result, she studied both Chinese literature and the Japanese kanji writing system, rare for women at that time. The little that is known of Lady Murasaki's life comes from the diary she kept from 1007 to 1010. She married and had a child. Her husband later died, after which she joined the imperial court. There, Lady Murasaki's intelligence helped her succeed. Several English translations of her diary are available. (See *Diary of Lady Murasaki* by Murasaki Shikibu, translated by Richard Bowring. New York, NY: Penguin, 1996.)

Did you know . . .

Lady Murasaki Shikibu's real name is unknown. The name *Murasaki* was a nickname she acquired based on a character in *The Tale of Genji. Shikibu* comes from her father's title as a government official.

Advanced/Gifted and Talented **Above Level**

1. Point out to students that because this story is written in the third person, readers must infer the characters' motivations based on the characters' words and actions or what is revealed about their thoughts and feelings.
2. Have each student rewrite the first two paragraphs of the excerpt in the first person. Students should use the characterization provided in the excerpt to infer what Genji is thinking and feeling during the events taking place.
3. Ask volunteers to read selections from their first-person versions aloud to the class.
LS Verbal/Linguistic

Alternative Assessment Handbook, Rubric 39: Writing to Create

Answers

Connecting Literature to History
1. *music, poetry, and dancing;*
2. *possible answers—The preparations for the party were elaborate and detailed, and the nobles enjoyed a variety of entertainment.* **3.** *possible answer—Japanese court life was filled with elaborate preparations; people wore beautiful clothing, enjoyed entertainment and luxuries, were waited upon, and had to do little themselves.*

Preteach

Bellringer

If YOU were there . . . Use the **Daily Bellringer Transparency** to help students answer the question.

Daily Bellringer Transparency, Section 3

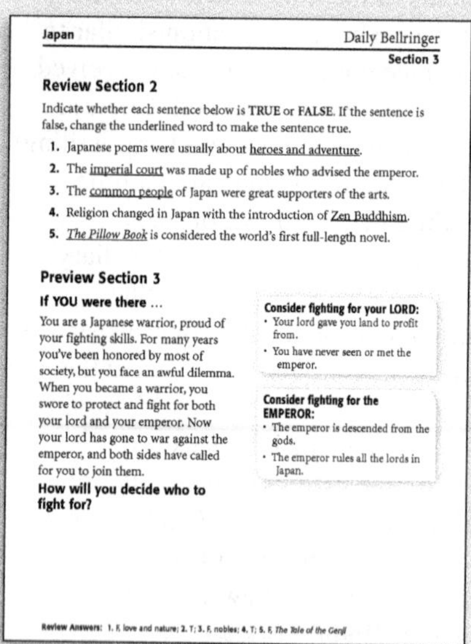

Japan — Daily Bellringer, Section 3

Review Section 2

Indicate whether each sentence below is TRUE or FALSE. If the sentence is false, change the underlined word to make the sentence true.

1. Japanese poems were usually about heroes and adventure.
2. The imperial court was made up of nobles who advised the emperor.
3. The common people of Japan were great supporters of the arts.
4. Religion changed in Japan with the introduction of Zen Buddhism.
5. *The Pillow Book* is considered the world's first full-length novel.

Preview Section 3

If YOU were there ...

You are a Japanese warrior, proud of your fighting skills. For many years you've been honored by most of society, but you face an awful dilemma. When you became a warrior, you swore to protect and fight for both your lord and your emperor. Now your lord has gone to war against the emperor, and both sides have called for you to join them.

How will you decide who to fight for?

Consider fighting for your LORD:
- Your lord gave you land to profit from.
- You have never seen or met the emperor.

Consider fighting for the EMPEROR:
- The emperor is descended from the gods.
- The emperor rules all the lords in Japan.

Review Answers: 1. F, love and nature; 2. T; 3. F, nobles; 4. T; 5. F, *The Tale of the Genji*

Academic Vocabulary

Review with students the high-use academic term in this section.

values ideas that people hold dear and try to live by (p. 457)

CRF: Vocabulary Builder Activity, Section 3

Taking Notes

Have students use the graphic organizer online to take notes on the section. This activity will prepare students for the Section Assessment, in which they will complete a graphic organizer that builds on the information using the Critical Thinking Skill: Analyzing.

SECTION 3

What You Will Learn...

Main Ideas

1. Samurai and shoguns took over Japan as emperors lost influence.
2. Samurai warriors lived honorably.
3. Order broke down when the power of the shoguns was challenged by invaders and rebellions.
4. Strong leaders took over and reunified Japan.

The Big Idea

Japan developed a military society led by generals called shoguns.

Key Terms and People

daimyo, *p. 454*
samurai, *p. 454*
figurehead, *p. 455*
shogun, *p. 455*
Bushido, *p. 456*

hmhsocialstudies.com TAKING NOTES

Use the graphic organizer online to take notes about the growth of a military society in Japan.

Growth of a Military Society

If YOU were there...

You are a Japanese warrior, proud of your fighting skills. For many years you've been honored by most of society, but you face an awful dilemma. When you became a warrior, you swore to protect and fight for both your lord and your emperor. Now your lord has gone to war against the emperor, and both sides have called for you to join them.

How will you decide whom to fight for?

BUILDING BACKGROUND Wars between lords and emperors were not uncommon in Japan after 1100. Closed off from society at Heian, emperors had lost touch with the rest of Japan. As a result, order broke down throughout the islands.

Samurai and Shoguns Take Over Japan

By the late 1100s, Heian was the great center of Japanese art and literature. But in the rest of Japan, life was very different. Powerful nobles fought each other over land. Rebels fought against imperial officials. This fighting destroyed land, which made it difficult for peasants to grow food. Some poor people became bandits or thieves. Meanwhile, Japan's rulers were so focused on courtly life, they didn't notice the many problems growing in their country.

The Rise of the Samurai

With the emperor distracted by life in his court, Japan's large landowners, or **daimyo** (DY-mee-oh), decided that they needed to protect their own lands. They hired **samurai** (SA-muh-ry), or trained professional warriors, to defend them and their property. The samurai wore light armor and fought with swords and bows. Most samurai came from noble families and inherited their positions from their fathers.

Teach the Big Idea

At Level

Growth of a Military Society

1. **Teach** Ask students the question in the Main Idea boxes to teach this section.
2. **Apply** Have each student list the main events of this section on a sheet of paper, along with their dates. Have students mark each event that strengthened the rule of the shoguns with a square, events that weakened their rule with a circle, and events that did not affect their rule with a triangle.
   LS **Verbal/Linguistic, Logical/Mathematical**
3. **Review** As a class, review students' lists. Make sure that students understand which events strengthened or weakened the rule of the shoguns and which events had no effect.
4. **Practice/Homework** Have each student create a time line for the events on his or her list. Have students compare their time lines with the time line at the beginning of the chapter to see what events took place in other parts of the world during this period.
   LS **Visual/Spatial**

The word *samurai* comes from the Japanese word for servant. Every samurai, from the weakest soldier to the most powerful warrior, was supposed to serve his lord. Because all lords in Japan were supposed to serve the emperor, all samurai were required to be loyal to him.

Samurai were expensive to support. Few lords could afford to buy armor and weapons for their warriors. As a result, lords paid their samurai with land or food. Historians call this exchange of land for military service a feudal system, after a similar system that developed in Europe.

Only the most powerful samurai got land for their service. Every year, the peasant farmers who worked on the land gave the samurai money or food. Samurai who received no land were given food—usually rice—as payment.

Shoguns Rule Japan

Many of the nobles outside Heian were unhappy with the way Japan's government was being run. Frustrated, these nobles wanted a change of leadership. Eventually a few very strong noble clans decided to try to take power for themselves.

Two of these powerful clans went to war with each other in the 1150s. For almost 30 years, the two clans fought. Their fighting was terrible, destroying land and property and tearing families apart.

In the end, the Minamoto clan won. Because he had a very powerful army, and because the emperor was still busy in Heian, the leader of the Minamoto clan was the most powerful man in Japan. He decided to take over ruling the country.

He didn't, however, want to get rid of the emperor. He kept the emperor as a **figurehead**, a person who appears to rule even though real power rests with someone else. As a samurai, the Minamoto leader was supposed to be loyal to the emperor, but he decided to rule in the emperor's place. In 1192 he took the title **shogun**, a general who ruled Japan in the emperor's name. When he died, he passed his title and power on to one of his children. For about the next 700 years, one shogun would rule in Japan.

READING CHECK **Sequencing** How did the shogun rise to power in Japan?

QUICK FACTS
Samurai Society
Emperor
The emperor was a figurehead for the powerful shogun.
Shogun
A powerful military leader, the shogun ruled in the emperor's name.
Daimyo and Samurai
Daimyo were powerful lords who often led armies of samurai. Samurai warriors served the shogun and daimyo.
Peasants
Most Japanese were poor peasants who had no power.
hmhsocialstudies.com
ANIMATED HISTORY

ANALYSIS SKILL **ANALYZING VISUALS**

Who was the most powerful person in Japan's samurai society?

Direct Teach

Main Idea

❶ Samurai and Shoguns Take Over Japan

Samurai and shoguns took over Japan as emperors lost influence.

Describe What was life like outside Heian in the late 1100s? *Fighting among nobles and rebels destroyed land, making it hard for peasants to grow food, so some resorted to theft.*

Define What was a daimyo? *a large landowner*

Explain What did samurai receive in return for their service? *Some got land from their lord; most received food or money from peasants.*

Contrast What was the difference between the emperor and the shogun? *The emperor appeared to rule, but was just a figurehead. The shogun actually ruled in the emperor's name.*

Quick Facts Transparency: Samurai Society

QUICK FACTS Samurai Society

Analyzing Visuals Point out to students that while the emperor is featured above the shogun in the diagram, in reality the shogun had more power than the emperor, who was merely a figurehead and did not actively rule the country.

Differentiating Instruction

English-Language Learners **At Level** Standard English Mastery

1. Review with students key terms from this section with which they may not be familiar: *daimyo, armor, samurai, figurehead, shogun, discipline, shame, Bushido,* and *isolation.*
2. Draw a tic-tac-toe diagram (nine-square grid) for students to see. Organize students into two groups: Xs and Os.
3. Determine which group will go first. Then select one student in that group to answer a question. Given one of the vocabulary words, the student is to define the term and use it in a sentence. Upon answering correctly, that group puts its mark in the square of its choosing. The first group to get three in a row wins. **LS Verbal/Linguistic, Visual/Spatial**

Alternative Assessment Handbook, Rubric 11: Discussions

CRF: Vocabulary Builder Activity, Section 3

Answers

Analyzing Visuals *the shogun*

Reading Check *The emperor was busy in Heian, and the leader of the Minamoto clan defeated another powerful clan and took control of the country.*

Direct Teach

Main Idea

❷ Samurai Live Honorably

Samurai warriors lived honorably.

Recall What were two things that samurai could *not* do? *attend certain types of entertainment, such as theater; take part in trade or commerce*

Explain What was Bushido, and who was expected to live by its rules? *samurai code of rules; both men and women from samurai families*

Summarize What samurai values are still admired in modern-day Japan? *loyalty, honor, dedication, discipline*

Info to Know

Japan's Samurai Young men and even some young women trained to become samurai warriors in feudal Japan. Their training included learning the art of warfare, and later, the ways of peace. To become a samurai demanded strict training in the martial arts. Many samurai developed great skill handling a sword. But a samurai also learned other lessons, such as the proper way to conduct a tea ceremony and how to write poetry. Above all, a samurai trained to overcome his or her fear of death.

Samurai Live Honorably

Focus on Reading
As you read this section, notice the facts and examples that support the main idea.

Under the shogun, who were military rulers, samurai warriors became more central to Japanese society. As a result, samurai enjoyed many social privileges. Common people had to treat the samurai with respect. Anyone who disrespected a samurai could be killed.

At the same time, tradition placed restrictions on samurai. For example, they couldn't attend certain types of entertainment, such as theater, which were considered beneath them. They also couldn't take part in trade or commerce.

Bushido

More importantly, all samurai had to follow a strict code of rules that taught them how to behave. The samurai code of rules was known as **Bushido** (BOOH-shi-doh). This name means "the way of the warrior." Both men and women from samurai families had to follow Bushido rules.

Bushido required samurai to be brave and honorable fighters. Both men and women of samurai families learned how to fight, though only men went to war. Women learned to fight so they could protect their homes from robbers.

Japan's Samurai

The samurai were bold, highly trained warriors. They followed a strict code of behavior called Bushido, or "the way of the warrior."

What equipment did samurai have to protect themselves?

Samurai wore armor and special helmets. Many carried two swords.

Samurai were often called on to fight, like in the scene above. They were expected to serve with honor and loyalty in battle. The samurai in the scene to the right is writing a poem on a cherry tree. Writing poetry helped train the samurai to concentrate.

Critical Thinking: Drawing Conclusions

Above Level

Samurai Brochures

Research Required

1. Organize the class into small groups. Have each group research the following topics relating to samurai:
   - definition of samurai
   - relationship between samurai and daimyo
   - how samurai were paid
   - description of samurai battle dress and equipment
   - rules regarding behavior
   - descriptions of customs and traditions in which samurai participated
   - significance to Japanese history
2. Have each group create a brochure that presents the information group members learned about samurai.
3. Ask groups to share their brochures with the class. **LS Interpersonal, Verbal/Linguistic, Visual/Spatial**

Alternative Assessment Handbook, Rubrics 14: Group Activity; and 42: Writing to Inform

Answers

Japan's Samurai *helmets, swords, and armor*

Samurai were expected to live simple, disciplined lives. They believed that self-discipline made them better warriors. To improve their discipline, many samurai participated in peaceful rituals that required great concentration. Some created intricate flower arrangements or grew miniature bonsai trees. Others held elaborate tea ceremonies. Many samurai also adopted Zen Buddhism, which stressed self-discipline and meditation.

More than anything else, Bushido required a samurai to be loyal to his lord. Each samurai had to obey his master's orders without hesitation, even if it caused the samurai or his family to suffer. One samurai expressed his duties in this way:

> "If one were to say in a word what the condition of being a samurai is, its basis lies first in seriously devoting one's body and soul to his master."
>
> –Yamamoto Tsunetomo, from *Hagakure*

Obeying his lord was important to the samurai's sense of honor. Honor was the most important thing in a samurai's life. If he did anything to lose honor, a samurai was expected to commit suicide rather than live with his shame. Such shame might be caused by disobeying an order, losing a fight, or failing to protect his lord.

Bushido and Modern Japan

Although it was created as a code for warriors, Bushido influenced much of Japanese society. Even today, many Japanese feel a connection to the samurai. For example, the samurai's dedication and discipline are still greatly admired in Japan. **Values** such as loyalty and honor, the central ideas of the samurai code, remain very important in modern Japan.

ACADEMIC VOCABULARY
values ideas that people hold dear and try to live by

READING CHECK **Finding Main Ideas** What customs did samurai follow?

HISTORY
VIDEO
Samurai in the Modern World
hmhsocialstudies.com

LINKING TO TODAY

Modern Samurai

Although the samurai class disappeared from Japan at the end of the 1800s, samurai images and values live on. Fierce samurai appear on posters, in advertisements and movies, and in video games, challenging foes with their sharp swords and deadly skills. Many people study the same martial arts, such as sword fighting, that the samurai practiced. In addition, the loyalty that samurai felt toward their lords is still a key part of Japanese society. Many Japanese feel that same loyalty toward other groups—their families, companies, or favorite sports teams. Samurai values such as hard work, honor, and sacrifice have also become deeply rooted in Japanese society.

ANALYSIS SKILL **ANALYZING INFORMATION**
How are Japan's samurai values still alive today?

Direct Teach

Linking to Today

Modern Samurai

The position of samurai officially ended in the 1870s when the Japanese government forbade them to wear their swords in public. Today samurai occupy a place in Japanese culture much like that held by the cowboys of the Old West in America. Samurai movies are the so-called westerns of Japanese entertainment.

Biography

Akira Kurasawa (1910–1998) Akira Kurasawa was one of Japan's leading film directors. He was influenced by American directors and American popular culture, especially westerns. However, Kurasawa's films often featured samurai heroes instead of cowboys.

Kurasawa's film *The Seven Samurai* (1954) is considered one of the best samurai movies ever made. It inspired the American western *The Magnificent Seven* (1960). Another western, *A Fistful of Dollars* (1967), was based on Kurasawa's film *Yojimbo* (1961). His film *The Hidden Fortress* (1958) influenced George Lucas's *Star Wars* (1977).

Kurasawa's films were popular in Europe and the United States. He received many awards, including an Academy Award for best picture (*Kagemusha,* 1980).

hmhsocialstudies.com
Online Resources
Activity: Japan's Samurai

Collaborative Learning

At Level

Presenting a Code of Rules

1. Divide the class into groups of four to six students. Have each group develop a code of rules similar to the samurai code of Bushido but geared to present-day life. Each group should come up with a list of 10 rules for proper behavior. Rules should be about general behavior in society.
2. Have each group read its rules to the class. Each member of the group should take a turn reading some of his or her group's rules.
3. After each group's rules have been read, lead the class in a discussion of them. Did some rules appear on every list? If so, what were they? Why did each group think they were important? Were there rules that appeared on only one list? Why?
4. Have each student write a paragraph explaining what this activity reveals about the importance of rules for behavior.
LS Verbal/Linguistic

Alternative Assessment Handbook, Rubrics 14: Group Activity; and 37: Writing Assignments

Answers

Analyzing Information *Loyalty, hard work, and sacrifice are still important parts of Japanese society.*

Reading Check *possible answers—followed code of Bushido; practiced rituals like flower arranging or growing bonsai trees; tea ceremonies*

Main Idea

3 Order Breaks Down

Order broke down when the power of the shoguns was challenged by invaders and rebellions.

Recall What help did the Japanese get in fighting off the two Mongol invasions? *Huge storms destroyed many of the Mongol ships.*

Analyze Why did the Japanese refer to the storms as kamikaze? *They believed the gods had sent the storms to protect Japan.*

Identify Who made laws and collected taxes in Japan during the 1400s? Why? *the daimyo; no central authority anymore*

- **CRF:** History and Geography Activity: The Winds that Saved Japan
- **CRF:** Primary Source Activity: The Mongol Invasion Scrolls
- Map Transparency: Mongol Invasions of Japan

Did you know . . .

The Japanese word *kamikaze* means "divine wind." The word was first used to describe the storm that destroyed the Mongol fleet in 1281, putting an end to the Mongol invasion of Japan. The term was revived in 1945 toward the end of World War II. It referred to the Japanese suicide pilots who flew airplanes loaded with explosives into American ships.

hmhsocialstudies.com INTERACTIVE MAP

Mongol Invasions of Japan

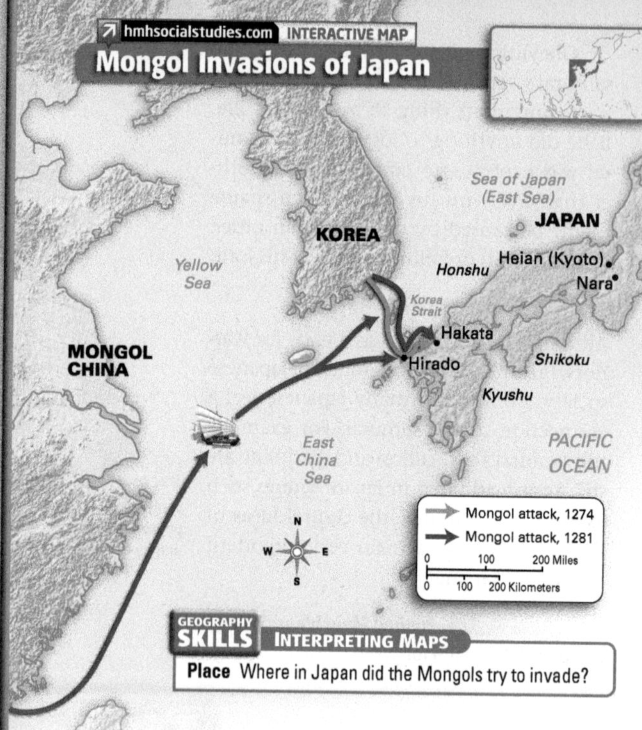

GEOGRAPHY SKILLS INTERPRETING MAPS

Place Where in Japan did the Mongols try to invade?

Order Breaks Down

For about a century, the shoguns kept order in Japan. Supported by the samurai, the shoguns were able to put down challenges to their authority. Eventually, however, more serious challenges arose that brought this order to an end.

Foreign Invasion

One of the greatest challenges to the shoguns was an invasion by the Mongols from China. China's emperor, Kublai Khan, sent an army to conquer the islands in 1274. Faced with invasion, the shogun sent troops to fight the Mongols. In addition, Japan's warring nobles put aside their differences to fight the enemy. The Japanese warriors were aided by a great storm. The storm sank many Mongol ships and forced the Mongols to flee.

In 1281 the Mongols invaded again. This time they sent two huge armies and threatened to overwhelm the Japanese warriors. For weeks, the two armies were locked in deadly combat.

Once again, though, the weather helped the Japanese. A huge storm swept over Japan, sinking most of the Mongol fleet. Many Mongol soldiers drowned, and many more returned to China. The grateful Japanese called the storm that had saved them the kamikaze (kah-mi-KAH-zee), or "divine wind." They believed the gods had sent the storm to save Japan.

But many nobles were left unhappy by the war. They didn't think the shogun gave them enough credit for their part in the fighting. Many came to resent the shogun's power over them.

Internal Rebellion

After the Mongol invasion, new problems arose for the shogun. The emperor, tired of having no say in the government, began to fight the shogun for control of the country. At the same time daimyo, the nobles who owned much of Japan's land, fought to break free of the shogun's control. During these struggles for power, small wars broke out all over Japan.

By the 1400s the shoguns had lost most of their authority. The emperor was still largely powerless, and daimyo ruled much of Japan. Each daimyo controlled his own territory. Within that territory, he made laws and collected taxes. There was no powerful central authority of any sort to impose order in Japan.

READING CHECK **Summarizing** What challenges appeared to the shogun's authority?

Cross-Discipline Activity: Arts and the Humanities

At Level

Mongol Invasion Skits

Prep Required

1. Before class, locate some of the images from the Mongol Invasion Scrolls.
2. Review with students the events surrounding the two attempted Mongol invasions of Japan. Share with students some of the images from the Japanese Mongol Invasion Scrolls.
3. Organize students into groups of four or five. Have each group prepare a short skit in which members depict the events surrounding the Mongol attack on Japan in 1274 and 1281. Remind students to present facts in their skits that explain who invaded, why they invaded, what actions the Japanese took, and what the outcome was of the invasion.
4. Each group should then write a script that includes a cast of characters and dialogue for each character.
5. Ask groups to volunteer to present their skits to the class. LS **Interpersonal, Kinesthetic**

Alternative Assessment Handbook, Rubric 33: Skits and Reader's Theater

Answers

Interpreting Maps *Hirado and Hakata*

Reading Check *Nobles were unhappy that the shogun did not give them credit for fighting the Mongols, the emperor wanted more control, and daimyo broke free of the shogun's control.*

Strong Leaders Take Over

Soon new leaders rose to power. They began as local rulers, but these men wanted more power. In the 1500s, each fought to unify all of Japan under his control.

Unification

The first such leader was Oda Nobunaga (ohd-ah noh-booh-nah-gah). Oda gave his soldiers guns that had been brought to Japan by Portuguese traders. This was the first time guns had been used in Japan. With these new weapons, Oda easily defeated his opponents.

After Oda died, other leaders continued his efforts to unify Japan. By 1600, one of them, Tokugawa Ieyasu (toh-koohg-ah-wuh ee-e-yahs-ooh), had conquered his enemies. In 1603 Japan's emperor made Tokugawa shogun. From his capital at Edo (AY-doh)—now Tokyo—Tokugawa ruled all of Japan.

Tokugawa's rise to power began the Tokugawa shogunate (SHOH-guhn-uht), or rule by shoguns of the Tokugawa family. Early in this period, which lasted until 1868, Japan traded with other countries and let Christian missionaries live in Japan.

Isolation

Not all of the shoguns who followed Tokugawa liked this contact with the world, though. Some feared that Japan would become too much like Europe, and the shoguns would lose their power. To prevent such a thing from happening, in the 1630s the ruling shogun closed Japan off from the rest of the world.

Japan's rulers also banned guns. They feared that peasants with guns could defeat their samurai armies. The combination of isolation from the world and limited technology helped extend the samurai period in Japan until the 1800s, far longer than it might have otherwise lasted.

READING CHECK **Drawing Conclusions** How did Japan change in the Tokugawa shogunate?

SUMMARY AND PREVIEW By the 1100s, the growing power of shoguns, daimyo, and samurai had turned Japan into a military society. Next you will read about societies that developed on the other side of the world—in the Americas.

Section 3 Assessment

hmhsocialstudies.com ONLINE QUIZ

Reviewing Ideas, Terms, and People

1. a. **Recall** What was the relationship between **samurai** and **daimyo**?
   b. **Elaborate** Why do you think the first **shogun** wanted to keep the emperor as a **figurehead**?
2. a. **Define** What was **Bushido**?
   b. **Explain** Why did samurai take up pursuits like flower arranging?
3. a. **Identify** Who invaded Japan in the 1270s and 1280s?
   b. **Summarize** How did the daimyo help weaken the shoguns?
4. **Identify** What strong leaders worked to unify Japan in the late 1500s?

Critical Thinking

5. **Analyzing** Draw a word web. In the center, write a sentence that describes the samurai. Using your notes about life in a military society, write one of the samurai's jobs, duties, or privileges in each outer circle.

FOCUS ON WRITING

6. **Describing the Samurai** A Japanese history museum will offer a special exhibit on the samurai warrior. Add notes about the samurai to encourage tourists to visit the exhibit. Tell who they were, what they did, and how they lived.

Direct Teach

Main Idea

4 Strong Leaders Take Over

Strong leaders took over and reunified Japan.

Identify Who finally reunified Japan about 1600? *Tokugawa Ieyasu*

Explain What caused the ruling shogun to close Japan off from the rest of the world in the 1630s? *fear that Japan would become too much like Europe and that the shoguns would lose their power*

CRF: Biography Activity: Tokugawa Ieyasu

Review & Assess

Close

Guide students in a review of Japanese government and society during this period of military rule.

Review

Online Quiz, Section 3

Assess

SE Section 3 Assessment

PASS: Section 3 Quiz

Alternative Assessment Handbook

Reteach/Classroom Intervention

Guided Reading Workbook, Section 3

Interactive Skills Tutor CD-ROM

Section 3 Assessment Answers

1. **a.** Daimyo hired the samurai to defend themselves and their property.
   b. possible answer—to prevent a revolt
2. **a.** samurai code of rules
   b. to improve their self-discipline
3. **a.** the Mongols
   b. Daimyo took control of their small piece of land, they collected taxes, made laws, and fought wars.
4. Oda Nobunaga and Tokugawa Ieyasu
5. possible answer: center circle—Samurai were professional warriors who served a daimyo; outer circles—follow Bushido; serve daimyo; paid with land or food
6. possible responses—Samurai were professional warriors; they tried to live simple, disciplined lives; samurai put great value in loyalty and honor.

Answers

Reading Check *Japan began to trade with other countries and let European missionaries live in Japan.*

Social Studies Skills

Solving Problems

Activity Problem-Solving Flow Chart Have each student create a flow chart that illustrates the problem-solving steps described under "Learn the Skill." Have volunteers share the information in their charts as you create a master chart for the class to see. Then have each student create a flow chart illustrating the problem-solving steps they took to complete the "Practice and Apply the Skill" activity.
LS **Logical/Mathematical, Visual/Spatial**

Alternative Assessment Handbook, Rubrics 13: Graphic Organizers; and 35: Solving Problems

Interactive Skills Tutor CD-ROM, Lessons 12: Identify Issues and Problems; and 16: Identify Possible Solutions and Predict Consequences

Answers

Practice and Apply the Skill
1. *deciding what action to take in the war between the lord and the emperor; It is a problem because I am bound by Bushido to serve my lord, but I have also pledged loyalty to the emperor.* **2.** *my lord going to war against the emperor; internal unrest in Japan, emperors' struggle against the shoguns for power, daimyo's efforts to free themselves from the shoguns' control, and the samurai code that I am must follow;* **3.** *Possible options include supporting the lord, supporting the emperor, trying to remain neutral, trying to be a peacemaker, or doing nothing. Students may think of other options as well. They should list realistic advantages and disadvantages for each option.* **4.** *Solutions will vary, but the one chosen should be based on an accurate and reasoned evaluation of the options identified in Question 3.*

Social Studies Skills

Analysis | Critical Thinking | Economics | Study

Solving Problems

Understand the Skill

Problem solving is a process for finding good solutions to difficult situations. It involves asking questions, identifying and evaluating information, comparing and contrasting, and making judgments. It is useful in studying history because it helps you better understand problems a person or group faced in the past and how they dealt with those issues.

The ability to understand and evaluate how people solved problems in the past also can help in solving similar problems today. The skill can be applied to many other kinds of difficulties besides historical ones. It is a method for thinking through almost any situation.

Learn the Skill

Using the following steps will help you to better understand and solve problems.

1. **Identify the problem.** Ask questions of yourself and others. This first step helps you to be sure you know exactly what the situation is. It also helps you understand why it is a problem.
2. **Gather information.** Ask other questions and do research to learn more about the problem. For example, what is its history? What caused the problem? What contributes to it?
3. **List options.** Based on the information you have gathered, identify possible options for solving the problem. It will be easier to find a good solution if you have several options.
4. **Evaluate the options.** Weigh each option you are considering. Think of the advantages it has as a solution. Then think of its potential disadvantages. It may help you to compare your options if you make a list of advantages and disadvantages for each possible solution.
5. **Choose and apply a solution.** After comparing the advantages and disadvantages of each possible solution, choose the one that seems best and apply it.
6. **Evaluate the solution.** Once the solution has been tried, evaluate how effective it is in solving the problem. This step will tell you if the solution was a good one, or if you should try another of the options instead. It will also help you know what to do in the future if you happen to face the same problem again.

Practice and Apply the Skill

Read again the "If you were there" in Section 3. Imagine that you are the warrior with this problem. You can apply the steps for solving problems to help you decide what to do. Review the information in the section about the samurai and this time period in Japan's history. Then, in the role of the samurai warrior, answer the questions below.

1. What is the specific problem that you face? Why is it a problem?
2. What events led to your problem? What circumstances and conditions have contributed to it?
3. What options can you think of to solve your problem? List the advantages and disadvantages of each.
4. Which of your options seems to be the best solution for your problem? Explain why. How will you know if it is a good solution?

Social Studies Skills Activity: Solving Problems

At Level

Problem-Solving in Japan

1. Have each student review the information in Section 3 under the headings "Order Breaks Down" and "Strong Leaders Take Over."
2. Ask students to imagine that they are an assistant to either Oda Nobunaga or Tokugawa Ieyasu. Have each student create a flow chart showing a hypothetical problem-solving process that either leader might have gone through when considering how to address the problems facing Japan at the time. Students might work independently or in pairs or small groups to complete the activity.
3. Have volunteers share their work with the class. Then have students discuss and evaluate each leader's solutions in solving Japan's problems. Students should consider any positive and negative results of each leader's actions. LS **Logical/Mathematical, Visual/Spatial**

Alternative Assessment Handbook, Rubrics 7: Charts; and 35: Solving Problems

CHAPTER 15

Chapter Review

History's Impact
▶ **video series**
Review the video to answer the focus question:
How did the samurai era end, and how is the samurai tradition felt in Japan today?

Visual Summary

Use the visual summary below to help you review the main ideas of the chapter.

QUICK FACTS

Japan's early culture was influenced by China and Korea.

A golden age of Japanese art and culture occurred during Japan's Heian Period.

After the Heian Period, the Japanese created a military society.

Reviewing Vocabulary, Terms, and People

Unscramble each group of letters below to spell a term that matches the given definition.

1. **etrgne**—a person who rules in someone else's name
2. **misaaru**—a Japanese warrior
3. **aclsn**—large, extended families
4. **elauvs**—ideas that people hold dear
5. **uctro**—a group of nobles who surround a ruler
6. **nguosh**—a great Japanese general who ruled instead of the emperor
7. **enz**—a form of Japanese Buddhism
8. **osnith**—a nature religion that began in Japan
9. **odmiya**—Japanese lords who gave land to samurai
10. **kosouth**—prince who introduced many Chinese ideas to Japan
11. **rctusrteu**—the way something is set up

Comprehension and Critical Thinking

SECTION 1 *(Pages 438–443)*

12. a. Identify Who was Prince Shotoku, and what did he do?

b. Compare and Contrast Why was Japan isolated from China and Korea? How did China and Korea still affect Japan?

c. Predict How would Japan's physical geography affect the development of Japanese government and society?

SECTION 2 *(Pages 444–448)*

13. a. Recall Why is Murasaki Shikibu a major figure in the history of Japanese culture?

b. Analyze What made the period between the 800s and the 1100s a golden age of the arts in Japan?

c. Evaluate Would you like to have been a member of the imperial court at Heian? Why or why not?

Answers

Visual Summary

Review and Inquiry Use the visual summary to review the chapter's main ideas. Ask students to provide supporting details for each main idea shown.

Quick Facts Transparency: Japan Visual Summary

Reviewing Vocabulary, Terms, and People

1. regent
2. samurai
3. clans
4. values
5. court
6. shogun
7. Zen
8. Shinto
9. daimyo
10. Shotoku
11. structure

Comprehension and Critical Thinking

12. a. served as regent of Japan from 593 to 622; influential in spreading Chinese ideas and culture, including Buddhism, throughout Japan

b. because Japan is located on islands; Japanese leaders helped bring Chinese and Korean culture to Japan, which influenced many areas of Japanese life, such as writing.

c. Because they lived on islands, the Japanese were separated from the other people of Asia, which allowed them to develop their own government and society.

Review and Assessment Resources

Review and Reinforce

- SE Chapter Review
- **CRF:** Chapter Review Activity
- Quick Facts Transparency: Japan Visual Summary
- Spanish Chapter Summaries Audio CD Program
- Online Chapter Summaries in Six Languages
- TOS Holt McDougal PuzzleView
- Quiz Game CD-ROM

Assess

- SE Standardized Test Practice
- PASS: Chapter Test
- Alternative Assessment Handbook
- TOS ExamView Assessment Suite, Chapter Test
- Differentiated Instruction Modified Worksheets and Tests CD-ROM: Chapter Test
- Online Assessment Program, in the Interactive Student Edition

Reteach/Intervene

- Guided Reading Workbook
- Differentiated Instruction Teacher Management System: Lesson Plans
- Differentiated Instruction Modified Worksheets and Tests CD-ROM
- Interactive Skills Tutor CD-ROM

hmhsocialstudies.com
Chapter Resources

Answers

13. a. She wrote *The Tale of Genji*, considered the world's first full-length novel as well as a great work of literature.

b. The imperial court at Heian was a great supporter of the arts. They created a center of culture and learning that included fashion, literature, visual arts, architecture, performing arts, and Buddhism.

c. Answers will vary, but students should correctly describe the imperial court's lifestyle of ease, privilege, beauty, and artistic culture.

14. a. the rule of Japan by shoguns of the Tokugawa family, which lasted from the early 1600s to the 1860s

b. A few strong nobles, unhappy with the government, vied for power. One clan gained control and its leader began ruling as shogun in the emperor's place. The groups of this society were the emperor, shogun, daimyo, samurai, and peasants.

c. served their lords and the emperor; led simple, disciplined lives according to a strict code of laws called Bushido; learned to fight; performed peaceful tasks that required great concentration, such as writing poetry

Reviewing Themes

15. The military ran the government through the system of shogun, daimyo, and samurai.

16. Nobles became less interested in art and more involved in war. Society broke apart, no longer unified under a single ruler.

17. Bushido values such as loyalty, honor, and self-discipline remain central to Japanese life.

Reading Skills

18. Prince Shotoku took steps to introduce Chinese culture into Japan.

19. Possible answers—stories or examples; Either method could have given specific examples of what Shotoku brought to Japan.

20. definition of *regent*; It explains Shotoku's position in Japan and his ability to change society.

SECTION 3 *(Pages 454–459)*

14. a. Define What was the Tokugawa shogunate?

b. Analyze How did Japan develop into a military society? What groups made up that society?

c. Elaborate What was daily life like for the samurai?

Reviewing Themes

15. Politics How did Prince Shototku try to change the political system in Japan?

16. Science and Technology What new technological advance did Japan's rulers ban, starting in the 1630s? Why?

17. Society and Culture How did Bushido affect modern Japanese culture?

Reading Skills 

Main Ideas and Their Support *The passage below is taken from this textbook. Read the passage and then answer the questions that follow.*

> "One of the people most influential in bringing Chinese ideas to Japan was Prince Shotoku. He served from 593 to 621 as regent for his aunt, the empress. A regent is a person who rules a country for someone who is unable to rule alone.
>
> All his life, Prince Shotoku admired Chinese culture. As regent, Shotoku saw a chance for Japan to adopt more Chinese ideas. He sent scholars to China to learn more about Chinese society."

18. Explain in your own words the main idea of this passage.

19. Which other method might the author have used to make the explanation more informative and interesting? What would this method have contributed to the passage's meaning?

20. What is a definition the author gives in this passage? How does it help support the main idea?

Using the Internet 

21. Activity: Drawing a Comic Strip A strong military influence affected the governing structure of Japan. Eventually, warriors and generals gained power in Japan as emperors lost some of it. Use your online textbook to conduct research and create a comic strip, similar in style to Japanese anime, about the people who held power. Your characters should include a shogun, a daimyo, a samurai, and an emperor.

hmhsocialstudies.com

Social Studies Skills 

22. Solving Problems Imagine that you are a samurai warrior who has been called upon to help fight the Mongol invasion. You are stationed in a small village that is directly in the path of the Mongol army. Some people in the village want to stay and fight the Mongols, but you know they will be killed if they try to fight. The town's leaders want your opinion about what they should do. Write down one or two ideas you might suggest for how to save the people of the village. For each idea, make notes about what consequences your proposed action may have.

Focus on Writing 

23. Creating Your Travel Brochure Look back over your notes from this chapter, and then create a travel brochure that describes Japan's historic attractions. Keep your writing brief—remember that you have to get your audience's attention with just a few words. To help get their attention, draw or find pictures to illustrate your travel brochure.

Using the Internet

21. Go to hmhsocialstudies.com to access a rubric for this activity.

Social Studies Skills

22. possible response—idea: join together with a nearby village; consequences:will have more warriors available to fight Mongols, will have better relations with neighbors

Focus on Writing

23. Rubric Students' travel brochures should:

- include facts that will interest an audience.
- describe Japanese art forms and samurai warriors.
- present drawings or images that would encourage people to visit Japan.
- be brief and to the point.

CRF: Focus on Writing: Writing a Travel Brochure

CHAPTER 15 Standardized Test Practice

DIRECTIONS: Read each question, and write the letter of the best response.

1

> I was brought up in a distant province which lies farther than the farthest end of the Eastern Road. I am ashamed to think that inhabitants of the Royal City will think me an uncultured girl.
>
> Somehow I came to know that there are such things as romances in the world and wished to read them. When there was nothing to do by day or at night, one tale or another was told me by my elder sister or stepmother, and I heard several chapters about the shining Prince Genji.

From the content of this passage, it can be concluded that its author was a

A samurai warrior.
B noble woman from Heian.
C farmer from northern Japan.
D daimyo.

2 **The importance of loyalty, honor, and discipline in Japanese society today are *mainly* the result of what influence in Japan's history?**

A the code of the samurai
B the teachings of Shinto
C the reforms of Prince Shotoku
D the spread of Chinese Buddhism

3 **Most great works of early Japanese literature were written by**

A Buddhist scholars.
B samurai warriors.
C Shinto priests.
D noble women.

4 **The influence of China and Korea on Japan's history, culture, and development is found in all of the following *except***

A Japan's first writing system.
B the traditional Japanese diet.
C early rules for family behavior.
D the practice of Buddhism.

5 **The main function of samurai in Japanese society was to**

A write poetry.
B manage farmland.
C defend lords.
D conquer China.

Connecting with Past Learnings

6 **Early Japanese society under the clans was not a single unified country but many small states. This type of government *most* resembled that of**

A the early city-states of ancient Greece.
B the Roman Empire during the Pax Romana.
C the Old Kingdom of ancient Egypt.
D the New Kingdom of ancient Egypt.

7 **The nobles of Heian placed great emphasis on art and learning, just like the people of which ancient Greek city-state that you learned about earlier?**

A Sparta
B Athens
C Macedonia
D Troy

Answers

Standardized Test Practice

1. B

Break Down the Question: Point out to students that the speaker is a girl who is interested in stories about Prince Genji. As the author of *Tale of Genji* was a noblewoman from Heian, students should be able to eliminate the other answer choices.

2. A

Break Down the Question: This question requires students to recall factual information from Section 3.

3. D

Break Down the Question: Point out to students that options A, B, and C can be eliminated because people who held those jobs had little interest in literature, while noblewomen had great interest and involvement in literature.

4. B

Break Down the Question: Remind students that the Japanese diet was based on their geography and location and was not influenced by Chinese or Korean contacts.

5. C

Break Down the Question: This question requires students to recall factual information from Section 3.

6. A

Break Down the Question: Students should recall that the ancient Greek city-states also formed small, separate governments.

7. B

Break Down the Question: Students should remember that the Greek city-state of Athens was known for its interest in art, architecture, and drama.

Intervention Resources

Reproducible

- Guided Reading Workbook
- Differentiated Instruction Teacher Management System: Lesson Plans

Technology

- Quick Facts Transparency: Japan Visual Summary
- Differentiated Instruction Modified Worksheets and Tests CD-ROM
- Interactive Skills Tutor CD-ROM

Tips for Test Taking

Negatives Do Not Fit Students should be sure to watch for negative words in the questions such as *never, unless, not,* and *except*. When a question contains one of these negative words, students should look for the answer that **does not fit** with the other answers.

Multimedia Classroom

The **HISTORY™ Multimedia Classroom** is a set of exciting new social studies teaching tools featuring award-winning program content. These comprehensive lesson plans, correlated to individual state and national curriculum standards, are easy to use for both teachers and students.

Each lesson contains the following:

- Short video segments that bring history topics to life
- Maps and visual materials
- Discussion and review questions
- Easily printable primary source documents
- Classroom activities and Internet-based activity links

The Multimedia Classroom has been specially designed to be versatile and easily adaptable to existing courses, lesson plans, and syllabi. Every lesson is designed to offer maximum flexibility. Teachers can select entire plans or only the elements they need, allowing them to individually tailor each lesson. Each multimedia lesson is available in CD-ROM format and is accompanied by full-length award-winning programs on DVD from HISTORY™.

For more information or to purchase go to hmhsocialstudies.com

Because some of these lessons may contain video material of a sensitive nature, we recommend that teachers and parents review these materials in their entirety before screening them to students.

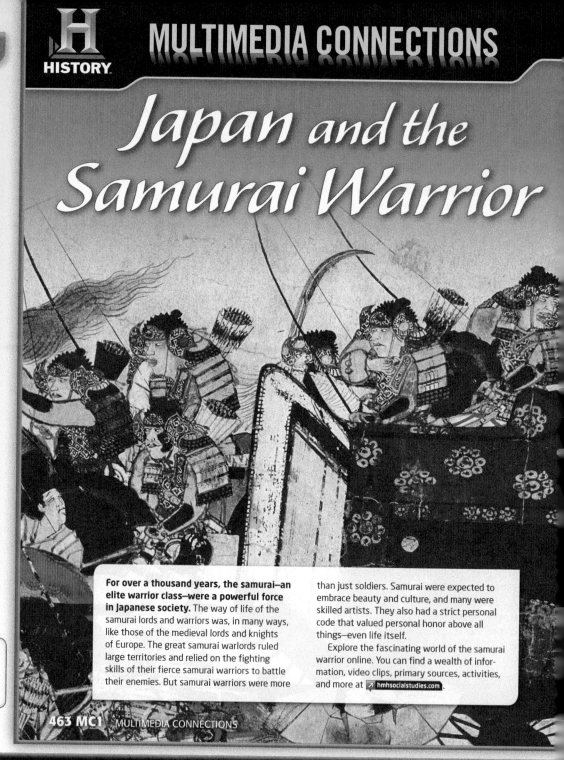

HISTORY

MULTIMEDIA CONNECTIONS

Japan and the Samurai Warrior

For over a thousand years, the samurai—an elite warrior class—were a powerful force in Japanese society. The way of life of the samurai lords and warriors was, in many ways, like those of the medieval lords and knights of Europe. The great samurai warlords ruled large territories and relied on the fighting skills of their fierce samurai warriors to battle their enemies. But samurai warriors were more than just soldiers. Samurai were expected to embrace beauty and culture, and many were skilled artists. They also had a strict personal code that valued personal honor above all things—even life itself.

Explore the fascinating world of the samurai warrior online. You can find a wealth of information, video clips, primary sources, activities, and more at hmhsocialstudies.com.

Japan and the Samurai Warrior

Resources 

The following resources come with printable introductions, comprehension and critical thinking questions, transcripts, and vocabulary support.

Full Length DVD

Samurai Warrior (45 minutes)

Video Clips

- The Symbol of the Warrior (1:44)
- The Rise of the Samurai Class (2:57)
- The Importance of Honor (4:41)
- The Sword and Soul Merge (3:05)
- Women and the Samurai Life (2:39)
- The Samurai's Two Sides (3:11)
- A New Way of Life in Japan (4:57)
- Death of the Samurai Class (1:38)
- Samurai in the Modern World (5:17)

Primary Sources

- A Code for Samurai Living
- Samurai Armor and War Coat
- The Kamakura Buddha
- A Discussion on Women
- An Edict Concerning Farmers
- Western Traders in Japan
- Excerpt from *In Search of Truth and Peace*

Lesson Preview

Rise of the Samurai Class

The samurai began as servants of the emperor, extending his power throughout the difficult, mountainous terrain of Japan. But once the samurai found they controlled the countryside, they realized they could rule it as well. The rise of samurai warlords with their private armies of fierce swordsmen coincides with the decline of the emperor's stature to little more than a figurehead. It was left to the samurai warlords to battle for dominion over Japan.

A New Way of Life in Japan

Japan had no contact with Europeans until 1542. Japanese warlords saw the value in European guns, but many samurai disdained their use. To the samurai, personal honor could only be maintained through face-to-face combat. In spite of this, guns played a major role in the Battle of Sekigahara, which led to a united Japan that was peaceful and isolated from the West for 250 years. In this peaceful time, the samurai became administrators and officials, whose honor depended on how well they could promote the welfare of society as a whole.

A Code for Samurai Living

The samurai way of life demanded a certain level of conduct and placed personal honor above everything else. The Samurai's Creed, supposedly written in the 14th century, uses poetic language to outline many of the behaviors, skills, and beliefs that defined the way of the samurai.

Death of the Samurai Class

In 1853, Japanese isolation came to an end abruptly, when an American naval fleet entered Tokyo Bay and demanded that Japan open itself to outside commerce. The Japanese were deeply humiliated but unable to resist. In the modernization movement that followed, the samurai's place in society vanished.

CLICK THROUGH
INTERACTIVITIES
hmhsocialstudies.com

Rise of the Samurai Class
Watch the video to learn how the samurai developed from armed tax collectors into warlords and armies that ruled Japan.

A New Way of Life in Japan
Watch the video to learn how peace and isolation took hold in Japan and changed the role of the samurai in society.

"I have no eyes;
I make the Flash of Lightning my Eyes.
I have no ears; I make Sensibility my Ears.
I have no limbs;
I make Promptitude my Limbs.
I have no laws;
I make Self-Protection my Laws."

A Code for Samurai Living
Read the document to learn about the strict but lyrical code of the samurai warrior.

Death of the Samurai Class
Watch the video to see how the end of Japan's isolation from the outside world signaled the beginning of the end of the samurai class.

JAPAN AND THE SAMURAI WARRIOR 463 MC2

Maps
- Japan's Empire, 1895–1942

Activities
- Warriors of the East and West
- Writing a Code of Honor
- Japanese Art and Culture
- Records of Samurai Life
- Japan and Western Culture
- Twentieth-Century Japan

General Review Questions

General Discussion Questions

Web Links

Bibliography

Chapter 16 Planning Guide

The Early Americas

Overview	Instructional Resources	
CHAPTER 16 **Essential Question:** What led to the development of complex societies in the Americas? **Focus on the Essential Question Podcast**	TOS **Differentiated Instruction Teacher Management System:** • Instructional Benchmarking Guides • Lesson Plans for Differentiated Instruction **Guided Reading Workbook** **Chapter Resource File:** • Chapter Review Activity • Focus on Writing Activity: A Newspaper Article • Social Studies Skills Activity: Accepting Social Responsibility	TOS **Calendar Planner** **Power Presentations with Media Gallery** **Differentiated Instruction Modified Worksheets and Tests CD-ROM** **Interactive Skills Tutor CD-ROM** **Student Edition on Audio CD Program** **The World's Music Audio Program** **Video:** Machu Picchu **Multimedia Connections:** The Maya
Section 1: **The Maya** **The Big Idea:** The Maya developed an advanced civilization that thrived in Mesoamerica from about 250 until the 900s.	TOS **Differentiated Instruction Teacher Management System:** Section 1 Lesson Plan **Guided Reading Workbook:** Section 1 **Chapter Resource File:** • Vocabulary Builder Activity, Section 1 • Biography Activity: Bishop Diego de Landa	**Daily Bellringer Transparency:** Section 1 **Map Transparency:** Maya Civilization **Internet Activity:** Adding the Maya Way **Video:** Maya: The Disappearance
Section 2: **The Aztecs** **The Big Idea:** The strong Aztec Empire, founded in central Mexico in 1325, lasted until the Spanish conquest in 1521.	TOS **Differentiated Instruction Teacher Management System:** Section 2 Lesson Plan **Guided Reading Workbook:** Section 2 **Chapter Resource File:** • Vocabulary Builder Activity, Section 2 • Biography Activity: Moctezuma I • Biography Activity: Tlacaelel • History and Geography Activity: The Aztec Empire • Primary Source Activity: Cortes's First Meeting with Moctezuma (1519)	**Daily Bellringer Transparency:** Section 2 **Map Transparency:** The Aztec Empire **Internet Activity:** Aztec Roles **Animated History:** Chinampas **Video:** Aztecs: Culture of Art and Death
Section 3: **The Incas** **The Big Idea:** The Incas controlled a huge empire in South America, but it was conquered by the Spanish.	TOS **Differentiated Instruction Teacher Management System:** Section 3 Lesson Plan **Guided Reading Workbook:** Section 3 **Chapter Resource File:** • Vocabulary Builder Activity, Section 3	**Daily Bellringer Transparency:** Section 3 **Map Transparency:** The Inca Empire **Internet Activity:** Brochure on Machu Picchu

Chart Key:

SE Student Edition  Presentation Resource 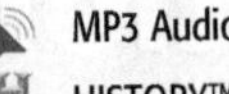 MP3 Audio
TOS Teacher One Stop 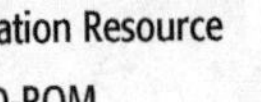 DVD/CD-ROM HISTORY™
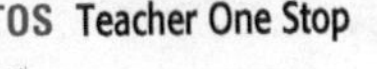 Printable Resource

Program Resources available on TOS and @  hmhsocialstudies.com

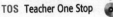

Review, Assessment, Intervention

 **Quick Facts Transparency:** The Early Americas Visual Summary

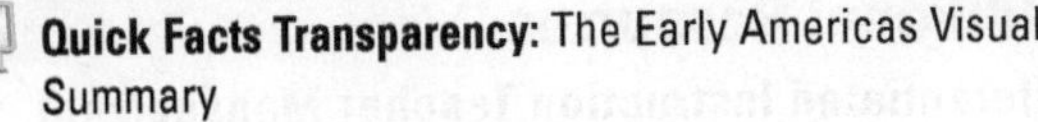 **Spanish Chapter Summaries Audio CD Program**

 **Quiz Game CD-ROM**

 **Progress Assessment Support System (PASS):** Chapter Test

 **Differentiated Instruction Modified Worksheets and Tests CD-ROM:** Modified Chapter Test

TOS **ExamView® Assessment Suite (English/Spanish)**

 **Online Assessment Program,** in the Interactive Student Edition

 **PASS:** Section 1 Quiz

 **Online Quiz:** Section 1

 **Alternative Assessment Handbook**

 **PASS:** Section 2 Quiz

 **Online Quiz:** Section 2

 **Alternative Assessment Handbook**

 **PASS:** Section 3 Quiz

 **Online Quiz:** Section 3

 **Alternative Assessment Handbook**

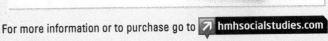

Supporting Resources

- Multimedia Classroom Global History Series
- Global History Teacher's Guide

Maps Globes Graphs Level F

- Student Workbook
- Teacher's Guide

Social Studies Trade Library Collections

- Premier Secondary World History Trade Collection

History's Impact

World History Video Program

- **Mayan Achievements in Science and Math**

For more information or to purchase go to  hmhsocialstudies.com

Power Presentations with Media Gallery

Power Presentations with Media Gallery are visual presentations of each chapter's main ideas. Presentations can be customized by including Quick Facts charts, images from the text, and video clips.

CHAPTER 16 PLANNING GUIDE

Differentiating Instruction

How do I address the needs of varied learners?

The Target Resource acts as your primary strategy for differentiated instruction.

ENGLISH-LANGUAGE LEARNERS & STRUGGLING READERS

Interactive Skills Tutor CD-ROM

The Interactive Skills Tutor CD-ROM contains lessons that provide additional practice for 20 different critical thinking skills.

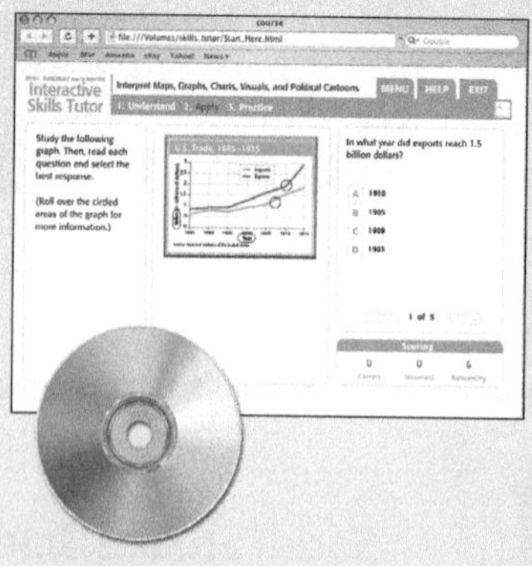

Additional Resources

Differentiated Instruction Teacher Management System: Lesson Plans for Differentiated Instruction

Chapter Resource File:

- Vocabulary Builder Activities
- Social Studies Skills Activity: Accepting Social Responsibility

Quick Facts Transparencies:

- The Early Americas Visual Summary

Student Edition on Audio CD Program

Spanish/English Guided Reading Workbook

SPECIAL NEEDS LEARNERS

Differentiated Instruction Modified Worksheets and Tests CD-ROM

- Vocabulary Flash Cards
- Vocabulary Builder Activities
- Chapter Review Activity
- Chapter Test

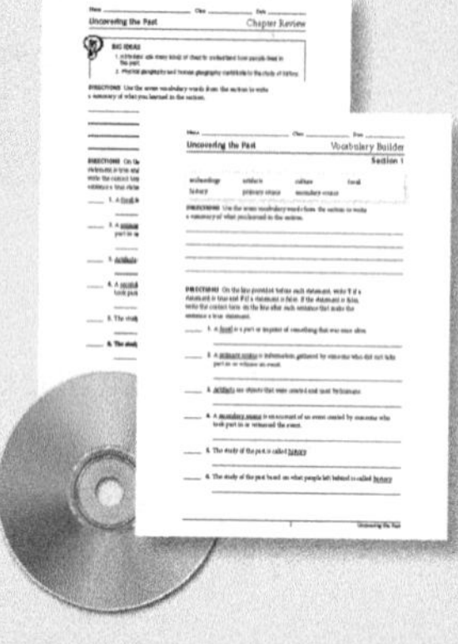

Additional Resources

Differentiated Instruction Teacher Management System: Lesson Plans for Differentiated Instruction

Guided Reading Workbook

Chapter Resource File: Social Studies Skills Activity: Accepting Social Responsibility

Student Edition on Audio CD Program

Interactive Skills Tutor CD-ROM

ADVANCED/GIFTED-AND-TALENTED STUDENTS

Primary Source Library CD-ROM for World History

The Library contains longer versions of quotations in the text, extra sources, and images. Included are point-of-view articles, journals, diaries, historical fiction, and political documents.

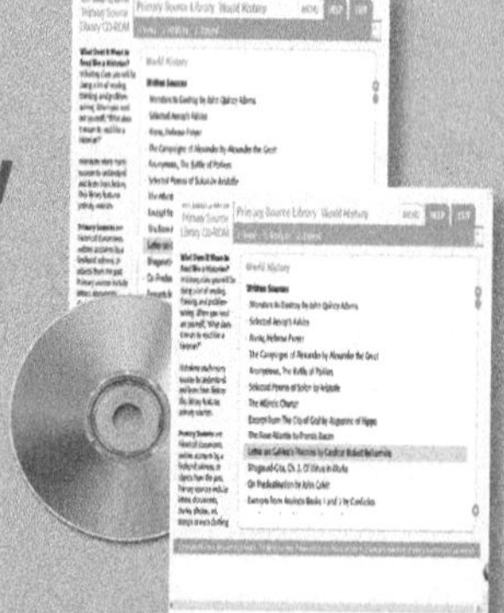

Additional Resources

Differentiated Instruction Teacher Management System: Lesson Plans for Differentiated Instruction

Chapter Resource File:

- Focus on Writing Activity A Newspaper Article

Document-Based Questions Activities

Differentiated Activities in the Teacher's Edition

- Creating Maya Artwork, p. 472
- Modeling the Inca Empire, p. 480

Differentiated Activities in the Teacher's Edition

- Chart Characteristics, p. 471
- Factors in Aztec Wealth, p. 475

Differentiated Activities in the Teacher's Edition

- Maya Classic Age Recipe, p. 470
- Step into the Picture, p. 471
- Making More Farmland, p. 476
- Looking at Inca Religion, p. 481
- The Spanish Conquest, p. 482

Teacher One Stop™

How can I manage the lesson plans and support materials for differentiated instruction?

With the Teacher One Stop, you can easily organize and print lesson plans, planning guides, and instructional materials for all learners. The Teacher One Stop includes the following materials to help you differentiate instruction:

- **Interactive Teacher's Edition**
- **Calendar Planner and pacing guides**
- **Editable lesson plans**
- **All reproducible ancillaries in Adobe Acrobat (PDF) format**
- **ExamView Assessment Suite (English & Spanish)**
- **Transparency and video previews**

Interactive Student Edition

Complete online student edition with interactive multimedia support for chapter content assessment and reporting

- Interactive Maps and Notebook
- Graphic Organizers
- Standardized Test Prep
- Online Homework Practice and Research Activities
- Current Events
- Chapter-based Internet Activities
- Animated History Activities
- and more!

Chapter Preview

Essential Question

Introduce the Essential Question

- Discuss the development of agriculture in Mesoamerica and the Andes.
- Explain that advances in society are only possible when a surplus of food allows people to work at jobs not related to food production.
- Tell students that the development of complex cities requires the creation of an advanced system of agriculture.

CHAPTER 16 500 BC–AD 1537

The Early Americas

Essential Question What led to the development of complex societies in the Americas?

South Carolina Performance Standards

6-4.3 Compare the contributions and the decline of the Maya, Aztec, and Inca civilizations in Central and South America, including their forms of government and their contributions in mathematics, astronomy, and architecture.

Literacy Skills for Social Studies

- Identify and explain the relationships among multiple causes and multiple effects.
- Apply economic decision making to understand how limited resources necessitate choices.
- Examine the costs and benefits of economic choices made by a particular society and explain how those choices affect overall economic well-being.

Partnership for the 21st Century Skills

Integrate information from a variety of media sources with print or digital text in an appropriate manner.

FOCUS ON WRITING

A Newspaper Article You are a writer for a European newspaper who is traveling with some explorers to the Americas. Your newspaper wants you to write an article to share what you have seen with readers back home in Europe. As you read this chapter, you will decide what to write about—the land, the people, or the events that occurred after the explorers arrived.

REGION EVENTS

c. AD 200 The Maya begin building large cities in the Americas.

c. 900 The Maya Classic Age ends.

500 BC

WORLD EVENTS

c. 500 BC Athens develops the world's first democracy.

Focus on Writing

The **Chapter Resource File** provides a Focus on Writing worksheet to help students organize their writing.

CRF: Focus on Writing Activity: A Travel Brochure

Key to Differentiating Instruction

Below Level

Basic-level activities designed for all students encountering new material

At Level

Intermediate-level activities designed for average students

Above Level

Challenging activities designed for honors and gifted and talented students

Standard English Mastery

Activities designed to improve standard English usage

LS Learning Styles

Introduce the Chapter

At Level

Lost Cities in the Jungle

1. Ask students to imagine that they are on an archaeological expedition in the jungles of Central America. They hack their way through the growth and, suddenly, there before them is a large, elaborately carved stone. Beyond are other ruins of an ancient lost city.
2. Have students discuss what they might feel at the sight of the ancient ruins. Encourage discussion.
3. Then ask students what they and other scientists might do to find out more about the people who lived in this ancient city. What questions might they ask? What objects might they study?
4. Explain to students that in this chapter they will be learning about the first people who came to the Americas and some of the early civilizations that developed.

LS Intrapersonal, Verbal/Linguistic

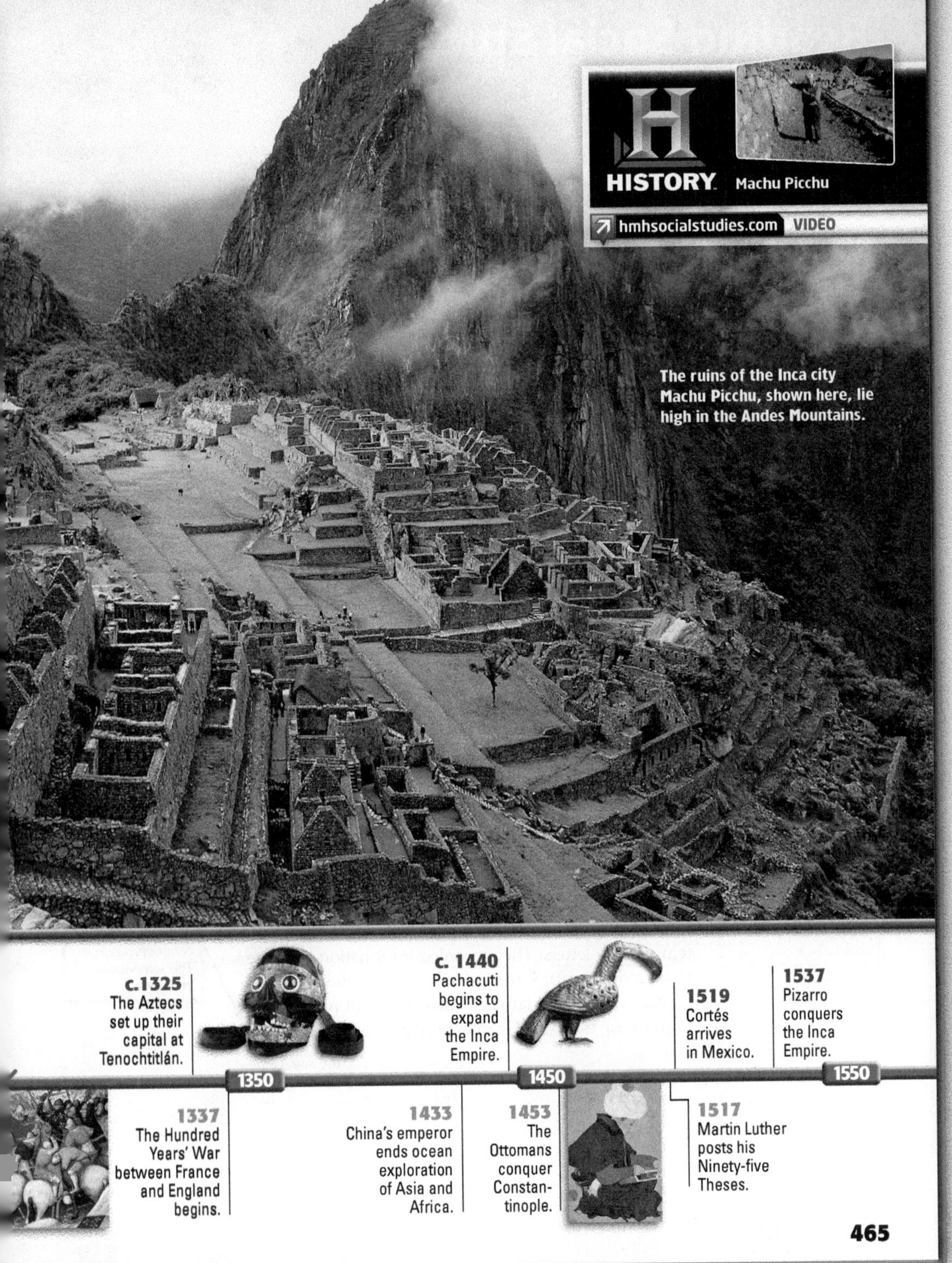
HISTORY
Machu Picchu
hmhsocialstudies.com VIDEO
c.1325 The Aztecs set up their capital at Tenochtitlán.
c. 1440 Pachacuti begins to expand the Inca Empire.
1519 Cortés arrives in Mexico.
1537 Pizarro conquers the Inca Empire.
1350
1450
1550
1337 The Hundred Years' War between France and England begins.
1433 China's emperor ends ocean exploration of Asia and Africa.
1453 The Ottomans conquer Constantinople.
1517 Martin Luther posts his Ninety-five Theses.
465

The ruins of the Inca city Machu Picchu, shown here, lie high in the Andes Mountains.

Chapter Preview

Explore the Picture

Inca City of Machu Picchu Machu Picchu was built as a royal sanctuary in a narrow canyon between two mountain peaks. Because it was so remote and no one lived there, the Spaniards ignored and later forgot about the site. In 1911, American explorer Hiram Bingham rediscovered it.

Analyzing Visuals What does the picture tell you about the region's geography? What can you tell about the structure of Machu Picchu? *The land is very mountainous. The city is laid out in terraces, with streets and buildings in neat rows.*

hmhsocialstudies.com
Teacher Resources

Explore the Time Line

1. How long after the Maya began building large cities did their Classic Age end? *700 years*
2. How many years passed between the establishment of Tenochtitlán by the Aztecs and the expansion of the Inca Empire by Pachacuti? *115 years*
3. What event related to religion happened in Europe just before Cortés arrived in Mexico? *Martin Luther announced his Ninety-five Theses.*

Info to Know

Amazing Lives, Dismal Deaths The Spanish conquerors of the Aztec and Inca empires, Hernán Cortés and Francisco Pizarro, had incredible successes and controlled great wealth for a while. However, neither ended his life in peace. Cortés was poor and in debt when he died. Pizarro was killed during a conflict with a rival family.

Reading Social Studies

Understanding Themes

Introduce the key themes of this chapter to the class by asking them what they know about the geography of Central and South America. Responses might include that it is isolated and has tropical jungles. Point out to students that the geography of Mesoamerica had a great effect on the way of life that developed there. Ask students to predict how geography affected life there. Then lead a discussion of how the people of Mesoamerica might have developed science and technology in response to their lifestyle.

Analyzing Historical Information

Focus on Reading Explain to students that sometimes writers include details and descriptions that add interest, but are not completely necessary to understand the main idea. Have students examine a magazine article or primary source document. Ask students to look for a paragraph that includes information that is incidental or irrelevant to the main idea or purpose. Ask each student to re-write the paragraph without the incidental information.

Reading Social Studies

Economics | **Geography** | Politics | Religion | Society and Culture | **Science and Technology**

Focus on Themes In this chapter, you will read about the development of civilizations in the Americas—in Mesoamerica, which is in the southern part of North America, and in the Andes, which is in South America. As you read about the Maya in Mesoamerica, the Aztecs in central Mexico, and the Incas in South America, you will see how the **geography** of the areas affected their way of life. You will learn that these ancient civilizations made interesting advancements in **science**.

Analyzing Historical Information

Focus on Reading History books are full of information. As you read, you are confronted with names, dates, places, terms, and descriptions on every page. Because you're faced with so much information, you don't want to have to deal with unimportant or untrue material in a history book.

Identifying Relevant and Essential Information Information in a history book should be relevant, or related to the topic you're studying. It should also be essential, or necessary, to understanding that topic. Anything that is not relevant or essential distracts from the important material you are studying.

The passage below comes from an encyclopedia, but some irrelevant and nonessential information has been added so that you can learn to identify it.

The Maya

The first sentence of the paragraph expresses the main idea. Anything that doesn't support this idea is nonessential.

Who They Were Maya were an American Indian people who developed a magnificent civilization in Mesoamerica, which is the southern part of North America. They built their largest cities between AD 250 and 900. Today, many people travel to Central America to see Maya ruins.

The last sentence does not support the main idea and is nonessential.

This paragraph discusses Maya communication. Any other topics are irrelevant.

Communication The Maya developed an advanced form of writing that used many symbols. Our writing system uses 26 letters. They recorded information on large stone monuments. Some early civilizations drew pictures on cave walls. The Maya also made books of paper made from the fig tree bark. Fig trees need a lot of light.

The needs of fig trees have nothing to do with Maya communication. This sentence is irrelevant.

Portions of this text and the one on the next page were taken from the 2004 World Book Online Reference Center.

Reading and Skills Resources

Reading Support

- Guided Reading Workbook
- Student Edition on Audio CD
- Spanish Chapter Summaries Audio CD Program

Social Studies Skills Support

- Interactive Skills Tutor CD-ROM

Vocabulary Support

- **CRF:** Vocabulary Builder Activities
- **CRF:** Chapter Review Activity
- Differentiated Instruction Modified Worksheets and Tests CD-ROM:
  - Vocabulary Flash Cards
  - Vocabulary Builder Activity
  - Chapter Review Activity

TOS Holt McDougal PuzzleView

You Try It!

The following passage has some sentences that aren't important, necessary, or relevant. Read the passage and identify those sentences.

The Maya Way of Life

Religion The Maya believed in many gods and goddesses. More than 160 gods and goddesses are named in a single Maya manuscript. Among the gods they worshipped were a corn god, a rain god, a sun god, and a moon goddess. The early Greeks also worshipped many gods and goddesses.

Family and Social Structure Whole families of Maya—including parents, children, and grandparents—lived together. Not many houses today could hold all those people. Each family member had tasks to do. Men and boys, for example, worked in the fields. Very few people are farmers today. Women and older girls made clothes and meals for the rest of the family. Now most people buy their clothes.

After you read the passage, answer the following questions.

1. Which sentence in the first paragraph is irrelevant to the topic? How can you tell?
2. Which three sentences in the second paragraph are not essential to learning about the Maya? Do those sentences belong in this passage?

Key Terms and People

Chapter 16

Section 1
maize *(p. 468)*
observatories *(p. 472)*

Section 2
causeways *(p. 474)*
conquistadors *(p. 477)*
Hernán Cortés *(p. 478)*
Moctezuma II *(p. 478)*

Section 3
Pachacuti *(p. 479)*
Quechua *(p. 480)*
masonry *(p. 481)*
Atahualpa *(p. 482)*
Francisco Pizarro *(p. 482)*

Academic Vocabulary

Success in school is related to knowing academic vocabulary—the words that are frequently used in school assignments and discussions. In this chapter, you will learn the following academic words:

aspect *(p. 471)*
rebel *(p. 472)*
motive *(p. 478)*
distribute *(p. 480)*

As you read Chapter 16, practice deteming what is relevant information for each section.

Reading Social Studies

Key Terms and People

Preteach the key terms and people from this chapter by first reviewing each term with the class. Then have students use the page numbers listed to locate each term or person in the chapter. Have each student write the word and the definition as it appears in the text on their own sheet of paper. Then have each student write a paragraph in which they use each key term or person. Remind students to use each term correctly.
LS Verbal/Linguistic

Focus on Reading

See the **Focus on Reading** questions in this chapter for more practice on reading social studies skills.

Reading Social Studies Assessment

See the **Chapter Review** at the end of this chapter for student assessment questions related to this reading skill.

Teaching Tip

Remind students that the easiest way to identify irrelevant and incidental information is to first identify the main idea of the paragraph. The main idea will be supported by specific facts and details. However, there will be other details as well. Have students identify which details support the main idea and which are not important to the main idea.

Answers

You Try It! 1. *"The early Greeks also worshipped many gods and goddesses;" possible answer—paragraph is not intended to compare and contrast Greek and Mayan religious systems.* **2.** *"Not many houses today could hold all those people;" "Very few people are farmers today;" "Now, most people buy their clothes;" no, those sentences belong in a paragraph that compares and contrasts Mayan life and modern life.*

Preteach

Bellringer

If YOU were there . . . Use the **Daily Bellringer Transparency** to help students answer the question.

Daily Bellringer Transparency, Section 1

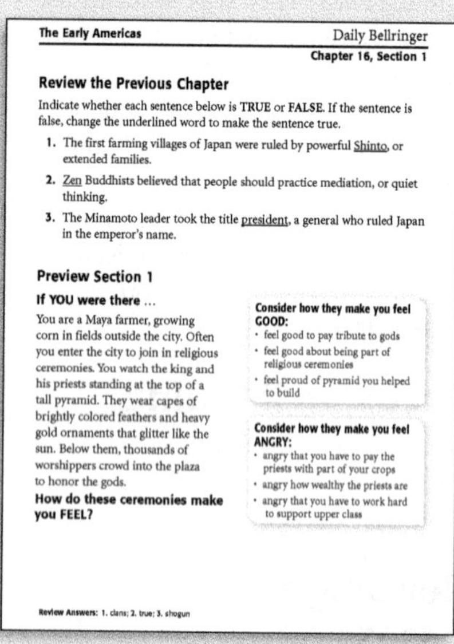

The Early Americas — Daily Bellringer

Chapter 16, Section 1

Review the Previous Chapter

Indicate whether each sentence below is TRUE or FALSE. If the sentence is false, change the underlined word to make the sentence true.

1. The first farming villages of Japan were ruled by powerful Shinto, or extended families.
2. Zen Buddhists believed that people should practice mediation, or quiet thinking.
3. The Minamoto leader took the title president, a general who ruled Japan in the emperor's name.

Preview Section 1

If YOU were there ...

You are a Maya farmer, growing corn in fields outside the city. Often you enter the city to join in religious ceremonies. You watch the king and his priests standing at the top of a tall pyramid. They wear capes of brightly colored feathers and heavy gold ornaments that glitter like the sun. Below them, thousands of worshippers crowd into the plaza to honor the gods.

How do these ceremonies make you FEEL?

Consider how they make you feel GOOD:
- feel good to pay tribute to gods
- feel good about being part of religious ceremonies
- feel proud of pyramid you helped to build

Consider how they make you feel ANGRY:
- angry that you have to pay the priests with part of your crops
- angry how wealthy the priests are
- angry that you have to work hard to support upper class

Review Answers: 1. clans; 2. true; 3. shogun

Academic Vocabulary

Review with students the high-use academic terms in this section.

aspect a part of something (p. 471)

rebel to fight against authority (p. 473)

CRF: Vocabulary Builder Activity, Section 1

Taking Notes

Have students use the graphic organizer online to take notes on the section. This activity will prepare students for the Section Assessment, in which they will complete a graphic organizer that builds on the information using the Critical Thinking Skill: Evaluating.

SECTION 1

The Maya

What You Will Learn...

Main Ideas

1. Geography helped shape the lives of the early Maya in Mesoamerica.
2. During the Classic Age, the Maya built great cities linked by trade.
3. Maya culture was influenced by social structure, religion, and achievements in science and the arts.
4. The decline of Maya civilization began in the 900s, for reasons that are still unclear.

The Big Idea

The Maya developed an advanced civilization that thrived in Mesoamerica from about 250 until the 900s.

Key Terms and People

maize, *p. 468*
Pacal, *p. 469*
observatories, *p. 472*

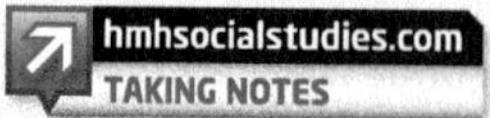

Use the graphic organizer online to take notes on different aspects of Maya civilization.

If YOU were there...

You are a Maya farmer, growing corn in fields outside a city. Often you enter the city to join in religious ceremonies. You watch the king and his priests standing at the top of a tall pyramid. They wear capes of brightly colored feathers and gold ornaments that glitter in the sun. Far below them, thousands of worshippers crowd into the plaza with you to honor the gods.

How do these ceremonies make you feel?

BUILDING BACKGROUND Religion was very important to the Maya, one of the early peoples in the Americas. The Maya believed the gods controlled everything in the world around them.

Geography and the Early Maya

The region known as Mesoamerica stretches from the central area of Mexico south to the northern part of Central America. It was in this region that a people called the Maya (MY-uh) developed a remarkable civilization.

Around 1000 BC the Maya began settling in the lowlands of what is now northern Guatemala. Thick tropical forests covered most of the land, but the people cleared areas to farm. They grew a variety of crops, including beans, squash, avocados, and **maize**, or corn. The forests provided valuable resources, too. Forest animals such as deer, rabbits, and monkeys were sources of food. In addition, trees and other plants made good building materials. For example, some Maya used wooden poles and vines, along with mud, to build their houses.

The early Maya lived in small, isolated villages. Eventually, though, these villages started trading with one another and with other groups in Mesoamerica. As trade increased, the villages grew. By about AD 200, the Maya had begun to build large cities in Mesoamerica.

READING CHECK **Finding Main Ideas** How did the early Maya make use of their physical environment?

Teach the Big Idea

At Level

The Maya

Prep Required

Materials: colored paper, colored markers, scissors, string, tape

1. **Teach** Ask students the questions in the Main Idea boxes to teach this section.
2. **Apply** Have students create Maya mobiles. The parts of the mobile should illustrate aspects of the Maya civilization and Classic Age. For example, students might include a map of the main Maya cities and trade routes. Provide students with instructions and materials for creating their mobiles.
   LS Kinesthetic, Visual/Spatial
3. **Review** As you review the section, have students share how they represented different aspects of Maya civilization in their mobiles.
4. **Practice/Homework** Have each student write a fictional obituary for the "death" of the Maya civilization. Encourage students to look at some real obituaries for models.
   LS Verbal/Linguistic

Alternative Assessment Handbook, Rubrics 3: Artwork; and 37: Writing Assignments

The Classic Age

The Maya civilization reached its height between about AD 250 and 900. This time in Maya history is known as the Classic Age. During this time, Maya territory grew to include more than 40 large cities.

Maya cities were really city-states. Each had its own government and its own king. No single ruler ever united the many cities into one empire. However, trade helped hold Maya civilization together. People exchanged goods for products that were not available locally. For example, Maya in the lowlands exported forest goods, cotton, and cacao (kuh-KOW) beans, which are used in making chocolate. In return, they received obsidian (a glasslike volcanic rock), jade, and colorful bird feathers.

Through trade, the Maya got supplies for construction. Maya cities had grand buildings, such as palaces decorated with carvings and paintings. The Maya also built stone pyramids topped with temples. Some temples honored local kings. For example, in the city of Palenque (pah-LENG-kay), the king **Pacal** (puh-KAHL) built a temple to record his achievements.

hmhsocialstudies.com INTERACTIVE MAP

Maya Civilization

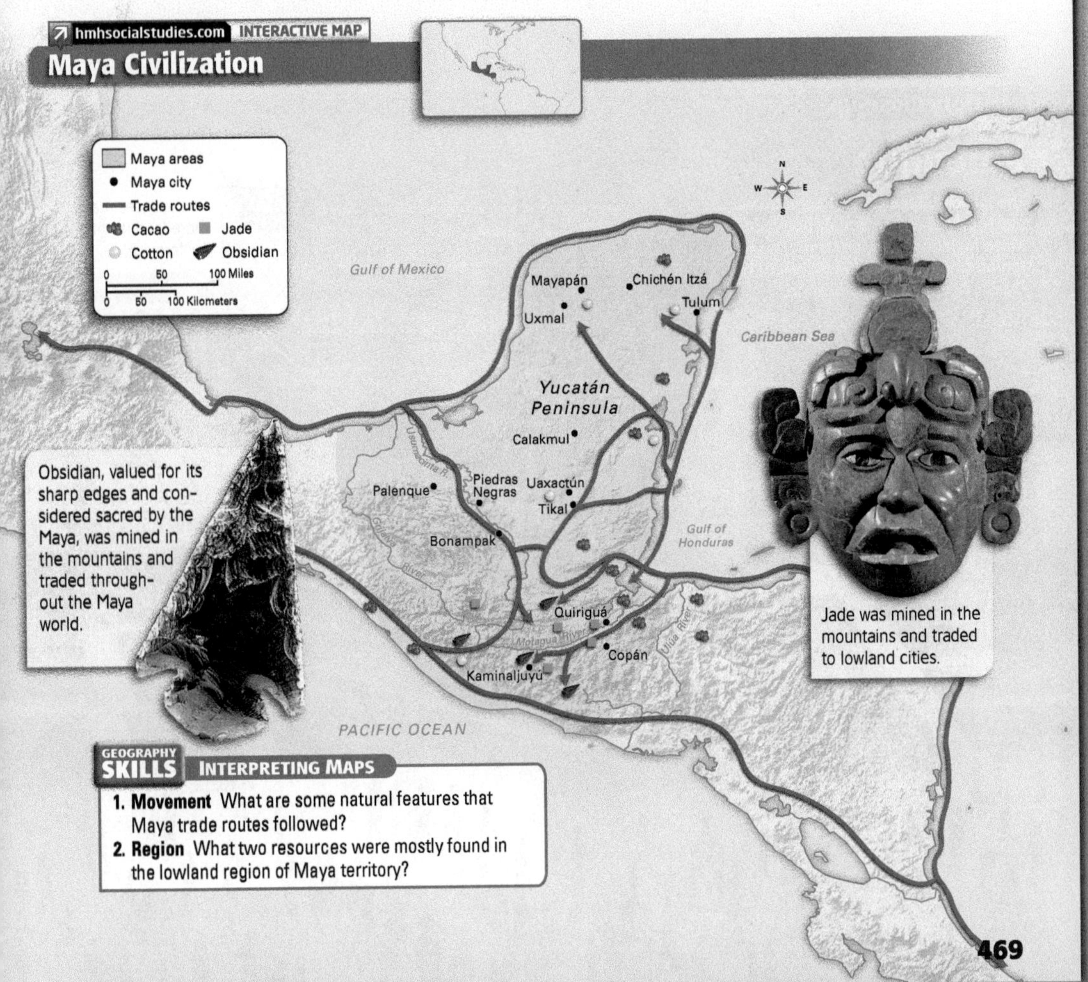

Obsidian, valued for its sharp edges and considered sacred by the Maya, was mined in the mountains and traded throughout the Maya world.

Jade was mined in the mountains and traded to lowland cities.

GEOGRAPHY SKILLS INTERPRETING MAPS

1. **Movement** What are some natural features that Maya trade routes followed?
2. **Region** What two resources were mostly found in the lowland region of Maya territory?

Direct Teach

Main Idea

1 Geography and the Early Maya

Geography helped shape the lives of the early Maya in Mesoamerica.

Describe How did the Maya adapt to and change their environment? *cleared wooded areas for farmland, used available resources for building materials, traded to obtain resources not available locally*

Make Inferences Why do you think the Maya expanded into the highlands? *needed more space as populations grew, to access resources*

Main Idea

2 The Classic Age

During the Classic Age, the Maya built great cities linked by trade.

Recall When did the Maya Classic Age occur, and what defined it? *between about AD 250 and 900; Maya civilization reached its height, growth of great cities, and trade*

Drawing Inferences Explain why trade led to Maya population growth. *Trade made more resources and food available, providing support for population growth.*

Map Transparency: Maya Civilization

Critical Thinking: Making Generalizations

At Level

Maya Civilization Regional Slogans

1. Ask students to summarize how geography affected early Maya civilization. Ask students to describe how the Maya both changed their environment and adapted to it.
2. Tell students that some of the states in our nation have state slogans that reflect the state's geography or the resources for which the state is known.
3. Then have students create similar types of slogans for different regions of Maya civilization, as shown on the map above. For example, students might describe the Maya highlands as the Land of Black Rock.
4. Close by having students explore how life for the Maya may have varied by region.

LS Verbal/Linguistic

Alternative Assessment Handbook, Rubric 34: Slogans and Banners

Answers

Reading Check (p. 468) *relied on land for farming, trees and plants for building, forest animals for food*

Interpreting Maps 1. *rivers, coastlines, regions where highlands met lowlands;* **2.** *cacao and cotton*

Direct Teach

Main Idea

2 The Classic Age

During the Classic Age, the Maya built great cities linked by trade.

Describe List some nouns and adjectives that describe Maya cities. *Nouns might include temples, palaces, plazas, canals, ball courts; adjectives might include grand, regal, decorated, terraced, and paved.*

Summarize How did the Maya change their environment to improve city life? *terraced land for farming, paved areas for public gatherings, built canals*

Main Idea

3 Maya Culture

Maya culture was influenced by social structure, religion, and achievements in science and the arts.

Recall What two forces influenced people's lives? *social structure and religion*

Identify Besides the king, who else made up the Maya upper classes? *priests, warriors, merchants*

In addition to palaces and temples, the Maya built canals and paved large plazas, or open squares, for public gatherings. Farmers used stone walls to shape hillsides into flat terraces so they could grow crops on them. Almost every Maya city also had a stone court for playing a special ball game. Using only their heads, shoulders, or hips, players tried to bounce a heavy, hard rubber ball through stone rings attached high on the court walls. The winners of these games received jewels and clothing.

READING CHECK **Analyzing** Why is Maya civilization not considered an empire?

Maya Culture

In Maya society, people's everyday lives were heavily influenced by two main forces. One was the social structure, and the other was religion.

Social Structure

The king held the highest position in Maya society. Because he was believed to be related to the gods, the king had religious as well as political authority. Priests, merchants, and noble warriors were also part of the upper class. Together with the king, they held all the power in Maya society.

History Close-up

Palenque

The ancient Maya city of Palenque was a major power on the border between the Maya highlands and lowlands. Its great temples and plazas were typical of the Classic Age of Maya civilization.

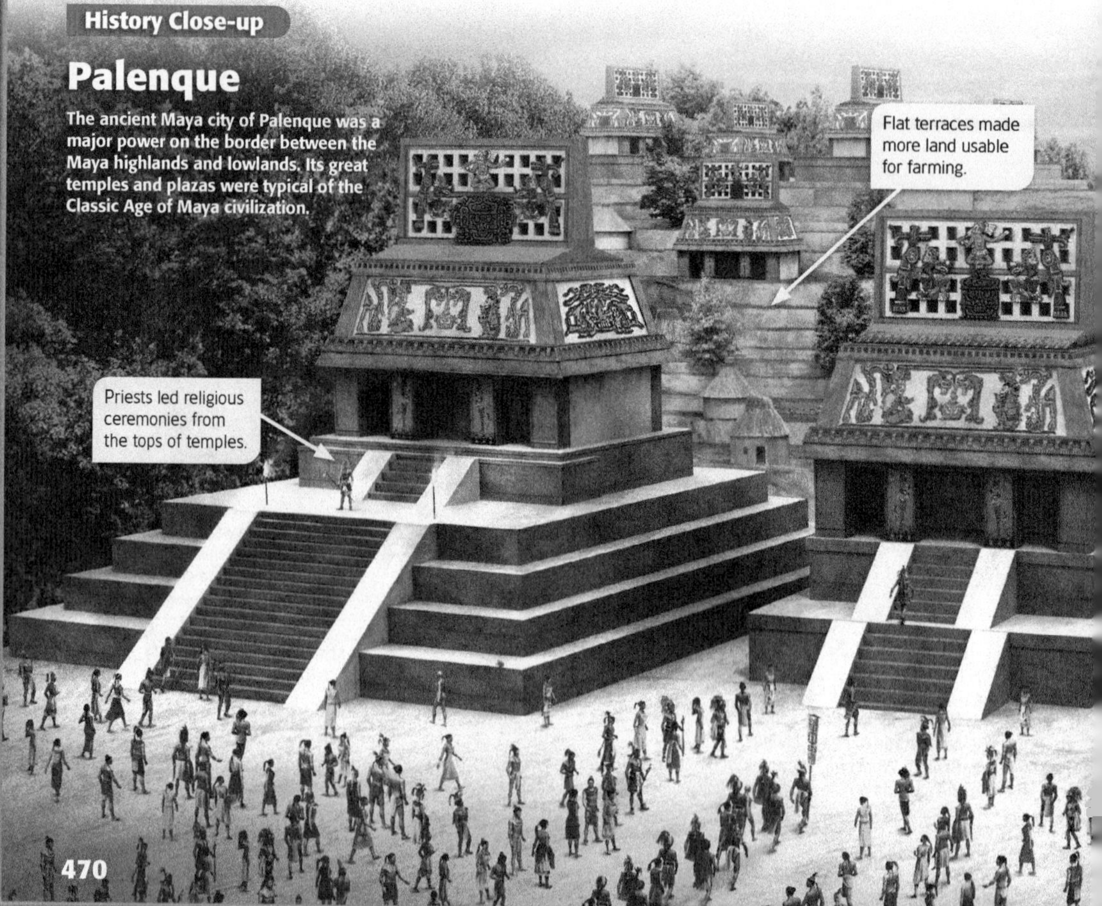

Flat terraces made more land usable for farming.
Priests led religious ceremonies from the tops of temples.

470

Critical Thinking: Synthesizing

Above Level

Maya Classic Age Recipe

1. Have students create an imaginary recipe for the Maya Classic Age. The recipe should include a list of ingredients and preparation steps. Students will specify the "dish" they want to make.
2. Explain that the recipe's ingredients should be the defining characteristics of the Maya Classic Age. Ingredient amounts should reflect the importance of each characteristic. Preparation or cooking instructions should be creative or symbolize aspects of the Maya Classic Age. For example, preparation might require actively beating two ingredients together to symbolize the warfare common to the Maya Classic Age. Or the recipe might include a warning not to overcook the dish to symbolize theories about the decline of the Maya civilization.
3. Encourage students to illustrate or decorate their recipes. **LS Verbal/Linguistic**

Alternative Assessment Handbook, Rubric 37: Writing Assignments

Answers

Reading Check *No single ruler united the many city-states into one empire.*

Most Maya, though, belonged to the lower class. This group was made up of farming families who lived outside the cities. The women cared for the children, cooked, made yarn, and wove cloth. The men farmed, hunted, and crafted tools.

Lower-class Maya had to "pay" their rulers by giving the rulers part of their crops and goods such as cloth and salt. They also had to help construct temples and other public buildings. If their city went to war, Maya men had to serve in the army, and if captured in battle, they usually became slaves. Slaves carried goods along trade routes or worked as servants or farmers for upper-class Maya.

Religion

The Maya worshipped many gods, including a creator, a sun god, a moon goddess, and a maize god. Each god was believed to control a different **aspect** of daily life.

According to Maya beliefs, the gods could be helpful or harmful, so people tried to please the gods to get their help. The Maya believed their gods needed blood to prevent disasters or the end of the world. Every person offered blood to the gods by piercing their tongue or skin. On special occasions, the Maya also made human sacrifices. They usually used prisoners captured in battle, offering their hearts to stone carvings of the gods.

Academic Vocabulary
aspect a part of something

Maya temples were shaped like mountains, which the Maya considered sacred because they allowed people to approach the gods.
BIOGRAPHY
Pacal
603–683
Pacal became king of the Maya city of Palenque when he was just 12 years old. As king, Pacal led many important community events, such as religious dances and public meetings. When he died he was buried at the bottom of the Temple of the Inscriptions shown to the near left.
HISTORY
VIDEO
Maya: The Disappearance
hmhsocialstudies.com
Maya buildings were covered with stucco and painted in bright colors.
ANALYSIS SKILL ANALYZING VISUALS
In what ways might Palenque's setting have helped the city? In what ways might it have hurt the city?
471

Differentiating Instruction

Advanced/Gifted and Talented — Above Level

Step Into the Picture Ask students to imagine that they are one of the people in the "History Close-up" image above. Have students use the information in this section and their historical imaginations to write a short narrative based on the picture. **LS Verbal/Linguistic, Visual/Spatial**

Alternative Assessment Handbook, Rubric 37: Writing Assignments

Struggling Readers — Below Level

Chart Characteristics To help students focus on the characteristics of Maya Culture, make a three-column chart for students to see. Label the columns *Social Structure, Religion,* and *Achievements.* Point out that these titles match the three red titles in the text under "Maya Culture." Have students copy and fill in the chart as they read. **LS Verbal/Linguistic**

Direct Teach

Main Idea

3 Maya Culture

Maya culture was influenced by social structure, religion, and achievements in science and the arts.

Contrast How did the roles of men and women differ in Maya society? *Men crafted tools, hunted, farmed; women cared for children, cooked, made yarn, wove cloth.*

Explain Why was blood significant in Maya religious beliefs and practices? *The Maya believed their gods needed blood to avoid disasters or to prevent the end of the world, so they frequently offered blood to the gods.*

Draw Conclusions How might Maya beliefs have contributed to frequent warfare? *Maya beliefs involved human sacrifices, which were often obtained through battle.*

CRF: Biography Activity: Bishop Diego de Landa

Biography

John Lloyd Stephens (1805–1852) In the 1830s John Lloyd Stephens, an American lawyer, was advised to travel for his health. He went to the Middle East and eastern Europe, where he toured ruins and archaeological sites. Having developed a passion for exploration, in 1839 Stephens went to Honduras. He was in search of ancient ruins said to exist deep in the Yucatán jungle. After struggling through dense tropical rain forest, Stephens came upon a magnificent carved stone. He had found the ruins of the ancient Maya city of Palenque. News of the find sparked interest in the Maya and led to modern historical study of Maya civilization. Today scientists and explorers continue to find Maya ruins hidden in the jungle.

Answers

Analyzing Visuals *helped—may have brought it power as an important stop on trade routes between the lowlands and the highlands; hurt—may have led it into conflict as other Maya cities fought to control it*

Direct Teach

Main Idea

3 Maya Culture

Maya culture was influenced by social structure, religion, and achievements in science and the arts.

Summarize What advances did the Maya make in astronomy? *built observatories, developed calendars, determined length of year*

Make Generalizations Why might builders today be impressed with Maya building methods? *The Maya built great cities without metal tools or wheeled vehicles.*

Connect to Science

Maya Astronomy The Maya considered stars and planets to be gods. They watched the stars to predict events on Earth that they believed the gods controlled. The planet Venus was one of the Maya's most important "stars." The Maya determined that Venus took about 584 days to reappear at the same point on the horizon.

hmhsocialstudies.com
Online Resources
Activity: Adding the Maya Way

Maya Astronomy and Writing

This photo (left) shows the observatory at the Maya city of Chichén Itzá. The stone carving (above) is an artistic and written record of a religious ceremony.

Achievements

Focus on Reading
Is any information in this paragraph irrelevant?

The Maya's religious beliefs led them to make impressive advances in science. They built **observatories**, or buildings from which people could study the sky, so their priests could watch the stars and plan the best times for religious festivals. With the knowledge they gained about astronomy, the Maya developed two calendars. One, with 365 days, guided planting, harvesting, and other farming activities. This calendar was more accurate than the calendar used in Europe at that time. The Maya also had a separate 260-day calendar that they used for keeping track of religious events.

The Maya could measure time accurately partly because they were skilled mathematicians. They created a number system that helped them make complex calculations, and they were among the first people with a symbol for zero. The Maya used their number system to record key dates in their history.

The Maya also developed a writing system. In a way, it was similar to Egyptian hieroglyphics, because symbols represented both objects and sounds. The Maya carved series of these symbols into large stone tablets to record their history and the achievements of their kings. They also wrote in bark paper books and passed down stories and poems orally.

The Maya created amazing art and architecture as well. Maya jade and gold jewelry was exceptional. Also, their huge temple-pyramids were masterfully built. The Maya had neither metal tools for cutting nor wheeled vehicles for carrying supplies. Instead, workers used obsidian tools to cut limestone into blocks. Then workers rolled the giant blocks over logs and lifted them with ropes. The Maya often decorated their buildings with paintings.

Reading Check **Categorizing** What groups made up the different classes in Maya society?

Differentiating Instruction

English-Language Learners

Below Level | Prep Required

Materials: butcher paper, art supplies

1. Ask students to imagine that they are Maya artists during the Classic Age and that the king has asked them to create a mural showing Maya achievements in science, math, writing, and architecture.
2. Organize students into small groups. If possible, place students who are proficient in English in the same groups with English learners.
3. Have students examine the examples of Maya artwork in this section and use the artwork as a model.
4. Then have each group create and display its mural. **LS Interpersonal, Visual/Spatial**

Alternative Assessment Handbook, Rubrics 3: Artwork; and 14: Group Activity

Answers

Reading Check *king, priests, merchants, noble warriors, farmers, and slaves*

Decline of Maya Civilization

Maya civilization began to collapse in the AD 900s. People stopped building temples and other structures. They left the cities and moved back to the countryside. What caused this collapse? Historians aren't sure, but they think a combination of factors was probably responsible.

One factor could have been the burden on the common people. Maya kings forced their subjects to farm for them or work on building projects. Perhaps people didn't want to work for the kings. They might have decided to **rebel** against their rulers' demands and abandon their cities.

Increased warfare between cities could also have caused the decline. Maya cities had always fought for power. But if battles became more widespread or destructive, they would have cost many lives and disrupted trade. People might have fled the cities for their safety.

A related theory is that perhaps the Maya could not produce enough to feed everyone. Growing the same crops year after year could have weakened the soil. In addition, as the population grew, the demand for food would have increased. To meet this demand, cities might have begun competing fiercely for new farmland. But the resulting battles would have ruined more crops, damaged more land, and created even greater food shortages.

Climate change could have played a role, too. Scientists know that Mesoamerica suffered from droughts during the period when the Maya were leaving their cities. Droughts would have made it hard to grow enough food for city dwellers.

Whatever the reasons, the collapse of Maya civilization happened gradually. The Maya scattered after 900, but they did not disappear entirely. In fact, the Maya civilization later revived in the Yucatán Peninsula. But by the time Spanish conquerors reached the Americas in the 1500s, Maya power had faded.

READING CHECK **Summarizing** What factors may have caused the end of Maya civilization?

SUMMARY AND PREVIEW The Maya built a civilization that peaked between about 250 and 900 but later collapsed for reasons still unknown. In Section 2, you will learn about another people of Mesoamerica, the Aztecs.

ACADEMIC VOCABULARY
rebel to fight against authority

Section 1 Assessment

hmhsocialstudies.com ONLINE QUIZ

Reviewing Ideas, Terms, and People

1. a. **Recall** What resources did the Maya get from the forest?
   b. **Elaborate** How do you think Maya villages grew into large cities?
2. a. **Describe** What features did Maya cities include?
   b. **Make Inferences** How did trade strengthen the Maya civilization?
3. a. **Identify** Who belonged to the upper class in Maya society?
   b. **Explain** How did the Maya try to please their gods?
   c. **Rank** What do you think was the most impressive cultural achievement of the Maya? Why?
4. a. **Describe** What happened to the Maya after 900?
   b. **Evaluate** What would you consider to be the key factor in the collapse of Maya civilization? Explain.

Critical Thinking

5. **Evaluating** Draw a diagram like the one to the right. Use your notes to rank Maya achievements, with the most important at the top.

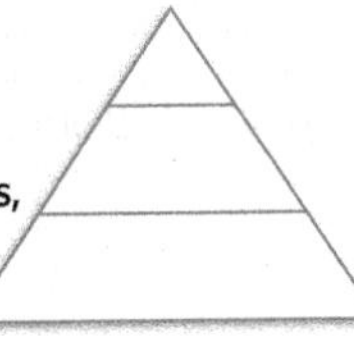

FOCUS ON WRITING

6. **Gathering Information about the Maya** Part of your article would likely be devoted to the Maya. Use the map and pictures in this section to help you decide which places to write about. How would you describe the land and the Maya cities? What would you add about the history and culture of the Maya?

Direct Teach

Main Idea

4 Decline of Maya Civilization

The decline of Maya civilization began in the 900s, for reasons that are still unclear.

Recall When did the Maya civilization decline, and what resulted? *In the AD 900s; the Maya stopped building temples and other structures and left their cities.*

Evaluate Which theory do you think best explains why the Maya civilization collapsed, and why? *Answers will vary, but students should accurately describe the theory they choose.*

Review & Assess

Close

Have students summarize and discuss the different theories for the decline of the Classic Age in Maya civilization.

Review

Online Quiz, Section 1

Assess

SE Section 1 Assessment
PASS: Section 1 Quiz
Alternative Assessment Handbook

Reteach/Classroom Intervention

Guided Reading Workbook, Section 1
Interactive Skills Tutor CD-ROM

Section 1 Assessment Answers

1. a. deer, rabbits, and monkeys for food; wood poles, vines, and mud for building materials
   b. Increased food supply and trade could support larger cities.
2. a. possible answers—temples, pyramids, palaces, plazas, canals, ball courts
   b. brought city-states into contact with each other, provided food and supplies that were not available locally, held civilization together
3. a. kings, priests, warriors, merchants
   b. offered blood to the gods by piercing themselves or by offering human sacrifices
   c. Students should exhibit an understanding of Maya contributions in art, mathematics, science, and writing and provide reasons to support their opinions.
4. a. They stopped building temples and went to live in the countryside.
   b. Answers will vary, but could include rebellion, food shortages, warfare, and climate change.
5. Answers should show Maya achievements in art, math, science, and writing.
6. Students should list some of the cities on the Maya Civilization map and describe some features of Maya cities that they want to include in their article.

Answers

Reading Check *rebellion by the common people, increased warfare, lack of food, climate change*

Preteach

Bellringer

If YOU were there . . . Use the **Daily Bellringer Transparency** to help students answer the question.

Daily Bellringer Transparency, Section 2

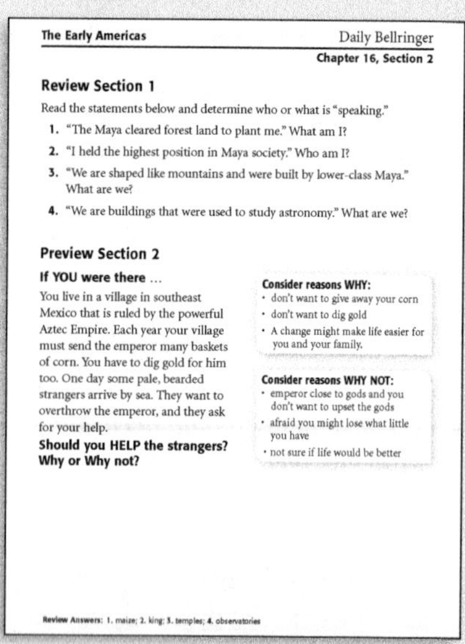

The Early Americas Daily Bellringer
Chapter 16, Section 2

Review Section 1

Read the statements below and determine who or what is "speaking."

1. "The Maya cleared forest land to plant me." What am I?
2. "I held the highest position in Maya society." Who am I?
3. "We are shaped like mountains and were built by lower-class Maya." What are we?
4. "We are buildings that were used to study astronomy." What are we?

Preview Section 2

If YOU were there ...

You live in a village in southeast Mexico that is ruled by the powerful Aztec Empire. Each year your village must send the emperor many baskets of corn. You have to dig gold for him too. One day some pale, bearded strangers arrive by sea. They want to overthrow the emperor, and they ask for your help.

Should you HELP the strangers? Why or Why not?

Consider reasons WHY:
- don't want to give away your corn
- don't want to dig gold
- A change might make life easier for you and your family.

Consider reasons WHY NOT:
- emperor close to gods and you don't want to upset the gods
- afraid you might lose what little you have
- not sure if life would be better

Review Answers: 1. maize; 2. king; 3. temples; 4. observatories

Academic Vocabulary

Review with students the high-use academic term in this section.

motive reason for doing something (p. 478)

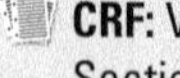
CRF: Vocabulary Builder Activity, Section 2

Taking Notes

Have students use the graphic organizer online to take notes on the section. This activity will prepare students for the Section Assessment, in which they will complete a graphic organizer that builds on the information using the Critical Thinking Skill: Evaluating.

SECTION 2

The Aztecs

What You Will Learn...

Main Ideas

1. The Aztecs built a rich and powerful empire in central Mexico.
2. Life in the empire was shaped by social structure, religion, and warfare.
3. Hernán Cortés conquered the Aztec Empire in 1521.

The Big Idea

The strong Aztec Empire, founded in central Mexico in 1325, lasted until the Spanish conquest in 1521.

Key Terms and People

causeways, *p. 474*
conquistadors, *p. 478*
Hernán Cortés, *p. 478*
Moctezuma II, *p. 478*

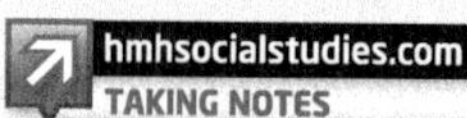

Use the graphic organizer online to take notes on the founding of the Aztec Empire, life in the empire at its height, and the fall of the Aztec Empire.

If YOU were there...

You live in a village in southeast Mexico that is ruled by the powerful Aztec Empire. Each year your village must send the emperor many baskets of corn. You have to dig gold for him, too. One day some pale, bearded strangers arrive by sea. They want to overthrow the emperor, and they ask for your help.

Should you help the strangers? Why or why not?

BUILDING BACKGROUND The Aztecs ruled a large empire in Mesoamerica. Each village they conquered had to contribute heavily to the Aztec economy. This system helped create a mighty state, but one that did not inspire loyalty.

The Aztecs Build an Empire

The first Aztecs were farmers who migrated from the north to central Mexico. Finding the good farmland already occupied, they settled on a swampy island in the middle of Lake Texcoco (tays-KOH-koh). There, in 1325, they began building their capital and conquering nearby towns.

War was a key factor in the Aztecs' rise to power. The Aztecs fought fiercely and demanded tribute payments from the people they conquered. The cotton, gold, and food that poured in as a result became vital to their economy. The Aztecs also controlled a huge trade network. Merchants carried goods to and from all parts of the empire. Many merchants doubled as spies, keeping the rulers informed about what was happening in their lands.

War, tribute, and trade made the Aztec Empire strong and rich. By the early 1400s the Aztecs ruled the most powerful state in Mesoamerica. Nowhere was the empire's greatness more visible than in its capital, Tenochtitlán (tay-NAWCH-teet-LAHN).

To build this amazing island city, the Aztecs first had to overcome many geographic challenges. One problem was difficulty getting to and from the city. The Aztecs addressed this challenge by building three wide **causeways**—raised roads across water or wet ground—to connect the island to the lake shore.

Teach the Big Idea

At Level

The Aztecs

1. **Teach** Ask students the questions in the Main Idea boxes to teach this section.
2. **Apply** Create a flowchart for students to see that lists, in order, the major events in Aztec history. The flowchart should have about five or six major events.
3. **Review** Pair students and have them copy the flowchart. One partner teaches the flowchart to the other person. The second person adds additional details.
LS Interpersonal, Visual/Spatial
4. **Practice/Homework** Instruct students to write down one or more causes for each event in the flowchart. *Possible answer: "The Aztecs built their capital on an island in Lake Texcoco." Cause: "because other tribes had already taken the good farmland in the area."*
LS Verbal/Linguistic, Visual/Spatial

The Aztec Empire

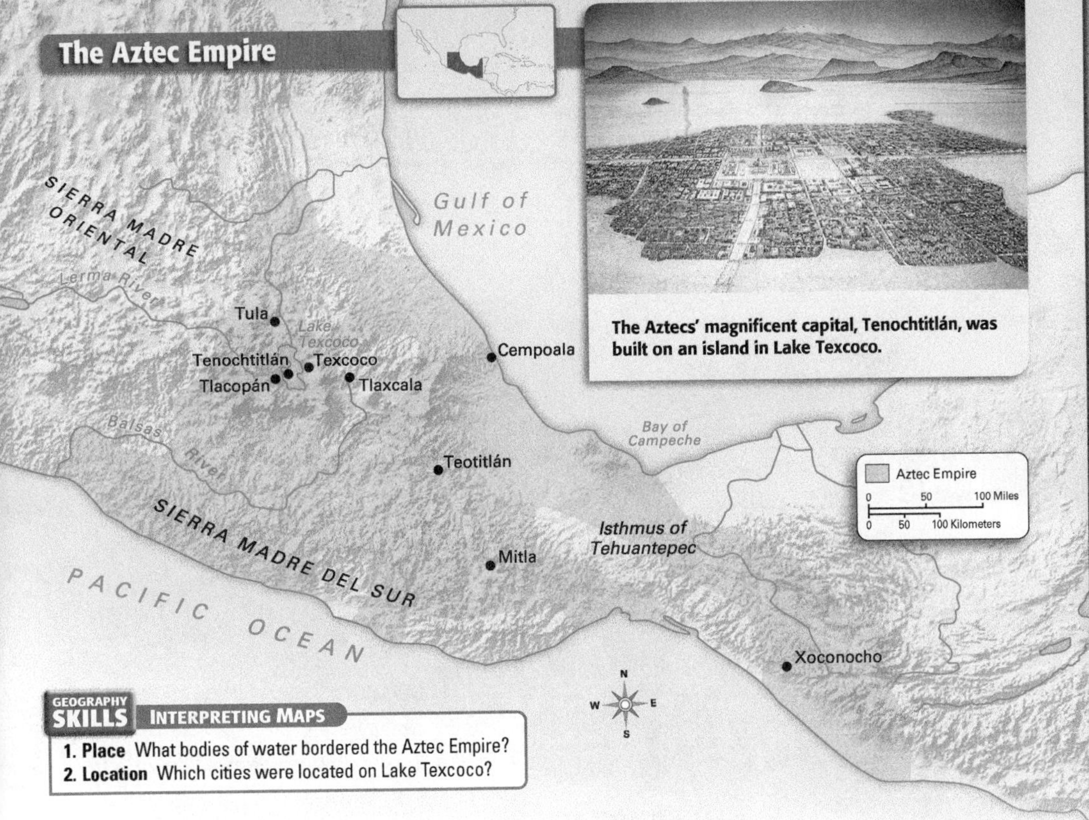

The Aztecs' magnificent capital, Tenochtitlán, was built on an island in Lake Texcoco.

GEOGRAPHY SKILLS INTERPRETING MAPS

1. **Place** What bodies of water bordered the Aztec Empire?
2. **Location** Which cities were located on Lake Texcoco?

They also built canals that crisscrossed the city. The causeways and canals made travel and trade much easier.

Tenochtitlán's island location also limited the amount of land available for farming. To solve this problem, the Aztecs created floating gardens called *chinampas* (chee-NAHM-pahs). They piled soil on top of large rafts, which they anchored to trees that stood in the water.

The Aztecs made Tenochtitlán a truly magnificent city. Home to some 200,000 people at its height, it had huge temples, a busy market, and a grand palace.

READING CHECK **Finding Main Ideas** How did the Aztecs rise to power?

Life in the Empire

The Aztecs' way of life was as distinctive as their capital city. They had a complex social structure, a demanding religion, and a rich culture.

ANIMATED HISTORY
Chinampas

Aztec Society

The Aztec emperor, like the Maya king, was the most important person in society. From his great palace, he attended to law, trade, tribute, and warfare. Trusted nobles helped him as tax collectors, judges, and other government officials. Noble positions were passed down from fathers to sons, and young nobles went to school to learn their responsibilities.

Mexico's capital, Mexico City, is located where Tenochtitlán once stood.

Direct Teach

Main Idea

1 The Aztecs Build an Empire

The Aztecs built a rich and powerful empire in central Mexico.

Recall About when did the Aztec Empire become the most powerful state in Mesoamerica? *early 1400s*

Analyze Why do you think merchants would make good spies for the emperor? *The merchants traveled widely and interacted with many different people.*

Identify How did visitors travel to and from Tenochtitlán? *across a causeway*

Map Transparency: The Aztec Empire

CRF: History and Geography: The Aztec Empire

Linking to Today

Mexica and Mexico The Aztecs were also called Mexica, probably from Metzliapán ("Moon Lake"), another name for Lake Texcoco. The name Mexica is the source of the name of the present-day country, Mexico.

Interpreting Maps

The Aztec Empire

Location How far was Tenochtitlán from the Gulf of Mexico? *about 150 miles*

Place What physical features surrounded Lake Texcoco? *mountains or hills*

Differentiating Instruction

Special Needs Learners **Below Level**

1. Draw a chart similar to the following for students to see and discuss what it means.

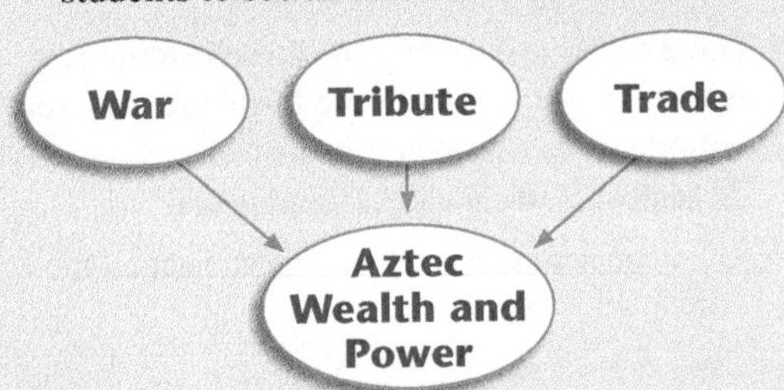

2. Explain that *tribute* means what one pays a ruler to show that you recognize his or her power over you, expecting protection in return. Ask what kind of protection those paying tribute to the Aztecs might have expected.
3. Ask students what people might have given as tribute. Also, ask what items might have been traded. LS **Visual/Spatial, Verbal/Linguistic**

Answers

Interpreting Maps **1.** *Gulf of Mexico, Pacific Ocean*; **2.** *Tenochtitlán, Texcoco, and Tlacopán*

Reading Check *war, tribute, and trade*

Direct Teach

History Close-up

Tenochtitlán

Ask students these questions based on the illustration of Tenochtitlán.

Identify What goods were traded at the market? *possible answers—crops, animals, rugs, gold, silver, cloaks, and precious stones*

Analyze How did people travel throughout the city? *by boat*

Draw Conclusions Because the best farmland was already taken when the Aztecs arrived in central Mexico, they had to work hard at making the swampy land usable. How do you think this affected their success? *Answers will vary; often when people must overcome difficulties, they work harder.*

Did you know . . .

A major reason the Aztecs were so prosperous was that they engaged in intensive agriculture. This means that the Aztecs farmed the available land to the greatest possible extent.

Connect to Geography

Land from the Sea In other parts of the world, people have claimed land from areas once covered by water. For example, for centuries the people of the Netherlands have built dikes and then used windmills to pump out the water. In this way the Dutch have created farmland where the North Sea once flowed.

History Close-up
Tenochtitlán
The Aztecs turned a swampy, uninhabited island into one of the largest and grandest cities in the world. The first Europeans to visit Tenochtitlán were amazed. At the time, the Aztec capital was about five times bigger than London.
The Great Temple stood at the heart of the city. On top of the temple were two shrines—a blue shrine for the rain god and a red shrine for the sun god.
HISTORY
VIDEO
Aztecs: Culture of Art and Death
hmhsocialstudies.com
Gold, silver, cloaks, and precious stones were among the many items sold at the market.
A network of canals linked different parts of the city.
Aztec farmers grew crops on "floating gardens" called *chinampas*.
ANALYSIS SKILL ANALYZING VISUALS
What is the most important building in this picture? How can you tell?
476

Critical Thinking: Solving Problems

Above Level

Making More Farmland

1. Organize students into small groups. Ask students to imagine they are Aztecs who have come to build a new home around Lake Texcoco. However, there is not enough farmland.
2. Each group should explore options for creating more farmland, such as building *chinampas*. Encourage students to brainstorm.
3. Once groups have decided how they are going to create additional farmland, have them list necessary materials and processes. For example: What tools will be needed? If they need rafts, what materials will be required? How will they move soil around?
4. Have students explain how these resources will be used to create more farmland. Ask for volunteers to share their solutions.

LS Logical/Mathematical, Interpersonal

Alternative Assessment Handbook, Rubric 14: Group Activity

Answers

Analyzing Visuals *the Great Temple*

Aztec Arts: Ceremonial Jewelry

Aztec artists were very skilled. They created detailed and brightly colored items. This double-headed serpent was probably worn during religious ceremonies. The man on the right is wearing it on his chest.

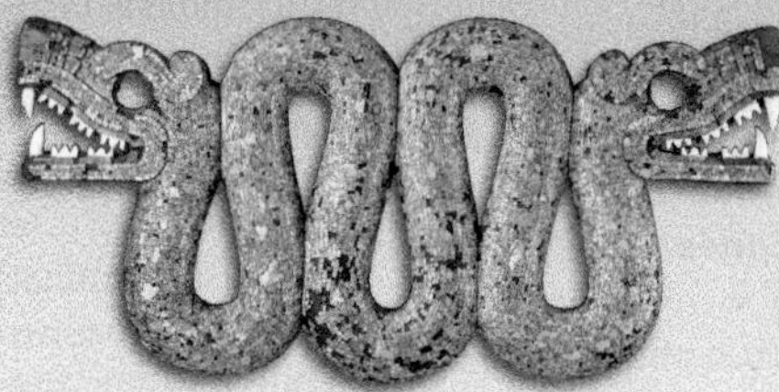

What are some features of Aztec art that you can see in these pictures?

Just below the emperor and his nobles was a class of warriors and priests. Warriors were highly respected and had many privileges, but priests were more influential. They led religious ceremonies, passed down history, and, as keepers of the calendars, decided when to plant and harvest.

The next level of Aztec society included merchants and artisans. Below them, in the lower class, were farmers and laborers, who made up the majority of the population. Many didn't own their land, and they paid so much in tribute that they often found it tough to survive. Only slaves, at the very bottom of society, struggled more.

Religion and Warfare

Like the Maya, the Aztecs worshipped many gods who were believed to control both nature and human activities. To please the gods, Aztec priests regularly made human sacrifices. Most victims were battle captives or slaves. In ritual ceremonies, priests would slash open their victims' chests to "feed" human hearts and blood to the gods. The Aztec sacrificed as many as 10,000 people a year. To supply enough victims, Aztec warriors waged frequent battles with neighboring peoples.

Cultural Achievements

As warlike as the Aztecs were, they also appreciated art and beauty. Architects and sculptors created fine stone pyramids and statues. Artisans used gold, gems, and bright feathers to make jewelry and masks. Women embroidered colorful designs on the cloth they wove.

The Aztecs valued learning as well. They studied astronomy and devised a calendar much like the Maya one. They developed a number system based on the number 20. Tax officials used geometry to calculate how much land people owned. The Aztecs also took pride in their history and kept detailed written records, as well as a strong oral tradition. They enjoyed fine speeches and riddles such as this one:

> "What is a little blue-green jar filled with popcorn? Someone is sure to guess our riddle: it is the sky."
>
> –Bernardino de Sahagún, from *Florentine Codex*

Knowing the answers to riddles showed that one had paid attention in school.

THE IMPACT TODAY Unlike the Aztecs, we use a number system based on 10. We think in terms of 10, 100, 1,000 and so on. They thought in terms of 20, 400, and 8,000.

READING CHECK **Identifying Cause and Effect** How did their religious practices influence Aztec warfare?

Direct Teach

Main Idea

❷ Life in the Empire

Life in the empire was shaped by social structure, religion, and warfare.

Analyze Why do you think priests were able to remain so powerful? *possible answer—People were afraid that if the priests did not pacify the gods with their rituals, terrible things would happen.*

Make an Inference If you were a young Aztec child, why would you be proud if you knew the answer to a riddle an adult asked? *because Aztecs believed that this showed you had been paying attention in school*

Activity **Advertisements** Have class members create a print advertisement that an Aztec artisan might use to sell his or her work. The ad should be attention-grabbing and colorful and contain at least one drawing of the artisan's work.

LS Visual/Spatial, Verbal/Linguistic

CRF: Biography Activity: Tlacaelel,

Linking to Today

From Mud to Museum In 1790 a 25-ton basalt object was unearthed in Mexico City. The object was a 12-foot circular Aztec sun stone with the Aztec sun god Tonatiuh at its center. The stone was originally painted in bright colors, but the paint has disappeared. Today the sun stone hangs in the National Museum of Anthropology in Mexico City.

Connect to Economics

Taking Care of Business The Aztecs used pictographs not only to record historical events but also for their number system, which was base 20. The ability to keep business records was essential to the Aztec economy.

Cross-Discipline Activity: Arts and the Humanities

Above Level

Prep Required

Aztecs at Work

Materials: examples of Mexican murals, butcher paper, art supplies

1. Display examples from art or history books of murals by great Mexican artists, including Diego Rivera and Jose Clemente Orozco. Point out that these artists have portrayed aspects of Mexican history in their murals.
2. Organize students into groups of three or four. Have each group conduct additional research on Aztec daily life, especially as it affected the various occupations of the Aztec people.
3. Ask each group to paint a mural, using Rivera or Orozco murals as models, showing the various levels of Aztec society performing the tasks assigned to that group.
4. Display the murals in the classroom.
LS Visual/Spatial, Interpersonal

Alternative Assessment Handbook, Rubric 3: Artwork

Answers

Aztec Arts *bright colors, stone sculpture, gems, mask with feathers*

Reading Check *Battle captives were used as human sacrifices.*

Direct Teach

Main Idea

3 Cortés Conquers the Aztecs

Hernán Cortés conquered the Aztec Empire in 1521.

Identify What were the Spanish soldiers called? *conquistadors*

Evaluate Do you think Moctezuma was too trusting of Cortés and his men? Explain your answer. *Students' answers should reflect the text.*

CRF: Primary Source Activity: Cortés's First Meeting with Moctezuma (1519)

CRF: Biography Activity: Moctezuma

Biography

Hernán Cortés (1485–1547) After conquering the Aztec Empire, Cortés became governor of New Spain in 1522. He then encouraged missionaries to convert the Aztecs to Christianity.

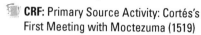

Review & Assess

Close

Ask students which factors that contributed to the Aztecs' defeat were the most and least important and to defend their choices.

Review

Online Quiz, Section 2

Assess

SE Section 2 Assessment

PASS: Section 2 Quiz

Alternative Assessment Handbook

Reteach/Classroom Intervention

Guided Reading Workbook, Section 2

Interactive Skills Tutor CD-ROM

Answers

Reading Check *alliances with other people in the region, better weapons, horses, disease*

Cortés Conquers the Aztecs

In the late 1400s the Spanish arrived in the Americas, seeking adventure, riches, and converts to Catholicism. One group of **conquistadors** (kahn-kees-tuh-DOHRZ), or Spanish conquerors, reached Mexico in 1519. Led by **Hernán Cortés** (er-NAHN kawr-TAYS), their motives were to find gold, claim land, and convert native peoples.

Academic Vocabulary
motive reason for doing something

The Aztec emperor, **Moctezuma II** (MAWK-tay-SOO-mah), cautiously welcomed the strangers. He believed Cortés to be the god Quetzalcoatl (ket-suhl-kuh-WAH-tuhl), whom the Aztecs believed had left Mexico long ago. According to legend, the god had promised to return in 1519.

Moctezuma gave the Spaniards gold and other gifts, but Cortés wanted more. He took the emperor prisoner, enraging the Aztecs, who attacked the Spanish. They managed to drive out the conquistadors, but Moctezuma was killed in the fighting.

Within a year, Cortés and his men came back. This time they had help from other Indians in the region who resented the Aztecs' harsh rule. In addition, the Spanish had better weapons, including armor, cannons, and swords. Furthermore, the Aztecs were terrified of the enemy's big horses—animals they had never seen before. The Spanish had also unknowingly brought deadly diseases such as smallpox to the Americas. These diseases weakened or killed thousands of native people. In 1521 the Aztecs surrendered. Their once mighty empire came to a swift end.

Reading Check **Summarizing** What factors helped the Spanish defeat the Aztecs?

Summary and Preview The Aztec Empire, made strong by warfare and tribute, fell to the Spanish in 1521. Next you will learn about another empire in the Americas, that of the Incas.

Section 2 Assessment

hmhsocialstudies.com ONLINE QUIZ

Reviewing Ideas, Terms, and People

1. a. **Recall** Where and when did Aztec civilization develop?
   b. **Explain** How did the Aztecs in Tenochtitlán adapt to their island location?
   c. **Elaborate** How might Tenochtitlán's location have been both a benefit and a hindrance to the Aztecs?
2. a. **Recall** What did the Aztecs feed their gods?
   b. **Rate** Consider the roles of the emperor, warriors, priests, and others in Aztec society. Who do you think had the hardest role? Explain.
3. a. **Identify** Who was **Moctezuma II**?
   b. **Make Generalizations** Why did allies help **Cortés** defeat the Aztecs?
   c. **Predict** The Aztecs vastly outnumbered the **conquistadors**. If the Aztecs had first viewed Cortés as a threat rather than a god, how might history have changed?

Critical Thinking

4. **Evaluating** Draw a diagram like the one shown. Use your notes to identify three factors that contributed to the Aztecs' power. Put the factor you consider most important first, and put the least important last. Explain your choices.

1.	2.	3.

Focus on Writing

5. **Describing the Aztec Empire** Tenochtitlán would certainly be described in your article. Make notes about how you would describe Tenochtitlán. Be sure to explain the causeways, *chinampas*, and other features. What activities went on in the city? Your article should also describe the events that occurred when the Spanish discovered the Aztec capital. Make notes on the fall of the Aztec Empire.

Section 2 Assessment Answers

1. a. in central Mexico in the early 1300s
   b. built causeways, canals, *chinampas*
   c. benefit—improved trade; hindrance—limited farmland, made Aztecs vulnerable to isolation
2. a. human hearts and blood
   b. possible answer—slaves, because they had to work for other people and could be sacrificed
3. a. the Aztec emperor conquered by Cortés
   b. They did not like losing battles and paying tribute to the Aztecs.
   c. possible answer—Aztecs would not have been conquered by the Spanish.
4. Aztecs were fierce warriors, demanded tribute from conquered people, controlled trade network; order of answers will vary.
5. Responses will vary. Students should use vivid, colorful language to describe Tenochtitlán, *chinampas,* and other features.

The Incas

SECTION 3

If YOU were there...

You live in the Andes Mountains, where you raise llamas. You weave their wool into warm cloth. Last year, soldiers from the powerful Inca Empire took over your village. They brought in new leaders, who say you must all learn a new language and send much of your woven cloth to the Inca ruler. They also promise that the government will provide for you in times of trouble.

How do you feel about living in the Inca Empire?

BUILDING BACKGROUND The Incas built their huge empire by taking over village after village in South America. They brought many changes to the people they conquered before they were themselves conquered by the Spanish.

What You Will Learn...

Main Ideas

1. The Incas created an empire with a strong central government in South America.
2. Life in the Inca Empire was influenced by social structure, religion, and the Incas' cultural achievements.
3. Francisco Pizarro conquered the Incas and took control of the region in 1537.

The Big Idea

The Incas controlled a huge empire in South America, but it was conquered by the Spanish.

Key Terms and People

Pachacuti, *p. 479*
Quechua, *p. 480*
masonry, *p. 481*
Atahualpa, *p. 482*
Francisco Pizarro, *p. 482*

Use the graphic organizer online to take notes about the geography, government, society, religion, achievements, and conquest of the Inca Empire.

The Incas Create an Empire

While the Aztecs were ruling Mexico, the Inca Empire arose in South America. The Incas began as a small tribe in the Andes. Their capital was Cuzco (KOO-skoh) in what is now Peru.

In the mid-1400s a ruler named **Pachacuti** (pah-chah-KOO-tee) began to expand Inca territory. Later leaders followed his example, and by the early 1500s the Inca Empire was huge. It stretched from modern Ecuador to central Chile and included coastal deserts, snowy mountains, fertile valleys, and thick forests. About 12 million people lived in the empire. To rule effectively, the Incas formed a strong central government.

The Incas lived in a region of high plains and mountains.

Preteach

Bellringer

If YOU were there . . . Use the **Daily Bellringer Transparency** to help students answer the question.

Daily Bellringer Transparency, Section 3

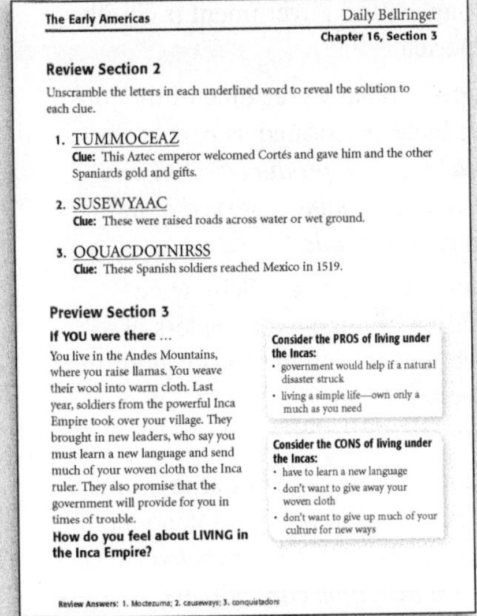

The Early Americas | Daily Bellringer | Chapter 16, Section 3

Review Section 2

Unscramble the letters in each underlined word to reveal the solution to each clue.

1. TUMMOCEAZ
   Clue: This Aztec emperor welcomed Cortés and gave him and the other Spaniards gold and gifts.
2. SUSEWYAAC
   Clue: These were raised roads across water or wet ground.
3. OQUACDOTNIRSS
   Clue: These Spanish soldiers reached Mexico in 1519.

Preview Section 3

If YOU were there ...

You live in the Andes Mountains, where you raise llamas. You weave their wool into warm cloth. Last year, soldiers from the powerful Inca Empire took over your village. They brought in new leaders, who say you must learn a new language and send much of your woven cloth to the Inca ruler. They also promise that the government will provide for you in times of trouble.

How do you feel about LIVING in the Inca Empire?

Consider the PROS of living under the Incas:
- government would help if a natural disaster struck
- living a simple life—own only a much as you need

Consider the CONS of living under the Incas:
- have to learn a new language
- don't want to give away your woven cloth
- don't want to give up much of your culture for new ways

Review Answers: 1. Moctezuma; 2. causeways; 3. conquistadors

Academic Vocabulary

Review with students the high-use academic terms in this section.

distribute to divide among a group of people (p. 480)

CRF: Vocabulary Builder Activity, Section 3

Taking Notes

Have students use the graphic organizer online to take notes on the section. This activity will prepare students for the Section Assessment, in which they will complete a graphic organizer that builds on the information using the Critical Thinking Skill: Analyzing.

Teach the Big Idea

At Level

The Incas

1. **Teach** Ask students the questions in the Main Idea boxes to teach this section.
2. **Apply** Create a two-column chart for students to see. Title the left column *Before the Spaniards Arrived* and the right column *After the Spaniards Arrived.* Title the whole chart *The Inca Empire.* Have students copy the chart. Call on volunteers to provide key words and phrases to describe the Inca Empire before and after the Spaniards' arrival. Place those words and phrases on the chart. LS **Visual/Spatial**
3. **Review** Ask students if any characteristics in the *Before* column may have continued after the conquest. *possible answer—aspects of daily life, such as farming techniques, use of llamas*
4. **Practice/Homework** Have each student write a paragraph about how the lives of the Inca people changed after the Spanish conquest. LS **Verbal/Linguistic**

Alternative Assessment Handbook, Rubric 37: Writing Assignments

Direct Teach

Main Idea

❶ The Incas Create an Empire

The Incas created an empire with a strong central government in South America.

Recall What were some of the jobs that Incas performed as part of the *mita*? *farmed, produced cloth and other goods, mined, served in the army, built roads*

Make Inferences Why were children of conquered leaders used to govern and teach the Inca way of life? *They would have been trusted and respected.*

Evaluate Was life better or worse for people after the Incas conquered them? *possible answers: better—The government took care of them; worse—They had to participate in the* mita.

Map Transparency: The Inca Empire

Interpreting Maps

The Inca Empire

Region How do the size, shape, and physical features of the Inca Empire compare to those of the Aztec Empire? *Inca Empire—long and narrow, located along Pacific coast, two major lakes, high mountains; Aztec Empire—coasts on two oceans, more compact, some mountains, Lake Texcoco*

Central Rule

Pachacuti did not want the people he conquered to have too much power. He began a policy of removing local leaders and replacing them with new officials he trusted. He also made the children of conquered leaders travel to Cuzco to learn about Inca government and religion. When the children were grown, they were sent back to govern their villages, where they taught people the Inca way of life.

As another means of unifying the empire, the Incas used an official Inca language, **Quechua** (KE-chuh-wuh). Although people spoke many other languages, all official business had to be done in Quechua. Even today, many people in Peru speak Quechua.

A Well-Organized Economy

The Inca government strictly controlled the economy and told each household what work to do. Most Incas had to spend time working for the government as well as themselves. Farmers tended government land in addition to their own. Villagers made cloth and other goods for the army. Some Incas served as soldiers, worked in mines, or built roads and bridges. In this way, the people paid taxes in the form of labor rather than money. This labor tax system was called the *mita* (MEE-tah).

Another feature of the Inca economy was that there were no merchants or markets. Instead, government officials would **distribute** goods collected through the *mita*. Leftover goods were stored in the capital for emergencies. If a natural disaster struck, or if people simply could not care for themselves, the government provided supplies to help them.

ACADEMIC VOCABULARY
distribute to divide among a group of people

READING CHECK **Summarizing** How did the Incas control their empire?

BIOGRAPHY

Pachacuti
Died 1471

Pachacuti became the Inca ruler in about 1438. Under his rule the Inca Empire began a period of great expansion. Pachacuti, whose name means "he who remakes the world," had the Inca capital at Cuzco rebuilt. He also established an official Inca religion.

Drawing Inferences Why do you suppose Pachacuti wanted an official religion for the empire?

hmhsocialstudies.com INTERACTIVE MAP

The Inca Empire

GEOGRAPHY SKILLS **INTERPRETING MAPS**

1. **Place** About how many miles did the Inca Empire stretch from north to south?
2. **Location** Why was Cuzco a better location for the Inca capital than Quito?

Answers

Biography *possible answers—to unify empire, to make conquered people easier to control*

Interpreting Maps **1.** *about 2,400 miles if measured in a straight line, about 2,700 if measured along the Pacific coast;* **2.** *centrally located, mountains provided protection from invaders*

Reading Check *brought in new leaders, educated leaders' children in the capital, established an official religion, established Quechua as the official language, imposed a labor tax, collected and distributed goods*

Differentiating Instruction

Struggling Readers Below Level Prep Required

Materials: heavy string or twine

1. Clear a space in the classroom about 6 feet by 20 feet or secure a space that size in the hallway.
2. Supply students with heavy string or twine. Have students use the string to create an outline of the Inca Empire. They can position chairs and desks to hold the string in place.
3. Have students determine the locations of major cities and place individuals at those locations.
4. Call on a volunteer to walk from one end of the "empire" to the other. Point out that if the same amount of area was in a different shape, such as a square or circle, the distance from end to end would be much shorter.
5. Ask students how they think the empire's shape affected travel and communication. **LS Kinesthetic, Visual/Spatial**

Alternative Assessment Handbook, Rubric 14: Group Activity

Most Incas were farmers. The Incas in this drawing from the mid-1500s are harvesting potatoes.

Life in the Inca Empire

Because the rulers controlled Inca society so closely, the common people had little personal freedom. At the same time, the government protected the general welfare of all in the empire. But that did not mean everyone was treated equally.

Social Divisions

Inca society had two main social classes. The emperor, priests, and government officials made up the upper class. Members of this class lived in stone houses in Cuzco and wore the best clothes. They didn't have to pay the labor tax, and they enjoyed many other privileges. Inca rulers, for example, could relax in luxury at Machu Picchu (MAH-choo PEEK-choo). This royal retreat lay nestled high in the Andes. Palaces and gardens could be found behind its gated wall.

The lower class in Inca society included farmers, artisans, and servants. There were no slaves, however, because the Incas did not practice slavery. Most Incas were farmers. In the warmer valleys, they grew crops like maize and peanuts. In the cooler mountains, they carved terraces into the hillsides and grew potatoes. High in the Andes, people raised llamas—South American animals related to camels—for meat and wool.

Lower-class Incas dressed in plain clothes and lived simply. By law, they couldn't own more goods than what they needed to survive. Most of what they produced went to the *mita* and the upper class.

Religion

The Inca social structure was partly related to religion. For example, the Incas thought that their rulers were related to the sun god and never really died. As a result, priests brought mummies of former kings to many ceremonies. People gave these royal mummies food and gifts.

Inca ceremonies often included sacrifices. But unlike the Maya and the Aztecs, the Incas rarely sacrificed humans. Instead they sacrificed llamas, cloth, or food.

In addition to practicing the official religion, people outside Cuzco worshipped other gods at local sacred places. The Incas believed certain mountaintops, rocks, and springs had magical powers. Many Incas performed sacrifices at these places as well as at the temple in Cuzco.

Achievements

Inca temples were grand buildings. The Incas were master builders, known for their expert **masonry**, or stonework. They cut stone blocks so precisely that they didn't need cement to hold them together. The Incas also built a network of roads. Two major highways ran the length of the empire and linked to many other roads.

The Incas produced works of art as well. Artisans made pottery and gold and silver jewelry. They even created a life-sized cornfield of gold and silver, crafting each cob, leaf, and stalk individually. Inca weavers also made some of the finest textiles in the Americas.

THE IMPACT TODAY

The ruins of Machu Picchu draw thousands of tourists to Peru every year.

Direct Teach

Main Idea

2 Life in the Inca Empire

Life in the Inca Empire was influenced by social structure, religion, and the Incas' cultural achievements.

Explain Why did the Inca believe their rulers never really died? *They believed rulers were related to the sun god.*

Analyze How do you think lower-class workers felt about having to work long and hard to pay the labor tax? *possible answer—may have felt that the Inca government was taking advantage of them*

Predict Why do you think Inca rulers allowed people to practice local religions in addition to the official religion? *possible answer—people may have become angry and rebelled if forced to give up their local religion*

Connect to Music

Ancient Instruments of the Andes Some musical instruments still popular in the Andes today may have been played at Machu Picchu. One example is the *quena*—a flute made from bone or cane. Large and small drums also date back many centuries. When the Spaniards arrived, the Andean peoples adapted Spanish instruments. Instead of guitars, the Andean natives made stringed instruments called *charangos* from armadillo shells.

Info to Know

Build It Like This! Because the Incas didn't have a written language, they couldn't write down verbal instructions when designing buildings. Instead, they created clay models before beginning construction.

hmhsocialstudies.com

Online Resources
Activity: Brochure on Machu Picchu

Differentiating Instruction

Advanced/Gifted and Talented

Above Level **Research Required**

Looking at Inca Religion Tell students that the Incas had many gods. Some of the gods were connected to the stars and other heavenly bodies. One god was Virachoca, the creator god. He had many names, including Old Man of the Sky and Lord Instructor of the World. Apu Illapu, the rain god, was believed to cause rain by drawing water from the Milky Way. The Incas also paid close attention to the waxing and waning of the moon when planning events such as religious observances.

1. Ask each student to choose and conduct research on a subject related to Inca religion in which they are interested.
2. Students should prepare brief oral presentations on their chosen subjects. Encourage students to make the presentation entertaining by including interesting myths and using visual aids.
3. Have students give their presentations to the class. **LS Verbal/Linguistic, Visual/Spatial**

Alternative Assessment Handbook, Rubric 24: Oral Presentations

Direct Teach

Main Idea

3 Pizarro Conquers the Incas

Francisco Pizarro conquered the Incas and took control of the region in 1537.

Identify Who was the Inca ruler when Pizarro arrived in the empire? *Atahualpa*

Make Inferences Why do you think the Spaniards killed Atahualpa? *possible answer—The Spaniards feared that the Inca would rally around their king and rebel against them.*

Primary Source

Pizarro In his book *History of the Conquest of Peru,* published in 1847, William H. Prescott quotes Pizarro as saying the following to get his men to leave Panama and head to Peru with him:

"On that side are toil, hunger, nakedness, the drenching storm, desertion, and death; on this side ease and pleasure. There lies Peru with its riches; here, Panama and its poverty. Choose, each man, what best becomes a brave Castilian. For my part, I go to the south."

Interpret Ask students if they think this is an exact quote and to support their opinions. *possible answer—depends on what sources Prescott used*

Answers

Analyzing Visuals *bright colors, intricate detail, gold and silver, animals, and people*

Reading Check *upper class—lived in stone houses, wore the best clothes, did not have to pay labor taxes; lower class—worked all day, lived outside of the city, had to pay labor taxes, were servants*

Inca Arts

Inca arts included beautiful textiles and gold and silver objects. While many gold and silver objects have been lost, some Inca textiles have survived for hundreds of years.

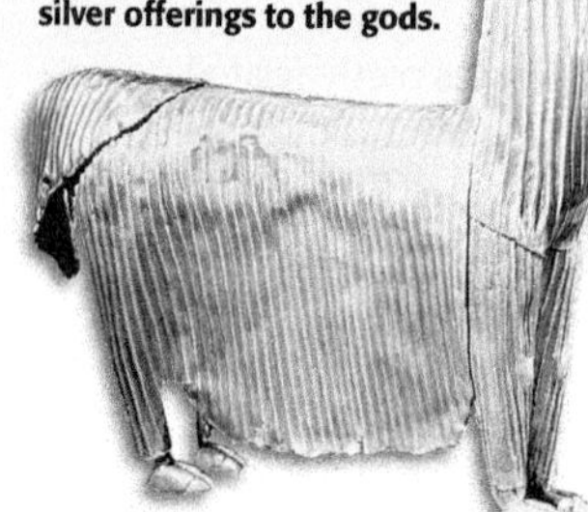

This llama is made of silver. Inca artisans made many silver offerings to the gods.

The Incas are famous for their textiles, which featured bright colors and detailed designs. Inca artists made cloth from cotton and from the wool of llamas.

Inca artisans also worked in gold. They made many beautiful objects such as this mask.

ANALYSIS SKILL ANALYZING VISUALS

What are some features of Inca art that you can see in these pictures?

While such artifacts tell us much about the Incas, nothing was written about their empire until the Spanish arrived. Indeed, the Incas had no writing system. Instead, they kept records with knotted cords called *quipus* (KEE-pooz). Knots in the cords represented numbers. Different colors stood for information about crops, land, and other important topics.

THE IMPACT TODAY

Archaeologists are still working to decipher the full meaning of *quipus*, but they believe the Incas used a number system based on 10, much as we do today.

The Incas also passed down their history orally. People sang songs and told stories about daily life and military victories. Official "memorizers" learned long poems about Inca legends and history. Eventually, after the conquistadors came, records were written in Spanish and Quechua. We know about the Incas from these records and from the stories that survive in the songs, dances, and religious practices of the people in the region today.

READING CHECK **Contrasting** How did daily life differ for upper- and lower-class Incas?

Pizarro Conquers the Incas

The arrival of conquistadors changed more than how the Incas recorded history. In the late 1520s, a civil war began in the Inca Empire after the death of the ruler. Two of the ruler's sons, **Atahualpa** (ah-tah-WAHL-pah) and Huáscar (WAHS-kahr), fought to claim the throne. Atahualpa won the war in 1532, but fierce fighting had weakened the Inca army.

On his way to be crowned as king, Atahualpa got news that a band of about 180 Spanish soldiers had arrived in the Inca Empire. They were conquistadors led by **Francisco Pizarro**. When Atahualpa came to meet the group, the Spanish attacked. They were greatly outnumbered, but they caught the unarmed Incas by surprise. They quickly captured Atahualpa and killed thousands of Inca soldiers.

To win his freedom, Atahualpa asked his people to fill a room with gold and silver for Pizarro. Incas brought jewelry,

Critical Thinking: Identifying Points of View

Above Level

The Spanish Conquest

Research Required

1. Have students conduct research on the arrival of the Spaniards, Atahualpa's meeting with them, and the subsequent Spanish attack.
2. Then have students write two journal entries. The first entry should present the events related to the conquest of the Inca Empire from the point of view of one of Pizarro's men. The second should describe the same events from an Inca point of view.
3. Each account should be written in the first person and begin by describing the author. Encourage students to be as descriptive and detailed as possible.
4. Ask for volunteers to share their journal entries with the class. **LS Verbal/Linguistic**

Alternative Assessment Handbook, Rubric 15: Journals

statues, and other valuable items from all parts of the empire. Melted down, the precious metals may have totaled 24 tons. They would have been worth millions of dollars today. Despite this huge payment, the Spaniards killed Atahualpa. They knew that if they let the Inca ruler live, he might rally his people and overpower their forces.

Some Incas fought back after the emperor's death. In 1537, though, Pizarro defeated the last of the Incas. Spain took control over the entire Inca Empire and ruled the region for the next 300 years.

READING CHECK **Identifying Cause and Effect** What events ended the Inca Empire?

SUMMARY AND PREVIEW The Incas built a huge empire with a strong central government, but they could not withstand the Spanish conquest in 1537. In the next chapter, you will turn to Europe in an earlier age—an age before the Spanish even learned of the Americas.

BIOGRAPHY

Atahualpa

1520–1533

Atahualpa was the last Inca emperor. He was brave and popular with the Inca army, but he didn't rule long. At his first meeting with Pizarro, he was offered a religious book to convince him to accept Christianity. Atahualpa held the book to his ear and listened. When the book didn't speak, Atahualpa threw it on the ground. The Spanish considered this an insult and a reason to attack.

Identifying Bias How do you think the Spanish viewed non-Christians?

BIOGRAPHY

Francisco Pizarro

1475–1541

Francisco Pizarro organized expeditions to explore the west coast of South America. His first two trips were mostly uneventful. But on his third trip, Pizarro met the Inca. With only about 180 men, he conquered the Inca Empire, which had been weakened by disease and civil war. In 1535 Pizarro founded Lima, the capital of modern Peru.

Predicting If Pizarro had not found the Inca Empire, what do you think might have happened?

Section 3 Assessment

hmhsocialstudies.com ONLINE QUIZ

Reviewing Ideas, Terms, and People

1. a. **Identify** Where was the Inca Empire located? What kinds of terrain did it include?
   b. **Explain** How did the Incas control their economy?
   c. **Evaluate** Do you think the *mita* system was a good government policy? Why or why not?
2. a. **Describe** What social classes existed in Inca society?
   b. **Make Inferences** How might the Inca road system have helped strengthen the empire?
3. a. **Recall** When did the Spanish gain full control over Inca lands?
   b. **Analyze** Why do you think **Pizarro** was able to defeat the much larger forces of the Incas?
   c. **Elaborate** What effect do you think the civil war with his brother had on **Atahualpa**'s kingship? How might history have been different if the Spanish had not arrived until a few years later?

Critical Thinking

4. **Analyzing** Draw a diagram like the one below. Using your notes, write a sentence in each box about how that topic influenced the topic its arrow points to.

Geography → Government → Society → Achievements

Focus on Writing

5. **Adding Information about the Inca Empire** Your article would also describe the lands where the Incas lived. How would you highlight the diversity of the geography? What specific sites would you describe? Include some comments about how the Incas' building activities related to their environment. You will also want to include information on what happened when the Spanish arrived.

Main Idea

❸ Pizarro Conquers the Incas

Francisco Pizarro conquered the Incas and took control of the region in 1537.

Recall When did the Spaniards defeat the last of the Incas? *1537*

Analyze Why did the Spaniards kill Atahualpa? *They believed he would lead his people to attack them.*

Review & Assess

Close

Lead a brief discussion about the major events leading to the fall of the Inca Empire. Ask students how these events might have interacted with one another.

Review

Online Quiz, Section 3

Assess

SE Section 3 Assessment

PASS: Section 3 Quiz

Alternative Assessment Handbook

Reteach/Classroom Intervention

Guided Reading Workbook, Section 3

Interactive Skills Tutor CD-ROM

Section 3 Assessment Answers

1. a. along the west coast of South America; coastal deserts, snowy mountains, fertile valleys, and thick forests
   b. collected a labor tax called a *mita,* distributed goods collected through the *mita*
   c. possible answers: yes—resources distributed effectively; no—limited freedoms
2. a. upper class of emperor, priests, and government officials; and lower class of farmers, artisans, and servants
   b. All parts of the empire were connected, simplifying travel and communication.
3. a. 1537
   b. internal problems, leader captured, Spanish advantage with guns and horses, disease
   c. possible answers—*weakened the Inca army and Atahualpa's power; Atahualpa may have been able to rebuild the army and defeat the Spaniards.*
4. Students' diagrams should reflect ideas in the text.
5. Student responses will vary, but should reflect text information accurately.

Answers

Biographies *Atahualpa: possible answers—as uncivilized and deserving conquest and death; Pizarro: possible answers—Inca empire would continue to control South America; weakened by civil war, empire might still have collapsed.*

Reading Check *war between Atahualpa and Huáscar, refusal of Atahualpa to convert to Christianity, capture and killing of Atahualpa*

History and Geography

Activity Pros and Cons of Mountain Living After students have reviewed the feature on these pages, ask each student to write a paragraph answering these questions: What advantages may the Inca have enjoyed by living in the mountains? What may have been some disadvantages? *possible answers—A major advantage is that a mountain empire is more isolated and easier to protect from intruders. However, isolation can also be a disadvantage, making it difficult to farm, communicate, and bring in supplies from outside.* **LS Verbal/Linguistic**

Linking to Today

Terracing Terracing is a conservation practice still in use around the world. It enables people to make use of hilly or mountainous land. Terraces also help retain the water necessary for growing rice in Asian countries such as China and the Philippines.

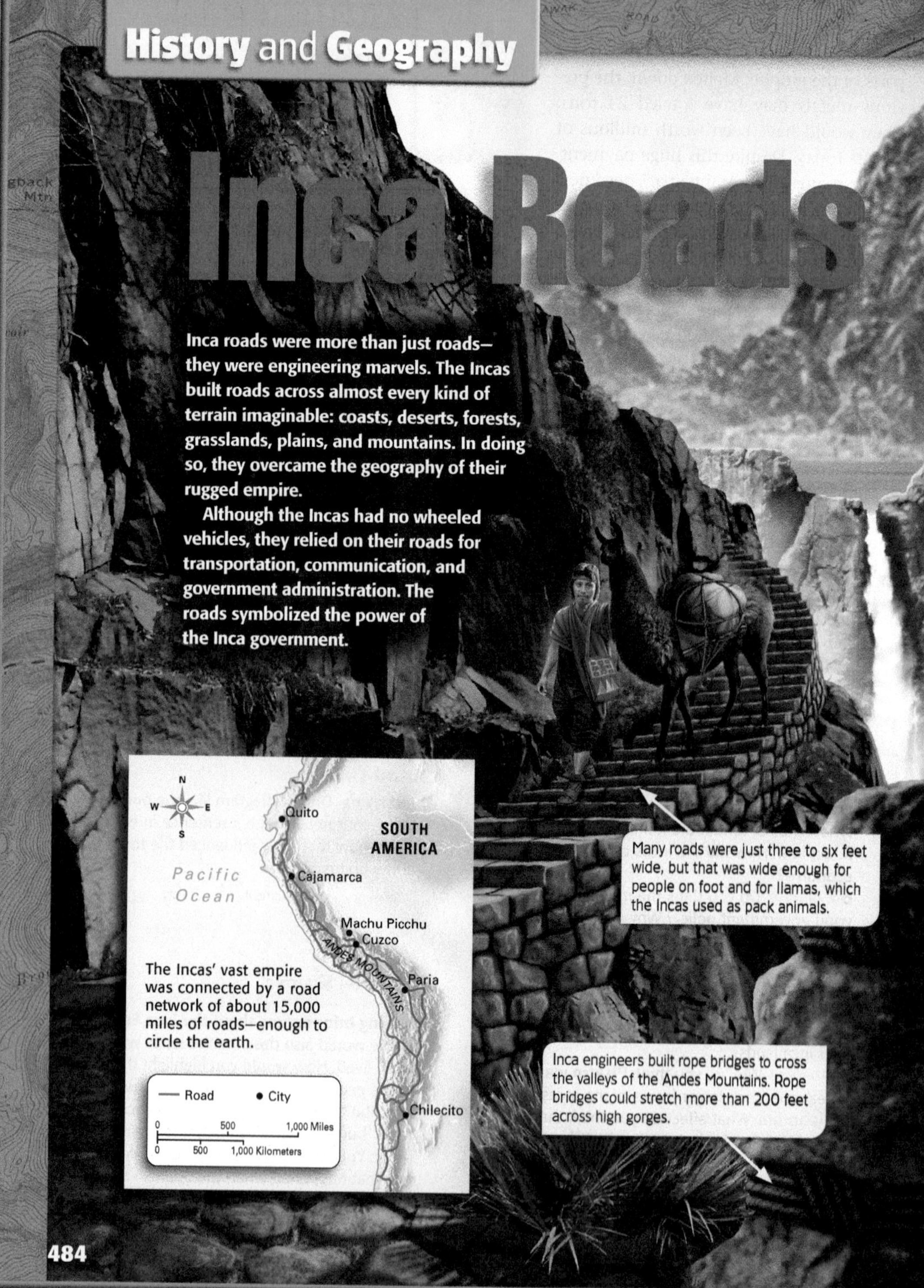

History and Geography
Inca Roads
Inca roads were more than just roads—they were engineering marvels. The Incas built roads across almost every kind of terrain imaginable: coasts, deserts, forests, grasslands, plains, and mountains. In doing so, they overcame the geography of their rugged empire.
Although the Incas had no wheeled vehicles, they relied on their roads for transportation, communication, and government administration. The roads symbolized the power of the Inca government.
Quito
SOUTH AMERICA
Pacific Ocean
Cajamarca
Machu Picchu
Cuzco
ANDES MOUNTAINS
Paria
Chilecito
The Incas' vast empire was connected by a road network of about 15,000 miles of roads—enough to circle the earth.
Road
City
0 500 1,000 Miles
0 500 1,000 Kilometers
Many roads were just three to six feet wide, but that was wide enough for people on foot and for llamas, which the Incas used as pack animals.
Inca engineers built rope bridges to cross the valleys of the Andes Mountains. Rope bridges could stretch more than 200 feet across high gorges.
484

Collaborative Learning

At Level

Building Roads and Bridges

Research Required

1. Remind students that the Inca never developed the wheel and that they could build thick stone walls without using cement.
2. Organize students into small groups. Have them conduct research on the tools and resources available to the Incas for construction of their roads and bridges.
3. Have each group choose a certain structure, such as a bridge or a road up a mountain slope. Have the group brainstorm how it might have been built using the available resources.
4. Have each group discuss specific obstacles faced in building the structure. For example, how would they build a bridge between mountains without modern equipment? Ask groups to present their ideas to the class.
   LS Interpersonal, Logical/Mathematical

Alternative Assessment Handbook, Rubric 14: Group Activity

Machu Picchu
Cuzco

Inca roads stretched from sea level to nearly 12,000 feet in elevation. Roads often followed natural features, such as valleys, ridgelines, and the coastline.

14,000 ft.
10,000 ft.
5,000 ft.
Sea Level
Pacific Ocean

Since the Incas had no wheeled vehicles, some of their roads had steps cut into the hillsides for people and animals.

The Incas were expert stone workers. They cut huge blocks of stone and fit them together so well that they didn't need any cement.

Important messages were carried by official runners. Each would run about two miles and then pass the message on to the next runner. Using this system, the Incas could send a message 150 miles in one day.

ANALYSIS SKILL ANALYZING VISUALS

1. What are some features of Inca roads that you can see in the illustration?
2. What challenges did the Incas face in building their roads?

485

History and Geography

Info to Know

Animals of the Inca Empire The llama, alpaca, and vicuña are members of the family of animals called *Camelidae.* These rugged, sure-footed animals have a high tolerance for thirst and can live on wild grasses. The Inca primarily used the llama as a pack animal, but it was also a source of food and wool. Both the vicuña's long, luxurious fur and the alpaca's shaggy, thick fur were reserved for use by the nobles.

Primary Source

Ciezo de Leon The Spanish conquistador Ciezo de Leon wrote that the Inca road system ran "through deep valleys and over mountains, through piles of snow, quagmires . . . in some places it ran smooth and paved, carefully laid out, in others over sierras [mountains], cut through the rock, with walls skirting the rivers . . . " Ask students how they think the Inca roads compared to other sights that Ciezo de Leon had seen. *possible answer—He probably had never seen anything like them in Spain.*

Critical Thinking: Analyzing Information

At Level

A Runner's Journal

1. Remind students that teams of runners transported official messages over the roads of the Inca Empire.
2. Have students imagine that they are official Inca runners. Ask each student to write a journal entry about his or her experiences in this job.
3. Students should pose at least three questions that they will answer in their journals. Examples: What were the roads and climate like? What did they eat? What kinds of messages were they carrying?
4. Encourage students to use both their imaginations and information in the feature when creating their journals.

LS Verbal/Linguistic

Alternative Assessment Handbook, Rubric 15: Journals

Answers

Inca Roads 1. *excellent stonework, steps up steep mountainsides, rope bridges across rivers* **2.** *high mountains, deep valleys, swift rivers; no wheeled vehicles*

Social Studies Skills

Analyzing Economic Effects

Activity Understanding Economic Choices and Effects Lead students in a discussion of how being able to analyze economic effects will help them to better understand historical events, as well as to make better personal decisions. Ask students to identify the best or the worst purchase they ever made. Then ask students to make a list of the positive and negative effects of their purchase. After students have completed their lists, ask students to consider the following questions: *What were the economic effects of your purchase? Who benefited from your purchase and how did they benefit? Were there any other effects—social, personal, or political—of your purchase? What, if any, were the unexpected effects of your purchase? How did these compare to the effects you had expected when you made the purchase? Would you make the same purchase again?*

Then, give students 15 minutes to write a paragraph about the best or worst purchase they ever made. Have volunteers read their responses to the class. Encourage discussion and feedback.

LS Verbal/Linguistic

Alternative Assessment Handbook, Rubric 37: Writing Assignment

Social Studies Skills

Analysis | Critical Thinking | **Economics** | Study

Analyzing Economic Effects

Understand the Skill

Most decisions people make or actions they take have several effects. Effects can be political, social, personal, or economic. For example, think about the effects of a decision you might make to get a summer job. A social effect might be that you make new friends at your job. A personal effect might be that you have less time for other activities that you enjoy. An economic effect would be that you have more money to spend.

Throughout history, many decisions have had economic effects—either intended or unintended. Even a decision made for a political, social, or environmental reason can have economic effects. Since economic circumstances have often been a factor in the rise and fall of civilizations, learning to analyze economic effects can be useful in your study of history.

Learn the Skill

Analyzing economic effects can help you to better understand and evaluate historical events. Follow these guidelines to understand economic effects of decisions and actions in history.

1. Determine who made the decision or took the action and decide what the goal was.
2. Consider whether the goal was to improve or change economic circumstances.
3. Sometimes an economic effect is not the main effect of a decision. Think about any unintended consequences of the decision or action. Consider whether any social or political effects are also economic effects.
4. Note that sometimes economic effects can be viewed either positively or negatively depending on whom they affect.

Practice and Apply the Skill

Review the information in the chapter about the Maya. Use that information to help you answer the following questions.

1. What was an economic effect of the Maya in lowland cities exporting forest goods and cotton? Was that effect expected or unexpected?
2. What might have been a positive economic effect of the Maya king's making lower-class Maya farm and work for him? What might have been a negative effect?
3. Do you think the development of the Maya calendar had any economic effects? Why or why not?
4. What economic effects did warfare have on Maya civilization? Were these effects expected or unexpected?

Social Studies Skills: Analyzing Economic Effects

At Level

Posters Promoting Responsible Economic Choices

Materials: art supplies, colored markers, poster board

1. Have students imagine that they have been asked to advise a Mayan king on whether he should use his resources to build a great pyramid, wage war, or construct terraces for farming. Have students create posters illustrating the economic, social, and political effects of each option.
2. Students' posters should include information and images for each option. Students might also include a paragraph explaining what they think is the best use of resources. Remind students that one or two large, emotionally charged images often are more powerful than many small images.
3. Display students' posters in public areas of the school. **LS Visual/Spatial**

Alternative Assessment Handbook, Rubrics 28: Posters

Answers

Practice and Apply the Skill

1. *possible answer—increased trade; expected* **2.** *The building of great temples and palaces could be a positive effect; mistreating workers could be a negative effect.* **3.** *Answers will vary, but students should clearly state and support their opinions.* **4.** *possible answer—may have ended Maya civilization; unexpected*

CHAPTER 16

Chapter Review

History's Impact

▶ **video series**

Review the video to answer the focus question:

Why do scholars today consider the Maya civilization to have been so advanced?

Visual Summary

Use the visual summary below to help you review the main ideas of the chapter.

QUICK FACTS

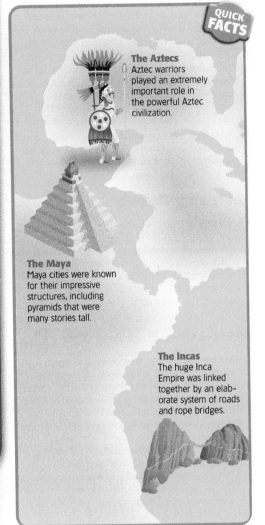

The Aztecs
Aztec warriors played an extremely important role in the powerful Aztec civilization.

The Maya
Maya cities were known for their impressive structures, including pyramids that were many stories tall.

The Incas
The huge Inca Empire was linked together by an elaborate system of roads and rope bridges.

Reviewing Vocabulary, Terms and People

For each statement below, write T if it is true and F if it is false. If the statement is false, replace the underlined term with one that would make the sentence a true statement.

1. The main crops of the Maya included **maize** and beans.
2. The **Quechua** came to the Americas to find land, gold, and converts to Catholicism.
3. The Aztecs mistook **Hernán Cortés** for the god Quetzalcoatl.
4. Maya priests studied the sun, moon, and stars from stone **observatories**.
5. **Francisco Pizarro** led a party of Spanish soldiers to Mexico in 1519.
6. **Atahualpa** tried to buy his freedom by having his people deliver great riches to the Spanish.
7. The official language of the Inca Empire was **Pachacuti**.
8. The Aztecs built raised roads called **masonry** to cross from Tenochtitlán to the mainland.
9. **Moctezuma II** was the Inca leader at the time of the Spanish conquest.
10. Many people in Mesoamerica died at the hands of the **conquistadors**.

Comprehension and Critical Thinking

SECTION 1 *(Pages 468–473)*

11. a. **Recall** Where did the Maya live, and when was their Classic Age?

 b. **Analyze** What was the connection between Maya religion and astronomy?

 c. **Elaborate** Why did Maya cities trade with each other? Why did they fight?

Answers

Visual Summary

Review and Inquiry Use the visual summary to review the chapter's main ideas. Ask students to explain the significance of each main idea. Then ask students to provide supporting details for each main idea.

Quick Facts Transparency: The Early Americas Visual Summary

Reviewing Vocabulary, Terms, and People

1. T
2. F; conquistadors
3. T
4. T
5. F; Hernán Cortés
6. T
7. F; Quechua
8. F; causeways
9. F; Atahualpa
10. T

Comprehension and Critical Thinking

11. a. northern Guatemala and the Yucatán Peninsula; AD 250 to 900

 b. Their priests studied the stars to plan the best times for religious festivals.

 c. to obtain goods that weren't available locally; for power and new farmland

Review & Assessment Resources

Review and Reinforce

- SE Chapter Review
- **CRF:** Chapter Review Activity
- Quick Facts Transparency: The Early Americas Visual Summary
- Spanish Chapter Summary Audio CD
- Online Chapter Summaries in Six Languages
- TOS Holt McDougal PuzzleView
- Quiz Game CD-ROM

Assess

- SE Standardized Test Practice
- PASS: Chapter Test
- Alternative Assessment Handbook
- TOS ExamView Assessment Suite, Chapter Test
- Differentiated Instruction Modified Worksheets and Tests CD-ROM: Chapter Test
- Online Assessment Program, in the Interactive Student Edition

Reteach/Intervene

- Guided Reading Workbook
- Differentiated Instruction Teacher Management System: Lesson Plans
- Differentiated Instruction Modified Material CD-ROM
- Interactive Skills Tutor CD-ROM

hmhsocialstudies.com
Chapter Resources

Answers

12. a. a magnificent city with 200,000 people, chinampas, huge temples, a busy market, and a grand palace; on an island in the middle of Lake Texcoco

b. War, tribute, and human sacrifices were important to Aztec power, and warriors were responsible for all these things.

c. possible answers—alliances, weapons and horses, geography, and disease. Students should give reasons for their answers.

13. a. Pachacuti—expanded the Inca Empire, rebuilt Cuzco, and established an official Inca religion; Atahualpa—fought Huáscar to claim the throne, was captured and killed by Francisco Pizarro

b. the empire's long, narrow shape, high Andes, coastal deserts, many different peoples and languages within the empire

c. possible answers—appreciated, because they knew the government would take care of them; resented, because they had no freedom

Social Studies Skills

14. For rubrics for this activity, see the ***Alternative Assessment Handbook*, Rubric 14: Group Activity and Rubric 11: Discussions.**

Using the Internet

15. Go to hmhsocialstudies.com to access a rubric for this activity.

Reading Skills

16. Cacao trees are evergreens.

17. In many parts of the world, access to clean water is still a problem.

18. Does that idea appeal to you?

SECTION 2 *(Pages 474–478)*

12. a. Describe What was Tenochtitlán like? Where was it located?

b. Make Inferences Why do you think warriors were such respected members of Aztec society?

c. Evaluate What factor do you think played the biggest role in the Aztecs' defeat? Defend your answer.

SECTION 3 *(Pages 479–483)*

13. a. Identify Name two Inca leaders and explain their roles in Inca history.

b. Draw Conclusions What geographic and cultural problems did the Incas overcome to rule their empire?

c. Predict Do you think most people in the Inca Empire appreciated or resented the *mita* system? Explain your answer.

Social Studies Skills

14. Analyzing Economic Effects Organize your class into groups. Choose one member of your group to represent the ruler of a Maya city. The rest of the group will be his or her advisers. As a group, decide on some policies for your city. For example, will you go to war, or will you trade? Will you build a new palace, or will you construct terraces for farming? Once you have determined policies for your city, share your ideas with representatives of other cities. As a class, discuss the economic effects of each policy you have chosen.

Using the Internet

15. Making Diagrams In this chapter you learned about the rise and fall of Maya civilization and of the Aztec and Inca empires. What you may not know is that the rise and fall of empires is a pattern that occurs again and again throughout history. Use your online textbook to learn more about this topic. Then create a diagram that shows factors that cause empires to form and factors that cause empires to fall apart.

hmhsocialstudies.com

Reading Skills

Analyzing Historical Information *In each numbered passage below, the first sentence expresses the main idea. One of the following sentences is irrelevant or nonessential to the main idea. Identify the irrelevant or nonessential sentence in each passage.*

16. Cacao beans had great value to the Maya. Cacao trees are evergreens. They were the source of chocolate, known as a favorite food of rulers and the gods. The Maya also used cacao beans as money.

17. Tenochtitlán was surrounded by water, but the water was undrinkable. As a result, the Aztecs built a stone aqueduct, or channel, to bring fresh water to the city. In many parts of the world, access to clean water is still a problem.

18. Most Inca children did not attend school. Does that idea appeal to you? Inca children learned skills by watching and helping their parents.

Reviewing Themes

19. Geography How did geography play a role in the Maya and Inca economies?

20. Science and Technology The people of Mesoamerica were skilled at civil engineering—that is, the building of public structures. Give examples from Maya, Aztec, and Inca civilization to support this statement.

Focus on Writing

21. Writing Your Article Your newspaper article will include information about your journey through the Americas. Choose at least one place of interest from the Maya civilization, the Aztec Empire, and the Inca Empire. For each site, use your notes to write several sentences to describe its location and how it looked at its height. Try to include details that would help a European reader imagine what life was like for the people who lived there. You will also want to explain to your readers what happened to these civilizations when the Spanish arrived.

Reviewing Themes

19. Maya—villages traded natural resources found locally throughout the region; Inca—long, narrow empire made it easier for government to control trade

20. possible answers: Maya—large cities, temples, canals, terraced farmland, observatories; Aztecs—causeways, *chinampas,* aqueduct; Incas—paved roads, rope bridges, terraced mountainsides

Focus on Writing

21. Rubric Students' articles should:

- describe ancient sites in the Americas.
- use vivid details to pique reader interest.
- be written clearly and concisely.

CHAPTER 16

Standardized Test Practice

DIRECTIONS: Read each question, and write the letter of the best response. Use the map below to answer question 1.

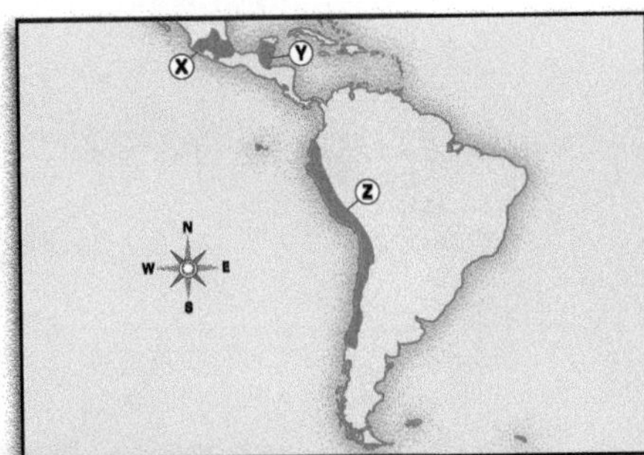

1 The Aztec and Inca empires are indicated on this map by

A X for the Inca and Y for the Aztec.
B Y for the Aztec and Z for the Inca.
C Y for the Inca and Z for the Aztec.
D X for the Aztec and Z for the Inca.

2 Maya, Aztec, and Inca societies were similar in many ways. Which of the following practices were common to all three civilizations?

A producing works of art and keeping written records
B engaging in trade and demanding tribute payments
C offering sacrifices to the gods and building stone temples
D practicing slavery and worshipping many gods

3 Farming was important to the Maya, the Aztecs, and the Incas. Which of the following is *not* a true statement?

A The Maya grew crops on *chinampas*.
B Farmers in all three civilizations grew maize, but only the Incas raised llamas.
C Maya farmers might not have been able to produce enough food for the entire population.
D Maya and Aztec priests decided the best times to plant and harvest.

4 The following factors all helped the Spanish to conquer the Aztecs and the Incas *except*

A European diseases.
B a greater number of soldiers.
C superior weapons.
D existing problems within the empires.

5 Which statement *best* describes the social structure in Maya, Aztec, and Inca civilizations?

A The ruler held the highest position in society, and slaves held the lowest.
B The Aztecs had a simpler class structure than the Maya or the Incas.
C Social divisions were very important to the Maya and the Aztecs, but power and wealth were equally distributed in the Inca Empire.
D Social class helped shape daily life, with the upper class enjoying special privileges made possible by the labor of the common people.

Connecting with Past Learnings

6 In this chapter you read that Maya civilization during the Classic Age included independent city-states. What other civilization that you have studied was organized into city-states?

A ancient Greece
B ancient Persia
C Han China
D the Roman Empire

7 The Maya and the Incas both believed their rulers were related to the gods. Which ancient people believed the same thing?

A Jews
B Indians
C Phoenicians
D Egyptians

Answers

Standardized Test Practice

1. D
Break Down the Question Refer students who miss the question to the maps in Sections 2 and 3. The area marked Y on the map was the area controlled by the Maya.

2. C
Break Down the Question Point out that every other answer has one true and one false statement. The Inca kept no written records and did not practice slavery, and the Aztecs demanded tribute.

3. A
Break Down the Question Remind students that italicized words in test questions often significantly affect the question's meaning.

4. B
Break Down the Question Point out that all but one of the answers was a factor in the defeat of the Aztecs. There were fewer Spanish soldiers, though, than Aztec soldiers.

5. D
Break Down the Question This question requires students to recall factual information. Refer students who miss the question to coverage of daily life in Sections 1, 2, and 3.

6. A
Break Down the Question This question connects to information in Chapter 8, Section 1.

7. D
Break Down the Question This question connects to information in Chapter 4, Section 2.

Intervention Resources

Reproducible

- Guided Reading Workbook
- Differentiated Instruction Teacher Management System: Lesson Plans

Technology

- Quick Facts Transparency The Early Americas Visual Summary
- Differentiated Instruction Modified Material CD-ROM
- Interactive Skills Tutor CD-ROM

Tips for Test Taking

I'm Stuck! If students come across a question that stumps them, tell them not to get frustrated or worried. Remind them to master the question to make sure they understand what is being asked. Then instruct students to go through the list of test-taking strategies they have learned. If still stuck, they should practice the 50/50 strategy and make an educated guess.

Multimedia Classroom

The **HISTORY™ Multimedia Classroom** is a set of exciting new social studies teaching tools featuring award-winning program content. These comprehensive lesson plans, correlated to individual state and national curriculum standards, are easy to use for both teachers and students.

Each lesson contains the following:

- Short video segments that bring history topics to life
- Maps and visual materials
- Discussion and review questions
- Easily printable primary source documents
- Classroom activities and Internet-based activity links

The Multimedia Classroom has been specially designed to be versatile and easily adaptable to existing courses, lesson plans, and syllabi. Every lesson is designed to offer maximum flexibility. Teachers can select entire plans or only the elements they need, allowing them to individually tailor each lesson. Each multimedia lesson is available in CD-ROM format and is accompanied by full-length award-winning programs on DVD from HISTORY™.

For more information or to purchase go to hmhsocialstudies.com

Because some of these lessons may contain video material of a sensitive nature, we recommend that teachers and parents review these materials in their entirety before showing them to students.

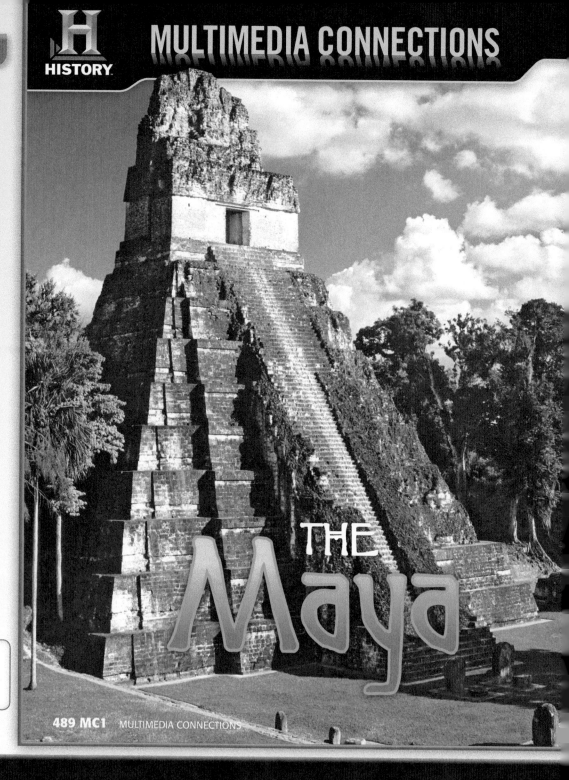

MULTIMEDIA CONNECTIONS

HISTORY

THE Maya

489 MC1 MULTIMEDIA CONNECTIONS

The Maya

Resources

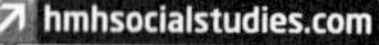

The following resources come with printable introductions, comprehension and critical thinking questions, transcripts, and vocabulary support.

Full Length DVD

The Maya (50 minutes)

Video Clips

- Who Were the Maya People? (1:43)
- The Beginnings of Maya Life (2:29)
- Finding the City of Palenque (2:37)
- The Builders of Palenque (2:38)
- Destroying the Maya's Past (1:47)
- The Mystery in the Temple (3:59)
- Inside King Pakal's Tomb (3:04)
- Tomb of an Unknown Woman (6:12)
- A Civilization Abandoned (3:29)
- Descendants of the Maya (2:09)

Primary Sources

- The Quiche Popol Vuh
- Chumayel Chilam Balam (i)
- Chumayel Chilam Balam (ii)
- Burial Remains from Tikal

CLICK THROUGH
INTERACTIVITIES
hmhsocialstudies.com

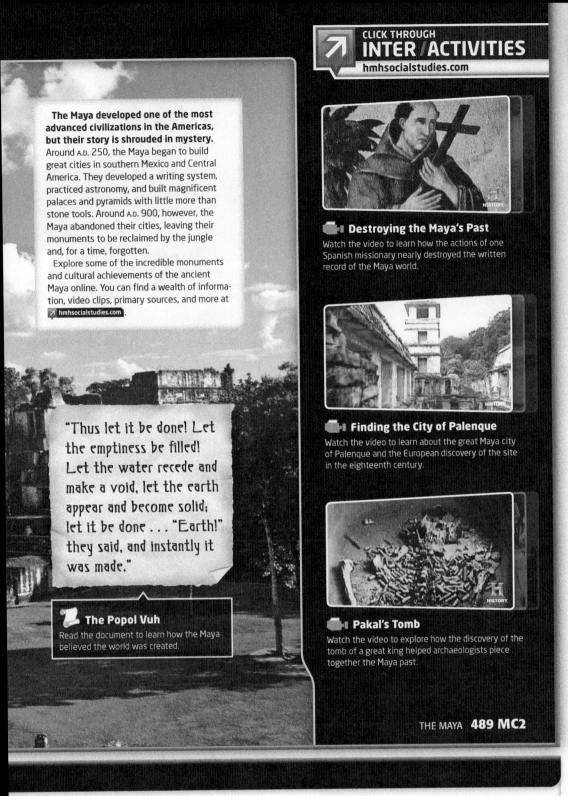

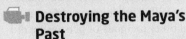

The Maya developed one of the most advanced civilizations in the Americas, but their story is shrouded in mystery. Around A.D. 250, the Maya began to build great cities in southern Mexico and Central America. They developed a writing system, practiced astronomy, and built magnificent palaces and pyramids with little more than stone tools. Around A.D. 900, however, the Maya abandoned their cities, leaving their monuments to be reclaimed by the jungle and, for a time, forgotten.

Explore some of the incredible monuments and cultural achievements of the ancient Maya online. You can find a wealth of information, video clips, primary sources, and more at hmhsocialstudies.com.

"Thus let it be done! Let the emptiness be filled! Let the water recede and make a void, let the earth appear and become solid; let it be done . . . "Earth!" they said, and instantly it was made."

The Popol Vuh
Read the document to learn how the Maya believed the world was created.

Destroying the Maya's Past
Watch the video to learn how the actions of one Spanish missionary nearly destroyed the written record of the Maya world.

Finding the City of Palenque
Watch the video to learn about the great Maya city of Palenque and the European discovery of the site in the eighteenth century.

Pakal's Tomb
Watch the video to explore how the discovery of the tomb of a great king helped archaeologists piece together the Maya past.

THE MAYA 489 MC2

Maps
- Palenque Site Plan

Activities
- At Home in the Rainforest
- Centers of the Maya World
- Opposite Sides of the Globe
- The Measurement of Time

General Review Questions

General Discussion Questions

Web Links

Bibliography

Lesson Preview

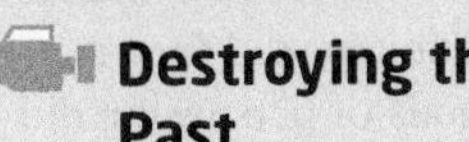

The Popol Vuh

The Popol Vuh tells the Maya creation story. In 1702, the Spanish priest Francisco Ximenez discovered the most complete Popol Vuh manuscript. The text is an invaluable resource for historians and linguists.

Destroying the Maya's Past

The Maya had a sophisticated writing system. However, the language of the Maya fell victim to colonizing forces. Spanish missionaries attempted to put an end to all non-Christian practices of the Maya by destroying all their written documents. Only four Maya manuscripts survived and they have proved invaluable to scholars.

Finding the City of Palenque

The Maya civilization flourished for more than 600 years in the jungles of what are now Mexico, Guatemala, Honduras, Belize, and El Salvador. Yet, at some point around the 10th century, the Maya abandoned their cities. It was not until the late 18th century that Palenque, one of the Maya's most important cities, was rediscovered by archaeologists.

Pakal's Tomb

At Palenque, archaeologist Alberto Ruz Lhuillier and his team discovered an elaborately decorated tomb. At first, they could only guess that the figure buried there was of great importance. Later, they discovered that the figure was Pakal, one of the Maya's greatest kings.

Preteach

Bellringer

Motivate Have students think of a time when they were successful in persuading someone to agree with something or do something (for example, in persuading their parents to let them stay up past their bedtime). Ask students how they managed to persuade the other person. What arguments did they use? What other methods of persuasion did they use? Explain that presenting logical, sound, and convincing reasons and evidence is the most effective method of persuasion—and a highly useful skill in life. Tell students that they will hone their persuasive skills in this workshop.

Direct Teach

Stating Your Opinion

Take a Stand Some students may not have a strong opinion about the assigned topic. Suggest that these students ask themselves what might have happened if things had been different—if the Spanish had never arrived in Peru or if the Aztecs had defeated Cortés and his army. Tell students to list the hypothetical consequences or effects. Next, have students list the effects of each event as it actually happened. Then have students examine their lists to determine whether the arrival of the Spanish was the only cause of the fall of the two empires. Have students consider whether other factors might have brought about the end of the civilizations.

Persuasion and Historical Issues

Assignment

Write an essay stating your opinion on this topic or another historical topic of your choice: All great empires are likely to end in the same way the Maya and Aztec empires did.

TIP **Fact vs. Opinion** A fact is a statement that can be proved true. Facts include
- measurements
- dates
- locations
- definitions

An opinion is a statement of a personal belief. Opinions often include judgmental words and phrases such as *better, should,* and *think.*

The study of history raises questions, or issues, that can be argued from both sides. Effective persuasive writing supports a point of view with evidence.

1. Prewrite

Taking a Position

Do you think all great empires will follow the same course as the Maya and Aztecs, or could an empire take a different course? Write a sentence that states your position, or opinion about, this topic or another topic.

Supporting Your Position

To convince your audience to agree with your position, you will need reasons and evidence. **Reasons** tell *why* a writer has a particular point of view. **Evidence** backs up, or helps prove, the reasons. Evidence includes facts, examples, and opinions of experts, like historians. You can find this evidence in this textbook or other books recommended by your teacher.

Organizing Reasons and Evidence

Try to present your reasons and evidence in order of importance, so that you can end with your most convincing points. Use transitions such as *mainly, last,* and *most important* to emphasize ideas.

2. Write

This framework can help you state your position clearly and present convincing reasons and evidence.

A Writer's Framework

Introduction	Body	Conclusion
■ Introduce the topic by using a surprising fact, quotation, or comparison to get your reader's attention. ■ Identify at least two differing positions on this topic. ■ State your own position on the topic.	■ Present at least two reasons to support your position. ■ Support each reason with evidence (facts, examples, expert opinions). ■ Organize your reasons and evidence in order of importance with your most convincing reason last.	■ Restate your position. ■ Summarize your supporting reasons and evidence. ■ Project your position into history by using it to predict the course of current and future events.

Differentiating Instruction

Special Needs Learners — Below Level

1. Some students may benefit from studying a spatial representation of the relationship among a position statement, reasons, and evidence.
2. Draw the pyramid at right for students to see. Explain how a position statement is supported by reasons, which are in turn supported by evidence. Have students copy the pyramid and use it to organize their ideas.
LS Visual/Spatial

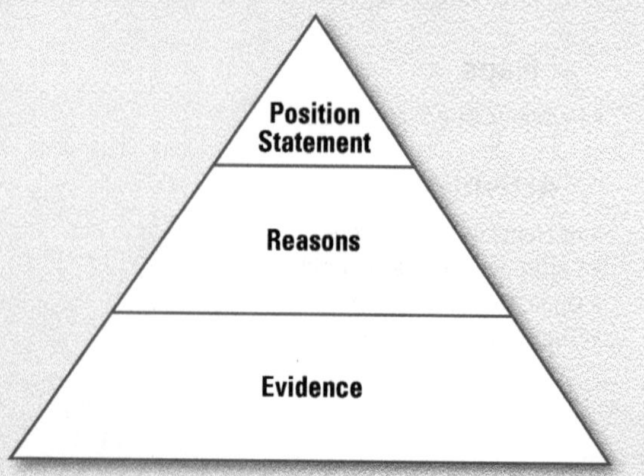

3. Evaluate and Revise

Evaluating

Use the following questions to evaluate your draft and find ways to make your paper more convincing.

Evaluation Questions for a Persuasive Essay

- Does your introduction include an opinion statement that clearly states your position?
- Have you given at least two reasons to support your position?
- Do you provide convincing evidence to back up your reasons?
- Are your reasons and evidence organized by order of importance, ending with the most important?
- Does your conclusion restate your position and summarize your reasons and evidence? Do you apply your opinion to future history?

TIP Using a Computer to Check Spelling in History Papers Whenever you can, use a spell-checker program to help you catch careless errors. However, keep in mind that it will not solve all your spelling problems.

- It will not catch misspellings that correctly spell other words, such as *their, they're,* and *there,* or *an* instead of *and.*
- It will highlight but not give the preferred spelling for many proper names.
- It cannot be relied upon for correct capitalization.

Revising

Strengthen your argument with loaded words. Loaded words are words with strong positive or negative connotations.

- Positive—leader
- Negative—tyrant, despot
- Neutral—ruler, emperor

Loaded words can add powerful emotional appeals to your reader's feelings and help convince them to agree with your opinion.

4. Proofread and Publish

Proofreading

Keep the following guidelines in mind as you reread your paper.

- Wherever you have added, deleted, or changed anything, make sure your revision fits in smoothly and does not introduce any errors.
- Double-check names, dates, and other factual information.

Publishing

Team up with one of your classmates who has taken the same position you have. Combine your evidence to create the most powerful argument you can. Challenge a team that has taken an opposing view to a debate. Ask the rest of the class for feedback: Which argument was more convincing? What were the strengths and weaknesses of each position?

Practice and Apply

Use the steps and strategies outlined in this workshop to write a persuasive composition.

Reteach

Evaluating

Map Structure On their drafts, have students make a rectangle around their opinion statement. It should appear in the first paragraph. Then have students circle each supporting reason. The paper should provide one reason at or near the beginning of each paragraph and at least three reasons. Finally, have students underline each piece of evidence. The paper should provide at least two pieces of evidence for each reason. Students should check to make sure that each piece of evidence supports the reason that is the topic of that paragraph. Then have students draw a wavy line under any sentence containing support for a different point of view than the position stated in the paper. Students should cut any support that does not fit.

MISCONCEPTION ALERT

More is Not Always Better

Students may try to include as many reasons as possible to support their positions, including weak reasons. Explain to students that a weak reason or piece of evidence can actually damage the overall strength of an argument by tainting the rest of it. Remind students to include only strong reasons and evidence in their papers.

Practice & Apply

Rubric

Students' persuasive essays should

- provide a clear position statement.
- include at least three reasons to support the position.
- provide supporting evidence for each reason.
- provide one paragraph for each reason and its evidence.
- present the reasons in order of importance.
- end with a summary and a restatement of the position.
- use correct grammar, punctuation, spelling, and capitalization.

English-Language Learners

Below Level **Standard English Mastery**

1. Have English learners demonstrate to the class or to a small group how the passive and active voices are formed in their primary languages.
2. Then have students practice forming the active voice. Write the sentences at right for students to see. Have students change each sentence from the passive to the active voice. Help English learners to understand how to construct the active voice in English.

LS Verbal/Linguistic

- The conquistadors in Peru were led by Francisco Pizarro.
- Many cities were abandoned by the Maya.
- Thousands of Aztec citizens were killed by disease.
- The city of Tenochtitlán was conquered by Hernán Cortés.
- The Maya, Aztec, and Inca civilizations were brought to an end by a combination of many factors.

Unit Preview

Introduce the Unit

Share the information in the chapter overviews with students.

Chapter 17 The period after the collapse of the Roman Empire—from about 500 to about 1500—is called the Middle Ages. During this period, barbarian tribes created many small kingdoms in Europe. As Christianity slowly spread north, invaders continued to threaten much of Europe during the 700s and 800s.

Chapter 18 During the later Middle Ages, the Christian Church was central to life and politics in Europe. Kings and popes dominated society, and Christians crusaded against Muslims. Europe's political, social, and economic systems underwent great changes.

Chapter 19 The Renaissance began in Italy in the 1300s and later spread to northern Europe. Interest in Greek and Roman culture revived, and a new emphasis was placed on people as individuals. Renaissance ideas led religious reformers to break away from the Catholic Church. This movement is called the Reformation, and its followers became known as Protestants.

Chapter 20 During the Scientific Revolution, brilliant individuals laid the foundations for modern science. They paved the way for the Age of Exploration in the late 1400s and 1500s. Plants, animals, and ideas were traded between the Old World and the New World, where a number of diverse cultures had developed.

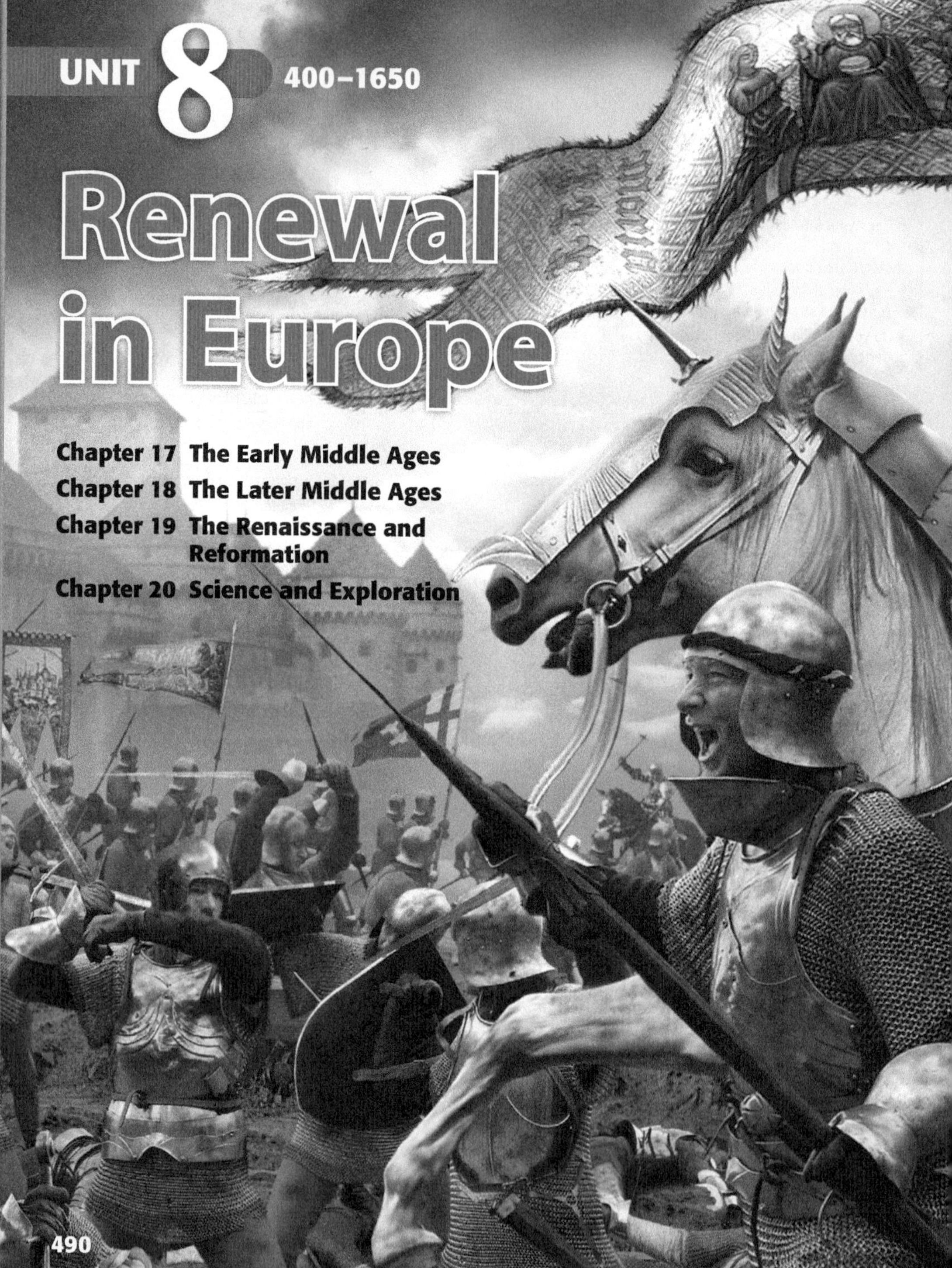

UNIT 8 400–1650
Renewal in Europe
Chapter 17 The Early Middle Ages
Chapter 18 The Later Middle Ages
Chapter 19 The Renaissance and Reformation
Chapter 20 Science and Exploration
490

Unit Resources

Planning

- Differentiated Instruction Teacher Management System: Unit Instructional Benchmarking Guides
- TOS Calendar Planner
- Power Presentations with Media Gallery
- A Teacher's Guide to Religion in the Public Schools

Differentiating Instruction

- Differentiated Instruction Teacher Management System: Lesson Plans for Differentiated Instruction

Enrichment

- **CRF 17:** Interdisciplinary Project
- **CRF 18:** Economics and History Activity: The Economic Impact of the Crusades
- **CRF 18:** Interdisciplinary Project
- **CRF 19:** Economics and History Activity: Funding the State: Progressive Taxes
- **CRF 19:** Interdisciplinary Project
- **CRF 20:** Interdisciplinary Project: Explorers: Brain Teasers
- Civic Participation Activities
- Primary Source Library CD-ROM

Assessment

- Progress Assessment System Solution: Unit Test
- TOS ExamView Assessment Suite: Unit Test
- Online Assessment Program, in the Interactive Student Edition
- Alternative Assessment Handbook

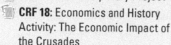

The **Differentiated Instruction Teacher Management System** provides a planning and instructional benchmarking guide for this unit.

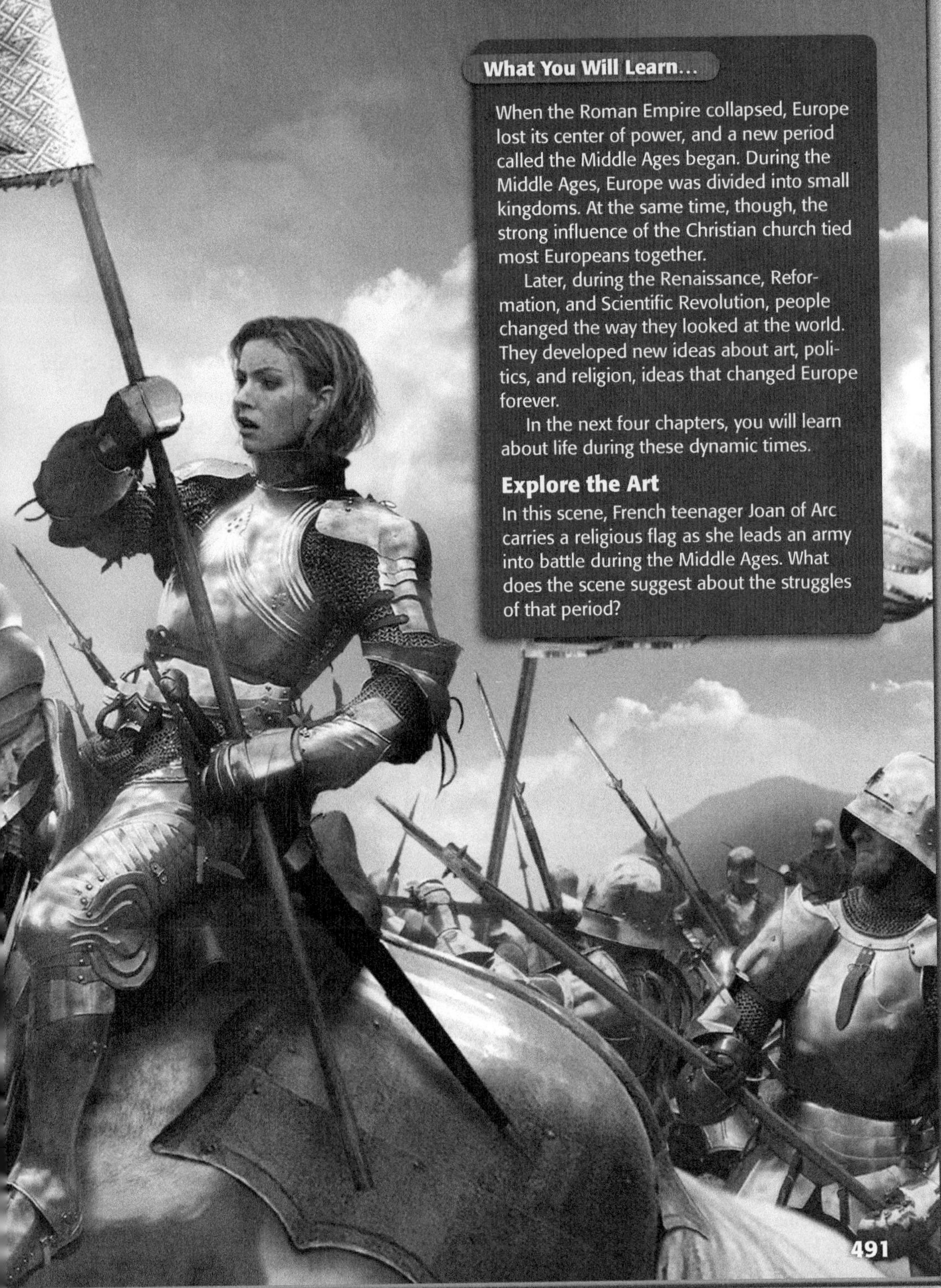

What You Will Learn...

When the Roman Empire collapsed, Europe lost its center of power, and a new period called the Middle Ages began. During the Middle Ages, Europe was divided into small kingdoms. At the same time, though, the strong influence of the Christian church tied most Europeans together.

Later, during the Renaissance, Reformation, and Scientific Revolution, people changed the way they looked at the world. They developed new ideas about art, politics, and religion, ideas that changed Europe forever.

In the next four chapters, you will learn about life during these dynamic times.

Explore the Art

In this scene, French teenager Joan of Arc carries a religious flag as she leads an army into battle during the Middle Ages. What does the scene suggest about the struggles of that period?

491

Unit Preview

Connect to the Unit

Activity Exploring the Middle Ages Ask students what they know about the Middle Ages based on books, television, movies, the Internet, and other sources. Have students discuss what they think life was like for knights, what it was like to live in a castle, and so on. Write students' responses for the class to see. Then have students make a list of five questions about the Middle Ages to which they would like to know the answers. At the end of the unit, have students review their initial list. How accurate were their ideas about the Middle Ages? Then have students discuss their questions and the answers. If students did not find the answer to a question, encourage them to conduct research to learn the answer.
LS Verbal/Linguistic

Explore the Art

Joan of Arc was a French peasant girl. When English forces invaded her town, she wanted to help defend it. Joan believed that God called her to drive the English from France. She asked many times to help fight, and at last was given a group of soldiers to lead. Joan of Arc's actions rallied the French troops. Although she was killed, the French were victorious.

About the Illustration

This illustration is an artist's conception based on available sources. However, historians are uncertain exactly what this scene looked like.

Democracy and Civic Education

At Level

Justice: Promoting Religious Tolerance

Background Explain that during the Middle Ages, Christians and Muslims fought a series of wars over control of holy sites, such as the region of Palestine. These wars led to increased tensions and distrust among Christians, Jews, and Muslims that still influences relations today.

1. Lead a discussion on the importance of tolerance and respect for other people's differences, and in particular for different religious beliefs and practices.
2. Ask students to identify examples of how a lack of tolerance can negatively affect society. Encourage student discussion.
3. Then have each student create a political cartoon or a poster promoting religious tolerance. Display students' work around the classroom. **LS Verbal/Linguistic, Visual/Spatial**

Alternative Assessment Handbook, Rubrics 27: Political Cartoons; and 28: Posters

Civic Participation Activities

Answers

Explore the Art *that soldiers wore armor, wielded swords and lances, sometimes fought on horseback, and fought in hand-to-hand combat*

Chapter 17 Planning Guide

The Early Middle Ages

Overview	Instructional Resources	
CHAPTER 17 **Essential Question:** How did life in Europe change after the fall of Rome? **Focus on the Essential Question Podcast**	TOS **Differentiated Instruction Teacher Management System:** • Instructional Benchmarking Guides • Lesson Plans for Differentiated Instruction **Guided Reading Workbook** **Chapter Resource File:** • Chapter Review Activity • Focus on Writing Activity: A Job Advertisement • Social Studies Skills Activity: Interpreting Diagrams	TOS **Calendar Planner** **Power Presentations with Media Gallery** **Differentiated Instruction Modified Worksheets and Tests CD-ROM** **Interactive Skills Tutor CD-ROM** **Student Edition on Audio CD Program** **The World's Music Audio Program**
Section 1: **Geography of Europe** **The Big Idea:** Because Europe has many types of landforms and climates, different ways of life have developed there.	TOS **Differentiated Instruction Teacher Management System:** Section 1 Lesson Plan **Guided Reading Workbook:** Section 1 **Chapter Resource File:** • Vocabulary Builder Activity, Section 1	**Daily Bellringer Transparency:** Section 1 **Map Transparency:** Europe: Physical
Section 2: **Europe After the Fall of Rome** **The Big Idea:** Despite the efforts of Christians to maintain order, Europe was a dangerous place after the fall of Rome.	TOS **Differentiated Instruction Teacher Management System:** Section 2 Lesson Plan **Guided Reading Workbook:** Section 2 **Chapter Resource File:** • Vocabulary Builder Activity, Section 2 • Biography Activity: Leif Eriksson • History and Geography Activity: Invasions of Europe, 800–1000	**Daily Bellringer Transparency:** Section 2 **Map Transparency:** The Spread of Christianity **Map Transparency:** Charlemagne's Empire **Map Transparency:** Invasions of Europe, AD 800–1000 **Internet Activity:** Charlemagne Biography
Section 3: **Feudalism and Manor Life** **The Big Idea:** A complex web of duties and obligations governed relationships between people in the Middle Ages.	TOS **Differentiated Instruction Teacher Management System:** Section 3 Lesson Plan **Guided Reading Workbook:** Section 3 **Chapter Resource File:** • Vocabulary Builder Activity, Section 3 • Biography Activity: Eleanor of Aquitaine • Primary Source Activity: Feudal Capitularies	**Daily Bellringer Transparency:** Section 3 **Quick Facts Transparency:** Feudal Society **Internet Activity:** Medieval Fashion Show **Animated History:** Europe, AD 1000
Section 4: **Feudal Societies** **The Big Idea:** Although the feudal systems of Europe and Japan were similar, their cultures were very different.	TOS **Differentiated Instruction Teacher Management System:** Section 4 Lesson Plan **Guided Reading Workbook:** Section 4 **Chapter Resource File:** • Vocabulary Builder Activity, Section 4	**Daily Bellringer Transparency:** Section 4 **Quick Facts Transparency:** Comparing and Contrasting Europe and Japan

Chart Key:

SE Student Edition  Presentation Resource 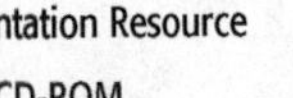  MP3 Audio

TOS Teacher One Stop  DVD/CD-ROM HISTORY™

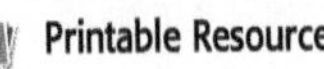 Printable Resource

Program Resources available on TOS and @  hmhsocialstudies.com

Review, Assessment, Intervention

 **Quick Facts Transparency:** The Early Middle Ages Visual Summary

 **Spanish Chapter Summaries Audio CD Program**

 **Quiz Game CD-ROM**

 **Progress Assessment Support System (PASS):** Chapter Test

 **Differentiated Instruction Modified Worksheets and Tests CD-ROM:** Modified Chapter Test

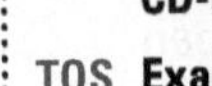 TOS **ExamView® Assessment Suite (English/Spanish)**

 **Holt Online Assessment Program,** in the Interactive Student Edition

 **PASS:** Section 1 Quiz

 **Online Quiz:** Section 1

 **Alternative Assessment Handbook**

 **PASS:** Section 2 Quiz

 **Online Quiz:** Section 2

 **Alternative Assessment Handbook**

 **PASS:** Section 3 Quiz

 **Online Quiz:** Section 3

 **Alternative Assessment Handbook**

 **PASS:** Section 4 Quiz

 **Online Quiz:** Section 4

 **Alternative Assessment Handbook**

Supporting Resources

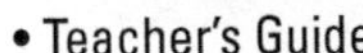

- Multimedia Classroom Global History Series
- Global History Teacher's Guide

Maps Globes Graphs Level F

- Student Workbook
- Teacher's Guide

Social Studies Trade Library Collections

- Premier Secondary World History Trade Collection

History's Impact

World History Video Program

- **The Legacy of the Feudal System in Europe**

For more information or to purchase go to hmhsocialstudies.com

Power Presentations with Media Gallery

Power Presentations with Media Gallery are visual presentations of each chapter's main ideas. Presentations can be customized by including Quick Facts charts, images from the text, and video clips.

Differentiating Instruction

How do I address the needs of varied learners?

The Target Resource acts as your primary strategy for differentiated instruction.

ENGLISH-LANGUAGE LEARNERS & STRUGGLING READERS

Interactive Skills Tutor CD-ROM

The interactive Skills tutor CD-ROM contains lessons that provide additional practice for 20 different critical thinking skills.

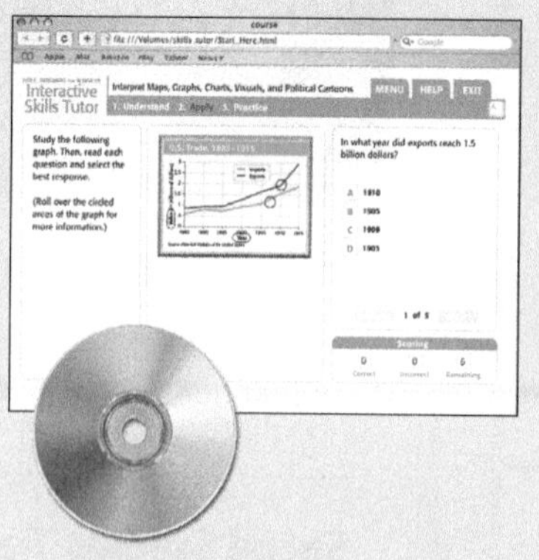

Additional Resources

Diffferentiated Instruction Teacher Management System: Lesson Plans for Differentiated Instruction

Chapter Resource File:
- Vocabulary Builder Activities
- Social Studies Skills Activity: Interpreting Diagrams

Quick Facts Transparencies:
- Comparing and Contrasting Europe and Japan
- Feudal Society

Student Edition on Audio CD Program

Spanish/English Guided Reading Workbook

SPECIAL NEEDS LEARNERS

Differentiated Instruction Modified Worksheets and Tests CD-ROM

- Vocabulary Flash Cards
- Vocabulary Builder Activities
- Chapter Review Activity
- Chapter Test

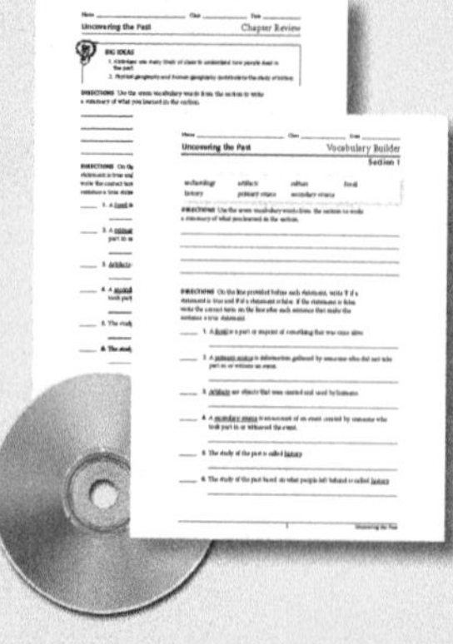

Additional Resources

Differentiated Instruction Teacher Management System: Lesson Plans for Differentiated Instruction

Guided Reading Workbook

Chapter Resource File: Social Studies Skills Activity: Interpreting Diagrams

Student Edition on Audio CD Program

Interactive Skills Tutor CD-ROM

ADVANCED/GIFTED-AND-TALENTED STUDENTS

Primary Source Library CD-ROM for World History

The Library contains longer versions of quotations in the text, extra sources, and images. Included are point-of-view articles, journals, diaries, historical fiction, and political documents.

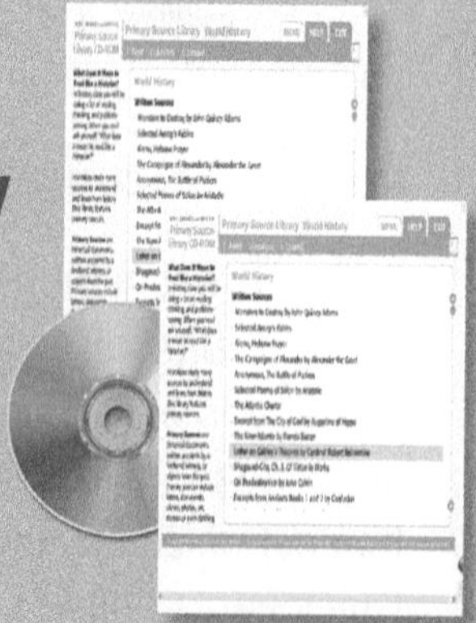

Additional Resources

Differentiated Instruction Teacher Management System: Lesson Plans for Differentiated Instruction

Chapter Resource File:
- Focus on Writing Activity: A Job Advertisement

Document-Based Questions Activities

Differentiated Activities in the Teacher's Edition

- Studying a Map of Europe, p. 497
- Writing a Newspaper Headline, p. 503

Teacher One Stop™

How can I manage the lesson plans and support materials for differentiated instruction?

With the Teacher One Stop, you can easily organize and print lesson plans, planning guides, and instructional materials for all learners. The Teacher One Stop includes the following materials to help you differentiate instruction:

- **Interactive Teacher's Edition**
- **Calendar Planner and pacing guides**
- **Editable lesson plans**
- **All reproducible ancillaries in Adobe Acrobat (PDF) format**
- **ExamView Assessment Suite (English & Spanish)**
- **Transparency and video previews**

Differentiated Activities in the Teacher's Edition

- Writing a Classified Advertisement, p. 507
- Feudal Societies, p. 514

Interactive Student Edition

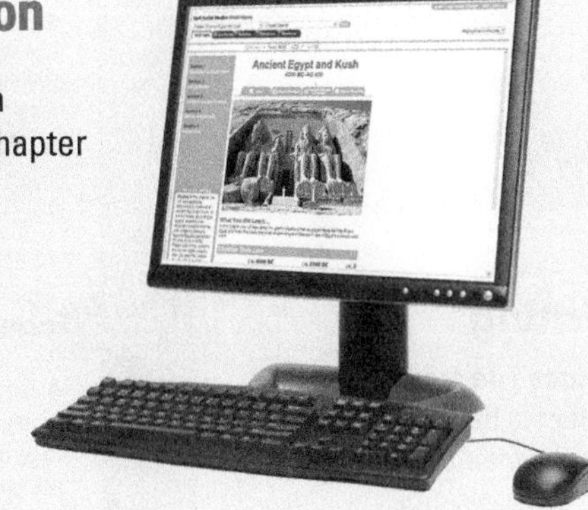

Complete online student edition with interactive multimedia support for chapter content assessment and reporting

- Interactive Maps and Notebook
- Graphic Organizers
- Standardized Test Prep
- Online Homework Practice and Research Activities
- Current Events
- Chapter-based Internet Activities
- Animated History Activities
- and more!

Differentiated Activities in the Teacher's Edition

- Regional Newspapers, p. 498
- Rewriting *The Song of Roland*, p. 513

Chapter Preview

Essential Question

Introduce the Essential Question

- Explain that after the Roman Empire fell, Europe became an unstable and violent place.
- Tell students that feudalism emerged as a new social order of the Middle Ages.
- Point out that Japan, like Europe, also developed a feudal society.

Focus on Writing

The **Chapter Resource File** provides a Focus on Writing worksheet to help students organize and describe their advertisements.

CRF: Focus on Writing: A Job Advertisement

Key to Differentiating Instruction

Below Level

Basic-level activities designed for all students encountering new material

At Level

Intermediate-level activities designed for average students

Above Level

Challenging activities designed for honors and gifted and talented students

Standard English Mastery

Activities designed to improve standard English usage

LS Learning Styles

CHAPTER 17 400–1200

The Early Middle Ages

Essential Question How did life in Europe change after the fall of Rome?

South Carolina Performance Standards

6-5.1 Explain feudalism and its relationship to the development of European monarchies and nation-states, including feudal relationships, the daily lives of peasants and serfs, and the economy under the manorial system; **6-5.4** Explain the role and influence of the Roman Catholic Church in medieval Europe.

Literacy Skills for Social Studies

- Analyze evidence, arguments, claims, and beliefs.
- Select or design appropriate forms of social studies resources to organize and evaluate social studies information.
- Interpret Earth's physical and human systems by using maps, mental maps, geographic models, and other social studies resources.
- Compare the locations of places, the conditions at places, and the connections between places.
- Explain how political, social, and economic institutions are similar or different across time and/or throughout the world.

Partnership for the 21st Century Skills

Cite specific textual evidence to support the analysis of primary and secondary sources.

Focus on Writing

A Job Advertisement In the 900s nobles needed knights, or warriors, to help protect their property. As you read this chapter, imagine what it would be like to be one of those nobles. Then you will write a job ad seeking knights to help you defend your land.

CHAPTER EVENTS

c. 430 Saint Patrick brings Christianity to Ireland.

400

WORLD EVENTS

476 Rome falls.

Introduce the Chapter — At Level

Samurai and Knights

1. Lead the class in a quick review of samurai society in medieval Japan. Ask students if they can think of a similar kind of system that existed in Europe at about the same time. (Provide hints if necessary to help students think of knights and knighthood.) What do students know of the society in which knighthood flourished? Write students' responses for the class to see.
2. Explain to students that in this chapter they will learn about European knighthood and the period during which it flourished. Have students predict how European knighthood might be similar to and different from the samurai system of Japan. Write students' predictions for the class to see.
3. Have students make a copy of their predictions. At the end of the chapter, have students review their lists to see how accurate they were. **LS Logical/Mathematical**

This photo shows Caernarfon Castle in Wales. Built in the late 1200s, the castle showed the king's power and provided defense from invasions.

600 — 800 — 1000 — 1200

700s–800s The Vikings raid Europe.

800 Charlemagne is crowned emperor of much of Europe.

1066 Feudalism is introduced into Britain.

613 Muhammad begins teaching people about Islam.

794 Heian becomes the capital of Japan.

1000s The Chinese invent gunpowder.

1076 Ghana falls to Muslim invaders.

THE EARLY MIDDLE AGES 493

• Chapter Preview •

Explore the Picture

Caernarfon Castle The English king Edward I had Caernarfon Castle, pictured at left, built after his conquest of Wales in the 1280s. Located in North Wales, the castle sits at the mouth of the Seiont River. The use of different types of stones in building the castle create the unusual colored bands on the walls.

Analyzing Visuals What clues does the photograph give about architecture during this period? *possible answers—The castle's thick, tall walls might indicate that people were concerned about protection and defense.*

hmhsocialstudies.com
Teacher Resources

Explore the Time Line

1. In what year did Saint Patrick take Christianity to Ireland? *c. 430*
2. When was feudalism introduced into Britain? *1066*
3. What event occurred in the year 800? *Charlemagne was crowned emperor of much of Europe.*
4. What happened in Japan shortly before this event? *Heian became the capital.*

Info to Know

A New Roman Empire The Roman Empire in Western Europe fell in 476, in part as a result of Germanic invasions. More than 300 years later, the leader of another Germanic tribe, the Franks, became a Roman emperor. Named Charlemagne, he had conquered much of the old Roman Empire. For that reason, on Christmas Day in 800, Pope Leo III crowned Charlemagne Emperor of the Romans.

Reading Social Studies

Understanding Themes

Explain to students that in this chapter, they will learn about Europe in the Middle Ages. Point out to students that the key themes of this chapter are religion, and society and culture. Have students write three to four questions for each theme that will add to their knowledge about Europe. For example, *what role did religion play in Europe in the Middle Ages?* Encourage students to look for answers to their questions as they read the chapter.

Evaluating Sources

Focus on Reading Fairy tales and movies have provided some information about medieval life for many children. Remind students that these are not always accurate sources of historical information. Ask students to name books, television programs, movies, or video games that have given them a mental picture of what European medieval life was like. Explain that, for a historian, it is important to rely only on the most accurate sources of information available. Write the headings, *Primary* and *Secondary* on the board. Ask students to name resources that would be good primary and secondary sources of information about the Middle Ages. Have volunteers record students' suggestions on the board.

Reading Social Studies

Economics | Geography | Politics | **Religion** | **Society and Culture** | Science and Technology

Focus on Themes In this chapter you will read about Europe during the early Middle Ages. You will learn how the geography of the land affected growth and trade and see how the Christian **religion** spread throughout northern Europe during this time. You will learn about the invaders who tried to conquer the land and see how the feudal system developed. As you read, you will understand how this feudal system shaped the entire **society and culture** of the people.

Evaluating Sources

Focus on Reading As you have already learned, historians study both primary and secondary sources to learn about the past. By studying both types, they can get a better picture of what life was like.

Assessing Primary and Secondary Sources However, not all sources are accurate or reliable. You need to be careful when you read historical sources. Checklists like the ones below can help you judge which sources are reliable and worth using in your research.

Checklist for Primary Sources

- ✔ Who is the author? Does he or she seem trustworthy?
- ✔ Was the author actually present for the event described in the source?
- ✔ How soon after the event occurred was the source written?
- ✔ Can the information in the source be verified in other primary or secondary sources?

Historians in the past were not always careful about what they put in their books. Some included rumors, gossip, or hearsay.

The more time that passed between the event and the writing, the greater the chance of errors or distortion in the description.

Not everyone who writes about history is a good historian. Try to use sources by qualified writers.

Good historians will always tell you where they got their information. If information isn't documented, you can't always trust that it is true or accurate.

Checklist for Secondary Sources

- ✔ Who is the author? What are his or her credentials, or qualifications for writing?
- ✔ Where did the author get his or her information?
- ✔ Is the information in the source properly documented?
- ✔ Has the author drawn valid conclusions from his or her sources?

Reading and Skills Resources

Reading Support

- Guided Reading Workbook
- Student Edition on Audio CD
- Spanish Chapter Summaries Audio CD Program

Social Studies Skills Support

- Interactive Skills Tutor CD-ROM

Vocabulary Support

- **CRF:** Vocabulary Builder Activities
- **CRF:** Chapter Review Activity
- Differentiated Instruction Modified Worksheets and Tests CD-ROM:
  - Vocabulary Flash Cards
  - Vocabulary Builder Activity
  - Chapter Review Activity

TOS Holt McDougal PuzzleView

You Try It!

The following passage of a primary source can be found in the chapter you are about to read. As you read this passage, ask yourself what you could learn from this source.

The Benedictine Rule

For bedding, a mattress, a blanket, a coverlet and a pillow are enough. The beds should be frequently inspected by the Abbot as a precaution against private possessions. If anyone is found to have anything which was not given him by the Abbot, he is to undergo the severest punishment; and that this vice of personal ownership may be totally eliminated, everything necessary should be given by the Abbot; namely a cowl, a tunic, stockings, shoes, a belt, a knife, a pen, a needle, a handkerchief and writing tablets, so that all excuses about necessity are removed.

From Chapter 17, page 502

After you read the passage, answer the following questions.

1. The passage you have just read is from a code of rules that monks lived by in the early 500s. If a historian wanted to study how monks lived at that time, would this be a good source to use? Why or why not?
2. Where else might a historian look to verify the information found in this source?
3. Would this be a good source to study to learn how monks live today? Why or why not?

Key Terms and People

Chapter 17

Section 1
Eurasia *(p. 496)*
topography *(p. 496)*

Section 2
Middle Ages *(p. 500)*
medieval *(p. 500)*
Patrick *(p. 501)*
monks *(p. 502)*
monasteries *(p. 502)*
Benedict *(p. 502)*
Charlemagne *(p. 503)*

Section 3
knights *(p. 506)*
vassal *(p. 507)*
feudalism *(p. 507)*
William the Conqueror *(p. 508)*
manor *(p. 509)*
serfs *(p. 509)*
Eleanor of Aquitaine *(p. 510)*

Section 4
chivalry *(p. 513)*
haiku *(p. 514)*

Academic Vocabulary

Success in school is related to knowing academic vocabulary—the words that are frequently used in school assignments and discussions. In this chapter, you will learn the following academic words:

role *(p. 510)*
elements *(p. 514)*

As you read Chapter 17, look at the primary sources included in the chapter. Why do you think these sources were chosen to be included?

Reading Social Studies

Key Terms and People

Review the terms and people with students. Ask students to choose five to eight terms with which they are unfamiliar. Then have students define the terms they selected. Have students create a crossword puzzle using the definitions they wrote as clues. If time permits, have students exchange their puzzle with a partner and complete the other person's crossword. Then have students check their answers.
LS Verbal/Linguistic, Visual/Spatial

Focus on Reading

See the **Focus on Reading** questions in this chapter for more practice on this reading social studies skill.

Reading Social Studies Assessment

See the **Chapter Review** at the end of this chapter for student assessment questions related to this reading skill.

Teaching Tip

Help students practice evaluating sources by providing them with a wide variety of sources. Examples might include diaries, Web sites, and encyclopedia entries. Have students answer the questions from checklists to determine if the source is reliable or not. Then have students exchange their answers with a partner. Ask students if they disagreed on any document. Help the students to understand why the disagreement occurred and whether the document is reliable and accurate.

Answers

You Try It! 1. *Yes, because these rules for behavior were used by monks in the early 500s to guide their lives and it gives specific information about their daily lives.* **2.** *possible answer—Original writings, such as diaries and letters written by people of the period;* **3.** *No, because the world has changed a great deal since medieval times.*

Preteach

Bellringer

If YOU were there . . . Use the **Daily Bellringer Transparency** to help students answer the question.

Daily Bellringer Transparency, Section 1

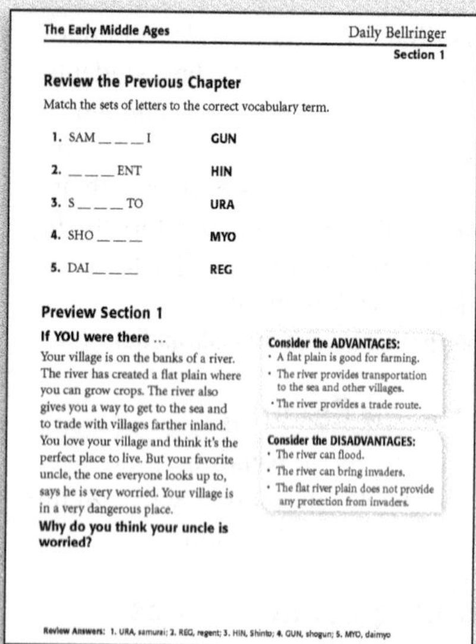

The Early Middle Ages — Daily Bellringer — **Section 1**

Review the Previous Chapter

Match the sets of letters to the correct vocabulary term.

1. SAM _ _ _ I — **GUN**
2. _ _ _ ENT — **HIN**
3. S _ _ _ TO — **URA**
4. SHO _ _ _ — **MYO**
5. DAI _ _ _ — **REG**

Preview Section 1

If YOU were there ...

Your village is on the banks of a river. The river has created a flat plain where you can grow crops. The river also gives you a way to get to the sea and to trade with villages farther inland. You love your village and think it's the perfect place to live. But your favorite uncle, the one everyone looks up to, says he is very worried. Your village is in a very dangerous place.

Why do you think your uncle is worried?

Consider the ADVANTAGES:
- A flat plain is good for farming.
- The river provides transportation to the sea and other villages.
- The river provides a trade route.

Consider the DISADVANTAGES:
- The river can flood.
- The river can bring invaders.
- The flat river plain does not provide any protection from invaders.

Review Answers: 1. URA, samurai; 2. REG, regent; 3. HIN, Shinto; 4. GUN, shogun; 5. MYO, daimyo

Building Vocabulary

Preteach or review the following term:

expanse a wide or open space (p. 497)

CRF: Vocabulary Builder Activity, Section 1

Taking Notes

Have students use the graphic organizer online to take notes on the section. This activity will prepare students for the Section Assessment, in which they will complete a graphic organizer that builds on the information using the Critical Thinking Skill: Categorizing.

SECTION 1

Geography of Europe

What You Will Learn...

Main Ideas

1. The physical features of Europe vary widely from region to region.
2. Geography has shaped life in Europe, including where and how people live.

The Big Idea

Because Europe has many types of landforms and climates, different ways of life have developed there.

Key Terms

Eurasia, *p. 496*
topography, *p. 496*

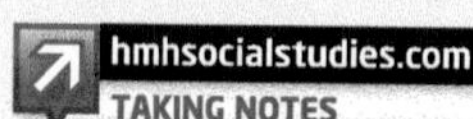

Use the graphic organizer online to take notes on the geography of three regions of Europe.

If YOU were there...

Your village is on the banks of a river. The river has created a flat plain where you can grow crops. The river also gives you a way to get to the sea and to trade with villages farther inland. You love your village and think it's the perfect place to live. But your favorite uncle, the one everyone looks up to, says he is very worried. Your village is in a very dangerous place.

Why do you think your uncle is worried?

BUILDING BACKGROUND Many villages in Europe were built on rivers. But rivers were only one of the physical features that affected where and how people lived in Europe. All of Europe's features—its landforms, its waterways, and its climates—played roles in shaping people's lives.

The Physical Features of Europe

Europe is a small continent, but it is very diverse. Many different landforms, water features, and climates can be found there.

Although we call Europe a continent, it is actually part of **Eurasia**, the large landmass that includes both Europe and Asia. Geographers consider the Ural Mountains to be the boundary between the two continents.

Landforms and Waterways

Look at the map of Europe. You can see that different parts of Europe have very different features. In other words, Europe's topography (tuh-PAH-gruh-fee) varies widely from place to place. **Topography** refers to the shape and elevation of land in a region.

Mountain ranges cover much of southern Europe. Some peaks in the Alps reach higher than 15,000 feet. The highest mountains have large snowfields and glaciers.

Teach the Big Idea

At Level

Geography of Europe

1. **Teach** Ask students the questions in the Main Idea boxes to teach this section.
2. **Apply** Draw a table with three columns and three rows for students to see. Label the columns *Southern Europe*, *Northern Europe*, and *Far Northern Europe*. Label the rows *Topography*, *Climate*, and *Ways of Life*. Have each student copy the table and complete it by identifying the characteristics for each region.
   LS **Verbal/Linguistic, Visual/Spatial**
3. **Review** As you review the geography of each region, have students share the information they listed. Guide students in a discussion of how geography has influenced life in Europe.
4. **Practice/Homework** Have students select one of the regions and create a postcard that depicts the region's geography and way of life. LS **Visual/Spatial**

Alternative Assessment Handbook, Rubrics 3: Artwork; and 7: Charts

GEOGRAPHY SKILLS INTERPRETING MAPS

1. **Region** What four peninsulas do you see labeled?
2. **Movement** How might the Alps have affected the movement of peoples?

North of the Alps, the land is much flatter than in southern Europe. In fact, most of northern Europe is part of the vast Northern European Plain. As you can see on the map, this plain stretches all the way from the Atlantic Ocean in the west to the Ural Mountains in the east. In the past, this huge expanse of land was covered with thick forests. Many types of trees grew well in the plain's rich, fertile soils.

The Northern European Plain is also the location of most of Europe's major rivers. Many of these rivers begin with melting snow in the southern mountains and flow out across the plain on their way northward to the sea.

If you travel even farther north from the Northern European Plain, the land starts to rise again. Far northern Europe has many rugged hills and low mountains.

Direct Teach

Main Idea

❶ The Physical Features of Europe

The physical features of Europe vary widely from region to region.

Identify What is the boundary between Europe and Asia? *the Ural Mountains*

Recall Where are most of Europe's major rivers located? *in the Northern European Plain*

Contrast How is the topography of southern Europe different from that of the Northern European Plain? *southern Europe—high mountains; Northern European Plain—large areas of flat land with many rivers*

Map Transparency: Europe: Physical

Interpreting Maps

Europe: Physical

Review the map with students and ask the following questions:

Location List the rivers located in the Northern European Plain. *Rivers include the Seine, Rhine, Po, Elbe, Danube, Vistula, and Dnieper.*

Movement Why might the Iberian Peninsula be isolated from the rest of Europe? *It is separated by the Pyrenees Mountains and is farther to the west.*

Map Transparency: Europe: Physical

Differentiating Instruction

Struggling Readers **Below Level**

1. Tell the class that Europe is often called a peninsula of peninsulas. On a wall map or transparency, trace the outline of Europe so that students can observe how the continent is a peninsula of the Eurasian landmass.
2. Have students refer to a political map of Europe to identify the modern-day countries that make up Europe. Then have students identify the countries that answer the following questions:

- What countries are located on peninsulas? *Norway, Sweden, Denmark, Portugal, Spain, Italy, Greece*
- What countries are islands? *United Kingdom, Ireland, Iceland*
- What country is farthest north? *Norway*
- What sea forms the southern border of Europe? *the Mediterranean* **LS Verbal/Linguistic, Visual/Spatial**

Alternative Assessment Handbook, Rubric 21: Map Reading

Answers

Interpreting Maps 1. *Scandinavian, Iberian, Italian, Balkan;* **2.** *possible answer—might have prevented or slowed people who wanted to move north or south through the area.*

Direct Teach

Main Idea

❷ Geography Shapes Life

Geography has shaped life in Europe, including where and how people live.

Identify What kinds of crops do people in southern Europe grow? *crops like grapes and olives that could survive the region's dry summers*

Recall What city was built on an island in a river to make it hard for raiders to reach? *Paris, France*

Draw Conclusions Why have so many different ways of life developed in Europe? *because it has so many types of landforms, waterways, and climates*

Activity **Create a Map** Have students use an outline map of Europe to identify the different regions within Europe and the characteristics of each region. **LS Verbal/Linguistic, Visual/Spatial**

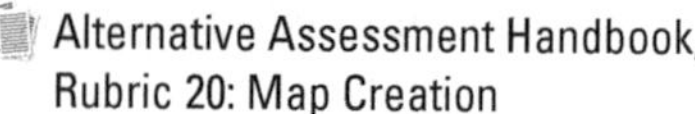

Alternative Assessment Handbook, Rubric 20: Map Creation

Did you know . . .

Scandinavia is a land of extremes. During the summer parts of Scandinavia north of the Arctic Circle experience days in which the sun never sets. In the winter those same regions experience 24 hours of darkness!

Geography and Living

Europe's geography has influenced the development of different ways of life. It has influenced, for example, what crops people have grown and where cities have developed.

❶ Farmers have long grown olives and other hardy crops in the drier, warmer areas along the Mediterranean in southern Europe.

You can see these hills and mountains in the northern part of the British Isles and in Scandinavia, Europe's largest peninsula. Scandinavia is only one of Europe's many peninsulas. Smaller peninsulas extend into the sea from many parts of Europe. These peninsulas give Europe a very long, jagged coastline.

Climate and Vegetation

Like its landforms, Europe's climates and vegetation vary widely from region to region. For example, southern Europe is largely warm and sunny. As a result, shrubs and trees that don't need a lot of water are common there.

Most of northwestern Europe, in contrast, has a mild and cooler, wetter climate. Cold winds from the north and northeast can bring freezing weather in winter.

Freezing weather is much more common in Scandinavia, though. That region is very cold throughout the year. Snow falls for much of the year, and few plants can survive the region's cold climates.

READING CHECK **Summarizing** How do Europe's landforms and climates vary by region?

Geography Shapes Life

As in other parts of the world, geography has affected history in Europe. It influenced where and how people lived.

Southern Europe

In southern Europe, most people lived on coastal plains or in river valleys where the land was flat enough to farm. People grew crops like grapes and olives that could survive the region's dry summers. In the mountains where the land was steep or rocky, people raised sheep and goats.

Because southern Europe has many peninsulas, people there don't live far from the sea. As a result, many became traders and seafarers.

Northern Europe

Most people in northern Europe lived farther from the sea. They still had access to the sea, however, through northern Europe's rivers. Because rivers were an easy method of transportation, towns grew up along them. Rivers also provided protection. The city of Paris, France, for example, was built on an island in a river to make the city hard for raiders to reach.

Collaborative Learning

Above Level

Regional Newspapers

1. Draw students' attention to the three photographs on these pages. Point out to students that each photograph depicts a different geographic region in Europe: Italy in southern Europe, Germany in the Northern European Plain, and Norway in far northern Europe.
2. Organize the class into three groups, one for each of the regions. Have each group plan and create a newspaper page that focuses on the geography and way of life for its assigned region. Have each group member write a newspaper article and an advertisement for the group newspaper.
3. Ask each group to share its newspaper page with the class.

LS Verbal/Linguistic,Visual/Spatial

Alternative Assessment Handbook, Rubric 23: Newspapers

Answers

Reading Check *In northern Europe, the land is flat with rivers that flow to the seas, and the climate is mild and cool. In southern Europe, there are more mountain ranges, and the climate is warm and sunny.*

2 Cities have grown along rivers such as the Rhine in Germany. Rivers have been routes for moving people and goods.

3 Many people in cold, snowy Scandinavia have settled on the coasts, looking to the sea and lands beyond for the resources they need.

In the fields around cities, farmers grew all sorts of crops. These fields were excellent farmlands, but the flat land also made an easy route for invaders to follow. No mountains blocked people's access to northern Europe, and as a result, the region was frequently invaded.

READING CHECK **Contrasting** How did geography influence where people lived in Europe?

SUMMARY AND PREVIEW You have just read about the role Europe's geography played in its history. Because Europe has so many types of landforms and climates, many different ways of life developed there. Also, northern Europe had few natural barriers to prevent invasions. In the next section, you will learn how Europe changed when invasions did occur.

Section 1 Assessment

hmhsocialstudies.com ONLINE QUIZ

Reviewing Ideas, Terms, and People

1. a. **Define** What is **topography**?
   b. **Compare and Contrast** How is southern Europe's climate like or unlike your climate?
2. a. **Describe** Where do most people in southern Europe live?
   b. **Draw Conclusions** Do you think Europe's major farming regions are in the north or the south? Why?
   c. **Elaborate** How might the region's climate affect how people live in Scandinavia?

Critical Thinking

3. **Categorizing** Draw a chart like the one to the right. Using your notes, list the landforms, climates, and vegetation of northern Europe, southern Europe, and Scandinavia.

	Landforms	Climates	Vegetation
Northern Europe			
Southern Europe			
Scandinavia			

FOCUS ON WRITING

4. **Thinking about Geography** If you were a noble living in northern Europe, what might your life be like? How would the landforms and climate affect people in your area? Why might you need the protection of knights? Write some ideas down in your notebook.

Direct Teach

Analyzing Visuals

Geography and Living

Point out to students that the photos in this feature reflect different regions in Europe.

1. Have students identify in what geographic region Germany is located. *the Northern European Plain*
2. Remind students that Scandinavia is in far northern Europe. What is the climate of Scandinavia? *very cold*
3. Lastly, ask students in which region of Europe they would most like to live. Have students explain why they chose that region. **LS Verbal/Linguistic**

Review & Assess

Close

Have students create an outline that summarizes the characteristics of European geography.

Review

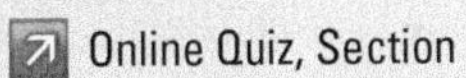

Online Quiz, Section 1

Assess

SE Section 1 Assessment

PASS: Section 1 Quiz

Alternative Assessment Handbook

Reteach/Classroom Intervention

Guided Reading Workbook, Section 1

Interactive Skills Tutor CD-ROM

Section 1 Assessment Answers

1. a. the shape and elevation of land in a region
   b. possible answer—Southern Europe is dry and warm.
2. a. coastal plains or river valleys where it is flat enough to farm
   b. north; flat land, fertile soil, and many rivers
   c. People will live where they can grow crops and be protected from the cold climate, so Scandinavians settled on coasts.
3. Northern Europe—landforms: Northern European Plain; climate: mild and cool; vegetation: forests; Southern Europe—landforms: mountains; climate: warm and sunny; vegetation: hardy shrubs and trees; Scandinavia—landforms: mountains and hills; climate: cold; vegetation: few plants
4. possible answer—You would own land that others farmed for you; you would probably live near rivers; because of the flat land, it was easy for invaders to enter the region.

Answers

Reading Check *southern Europe—cities near the coast and river valleys; northern Europe—cities away from oceans and near rivers*

Preteach

Bellringer

If YOU were there . . . Use the **Daily Bellringer Transparency** to help students answer the question.

Daily Bellringer Transparency, Section 2

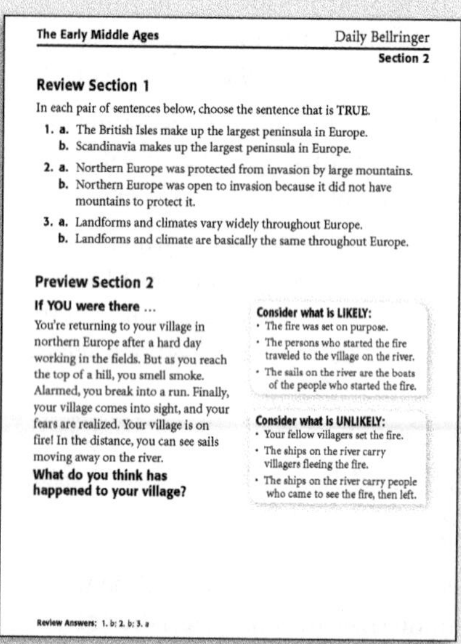

The Early Middle Ages — Daily Bellringer, **Section 2**

Review Section 1

In each pair of sentences below, choose the sentence that is TRUE.

1. a. The British Isles make up the largest peninsula in Europe.
   b. Scandinavia makes up the largest peninsula in Europe.
2. a. Northern Europe was protected from invasion by large mountains.
   b. Northern Europe was open to invasion because it did not have mountains to protect it.
3. a. Landforms and climates vary widely throughout Europe.
   b. Landforms and climate are basically the same throughout Europe.

Preview Section 2

If YOU were there ...

You're returning to your village in northern Europe after a hard day working in the fields. But as you reach the top of a hill, you smell smoke. Alarmed, you break into a run. Finally, your village comes into sight, and your fears are realized. Your village is on fire! In the distance, you can see sails moving away on the river.

What do you think has happened to your village?

Consider what is LIKELY:
- The fire was set on purpose.
- The persons who started the fire traveled to the village on the river.
- The sails on the river are the boats of the people who started the fire.

Consider what is UNLIKELY:
- Your fellow villagers set the fire.
- The ships on the river carry villagers fleeing the fire.
- The ships on the river carry people who came to see the fire, then left.

Review Answers: 1. b; 2. b; 3. a

Building Vocabulary

Preteach or review the following terms:

looted to have taken goods by force (p. 503)

scribe one who copies manuscripts or documents (p. 502)

CRF: Vocabulary Builder Activity, Section 2

Taking Notes

Have students use the graphic organizer online to take notes on the section. This activity will prepare students for the Section Assessment, in which they will complete a graphic organizer that builds on the information using the Critical Thinking Skill: Analyzing.

SECTION 2

Europe after the Fall of Rome

What You Will Learn...

Main Ideas

1. Christianity spread to northern Europe through the work of missionaries and monks.
2. The Franks, led by Charlemagne, created a huge Christian empire and brought together scholars from around Europe.
3. Invaders threatened much of Europe in the 700s and 800s.

The Big Idea

Despite the efforts of Christians to maintain order, Europe was a dangerous place after the fall of Rome.

Key Terms and People

Middle Ages, *p. 500*
medieval, *p. 500*
Patrick, *p. 501*
monks, *p. 502*
monasteries, *p. 502*
Benedict, *p. 502*
Charlemagne, *p. 503*

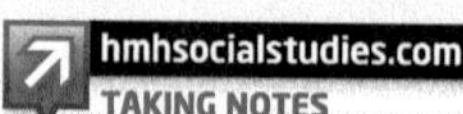

Use the graphic organizer online to record information about how events and people in the Middle Ages affected Europe.

If YOU were there...

You're returning to your village in northern Europe after a hard day working in the fields. But as you reach the top of a hill, you smell smoke. Alarmed, you break into a run. Finally, your village comes into sight, and your fears are realized. Your village is on fire! In the distance, you can see sails moving away on the river.

What do you think has happened to your village?

BUILDING BACKGROUND Europe was a dangerous place after Rome fell. Without the Roman government, Europe had no central authority to keep order. As a result, outlaws and bandits became common. At the same time, new groups of people were moving into Europe. Violence was common. Distressed, people looked for ways to bring order and comfort into their lives.

Christianity Spreads to Northern Europe

As the Roman Empire fell, various groups from the north and east moved into former Roman lands. As they moved in, these groups created their own states. The rulers of these states, usually powerful warlords, began to call themselves kings. These kings often fought among themselves. As a result, by the early 500s Europe was divided into many small kingdoms.

The creation of these kingdoms marked the beginning of the **Middle Ages**, a period that lasted from about 500 to about 1500. We call this time the "middle" ages because it falls between ancient times and modern times. Another name for the Middle Ages is the **medieval** (mee-DEE-vuhl) period, from the Latin words for "middle age."

At the beginning of the Middle Ages, many of the kingdoms of northern Europe were not Christian. Christianity was only common in places that had been part of the Roman Empire, such as Italy and Spain. As time passed, however, Christianity

Teach the Big Idea

At Level

Europe after the Fall of Rome

1. **Teach** Ask students the questions in the Main Idea boxes to teach this section.
2. **Apply** Have students identify the main events in this section and create a time line showing the correct sequence of events. (Most dates will be approximate.) **LS Verbal/Linguistic, Visual/Spatial**
3. **Review** As a class, review students' time line entries. Have students identify the events they feel are most important or most interesting. Guide students in a discussion of the history of Europe after the fall of Rome.
4. **Practice/Homework** Ask students to imagine that they live in the time of the Vikings. Have each student write a brief journal entry about a Viking raid on his or her village. **LS Intrapersonal, Verbal/Linguistic**

Alternative Assessment Handbook, Rubrics 15: Journals; and 36: Time Lines

BIOGRAPHY

Saint Patrick

AD 400s

Patrick was a monk who helped convert the Irish to Christianity. As a teenager, Patrick was kidnapped in Britain and taken to Ireland, where he was forced to work as a shepherd. After six years, he escaped. But later he returned to Ireland to spread Christianity. According to legend, he won favor with the Irish by driving all of the snakes in Ireland into the sea. After Patrick died, he was declared a saint by the people of Ireland.

GEOGRAPHY **SKILLS** INTERPRETING MAPS

Place How far north had Christianity spread by AD 600?

slowly spread farther north. This spread was largely through the efforts of two groups of Christians—missionaries and monks.

Missionaries

Perhaps the most powerful force that helped spread Christianity into northern Europe was the pope. Over the years, many popes sent missionaries to teach people in northern kingdoms about Christianity. Missionaries are people who try to convert others to a particular religion. Some missionaries traveled great distances to spread Christianity to new lands.

One of the first places to which popes sent missionaries was Britain. These missionaries traveled all over the island, and eventually most people in Britain became Christian. From Britain, other missionaries carried Christianity into what are now France and Germany.

Not all missionaries, though, were sent by the pope. In fact, one of the first missionaries to travel to northern Europe was **Patrick**, who took it upon himself to teach people about Christianity. In the mid-400s Patrick traveled from Britain to Ireland to convert the people there.

Direct Teach

Main Idea

1 Christianity Spreads to Northern Europe

Christianity spread to northern Europe through the work of missionaries and monks.

Recall In what parts of Europe was Christianity common at the beginning of the Middle Ages? *in places that had been part of the Roman Empire, such as Italy and Spain*

Define What are missionaries? *people sent to convert others to a particular religion*

Analyze Why was Saint Patrick important? *He converted the Irish to Christianity.*

Map Transparency: The Spread of Christianity

Interpreting Maps

The Spread of Christianity

Review the map with students and ask the following questions:

Location What rivers served as the eastern boundaries for the spread of Christianity in Europe? *the Danube and the Rhine*

Place What were the centers of Christianity in Britain? *Whitby and Canterbury*

Map Transparency: The Spread of Christianity

Critical Thinking: Comparing and Contrasting

At Level

Missionary Journal Entries

1. Review with the class what life was like in northern Europe in the early Middle Ages. Remind students that small kingdoms fought for power. Next, review with students the role that missionaries played in the spread of Christianity throughout Europe.
2. Then have each student create a chart comparing and contrasting medieval missionaries and monks. Students' charts should describe or explain each group's purpose, way of life, and role in the spread of Christianity. LS **Verbal/Linguistic, Visual/Spatial**

Alternative Assessment Handbook, Rubrics 7: Charts; and 9: Comparing and Contrasting

Answers

Interpreting Maps *as far as Ireland and Britain*

Direct Teach

Main Idea

1 Christianity Spreads to Northern Europe

Christianity spread to northern Europe through the work of missionaries and monks.

Contrast How were medieval monks and missionaries different? *monks—lived apart from society and provided services for the community and the poor; missionaries—traveled to distant lands to convert people to Christianity*

Make Inferences How did monks influence life outside of the monasteries? *by providing health care, running schools, saving ancient writings, and serving as scribes and advisers to local rulers*

Info to Know

Monasteries and Convents A monastery is a community of monks, but men were not the only ones who entered religious communities during the Middle Ages. Many women became nuns and lived and worked together in convents or abbeys. Women who were known as abbesses supervised the nuns. Although they focused on religious study, medieval nuns also taught, provided nursing, or did charitable work with the poor.

Unlike most missionaries, Patrick traveled alone. Although he faced resistance to his teachings, he eventually converted the Irish people to Christianity.

Monks

While missionaries traveled to spread Christian teachings, men called monks were equally dedicated to their faith. **Monks** were religious men who lived apart from society in isolated communities. In these communities, monks spent their time in prayer, work, and meditation.

Communities of monks, or **monasteries**, were built all over Europe in the Middle Ages. Life in a monastery was strictly organized. The monks had to follow rules that were intended to help them live as good Christians. These rules outlined the day-to-day affairs of the monastery, including how monks should dress and what they should eat.

Most European monasteries followed a set of rules created in the early 500s by an Italian monk named **Benedict**. His code was called the Benedictine Rule, and those who followed it were called Benedictine monks. But not all monks in Europe were Benedictines. Different groups of monks created their own rules. For example, monks in Ireland were very different from monks in France or Germany.

Even though they lived apart from society, monks had a big influence on Europe. Monks performed many services, both inside and outside of monasteries. Monasteries sometimes provided basic services, such as health care, that were unavailable to many members of their communities. The poor and needy would arrive at a monastery and the monks would give them aid.

In addition to giving aid to people in their communities, monks

- ran schools and copied books for those who couldn't read or write,
- collected and saved ancient writings from Greece and Rome,
- served as scribes and advisors to local rulers.

Monks also helped spread Christian teachings into new areas. Many monasteries were built in remote locations where Christians had never traveled before. People living near the monasteries learned about Christianity from the monks.

READING CHECK **Summarizing** How did missionaries and monks help spread Christianity into new areas?

Primary Source

HISTORIC DOCUMENT

The Benedictine Rule

The Benedictine Order was the largest group of monks in Europe in the early Middle Ages. In his rule, Benedict listed the guidelines monks had to follow. Here he describes what each monk was allowed to own.

"For bedding, a mattress, a blanket, a coverlet and a pillow are enough. The beds should be frequently inspected by the Abbot as a precaution against private possessions. If anyone is found to have anything which was not given him by the Abbot, he is to undergo the severest punishment; and that this vice [wickedness] of personal ownership may be totally eliminated, everything necessary should be given by the Abbot; namely, a cowl [hood], a tunic [long shirt], stockings, shoes, a belt, a knife, a pen, a needle, a handkerchief and writing tablets, so that all excuses about necessity are removed."

—from *The Rule of Saint Benedict*, translated by Abbot Parry

Monks were not allowed to own any property.

An abbot is the head of a monastery.

ANALYSIS SKILL **ANALYZING PRIMARY SOURCES**

Why do you think Benedictine monks were only allowed a few simple possessions?

Critical Thinking: Sequencing

Above Level

Research Required

A Monk's Daily Schedule

1. Ask students if they have a daily schedule or routine that they follow. Ask students for examples of activities and times in their school day schedule. Then explain that monks also followed a set schedule.
2. Have students use the library, the Internet, or other resources to conduct research on the daily lives of medieval monks. Students may want to examine the Benedictine Rule for further information.
3. Then have students work in pairs to develop schedules that reflect a typical day for a medieval monk. Have students put down approximate times for activities on the list.
4. Ask volunteers to share their schedules with the class. **LS Interpersonal, Verbal/Linguistic**

Alternative Assessment Handbook, Rubrics 30: Research; and 42: Writing to Inform

Answers

Analyzing Primary Sources *possible answers—to avoid wanting more things; to prevent distractions*

Reading Check *Missionaries traveled to spread Christianity, while monks built monasteries in remote locations where they taught about Christianity.*

The Franks Build an Empire

As Christianity was spreading into northern Europe, political changes were also taking place. In the 480s a powerful group called the Franks conquered Gaul, the region we now call France. Under a ruler named Clovis, the Franks became Christian and created one of the strongest kingdoms in Europe.

As strong as the Franks were under Clovis, though, they had yet to reach their greatest power. That power would not come until the late 700s, when a leader named **Charlemagne** (SHAHR-luh-mayn) appeared. Charlemagne was a brilliant warrior and a strong king, and he led the Franks in building a huge empire.

To build this empire, Charlemagne spent much of his time at war. He led his armies into battle against many neighboring kingdoms and conquered them. By the time he was finished, Charlemagne's empire included all of what is now France. It also stretched into modern Germany, Austria, Italy, and northern Spain.

Charlemagne, a Christian king, had conquered parts of the former Roman Empire. For that reason, on Christmas Day in 800, Pope Leo III crowned Charlemagne Emperor of the Romans. This title symbolized a return to the greatness of the Roman Empire.

Charlemagne didn't spend all of his energy on warfare, however. A great admirer of education, he built schools across Europe. He also brought scholars to teach in his capital at Aachen (AH-kuhn), now in western Germany. Among these scholars were some of the greatest religious scholars and teachers of the Middle Ages. Their teachings helped shape religious and social life in Europe for centuries.

READING CHECK **Finding Main Ideas** What were Charlemagne's major accomplishments?

Charlemagne's Empire

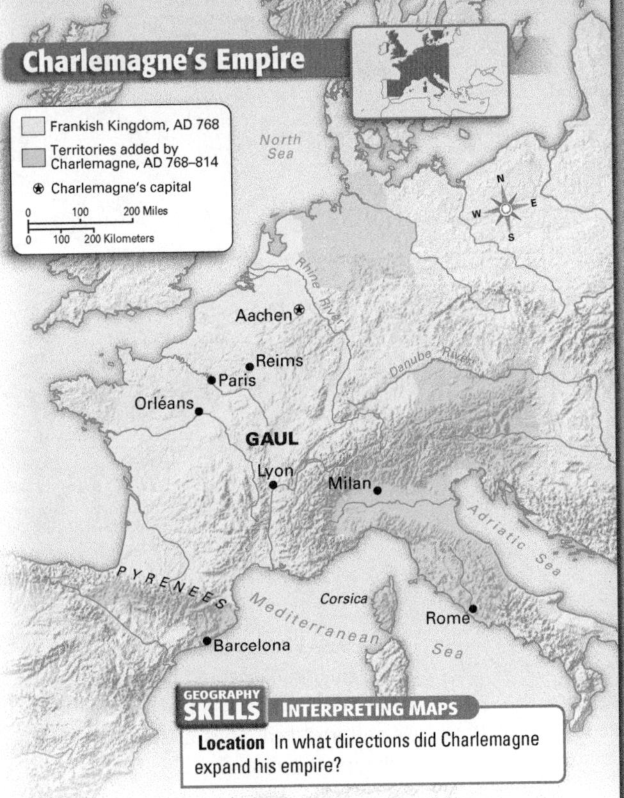

GEOGRAPHY SKILLS **INTERPRETING MAPS**

Location In what directions did Charlemagne expand his empire?

Invaders Threaten Europe

Even while Charlemagne was building his empire, though, new threats appeared in Europe. Invaders began to attack settlements all over the continent. Muslim armies poured into southern France and northern Italy. Fierce warriors called the Magyars swept into Europe from the east, attacking towns and destroying fields. From Scandinavia came perhaps the most frightening invaders of all, the Vikings.

The Vikings raided Britain, Ireland, and other parts of western Europe. They looted towns and monasteries and took prisoners to sell into slavery. The attacks were swift and savage, and Europeans lived in terror of Viking raids.

Direct Teach

Main Idea

2 The Franks Build an Empire

The Franks, led by Charlemagne, created a huge Christian empire and brought together scholars from around Europe.

Analyze What changes did the Franks make under Clovis? *converted to Christianity and became one of the strongest kingdoms in Europe*

Explain How did Charlemagne create a large empire? *He spent much of his time at war and defeated many neighboring kingdoms.*

Evaluate Which of Charlemagne's accomplishments do you think had the most lasting effect? Why? *possible answer—He built schools across Europe; the scholars he brought together helped shape religious and social life in Europe for centuries.*

- **CRF:** Biography Source Activity: Charles Martel
- **CRF:** Primary Source Activity: The End of Charlemagne's Life
- Map Transparency: Charlemagne's Empire

Did you know . . .

Charlemagne's given name was Charles. The name *Charlemagne* comes from his Latin name, *Carolus Magnus*, which means "Charles the Great."

hmhsocialstudies.com

Online Resources
Activity: Charlemagne Biography

Differentiating Instruction

Struggling Readers

Below Level Research Required

1. Review with the class the Viking invasions. Remind students that the Vikings were one of the most feared groups of the Middle Ages.
2. Have students use the library, the Internet, or other resources to conduct research on the Vikings. Guide students in their research by asking them to search for information on the following topics: warfare, exploration, ships, society, and mythology.
3. After students have completed their research, have them write one newspaper headline for each of the topics listed. Remind students that their headlines should try to capture the attention of the reader and provide basic information.
4. Have students share their headlines with the class. Have students select their favorite headlines and explain why they liked particular headlines. **LS Verbal/Linguistic**

Alternative Assessment Handbook, Rubric 30: Research

Answers

Interpreting Maps *to the east and south*

Reading Check *built a huge empire that included schools to teach many subjects, including Christianity*

Preteach

Main Idea

❸ Invaders Threaten Europe

Invaders threatened much of Europe in the 700s and 800s.

Identify Of the groups that invaded Europe in the 700s and 800s, which was the most feared? *the Vikings*

Summarize What damage did the invasions cause? *Settlements were attacked, fields were destroyed, towns and monasteries were looted, and prisoners were sold into slavery.*

Activity Viking Song Have students write a song or poem that tells of the raids by the Vikings.

LS Auditory/Musical, Verbal/Linguistic

CRF: Biography Activity: Leif Eriksson

CRF: History and Geography Activity: Invasions of Europe, 800–1000

Map Transparency: Invasions of Europe, AD 800–1000

Review & Assess

Close

Have students summarize the main points of this section.

Review

Online Quiz, Section 2

Assess

SE Section 2 Assessment

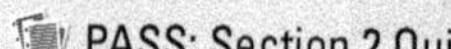
PASS: Section 2 Quiz

Alternative Assessment Handbook

Reteach/Classroom Intervention

Guided Reading Workbook, Section 2

Interactive Skills Tutor CD-ROM

Answers

Interpreting Maps *the Vikings*

Reading Check *the Magyars, Muslims, and Vikings*

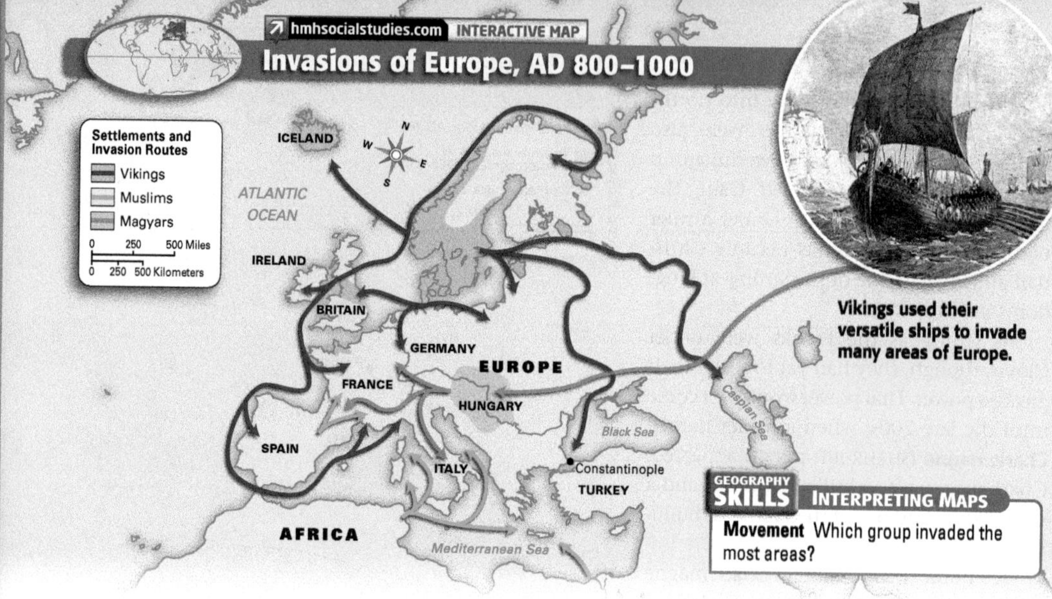

Vikings used their versatile ships to invade many areas of Europe.

GEOGRAPHY SKILLS INTERPRETING MAPS

Movement Which group invaded the most areas?

Because Vikings could sail their ships up rivers, their raids weren't limited to coastal areas. The Vikings also reached inland cities and attacked cities in the Iberian and Italian peninsulas.

READING CHECK Finding Main Ideas What groups invaded Europe in the 700s and 800s?

SUMMARY AND PREVIEW After the fall of Rome, northern Europe gradually became Christian. But Europe could still be a dangerous place. Invaders threatened Europeans constantly. In the next section, you will learn about ways people tried to protect themselves from invaders.

Section 2 Assessment

hmhsocialstudies.com ONLINE QUIZ

Reviewing Ideas, Terms, and People

1. a. **Describe** How are **monks** and **monasteries** related?
   b. **Explain** Why did missionaries travel to northern Europe?
   c. **Elaborate** Why do you think monks followed such strict rules?
2. a. **Recall** What is **Charlemagne** famous for?
   b. **Evaluate** What do you think Charlemagne's greatest accomplishment was? Why?
3. a. **Identify** What areas of Europe did the Vikings raid?
   b. **Make Generalizations** Why were people in Europe so frightened of Viking raids?

Critical Thinking

4. **Analyzing** Using your notes, determine which events brought unity to Europe and which brought division or disruption. Write your answers in a diagram like this one.

Unity | Disruption

Focus on Writing

5. **Considering Life Then** Now you see why you might need the protection of knights. Look back at your list and add to it. What services might you hire knights to perform?

Section 2 Assessment Answers

1. a. Monks lived in communities called monasteries.
   b. to convert people to Christianity
   c. possible answer—to help them live as good Christians
2. a. uniting much of Europe in an empire
   b. possible answer—creating schools; it helped spread Christianity
3. a. Britain, Ireland, France, Iceland, Germany, Spain, and the Iberian and Italian peninsulas
   b. Viking raids were fast, unpredictable, and very fierce.
4. possible answers: Unity—the spread of Christianity, the rule of Charlemagne; Disruption—Viking, Muslim, and Magyar invasions
5. possible responses—to protect from invasions, to protect monasteries

BIOGRAPHY

Charlemagne

What would you do if you ruled much of Europe?

When did he live? 742–814

Where did he live? Charlemagne, or Charles the Great, ruled most of what are now France and Germany. He lived mainly in his capital, Aachen, near the modern city of Cologne, Germany.

What did he do? Through his wars of conquest, Charlemagne united many of the tribes of central and western Europe into a single empire.

Why is he important? While Europe was still reeling from the collapse of Rome, Charlemagne brought people together. He helped Europeans realize that they shared common bonds, such as Christianity, that linked them. In other words, he helped people see themselves as Europeans, not members of tribes.

Drawing Conclusions How did this change in view affect later European society?

KEY EVENTS

- **771** Charlemagne becomes king of the Franks.
- **773** Charlemagne becomes an ally of the pope after rescuing him from invaders.
- **794** Charlemagne makes Aachen his capital.
- **800** Pope Leo III names Charlemagne emperor.

This painting shows Charlemagne being crowned by the pope in AD 800.

505

Biography

Reading Focus Question

Have students briefly discuss the introductory question. Ask students to consider their goals as ruler as well as difficulties they might face. Then tell students to keep this question in mind as they read the biography. When students have completed the reading, have them describe what Charlemagne accomplished as ruler over much of Europe.

Primary Source

Einhard on Charlemagne

Einhard, who lived at Charlemagne's court, describes the king's appearance and character in this excerpt from *Vita Karoli Magni*: "He had a broad and strong body of unusual height, but well-proportioned; for his height measured seven times his feet. His skull was round, the eyes were lively and rather large, the nose of more than average length, the hair gray but full, the face friendly and cheerful. . . He strode with firm step and held himself like a man; he spoke with a higher voice than one would have expected of someone of his build."

Linking to Today

European Unity Today European unity is an idea that still exists today. One example is the euro. This unit of money serves as the standard currency for all nations in the European Union.

About the Illustration

This illustration of Charlemagne is an artist's conception based on available sources. However, historians are uncertain exactly what Charlemagne looked like.

Critical Thinking: Evaluating

At Level

Evaluating Charlemagne

1. Explain to students that Charlemagne served as the model of the ideal king throughout the Middle Ages and into modern times.
2. Have students make a list of the characteristics of the ideal king based on Charlemagne's life, actions, and character. Students should refer to the biography on this page and to the information in Section 2 to complete the activity.
3. Have students share the characteristics they noted. List them for students to see.
4. Then ask students to indicate how this list differs from the characteristics that they personally think an ideal ruler should have. Have students share and discuss their points of view. LS **Verbal/Linguistic**

Alternative Assessment Handbook, Rubric 11: Discussions

Answers

Drawing Conclusions *Answers will vary, but students might say that people in Europe continued to see themselves as Europeans.*

Preteach

Bellringer

If YOU were there . . . Use the **Daily Bellringer Transparency** to help students answer the question.

Daily Bellringer Transparency, Section 3

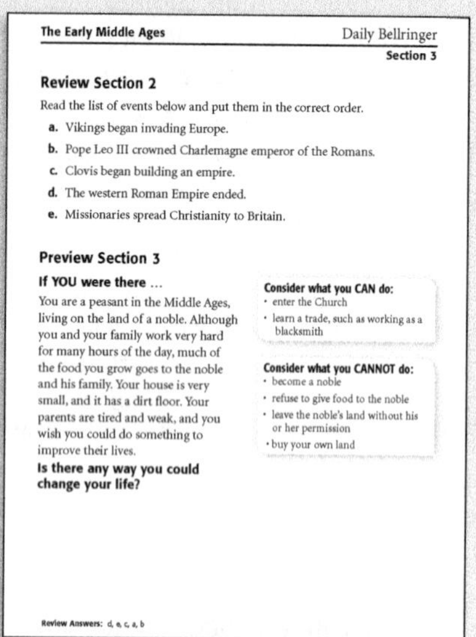

The Early Middle Ages Daily Bellringer **Section 3**

Review Section 2

Read the list of events below and put them in the correct order.

a. Vikings began invading Europe.
b. Pope Leo III crowned Charlemagne emperor of the Romans.
c. Clovis began building an empire.
d. The western Roman Empire ended.
e. Missionaries spread Christianity to Britain.

Preview Section 3

If YOU were there ...

You are a peasant in the Middle Ages, living on the land of a noble. Although you and your family work very hard for many hours of the day, much of the food you grow goes to the noble and his family. Your house is very small, and it has a dirt floor. Your parents are tired and weak, and you wish you could do something to improve their lives.

Is there any way you could change your life?

Consider what you CAN do:
- enter the Church
- learn a trade, such as working as a blacksmith

Consider what you CANNOT do:
- become a noble
- refuse to give food to the noble
- leave the noble's land without his or her permission
- buy your own land

Review Answers: d, e, c, a, b

Academic Vocabulary

Review with students the high-use academic term in this section.

role assigned behavior (p. 510)

CRF: Vocabulary Builder Activity, Section 3

Taking Notes

Have students use the graphic organizer online to take notes on the section. This activity will prepare students for the Section Assessment, in which they will complete a graphic organizer that builds on the information using the Critical Thinking Skill: Analyzing.

SECTION 3

Feudalism and Manor Life

What You Will Learn...

Main Ideas

1. Feudalism governed how knights and nobles dealt with each other.
2. Feudalism spread through much of Europe.
3. The manor system dominated Europe's economy.
4. Towns and trade grew and helped end the feudal system.

The Big Idea

A complex web of duties and obligations governed relationships between people in the Middle Ages.

Key Terms and People

knights, *p. 506*
vassal, *p. 507*
feudalism, *p. 507*
William the Conqueror, *p. 508*
manor, *p. 509*
serfs, *p. 509*
Eleanor of Aquitaine, *p. 510*

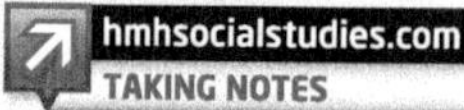

Use the graphic organizer online to take notes on the duties and obligations of different people in the Middle Ages.

If YOU were there...

You are a peasant in the Middle Ages, living on the land of a noble. Although you and your family work very hard for many hours of the day, much of the food you grow goes to the noble and his family. Your house is very small, and it has a dirt floor. Your parents are tired and weak, and you wish you could do something to improve their lives.

Is there any way you could change your life?

BUILDING BACKGROUND Hard work was a constant theme in the lives of peasants in the Middle Ages. They worked long hours and had to obey the wishes of nobles. But most nobles weren't free to live as they chose either. They were sworn to obey more powerful nobles, who had to obey the wishes of the king. Life in the Middle Ages was one big web of duties and obligations.

Feudalism Governs Knights and Nobles

When the Vikings, Magyars, and Muslims began their raids in the 800s, the Frankish kings were unable to defend their empire. Their army was too slow to defend against the lightning-fast attacks of their enemies. Because they couldn't depend on protection from their kings, nobles had to defend their own lands. As a result, the power of nobles grew, and kings became less powerful. In fact, some nobles became as powerful as the kings themselves. Although these nobles remained loyal to the king, they ruled their lands as independent territories.

Knights and Land

To defend their lands, nobles needed soldiers. The best soldiers were **knights**, warriors who fought on horseback. However, knights needed weapons, armor, and horses. This equipment was expensive, and few people had money in the early Middle Ages.

Teach the Big Idea

At Level

Feudalism and Manor Life

1. **Teach** Ask students the questions in the Main Idea boxes to teach this section.
2. **Apply** Have students create an outline of this section using the main idea points listed above as headings. Ask students to identify at least two supporting details for each main idea statement. **LS Verbal/Linguistic**
3. **Review** Have students exchange outlines with a partner. Ask students to identify the points in their partners' outlines that they feel are most important or most interesting. Review these main points as a class.
4. **Practice/Homework** Have students write a paragraph that summarizes the different elements of the feudal system and manor life. **LS Verbal/Linguistic**

Alternative Assessment Handbook, Rubrics 38: Writing to Classify; and 42: Writing to Inform

As a result, nobles gave knights fiefs (FEEFS), or pieces of land, instead of money for their military service. A noble who gave land to a knight in this way was called a lord.

In return for the land, a knight promised to support the noble in battle or in other matters. A knight who promised to support a lord in exchange for land was called a **vassal**. The vassal swore that he would always remain loyal to his lord. Historians call this system of promises that governed the relationships between lords and vassals **feudalism** (FYOO-duh-lih-zuhm).

A Lord's Duties

The ties between lords and vassals were the heart of feudalism. Each group had certain responsibilities toward the other. A lord had to send help to his vassals if an enemy attacked. In addition, he had to be fair toward his vassals. He couldn't cheat them or punish them for no reason. If a lord failed to do what he was supposed to, his vassals could break all ties with him.

To defend their lands, many lords built castles. A castle is a large building with strong walls that can easily be defended against attacks. Early castles didn't look like the towering structures we see in movies and storybooks. Those great castles were built much later in the Middle Ages. Most early castles were made of wood, not stone. Nevertheless, these castles provided security in times of war.

A Vassal's Duties

When a lord went to war, he called on his vassals to fight with him. But fighting wasn't a vassal's only duty. For example, vassals had to give their lords money on special occasions, such as when a lord's son became a knight or when his daughter got married. A vassal also had to give his lord food and shelter if he came to visit. If a vassal gained enough land, he could become a lord. In this way a person might be both a lord and a vassal. A knight could also accept fiefs from two different lords and become a vassal to both. Feudal obligations could become confusing.

READING CHECK **Sequencing** What led to the creation of feudalism?

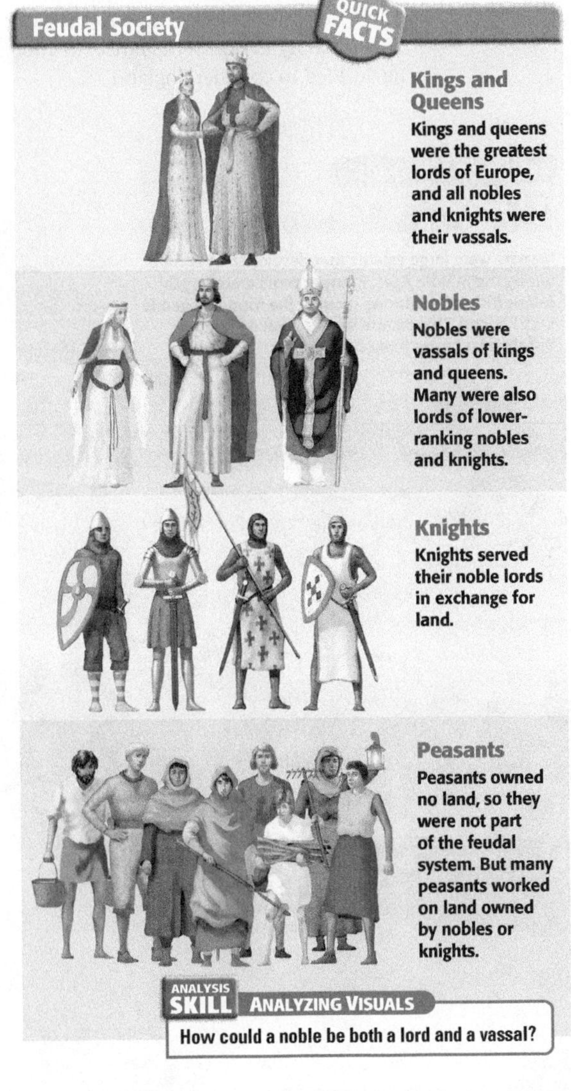

Feudal Society
QUICK FACTS
Kings and Queens
Kings and queens were the greatest lords of Europe, and all nobles and knights were their vassals.
Nobles
Nobles were vassals of kings and queens. Many were also lords of lower-ranking nobles and knights.
Knights
Knights served their noble lords in exchange for land.
Peasants
Peasants owned no land, so they were not part of the feudal system. But many peasants worked on land owned by nobles or knights.

ANALYSIS SKILL **ANALYZING VISUALS**

How could a noble be both a lord and a vassal?

Direct Teach

Main Idea

1 Feudalism Governs Knights and Nobles

Feudalism governed how knights and nobles dealt with each other.

Describe Under the feudal system, what type of exchange took place between lords and vassals? *Vassals gave their support and loyalty to their lords in exchange for a fief, or piece of land.*

Explain How could a vassal become a lord? *If a vassal gained enough land, he could give some to other knights and become a lord himself.*

Make Inferences Why were the Frankish kings unable to defend their empire against invaders, such as the Vikings, Magyars, and Muslims? *because the invaders made quick attacks and the Frankish army was too slow to react*

Quick Facts Transparency: Feudal Society

Checking for Understanding

Select the best answer for each of the following:

1. Nobles who gave land in return for military service were called
   a. knights c. serfs
   b. *lords* d. kings
2. Which of the following duties did a vassal owe his lord?
   a. land
   b. *military service*
   c. servants
   d. horses
3. The system of promises that governed lords and vassals is known as
   a. obligations c. fief
   b. manorialism d. *feudalism*

Differentiating Instruction

Special Needs Learners **Below Level**

1. Have students look at the illustration above. Ask students what the diagram represents.
2. Ask students how many social classes the diagram shows *(four)*. Have them identify the different classes *(kings and queens, nobles, knights, peasants)*.
3. Ask students to read and identify which levels served as lords *(kings and queens, nobles)*. Then ask them to identify which levels served as vassals *(nobles and knights)*.
4. Ask students to identify which levels were outside the feudal system *(peasants)*.
5. Have students select one of the social classes from the illustration. Have each student write a brief classified advertisement that identifies the qualifications expected of someone from that social class.

LS Verbal/Linguistic, Visual/Spatial

Alternative Assessment Handbook, Rubric 16: Judging Information

Answers

Analyzing Visuals *A noble could receive land from a lord or king and in turn grant land to a lower-ranking noble.*

Reading Check *Nobles needed to defend their lands from invaders and from other nobles or kings.*

Direct Teach

Main Idea

2 Feudalism Spreads

Feudalism spread through much of Europe.

Recall Where did feudalism first emerge? *among the Franks*

Identify Who was William the Conqueror? *the duke of Normandy who conquered England and made himself the new king of England*

Sequence How did feudalism spread in the 1000s? *Frankish knights introduced it to northern Italy, Spain, Germany, and England. From Germany, they spread it to eastern Europe.*

Activity **Writing Headlines**
Have students write a newspaper headline that describes William the Conqueror's conquest of England.

CRF: Biography Activity: William the Conqueror

CRF: Primary Source Activity: Feudal Capitularies

Info to Know

The Normans The people of Normandy are referred to as Normans. They get their name from the word *Nortmanni,* or "north men." The Normans were descendants of the Vikings. The Vikings invaded the northern coast of France and took it over by about 900. In 1066, William the Conqueror became king of England as a result of the Norman Conquest.

THE IMPACT TODAY
Though many people have tried to invade England since, William's invasion in 1066 was the last time England was conquered.

Feudalism Spreads

Feudalism was first created by the Franks. Before long the system began to spread into other kingdoms. In the 1000s, Frankish knights introduced feudalism into northern Italy, Spain, and Germany. Feudalism then spread into eastern Europe.

Feudalism also reached Britain in the 1000s. It was brought there by a French noble named William, who was the duke of Normandy in northern France. In 1066, he decided to conquer England.

William and his knights sailed into England and defeated the English king in a battle near the town of Hastings. After winning the battle, William declared himself the new king of England. He became known as **William the Conqueror**. To reward his knights for their part in the victory, William gave them large estates of land in his new country. This was the beginning of feudalism in England.

READING CHECK **Sequencing** How did feudalism spread to England?

History Close-up

Life on a Manor

Manors were large estates that developed in Europe during the Middle Ages. Many manors were largely self-sufficient, producing most of the food and goods they needed. This picture shows what a manor in Britain might have looked like.

The lord of the manor lived in a large stone house called the manor house.
Peasants grew vegetables in small gardens near their houses.
In the fall, peasants worked to harvest crops like wheat.

508

Differentiating Instruction

Struggling Readers **Below Level**

1. Have students look at the picture above. Help them locate the manor house and church. Explain that the lord owned the manor house and all the land surrounding it, including the land on which the church was built.
2. Help students locate peasants' homes. Explain that the peasants were people who worked on farms. Have the students locate peasants in the picture. Ask them what the peasants are doing *(harvesting crops).*
3. Help students locate sheep. Explain that in the Middle Ages most clothes were made from wool and that people got wool from sheep.
4. Help students locate the mill and blacksmith shop. Explain that the mill is a place where grain was made into flour and that flour is used to make bread. Explain that a blacksmith shop was a place where iron tools were made and that farmers used iron tools for farming.
LS **Verbal/Linguistic, Visual/Spatial**

Answers

Reading Check *It was carried there by William the Conqueror.*

The Manor System

When a knight received a fief from his lord, he needed a way to farm it. Knights were fighters who didn't have time to work in the fields. At the same time, peasants, or small farmers, needed to grow food to live. Very few peasants, however, owned any land.

As a result, a new economic system developed. Under this system, knights allowed peasants to farm land on their large estates. In return, the peasants had to give the knights food or other payment.

The large estate owned by a knight or lord was called a **manor**. In general, each manor included a large house or castle, pastures, fields, and forests. It also had a village where the peasants who worked on the manor lived.

Peasants, Serfs, and Other Workers

Most medieval lords kept about one-fourth to one-third of their land for their own use. The rest of the land was divided among peasants and **serfs**—workers who were tied to the land on which they lived.

The village church was built on a small piece of land that belonged to the lord.
Sheep grazed on grassy fields, and villagers used sheep's wool to make clothes.
The village blacksmith made iron tools for farming.
Harvested wheat was taken to the mill and ground into flour, which was used to make bread.

ANALYSIS SKILL ANALYZING VISUALS

What goods can you see being produced on this manor?

Direct Teach

Main Idea

3 The Manor System

The manor system dominated Europe's economy.

Define What was a manor? *a large estate owned by a knight or lord*

Explain Why didn't knights farm the land they received? *because they provided protection and had peasants to farm the land*

Contrast How did peasants differ from serfs? *serfs—workers tied to the land on which they lived, could not leave without lord's permission; peasants—farmers who paid knights for the use of their land.*

Checking for Understanding

Select the best answer for each of the following:

1. Who first created feudalism?
   a. Spanish
   b. Germans
   c. *Franks*
   d. Italians
2. Knights did not have time to
   a. support nobles
   b. fight battles
   c. serve their lords
   d. *work in the fields*
3. In return for farming knights' land, peasants had to
   a. *give knights food*
   b. fight for knights
   c. care for knights' children
   d. provide weapons

Critical Thinking: Comparing and Contrasting

At Level

The Manor System

1. Review with students the characteristics of the manor system.
2. To help the students compare and contrast the manor system with modern-day life, copy the graphic organizer for students to see. Omit the blue answers.
3. Have students copy the graphic organizer and complete it by identifying the similarities and differences between the medieval manor system and modern-day life.

LS Verbal/Linguistic, Visual/Spatial

Manor	Similarities	Modern
-peasants tied to land *-live in small villages* *-knights and lords* *-most people farmers*	*-gardens near homes* *-harvest crops* *-wealthy live in large homes*	*-people free to move* *-live in cities and towns* *-no knights or lords* *-variety of jobs* *-no manors*

Answers

Analyzing Visuals *foods (vegetables, wheat, flour, and bread), wool for clothing, tools for farming*

Direct Teach

Main Idea

❸ The Manor System

The manor system dominated Europe's economy.

Explain What did serfs get in return for working the fields on their lords' land? *protection and a small piece of land to farm for themselves*

Summarize What responsibilities did the lord have in running his manor? *punished misbehavior, settled disputes, and collected taxes*

Analyze What role did women play in medieval society? *worked to support families, ran households, supervised servants, obeyed fathers and husbands, governed manors when husbands went to war*

CRF: Biography Activity: Eleanor of Aquitaine

CRF: Interdisciplinary Project: Person, Place, and Problem: Group Stories

Did you know . . .

Eleanor of Aquitaine was the wife of two different kings in turn, Louis VII of France and Henry II of England, and the mother of two kings, Richard I and John I of England.

hmhsocialstudies.com

Online Resources
Activity: Medieval Fashion Show

About the Illustration
This illustration of Eleanor of Aquitaine is an artist's conception based on available sources. However, historians are uncertain exactly what Eleanor of Aquitaine looked like.

Although they weren't slaves, serfs weren't allowed to leave their land without the lord's permission. Serfs spent much of their time working in their lords' fields. In return for this work, they got a small piece of land to farm for themselves. They also received their lords' protection against outlaws and raiders.

The lives of serfs and peasants weren't easy. Farm labor was hard, and they often worked in the fields late into the night. Men did most of the farming. Women made clothing, cooked, grew vegetables, and gathered firewood. Even children worked, tending sheep and chickens.

In addition to peasants and serfs, most manors had several skilled workers. These workers traded their goods and services to the peasants in exchange for food. Lords wanted the people who lived on the manor to produce everything they needed, including food and clothing.

Academic Vocabulary
role assigned behavior

Biography

Eleanor of Aquitaine
c. 1122–1204

Eleanor of Aquitaine was one of the most powerful people of the Middle Ages. She ruled Aquitaine, a region in southwestern France, as the king's vassal. In 1137 Eleanor became queen of France when she married King Louis VII. Later, she divorced Louis and became queen of England by marrying King Henry II of England. Even while she was queen of England, she spent much of her time ruling her own territory. Eleanor had many children, and two of her sons later became kings of England.

Drawing Conclusions
Why do you think Eleanor had more power than other women in the Middle Ages?

Manor Lords

The lord of a manor controlled everything that happened on his lands. His word was law. The lord resolved any disputes that arose on the manor and punished people who misbehaved. He also collected taxes from the people who lived on his manor.

As you would expect, manor lords and ladies lived more comfortably than other people on the manor. They had servants and large houses. Still, their lives weren't easy. Lords who survived diseases faced the possibility of being killed in war.

Women in the Middle Ages

Regardless of their social class, women in the Middle Ages had fewer rights than men. Women generally had to obey the wishes of their fathers or husbands. But women still had important **roles** in society. As you have read, peasant women worked to support their families. Noblewomen also had duties. They ran manor households and supervised servants. Women governed manors when their husbands went to war. Some noblewomen, like the French woman **Eleanor of Aquitaine**, had great political power. Other women who wanted power and influence joined the most powerful of institutions, the Christian Church.

Reading Check **Contrasting** How were the lives of nobles and peasants different?

Towns and Trade Grow

In the Middle Ages, most people lived on manors or on small farms, not in towns. As a result, most towns were small. After about 1000, however, this situation began to change. Some towns became big cities. At the same time, new towns appeared.

What led to the growth of medieval towns? For one thing, Europe's population increased, partly because more food was

Cross-Discipline Activity: Science

At Level

Medieval Technology Fair

Research Required

Materials: poster board, art supplies

1. Review with students the new technology that improved life in the Middle Ages.
2. Have students use the library, Internet, or other resources to research some of these technological developments of the early Middle Ages. Ask students to select one invention or example of technology that made life easier.
3. Have each student create a poster that explains how the invention or method worked. If possible, have students include a photo or illustration in their poster.
4. Have students hold a technology fair in which they display their posters and explain to visitors the function and purpose of the invention they researched.

LS Verbal/Linguistic, Visual/Spatial

Alternative Assessment Handbook, Rubrics 28: Posters; and 30: Research

Answers

Biography *She ruled Aquitaine, was a vassal of the king, and was married to two kings.*

Reading Check *nobles—lived more comfortably than peasants, had larger houses and servants; peasants—worked hard, lived in small houses, little freedom*

available. New technology helped farmers produce larger harvests than ever before. Among these improvements was a heavier plow. With this plow farmers could dig deeper into the soil, helping their plants grow better. Another new device, the horse collar, allowed farmers to plow fields using horses. In times past, farmers had used oxen, which were strong but slow. With horses, farmers could tend larger fields, grow more food, and feed more people.

Towns also grew because trade increased. As Europe's population grew, so did trade. Trade routes spread all across Europe. Merchants also brought goods from Asia and Africa to sell in markets in Europe. The chance to make money in trade led many people to leave their farms and move to cities, causing cities to grow even larger.

In time, the growth of trade led to the decline of feudalism. Knights began to demand money for their services instead of land. At the same time, serfs and peasants left their manors for towns, slowly weakening the manor system.

READING CHECK **Identifying Cause and Effect** Why did towns and trade grow in the Middle Ages?

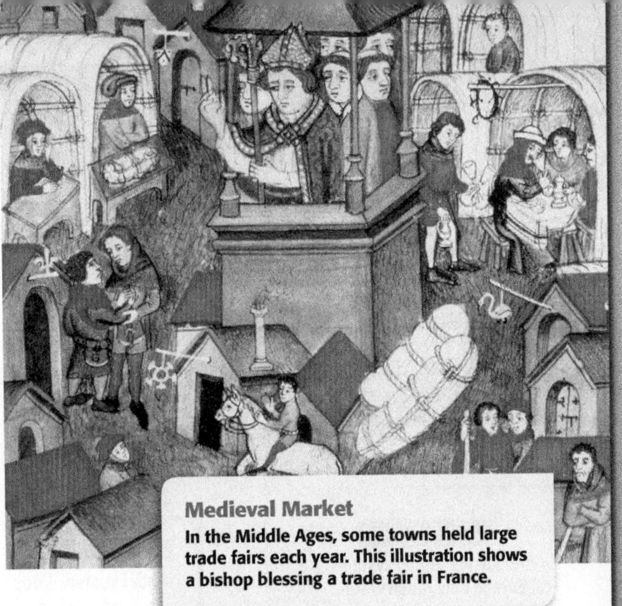

Medieval Market
In the Middle Ages, some towns held large trade fairs each year. This illustration shows a bishop blessing a trade fair in France.

SUMMARY AND PREVIEW In this section, you learned about European feudalism and the social and economic relationships it created among people. In the next section, you'll read about how this system compares to one that developed halfway around the world in Japan.

hmhsocialstudies.com
ANIMATED HISTORY
Europe, AD 1000

Section 3 Assessment

hmhsocialstudies.com ONLINE QUIZ

Reviewing Ideas, Terms, and People

1. a. **Define** What was a **knight**?
   b. **Explain** Why did **vassals** have to serve lords?
   c. **Elaborate** Do you think knights or lords benefited more from **feudalism**? Why?
2. **Explain** How did **William the Conqueror** help spread feudalism?
3. a. **Describe** What was a typical **manor** like?
   b. **Elaborate** How do you think most **serfs** felt about the manor system?
4. a. **Recall** What led to the growth of Europe's population in the Middle Ages?
   b. **Draw Conclusions** Why do you think many peasants left their farms for cities?

Critical Thinking

5. **Analyzing** Draw a flow chart like the one below. Review your notes and then, in each box, list the duties and obligations that each group had toward the other.

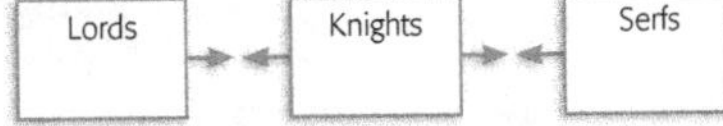

Focus on Writing

6. **Writing about Knights** Take notes on the knights described in this section and how what you've learned will affect your search for knights. What kinds of people will you hire? How will you pay them? Write your answers in your notebook.

Direct Teach

Main Idea

4 Towns and Trade Grow

Towns and trade grew and helped end the feudal system.

Identify What is trade? *possible answer—an exchange of goods between different communities or regions*

Recall When did towns start becoming cities and new towns start appearing? *about 1000*

Make Inferences Why did Europe's population increase? *The development of new technology helped farmers plant larger fields, grow more food, and feed more people.*

Review & Assess

Close

Have students review this section by creating an outline that uses the main ideas as headings.

Review

Online Quiz, Section 3

Assess

SE Section 3 Assessment
PASS: Section 3 Quiz
Alternative Assessment Handbook

Reteach/Classroom Intervention

Guided Reading Workbook, Section 3
Interactive Skills Tutor CD-ROM

Section 3 Assessment Answers

1. a. warriors who fought on horseback
   b. because they had received land from the lord
   c. Answers will vary, but students should note that lords received protection and loyalty while knights received land.
2. He introduced feudalism to England after he conquered it in 1066.
3. a. It had a large house or castle, fields, forests, pastures, and a village.
   b. Answers will vary, but students should indicate that a serf's life was very difficult.
4. a. new technology that produced larger harvests
   b. They had more opportunities to make more money in cities than on the manor.
5. lord to knight—military aid, gift of land; knight to lord—military service, money on special occasions; knight to serf—land to farm on, protection; serf to knight—food or other payment
6. possible responses—look for brave, dedicated knights; pay them with land or money

Answers

Reading Check *The production of more food meant that more people could be fed, which caused the population to grow. This growth in population caused towns to grow. The growth of towns led to an increase in trade, which in turn led people to move to cities in search of jobs, causing cities to grow even more.*

Preteach

Bellringer

If YOU were there . . . Use the **Daily Bellringer Transparency** to help students answer the question.

Daily Bellringer Transparency, Section 4

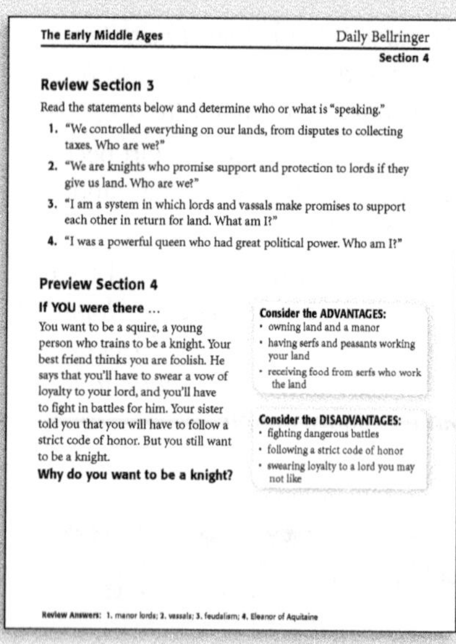

The Early Middle Ages — Daily Bellringer — Section 4

Review Section 3

Read the statements below and determine who or what is "speaking."

1. "We controlled everything on our lands, from disputes to collecting taxes. Who are we?"
2. "We are knights who promise support and protection to lords if they give us land. Who are we?"
3. "I am a system in which lords and vassals make promises to support each other in return for land. What am I?"
4. "I was a powerful queen who had great political power. Who am I?"

Preview Section 4

If YOU were there ...

You want to be a squire, a young person who trains to be a knight. Your best friend thinks you are foolish. He says that you'll have to swear a vow of loyalty to your lord, and you'll have to fight in battles for him. Your sister told you that you will have to follow a strict code of honor. But you still want to be a knight.

Why do you want to be a knight?

Consider the ADVANTAGES:
- owning land and a manor
- having serfs and peasants working your land
- receiving food from serfs who work the land

Consider the DISADVANTAGES:
- fighting dangerous battles
- following a strict code of honor
- swearing loyalty to a lord you may not like

Review Answers: 1. manor lords; 2. vassals; 3. feudalism; 4. Eleanor of Aquitaine

Academic Vocabulary

Review with students the high-use academic term in this section.

elements parts (p. 514)

Building Vocabulary

Preteach or review the following terms:

literary of or relating to literature (p. 513)

CRF: Vocabulary Builder Activity, Section 4

Taking Notes

Have students use the graphic organizer online to take notes on the section. This activity will prepare students for the Section Assessment, in which they will complete a graphic organizer that builds on the information using the Critical Thinking Skill: Comparing and Contrasting.

SECTION 4

Feudal Societies

If YOU were there...

You want to be a squire, a young person who trains to be a knight. Your best friend thinks you are foolish. He says that you'll have to swear a vow of loyalty to your lord, and you'll have to fight in battles for him. Your sister told you that you will have to follow a strict code of honor. But you still want to be a knight.

Why do you want to be a knight?

What You Will Learn...

Main Ideas

1. Feudal societies shared common elements in Europe and Japan.
2. Europe and Japan differed in their cultural elements such as religion and art.

The Big Idea

Although the feudal systems of Europe and Japan were similar, their cultures were very different.

Key Terms

chivalry, *p. 513*
haiku, *p. 514*

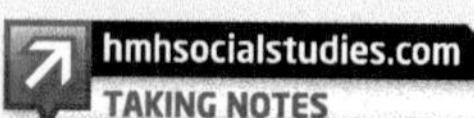

Use the graphic organizer online to take notes on the feudal systems and cultures of Europe and Japan in the Middle Ages.

BUILDING BACKGROUND Knights were an important part of feudal society. People who wanted to be knights did have to swear vows of loyalty, fight in battles, and follow a code of honor. But European knights were not the only people who had to live by these rules. Half a world away, Japanese samurai lived under similar obligations. In fact, if you look at these two societies, you will see that many striking similarities existed between them.

Feudal Societies Share Common Elements

Feudalism was not unique to Europe. As you have already read, the Japanese developed a very similar system halfway around the world from Europe at about the same time. But how similar were the two societies?

Lords and Vassals

In Europe, the basis for the feudal system was land. Kings and lords gave land to knights. In return, the knights promised to serve their lords and fight for them when necessary. Many knights owned large manors. Peasants and serfs worked on the manors and paid the lords in food.

A very similar system existed in Japan. There, the emperor gave land to great lords who were later called daimyo. In turn, these lords employed warriors called samurai. Like European knights, the samurai promised to serve and fight for their lords. In exchange, the samurai received rice and grain. Lords got the grain from peasants who farmed their land. Peasants had to pay their lords in grain.

512

Teach the Big Idea

At Level

Feudal Societies

1. **Teach** Ask students the questions in the Main Idea boxes to teach this section.
2. **Apply** Draw a large Venn diagram for students to see. Label one circle *Medieval Europe* and the other *Feudal Japan*. In the overlapping area, write the label *Similarities*. Have students copy the Venn diagram and complete it by identifying the similarities and differences between medieval Europe and feudal Japan. **LS Verbal/Linguistic, Visual/Spatial**
3. **Review** Have students summarize the similarities and differences they identified.
4. **Practice/Homework** Have students create collages that identify similarities and differences between Europe and Japan. **LS Visual/Spatial**

Alternative Assessment Handbook, Rubrics 8: Collages; and 13: Graphic Organizers

Samurai and Knights

Although Japanese samurai and European knights never actually met, they had much in common. Both were the elite warriors of their time and place.

ANALYSIS SKILL ANALYZING VISUALS

How are the samurai and knight similar? How are they different?

Knights and Samurai

The lives of knights and samurai were, in many ways, very similar. Both had to swear vows of loyalty to their lords. These lords expected them to fight well and to be fearless in battle. The lords also expected their knights or samurai to live disciplined and honorable lives.

Both European knights and Japanese samurai had to follow strict codes of honor that governed how they behaved. You have already learned about Bushido, the Japanese code of the samurai. Europeans called their code of honorable behavior for knights **chivalry** (SHIV-uhl-ree). Like Bushido, chivalry required knights to be brave and loyal but humble and modest at the same time. It also required them to be kind and generous when dealing with people, especially women.

Because of their loyalty and dedication, both knights and samurai were greatly admired by other members of their societies. This admiration can often be seen in literary descriptions of the men, such as this description of the French knight Roland and his comrades who are greatly outnumbered by their enemies:

> "The battle is fearful and full of grief.
> Oliver and Roland strike like good men,
> the Archbishop, more than a thousand blows,
> and the Twelve Peers do not hang back, they strike!
> the French fight side by side, all as one man.
> The pagans die by hundreds, by thousands:
> whoever does not flee finds no refuge from death,
> like it or not, there he ends his days."
>
> –from *The Song of Roland*, translated by Frederick Goldin

FOCUS ON READING
Why do you think a primary source is included here?

Even though Roland and the others were almost certain that they would die, they continued to fight. They became heroes, admired for their courage and bravery.

Direct Teach

Main Idea

❶ Feudal Societies Share Common Elements

Feudal societies shared common elements in Europe and Japan.

Explain According to the code of chivalry, how were knights required to behave? *be brave and loyal, humble and modest, and kind and generous, especially with women*

Make Generalizations How did knights and samurai react when faced with difficult odds? *with courage*

Compare How were the feudal systems of Europe and Japan similar? *In both societies, lords gave land to people who promised to serve them and fight for them. These estates were farmed by peasants.*

 **CRF:** Literature Activity: Europe and Japan: Comparing Poetry of the Middle Ages

Linking to Today

Chivalry The word *chivalry* comes from the French word *chevalier*, or "knight," which in turn comes from the word *cheval*, or "horse." The English word *cavalry* is related to *cheval* as well. Cavalry, knights, and chevaliers all fought on horseback.

The word *chivalrous* is also related to *chivalry*. Today when we say people are chivalrous, we mean they are honorable or courteous, not that they follow the code of chivalry. Chivalrous behavior today has nothing to do with horses.

Differentiating Instruction

Advanced/Gifted and Talented **Above Level**

1. Provide students with the following background information to help them understand the excerpt from *The Song of Roland*.
   - The battle referred to is the Battle of Roncesvalles, which took place as Charlemagne and his troops were returning to France from Spain. They were attacked by the Basques, who wiped out much of Charlemagne's force.
   - Roland is Charlemagne's favorite nephew. Oliver is Roland's best friend.
   - Roland and Oliver are two of the Twelve Peers of France. A peer is a nobleman.
2. Have students reread the passage from *The Song of Roland* now that they have this additional information, then rewrite the passage in their own words.
3. Ask volunteers to read their rewritten passages. How did rewriting help them understand what the author is saying?
   LS Verbal/Linguistic

Alternative Assessment Handbook, Rubric 37: Writing Assignments

Answers

Samurai and Knights *similarities—wore armor, rode horses, trained soldiers, fought with swords; differences—knight carried a banner and shields; armor made of different materials*

Focus on Reading *because it provides a firsthand account of the lives of knights*

Direct Teach

Main Idea

❷ Europe and Japan Differ

Europe and Japan differed in their cultural elements such as religion and art.

Recall What was the main difference between medieval Europeans and Japanese? *religion; Europeans were Christian, while Japanese blended Buddhism, Shinto, and Confucianism*

Analyze How did the subjects of European art and Japanese art differ during the Middle Ages? *European—dealt mostly with religious themes; Japanese—dealt with natural themes*

Evaluate Which were greater, the similarities or the differences between European and Japanese societies in the Middle Ages? Why? *Answers will vary, but students should provide examples to support either similarities or differences.*

CRF: Literature Activity: Europe and Japan: Comparing Poetry

Quick Facts Transparency: Comparing and Contrasting Europe and Japan

Info to Know

Feudalism in Europe and Japan In Europe, feudalism did not become part of the law code until the 1200s, but it was already becoming obsolete by the 1300s. Feudalism continued in Japan until 1869, when it was abolished by law.

Answers

Art in Europe and Japan *The European painting has a religious theme, while the Japanese painting emphasizes nature.*

Reading Check *Both had to swear vows of loyalty to their lords. Both were expected to live disciplined and honorable lives. Both were admired for their courage and bravery.*

The Japanese also admired their warriors for their courage. A passage from a Japanese text shows a similar admiration for warriors fighting impossible odds:

ACADEMIC VOCABULARY
elements parts

> "Where Naozane galloped, Sueshige followed; where Sueshige galloped, Naozane followed. Neither willing to be outdone, they dashed in by turns, whipping their horses and attacking until the sparks flew... Naozane pulled out the arrows that were lodged in his own armor, tossed them aside, faced the stronghold with a scowl, and shouted in a mighty voice, 'I am Naozane, the man who left Kamakura last winter determined to give his life for Lord Yoritomo... Confront me! Confront me!'"
>
> –from *The Tale of the Heike*, translated by Helen Craig McCullough

READING CHECK **Comparing** How were European knights and Japanese samurai similar?

Europe and Japan Differ

Although European and Japanese societies were the same in some ways, in most ways they were not. Their two cultures were also very different.

Perhaps the main difference between medieval Europeans and Japanese was religion. Nearly all Europeans were Christian, while the Japanese blended **elements** of Buddhism, Shinto, and Confucianism. European and Japanese religions taught very different ways of looking at the world. People in those places, therefore, did not act the same way.

The differences between Europe and Japan can also be seen in the artistic forms popular in each place. European art in the Middle Ages dealt mostly with religious themes. Paintings showed scenes from the Bible, and writers tried to inspire people with stories about great Christians.

In Japan, on the other hand, most art dealt with natural themes. Paintings of nature were common, and people built many gardens. Buildings blended with nature, rather than standing out. Japanese literature also celebrated nature. For example, Japanese poets in the 1600s created **haiku** (HY-koo), short, three-line poems of 17 syllables that describe nature scenes.

Art in Europe and Japan

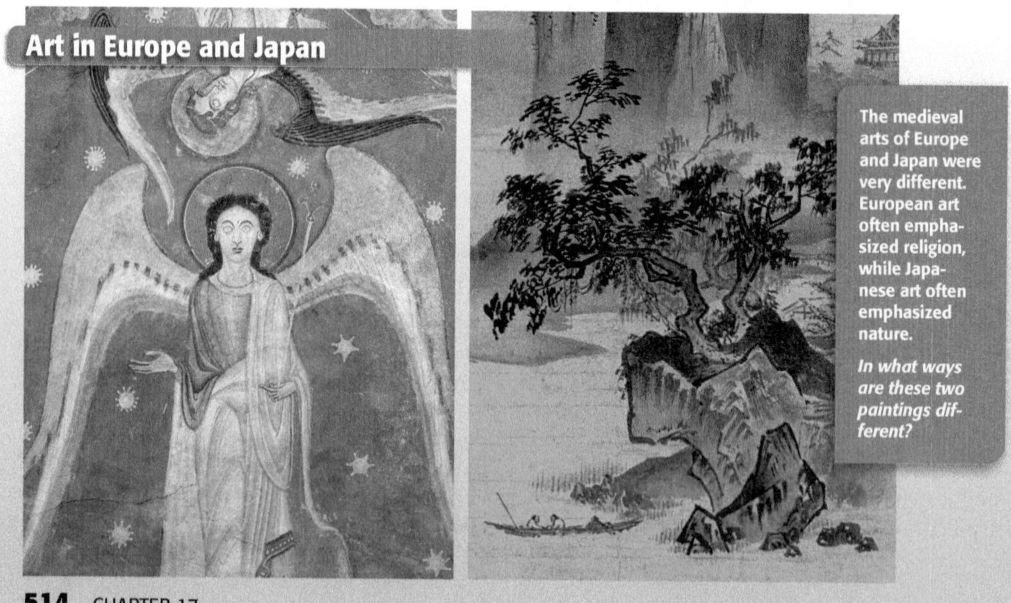

The medieval arts of Europe and Japan were very different. European art often emphasized religion, while Japanese art often emphasized nature.

In what ways are these two paintings different?

Critical Thinking: Comparing and Contrasting

At Level

Compare-Contrast Posters

Research Required

1. Review with the class the similarities and differences between the feudal societies of medieval Europe and Japan.
2. Have students use the library, Internet, or other resources to find illustrations that depict both feudal Europe and Japan. Remind students to look for images that represent feudalism, art, religion, and warfare.
3. Have students create posters in which they use the illustrations to depict the similarities and differences between these two societies. Ask students to include a title for their poster as well as captions that explain their illustrations.
4. Have students present their posters to the class. Lead a discussion on the key similarities and differences that existed between feudal Europe and Japan.

LS Verbal/Linguistic, Visual/Spatial

Alternative Assessment Handbook, Rubric 28: Posters

Comparing and Contrasting Europe and Japan 

Feudal Europe	Both	Feudal Japan
■ Christianity ■ Religious themes in art and literature	■ Feudal government ■ Royalty (kings and queens, emperor) ■ Nobles (lords, daimyo) ■ Warriors (knights, samurai) ■ Warrior codes of honor (chivalry, Bushido) ■ Peasants worked land	■ Buddhism, Shinto, Confucianism ■ Nature themes in art and literature

Here is one example of haiku:

Very soon they die—
but of that there is no sign
in the locust-cry.

–Matsuo Basho, from *Anthology of Japanese Literature*, edited by Donald Keene

Although European and Japanese feudal systems seemed similar, the cultures that lay behind them were different. Still, it is remarkable to think that feudal systems so similar could exist so far apart.

READING CHECK **Contrasting** How were feudal European and Japanese cultures different?

SUMMARY AND PREVIEW In this section you learned how to compare feudalism in Europe and Japan. Although both Europe and Japan had feudal societies, there were many differences in the two societies. Feudalism lasted much longer in Japan than it did in Europe, not disappearing until the 1800s. In the next chapter you will learn about how European society changed after feudalism disappeared in the later Middle Ages. One major change was the growing importance of religion.

Section 4 Assessment

hmhsocialstudies.com ONLINE QUIZ

Reviewing Ideas, Terms, and People

1. a. **Define** What was **chivalry**?
   b. **Compare** What were three characteristics knights and samurai shared?
   c. **Develop** Why do you think feudal systems developed in both Europe and Japan?
2. a. **Identify** What was the religion of most people in medieval Europe? What religions influenced most people in Japan?
   b. **Contrast** How were the subjects of **haiku** different from medieval European poems?
   c. **Evaluate** In your opinion, were European and Japanese societies more similar to or different from each other? Explain your answer.

Critical Thinking

3. **Comparing and Contrasting** Draw a chart like the one below. Using your notes, list two similarities and one key difference between knights and samurai.

Similarities	Difference
1.	1.
2.	

FOCUS ON WRITING

4. **Describing Chivalry** Think about what you've just learned about chivalry. What kinds of rules will you expect your knights to follow? How will you explain these rules to them?

Direct Teach

Info to Know

Medieval Castles During the feudal age, both European and Japanese lords constructed castles built of wood to protect themselves and their families from attack. As time went on, castles in both Europe and Japan became larger and more elaborate and came to symbolize the power and importance of their owners.

Review & Assess

Close

Have students write a paragraph that summarizes the similarities and differences between feudal Japan and Europe.

Review

Online Quiz, Section 4

Assess

SE Section 4 Assessment

PASS: Section 4 Quiz

Alternative Assessment Handbook

Reteach/Classroom Intervention

Guided Reading Workbook, Section 4

Interactive Skills Tutor CD-ROM

Section 4 Assessment Answers

1. a. a code of behavior that knights were expected to follow
   b. swore oaths of loyalty, fought, followed codes of honor, received some type of reward for services, greatly admired for bravery
   c. Local lords needed the support of warriors to defend their lands in the absence of central order.
2. a. Christian; a blend of Buddhism, Shinto, and Confucianism
   b. Haiku were about nature, while medieval European poems were about religion.
   c. Answers will vary, but students should indicate that medieval Europe and feudal Japan both had a system of feudalism.
3. similarities—professional warriors; received land; loyal to lords; followed codes of honor; differences—religion; type of armor worn
4. possible responses—to swear an oath of loyalty, to be obedient, to be brave; through conversation, provide written laws

Answers

Reading Check *Europe—Christianity influenced almost all artistic forms; Japan—blend of Shinto, Buddhism, and Confucianism; art based on themes of nature*

Social Studies Skills

Interpreting Diagrams

Activity **Sample Diagrams**

Materials: photocopies of sample diagrams

Make photocopies of two to four diagrams. You might ask the librarian to suggest books that contain diagrams related to the Middle Ages. Provide each student with copies of the diagrams. Go through the diagrams as a class. Have students identify labeled items and other important features. Then have each student select one diagram and write a paragraph describing what it shows. Have volunteers read their paragraphs to the class. Correct any student errors. **LS Visual/Spatial**

- Alternative Assessment Handbook, Rubric 37: Writing Assignments
- Interactive Skills Tutor CD-ROM, Lesson 6: Interpret Maps, Graphs, Charts, Visuals, and Political Cartoons

Social Studies Skills

Analysis | Critical Thinking | Economics | **Study**

Interpreting Diagrams

Understand the Skill

Diagrams are drawings that use lines and labels to explain or illustrate something. Different types of diagrams have different purposes. *Pictorial diagrams* show an object in simple form, much like it would look if you were viewing it. *Cutaway diagrams* show the "insides" of an object. *Component diagrams* show how an object is organized by separating it into parts. Such diagrams are sometimes also called *schematic drawings*. The ability to interpret diagrams will help you to better understand a historical object, its function, and how it worked.

Learn the Skill

Use these basic steps to interpret a diagram:

1. Determine what type of diagram it is.
2. Read the diagram's title or caption to find out what it represents.
3. Look for any labels and read them carefully. Most diagrams include text that identifies the object's parts or explains relationships between the parts.
4. If a legend is present, study it to identify and understand any symbols and colors that are used in the diagram.
5. Look for numbers or letters that might indicate a sequence of steps. Also look for any arrows that might show direction or movement.

An Early Castle

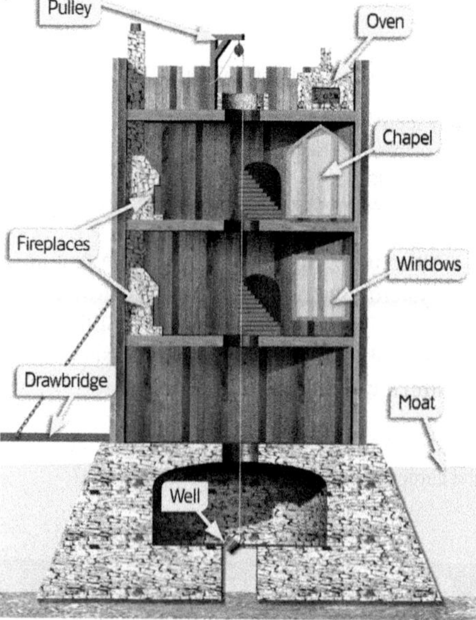

Practice and Apply the Skill

Interpret the diagram above, of an early castle, and answer the following questions.

1. What type of diagram is this?
2. What labels in diagram suggest how the castle was heated?
3. What was the purpose of the pulley?
4. Of what materials was the castle made?
5. What features of the castle helped make it secure against attack?

Social Studies Skills Activity: Interpreting Diagrams

At Level

Creating Diagrams

Research Required

Materials: art supplies, poster board

1. Have each student conduct research to find a diagram of a historical structure from the Middle Ages. For example, students might look for a diagram of a cathedral, a castle, a mill, or a manor (as shown in this chapter).
2. Each student should create a large copy of the diagram on poster board. Below the diagram, students should provide captions explaining the information in the diagram and providing background information about the structure.
3. Ask for volunteers to share their diagrams with the class. Give other students a chance to interpret the diagrams and to ask questions. Then have volunteers explain their diagrams.
4. Display students' diagrams around the classroom. **LS Visual/Spatial**

- Alternative Assessment Handbook, Rubric 3: Artwork; and 30: Research

Answers

Practice and Apply the Skill

1. *a cutaway diagram;* **2.** *fireplaces;* **3.** *to draw water from the well;* **4.** *wood and some stone above the waterline and stone below the waterline;* **5.** *the water-filled moat surrounding the castle; the single entrance and drawbridge; the high, narrow windows*

CHAPTER 17 Chapter Review

History's Impact
▶ **video series**
Review the video to answer the focus question:
What do you think were some benefits and consequences of living in feudal societies?

Visual Summary

Use the visual summary below to help you review the main ideas of the chapter.

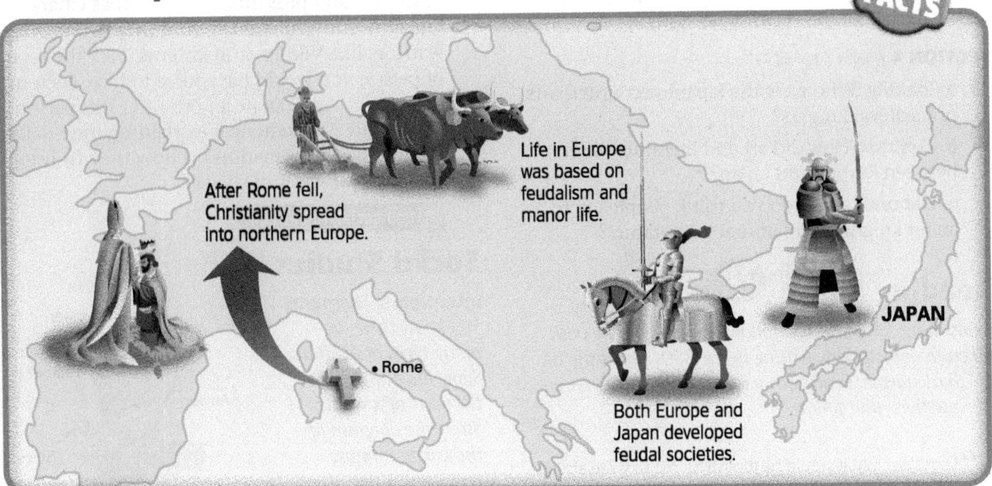

Reviewing Vocabulary, Terms, and People

Write each word defined below, circling each letter that is marked by a star. Then write the word these letters spell.

1. * _ _ _ _—religious men who lived in isolated communities
2. * _ _ _ _ _ _ of Aquitaine—one of the most powerful women of the Middle Ages
3. _ _ _ * _ _ _ _ _—a political system in which land is given for military service
4. _ _ * _ _ _ _ _—a code of behavior that knights had to follow
5. _ * _ _ _—farm workers who were tied to the land they worked
6. * _ _ _ _ _—someone who received land in exchange for military service
7. _ * _ _ _—a large estate
8. _ _ _ _ * _ _ _ _ _ _—Frankish king who created a huge empire

Comprehension and Critical Thinking

SECTION 1 *(Pages 496–499)*

9. **a. Identify** What region of Europe has the best land for farming?
   b. Analyze How have rivers and seas influenced life in Europe?
   c. Evaluate Based on its geography, in which part of Europe would you want to live? Why would you want to live there?

SECTION 2 *(Pages 500–504)*

10. **a. Identify** What two groups of people were largely responsible for the northern spread of Christianity?
    b. Compare In what way was the empire of the Franks under Charlemagne like the Roman Empire?
    c. Elaborate How do you think the building of new monasteries helped spread Christianity?

Answers

Visual Summary

Review and Inquiry Use the visual summary to review the chapter's main ideas and supporting details.

Quick Facts Transparency: The Early Middle Ages Visual Summary

Reviewing Vocabulary, Terms, and People

1. **m**onks
2. **E**leanor
3. feu**d**alism
4. ch**i**valry
5. s**e**rfs
6. **v**assal
7. m**a**nor
8. Char**l**emagne

mystery word—**medieval**

Comprehension and Critical Thinking

9. **a.** Northern European Plain
   b. rivers—transportation routes; seas—transportation, protection from attack, food
   c. Answers will vary, but students should exhibit an understanding of the Europe's diverse geography.
10. **a.** missionaries and monks
    b. covered much of the same territory
    c. possible answer—Monks in these monasteries worked to convert the people living nearby to Christianity.

Review and Assessment Resources

Review and Reinforce

SE Chapter Review
CRF: Chapter Review Activity
Quick Facts Transparency: The Early Middle Ages Visual Summary
Spanish Chapter Summaries Audio CD Program
Online Chapter Summaries in Six Languages
TOS Holt McDougal PuzzleView

Assess

SE Standardized Test Practice
PASS: Chapter Test, Forms A and B
Alternative Assessment Handbook
TOS ExamView Assessment Suite,
Differentiated Instruction Modified Worksheets and Tests CD-ROM: Chapter Test
Online Assessment Program, in the Interactive Student Edition

Reteach/Intervene

Guided Reading Workbook
Differentiated Instruction Teacher Management System: Lesson Plans
Differentiated Instruction Modified Worksheets and Tests CD-ROM
Interactive Skills Tutor CD-ROM

hmhsocialstudies.com
Chapter Resources

Answers

11. a. fewer rights than men, had to obey fathers or husbands, worked in the home

b. They brought skilled workers to the manors to build everything people would need to live.

c. Limited amounts of money led to the development of feudalism, and feudalism in part led to the system of manorialism.

12. a. samurai

b. European art and literature dealt mainly with religious themes, whereas Japanese art and literature dealt mainly with natural themes.

c. They were heroes who were greatly admired for their courage, loyalty, and exciting deeds.

Reading and Analysis Skills

13. The first passage is a secondary source, because it says that no one is alive who has personal knowledge of the events. The second is a primary source, because the author had known Charlemagne personally.

14. the second because he knew and spoke with Charlemagne

Reviewing Themes

15. Answers will vary, but students should indicate an understanding that most Europeans were Christians.

16. Answers will vary, but students should provide examples from the text to support their opinions.

Using the Internet

17. Go to hmhsocialstudies.com to access a rubric for this activity.

Social Studies Skills

18. protection—armor, helmet, shield; recognition—banner, cloth trappings

19. sword

20. to identify the lord for whom he fought

Focus on Writing

21. Rubric Students' job advertisements should:

- explain why knights are needed.
- describe the skills or traits of the people best suited for the job.
- list the rules for behavior.
- tell how knights will be paid and emphasize the benefits of the job.

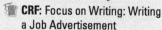

CRF: Focus on Writing: Writing a Job Advertisement

SECTION 3 *(Pages 506–511)*

11. a. Describe What were women's lives like during the Middle Ages?

b. Analyze How did knights and lords try to make their manors self-sufficient?

c. Elaborate How was feudalism related to medieval Europe's economic system?

SECTION 4 *(Pages 512–515)*

12. a. Identify Who were the Japanese counterparts of medieval knights?

b. Contrast How did art and literature differ between Europe and Japan?

c. Elaborate Why do you think people wrote about knights and samurai in literature?

Reading Skills

Evaluating Sources *The following passages are both taken from historians writing in the 800s about the life of Charlemagne. Read both passages and then answer the questions that follow.*

> "I consider that it would be foolish for me to write about Charlemagne's birth and childhood . . . for nothing is set down in writing about this and nobody can be found still alive who claims to have any personal knowledge of these matters. I have therefore decided to leave out what is not really known . . ."
>
> –Einhard, from *Two Lives of Charlemagne,* translated by Lewis Thorpe

> "When I was a child, he was already a very old man. He brought me up and used to tell me about these events. I was a poor pupil, and I often ran away, but in the end he forced me to listen."
>
> –Notker, from *Two Lives of Charlemagne,* translated by Lewis Thorpe

13. Are these passages primary or secondary sources?

14. Which historian do you think would be the most credible, or believable?

Reviewing Themes

15. Religion Do you think religion helped to unify or divide Europeans in the Middle Ages? Why?

16. Society and Culture Do you think religion or government had more influence on medieval societies? Why?

Using the Internet

17. Activity: Researching Daily Life Feudalism created a web of relationships and duties between different people in medieval Europe. Use your online book to research the lives of monks and peasants, rulers such as Charlemagne and William the Conqueror, and warriors like Vikings and knights. Pick the type of person you would have liked to have been in the Middle Ages. Draw a portrait of this person. Then write 5–6 sentences explaining their daily life. Include information on how they fit into the political order of society.

hmhsocialstudies.com

Social Studies Skills

Interpreting Diagrams *You know there are many types of diagrams. Some diagrams show the parts of a whole. Study the diagram of the knight and use it to answer the questions that follow.*

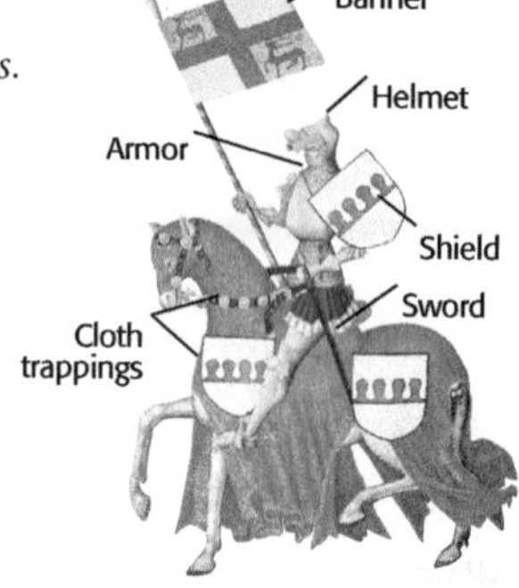

18. Which parts of a knight's outfit were used for protection? Which might help him be recognized in battle?

19. What did a knight use as a weapon?

20. Why might a knight carry a banner?

Focus on Writing

21. Writing a Job Ad "Wanted: Brave and Loyal Knights." Use your notes from this chapter to write a job ad. Start your ad by explaining why you need knights to help you. Then write a description of the type of people who will be suitable for the job and how they will be expected to behave. Be sure to mention in your ad what knights will receive in exchange for their service.

CHAPTER 17

Standardized Test Practice

DIRECTIONS: Read each question, and write the letter of the best response.

1

PERSON A
Obligations to Person B
■ Provide Protection
■ Provide Land

PERSON B
Obligations to Person A
■ Provide Loyalty
■ Provide Military Service

In this diagram, Person B is probably a

A lord.
B vassal.
C serf.
D peasant.

2 **One thing that continued to grow and spread across Europe after the fall of the Roman Empire was**

A Christianity.
B Roman culture.
C Bushido.
D republican government.

3 **Why would feudalism have taken hold more strongly in northern Europe than in southern Europe?**

A Fewer geographic barriers protected northern Europeans from invasion by enemies.
B Southern Europeans were more interested in fishing than in farming.
C A larger number of towns grew up along the rivers of northern Europe.
D Most people in southern Europe lived along the region's long coastlines.

4 **Which of these descriptions does *not* apply to feudalism as it developed in Europe?**

A growing power of kings
B powerful nobles
C clearly defined roles in society
D duties and obligations

5 **One way in which society developed *differently* in Europe and Japan was in**

A the relationship between lords and vassals.
B the duties and obligations in each system.
C the themes of their art and literature.
D the behavior of knights and samurai.

Connecting with Past Learnings

6 **Charlemagne was a brilliant warrior and a strong king. The achievements of which ancient figure have the *least* in common with those of Charlemagne?**

A Julius Caesar
B Alexander the Great
C Aristotle
D Shi Huangdi

7 **Serfs were tied to the land on which they worked. A serf in medieval Europe held a place in society that was *most* like**

A a Brahman in ancient India.
B a peasant in ancient China.
C a Christian in ancient Rome.
D a trader in ancient Egypt.

Answers

Standardized Test Practice

1. B
Break Down the Question: Remind students to examine charts closely, including any arrows or other items indicating direction or sequence.

2. A
Break Down the Question: Remind students that in the early Middle Ages Christianity was spread by missionaries to Northern Europe.

3. A
Break Down the Question: Point out to students that feudalism developed in response to the need for more protection from attacks by invaders.

4. A
Break Down the Question: Remind students that they are looking for the false answer. Options B, C, and D can be eliminated as answer choices because they are all true of feudalism.

5. C
Break Down the Question: This question requires students to recall factual information from Section 4.

6. C
Break Down the Question: Students should remember that Aristotle was a famous Greek philosopher, not a warrior or king.

7. B
Break Down the Question: Students should recall that peasants in ancient China were also bound to the land they farmed.

Intervention Resources

Reproducible

- Guided Reading Workbook
- Differentiated Instruction Teacher Management System: Lesson Plans

Technology

- Quick Facts Transparency: The Early Middle Ages Visual Summary
- Differentiated Instruction Modified Worksheets and Tests CD-ROM
- Interactive Skills Tutor CD-ROM

Tips for Test Taking

Getting the Full Picture When a question refers to a table or a chart, such as Question 1 above, students should carefully read all the information in the table or chart, including headings and labels, before answering the question. When a question refers to a graph, encourage students to first carefully study the data plotted on the graph to determine any trends or oddities before answering the question.

Chapter 18 Planning Guide

The Later Middle Ages

Overview	Instructional Resources	
CHAPTER 18 **Essential Question:** How did religion affect Europe's political and social life during the later Middle Ages? **Focus on the Essential Question Podcast**	TOS **Differentiated Instruction Teacher Management System:** • Instructional Benchmarking Guides • Lesson Plans for Differentiated Instruction **Guided Reading Workbook** **Chapter Resource File:** • Chapter Review Activity • Focus on Writing Activity: A Historical Article • Social Studies Skills Activity: Understanding Transportation Maps **Multimedia Connections:** The Crusades	TOS **Calendar Planner** **Power Presentations with Media Gallery** **Differentiated Instruction Modified Worksheets and Tests CD-ROM** **Interactive Skills Tutor CD-ROM** **Student Edition on Audio CD Program** **The World's Music Audio Program** **Video:** Motivations for the First Crusade
Section 1: **Popes and Kings** **The Big Idea:** Popes and kings dominated European society in the Middle Ages.	TOS **Differentiated Instruction Teacher Management System:** Section 1 Lesson Plan **Guided Reading Workbook:** Section 1 **Chapter Resource File:** • Vocabulary Builder Activity, Section 1	**Daily Bellringer Transparency:** Section 1 **Map Transparency:** Europe, 1000
Section 2: **The Crusades** **The Big Idea:** The Christian and Muslim cultures fought over holy sites during a series of medieval wars.	TOS **Differentiated Instruction Teacher Management System:** Section 2 Lesson Plan **Guided Reading Workbook:** Section 2 **Chapter Resource File:** • Vocabulary Builder Activity, Section 2 • Primary Source: The Siege and Capture of Nicea	**Daily Bellringer Transparency:** Section 2 **Map Transparency:** The Major Crusades, AD 1096–1204 **Quick Facts Transparency:** The Crusades **Internet Activity:** Crusader Propaganda Posters
Section 3: **Christianity and Medieval Society** **The Big Idea:** The Christian Church was central to life in the Middle Ages.	TOS **Differentiated Instruction Teacher Management System:** Section 3 Lesson Plan **Guided Reading Workbook:** Section 3 **Chapter Resource File:** • Vocabulary Builder Activity, Section 3	**Daily Bellringer Transparency:** Section 3
Section 4: **Political and Social Change** **The Big Idea:** Europe's political and social systems underwent great changes in the late Middle Ages.	TOS **Differentiated Instruction Teacher Management System:** Section 4 Lesson Plan **Guided Reading Workbook:** Section 4 **Chapter Resource File:** • Vocabulary Builder Activity, Section 4	**Daily Bellringer Transparency:** Section 4 **Quick Facts Transparency:** Beginnings of Democracy in England **Internet Activity:** Joan of Arc Biography **Video:** Traders Carry the Plague
Section 5: **Challenges to Church Authority** **The Big Idea:** In the Middle Ages, the Christian Church dealt harshly with people who did not respect its authority.	TOS **Differentiated Instruction Teacher Management System:** Section 5 Lesson Plan **Guided Reading Workbook:** Section 5 **Chapter Resource File:** • Vocabulary Builder Activity, Section 5	**Daily Bellringer Transparency:** Section 5 **Map Transparency:** The Reconquista, 1000–1300

Chart Key:

SE Student Edition  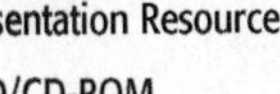 Presentation Resource  MP3 Audio

TOS Teacher One Stop 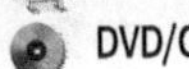 DVD/CD-ROM HISTORY™

 Printable Resource

Program Resources available on TOS and @  hmhsocialstudies.com

Review, Assessment, Intervention

 **Quick Facts Transparency:** The Later Middle Ages Visual Summary

 **Spanish Chapter Summaries Audio CD Program**

 **Quiz Game CD-ROM**

 **Progress Assessment Support System (PASS):** Chapter Test

 **Differentiated Instruction Modified Worksheets and Tests CD-ROM:** Modified Chapter Test

TOS **ExamView® Assessment Suite (English/Spanish)**

 **PASS:** Section 1 Quiz

 **Online Quiz:** Section 1

 **Alternative Assessment Handbook**

 **PASS:** Section 2 Quiz

 **Online Quiz:** Section 2

 **Alternative Assessment Handbook**

 **PASS:** Section 3 Quiz

 **Online Quiz:** Section 3

 **Alternative Assessment Handbook**

 **PASS:** Section 4 Quiz

 **Online Quiz:** Section 4

 **Alternative Assessment Handbook**

 **PASS:** Section 5 Quiz

 **Online Quiz:** Section 5

 **Alternative Assessment Handbook**

Supporting Resources

- Multimedia Classroom Global History Series
- Global History Teacher's Guide

Maps Globes Graphs Level F

- Student Workbook
- Teacher's Guide

Social Studies Trade Library Collections

- Premier Secondary World History Trade Collection

History's Impact

World History Video Program

- **The Bubonic Plague**

For more information or to purchase go to  hmhsocialstudies.com

Power Presentations with Media Gallery

Power Presentations with Media Gallery are visual presentations of each chapter's main ideas. Presentations can be customized by including Quick Facts charts, images from the text, and video clips.

CHAPTER 18 PLANNING GUIDE

Differentiating Instruction

How do I address the needs of varied learners?

The Target Resource acts as your primary strategy for differentiated instruction.

ENGLISH-LANGUAGE LEARNERS & STRUGGLING READERS

Interactive Skills Tutor CD-ROM

The Interactive Skills Tutor CD-ROM contains lessons that provide additional practice for 20 different critical thinking skills.

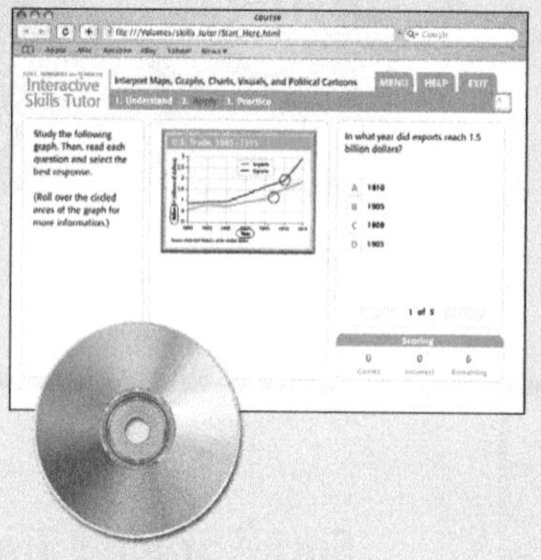

Additional Resources

Differentiated Instruction Teacher Management System: Lesson Plans for Differentiated Instruction

Chapter Resource File:
- Vocabulary Builder Activities
- Social Studies Skills Activity: Interpreting Maps: Cultural Features

Quick Facts Transparencies:
- The Crusades
- Beginnings of Democracy in England
- The Later Middle Ages Visual Summary

Student Edition on Audio CD Program

Interactive Skills Tutor CD-ROM

Spanish/English Guided Reading Workbook

SPECIAL NEEDS LEARNERS

Differentiated Instruction Modified Worksheets and Tests CD-ROM

- Vocabulary Flash Cards
- Vocabulary Builder Activities
- Chapter Review Activity
- Chapter Test

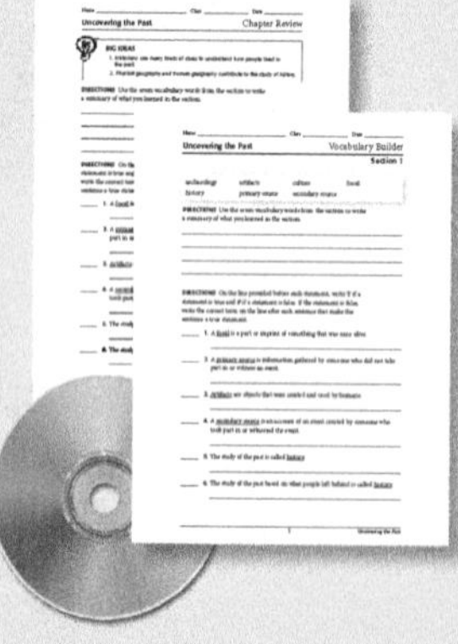

Additional Resources

Differentiated Instruction Teacher Management System: Lesson Plans for Differentiated Instruction

Guided Reading Workbook

Chapter Resource File: Social Studies Skills Activity: Interpreting Maps: Cultural Features

Student Edition on Audio CD Program

Interactive Skills Tutor CD-ROM

ADVANCED/GIFTED-AND-TALENTED STUDENTS

Primary Source Library CD-ROM for World History

The Library contains longer versions of quotations in the text, extra sources, and images. Included are point-of-view articles, journals, diaries, historical fiction, and political documents.

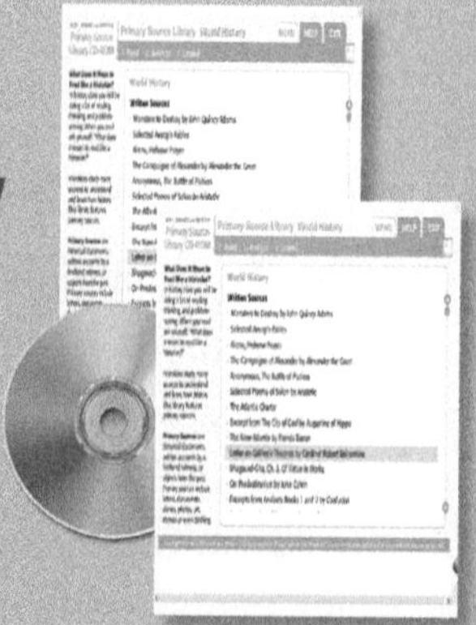

Additional Resources

Differentiated Instruction Teacher Management System: Lesson Plans for Differentiated Instruction

Chapter Resource File:
- Focus on Writing Activity: A Historical Article

Document-Based Questions Activities

Differentiated Activities in the Teacher's Edition

- Listing Reasons to Join the Crusade, p. 529
- Translating *The Canterbury Tales*, p. 534

Differentiated Activities in the Teacher's Edition

- Mapping Change, p. 525
- Creating Political Signs, p. 526

Differentiated Activities in the Teacher's Edition

- Debate on Schism of 1054, p. 526
- The Legend of Robin Hood, p. 530

Teacher One Stop™

How can I manage the lesson plans and support materials for differentiated instruction?

With the Teacher One Stop, you can easily organize and print lesson plans, planning guides, and instructional materials for all learners. The Teacher One Stop includes the following materials to help you differentiate instruction:

- Interactive Teacher's Edition
- Calendar Planner and pacing guides
- Editable lesson plans
- All reproducible ancillaries in Adobe Acrobat (PDF) format
- ExamView Assessment Suite (English & Spanish)
- Transparency and video previews

Interactive Student Edition

Complete online student edition with interactive multimedia support for chapter content assessment and reporting

- Interactive Maps and Notebook
- Graphic Organizers
- Standardized Test Prep
- Online Homework Practice and Research Activities
- Current Events
- Chapter-based Internet Activities
- Animated History Activities
- and more!

Chapter Preview

Essential Question

Introduce the Essential Question

- Explain that during feudalism popes of the Roman Catholic Church and kings dominated society.
- Talk about the Crusades, the bubonic plague, and the Hundred Years' War as important events that shook European society. These events also moved Europe slowly away from feudalism.

Focus on Writing

The **Chapter Resource File** provides a Focus on Writing work sheet to help students organize and write their historical articles.

CRF: Focus on Writing Activity: A Historical Article

Key to Differentiating Instruction

Below Level
Basic-level activities designed for all students encountering new material

At Level
Intermediate-level activities designed for average students

Above Level
Challenging activities designed for honors and gifted and talented students

Standard English Mastery
Activities designed to improve standard English usage

LS Learning Styles

CHAPTER 18 1000–1500

The Later Middle Ages

Essential Question How did religion affect Europe's political and social life during the later Middle Ages?

South Carolina Performance Standards

6-5.1 Explain feudalism and its relationship to the development of European monarchies and nation-states, including feudal relationships, the daily lives of peasants and serfs, and the economy under the manorial system; **6-5.2** Explain the effects of the Magna Carta on European society, its effect on the feudal system, and its contribution to the development of representative government in England; **6-5.3** Summarize the course of the Crusades and explain their effects on feudalism and their role in spreading Christianity; **6-5.4** Explain the role and influence of the Roman Catholic Church in medieval Europe; **6-5.5** Summarize the origins and impact of the bubonic plague (Black Death) on feudalism.

Literacy Skills for Social Studies

- Evaluate multiple points of view or biases and attribute the perspectives to the influences of individual experiences, societal values, and cultural traditions.

Partnership for the 21st Century Skills
Articulate his or her own ideas and those of others objectively through speaking and writing.

Focus on Writing

A Historical Article Your friend is the editor of a magazine for young children. He wants you to write an article on the most important people in Europe in the Middle Ages. As you read, collect information to help you write this article.

520 CHAPTER 18

This photo shows the monastery at Mont St. Michel in France.

CHAPTER EVENTS

1066 Feudalism is introduced into Britain.

1000

WORLD EVENTS

1055 The Seljuk Turks take control of Baghdad.

Introduce the Chapter

At Level

The Later Middle Ages

1. In this chapter students will learn how influential the Christian Church was in all areas of life in the late Middle Ages.
2. To introduce students to the topic, ask them to imagine that all aspects of their lives are influenced by one institution. The class might select their school, the National Football League, or a popular TV network.
3. Ask, "What would your life be like if all your social activities revolved around this institution? What would it be like if the leaders of this institution had the most power in society?" Help students see ways that their lives might be different in such a situation.
4. Tell students that in this chapter they will learn that the Christian Church influenced politics, education, art, architecture, and even travel in Europe during the later Middle Ages. **LS Verbal/Linguistic**

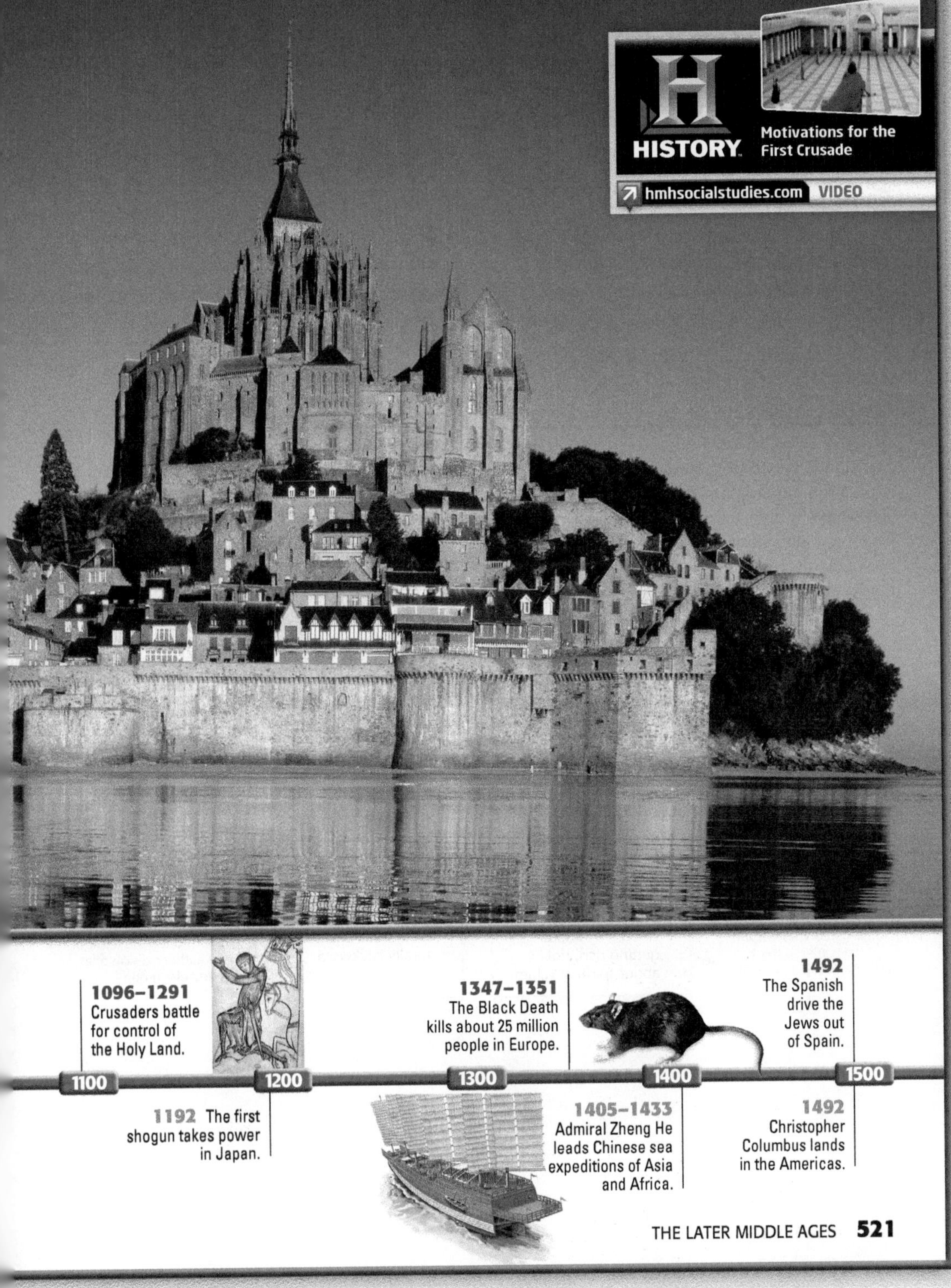

HISTORY
Motivations for the First Crusade
hmhsocialstudies.com VIDEO
1096–1291 Crusaders battle for control of the Holy Land.
1192 The first shogun takes power in Japan.
1347–1351 The Black Death kills about 25 million people in Europe.
1405–1433 Admiral Zheng He leads Chinese sea expeditions of Asia and Africa.
1492 The Spanish drive the Jews out of Spain.
1492 Christopher Columbus lands in the Americas.
1100
1200
1300
1400
1500
THE LATER MIDDLE AGES 521

Chapter Preview

Explore the Picture

Mont St. Michel Pictured at left, Mont St. Michel is an islet off the northern coast of France. It's named after the archangel, Michael, also known as Saint Michael. The small chapel was a popular pilgrimage destination. In 966, a medieval monastery was built on the site. At the island's peak you can see the monastery's abbey church.

Analyzing Visuals What does this photograph convey about the Middle Ages? *possible answer—Churches must have been important because of their size and prominent locations.*

hmhsocialstudies.com
Teacher Resources

Explore the Time Line

1. About how long did the Crusades last? *200 years*
2. While Crusaders fought for control of the Holy Land, what was happening in Japan? *The first shogun took power in 1192.*
3. About how long did the Black Death last? Approximately how many Europeans died as a result of the Black Death? *4 years; 25 million people*

Info to Know

The Holy Land Also known as Palestine, the Holy Land is sacred to three major world religions—Judaism, Islam, and Christianity. The Holy Land lies along the eastern shore of the Mediterranean Sea, joining Africa and Southwestern Asia. Today the Holy Land, or ancient Palestine, includes the modern nation of Israel and parts of Jordan and Syria.

Reading Social Studies

Understanding Themes

This chapter deals with the enormous influence religion had on the development of society and culture in Europe. Ask students to recall from the last chapter the influence of religion in Europe. Ask students to discuss some possible effects that this religious influence might have had on society and culture. Point out to students that religion in the late Middle Ages influenced everything from architecture to who ruled a country. Make a list of students' suggestions for the class to see.

Causes and Effects in History

Focus on Reading Ask students to think of events in their daily lives that have causes or effects. Write students' suggestions for the class to see. Remind students that there might be multiple causes of one effect, or that one cause might lead to several effects. Have each student write a short paragraph that contains at least three cause-and-effect relationships. Then ask students to exchange paragraphs with a partner. Have each student identify the causes and effects. Then have students create graphic organizers that express the cause-and-effect relationships that they identified in the paragraph.

Reading Social Studies

Economics | Geography | Politics | **Religion** | **Society and Culture** | Science and Technology

Focus on Themes In this chapter, you will learn about Europe in the late Middle Ages, a period of important change and new developments. You will see how the Christian **religion** was a major influence on people's lives. You will also read about the conflict between religious and political leaders and how this conflict shaped **society and culture**. Finally, you will learn about important events that changed medieval society and opened up the way towards the development of modern life.

Stereotypes and Bias in History

Focus on Reading Historians today try to be impartial in their writing. They don't let their personal feelings affect what they write. Writers in the past, however, didn't always feel the need to be impartial. Their writings were sometimes colored by their attitudes about other people, places, and ideas.

Identifying Stereotypes and Bias Two ways in which writing can be colored by the author's ideas are stereotypes and bias. A **stereotype** is a generalization about whole groups of people. **Bias** is an attitude that one group is superior to another. The examples below can help you identify stereotypes and bias in the things you read.

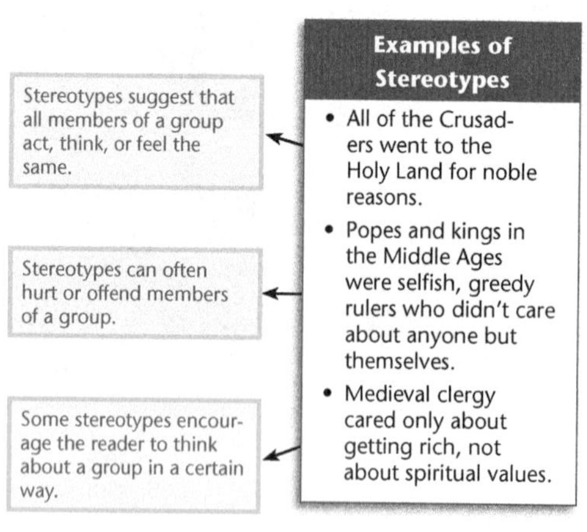

Examples of Stereotypes
• All of the Crusaders went to the Holy Land for noble reasons.
• Popes and kings in the Middle Ages were selfish, greedy rulers who didn't care about anyone but themselves.
• Medieval clergy cared only about getting rich, not about spiritual values.
Stereotypes suggest that all members of a group act, think, or feel the same.
Stereotypes can often hurt or offend members of a group.
Some stereotypes encourage the reader to think about a group in a certain way.

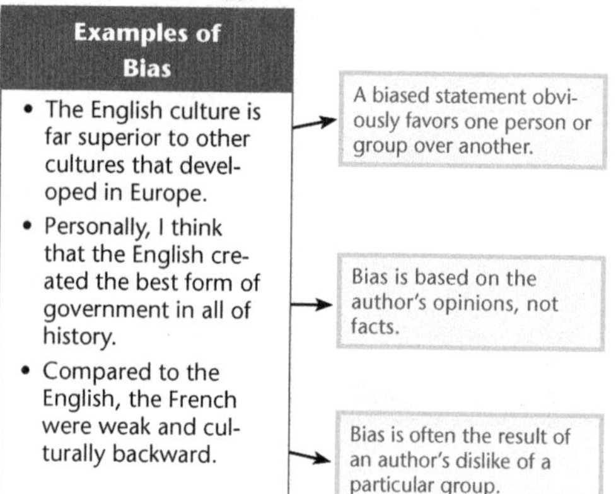

Examples of Bias
• The English culture is far superior to other cultures that developed in Europe.
• Personally, I think that the English created the best form of government in all of history.
• Compared to the English, the French were weak and culturally backward.
A biased statement obviously favors one person or group over another.
Bias is based on the author's opinions, not facts.
Bias is often the result of an author's dislike of a particular group.

Reading and Skills Resources

Reading Support

- Guided Reading Workbook
- Student Edition on Audio CD
- Spanish Chapter Summaries Audio CD Program

Social Studies Skills Support

- Interactive Skills Tutor CD-ROM

Vocabulary Support

- **CRF:** Vocabulary Builder Activities
- **CRF:** Chapter Review Activity
- Differentiated Instruction Modified Worksheets and Tests CD-ROM:
  - Vocabulary Flash Cards
  - Vocabulary Builder Activity
  - Chapter Review Activity
- TOS Holt McDougal PuzzleView

You Try It!

The following passage was written by a French poet and knight named Rutebeuf. Rutebeuf, who lived from about 1245 to 1285, explains his reasons for not wanting to join the Crusades. As you read the passage, look for examples of stereotypes and bias in his writing.

A Knight Speaks

Am I to leave my wife and children, all my goods and inheritance, to go and conquer a foreign land which will give me nothing in return? I can worship God just as well in Paris as in Jerusalem . . . . Those rich lords and prelates [priests] who have grabbed for themselves all the treasure on earth may well need to go on Crusade. But I live at peace with my neighbors. I am not bored with them yet and so I have no desire to go looking for a war at the other end of the world. If you like heroic deeds, you can go along and cover yourself with glory: tell the Sultan from me that if he feels like attacking me I know very well how to defend myself. But so long as he leaves me alone, I shall not bother my head about him. All you people, great and small, who go on pilgrimage to the Promised Land, ought to become very holy there: so how does it happen that the ones who come back are mostly bandits?

–Rutebeuf, from *The Medieval World* by Freidrich Heer, translated by Janet Sondheimer

Review the graphic organizer on the previous page. Then answer the following questions about the passage you just read.

1. Does the author show a bias against any groups in medieval society?
2. What is the author's opinion about rich lords and prelates? Do you think his opinion is justified? Why or why not?
3. What stereotype about Crusaders does the writer include in the passage?
4. How do you think a Crusader would feel about this passage? Why?

As you read Chapter 18, notice how the authors of this book have avoided making stereotypes and expressing bias about European society and culture.

Key Terms and People

Chapter 18

Section 1
excommunicate *(p. 525)*
Pope Gregory VII *(p. 527)*
Emperor Henry IV *(p. 527)*

Section 2
Crusades *(p. 528)*
Holy Land *(p. 528)*
Pope Urban II *(p. 528)*
King Richard I *(p. 530)*
Saladin *(p. 530)*

Section 3
clergy *(p. 533)*
religious order *(p. 536)*
Francis of Assisi *(p. 536)*
friars *(p. 536)*
Thomas Aquinas *(p. 537)*
natural law *(p. 538)*

Section 4
Magna Carta *(p. 540)*
Parliament *(p. 541)*
Hundred Years' War *(p. 542)*
Joan of Arc *(p. 542)*
Black Death *(p. 543)*

Section 5
heresy *(p. 546)*
Reconquista *(p. 547)*
King Ferdinand *(p. 548)*
Queen Isabella *(p. 548)*
Spanish Inquisition *(p. 548)*

Academic Vocabulary

Success in school is related to knowing academic vocabulary—the words that are frequently used in school assignments and discussions. In this chapter, you will learn the following academic words:

authority *(p. 526)*
policy *(p. 548)*

Reading Social Studies

Key Terms and People

Preteach the key terms and people from this chapter by asking students what they think each term means or who each person was. Review with the class the meaning or description of each term or person. Ask the class to select six of the terms or people. Have each student define or identify the six terms or people they chose. Then have students draw an illustration that best represents each term or person. Ask volunteers to share their illustrations with the class.
LS Verbal/Linguistic, Visual/Spatial

Focus on Reading

See the **Focus on Reading** questions in this chapter for more practice on this reading social studies skill.

Reading Social Studies Assessment

See the **Chapter Review** at the end of this chapter for student assessment questions related to this reading skill.

Teaching Tip

Explain to students that they can often identify causes and effects by looking out for certain signal words. Review the words that signal cause and effect with students. Ask the class if there are other words that serve the same purpose. Create a class list of words that signal cause and words that signal effect. Then have each student write three sentences that illustrate cause and effect. Have students exchange sentences with a partner. Have students circle the cause and underline the effect in each sentence.

Answers

You Try It! **1.** *yes, rich lords, prelates, conquerors* **2.** *possible answer—author thinks they are greedy and bored; yes, because they seem to want adventure* **3.** *they like heroic deeds, they come back as bandits* **4.** *possible answer—offended, because the author is insulting Crusaders*

Preteach

Bellringer

If YOU were there . . . Use the **Daily Bellringer Transparency** to help students answer the question.

Daily Bellringer Transparency, Section 1

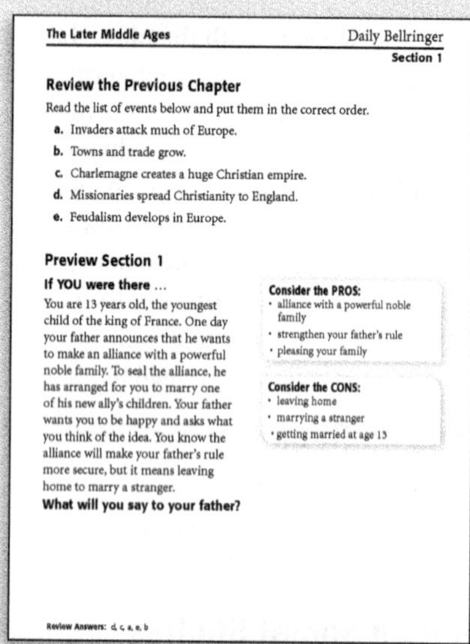

The Later Middle Ages — Daily Bellringer — Section 1

Review the Previous Chapter

Read the list of events below and put them in the correct order.

a. Invaders attack much of Europe.
b. Towns and trade grow.
c. Charlemagne creates a huge Christian empire.
d. Missionaries spread Christianity to England.
e. Feudalism develops in Europe.

Preview Section 1

If YOU were there ...

You are 13 years old, the youngest child of the king of France. One day your father announces that he wants to make an alliance with a powerful noble family. To seal the alliance, he has arranged for you to marry one of his new ally's children. Your father wants you to be happy and asks what you think of the idea. You know the alliance will make your father's rule more secure, but it means leaving home to marry a stranger.

What will you say to your father?

Consider the PROS:
- alliance with a powerful noble family
- strengthen your father's rule
- pleasing your family

Consider the CONS:
- leaving home
- marrying a stranger
- getting married at age 13

Review Answers: d, c, a, e, b

Academic Vocabulary

Review with students the high-use academic term in this section.

authority power, right to rule (p. 526)

CRF: Vocabulary Builder Activity, Section 1

Taking Notes

Have students use the graphic organizer online to take notes on the section. This activity will prepare students for the Section Assessment, in which they will complete a graphic organizer that builds on the information using the Critical Thinking Skill: Comparing.

SECTION 1

Popes and Kings

What You Will Learn...

Main Ideas

1. Popes and kings ruled Europe as spiritual and political leaders.
2. Popes fought for power, leading to a permanent split within the church.
3. Kings and popes clashed over some issues.

The Big Idea

Popes and kings dominated European society in the Middle Ages.

Key Terms and People

excommunicate, *p. 525*
Pope Gregory VII, *p. 527*
Emperor Henry IV, *p. 527*

Use the graphic organizer online to help you keep track of the powers popes claimed and the powers kings claimed.

If YOU were there...

You are 13 years old, the youngest child of the king of France. One day your father announces that he wants to make an alliance with a powerful noble family. To seal the alliance, he has arranged for you to marry one of his new ally's children. Your father wants you to be happy and asks what you think of the idea. You know the alliance will make your father's rule more secure, but it means leaving home to marry a stranger.

What will you say to your father?

BUILDING BACKGROUND In the Middle Ages, kings were some of the most powerful men in Europe. Many kings, like the one described above, looked for ways to increase their power. But in their search for power, these kings had to deal with other powerful leaders, including popes. These other leaders had their own plans and goals.

Popes and Kings Rule Europe

In the early Middle Ages, great nobles and their knights held a great deal of power. As time passed, though, this power began to shift. More and more, power came into the hands of two types of leaders, popes and kings. Popes had great spiritual power, and kings had political power. Together, popes and kings controlled most of European society.

The Power of the Popes

In the Middle Ages, the pope was the head of the Christian Church in Western Europe. Since nearly everyone in the Middle Ages belonged to this church, the pope had great power. People saw the pope as God's representative on Earth. They looked to him for guidance about how to live and pray.

Because the pope was seen as God's representative, it was his duty to decide what the church would teach. From time to time, a pope would write a letter called a bull to explain a religious teaching or outline a church policy. In addition, the pope decided when someone was acting against the church.

Teach the Big Idea

At Level

Popes and Kings

1. **Teach** Ask students the questions in the Main Idea boxes to teach this section.
2. **Apply** Have students create an outline of the section using the blue heads as main points. Help students identify at least two supporting details for each main point. **LS Verbal/Linguistic**
3. **Review** As you review the section, have students identify the points in their outlines that they feel are most important or most interesting. Guide students in a discussion of the growth of the power of popes and kings during the late Middle Ages.
4. **Practice/Homework** Have each student write a brief newspaper article that explains the conflict between Pope Gregory VII and Emperor Henry IV. **LS Verbal/Linguistic**

Alternative Assessment Handbook, Rubric 37: Writing Assignments

If the pope felt someone was working against the church, he could punish the person in many ways. For serious offenses, the pope or other bishops could choose to **excommunicate**, or cast out from the church, the offender. This punishment was deeply feared because Christians believed that a person who died while excommunicated would not get into heaven.

In addition to spiritual power, many popes had great political power. After the Roman Empire collapsed, many people in Italy looked to the pope as their leader. As a result, some popes began to live like royalty. They became rich and built huge palaces. At the same time, they came into conflict with Europe's other political leaders, kings.

The Power of Kings

As you can see on the map below, Europe in 1000 was divided into many small states. Most of these states were ruled by kings, some of whom had little real power. In a few places, though, kings had begun to take firm control of their countries. Look at the map to find England, France, and the Holy Roman Empire. At this time, Europe's most powerful kings ruled those three countries.

In England and France, kings inherited their thrones from their fathers. At times, nobles rebelled against the kings, but the kings usually reestablished order fairly quickly. They maintained this order through alliances as well as warfare.

THE IMPACT TODAY

Hundreds of millions of people around the world consider the pope their spiritual leader.

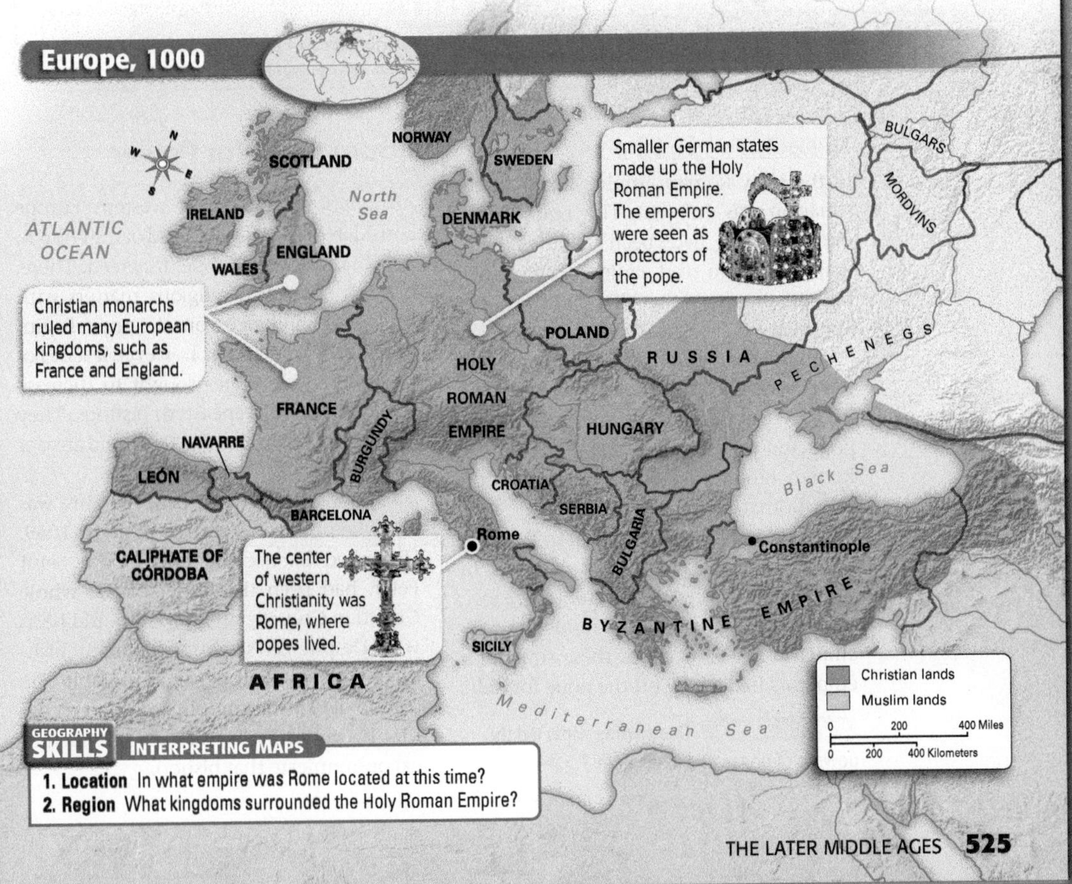

GEOGRAPHY SKILLS INTERPRETING MAPS

1. **Location** In what empire was Rome located at this time?
2. **Region** What kingdoms surrounded the Holy Roman Empire?

Direct Teach

Main Idea

1 Popes and Kings Rule Europe

Popes and kings ruled Europe as spiritual and political leaders.

Identify Whom might a pope choose to excommunicate? *people he felt were working against the church*

Identify Cause and Effect Why did some popes eventually begin to live like royalty? *They had great political power after the Roman Empire collapsed; many people in Italy looked to the pope as their leader.*

Contrast How did becoming king in England and France differ from how it was done in the Holy Roman Empire? *England and France—inherited thrones; Holy Roman Empire—elected*

CRF: Literature Activity: Guinevere and the Round Table

Map Transparency Europe, 1000

Info to Know

Excommunication A person who was excommunicated was denied the sacraments of the church, including mass and confession. Because rulers were believed to rule by the authority of God, an excommunicated king or emperor had no right to rule.

Critical Thinking: Comparing and Contrasting

At Level

Mapping Change

Materials: tracing paper or transparency sheets, colored markers

1. Give each student tracing paper (or a transparency sheet) and a set of colored markers.
2. Have students trace the map above, outlining only the borders of Christian and Muslim lands.
3. Next, ask students to overlay their traced maps onto "The Spread of Christianity" map in the previous chapter.
4. Based on the differences in the two maps, ask students what generalizations they can make about the spread of Christianity and the spread of Islam. *possible answers—Both religions were spreading. Islam was replacing Christianity in many places around the Mediterranean, while Christianity was extending north and eastward.*

LS Logical/Mathematical, Visual/Spatial

Alternative Assessment Handbook, Rubrics 9: Comparing and Contrasting; and 21: Map Reading

Answers

Interpreting Maps 1. *Holy Roman Empire;* **2.** *Poland, Hungary, Croatia, Burgundy, France, Denmark*

Direct Teach

Main Idea

❷ Popes Fight for Power

Popes fought for power, leading to a permanent split within the church.

Identify In what region did many bishops not recognize the pope's authority? *eastern Europe*

Explain Why did Leo IX believe that all church officials should answer to him? *His argument was that the first pope, Saint Peter, had been the leader of the whole Christian Church.*

Predict What might have happened if Leo IX had not excommunicated the bishop of Constantinople? *possible answers—The church might have stayed united; the pope's power might have been weakened.*

Primary Source

Reading Like a Historian

Views of Power Help students practice reading the documents like historians. Ask the following:

- Who wrote these two letters? When were they written? To whom were they written?
- Why do the writers matter to history? How do their points of view differ? Why?

Primary Source

POINTS OF VIEW

Views of Power

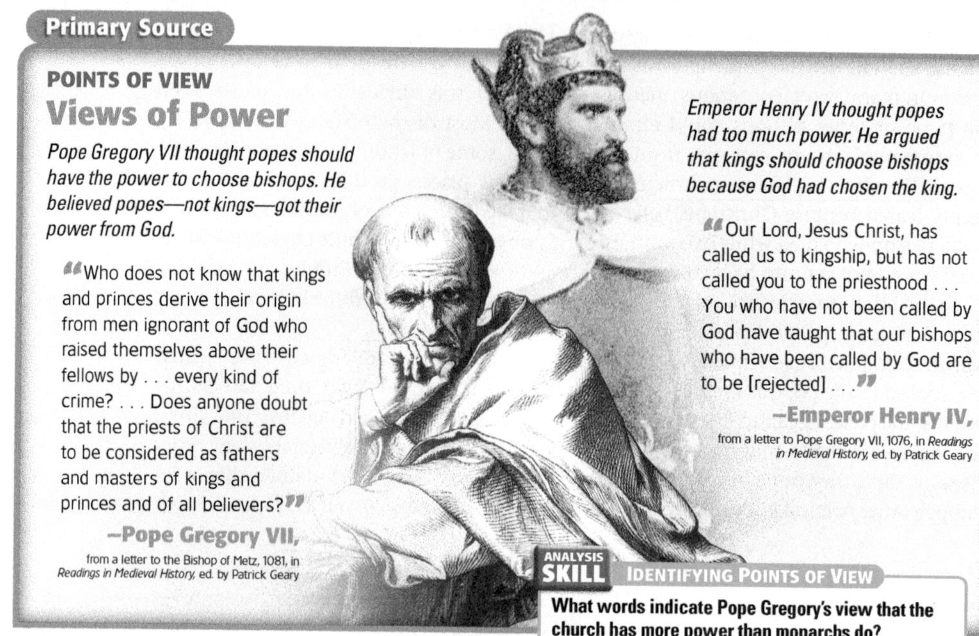

Pope Gregory VII thought popes should have the power to choose bishops. He believed popes—not kings—got their power from God.

"Who does not know that kings and princes derive their origin from men ignorant of God who raised themselves above their fellows by . . . every kind of crime? . . . Does anyone doubt that the priests of Christ are to be considered as fathers and masters of kings and princes and of all believers?"

—Pope Gregory VII,

from a letter to the Bishop of Metz, 1081, in *Readings in Medieval History*, ed. by Patrick Geary

Emperor Henry IV thought popes had too much power. He argued that kings should choose bishops because God had chosen the king.

"Our Lord, Jesus Christ, has called us to kingship, but has not called you to the priesthood . . . You who have not been called by God have taught that our bishops who have been called by God are to be [rejected] . . ."

—Emperor Henry IV,

from a letter to Pope Gregory VII, 1076, in *Readings in Medieval History*, ed. by Patrick Geary

ANALYSIS SKILL IDENTIFYING POINTS OF VIEW

What words indicate Pope Gregory's view that the church has more power than monarchs do?

The Holy Roman Empire

In the Holy Roman Empire, however, the situation was different. This empire grew out of what had been Charlemagne's empire. As you read earlier, Charlemagne built his empire in the 700s with the pope's approval.

In the mid-900s, another emperor took the throne with the approval of the pope. Because the empire was approved by the pope and people saw it as a rebirth of the Roman Empire, it became known as the Holy Roman Empire.

Holy Roman emperors didn't inherit their crowns. Instead, they were elected by the empire's nobles. Sometimes, these elections led to fights between nobles and the emperor. In the worst of these squabbles, emperors had to call on the pope for help.

READING CHECK **Contrasting** How did the powers of popes and kings differ?

ACADEMIC VOCABULARY

authority power, right to rule

Popes Fight for Power

Although the people of western Europe considered the pope the head of the church, people in eastern Europe disagreed. There, bishops controlled religious matters with little or no guidance from the pope. Beginning in the mid-1000s, however, a series of clever and able popes sought to increase their **authority** over eastern bishops. They believed all religious officials should answer to the pope.

Among those who believed this was Pope Leo IX, who became pope in 1049. He argued that because the first pope, Saint Peter, had been the leader of the whole Christian Church, later popes should be as well. Despite Leo's arguments, many bishops in eastern Europe, most notably the bishop of Constantinople, wouldn't recognize his authority. In 1054, Leo decided to excommunicate that bishop.

Differentiating Instruction

Special Needs Learners

Below Level

1. Ask students to imagine that they are medieval residents of Constantinople.
2. Have each student create two or three political signs, either supporting or opposing the excommunication of the bishop of Constantinople. LS **Visual/Spatial**

Alternative Assessment Handbook, Rubric 34: Slogans and Banners

Advanced/Gifted and Talented

Above Level

Research Required

1. Divide students into two groups to conduct research on the Schism of 1054. Then conduct a historical debate.
2. Groups should argue either for or against the excommunication of the bishop of Constantinople. LS **Verbal/Linguistic**

Alternative Assessment Handbook, Rubric 10: Debates

Answers

Identifying Points of View *"the priests of Christ are to be considered as fathers and masters of kings and princes and of all believers"*

Reading Check *popes—religious and sometimes political power; kings—political power*

Leo's decision created a permanent split within the church. Christians who agreed with the bishop of Constantinople formed the Orthodox Church. Those who supported Leo's authority became known as Roman Catholics. With their support, the pope became head of the Roman Catholic Church and one of the most powerful figures in western Europe.

READING CHECK **Generalizing** How did Leo IX try to increase popes' authority?

Kings and Popes Clash

As popes worked to increase their power, they often came into conflict with kings. For example, kings thought they should be able to select bishops in their countries. Popes, on the other hand, argued that only they could choose religious officials.

In 1073 a new pope came to power in Rome. His name was **Pope Gregory VII**. Trouble arose when Gregory disapproved of a bishop chosen by the Holy Roman **Emperor Henry IV**. Angry because the pope questioned his authority, Henry convinced Germany's bishops that they should remove Gregory as pope. In response, the pope excommunicated Henry. He called on the empire's nobles to overthrow Henry.

Desperate to stay in power, Henry went to Italy to ask the pope for forgiveness. Gregory refused to see him. For three days Henry stood barefoot in the snow outside the castle where Pope Gregory was staying. Eventually, Gregory accepted Henry's apology and allowed the emperor back into the church. Gregory had proven himself more powerful than the emperor, at least for that moment.

The fight over the right to choose bishops continued even after Henry and Gregory died. In 1122 a new pope and emperor reached a compromise. They decided that church officials would choose all bishops and abbots. The bishops and abbots, however, would still have to obey the emperor.

This compromise did not end all conflict. Kings and popes continued to fight for power throughout the Middle Ages, changing lives all over Europe.

READING CHECK **Identifying Causes and Effects** What caused Gregory and Henry's power struggle?

SUMMARY AND PREVIEW In this section you read about the powers of popes and kings. In many cases, these powers led to conflict between the two. In the next section, though, you will read about popes and kings working together against a common enemy.

Section 1 Assessment

hmhsocialstudies.com ONLINE QUIZ

Reviewing Ideas, Terms, and People

1. a. **Describe** What was the pope's role in the Roman Catholic Church?
   b. **Draw Conclusions** How did cooperation with the pope help kings like Charlemagne and the early Holy Roman Emperors?
2. **Explain** Why did Pope Leo IX **excommunicate** the bishop of Constantinople?
3. a. **Identify** With whom did **Pope Gregory VII** clash?
   b. **Elaborate** Why do you think the pope made **Emperor Henry IV** wait for three days before forgiving him?

Critical Thinking

4. **Comparing** Draw a diagram like the one shown here. Use it and your notes to compare the power of popes to the power of kings.

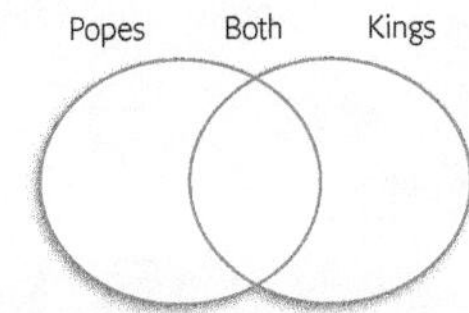

FOCUS ON WRITING

5. **Taking Notes on the Popes and Kings** Who were the popes and kings you read about in this section? Why were they important? Start a list of important people.

Direct Teach

Main Idea

3 Kings and Popes Clash

Kings and popes clashed over some issues.

Recall What compromise solved the conflict over who had the right to choose bishops? *Church officials would appoint all bishops; bishops would still have to obey the emperor.*

Evaluate Why do you think a king would want to select bishops himself? *possible answer—so that the bishops would be loyal to him*

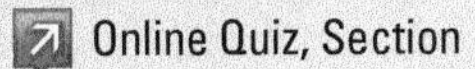

Review & Assess

Close

Have students briefly trace the events that led to the growing power of kings and popes in medieval Europe.

Review

Online Quiz, Section 1

Assess

SE Section 1 Assessment

PASS: Section 1 Quiz

Alternative Assessment Handbook

Reteach/Classroom Intervention

Guided Reading Workbook, Section 1

Interactive Skills Tutor CD-ROM

Section 1 Assessment Answers

1. a. head of the Roman Catholic Church
   b. The pope's approval increased the kings' standing in people's eyes and legitimized their reigns.
2. The bishop refused to recognize Leo's authority as pope.
3. a. Emperor Henry IV
   b. possible answer—to show that he had enough power even to make kings wait
4. popes—spiritual power, could excommunicate enemies of church; both—powerful leaders, respected and admired; kings—political power, governed countries
5. Charlemagne—ruled empire that would eventually be the Holy Roman Empire; Pope Gregory VII—excommunicated Emperor Henry IV; Emperor Henry IV—apologized to Pope Gregory VII; Pope Leo IX—excommunicated the bishop of Constantinople, created permanent split between Orthodox Church and Roman Catholic Church

Answers

Reading Check (left) *He excommunicated the bishop of Constantinople.*

Reading Check (right) *Henry thought he should be able to select bishops; Gregory thought only the pope should be able to select them.*

Preteach

Bellringer

If YOU were there . . . Use the **Daily Bellringer Transparency** to help students answer the question.

Daily Bellringer Transparency, Section 2

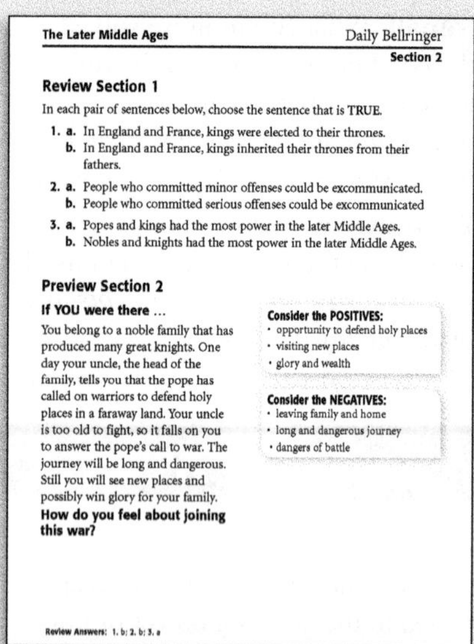

The Later Middle Ages Daily Bellringer **Section 2**

Review Section 1

In each pair of sentences below, choose the sentence that is TRUE.

1. a. In England and France, kings were elected to their thrones.
   b. In England and France, kings inherited their thrones from their fathers.
2. a. People who committed minor offenses could be excommunicated.
   b. People who committed serious offenses could be excommunicated
3. a. Popes and kings had the most power in the later Middle Ages.
   b. Nobles and knights had the most power in the later Middle Ages.

Preview Section 2

If YOU were there ...
You belong to a noble family that has produced many great knights. One day your uncle, the head of the family, tells you that the pope has called on warriors to defend holy places in a faraway land. Your uncle is too old to fight, so it falls on you to answer the pope's call to war. The journey will be long and dangerous. Still you will see new places and possibly win glory for your family.
How do you feel about joining this war?

Consider the POSITIVES:
- opportunity to defend holy places
- visiting new places
- glory and wealth

Consider the NEGATIVES:
- leaving family and home
- long and dangerous journey
- dangers of battle

Review Answers: 1. b; 2. b; 3. a

Building Vocabulary

Preteach or review the following term:

vassal a person who held land under a feudal lord, exchanging loyalty and service for protection (p. 530)

CRF: Vocabulary Builder Activity, Section 2.

Taking Notes

Have students use the graphic organizer online to take notes on the section. This activity will prepare students for the Section Assessment, in which they will complete a graphic organizer that builds on the information using the Critical Thinking Skill: Comparing and Contrasting.

SECTION 2

The Crusades

What You Will Learn...

Main Ideas

1. The pope called on Crusaders to invade the Holy Land.
2. Despite some initial success, the later Crusades failed.
3. The Crusades changed Europe forever.

The Big Idea

The Christian and Muslim cultures fought over holy sites during a series of medieval wars.

Key Terms and People

Crusades, *p. 528*
Holy Land, *p. 528*
Pope Urban II, *p. 528*
King Richard I, *p. 530*
Saladin, *p. 530*

Use the graphic organizer online to take notes on what happened in Europe before, during, and after the Crusades.

If YOU were there...

You belong to a noble family that has produced many great knights. One day your uncle, the head of the family, tells you that the pope has called on warriors to defend holy places in a faraway land. Your uncle is too old to fight, so it falls on you to answer the pope's call to war. The journey will be long and dangerous. Still, you will see new places and possibly win glory for your family.

How do you feel about joining this war?

BUILDING BACKGROUND In the early Middle Ages few people traveled far from home. They spent most of their lives in a single village or farm. As time passed, however, Europeans learned of other people and places. Their contacts with some of these people were peaceful. With others, though, the contact was not peaceful. Wars broke out. The most famous of these wars were the Crusades.

Crusaders Invade the Holy Land

The **Crusades** were a long series of wars between Christians and Muslims in Southwest Asia. They were fought over control of Palestine, a region of Southwest Asia. Europeans called Palestine the **Holy Land** because it was the region where Jesus had lived, preached, and died.

Causes of the Crusades

For many years, Palestine had been in the hands of Muslims. In general, the Muslims did not bother Christians who visited the region. In the late 1000s, though, a group of Turkish Muslims entered the area and captured the city of Jerusalem. Pilgrims returning to Europe said that these Turks had attacked them in the Holy Land, which was no longer safe for Christians.

Before long, the Turks began to raid the Byzantine Empire. The Byzantine emperor, fearing an attack on Constantinople, asked **Pope Urban II** of the Roman Catholic Church for help. Although the Byzantines were Orthodox Christians and not Catholic, the pope agreed to the request.

Teach the Big Idea

At Level

The Crusades

1. **Teach** Ask students the questions in the Main Idea boxes to teach this section.
2. **Apply** Have students work in pairs to create a chart about the Crusades, with boxes for each of the four Crusades discussed in this section. Students should list important details from each Crusade, such as answers to who, what, when, where, how, and why.
   LS Verbal/Linguistic, Visual/Spatial
3. **Review** As you review, have students draw conclusions about the causes and effects of the Crusades from the details in their charts. Have students discuss the long term results of the Crusades.
4. **Practice/Homework** Have each student write a 30-second radio commercial to recruit knights to fight in a Crusade. Encourage students to come up with a slogan to persuade knights to fight.
   LS Verbal/Linguistic

Alternative Assessment Handbook, Rubrics 7: Charts; 34: Slogans and Banners; and 43: Writing to Persuade

Crusader Battlefield

The Holy Land was the scene of many bloody battles during the Crusades, like the one near the city of Antioch shown in this medieval painting. The men at right show what Crusaders may have worn.

What was the goal of the Crusaders?

The Call to Arms

Pope Urban called on Christians from all over Europe to retake the Holy Land from the Muslim Turks. He challenged Europe's kings and nobles to quit fighting among themselves and fight together against the Turks. In response, people joined the pope's army by the thousands.

Crusaders from all over Europe flocked to France to prepare for their long journey. They sewed crosses onto their clothing to show that they were fighting for God. In fact, the word *crusade* comes from the Latin for "marked with a cross." As they marched off to war, the Crusaders yelled their rallying cry, "God wills it!"

Why would people leave home to fight in a distant land? Some just hoped to save their souls or to do what they thought God wanted. They thought that God would look favorably on them for fighting his enemies, as one French abbot noted:

> "What a glory to return in victory from such a battle! . . . if they are blessed who die in the Lord, how much more are they who die for the Lord!"
>
> —Saint Bernard of Clairvaux, from *In Praise of the New Knighthood*

Other Crusaders wanted land and treasure. Still others were looking for something to do. Adventure called to them.

The First Crusade

About 5,000 Crusaders left Europe for the Holy Land in 1096. Some of the first ones to set out were peasants, not soldiers. On their way to the Holy Land, these peasant Crusaders attacked Jews in Germany. They blamed the Jews for Jesus's death.

Direct Teach

Main Idea

1 Crusaders Invade the Holy Land

The pope called on Crusaders to invade the Holy Land.

Recall Why did the Byzantine emperor ask Pope Urban II for help? *He was afraid Muslim Turks would attack Constantinople.*

Define Where does the word crusade come from? *Latin for "marked with a cross"*

Predict What states might Pope Urban II call on to retake the Holy Land? *possible answers—those in the Holy Roman Empire, England, France*

CRF: Primary Source Activity: The Siege and Capture of Nicea

MISCONCEPTION ALERT

Heavy Metal The idea that knights in armor had to use cranes to hoist themselves onto their horses actually started out as a joke in the 1800s and slowly worked its way into popular fiction. Typical armor was by no means too heavy or awkward to inhibit movement. At most, a stool or squire might aid a knight in getting on his horse more quickly, but the typical knight could get in the saddle without any help.

hmhsocialstudies.com

Online Resources
Activity: Crusader Propaganda Posters

Differentiating Instruction

Struggling Readers — Below Level

1. With students, create a numbered list with the heading *Reasons to join the Crusades.*
2. Have students reread the third paragraph above and list the reasons given. (*Answers include to save their souls, to do what they thought God wanted, or because they wanted land, treasure, or adventure*)

LS Interpersonal, Verbal/Linguistic

Advanced/Gifted and Talented — Above Level, Research Required

1. Have students conduct research on a topic related to the Crusades, such as key leaders, weaponry, armor, cities, or trade. Students should write questions to guide their research.
2. Have students create a traditional or software presentation to present their findings.

LS Verbal/Linguistic

Alternative Assessment Handbook, Rubrics 29: Presentations; and 30: Research

Answers

Crusader Battlefield *to retake the Holy Land from the Muslim Turks*

Direct Teach

Main Idea

❷ Later Crusades Fail

Despite some initial success, the later Crusades failed.

Identify Which countries took part in the Third Crusade? *England, France, and the Holy Roman Empire*

Evaluate Which Crusade do you think was more successful: the Second or the Third? Why? *possible answer—the Third Crusade, because Richard was able to capture a few towns and get safe passage for Christian pilgrims*

Draw Conclusions How do you think the Crusades affected Muslim attitudes toward the Christian West? *possible answer—Muslims may have seen Christians as aggressive invaders and have grown to fear and distrust Christians.*

CRF: Biography Activity: Blanche of Castile

Map Transparency: The Major Crusades, AD 1096–1204

Answers

Reading Check *Christians took Jerusalem, set up four small kingdoms, a lord and vassal system, and began trade with Europe.*

Before they even reached the Holy Land, Turkish troops killed most of these untrained, poorly equipped peasants.

The nobles and knights fared better. When they reached Jerusalem in 1099, they found the Muslim army disorganized and unready to fight. After about a month of fighting, the Crusaders took Jerusalem.

After the Europeans took Jerusalem, they set up four small Christian kingdoms in the Holy Land. The rulers of these kingdoms built churches and created lord and vassal systems like they had known at home. They also began to trade with Europe.

READING CHECK **Summarizing** What did the First Crusade accomplish?

Later Crusades Fail

The kingdoms the Christians created in the Holy Land didn't last, though. Within 50 years the Muslims had started taking land back from the Christians. In response, the Europeans launched more Crusades.

The Second and Third Crusades

French and German kings set off in 1147 to retake land from the Muslims. This Second Crusade was a terrible failure. Poor planning and heavy losses on the journey to the Holy Land led to the Christians' total defeat. Ashamed, the Crusaders returned to Europe in less than a year.

The Third Crusade began after the Muslims retook Jerusalem in 1189. The rulers of England, France, and the Holy Roman Empire led their armies to the Holy Land to fight for Jerusalem, but problems soon arose. The German king died, and the French king left. Only **King Richard I** of England stayed in the Holy Land.

King Richard's main opponent in the Third Crusade was **Saladin**, the leader of the Muslim forces. Saladin was a brilliant leader. Even Crusaders respected his kindness toward fallen enemies. In turn, the Muslims admired Richard's bravery.

For months, Richard and Saladin fought and negotiated. Richard captured a few towns and won protection for Christian pilgrims. In the end, however, he returned home with Jerusalem still in Muslim hands.

BIOGRAPHY

Richard I

1157–1199

Called "Lion Heart" for his courage, Richard I was a skilled soldier and a great general. He did not succeed in taking Jerusalem during the Third Crusade, but he earned the respect of Muslims and Christians alike. Since his death, he has become the hero of countless stories and legends.

ATLANTIC OCEAN

The Fourth Crusade

In 1201 French knights arrived in Venice ready to sail to the Holy Land to begin a Fourth Crusade. However, the knights didn't have money to pay for the voyage. For payment the Venetians asked the knights to conquer Zara, a rival trade city. The knights agreed. Later they also attacked Constantinople and carried off many treasures. The city that had been threatened by Muslims before the Crusades had been sacked by Christians!

The End of the Crusades

Other Crusades followed, but none was successful. By 1291 the Muslim armies had taken back all of the Holy Land, and the

Cross-Discipline Activity: Literature

Above Level

The Legend of Robin Hood

Research Required

Background Most versions of the Robin Hood legend take place during the time of the Third Crusade. Robin is faithful to King Richard I who has gone to fight. During his absence, his younger brother Prince John, who is left in charge, attempts to steal the throne. The sheriff of Nottingham supports Prince John.

1. Ask the class to share anything they know about the legend of Robin Hood. Provide students with some background about the legend.
2. Organize students into small groups. Have each group use the library and other resources to conduct research on the legend of Robin Hood. Tell students to pay special attention to any historical details that relate to the legend, such as what was going on in England and in the Holy Land during that time. Ask students to look as well for any evidence that the legend of Robin Hood is based on fact.
3. Have students share what they learned by giving short group presentations.
LS Interpersonal, Verbal/Linguistic

Alternative Assessment Handbook, Rubrics 29: Presentations; and 30: Research

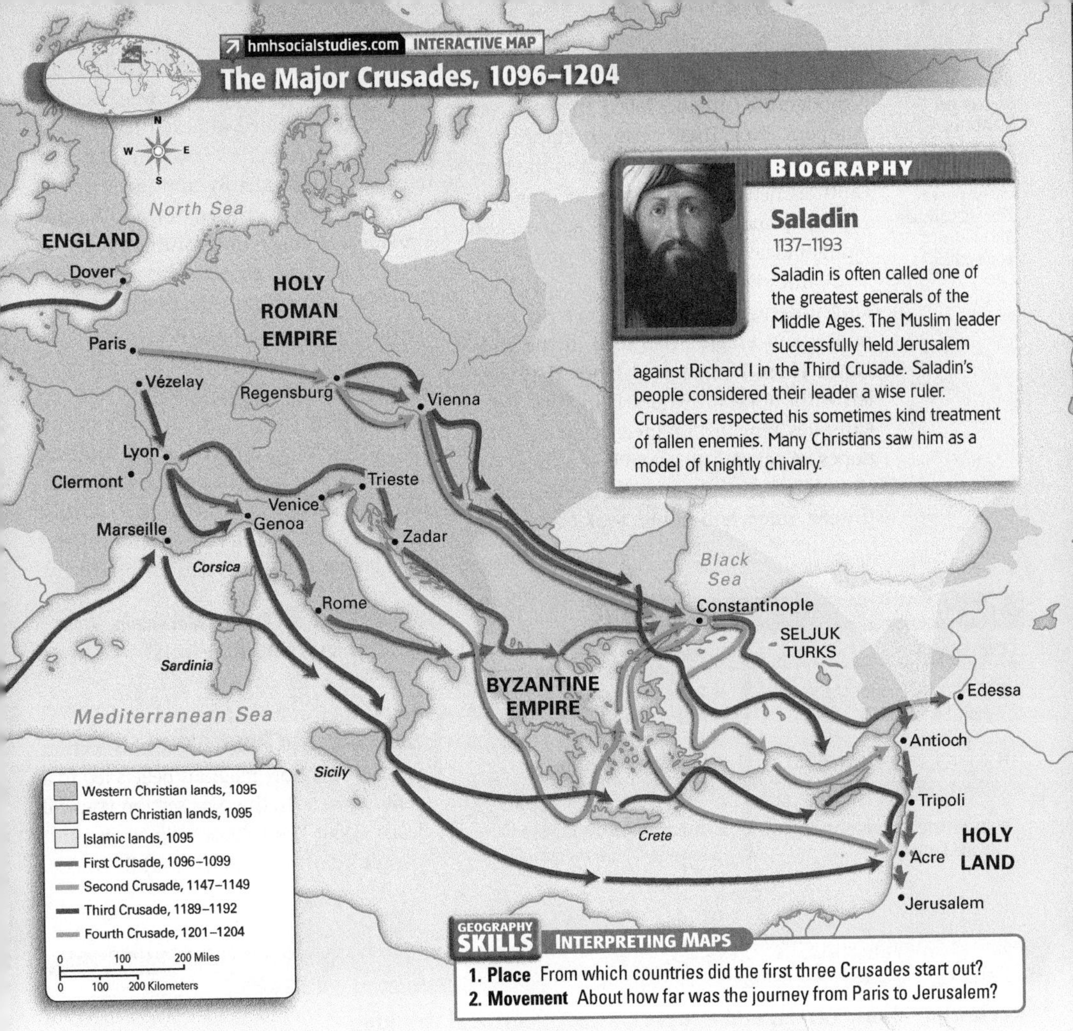

BIOGRAPHY

Saladin

1137–1193

Saladin is often called one of the greatest generals of the Middle Ages. The Muslim leader successfully held Jerusalem against Richard I in the Third Crusade. Saladin's people considered their leader a wise ruler. Crusaders respected his sometimes kind treatment of fallen enemies. Many Christians saw him as a model of knightly chivalry.

GEOGRAPHY SKILLS INTERPRETING MAPS

1. **Place** From which countries did the first three Crusades start out?
2. **Movement** About how far was the journey from Paris to Jerusalem?

Crusades had ended. Why did the Crusades fail? There were many reasons.

- The Crusaders had to travel huge distances just to reach the war. Many died along the way.
- Crusaders weren't prepared to fight in Palestine's desert climate.
- The Christians were outnumbered by their well-led and organized Muslim foes.
- Christian leaders fought among themselves and planned poorly.

Whatever the reasons for their failure, the Crusades ended just as they had begun so many years before, with the Holy Land under Muslim control.

READING CHECK **Analyzing** How did geography limit the success of the Crusades?

Direct Teach

Info to Know

Women Crusaders Not all Crusaders were men. Eleanor of Aquitaine accompanied her first husband, King Louis VII of France, on the Second Crusade. Her son was Richard I of England, the leader of the Third Crusade.

History Humor

When a knight was killed in battle, what did they put on his tombstone? *Rust in peace.*

Teaching Tip

Link it to Today Display or provide students with a copy of a modern political map of the region shown in the map at left. Have students compare the two maps to understand better where the Crusades took place and through what regions the Crusaders traveled.

Critical Thinking: Evaluating Information

At Level

Crusader Journal

1. Have students compare a physical map of Europe with the map above.
2. Ask students to identify geographic features that may have made travel difficult between Europe and the Holy Land. *many mountains in southern Europe and the Balkan Peninsula*
3. Ask students to think of reasons why some routes were partly or entirely made up of water. (*possible answers—It might be easier or safer to sail than to cross the mountains.*)
4. Ask students to imagine that they are English Crusaders going to the Holy Land on the Third Crusade. Have them write a journal entry for a rough day of travel, taking into account difficulties discussed in this exercise. **LS Verbal/Linguistic, Visual/Spatial**

Alternative Assessment Handbook, Rubrics 15: Journals; and 21: Map Reading

Answers

Interpreting Maps 1. *France, Holy Roman Empire, England;* **2.** *1,400 miles*

Reading Check *The Crusaders had to travel a long way, and many died on the hard journey. Crusaders were not prepared to fight in Palestine's desert climate.*

Direct Teach

Main Idea

3 Crusades Change Europe

The Crusades changed Europe forever.

List Name three products Europeans learned about in the Holy Land. *apricots, rice, and cotton cloth*

Identify Cause and Effect How did the Crusades affect relations between Christians and Jews? *Many Jews grew to distrust Christians.*

Economics and History Activity: The Economic Impact of the Crusades

Quick Facts Transparency: The Crusades

Review & Assess

Close

Have students summarize the Christian and Muslim conflict over the Holy Land and its affect on relationships among Christians, Jews, and Muslims.

Review

Online Quiz, Section 2

Assess

SE Section 2 Assessment

PASS: Section 2 Quiz

Alternative Assessment Handbook

Reteach/Classroom Intervention

Guided Reading Workbook, Section 2

Interactive Skills Tutor CD-ROM

Crusades Change Europe

Focus on Reading
How might stereotype and bias have affected Christian and Muslim relationships?

Although the Crusades failed, they changed Europe forever. Trade between Europe and Asia grew. Europeans who went to the Holy Land learned about products such as apricots, rice, and cotton cloth. Crusaders also brought ideas of Muslim thinkers to Europe.

Politics in Europe also changed. Some kings increased their power because many nobles and knights had died in the Holy Land. These kings seized lands that were left without clear owners. During the later Crusades, kings also gained influence at the popes' expense. The popes had wanted the church to be in charge of all the Crusades. Instead, rulers and nobles took control.

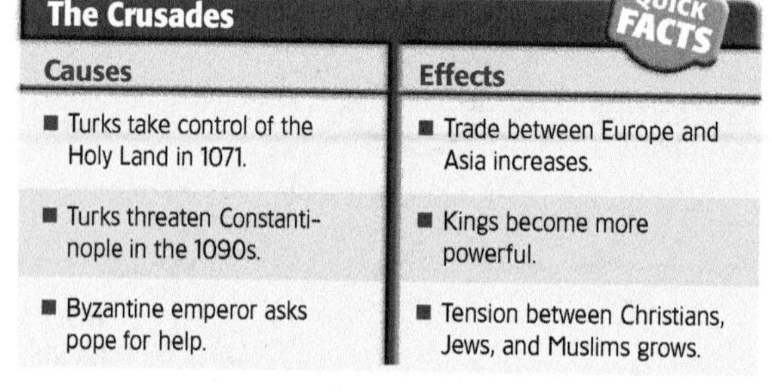

The Crusades — Quick Facts

Causes	Effects
■ Turks take control of the Holy Land in 1071.	■ Trade between Europe and Asia increases.
■ Turks threaten Constantinople in the 1090s.	■ Kings become more powerful.
■ Byzantine emperor asks pope for help.	■ Tension between Christians, Jews, and Muslims grows.

The Crusades had lasting effects on relations among peoples as well. Because some Crusaders had attacked Jews, many Jews distrusted Christians. In addition, tension between the Byzantines and western Christians increased, especially after Crusaders attacked Constantinople.

The greatest changes occurred with Christian and Muslim relationships. Each group learned about the other's religion and culture. Sometimes this led to mutual respect. In general, though, the Crusaders saw Muslims as unbelievers who threatened innocent Christians. Most Muslims viewed the Crusaders as vicious invaders. Some historians think that the distrust that began during the Crusades still affects Christian and Muslim relationships today.

Reading Check **Finding Main Ideas** What were some results of the Crusades?

Summary and Preview In this section you learned how religious beliefs led to a series of wars. In the next section you will learn about the role of religion in most people's daily lives in the Middle Ages.

Section 2 Assessment

hmhsocialstudies.com ONLINE QUIZ

Reviewing Ideas, Terms, and People

1. a. **Recall** What did **Pope Urban II** ask Christians to do?
   b. **Elaborate** Why do you think so many people were willing to go on a Crusade?
2. a. **Identify** In which Crusade did **Saladin** and **King Richard I** fight?
   b. **Rank** Which Crusade do you think was the least successful? Why?
3. a. **Identify** What new products were introduced to Europe after the Crusades?
   b. **Draw Conclusions** Why did the Crusades change relationships between Christians and other groups?

Critical Thinking

4. **Comparing and Contrasting** Draw a diagram like the one here. Use it and your notes to compare and contrast Europe before and after the Crusades.

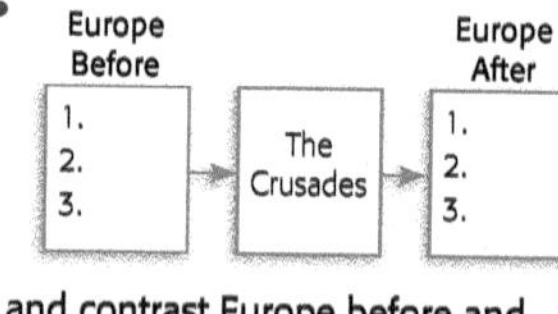

Focus on Writing

5. **Thinking about the Crusades** Look back through what you've just read and make a list of people who were important in the Crusades. What made them important?

Section 2 Assessment Answers

1. a. free the Holy Land from Muslim Turks
   b. possible answers—to save their souls; thought God would look favorably upon them; for land, treasure, or adventure
2. a. Third Crusade
   b. Answers will vary; possible answer—the Second Crusade, because Crusaders returned home totally defeated after less than one year.
3. a. apricots, rice, cotton cloth
   b. because some Christian Crusaders had attacked other groups, such as Jews, relations between Christians and others worsened in some ways; close contact also led to some mutual respect.
4. before—kings and nobles fought among themselves; after—trade between Europe and Asia grew, ideas of Muslim thinkers were brought to Europe, politics changes, Jews' distrust of Christians grows, Christian-Muslim relationship changed.
5. Pope Urban II—pope of the First Crusade; King Richard I—led English forces in Third Crusade; Saladin—leader of Muslim forces in Third Crusade.

Answers

Reading Check *Trade between Europe and Asia increased; kings became more powerful; tension between Christians, Jews, and Muslims grew.*

Christianity and Medieval Society

SECTION 3

If YOU were there...

You are a stone carver, apprenticed to a master builder. The bishop has hired your master to design a huge new church. He wants the church to inspire and impress worshippers with the glory of God. Your master has entrusted you with the decoration of the outside of the church. You are excited by the challenge.

What kind of art will you create for the church?

BUILDING BACKGROUND Thousands of churches were built across Europe in the Middle Ages. People took great pride in their churches because religion was very important to them. In fact, Christianity was a key factor in shaping medieval society.

The Church Shapes Society and Politics

Nearly everyone who lived in Europe during the Middle Ages was Roman Catholic. In fact, religion was central to every part of life. Church officials, called **clergy**, and their teachings were very influential in European culture and politics.

The towers of old Christian churches still rise above many European towns and cities. Christianity became a strong influence on European life in the Middle Ages.

What You Will Learn...

Main Ideas

1. The Christian Church shaped both society and politics in medieval Europe.
2. Orders of monks and friars did not like the church's political nature.
3. Church leaders helped build the first universities in Europe.
4. The church influenced the arts in medieval Europe.

The Big Idea

The Christian Church was central to life in the Middle Ages.

Key Terms and People

clergy, *p. 533*
religious order, *p. 536*
Francis of Assisi, *p. 536*
friars, *p. 536*
Thomas Aquinas, *p. 537*
natural law, *p. 538*

Use the graphic organizer online to take notes on the many roles the Catholic Church played in Europe in the Middle Ages.

...ch the Big Idea

At Level

Christianity and Medieval Society

1. **Teach** Ask students the questions in the Main Idea boxes to teach this section.
2. **Apply** Draw a cluster diagram for students to see. In the center circle, write *The Church.* In the surrounding circles write the subtopics *Society and Politics, Monks and Friars, Universities,* and *The Arts.* Have students copy the diagram and list two or three facts for each subtopic. **LS Visual/Spatial**
3. **Review** As you review the section's main ideas, have volunteers share the information they listed. Link facts to the appropriate subtopic circles.
4. **Practice/Homework** Have students use the information in their cluster diagrams to write a one-paragraph summary of this section. **LS Verbal/Spatial**

Alternative Assessment Handbook, Rubric 13: Graphic Organizers

Preteach

Bellringer

If YOU were there . . . Use the **Daily Bellringer Transparency** to help students answer the question.

Daily Bellringer Transparency, Section 3

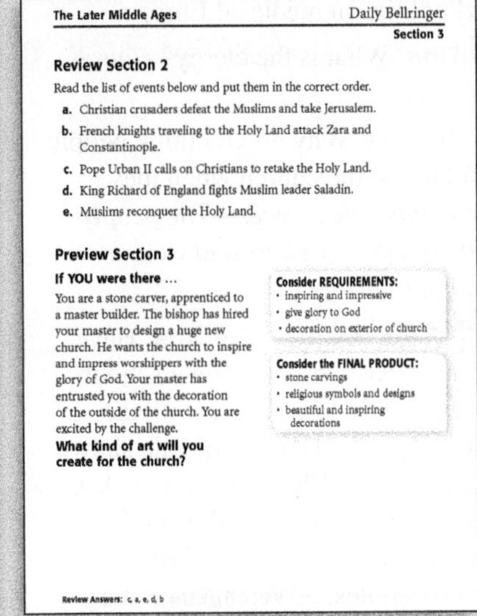

The Later Middle Ages — Daily Bellringer — **Section 3**

Review Section 2

Read the list of events below and put them in the correct order.

- **a.** Christian crusaders defeat the Muslims and take Jerusalem.
- **b.** French knights traveling to the Holy Land attack Zara and Constantinople.
- **c.** Pope Urban II calls on Christians to retake the Holy Land.
- **d.** King Richard of England fights Muslim leader Saladin.
- **e.** Muslims reconquer the Holy Land.

Preview Section 3

If YOU were there ...

You are a stone carver, apprenticed to a master builder. The bishop has hired your master to design a huge new church. He wants the church to inspire and impress worshippers with the glory of God. Your master has entrusted you with the decoration of the outside of the church. You are excited by the challenge.

What kind of art will you create for the church?

Consider REQUIREMENTS:
- inspiring and impressive
- give glory to God
- decoration on exterior of church

Consider the FINAL PRODUCT:
- stone carvings
- religious symbols and designs
- beautiful and inspiring decorations

Review Answers: c, a, e, d, b

Building Vocabulary

Preteach or review the following terms:

convent a community of nuns (p. 536)
fief land given in exchange for loyalty or service (p. 535)
monastery a residence for monks (p. 535)
pilgrimage a journey to a religious location (p. 534)
tapestry a heavy, woven cloth decorated with designs and pictures, often hung on a wall (p. 538)

CRF: Vocabulary Builder Activity, Section 3

Taking Notes

Have students use the graphic organizer online to take notes on the section. This activity will prepare students for the Section Assessment, in which they will complete a graphic organizer that builds on the information using the Critical Thinking Skill: Categorizing.

Direct Teach

Main Idea

1 The Church Shapes Society and Politics

The Christian Church shaped society and politics in medieval Europe.

Define What is the clergy? *church officials*

Elaborate Why do you think people left land to the church when they died? *possible answer—The people were deeply religious and wanted the church to prosper.*

Activity **Daily Schedule** Have students write out their own school-day schedule to compare with the Cluny Monk's Daily Schedule shown in the History Close-up feature. Ask students to think about the similarities and differences they note between the two schedules. LS **Verbal/Linguistic**

Alternative Assessment Handbook, Rubric 9: Comparing and Contrasting

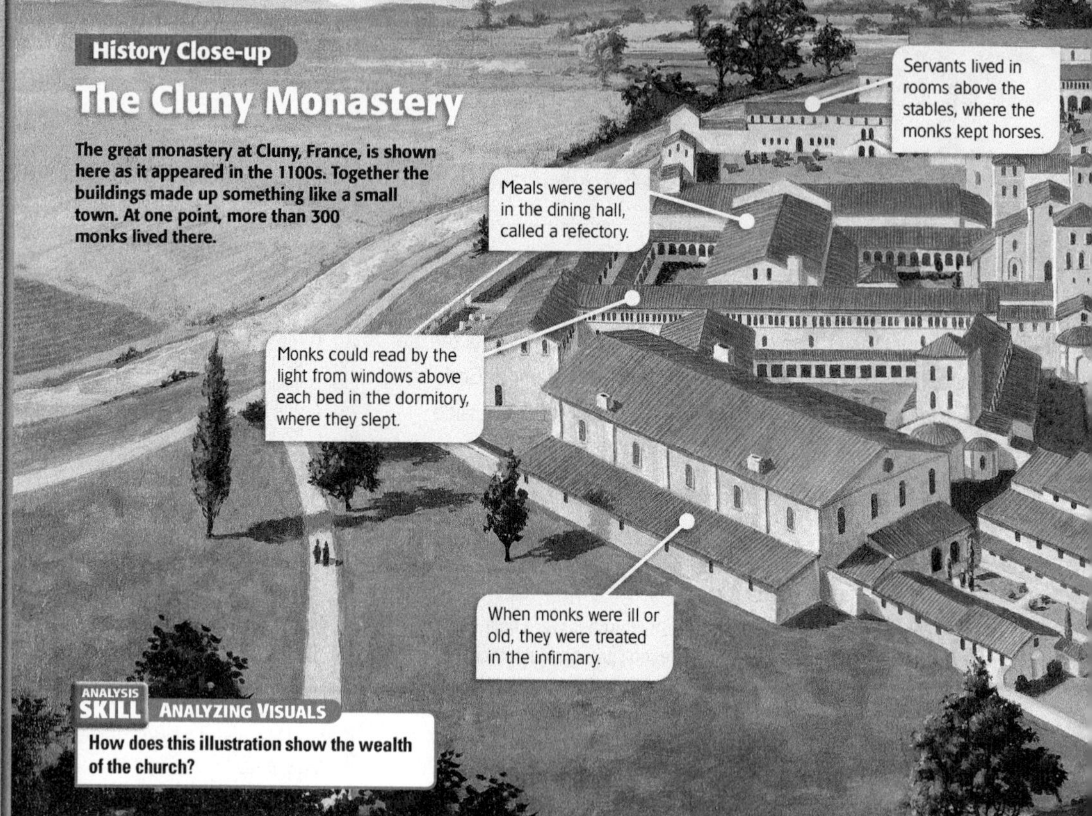

Servants lived in rooms above the stables, where the monks kept horses.
Meals were served in the dining hall, called a refectory.
Monks could read by the light from windows above each bed in the dormitory, where they slept.
When monks were ill or old, they were treated in the infirmary.

History Close-up

The Cluny Monastery

The great monastery at Cluny, France, is shown here as it appeared in the 1100s. Together the buildings made up something like a small town. At one point, more than 300 monks lived there.

ANALYSIS SKILL **ANALYZING VISUALS**

How does this illustration show the wealth of the church?

The Church and Society

In the Middle Ages, life revolved around the local church. Markets, festivals, and religious ceremonies all took place there.

For some people, however, the local church was not enough. They wanted to see important religious sites—the places where Jesus lived, where holy men and women died, and where miracles happened. The church encouraged these people to go on pilgrimages, journeys to religious locations. Among the most popular destinations were Jerusalem, Rome, and Compostela, in northwestern Spain. Each of these cities had churches that Christians wanted to visit.

Another popular pilgrimage destination was Canterbury, near London in England. Hundreds of visitors went to the cathedral in Canterbury each year. One such visit is the basis for one of the greatest books of the Middle Ages, *The Canterbury Tales* by Geoffrey Chaucer (CHAW-suhr). Chaucer's book tells of a group of pilgrims who feel drawn, like many people, to Canterbury:

> "When in April the sweet showers fall
> And pierce the drought of March to the root . . .
> Then people long to go on pilgrimages
> And palmers long to seek the stranger strands
> Of far-off saints, hallowed in sundry lands
> And specially, from every shire's end
> Of England, down to Canterbury they wend."
>
> —Geoffrey Chaucer, from *The Canterbury Tales*

Answers

Analyzing Visuals *possible answers—many buildings, servant quarters, elaborate abbey, farm land*

Differentiating Instruction

Struggling Learners

Below Level Standard English Mastery

1. If students had difficulty understanding the passage from *The Canterbury Tales* on this page, explain that Chaucer originally wrote in Middle English, which is very different from the language we speak today. The translation above is in modern English; however, it uses some archaic wording to retain Chaucer's style and sound.
2. Write the definitions listed to the right for students to see.

- **drought** period of dry weather
- **palmer** pilgrim
- **long** to want badly
- **stranger** foreign
- **strand** shore
- **hallowed** blessed
- **sundry** various
- **shire** county in England
- **wend** to travel

3. Have students rewrite the passage in their own words—*not* by just substituting the definitions given here. Remind students to use standard English.
4. Ask volunteers to read their rewritten passages. How did rewriting help them understand what Chaucer is saying? LS **Verbal/Linguistic**

Alternative Assessment Handbook: Rubric 1: Acquiring Information

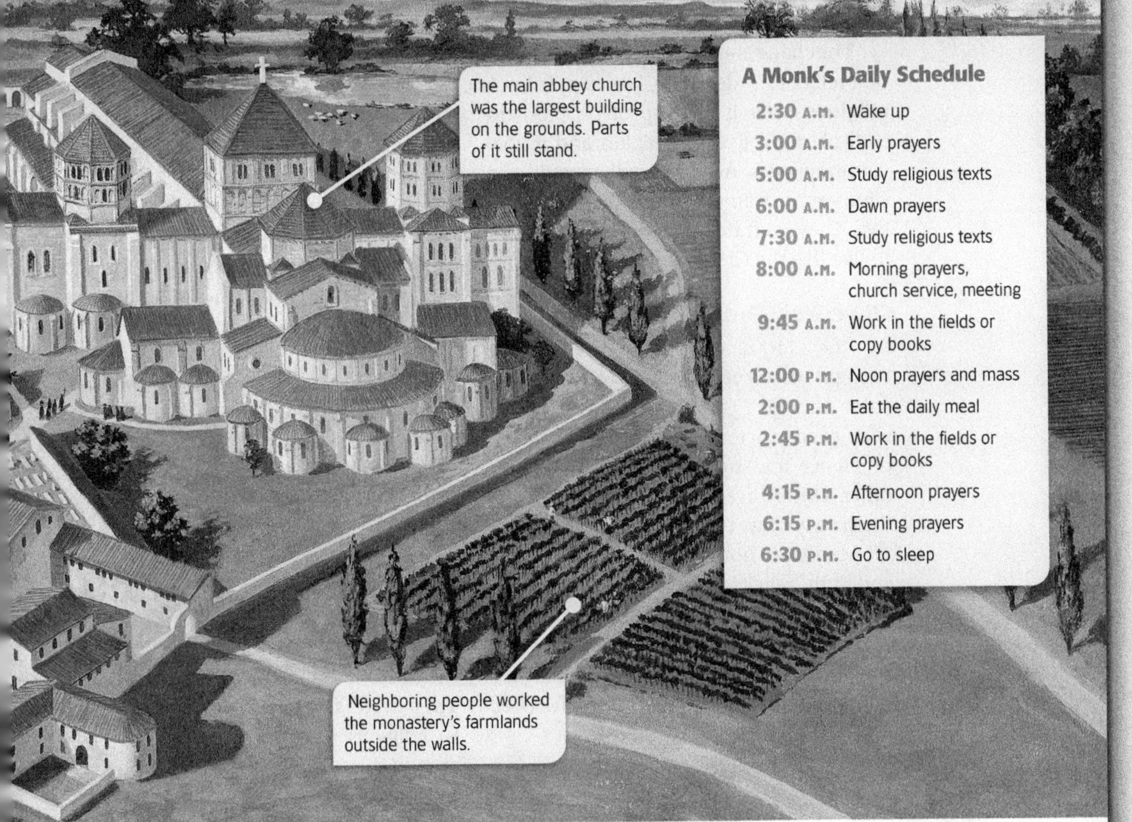

The main abbey church was the largest building on the grounds. Parts of it still stand.
A Monk's Daily Schedule
2:30 A.M. Wake up
3:00 A.M. Early prayers
5:00 A.M. Study religious texts
6:00 A.M. Dawn prayers
7:30 A.M. Study religious texts
8:00 A.M. Morning prayers, church service, meeting
9:45 A.M. Work in the fields or copy books
12:00 P.M. Noon prayers and mass
2:00 P.M. Eat the daily meal
2:45 P.M. Work in the fields or copy books
4:15 P.M. Afternoon prayers
6:15 P.M. Evening prayers
6:30 P.M. Go to sleep
Neighboring people worked the monastery's farmlands outside the walls.

The Church and Politics

The church also gained political power during the Middle Ages. Many people left land to the church when they died. In fact, the church was one of the largest landholders in Europe. Eventually, the church divided this land into fiefs. In this way, it became a feudal lord.

Of all the clergy, bishops and abbots were most involved in political matters. They often advised local rulers. Some clergy got so involved with politics that they spent little time dealing with religious affairs.

READING CHECK **Analyzing** In what ways were clergy members important political figures?

Monks and Friars

Some people were unhappy with the political nature of the church. They thought the clergy should focus only on spiritual matters. These people feared that the church had become obsessed with wealth and power.

The Monks of Cluny

Among those unhappy with the church were a group of French monks. In the early 900s they started a monastery in the town of Cluny (KLOO-nee). The monks of Cluny followed a strict schedule of prayers and religious services. They paid little attention to the world, concerning themselves only with religious matters.

Direct Teach

Main Idea

❷ Monks and Friars

Orders of monks and friars did not like the church's political nature.

Define What is a religious order? *a group of people who dedicate their lives to religion and follow common rules*

Make Inferences Why do you think monks and friars owned no property? *They wanted to focus on religion, not on worldly goods.*

Make Judgments Would you rather be a monk or a friar? Why? *possible answers—a friar, because monks' schedules and regimens are too strict; a monk, because I would rather read and study than travel and beg*

Info to Know

Giant Churches The main abbey church at Cluny was called the Basilica of St. Peter and St. Paul. Built between 1088 and 1130, it was not only the largest building on the grounds but also the largest church in the world. It remained the largest church until St. Peter's Basilica in Rome was built between 1506 and 1615. Much of the Cluny basilica was destroyed early in the 1800s, after the abbey was closed during the French Revolution.

Cross-Discipline Activity: English-Language Arts

At Level

Visiting Cluny Monastery

Standard English Mastery

1. Ask students to imagine that they live in France in the 1100s. Although they do not live at Cluny Monastery they have heard a great deal about it. Tell students that they have been invited to visit the monastery.
2. Have students write journal entries that record their impressions of the monastery as a monk guides them through the buildings and grounds. Students may choose to keep their journal entry descriptive or to contrast their imaginary medieval life with the lives of the Cluny monks. Remind students to use standard English in their journal entries.
2. Have volunteers read their journal entries to the class. Help students revise their entries to improve their use of Standard English.

LS Verbal/Linguistic

Alternative Assessment Handbook, Rubric 37: Writing Assignments

Answers

Reading Check *They owned land and advised local rulers.*

Direct Teach

Did you know . . .

The word *friar* comes from the French word *frère,* which means "brother."

Connect to Music

"Frère Jacques" You may be familiar with the song "Frère Jacques," known in English as "Are You Sleeping?" Here are the English words of the song:

Are you sleeping,
Are you sleeping,
Brother John,
Brother John?
Morning bells are ringing,
Morning bells are ringing,
Ding, ding, dong,
Ding, ding, dong!

The morning bells referred to in the song are those calling people to matins, the morning church service.

Answers

Biography *possible answer—He lived simply, helped the poor and ill, and treated everyone fairly, which might inspire other people to do the same.*

Reading Check *They felt that the church had become too political and obsessed with wealth and power, and they wanted to focus instead on God.*

The changes at Cluny led to the creation of a religious order, the Cluniac monks. A **religious order** is a group of people who dedicate their lives to religion and follow common rules. Across Europe, people saw Cluny as an example of how monks should live. They built new monasteries and tried to live like the Cluniacs.

Other New Orders

By the 1100s, though, some monks thought that even Cluny's rules weren't strict enough. They created new orders with even stricter rules. Some took vows of silence and stopped speaking to each other. Others lived in tiny rooms and left them only to go to church services.

Men were not the only ones to create and join religious orders. Women were allowed to join these kinds of orders as well. Communities of nuns called convents appeared across Europe. Like monks, these nuns lived according to a strict set of rules. The nuns of each convent prayed and worked together under the watchful eyes of an abbess, the convent's leader.

Although monks and nuns lived apart from other people, they did a great deal for society. For example, they collected and stored texts that explained Christian teachings. Monks spent hours copying these documents, and they sent copies to monasteries across Europe.

BIOGRAPHY

Saint Francis of Assisi

c. 1182–1226

Born in Assisi, Italy, Francis was the son of a wealthy merchant. As a young man, however, Francis gave all his money and possessions away and left his father's house. He lived a simple life, preaching and tending to people who were poor or ill. Francis considered everyone his brother or sister, including animals. He encouraged people to take care of animals just as they would take care of other people. Within a few years other people had begun to copy his lifestyle. In 1210 they became the first members of the Franciscan Order.

Making Generalizations How do you think Francis's generosity and compassion might inspire Christians to follow the church's teachings?

The Friars

Not everyone who joined a religious order wanted to live apart from society. Some wanted to live in cities and spread Christian teachings. As a result, two new religious orders were begun in the early 1200s.

These orders were the Dominicans and the Franciscans, named for their founders, Dominic de Guzmán and **Francis of Assisi**. Because they didn't live in monasteries, members of these orders were not monks. They were **friars**, people who belonged to religious orders but lived and worked among the general public.

Friars lived simply, wearing plain robes and no shoes. Like monks, they owned no property. They roamed about, preaching and begging for food. For that reason, friars were also called mendicants, from a Latin word for beggars.

The main goal of the friars was to teach people how to live good Christian lives. They taught people about generosity and kindness. A prayer credited to Francis illustrates what the friars hoped to do:

> "Lord, make me an instrument of your peace. Where there is hatred, let me sow love; where there is injury, pardon; where there is doubt, faith; where there is despair, hope; where there is darkness, light; and where there is sadness, joy."
>
> –Francis of Assisi, from *The Prayer of Saint Francis*

READING CHECK **Summarizing** Why did people create new religious orders?

Collaborative Learning

At Level

Monks and Friars Venn Diagram

1. To help students compare and contrast monks and friars, draw the graphic organizer for students to see. Omit the blue, italicized answers.
2. Have students copy and complete the graphic organizer. Instruct students to refer to the part of the text titled "Monks and Friars" to complete the activity. **LS Visual/Spatial**

Alternative Assessment Handbook, Rubric 13: Graphic Organizers

Monks	Both	Friars
• *lived apart from people* • *built monasteries* • *collected, stored,and copied Christian texts*	• *unhappy with politics in church* • *members of religious order*	• *lived and worked among people* • *owned no property* • *preached and begged*

LINKING TO TODAY

School Days

Did you know that many customs that schools and universities follow today began in the Middle Ages? For example, medieval teachers taught groups of students instead of individuals. Classes ran according to a fixed schedule, and students had to take tests. At night, students went to their rooms to study and complete assignments. Many students participated in sports such as races and ball games after classes. At graduation, students dressed up in caps and gowns. All of these customs are still common today.

Medieval universities were not exactly the same as universities are now, however. Medieval students entered the university at age 14, and only boys could attend.

ANALYSIS SKILL ANALYZING INFORMATION

Why do you think some customs followed by universities in the Middle Ages have lasted until today?

Universities Are Built

While some people were drawing away from the world in monasteries and convents, others were looking for ways to learn more about it. In time, their search for knowledge led to the creation of Europe's first universities.

Some of the earliest universities were created by the church. The church's goal was to teach people about religion. Other universities were created by groups of students who went searching for teachers who could tell them about the world.

Most teachers in these universities were members of the clergy. Besides religion, schools taught law, medicine, astronomy, and other courses. All classes were taught in Latin. Although relatively few people in Europe spoke Latin, it was the language of scholars and the church.

As people began to study new subjects, some of them developed new ideas about the world. In particular, they wondered how human reason and Christian faith were related. In the past, people had believed that some things could be proven with reason, but other things had to be taken on faith. Some people in universities, though, began to wonder if the two ideas could work together.

One such person was the Dominican philosopher **Thomas Aquinas** (uh-KWY-nuhs). Thomas was a teacher at the University of Paris. He argued that rational thought could be used to support Christian beliefs. For example, he wrote an argument to prove the existence of God.

Direct Teach

Main Idea

3 Universities Are Built

Church leaders helped build the first universities in Europe.

Recall Why were the first universities created? *The church created some to teach religion; other universities were created by students who wanted to learn about the world.*

Make Inferences How did teaching university classes in Latin help international relationships? *All educated people from different countries could communicate in Latin.*

Elaborate How did Thomas Aquinas think understanding natural law could help people? *He thought that if people studied and learned more about this law they could learn to live the way God wanted.*

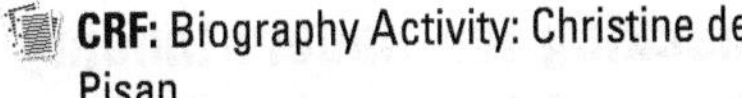

CRF: Biography Activity: Christine de Pisan

Info to Know

Scholasticism In the Middle Ages, there was an attempt to bridge the gap between faith and reason, or between religion and science. This led to the philosophical movement known as Scholasticism. Scholars such as Thomas Aquinas tried to combine the wisdom of the ancient Greeks and Romans with the religion of Christianity. The movement became popular in the monastic and cathedral schools, and led to the development of universities.

Collaborative Learning

At Level

Research Required

Medieval Universities

1. Organize the class into five small groups. Have each group conduct research on one of the following early European universities: Salerno, Montpellier, Bologna, Paris, and Oxford. Have students look for information, including answers to the following questions:
   - What country was it in?
   - When was it founded?
   - What subjects did it specialize in?
   - Does it still exist?
2. Have each group share its findings with the class. What similarities were there in these early universities? What differences were there?
3. Have students compare what they've learned about medieval universities with what they know about modern universities.
   LS Interpersonal, Verbal/Linguistic

Alternative Assessment Handbook, Rubrics 9: Comparing and Contrasting; 14: Group Activity; and 30: Research

Answers

Linking to Today *possible answer—People have strong feelings about established traditions.*

Direct Teach

Main Idea

4 The Church and the Arts

The church influenced the arts in medieval Europe.

Define What is a cathedral? *a large church in which bishops lead religious services*

Contrast How did Gothic churches differ from earlier churches? *They were much taller and had huge stained-glass windows.*

Summarize How did the church influence art and architecture? *Many churches were works of art. They were also filled with beautiful objects such as paintings and tapestries that showed respect for God.*

Checking for Understanding

True or False Answer each statement *T* if it is true or *F* if it is false. If false, explain why.

1. Women were not allowed to join religious orders. *F; Women lived in convents as nuns.*
2. Markets and festivals were held at the local church. *T*
3. The grandest of Europe's medieval churches were called chapels. *F; cathedrals*

Thomas also believed that God had created a law that governed how the world operated. He called it **natural law**. If people could study and learn more about this law, he argued, they could learn to live the way God wanted.

READING CHECK **Generalizing** How did universities help create new ideas?

The Church and the Arts

In addition to politics and education, the church was also a strong influence on art and architecture. Throughout the Middle Ages, religious feeling inspired artists and architects to create beautiful works of art.

Religious Architecture

Many of Europe's churches were incredible works of art. The grandest of these churches were cathedrals, large churches in which bishops led religious services. Beginning in the 1100s Europeans built their cathedrals using a dramatic new style called Gothic architecture.

Gothic cathedrals were not only places to pray, but also symbols of people's faith.

Gothic Architecture

One of the most beautiful of all Gothic cathedrals is in Chartres (SHAHRT), near Paris, France. At 112 feet high it is about as tall as a 10-story building.

As a result, they were towering works of great majesty and glory.

What made these Gothic churches so unusual? For one thing, they were much taller than older churches. The walls often rose up hundreds of feet, and the ceilings seemed to reach to heaven. Huge windows of stained glass let sunlight pour in, filling the churches with dazzling colors. Many of these amazing churches still exist. People continue to worship in them and admire their beauty.

BIOGRAPHY

Saint Thomas Aquinas

1225–1274

Though he was born in Italy, Thomas Aquinas lived most of his life in France. As a student and then a teacher at the University of Paris, Thomas spent most of his time in study. He wrote a book called the *Summa Theologica*, in which he argued that science and religion were related.

Although some people did not like Thomas's ideas, most considered him the greatest thinker of the Middle Ages. Later teachers modeled their lessons after his ideas.

Making Generalizations Why might people believe someone is a great thinker even if they disagree with his or her ideas?

Religious Art

Medieval churches were also filled with beautiful objects created to show respect for God. Ornate paintings and tapestries covered the walls and ceilings. Even the clothing priests wore during religious services was attractive. Their robes were often highly decorated, sometimes with threads made out of gold.

Many of the books used during religious ceremonies were beautiful objects. Monks had copied these books carefully.

Critical Thinking: Analyzing Information

At Level

Historical Marker

1. Have students study the pictures on this page and the next. Tell students that the building shown is an example of Gothic architecture.
2. Explain to students that the Chartres Cathedral was built between 1149 and 1260. Ask students how many years it took to build the cathedral *(about 111 years)*.
3. Next, ask students to imagine they are on the committee for historical preservation in Chartres.
4. Have each student write a historical marker to be placed on or near the cathedral. Markers should include a very short history of the structure and a sentence or two to describe the architectural style.

LS Visual/Spatial, Verbal/Linguistic

Alternative Assessment Handbook: Rubric 37: Writing Assignments

Answers

Biography *They may have valid arguments or a unique viewpoint.*

Reading Check *As people began to study new subjects, they developed new ideas about the world*

Pointed arches support the high ceilings.
Flying buttresses support heavy walls.
Huge stained glass windows called rose windows are found in many Gothic cathedrals.

ANALYSIS SKILL **ANALYZING VISUALS**

What would it have been like to travel from a small farm and see this cathedral for the first time?

They also decorated them using bright colors to adorn the first letters and the borders of each page. Some monks added thin sheets of silver and gold to the pages. Because the pages seem to glow, we use the word *illuminated* to describe them.

READING CHECK **Generalizing** How were medieval art and religion related?

SUMMARY AND PREVIEW Besides its religious role, the church played important roles in politics, education, and the arts. The church changed as time passed. In the next section, you will learn about other changes that took place in Europe at the same time. These changes created new political systems around the continent.

Section 3 Assessment

hmhsocialstudies.com ONLINE QUIZ

Reviewing Ideas, Terms, and People

1. a. **Recall** What are church officials called?
   b. **Explain** Why did people go on pilgrimages?
2. a. **Identify** What new monastery founded in France in the 900s served as an example to people around Europe?
   b. **Contrast** How were **friars** different from monks?
3. **Analyze** How did **Thomas Aquinas** think reason and faith could work together?
4. a. **Identify** What new style of religious architecture developed in Europe in the 1100s?
   b. **Elaborate** Why do you think so much of the art created in the Middle Ages was religious?

Critical Thinking

5. **Categorizing** Draw a chart like the one below. Using your notes, decide which of the church's roles were political, which were intellectual, and which were artistic. List each role in the appropriate column of your chart.

The Church in the Middle Ages		
Political	Intellectual	Artistic

FOCUS ON WRITING

6. **Taking Notes on Church Leaders** In this section, you've read about at least two people who became saints. Add them to your list and note why they're important.

Section 3 Assessment Answers

1. a. clergy
   b. to visit holy sites
2. a. Cluny
   b. Unlike monks, friars did not live in monasteries. They lived among the people and roamed about preaching and begging.
3. He thought people could use reason to prove things they believed in.
4. a. Gothic architecture
   b. possible answer—because most of the art was inspired by religious feelings
5. possible answers: Politics—acted as feudal lord; advised rulers; Education—clergy acted as teachers; helped create universities; The Arts—built cathedrals; inspired artists and architects
6. Saint Francis of Assisi—gave all his money and possessions away; Saint Thomas Aquinas—argued science and religion are related

Direct Teach

Did you know . . .

The term *Gothic* was somewhat of an insult originally. Historians of the Renaissance thought the architecture of the Middle Ages was unattractive and decided that it must have come from the barbarian Goths. The Goths had helped destroy the Roman Empire and classical art with it. It wasn't until the 1800s century that critics began re-evaluating Gothic architecture in a more positive light, and *Gothic* lost its negative implications.

Review & Assess

Close

Guide students in a discussion of the church's role in medieval society.

Review

Online Quiz, Section 3

Assess

SE Section 3 Assessment

PASS: Section 3 Quiz

Alternative Assessment Handbook

Reteach/Classroom Intervention

Guided Reading Workbook, Section 3

Interactive Skills Tutor CD-ROM

Answers

Analyzing Visuals *possible answer—the building's size would be impressive and awe-inspiring*

Reading Check *religious feelings inspired most medieval art*

Preteach

Bellringer

If YOU were there . . . Use the **Daily Bellringer Transparency** to help students answer the question.

Daily Bellringer Transparency, Section 4

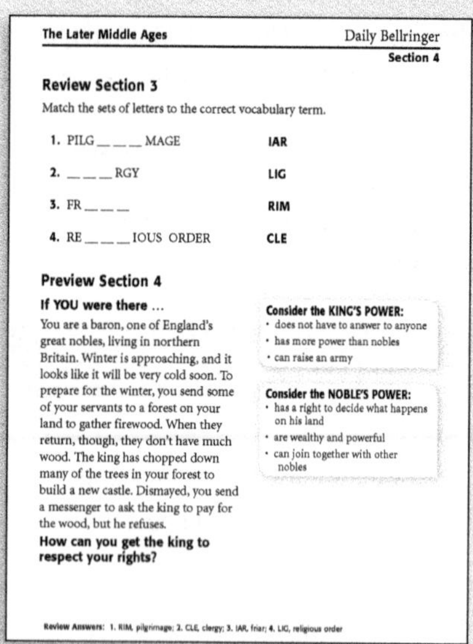

The Later Middle Ages — Daily Bellringer **Section 4**

Review Section 3

Match the sets of letters to the correct vocabulary term.

1. PILG _ _ _ MAGE — **IAR**
2. _ _ _ RGY — **LIG**
3. FR _ _ _ — **RIM**
4. RE _ _ _ IOUS ORDER — **CLE**

Preview Section 4

If YOU were there ...

You are a baron, one of England's great nobles, living in northern Britain. Winter is approaching, and it looks like it will be very cold soon. To prepare for the winter, you send some of your servants to a forest on your land to gather firewood. When they return, though, they don't have much wood. The king has chopped down many of the trees in your forest to build a new castle. Dismayed, you send a messenger to ask the king to pay for the wood, but he refuses.

How can you get the king to respect your rights?

Consider the KING'S POWER:
- does not have to answer to anyone
- has more power than nobles
- can raise an army

Consider the NOBLE'S POWER:
- has a right to decide what happens on his land
- are wealthy and powerful
- can join together with other nobles

Review Answers: 1. RIM, pilgrimage; 2. CLE, clergy; 3. IAR, friar; 4. LIG, religious order

Building Vocabulary

Preteach or review the following terms:

principles rules that form the basis for other rules (p. 541)

rallied bring back to action or strength (p. 542)

CRF: Vocabulary Builder Activity, Section 4

Taking Notes

Have students use the graphic organizer online to take notes on the section. This activity will prepare students for the Section Assessment, in which they will complete a graphic organizer that builds on the information using the Critical Thinking Skill: Evaluating.

SECTION 4

Political and Social Change

What You Will Learn...

Main Ideas

1. Magna Carta caused changes in England's government and legal system.
2. The Hundred Years' War led to political changes in England and France.
3. The Black Death, which swept through Europe in the Middle Ages, led to social changes.

The Big Idea

Europe's political and social systems underwent great changes in the late Middle Ages.

Key Terms and People

Magna Carta, *p. 540*
Parliament, *p. 541*
Hundred Years' War, *p. 542*
Joan of Arc, *p. 542*
Black Death, *p. 543*

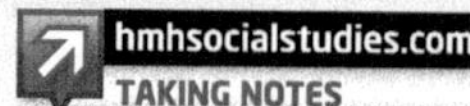

Use the graphic organizer online to take notes on the major events of the later Middle Ages and the political and social changes surrounding them.

If YOU were there...

You are a baron, one of England's great nobles, living in northern Britain. Winter is approaching, and it looks like it will be very cold soon. To prepare for the winter, you send some of your servants to a forest on your land to gather firewood. When they return, though, they don't have much wood. The king has chopped down many of the trees in your forest to build a new castle. Dismayed, you send a messenger to ask the king to pay a fair price for the wood, but he refuses.

How can you get the king to respect your rights?

BUILDING BACKGROUND Beginning with William the Conqueror, the kings of England fought to increase their power. By the 1200s, the kings felt that they could do as they pleased, whether their nobles agreed with them or not. The kings' attitudes upset many nobles, especially when kings began to create new taxes or take the nobles' property. Some nobles began to look for ways to limit kings' powers and protect their own rights.

Magna Carta Causes Change in England

In 1215 a group of nobles decided to force the king to respect their rights. In the middle of a field called Runnymede near London, they made King John approve a document they had written. This document listing rights that the king could not ignore was called **Magna Carta**. Its name is a Latin phrase meaning "Great Charter."

William the Conqueror

Teach the Big Idea

At Level

Political and Social Change

1. **Teach** Ask students the questions in the Main Idea boxes to teach this section.
2. **Apply** Draw a table with three columns for students to see. Label the columns *Magna Carta, Hundred Years' War,* and *Black Death.* Have each student copy the table and enter three or more facts under each heading. **LS Verbal/Linguistic, Visual/Spatial**
3. **Review** As you review the section's main ideas, have volunteers share the information they listed in each column.
4. **Practice/Homework** Have students imagine that they are reporters witnessing King John being forced to sign Magna Carta. Have each student write an article describing the historic event and its significance. **LS Verbal/Linguistic**

Alternative Assessment Handbook, Rubrics 7: Charts; and 42: Writing to Inform

Primary Source

HISTORIC DOCUMENT

Magna Carta

Magna Carta was one of the first documents to protect the rights of the people. Magna Carta was so influential that the British still consider it part of their constitution. Some of its ideas are also in the U.S. Constitution. Included in Magna Carta were 63 demands that English nobles made King John agree to follow. A few of these demands are listed here.

To all free men of our kingdom we have also granted, for us and our heirs for ever, all the liberties written out below, to have and to keep for them and their heirs, of us and our heirs.

(16) No man shall be forced to perform more service for a knight's 'fee,' or other free holding of land, than is due from it.

(31) Neither we nor any royal official will take wood for our castle, or for any other purpose, without the consent [permission] of the owner.

(38) In future no official shall place a man on trial upon his own unsupported statement, without producing credible [believable] witnesses to the truth of it.

—Magna Carta, from a translation by the British Library

Demand 31 defended people's right to own any property, not just wood.

Magna Carta guaranteed that everyone had the right to a fair trial.

ANALYSIS SKILL ANALYZING PRIMARY SOURCES

In what ways do you think the ideas listed above influenced modern democracy?

The Effects of Magna Carta

Magna Carta required the king to honor certain rights. Among these rights was habeas corpus (HAY-bee-uhs KOHR-puhs), a Latin phrase meaning "you have the body." The right of habeas corpus meant that people could not be kept in jail without a reason. They had to be charged with a crime and convicted at a jury trial before they could be sent to prison. Before, kings could arrest people for no reason at all.

More importantly, Magna Carta required that everyone—even the king—had to obey the law. The idea that everyone must follow the law became one of the basic principles of English government.

Changes after Magna Carta

Magna Carta inspired the English to find more ways to limit the king's power. A council of nobles was created to advise the king. In time, the council developed into **Parliament** (PAHR-luh-muhnt), the law-making body that governs England today. Over the years, membership in Parliament was opened to knights and town leaders. By the late Middle Ages, kings could do little without Parliament's support.

The English continued to work to secure and protect their rights. To ensure that everyone was treated fairly, people demanded that judges be free of royal control. Many people believed judges chosen by the king would always side with him. Eventually, in the late 1600s, the king agreed to free the courts of his control. This creation of an independent judicial system was a key step in bringing democracy to England.

READING CHECK **Summarizing** How did Magna Carta and Parliament limit the king's power?

THE IMPACT TODAY

Although we usually think of Magna Carta as a democratic document, it was originally written to protect nobles' feudal rights and preserve the feudal system. Its interpretation has changed greatly over the years.

Direct Teach

Main Idea

1 Magna Carta Causes Change in England

Magna Carta caused changes in England's government and legal system.

Explain How did habeas corpus affect the rights of citizens? *For the first time, people could not be jailed without a reason.*

Recall Under Magna Carta, who had to obey the law? *everyone, even the king*

Elaborate Why was the signing of Magna Carta so important? *It inspired the English to find more ways to limit the king's power and led to constitutional law and representative government.*

Activity **Summarize** Have each student choose one of the three demands from Magna Carta listed in the Primary Source feature at left. Ask students to summarize the demand in their own words and explain why it is important. **LS Verbal/Linguistic**

Alternative Assessment Handbook, Rubric 37: Writing Assignment

Collaborative Learning

At Level

Student Magna Carta

1. Have students read the Primary Source feature at the top of this page. Discuss the provisions made in Magna Carta and be sure students understand why the document is important.
2. Organize the class into groups of five or six. Ask the groups to imagine that they are nobles in the time of King John. Each group will write its own Magna Carta with 10 demands that students would impose on the king. The demands should be patterned after those of Magna Carta.
3. Have group representatives read some of the groups' demands to the class. Write the demands for students to see. What are some common demands? Are there any demands that appear on all lists? Only one list? Ask students to compare and contrast their lists with the demands in Magna Carta.

LS Interpersonal, Verbal/Linguistic

Alternative Assessment Handbook: Rubric 14: Group Activity

Answers

Analyzing Primary Sources *possible answer—They influenced the constitutional form of government in the United States.*

Reading Check *Magna Carta—The King had to obey the law, just as common citizens; Parliament—The King could do little without Parliament's support.*

Direct Teach

Main Idea

❷ The Hundred Years' War

The Hundred Years' War led to political changes in England and France.

Describe How did Magna Carta affect the way kings ruled outside of England? *It had little effect. They continued to rule as they always had.*

Explain What changed the course of the Hundred Years' War? *Joan of Arc inspired the French troops.*

Make Inferences Why do you think fighting the English created a bond between the king and nobles in France? *possible answer—because they faced a common enemy and protection of their homeland, which drew them together*

Quick Facts Transparency: Beginnings of Democracy in England

Online Resources
Activity: Joan of Arc Biography

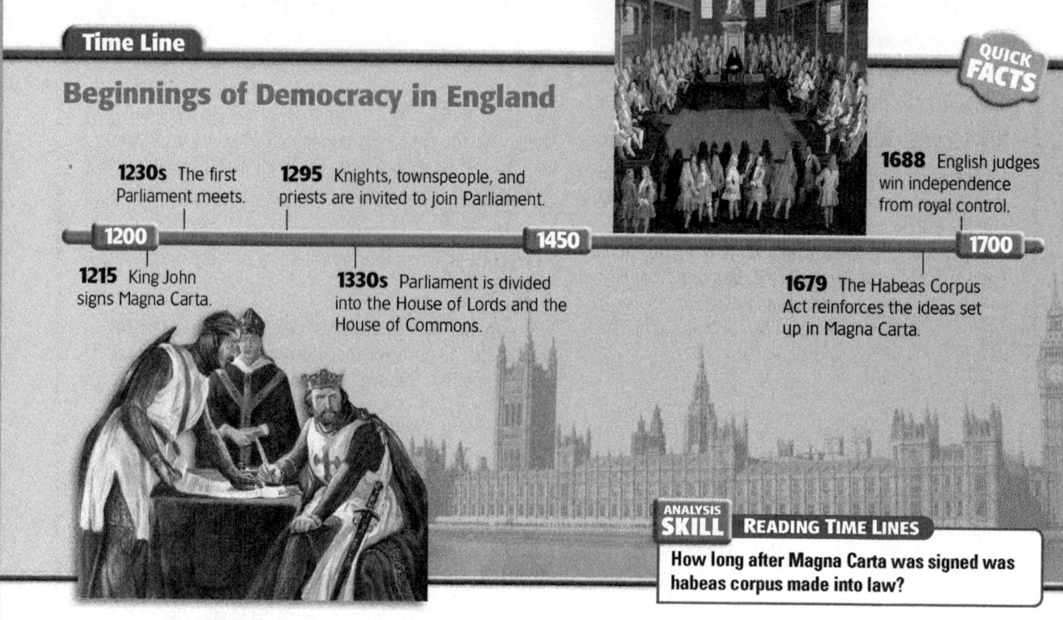

Time Line
Beginnings of Democracy in England
QUICK FACTS
1230s The first Parliament meets.
1295 Knights, townspeople, and priests are invited to join Parliament.
1688 English judges win independence from royal control.
1200
1450
1700
1215 King John signs Magna Carta.
1330s Parliament is divided into the House of Lords and the House of Commons.
1679 The Habeas Corpus Act reinforces the ideas set up in Magna Carta.

ANALYSIS SKILL **READING TIME LINES**

How long after Magna Carta was signed was habeas corpus made into law?

The Hundred Years' War

Although Magna Carta changed England's government, it had no effect outside of that country. Kings in other parts of Europe continued to rule as they always had. Eventually, however, these kings also had to face great political changes.

The Course of the War

In 1328 the king of France died with no sons, and two men claimed his throne. One was French. The other was the king of England. In the end, the French man became king.

This did not sit well with the English king, and a few years later he invaded France. This invasion began a long conflict between England and France that came to be called the **Hundred Years' War**.

At first the English armies did well, winning most of the battles. After nearly 100 years of fighting, however, a teenage peasant girl, **Joan of Arc**, rallied the French troops. Although the English captured and killed Joan, it was too late. The French defeated the English in 1453.

THE IMPACT TODAY Joan of Arc is still a national hero in France.

Results of the War

The war changed the governments of both England and France. In England, Parliament's power grew because the king needed its approval to raise money to pay for the war. As a result, the king lost power.

In France, on the other hand, the king's power grew. Fighting the English had created a bond between the king and nobles. As a result, the nobles came to accept the king as their absolute ruler. France became one of Europe's first nation-states. A nation-state is a country in which a strong leader has power and the people share one country. The rise of nation-states in the 1400s marked the decline of feudalism.

READING CHECK **Contrasting** How did the governments of England and France change after the war?

Critical Thinking: Identifying Points of View

At Level

Hundred Years' War Newspaper Article

1. Divide the class into two halves. Ask students to imagine that they are citizens during the Hundred Years' War. Ask one half of the students to imagine they are French citizens and the other half to imagine they are English citizens.
2. Have each student write a newspaper article reporting on the end of the Hundred Years' War and the political changes that resulted. Remind students to maintain a consistent point of view according to the country they represent.
3. Ask volunteers to read their articles to the class. How successfully have they put themselves into the place of either the English or the French? Have students discuss how the French and English views of the war and its effects differed. **LS Verbal/Linguistic**

Alternative Assessment Handbook, Rubrics 11: Discussions; and 23: Newspapers

Answers

Reading Time Lines *about 464 years*

Reading Check *England—Parliament gained power because the king needed its approval to raise money for the war; France—the king grew in power because of the support of his nobles.*

The Black Death

While the English and French fought the Hundred Years' War, an even greater crisis arose. This crisis was the **Black Death**, a deadly plague that swept through Europe between 1347 and 1351.

The plague originally came from central and eastern Asia. Unknowingly, traders brought rats carrying the disease to Mediterranean ports in 1347. From there it quickly swept throughout much of Europe. Fleas that feasted on the blood of infected rats passed on the plague to people.

The Black Death was not caused by one disease but by several different forms of plague. One form called bubonic plague (byoo-BAH-nik PLAYG) could be identified by swellings called buboes that appeared on victims' bodies. Another even deadlier form could spread through the air and kill people in less than a day.

The Black Death killed so many people that many were buried quickly without priests or ceremonies. In some villages nearly everyone died or fled as neighbors fell ill. In England alone, about 1,000 villages were abandoned.

The plague killed millions of people in Europe and millions more around the world. Some historians think Europe lost about a third of its population—perhaps 25 million people. This huge drop in population caused sweeping changes in Europe.

In most places, the manor system fell apart completely. There weren't enough people left to work in the fields. Those peasants and serfs who had survived the plague found their skills in high demand. Suddenly, they could demand wages for their labor. Once they had money, many fled their manors completely, moving instead to Europe's growing cities.

READING CHECK **Identifying Cause and Effect** What effects did bubonic plague have in Europe?

SUMMARY AND PREVIEW Magna Carta, the Hundred Years' War, and the Black Death changed European society. In the next section, you will learn about other changes in society, changes brought about by religious differences.

Section 4 Assessment

hmhsocialstudies.com ONLINE QUIZ

Reviewing Ideas, Terms, and People

1. **a. Identify** What document did English nobles hope would limit the king's power?
   b. Explain How was the creation of **Parliament** a step toward the creation of democracy in England?
2. **a. Identify** Who rallied the French troops during the **Hundred Years' War**?
   b. Elaborate The Hundred Years' War caused much more damage in France than in England. Why do you think this was the case?
3. **a. Describe** What was the **Black Death**?
   b. Explain How did the Black Death contribute to the decline of the manor system?
   c. Elaborate Why do you think the Black Death was able to spread so quickly through Europe?

Critical Thinking

4. **Evaluating** Copy the diagram below. Use it to rank the significance of the effects of Magna Carta, the Hundred Years' War, and the Black Death. Next to the diagram, write a sentence to explain your choices.

Most Significant
1.
2.
3.
Least Significant

FOCUS ON WRITING

5. **Rating Importance** After reading this section, you'll probably want to add King John to your list. You should also start to think about which people were the most important. Rank the people on your list from most to least important.

Section 4 Assessment Answers

1. **a.** Magna Carta
   b. It limited the king's power and gave some people a say in how the government was run.
2. **a.** Joan of Arc
   b. Most of the war was fought in France.
3. **a.** a deadly plague that swept through Europe between 1347 and 1351
   b. The surviving peasants and serfs were in high demand, asking wages for their work instead of just land to work on. Many moved to the cities.
   c. possible answers—People didn't know what caused the plague, so they didn't know how to stop it. Traders carried the plague from city to city.
4. 1. Black Death; The Black Death killed 25 million people and caused the manor system to fall apart. 2. Magna Carta; The Magna Carta is a big influence on modern democracy. 3. Hundred Years' War; The Hundred Years' War changed the governments of England and France.
5. Students should mention King John and Joan of Arc.

Direct Teach

Main Idea

3 The Black Death

The Black Death which swept through Europe in the Middle Ages, led to social changes.

Recall Where in Europe did the Black Death first appear? *in Mediterranean ports*

Evaluate Which do you think had the greater effect on Europe—the Hundred Years' War or the Black Death? Why? *possible answers—the Black Death, because the deaths of so many people caused the economic system to change; Hundred Years' War, because it changed the amount of power kings had in both England and France.*

CRF: History and Geography Activity: The Black Death

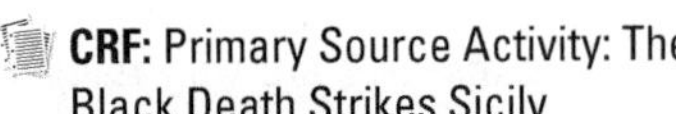

CRF: Primary Source Activity: The Black Death Strikes Sicily

Review & Assess

Close

Guide students in a review of Magna Carta, the Hundred Years' War, and the Black Death.

Review

Online Quiz, Section 4

Assess

SE Section 4 Assessment

PASS: Section 4 Quiz

Alternative Assessment Handbook

Reteach/Classroom Intervention

Guided Reading Workbook, Section 4

Interactive Skills Tutor CD-ROM

Answers

Reading Check *millions died; manor system fell apart; Europe's cities grew*

History and Geography

Activity **Calculating Percentages** Although estimates of the death toll from the plague vary, many historians agree that Europe's population was reduced by about one third. Have students use almanacs or other reference works to find population figures for your state or city. Then have students calculate how many people in the state or city would have died from the Black Death if the disease claimed the same percentage of victims. For example, if California's population is about 36 million, 12 million people would have died. **LS Logical/Mathematical**

Linking to Today

Epidemic Diseases Lead a discussion about how the effects of modern-day epidemic diseases differ from the results of the Black Death. For example, although some diseases are very dangerous, because we now know more about what causes disease, and we can treat many of them, people are seldom as terrified as they were in the mid-1300s.

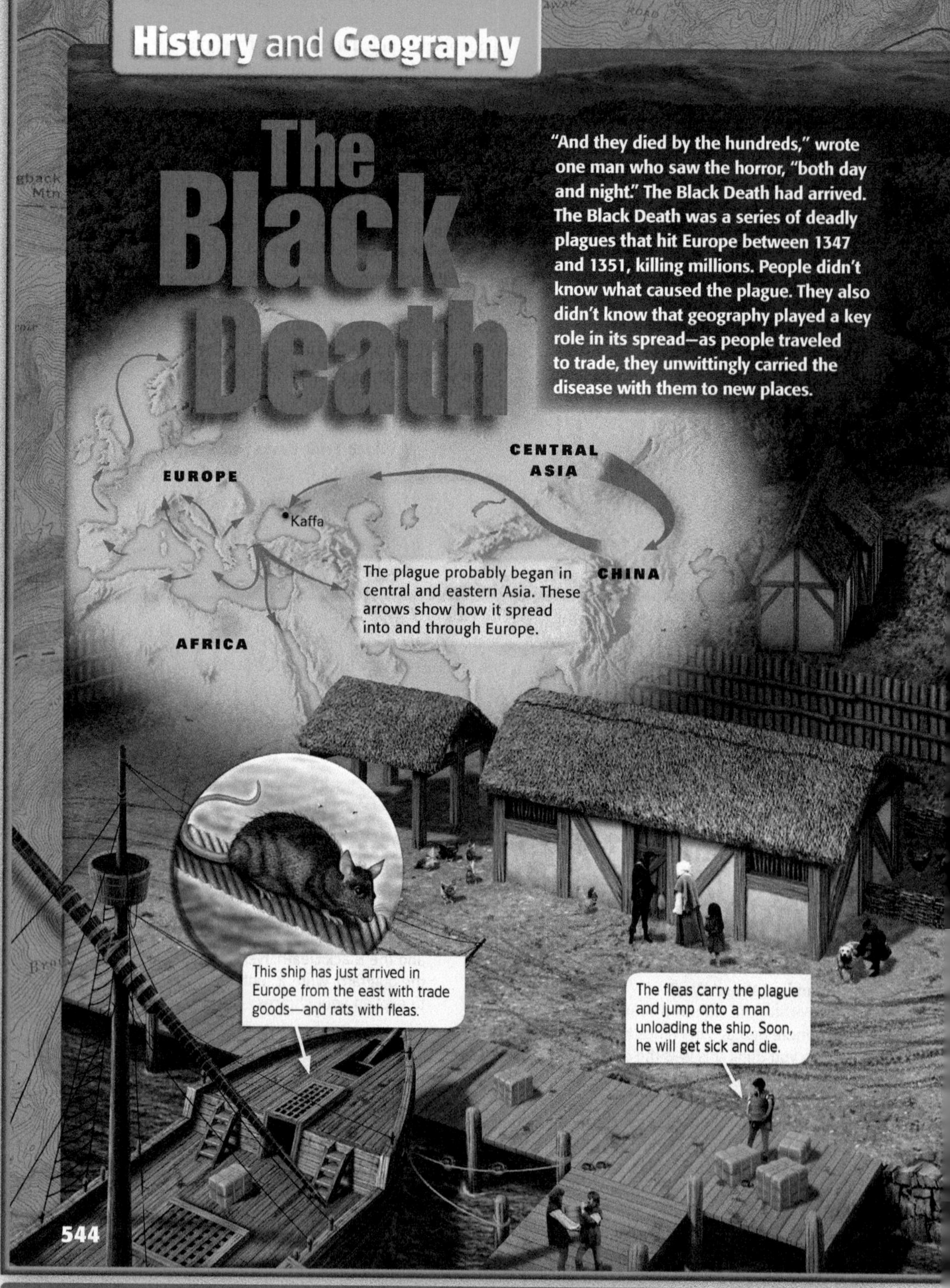

History and Geography
The Black Death
"And they died by the hundreds," wrote one man who saw the horror, "both day and night." The Black Death had arrived. The Black Death was a series of deadly plagues that hit Europe between 1347 and 1351, killing millions. People didn't know what caused the plague. They also didn't know that geography played a key role in its spread—as people traveled to trade, they unwittingly carried the disease with them to new places.
EUROPE
CENTRAL ASIA
Kaffa
CHINA
AFRICA
The plague probably began in central and eastern Asia. These arrows show how it spread into and through Europe.
This ship has just arrived in Europe from the east with trade goods—and rats with fleas.
The fleas carry the plague and jump onto a man unloading the ship. Soon, he will get sick and die.
544

Differentiating Instruction

Struggling Readers

Below Level

Standard English Mastery

Have students review the feature on these pages. Then ask students to assign names, occupations, and personalities to the people in the picture. Have students write brief stories about the roles these people are playing in the Black Death. Supply thesauri and dictionaries so that students can choose words that reflect standard English mastery. **LS Visual/Spatial**

Advanced/Gifted and Talented

Above Level

Predicting the Plague's Effects

Have students imagine one third of the people in your state have died from the plague. What would be the short- and long-term effects? Could there be any positive results? Have students apply their ideas to Europe to infer the plague's effects. Ask students to keep their ideas in mind when the long-term effects are discussed in the next chapter. **LS Verbal/Linguistic**

HISTORY
VIDEO
Traders Carry the Plague
hmhsocialstudies.com
The plague is so terrifying that many people think it's the end of the world. They leave town for the country, spreading the Black Death even farther.
People dig mass graves to bury the dead. But often, so many victims are infected that there is no one left to bury them.
The garbage and dirty conditions in the town provide food and a home for the rats, allowing the disease to spread even more.
So many people die so quickly that special carts are sent through the streets to gather the bodies.
GEOGRAPHY SKILLS INTERPRETING MAPS
1. How did the Black Death reach Europe from Asia?
2. What helped spread the plague within Europe?
545

History and Geography

Activity **Plague Cities** Point out that big cities were struck especially hard by the Black Death. Have students compare the map on the opposite page with other maps in this unit. Call on students to correspond major cities with points from which the Black Death spread. **LS Visual/Spatial**

Connect to Science

Types of Plague Remind students that the diseases grouped together as the Black Death spread in different ways and killed their victims at varying speeds. Doctors now call the worst form septicemic plague. With this disease, a victim's entire bloodstream was infected with bacteria. Death could come within 24 hours. Stories endure from the Black Death years of people seemingly healthy in the morning and dead by nightfall. They were probably victims of the septicemic type of plague.

Critical Thinking: Evaluating Information

At Level

Prep Required

Just a Nursery Rhyme?

1. Explain to students that some historians think the nursery rhyme *Ring Around the Rosie* refers to symptoms of the Black Death. Some accounts, however, dispute this claim.
2. In advance, locate and duplicate Internet sources that argue both sides of the *Ring Around the Rosie* question. Make a copy for each student.
3. Have students read the articles. Then create a *For* and *Against* chart for students to see. Ask students to summarize each side's arguments. List them in the appropriate columns.
4. Call on volunteers to tell why they thought some arguments were more reliable than others. Discuss how the sources of information were related to the reliability of the information.

LS Interpersonal, Logical/Mathematical

Alternative Assessment Handbook, Rubric 11: Discussions

Answers

Analyzing Visuals **1.** *by means of fleas carried by rats that traveled on traders' ships from Asia* **2.** *fast transmission of plague from person to person and flea to person, crowded living conditions, travel by people afraid of the disease, traders spreading it from town to town*

Preteach

Bellringer

If YOU were there . . . Use the **Daily Bellringer Transparency** to help students answer the question.

Daily Bellringer Transparency, Section 5

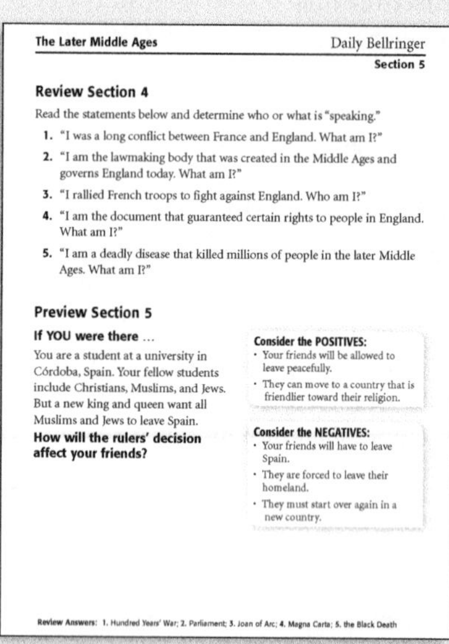

The Later Middle Ages — Daily Bellringer — Section 5

Review Section 4

Read the statements below and determine who or what is "speaking."

1. "I was a long conflict between France and England. What am I?"
2. "I am the lawmaking body that was created in the Middle Ages and governs England today. What am I?"
3. "I rallied French troops to fight against England. Who am I?"
4. "I am the document that guaranteed certain rights to people in England. What am I?"
5. "I am a deadly disease that killed millions of people in the later Middle Ages. What am I?"

Preview Section 5

If YOU were there ...

You are a student at a university in Córdoba, Spain. Your fellow students include Christians, Muslims, and Jews. But a new king and queen want all Muslims and Jews to leave Spain.

How will the rulers' decision affect your friends?

Consider the POSITIVES:
- Your friends will be allowed to leave peacefully.
- They can move to a country that is friendlier toward their religion.

Consider the NEGATIVES:
- Your friends will have to leave Spain.
- They are forced to leave their homeland.
- They must start over again in a new country.

Review Answers: 1. Hundred Years' War; 2. Parliament; 3. Joan of Arc; 4. Magna Carta; 5. the Black Death

Academic Vocabulary

Review with students the high-use academic term in this section.

policy rule, course of action (p. 548)

CRF: Vocabulary Builder Activity, Section 5

Taking Notes

Have students use the graphic organizer online to take notes on the section. This activity will prepare students for the Section Assessment, in which they will complete a graphic organizer that builds on the information using the Critical Thinking Skill: Categorizing.

SECTION 5

Challenges to Church Authority

What You Will Learn...

Main Ideas

1. The church reacted to challengers by punishing people who opposed its teachings.
2. Christians fought Moors in Spain and Portugal in an effort to drive all Muslims out of Europe.
3. Jews faced discrimination across Europe in the Middle Ages.

The Big Idea

In the Middle Ages, the Christian Church dealt harshly with people who did not respect its authority.

Key Terms and People

heresy, *p. 546*
Reconquista, *p. 547*
King Ferdinand, *p. 548*
Queen Isabella, *p. 548*
Spanish Inquisition, *p. 548*

Use the graphic organizer online to record information about groups of people who challenged the authority of the Catholic Church or were seen as the church's enemies.

If YOU were there...

You are a student at a university in Córdoba, Spain. Your fellow students include Christians, Muslims, and Jews. But a new king and queen want all Muslims and Jews to leave Spain.

How will the rulers' decision affect your friends?

BUILDING BACKGROUND As you have read, most Europeans in the Middle Ages belonged to the Catholic Church. As Christianity spread in Europe, many Jews and Muslims were pressured to become Christian or leave their homes. At the same time, others openly challenged the church's authority.

The Church Reacts to Challengers

By around 1100, some Christians had begun to question church teachings. They felt that the clergy focused more on money and land than on God. Others didn't agree with the church's ideas. They began to preach their own ideas about religion.

Religious ideas that oppose accepted church teachings are called **heresy** (HER-uh-see). People who hold such ideas are called heretics. Church officials sent priests and friars throughout Europe to find possible heretics. Most of these priests and friars tried to be fair. A few tortured people until they confessed to heresy, even if they were innocent. Most people found guilty in these trials were fined or put in prison. Others were killed.

In the early 1200s, Pope Innocent III decided that heresy was too great a threat to ignore. He called a crusade against heretics in southern France. With this call, the pope encouraged the king of France and his knights to rid their country of heretics. The result was a bloody war that lasted about 20 years. The war destroyed towns and cost thousands of people their lives.

READING CHECK **Finding Main Ideas** How did church leaders try to fight heresy?

Teach the Big Idea

At Level

Challenges to Church Authority

1. **Teach** Ask students the questions in the Main Idea boxes to teach this section.
2. **Apply** Have students help you create a list of the main people, events, and ideas covered in this section. Then ask students to imagine they are medieval town criers, and it is their job to walk the streets proclaiming the day's news. Have each student write out one "headline" for each of the section's main events. **LS Verbal/Linguistic**
3. **Review** As you review the section's main ideas, have volunteers share their headlines.
4. **Practice/Homework** Distribute headlines, one per student, and have each student write a short news proclamation to accompany their headline. Students should be prepared to "cry out" their news. **LS Verbal/Linguistic**

Alternative Assessment Handbook, Rubric 42: Writing to Inform

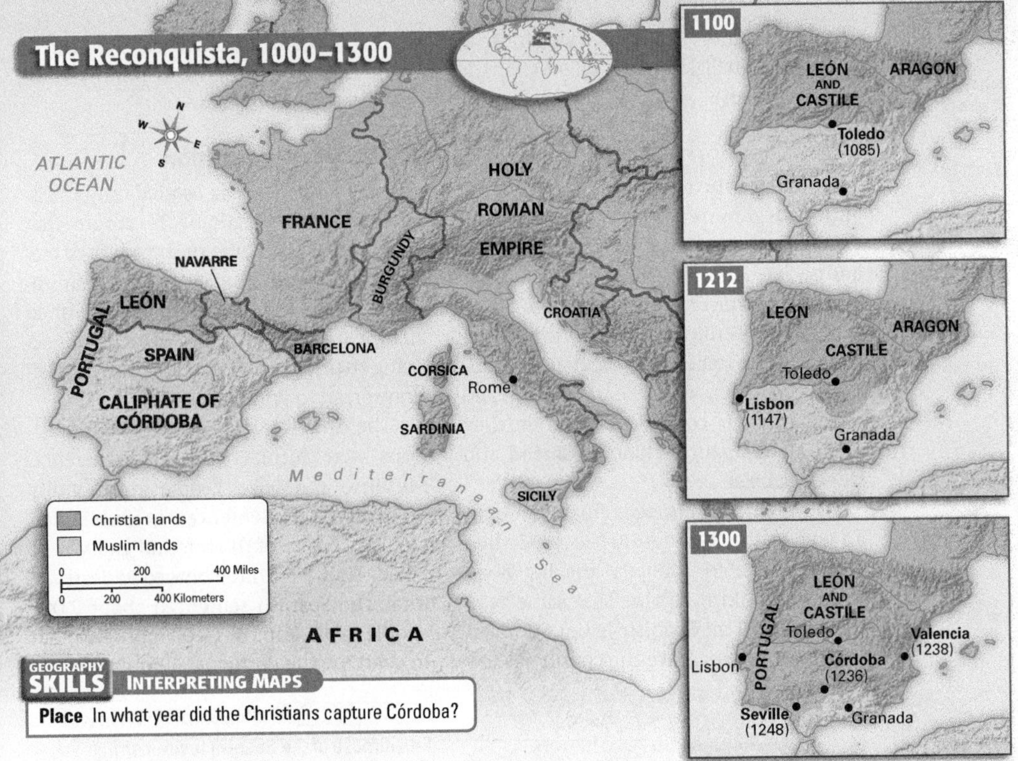

GEOGRAPHY SKILLS INTERPRETING MAPS

Place In what year did the Christians capture Córdoba?

Christians Fight the Moors

France was not the only place where Christians fought people they saw as the church's enemies. In Spain and Portugal, armed Christian warriors fought to drive the Muslim Moors out of their lands.

The Weakening of Muslim Control

By the late 900s the once powerful Muslim government of Spain had begun to weaken. Political and religious leaders fought each other for power. Various ethnic groups also fought each other.

In 1002 the Muslim government fell apart completely. Caught up in fighting among themselves, Muslim leaders were too busy to guard against the Christian kingdoms of northern Spain.

The Fight against the Moors

For centuries, the kingdoms of northern Spain had been small and weak. But as the Moors' power declined, these little Christian kingdoms seized the opportunity to attack. Slowly, they took land away from the Moors. They called their efforts to retake Spain from the Moors the **Reconquista** (reh-kahn-KEES-tuh), or reconquest.

In 1085 Castile (ka-STEEL), the largest of the Spanish kingdoms, won a great victory against the Moors. The Castilian victory inspired other Christian kingdoms to fight the Moors. The kingdoms of Aragon and Portugal soon joined the fight.

The Christian armies won victory after victory. By the 1250s, the victorious Christian armies had nearly pushed the Moors completely out of Europe.

THE IMPACT TODAY

Although the Moors were driven out, many places in Spain and Portugal still bear names that came from Arabic, the language the Moors spoke.

Direct Teach

Main Idea

❶ The Church Reacts to Challengers

The church reacted to challengers by punishing people who opposed its teachings.

Identify In what ways did Christians begin to challenge the church in the late Middle Ages? *questioning church teachings, thinking the clergy was too worldly, preaching their own ideas about religion*

Make Inferences Why were church officials interested in finding heretics? *possible answers—concerned that heretics might lead others to question church's teachings.*

Main Idea

❷ Christians Fight the Moors

Christians fought Moors in Spain and Portugal in an effort to drive all Muslims out of Europe.

Explain How did Castile and Aragon unite to form Spain? *Ferdinand, the prince of Aragon married Princess Isabella of Castile, and 10 years later they became king and queen of their countries.*

Summarize How did the Reconquista affect Spanish Jews and Muslims? *Jews had to convert to Christianity or leave the country. A few years later, Islam was banned.*

Map Transparency: The Reconquista, 1000–1300

Differentiating Instruction

English-Language Learners **At Level**

1. Guide students through the maps above. Explain that the large map shows Europe in 1000, while the three smaller maps show the Iberian Peninsula through later centuries, as land was retaken from the Moors in the Reconquista.
2. Ask students what color shows Christian lands *(purple)* and Muslim lands *(gold)*. What parts of the peninsula did Christians control in 1000? *(León, Navarre, Barcelona)*
3. Explain that in the smaller maps, the parenthetical dates show when Christians took over certain cities. Ask students which city was taken over first *(Toledo)*, and when *(1085)*. Then ask which city was taken last, *(Seville)*, and when *(1248)*.
4. Ask students what part of Spain was still Muslim land in 1300 *(very southern part)*.

LS Visual/Spatial

Alternative Assessment Handbook, Rubric 21: Map Reading

Answers

Interpreting Maps *1236*

Reading Check (previous page) *People found guilty of heresy were fined, imprisoned, or killed.*

Direct Teach

Main Idea

❸ Jews Face Discrimination

Jews faced discrimination across Europe in the Middle Ages.

Identify What three groups were punished for their beliefs in the Middle Ages? *heretics, Muslims, and Jews*

Make Inferences Why did some Christians discriminate against Jews? *They blamed Jews for the death of Jesus.*

Predict Where do you think European Jews went when they were forced out of their countries? *European countries where Jews were allowed; Asia, Africa*

MISCONCEPTION ALERT

Isabella's Jewels Some students may have heard the story that Queen Isabella sold her jewels to pay for Christopher Columbus's voyages. Explain that this tale is actually from a popular biography of Columbus (1828) written by the American author Washington Irving.

ACADEMIC VOCABULARY
policy rule, course of action

The only territory still under Muslim control was a small kingdom called Granada (grah-NAH-dah).

The Rise of Portugal and Spain

As a result of their victories, both Portugal and Spain grew more powerful than before. Portugal, once a part of Castile, broke free and declared its independence. Meanwhile, Castile and Aragon decided to unite.

In 1469 Ferdinand, the prince of Aragon, married Isabella, a Castilian princess. Ten years later, they became king and queen of their countries. Together, they ruled all of Spain as **King Ferdinand** and **Queen Isabella**.

Ferdinand and Isabella finally brought an end to the Reconquista. In 1492 their army conquered Granada, the last Muslim stronghold in Spain. That same year, they required all Spanish Jews to convert to Christianity or leave the country. A few years later, they banned the practice of Islam as well. Through this policy, all of Spain became Christian.

The Spanish Inquisition

Ferdinand and Isabella wanted only Christians in their kingdom. To ensure that Christianity alone was practiced, they created the **Spanish Inquisition**, an organization of priests that looked for and punished anyone in Spain suspected of secretly practicing their old religion. Later, the Inquisition spread to Portugal as well.

The Spanish and Portuguese Inquisitions were ruthless in seeking heretics, Muslims, and Jews. People found guilty of heresy were sentenced in public ceremonies. Many of those found guilty were killed. They were often burned to death. In total, the Spanish sentenced about 2,000 people to die. Almost 1,400 more were put to death by the Portuguese Inquisition.

READING CHECK **Summarizing** What was the purpose of the Spanish Inquisition?

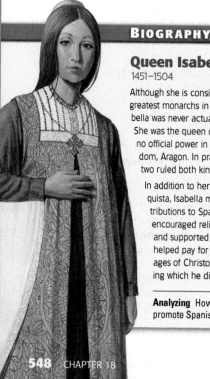

BIOGRAPHY

Queen Isabella
1451–1504

Although she is considered one of the greatest monarchs in Spanish history, Isabella was never actually the queen of Spain. She was the queen of Castile, but she had no official power in her husband's kingdom, Aragon. In practice, however, the two ruled both kingdoms together.

In addition to her role in the Reconquista, Isabella made great contributions to Spanish society. She encouraged religion and education and supported many artists. She also helped pay for the transatlantic voyages of Christopher Columbus, during which he discovered America.

Analyzing How did Isabella help promote Spanish culture?

Jews Face Discrimination

Heretics and Muslims were not the only groups punished for their beliefs in the Middle Ages. European Jews also suffered. This suffering was caused by Christians who believed that the Jews had been responsible for the death of Jesus. These Christians thought Jews should be punished.

You have already read about how Jews were killed during the Crusades. You have also read that Jews were forced to leave their homes in Spain. Similar things happened all over Europe. Rulers, supported by the church, forced Jews to leave their countries. For example, in 1290, the king of England arrested all English Jews and forced them to leave the country. The same thing happened in France in 1306 and again in 1394.

Critical Thinking: Identifying Points of View

Above Level

Alternative Textbook Entries

1. Lead students in a discussion of ways in which the world views of Ferdinand and Isabella differed from those of Jews and Muslims being forced to convert to Christianity or to leave Spain.
2. Ask students to think about how the Reconquista and the Spanish Inquisition might be treated in a world history book published in a Muslim country. Then have each student write a brief history of the Reconquista and Inquisition from the Muslim point of view.
3. Ask volunteers to read their entries to the class. Encourage student feedback and discussion. **LS Verbal/Linguistic**

Alternative Assessment Handbook, Rubrics 11: Discussions; and 37: Writing Assignments

Answers

Biography *She encouraged many artists and the spread of religion and education throughout the country.*

Reading Check *to ensure that Christianity was the only religion practiced in Spain*

The Spanish Inquisition

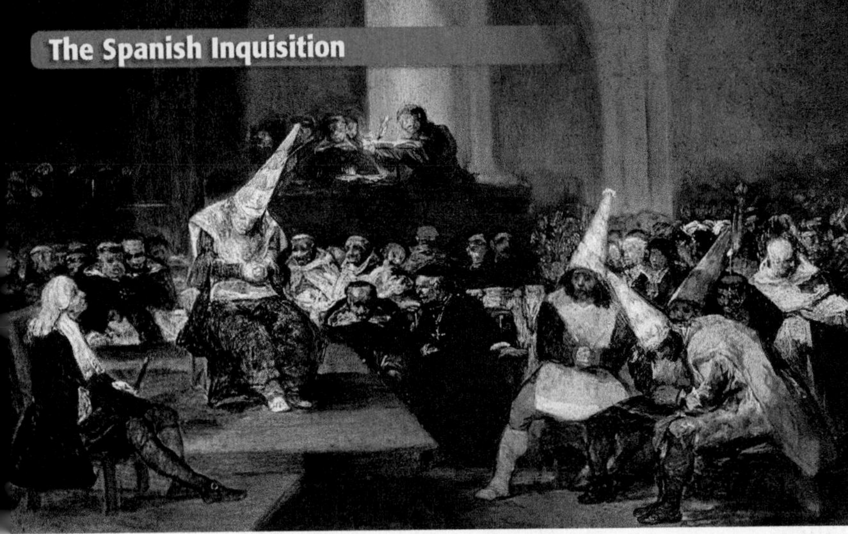

The painting shows accused heretics, in the pointed hats, before the Spanish Inquisition. The Spanish artist Francisco Goya painted it in the early 1800s.

How did the artist show what the accused heretics are feeling?

In the Holy Roman Empire, frightened people blamed Jews for the arrival of the Black Death. Many Jews had to flee their homes to escape angry mobs. Because the Jews were not Christian, many Europeans didn't want them in their towns.

READING CHECK **Summarizing** How were Jews discriminated against in the Middle Ages?

SUMMARY AND PREVIEW During the Middle Ages, religion shaped how people thought, what they did, and where they lived. In some places religion led to wars and punishment for those who didn't agree with the Catholic Church. In the next chapter, you will learn about the era that followed the Middle Ages.

Section 5 Assessment

hmhsocialstudies.com ONLINE QUIZ

Reviewing Ideas, Terms, and People

1. a. **Define** What is **heresy**?
   b. **Explain** Why did the church send priests and friars to find heretics?
2. a. **Identify** Who did Spanish Christians try to drive out of their lands?
   b. **Explain** What was the purpose of the **Spanish Inquisition**?
   c. **Predict** How might Spanish history have been different if the Spanish had not defeated the Moors?
3. **Summarize** How did kings and other rulers punish Jews in the Middle Ages?

Critical Thinking

4. **Categorizing** Draw a chart like the one here. Use your notes to help you fill in each box with a description of Christians' reactions to that group.

Heretics	Moors	Jews

Focus on Writing

5. **Choosing Important People** There are two more people in this section to add to your list. How do you rank them on the list of most-to-least important? Who do you feel is most important?

Section 5 Assessment Answers

1. a. ideas that oppose accepted church teachings
   b. They thought heresy was a danger to the church and to Christians.
2. a. the Muslim Moors
   b. to find and punish non-Christians in Spain
   c. possible answer—Spain might have become a Muslim country.
3. Jews were forced out of many countries.
4. Heretics—tortured, fined, imprisoned, killed; Moors—launched Reconquista to retake Spain from the Moors, forced Muslims out of Spain; Jews— forced Jews out of many countries.
5. possible answer—Ferdinand and Isabella

Direct Teach

Connect to Literature

Song of the Cid Just as France had its epic *Song of Roland,* Spain had a great epic poem called the *Song of the Cid.* It tells of the adventures of a Castilian hero who served under the Moors. The poem is based on the real-life exploits of Ruy Díaz de Vivar, who was known as the Cid (from a Spanish Arabic word for "lord"). Because of his chivalric behavior, the Cid remained the ideal model of Spanish knighthood long after the Moors came to be seen as Spain's enemy.

Review & Assess

Close

Review with students how the Christian Church and Christian rulers dealt with heretics, Moors, and Jews.

Review

Online Quiz, Section 5

Assess

SE Section 5 Assessment

PASS: Section 5 Quiz

Alternative Assessment Handbook

Reteach-Classroom Intervention

Guided Reading Workbook, Section 5

Interactive Skills Tutor CD-ROM

Answers

The Spanish Inquisition *possible answer—by showing them looking downcast with heads bowed and shoulders slumped*

Reading Check *blamed for the death of Jesus and the arrival of the Black Death, forced to leave their countries, sometimes killed*

Understanding Transportation Maps

Activity **Interpreting Local Maps**

Materials: local community or city cultural map

Have students examine a map of their community or of a nearby city that includes cultural features, such as the locations of airports, churches, parks, and other sites. Ask students to identify various features on the map. Then have students use the scale to calculate distances between some of the cultural features. Finally, have students summarize why including such information on a map might be useful in daily life as well as in the study of history.

LS Visual/Spatial

Alternative Assessment Handbook, Rubric 21: Map Reading

Interactive Skills Tutor CD-ROM, Lesson 6: Interpret Maps, Graphs, Charts, Visuals, and Political Cartoons

Social Studies Skills

Analysis | Critical Thinking | Economics | Study

Understanding Transportation Maps

Define the Skill

Transportation maps show routes of travel and trade. These maps help you understand about the movement of people, products, and ideas between places in the world.

Learn the Skill

Follow these steps to interpret a transportation map.

1. Read the map's title. This will tell you what general information is shown on the map. Study the legend. Look for any symbols that relate to routes or methods of transportation.
2. Note any lines or arrows on the map. These lines and arrows often indicate routes of movement. Study these carefully. Note their starting and ending points and where they pass in between.
3. Study the whole map. Read all the labels. Transportation maps can tell you about the history of an area. For example, they can show how geography influenced the area's development.

Practice the Skill

Use the map below to answer the questions.

1. Which Crusade passed through Rome?
2. Which city did three Crusades travel through?
3. How did the later Crusades differ from the earlier ones in type of transportation used?
4. Why do you think all four Crusades passed through territory of the Byzantine Empire?

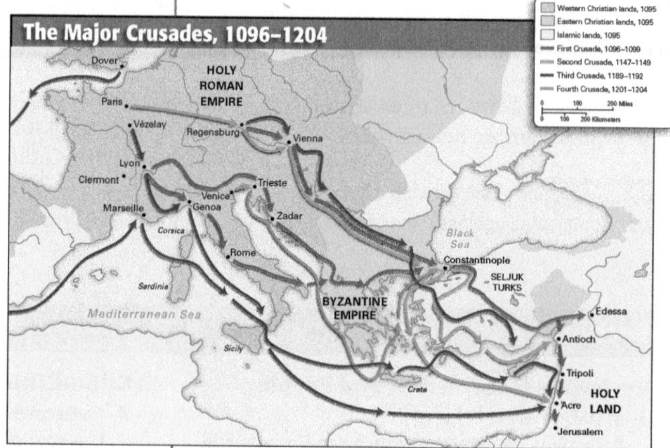

Social Studies Skills Activity: Understanding Transportation Maps

Interpreting a Map of the Vatican City

At Level | Prep Required

Materials: modern cultural map of the Holy See (Vatican City)

1. Show students a cultural map of the modern-day Vatican City. A number of different maps are available online. A useful site is the CIA's World Factbook (http://www.cia.gov/cia/publications/factbook/index.html).
2. Ask students to identify the cultural features and political boundaries shown on the map.
3. Next, ask students to use the map scale, if the map includes one, to calculate the size of the Vatican and the distances between various features shown on the map.
4. Then have each student write a paragraph describing the Vatican City based on the information in the map.

LS Verbal/Linguistic, Visual/Spatial

Alternative Assessment Handbook, Rubric 21: Map Reading; and 40: Writing to Describe

Answers

Practice and Apply the Skill

1. *First Crusade* **2.** *Vienna* **3.** *went by sea* **4.** *bordered Islamic lands*

CHAPTER 18 # Chapter Review

History's Impact
▶ **video series**
Review the video to answer the focus question:
What is plague, and how did it spread through medieval Europe?

Visual Summary

Use the visual summary below to help you review the main ideas of the chapter.

QUICK FACTS

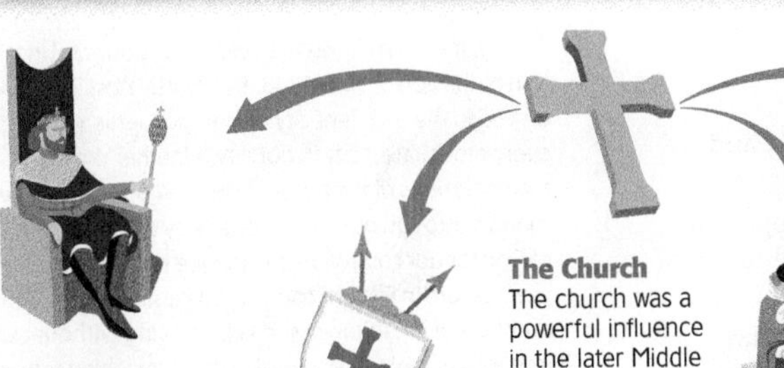

The Church
The church was a powerful influence in the later Middle Ages.

Government
The church and monarchy often worked together but sometimes were rivals.

Crusades
The pope called for Christians to retake the Holy Land.

Education and Society
The church helped guide learning and reacted to challenges to its authority.

Art and Architecture
Christianity inspired great forms of art and architecture.

Reviewing Vocabulary, Terms, and People

Match the words with their definitions.

1. excommunicate
2. religious order
3. Crusades
4. clergy
5. heresy
6. Thomas Aquinas
7. Magna Carta
8. Spanish Inquisition

a. church officials
b. punished non-Christians in Spain
c. religious ideas that oppose church teachings
d. an English document limiting the king's powers
e. cast out from the church
f. thought faith and reason could be used together
g. a group of people who dedicate their lives to religion, live together, and follow the same rules
h. wars fought to regain the Holy Land

Comprehension and Critical Thinking

SECTION 1 *(Pages 524–527)*

9. a. Describe What was the relationship between Charlemagne and the pope like?

b. Contrast How did the opinions of popes like Gregory VII about power differ from those of kings like Henry IV?

c. Evaluate Do you think conflict with kings strengthened or weakened medieval popes? Why?

SECTION 2 *(Pages 528–532)*

10. a. Identify What was the main goal of the Crusades?

b. Draw Conclusions Why do you think the Crusades changed the relationships between Christians and other groups?

c. Evaluate Which Crusade do you think was most successful? Which was least successful? Why?

Answers

Visual Summary

Review and Inquiry Have students use the visual summary to explain the causes and effects of the major events of the later Middle Ages.

Quick Facts Transparency: The Later Middle Ages Visual Summary

Reviewing Vocabulary, Terms, and People

1. e
2. g
3. h
4. a
5. c
6. f
7. d
8. b

Comprehension and Critical Thinking

9. a. The pope approved of Charlemagne's empire.

b. They disagreed about whether kings or popes should have the right to choose bishops.

c. possible answer—strengthened, because popes usually kept the upper hand when dealing with kings

10. a. to take control of the Holy Land away from Muslims

b. possible answer—Christian attacks increased tensions with Jews and Byzantines. Losses may have left Christians feeling resentful toward Muslims. Muslims saw Christians as invaders.

Review and Assessment Resources

Review and Reinforce

SE Chapter Review
CRF: Chapter Review Activity
Quick Facts Transparency: The Later Middle Ages Visual Summary
Spanish Chapter Summaries Audio CD Program
Online Chapter Summaries in Six Languages
TOS Holt McDougal PuzzleView

Assess

SE Standardized Test Practice
PASS: Chapter Test, Forms A and B
Alternative Assessment Handbook
TOS ExamView Assessment Suite,
Differentiated Instruction Modified Worksheets and Tests CD-ROM: Chapter Test
Online Assessment Program, in the Interactive Student Edition

Reteach/Intervene

Guided Reading Workbook
Differentiated Instruction Teacher Management System: Lesson Plans
Differentiated Instruction Modified Worksheets and Tests CD-ROM
Interactive Skills Tutor CD-ROM

hmhsocialstudies.com
Chapter Resources

Answers

c. possible answers—most: the first Crusade, because the Christians took control of the Holy Land and opened trade between Europe and the Middle East; least: the second Crusade, because poor planning and heavy losses on the journey to the Holy Land led to the Christians' total defeat.

11. a. art—Beautiful objects were created and put in churches to show respect for God; education—Most teachers in the universities were members of the clergy. Art and architecture were created out of respect for God.

b. People had more faith and trust in the church than in kings; the church owned much land and had political power.

c. Some thought the church was becoming too concerned with worldly things and needed to focus more on spiritual matters.

12. a. a plague; killed millions, caused a collapse of the manor system

b. because for the first time everyone (even the king) had to obey the law, an idea that became the foundation of English government

c. possible answer—England would have had more influence on mainland Europe; for example, English law would have been the rule in France.

13. a. The Christian armies pushed the Moors out of Europe.

b. Thousands of people were killed, many burned in public.

c. possible answer—Heretics did not respect the authority of the church, which to many people represented God on earth.

Reviewing Themes

14. possible answer—The church was able to unify Europe to fight Muslims in the Holy Land.

15. possible answer—The church was involved in education, politics, the arts, and other aspects of daily life.

Using the Internet

16. Go to hmhsocialstudies.com to access a rubric for this activity.

Reading Skills

17. yes

18. excellent, surpass . . . in nobility

Social Studies Skills

19. started in Lyon, went east over land and sea to Constantinople and then to the Holy Land

Focus on Writing

20. Rubric Students' historical articles should:

- include one or two sentences to introduce the topic.
- name three important people and describe why they were important.
- offer accurate information and present it clearly.
- contain a one- or two-sentence conclusion.

CRF: Focus on Writing: A Historical Article

SECTION 3 *(Pages 533–539)*

11. a. Describe How did Christianity shape art and education in the Middle Ages?

b. Analyze Why was Christianity so influential in so many areas of medieval life?

c. Elaborate How were the changes that took place in the medieval church related to its growing power and wealth?

SECTION 4 *(Pages 540–543)*

12. a. Describe What was the Black Death, and how did it affect Europe?

b. Make Inferences Why do some people consider Magna Carta to represent the beginning of democracy in England?

c. Predict How might Europe's history have been different if England had won the Hundred Years' War?

SECTION 5 *(Pages 546–549)*

13. a. Identify What were the results of the Reconquista?

b. Draw Conclusions Why were the Spanish and Portuguese Inquisitions so feared?

c. Elaborate Why do you think some Christians considered heresy such a threat?

Reviewing Themes

14. Religion In what ways did the Crusades demonstrate the power of the church in Europe?

15. Society and Culture How did the church affect the lives of ordinary people?

Using the Internet 

16. Activity: Evaluating Sources A challenge for anyone trying to understand the Middle Ages is evaluating the primary and secondary sources. Use your online book to rate the listed sources. Explain whether the source is a primary or secondary source, whether you think it is believable, and your reasoning.

hmhsocialstudies.com

Reading Skills 

Stereotypes and Bias in History *The passage below is taken from a collection of stories called the* Decameron *by the Italian writer Boccaccio. In it, he describes the arrival of the Black Death in his home city of Florence. Read the passage and then answer the questions that follow.*

> "I say, then, that it was the year of the bountiful Incarnation of the Son of God, 1348. The mortal pestilence then arrived in the excellent city of Florence, which surpasses every other Italian city in nobility. Whether through the operations of the heavenly bodies, or sent upon us mortals through our wicked deeds by the just wrath of God for our correction, the plague had begun some years before in Eastern countries. It carried off uncounted numbers of inhabitants, and kept moving without cease from place to place. It spread in piteous fashion towards the West."

17. Do you think Boccaccio expresses any bias about the city of Florence in this passage?

18. Do any words or phrases in the passage indicate stereotypes or bias about the people of Florence?

Social Studies Skills

19. Understanding Transportation Maps Look at the map on page 550. Then describe the route taken by members of the First Crusade. Include information on directions traveled and method of transportation.

Focus on Writing

20. Writing Your Article Review your notes. Be sure you've identified the three people you think are the most important and why they're important. Now write an article explaining why these people were so important to Europe in the Middle Ages. Keep your article short: one or two sentences to introduce your topic, a sentence or two about each important person, and a one- or two-sentence conclusion.

CHAPTER 18 Standardized Test Practice

DIRECTIONS: Read each question, and write the letter of the best response.

1

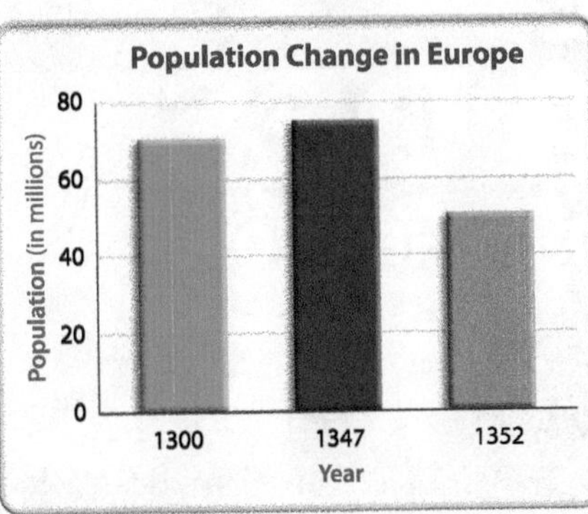

What historical event was responsible for the population trend shown in the graph?

A the Crusades
B the Black Death
C the Hundred Years' War
D the Spanish Inquisition

2 Which of the following had the *greatest* influence on the lives of most Europeans during the Middle Ages?

A towns and trade
B the king
C religion and the church
D universities

3 One reason the Crusades failed to conquer the Holy Land permanently was because

A the fighting was a long distance from Europe.
B Crusader armies had better weapons than the Muslims did.
C religion was not important to most Europeans.
D the power of the popes declined.

4 Which statement *best* describes the relationship between popes and kings during Europe's Middle Ages?

A Popes became more powerful than kings.
B Many popes became kings, and many kings became popes.
C Popes and kings often disagreed with each other.
D Kings had more power than popes did.

5 Before the Reconquista, most of the Iberian Peninsula was controlled by

A Spaniards.
B Portuguese.
C Crusaders.
D Muslims.

Connecting with Past Learnings

6 Muslim culture spread all the way to Spain through conquest and trade. Which culture spread across much of the ancient world in the same way?

A Japanese
B Harappan
C Roman
D Sumerian

7 Magna Carta helped introduce democratic ideas to England. The first democracy in the ancient world arose in

A Greece.
B China.
C India.
D Rome.

Answers

Standardized Test Practice

1. B
Break Down the Question Students should see a marked population decline between 1347 and 1352 on the graph and recall that these were the approximate dates of the Black Death.

2. C
Break Down the Question Point out that the word *greatest* means that more than one answer may be correct and that students must choose the one that provides the best answer.

3. A
Break Down the Question This question requires students to recall factual information. Refer students who miss the question to the material "The End of the Crusades" in Section 2.

4. C
Break Down the Question Point out that the italicized word *best* means that more than one answer may be correct and that students must choose the one that provides the best answer.

5. D
Break Down the Question This question requires students to recall factual information. Refer students who miss the question to the material "Christians Fight the Moors" in Section 5.

6. C
Break Down the Question This question requires students to recall information covered in Chapters 10 and 11.

7. A
Break Down the Question This question requires students to recall information covered in Chapter 8.

Intervention Resources

Reproducible

- Guided Reading Workbook
- Differentiated Instruction Teacher Management System: Lesson Plans

Technology

- Quick Facts Transparency: The Later Middle Ages Visual Summary
- Differentiated Instruction Modified Worksheets and Tests CD-ROM
- Interactive Skills Tutor CD-ROM

Tips for Test Taking

Anticipate the Answers Provide this tip to students: Before you read the answer choices, **answer the question yourself. Then, read the choices.** If the answer you gave is among the choices listed, it is probably correct!

Multimedia Classroom

The **HISTORY™ Multimedia Classroom** is a set of exciting new social studies teaching tools featuring award-winning program content. These comprehensive lesson plans, correlated to individual state and national curriculum standards, are easy to use for both teachers and students.

Each lesson contains the following:

- Short video segments that bring history topics to life
- Maps and visual materials
- Discussion and review questions
- Easily printable primary source documents
- Classroom activities and Internet-based activity links

The Multimedia Classroom has been specially designed to be versatile and easily adaptable to existing courses, lesson plans, and syllabi. Every lesson is designed to offer maximum flexibility. Teachers can select entire plans or only the elements they need, allowing them to individually tailor each lesson. Each multimedia lesson is available in CD-ROM format and is accompanied by full-length award-winning programs on DVD from HISTORY™.

For more information or to purchase go to hmhsocialstudies.com

Because some of these lessons may contain video material of a sensitive nature, we recommend that teachers and parents review these materials in their entirety before screening them to students.

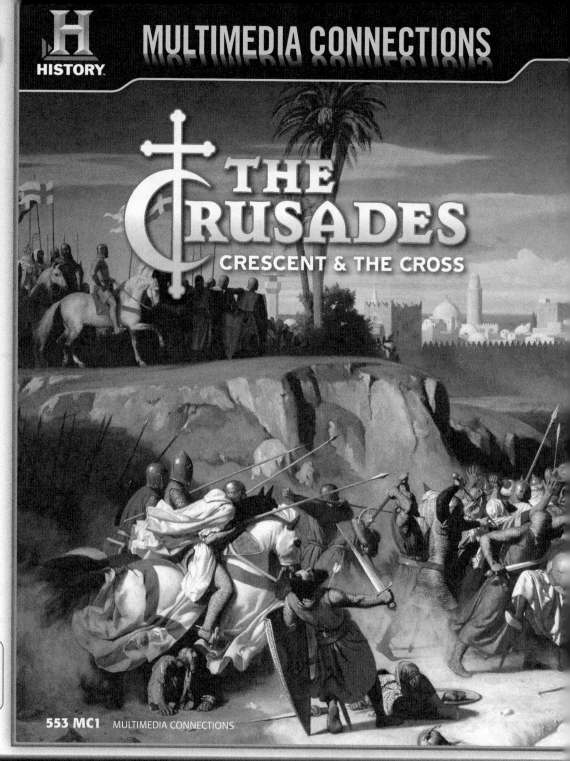

HISTORY

MULTIMEDIA CONNECTIONS

THE CRUSADES
CRESCENT & THE CROSS

553 MC1 MULTIMEDIA CONNECTIONS

The Crusades: Crescent & the Cross

Resources 

The following resources come with printable introductions, comprehension and critical thinking questions, transcripts, and vocabulary support.

 Full Length DVD

The Crusades (3 hrs)

 Video Clips

- The Spiritual Life of Europe (3:29)
- Byzantium's Call for Help (3:12)
- Journey to the Holy Land (3:06)
- Alexius Makes a Double Deal (3:38)
- Shaping a Violent Legacy (3:45)
- The Siege of Jerusalem (3:21)
- Crusaders Take the Holy City (3:17)
- Zengi Launches a Jihad (3:14)
- Call for a Second Crusade (3:26)
- Defeat of the Crusaders (2:25)
- Appeal for a Third Crusade (1:07)
- King Richard I and Saladin (5:12)
- The Crusades' Aftermath (2:14)

 Primary Sources

- A Letter to the Crusaders
- An Excerpt from the *Alexiad*
- Medieval Map of Jerusalem
- Dome of the Rock
- On Divisions among Muslims
- On Traveling Through Tyre
- A Talk Between Friends

CLICK THROUGH
INTER/ACTIVITIES
hmhsocialstudies.com

Fought over nearly two centuries, the Crusades were a violent struggle between soldiers of two religions. In a series of nine wars, European Christians battled Turkish and Arabic Muslims for control of the city of Jerusalem and the surrounding areas, considered sacred by both religions. Thousands died in the fighting—both soldiers and civilians—and whole cities were destroyed. The brutality of the Crusades created strong feelings of resentment between Christians and Muslims. This resentment lingered for centuries after the wars themselves had ended.

Explore the causes, events, and results of the Crusades online. You can find a wealth of information, video clips, primary sources, activities, and more at hmhsocialstudies.com.

Siege of Jerusalem

Watch the video to learn how the Christian army captured Jerusalem from the Turks in 1099.

The First Four Crusades

Explore the map to see the different routes followed by Crusaders from Europe to the Holy Land.

Defeat of the Crusaders

Watch the video to understand how Muslim leaders rallied after the Second Crusade to drive Christians out of the Holy Land.

Lesson Preview

Siege of Jerusalem

The first Crusaders did not reach Jerusalem until 1099. After months of difficult travel—and sporadic but fierce fighting—some Crusaders were so overwhelmed by the sight of the holy city that they broke down in tears. Before they could enter the city, however, they had to face the Muslims who controlled it. The Crusaders did not have enough soldiers or supplies to establish a long siege to wear the city's defenders down, and so they determined that they would have to take Jerusalem by force. The battle was on.

The First Four Crusades

Of all the Crusades, the first four were the largest and best organized. The journey from western Europe to Southwest Asia was a long and difficult one, costly in terms of soldiers and supplies. Crusade leaders sought various routes to ease the strain on their armies with little success. Some marched their armies overland through rugged terrain and hostile kingdoms. Others set sail with their armies, but sailing in the Middle Ages was a risky venture. For the Fourth Crusade, the journey provided a new challenge: the lure of treasure. The soldiers of that Crusade never reached the Holy Land. Instead, they stopped to attack and loot the Christian city of Constantinople.

Defeat of the Crusaders

The Second Crusade was a dismal failure. The Crusaders failed in their goal, which was to retake the city of Edessa from the Turks. Even worse, their actions during the Crusade led to increased hostility against Christians in the Holy Land. During the war, the Christians besieged the Muslim city of Damascus, formerly an ally of the Kingdom of Jerusalem. The people of Damascus invited a general, Nur al-Din, to defend them, and he quickly took control of the city. His power in Damascus soon became a threat to those Crusaders who remained in the Holy Land.

Activities

- An Unlikely Crusader Army
- A Byzantine Perspective
- News Story on the Crusades
- Women and the Holy Wars
- Report from the Front Lines
- Profiles in Power and Politics
- Charting the Crusades

Maps

- The Third Crusade
- The First Four Crusades

General Review Questions

General Discussion Questions

Web Links

Bibliography

Chapter 19 Planning Guide

The Renaissance and Reformation

Overview	Instructional Resources	
CHAPTER 19 **Essential Question:** What political and economic changes led to the Renaissance? **Focus on the Essential Question Podcast**	TOS **Differentiated Instruction Teacher Management System:** • Instructional Benchmarking Guides • Lesson Plans for Differentiated Instruction **Guided Reading Workbook** **Chapter Resource File:** • Chapter Review Activity • Focus on Writing Activity: A Book Jacket • Social Studies Skills Activity: Understanding Graphs	TOS **Calendar Planner** **Power Presentations with Media Gallery** **Differentiated Instruction Modified Worksheets and Tests CD-ROM** **Primary Source Library CD-ROM for World History** **Interactive Skills Tutor CD-ROM** **Student Edition on Audio CD Program** **Video:** Humanism Triggers the Renaissance
Section 1: **The Italian Renaissance** **The Big Idea:** The growth of wealthy trading cities in Italy led to a rebirth of the arts and learning called the Renaissance.	TOS **Differentiated Instruction Teacher Management System:** Section 1 Lesson Plan **Guided Reading Workbook:** Section 1 **Chapter Resource File:** • Vocabulary Builder Activity, Section 1 • Primary Source Activity: Portrait of Giuliano de' Medici by Botticelli • History and Geography: Major Trading Cities in Italy	**Daily Bellringer Transparency:** Section 1 **Map Transparency:** Major Trading Cities **Animated History:** Renaissance Artists
Section 2: **The Renaissance beyond Italy** **The Big Idea:** The Renaissance spread far beyond Italy, and as it spread, it changed.	TOS **Differentiated Instruction Teacher Management System:** Section 2 Lesson Plan **Guided Reading Workbook:** Section 2 **Chapter Resource File:** • Vocabulary Builder Activity, Section 2 • Biography Activity: Johann Gutenberg • Biography Activity: Miguel de Cervantes	**Daily Bellringer Transparency:** Section 2 **Internet Activity:** Gutenberg's Printing Press **Internet Activity:** Renaissance Writers Biography **Animated History:** Renaissance Europe, c. 1500
Section 3: **The Reformation of Christianity** **The Big Idea:** Efforts to reform the Roman Catholic Church led to changes in society and the creation of new churches.	TOS **Differentiated Instruction Teacher Management System:** Section 3 Lesson Plan **Guided Reading Workbook:** Section 3 **Chapter Resource File:** • Vocabulary Builder Activity, Section 3 • Biography Activity: Jeanne d'Albret • Biography Activity: Junípero Serra	**Daily Bellringer Transparency:** Section 3 **Quick Facts Transparency:** Results of the Council of Trent **Quick Facts Transparency:** Some Results of the Reformation **Internet Activity:** Pamphlet on Reformation Leaders **Animated History:** Spread of Protestantism, 1500s

Chart Key:

SE Student Edition  Presentation Resource  MP3 Audio

TOS Teacher One Stop 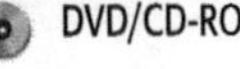 DVD/CD-ROM  HISTORY™

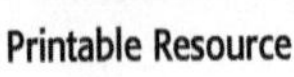 Printable Resource

Program Resources available on TOS and @  hmhsocialstudies.com

Review, Assessment, Intervention

- **Quick Facts Transparency:** The Renaissance and Reformation Visual Summary
- **Spanish Chapter Summaries Audio CD Program**
- **Quiz Game CD-ROM**
- **Progress Assessment Support System (PASS):** Chapter Test
- **Differentiated Instruction Modified Worksheets and Tests CD-ROM:** Modified Chapter Test
- TOS **ExamView® Assessment Suite (English/Spanish)**
- **Holt Online Assessment Program,** in the Interactive Student Edition

 **PASS:** Section 1 Quiz

 **Online Quiz:** Section 1

 **Alternative Assessment Handbook**

 **PASS:** Section 2 Quiz

 **Online Quiz:** Section 2

 **Alternative Assessment Handbook**

 **PASS:** Section 3 Quiz

 **Online Quiz:** Section 3

 **Alternative Assessment Handbook**

Supporting Resources

- Multimedia Classroom Global History Series
- Global History Teacher's Guide

Maps Globes Graphs Level F

- Student Workbook
- Teacher's Guide

Social Studies Trade Library Collections

- Premier Secondary World History Trade Collection

History's Impact

World History Video Program

- **The Renaissance and the Reformation**

For more information or to purchase go to  hmhsocialstudies.com

Power Presentations with Media Gallery

Power Presentations with Media Gallery are visual presentations of each chapter's main ideas. Presentations can be customized by including Quick Facts charts, images from the text, and video clips.

Differentiating Instruction

How do I address the needs of varied learners?

The Target Resource acts as your primary strategy for differentiated instruction.

ENGLISH-LANGUAGE LEARNERS & STRUGGLING READERS

Interactive Skills Tutor CD-ROM

The Interactive Skills Tutor CD-ROM contains lessons that provide additional practice for 20 different critical thinking skills.

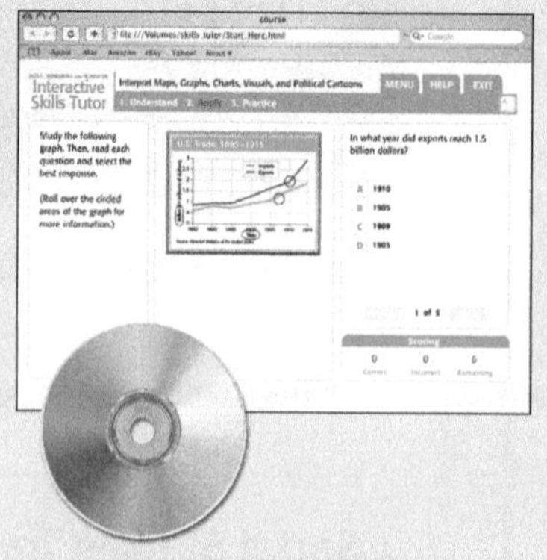

Additional Resources

Differentiated Instruction Teacher Management System: Lesson Plans for Differentiated Instruction

Chapter Resource File:

- Vocabulary Builder Activities
- Social Studies Skills Activity: Understanding Graphs

Quick Facts Transparencies: The Renaissance and Reformation Visual Summary

Student Edition on Audio CD Program

Spanish/English Guided Reading Workbook

SPECIAL NEEDS LEARNERS

Differentiated Instruction Modified Worksheets and Tests CD-ROM

- Vocabulary Flash Cards
- Vocabulary Builder Activities
- Chapter Review Activity
- Chapter Test

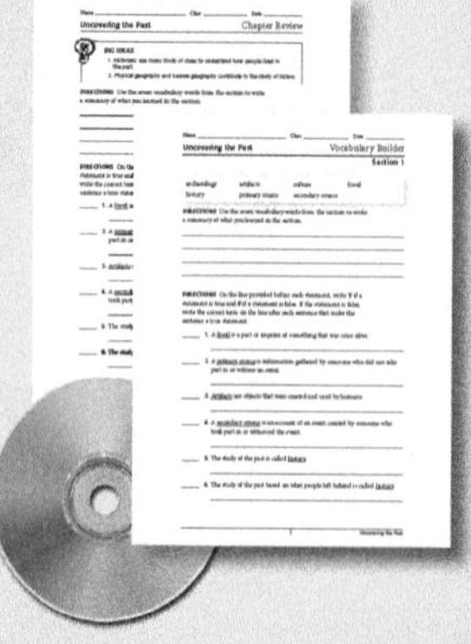

Additional Resources

Differentiated Instruction Teacher Management System: Lesson Plans for Differentiated Instruction

Guided Reading Workbook

Chapter Resource File: Social Studies Skills Activity: Understanding Graphs

Student Edition on Audio CD Program

Interactive Skills Tutor CD-ROM

ADVANCED/GIFTED-AND-TALENTED STUDENTS

Primary Source Library CD-ROM for World History

The Library contains longer versions of quotations in the text, extra sources, and images. Included are point-of-view articles, journals, diaries, historical fiction, and political documents.

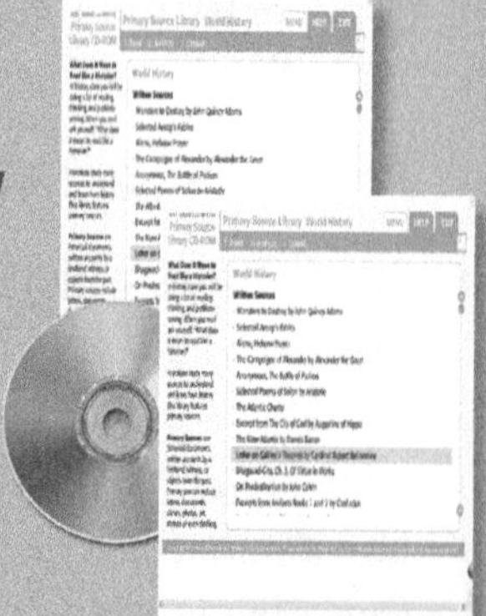

Additional Resources

Differentiated Instruction Teacher Management System: Lesson Plans for Differentiated Instruction

Chapter Resource File:

- Focus on Writing Activity: A Book Jacket
- Literature Activity: *Don Quixote*

Document-Based Questions Activities

Differentiated Activities in the Teacher's Edition

- Using Journals to Travel through Time, p. 560
- Getting to Know Major Figures of the Renaissance, p. 562

Differentiated Activities in the Teacher's Edition

- Exploring the Printing Process, p. 566
- Finding Meaning of Words and Phrases, p. 576

Differentiated Activities in the Teacher's Edition

- Researching Marco Polo, p. 559
- Humanism in Art, p. 563

Teacher One Stop™

How can I manage the lesson plans and support materials for differentiated instruction?

With the Teacher One Stop, you can easily organize and print lesson plans, planning guides, and instructional materials for all learners. The Teacher One Stop includes the following materials to help you differentiate instruction:

- Interactive Teacher's Edition
- Calendar Planner and pacing guides
- Editable lesson plans
- All reproducible ancillaries in Adobe Acrobat (PDF) format
- ExamView Assessment Suite (English & Spanish)
- Transparency and video previews

Interactive Student Edition

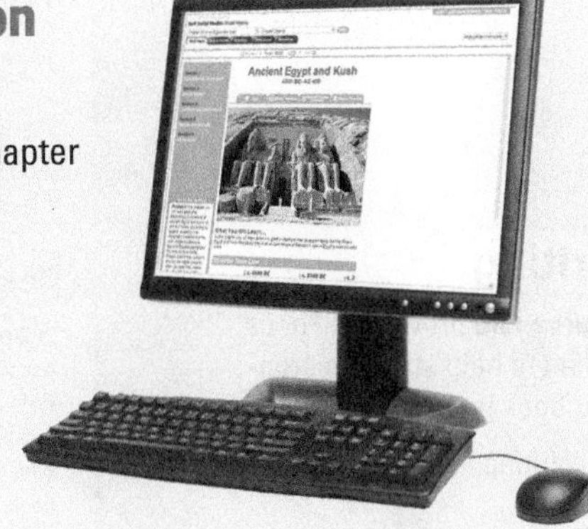

Complete online student edition with interactive multimedia support for chapter content assessment and reporting

- Interactive Maps and Notebook
- Graphic Organizers
- Standardized Test Prep
- Online Homework Practice and Research Activities
- Current Events
- Chapter-based Internet Activities
- Animated History Activities
- and more!

Chapter Preview

Essential Question

Introduce the Essential Question

- Point out that feudalism provided a social and political structure in Europe during the Middle Ages.
- Remind students that throughout Europe, Roman Catholicism was the dominant religion.
- Explain to students that *renaissance* means *rebirth*. Discuss what sort of rebirth Europe might have experienced after the Middle Ages.

Focus on Writing

The **Chapter Resource File** provides a Focus on Writing worksheet to help students organize and write their book jackets.

CRF: Focus on Writing Activity: A Book Jacket

Key to Differentiating Instruction

Below Level
Basic-level activities designed for all students encountering new material

At Level
Intermediate-level activities designed for average students

Above Level
Challenging activities designed for honors and gifted and talented students

Standard English Mastery
Activities designed to improve standard English usage

LS Learning Styles

CHAPTER 19 1270–1650

The Renaissance and Reformation

Essential Question What political and economic changes led to the Renaissance?

South Carolina Performance Standards

6-6.1 Summarize the contributions of the Italian Renaissance, including the importance of Florence, the influence of humanism and the accomplishments of the Italians in art, music, literature, and architecture; **6-6.2** Identify key figures of the Renaissance and the Reformation and their contributions (e.g., Leonardo da Vinci, Michelangelo, Johannes Gutenberg, John Calvin, and Martin Luther); **6-6.3** Explain the causes, events, and points of contention and denominational affiliations (of nations) of the Reformation and the Catholic Reformation (Counter Reformation).

Literacy Skills for Social Studies

- Select or design appropriate forms of social studies resources to organize and evaluate social studies information.
- Explain why trade occurs and how historical patterns of trade have contributed to global interdependence.

Partnership for the 21st Century Skills
Integrate information from a variety of media sources with print or digital text in an appropriate manner.

Focus on Writing

A Book Jacket You work at a publishing company, and you've been asked to design a book jacket for a book about the Renaissance and Reformation. As you read this chapter, consider which main ideas and important details you should include in the description on the back page, which image you might pick for the front, and what you should call the book.

CHAPTER EVENTS
1271 Marco Polo travels to China.

1200

WORLD EVENTS
1201 The Fourth Crusade begins.

Introduce the Chapter

At Level

Focus on Trade

1. Remind students that during the Middle Ages most people knew little about the world beyond their immediate area.
2. Ask, "What would your life be like if everything you had came from no more than 100 miles away? Would you have ever eaten an orange? Would you have seen a Japanese animated film?" As a class, list ways that students' lives would be different under those circumstances.
3. Point out that during the period they will study in this chapter, the Renaissance, Europeans began seeing more trade goods from Asia in their markets. These goods included exotic spices and silk.
4. Lead a class discussion about ways that seeing and buying such foreign items could affect people. Point out that the expansion of trade would have widespread commercial, educational, and cultural effects.
LS Interpersonal, Verbal/Linguistic

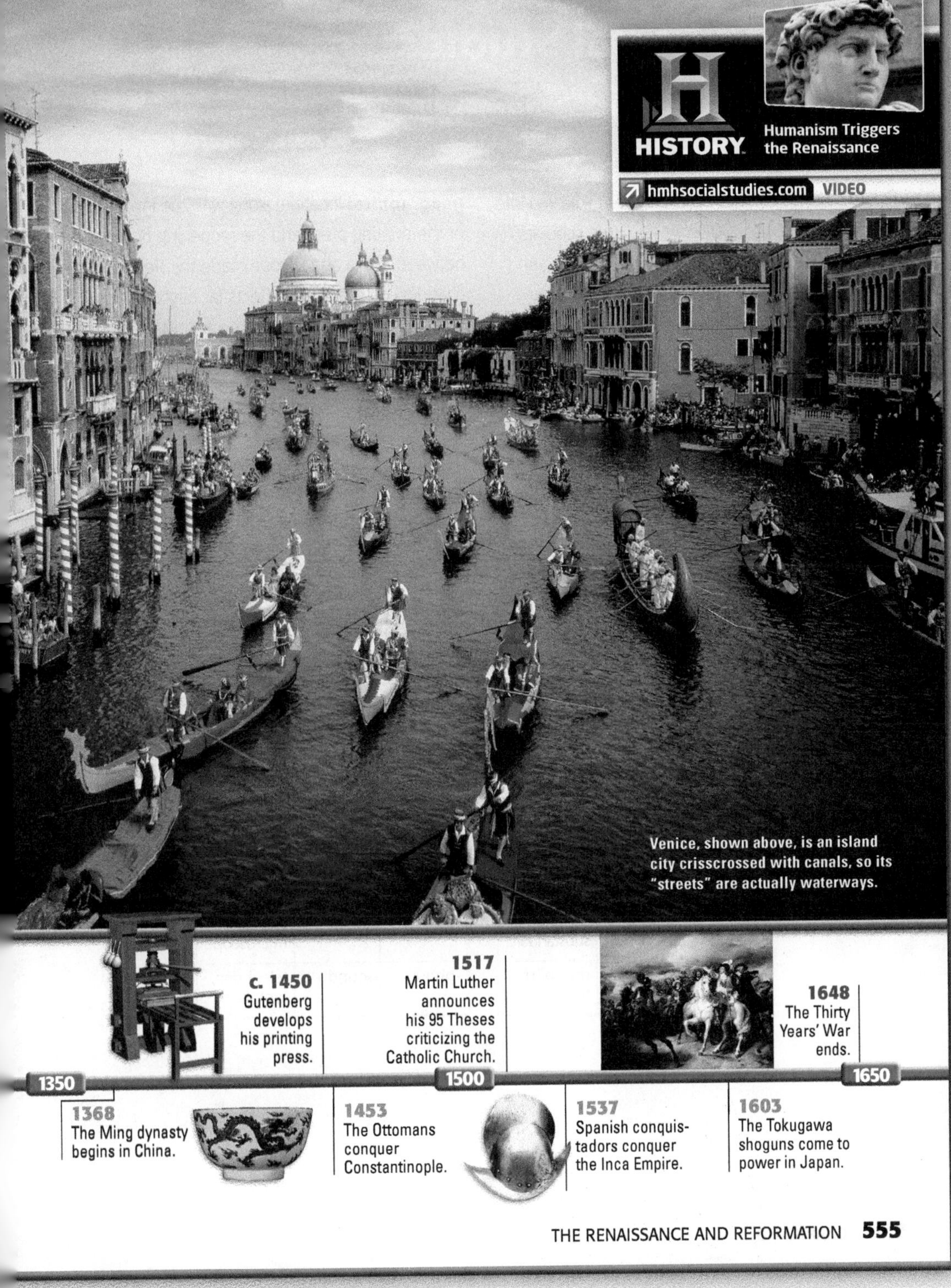
HISTORY
Humanism Triggers the Renaissance
hmhsocialstudies.com VIDEO
Venice, shown above, is an island city crisscrossed with canals, so its "streets" are actually waterways.
c. 1450 Gutenberg develops his printing press.
1517 Martin Luther announces his 95 Theses criticizing the Catholic Church.
1648 The Thirty Years' War ends.
1350
1500
1650
1368 The Ming dynasty begins in China.
1453 The Ottomans conquer Constantinople.
1537 Spanish conquistadors conquer the Inca Empire.
1603 The Tokugawa shoguns come to power in Japan.
THE RENAISSANCE AND REFORMATION 555

• Chapter Preview •

Explore the Picture

The Island City of Venice The only ways to get around Venice are to walk or take a boat. Even police, emergency medical technicians, garbage collectors, and other public service personnel all use boats to move about the city. For residents and tourists, large boats take the place of busses. The long, narrow boats called gondolas are the local taxis. The striped poles in the picture are for tying up the gondolas.

Analyzing Visuals How may Venice's island location have affected the daily lives of the city's residents? *possible answers—more difficult to move about, especially to move large objects; building construction more complicated; potential for flooding; possible protection from enemies*

hmhsocialstudies.com
Teacher Resources

Explore the Time Line

1. How long after Marco Polo traveled to China did the Ming Dynasty begin? *97 years*
2. What event happened in Europe at about the same time as the Ottoman conquest of Constantinople? *Gutenberg developed his printing press.*
3. How many years separated Martin Luther's criticism of the Catholic Church in the Ninety-Five Theses and the Spanish conquest of the Inca Empire? *20 years*

Connect to Geography

The Power of Water Being surrounded by water has affected not only Venice, but also much of Italy. A major reason why Italy became an important trade center was its location near the middle of the Mediterranean Sea. Lead a brief discussion about the impact that bodies of water may have had on your community's development. For example the bay was an essential element of San Francisco's growth.

Reading Social Studies

Understanding Themes

Introduce the themes of this chapter to students by pointing out to students that the Renaissance was a time of new advances in science and technology. Ask students what science and technology Europeans did not have that other civilizations did. Answers might include the compass and medical knowledge. Then ask students how Italy's geography might play a role in improving contact between Europe and other civilizations.

Vocabulary Clues

Focus on Reading Organize students into small groups. Have each group create a two-column chart. Ask students to label the first column *Words* and the second column *Meaning*. Then have each group list as many words as they can that use each of the roots listed in the two tables at right. Ask students to underline the root in each word and provide the meaning of each word. Ask groups to share their lists with the class.

Reading Social Studies

Economics | Geography | Politics | Religion | Society and Culture | Science and Technology

Focus on Themes This chapter takes you into Italy in the 1300s to 1600s. At that time scholars, artists, and scientists built on classical Greek and Roman roots to make new advances in **society and culture** and the arts. You will read how Italy's **geographical** location, along with the invention of the printing press and the reopening of routes between China and Europe made the Renaissance a worldwide event with effects far beyond Italy.

Greek and Latin Word Roots

Focus on Reading During the Renaissance, scientists and scholars became interested in the history and languages of ancient Greece and Rome. Many of the words we use every day are based on words spoken by people in these ancient civilizations.

Common roots The charts below list some Greek and Latin roots found in many English words. As you read the charts, try to think of words that include each root. Then think about how the words' meanings are related to their roots.

Common Latin Roots

Root	Meaning	Sample words
-aud-	hear	audience, audible
liter-	writing	literature, literary
re-	again	repeat, redo
-script-	write	script, manuscript
sub-	below	submarine, substandard
trans-	across	transport, translate

Common Greek Roots

Root	Meaning	Sample words
anti-	against	antifreeze, antiwar
astr-	star	asteroid, astronaut
-chron-	time	chronicle, chronology
dia-	across, between	diagonal, diameter
micr-	small	microfilm, microscope
-phono-	sound	telephone, symphony

Reading and Skills Resources

Reading Support

- Guided Reading Workbook
- Student Edition on Audio CD
- Spanish Chapter Summaries Audio CD Program

Social Studies Skills Support

- Interactive Skills Tutor CD-ROM

Vocabulary Support

- **CRF:** Vocabulary Builder Activities
- **CRF:** Chapter Review Activity
- Differentiating Instruction Modified Worksheets and Tests CD-ROM:
  - Vocabulary Flash Cards
  - Vocabulary Builder Activity
  - Chapter Review Activity

TOS Holt McDougal PuzzleView

You Try It!

Each of the following sentences is taken from the chapter you are about to read. After you've read the sentences, answer the questions at the bottom of the page.

Getting to the Root of the Word

1. Many Italian writers contributed great works of literature to the Renaissance. (*p. 562*)
2. As Protestantism spread in the later 1500s and 1600s, Catholic leaders responded. (*p. 572*)
3. They studied astronomy to learn about the sun, stars, and planets. (*p. 566*)
4. In 1456 Gutenberg printed the Bible in Latin. It was later translated and printed in other languages. (*p. 566*)
5. Also, parallel lines, such as on floor tiles, are drawn diagonally. (*p. 563*)

Answer the following questions about the underlined words. Use the Common Roots charts on the opposite page for help.

1. Which of the underlined words has a root word that means "writing?" How does knowing the root word help you figure out what the word means?
2. What does the root word *astr-* mean? How does that help you figure out the meaning of *astronomy?*
3. In the second sentence, what do you think *responded* means? How could this be related to the root *re-*?
4. What's the root word in *translated*? What does *translated* mean? How is that definition related to the meaning of the root word?
5. What does the word *diagonally* mean? How is that meaning related to the meaning of *dia-*?
6. How many more words can you think of that use the roots in the charts on the opposite page? Make a list and share it with your classmates.

Key Terms and People

Chapter 19

Section 1
Marco Polo (*p. 559*)
Renaissance (*p. 561*)
humanism (*p. 561*)
Dante Alighieri (*p. 562*)
Niccolo Machiavelli (*p. 562*)
Michelangelo (*p. 563*)
Leonardo da Vinci (*p. 563*)

Section 2
Petrarch (*p. 566*)
Johann Gutenberg (*p. 566*)
Christian humanism (*p. 567*)
Desiderius Erasmus (*p. 567*)
Albrecht Dürer (*p. 568*)
Miguel de Cervantes (*p. 568*)
William Shakespeare (*p. 568*)

Section 3
Reformation (*p. 569*)
Martin Luther (*p. 570*)
Protestants (*p. 570*)
John Calvin (*p. 571*)
Catholic Reformation (*p. 572*)
Jesuits (*p. 572*)
federalism (*p. 575*)

Academic Vocabulary

Success in school is related to knowing academic vocabulary—the words that are frequently used in school assignments and discussions. In this chapter, you will learn the following academic words:

classical (*p. 562*)
affect (*p. 566*)
agreement (*p. 575*)

As you read Chapter 19, be on the lookout for words with Greek and Latin root words like those listed in the chart on the opposite page. Use the chart to help you figure out what the words mean.

Reading Social Studies

Key Terms and People

Read the list aloud so that students will know how to pronounce each term or name. Then organize the students in pairs and assign each pair a person or term from the list. Have each pair identify the importance of the person or term. Have each group draw a picture that represents the significance of that term or person. Have students present their term, a description of the term or person, and their illustration to the class. Encourage students to take notes on the presentations.
LS Verbal/Linguistic, Visual/Spatial

Focus on Reading

See the **Focus on Reading** questions in this chapter for more practice on reading social studies skills.

Reading Social Studies Assessment

See the **Chapter Review** at the end of this chapter for student assessment questions related to this reading skill.

Teaching Tip

Remind students that knowing some common Greek and Latin roots can help them to determine the meanings of unfamiliar words. For example, the root *geo-* in *geography* means "earth" and the root *-logy* in *biology* means "study." Have students create a chart that lists roots and their meaning from commonly used words. Have students look in a dictionary for word origins. Some roots might be *aud-*, hear; *philo-*, loving; *anthro-*, man, and *med-*, middle. Then have students think of words in which those roots are used.

Answers

You Try It! 1. *literature; The meaning of the word in English is often related to the meaning of its root.* **2.** *star; We can figure out that astronomy is the study of stars based on the root and the context of the sentence.* **3.** *acted again; because the root* re- *means again* **4.** trans-; *It means the process of changing words from one language to another;* trans- *refers to going across languages.* **5.** *joining two non-adjacent angles;* dia- *refers to going across from one angle to another;* **6.** *Students' answers will vary, but the words they list should contain one of the Greek or Latin roots.*

Preteach

Bellringer

If YOU were there . . . Use the **Daily Bellringer Transparency** to help students answer the question.

Daily Bellringer Transparency, Section 1

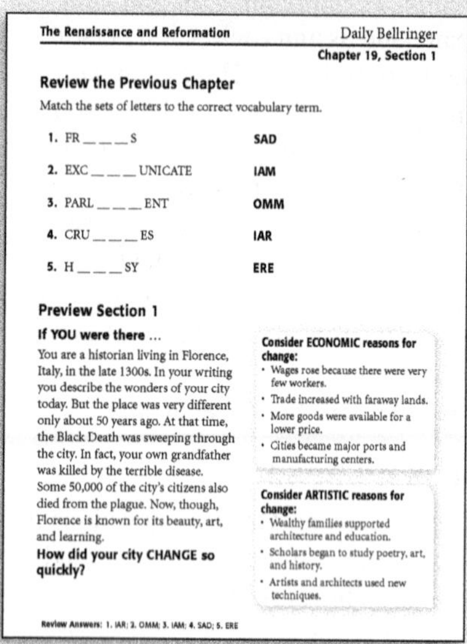

The Renaissance and Reformation — Daily Bellringer

Chapter 19, Section 1

Review the Previous Chapter

Match the sets of letters to the correct vocabulary term.

1. FR ___ ___ ___ S	SAD
2. EXC ___ ___ ___ UNICATE	IAM
3. PARL ___ ___ ___ ENT	OMM
4. CRU ___ ___ ___ ES	IAR
5. H ___ ___ ___ SY	ERE

Preview Section 1

If YOU were there ...

You are a historian living in Florence, Italy, in the late 1300s. In your writing you describe the wonders of your city today. But the place was very different only about 50 years ago. At that time, the Black Death was sweeping through the city. In fact, your own grandfather was killed by the terrible disease. Some 50,000 of the city's citizens also died from the plague. Now, though, Florence is known for its beauty, art, and learning.

How did your city CHANGE so quickly?

Consider ECONOMIC reasons for change:
- Wages rose because there were very few workers.
- Trade increased with faraway lands.
- More goods were available for a lower price.
- Cities became major ports and manufacturing centers.

Consider ARTISTIC reasons for change:
- Wealthy families supported architecture and education.
- Scholars began to study poetry, art, and history.
- Artists and architects used new techniques.

Review Answers: 1. IAR; 2. OMM; 3. IAM; 4. SAD; 5. ERE

Academic Vocabulary

Review with students the high-use academic terms in this section.

classical referring to the cultures of ancient Greece or Rome (p. 562)

CRF: Vocabulary Builder Activity, Section 1

Taking Notes

Have students use the graphic organizer online to take notes on the section. This activity will prepare students for the Section Assessment, in which they will complete a graphic organizer that builds on the information using the Critical Thinking Skill: Sequencing.

SECTION 1

The Italian Renaissance

What You Will Learn...

Main Ideas

1. Increased trade with Asia brought wealth to Italian trade cities, leading to the Renaissance.
2. Italian writers and artists contributed great works during the Renaissance.

The Big Idea

The growth of wealthy trading cities in Italy led to a rebirth of the arts and learning called the Renaissance.

Key Terms and People

Marco Polo, *p. 559*
Renaissance, *p. 561*
humanism, *p. 561*
Dante Alighieri, *p. 562*
Niccolo Machiavelli, *p. 562*
Michelangelo, *p. 563*
Leonardo da Vinci, *p. 563*

Use the graphic organizer online to record information about the growth of trade and cities. Note how this growth influenced writers and artists.

If YOU were there...

You are a historian living in Florence, Italy, in the late 1300s. In your writing you describe the wonders of your city today. But the place was very different only about 50 years ago. At that time, the Black Death was sweeping through the city. In fact, your own grandfather was killed by the terrible disease. Some 50,000 of the city's other citizens also died from the plague. Now, though, Florence is known for its beauty, art, and learning.

How did your city change so quickly?

BUILDING BACKGROUND By the late 1300s the Black Death's horrors had passed. Europeans could worry less about dying and concentrate more on living. They wanted to enjoy some of life's pleasures—art, literature, and learning. Increased trade with faraway lands would help spark new interest in these activities.

Trade with Asia

It seems strange that the Black Death had any positive results, but that is what happened. Though the death toll was terrible, the disease didn't damage farmland, buildings, ships, machines, or gold. People who survived used these things to raise more food and make new products. Wages rose as workers, now in short supply, demanded higher pay. Europe's economy began to grow again.

As more goods became available, prices went down. Trade increased, and new products appeared in the markets. Some of these goods came from thousands of miles away. To learn how these items ended up in Europe, we need to go back in time.

The Silk Road Reopens

The Chinese and Romans did business together from about AD 1 to 200. Products moved between East and West along the Silk Road. This was a caravan route that started in China and ended at the

Teach the Big Idea

At Level

The Italian Renaissance

1. **Teach** Ask students the questions in the Main Idea boxes to teach this section.
2. **Apply** Draw a two-column chart for students to see. Title the chart *Setting the Scene for the Renaissance.* Title the columns *Causes* and *Results.* To begin the chart, write "Black Death" in the *Causes* column.
3. **Organize** the class into small groups. Each group should copy the chart and skim the section to find how various events led to or resulted from the Renaissance.
   LS Visual/Spatial
4. **Review** Have each group share its answers. Write the responses for students to see. Then have students discuss which causes had the biggest results.
5. **Practice/Homework** Instruct students to write a paragraph on what they think would have happened if the Silk Road had not reopened when it did and how this might have affected the Renaissance.
   LS Logical/Mathematical, Verbal/Linguistic

Alternative Assessment Handbook, Rubrics 7: Charts; and 37: Writing Assignments

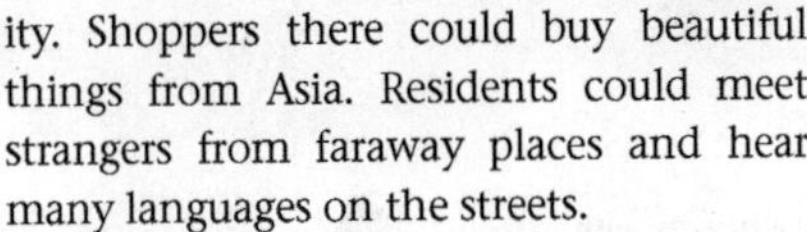

Mediterranean Sea. When the Roman Empire and the Han dynasty fell, soldiers no longer protected travelers. As a result, use of the Silk Road declined. Then in the 1200s the Mongols took over China. They once again made the roads safer for travelers and traders. Among these traders were a remarkable man from Venice named **Marco Polo** and his family.

The Polos traveled from Europe to China, where they saw many amazing things, such as paper money, and coal used for fuel. In China they also met with the Mongol emperor Kublai Khan. He invited them to stay in his court and made Marco Polo a government official. The Polos spent 20 years in Asia before returning to Venice. There, a writer helped Polo record his journey. Polo's descriptions made many Europeans curious about Asia. People began to desire Asian goods, and trade between Asia and Europe grew. Italian merchants organized much of this trade.

Trade Cities in Italy

By the 1300s four northern Italian cities had become trading centers—Florence, Genoa (JEN-uh-wuh), Milan (muh-LAHN), and Venice. These cities bustled with activity. Shoppers there could buy beautiful things from Asia. Residents could meet strangers from faraway places and hear many languages on the streets.

Italian cities played two important roles in trade. One role was as ports on the Mediterranean Sea. Venice and Genoa were the main port cities. Merchant ships brought spices and other luxuries from Asia into the cities' harbors. Merchants then shipped the goods all across Europe.

Major Trading Cities

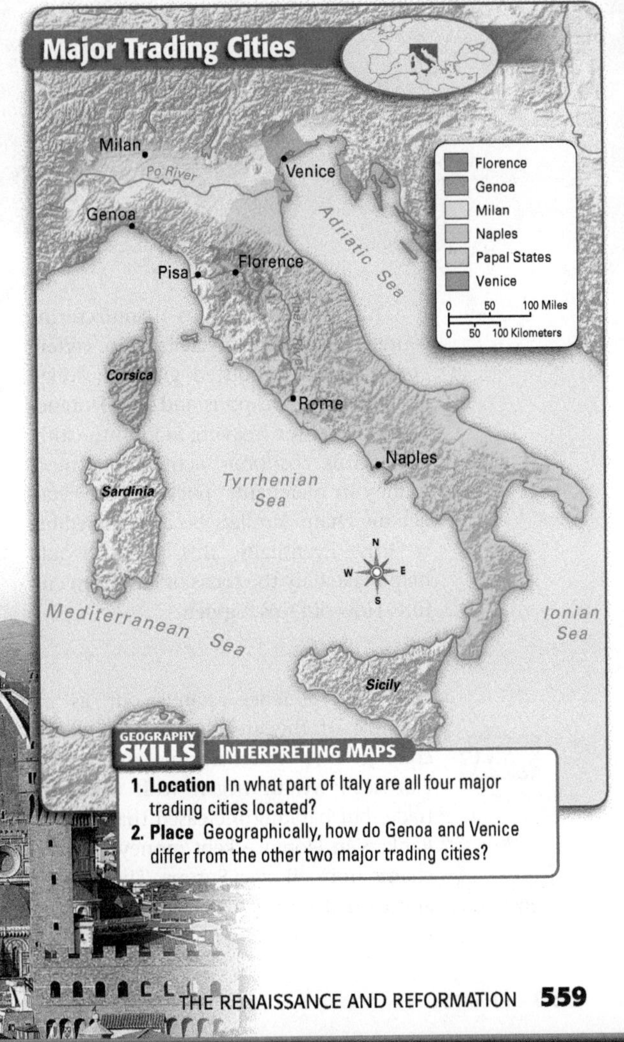

GEOGRAPHY SKILLS **INTERPRETING MAPS**

1. **Location** In what part of Italy are all four major trading cities located?
2. **Place** Geographically, how do Genoa and Venice differ from the other two major trading cities?

Florence was a banking and trade center. The city's wealthy leaders used their money to beautify the city with impressive buildings and art.

Differentiating Instruction

Advanced/Gifted and Talented

Above Level Research Required

1. Discuss with students that some people did not believe Marco Polo's stories about his journeys. Even today, there is discussion on this issue among scholars.
2. Have students begin by asking a specific question about Marco Polo on which they wish to conduct research. An example is "What did Polo say in his writings that led some to disbelieve his stories?"
3. Students should conduct research to answer their questions.
4. Students should write a short paper with their findings and state their opinion on whether Polo actually made his journey.
5. Have students read and discuss one another's papers. Encourage students to defend the positions they took in their papers.

LS Logical/Mathematical, Verbal/Linguistic

Alternative Assessment Handbook, Rubric 30: Research

Direct Teach

Main Idea

1 Trade with Asia

Increased trade with Asia brought wealth to Italian trade cities, leading to the Renaissance.

Define Create a definition for trade city. *possible answer—a bustling urban area that sells goods from faraway places*

Analyze Why did the location of Genoa and Venice on the seacoast give them a commercial advantage over most inland cities? *Ships could easily unload goods at their harbors, saving transportation costs.*

Predict How might people living in Italy's trade cities have been affected by seeing people from different lands and hearing a variety of languages on the streets? *possible answer—When people interact with others from different cultures, they are more aware of the variety in the world and learn new ideas.*

Map Transparency: Major Trading Cities

CRF: History and Geography: Major Trading Cities in Italy

MISCONCEPTION ALERT

Europeans in East Asia The Polos were not the first Europeans to visit the Mongol court. Among earlier travelers was William of Rubruck, a French friar, who headed east in 1253 and stayed in the Mongol capital for several months. He found a few other Europeans living in Mongol lands. Rubruck wrote a vivid description of Mongol daily life. However, he is not as well known as Marco Polo because few people read Rubruck's account of his travels.

Interpreting Maps

Major Trading Cities in Renaissance Italy

Location What bodies of water surround Italy? *Adriatic, Ionian, Mediterranean, and Tyrrhenian seas*

Answers

Interpreting Maps 1. *northern part* **2.** *They are port cities.*

Direct Teach

Main Idea

1 Trade with Asia

Increased trade with Asia brought wealth to Italian trade cities, leading to the Renaissance.

Explain Why were the bankers in Florence so powerful? *They kept money for merchants from all over Europe and made money from interest on loans.*

Analyze The wealth generated by trading was used to support education and cultural activities that led to the Renaissance. Do you think that only wealthy societies can support these things? Why? *possible answer—yes; because wealthy societies have more time and opportunity for leisure activities and more resources to support education and culture*

Predict How do you think your life might be different if a single family controlled your community? *possible answer—People might have less freedom to do as they wish and less input into the way that institutions such as schools are run.*

CRF: Primary Source Activity: Portrait of Giuliano de' Medici by Botticelli

Connect to Economics

Renaissance Accounting During the Renaissance, accountants developed double-entry bookkeeping. In this process, debits (withdrawals) are listed in the left column and credits (deposits) in the right. This accounting method enabled merchants to keep track of income and expenditures more accurately.

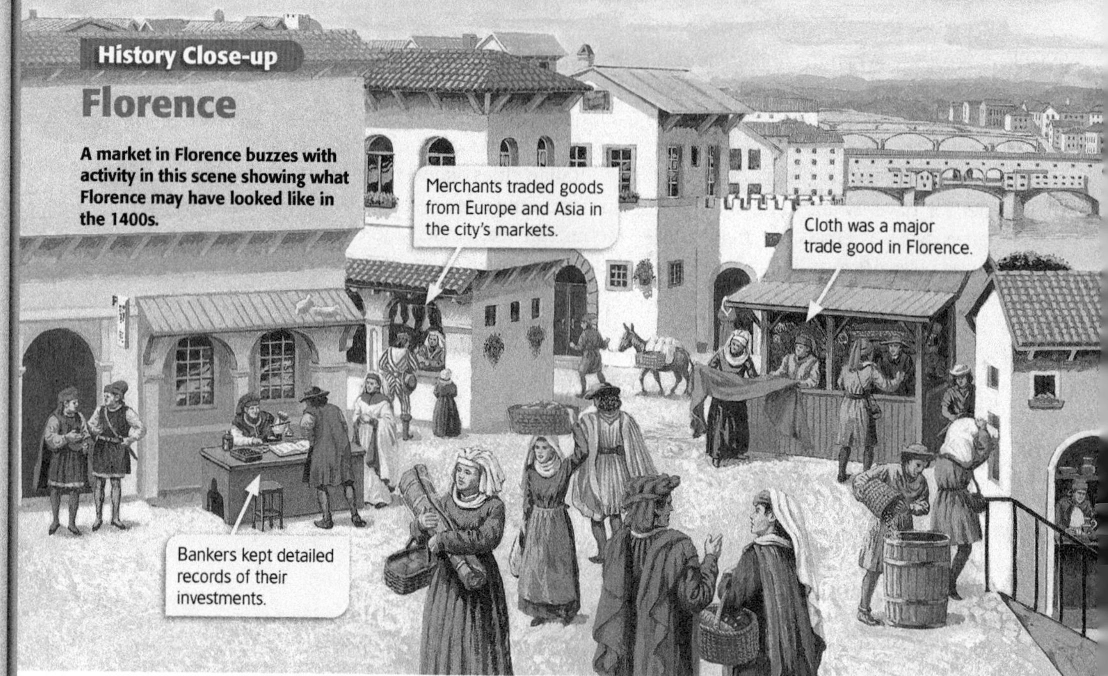

History Close-up
Florence
Merchants traded goods from Europe and Asia in the city's markets.
Cloth was a major trade good in Florence.
Bankers kept detailed records of their investments.

A market in Florence buzzes with activity in this scene showing what Florence may have looked like in the 1400s.

The other role was as manufacturing centers. Each city specialized in certain crafts. Venice produced glass. In Milan workers made weapons and silk. Florence was a center for weaving wool into cloth. All of this economic activity put more money in merchants' pockets. Some Italian merchant families became incredibly wealthy. Eventually, this wealth would help make Italy the focus of European culture. How did this happen?

Florence

Bankers in Florence during this time developed a bookkeeping system that is still used today.

One city—Florence—stands out as an example of the great trade and wealth coming into Italy during the 1300s. Florence's wealth began with the wool trade, but banking increased that wealth. Bankers in Florence kept money for merchants from all over Europe. The bankers also earned money by making loans and charging interest. Interest is a fee that lenders charge people who borrow money from them. This fee is usually a certain percentage of the loan.

The greatest of the Florence bankers were the Medici (MED-i-chee) family. In the early 1400s they were the richest family in the city. Their fortune gave the Medicis political power too. You see, in most big Italian cities, a single rich family controlled the government. The head of the family ruled the city. By 1434 Cosimo de' Medici (KOH-zee-moh day MED-i-chee) ruled Florence.

Cosimo de' Medici wanted Florence to be the most beautiful city in the world. He hired artists to decorate his palace. He also paid architects to redesign many of Florence's buildings.

Cosimo de' Medici also valued education. After all, his banks needed workers who could read, write, and understand math.

Differentiating Instruction

English-Language Learners — Below Level — Standard English Mastery

1. Ask students to imagine that they are average 50-year-old men or women living in Florence in about 1400. They have decided to begin writing journals.
2. The journal should include major changes they see in the world around them. Have students use their textbook as a guideline for changes that are taking place during this time.
3. Write the first entry as a group to model the activity.
4. Encourage students to use their imaginations to create stories about specific events. Perhaps they see people dressed in strange clothing in the marketplace or hear Silk Road travelers bragging about their journey.
5. The journal should contain at least five entries written with correct grammar and using standard English. **LS Verbal/Linguistic**

Alternative Assessment Handbook, Rubric 15: Journals

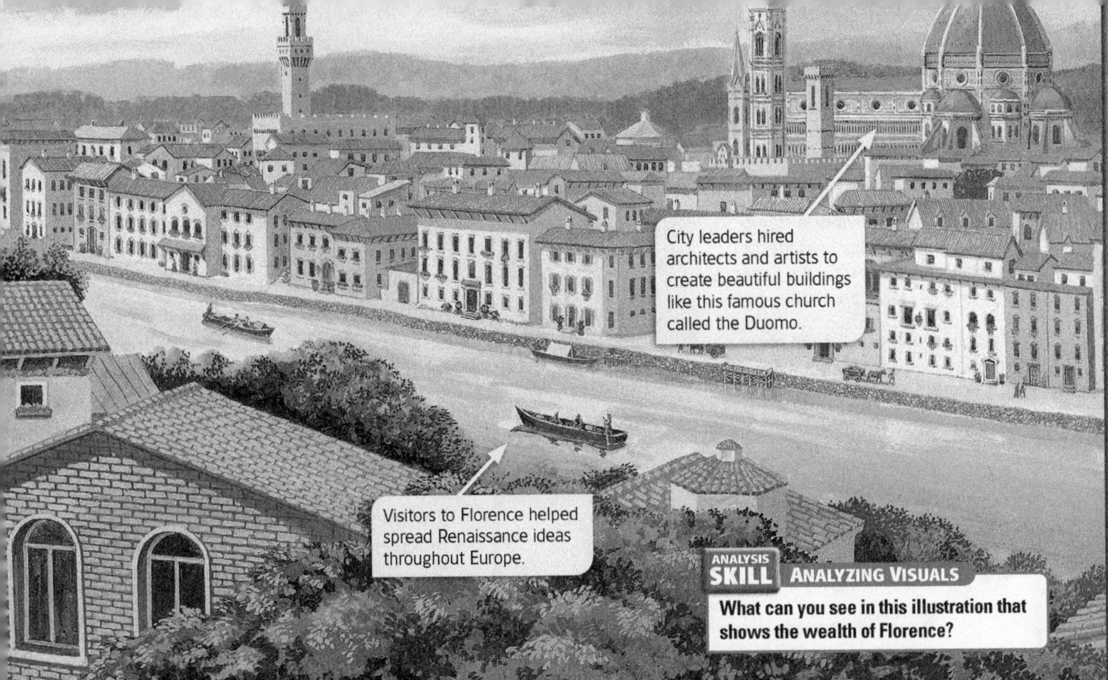
City leaders hired architects and artists to create beautiful buildings like this famous church called the Duomo.
Visitors to Florence helped spread Renaissance ideas throughout Europe.
ANALYSIS SKILL ANALYZING VISUALS
What can you see in this illustration that shows the wealth of Florence?

To improve education, he built libraries and collected books. Under the Medicis, Florence became the center of Italian art, literature, and culture. In other Italian cities, rich families tried to outdo each other in their support of the arts and learning.

Beginning of the Renaissance

This love of art and education was a key feature of a time we call the Renaissance (re-nuh-SAHNS). The word ***Renaissance*** means "rebirth" and refers to the period that followed Europe's Middle Ages.

What was being "reborn"? Interest in art and literature revived, especially in ancient Greek and Roman works. Appreciation also developed for the importance of people as individuals. These ideas were very different from those of the Middle Ages.

READING CHECK **Summarizing** How did trade lead to the Renaissance in Italy?

Italian Writers and Artists

New ways of thinking emerged during the Renaissance. At the same time, the period brought a renewed emphasis on the past. These trends inspired Italian writers and artists to produce many brilliant works.

FOCUS ON READING
What word in this paragraph, besides *Renaissance*, uses a Latin root that means "again"? How does the meaning of the word reflect the meaning of the Latin root?

Sources of Inspiration

During the Middle Ages, most thinkers in Europe had devoted themselves to religious study. By the 1300s, however, scholars had begun to broaden their interests. They studied poetry, history, art, and the Greek and Latin languages. Together, these subjects are known as the humanities because they explore human activities rather than the physical world or the nature of God. The study of the humanities led to a movement called **humanism**, a way of thinking and learning that stresses the importance of human abilities and actions.

Direct Teach

Main Idea

2 Italian Writers and Artists

Italian writers and artists contributed great works during the Renaissance.

Recall What new subjects did scholars study in the 1300s? *poetry, history, art, and Greek and Latin languages*

Explain Why is the word *human* contained in the term *humanism*? *because humanism centered around human activities*

Activity **Renaissance vs. renaissance** Have a member of the class read the definition of the word *renaissance* (with a lowercase *r*) from a dictionary. Ask students to compare this use of the word *renaissance* with the historical period we call the Renaissance. Give examples of "renaissances," such as the Harlem Renaissance. Ask students for other situations in which this term might be appropriately used.
LS Verbal/Linguistic

Collaborative Learning

At Level

Studying at a Renaissance University

1. Organize the class into groups of three or four. Ask group members to imagine that they are students at an Italian university during the Renaissance.
2. Have each group create a list of humanities classes that might be offered at that university. Students should base their lists on what they have learned in this section about sources of inspiration. For example, there might be classes on the Greek and Latin languages, Greek sculpture, Roman architecture, and so forth.
3. The group should then come up with a "class schedule" for each group member depending upon that person's interests and the available courses.
4. Depending upon the time available, ask for volunteers to share their "schedules" with the class. **LS Interpersonal, Verbal/Linguistic**

Alternative Assessment Handbook, Rubric 14: Group Activity

Answers

Reading Check *Trade made merchants wealthy; wealthy merchants and bankers spent money on art and education.*

Direct Teach

Main Idea

❷ Italian Writers and Artists

Italian writers and artists contributed great works during the Renaissance.

Describe How did the Turkish conquest of the Byzantine Empire cause many ancient classical writings to arrive in Italy? *Scholars who fled that empire brought ancient literary works with them.*

Explain Why did Dante write in Italian instead of in Latin? *He considered Italian, the people's language, as good as Latin.*

Analyze Why do you think a politician who is cunning and uses excessive force may be referred to as *Machiavellian*? *possible answer—Machiavelli advised rulers to do whatever was necessary to keep order.*

Linking to Today

The Vernacular and Catholic Mass

Although Renaissance authors increasingly wrote in the vernacular, masses, or worship services in the Roman Catholic Church, were still performed in Latin. It was not until the 1960s that the Second Vatican Council stated that masses should be presented in the vernacular.

Analyze What advantages can you see for religious ceremonies, such as masses, being in the vernacular? Why may some people prefer that masses be in Latin? *If masses are in the vernacular, more people can understand the words. However, some people believe that Latin has historic value and adds beauty and spiritualism to the mass.*

Answers

Analyzing Primary Sources *possible answers—yes, because it would help rulers in power; no, because rulers may abuse their power*

Primary Source

BOOK

The Prince

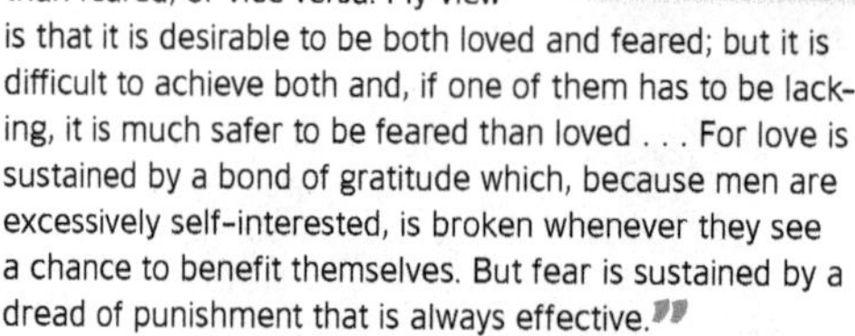

In The Prince, *Machiavelli offers advice for rulers on how to stay in power. In this famous passage, he explains why in his view it is better for rulers to be feared than to be loved.*

"A controversy has arisen about this: whether it is better to be loved than feared, or vice versa. My view is that it is desirable to be both loved and feared; but it is difficult to achieve both and, if one of them has to be lacking, it is much safer to be feared than loved . . . For love is sustained by a bond of gratitude which, because men are excessively self-interested, is broken whenever they see a chance to benefit themselves. But fear is sustained by a dread of punishment that is always effective."

ANALYSIS SKILL **ANALYZING PRIMARY SOURCES**

Do you think that Machiavelli gave good advice in this passage? Why or why not?

This interest in the humanities was linked to the rediscovery of ancient writings. In the 1300s Turks conquered much of the Byzantine Empire. Scholars seeking to escape the Turks fled to Italy. With them they carried rare works of literature.

ACADEMIC VOCABULARY
classical referring to the cultures of ancient Greece or Rome

Many of the works they brought to Italy were ancient classical writings, such as works by Greek thinkers. Scholars were excited by the return of these writings and went looking for ancient Latin texts too. They found many in monasteries, where monks had preserved works by Roman writers. As scholars rediscovered the glories of Greece and Rome, they longed for a renewal of classical culture.

Renaissance artists and architects were also drawn to the past. Classical statues and ruins of Roman buildings still stood in Italy. These ancient ruins and statues inspired painters and sculptors.

Italian Writers

Many Italian writers contributed great works of literature to the Renaissance. The earliest was the politician and poet **Dante Alighieri** (DAHN-tay ahl-eeg-YEH-ree). Before Dante, most medieval authors had written in Latin, the language of the church. Dante wrote in Italian, which was the common language of the people. This showed that he considered Italian, the people's language, to be as good as Latin.

A later Italian writer, **Niccolo Machiavelli** (neek-koh-LOH mahk-yah-VEL-lee), was also a politician. In 1513 he wrote a short book called *The Prince*. It gave leaders advice on how they should rule.

Machiavelli didn't care about theories or what *should* work. He was only interested in what really happened in war and peace. He argued that to be successful, rulers had to focus on the "here and now," not on theories. Machiavelli thought that rulers sometimes had to be ruthless to keep order. In this way, Machiavelli serves as a good example of Renaissance interest in human behavior and society.

Two Masters

Michelangelo
1475–1564

Michelangelo produced some the most famous works of art in world history. Like many of his masterpieces, his powerful statue of the Hebrew king David and his remarkable painting for the Sistine Chapel (both at right) were created for the Roman Catholic Church.

Differentiating Instruction

Struggling Readers Below Level

1. The names of the people and places of the Renaissance can be difficult to pronounce. By practicing the names, students can become more comfortable with them.
2. As a class, go through this section, writing down the names of artists, writers, and other important figures for students to see.
3. Have the students copy the names. Then say each name and have students repeat the name as a group.
4. Organize the class into pairs. Have the pairs practice speaking the names to one another.
5. Then have each pair go through the section to find one fact about each place or person. For example: Dante Alighieri wrote the *Divine Comedy*. **LS Auditory/Musical, Verbal/Linguistic**

Alternative Assessment Handbook, Rubric 18: Listening

Italian Art and Artists

During the Renaissance, Italian artists created some of the most beautiful paintings and sculptures in the world. Ideas about the value of human life affected the art of the time. Artists showed people in a more realistic way than medieval artists had done. Renaissance artists studied the human body and drew what they saw.

Artists also used a new technique called perspective—a way of showing depth and distance on a flat surface. Perspective is created by various means. For example, people in the background of a painting are shown smaller than people in the front to make them look farther away.

Architects developed new techniques to improve their works as well. For example, Filippo Brunelleschi (broo-nayl-LAYS-kee) designed a dome for the main cathedral in Florence. He developed new construction methods that allowed the dome to be larger than people had been able to build before.

Music also advanced in the Renaissance. Composers wove complex harmonies into stirring melodies. Their works deal with both religious and secular themes.

Two Masters

There were several great Italian Renaissance artists. But two stand out above the rest. Each is an example of what we call a Renaissance person—someone who can do practically anything well.

hmhsocialstudies.com
ANIMATED HISTORY
Renaissance Artists

One of these great Italian masters was **Michelangelo** (mee-kay-LAHN-jay-loh). He had many talents. Michelangelo designed buildings, wrote poetry, carved sculptures, and painted magnificent pictures. Perhaps his most famous work is a painting that covers the ceiling of the Sistine Chapel in the Vatican.

The true genius of the Renaissance was **Leonardo da Vinci**. In addition to being an expert painter, Leonardo was a sculptor, architect, inventor, engineer, town planner, and mapmaker. Both nature and technology fascinated Leonardo. Detailed drawings of plants, animals, and machines fill the sketchbooks that he left behind.

THE IMPACT TODAY

The ancestors of many modern musical instruments, including the trombone and the violin, were developed in the Renaissance.

Leonardo da Vinci

1452–1519

Leonardo showed artistic talent at a young age, but no one could have known that he would become one of the great geniuses of history. His Mona Lisa (far right) is one of the most famous paintings in the world. Leonardo also left behind notebooks that were filled with examples of his other interests. His self-portrait (above right) and anatomical sketches (right) reveal his attention to detail and study of the human body. His ideas for a human-powered flying machine are reflected in the model above.

563

Direct Teach

Main Idea

❷ Italian Writers and Artists

Italian writers and artists contributed great works during the Renaissance.

Identify Who painted the ceiling of the Sistine Chapel in the Vatican? *Michelangelo*

Recall List four of Leonardo da Vinci's areas of interest. *possible answers—painting, sculpture, anatomy, writing, architecture, invention, engineering, town planning, and mapmaking*

Make Inferences What does it mean if someone is called a Renaissance man or woman? *He or she is very intelligent and has skills and knowledge in a wide range of areas.*

Info to Know

Fooling the Eye With the increasing realism in art, the technique called *trompe l'oeil* ("fool the eye") flourished. One Renaissance master of the technique was Andrea Mantegna (c. 1431-1506), who is famous for his paintings in the palace at Mantua. In the *Camera degli sposi*, Mantegna painted the walls so skillfully that the room appears to be open to the outdoors. Even more impressive is the room's ceiling. Though the ceiling is mostly flat, Mantegna created the illusion of a tall dome open to the sky through which cupids and people peer down on the room's occupants.

Critical Thinking: Analyzing Information

Above Level

Humanism in Art

Prep Required

1. Discuss with students that, in general, Renaissance artists expressed the concept of humanism in their work. Artists thought that art should follow three fundamental principles: balance, harmony, and perspective.
2. Discuss with the class what humanism meant to the Renaissance artist. Show the class works of art that illustrate this principle. Also show examples of works that demonstrate balance, harmony, and perspective.
3. Have students choose a piece of Renaissance artwork to study.
4. Then ask them to write a short essay discussing how the work illustrates humanism.
5. Ask for volunteers to share their analyses of their artwork with the class.

LS Verbal/Linguistic, Visual/Spatial

Alternative Assessment Handbook, Rubric 40: Writing to Describe

Direct Teach

Main Idea

❷ Italian Writers and Artists

Italian writers and artists contributed great works during the Renaissance.

Recall Why did Leonardo da Vinci study anatomy, the structure of the human body? *to make his art more realistic*

Evaluate Do you prefer to see a painting of a landscape that uses perspective or one that does not use perspective? Why? *Answers will vary. Not using perspective gives a painting a more "primitive" look that some people find appealing. Using perspective makes the painting look more realistic.*

Review & Assess

Close

Have students list at least four changes that occurred at the beginning of the Renaissance. Write these changes for students to see.

Review

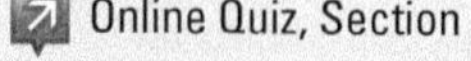

Online Quiz, Section 1

Assess

SE Section 1 Assessment

PASS: Section 1 Quiz

Alternative Assessment Handbook

Reteach/Classroom Intervention

Guided Reading Workbook, Section 1

Interactive Skills Tutor CD-ROM

Answers

Renaissance Art *possible answers: similar—Both paintings show Mary and the infant Jesus; different—the medieval painting is less realistic and does not use perspective; the Renaissance painting shows realistic people in a real-looking place.*

Reading Check *Dante, Machiavelli, Michelangelo, Leonardo da Vinci*

Renaissance Art

Renaissance art was very different from medieval art. Renaissance artists used new techniques to make their paintings more realistic.

How are these two paintings similar and different?

The people in this painting appear larger and have more detail than the mountains in the distance, creating a sense of depth.

Artists in the Middle Ages didn't use perspective, so their art looked flat.

To make his art more real, Leonardo studied anatomy, the structure of human bodies. He also showed human emotions in his work. His famous portrait of Mona Lisa, for example, shows the lady smiling.

READING CHECK **Summarizing** Who were some of the great Renaissance writers and artists?

SUMMARY AND PREVIEW Changes in Italy led to the beginning of an era called the Renaissance. During the late 1300s, a great rebirth of art, literature, and learning occurred in Italy. In the next section, you will learn how Renaissance ideas changed as they spread across Europe.

Section 1 Assessment

hmhsocialstudies.com ONLINE QUIZ

Reviewing Ideas, Terms, and People

1. a. **Identify** Who was **Marco Polo** and how was he influential?
   b. **Analyze** Why were the four major trade cities of Italy important economically?
   c. **Elaborate** How did the city of Florence rise to its position of fame?
2. a. **Describe** What sources inspired Renaissance artists and scholars?
   b. **Compare** Which artist would you rather have met in real life—**Michelangelo** or **Leonardo da Vinci**? What is the reason for your choice?
   c. **Evaluate** Why do you think **Dante Alighieri** chose to write in Italian, rather than Latin, the language used by most scholars?

Critical Thinking

3. **Sequencing** Draw a diagram like the one below. Using your notes, put the events in the correct order.

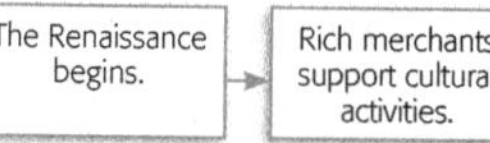
The Renaissance begins.
Rich merchants support cultural activities.
Trade between Europe and Asia increases.

Focus on Writing

4. **Finding Key Details** The main idea of this section might be stated, "Due to contact with Asia and the wealth that resulted from trade, the Renaissance began in Italy." Write this main idea in your notebook. What key details in this section support this idea? Write them in your notebook as well.

Section 1 Assessment Answers

1. a. trader who traveled to China; increased interest in trade with Asia
   b. as ports and manufacturing centers
   c. by being the center of Italian art, literature, and culture
2. a. ancient Greek and Latin literature, statues, and ruins
   b. Answers will vary, but students should support their choices.
   c. to make his work accessible to the common reader
3. Trade between Europe and Asia increases; rich merchants support cultural activities; the Renaissance begins.
4. possible answers—Trade goods from Asia poured into Europe; merchant families became rich and powerful; wealthy families contributed to the arts and learning.

The Renaissance beyond Italy

SECTION 2

If YOU were there...

You are a student from Holland, studying law at the university in Bologna, Italy. Life in Renaissance Italy is so exciting! You've met artists and writers and learned so much about art and literature. You can hardly wait to tell people at home about everything you've learned. But now a lawyer in Bologna has offered you a chance to stay and work in Italy.

Will you stay in Italy or return to Holland?

BUILDING BACKGROUND By the late 1400s the Renaissance spirit was spreading from Italy to other parts of Europe. Artists, writers, and scholars came to Italy to study. Then they taught others what they had learned and brought paintings and sculptures from Italy back home. They also picked up new ideas. Soon, printing and books made these new ideas available to even more people.

Advances in Science and Education

Many of the texts rediscovered in the 1300s dealt with science. Europeans could once again read works by ancient scientists in the original Greek. After learning from these works, Renaissance scholars went on to make their own scientific advances.

Mathematics and the Sciences

Some Renaissance scientists thought mathematics could help them understand the universe. They studied ancient math texts and built on the ideas in them. In the process, they created many of the symbols we use in math today. These include the symbols for the square root ($\sqrt{\ }$) and for positive (+) and negative (-) numbers.

Advances in mathematics led to advances in other fields of science. Engineers and architects, for example, used new mathematical formulas to design ways to strengthen buildings.

What You Will Learn...

Main Ideas

1. During the Renaissance, advances in science and education were made.
2. New ideas from the Renaissance spread across Europe through the development of paper, printing, and new universities.

The Big Idea

The Renaissance spread far beyond Italy, and as it spread, it changed.

Key Terms and People

Petrarch, *p. 566*
Johann Gutenberg, *p. 566*
Christian humanism, *p. 567*
Desiderius Erasmus, *p. 567*
Albrecht Dürer, *p. 568*
Miguel de Cervantes, *p. 568*
William Shakespeare, *p. 568*

Use the graphic organizer online to describe the ideas, art, and literature of the Renaissance outside of Italy.

Teach the Big Idea

At Level

The Renaissance beyond Italy

1. **Teach** Ask students the questions in the Main Idea boxes to teach this section.
2. **Apply** Display a map of Europe during the Renaissance for students to see. Attach labels with the names of individuals who were important to the Italian Renaissance to the map. Include Johann Gutenberg (Germany), Desiderius Erasmus (Netherlands), Albrecht Dürer (Germany), Miguel de Cervantes (Spain), and William Shakespeare (England). LS **Visual/Spatial**
3. **Review** As you review each of these individuals, discuss their accomplishments.
4. **Practice/Homework** Have students create a chart listing each individual in the left column and one of his accomplishments in the right column. LS **Visual/Spatial**

Alternative Assessment Handbook, Rubric 7: Charts

Preteach

Bellringer

If YOU were there . . . Use the **Daily Bellringer Transparency** to help students answer the question.

Daily Bellringer Transparency, Section 2

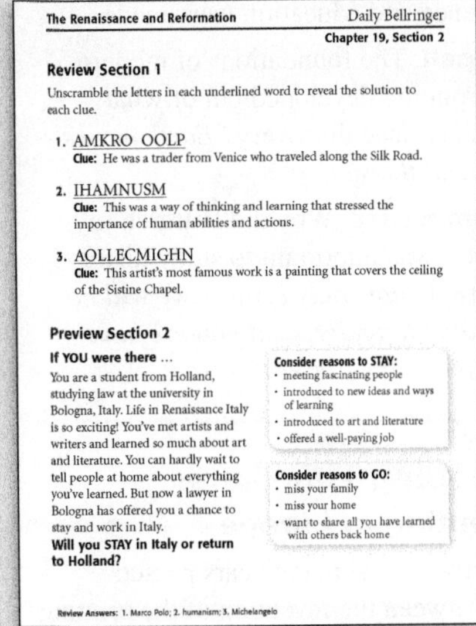

The Renaissance and Reformation — Daily Bellringer
Chapter 19, Section 2

Review Section 1

Unscramble the letters in each underlined word to reveal the solution to each clue.

1. AMKRO OOLP
   Clue: He was a trader from Venice who traveled along the Silk Road.
2. IHAMNUSM
   Clue: This was a way of thinking and learning that stressed the importance of human abilities and actions.
3. AOLLECMIGHN
   Clue: This artist's most famous work is a painting that covers the ceiling of the Sistine Chapel.

Preview Section 2

If YOU were there ...

You are a student from Holland, studying law at the university in Bologna, Italy. Life in Renaissance Italy is so exciting! You've met artists and writers and learned so much about art and literature. You can hardly wait to tell people at home about everything you've learned. But now a lawyer in Bologna has offered you a chance to stay and work in Italy.

Will you STAY in Italy or return to Holland?

Consider reasons to STAY:
- meeting fascinating people
- introduced to new ideas and ways of learning
- introduced to art and literature
- offered a well-paying job

Consider reasons to GO:
- miss your family
- miss your home
- want to share all you have learned with others back home

Review Answers: 1. Marco Polo; 2. humanism; 3. Michelangelo

Academic Vocabulary

Review with students the high-use academic term in this section.

affect to change or influence (p. 566)

CRF: Vocabulary Builder Activity, Section 2

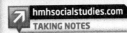

hmhsocialstudies.com

Online Resources
Activity: Gutenberg's Printing Press

Taking Notes

Have students use the graphic organizer online to take notes on the section. This activity will prepare students for the Section Assessment, in which they will complete a graphic organizer that builds on the information using the Critical Thinking Skill: Comparing and Contrasting.

Direct Teach

Main Idea

1 Advances in Science and Education

During the Renaissance, advances in science and education were made.

Recall The foundations of modern astronomy developed out of what Renaissance discovery? *Earth moves around the sun.*

Summarize Why did Petrarch say that it was important to study history? *If we do not study history, we will not be able to understand how we have gotten to the present.*

Reading Time Lines

Printing in Europe

1. About how many years passed between the invention of the printing press and the introduction of steam engines to make printing faster and cheaper? *about 350 years*
2. During what period did the printing press help to spread ideas and information through Europe? *the 1500s and 1600s*
3. How do you think the printing press affected people involved in making books? *Books had been copied mainly by monks. Later, trained workers probably performed printing tasks, which removed the process from the religious world.*

Answers

Reading Check *mathematics, engineering, architecture, astronomy*

Other Renaissance scientists wanted to know more about the sky and what was in it. They studied astronomy to learn about the sun, stars, and planets. Through their efforts, Renaissance scientists learned that the earth moves around the sun.

Changes in Education

THE IMPACT TODAY

American universities grant degrees in the humanities.

During the Renaissance, students continued to study religious subjects, but they learned about the humanities as well. History became especially important. The Renaissance scholar **Petrarch** (PE-trahrk) warned against ignoring history:

> "O inglorious age! that scorns antiquity, its mother, to whom it owes every noble art ... What can be said in defense of men of education who ought not to be ignorant of antiquity [ancient times] and yet are plunged in ... darkness and delusion?"
>
> —Francesco Petrarch, from a 1366 letter to Boccaccio

ACADEMIC VOCABULARY
affect to change or influence

Petrarch's ideas would **affect** education for many years. Education and new ways of spreading information would take the Renaissance far beyond Italy.

READING CHECK **Summarizing** What fields of study advanced during the Renaissance?

The Spread of New Ideas

Travelers and artists helped spread Renaissance ideas throughout Europe. But the development of printing played a giant role. It allowed thousands of people to read books for the first time ever.

Paper and Printing

Papermaking spread from China to the Middle East, and then to Europe. Several European factories were making paper by the 1300s. Cheaper and easier to prepare, paper soon replaced the processed animal skins on which people had written before.

In the mid-1400s a German named **Johann Gutenberg** (GOOT-uhn-berk) developed a printing press that used movable type. That is, each letter was on a separate piece of metal. A worker fitted letters into a frame, spread ink on the letters, and then pressed a sheet of paper against the letters. An entire page was printed at once. The worker could then rearrange the letters in the frame to create a new page.

In 1456 Gutenberg printed the Bible in Latin. It was later translated and printed

Time Line

Printing in Europe

1000 Printing has not developed in Europe yet. Books are copied by hand, usually by monks.

c. 1455 Johann Gutenberg develops the printing press. It uses movable type, which makes the mass production of books possible and allows ideas to spread more quickly.

1000 — 1300

1300s Factories in Europe begin making paper using techniques introduced from Asia.

Differentiating Instruction

Special Needs Learners

Below Level | Prep Required

Materials: ink or paint, small roller, dense foam, thick cardboard, scissors, glue, paper

1. Review the printing process with students.
2. Write a sentence for students to see. Example: *After many years, Marco Polo returned from the court of Kublai Khan.* Tell students that they are going to "print" this sentence.
3. As a group, create a chart listing the needed letters. For example, how many letter *E*'s will be needed? Assign letters to students.
4. Point out that the letters must be created backwards as if looking in a mirror. Have students create their assigned letters. Have students position the letters inside a cardboard frame. Place blanks for spaces.
5. Have one student use a small roller to roll the "ink" onto the type's surface. Have another student press the paper onto the type. Have students correct any errors.
6. Let students trade jobs and repeat the printing process several times.

LS **Kinesthetic, Visual/Spatial**

in other languages. As the Bible became increasingly available, more people learned to read. They then wanted more education.

New Universities

Students from around Europe traveled to Italy to study. At Italian universities, they picked up humanist ideas, which they took back to their own countries.

Over time, new universities opened in France, Germany, and the Netherlands. Because they were set up by humanists, Renaissance ideas about the value of individuals spread throughout Europe.

Although only men could attend universities, many noble families in Italy educated their daughters at home. Some of these women married nobles from other parts of Europe and became influential. They used their positions to encourage the spread of Renaissance ideas in the lands that their husbands ruled.

The Northern Renaissance

As humanism spread into northern Europe, it took on a more religious form. Scholars there focused on the history of Christianity, not Greece or Rome. This **Christian humanism** was a blend of humanist and religious ideas.

Many northern scholars came to feel that the church was corrupt and did not follow Jesus's teachings. A Dutch priest named **Desiderius Erasmus** (des-i-DEER-ee-uhs i-RAZ-mus) was the most important voice for reform. Erasmus criticized corrupt clergy and wanted to get rid of some church rituals that he considered meaningless. Instead of rituals, he emphasized devotion to God and the teachings of Jesus.

Northern Europeans also brought key changes to Renaissance art. For example, they used a more realistic style than Italian artists did. People in northern paintings don't look like Greek gods. Instead, they are more lifelike, with physical flaws. Northern artists also worked on a broader range of subjects. Many painted scenes of daily life, rather than the biblical scenes and classical myths favored by Italian artists.

One of the most famous artists of the northern Renaissance was a gifted German.

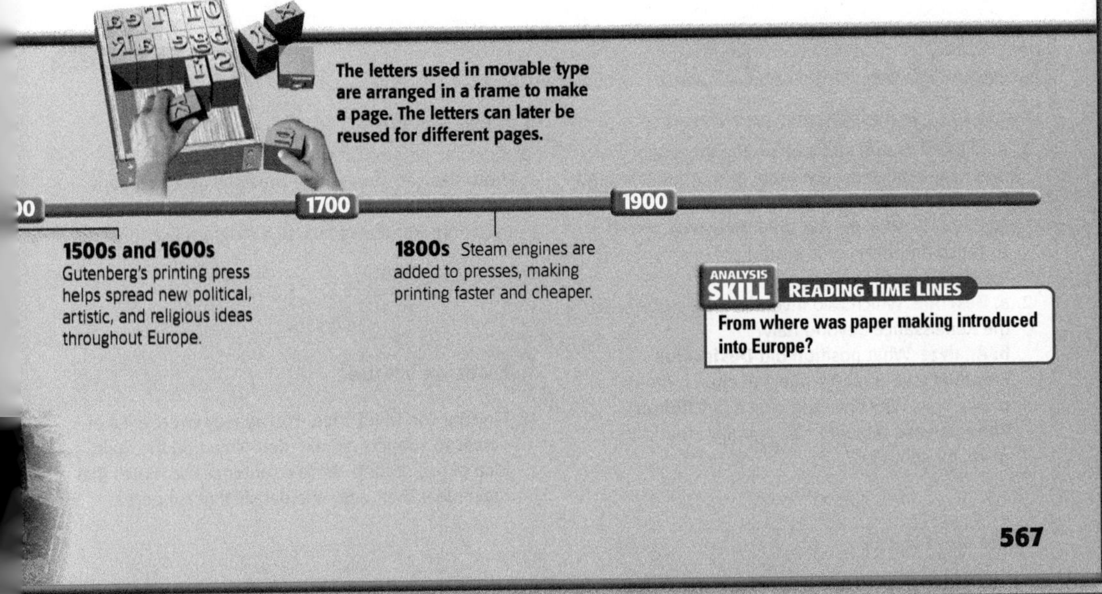

The letters used in movable type are arranged in a frame to make a page. The letters can later be reused for different pages.
00
1700
1900
1500s and 1600s Gutenberg's printing press helps spread new political, artistic, and religious ideas throughout Europe.
1800s Steam engines are added to presses, making printing faster and cheaper.

ANALYSIS SKILL READING TIME LINES

From where was paper making introduced into Europe?

Direct Teach

Main Idea

❷ The Spread of New Ideas

New ideas from the Renaissance spread across Europe through the development of paper, printing, and new universities.

Recall What did Erasmus criticize? *corrupt clergy and meaningless church rituals*

Analyze How do you think young women who lived during the Renaissance felt about the changes occurring in Europe? *Answers will vary. Some women may have resented being excluded from the universities but glad that they could influence change in other ways.*

Predict How do you think the availability of paper and the printing press would have changed students' lives? *possible answers—They could afford to own books; they could read things for themselves instead of depending on the teacher; they could carry books back to their home countries.*

CRF: Biography Activity: Johann Gutenberg

Critical Thinking: Finding Main Ideas

At Level

Art Gallery Advertisement

1. Ask students to imagine that they are the marketing manager for an art gallery that specializes in Northern European Renaissance artwork.
2. Organize students in pairs. Have each pair create an advertisement for the local newspaper. The ad should contain the name of an artist whose work the gallery sells.
3. The ad should also describe the available artwork. Students should use what they have learned in this section to write these descriptions.
4. Encourage students to choose an interesting name for their gallery and to use attention-getting phrases in their ads. The ad should include at least one original graphic.

LS Verbal/Linguistic, Visual/Spatial

Alternative Assessment Handbook, Rubric 2: Advertisements

Answers

Reading Time Lines *Asia*

Direct Teach

Main Idea

2 The Spread of New Ideas

New ideas from the Renaissance spread across Europe through the development of paper, printing, and new universities.

Explain What is a print? *a work of art reproduced from an original*

Identify What kinds of plays did Shakespeare write? *comedies, tragedies, and histories*

Analyze Why did Cervantes think his time was better than the Middle Ages? *Possible answers—the love of learning; the sharing of ideas.*

CRF: Biography Activity: Miguel de Cervantes

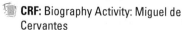

Online Resources
Activity: Renaissance Writers Biography

Review & Assess

Close

Ask students if they would rather have lived in the Middle Ages or the Renaissance and to explain their choices.

Review

Online Quiz, Section 2

Assess

SE Section 2 Assessment
PASS: Section 2 Quiz
Alternative Assessment Handbook

Reteach/Classroom Intervention

Guided Reading Workbook, Section 2
Interactive Skills Tutor CD-ROM

Answers

Biography *possible answer—He may have drawn on current words to create new words and phrases.*

Reading Check *People who traveled to Italy or married Italians spread Renaissance ideas.*

BIOGRAPHY

William Shakespeare
1564–1616

Many people consider William Shakespeare the greatest playwright of all time. His plays are still hugely popular around the world. Shakespeare was such an important writer that he even influenced the English language. He invented common phrases such as *fair play* and common words such as *lonely*. In fact, Shakespeare is probably responsible for more than 2,000 English words.

Drawing Inferences How do you think Shakespeare invented new words and phrases?

His name was **Albrecht Dürer** (AWL-brekt DYUR-uhr). Dürer studied anatomy so that he could paint people more realistically. He showed objects in great detail. Dürer is most famous for his prints. A print is a work of art that is reproduced from an original.

hmhsocialstudies.com
ANIMATED HISTORY
Renaissance Europe, c. 1500

Literature beyond Italy

Writers in other countries besides Italy also included Renaissance ideas in their works. Like Dante, they wrote in the languages of their home countries. In Spain **Miguel de Cervantes** (mee-GEL day ser-VAHN-tays) wrote *Don Quixote* (kee-HOH-tay). In this book Cervantes poked fun at the romantic tales of the Middle Ages. Like many writers of his day, Cervantes thought that his own time was much better than the Middle Ages.

Many readers consider **William Shakespeare** the greatest writer in the English language. Although he also wrote poems, Shakespeare is most famous for his plays. He wrote more than 30 comedies, tragedies, and histories. London audiences of the late 1500s and early 1600s packed the theatre to see his works performed. Ever since then, people have enjoyed Shakespeare's language and his understanding of humanity.

READING CHECK **Analyzing** How did travel and marriage spread Renaissance ideas?

SUMMARY AND PREVIEW The development of paper, the printing press, and new universities helped spread the Renaissance beyond Italy. Northern artists and writers altered Renaissance ideas. Next, you will learn about new religious ideas that swept through Europe at about the same time.

Section 2 Assessment

hmhsocialstudies.com ONLINE QUIZ

Reviewing Ideas, Terms, and People

1. a. **Identify** Name and explain the importance of one Renaissance achievement in mathematics and one achievement in astronomy.
   b. **Evaluate** Why do you think **Petrarch** placed so much emphasis on the study of history during the Renaissance?
2. a. **Describe** Which two inventions helped spread the Renaissance beyond Italy?
   b. **Analyze** What position did **Desiderius Erasmus** take on the subject of church rituals?
   c. **Evaluate** Why have the works of **William Shakespeare** remained so popular around the world for centuries?

Critical Thinking

3. **Comparing and Contrasting** Using your notes from this section and the previous one, compare and contrast the Italian Renaissance and the Northern Renaissance. Use a diagram like this one.

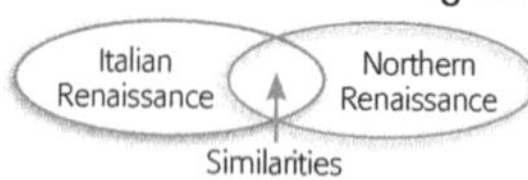

FOCUS ON WRITING

4. **Finding the Main Idea** You already wrote a list of details to support a main idea. Now find the main idea of this section. Write a sentence that states that main idea. Then write the details that support it.

Section 2 Assessment Answers

1. a. possible answers: mathematics—symbols, helped explain new ideas; astronomy—learned that the Earth moves around the sun
   b. The rediscovery of ancient Greek and Latin texts made him appreciate the value of history.
2. a. paper and printing
   b. He wanted to get rid of those that he thought were meaningless.
   c. possible answer—the beauty of his language and his understanding of humanity
3. possible answers: similarities—advances in science and art; differences—in Northern Renaissance, Christian humanism blended humanism and religion; artists painted scenes and classical myths rather than scenes and people from daily life in art
4. Answers will vary, but should demonstrate understanding of how the Renaissance spread beyond Italy.

The Reformation of Christianity

SECTION 3

If YOU were there...

You live in a small town in Germany in the 1500s. The Catholic Church has a lot of influence here. Often, church officials clash with local nobles over who has the final say in certain political issues. The church also demands that the nobles pay high taxes. Lately, however, a local priest has been openly criticizing church leaders. He wants to make some changes.

How do you think the nobles will respond to him?

BUILDING BACKGROUND By the early 1500s Renaissance ideas had caused many Europeans to view their lives with a more critical eye. They thought their lives could be changed for the better. One area that some people thought needed improvement was religion.

What You Will Learn...

Main Ideas

1. Reformers called for change in the Catholic Church, but some broke away to form new churches.
2. The Catholic Reformation was an attempt to reform the church from within.
3. The political impact of the Reformation included religious wars and social change.

The Big Idea

Efforts to reform the Roman Catholic Church led to changes in society and the creation of new churches.

Key Terms and People

Reformation, *p. 569*
Martin Luther, *p. 570*
Protestants, *p. 570*
John Calvin, *p. 571*
Catholic Reformation, *p. 572*
Jesuits, *p. 572*
federalism, *p. 575*

hmhsocialstudies.com
TAKING NOTES

Use the graphic organizer online to take notes on efforts to reform the Catholic Church, both by Protestants—people who broke away from the church—and by Catholics.

Reformers Call for Change

By the late Renaissance some people had begun to complain about problems in the Catholic Church. They called on its leaders to end corruption and focus on religion. Their calls led to the **Reformation**, a reform movement against the Roman Catholic Church.

Unpopular Church Practices

Those who wanted to reform the church had many complaints. Some thought that priests and bishops weren't religious anymore. Others felt that the pope was too involved in politics, neglecting his religious duties. Many thought the church had grown too rich. The Roman Catholic Church had become one of the richest institutions in Europe because it didn't have to pay taxes.

Many people objected to the ways the church earned its money. One common method was the sale of indulgences. An indulgence was a document given by the pope that excused a person from penalties for the sins that he or she had committed.

Preteach

Bellringer

If YOU were there . . . Use the **Daily Bellringer Transparency** to help students answer the question.

Daily Bellringer Transparency, Section 3

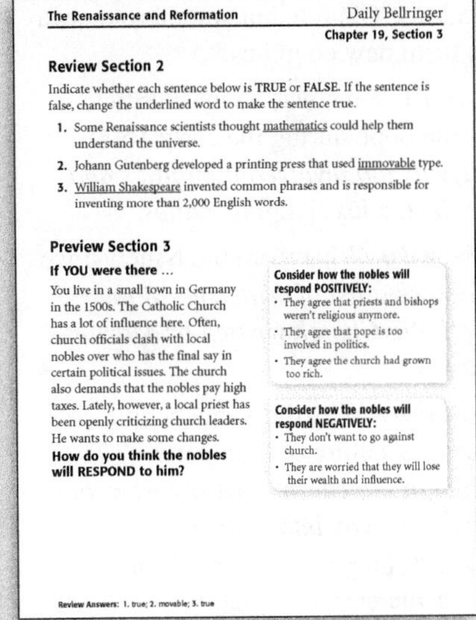

The Renaissance and Reformation — Daily Bellringer
Chapter 19, Section 3

Review Section 2

Indicate whether each sentence below is **TRUE** or **FALSE**. If the sentence is false, change the underlined word to make the sentence true.

1. Some Renaissance scientists thought mathematics could help them understand the universe.
2. Johann Gutenberg developed a printing press that used immovable type.
3. William Shakespeare invented common phrases and is responsible for inventing more than 2,000 English words.

Preview Section 3

If YOU were there ...

You live in a small town in Germany in the 1500s. The Catholic Church has a lot of influence here. Often, church officials clash with local nobles over who has the final say in certain political issues. The church also demands that the nobles pay high taxes. Lately, however, a local priest has been openly criticizing church leaders. He wants to make some changes.

How do you think the nobles will RESPOND to him?

Consider how the nobles will respond POSITIVELY:
- They agree that priests and bishops weren't religious anymore.
- They agree that pope is too involved in politics.
- They agree the church had grown too rich.

Consider how the nobles will respond NEGATIVELY:
- They don't want to go against church.
- They are worried that they will lose their wealth and influence.

Review Answers: 1. true; 2. movable; 3. true

Academic Vocabulary

Review with students the high-use academic term in this section.

agreement a decision reached by two or more people or groups (p. 575)

CRF: Vocabulary Builder Activity, Section 3

Taking Notes

Have students use the graphic organizer online to take notes on the section. This activity will prepare students for the Section Assessment, in which they will complete a graphic organizer that builds on the information using the Critical Thinking Skill: Analyzing.

Teach the Big Idea

At Level

The Reformation of Christianity

1. **Teach** Ask students the questions in the Main Idea boxes to teach this section.
2. **Apply** Lead a discussion about the changes that the Protestant Reformation sought to make in the Catholic Church. Then discuss how the Catholic Reformation sought to strengthen the Church. During the discussion, list the key people, events, and ideas of the movement for students to see. **LS Verbal/Spatial**
3. **Review** As you review the section, have students identify the major figures of both Reformations and describe their ideas.
4. **Practice/Homework** Ask half the students to imagine that they have heard a Protestant leader speak about problems in the Catholic Church. Ask the other students to imagine that they have heard a Catholic leader speak about the Reformation. Have each student write a brief news article about the speech he or she heard. **LS Verbal/Linguistic**

Alternative Assessment Handbook, Rubrics 11: Discussions; and 40: Writing to Describe

Direct Teach

Main Idea

1 Reformers Call for Change

Reformers called for change in the Catholic Church, but some broke away to form new churches.

Recall What was a major criticism of the pope during the early 1500s? *He was too involved in politics and neglected his religious duties.*

Identify What were the Ninety-Five Theses? *a list of criticisms of the Catholic Church written by Martin Luther*

Analyze Why did some people criticize the selling of indulgences? *They thought the church was letting people buy their way into heaven.*

CRF: Biography Activity: Jeanne d' Albret

Activity **Interviewing the Clergy** Have students imagine they are television reporters interviewing a member of the Catholic clergy. Have them write a one-page list of the questions and answers from the interview. The questions should concern the issues raised by Protestant reformers. **LS Verbal/Linguistic**

Alternative Assessment Handbook, Rubric 37: Writing Assignments

Online Resources
Activity: Pamphlet on Reformation Leaders

According to the church, an indulgence reduced the time that a person would serve in purgatory. In Catholic teachings, purgatory was a place where souls went to make up for their sins before they went to heaven. Many Christians thought that by selling indulgences, the church was letting people buy their way into heaven.

Martin Luther

By the early 1500s scholars in northern Europe were calling for church reforms. On October 31, 1517, a priest named **Martin Luther** added his voice to the call for reform. He nailed a list of complaints about the church to the door of a church in Wittenberg (VIT-uhn-berk) in the German state of Saxony. Luther's list is called the Ninety-Five Theses (THEE-seez). Thanks to the newly invented printing press, copies of this list spread to neighboring states.

Luther's complaints angered many Catholics. Pope Leo X called Luther a heretic and excommunicated him. Germany's ruler, the Holy Roman Emperor, ordered Luther to appear before a diet, or council of nobles and church officials, in the German city of Worms (VOHRMS). The emperor called Luther an outlaw and ordered him to leave the empire. But one noble secretly supported Luther and helped him to hide from the emperor.

Luther's ideas eventually led to a split in the church. Those who protested against the Roman Catholic church became known as **Protestants** (PRAH-tuhs-tuhnts). Those Protestants who followed Luther's teachings were specifically known as Lutherans.

Luther taught that anyone could have a direct relationship with God. They didn't need priests to talk to God for them. This idea is called the priesthood of all believers.

When Martin Luther nailed his Ninety-Five Theses to a church door in Wittenberg, Germany, the Reformation began. Soon, others unhappy with church practices also began to criticize the church.

BIOGRAPHY

Martin Luther
1483–1546

Martin Luther is credited with starting the Reformation, but he never wanted to leave the Catholic Church. He just wanted to correct what he saw as the church's mistakes. After he was excommunicated, Luther began to depart more and more from church teachings. For example, although the Roman Catholic Church didn't let priests get married, Luther married a former nun in 1525. Still, as an old man Luther regretted that his actions had caused a split in the church.

Drawing Inferences Why do you think Luther regretted causing a split in the church?

Critical Thinking: Comparing

At Level

Comparing Reformers

Research Required

1. Lead a discussion about what it takes to be a reformer. Remind students that famous reformers are often inspired by the actions of reformers who came before them.
2. Have students compare and contrast the reformers Martin Luther and Dr. Martin Luther King Jr. Have students use library or Internet resources to learn more about each man and his reform efforts.
3. Have students take notes on each reformer. The notes should include what motivated each man to act and what each accomplished.
4. Have students write brief essays comparing and contrasting the two reformers. Ask for volunteers to read their work to the class. **LS Verbal/Linguistic**

Alternative Assessment Handbook, Rubrics 9: Comparing and Contrasting; and 37: Writing Assignments

Answers

Biography *possible answer—He wanted to improve the Catholic Church, not cause it to split.*

It challenged the traditional structure and power of the church. But Luther encouraged people to live as the Bible, not priests or the pope, said.

To help people understand how God wanted them to live, Luther translated the Bible's New Testament into German, his native language. For the first time many Europeans who didn't know Greek or Latin could read the Bible for themselves. In addition to translating the Bible, Luther wrote pamphlets, essays, and songs about his ideas, many of them in German.

Many German nobles liked Luther's ideas. They particularly supported Luther's position that the clergy should not interfere with politics. Because these nobles allowed the people who lived on their lands to become Lutheran, the Lutheran Church soon became the dominant church in most of northern Germany.

Other Reformers

Even before Luther died in 1546, other reformers across Europe had begun to follow his example. William Tyndale (TIN-duhl), an English professor, thought that everyone should be able to read and interpret the Bible. This belief went against the teachings of the Catholic Church, which held that only the clergy could interpret the Bible. When Tyndale translated the Bible into English, Catholic authorities had him executed.

A more influential reformer than Tyndale was **John Calvin**. One of Calvin's main teachings was predestination, the idea that God knew who would be saved even before they were born. Nothing people did during their lives would change God's plan. However, Calvin also thought that it was important to live a good life and obey God's laws.

THE IMPACT TODAY

Many of the songs Luther wrote are still sung in Protestant churches around the world.

Primary Source

HISTORIC DOCUMENT

Luther's Ninety-Five Theses

In Wittenberg, nailing documents to the church door was a common way of sharing ideas with the community. The Ninety-Five Theses Martin Luther posted, however, created far more debate than other such documents. The items listed here, selected from Luther's list, argued against the sale of indulgences.

(5) The pope will not, and cannot, remit [forgive] other punishments than those which he has imposed by his own decree [ruling] or according to the canons [laws].

(21) Therefore, those preachers of indulgences err [make a mistake] who say that, by the pope's indulgence, a man may be exempt from all punishments, and be saved.

(30) Nobody is sure of having repented [been sorry] sincerely enough; much less can he be sure of having received perfect remission of sins.

Luther thought that only God—not the pope—could grant forgiveness.

(43) Christians should be taught that he who gives to the poor, or lends to a needy man, does better than buying indulgences.

(52) It is a vain and false thing to hope to be saved through indulgences, though the commissary [seller]—nay, the pope himself—was to pledge his own soul therefore.

Luther thought buying indulgences was useless.

—Martin Luther, *Ninety-Five Theses*

ANALYSIS SKILL ANALYZING PRIMARY SOURCES

Why did Martin Luther argue against the sale of indulgences?

Direct Teach

Primary Source

Luther's Ninety-Five Theses

Interpret Martin Luther's Ninety-Five Theses caused quite a controversy. Why might number 52 in particular have angered the Catholic Church? *possible answer—because its claim that the pope did not have the power to get anyone into heaven was a direct challenge to the pope's authority*

Linking to Today

Lutherans in the United States Today there are thousands of Lutheran churches in the United States. Because Lutheranism became the main form of Christianity in Scandinavia and northern Germany, when immigrants from these regions came to this country they brought their faith with them.

Info to Know

A Failed Plan The Catholic clergy of England did not want people to read William Tyndale's English translation of the New Testament. To keep the translation away from readers, the Bishop of London bought all the available copies and burned them. However, more copies appeared on the market. Money from the bishop's purchases had reached Tyndale, who used the cash to pay for more copies of his New Testament. The bishop's efforts to stamp out the English translation had backfired!

Critical Thinking: Supporting a Point of View

At Level

Writing Your Nine Theses

1. Guide students in a discussion of the importance of critical thinking and courage and how those qualities relate to reform.
2. Review with students Martin Luther's Ninety-Five Theses and their significance.
3. Work with students to write Nine Theses criticizing a modern-day topic. Examples might include popular culture (television, movies, music, fashion), a school policy, or local government.
4. Have students refer to the examples from Martin Luther's Ninety-Five Theses on this page as a model.
5. Have students write their Nine Theses in large print on legal-size sheets of paper and allow students to "nail" them to the bulletin board with thumbtacks. LS **Verbal/Linguistic**

Alternative Assessment Handbook, Rubric 41: Writing to Express

Answers

Analyzing Primary Sources *He thought they were useless and a waste of money because he believed that only God could grant forgiveness.*

Direct Teach

Main Idea

1 Reformers Call for Change

Reformers called for change in the Catholic Church, but some broke away to form new churches.

Identify What did Calvinist leaders do in Geneva in 1541? *They passed laws to make people live according to John Calvin's teachings.*

Draw Conclusions Why was the creation of the Church of England a significant event? *possible answers—It changed the religious authority of an entire country; it opened the door for other Protestant beliefs in England.*

Main Idea

2 The Catholic Reformation

The Catholic Reformation was an attempt to reform the church from within.

Explain What was the job of the Spanish Inquisition? *finding and punishing converted Muslims and Jews who were suspected of keeping their old beliefs; later punished Protestants, too*

Summarize What was the purpose of the Society of Jesus, or the Jesuits? *to serve the pope and the church, particularly by teaching Catholic ideas*

Did you know . . .

The Spanish Inquisition was so harsh in its pursuit of non-Catholics that it went beyond what the Roman Catholic Church leadership wanted. While the Vatican had some control over the Inquisition, it didn't fully approve of everything that was done.

Answers

Biography *He taught that they could make a profit and still be saved.*

Reading Check *He believed that all people could have a direct relationship with God, and that their beliefs should be based on the Bible.*

BIOGRAPHY

John Calvin

1509–1564

Calvin was probably the most influential figure of the Reformation after Luther. Through his writings and preaching, Calvin spread basic Reformation ideas such as the right of the common people to make church policy. Unlike many other religious leaders, Calvin didn't think that the pursuit of profits would keep businesspeople from being saved. This idea would eventually help lead to the growth of capitalism.

Making Inferences Why might Calvin's economic ideas have been popular with the people of Geneva?

In 1541 the people of Geneva, Switzerland, made Calvin their religious and political leader. He and his followers, called Calvinists, passed laws to make people live according to Calvin's teachings. Calvin hoped to make Geneva an example of a good Christian city.

In England the major figure of the Reformation was King Henry VIII. Henry asked the pope to officially end his marriage, but the pope refused. Furious, Henry decided that he was not going to obey the pope anymore. In 1534 he declared himself the head of a new church, called the Church of England, or Anglican Church.

Henry broke from the Catholic Church for personal reasons, not religious ones. As a result, he didn't change many church practices. The rituals and beliefs of the Anglican Church stayed very much like those of the Catholic Church. But Henry's actions opened the door for other Protestant beliefs to take hold in England.

THE IMPACT TODAY The Jesuit Order runs Catholic schools and universities all around the world.

READING CHECK **Summarizing** What were Martin Luther's main religious teachings?

The Catholic Reformation

As Protestantism spread in the later 1500s and 1600s, Catholic leaders responded. Their effort to stop the spread of Protestantism and to reform the Catholic Church from within was known as the **Catholic Reformation**, or the Counter-Reformation.

Catholic Culture in Spain

Even before the Catholic Reformation, Spain's rulers had been battling to drive non-Catholics from their lands. In 1492 the king and queen defeated the last Muslim forces in Spain. They then forced all Muslims and Jews remaining in the country to convert to Catholicism.

The Spanish monarchs also ordered the Spanish Inquisition to find and punish any Muslims or Jews who had converted to Catholicism but still secretly kept their old beliefs.

The Inquisition was ruthless in carrying out this duty. It later sought out Protestants. Once the Inquisition had punished all Muslim, Jewish, and Protestant believers, Spain's Catholic Church had no opposition.

Catholic Reforms

In other parts of Europe, Catholic leaders were responding to the criticisms of Protestants. Catholic reformers created new religious orders, or communities, in southern Europe. These orders wanted to win people back to the Catholic Church.

The first of the new orders was founded in 1534 by a Spanish noble, Saint Ignatius (ig-NAY-shuhs) of Loyola. This new order was the Society of Jesus, or the Jesuits. The **Jesuits** were a religious order created to serve the pope and the church. Ignatius had fought as a knight, and the Jesuits were trained to be as disciplined as soldiers in their religious duties. By teaching people about Catholic ideas, Jesuits hoped to turn people against Protestantism.

Critical Thinking: Identifying Points of View

At Level

A Dialogue between Calvin and Loyola

Research Required

Background: John Calvin and Ignatius of Loyola lived about the same time.

1. Have students use encyclopedias and other library resources to learn more about each religious leader.
2. Have students imagine that Calvin and Ignatius met at some point in their lives. Ask students to use what they have learned to write a brief dialogue between the two men.
3. Call on volunteers to read their dialogues to the class. LS **Verbal/Linguistic**

Alternative Assessment Handbook, Rubric 37: Writing Assignments

The Council of Trent

Many Catholic leaders felt more change was needed. They called together the Council of Trent, a meeting of church leaders in Trent, Italy. Clergy from across Europe came to discuss, debate, and eventually reform Catholic teachings.

The council restated the importance of the clergy in interpreting the Bible, but it created new rules that clergy had to follow. One rule ordered bishops to live in the areas they oversaw. The council also officially rejected the ideas of the Protestant leaders.

Some Catholic Reformation leaders wanted to punish Protestants as heretics. To lead this campaign, the pope created religious courts to punish any Protestants found in Italy. He also issued a list of books considered dangerous for people to read, including many by Protestant leaders. People reading books on this list could be excommunicated from the Catholic Church.

Catholic Missionaries

Many Catholics dedicated their lives to helping the church grow. They became missionaries, traveling to foreign countries to spread their faith. As this missionary activity greatly increased during the Catholic Reformation, Catholic teachings spread around the world.

Many of the new missionaries were Jesuits. Jesuit priests went to Africa, Asia, and America. Probably the most important missionary of the period was the Jesuit priest Saint Francis Xavier (ZAYV-yuhr). He brought Catholicism to parts of India and Japan in the mid-1500s.

Around the world Catholic missionaries baptized millions of people. Through their efforts the Catholic Reformation reached far beyond Europe.

READING CHECK **Finding Main Ideas** What were the goals of Catholic Reformation leaders?

The Council of Trent

Results of the Council of Trent

- The selling of indulgences is banned
- Bishops must live in the areas they oversee
- The ideas of Luther, Calvin, and other Reformation leaders are rejected

The Council of Trent met between 1545 and 1563 to clarify church teachings that had been criticized by Protestants. The council played a key role in revitalizing the Catholic Church in Europe.

Direct Teach

Main Idea

❷ The Catholic Reformation

The Catholic Reformation was an attempt to reform the church from within.

Recall What did Saint Francis Xavier accomplish in his missionary work? *He brought Catholicism to parts of India and Japan.*

Analyze Why was the Council of Trent important? *Catholic clergy met to debate and reform Catholic teachings. Decisions made at the council led to major reforms in the church.*

Draw Conclusions How much of an impact do you think Catholic missionary work had on the growth of the church during this period? *possible answer—important, because millions of people converted and Catholicism was spread around the world*

CRF: Biography Activity: Junípero Serra

Quick Facts Transparency: Results of the Council of Trent

Biography

Junipero Serra (1713-1784) Among the many missionaries who spread Catholicism in the Americas was a member of the Franciscan order who became known as Father Junipero Serra. After teaching in Mexico, Serra went to California, where in 1769 he founded Mission San Diego, the first mission in California. Serra went on to found eight more California missions.

Info to Know

Council of Trent In 1547, the council agreed to meet in Trent, but a fear of plague sent many of the attendees away. Later, Pope Paul IV lost interest in the meetings. Also, political unrest in Germany led to delays. Eventually, however, the Council of Trent got to work and approved changes that helped revitalize the Catholic Church.

Critical Thinking: Analyzing Information

At Level

A Reporter on the Scene

1. Ask students to imagine that they are newspaper reporters taking notes during a meeting of the Council of Trent. Emphasize that reporters should remain neutral about an issue.
2. For the meeting that the "reporters" will write about, two groups are debating the issues. One group wants the Catholic Church to change to win back Protestants; the other side does not want change and is defending the Catholic Church as it is.
3. Have students write newspaper articles about the meeting, using what they have learned about the Council of Trent.
4. Ask volunteers to read their articles aloud to the class. Discuss the articles' accuracy and neutrality with the class. **LS Verbal/Linguistic**

Alternative Assessment Handbook, Rubrics 11: Discussions; and 23: Newspapers

Answers

Reading Check *to stop the spread of Protestantism and to strengthen the Catholic Church*

Direct Teach

Main Idea

❸ The Political Impact

The political impact of the Reformation included religious wars and social change.

Identify Who were the Huguenots? *French Protestants*

Explain How did the war between French Catholics and Huguenots end? *with the Edict of Nantes of 1598, which granted religious freedom in most of France*

Analyze What was the result of the Treaty of Westphalia? *The Thirty Years' War ended, rulers could determine whether their countries would be Catholic or Protestant, and the states of Germany became independent of the Holy Roman Empire.*

Quick Facts Transparency: Some Results of the Reformation

Connect to English-Language Arts

Out the Window Events in Prague have popularized an unusual word. It is *defenestration,* which means "to throw someone or something out of a window." The word comes from the Latin word for "window," *fenestra.* In 1419 religious reformers in Bohemia tossed the entire Prague city council out the window. Then, when in 1618 two Catholics were thrown from a Prague window, the incident became known as the Second Defenestration of Prague. This event was the spark that started the Thirty Years' War.

Other People, Other Places

Government in America One year after the violent incident in Prague, self-government was beginning in the New World. In 1619 in Virginia, colonists gathered to form their first governing body, the House of Burgesses. Virginia still had a royal governor from England, but the establishment of this group was an important development for democracy in the American colonies.

Protestant Self-Government

This painting from the 1600s shows a Protestant church in France. Members of a congregation like this one would elect leaders and make their own rules. The rise of self-government was one result of the Reformation.

Some Results of the Reformation (Quick Facts)

- Religious conflicts spread across Europe
- Church leaders reform the Catholic Church
- Missionaries spread Catholicism around the world
- Northern Europe becomes largely Protestant
- Local Protestant churches practice self-government

The Political Impact

THE IMPACT TODAY The religious division in Europe created by the Reformation is still largely in place today. France, Spain, Portugal, and Italy are still largely Roman Catholic, while England, Germany, and other northern European countries are mostly Protestant.

The Reformation created division within Europe. In Spain most people were Catholic. In the northern countries most people were Protestant. The Holy Roman Empire was a patchwork of small kingdoms, some Catholic and some Protestant. These divisions often led to political conflicts.

Religious Wars

Although most people in France were Catholic, some became Protestants. French Protestants were called Huguenots (HYOO-guh-nahts). Tensions increased between the two religious groups after the French king, who was Catholic, banned all Protestant religions. In 1562 violence broke out.

The war between French Catholics and Huguenots continued off and on for decades. The conflict finally ended in 1598. In that year King Henry IV issued the Edict of Nantes (NAHNT), a law granting religious freedom in most of France. Protestants could worship anywhere except in Paris and a few other cities.

Religious wars caused even more destruction in the Holy Roman Empire. There, the king of Bohemia sparked a conflict when he forced everyone in his kingdom to become Catholic. In 1618 Protestants rose up in revolt. The rebellion spread through the Holy Roman Empire, starting what is known as the Thirty Years' War.

The Holy Roman Emperor sought help from other Catholic countries. The Protestants also sought allies. The Catholic king of France agreed to help them because he didn't like the Holy Roman Emperor.

Collaborative Learning

At Level

Issuing a Travel Warning

Prep Required

Materials: sample U.S. State Department travel warnings

1. First, lead a discussion about how war disrupts the lives of people where the fighting is happening. Point out that warfare can damage people on both sides of a conflict.
2. Locate samples of U.S. State Department travel warnings for students to examine. Circulate the printouts or pamphlets around the classroom.
3. Organize students into groups. Have each group create a travel warning for either France or the Holy Roman Empire based on information in the section. **LS Visual/Spatial**

Alternative Assessment Handbook, Rubrics 14: Group Activity; and 42: Writing to Inform

After 30 years of fighting, Europe's rulers worked out a peace agreement in 1648. This agreement, the Treaty of Westphalia, allowed rulers to determine whether their countries would be Catholic or Protestant. The treaty also made the states of Germany independent of the Holy Roman Empire.

Social Changes

The Reformation led not only to political changes but to social changes too. Before the Reformation, most Europeans had no voice in governing the Catholic Church. They simply followed the teachings of their priests and bishops. However, many Protestant churches didn't have priests, bishops, or other clergy. Instead each congregation, or community of worshippers, made its own rules and elected its own leaders. People began to think that their own ideas, not just the clergy's, were important.

Once people began to govern their own churches, they also wanted political power. In some places congregations ruled their towns, not just their churches. In the American colonies of New England, for instance, congregations met to decide how their towns would be run. These town meetings were an early form of self-government, in which people rule themselves.

As time passed, some congregations gained even more power. Their decisions came to affect more aspects of people's lives or to control events in larger areas. The power of these congregations didn't replace national governments, but national rulers began to share some power with local governments. The sharing of power between local governments and a strong central government is called **federalism**.

Once people began to think that their ideas were important, they began to raise questions. They wanted to know more about the world around them. In addition, many people refused to accept information based on someone else's authority. They didn't care if the person was an ancient writer or a religious leader. The desire to investigate led people to turn to science.

ACADEMIC VOCABULARY
agreement a decision reached by two or more people or groups

READING CHECK **Analyzing** How did Europe change after the Thirty Years' War?

SUMMARY AND PREVIEW In the 1500s Protestants challenged the Catholic Church. Catholic leaders adopted religious reforms to preserve the church's influence. The religious changes of the Reformation led to conflict and social changes. In the next chapter, you'll learn about the growth of science and the Scientific Revolution.

hmhsocialstudies.com
ANIMATED HISTORY
Spread of Protestantism, 1500s

Section 3 Assessment

hmhsocialstudies.com ONLINE QUIZ

Reviewing Ideas, Terms, and People

1. a. **Recall** What were three complaints people had about the Catholic Church in the early 1500s?
   b. **Contrast** How did **Martin Luther's** ideas about interpreting the Bible differ from Catholics' ideas?
2. a. **Define** What was the **Catholic Reformation**?
   b. **Analyze** What was the goal of the Spanish Inquisition?
3. a. **Identify** Where did the Thirty Years' War begin?
   b. **Sequence** How did the **Reformation** lead to the growth of **federalism**?

Critical Thinking

4. **Analyzing** Using your notes on the reformers and a diagram like the one below, explain how tensions between Protestants and Catholics led to conflict and violence in Europe.

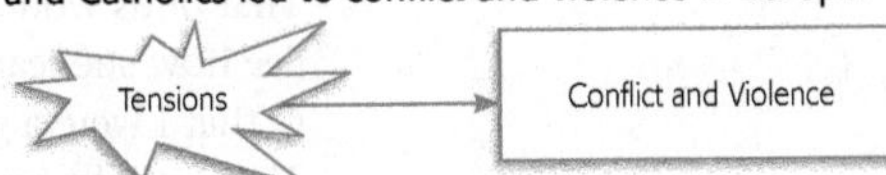

FOCUS ON WRITING

5. **Choosing Important Details** Write the main idea and supporting details of the section in your notebook. Then go over your notes to choose the most important or intriguing details to include on your book jacket. Put a check mark next to the details you think you'll include.

Direct Teach

Main Idea

3 The Political Impact

The political impact of the Reformation included religious wars and social change.

Identify Who led many Protestant churches? *the congregation, or church assembly*

Explain How was new religious freedom related to increasing political freedom? *As people gained more of a voice in their religion, they wanted more voice in their government too.*

Elaborate How did religious reform lead to increased interest in science? *As church authority was taken away from a small group of leaders, people began to value their own ideas more. This led them to question authority and investigate the world around them.*

Review & Assess

Close

Ask students how religion, politics, and social change were connected during this period.

Review

Online Quiz, Section 3

Assess

SE Section 3 Assessment
PASS: Section 3 Quiz
Alternative Assessment Handbook

Reteach/Classroom Intervention

Guided Reading Workbook, Section 3
Interactive Skills Tutor CD-ROM

Section 3 Assessment Answers

1. a. behavior of the clergy, wealth of the church, sale of indulgences
   b. Luther thought people could interpret the Bible for themselves. Catholics thought only clergy could interpret it.
2. a. internal effort to reform Catholic Church from within
   b. to find and punish Muslims, Jews, Protestants who kept their beliefs
3. a. Bohemia, in the Holy Roman Empire
   b. Congregations began to govern their own churches, then gained political power. In time, this power increased and national governments began to share power with local governments.
4. possible answers: tensions—Catholic-Protestant disagreements over freedom of worship, authority, who could interpret the Bible, who had a voice in church government; conflict and violence—Spanish Inquisition, war in France, Thirty Years' War; students should be able to explain how tensions led to conflict and violence.
5. Students should record information and add check marks.

Answers

Reading Check *The states of Germany became independent; rulers could determine their countries' religion, and the Holy Roman Empire ceased to exist.*

Literature in History

Romeo and Juliet

As You Read Tell students as they read to record three lines in which Romeo describes Juliet. Then have them rewrite the lines, substituting modern language for Shakespeare's phrases.

Meet the Writer

William Shakespeare Shakespeare grew up in Stratford, England. When he was 18, he married Anne Hathaway, who was 26. Shakespeare became both an actor and a playwright. However, we really know very little about his life. In fact, some scholars think that another person or persons wrote some or all of the plays that now bear Shakespeare's name.

Info to Know

Same Story, Many Forms The tragic tale of Romeo and Juliet first appeared in an Italian short story. An English poet then took a French translation of that story and wrote his own poem about the doomed couple. Shakespeare based his play on that poem. In turn, Shakespeare's play has inspired many other artistic creations. They include an overture by Russian composer Peter Tchaikovsky, a ballet, a stage musical called *West Side Story,* and a film adaptation of the musical. American composer Leonard Bernstein wrote the music for *West Side Story.*

Literature in History

from Romeo and Juliet

by William Shakespeare

About the Reading *Shakespeare's plays spotlight an enormous range of human experiences—including love, loss, and everything in between. Even though* Romeo and Juliet *ends in disaster, its message is a hopeful one. Its main characters, two teenaged members of warring families, meet at a party and fall instantly in love. In this scene, which takes place later that evening, a troubled Romeo sees Juliet on her balcony.*

AS YOU READ **Notice the words Romeo uses to describe Juliet's beauty.**

Rom. But soft, what light through yonder window breaks?
It is the east, and Juliet is the sun. ❶
Arise, fair sun, and kill the envious moon,
Who is already sick and pale with grief
That thou, her maid, art far more fair than she . . .
Two of the fairest stars in all the heaven,
Having some business, do entreat her eyes
To twinkle in their spheres till they return.
What if her eyes were there, they in her head?
The brightness of her cheek would shame those stars,
As daylight doth a lamp; her eyes in heaven
Would through the airy region stream so bright
That birds would sing and think it were not night.
See how she leans her cheek upon her hand!
O that I were a glove upon that hand,
That I might touch that cheek!
Jul. Ay me!
Rom. She speaks!
O, speak again, bright angel, for thou art
As glorious to this night, being o'er my head,
As is a winged messenger of heaven
Unto the white-upturned wond'ring eyes
Of mortals that fall back to gaze on him,

GUIDED READING

WORD HELP

envious jealous
entreat beg

❶ Romeo compares Juliet to the sun and claims that even the moon will be jealous of her beauty.

To what else does he compare her in this speech?

Differentiating Instruction

Special Needs Learners

Below Level

Have each student create a two-column chart on a piece of paper. In the left column, they should write the words or phrases from the excerpt that they do not understand. Then have them use resources such as an unabridged dictionary or the Internet to find the meanings of the words and phrases and write them down in the right column. Call on volunteers to read their lists aloud. Help with any pronunciation problems. **LS Verbal/Linguistic**

Struggling Readers

Below Level

After students have read the passage, call on volunteers to read portions of the scene aloud. Point out that different actors may interpret the speeches differently. Have more than one pair of students read the excerpts aloud. You may want them to move about the room and use dramatic gestures. After the class has heard and seen more than one performance, lead a discussion about how hearing the words spoken in different ways can help the audience understand the speeches. **LS Auditory/Musical**

Answers

1. *stars, an angel*

When he bestrides the lazy puffing clouds,
And sails upon the bosom of the air.
Jul. O Romeo, Romeo, wherefore art thou Romeo? ❷
Deny thy father and refuse thy name;
Or, if thou wilt not, be but sworn my love,
And I'll no longer be a Capulet.
Rom. [Aside.] Shall I hear more, or shall I speak at this?
Jul. 'Tis but thy name that is my enemy;
Thou art thyself, though not a Montague.
What's Montague? It is nor hand nor foot,
Nor arm nor face, nor any other part
Belonging to a man. O, be some other name!
What's in a name? That which we call a rose
By any other word would smell as sweet;
So Romeo would, were he not Romeo call'd,
Retain that dear perfection which he owes
Without that title. Romeo, doff thy name,
And for thy name, which is no part of thee,
Take all myself. ❸
Rom. I take thee at thy word.
Call me but love, and I'll be new baptized;
Henceforth I never will be Romeo.
Jul. What man art thou that thus bescreen'd in night
So stumblest on my counsel?
Rom. By a name
I know not how to tell thee who I am.
My name, dear saint, is hateful to myself,
Because it is an enemy to thee;
Had I it written, I would tear the word.
Jul. My ears have not yet drunk a hundred words
Of thy tongue's uttering, yet I know the sound.
Art thou not Romeo, and a Montague?
Rom. Neither, fair maid, if either thee dislike.

GUIDED READING

WORD HELP

bestrides mounts
wherefore why
doff remove
counsel secret thoughts

❷ Juliet is not asking where Romeo is. She is asking why he is Romeo, her family's enemy.

❸ Juliet says that she could be with Romeo if he were from a different family.

What does she ask him to do?

A painting of Romeo and Juliet from the 1800s

CONNECTING LITERATURE TO HISTORY

1. **Evaluating** Renaissance humanists explored human activities and focused on human actions. Why do you think the actions of Romeo and Juliet are still important to audiences today?
2. **Analyzing** Medieval writings often focused on religious topics. But the Renaissance humanists believed that people could write about many subjects other than religion. Based on this passage, what new topic did some humanist writers explore?

Literature in History

Reading Skills

Drawing Conclusions Ask students to recall some of their favorite fiction books. Write several of the titles for the students to see. Ask what these books' major themes were. Were any of them about love and loss? Ask students why these themes are popular in literature. *Answers will vary. Most people experience the loss of a loved one some time in their lives.*

Did you know . . .

Romeo and Juliet have been called "star-crossed lovers." This phrase comes from the ancient belief that the planets and stars control people's lives. Astrology is based on this idea.

Differentiating Instruction

Advanced/Gifted and Talented **Above Level**

1. Discuss with students how some of the themes in *Romeo and Juliet* have appeared in literature ever since people began recording their thoughts and feelings.
2. Call on students to suggest movies they have seen that contain the themes of love, loss, or how prejudice keeps people apart.
3. Then have them write a paragraph comparing the movie's themes with those of *Romeo and Juliet.* Students should discuss how the themes are similar and how they are different.
4. Have students share their paragraphs with the class.

LS Verbal/Linguistic

Answers

Guided Reading *She asks him to give up his name and take her in exchange for it.*

Connecting Literature to History
1. *They seem willing to overcome obstacles to be together.* **2.** *romantic love*

Social Studies Skills

Understanding Graphs

Materials: copies of various graphs from magazines and newspapers

Activity Graphs in the Media Before class, find at least one example of a bar graph, a line graph, and a circle graph in a magazine or newspaper. Display the graphs for the class to see. Have students identify each type of graph. Then ask students to describe the information shown in the graph legend. Have students identify what each color in the graph represents. Next, ask students to identify the labels in the graph and use them to explain what information the graph is showing. To test students' understanding, ask one to two questions about each graph that require students to interpret the information in the graph and to identify relationships or trends shown. LS **Visual/Spatial**

Alternative Assessment Handbook, Rubric 7: Charts

Interactive Skills Tutor CD-ROM, Lesson 6: Interpret Maps, Graphs, Charts, Visuals, and Political Cartoons

Answers

Practice and Apply the Skill **1.** *bar graph* **2.** *to show what percentages of the populations in France, Germany, and Spain were Catholic and Protestant in 2004* **3.** *about 85 percent* **4.** *Germany*

Social Studies Skills

Analysis | Critical Thinking | Economics | **Study**

Understanding Graphs

Understand the Skill

Graphs are drawings that display information in a clear, visual form. There are three main types of graphs. *Line graphs* show changes in something over time. *Bar graphs* compare quantities within a category. Some bar graphs may illustrate changes over time as well. *Circle graphs*, also called *pie graphs*, represent the parts that make up a whole of something. Each piece of the circle, or "pie," shows what proportion that part is of the whole.

Graphs let you see relationships more quickly and easily than tables or written explanations do. The ability to read and interpret graphs will help you to better understand and use statistical information in history.

Learn the Skill

Use the following guidelines to understand and interpret data presented in a graph.

1. Read the graph's title to identify the subject. Note the type of graph. This will give you clues about its purpose.
2. Study the graph's parts and read its labels. Note the subjects or categories that are graphed. Also note the units of measure. If the graph uses different colors, determine what each means.
3. Analyze the data. Note any increases or decreases in quantities. Look for trends or changes over time. Determine any other relationships in the data that is graphed.

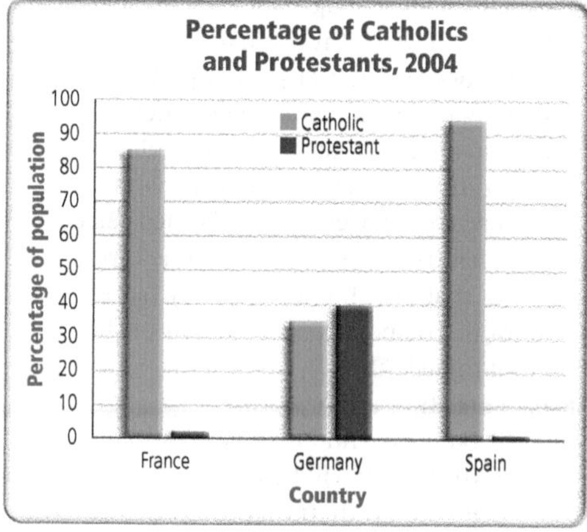

Practice and Apply the Skill

The Reformation brought changes to Christianity in Europe. The effects of these changes can still be seen there today. Use the graph to answer the following questions.

1. What kind of graph is this?
2. What is the purpose of the graph?
3. What percentage of the population in France is Catholic?
4. In what country are there more Protestants than Catholics?

Social Studies Skills Activity: Understanding Graphs — At Level

Graph Quiz

1. To extend the "Practice and Apply the Skill" activity, have each student create a five-question quiz based on the graph shown above. Assign students the type of questions to create such as multiple choice, short answer, or true-false.
2. Have each student create a separate answer key for his or her quiz.
3. Then have students exchange quizzes with a partner. Students should answer the quiz they receive and return it to its author for grading.
4. Then have each student write a few sentences summarizing the information shown in the graph above. Ask for volunteers to read their summaries to the class.
LS **Interpersonal, Verbal/Linguistic**

Alternative Assessment Handbook, Rubric 37: Writing Assignment

CHAPTER 19

Chapter Review

History's Impact

▶ **video series**

Review the video to answer the focus question:

Where did the Renaissance begin, and what impact did it have on the rest of Europe?

Visual Summary

Use the visual summary below to help you review the main ideas of the chapter.

QUICK FACTS

Italian trade wealth supported a rebirth of the arts and learning, inspiring great works of Renaissance genius.

The printing press played a key role in spreading the ideas of the Renaissance beyond Italy.

Reformers criticized practices of the Catholic Church and eventually broke away to form Protestant churches.

Reviewing Vocabulary, Terms, and People

Copy each sentence onto your own paper and fill in the blank with the word or name in the word pair that best completes the sentence.

1. The trader from Venice who traveled to China and met with Kublai Khan was ______________________ (Cosimo de Medici/Marco Polo).
2. A way of thinking and learning that stresses the importance of human abilities and actions is called ______________ (humanism/the Renaissance).
3. ______________ (Leonardo da Vinci/Michelangelo) was a painter, sculptor, inventor, engineer, and mapmaker.
4. ______________ (Albrecht Dürer/Johann Gutenberg) developed a printing press that used movable type.
5. Poet ______________ (Miguel de Cervantes/William Shakespeare) also wrote more than 30 plays.
6. The ______________ (Spanish Inquisition/Reformation) was a movement to reform the Catholic Church during the late Renaissance.
7. The priest who posted a list of 95 complaints about the church was ______________ (Pope Leo X/Martin Luther).
8. ______________ (John Calvin/Dante Alighieri) believed in predestination, as well as in the importance of living a good life and obeying God's laws.
9. The ______________ (congregation/Council of Trent) was a meeting held to discuss and reform practices of the Catholic Church.
10. Sharing power between local governments and a strong central government is called ______________ (federalism/indulgences).

Answers

Visual Summary

Review and Inquiry Use the visual summary to review the main ideas of the chapter. Ask students to identify the person in each panel. Then ask students to explain the significance of each main idea.

Quick Facts Transparency: The Renaissance and Reformation Visual Summary

Reviewing Vocabulary, Terms, and People

1. Marco Polo
2. humanism
3. Leonardo da Vinci
4. Johann Gutenberg
5. William Shakespeare
6. Reformation
7. Martin Luther
8. John Calvin
9. Council of Trent
10. federalism

Review & Assessment Resources

Review and Reinforce

SE Chapter 19 Chapter Review

CRF 19: Chapter Review Activity

Quick Facts Transparency: The Renaissance and Reformation Visual Summary

Spanish Chapter Summary Audio CD

Online Chapter Summaries in Six Languages

TOS Holt McDougal PuzzleView

Assess

SE Chapter 19 Standardized Test Practice

Progress Assessment: Chapter 19 Test

Alternative Assessment Handbook

TOS ExamView Assessment Suite, Chapter Test

Differentiating Instruction Modified Material CD-ROM: Chapter 19 Test, Form C

Online Assessment Program, in the Interactive Student Edition

Reteach/Intervene

Guided Reading Workbook, Chapter 19

Differentiating Instruction Teacher Management System: Lesson Plans for ELL, Special Education, and Advanced Learners

Differentiating Instruction Modified Material CD-ROM

Interactive Skills Tutor CD-ROM

Chapter Resources

Answers

Comprehension and Critical Thinking

11. a. Florence, Genoa, Milan, and Venice

b. There was a revival of interest in art and literature, especially ancient Greek and Roman works.

12. a. printing and universities

b. People shown in Northern European art were more realistic, with flaws; objects painted in great detail; subject matter included daily lives of ordinary people.

c. possible answers—electric light, telephone, automobile, computer

13. a. northern

b. Martin Luther and other reformers objected to corruption in the Catholic Church. Their followers broke off from the Catholic Church and founded new churches.

Reviewing Themes

14. Because of their location on the Mediterranean Sea, ships brought goods into the cities' harbors. From these cities, goods were shipped all across Europe.

15. possible answers—Wars broke out; the Holy Roman Empire ended; interest in self-government and science increased.

Using the Internet

16. Go to hmhsocialstudies.com to access a rubric for this activity.

Comprehension and Critical Thinking

SECTION 1 *(Pages 558–564)*

11. a. Identify What were the four main trade cities of Italy during the 1300s?

b. Analyze In what sense was the Renaissance a rebirth?

SECTION 2 *(Pages 565–568)*

12. a. Recall How did new ideas about education spread beyond Italy?

b. Contrast How was Northern European art different from Italian art?

c. Elaborate The printing press significantly changed the history of the world. In your opinion, what other inventions have had a major impact on world history?

SECTION 3 *(Pages 569–575)*

13. a. Recall Where did more Protestants live, in northern or southern Europe?

b. Draw Conclusions How did Protestant religions come into being?

Reviewing Themes

14. Geography How did their location help Italy's major port cities develop trade networks?

15. Society and Culture Give three non-religious effects of the Renaissance and Reformation.

Using the Internet 

16. Activity: Supporting a Point of View The Renaissance was a time of great advances in literature, the arts, science, and math. Individuals such as Marco Polo, William Shakespeare, Leonardo da Vinci, and Johann Gutenberg helped change people's view of the world. Through your online book, learn about the important people and events of the Renaissance. Then create a political cartoon about an event or person in the chapter. Pick the point of view of a supporter or critic and use your cartoon to explain how he or she would have viewed your topic.

hmhsocialstudies.com

Reading Skills 

Greek and Latin Word Roots *Answer the following questions about the Greek and Latin roots of words from this chapter.*

17. Based on the definition of *perspective,* what do you think the Latin root *spec-* means. *Hint:* Think about other words that use this root, such as *spectator* and *spectacles.*

a. to feel
b. to see
c. to hear
d. to understand

18. The prefix *per-* in perspective means "through." Based on this meaning, what do you think the word *permeate* means?

a. to spread through
b. to dissolve in
c. to disappear from
d. to climb over

Social Studies Skills

19. Understanding Graphs What kind of graph (line, bar, or circle) would you create to show how the number of Protestants in the Netherlands rose and fell during the 1600s? Explain your answer.

Focus on Writing

20. A Book Jacket Now that you have all the main ideas and supporting details, it is time to create your book jacket. Remember to put the title on the front cover. Illustrate the front page with a picture that you feel best illustrates the Renaissance and Reformation. On the back cover, list the main ideas and supporting details that you have already identified. What do you think will attract people to your book?

Reading Skills

17. b

18. a

Social Studies Skills

19. A line graph would best show how the number changed over time.

Focus on Writing

20. Rubric Students' book jackets should:

- include a title.
- include a relevant illustration.
- list main ideas and supporting details on the back.

CRF 19: Focus on Writing Activity: A Book Jacket.

CHAPTER 19

Standardized Test Practice

DIRECTIONS: Read each question, and write the letter of the best response. Use the primary source below to answer question 1.

> "I realize that women have accomplished many good things and that even if evil women have done evil, … the benefits accrued [gained] … because of good women—particularly the wise and literary ones … outweigh the evil. Therefore, I am amazed by the opinion of some men who claim they do not want their daughters, wives, or kinswomen [female relatives] to be educated because their mores [morals] will be ruined as a result."
>
> —Christine de Pizan, from the *Book of the City of Ladies*, 1405

1 The content of this passage suggests that the person who wrote it was

A a rich Italian merchant.
B Niccolo Machiavelli.
C a supporter of humanism.
D Marco Polo.

2 Which person's contribution was *most* important in spreading the ideas of the Renaissance beyond Italy?

A Cosimo de' Medici
B Johann Gutenberg
C Leonardo da Vinci
D Dante Alighieri

3 In general, the artists and architects of the Renaissance were financially supported by

A rich families and church leaders.
B large European universities.
C the most powerful nations in Europe.
D the printing industry.

4 Reformers found fault with all the following practices of the Catholic Church *except*

A its sale of indulgences.
B its support of monotheism.
C the clergy's involvement in corruption.
D the church owning vast wealth.

5 Which person is generally credited with starting the Reformation?

A Desiderius Erasmus
B Martin Luther
C John Calvin
D King Henry VIII

Connecting with Past Learning

6 Italy in the Renaissance was not a unified country, but several small independent states. Which of the following cultures had a similar structure?

A ancient Greece during the Golden Age
B the Fertile Crescent during the Stone Age
C the New Kingdom of ancient Egypt
D Rome during the Pax Romana

7 In many places in Europe in the 1500s, Protestants were persecuted for their beliefs. Other people that you have studied who were persecuted for what they believed were

A Egyptians under Alexander the Great.
B Hindus in India.
C Christians in the early Roman Empire.
D Buddhists in China.

Intervention Resources

Reproducible

- Guided Reading Workbook, Chapter 19
- Differentiating Instruction Teacher Management System: Lesson Plans for ELL, Special Education, and Advanced Learners, Chapter 19

Technology

- Quick Facts Transparency: The Renaissance and Reformation Visual Summary
- Modified Material for Struggling Students CD-ROM
- Interactive Skills Tutor CD-ROM

Tips for Test Taking

Find the Main Idea The main goal of a reading comprehension section is to test a student's understanding of a reading passage. Advise students to keep these suggestions in mind when they read a selection on a test:

- Read the passage once to get a general overview of the topic.
- If you don't understand the passage at first, keep reading. Try to find the main idea.
- Then, read the questions so that you'll know what information to look for when you re-read the passage.

Answers

Standardized Test Practice

1. C
Break Down the Question The passage was written by someone interested in education, as were the supporters of humanism. A rich Italian merchant may or may not have agreed. Moreover, the names in both B and D are men. The passage was written by Christine de Pizan, whose name indicates that she was a woman.

2. B
Break Down the Question Although all the people listed contributed to the Renaissance, Gutenberg's development of the printing press helped spread the ideas.

3. A
Break Down the Question This question requires students to recall factual information. Refer students who miss the question to the information on Florence in Section 1.

4. B
Break Down the Question Point out to students that the word *except* means that they need to identify which of the answers is not something for which Reformers faulted the Catholic Church.

5. B
Break Down the Question This question requires students to recall factual information. Refer students who missed it to Section 3.

6. A
Break Down the Question This question connects to information in Chapter 8.

7. C
Break Down the Question This question requires students to recall information covered in Chapter 11, Section 2.

Preteach

Bellringer

Motivate Now that students have read about Europe during the Middle Ages, they can use what they learned to write a historical narrative. Have students decide who will be the narrator of their story. Next, have students choose the event or incident their narrator will tell about. Finally, have them choose a setting in Europe during the Middle Ages. Tell students that these steps are similar to how authors write books and screenwriters create scripts for movies.

Direct Teach

Finding Historical Information

Perform Research Tell students that in addition to what they learned in their textbooks about the Middle Ages, they can perform research at home, the media center, or the local library to find information in books, in encyclopedias, and on the internet. Explain to students that as they perform research, they should take notes as well. Notes might include important dates, people's names, or interesting facts. Point out that they can use the notes to help them write their historical narrative and to make it more interesting.

A Historical Narrative

Assignment

A narrative is a story that may be true or fictional. Write a fictional historical narrative set in Europe during the Middle Ages.

What was life like in Europe in the Middle Ages? Where did people live? How did they spend their days? You can learn more about history by researching and writing a narrative that is set in a different time and place.

1. Prewrite

Planning Character and Setting

You should write your narrative from the point of view of someone who lived during that time.

- **The Narrator** Is the person telling your story a knight, a peasant, or a priest? A lady or a lady's maid?
- **The Event** What event or incident will your narrator experience? A jousting tournament? A Viking invasion? A religious pilgrimage? A famine or fire in the village?
- **The Setting** How will the time, between 800 and 1200 AD, and place, somewhere in Europe, affect this person? What will he or she want out of life or would fear or admire?

TIP **Adding Details** Help your audience get a feel for the setting by using sensory details. As you think about everyday life in the Middle Ages, make note of details that describe how things might have looked, felt, sounded, smelled, or tasted.

Developing a Plot

Select an event or incident, and then ask yourself these questions.

- How would the event have unfolded? In other words, what would have happened first, second, third, and so on?
- What problem might face your narrator during this event? How could your narrator solve this problem?

2. Write

Have your narrator tell what happened in the first person, using *I, me, we, us,* etc. For example, *I woke up early. We stopped by a stream.* Then use the framework below to help you write your first draft.

A Writer's Framework

Introduction	Body	Conclusion
■ Grab the reader's attention. ■ Offer needed background information about the place and the people involved in the event.	■ Start with the beginning of the incident or event, and present the actions in the order they happen. ■ Build to a suspenseful moment when the outcome is uncertain.	■ Show how the narrator solves his or her problem. ■ Explain how the narrator changes or how his or her life changes.

Differentiating Instruction

Special Needs Learners

Below Level

Standard English Mastery

1. Provide or assign students who choose to perform research with one appropriate source. Otherwise, they may be overwhelmed with all the options.
2. A book in the classroom might be an ideal source for those students whose research needs monitoring. LS **Verbal/Linguistic**

Advanced/Gifted and Talented

Above Level

1. Encourage students to perform research using at least three additional sources.
2. Have students rank the reliability of the sources and summarize any differences among them. LS **Verbal/Linguistic**

3. Evaluate and Revise

Evaluating

Read through the first draft of your narrative. Then use the guidelines below to consider its content and organization.

Evaluation Questions for a Fictional Historical Narrative

■ Do you grab the reader's attention at the very beginning? ■ Do you include background information to explain the time, place, and people involved in the event? ■ Do you use first-person pronouns to show that your narrator is the central person in the event?	■ Do you tell the actions in the order they happen or happened? ■ Do you show how the narrator solves the problem or how it is solved for him or her? ■ Do you explain how the narrator changes as a result of the event?

Revising

Before you share your narrative with others, have a classmate read it and retell the narrative to you. Add details at any point where his or her retelling seems uncertain or dull. Add transitions to show how events are connected in time.

4. Proofread and Publish

Proofreading

Weak word choice can drain the life from your narrative. Vague nouns and adjectives do little to spark the interest and imagination of readers. In contrast, precise words make your story come alive. They tell readers exactly what the characters and setting are like.

- **Vague Nouns or Pronouns** Words like *man* and *it* tell your readers little. Replace them with precise words, like *peasant* or *cottage*.
- **Vague adjectives** Would you prefer an experience that is *nice* or *fun*, or one that is *thrilling, exhilarating, or stirring?*

Publishing

You can publish your historical narrative by reading it aloud in class or by posting it on a class authors' wall. You may also publish all the narratives in your class as an Internet page or in a photocopied literary magazine.

Practice and Apply

Use the steps and strategies outlined in this workshop to write your historical narrative.

TIP Describing Actions We communicate not only with our words but also with our actions. By describing specific actions—movements, gestures, and facial expressions—you can make people in your narrative live and breathe.

TIP Connecting Events To improve your narrative, use transitions such as *next, later,* and *finally* to show the order in which the events and actions happen or happened.

Reteach

Proofreading

Use Technology Word processing skills will allow students to revise their sentence structure very easily. Tell students that using the grammar check tool can save them time because as they read the explanations they will learn to avoid those errors in the future and they will spend less time rewriting their sentences.

Teaching Tip

Personal Writing Style Tell students that grammar checkers do not appreciate creative sentence structure. Students should resist using these structures, such as fragments, which technically are grammatically incorrect. Students will see this creative style in their literature reading, but they should avoid breaking grammar rules in their own writing.

Practice & Apply

Rubric

Students' historical narratives should

- introduce the event or incident.
- include background information about the place and people in the event.
- describe how the narrator is connected.
- follow a chronological order
- include people's reactions to the event, and how their reactions affected history.
- use correct grammar, punctuation, spelling, and capitalization.

English-Language Learners

At Level

Standard English Mastery

1. Students may be far more comfortable performing research using sources written in their first language. When their research is complete, students will need to translate the notes use into English.
2. Remind students to use a dictionary to find the correct meaning of a word they translate so it conveys the same meaning as in their native language.
3. Tell students who have difficulties writing in English to first write their entire historical narrative in their native language and then translate it into English. **LS Verbal/Linguistic**

Preteach

Bellringer

Motivate Now that students have read about Europe during the Middle Ages, they can use what they learned to write a historical narrative. Have students decide who will be the narrator of their story. Next, have students choose the event or incident their narrator will tell about. Finally, have them choose a setting in Europe during the Middle Ages. Tell students that these steps are similar to how authors write books and screenwriters create scripts for movies.

Direct Teach

Finding Historical Information

Perform Research Tell students that in addition to what they learned in their textbooks about the Middle Ages, they can perform research at home, the media center, or the local library to find information in books, in encyclopedias, and on the internet. Explain to students that as they perform research, they should take notes as well. Notes might include important dates, people's names, or interesting facts. Point out that they can use the notes to help them write their historical narrative and to make it more interesting.

Writing Workshop

21st Century

A Historical Narrative

Assignment

A narrative is a story that may be true or fictional. Write a fictional historical narrative set in Europe during the Middle Ages.

What was life like in Europe in the Middle Ages? Where did people live? How did they spend their days? You can learn more about history by researching and writing a narrative that is set in a different time and place.

1. Prewrite

Planning Character and Setting

You should write your narrative from the point of view of someone who lived during that time.

- **The Narrator** Is the person telling your story a knight, a peasant, or a priest? A lady or a lady's maid?
- **The Event** What event or incident will your narrator experience? A jousting tournament? A Viking invasion? A religious pilgrimage? A famine or fire in the village?
- **The Setting** How will the time, between 800 and 1200 AD, and place, somewhere in Europe, affect this person? What will he or she want out of life or would fear or admire?

TIP **Adding Details** Help your audience get a feel for the setting by using sensory details. As you think about everyday life in the Middle Ages, make note of details that describe how things might have looked, felt, sounded, smelled, or tasted.

Developing a Plot

Select an event or incident, and then ask yourself these questions.

- How would the event have unfolded? In other words, what would have happened first, second, third, and so on?
- What problem might face your narrator during this event? How could your narrator solve this problem?

2. Write

Have your narrator tell what happened in the first person, using *I, me, we, us,* etc. For example, *I woke up early. We stopped by a stream.* Then use the framework below to help you write your first draft.

A Writer's Framework

Introduction	Body	Conclusion
■ Grab the reader's attention. ■ Offer needed background information about the place and the people involved in the event.	■ Start with the beginning of the incident or event, and present the actions in the order they happen. ■ Build to a suspenseful moment when the outcome is uncertain.	■ Show how the narrator solves his or her problem. ■ Explain how the narrator changes or how his or her life changes.

Differentiating Instruction

Special Needs Learners

Below Level

Standard English Mastery

1. Provide or assign students who choose to perform research with one appropriate source. Otherwise, they may be overwhelmed with all the options.
2. A book in the classroom might be an ideal source for those students whose research needs monitoring. LS **Verbal/Linguistic**

Advanced/Gifted and Talented

Above Level

1. Encourage students to perform research using at least three additional sources.
2. Have students rank the reliability of the sources and summarize any differences among them. LS **Verbal/Linguistic**

3. Evaluate and Revise

Evaluating

Read through the first draft of your narrative. Then use the guidelines below to consider its content and organization.

Evaluation Questions for a Fictional Historical Narrative

- Do you grab the reader's attention at the very beginning?
- Do you include background information to explain the time, place, and people involved in the event?
- Do you use first-person pronouns to show that your narrator is the central person in the event?
- Do you tell the actions in the order they happen or happened?
- Do you show how the narrator solves the problem or how it is solved for him or her?
- Do you explain how the narrator changes as a result of the event?

Revising

Before you share your narrative with others, have a classmate read it and retell the narrative to you. Add details at any point where his or her retelling seems uncertain or dull. Add transitions to show how events are connected in time.

4. Proofread and Publish

Proofreading

Weak word choice can drain the life from your narrative. Vague nouns and adjectives do little to spark the interest and imagination of readers. In contrast, precise words make your story come alive. They tell readers exactly what the characters and setting are like.

- **Vague Nouns or Pronouns** Words like *man* and *it* tell your readers little. Replace them with precise words, like *peasant* or *cottage*.
- **Vague adjectives** Would you prefer an experience that is *nice* or *fun*, or one that is *thrilling, exhilarating, or stirring*?

Publishing

You can publish your historical narrative by reading it aloud in class or by posting it on a class authors' wall. You may also publish all the narratives in your class as an Internet page or in a photocopied literary magazine.

Practice and Apply

Use the steps and strategies outlined in this workshop to write your historical narrative.

TIP **Describing Actions** We communicate not only with our words but also with our actions. By describing specific actions—movements, gestures, and facial expressions—you can make people in your narrative live and breathe.

TIP **Connecting Events** To improve your narrative, use transitions such as *next, later,* and *finally* to show the order in which the events and actions happen or happened.

Reteach

Proofreading

Use Technology Word processing skills will allow students to revise their sentence structure very easily. Tell students that using the grammar check tool can save them time because as they read the explanations they will learn to avoid those errors in the future and they will spend less time rewriting their sentences.

Teaching Tip

Personal Writing Style Tell students that grammar checkers do not appreciate creative sentence structure. Students should resist using these structures, such as fragments, which technically are grammatically incorrect. Students will see this creative style in their literature reading, but they should avoid breaking grammar rules in their own writing.

Practice & Apply

Rubric

Students' historical narratives should

- introduce the event or incident.
- include background information about the place and people in the event.
- describe how the narrator is connected.
- follow a chronological order
- include people's reactions to the event, and how their reactions affected history.
- use correct grammar, punctuation, spelling, and capitalization.

English-Language Learners

At Level

Standard English Mastery

1. Students may be far more comfortable performing research using sources written in their first language. When their research is complete, students will need to translate the notes use into English.
2. Remind students to use a dictionary to find the correct meaning of a word they translate so it conveys the same meaning as in their native language.
3. Tell students who have difficulties writing in English to first write their entire historical narrative in their native language and then translate it into English. LS **Verbal/Linguistic**

Chapter 20 Planning Guide

Science and Exploration

Overview	Instructional Resources	
CHAPTER 20 **Essential Question:** How did new ideas lead to exploration and cultural and economic changes? **Instructional Resources for Chapter 20 can be found online via the State Specific Resources link in the Teacher One Stop.**	TOS **Differentiated Instruction Teacher Management System:** • Instructional Benchmarking Guides • Lesson Plans for Differentiated Instruction **Guided Reading Workbook** **Chapter Resource File:** • Chapter Review Activity • Focus on Speaking Activity: An Informative Report • Social Studies Skills Activity: Analyzing Tables	TOS **Calendar Planner** **Power Presentations** **Primary Source Library CD-ROM for World History** **Interactive Skills Tutor CD-ROM**
Section 1: The Scientific Revolution **The Big Idea:** Europeans developed a new way of gaining knowledge, leading to a Scientific Revolution that changed the way people thought about the world.	TOS **Differentiated Instruction Teacher Management System:** Section 1 Lesson Plan **Guided Reading Workbook:** Section 1 **Chapter Resource File:** • Vocabulary Builder Activity, Section 1 • Biography Activity: Galileo Galilei • Primary Source Activity: Galileo's Testimony Before the Catholic Church	**Daily Bellringer Transparency:** Section 1
Section 2: Great Voyages of Discovery **The Big Idea:** European explorers made discoveries that brought knowledge, wealth, and influence to their countries.	TOS **Differentiated Instruction Teacher Management System:** Section 2 Lesson Plan **Guided Reading Workbook:** Section 2 **Chapter Resource File:** • Vocabulary Builder Activity, Section 2 • Biography Activity: Ferdinand Magellan • Primary Source Activity: *From the Report of the Expedition* by Christopher Columbus	**Daily Bellringer Transparency:** Section 2 **Map Transparency:** European Exploration, 1487–1580
Section 3: New Systems of Trade **The Big Idea:** Exchanges between the Old World and the New World influenced the development of new economic systems: mercantilism and capitalism.	TOS **Differentiated Instruction Teacher Management System:** Section 3 Lesson Plan **Guided Reading Workbook:** Section 3 **Chapter Resource File:** • Vocabulary Builder Activity, Section 3	**Daily Bellringer Transparency:** Section 3 **Quick Facts Transparency:** The Columbian Exchange **Quick Facts Transparency:** Supply and Demand
Section 4: Native American Cultures **The Big Idea:** Many diverse Native American cultures developed across the different geographic regions of North America.	TOS **Differentiated Instruction Teacher Management System:** Section 4 Lesson Plan **Guided Reading Workbook:** Section 4 **Chapter Resource File:** • Vocabulary Builder Activity, Section 4	**Daily Bellringer Transparency:** Section 4 **Map Transparency:** Native American Culture Areas

Chart Key:

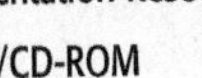
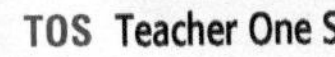

SE Student Edition — Presentation Resource — MP3 Audio
TOS Teacher One Stop — DVD/CD-ROM — HISTORY™
Printable Resource

Program Resources available on TOS and @  hmhsocialstudies.com

Review, Assessment, Intervention

Quick Facts Transparency: Science and Exploration Visual Summary

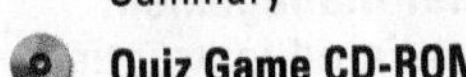
Quiz Game CD-ROM

Progress Assessment Support System (PASS): Chapter Test

TOS **ExamView® Assessment Suite (English/Spanish)**

PASS: Section 1 Quiz

Alternative Assessment Handbook

PASS: Section 2 Quiz

Alternative Assessment Handbook

PASS: Section 3 Quiz

Alternative Assessment Handbook

PASS: Section 4 Quiz

Alternative Assessment Handbook

Supporting Resources

- Multimedia Classroom Global History Series
- Global History Teacher's Guide

Maps Globes Graphs Level F

- Student Workbook
- Teacher's Guide

Social Studies Trade Library Collections

- Premier Secondary World History Trade Collection
- Modern World History Trade Collection

History's Impact

World History Video Program

- **The Columbian Exchange**

For more information or to purchase go to  hmhsocialstudies.com

Power Presentations

Power Presentations are visual presentations of each chapter's main ideas. Presentations can be customized by including Quick Facts charts, images from the text, and video clips.

CHAPTER 20 PLANNING GUIDE

Differentiating Instruction

How do I address the needs of varied learners?

The Target Resource acts as your primary strategy for differentiated instruction.

ENGLISH-LANGUAGE LEARNERS & STRUGGLING READERS

Interactive Skills Tutor CD-ROM

The Interactive Skills Tutor CD-ROM contains lessons that provide additional practice for 20 different critical thinking skills.

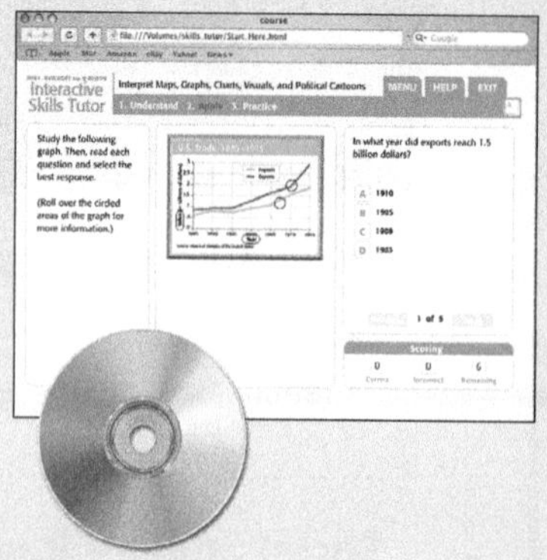

Additional Resources

Differentiated Instruction Teacher Management System: Lesson Plans for Differentiated Instruction

Chapter Resource File:

- Vocabulary Builder Activities
- Social Studies Skills Activity: Analyzing Tables

Quick Facts Transparencies:

- The Columbian Exchange
- Supply and Demand
- Science and Exploration Visual Summary

Spanish/English Guided Reading Workbook

SPECIAL NEEDS LEARNERS

Differentiated Instruction Modified Worksheets and Tests

- Vocabulary Flash Cards
- Vocabulary Builder Activities
- Chapter Test

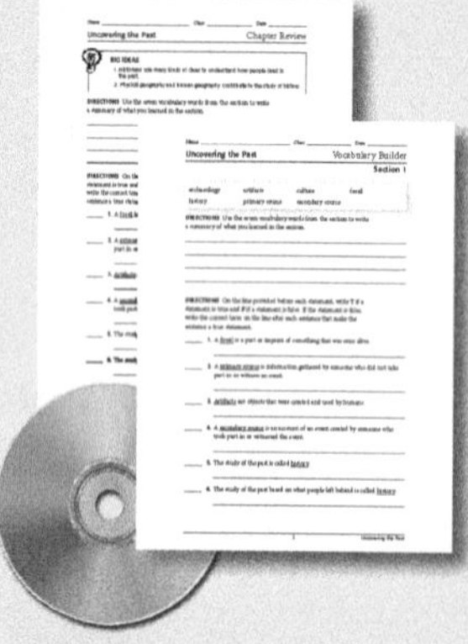

Additional Resources

Differentiated Instruction Teacher Management System: Lesson Plans for Differentiated Instruction

Guided Reading Workbook

Chapter Resource File: Social Studies Skills Activity: Analyzing Tables

Interactive Skills Tutor CD-ROM

ADVANCED/GIFTED-AND-TALENTED STUDENTS

Primary Source Library CD-ROM for World History

The Library contains longer versions of quotations in the text, extra sources, and images. Included are point-of-view articles, journals, diaries, historical fiction, and political documents.

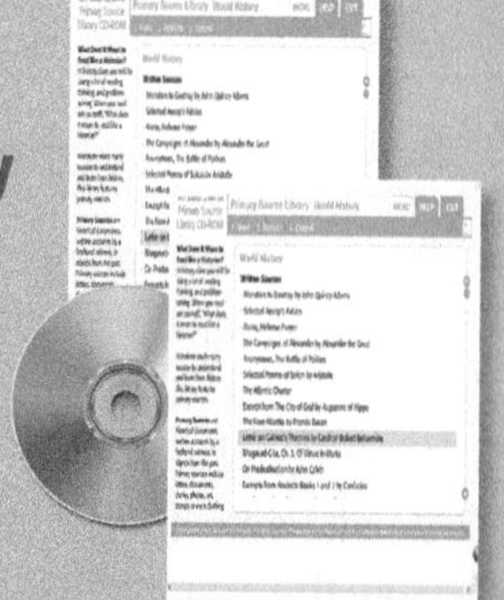

Additional Resources

Differentiated Instruction Teacher Management System: Lesson Plans for Differentiated Instruction

Chapter Resource File:

- Focus on Writing Activity: An Informative Report

Document-Based Questions Activities

Differentiated Activities in the Teacher's Edition

- Bringing Copernicus, Kepler, Galileo, and Newton to Life, p. 590

Teacher One Stop™

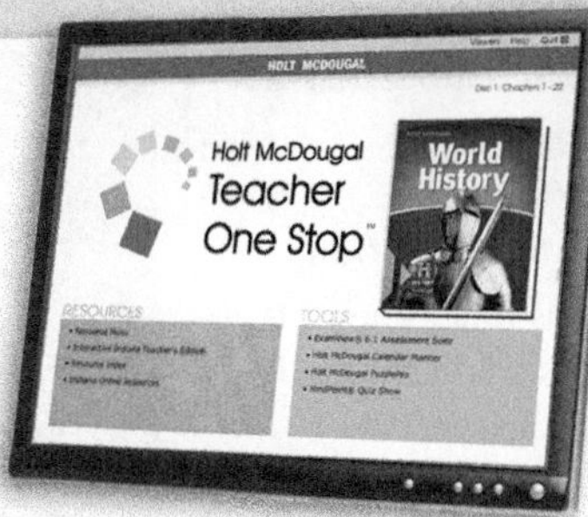

How can I manage the lesson plans and support materials for differentiated instruction?

With the Teacher One Stop, you can easily organize and print lesson plans, planning guides, and instructional materials for all learners. The Teacher One Stop includes the following materials to help you differentiate instruction:

- **Interactive Teacher's Edition**
- **Calendar Planner and pacing guides**
- **Editable lesson plans**
- **All reproducible ancillaries in Adobe Acrobat (PDF) format**
- **ExamView Assessment Suite (English & Spanish)**
- **Transparency and video previews**

Differentiated Activities in the Teacher's Edition

- Old World/New World Menus, p. 598
- Describing Home, p. 602
- Mapping Native American Culture Groups, p. 605

Interactive Student Edition

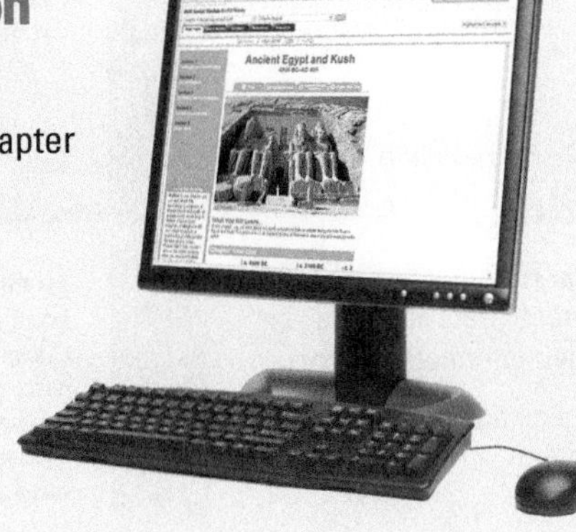

Complete online student edition with interactive multimedia support for chapter content assessment and reporting

- Interactive Maps and Notebook
- Graphic Organizers
- Standardized Test Prep
- Online Homework Practice and Research Activities
- Current Events
- Chapter-based Internet Activities
- Animated History Activities
- and more!

Differentiated Activities in the Teacher's Edition

- Writing Biographies of Greek Thinkers, p. 589
- Explorer Role Playing, p. 594
- Anasazi Presentations, p. 603
- Joining the Iroquois League, p. 606

• Chapter Preview •

Essential Question

Introduce the Essential Question

- Point out that at this time, scientists, artists, and scholars were constantly producing innovations.
- Explain that inventions, theories, and voyages of discovery resulted from these innovations.
- Discuss how the relationship between the Church and society changed and how economic systems were altered by colonies and new economic ideas.

Focus on Writing

The **Chapter Resource File** provides a Focus on Speaking worksheet to help students organize and write their informative report.

CRF: Focus on Speaking Activity: An Informative Report

Key to Differentiating Instruction

Below Level

Basic-level activities designed for all students encountering new material

At Level

Intermediate-level activities designed for average students

Above Level

Challenging activities designed for honors and gifted and talented students

Standard English Mastery

Activities designed to improve standard English usage

LS Learning Styles

CHAPTER 20 1400–1700

Science and Exploration

Essential Question How did new ideas lead to exploration and cultural and economic changes?

South Carolina Performance Standards

6-4.4 Explain the contributions, features, and rise and fall of the North American ancestors of the numerous Native American tribes, including the Adena, Hopewell, Pueblo, and Mississippian cultures; **6-6.4** Compare the economic, political, and religious incentives of the various European countries to explore and settle new lands; **6-6.5** Identify the origin and destinations of the voyages of major European explorers; **6-6.6** Explain the effects of the exchange of plants, animals, diseases, and technology throughout Europe, Asia, Africa, and the Americas (known as the Columbian Exchange).

Literacy Skills for Social Studies

- Explain why trade occurs and how historical patterns of trade have contributed to global interdependence.
- Examine the costs and benefits of economic choices made by a particular society and explain how those choices affect overall economic well-being.

Partnership for the 21st Century Skills

Demonstrate the ability and willingness to make compromises to accomplish a common team goal.

Focus on Speaking

An Informative Report A teacher at an elementary school has asked you to create an informative oral report for fifth graders about changes in Europe, Africa, Asia, and the Americas during the Scientific Revolution and the Age of Exploration. As you read this chapter, look for the important people and events that you will discuss. After you have finished the chapter, you will prepare a short speech and create a simple visual aid to refer to during your presentation.

Chapter Events

1416 Henry the Navigator sets up his school of navigation.

1492 Columbus arrives in the Americas.

1400

World Events

1431 Joan of Arc is burned at the stake.

Introduce the Chapter

At Level

Is Seeing Always Believing?

1. Call on a volunteer to describe where the sun is in the morning, at noon, and in the evening. *in the east, close to overhead, in the west*
2. Ask another student how he or she knows that the sun is not circling Earth. Point out that if one depended on observation alone, this would be a logical conclusion.
3. Tell students that, although during the Scientific Revolution scientists relied on observation, they also went beyond what they could see to prove their ideas about the natural world. Some of these scientists even risked their lives to defend their ideas.
4. Return to the original question by pointing out that it took a leap of imagination to figure out that Earth revolves around the sun, since our senses tell us otherwise.

LS Verbal/Linguistic, Logical/Mathematical

This photo shows a powerful telescope that astronomers use to study the skies.

1519 Magellan sails around the tip of South America.

1530s Copernicus develops his theory of the sun-centered solar system.

1609 Galileo uses his telescope to study planets.

1687 Sir Isaac Newton publishes *Principia Mathematica.*

1600

1700

c. 1500 Askia the Great rules Songhai.

1649 Shah Jahan finishes building the Taj Mahal.

1690 John Locke argues that people have certain natural rights.

• Chapter Preview •

Explore the Picture

Telescopes Students will learn that scientists developed telescopes for learning about the universe. Telescopes have changed quite a bit since the 1600s—in both size and function. Traditional telescopes depend on gathering visible light for their data. A telescope of this type is in the picture. It is at Mount Palomar, California. Now, however, there are also telescopes that gather invisible infrared light, radio waves, and x-rays.

Analyzing Visuals What are the curved lines in the sky? *tracks made by stars as Earth revolves, as revealed in a long-exposure photograph*

Explore the Time Line

1. When did Columbus arrive in the Americas? *1492*
2. Approximately how much time passed between Columbus's arrival in the Americas and Magellan's voyage around the southern tip of South America? *about 27 years*
3. What theory did Copernicus develop in the 1530s? *his theory of a sun-centered solar system*
4. Is there a possibility that Sir Isaac Newton and John Locke knew each other? How can you tell? *yes; they were publishing their ideas at about the same time*

Other People, Other Places

Astronomy in Mughal India The Taj Mahal was built while the Mughals ruled northern India. Some Mughal rulers also built observatories for watching the skies. One ruler who was particularly interested in astronomy built five such observatories. He also built an enormous sundial that is accurate to within two seconds. Another ruler had instruments for studying the heavens built right into the walls of his capital city.

Reading Social Studies

Understanding Themes

Introduce the themes of this chapter by explaining that advances in science often lead to changes in society. Ask for examples of recent advances in technology, such as cell phones and the Internet, which have changed society. Then discuss ways in which these advances have affected how people do business.

Vocabulary Clues

Focus on Reading Give students one or two minutes to make a list of words and phrases they know from their interests and activities but which might be unfamiliar to others. Provide examples, such as balk (from baseball), forte (from music), or fettuccine. When time is up, ask volunteers to give examples of words from their lists. Write the words on the board. As a class, brainstorm sentences which give context clues for each word, as a direct definition, restatement, and comparison or contrast.

Reading Social Studies

Economics | Geography | Politics | Religion | Society and Culture | Science and Technology

Focus on Themes In this chapter you will read about how a new way of looking at science was developed, as well as how the Scientific Revolution led to profound changes in **society and culture**. You will also learn about the European explorers who sailed to the Americas and the routes they followed to get there, as well as the people who lived there. You will also learn how their explorations led to the creation of a new **economic** system called capitalism.

Vocabulary Clues

Focus on Reading When you are reading your history textbook, you may often come across a word you do not know. If that word isn't listed as a key term, how do you find out what it means?

Using Context Clues Context means surroundings. Authors often include clues to the meaning of a difficult word in its context. You just have to know how and where to look.

Clue	How It Works	Example	Explanation
Direct Definition	Includes a definition in the same or a nearby sentence	European countries practiced mercantilism, in which a government controls all economic activity in a country and its colonies to make the government stronger and richer.	The phrase *"in which a government controls all economic activity in a country and its colonies to make the government stronger and richer"* defines *mercantilism*.
Restatement	Uses different words to say the same thing	Observation of the real world had disproved, or shown to be false, the teachings of an ancient authority.	The word *disproved* is another way to say *shown to be false*.
Comparisons or Contrasts	Compares or contrasts the unfamiliar word with a familiar one	Kepler discovered that the planets moved in elliptical, rather than in circular, orbits.	The word *rather* indicates that *elliptical* means something different from *circular*.

Reading and Skills Resources

Reading Support

- Guided Reading Workbook

Social Studies Skills Support

- Interactive Skills Tutor CD-ROM

Vocabulary Support

- **CRF:** Vocabulary Builder Activities
- **CRF:** Chapter Review Activity
- Differentiated Instruction Modified Worksheets and Tests:
  - Vocabulary Flash Cards
  - Vocabulary Builder Activity
  - Chapter Review Activity

TOS Holt McDougal PuzzleView

You Try It!

The following sentences are from this chapter. Each uses a definition or restatement clue to explain unfamiliar words. See if you can use the context to figure out the meaning of the words in italics.

Vocabulary Clues

1. These thinkers were *rationalists*, people who looked at the world in a rational, or reasonable and logical, way. (p. 589)
2. Its author was Polish astronomer Nicolaus Copernicus. The book was called *On the Revolution of the Celestial Spheres*. (p. 590)
3. Although Magellan was killed before he could complete the voyage, his crew became the first to *circumnavigate*, or go all the way around, the globe. (p. 595)
4. Capitalism is an economic system in which individuals and private businesses run most industries. (p. 601)

After you read the sentences, answer the following questions.

1. In example 1, what does the word *rationalists* means? What hints did you find in the sentence to figure that out?
2. In example 2, what is the meaning of *Celestial Spheres*? What hint helps you understand what this phrase means?
3. What is the definition of *circumnavigate* in example 3? What kind of context clues did you find in that sentence?
4. In example 4, what does *capitalism* mean? How do you know?

As you read Chapter 20, look for phrases between commas or dashes. Those phrases might be the definition or restatement of an unfamiliar word or term.

Key Terms and People

Chapter 20

Section 1

Scientific Revolution *(p. 588)*
theories *(p. 588)*
Ptolemy *(p. 589)*
Nicolaus Copernicus *(p. 590)*
Johannes Kepler *(p. 590)*
Galileo Galilei *(p. 591)*
Sir Isaac Newton *(p. 591)*
scientific method *(p. 592)*

Section 2

Henry the Navigator *(p. 595)*
Vasco da Gama *(p. 595)*
Christopher Columbus *(p. 595)*
Ferdinand Magellan *(p. 595)*
circumnavigate *(p. 595)*
Sir Francis Drake *(p. 596)*
Spanish Armada *(p. 596)*

Section 3

plantations *(p. 598)*
mercantilism *(p. 599)*
capitalism *(p. 601)*
market economy *(p. 601)*

Section 4

pueblos *(p. 603)*
kivas *(p. 603)*
totems *(p. 604)*
teepees *(p. 606)*
matrilineal *(p. 606)*

Academic Vocabulary

Success in school is related to knowing academic vocabulary—the words that are frequently used in school assignments and discussions. In this chapter, you will learn the following academic words:

logical *(p. 589)*
principles *(p. 592)*

Reading Social Studies

Key Terms and People

Preteach these terms and people to the class. Then organize students into pairs and assign each pair a person or term from the list. Have each pair develop an advertising slogan for their person or term, referring to the chapter for more information. Ask for volunteers to present their slogans to the class.
LS Verbal/Linguistic

Focus on Reading

See the **Focus on Reading** questions in this chapter for more practice on reading social studies skills.

Reading Social Studies Assessment

See the **Chapter Review** at the end of this chapter for student assessment questions related to this reading skill.

Teaching Tip

Explain to students that context clues may be found in sentences that precede or follow the sentence they are reading. For example, in reading about navigation, if the word *astrolabe* comes up, they should be able to recognize it as a navigational instrument, even if they don't know anything else about it. Remind them that illustrations are another good source for context clues. For example, the illustration of Galileo depicts him holding a telescope.

Answers

You Try It! 1. *people who look at the world in a logical way; direct definition* **2.** *planets; previous knowledge about Copernicus* **3.** *go around the globe; restatement* **4.** *an economic system of private ownership; direct definition*

Preteach

Bellringer

If YOU were there . . . Use the **Daily Bellringer Transparency** to help students answer the question.

Daily Bellringer Transparency, Section 1

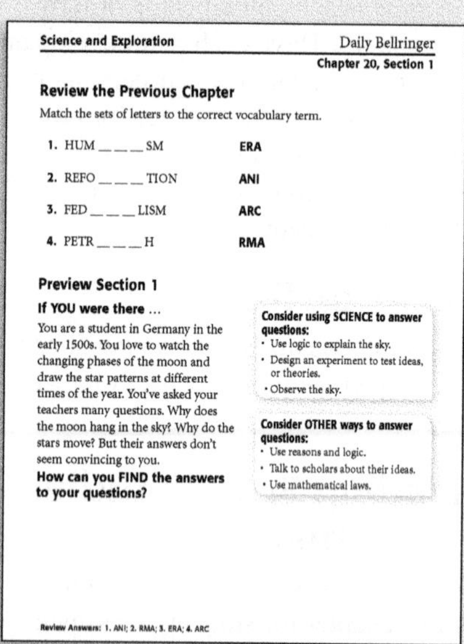

Science and Exploration — Daily Bellringer
Chapter 20, Section 1

Review the Previous Chapter

Match the sets of letters to the correct vocabulary term.

1. HUM _ _ _ SM — **ERA**
2. REFO _ _ _ TION — **ANI**
3. FED _ _ _ LISM — **ARC**
4. PETR _ _ _ H — **RMA**

Preview Section 1

If YOU were there ...

You are a student in Germany in the early 1500s. You love to watch the changing phases of the moon and draw the star patterns at different times of the year. You've asked your teachers many questions. Why does the moon hang in the sky? Why do the stars move? But their answers don't seem convincing to you.

How can you FIND the answers to your questions?

Consider using SCIENCE to answer questions:
- Use logic to explain the sky.
- Design an experiment to test ideas, or theories.
- Observe the sky.

Consider OTHER ways to answer questions:
- Use reasons and logic.
- Talk to scholars about their ideas.
- Use mathematical laws.

Review Answers: 1. ANI; 2. RMA; 3. ERA; 4. ARC

Instructional Resources for Chapter 20 can be found online via the State Specific Resources link in the Teacher One Stop.

Academic Vocabulary

Review with students the high-use academic terms in this section.

logical reasoned, well thought out (p. 589)

principles basic beliefs, rules, or laws (p. 592)

CRF: Vocabulary Builder Activity, Section 1

Taking Notes

Have students use a graphic organizer to take notes on the section. This activity will prepare students for the Section Assessment, in which they will complete a graphic organizer that builds on the information using the Critical Thinking Skill: Identifying Effects.

SECTION 1

The Scientific Revolution

What You Will Learn...

Main Ideas

1. The Scientific Revolution marked the birth of modern science.
2. Discoveries and inventions helped scientists study the natural world.
3. The Scientific Revolution had broad effects on society, changing ideas about the physical world, human behavior, and religion.

The Big Idea

Europeans developed a new way of gaining knowledge, leading to a Scientific Revolution that changed the way people thought about the world.

Key Terms and People

Scientific Revolution, *p. 588*
theories, *p. 588*
Ptolemy, *p. 589*
Nicolaus Copernicus, *p. 590*
Johannes Kepler, *p. 590*
Galileo Galilei, *p. 591*
Sir Isaac Newton, *p. 591*
scientific method, *p. 592*

Create a graphic organizer to take notes on the new ideas, inventions, and thinkers of the Scientific Revolution.

If YOU were there...

You are a student in Germany in the early 1500s. You love to watch the changing phases of the moon and draw the star patterns at different times of the year. You've asked your teachers many questions. Why does the moon hang in the sky? Why do the stars move? But their answers don't seem convincing to you.

How can you find the answers to your questions?

BUILDING BACKGROUND In the 1500s, Europe was undergoing dramatic changes. The Renaissance was well under way. During the Renaissance, educated people began to focus more on the world they lived in. It was a time of great advancements in art, writing, and education. The stage was set for another revolution in thinking.

The Birth of Modern Science

The series of events that led to the birth of modern science is called the **Scientific Revolution**. It occurred in Europe between about 1540 and 1700. Before the Scientific Revolution, most educated people who studied the world relied on explanations from authorities like ancient Greek writers or Catholic Church officials. After the Scientific Revolution, educated people felt freer to question old beliefs. They gained knowledge by studying the world around them and using logic to explain what they saw.

Understanding Science

The word *science* comes from a Latin word meaning "knowledge" or "understanding." So it is not surprising that science involves a particular way of gaining knowledge about the world. Science starts with observation. Scientists observe, or look at, the world. By observing the world they can identify facts about it. But scientists do more than identify facts. They use logic to explain what they have observed. The explanations scientists develop to explain observed facts are called **theories**.

Teach the Big Idea

At Level

The Scientific Revolution

1. **Teach** Ask students the questions in the Main Idea boxes to teach this section.
2. **Apply** Create a chart with five columns for the students to see. Label the columns with the names of key people from this section: *Copernicus, Brahe, Kepler, Galileo,* and *Newton.* Have students copy the chart and list the contributions of each of these people to the Scientific Revolution. **LS Visual/Spatial**
3. **Review** As you review the main idea of each section, have students share information from their charts and discuss the significance of these scientists' theories.
4. **Practice/Homework** Ask students to select one key invention made during the Scientific Revolution and write a short essay on the use of the invention and its significance today. **LS Verbal/Linguistic, Visual/Spatial**

Scientists design experiments to test whether their theories are correct. If the experiments show that the theory makes sense, the theory is accepted. If the experiments do not support the theory, scientists develop a new theory.

As you can see, scientific knowledge is based on observations, facts, and logical ideas, or theories, about them. Before the Scientific Revolution, this method of gaining knowledge was uncommon.

Roots of the Revolution

Many scientific ideas had been expressed in ancient times. Greek thinkers, such as Aristotle and **Ptolemy** (TAHL-uh-mee), wrote about astronomy, geography, and logic. These thinkers were rationalists, people who looked at the world in a rational, or reasonable and logical, way.

Muslim scholars translated the works of Greek thinkers into Arabic. They also added their own ideas about how the world worked. Arabic writings were later translated into Latin, allowing Europeans to study past rational thought. As the Europeans learned from these writings, their own view of the world became more rational.

Developments in Europe also helped bring about the Scientific Revolution. One such development was the growth of humanism during the Renaissance. Humanist artists and writers encouraged study of the natural world. Another development was the popularity of alchemy (AL-kuh-mee). A forerunner of chemistry, alchemy involved experiments whose aim was to turn common metals into gold.

READING CHECK **Finding Main Ideas** What was the Scientific Revolution?

ACADEMIC VOCABULARY
logical reasoned, well thought out

Philosophers like Plato and Aristotle used reason and logic to understand the world.
Pythagoras studied numbers and believed that things could be predicted and measured.
Euclid discovered basic mathematical laws that helped explain the natural world.

Greek Thinkers
The ancient Greeks developed theories about how the world worked that influenced later scientific thinkers. This famous painting from the early 1500s by the Italian artist Raphael shows some influential Greek thinkers.

Direct Teach

Main Idea

1 The Birth of Modern Science

The Scientific Revolution marked the birth of modern science.

Define What are theories? *explanations that scientists develop based on what they have observed*

Draw Conclusions How does a scientist prove a theory? *by performing tests and experiments to see if the theory holds true*

Evaluate Why would an experiment performed many times be more reliable than one performed only once? *possible answer—because repetition would probably eliminate accidents or prejudices that could affect an experiment's outcome*

Analyzing Visuals

Greek Thinkers What do you think inspired the artist Raphael to paint this picture? *possible answer—He was inspired by these Greek thinkers and wanted to honor their ideas.* Who do you think Raphael saw as the most important Greek philosophers? How can you tell? *Plato and Aristotle, because they are at the center of the picture and the other philosophers surround them*

Differentiating Instruction

Advanced/Gifted and Talented

Above Level | Research Required

1. Have students select one of the Greek thinkers discussed in the text or portrayed in *The School of Athens*, the painting on this page.
2. Then have each student use Internet or library resources to write a short biography of his or her chosen Greek person. Ask students to pay particular attention to information that relates to the Scientific Revolution.
3. Ask volunteers to share their biographies with the class.
4. Conclude by asking students what they feel are these philosophers' greatest contributions. LS **Verbal/Linguistic**

Alternative Assessment Handbook, Rubrics 30: Research; and 42: Writing to Inform

Answers

Reading Check *the series of events from the 1540s to about 1700 that led to the birth of modern science*

Direct Teach

Main Idea

❷ Discoveries and Inventions

Discoveries and inventions helped scientists study the natural world.

Draw Conclusions How did learning of the existence of the Americas alter the views European scholars had of other Greek authorities? *If Ptolemy's long-held beliefs were wrong, other Greek thinkers might be wrong too.*

Predict Do you think Columbus changed his mind about the accuracy of Ptolemy's map? Why or why not? *possible answer—no, because he didn't realize he had not reached Asia*

Identify Who was the first astronomer to say that planets orbit the sun? *Copernicus*

Info to Know

Ptolemy's Map Although Ptolemy's map of the world contained inaccuracies, it displays a significant contribution to mapmaking. Ptolemy used lines of latitude and longitude on his map. The addition of this grid helped later mapmakers create duplicates of Ptolemy's map. Such a feat would have been extremely difficult otherwise, because Ptolemy's map showed about 8,000 locations.

Discoveries and Inventions

During the Renaissance, European scholars eagerly studied the works of Greek rationalists. Then an event took place that caused Europeans to doubt the Greeks. In 1492 Christopher Columbus sailed west across the Atlantic Ocean in hopes of reaching Asia. To navigate, he relied in part on a map of the world that Ptolemy had created.

Columbus never reached Asia. He ran into North America instead, a land mass Ptolemy knew nothing about. Europeans were stunned that observation of the real world had disproved the teachings of an ancient authority. Soon scholars began to question the accuracy of other authorities. They also began to make important discoveries of their own.

Advances in Astronomy

In 1543 an astronomer published a book that contradicted Ptolemy on another matter. Many historians think the publication of this book marks the beginning of the Scientific Revolution. The book was called *On the Revolution of the Celestial Spheres.* Its author was Polish astronomer **Nicolaus Copernicus** (kuh-PUHR-ni-kuhs).

Nearly 1,400 years before Copernicus, Ptolemy had written that the sun and planets orbited, or circled around, the earth. As Copernicus studied the movements of the planets, however, he learned that Ptolemy's theory made little sense.

So Copernicus came up with a different explanation for what he observed. His theory was that the planets moved around the sun in circular orbits. Though he never proved this theory, Copernicus inspired fresh thinking about science.

Another leading astronomer, Tycho Brahe (TEE-koh BRAH-huh), worked in Denmark. In the late 1500s, he charted the positions of more than 750 stars. In his work, Brahe set an example by emphasizing careful observation and detailed, accurate records. Careful recording of information is necessary so that other scientists can use what has previously been learned.

Brahe was assisted by German astronomer **Johannes Kepler**. Later, Kepler tried to map the orbits of the planets. But Kepler

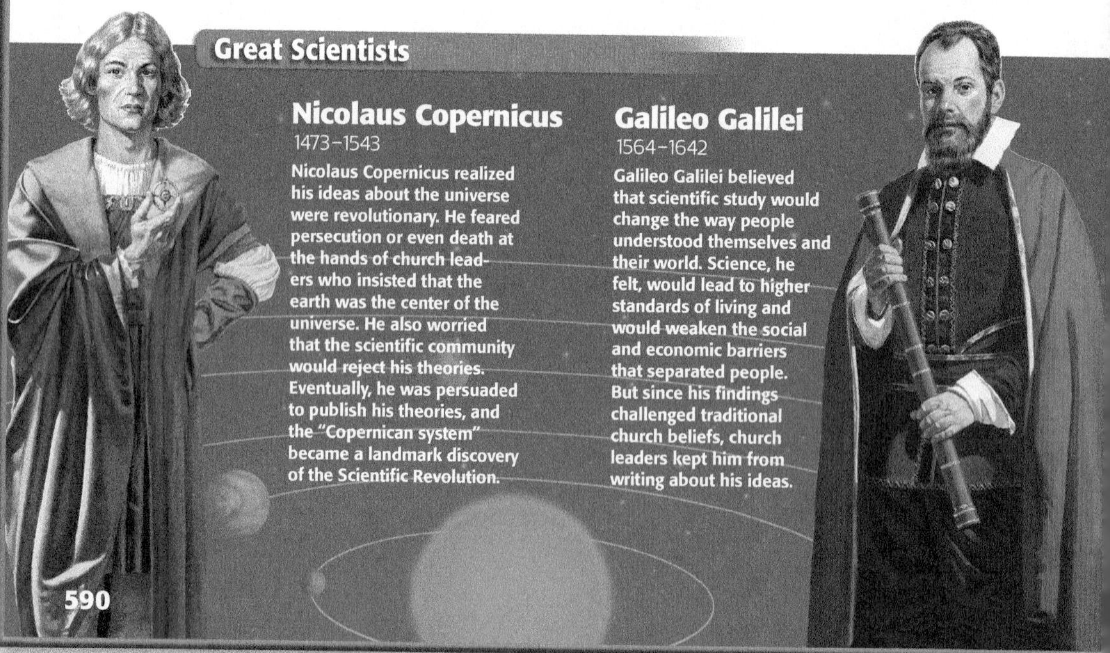

Great Scientists
Nicolaus Copernicus
1473–1543
Nicolaus Copernicus realized his ideas about the universe were revolutionary. He feared persecution or even death at the hands of church leaders who insisted that the earth was the center of the universe. He also worried that the scientific community would reject his theories. Eventually, he was persuaded to publish his theories, and the "Copernican system" became a landmark discovery of the Scientific Revolution.
Galileo Galilei
1564–1642
Galileo Galilei believed that scientific study would change the way people understood themselves and their world. Science, he felt, would lead to higher standards of living and would weaken the social and economic barriers that separated people. But since his findings challenged traditional church beliefs, church leaders kept him from writing about his ideas.
590

Differentiating Instruction

English Language Learners **Below Level** **Standard English Mastery**

1. Organize the class into groups of four. Assign one of these roles to each student within a group: Copernicus, Kepler, Galileo, or Newton.
2. Ask students to imagine that the four astronomers are having dinner together. Ask students what the men's conversation would be like.
3. Then ask each student to write at least three sentences that his or her assigned character might have contributed to such a conversation. Sentences could be about the astronomer's own discoveries, about the other scientists' ideas, or similar topics. Students should share their sentences within the group.
4. Then have each group edit its sentences to create a realistic conversation. Ask each group to read its conversation aloud while class members help ensure that all sentences are in standard English.

LS Verbal/Linguistic, Auditory/Musical

Alternative Assessment Handbook, Rubric 14: Group Activity

ran into a problem. He discovered that the planets did not move in circular orbits as Copernicus had thought. The planets instead move in elliptical, or oval, orbits around the sun. Kepler's basic ideas about the planets' movements are still accepted by scientists today.

Italian scientist **Galileo Galilei** (gal-uh-LEE-oh gal-uh-LAY) was the first person to study the sky with a telescope. Galileo saw craters and mountains on the moon and discovered that moons orbit Jupiter.

Galileo was also interested in how falling objects behave. Today, we use the term *mechanics* for the study of objects and motion. Galileo's biggest contribution to science was the way he learned about mechanics. Instead of just observing things in nature, he set up experiments. In fact, Galileo was the first scientist to routinely use experiments to test his theories.

Sir Isaac Newton

The high point of the Scientific Revolution came with the publication of *Principia Mathematica*. The author of this book, published in 1687, was the English scientist **Sir Isaac Newton**. Newton was one of the greatest scientists who ever lived. Some of his theories have been proven so many times that they are now called laws.

One of Newton's laws is called the law of gravity. You may know that gravity is the force that attracts objects to each other. It's the force that makes a dropped apple fall to the ground and that keeps the planets in orbit around the sun.

Newton's other three laws are called the laws of motion. They describe how objects move in space. Newton went on to explain how much of the physical world worked. His laws became the foundation of nearly all scientific study until the 1900s.

THE IMPACT TODAY

Astronomers still study Kepler's ideas, which they call his laws of planetary motion.

New Inventions

During the Scientific Revolution, scientists made dramatic advances in technology. Around 1590 a Dutch lens maker invented a simple microscope. By the mid-1600s, a microscope was used to observe tiny plants and animals living in drops of pond water.

In 1593 Galileo invented the thermometer to measure temperature. In 1609 he built a much-improved telescope that he used to make his important observations and discoveries.

In 1643, an Italian scientist invented the barometer, a device that measures air pressure. Used to help forecast the weather, the barometer, like other inventions of the time, gave scientists new ways to learn about their world.

FOCUS ON READING

Which sentence in this paragraph contains a direct definition of an unfamiliar word?

READING CHECK

Summarizing What were two major achievements in astronomy during this era?

Sir Isaac Newton

1642–1727

Sir Isaac Newton was interested in learning about the nature of light, so he conducted a series of experiments. In Newton's time, most people assumed that light was white. Newton proved, however, that light is actually made up of all of the colors of the rainbow. His research on light became the basis for his invention of the reflecting telescope—the type of telescope that is found in most large observatories today.

Direct Teach

Main Idea

❷ Discoveries and Inventions

Discoveries and inventions helped scientists study the natural world.

Identify Who was Galileo Galilei? *the first person to study the sky with a telescope*

Summarize What was Galileo's key contribution to the development of science? *the practice of routinely using experiments to test theories*

Draw Conclusions How was Newton's law of gravity connected to discoveries about the planets' orbits? *Gravity attracts objects to each other and thus keeps the planets in motion around the sun.*

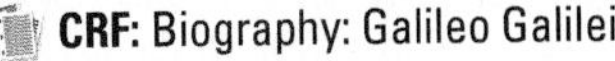

CRF: Biography: Galileo Galilei

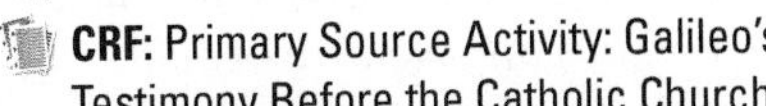

CRF: Primary Source Activity: Galileo's Testimony Before the Catholic Church

Connect to Science

The Kepler Mission In 2001 NASA created a mission that honors astronomer Johannes Kepler. The purpose of the Kepler Mission is to find planets that could support life orbiting stars beyond our solar system. NASA searches for these planets in what is called the habitable zone—the area around a star in which liquid water can exist on a planet's surface.

Critical Thinking: Summarizing

At Level

Scientific Revolution Newspaper Articles

1. Ask students to imagine they are newspaper reporters who have been given an assignment to write about one of the main discoveries or inventions of the Scientific Revolution.
2. Ask students to select one major discovery or invention and write a headline for it.
3. Then have students write the first paragraph for the article that would follow their headline. The paragraph should answer the basic who, where, what, when, and why questions about the topic.
4. Call on volunteers to read their headlines and paragraphs. Then ask students which headlines should go "above the fold," the most prominent spots on a newspaper's front page. Students should defend their choices about which topics are more important than others. **LS Verbal/Linguistic**

Alternative Assessment Handbook, Rubric 23: Newspapers

Answers

Reading Check *the discovery of the orbit of the planets and the use of a telescope to study the sky*

Direct Teach

Main Idea

❸ Effects on Society

The Scientific Revolution had broad effects on society, changing ideas about the physical world, human behavior, and religion.

Summarize What is the scientific method? *a step-by-step method for performing experiments and other scientific research*

Recall How did philosophers try to improve society? *by using logic and reason to solve problems in society and government*

Analyze How were science and fundamental democratic ideas connected, according to philosophers of the Scientific Revolution? *If the natural world is governed by laws, human behavior may be governed by laws also, and perhaps all people are equal.*

Review & Assess

Close

Challenge students to formulate questions about the illustrations in this section.

Assess

SE Section 1 Assessment

PASS: Section 1 Quiz

Alternative Assessment Handbook

Reteach/Classroom Intervention

Guided Reading Workbook, Section 1

Interactive Skills Tutor CD-ROM

Effects on Society

The Scientific Revolution changed the way we learn about the world. People started to pursue science in a systematic fashion. Two men in particular, Francis Bacon and Rene Descartes (ruh-NAY day-CART), encouraged the use of orderly experiments and clear reasoning. Their ideas helped shape the **scientific method**, a step-by-step process for performing experiments and other scientific research. The basics of this method—observation and experimentation—are the main principles of modern science.

ACADEMIC VOCABULARY
principles basic beliefs, rules, or laws

The Scientific Revolution affected other areas of life too. Philosophers thought observation and logic could explain problems like poverty and war. By using reason, they hoped to find ways to improve society.

As scientists discovered laws that governed nature, some thinkers began to believe that certain laws governed human behavior as well. If all people were governed by the same laws, then it stood to reason that all people must be equal. This idea of equality was important in the development of democratic ideas in Europe.

Science also created conflict as some scientific discoveries raised questions about church teachings. Church officials feared that science might lead people to doubt key elements of their faith, undermining the church's influence.

Catholic leaders tried to force scientists to reject any findings that contradicted church teachings. For example, they threatened Galileo with torture unless he accepted the church's belief that the earth did not move. Despite such conflicts, science continued to develop rapidly.

READING CHECK **Analyzing** Why was the church troubled by the Scientific Revolution?

SUMMARY AND PREVIEW The Scientific Revolution was the birth of modern science. Scientists developed new methods and inventions to make key discoveries. Next, you will learn about the age of European exploration.

Section 1 Assessment

Reviewing Ideas, Terms, and People

1. a. **Recall** When did the **Scientific Revolution** take place?
   b. **Analyze** Why was the Scientific Revolution important in world history?
   c. **Predict** What might cause scientists to reject a popular **theory**?
2. a. **Recall** What event caused Europeans to doubt the ideas of ancient Greek authorities?
   b. **Analyze** What was the most important contribution **Galileo Galilei** made to modern science?
   c. **Evaluate** Why do you think **Sir Isaac Newton** is considered to be one of the greatest scientists of all time?
3. a. **Describe** What is the **scientific method**?
   b. **Contrast** How did the views of science and the church differ?
   c. **Elaborate** What effect did the Scientific Revolution have on some philosophers?

Critical Thinking

4. **Identifying Effects** Based on your notes, list four major thinkers of the Scientific Revolution and their greatest achievements. Then write a statement that summarizes their effects on society.

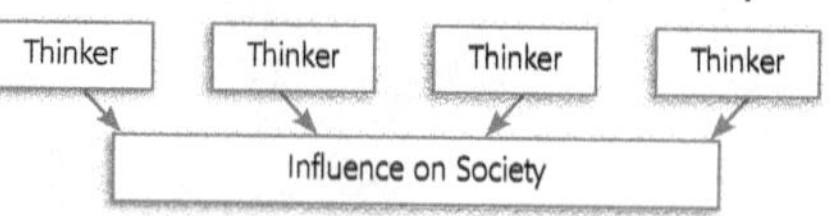

Focus on Speaking

5. **Organizing Information** To prepare for your presentation, create a two-column chart. Label one column "Scientific Revolution," and the other "Exploration." From your notes, select the key people and events that you will discuss in your report. Put these in your first column.

Section 1 Assessment Answers

1. a. between 1540 and 1700
   b. It was a radical new way of looking at the world, marked the birth of modern science, and taught people to believe what they observed through experiments rather than what they had been told.
   c. if experiments to prove the theory failed
2. a. learning of the existence of the Americas
   b. the practice of routinely using experiments to test theories
   c. His laws became the foundation for nearly all modern scientific study until the 1900s.
3. a. a step-by-step process for performing experiments and other scientific research
   b. science—ideas that can be tested and proved; church—ideas based on faith
   c. They began to believe that laws governed human behavior, so all people must be equal.
4. Students should list Copernicus, Kepler, Galileo, and Newton and their achievements. Students' statements will vary.
5. Answers should exhibit understanding of scientists and their achievements.

Answers

Reading Check *Science contradicted what the Catholic Church taught, and church officials were concerned that they would lose their authority.*

Great Voyages of Discovery

SECTION 2

What You Will Learn...

Main Ideas

1. Europeans had a desire and opportunity to explore in the 1400s and 1500s.
2. Portuguese and Spanish explorers discovered new trade routes, lands, and people.
3. The English and French claimed land in North America.

The Big Idea

European explorers brought knowledge, wealth, and influence to their countries.

Key Terms and People

Henry the Navigator, *p. 595*
Vasco da Gama, *p. 595*
Christopher Columbus, *p. 595*
Ferdinand Magellan, *p. 595*
circumnavigate, *p. 595*
Sir Francis Drake, *p. 596*
Spanish Armada, *p. 596*

Create a graphic organizer to take notes about the major explorers of the Age of Exploration and their discoveries.

If YOU were there...

Your uncle is a Portuguese ship captain who has just come back from a long sea voyage. He shows you a map of the new lands he has seen. He tells wonderful stories about strange plants and animals. You are studying to become a carpenter, but you wonder if you might like to be an explorer like your uncle instead.

How would you decide which career to choose?

BUILDING BACKGROUND A spirit of adventure swept across Europe in the 1400s. Improved maps showed new lands. Travelers' tales encouraged people to dream of finding riches and adventure.

Desire and Opportunity to Explore

Why did people seek to explore the world in the 1400s? First, they wanted Asian spices. Italy and Egypt controlled the trade routes to Asia, charging very high prices for spices. As a result, many countries wanted to find a direct sea route that led to Asia.

This photo shows replicas of the three ships that Christopher Columbus used to sail to the Americas in 1492.

Teach the Big Idea

At Level

Great Voyages of Discovery

1. **Teach** Ask students the questions in the Main Idea boxes to teach this section.
2. **Apply** Have students use the "Five Ws" to analyze voyages of discovery. Create a chart with columns labeled *who, what, when, where,* and *why* for the class to see. Have students use information from the section to complete the chart.
   LS Verbal/Linguistic, Visual/Spatial
3. **Review** As you review the section's main ideas, have students look for answers to these five questions.
4. **Practice/Homework** Have students create an advertisement for a voyage of discovery to search for new trade routes to India, China, and Southeast Asia. The ad should persuade people to join the adventure and provide information about the trip.
   LS Verbal/Linguistic

Alternative Assessment Handbook, Rubrics 2: Advertisements; 7: Charts; and 43: Writing to Persuade

Preteach

Bellringer

If YOU were there . . . Use the **Daily Bellringer Transparency** to help students answer the question.

Daily Bellringer Transparency, Section 2

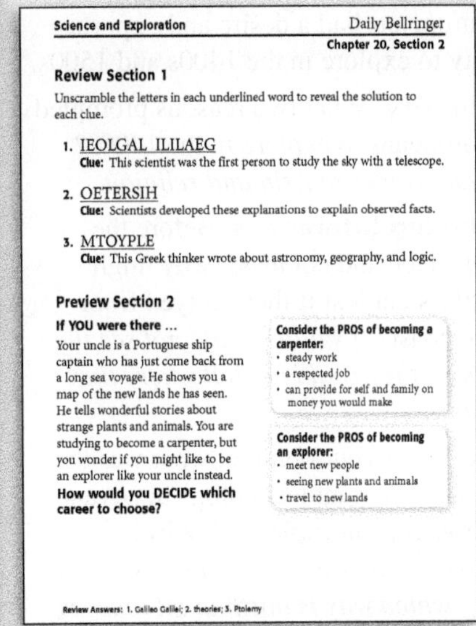

Science and Exploration Daily Bellringer
Chapter 20, Section 2

Review Section 1

Unscramble the letters in each underlined word to reveal the solution to each clue.

1. IEOLGAL ILILAEG
   Clue: This scientist was the first person to study the sky with a telescope.
2. OETERSIH
   Clue: Scientists developed these explanations to explain observed facts.
3. MTOYPLE
   Clue: This Greek thinker wrote about astronomy, geography, and logic.

Preview Section 2

If YOU were there ...

Your uncle is a Portuguese ship captain who has just come back from a long sea voyage. He shows you a map of the new lands he has seen. He tells wonderful stories about strange plants and animals. You are studying to become a carpenter, but you wonder if you might like to be an explorer like your uncle instead.

How would you DECIDE which career to choose?

Consider the PROS of becoming a carpenter:
- steady work
- a respected job
- can provide for self and family on money you would make

Consider the PROS of becoming an explorer:
- meet new people
- seeing new plants and animals
- travel to new lands

Review Answers: 1. Galileo Galilei; 2. theories; 3. Ptolemy

Instructional Resources for Chapter 20 can be found online via the State Specific Resources link in the Teacher One Stop.

Building Vocabulary

Preteach or review the following terms:

astrolabe a device used by sailors to navigate using the positions of stars and planets (p. 594)

caravel a fast, maneuverable ship originally designed by the Portuguese (p. 594)

Taking Notes

Have students use a graphic organizer to take notes on the section. This activity will prepare students for the Section Assessment, in which they will complete a graphic organizer that builds on the information using the Critical Thinking Skill: Drawing Conclusions.

Direct Teach

Main Idea

1 Desire and Opportunity to Explore

Europeans had a desire and opportunity to explore in the 1400s and 1500s.

Identify What two reasons prompted Europeans to explore in the 1400s? *trade routes to Asia and religion*

Making Inferences Before the astrolabe and compass, why might sailors get lost if they strayed from the coast? *If sailors could not see the coast, they could not tell where they were.*

Rank In your opinion, what was the most important technological advance for European explorers? Why? *possible answer—the compass; knowing which way is north at all times is important to navigation.*

Map Transparency: European Exploration, 1487–1580

Connect to Science

Compasses In the 1100s, navigators discovered that they could magnetize an iron needle. When they floated the needle in a bowl of water, it would point north. At some point during the 1200s or 1300s, navigators fixed magnetized needles to a card marked with directions. The true compasses were born. No longer would sailors need to keep sight of land to keep from getting lost!

Answers

Reading Check: *the astrolabe, compass, and caravel*

European Exploration, 1487–1580

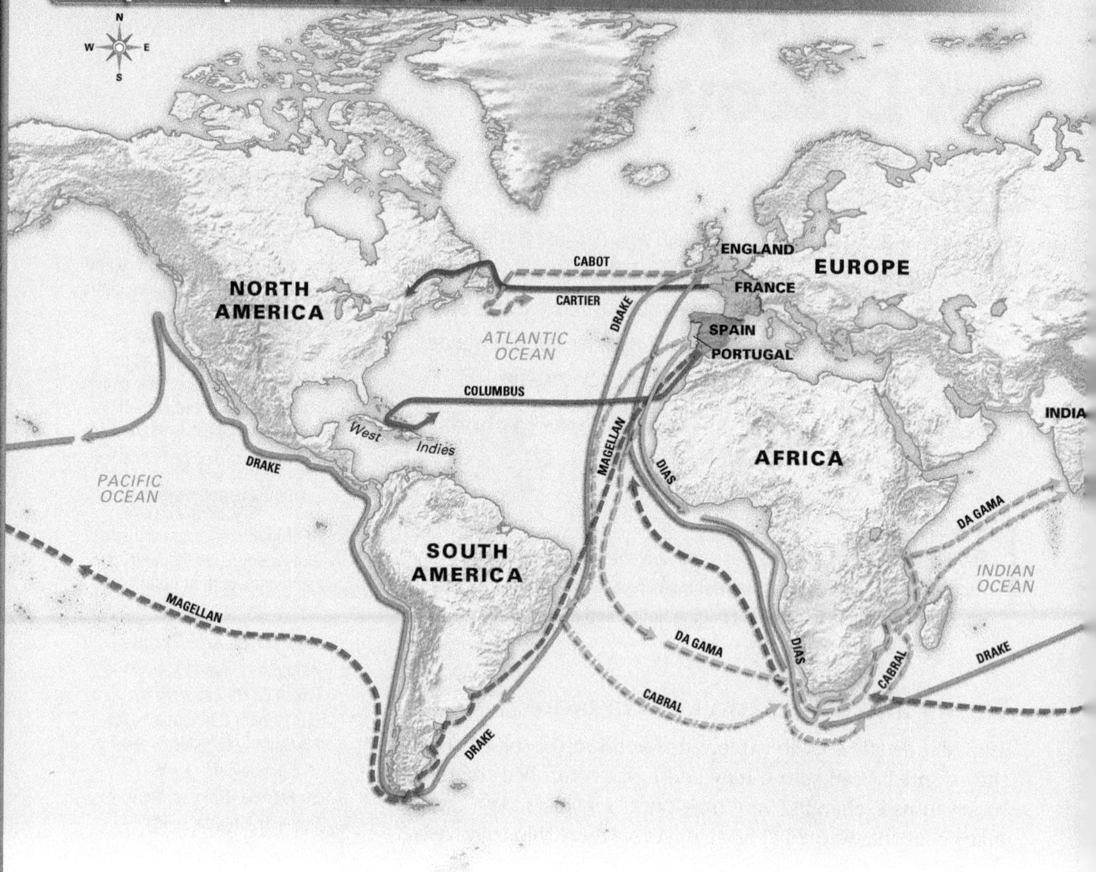

This way they could get spices without having to buy from Italian or Egyptian traders.

Religion gave explorers another reason to set sail. European Christians wanted to convert more people to their religion to counteract the spread of Islam in Europe, Africa, and Asia.

Advances in technology made exploration possible. Sailors used the astrolabe and the compass to find routes to faraway places. More accurate maps allowed sailors to sail from port to port without having to stay right along the coast the entire way.

Other advances came in shipbuilding. The Portuguese began building ships called caravels (KER-uh-velz). Caravels used triangular sails that, unlike traditional square sails, allowed ships to sail against the wind. By replacing oars on the ship's sides with rudders at the back of the ship, the Portuguese also greatly improved steering. The new caravels helped Portugal take the lead in the European Age of Exploration.

READING CHECK **Finding Main Ideas** What advances in technology aided exploration?

Collaborative Learning

Above Level

Explorer Role Playing

1. Ask students to imagine the following scenario: "You are the captain of a ship in the 1400s, about to leave on a year-long voyage. Just as you are about to set sail, you learn that your child is very sick and you must stay home. Because of the tides and the weather, the boat must leave right away. Tell Lieutenant Garcia, the second-in-command, everything he needs to know."
2. Remind students to detail the purpose of the voyage, where to go, and what to take.
3. Organize the class into pairs who will act out the exchange between the captain and Lieutenant Garcia. The lieutenant should ask questions if the captain leaves out any information. Students should write out their scripts. Ask volunteers to present their skits to the class. **LS Interpersonal; Verbal/Linguistic**

Alternative Assessment Handbook, Rubrics 33: Skits and Reader's Theater; and 42: Writing to Inform

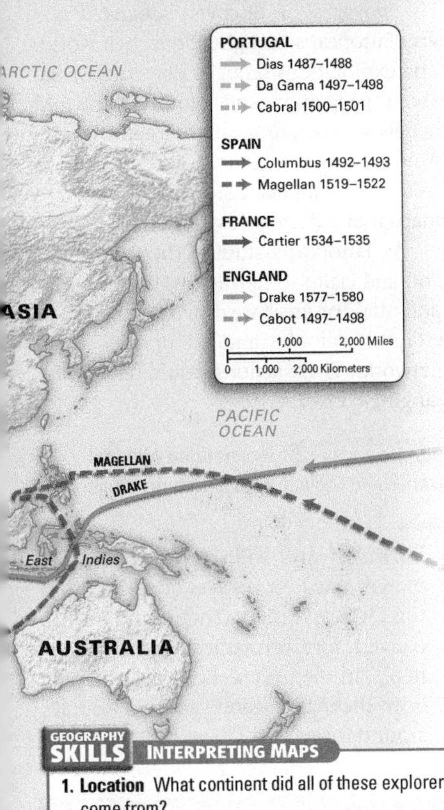

GEOGRAPHY SKILLS INTERPRETING MAPS

1. **Location** What continent did all of these explorers come from?
2. **Movement** Which explorers' expeditions went all the way around the world?

Portuguese and Spanish Explorations

Prince **Henry the Navigator** was responsible for much of Portugal's success on the seas. He built an observatory and a navigation school to teach sailors how to find their way on long ocean voyages. Some Portuguese sailors sailed south along the coast of Africa. In 1498 **Vasco da Gama** sailed around Africa and landed on the west coast of India. A sea route to Asia had been found.

Reaching the Americas

An Italian sailor, **Christopher Columbus**, thought he had already figured out a shorter way to Asia—sailing west across the Atlantic. He told the Spanish monarchs Ferdinand and Isabella his plan and promised them riches, new territory, and Catholic converts if they funded his journey. Isabella agreed.

In August 1492 Columbus set sail with 88 men and three small ships. On October 12, he and his crew landed on an island in the Bahamas. Columbus believed he had reached Asia. He didn't realize the continent of North America lay in front of him.

A Portuguese explorer later discovered South America by accident while trying to sail around Africa. Then, in 1519, **Ferdinand Magellan** (muh-JEHL-uhn) led a voyage around South America's southern tip. He continued sailing into the Pacific even though his ships were low on food and water. Although Magellan was killed before he could complete the voyage, his crew became the first to **circumnavigate**, or go all the way around, the globe.

Conquest of the "New World"

Spanish explorers called the Americas the "New World." When they arrived in these lands in the early 1500s, the Aztec Empire in Mexico and the Inca Empire in Peru were at the height of their powers. The Spanish saw these empires as good sources of gold and silver. They also wanted to convert the native peoples to Christianity.

Having better weapons, the Spanish quickly conquered the Aztecs and Incas. The Spanish also brought new diseases that over time killed possibly three-quarters of the native peoples. Soon, Spain ruled large parts of North and South America.

READING CHECK **Identifying Points of View** Why do you think European explorers called the Americas the "New World"?

Direct Teach

Main Idea

2 Portuguese and Spanish Explorations

Portuguese and Spanish explorers discovered new trade routes, lands, and people.

Recall What did Henry the Navigator contribute to world exploration? *built an observatory and navigation school, sponsored voyages*

Identify Who was the first European to sail around Africa and land in India? *Vasco da Gama*

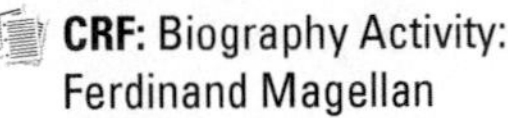

CRF: Biography Activity: Ferdinand Magellan

CRF: Primary Source Activity: From the *Report of the Expedition* by Christopher Columbus

Linking to Today

Circumnavigation In 1986, two American pilots were the first private individuals to circumnavigate the globe without touching the ground. Flying in an experimental airplane called *Voyager*, Dick Rutan and Jeana Yeager spent nine days in the airplane traveling 25,012 miles (40,251 km). The plane was lightweight but was able to carry enough fuel to circle Earth without landing. Fortunately for the pilots, unlike Magellan, they lived to tell the tale!

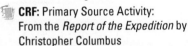

Critical Thinking: Interpreting Maps

At Level

Great Voyages Postcard

Materials: blank note cards, markers

1. Tell students that there is a long history of travelers sending postcards home. Ask them to imagine that they are explorers on one of the voyages illustrated on the map above.
2. Have each student select a voyage and route from which they would like to imagine writing a postcard home to friends or family.
3. On one side of the postcard, students should illustrate a scene from their current location. On the other side, they should write details about where they are, whom they are with, and what they are doing. They should also make up an address for where they are sending the postcard.
4. Have students describe and explain their postcard to the class. LS **Visual/Spatial**

Alternative Assessment Handbook, Rubric 3: Artwork; Rubric 40: Writing to Describe

Answers

Interpreting Maps **1.** *Europe* **2.** *Magellan, Drake*

Reading Check *To Europeans, the Americas were new territory.*

Direct Teach

Main Idea

❸ The English and French in America

The English and French claimed land in North America.

Identify What belief about geography was disproved by new explorations? *the Americas were part of Asia*

Make Judgements How would you feel about the discovery of a new continent? Why? *possible answers—excited: new places mean new opportunities; frightened: strange dangers might be discovered there.*

Review & Assess

Close

Have students summarize how technology and trade led to increased exploration.

Assess

SE Section 2 Assessment

PASS: Section 2 Quiz

Alternative Assessment Handbook

Reteach/Classroom Intervention

Guided Reading Workbook, Section 2

Interactive Skills Tutor CD-ROM

The English and French in America

England and France also wanted to find a new route to Asia. After Spain and Portugal gained control of the southern routes, the English and French sent explorers to look for a waterway through North America. Though these explorers did not find such a passage, they claimed land in North America for England and France.

Competing for Land and Wealth

Besides looking for a route to Asia, England hoped to find riches in the New World. But Spain controlled the gold and silver of the former Aztec and Inca empires. When English sailors, such as **Sir Francis Drake**, began stealing treasure from Spanish transport ships, Spain became furious.

In 1588 Spain sent 130 ships to attack England. This fleet, called the **Spanish Armada**, was part of Spain's large navy. But the English had faster ships and better guns. They defeated the Armada and saved England from invasion. Spain now had a rival for rule of the seas.

A New European Worldview

The voyages of discovery changed the way Europeans thought about their world. The explorations brought new knowledge about geography and proved some old beliefs wrong. Europeans learned that the Americas were a separate landmass from Asia. Geographers made more accurate maps that reflected this new knowledge.

As Europeans studied the new maps and laid claim to new lands, they saw the potential for great wealth. They began to establish colonies and set up new trade networks. These actions would have wide-ranging consequences.

READING CHECK **Generalizing** Why did France and England send explorers to America?

SUMMARY AND PREVIEW European explorers sailed on voyages of discovery in the 1400s and 1500s. They found wealth, converts for Christianity, and new continents. In the next section, you will read how these discoveries affected peoples around the world.

Section 2 Assessment

Reviewing Ideas, Terms, and People

1. a. **Describe** What were caravels? How were they better than what they replaced?
   b. **Explain** What motivated Europeans to explore the world in the 1400s and 1500s?
2. a. **Identify** Who led the first voyage to **circumnavigate** the globe?
   b. **Analyze** How did the Spanish conquer the Aztec and Inca empires?
3. a. **Recall** Where did the English and French look for a route to Asia?
   b. **Draw Conclusions** How did power shift in Europe after the defeat of the **Spanish Armada**?
   c. **Evaluate** When claiming land in the New World for themselves, Europeans ignored the ownership rights of native peoples. What is your opinion of this?

Critical Thinking

4. **Drawing Conclusions** Add another column to the chart you created. In this last column, write a statement drawing a conclusion about the significance of each discovery.

Explorer	Discovery	Significance

Focus on Speaking

5. **Collecting Information** Review your notes and this section. Select what you consider to be the three most important events of the European Age of Exploration. Describe these in the second column of your chart.

Section 2 Assessment Answers

1. a. Portuguese ships with triangular sails and rudder at the back; allowed ships to sail against the wind
   b. new trade routes and religion
2. a. Ferdinand Magellan
   b. had better weapons, brought new diseases
3. a. North America
   b. England took Spain's position as the world's greatest naval power.
   c. Student opinions will vary.
4. a. Gama—sea route to Asia; Columbus—Americas; Magellan—route around world
5. Answers will vary but should exhibit knowledge of the people and events discussed in this section.

Answers

Reading Check *wanted trade route to Asia and New World riches*

New Systems of Trade

SECTION 3

If YOU were there...

You live in a coastal town in Spain in the 1500s. This week, several ships have returned from the Americas, bringing silver for the royal court. But that's not all. The crew has also brought back some strange foods. One sailor offers you a round, red fruit. Natives in the Americas call it a "tomatl," he tells you. He dares you to taste it, but you are afraid it might be poison.

Will you taste the tomato? Why or why not?

BUILDING BACKGROUND New fruits and vegetables such as tomatoes and potatoes looked very strange to Europeans in the 1500s. But new foods were only one part of a much larger exchange of products and ideas that resulted from the voyages of discovery.

What You Will Learn...

Main Ideas

1. Europe, Asia, Africa, and the Americas exchanged plants, animals, and ideas.
2. In the 1600s and 1700s, new trade patterns developed and power shifted in Europe.
3. Market economies changed business in Europe.

The Big Idea

Exchanges between the Old World and the New World influenced the development of new economic systems: mercantilism and capitalism.

Key Terms

plantations, *p. 598*
mercantilism, *p. 599*
capitalism, *p. 601*
market economy, *p. 601*

Create a graphic organizer to take notes about the changes in Europe during the 1500s and 1600s.

Exchanging Plants, Animals, and Ideas

The exchange of plants, animals, and ideas between the New World (the Americas) and the Old World (Europe) is known as the **Columbian Exchange.** It changed lives around the world.

European manufactured goods, like this mirror, were new to the Americas.

Europeans brought new ideas and technologies when they settled new lands. This illustration shows a scene in what is now New Mexico.

Missions and settlements helped spread Christianity and European languages.

Europeans brought animals like oxen to pull carts.

Teach the Big Idea

At Level

New Systems of Trade

1. **Teach** Ask students the questions in the Main Idea boxes to teach this section.
2. **Apply** Tell students that the Greek philosopher Socrates taught his students by having them answer questions. After students have skimmed the chapter, have them write 10 questions about trade and economics. For example, students may ask how increased trade may lead to a stronger economy. **LS Verbal/Linguistic**
3. **Review** As you review the section, have students add questions to their lists or change their questions.
4. **Practice/Homework** Have students write a short answer to each question they wrote. Instruct students to review their questions and answers before completing the Section Assessment. **LS Verbal/Linguistic**

Alternative Assessment Handbook, Rubric 1: Acquiring Information

Preteach

Bellringer

If YOU were there . . . Use the **Daily Bellringer Transparency** to help students answer the question.

Daily Bellringer Transparency, Section 3

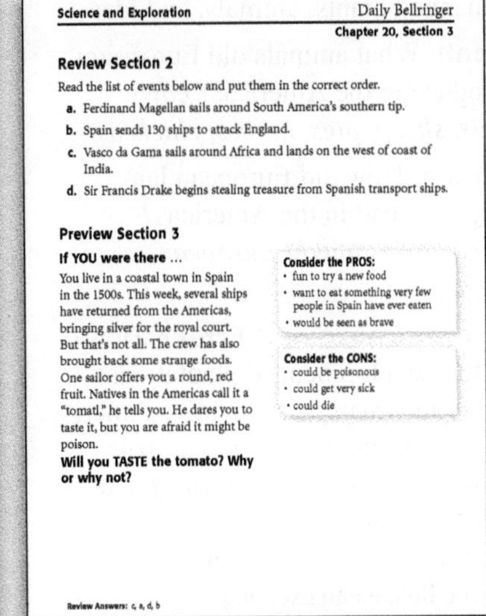

Science and Exploration — Daily Bellringer
Chapter 20, Section 3

Review Section 2

Read the list of events below and put them in the correct order.

a. Ferdinand Magellan sails around South America's southern tip.
b. Spain sends 130 ships to attack England.
c. Vasco da Gama sails around Africa and lands on the west of coast of India.
d. Sir Francis Drake begins stealing treasure from Spanish transport ships.

Preview Section 3

If YOU were there ...

You live in a coastal town in Spain in the 1500s. This week, several ships have returned from the Americas, bringing silver for the royal court. But that's not all. The crew has also brought back some strange foods. One sailor offers you a round, red fruit. Natives in the Americas call it a "tomatl," he tells you. He dares you to taste it, but you are afraid it might be poison.

Will you TASTE the tomato? Why or why not?

Consider the PROS:
- fun to try a new food
- want to eat something very few people in Spain have ever eaten
- would be seen as brave

Consider the CONS:
- could be poisonous
- could get very sick
- could die

Review Answers: c, a, d, b

Instructional Resources for Chapter 20 can be found online via the State Specific Resources link in the Teacher One Stop.

Building Vocabulary

Preteach or review the following terms:

manufactured made by hand or machine (p. 597)

commerce buying and selling goods (p. 600)

CRF: Vocabulary Builder Activity, Section 3

Taking Notes

Have students use the graphic organizer online to take notes on the section. This activity will prepare students for the Section Assessment, in which they will complete a graphic organizer that builds on the information using the Critical Thinking Skill: Analyzing.

Direct Teach

Main Idea

1 Exchanging Plants, Animals, and Ideas

Europe, Asia, Africa, and the Americas exchanged plants, animals, and ideas.

Recall What animals did Europeans introduce to the Americas? *cows, goats, sheep, pigs, horses, chickens*

Explain How did European languages spread in the Americas? *Missionaries taught European languages.*

Identify Cause and Effect How did the development of plantations lead to mistreatment of Native Americans? *Plantations required a large labor force, which Europeans filled with Native Americans.*

Quick Facts Transparency: The Columbian Exchange

Did you know. . .

The horse was new to Native Americans, but not to North and South America. An early relative of the horse was common in the Americas during the Pleistocene Epoch (from 2,500,000 until 10,000 years ago). However, this animal became extinct in the Americas about 8,000 years ago. Spanish explorers then re-introduced horses to the Americas.

Answers

Interpreting Maps 1. *See list on map* **2.** *See list on map.*

Reading Check *Explorers spread and collected new plants, animals, and ideas around the globe as they traveled.*

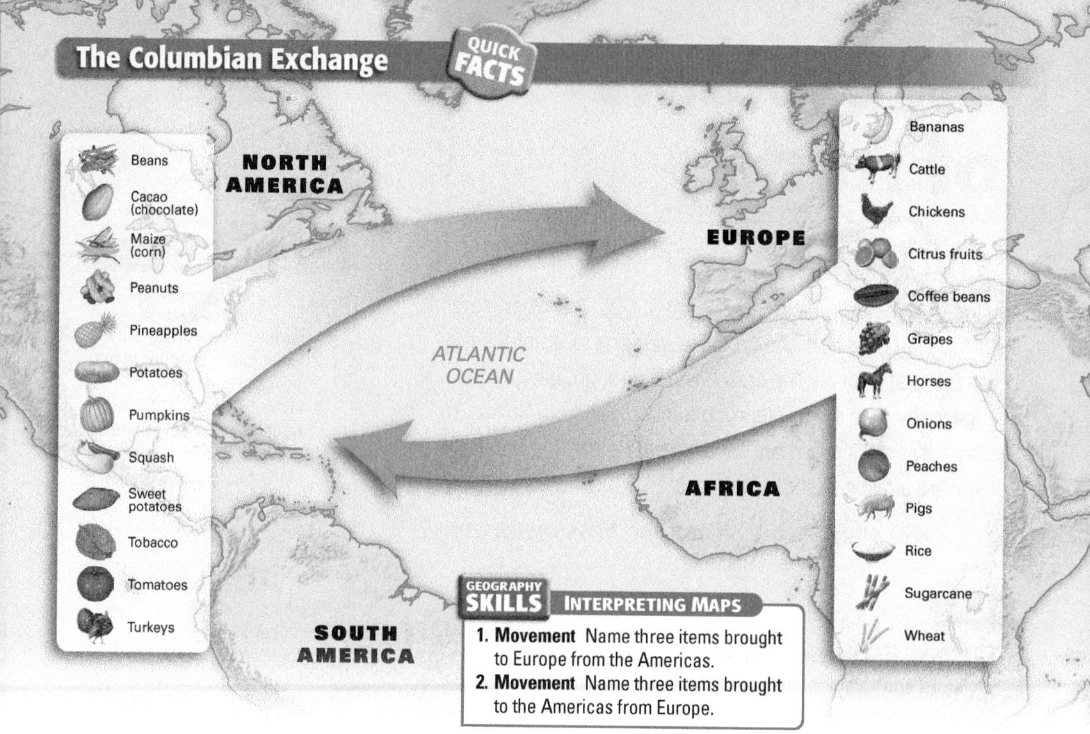

GEOGRAPHY SKILLS INTERPRETING MAPS

1. **Movement** Name three items brought to Europe from the Americas.
2. **Movement** Name three items brought to the Americas from Europe.

Europeans introduced many new plants to the Americas, including bananas, sugarcane, oranges, onions, and lettuce. Europeans also brought new animals such as cows, goats, sheep, pigs, horses, and chickens to the New World.

In the Americas, Europeans found plants and animals they had never seen. They took some back to Europe, as well as to Africa and Asia. This exchange of plants changed the eating habits of people around the world. Some of the foods new to Europeans were tomatoes, potatoes, beans, squash, and chocolate.

In addition, Europeans introduced their culture to the places they explored. Missionaries went to Asia, Africa, and the Americas to convert the peoples there to Christianity. Missionaries taught European languages to native peoples as well.

Europeans also brought technologies such as guns and steel to the New World. The introduction of sheep and sugarcane created new industries. Artisans made new kinds of textiles from the wool that the sheep provided. Colonists also began to grow sugarcane on **plantations**, or large farms.

Plantations and mines in the Americas made money for Portugal and Spain. However, many American Indians who were forced to work on the land died from harsh treatment and European diseases. Europeans then started using enslaved Africans as workers. Soon, thousands of Africans were being shipped to the Americas as slave labor. The use of slave labor continued in parts of the Americas until the late 1800s.

READING CHECK **Identifying Cause and Effect** What caused the Columbian Exchange?

Collaborative Learning

Below Level

Old World/New World Menus

Prep Required

Materials: photocopies of restaurant menus

1. To help students understand the impact of the Columbian Exchange, have them examine photocopies of modern restaurant menus featuring regional fare such as Chinese, Italian, Tex-Mex, French, or Moroccan.
2. Have students form small groups of three or four and give each group a menu. Using the information on the map, have students circle ingredients on their menus that would have been new to the menu's region after the Columbian Exchange (e.g., the tomatoes in a spaghetti sauce were new to Italy). Also, have them list where the new ingredients originated.
3. Ask volunteers to share their findings. Lead students in a short discussion of which region's menu probably changed the most due to the Columbian Exchange. **LS Interpersonal**

Alternative Assessment Handbook, Rubric 14: Group Activity

Trade and Economic Power

The exchange of products between European countries and their colonies changed economic relations around the world. European countries saw their colonies as a way to get rich.

This view of the colonies was part of an economic system called **mercantilism**—a system in which a government controls all economic activity in a country and its colonies to make the government stronger and richer. Mercantilism was the main economic policy in Europe between 1500 and 1800.

Under mercantilism, governments did everything they could to get more gold and silver, which were considered to be the measure of a country's strength. Countries also tried to export more goods than they imported. In this way, they could keep a favorable balance of trade—the relationship between the value of imports and exports.

New Trading Patterns

Mercantilism created new patterns of global trade. One involved the exchange of raw materials from colonies in the Americas, manufactured products from Europe, and slaves from Africa. This three-pronged network was known as the triangular trade.

The Atlantic slave trade was a major part of the triangular trade. European traders crammed enslaved Africans on ships for the long voyage to the Americas. Chained together without enough food and water, many slaves got sick and died. Between the late 1500s and early 1800s Europeans shipped millions of enslaved Africans to colonies in the New World.

Power Shifts in Europe

In the 1500s Portugal and Spain, the early leaders in exploration, were also the leading economic powers. That changed as the Dutch and English became stronger.

LINKING TO TODAY

Effects of the Columbian Exchange

Many of the foods you eat today didn't exist in America before 1492. Think of a cheeseburger, for example. Without foods from the Old World, you would have no bun, no patty, no cheese, and no lettuce. European explorers brought to the New World wheat for bread, cattle for beef and cheese, and lettuce.

They also brought many other vegetables, grains, and fruits. Now, of course, you can find foods from all over the world in your local grocery store. People in other countries also can get foods that originally were found only in America. The Columbian Exchange affects what you have for dinner nearly every day.

ANALYSIS SKILL ANALYZING INFORMATION

How does the Columbian Exchange affect one of your favorite dinners?

Direct Teach

Main Idea

❷ Trade and Economic Power

In the 1600s and 1700s, new trade patterns developed and power shifted in Europe.

Define What is mercantilism? *a system in which a government controls all economic activity in a country and its colonies*

Explain Why is exporting goods better for a country's economy than importing goods? *Selling exports brings in money; buying imports sends money to another country.*

Identify What was the triangular trade? *the trade network among Europe, Africa, and the Americas*

Linking to Today

Globalization and Trade Have students check the label on an article of clothing they are wearing. Most likely it has been made overseas. Explain that international trade has increased a great deal over time. Economic resources are constantly being shifted around the globe so that businesses can gain an advantage over their competitors. This process is called globalization.

Critical Thinking: Analyzing Primary Sources

Above Level

The Slave Trade

1. Organize the class into small groups. Half of the groups will research anti-slavery activities in the United States prior to the Civil War. The other groups will examine defenses of slavery put forth by slave holders and other people.
2. Have groups use library and Internet resources to find primary sources about the slave trade in the United States. Examples may include diaries, advertisements, newspaper articles, trial transcripts, posters, and speeches.
3. Ask all students to look for how both sides of the slavery issue used emotion to gain support for their positions. Have groups report their findings to the class.
4. Extend the activity by leading a discussion about the use of emotional appeals in present-day political issues. **LS Interpersonal**

Alternative Assessment Handbook, Rubric 14: Group Activity

Answers

Analyzing Information *possible answer—A pizza would be very different without tomato sauce, cheese, or a crust made from wheat.*

Direct Teach

Main Idea

❷ Trade and Economic Power

In the 1600s and 1700s, new trade patterns developed and power shifted in Europe.

Identify Economic power shifted from Spain and Portugal to what part of Europe? *Netherlands and England*

Summarize How did banks improve business? *exchanged money from different countries, loaned money to new businesses*

Quick Facts Transparency: Supply and Demand

Teaching Tip

To help students understand how a market economy works, point out that they can see examples of the law of supply and demand every day. Ask students to think of products that were very expensive when they first appeared on the market but dropped in price as supplies increased and demand decreased. Electronic devices such as DVD players are good examples.

Supply and Demand

QUICK FACTS

Market economies are based on the idea of supply and demand. This idea states that people will produce goods that other people want. In Europe, market economies developed as populations grew and the world economy developed.

❶ Population grew in Europe. With more people, there was a greater demand for goods.

❷ Since people wanted more goods, companies worked to make, or supply, more goods.

The Netherlands became a great trading power in the 1600s as the Dutch used their shipbuilding, sailing, and business skills to boost their overseas commerce. Dutch merchants formed a company to trade directly with Asia. The Dutch soon controlled many islands in Southeast Asia and trading posts in India, Japan, and southern Africa.

England also benefited greatly from increased trade. New trading posts in India and China, along with its colonies in North America, gave England access to huge markets and many resources.

Banking

Increased trade created a need for banks. Realizing this, the Dutch and the English each set up banks. Banking improved business in a number of ways. For example, with the growth of international trade, merchants had to deal with money from different countries. At banks, merchants could exchange money from one country for money from another and be certain that they were getting the proper value. Banks also loaned money to people who wanted to start new businesses. In doing so, banks contributed to economic growth.

Banking and new trade routes, along with increased manufacturing, brought wealth to England and the Netherlands. The economic power in Europe shifted.

READING CHECK **Identifying Cause and Effect** Why did power shift from Spain and Portugal to England and the Netherlands in the 1600s?

Market Economies

Economic growth and new wealth changed business in Europe. Because more people had wealth, they started buying more manufactured goods.

There were several reasons for the increased demand for manufactured goods. First, Europe's population was growing. More people meant a need for more goods. Second, farmers were growing food at lower costs. With lower expenses for food, people had more money to spend on manufactured goods. A third reason was that newly founded colonies had to get their manufactured goods from Europe.

As the demand rose, businesspeople realized they could make more money by finding better ways to make manufactured

Collaborative Learning

At Level

Banking Role Play

1. Have students read the text on this page closely. Organize the class into pairs and tell them they will be role playing a trader and banker.
2. The trader should be seeking money to finance a trip. The banker should be seeking interest, or a fee, for loaning the money. Each person should be asking questions so that he or she feels good about the deal. The banker deserves to know the details of the trader's plan. The trader deserves to know how much the banker expects in interest.
3. Ask for volunteers to discuss their role play, including what they learned about the relationship between a businessperson and a banker. **LS Interpersonal**

Alternative Assessment Handbook, Rubric 14: Group Activity

Answers

Reading Check *because England and the Netherlands developed new sources of wealth such as new trade routes, banks, and manufacturing*

3 Finally, the supply of goods met the demand for goods.

goods. They wanted to increase the supply of goods offered to meet the demand. This new way of doing business can be considered the beginning of capitalism. **Capitalism** is an economic system in which individuals and private businesses run most industries. Competition among these businesses affects how much goods cost.

Competition among different businesses is most successful in a market economy. In a **market economy**, individuals decide what goods and services they will buy and sell. The government does not make these decisions for people. A market economy works on a balance between supply and demand. If there is a great demand for a product, a seller will increase the supply in order to make more money.

The ability of individuals to control how they make and spend money is a benefit of a market economy and capitalism. In the 1800s capitalism would become the basis for most economic systems in western Europe and the Americas.

READING CHECK **Summarizing** What is a market economy?

SUMMARY AND PREVIEW The Columbian Exchange brought new plants, animals, and technology, as well as social and cultural changes, to Europe, Africa, Asia, and the Americas. New economic systems were developed too—mercantilism and, later, capitalism. Next, you'll learn about political changes in Europe.

Section 3 Assessment

Reviewing Ideas, Terms, and People

1. a. **Identify** Name some plants and animals that were part of the Columbian Exchange.
   b. **Evaluate** Who do you think benefitted more from the Columbian Exchange–Europeans or people in the Americas?
2. a. **Describe** What was the triangular trade?
   b. **Analyze** How did economic power shift in Europe in the 1600s?
   c. **Elaborate** How were colonies important to a country that was following the economic policy of **mercantilism**?
3. a. **Recall** In what kind of an economic system do individuals and private businesses run most of the industries?
   b. **Explain** How do supply and demand work in a market economy?

Critical Thinking

4. **Analyzing** Using your notes, explain how the availability of new products led to new trade patterns and new economic systems in Europe. Write your explanations in the arrows of a diagram like the one below.

FOCUS ON SPEAKING

5. **Understanding Economics** From your notes and reading, select the three most important effects of the interaction between the Old and New Worlds. Describe these in your chart.

Section 3 Assessment Answers

1. a. tomatoes, potatoes, beans, squash, chocolate, maize, bananas, cows, goats, horses, sheep, pigs, chickens
   b. possible answer—the Americas; because horses helped people travel farther and made work easier
2. a. exchange of raw materials from colonies, manufactured products from Europe, slaves from Africa
   b. It shifted from Spain and Portugal to England and the Netherlands.
   c. Colonies provided raw materials, gold and silver, and a place to sell European goods.
3. a. capitalism
   b. Sellers try to create supply to meet demand for products in order to make money.
4. first arrow—new trading posts in other countries; second arrow—need for banks and dealing with money from other countries
5. Answers will vary, but should demonstrate knowledge of new products, trade patterns, and economic systems that affected trade.

Direct Teach

Main Idea

3 Market Economies

Market economies changed business in Europe.

Recall What determines how much goods cost in a capitalist economy? *competition among businesses*

Finding Main Ideas Name one factor that led to increased demand for manufactured goods. *possible answers—increased population, increased income, demand from colonies*

Info to Know

Mercantile System The term *mercantile system* was not coined until 1776. Philosopher Adam Smith came up with the idea to describe a system that had been in practice for nearly two hundred years already. Smith, himself, advocated a *laissez faire*, or free trade, market system in which the government does not interfere with private business. Such a system is a pure form of capitalism.

Review & Assess

Close

Have students summarize the effects, both positive and negative, of the Columbian Exchange throughout the world.

Assess

SE Section 3 Assessment
PASS: Section 3 Quiz
Alternative Assessment Handbook

Reteach/Classroom Intervention

Guided Reading Workbook, Section 3
Interactive Skills Tutor CD-ROM

Answers

Reading Check *an economic system in which individuals (not the government) decide what goods and services they will buy and sell*

Preteach

Bellringer

If YOU were there . . . Use the **Daily Bellringer Transparency** for this section to help students answer the question.

Daily Bellringer Transparency

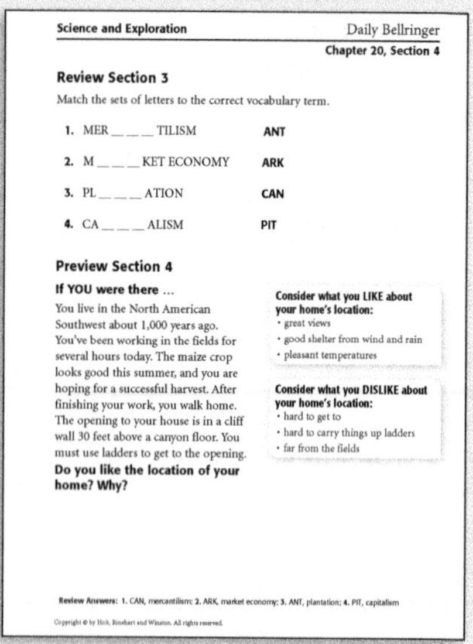

Science and Exploration — Daily Bellringer
Chapter 20, Section 4

Review Section 3

Match the sets of letters to the correct vocabulary term.

1. MER___TILISM — **ANT**
2. M___KET ECONOMY — **ARK**
3. PL___ATION — **CAN**
4. CA___ALISM — **PIT**

Preview Section 4

If YOU were there ...

You live in the North American Southwest about 1,000 years ago. You've been working in the fields for several hours today. The maize crop looks good this summer, and you are hoping for a successful harvest. After finishing your work, you walk home. The opening to your house is in a cliff wall 30 feet above a canyon floor. You must use ladders to get to the opening. **Do you like the location of your home? Why?**

Consider what you LIKE about your home's location:
- great views
- good shelter from wind and rain
- pleasant temperatures

Consider what you DISLIKE about your home's location:
- hard to get to
- hard to carry things up ladders
- far from the fields

Review Answers: 1. CAN, mercantilism; 2. ARK, market economy; 3. ANT, plantation; 4. PIT, capitalism

Instructional Resources for Chapter 20 can be found online via the State Specific Resources link in the Teacher One Stop.

Building Vocabulary

Preteach or review the following terms:

confederation alliance (p. 606)

nomadic traveling (p. 606)

raid attack, invade (p. 606)

CRF: Vocabulary Builder Activity, Section 4

Taking Notes

Have students use a graphic organizer to take notes on the section. This activity will prepare students for the Section Assessment, in which they will complete a graphic organizer that builds on the information using the Critical Thinking Skill: Comparing and Contrasting.

SECTION 4

Native American Cultures

What You Will Learn...

Main Ideas

1. Several early societies developed in North America long before Europeans explored the continent.
2. Geographic areas influenced Native American cultures.
3. Native American cultures shared beliefs about religion and land ownership.

The Big Idea

Many diverse Native American cultures developed across the different geographic regions of North America.

Key Terms and People

pueblos, *p. 603*
kivas, *p. 603*
totems, *p. 604*
teepees, *p. 606*
matrilineal, *p. 606*

Create a graphic organizer to take notes on Native American cultures of North America.

If YOU were there...

You live in the North American Southwest about 1,000 years ago. You've been working in the fields for several hours today. The maize crop looks good this summer, and you are hoping for a successful harvest. After finishing your work, you walk home. The opening to your house is in a cliff wall 30 feet above a canyon floor. You must use ladders to get to the opening.

Do you like the location of your home? Why?

BUILDING BACKGROUND The Europeans who reached the Americas in the 1400s and 1500s encountered a number of groups already living there. Many diverse cultures existed where Native Americans had adapted to their different environments.

Early Societies

The earliest people in North America were hunter-gatherers. After 5000 BC some of these people learned how to farm, and they settled in villages. Although less populated than South America and Mesoamerica, North America had many complex societies long before Europeans reached the continent.

Anasazi

By 1500 BC the people who lived in the North American Southwest, like those who lived in Mesoamerica, were growing maize. One of the early farm cultures in the Southwest was the Anasazi (ah-nuh-SAH-zee), or ancestral Pueblo. The Anasazi lived in the Four Corners region, where present-day Arizona, Colorado, New Mexico, and Utah meet. Anasazi farmers adapted to their dry environment and grew maize, beans, and squash. Over time, they began to use irrigation to increase food production. By the time the Anasazi settled in the area, they were already skilled basket makers. They wove straw, vines, and yucca to make containers for food and other items, and they eventually became skilled potters as well.

Teach the Big Idea

At Level

Native American Cultures

1. **Teach** To teach the main ideas in the section, use the questions in the Direct Teach boxes.
2. **Apply** Create a table with the following headings for students to see: *Arctic, Subarctic, Northwest Coast, Plateau, Great Plains, Northeast, Great Basin, California, Southwest,* and *Southeast.* Have students copy the table onto their own paper. As students read the section, have them list the Native American groups that lived in each region and explain how each group adapted to its environment.
3. **Review** Ask students to compare and contrast the information in their charts. Have students share their ideas about similarities and differences among the Native American groups.
4. **Practice/Homework** Have students create a Venn diagram that illustrates the similarities and differences among the groups discussed in this section. **LS Verbal/Linguistic**

Alternative Assessment Handbook, Rubric 11: Discussions

Dwellings like these were built into cliffs for safety. Often, ladders were needed to reach the buildings. The ladders could be removed, keeping invaders from reaching the dwelllings.

The early Anasazi lived in pit houses dug into the ground. After about AD 750 they built **pueblos**, or aboveground houses made of a heavy clay called adobe. The Anasazi built these houses on top of each other, creating large multistoried complexes. Some pueblos had several hundred rooms and could house 1,000 people.

The Anasazi often built their houses in canyon walls and had to use ladders to enter their homes. These cliff dwellings provided a strong defense against enemies. The Anasazi also built **kivas**, underground ceremonial chambers, at the center of each community. Kivas were sacred areas used for religious ceremonies. Some of these rituals focused on the life-giving forces of rain and maize.

The Anasazi thrived for hundreds of years. After AD 1300, however, they began to abandon their villages. Scholars believe that drought, disease, or raids by nomadic tribes from the north may have caused the Anasazi to move away from their pueblos.

Mound Builders

Several farming societies developed in the eastern part of North America after 1000 BC. The Hopewell lived along the Mississippi, Ohio, and lower Missouri river valleys. They supported their large population with agriculture and trade. They built large burial mounds to honor their dead.

The Hopewell culture had declined by AD 700. Other cultures, first the Adena and then the Mississippian, began to thrive in the same area. Skilled farmers and traders, the Mississippian built large settlements. Their largest city, Cahokia, was located in present-day Missouri. It had a population of 30,000.

Both the Adena and the Mississippian built hundreds of mounds for religious ceremonies. Cahokia alone had more than 100 temple and burial mounds. These mounds had flat tops, and temples were built on top. Many were gigantic. Monks Mound, near Collinsville, Illinois, for example, was 100 feet high and covered 16 acres.

Several other mound-building cultures thrived in eastern North America. More than 10,000 mounds have been found in the Ohio River valley alone. Some of these mounds are shaped like birds and snakes. The mound-building cultures had declined by the time European explorers reached the Southeast. Their societies no longer existed by the early 1700s.

READING CHECK **Summarizing** Why did some Native American groups build mounds?

Direct Teach

Main Idea

1 Early Societies

Several early societies developed in North America long before Europeans explored the continent.

Recall How did Anasazi houses change over time? *at first they were pit houses dug in the ground; later they were pueblos, with houses on top of each other; also cliff dwellings*

Summarize What was the purpose of the mounds built by the Mississippians? *used for religious ceremonies*

Generalize What did the Anasazi, Hopewell, and Mississippian societies have in common? *All were farming cultures.*

Info to Know

A Mississippian Game The Mississippians often played games, including a game called chunkey. This game involved one player rolling a stone disk down a court, while other players threw poles at the spot where they thought the stone would stop. The player whose pole landed closest to where the stone stopped scored points.

Analyzing Visuals

Adobe Pueblos were made out of adobe, or dried earth. Do you think adobe would have been a good building material for the Mississippians, considering that they lived in a humid, and often wet, environment? *possible answer—no, because adobe homes might turn to mud and collapse in wet environments*

Differentiating Instruction

Above Level

Advanced/Gifted and Talented

Research Required

Materials: art supplies and poster boards

1. Organize students into pairs.
2. Begin by reminding students of the unusual structure and location of Anasazi pueblos. Also, discuss the significance of the kivas located at the centers of the communities.
3. Instruct students to prepare a presentation in which they discuss the pueblo's structure and purpose.
4. Have students conduct research on the Internet or other resources to learn more about Anasazi communities. Then have students prepare their presentations, which should include drawings or paintings.
5. If time permits, allow students to give their presentations to the class. LS **Visual/Spatial, Interpersonal**

Alternative Assessment Handbook, Rubrics 14: Group Activity; and 29: Presentations

Answers

Reading Check *to honor their dead and for religious purposes*

Direct Teach

Main Idea

❷ Native American Culture Areas

Geographic areas influenced Native American cultures.

Explain How did the Inuit adapt to the harsh climate of Alaska and Canada? *built igloos, homes partially underground, fished and hunted for food, used dogs to pull sleds*

Draw Inferences Why did Subarctic peoples live in different types of shelters at different times? *When following the seasonal migrations of deer, these peoples needed shelters they could move easily. The rest of the time, they could live in more permanent dwellings.*

Summarize What different methods did Native American groups of the Southwest use to adapt to their dry climate? *learned to irrigate to grow crops, especially maize, squash, and beans; Apache and Navajo hunted small animals and foraged for food*

Map Transparency: Native American Culture Areas

Linking to Today

Potlatches In the Chinook language, the word *potlatch* means "to give." Potlatches were often associated with funerals. Even today, in some cultural groups, families may host a potlatch in honor of a deceased member on the one-year anniversary of that person's death.

Info to Know

Getting Around in the Far North In addition to dogsleds, the Inuit and Aleut used kayaks, or one-person canoes covered with skins. Kayaks enabled the Inuit to cross icy Arctic waters.

Native American Culture Areas

Researchers use culture areas—the geographic locations that influenced societies—to help them describe ancient Native American peoples. North America is divided into several culture areas.

North and Northwest

The far north of North America is divided into the Arctic and Subarctic culture areas. Few plants grow in the Arctic because the ground is always frozen beneath a thin top layer of soil. This harsh environment was home to two groups of people, the Inuit and the Aleut. The Inuit lived in present-day northern Alaska and Canada. Their homes were igloos, hide tents, and huts. The Aleut, whose home was in western and southern Alaska, lived in multifamily houses that were partially underground. The two groups shared many cultural features, including language. Both groups survived by fishing and hunting large mammals. The Aleut and Inuit also depended on dogs for many tasks, such as hunting and pulling sleds.

South of the Arctic lies the Subarctic, home to groups such as the Dogrib and Montagnais peoples. While they followed the seasonal migrations of deer, these peoples lived in shelters made of animal skins. At other times, they lived in villages made up of log houses. Farther south, the Kwakiutl and the Chinook thrived, thanks to the rich supply of game animals, fish, and wild plants that allowed large populations to increase without the need for farming.

Native Americans in the Pacific Northwest carved images of **totems**—ancestor or animal spirits—on tall, wooden poles. Totem poles held great religious and historical significance for Native Americans of the Northwest. Feasts called potlatches were another unique, or unusual, aspect of these Native Americans' culture. At these gatherings, hosts, usually chiefs or wealthy people, gave away most of their belongings as gifts. In this way, the hosts increased their social importance.

Focus on Reading
What is the definition of **totems** according to this sentence?

West and Southwest

Farther south along the Pacific coast was the California region, which included the area between the Pacific and the Sierra Nevada mountain range. Food sources were plentiful, so farming was not necessary. One major plant food was acorns, which were ground into flour. People also fished and hunted deer and other game. Most Native Americans in the California region lived in groups of families of about 50 to 300. Among these groups, including the Hupa, Miwok, and Yokuts, more than 100 languages were spoken.

The area east of the Sierra Nevada Mountains, the Great Basin, received little rain. To survive, Native Americans adapted to the drier climate by gathering seeds, digging roots, and trapping small animals for food. Most groups in this area, including the Paiute, Shoshone, and Ute, spoke the same language.

The Southwest culture region included the present-day states of Arizona and New Mexico, and parts of Colorado and Texas. Pueblo groups, such as the Hopi and Zuni, lived there. Like the Anasazi, these Native Americans also adapted to a dry climate. The Pueblo irrigated the land and grew maize, squash, and beans. These crops were vital to southwestern peoples. The Pueblo religion focused on two key areas of Pueblo life, rain and maize. The Pueblo performed religious rituals hoping to bring rain and a successful maize crop to their peoples.

Pueblo peoples were settled and built multistoried houses out of adobe bricks. Over time their towns grew larger, and some towns had more than 1,000 residents. Pueblo peoples made fine pottery that featured beautifully painted designs.

Bering Sea

Inu

Collaborative Learning

At Level

Early North American Societies Flash Cards

1. Have each student divide a sheet of paper into six parts, creating six note cards.
2. Ask students to label each of the cards with the name of one of the Native American societies discussed in this section.
3. On each card, have students write one question about an aspect of the Native American society they listed on the card. Encourage students to make the questions as specific as possible. Have students write the answers on the back of the cards.
4. Pair students and have partners use their cards to quiz each other.
5. When students are done, have them switch partners and repeat the process.
LS Verbal/Linguistic, Interpersonal

Alternative Assessment Handbook, Rubric 14: Group Activity

Answers

Focus on Reading *ancestor or animal spirits*

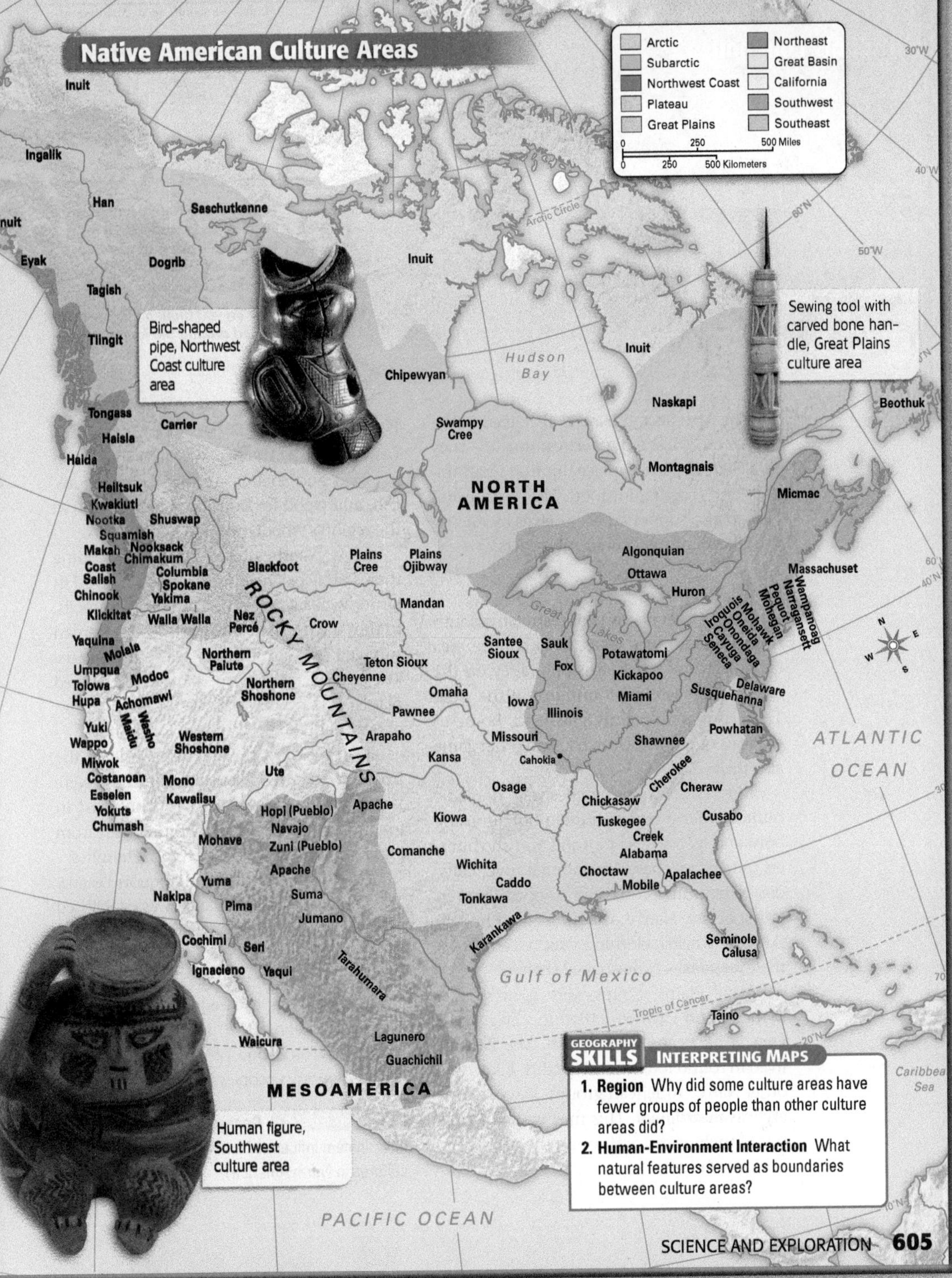

Bird-shaped pipe, Northwest Coast culture area

Sewing tool with carved bone handle, Great Plains culture area

Human figure, Southwest culture area

GEOGRAPHY SKILLS INTERPRETING MAPS

1. **Region** Why did some culture areas have fewer groups of people than other culture areas did?
2. **Human-Environment Interaction** What natural features served as boundaries between culture areas?

Direct Teach

Main Idea

❷ Native American Culture Areas

Geographic areas influenced Native American cultures.

Explain Why did the Pueblo peoples adopt a sedentary lifestyle? *They learned to grow crops and irrigate their land so they did not need to travel in search of food.*

Analyze Why do you think so many Native American groups lived along the Pacific coast of the present-day United States? *They could catch plenty of food, and the climate was mild.*

Map Transparency: Native American Culture Areas

Teaching Tip

Arctic vs. Subarctic
Explain to students that arctic relates to the North Pole or the region around it. Subarctic refers to the regions immediately outside of the arctic circle or regions that have similar conditions.

Cross-Discipline Activity: Geography

At Level

Mapping Native American Culture Groups

Materials: colored pencils

1. Have students examine the map, Native American Culture Areas.
2. Have students create their own outline maps of North America. Then, have students fill in the following on their maps:
   - Native American culture areas and groups covered in this section;
   - three distinguishing features about each culture area, such as methods of obtaining food, types of shelter, types of government, and religious rituals;
   - major geographical features, such as mountain ranges and bodies of water.
3. Maps should include a title and a legend.
4. Have students refer to their maps as you review how the environment influenced culture in North America. **LS Visual/Spatial**

Alternative Assessment Handbook, Rubric 20: Map Creation

Answers

Interpreting Maps 1. *Geographical and climatic conditions may have limited the size of groups; ability to grow food or hunt also affected the size of the population;* **2.** *mountains, rivers, lakes*

Direct Teach

Main Idea

❷ Native American Culture Areas

Geographic areas influenced Native American cultures.

Recall Explain how the Iroquois lived. *They were farmers, hunters, and traders who lived in rectangular homes, called longhouses, that housed 8 to 10 families.*

Compare and Contrast What were some of the similarities and differences between Native American cultures in the Great Plains and the East? *While both farmed, most Plains peoples depended on buffalo for food, clothing, and shelter. Plains peoples were nomadic; eastern groups had wood for housing, fished, and developed the Iroquois League.*

Predict What might be the differences between a matrilineal society, like the Pawnee, and a patrilineal society? *possible answers—In a matrilineal society, ties to the mother's side of the family might be stronger; women might be held in higher esteem.*

Map Transparency: Native American Culture Areas

MISCONCEPTION ALERT

What about Horses? When reading about Native Americans of the Great Plains, you may picture scenes from movies or television showing Plains peoples on horses. Actually, horses did not exist in North America until European explorers brought horses to the Americas.

Northeastern Native Americans such as the Iroquois lived in longhouses made of tree bark. The drawing shows the longhouses in one Iroquois village.

Why do you think a fence was placed around the longhouses?

The Apache and Navajo also lived in the Southwest. These groups were nomadic—they moved from place to place hunting small animals and foraging for food. The Apache and Navajo also supported themselves by raiding the villages of the Pueblo and others.

Great Plains

The huge Great Plains region stretches south from Canada into Texas. This culture area is bordered by the Mississippi Valley on the east and the Rocky Mountains on the west. The Plains were mainly grassland, home to millions of buffalo. Deer, elk, and other game also thrived there.

Most Great Plains peoples were nomadic hunters. Many groups hunted buffalo using bows and spears. Blackfoot and Arapaho hunters sometimes chased the animals over cliffs, drove them into corrals, or trapped them in a ring of fire. Native Americans used buffalo skins for shields, clothing, and coverings for their **teepees**—cone-shaped shelters.

Some Plains groups were farmers. The Mandan and Pawnee settled in villages and grew corn, beans, and squash. The Pawnee lived in round lodges made of dirt. Like some other Native American groups, Pawnee society was **matrilineal**. This means that people traced their ancestry through their mothers, not their fathers.

Northeast and Southeast

Eastern North America was rich in sources for food and shelter. Animals, plant foods, fish, and wood for housing were plentiful in the region's woodlands and river valleys.

Most southeastern groups, including the Cherokee, Creek, and Seminole, lived in farming villages governed by village councils. In the Northeast, groups like the Algonquian survived by hunting and gathering plants. Those in the south farmed, hunted, gathered plants, and fished. Many tribes used strings of beads known as wampum for money.

To the east of the Algonquian lived the Iroquois (or Haudenosaunee). They were farmers, hunters, and traders who lived in longhouses, or rectangular homes made from logs and bark, that housed 8 to 10 families.

The Iroquois created the Iroquois League. This confederation, or alliance, was established by the Cayuga, Mohawk, Oneida, Onondaga, and Seneca. The league waged war against and made peace with non-Iroquois peoples. Its goal was to strengthen the alliance against invasion. The league helped the Iroquois become one of the most powerful Native American peoples in North America.

READING CHECK **Generalizing** How did environment influence Native American cultures in North America?

Critical Thinking: Supporting a Point of View

Above Level

Joining the Iroquois League

1. Review with students the significance of the Iroquois League.
2. Ask students to imagine that they are leaders in a Native American group that is considering joining the league. Each student should write a short essay explaining why the group should join the league. The essay should contain specific reasons.
3. You may wish to instruct students to conduct additional research on the Iroquois League to obtain more information to use in their essays.
4. Ask volunteers to share their essays with the class. Encourage the class to discuss the essays. **LS Verbal/Linguistic**

Alternative Assessment Handbook, Rubrics 37: Writing Assignments; and 43: Writing to Persuade

Answers

Analyzing Visuals *to protect their homes from intruders*

Reading Check *Different groups had to adapt to their environment; people who lived in cold climates could not farm; those who could gather food did not have to farm; those who lived near oceans fished; those on the Plains hunted. The environment affected the type of housing that was built.*

Shared Beliefs

Although they were different culturally and geographically, Native American groups of North America shared certain beliefs. The religion of most Native American peoples, for example, was linked to nature. Native Americans believed that spiritual forces were everywhere, dwelling in heavenly bodies and in sacred places on the earth. Spirits even lived within animals and plants. Native Americans tried to honor the spirits in their daily lives.

Ceremonies maintained the group's relationship with Earth and Sky, which were believed to be the sustainers of life. In addition, individuals who wanted help prayed to their spirit protector.

Native Americans also shared beliefs about property. They believed that individual ownership only applied to the crops one grew. The land itself was for the use of everyone in the village, and a person's right to use it was temporary. Native Americans also thought they should preserve the land for future generations. These beliefs contrasted sharply with those of Europeans— a difference that would cause conflict.

Despite their shared beliefs, the diverse culture groups of North America had little interest in joining together into large political units. As a result, Native Americans on the North American continent did not form large empires like the Aztec and Inca of Meso- and South America did.

READING CHECK **Identifying Points of View** What religious beliefs did Native American groups share?

SUMMARY People of North America had formed many complex societies long before the first European explorers crossed the Atlantic Ocean.

Section 4 Assessment

Reviewing Ideas, Terms, and People

1. a. **Recall** Why did the Anasazi build **kivas**?
   b. **Summarize** What different types of housing were built by the Anasazi?
   c. **Draw Conclusions** Why do you think that some mounds were built in the shape of birds and snakes?
2. a. **Identify** What are culture areas?
   b. **Contrast** How did food sources for Native Americans of the North and Northwest differ from those of Native Americans living in the West and Southwest?
   c. **Elaborate** Why was the formation of the **Iroquois League** considered to be a significant political development?
3. a. **Recall** How did Native Americans view land ownership?
   b. **Analyze** What role did religion play in the lives of Native Americans?
   c. **Predict** Why do you think most Native American groups did not form large empires like the Aztec and the Inca did?

Critical Thinking

4. **Comparing and Contrasting** Review your notes on early societies and culture areas. Then use a Venn diagram like this one to identify similarities and differences among Native American culture groups.

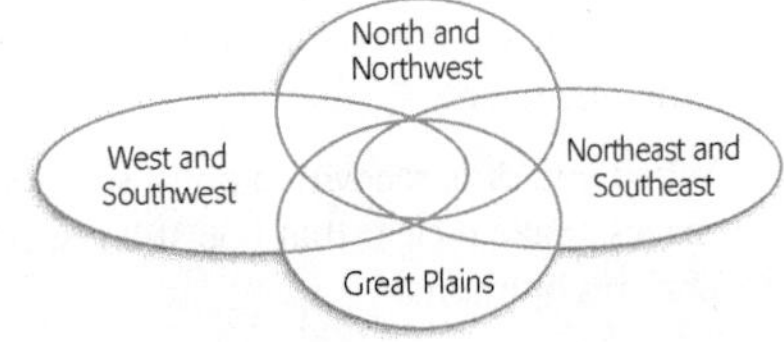

FOCUS ON SPEAKING

5. **Describing Culture** Look back through this section to discover ways in which a group's beliefs, environment, and practices can be described. Write down phrases that you think are especially useful in understanding Native American cultures.

Direct Teach

Main Idea

❸ Shared Beliefs

Native American cultures shared beliefs about religion and land ownership.

Compare What views about land ownership were shared by Native American groups? *Individual ownership applied only to crops and was temporary.*

Analyze Why do you think the religion of most Native American peoples related to nature? *possible answer—because their culture and lifestyle were deeply rooted in nature*

Review & Assess

Close

Have students refer to their culture maps of North America and briefly review the development of early North American societies.

Assess

SE Section 4 Assessment

PASS: Section 4 Quiz

Alternative Assessment Handbook

Reteach/Classroom Intervention

Guided Reading Workbook, Section 4

Interactive Skills Tutor CD-ROM

Section 2 Assessment Answers

1. a. for religious ceremonies
   b. pit houses, stacked pueblos, cliff dwellings
   c. possible answer—had religious or cultural significance to the group of Native Americans
2. a. geographic locations that influenced societies
   b. North and Northwest—hunted large animals, fished, ate wild plants; West and Southwest—hunted, farmed, gathered plants, trapped small animals
   c. It united and strengthened politically different Native American groups among other Native American groups.
3. a. Individuals did not own the land, only the crops that they grew.
   b. Native Americans believed spirits were everywhere; they honored the spirits in their daily lives.
   c. possible answers—geographic barriers made uniting difficult; wanted to maintain independence; lifestyles were too diverse
4. Students' answers should show the similarities and differences of Native American cultural groups discussed in this section.
5. Students' answers should include phrases from Section 4 that capture the Native American culture.

Answers

Reading Check *Spiritual forces were everywhere and should be honored; beliefs were linked to nature.*

Social Studies Skills

Making Group Decisions

Planning a School Store Ask students to imagine that their school is starting a school store and that they are going to be given $200 to purchase goods to be sold at the store. Organize students into small groups. Have each group brainstorm a list of five goods that the store should carry, such as school supplies or snack foods. Suggest that students prioritize their lists based on which goods would be in the highest demand by their fellow students. Allow students enough time to research the costs of the items that they have selected. Then, ask students to determine a price for each item. Groups should also discuss how setting prices too high or too low might affect demand for the goods or the store's ability to supply goods. Then have each group present their list and explain their prices to the class.

Alternative Assessment Handbook, Rubric 35: Solving Problems

Social Studies Skills

Analysis | Critical Thinking | **Economics** | Study

Making Group Decisions

Understand the Skill

Making decisions as a group is a complicated and difficult skill to learn. However, it is an important skill at all levels of society—from governing a nation to choosing a movie to see with friends. At every level, success is based on the ability of group members to work together in effective and cooperative ways.

Learn the Skill

Being part of an effective group requires certain behaviors.

1. Be an active member. Take part in setting the group's goals and in making its decisions.
2. Take a position. State your views and work to persuade other members to accept them. However, also be open to negotiating and compromising to settle differences within the group.
3. Be willing to take charge if leadership is needed. But also be willing to follow the leadership of other members.
4. When you disagree with a point someone makes, make it clear that you still respect that person's opinion.
5. Never make another member feel that his or her comments are stupid, unwanted, or not valuable. But let people know if you think they're not respecting your opinions.

Practice and Apply the Skill

Divide into a small group of four or five students. Imagine you are all members of a family living in the Spanish countryside in the early 1500s. Your family has farmed the same piece of land for many generations, but your life is hard and you have little money for anything more than food and shelter. Now you have heard that, in a nearby city, a captain is looking for sailors for an expedition to the New World. It would be a great adventure with the chance to make great wealth, but it may be dangerous. There is a chance you may never see your family again. In addition, life on a ship and in the Americas would be very different from what you are used to. Together, decide what to do. Make a plan with roles for all family members. After your group has made its plan, answer the following questions.

1. Did your group create a plan to improve the family's life and financial situation? Did you take into account both benefits and disadvantages? What did you contribute toward the plan?
2. How well did your group work together? What role did you play in that?
3. Was your group able to make a decision? If not, why? If so, was compromise involved? Explain why or why not.

Differentiating Instruction

Struggling Readers

Below Level

Have students create illustrated storybooks about a young man or woman who is considering leaving the farm to sail to the New World. Students' stories and pictures should describe how the family decides what to do. Provide colored paper and markers for drawing.

LS Intrapersonal, Visual/Spatial

Alternative Assessment Handbook, Rubrics 3: Artwork; and 39: Writing to Create

Answers

1. *Answers will vary based on group experiences.* **2.** *Answers will vary based on group experiences.* **3.** *Answers will vary based on group experiences.*

CHAPTER 20

Chapter Review

History's Impact
▶ **video series**
Review the video to answer the focus question:
What were some effects of the Columbian Exchange?

Visual Summary

Use the visual summary below to help you review the main ideas of the chapter.

QUICK FACTS

During the Scientific Revolution, scientists used observation, experimentation, and new inventions to greatly increase their knowledge of the world. This knowledge was also expanded by the European exploration of distant lands, made possible by technical advances in shipbuilding.

Reviewing Vocabulary, Terms, and People

For each statement below, write T if it is true and F if it is false. If the statement is false, write the correct term that would make the sentence a true statement.

1. **Galileo Galilei** was the first person to study the sky with a telescope.
2. An explanation that a scientist develops to explain observed facts is called a **scientific method**.
3. **Sir Isaac Newton** developed the theory that the planets orbit around the sun.
4. **Christopher Columbus** led the first voyage to **circumnavigate** the globe.
5. In 1588 an English navy was sent to destroy a fleet of ships called the **Spanish Armada**.
6. **Henry the Navigator** was responsible for much of Portugal's success on the seas.
7. The Anasazi built aboveground homes called **pueblos** in the Southwest.

Comprehension and Critical Thinking

SECTION 1 *(Pages 588–592)*

8. a. **Recall** When did the Scientific Revolution occur?
   b. **Compare and Contrast** How were Copernicus's and Kepler's theories about the movement of the planets similar? How were they different?
   c. **Elaborate** Choose one new invention from the period of the Scientific Revolution and explain how it affects your life.

SECTION 2 *(Pages 593–596)*

9. a. **Recall** What did these people achieve: Vasco da Gama, Christopher Columbus, and Ferdinand Magellan?
   b. **Draw Conclusions** How did new navigation tools, caravels, and better maps affect travel by sea?
   c. **Predict** If the Spanish Armada had defeated the English, how might history have changed?

Answers

Visual Summary

Review and Inquiry Have students use the visual summary to explain the roots, development, and results of the Scientific Revolution and European exploration.

Quick Facts Transparency: Science and Exploration Visual Summary

Reviewing Vocabulary, Terms, and People

1. T
2. F; theory
3. F; Nicolaus Copernicus
4. F; Ferdinand Magellan
5. T
6. T
7. T

Comprehension and Critical Thinking

8. a. between about 1540 and 1700
   b. Both Copernicus and Kepler thought that Earth and other planets orbited the sun, but Kepler proved that the planets' orbits were elliptical instead of circular.
   c. Answers will vary, but students should describe the invention's effects on their lives logically.

Review & Assessment Resources

Review and Reinforce

SE Chapter Review
Quick Facts Transparency: Science and Exploration Visual Summary
Quiz Game CD-ROM
TOS Holt McDougal PuzzleView

Assess

SE Standardized Test Practice
PASS: Chapter Test
Alternative Assessment Handbook
TOS ExamView Assessment Suite, Chapter Test

Reteach/Intervene

Guided Reading Workbook
Differentiated Instruction Teacher Management System: Lesson Plans
Interactive Skills Tutor CD-ROM

Answers

9. **a.** Vasco da Gama—first to sail around Africa to India; Christopher Columbus—"discovered" America; Ferdinand Magellan—led first voyage to circumnavigate the globe **b.** allowed sailors to know where they were when out of sight of land and sail against the wind **c.** possible answer—Spain would have continued to rule the seas and might possibly have claimed all of North America.
10. **a.** possible answers—banana trees, grape vines, lettuce, onions, sugar cane, cows, chickens, pigs, sheep, horses **b.** possible answers—positive: many European and African foods were introduced to the Americas and vice versa; negative: Native Americans and Africans were forced to work on plantations. **c.** Colonies provided raw materials and a market for manufactured goods.
11. **a.** Anasazi, cliff dwellings; Hopewell and Mississippian, mounds **b.** Because Native Americans believed that spirits controlled every aspect of their beliefs, they honored the spirits every day. **c.** Each group had geographic challenges, and life would not have been easy for either group.

Social Studies Skills

12. Group decisions will vary.

Using the Internet

13. Go to hmhsocialstudies.com to access a rubric for this activity.

Reading Skills

14. force; The sentence implies that the Church put pressure on scientists to follow its guidance.
15. to say the opposite; Church leaders wanted scientists to reject these findings, which implies the findings did not agree with Church teachings; could use words and phrases like *disagreed with* or *opposed.*

Reviewing Themes

16. Scientists discovered laws that governed nature, and some thinkers began to believe laws governed human behavior also. If all people were governed by the same laws, they must be equal.
17. an increase in manufacturing and the chance for individuals to make more money
18. Answers will vary.

Focus on Writing

19. **Rubric** Students' poems should:
    - clearly explain the topic in a way fifth graders will understand.
    - include an informative and useful visual aid.
    - be presented using proper eye contact, volume, rate and tone.

CRF: Focus on Speaking: An Informative Report

SECTION 3 *(Pages 597–601)*

10. **a. Identify** Name three plants and three animals that Europeans brought to the Americas.
    b. Compare and Contrast What were some positive and negative results of the Columbian Exchange?
    c. Evaluate How did the founding of colonies affect manufacturing?

SECTION 4 *(Pages 602–607)*

11. **a. Identify** Which early Native American society built cliff dwellings, and which built mounds?
    b. Analyze How did Native Americans' religious beliefs affect their lives in North America?
    c. Evaluate Do you think it was easier for Native Americans to live in the dry climates of the Southwest, where rainfall was unpredictable, or in the North, where the cold climate presented a constant challenge?

Social Studies Skills

12. **Making Group Decisions** Working with a small group of classmates, imagine you are the leaders of a North American Native American group. European explorers have just arrived in your area, and you must decide how to deal with the strangers. Remember to look at the benefits and costs of each course of action before you decide.

Using the Internet 

13. **Activity: Researching Scientists and Their Discoveries** Amazing discoveries were made during the Scientific Revolution. Go online to conduct research on important scientists of that time. Then create a chart of their key discoveries or inventions, the way the discoveries influenced society, and how information about the discoveries has evolved over time.

Reading Skills

Vocabulary Clues *Read the sentence, then answer the questions.*

> Catholic Church leaders tried strongly to impel scientists to reject any findings that contradicted church teachings.

14. What is the meaning of the word *impel*? What clues tell you its meaning?
15. What does the word *contradict* mean? How can you tell from the sentence? How could you restate the meaning by using words you know?

Reviewing Themes

16. **Society and Culture** How did the birth of science lead to the growth of democratic ideas?
17. **Economics** What led to the shift from mercantilism to capitalism?
18. **Economics** To make wise buying decisions in a market economy, individuals must know how to analyze advertisements, determine if they can afford a particular item, and judge whether their money might be better spent in other ways. Think of an item that you might like to buy. Describe the steps you would take in deciding whether to make the purchase.

FOCUS ON SPEAKING

19. **Giving Your Report** Look over the notes you made in your chart. Decide on an organized way to present your information. Then write your speech. Remember that your audience is young, so keep your content simple. Support your key points with interesting details. Use plenty of expressive language to keep your audience interested. Create a colorful, easy-to-follow visual to refer to as you speak.

CHAPTER 20

Standardized Test Practice

DIRECTIONS: Read each question, and write the letter of the best response.

1 Use the diagram to answer the following question.

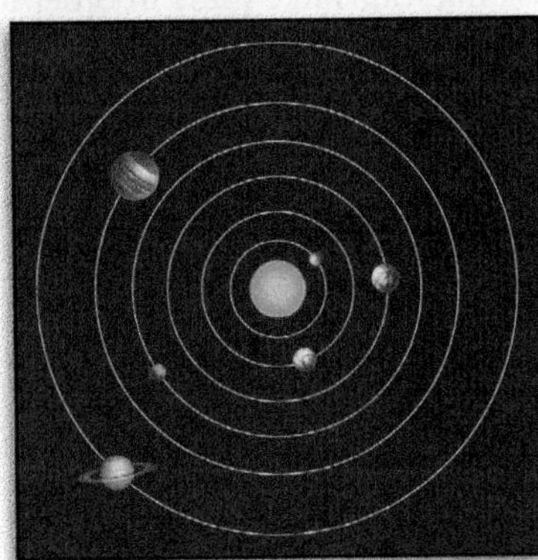

The pioneering work of which early scientist produced this understanding of the solar system?

A Francis Bacon
B Nicolaus Copernicus
C Ptolemy
D Isaac Newton

2 The fundamental principles of the modern scientific method are

A logic and mathematical theories.
B common beliefs of science and religion.
C very detailed record keeping.
D observation and experimentation.

3 Which North American groups lived in the Southeast and built mounds?

A Cherokee and Seminole
B Adena and Hopewell
C Anasazi and Pueblo
D Iroquois and Mohawk

4 The Columbian Exchange is responsible for all of the following *except*

A the spread of disease from Europe to America.
B the introduction of the horse to Europe.
C the spread of American crops to Africa and Asia.
D the introduction of firearms to America.

5 According to the policy of mercantilism, what was the main purpose of colonies?

A to be a source of slaves to work in the ruling country
B to provide a place where the ruling country could send undesirable people
C to help the ruling country have a favorable balance of trade
D to serve as bases from which the ruling country could launch attacks on enemies

Connecting with Past Learnings

6 The event you learned about earlier in this course that was *most* responsible for the Scientific Revolution was

A the Renaissance.
B the fall of Rome.
C the development of feudalism.
D the invention of the printing press.

7 One result of the Columbian Exchange was the spread of Christianity. What other reason for Christianity's spread have you learned about this year?

A the Crusades
B the Spanish Inquisition
C the Reformation
D the Catholic Reformation

Answers

Standardized Test Practice

1. B
Break Down the Question Students should recognize the basic structure of the solar system. Point out that the orbits shown are circular, so Copernicus is the correct answer.

2. D
Break Down the Question This question requires students to distinguish between the value of record keeping, which is important, and the greater contribution of observation and experimentation to the scientific method.

3. B
Break Down the Question This question requires students to recall factual information. Refer students who miss the question to the material in Section 4.

4. B
Break Down the Question Point out to students that the word *except* means that they need to identify which of the answers is not something for which the Columbian Exchange is responsible.

5. C
Break Down the Question Point out that the word *main* means that more than one response may be correct and that students must choose the one that provides the best answer.

6. A
Break Down the Question This question links humanism as discussed in the chapter on the Renaissance and humanism as discussed in this chapter.

7. D
Break Down the Question This question requires students to recall information covered in Chapter 19, Section 3.

Intervention Resources

Reproducible

- Guided Reading Workbook
- Differentiated Instruction Teacher Management System: Lesson Plans

Technology

- Quick Facts Transparency: Science and Exploration Visual Summary
- Interactive Skills Tutor CD-ROM

Tips for Test Taking

Rely on 50/50 Give students these pointers:

- Watch out for distracters—choices that may be true, but are too broad, too narrow, or not relevant to the question.
- Eliminate the least likely choice.
- Then, eliminate the next, and so on until you find the best one.
- If two choices seem equally correct, look to see if "All of the above" is an option. If it is, that might be the best choice.
- If no choice seems correct, look for "None of the above."

Preteach

Bellringer

Motivate Write the following for students to see: "Fred was excited because he got a role in the school play." Ask students to brainstorm causes and effects of the event. Then have students consider the effects they listed as causes and list further effects. Help students build a cause-and-effect chain. Explain that in this workshop students will write a paper explaining causes or effects of a historical event.

Direct Teach

Determining Causes

Get Your Reasons Straight Remind students that not all the details they will read about as they study the Columbian Exchange and the development of North American cultures will be causes or effects. Have students double-check the causes or effects they identified by asking the following questions:

- **Causes:** How did this action or situation contribute to the event I am studying
- **Effects:** How did the event I am studying lead to this event or situation?

Organizing

How Important Is It? Explain to students that they have two choices when organizing information by importance—from least to most important, and from most to least important. Suggest that students who are organizing by order of importance make two outlines, one using each option. Then have students choose the option that works best.

Cause and Effect in History

Assignment
Write a paper explaining one of the following topics:
(1) The effects of the Columbian exchange
(2) The development of many North American cultures

"Why did it happen?" "What happened as a result?" Historians ask questions like these in order to study the causes and effects of historical events. In this way, they learn more about historical events and the links that form the chain between them.

TIP Adding Facts and Details For each cause or effect you identify, you need supporting facts and examples.
Example
Effect: New plants and animals introduced to Americas
- European seeds
- Bananas, sugarcane, onions
- Domesticated animals
- Cows, goats, sheep

1. Prewrite

Identifying Causes and Effects

A **cause** is an action or event that causes another event or situation to happen. An **effect** is what happens as a result of an event or situation. To understand historical events, we sometimes look at causes, sometimes look at effects, and sometimes look at both. For example, we could look at the causes behind Columbus's discovery of a new land, but we could also limit our discussion to the effects.

Collecting and Organizing Information

After choosing the topic you want to write about, gather information from the chapter in this textbook, an encyclopedia, or another library source. You can use graphic organizers like the ones below to organize your information:

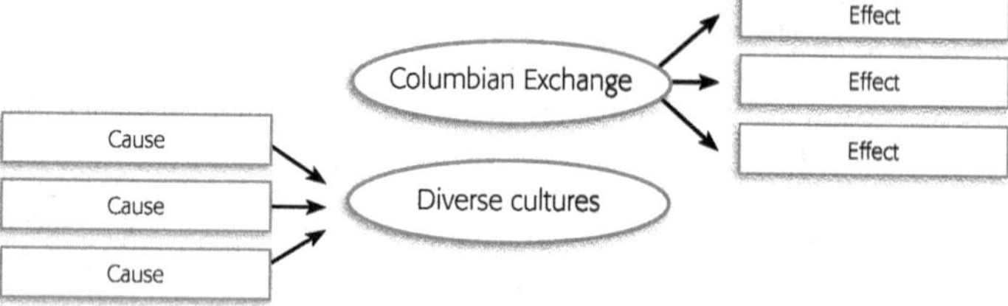

2. Write

You can use this framework to help you write your first draft.

A Writer's Framework

Introduction	Body	Conclusion
■ Briefly identify the event that you will discuss. [Columbian Exchange or North American cultures] ■ Identify at least three causes or effects you will discuss.	■ Explain the causes or effects one at a time, providing supporting facts and examples for each. ■ Present the causes or effects in order of importance, placing the most important point last.	■ Summarize your ideas about the causes or effects of the event.

Differentiating Instruction

English-Language Learners

Below Level | Standard English Mastery

1. Students may not be familiar with the transitional cause-and-effect words and phrases listed in the second Tip on the next page.
2. List the words and phrases and help students define each one. Then have the class use each word or phrase in a sentence.
3. Some students may be confused by the way that placement of transitions within a sentence can vary in English. Some appear before the ideas to which they connect, and some after. Illustrate this point by having students identify the idea to which each cause-and-effect transition connects.
4. Last, have students scan the text on the Columbian Exchange and look for cause-and-effect transitions. Help students identify the ideas to which each one connects.
LS Verbal/Linguistic

3. Evaluate and Revise

Evaluating

Use the following questions to discover ways to improve your draft.

Evaluation Questions for an Explanation of Causes or Effects

- Does your introduction identify the event you are going to explain?
- Does your introduction identify the causes or effects you will discuss?
- Do you explain the causes or effects one at a time, using facts and examples to support each one?
- Do you present the causes or effects in order of importance? Do you discuss the most important cause or effect last?
- Does the conclusion summarize causes or effects and their importance?

Revising

Keep a sharp eye out for false cause-and-effect relationships. The fact that one event happened after another does not mean that the first event caused the second.

Historical events: Columbus sailed to America in 1492. John Cabot sailed to Canada in 1497.

False cause-and-effect relationship: Because Columbus sailed to America in 1492, John Cabot sailed to Canada in 1497. [Although Columbus's voyage happened before Cabot's discovery, it was not a cause.]

4. Proofread and Publish

Proofreading

As you proofread your paper, check to see whether you have unclear pronoun references. They occur when you have two different nouns or phrases the pronoun might refer to.

Unclear After the explorers conquered the native peoples, many of *them* died. [Does *them* refer to the explorers or the native peoples?]

Clear After the explorers conquered the native peoples, many of the native peoples died.

Publishing

With classmates who wrote about the same topic, create a booklet of essays to display in your classroom or in the school library.

Practice and Apply

Use the steps and strategies outlined in this workshop to write an explanation of causes or effects.

TIP Saving the Best for the Last Why would you place the most important cause or effect at the end of your paper, rather than at the beginning? Think about your own experience. When you read something, what part do you remember best—the first or the last? When you hear a speech or your teacher presents a lesson, what sticks in your mind?

Most of the time, we remember what we heard last or read last. That is why it is often a good idea to "save the best for last."

TIP Signaling Causes and Effects Signal that you are about to discuss a cause or an effect with words and phrases like these:

- **Words and phrases that signal causes:** *because, due to, given that, since*
- **Words and phrases that signal effects:** *therefore, thus, consequently, so, as a result, for that reason*

Reteach

Check Organization

Sort It Out Have students trade papers. In the margin next to each paragraph, have students write a word or a phrase identifying the cause or effect discussed. Have them write "divide paragraph" next to any paragraph with more than one cause or effect. Have them write "combine paragraphs" next to any paragraphs that discuss the same cause or effect and then draw an arrow linking the two paragraphs to combine.

Teaching Tip

Stay on Topic Remind students that each paragraph must have a topic sentence. In most cases, it should be the first sentence of the paragraph. Check students' papers as they write and point out any paragraphs without topic sentences.

Practice & Apply

Rubric

Students' explanations of causes or effects should

- begin with an interesting quote or fact about the Columbian Exchange or North American cultures.
- clearly identify the topic.
- accurately explain the causes or effects of the event chosen.
- provide a paragraph and support for each cause or effect.
- follow either chronological order or order of importance.
- end with a summary.
- use correct grammar, punctuation, spelling, and capitalization.

Advanced/Gifted and Talented — Above Level

1. Have students prepare their papers as if they are making a presentation to French government either during or after the French Revolution.
2. Students writing a paper on the war's causes should present an analysis of the causes and recommend ways that war might have been avoided. Students writing a paper on the war's effects should provide solutions for addressing the negative effects. **LS Verbal/Linguistic**

Struggling Readers — Below Level

1. If students have trouble identifying cause and effect, have them practice the skill on an easier selection. Choose an applicable selection from a fifth or sixth grade history text.
2. Have students work in pairs to create a cause-and-effect chart for the selection. Tell students to look for the cause-and-effect transitions listed above to help them. Correct any student errors. **LS Logical/Mathematical**

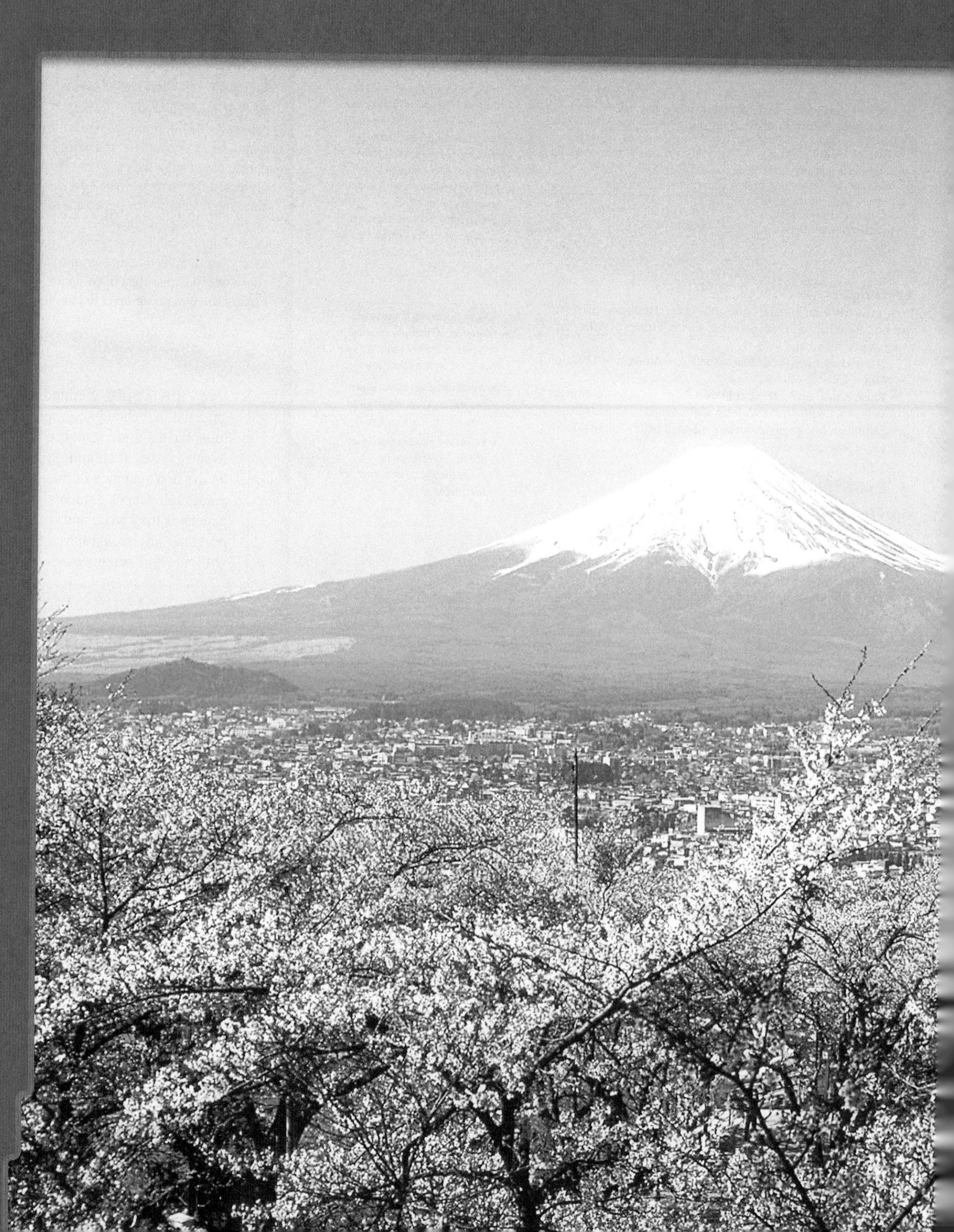

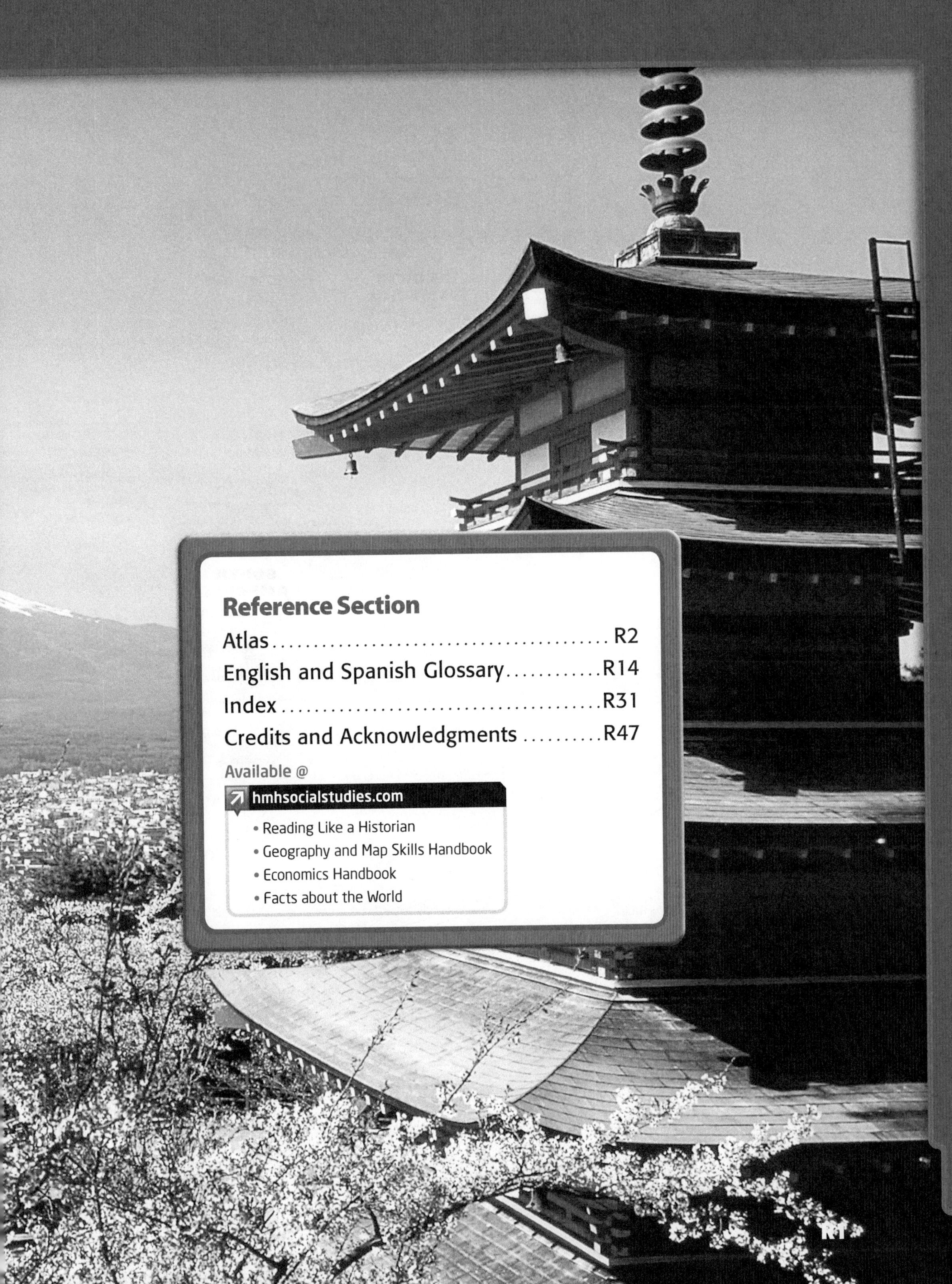

Reference Section

Available @

hmhsocialstudies.com

- Reading Like a Historian
- Geography and Map Skills Handbook
- Economics Handbook
- Facts about the World

ATLAS

World: Political

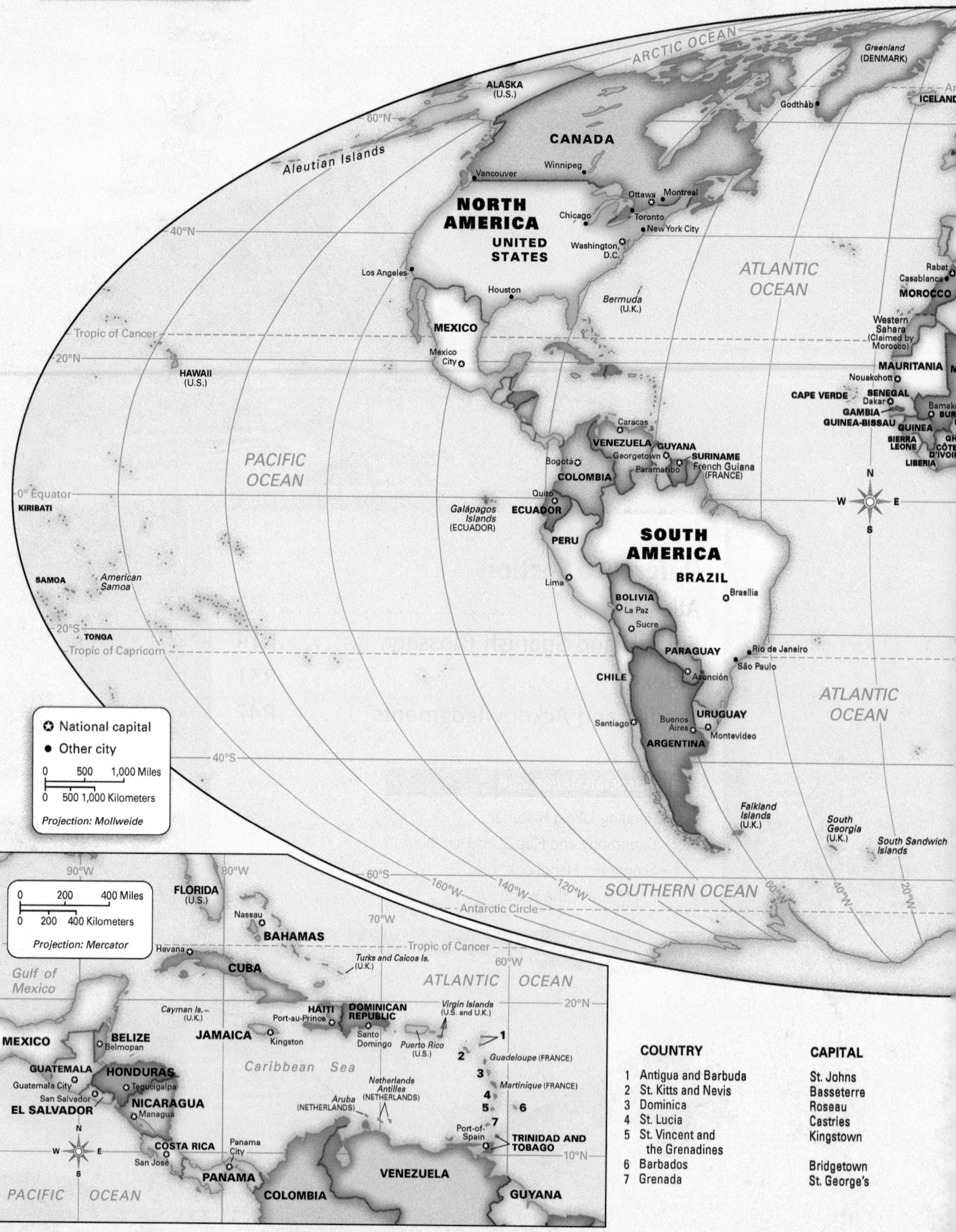

	COUNTRY	CAPITAL
1	Antigua and Barbuda	St. Johns
2	St. Kitts and Nevis	Basseterre
3	Dominica	Roseau
4	St. Lucia	Castries
5	St. Vincent and the Grenadines	Kingstown
6	Barbados	Bridgetown
7	Grenada	St. George's

ATLAS

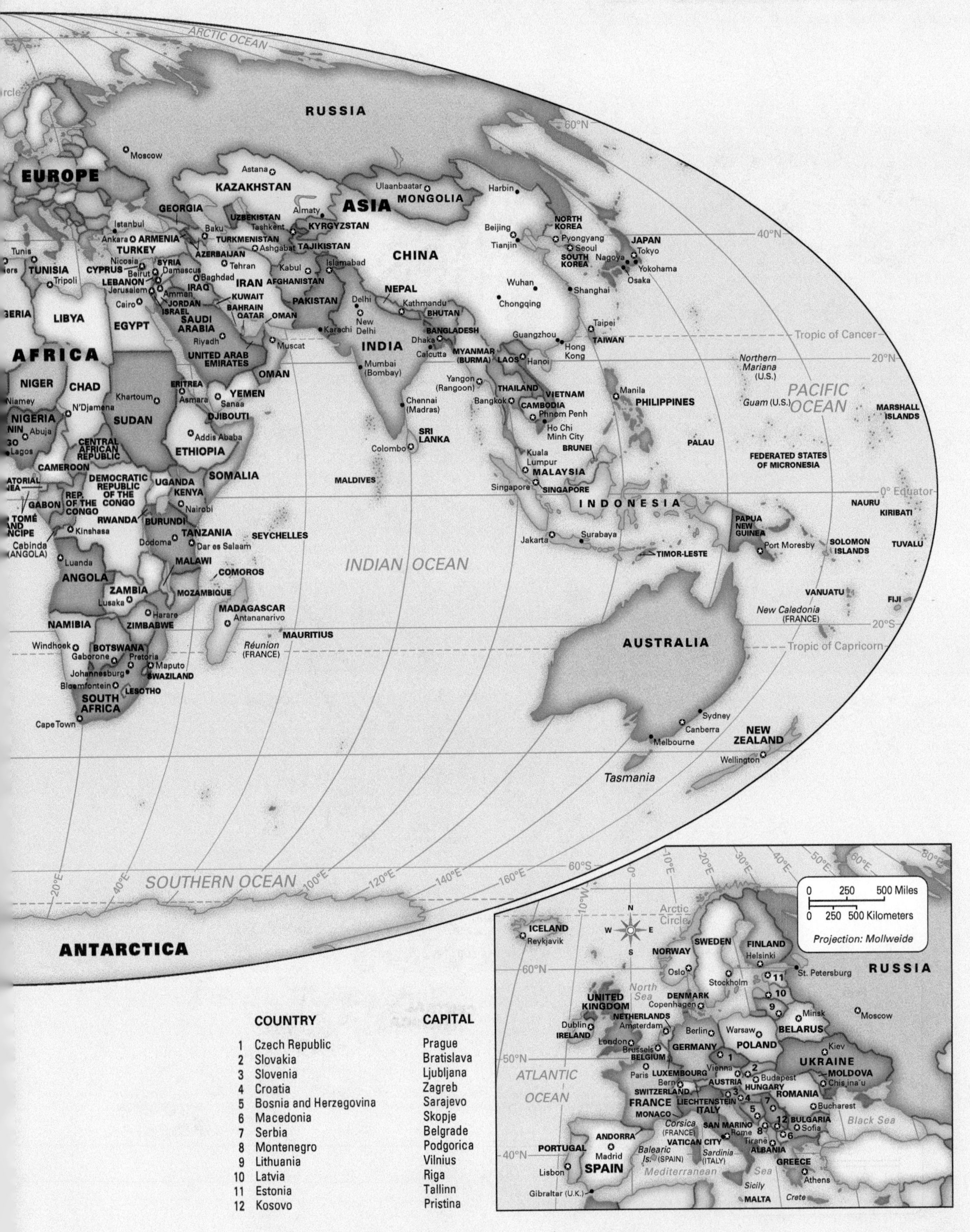

	COUNTRY	CAPITAL
1	Czech Republic	Prague
2	Slovakia	Bratislava
3	Slovenia	Ljubljana
4	Croatia	Zagreb
5	Bosnia and Herzegovina	Sarajevo
6	Macedonia	Skopje
7	Serbia	Belgrade
8	Montenegro	Podgorica
9	Lithuania	Vilnius
10	Latvia	Riga
11	Estonia	Tallinn
12	Kosovo	Pristina

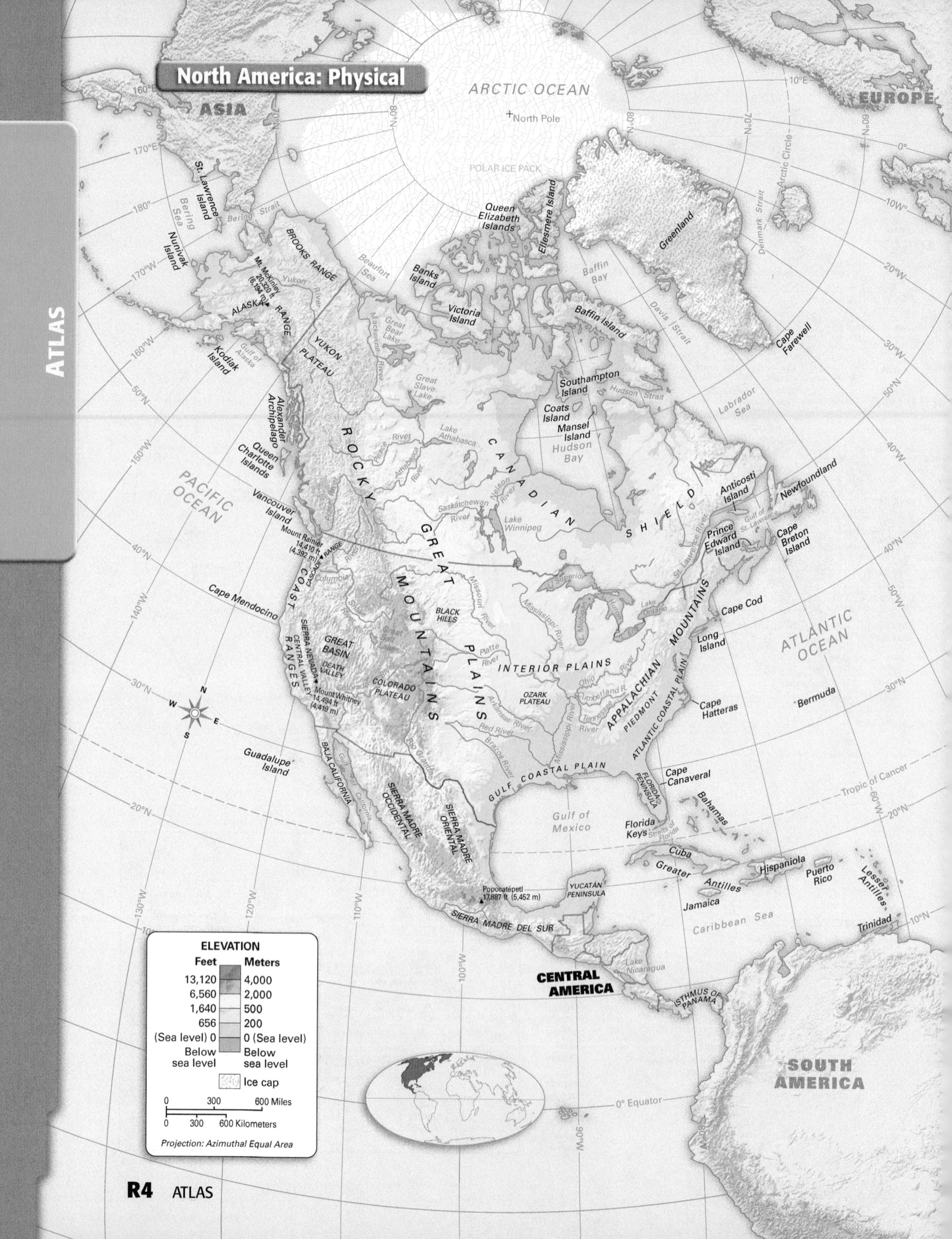
North America: Physical
ATLAS
ARCTIC OCEAN
North Pole
POLAR ICE PACK
ASIA
EUROPE
St. Lawrence Island
Bering Sea
Bering Strait
Nunivak Island
BROOKS RANGE
Mt. McKinley 20,320 ft (6,194 m)
ALASKA RANGE
Yukon River
Kodiak Island
Gulf of Alaska
Beaufort Sea
Banks Island
Victoria Island
Queen Elizabeth Islands
Ellesmere Island
Greenland
Baffin Bay
Baffin Island
Davis Strait
Denmark Strait
Arctic Circle
Cape Farewell
YUKON PLATEAU
Mackenzie River
Great Bear Lake
Great Slave Lake
Southampton Island
Hudson Strait
Coats Island
Mansel Island
Hudson Bay
Labrador Sea
Alexander Archipelago
Queen Charlotte Islands
ROCKY
Peace River
Lake Athabasca
Athabasca River
CANADIAN
SHIELD
PACIFIC OCEAN
Vancouver Island
Saskatchewan River
Nelson River
Lake Winnipeg
Anticosti Island
Newfoundland
Gulf of St. Lawrence
Prince Edward Island
Cape Breton Island
St. Lawrence River
Mount Rainier 14,410 ft (4,392 m)
CASCADE RANGE
GREAT
Columbia River
COAST RANGES
MOUNTAINS
Missouri River
Superior
Cape Mendocino
Snake River
BLACK HILLS
PLAINS
Mississippi River
Michigan
Huron
Lake Ontario
Erie
MOUNTAINS
Cape Cod
Long Island
ATLANTIC OCEAN
SIERRA NEVADA
CENTRAL VALLEY
GREAT BASIN
Great Salt Lake
DEATH VALLEY
Platte River
INTERIOR PLAINS
Ohio River
Cumberland R.
COLORADO PLATEAU
Colorado River
Mount Whitney 14,494 ft (4,419 m)
OZARK PLATEAU
Arkansas River
Tennessee River
APPALACHIAN
PIEDMONT
ATLANTIC COASTAL PLAIN
Cape Hatteras
Bermuda
Red River
Brazos River
Rio Grande
Guadalupe Island
BAJA CALIFORNIA
Gulf of California
GULF COASTAL PLAIN
FLORIDA PENINSULA
Cape Canaveral
Tropic of Cancer
Bahamas
SIERRA MADRE OCCIDENTAL
SIERRA MADRE ORIENTAL
Gulf of Mexico
Florida Keys
Straits of Florida
Cuba
Greater Antilles
Hispaniola
Puerto Rico
Lesser Antilles
Jamaica
Popocatépetl 17,887 ft (5,452 m)
YUCATÁN PENINSULA
SIERRA MADRE DEL SUR
Caribbean Sea
Trinidad
Lake Nicaragua
CENTRAL AMERICA
ISTHMUS OF PANAMA
SOUTH AMERICA
0° Equator
N
S
E
W
ELEVATION
Feet
Meters
13,120
4,000
6,560
2,000
1,640
500
656
200
(Sea level) 0
0 (Sea level)
Below sea level
Below sea level
Ice cap
0 300 600 Miles
0 300 600 Kilometers
Projection: Azimuthal Equal Area

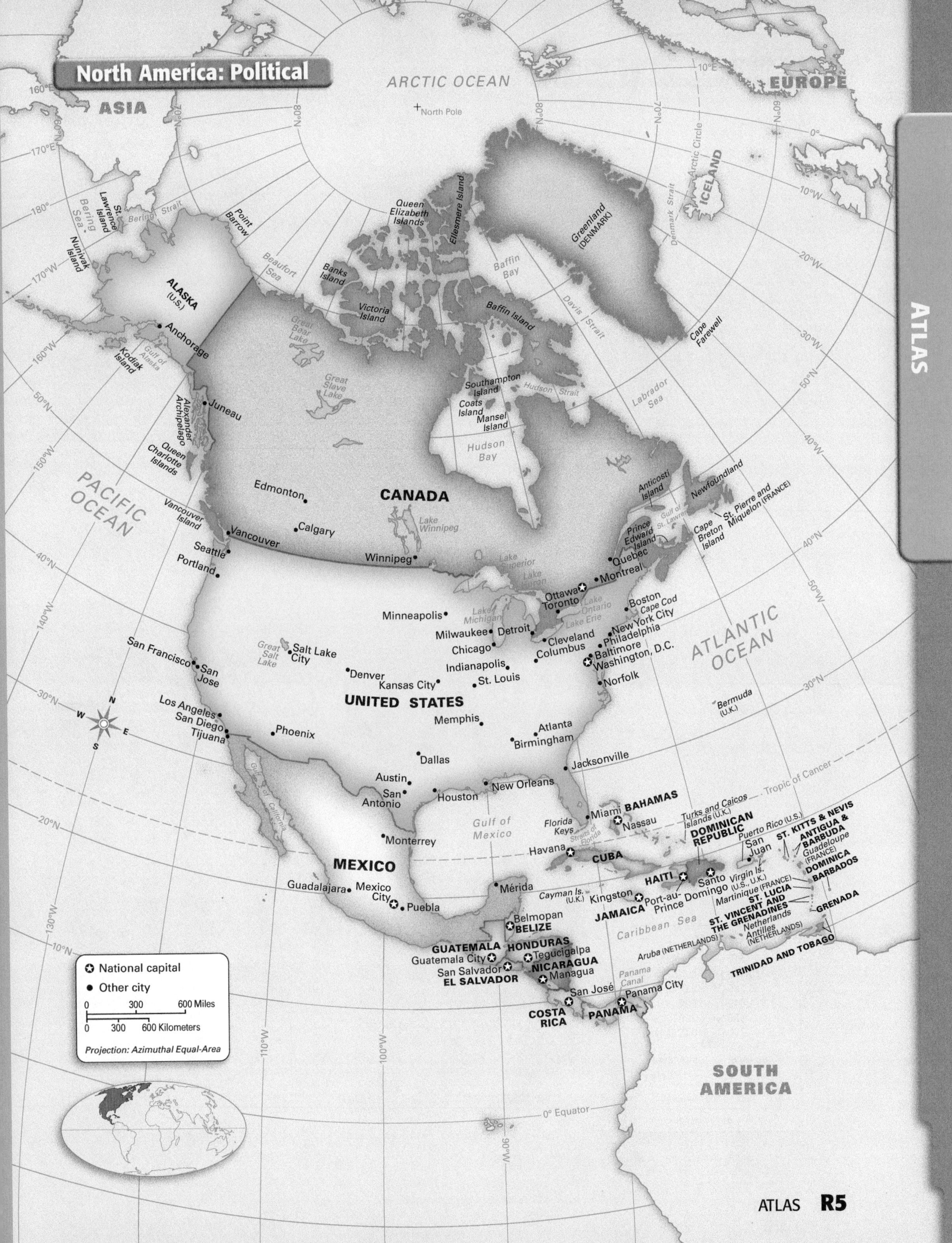
North America: Political
ARCTIC OCEAN
North Pole
ASIA
EUROPE
ATLAS
Arctic Circle
ICELAND
Denmark Strait
Greenland (DENMARK)
Queen Elizabeth Islands
Ellesmere Island
Baffin Bay
Baffin Island
Davis Strait
Cape Farewell
Labrador Sea
Hudson Strait
Southampton Island
Coats Island
Mansel Island
Hudson Bay
Banks Island
Victoria Island
Beaufort Sea
Point Barrow
Bering Strait
Bering Sea
St. Lawrence Island
Nunivak Island
ALASKA (U.S.)
Anchorage
Gulf of Alaska
Kodiak Island
Great Bear Lake
Great Slave Lake
Juneau
Alexander Archipelago
Queen Charlotte Islands
PACIFIC OCEAN
Vancouver Island
Edmonton
CANADA
Calgary
Vancouver
Lake Winnipeg
Winnipeg
Seattle
Portland
Anticosti Island
Newfoundland
Gulf of St. Lawrence
St. Pierre and Miquelon (FRANCE)
Cape Breton Island
Prince Edward Island
Quebec
Montreal
Lake Superior
Lake Huron
Ottawa
Toronto
Lake Ontario
Lake Erie
Lake Michigan
Boston
Cape Cod
New York City
Philadelphia
Baltimore
Washington, D.C.
Norfolk
ATLANTIC OCEAN
Bermuda (U.K.)
Minneapolis
Milwaukee
Detroit
Cleveland
Columbus
Chicago
Indianapolis
St. Louis
Kansas City
Denver
Great Salt Lake
Salt Lake City
San Francisco
San Jose
UNITED STATES
Los Angeles
San Diego
Tijuana
Phoenix
Memphis
Atlanta
Birmingham
Dallas
Jacksonville
Austin
San Antonio
Houston
New Orleans
Tropic of Cancer
Gulf of California
Gulf of Mexico
Monterrey
MEXICO
Guadalajara
Mexico City
Puebla
Mérida
Miami
BAHAMAS
Nassau
Florida Keys
Straits of Florida
Havana
CUBA
Turks and Caicos Islands (U.K.)
DOMINICAN REPUBLIC
Puerto Rico (U.S.)
San Juan
ST. KITTS & NEVIS
ANTIGUA & BARBUDA
Guadeloupe (FRANCE)
DOMINICA
BARBADOS
HAITI
Santo Domingo
Virgin Is. (U.S., U.K.)
Martinique (FRANCE)
ST. LUCIA
ST. VINCENT AND THE GRENADINES
GRENADA
Netherlands Antilles (NETHERLANDS)
Cayman Is. (U.K.)
Kingston
JAMAICA
Port-au-Prince
Caribbean Sea
Aruba (NETHERLANDS)
TRINIDAD AND TOBAGO
Belmopan
BELIZE
GUATEMALA
HONDURAS
Guatemala City
Tegucigalpa
San Salvador
NICARAGUA
EL SALVADOR
Managua
Panama Canal
San José
Panama City
COSTA RICA
PANAMA
SOUTH AMERICA
0° Equator
National capital
Other city
0 300 600 Miles
0 300 600 Kilometers
Projection: Azimuthal Equal-Area

South America: Physical

ATLAS
CENTRAL AMERICA
Caribbean Sea
Panama Canal
Gulf of Panama
Lake Maracaibo
Margarita Island
Tobago
Trinidad
Orinoco River Delta
LLANOS
Orinoco River
Meta River
Angel Falls
GUIANA
HIGHLANDS
ATLANTIC OCEAN
Devil's Island
Cape Orange
Amazon River Delta
Malpelo Island
Mount Tolima 18,425 ft (5,616 m)
Cauca River
Magdalena River
Caqueta River
Japurá River
Rio Negro
AMAZON BASIN
Amazon River
0° Equator
Mount Chimborazo 20,561 ft (6,267 m)
Galápagos Islands
Gulf of Guayaquil
Marañón River
Amazon River
Juruá River
Purus River
Madeira River
Tapajós River
Xingu River
Tocantins River
Parnaíb River
Ucayali
ANDES
Mount Huascarán 22,205 ft (6,768 m)
MATO GROSSO PLATEAU
BRAZILIAN HIGHLANDS
Araguaia River
São Francisco River
Beni River
Mamoré River
Ancohuma Peak 20,958 ft (6,388 m)
PACIFIC OCEAN
Lake Titicaca
Lake Poopó
ATACAMA DESERT
CHACO
Paraguay River
BRAZILIAN PLATEAU
Tropic of Capricorn
ANDES
San Ambrosio Island
San Félix Island
Salado River
Paraná River
Uruguay River
Mount Aconcagua 22,834 ft (6,960 m)
Juan Fernández Islands
Salado River
PAMPAS
Rio de la Plata
ATLANTIC OCEAN
Colorado River
Gulf of San Matías
PATAGONIA
Chiloé Island
Chonos Archipelago
Gulf of San Jorge
Cape Tres Puntas
Bahía Grande
Strait of Magellan
Falkland Islands
Tierra del Fuego
Cape Horn
South Georgia Islands
ELEVATION
Feet / Meters
13,120 / 4,000
6,560 / 2,000
1,640 / 500
656 / 200
(Sea level) 0 / 0 (Sea level)
Below sea level / Below sea level
0 250 500 Miles
0 250 500 Kilometers
Projection: Azimuthal Equal Area
N W E S
20°N 10°N 0° Equator 10°S 20°S 30°S 40°S 50°S
90°W 80°W 70°W 60°W 50°W 40°W 30°W 20°W 100°W

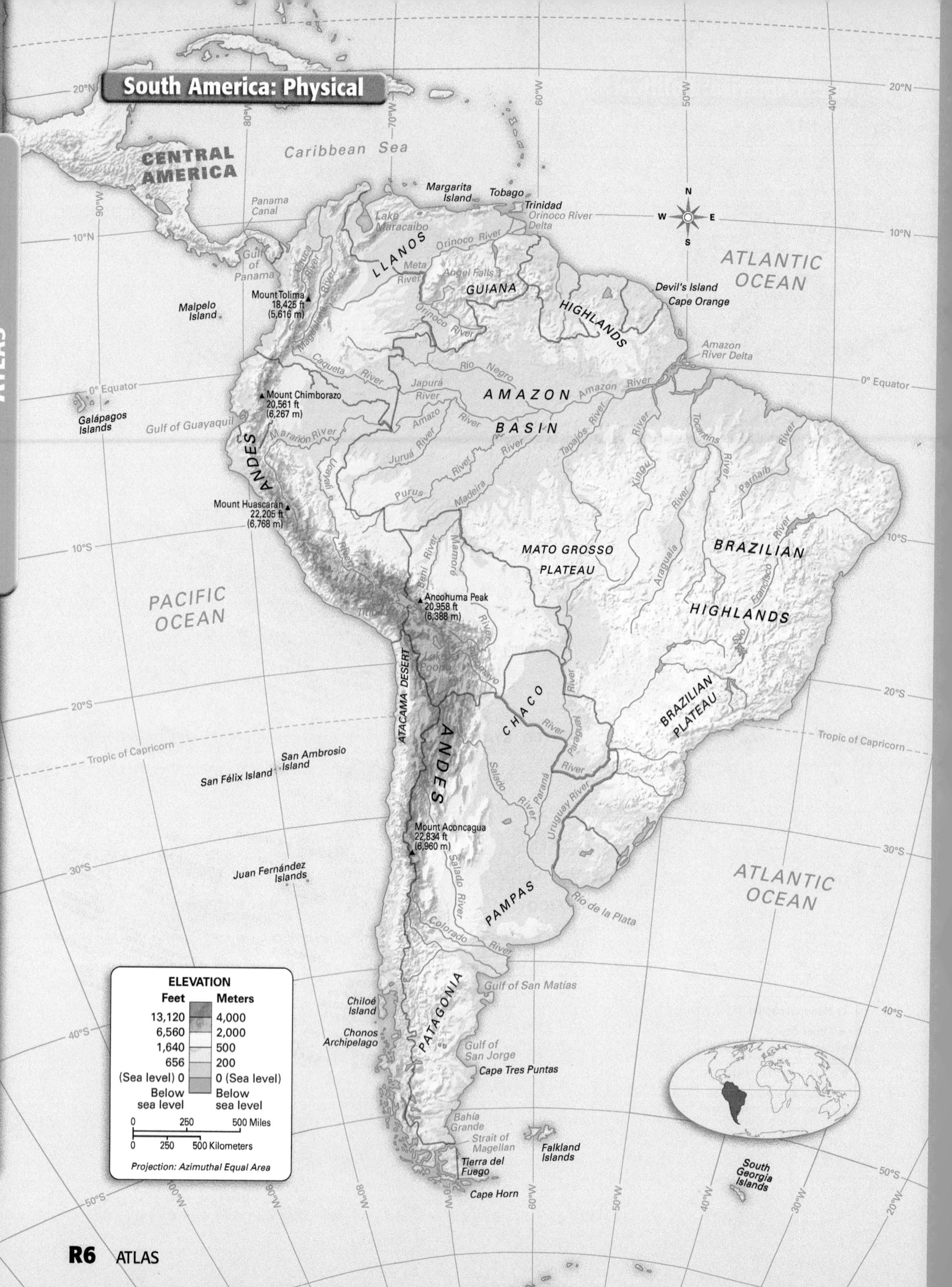

South America: Political
ATLAS
Caribbean Sea
CENTRAL AMERICA
Barranquilla
Cartagena
Caracas
Lake Maracaibo
VENEZUELA
Georgetown
Paramaribo
GUYANA
SURINAME
Cayenne
French Guiana (FRANCE)
ATLANTIC OCEAN
Medellín
Bogotá
COLOMBIA
Cali
Malpelo Island (COLOMBIA)
Quito
ECUADOR
Guayaquil
Galápagos Islands (ECUADOR)
0° Equator
Belém
PERU
BRAZIL
Recife
Trujillo
Callao
Lima
Salvador
Brasília
PACIFIC OCEAN
Lake Titicaca
La Paz
Arequipa
Lake Poopó
BOLIVIA
Sucre
Belo Horizonte
Campinas
São Paulo
Rio de Janeiro
PARAGUAY
Asunción
Curitiba
Tropic of Capricorn
San Ambrosio Island (CHILE)
San Félix Island (CHILE)
CHILE
Pôrto Alegre
Córdoba
Rosario
URUGUAY
Juan Fernández Islands (CHILE)
Valparaíso
Santiago
Buenos Aires
Montevideo
ATLANTIC OCEAN
ARGENTINA
National capital
Other city
0 250 500 Miles
0 250 500 Kilometers
Projection: Azimuthal Equal-Area
Strait of Magellan
Falkland Islands (U.K.)
Tierra del Fuego
South Georgia Island (U.K.)
N
S
E
W
20°N
10°N
10°S
20°S
30°S
40°S
50°S
90°W
80°W
70°W
60°W
50°W
40°W
30°W
20°W
100°W

Europe: Physical

ELEVATION

Feet	Meters
13,120	4,000
6,560	2,000
1,640	500
656	200
(Sea level) 0	0 (Sea level)
Below sea level	Below sea level

Ice cap

0 150 300 Miles
0 150 300 Kilometers

Projection: Azimuthal Equal Area

ARCTIC OCEAN
ATLANTIC OCEAN
Norwegian Sea
North Sea
Barents Sea
White Sea
Baltic Sea
Gulf of Bothnia
Gulf of Finland
Kattegat
Skagerrak
English Channel
Irish Sea
Bay of Biscay
Mediterranean Sea
Tyrrhenian Sea
Adriatic Sea
Aegean Sea
Sea of Marmara
Black Sea
Sea of Azov
Caspian Sea
Strait of Gibraltar
Arctic Circle
ASIA
SOUTHWEST ASIA
AFRICA
URAL MOUNTAINS
NORTHERN EUROPEAN PLAIN
BALTIC PLAINS
KJOLEN MOUNTAINS
KOLA PENINSULA
CRIMEAN PENINSULA
CAUCASUS MTS.
Mt. Elbrus 18,510 ft. (5,642 m)
CARPATHIAN
TRANSYLVANIAN ALPS
BALKAN PENINSULA
DINARIC ALPS
APENNINES
ALPS
Mont Blanc 15,781 ft. (4,810 m)
PYRENEES
IBERIAN PENINSULA
PENNINES
British Isles
Hebrides
Shetland Islands
Orkney Islands
Faeroe Islands
Iceland
North Cape
Cape Finisterre
Corsica
Sardinia
Sicily
Malta
Crete
Rhodes
Balearic Islands
Lake Onega
Lake Ladoga
Rybinsk Reservoir
Lake Vänern
Lake Vättern
Lake Geneva
Pechora River
Ural River
Kama River
Volga River
Don River
North Dvina River
Dnipro River
Daugava R.
Dvina River
Dnestr River
Nistru River
Danube River
Vistula River
Oder River
Elbe River
Rhine River
Po River
Tiber River
Rhone River
Seine River
Loire River
Garonne River
Thames River
Ebro River
Douro River
Tagus River
Guadiana River
Guadalquivir River
70°N
60°N
50°N
40°N
30°N
20°W
10°W
0°
10°E
20°E
30°E
40°E
50°E

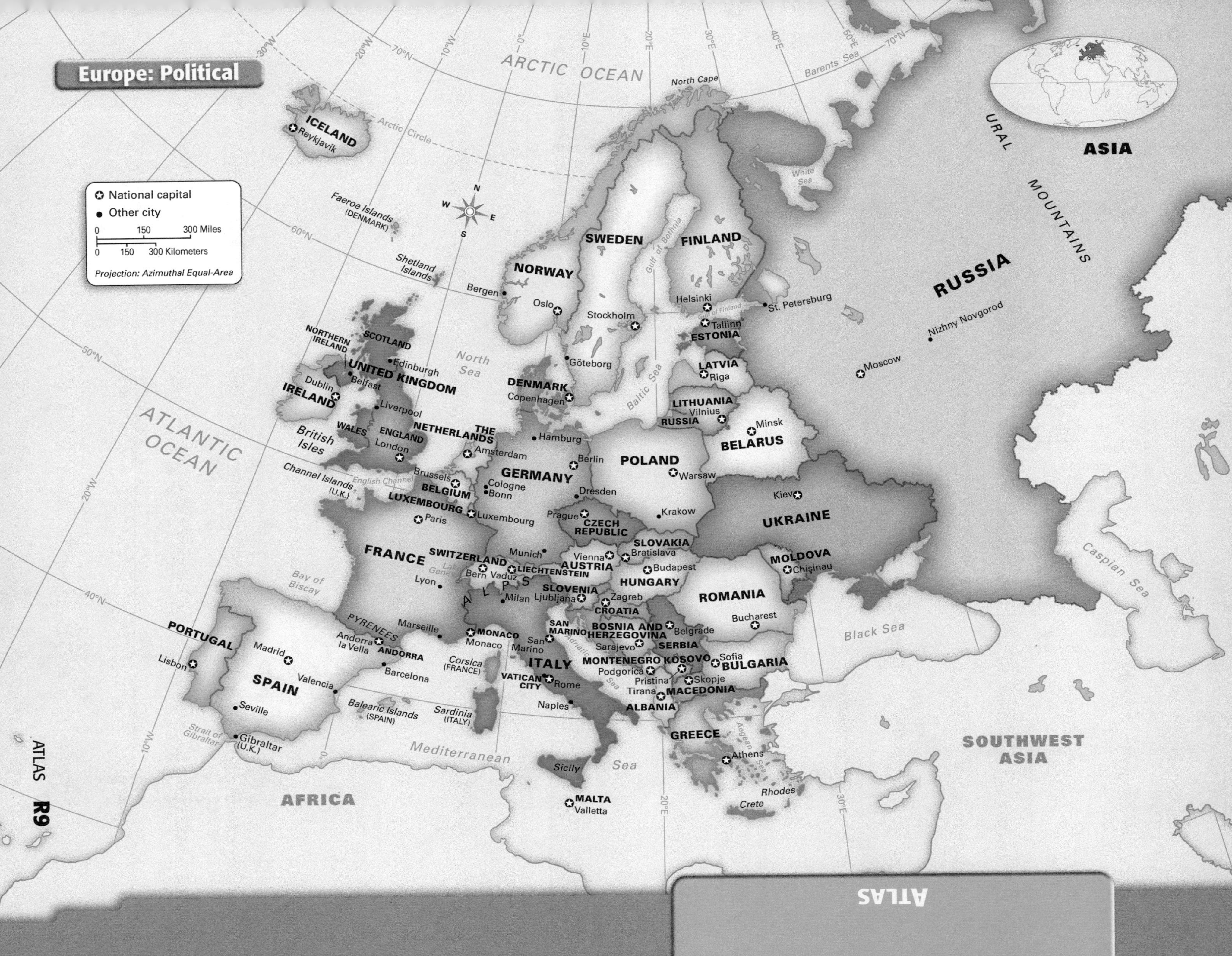
Europe: Political
National capital
Other city
0 150 300 Miles
0 150 300 Kilometers
Projection: Azimuthal Equal-Area
ARCTIC OCEAN
ATLANTIC OCEAN
North Sea
Baltic Sea
Gulf of Bothnia
Gulf of Finland
Barents Sea
White Sea
North Cape
Arctic Circle
Bay of Biscay
English Channel
Strait of Gibraltar
Mediterranean Sea
Adriatic Sea
Aegean Sea
Black Sea
Caspian Sea
URAL MOUNTAINS
ALPS
PYRENEES
ASIA
SOUTHWEST ASIA
AFRICA
ICELAND
Reykjavik
Faeroe Islands (DENMARK)
Shetland Islands
British Isles
Channel Islands (U.K.)
NORTHERN IRELAND
SCOTLAND
UNITED KINGDOM
WALES
ENGLAND
IRELAND
Dublin
Belfast
Edinburgh
Liverpool
London
NORWAY
Bergen
Oslo
SWEDEN
Stockholm
Göteborg
FINLAND
Helsinki
RUSSIA
St. Petersburg
Moscow
Nizhny Novgorod
ESTONIA
Tallinn
LATVIA
Riga
LITHUANIA
Vilnius
BELARUS
Minsk
DENMARK
Copenhagen
THE NETHERLANDS
Amsterdam
BELGIUM
Brussels
LUXEMBOURG
Luxembourg
GERMANY
Hamburg
Berlin
Cologne
Bonn
Dresden
Munich
POLAND
Warsaw
Krakow
UKRAINE
Kiev
MOLDOVA
Chişinau
CZECH REPUBLIC
Prague
SLOVAKIA
Bratislava
AUSTRIA
Vienna
HUNGARY
Budapest
ROMANIA
Bucharest
FRANCE
Paris
Lyon
Marseille
SWITZERLAND
Bern
Lake Geneva
LIECHTENSTEIN
Vaduz
SLOVENIA
Ljubljana
CROATIA
Zagreb
BOSNIA AND HERZEGOVINA
Sarajevo
SERBIA
Belgrade
MONTENEGRO
Podgorica
KOSOVO
Pristina
MACEDONIA
Skopje
ALBANIA
Tirana
BULGARIA
Sofia
GREECE
Athens
Rhodes
Crete
MONACO
Monaco
SAN MARINO
San Marino
ITALY
Milan
Rome
Naples
VATICAN CITY
Corsica (FRANCE)
Sardinia (ITALY)
Sicily
MALTA
Valletta
ANDORRA
Andorra la Vella
SPAIN
Madrid
Barcelona
Valencia
Seville
Balearic Islands (SPAIN)
Gibraltar (U.K.)
PORTUGAL
Lisbon
70°N
60°N
50°N
40°N
30°W
20°W
10°W
0°
10°E
20°E
30°E
40°E
50°E
N
S
E
W

Asia: Physical

ELEVATION

Feet	Meters
13,120	4,000
6,560	2,000
1,640	500
656	200
(Sea level) 0	0 (Sea level)
Below sea level	Below sea level

Ice cap

0 250 500 750 Miles
0 250 500 750 Kilometers

Projection: Two-Point Equidistant

North Pole
Arctic Circle
Tropic of Cancer
0° Equator
EUROPE
AFRICA
AUSTRALIA
PACIFIC OCEAN
INDIAN OCEAN
SIBERIA
URAL MOUNTAINS
WEST SIBERIAN PLAIN
CENTRAL SIBERIAN PLATEAU
CHERSKIY RANGE
VERKHOYANSKIY RANGE
KOLYMA MTS.
CENTRAL RANGE
KAMCHATKA PENINSULA
STANOVOY MOUNTAINS
YABLONOVY RANGE
SAYAN MOUNTAINS
ALTAY MOUNTAINS
MONGOLIAN PLATEAU
GREATER KHINGAN RANGE
GOBI
KAZAKH UPLANDS
TURAN LOWLAND
USTYURT PLATEAU
KYZYL KUM
KARA KUM
TIAN SHAN
TARIM BASIN
TAKLIMAKAN DESERT
HINDU KUSH
KUNLUN MOUNTAINS
PLATEAU OF TIBET
HIMALAYAS
Mount Everest 29,035 ft (8,850 m)
INDO-GANGETIC PLAIN
THAR DESERT
DECCAN PLATEAU
EASTERN GHATS
WESTERN GHATS
QIN LING
NORTH CHINA PLAIN
BOHEA HILLS
INDOCHINA PENINSULA
MALAY PENINSULA
CAUCASUS MTS.
Mount Ararat 16,945 ft (5,165 m)
ANATOLIAN PLATEAU
SYRIAN DESERT
AN-NAFUD
RUB' AL-KHALI
ZAGROS MTS.
GREAT SALT DESERT
SINAI PENINSULA
TAYMYR PENINSULA
MAOKE MOUNTAINS
Franz Josef Land
Novaya Zemlya
North Land
New Siberian Islands
Wrangel Island
Aleutian Islands
Sakhalin Island
Kuril Islands
Hokkaido
Honshu
Shikoku
Kyushu
Okinawa
Ryukyu Islands
Taiwan
Hainan
Luzon
Philippines
Mindanao
Celebes
Moluccas
New Guinea
Borneo
Bangka
Sumatra
Java
Mentawai Islands
Andaman Islands
Nicobar Islands
Sri Lanka
Maldives
Lakshadweep Islands
Socotra Island
Cyprus
Barents Sea
Kara Sea
Laptev Sea
Bering Sea
Sea of Okhotsk
Sea of Japan (East Sea)
Korea Strait
Yellow Sea
East China Sea
South China Sea
Luzon Strait
Gulf of Tonkin
Gulf of Thailand
Celebes Sea
Banda Sea
Arafura Sea
Java Sea
Strait of Malacca
Andaman Sea
Bay of Bengal
Arabian Sea
Gulf of Oman
Strait of Hormuz
Persian Gulf
Gulf of Aden
Red Sea
Mediterranean Sea
Black Sea
Bosporus
Caspian Sea
Aral Sea
Balqash Lake
Lake Baykal
Ob River
Irtysh River
Ishim River
Ural River
Yenisey River
Lower Tunguska River
Angara River
Lena River
Aldan River
Amur River
Shilka River
Syr Darya
Amu Darya
Huang He (Yellow River)
Chang Jiang (Yangzi River)
Xi River
Hong River
Mekong River
Chao Phraya River
Irrawaddy River
Ganges River
Sutlej River
Indus River
Godavari River
Tigris River
Euphrates River
170°W 180° 170°E 160°E 150°E 140°E 130°E 120°E 110°E 100°E 90°E 80°E 70°E 60°E 50°E 40°E 30°E 20°E 10°E 0°
80°N 70°N 60°N 50°N 40°N 30°N 20°N 10°N 10°S
N S E W

Asia: Political

National capitals
Other cities
0 250 500 750 Miles
0 250 500 750 Kilometers
Projection: Two-Point Equidistant
North Pole
Arctic Circle
Tropic of Cancer
0° Equator
EUROPE
RUSSIA
URAL MOUNTAINS
Moscow
Yekaterinburg
Chelyabinsk
Omsk
Novosibirsk
Irkutsk
Yakutsk
Vladivostok
Lake Baykal
Barents Sea
Kara Sea
Laptev Sea
Bering Sea
Sea of Okhotsk
Sakhalin Island
Kuril Islands (RUSSIA)
Aleutian Islands
KAZAKHSTAN
Astana
Almaty
Lake Balkhash
Aral Sea
Caspian Sea
Black Sea
Mediterranean Sea
Red Sea
Persian Gulf
Gulf of Aden
TURKEY
Istanbul
Izmir
Ankara
CYPRUS
Nicosia
LEBANON
Beirut
ISRAEL
Tel Aviv
Jerusalem
SYRIA
Damascus
JORDAN
Amman
GEORGIA
Tbilisi
ARMENIA
Yerevan
AZERBAIJAN
Baku
IRAQ
Mosul
Baghdad
Basra
KUWAIT
Kuwait City
SAUDI ARABIA
Riyadh
Jidda
Mecca
BAHRAIN
Manama
QATAR
Doha
UNITED ARAB EMIRATES
Abu Dhabi
OMAN
Masqat (Muscat)
YEMEN
Sanaa
Socotra (YEMEN)
IRAN
Tehran
Shiraz
TURKMENISTAN
Ashgabat
UZBEKISTAN
Tashkent
KYRGYZSTAN
Bishkek
TAJIKISTAN
Dushanbe
AFGHANISTAN
Kabul
PAKISTAN
Islamabad
Lahore
Karachi
INDIA
New Delhi
Delhi
Jaipur
Ahmadabad
Mumbai (Bombay)
Bangalore
Chennai (Madras)
Kolkata (Calcutta)
NEPAL
Kathmandu
BHUTAN
Thimphu
BANGLADESH
Dhaka
SRI LANKA
Colombo
MALDIVES
Male
Lakshadweep Islands (INDIA)
Andaman Islands (INDIA)
Nicobar Islands (INDIA)
Arabian Sea
Bay of Bengal
Andaman Sea
INDIAN OCEAN
AFRICA
MONGOLIA
Ulaanbaatar
CHINA
Beijing
Harbin
Fushun
Dalian
Qingdao
Nanjing
Shanghai
Wuhan
Chengdu
Chongqing
Guangzhou
Hong Kong
Macao
Hainan (CHINA)
NORTH KOREA
Pyongyang
SOUTH KOREA
Seoul
Pusan
Yellow Sea
East China Sea
JAPAN
Sapporo
Tokyo
Yokohama
Kyoto
Osaka
Hiroshima
Nagasaki
Ryukyu Islands (JAPAN)
TAIWAN
Taipei
Luzon Strait
South China Sea
PHILIPPINES
Manila
MYANMAR (BURMA)
Mandalay
Yangon (Rangoon)
LAOS
Vientiane
VIETNAM
Hanoi
Ho Chi Minh City
THAILAND
Bangkok
CAMBODIA
Phnom Penh
Gulf of Thailand
MALAYSIA
Kuala Lumpur
SINGAPORE
Singapore
BRUNEI
Bandar Seri Begawan
INDONESIA
Medan
Jakarta
Bandung
Surabaya
Ujung Pandang
Java Sea
Celebes Sea
TIMOR-LESTE
Dili
New Guinea
Arafura Sea
AUSTRALIA
PACIFIC OCEAN
N
S
E
W

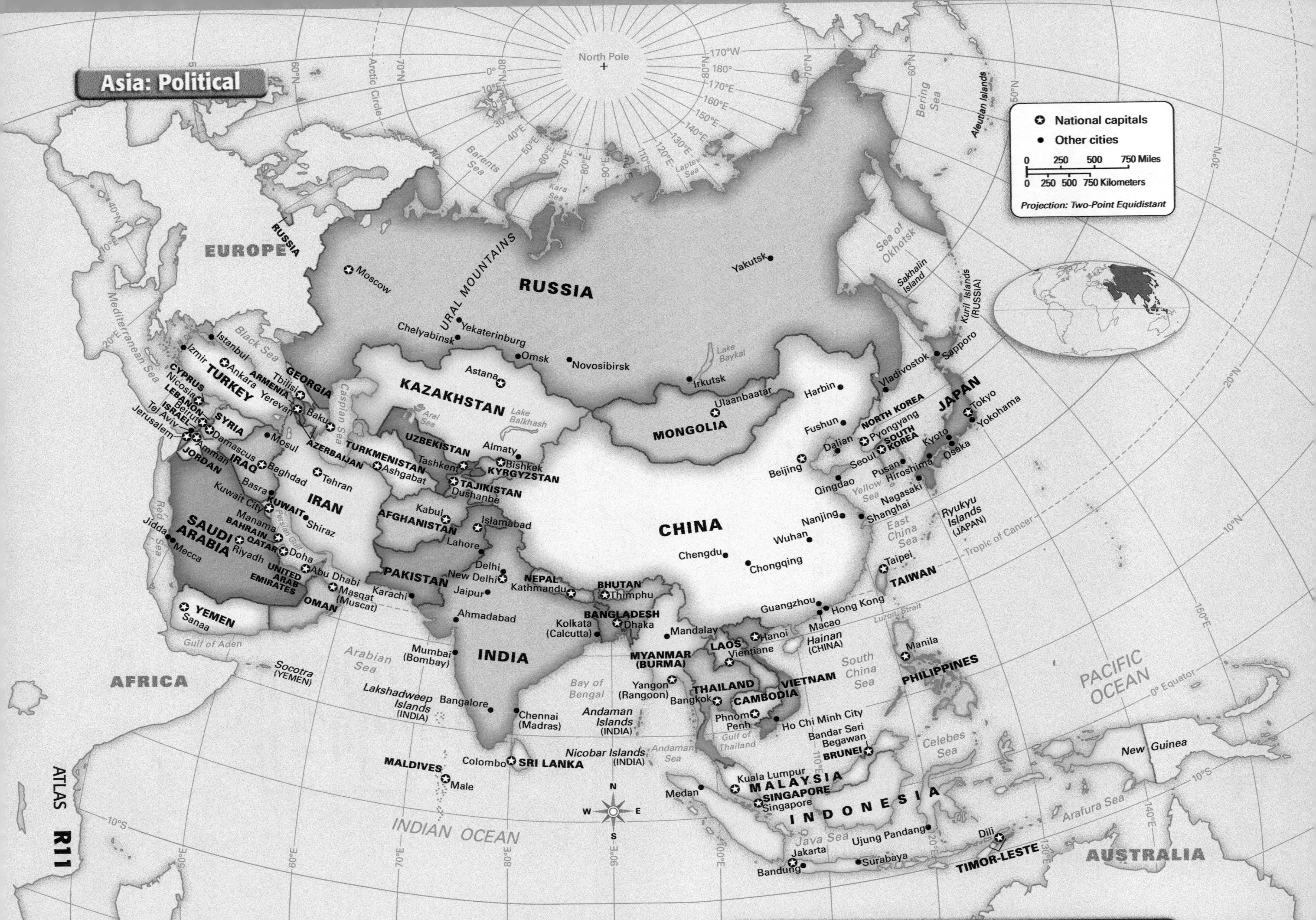

Africa: Physical

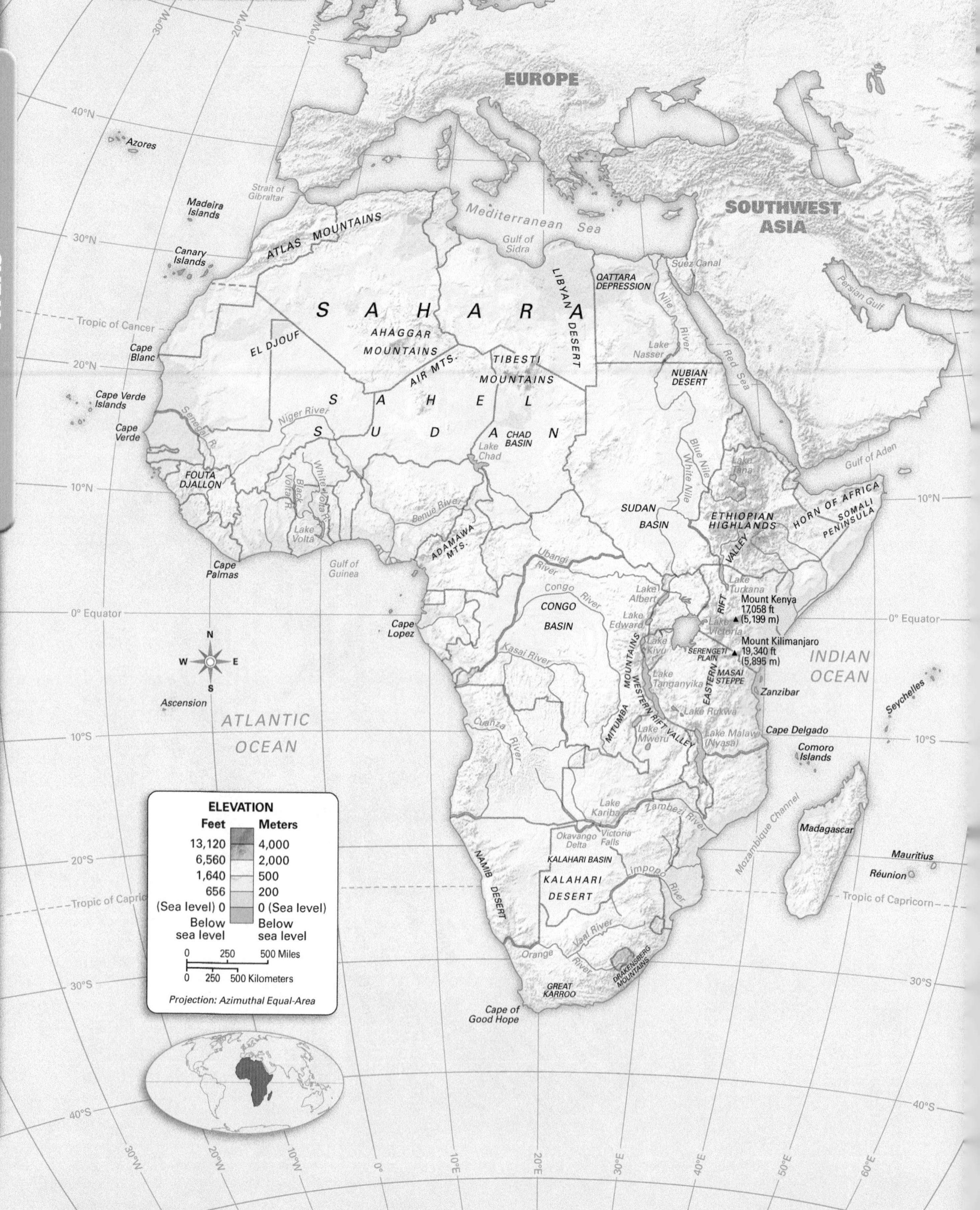

ATLAS

EUROPE
SOUTHWEST ASIA
Azores
Madeira Islands
Canary Islands
Strait of Gibraltar
ATLAS MOUNTAINS
Mediterranean Sea
Gulf of Sidra
Suez Canal
QATTARA DEPRESSION
Persian Gulf
S A H A R A
LIBYAN DESERT
AHAGGAR MOUNTAINS
EL DJOUF
AIR MTS.
TIBESTI MOUNTAINS
Nile River
Lake Nasser
Red Sea
NUBIAN DESERT
Cape Blanc
Cape Verde Islands
Cape Verde
S A H E L
S U D A N
Senegal R.
Niger River
CHAD BASIN
Lake Chad
Blue Nile
White Nile
Lake Tana
Gulf of Aden
FOUTA DJALLON
Black Volta R.
White Volta R.
Lake Volta
Benue River
ADAMAWA MTS.
SUDAN BASIN
ETHIOPIAN HIGHLANDS
HORN OF AFRICA
SOMALI PENINSULA
Cape Palmas
Gulf of Guinea
Ubangi River
Congo River
CONGO BASIN
Lake Albert
Lake Edward
Lake Turkana
Lake Victoria
RIFT VALLEY
Mount Kenya 17,058 ft (5,199 m)
Mount Kilimanjaro 19,340 ft (5,895 m)
SERENGETI PLAIN
MASAI STEPPE
EASTERN RIFT VALLEY
Cape Lopez
Kasai River
Lake Kivu
MITUMBA MOUNTAINS
WESTERN RIFT VALLEY
Lake Tanganyika
Lake Rukwa
Lake Mweru
Lake Malawi (Nyasa)
INDIAN OCEAN
Zanzibar
Seychelles
Ascension
ATLANTIC OCEAN
Cuanza River
Cape Delgado
Comoro Islands
Lake Kariba
Zambezi River
Mozambique Channel
Madagascar
Okavango Delta
Victoria Falls
KALAHARI BASIN
KALAHARI DESERT
NAMIB DESERT
Limpopo River
Mauritius
Réunion
Vaal River
Orange River
DRAKENSBERG MOUNTAINS
GREAT KARROO
Cape of Good Hope
Tropic of Cancer
Tropic of Capricorn
0° Equator
40°N
30°N
20°N
10°N
10°S
20°S
30°S
40°S
30°W
20°W
10°W
0°
10°E
20°E
30°E
40°E
50°E
60°E
N
S
E
W

ELEVATION

Feet	Meters
13,120	4,000
6,560	2,000
1,640	500
656	200
(Sea level) 0	0 (Sea level)
Below sea level	Below sea level

0 250 500 Miles
0 250 500 Kilometers

Projection: Azimuthal Equal-Area

Africa: Political

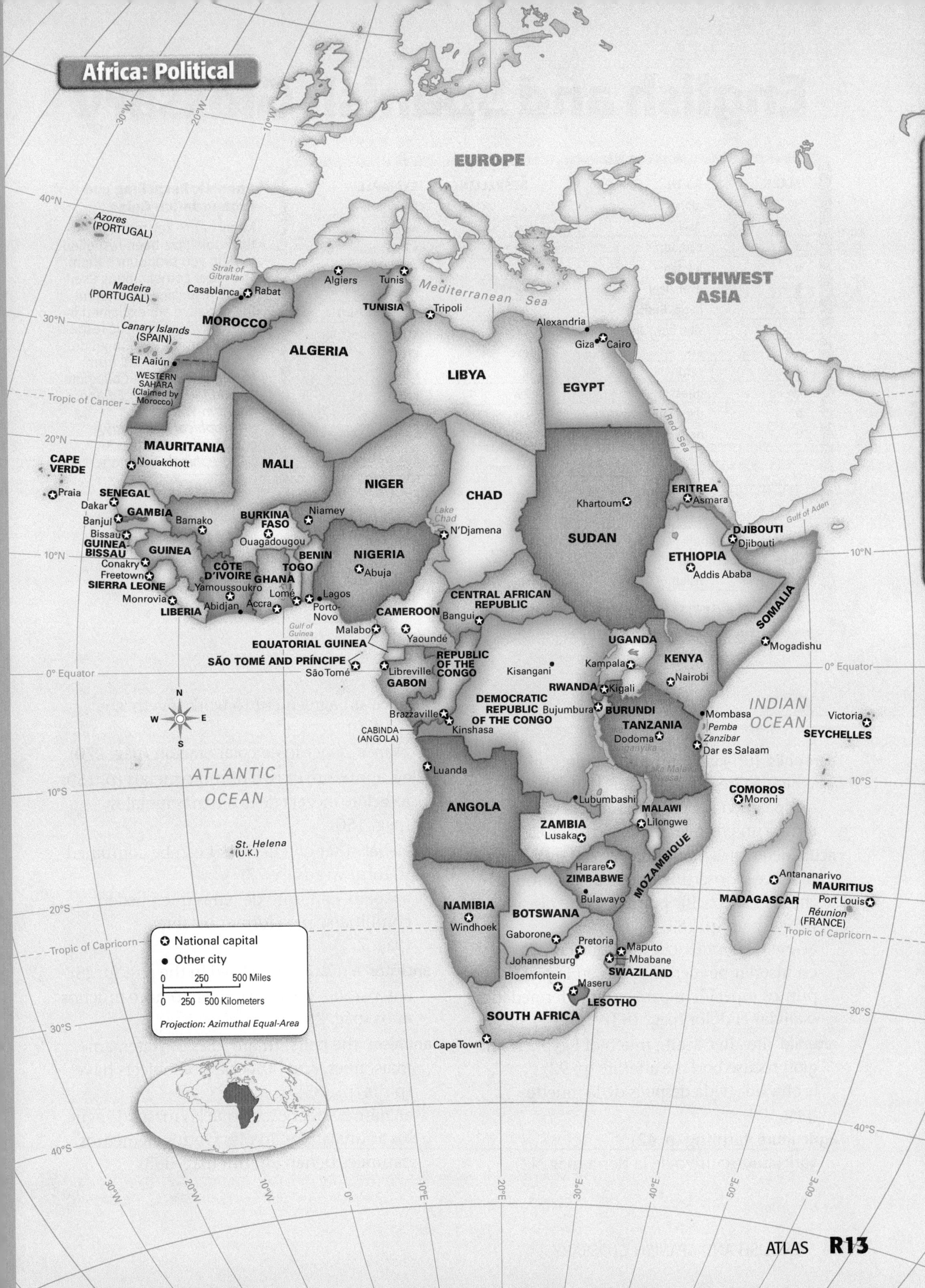

EUROPE

SOUTHWEST ASIA

Azores (PORTUGAL)

Madeira (PORTUGAL)

Strait of Gibraltar

Casablanca

Rabat

Algiers

Tunis

Mediterranean Sea

TUNISIA

Tripoli

Alexandria

Giza

Cairo

MOROCCO

Canary Islands (SPAIN)

El Aaiún

WESTERN SAHARA (Claimed by Morocco)

ALGERIA

LIBYA

EGYPT

Red Sea

Tropic of Cancer

MAURITANIA

Nouakchott

MALI

NIGER

CHAD

SUDAN

Khartoum

ERITREA

Asmara

CAPE VERDE

Praia

SENEGAL

Dakar

GAMBIA

Banjul

Bamako

BURKINA FASO

Ouagadougou

Niamey

Lake Chad

N'Djamena

Gulf of Aden

DJIBOUTI

Djibouti

Bissau

GUINEA-BISSAU

GUINEA

Conakry

Freetown

SIERRA LEONE

CÔTE D'IVOIRE

Yamoussoukro

GHANA

TOGO

BENIN

NIGERIA

Abuja

ETHIOPIA

Addis Ababa

Monrovia

LIBERIA

Abidjan

Accra

Lomé

Lagos

Porto-Novo

CENTRAL AFRICAN REPUBLIC

Bangui

SOMALIA

CAMEROON

Gulf of Guinea

Malabo

Yaoundé

EQUATORIAL GUINEA

UGANDA

Mogadishu

SÃO TOMÉ AND PRÍNCIPE

São Tomé

Libreville

GABON

REPUBLIC OF THE CONGO

Kisangani

Kampala

KENYA

Nairobi

0° Equator

RWANDA

Kigali

DEMOCRATIC REPUBLIC OF THE CONGO

Bujumbura

BURUNDI

Mombasa

INDIAN OCEAN

Victoria

SEYCHELLES

N

W

E

S

Brazzaville

Kinshasa

CABINDA (ANGOLA)

TANZANIA

Dodoma

Lake Tanganyika

Pemba

Zanzibar

Dar es Salaam

ATLANTIC OCEAN

Luanda

Lake Malawi (Nyasa)

COMOROS

Moroni

Lubumbashi

ANGOLA

MALAWI

Lilongwe

ZAMBIA

Lusaka

St. Helena (U.K.)

MOZAMBIQUE

Harare

ZIMBABWE

Bulawayo

Antananarivo

MAURITIUS

MADAGASCAR

Port Louis

Réunion (FRANCE)

NAMIBIA

Windhoek

BOTSWANA

Gaborone

Pretoria

Johannesburg

Maputo

Mbabane

SWAZILAND

Bloemfontein

Maseru

LESOTHO

SOUTH AFRICA

Cape Town

Tropic of Capricorn

National capital

Other city

0 250 500 Miles

0 250 500 Kilometers

Projection: Azimuthal Equal-Area

40°N 30°N 20°N 10°N 0° 10°S 20°S 30°S 40°S

30°W 20°W 10°W 0° 10°E 20°E 30°E 40°E 50°E 60°E

ATLAS

English and Spanish Glossary

MARK	AS IN	RESPELLING	EXAMPLE
a	alphabet	a	*AL-fuh-bet
ā	Asia	ay	AY-zhuh
ä	cart, top	ah	KAHRT, TAHP
e	let, ten	e	LET, TEN
ē	even, leaf	ee	EE-vuhn, LEEF
i	it, tip, British	i	IT, TIP, BRIT-ish
ī	site, buy, Ohio	y	SYT, BY, oh-HY-oh
	iris	eye	EYE-ris
k	card	k	KAHRD
kw	quest	kw	KWEST
ō	over, rainbow	oh	OH-vuhr, RAYN-boh
u̇	book, wood	ooh	BOOHK, WOOHD
ȯ	all, orchid	aw	AWL, AWR-kid
ȯi	foil, coin	oy	FOYL, KOYN
au̇	out	ow	OWT
ə	cup, butter	uh	KUHP, BUHT-uhr
ü	rule, food	oo	ROOL, FOOD
yü	few	yoo	FYOO
zh	vision	zh	VIZH-uhn

*A syllable printed in small capital letters receives heavier emphasis than the other syllable(s) in a word.

Phonetic Respelling and Pronunciation Guide

Many of the key terms in this textbook have been respelled to help you pronounce them. The letter combinations used in the respelling throughout the narrative are explained in the following phonetic respelling and pronunciation guide. The guide is adapted from *Merriam-Webster's Collegiate Dictionary, Eleventh Edition; Merriam-Webster's Biographical Dictionary;* and *Merriam-Webster's Geographical Dictionary.*

A

acropolis (uh-KRAH-puh-luhs) a high hill upon which a Greek fortress was built (p. 232)
acrópolis colina elevada sobre la que se construyó una fortaleza griega (pág. 232)

acupuncture (AK-yoo-punk-cher) the Chinese practice of inserting fine needles through the skin at specific points to cure disease or relieve pain (p. 183)
acupuntura práctica china que consiste en insertar pequeñas agujas en la piel en puntos específicos para curar enfermedades o aliviar el dolor (pág. 183)

afterlife life after death, much of Egyptain religion focused on the afterlife (p. 92)
la otra vida vida después de la muerte (pág. 92)

agriculture farming (p. 42)
agricultura cultivo de la tierra (pág. 42)

alliance an agreement to work together (p. 270)
alianza acuerdo de colaboración (pág. 270)

alloy a mixture of two or more metals (p. 150)
aleación mezcla de dos o más metales (pág. 150)

alphabet a set of letters that can be combined to form words (p. 77)
alfabeto conjunto de letras que pueden combinarse para formar palabras (pág. 77)

ancestor a relative who lived in the past (p. 28)
antepasado pariente que vivió hace muchos años (pág. 28)

animism the belief that bodies of water, animals, trees, and other natural objects have spirits (p. 383)
animismo creencia de que las masas de agua, los animales, los árboles y otros elementos naturales tienen espíritu (pág. 383)

Apostles (uh-PAHS-uhls) the 12 chosen disciples of Jesus who spread his teachings (p. 337)
apóstoles los 12 discípulos elegidos por Jesucristo que difundieron sus enseñanzas (pág. 337)

aqueduct (A-kwuh-duhkt) a human-made raised channel that carries water from distant places (p. 327)
acueducto canal hecho por el ser humano que transporta agua desde lugares alejados (pág. 327)

archaeology (ar-kee-AH-luh-jee) the study of the past based on what people left behind (p. 7)
arqueología estudio del pasado a través de los objetos que dejaron las personas tras desaparecer (pág. 7)

architecture the science of building (p. 68)
arquitectura ciencia de la construcción (pág. 68)

aristocrat (uh-RIS-tuh-krat) a rich landowner or noble (p. 237)
aristócrata propietario de tierras o noble rico (pág. 237)

artifact an object created and used by humans (p. 10)
artefacto objeto creado y usado por los humanos (pág. 10)

astronomy the study of stars and planets (p. 151)
astronomía estudio de las estrellas y los planetas (pág. 151)

B

Black Death a deadly plague that swept through Europe between 1347 and 1351 (p. 543)
Peste Negra plaga mortal que azotó Europa entre 1347 y 1351 (pág. 543)

Buddhism a religion based on the teachings of the Buddha that developed in India in the 500s BC (p. 138)
budismo religión basada en las enseñanzas de Buda, originada en la India en el siglo VI a. C. (pág. 138)

bureaucracy a body of unelected government officials (p. 422)
burocracia cuerpo de empleados no electos del gobierno (pág. 422)

Bushido (BOOH-shi-doh) the code of honor followed by the samurai in Japan (p. 456)
Bushido código de honor por el que se regían los samuráis en Japón (pág. 456)

Byzantine Empire the society that developed in the eastern Roman Empire after the fall of the western Roman Empire (p. 343)
Imperio bizantino sociedad que surgió en el Imperio romano de oriente tras la caída del Imperio rhomano de occidente (pág. 343)

C

caliph (KAY-luhf) a title that Muslims use for the highest leader of Islam (p. 362)
califa título que los musulmanes le dan al líder supremo del Islam (pág. 362)

calligraphy decorative writing (p. 371)
caligrafía escritura decorativa (pág. 371)

canal a human-made waterway (p. 56)
canal vía de agua hecha por el ser humano (pág. 56)

capitalism an economic system in which individuals and private businesses run most industries (p. 601)
capitalismo sistema económico en el que los individuos y las empresas privadas controlan la mayoría de las industrias (pág. 601)

caravan a group of traders that travel together (p. 355)
caravana grupo de comerciantes que viajan juntos (pág. 355)

caste system the division of Indian society into groups based on rank, wealth, or occupation (p. 131)
sistema de castas división de la sociedad india en grupos basados en la clase social, el nivel económico o la profesión (pág. 131)

cataracts rapids along a river, such as those along the Nile in Egypt (p. 87)
rápidos fuertes corrientes a lo largo de un río, como las del Nilo en Egipto (pág. 87)

Catholic Reformation the effort of the late 1500s and 1600s to reform the Catholic Church from within; also called the Counter-Reformation (p. 572)
Reforma católica iniciativa para reformar la Iglesia católica desde dentro que tuvo lugar a finales del siglo XVI y en el XVII; también conocida como Contrarreforma (pág. 572)

causeway a raised road across water or wet ground (p. 474)
carretera elevada carretera construida sobre agua o terreno pantanoso (pág. 474)

cavalry a unit of soldiers who ride horses (p. 262)
caballería grupo de soldados a caballo (pág. 262)

chariot a wheeled, horse-drawn cart used in battle (p. 74)
cuadriga carro tirado por caballos usado en las batallas (pág. 74)

checks and balances a system that balances the distribution of power in a government (p. 305)
pesos y contrapesos sistema creado para equilibrar la distribución del poder en un gobierno (pág. 305)

chivalry (SHIV-uhl-ree) the code of honorable behavior for medieval knights (p. 513)
caballería código de comportamiento y honor de los caballeros medievales (pág. 513)

Christian humanism the combination of humanist and religious ideas (p. 567)
humanismo cristiano combinación de ideas humanistas y religiosas (pág. 567)

Christianity a religion based on the teachings of Jesus of Nazareth that developed in Judea at the beginning of the first century AD (p. 334)
cristianismo religión basada en las enseñanzas de Jesús de Nazaret que se desarrolló en Judea a comienzos del siglo I d. C. (pág. 334)

circumnavigate to go all the way around (p. 595)
circunnavegar rodear por completo (pág. 595)

citizen a person who has the right to participate in government (p. 237)
ciudadano persona que tiene el derecho de participar en el gobierno (pág. 237)

city-state a political unit consisting of a city and its surrounding countryside (p. 60)
ciudad estado unidad política formada por una ciudad y los campos que la rodean (pág. 60)

civil law a legal system based on a written code of laws (p. 328)
derecho civil sistema jurídico basado en un código de leyes escritas (pág. 328)

civil service service as a government official (p. 422)
administración pública servicio como empleado del gobierno (pág. 422)

clan an extended family (p. 442)
clan familia extensa (pág. 442)

classical an age marked by great achievements (p. 232)
clásica época marcada por grandes logros (pág. 232)

clergy church officials (p. 533)
clero funcionarios de la Iglesia (pág. 533)

climate the average weather conditions in a certain area over a long period of time (p. 12)
clima condiciones del tiempo medias de una zona específica durante un largo período de tiempo (pág. 12)

compass an instrument that uses the earth's magnetic field to indicate direction (p. 418)
brújula instrumento que utiliza el campo magnético de la Tierra para indicar la dirección (pág. 418)

Confucianism a philosophy based on the ideas of Confucius that focuses on morality, family order, social harmony, and government (p. 169)
confucianismo filosofía basada en las ideas de Confucio que se basa en la moralidad, el orden familiar, la armonía social y el gobierno (pág. 169)

conquistadors (kahn-kees-tuh-DOHRS) Spanish soldiers (p. 478)
conquistadores soldados españoles (pág. 478)

consuls (KAHN-suhlz) the two most powerful officials in Rome (p. 303)
cónsules los dos funcionarios más poderosos en Roma (pág. 303)

corruption the decay of people's values (p. 342)
corrupción decadencia de los valores de las personas (pág. 342)

court a group of nobles who live near and serve or advise a ruler (p. 448)
corte grupo de nobles que viven cerca de un gobernante y lo sirven o aconsejan (pág. 448)

crucifixion (kroo-suh-FIK-shuhn) a type of execution in which a person was nailed to a cross (p. 336)
crucifixión tipo de ejecución en la que se clavaba a una persona en una cruz (pág. 336)

Crusades a long series of wars between Christians and Muslims in Southwest Asia fought for control of the Holy Land from 1096 to 1291 (p. 528)
cruzadas larga sucesión de guerras entre cristianos y musulmanes en el sudoeste de Asia para conseguir el control de la Tierra Santa; tuvieron lugar entre el año 1096 y el año 1291 (pág. 528)

culture the knowledge, beliefs, customs, and values of a group of people (p. 7)
cultura el conocimiento, las creencias, las costumbres y los valores de un grupo de personas (pág. 7)

cuneiform (kyoo-NEE-uh-fohrm) the world's first system of writing; developed in Sumer (p. 65)
cuneiforme primer sistema de escritura del mundo; desarrollado en Sumeria (pág. 65)

currency money (p. 326)
moneda dinero (pág. 326)

D

daimyo (DY-mee-oh) large landowners of feudal Japan (p. 454)
daimyo grandes propietarios de tierras del Japón feudal (pág. 454)

Daoism (DOW-ih-zum) a philosophy that developed in China and stressed the belief that one should live in harmony with the Dao, the guiding force of all reality (p. 170)
taoism filosofía que se desarrolló en China y que enfatizaba la creencia de que se debe vivir en armonía con el Tao, la fuerza que guía toda la realidad (pág. 170)

Dead Sea Scrolls writings about Jewish beliefs created about 2,000 years ago (p. 212)
manuscritos del mar Muerto escritos sobre las creencias judías, redactados hace unos 2,000 años (pág. 212)

delta a triangle-shaped area of land made from soil deposited by a river (p. 87)
delta zona de tierra de forma triangular creada a partir de los sedimentos que deposita un río (pág. 87)

democracy a type of government in which people rule themselves (p. 236)
democracia tipo de gobierno en el que el pueblo se gobierna a sí mismo (pág. 236)

Diaspora (dy-AS-pruh) the dispersal of the Jews outside of Judah after the Babylonian Captivity (p. 206)
diáspora la dispersión de los judíos desde Judá tras el cautiverio en Babilonia (pág. 206)

dictator a ruler who has almost absolute power (p. 298)
dictador gobernante que tiene poder casi absoluto (pág. 298)

diffusion the spread of ideas from one culture to another (p. 189)
difusión traspaso de ideas de una cultura a otra (pág. 189)

division of labor an arrangement in which each worker specializes in a particular task or job (p. 56)
división del trabajo organización mediante la que cada trabajador se especializa en un trabajo o tarea en particular (pág. 56)

domestication the process of changing plants or animals to make them more useful to humans (p. 41)
domesticación proceso en el que se modifican los animales o las plantas para que sean más útiles para los humanos (pág. 41)

dynasty a series of rulers from the same family (p. 89)
dinastía serie de gobernantes pertenecientes a la misma familia (pág. 89)

E

elite (AY-leet) people of wealth and power (p. 93)
élite personas ricas y poderosas (pág. 93)

empire land with different territories and peoples under a single rule (p. 61)
imperio zona que reúne varios territorios y pueblos bajo un mismo gobierno (pág. 61)

engineering the application of scientific knowledge for practical purposes (p. 94)
ingeniería aplicación del conocimiento científico para fines prácticos (pág. 94)

environment all the living and nonliving things that affect life in an area (p. 13)
medio ambiente todos los seres vivos y elementos inertes que afectan la vida de un área (pág. 13)

epics long poems that tell the stories of heroes (p. 66)
poemas épicos poemas largos que narran hazañas de héroes (pág. 66)

ethics moral values (p. 169)
ética valores morales (pág. 169)

excommunicate to cast out from the church (p. 525)
excomulgar expulsar de la Iglesia (pág. 525)

Exodus the journey of the Israelites, led by Moses, from Egypt to Canaan after they were freed from slavery (p. 203)
Éxodo viaje de los Israelita, guiados por Moisés, desde Egipto hasta Canaán después de su liberación de la esclavitud (pág. 203)

exports items sent to other regions for trade (p. 111)
exportaciones productos enviados a otras regiones para el intercambio commercial (pág. 111)

extended family a family group that includes the father, mother, children, and close relatives (p. 382)
familia extensa grupo familiar que incluye al padre, la madre, los hijos y los parientes cercanos (pág. 382)

F

fable a short story that teaches a lesson about life or gives advice on how to live (p. 247)
fábula relato breve que presenta una enseñanza u ofrece algún consejo sobre la vida (pág. 247)

fasting going without food for a period of time (p. 137)
ayunar dejar de comer durante un período de tiempo (pág. 137)

federalism the sharing of power between local governments and a strong central government (p. 575)
federalismo sistema de distribución del poder entre los gobiernos locales y un gobierno central fuerte (pág. 575)

Fertile Crescent an area of rich farmland in Southwest Asia where the first civilizations began (p. 55)
Media Luna de las tierras fértiles zona de ricas tierras de cultivo situada en el sudoeste de Asia, en la que comenzaron las primeras civilizaciones (pág. 55)

feudalism (FYOO-duh-lih-zuhm) the system of obligations that governed the relationships between lords and vassals in medieval Europe (p. 507)
feudalismo sistema de obligaciones que gobernaba las relaciones entre los señores feudales y los vasallos en la Europa medieval (pág. 507)

figurehead a person who appears to rule even though real power rests with someone else (p. 455)
títere persona que aparentemente gobierna aunque el poder real lo ostenta otra persona (pág. 455)

Five Pillars of Islam five acts of worship required of all Muslims (p. 360)
los cinco pilares del Islam cinco prácticas religiosas que los musulmanes tienen que observar (pág. 360)

Forum a Roman public meeting place (p. 305)
foro lugar público de reuniones en Roma (pág. 305)

fossil a part or imprint of something that was once alive (p. 10)
fósil parte o huella de un ser vivo ya desaparecido (pág. 10)

friar a member of a religious order who lived and worked among the public (p. 536)
fraile miembro de una orden religiosa que vivía y trabajaba entre la gente (pág. 536)

G

geography the study of Earth's physical and cultural features (p. 12)
geografía estudio de las características físicas y culturales de la Tierra (pág. 12)

Grand Canal a canal linking northern and southern China (p. 411)
canal grande un canal que conecta el norte con el sur de China (pág. 411)

Great Wall a barrier made of walls across China's northern frontier (p. 175)
Gran Muralla barrera formada por muros situada a lo largo de la frontera norte de China (pág. 175)

griot a West African storyteller (p. 396)
griot narrador de relatos de África occidental (pág. 396)

gunpowder a mixture of powders used in guns and explosives (p. 418)
pólvora mezcla de polvos utilizada en armas de fuego y explosivos (pág. 418)

haiku a type of Japanese poem with three lines and 17 syllables that describes nature scenes (p. 514)
haiku tipo de poema japonés de tres líneas y 17 sílabas en el que se describen escenas de la naturaleza (pág. 514)

Hammurabi's Code a set of 282 laws governing daily life in Babylon; the earliest known collection of written laws (p. 73)
Código de Hammurabi conjunto de 282 leyes que regían la vida cotidiana en Babilonia; la primera colección de leyes escritas conocida (pág. 73)

Hellenistic Greek-like; heavily influenced by Greek ideas (p. 275)
helenístico al estilo griego; muy influido por las ideas de la Grecia clásica (pág. 275)

heresy (HER-uh-see) religious ideas that oppose accepted church teachings (p. 546)
herejía ideas religiosas que se oponen a la doctrina oficial de la Iglesia (pág. 546)

hieroglyphics (hy-ruh-GLIH-fiks) the ancient Egyptian writing system that used picture symbols (p. 102)
jeroglíficos sistema de escritura del antiguo Egipto, en el cual se usaban símbolos ilustrados (pág. 102)

ENGLISH AND SPANISH GLOSSARY

High Holy Days the two most sacred of all Jewish holidays—Rosh Hashanah and Yom Kippur (p. 219)
Supremos Días Santos los dos días más sagrados de las festividades judías, Rosh Hashanah y Yom Kippur (pág. 219)

Hindu-Arabic numerals the number system we use today; it was created by Indian scholars during the Gupta dynasty (p. 150)
numerales indoarábigos sistema numérico que usamos hoy en día; fue creado por estudiosos de la India durante la dinastía Gupta (pág. 150)

Hinduism the main religion of India; it teaches that everything is part of a universal spirit called Brahman (p. 133)
hinduismo religión principal de la India; sus enseñanzas dicen que todo forma parte de un espíritu universal llamado Brahman (pág. 133)

history the study of the past (p. 6)
historia el estudio del pasado (pág. 6)

Holy Land the region on the eastern shore of the Mediterranean Sea where Jesus lived, preached, and died (p. 528)
Tierra Santa región de la costa este del mar Mediterráneo en la que Jesús vivió, predicó y murió (pág. 528)

hominid an early ancestor of humans (p. 28)
homínido antepasado primitivo de los humanos (pág. 28)

humanism the study of history, literature, public speaking, and art that led to a new way of thinking in Europe in the late 1300s (p. 561)
humanismo estudio de la historia, la literatura, la oratoria y el arte que produjo una nueva forma de pensar en Europa a finales del siglo XIV (pág. 561)

Hundred Years' War a long conflict between England and France that lasted from 1337 to 1453 (p. 542)
Guerra de los Cien Años largo conflicto entre Inglaterra y Francia que tuvo lugar entre 1337 y 1453 (pág. 542)

hunter-gatherers people who hunt animals and gather wild plants, seeds, fruits, and nuts to survive (p. 33)
cazadores y recolectores personas que cazan animales y recolectan plantas, semillas, frutas y nueces para sobrevivir (pág. 33)

I

ice ages long periods of freezing weather (p. 36)
eras glaciales largos períodos de clima helado (pág. 36)

imports goods brought in from other regions (p. 111)
importaciones bienes que se introducen en un país procedentes de otras regiones (pág. 111)

inoculation (i-nah-kyuh-LAY-shuhn) injecting a person with a small dose of a virus to help build up defenses to a disease (p. 150)
inoculación acto de inyectar una pequeña dosis de un virus a una persona para ayudarla a crear defensas contra una enfermedad (pág. 150)

irrigation a way of supplying water to an area of land (p. 56)
irrigación método para suministrar agua a un terreno (pág. 56)

Islam a religion based on the messages Muhammad is believed to have received from God (p. 356)
Islam religión basada en los mensajes que se cree que Mahoma recibió de Dios (pág. 356)

isolationism a policy of avoiding contact with other countries (p. 430)
aislacionismo política de evitar el contacto con otros países (pág. 430)

J

jade a hard gemstone often used in jewelry (p. 163)
jade piedra preciosa de gran dureza que se suele utilizar en joyería (pág. 163)

Jainism an Indian religion based on the teachings of Mahavira that teaches all life is sacred (p. 134)
jainismo religión de la India basada en las enseñanzas de Mahavira, que proclama que toda forma de vida es sagrada (pág. 135)

Janissary an Ottoman slave soldier (p. 364)
jenízaro soldado esclavo otomano (pág. 364)

Jesuits members of a Catholic religious order created to serve the pope and the church (p. 572)
jesuitas miembros de una orden religiosa católica creada para servir al Papa y a la Iglesia (pág. 572)

jihad (ji-HAHD) to make an effort or to struggle; has also been interpreted to mean holy war (p. 359)
yihad esforzarse o luchar; se ha interpretado también con el significado de guerra santa (pág. 359)

Judaism (JOO-dee-i-zuhm) the religion of the Hebrews (practiced by Jews today); it is the world's oldest monotheistic religion (p. 202)
judaísmo religión de los hebreos (practicada por los judíos hoy en día); es la religión monoteísta más antigua del mundo (pág. 202)

K

karma in Buddhism and Hinduism, the effects that good or bad actions have on a person's soul (p. 134)
karma en el budismo y el hinduismo, los efectos que las buenas o malas acciones producen en el alma de una persona (pág. 134)

kente a hand-woven, brightly colored West African fabric (p. 399)
kente tela muy colorida, tejida a mano, característica de África occidental (pág. 399)

kivas underground ceremonial chambers at the center of Anasazi communities (p. 603)
kivas cámaras ceremoniales subterráneas en el centro de las comunidades anasazi (pág. 603)

knight a warrior in medieval Europe who fought on horseback (p. 506)
caballero guerrero de la Europa medieval que luchaba a caballo (pág. 506)

L

land bridge a strip of land connecting two continents (p. 36)
puente de tierra franja de tierra que conecta dos continentes (pág. 36)

landforms the natural features of the land's surface (p. 12)
accidentes geográficos características naturales de la superficie terrestre (pág. 12)

Latin the language of the Romans (p. 304)
latín idioma de los romanos (pág. 304)

Legalism the Chinese belief that people were bad by nature and needed to be controlled (p. 170)
legalismo creencia china de que las personas eran malas por naturaleza y debían ser controladas (pág. 170)

legion (LEE-juhn) a group of up to 6,000 Roman soldiers (p. 309)
legión grupo que podía incluir hasta 6,000 soldados romanos (pág. 309)

lord a person of high rank who owned land but owed loyalty to his king (p. 167)
señor feudal persona de alto nivel social que poseía tierras y debía lealtad al rey (pág. 167)

M

magistrate (MA-juh-strayt) an elected official in Rome (p. 303)
magistrado funcionario electo en Roma (pág. 303)

Magna Carta a document signed in 1215 by King John of England that required the king to honor certain rights (p. 540)
Carta Magna documento firmado por el rey Juan de Inglaterra en 1215 que exigía

que el rey respetara ciertos derechos (pág. 540)

maize (MAYZ) corn (p. 468)
maíz cereal también conocido como elote o choclo (pág. 468)

manor a large estate owned by a knight or lord (p. 509)
señorío gran finca perteneciente a un ca-ballero o señor feudal (pág. 509)

market economy an economic system in which individuals decide what goods and services they will buy (p. 601)
economía de mercado sistema económico en el que los individuos deciden qué tipo de bienes y servicios desean comprar (pág. 601)

masonry stonework (p. 481)
mampostería obra de piedra (pág. 481)

matrilineal related to ancestry traced through the maternal, or mother's, line (p. 606)
materno basado en linaje seguido por línea maternal, o de la madre (pág. 606)

medieval (mee-DEE-vuhl) referring to the Middle Ages (p. 500)
medieval relativo a la Edad Media (pág. 500)

meditation deep, continued thought that focuses the mind on spiritual ideas (p. 137)
meditación reflexión profunda y continua, durante la cual la persona se concentra en ideas espirituales (pág. 137)

megalith a huge stone monument (p. 42)
megalito enorme monumento de piedra (pág. 42)

mercantilism a system in which a government controls all economic activity in a country and its colonies to make the government stronger and richer (p. 599)
mercantilismo sistem en el que el gobierno controla toda la actividad económica de un país y sus colonias con el fin de hacerse más fuerte y más rico (pág. 599)

merchant a trader (p. 111)
mercader comerciante (pág. 111)

Mesolithic Era the middle part of the Stone Age; marked by the creation of smaller and more complex tools (p. 38)
Mesolítico período central de la Edad de Piedra, caracterizado por la creación de herramientas más pequeñas y complejas (pág. 38)

Messiah (muh-SY-uh) in Judaism, a new leader that would appear among the Jews and restore the greatness of ancient Israel (p. 334)
Mesías en el judaísmo, nuevo líder que aparecería entre los judíos y restablecería la grandeza del antiguo Israel (pág. 334)

metallurgy (MET-uhl-uhr-jee) the science of working with metals (p. 150)
metalurgia ciencia de trabajar los metales (pág. 150)

Middle Ages a period that lasted from about 500 to 1500 in Europe (p. 500)
Edad Media nombre con el que se denomina el período que abarca aproximadamente desde el año 500 hasta el 1500 en Europa (pág. 500)

Middle Kingdom the period of Egyptian history from about 2050 to 1750 BC and marked by order and stability (p. 96)
Reino Medio período de la historia de Egipto que abarca aproximadamente del 2050 al 1750 a. C. y que se caracterizó por el orden y la estabilidad (pág. 96)

migrate to move to a new place (p. 36)
migrar desplazarse a otro lugar (pág. 36)

minaret a narrow tower from which Muslims are called to prayer (p. 371)
minarete torre fina desde la que se llama a la oración a los musulmanes (pág. 371)

missionary someone who works to spread religious beliefs (p. 140)
misionero alguien que trabaja para difundir sus creencias religiosas (pág. 140)

monarch (MAH-nark) a ruler of a kingdom or empire (p. 72)
monarca gobernante de un reino o imperio (pág. 72)

monastery a community of monks (p. 502)
monasterio comunidad de monjes (pág. 502)

monk a religious man who lived apart from society in an isolated community (p. 502)
monje religioso que vivía apartado de la sociedad en una comunidad aislada (pág. 502)

monotheism the belief in only one God (p. 208)
monoteísmo creencia en un solo Dios (pág. 208)

monsoon a seasonal wind pattern that causes wet and dry seasons (p. 125)
monzón viento estacional cíclico que causa estaciones húmedas y secas (pág. 125)

mosque (MAHSK) a building for Muslim prayer (p. 357)
mezquita edificio musulmán para la oración (pág. 357)

mummy a specially treated body wrapped in cloth for preservation (p. 93)
momia cadáver especialmente tratado y envuelto en tela para su conservación (pág. 93)

Muslim a follower of Islam (p. 356)
musulmán seguidor del Islam (pág. 356)

mythology stories about gods and heroes that try to explain how the world works (p. 243)
mitología relatos sobre dioses y héroes que tratan de explicar cómo funciona el mundo (pág. 243)

N

natural law a law that people believed God had created to govern how the world operated (p. 538)
ley natural ley que las personas pensaban que Dios había creado para controlar el funcionamiento del mundo (pág. 538)

Neolithic Era the New Stone Age; when people learned to make fire and tools such as saws and drills (p. 41)
Neolítico Nueva Edad de Piedra; el ser humano aprendió a producir fuego y a fabricar herramientas como sierras y taladros manuales (pág. 41)

New Kingdom the period from about 1550 to 1050 BC in Egyptian history when Egypt reached the height of its power and glory (p. 97)
Reino Nuevo período de la historia egipcia que abarca aproximadamente desde el 1550 hasta el 1050 a. C., en el que Egipto alcanzó la cima de su poder y su gloria (pág. 97)

nirvana in Buddhism, a state of perfect peace (p. 138)
nirvana en el budismo, estado de paz perfecta (pág. 138)

noble a rich and powerful person (p. 91)
noble persona rica y poderosa (pág. 91)

nonviolence the avoidance of violent actions (p. 135)
no violencia rechazo de las acciones violentas (pág. 135)

oasis a wet, fertile area within a desert (p. 354)
oasis zona húmeda y fértil en un desierto (pág. 354)

obelisk (AH-buh-lisk) a tall, pointed, four-sided pillar in ancient Egypt (p. 104)
obelisco pilar alto, de cuatro caras y acabado en punta, propio del antiguo Egipto (pág. 104)

observatories buildings used to study astronomy; Mayan priests watched the stars from these buildings (p. 472)
observatorios edificios que sirven para estudiar la astronomía; los sacerdotes mayas observaban las estrellas desde estos edificios (pág. 472)

Old Kingdom the period from about 2700 to 2200 BC in Egyptian history that began shortly after Egypt was unified (p. 90)
Reino Antiguo período de la historia egipcia que abarca aproximadamente del 2700 hasta el 2200 a. C. y comenzó poco después de la unificación de Egipto (pág. 90)

oligarchy (AH-luh-gar-kee) a government in which only a few people have power (p. 237)
oligarquía gobierno en el que sólo unas pocas personas tienen el poder (pág. 237)

oracle a prediction by a wise person, or a person who makes a prediction (p. 164)
oráculo predicción de un sabio o de alguien que hace profecías (pág. 164)

oral history a spoken record of past events (p. 396)
historia oral registro hablado de hechos ocurridos en el pasado (pág. 396)

P

Paleolithic Era (pay-lee-uh-LI-thik) the first part of the Stone Age; when people first used stone tools (p. 31)
Paleolítico primera parte de la Edad de Piedra; cuando el ser humano usó herramientas de piedra por primera vez (pág. 31)

papyrus (puh-PY-ruhs) a long-lasting, paper-like material made from reeds that the ancient Egyptians used to write on (p. 102)
papiro material duradero hecho de juncos, similar al papel, que los antiguos egipcios utilizaban para escribir (pág. 102)

Parliament (PAHR-luh-muhnt) the lawmaking body that governs England (p. 541)
Parlamento órgano legislador que gobierna Inglaterra (pág. 541)

Passover a holiday in which Jews remember the Exodus (p. 219)
Pascua judía festividad en la que los judíos recuerdan el Éxodo (pág. 219)

patricians (puh-TRI-shunz) the nobility in Roman society (p. 299)
patricios nobles de la sociedad romana (pág. 299)

patron a sponsor (p. 371)
mecenas patrocinador (pág. 371)

Pax Romana Roman Peace; a period of general peace and prosperity in the Roman Empire that lasted from 27 BC to AD 180 (p. 326)
Pax Romana Paz Romana; período de paz y prosperidad generales en el Imperio romano que duró del 27 a. C. al 180 d. C. (pág. 326)

peasant a farmer with a small farm (p. 167)
campesino agricultor dueño de una pequeña granja (pág. 167)

Peloponnesian War a war between Athens and Sparta in the 400s BC (p. 270)
guerra del Peloponeso guerra entre Atenas y Esparta en el siglo V a. C. (pág. 270)

Period of Disunion the time of disorder following the collapse of the Han Dynasty (p. 410)
período de desunión la época de desorden que siguió el derrumbe de la dinastía Han (pág. 410)

Persian Wars a series of wars between Persia and Greece in the 400s BC (p. 263)
guerras persas serie de guerras entre Persia y Grecia en el siglo V a. C. (pág. 263)

phalanx (FAY-langks) a group of Greek warriors who stood close together in a square formation (p. 273)
falange grupo de guerreros griegos que se mantenían unidos en formación compacta y cuadrada (pág. 273)

pharaoh (FEHR-oh) the title used by the rulers of Egypt (p. 89)
faraón título usado por los gobernantes de Egipto (pág. 89)

pictograph a picture symbol (p. 66)
pictograma símbolo ilustrado (pág. 66)

pilgrimage a journey to a sacred place (p. 356)
peregrinación viaje a un lugar sagrado (pág. 356)

plantation a large farm (p. 598)
plantación hacienda de grandes dimensiones (pág. 598)

plebeians (pli-BEE-uhnz) the common people of ancient Rome (p. 299)
plebeyos gente común de la antigua Roma (pág. 299)

polis (PAH-luhs) the Greek word for a city-state (p. 232)
polis palabra griega para designar una ciudad estado (pág. 232)

polytheism the worship of many gods (p. 62)
politeísmo culto a varios dioses (pág. 62)

porcelain a thin, beautiful pottery invented in China (p. 417)
porcelana cerámica bella y delicada creada en China (pág. 417)

prehistory the time before there was writing (p. 28)
prehistoria período anterior a la existencia de la escritura (pág. 28)

priest a person who performs religious ceremonies (p. 63)
sacerdote persona que lleva a cabo ceremonias religiosas (pág. 63)

primary source an account of an event by someone who took part in or witnessed the event (p. 10)
fuente primaria relato de un hecho por parte de alguien que participó o presenció el hecho (pág. 10)

prophet someone who is said to receive messages from God to be taught to others (p. 211)
profeta alguien del que se cree que recibe mensajes de Dios para transmitírselos a los demás (pág. 211)

Protestant a Christian who protested against the Catholic Church (p. 570)
protestante cristiano que protestaba en contra de la Iglesia católica (pág. 570)

proverb a short saying of wisdom or truth (p. 397)
proverbio refrán breve que expresa sabiduría o una verdad (pág. 397)

pueblos above ground houses made of a heavy clay called adobe that were built by Native Americans of the southwestern United States (p. 603)
pueblos casas de arcilla gruesa, llamada adobe, construidas más arriba de la superficie por indígenas del suroeste de Estados Unidos (pág. 603)

Punic Wars a series of wars between Rome and Carthage in the 200s and 100s BC (p. 309)
guerras púnicas sucesión de guerras entre Roma y Cartago en los siglos III y II a. C. (pág. 309)

pyramid a huge triangular tomb built by the Egyptians and other peoples (p. 94)
pirámide tumba triangular y gigantesca construida por los egipcios y otros pueblos (pág. 94)

Q

Quechua (KE-chuh-wuh) the language of the Inca (p. 480)
quechua idioma de los incas (pág. 480)

Qur'an (kuh-RAN) the holy book of Islam (p. 356)
Corán libro sagrado del Islam (pág. 356)

R

rabbi (RAB-eye) a Jewish religious leader and teacher (p. 216)
rabino líder y maestro religioso judío (pág. 216)

rain forest a moist, densely wooded area that contains many different plants and animals (p. 382)
selva tropical zona húmeda y con muchos árboles que contiene muchas variedades de plantas y animales (pág. 382)

reason clear and ordered thinking (p. 281)
razón pensamiento claro y ordenado (pág. 281)

Reconquista (re-kahn-KEES-tuh) the effort of Christian kingdoms in northern Spain to retake land from the Moors during the Middle Ages (p. 547)
Reconquista esfuerzo de los reinos cristianos del norte de España por recuperar los territorios en posesión de los moros durante la Edad Media (pág. 547)

Reformation (re-fuhr-MAY-shuhn) a reform movement against the Roman Catholic Church that began in 1517; it resulted in the creation of Protestant churches (p. 569)
Reforma movimiento de reforma contra la Iglesia católica romana que comenzó en 1517; resultó en la creación de las iglesias protestantes (pág. 569)

regent a person who rules a country for someone who is unable to rule alone (p. 444)
regente persona que gobierna un país en lugar de alguien que no puede hacerlo por su cuenta (pág. 444)

region an area with one or more features that make it different from surrounding areas (p. 15)
región zona con una o varias características que la diferencian de las zonas que la rodean (pág. 15)

reincarnation a Hindu and Buddhist belief that souls are born and reborn many times, each time into a new body (p. 133)
reencarnación creencia hindú y budista de que las almas nacen y renacen muchas veces, siempre en un cuerpo nuevo (pág. 133)

religious order a group of people who dedicate their lives to religion and follow common rules (p. 536)
orden religiosa grupo de personas que dedican su vida a la religión y respetan una serie de normas comunes (pág. 536)

Renaissance (re-nuh-SAHNS) the period of "rebirth" and creativity that followed Europe's Middle Ages (p. 561)
Renacimiento período de "volver a nacer" y creatividad posterior a la Edad Media en Europa (pág. 561)

republic a political system in which people elect leaders to govern them (p. 298)
república sistema político en el que el pueblo elige a los líderes que lo gobernarán (pág. 298)

resources the materials found on Earth that people need and value (p. 16)
recursos materiales de la Tierra que las personas necesitan y valoran (pág. 16)

Resurrection in Christianity, Jesus's rise from the dead (p. 336)
Resurrección en el cristianismo, la vuelta a la vida de Jesús (pág. 336)

rift a long, deep valley formed by the movement of the earth's crust (p. 380)
fisura valle largo y profundo formado por el movimiento de la corteza terrestre (pág. 380)

Roman Senate a council of wealthy and powerful citizens who advised Rome's leaders (p. 303)
Senado romano consejo de ciudadanos ricos y poderosos que aconsejaba a los gobernantes de Roma (pág. 303)

Romance languages languages that developed from Latin, such as Italian, French, Spanish, Portuguese, and Romanian (p. 328)
lenguas romances lenguas que surgieron del latín, como el italiano, el francés, el español, el portugués y el rumano (pág. 328)

Rosetta Stone a huge stone slab inscribed with hieroglyphics, Greek, and a later form of Egyptian that allowed historians to understand Egyptian writing (p. 103)
piedra Roseta gran losa de piedra en la que aparecen inscripciones en jeroglíficos, en griego y en una forma tardía del idioma egipcio que permitió a los historiadores descifrar la escritura egipcia (pág. 103)

rural a countryside area (p. 60)
rural zona del campo (pág. 60)

Sahel (sah-HEL) a semiarid region in Africa just south of the Sahara that separates the desert from wetter areas (p. 382)
Sahel región semiárida de África, situada al sur del Sahara, que separa el desierto de otras zonas más húmedas (pág. 382)

samurai (SA-muh-rye) a trained professional warrior in feudal Japan (p. 454)
samurai guerrero profesional del Japón feudal (pág. 454)

Sanskrit the most important language of ancient India (p. 129)
sánscrito el idioma más importante de la antigua India (pág. 129)

savannah an open grassland with scattered trees (p. 382)
sabana pradera abierta con árboles dispersos (pág. 382)

scholar-official an educated member of the government (p. 422)
funcionario erudito miembro culto del gobierno (pág. 422)

scientific method a step-by-step method for performing experiments and other scientific research (p. 592)
método científico método detallado para realizar experimentos y otros tipos de investigaciones científicas (pág. 592)

Scientific Revolution a series of events that led to the birth of modern science; it lasted from about 1540 to 1700 (p. 588)
Revolución científica serie de acontecimientos que condujeron al nacimiento de la ciencia moderna; se extendió desde alrededor del 1540 hasta el 1700 (pág. 588)

scribe a writer (p. 66)
escriba escritor (pág. 66)

secondary source information gathered by someone who did not take part in or witness an event (p. 10)
fuente secundaria información recopilada por alguien que no participó ni presenció un hecho (pág. 10)

seismograph a device that measures the strength of an earthquake (p. 182)
sismógrafo aparato que mide la fuerza de un terremoto (pág. 182)

serf a worker in medieval Europe who was tied to the land on which he or she lived (p. 509)
siervo trabajador de la Europa medieval que estaba atado al territorio en el que vivía (pág. 509)

Shia (SHEE-ah) a member of the second-largest branch of Islam (p. 365)
shia miembro de la segunda rama más importante del Islam (pág. 365)

Shinto the traditional religion of Japan (p. 442)
sintoísmo religión tradicional de Japón (pág. 442)

shogun a general who ruled Japan in the emperor's name (p. 455)
shogun general que gobernaba Japón en nombre del emperador (pág. 455)

Sikhism a monotheistic religion that developed in India in the 1400s (p. 135)
sijismo una religion monoteísta que se desarrolló en la India en el siglo XV (pág. 135)

silent barter a process in which people exchange goods without contacting each other directly (p. 386)
trueque silencioso proceso mediante el que las personas intercambian bienes sin entrar en contacto directo (pág. 386)

silk a soft, light, and highly valued fabric developed in China (p. 187)
seda tejido suave, ligero y muy apreciado que se originó en China (pág. 187)

Silk Road a network of trade routes that stretched across Asia from China to the Mediterranean Sea (p. 187)
Ruta de la Seda red de rutas comerciales que se extendían a lo largo de Asia desde China hasta el mar Mediterráneo (pág. 187)

silt a mixture of fertile soil and tiny rocks that can make land ideal for farming (p. 55)
cieno mezcla de tierra fértil y piedrecitas que pueden crear un terreno ideal para el cultivo (pág. 55)

social hierarchy the division of society by rank or class (p. 63)
jerarquía social división de la sociedad en clases o niveles (pág. 63)

society a community of people who share a common culture (p. 33)
sociedad comunidad de personas que comparten la misma cultura (pág. 33)

Spanish Armada a large fleet of Spanish ships that was defeated by England in 1588 (p. 596)
Armada española gran flota de barcos españoles que fue derrotada por Inglaterra en 1588 (pág. 596)

Spanish Inquisition an organization of priests in Spain that looked for and punished anyone suspected of secretly practicing their old religion (p. 548)
Inquisición española organización de sacerdotes que perseguía y castigaba a las personas que no eran cristianas en España (pág. 548)

sphinx (sfinks) an imaginary creature with a human head and the body of a lion that was often shown on Egyptian statues (p. 104)
esfinge criatura imaginaria con cabeza humana y cuerpo de león que aparecía re-presentada a menudo en las estatuas egipcias (pág. 104)

subcontinent a large landmass that is smaller than a continent, such as India (p. 124)
subcontinente gran masa de tierra menor que un continente, como la India (pág. 124)

sub-Saharan Africa Africa south of the Sahara (p. 380)
África subsahariana parte de África que queda al sur del Sahara (pág. 380)

Sufism (SOO-fi-zuhm) a movement in Islam that taught people they can find God's love by having a personal relationship with God (p. 369)
sufismo movimiento perteneciente al Islam que enseñaba a las personas que pueden hallar el amor de Dios si establecen una relación personal con Él (pág. 369)

sundial a device that uses the position of shadows cast by the sun to tell the time of day (p. 182)
reloj de sol dispositivo que utiliza la posición de las sombras que proyecta el sol para indicar las horas del día (pág. 182)

Sunnah (SOOH-nuh) a collection of writings about the way Muhammad lived that provides a model for Muslims to follow (p. 359)
Sunna conjunto de escritos sobre la vida de Mahoma que proporciona un modelo de comportamiento para los musulmanes (pág. 359)

Sunni a member of the largest branch of Islam (p. 365)
suní miembro de la rama más importante del Islam (pág. 365)

surplus more of something than is needed (p. 56)
excedente cantidad que supera lo que se necesita (pág. 56)

synagogue (SI-nuh-gawg) a Jewish house of worship (p. 210)
sinagoga lugar de culto judío (pág. 210)

Talmud (TAHL-moohd) a set of commentaries and lessons for everyday life in Judaism (p. 212)
Talmud Conjunto de comentarios y lecciones para la vida diaria en el judaísmo (pág. 212)

teepees cone-shaped shelters made of buffalo skins used by Native Americans in the Plains region (p. 606)
tipis viviendas en forma de cono hechas de piel de búfalo que usaban los indígenas norteamericanos en la región de las Planicies (pág. 606)

Ten Commandments in the Bible, a code of moral laws given to Moses by God (p. 204)
los Diez Mandamientos en la Biblia, código de leyes morales que Dios le entregó a Moisés (pág. 204)

theory an explanation a scientist develops based on facts (p. 588)
teoría explicación que desarrolla un científico basándose en hechos (pág. 588)

tolerance acceptance (p. 364)
tolerancia aceptación (pág. 364)

tool an object that has been modified to help a person accomplish a task (p. 30)
herramienta objeto que ha sido modificado para ayudar a una persona a realizar una tarea (pág. 30)

topography the shape and elevation of land in a region (p. 496)
topografía forma y elevación del terreno en una región (pág. 496)

Torah the most sacred text of Judaism (p. 210)
Torá el texto más sagrado del judaísmo (pág. 210)

totems images of ancestors or animal spirits; often carved onto tall, wooden poles by Native American peoples of the Pacific Northwest (p. 604)
tótems imágenes de antepasados o espíritus de animales; a menudo talladas en altos troncos de madera por los indígenas americanos de la costa noroeste del Pacifico (pág. 604)

trade network a system of people in different lands who trade goods back and forth (p. 111)
red comercial sistema de personas en diferentes lugares que comercian productos entre sí (pág. 111)

trade route a path followed by traders (p. 97)
ruta comercial itinerario seguido por los comerciantes (pág. 97)

tyrant an ancient Greek leader who held power through the use of force (p. 237)
tirano gobernante de la antigua Grecia que mantenía el poder mediante el uso de la fuerza (pág. 237)

urban a city area (p. 60)
urbano zona de ciudad (pág. 60)

vassal a knight who promised to support a lord in exchange for land in medieval Europe (p. 507)
vasallo caballero de la Europa medieval que prometía apoyar a un señor feudal a cambio de tierras (pág. 507)

veto (VEE-toh) to reject or prohibit actions and laws of other government officials (p. 304)
vetar rechazar o prohibir acciones y leyes de otros funcionarios del gobierno (pág. 304)

woodblock printing a form of printing in which an entire page is carved into a block of wood, covered with ink, and pressed to a piece of paper to create a printed page (p. 418)
xilografia forma de impresión en la que una página completa se talla en una plancha de madera, se cubre de tinta y se presiona sobre un papel para crear la página impresa (pág. 418)

ENGLISH AND SPANISH GLOSSARY

X, Y, Z

Zealots (ZE-luhts) radical Jews who supported rebellion against the Romans (p. 214)
zelotes judíos radicales que apoyaron la rebelión contra los romanos (pág. 214)

Zen a form of Buddhism that emphasizes meditation (p. 452)
zen forma del budismo que se basa en la meditación (pág. 452)

ziggurat a pyramid-shaped temple in Sumer (p. 68)
zigurat templo sumerio en forma de pirámide (pág. 68)

Index

KEY TO INDEX

c = chart	m = map
f = feature	p = photo

A

INDEX

B

C

INDEX

M

INDEX

N

INDEX

Q

R

S

U

V

INDEX

Credits and Acknowledgments

Grateful acknowledgment is made to the following sources for permission to reproduce copyrighted material:

Cesar E. Chavez Foundation: Quote from "Core Values of Cesar E. Chavez' from *Cesar E. Chavez Foundation* Web site; accessed September 24, 2004, at http://www.cesar-chavezfoundation.org. Copyright © by Cesar E. Chavez Foundation.

Columbia University Press: From *Records of the Grand Historian of China, Vol. II: The Age of Emperor Wu* by Burton Watson. Copyright © 1961 by Columbia University Press. From "Heinrich Von Treitschke" from *Introduction to Contemporary Civilization in the West* by the staff of Columbia College. Copyright © 1946, 1954, 1960 by Columbia University Press.

Benedict Fitzgerald for the Estate of Robert Fitzgerald: From *The Iliad* by Homer, translated by Robert Fitzgerald. Copyright © 1974 by Robert Fitzgerald. From *The Odyssey* by Homer, translated by Robert Fitzgerald. Copyright © 1961, 1963, by Robert Fitzgerald; copyright renewed © 1989 by Benedict R. C. Fitzgerald, on behalf of the Fitzgerald Children.

Penelope Fitzgerald for the Estate of Robert Fitzgerald: From *The Aeneid* by Virgil, translated by Robert Fitzgerald. Translation copyright © 1980, 1982, 1983 by Robert Fitzgerald.

Grove Press, Inc.: From "Poetry from the Six Collections" by Ki no Tomonori from *Anthology of Japanese Literature: From the earliest era to the mid-nineteenth century,* compiled and edited by Donald Keene. Copyright © 1955 by Grove Press.

Kendall/Hunt Publishing Company: From *Kings, Saints, and Parliaments: A Sourcebook for Western Civilization, 1050–1700,* edited by Sears McGee, et al. Copyright © 1994 by Kendall/Hunt Publishing Company.

Alfred A. Knopf, a division of Random House, Inc., www.randomhouse.com: From *The Tale of Genji* by Lady Murasaki Shikibu, translated by Edward G. Seidensticker. Copyright © 1976 by Edward G. Seidensticker.

Moznaim Publishing Corporation: From "10 Commandments," "The Story of Noah," and "The Story of the Tower of Babel" from *The Living Torah,* edited by Rabbi Aryeh Kaplan. Copyright © 1981 by Moznaim Publishing Corporation. Psalms 23:1–3 from *The Book of Tehillim,* edited by Rabbi Shmuel Yerushalmi, translated and adapted by Dr. Zvi Faier. Copyright © 1989 by Moznaim Publishing Corporation.

Penguin Books Ltd.: "Quiet Night Thoughts" by Li Po from *Li Po and Tu Fu: Poems,* translated by Arthur Cooper. Copyright © 1973 by Arthur Cooper. From *The Epic of Gilgamesh: an English version with an Introduction by N. K. Sandars.* Copyright © 1960, 1964, 1972 by N. K. Sandars.

John Porter: From *Polybius 6.11–18: The Constitution of the Roman Republic,* translated by John Porter. Copyright © 1995 by John Porter, University of Saskatchewan.

Simon & Schuster Adult Publishing Group: From *Popol Vuh: The Definitive Edition of the Mayan Book of the Dawn of Life and the Glories of Gods and Kings* by Dennis Tedlock. Copyright © 1985, 1996 by Dennis Tedlock.

The University of Chicago Press: From *The Panchatantra,* translated from the Sanskrit by Arthur William Ryder. Copyright 1925 by the University of Chicago Press.

The Arthur Waley Estate: From *The Pillow Book of Sei Shonagon,* translated by Arthur Waley. Copyright 1928, 1929, 1949, 1957 by The Arthur Waley Estate.

Weidenfeld & Nicolson, Ltd.: Excerpt (Retitled "A Knight Speaks") by Rutebeuf from *The Medieval World: Europe 1100–1350* by Friedrich Heer, translated from the German by Janet Sondheimer. Copyright © 1961 by George Weidenfeld and Nicolson Ltd. English translation copyright © 1962 by George Weidenfeld and Nicolson Ltd.

Sources Cited:

From "Richard the Lionheart Massacres the Saracens, 1191" from the *Eyewitness to History* Web site, accessed November 1, 2004, at www.eyewitnesstohistory.com.

From "Saladin and the Third Crusade" from *Arab Historians of the Crusades—Selected and Translated from the Arabic Sources* by Francesco Gabrieli, translated and edited by E. J. Costello. Published by University of California Press, 1969.

Illustrations and Photo Credits

Cover: ©Time Life Pictures/Getty Images

Front Matter: ii (t), Seth Joel/Getty Images/HMH Photo; ii (b), Clay McClachlan/Getty Images/HMH Photo.

Table of Contents: v, Réunion des Musées Nationaux/Art Resource, NY; vi, Ronald Sheridan @ Ancient Art & Architecture Collection Ltd.; vii, DEA/G. Dagli Orti/Getty Images; viii, ©Hemis/Alamy; ix, ©Anders Blomqvist/Lonely Planet Images; x, Richard T. Nowitz/National Geographic Image Collection; xi, Private Collection/Photo ©Heini Schneebeli/The Bridgeman Art Library; xii, Snark/Art Resource, NY; xiii, ©Angelo Cavalli/SuperStock; xiv, ©World History Cathedral Treasury, Aachen, Germany/E.T. Archive, London/SuperStock; H9, ©Alamy Images.

Chapter 1: 2-3 (t), O. Louis Mazzatenta/National Geographic Image Collection; 6-7, Rohan/Stone/Getty Images; 8 (b), Garry Gay/Alamy Images; 10-11 (t), ©STR/Reuters/Corbis; 11 (tc), Instituto Nacional de Antropología y Historia, Mexico (Detail)/All Rights Reserved, Image Archives, Denver Museum of Nature & Science; 11 (tr), ©Bojan Brecelj/Corbis; 11 (tl), Instituto Nacional de Antropología y Historia, Mexico (Detail)/All Rights Reserved, Image Archives, Denver Museum of Nature & Science; 13 (tl), Anne Rippy/Image Bank/Getty Images; 13 (tr), ©Royalty-Free/CORBIS; 16-17 (t), Gavin Hellier/Robert Harding World Imagery/Getty Images; 19 (tr), ©Kevin Schafer/CORBIS; 23, ©Egyptian National Museum, Cairo, Egypt/ET Archive, London/SuperStock.

Chapter 2: 24-25 (t), ©Pierre Vauthey/Sygma/CORBIS; 24 (b), ©Michael Holford Photographs; 24 (bc), Kenneth Garrett/National Geographic Image Collection; 25 (bl), Pascal Goetgheluck/Photo Researchers, Inc.; 25 (c), Réunion des Musées Nationaux/Art Resource, NY; 25 (br), Photodisc/Getty Images; 29 (b), Robert I.M. Campbell/National Geographic Image Collection; 29 (t), ©Ferorelli 2005; 30 (l), Pascal Goetgheluck/Photo Researchers, Inc.; 30 (tr), Pascal Goetgheluck/Photo Researchers, Inc.; 30 (br), ©Michael Holford Photographs; 31 (tr), Pascal Goetgheluck/Photo Researchers, Inc.; 31 (tl), Pascal Goetgheluck/Photo Researchers, Inc.; 31 (br), Erich Lessing/Art Resource, NY; 31 (bl), John Reader/Photo Researchers, Inc.; 33 (r), Taxi/Getty Images; 33 (l), ©David R. Frazier Photolibrary, Inc./Alamy; 34, Robert Harding Picture Library Ltd/Alamy Images; 35 (tr), South Tyrol Museum of Archaeology, Bolzano, Italy/Wolfgang Neeb/The Bridgeman Art Library; 35 (br), ©Vienna Report Agency/Sygma/Corbis; 38 (r), ©Photo courtesy of Dr. James Dixon/Photograph by Eric Parrish; 38 (l), Sisse Brimberg/National Geographic Image Collection.

Chapter 3: 50-51 (t), Georg Gerster/Photo Researchers, Inc.; 50 (b), Scala/Art Resource, NY; 51 (br), Erich Lessing/Art Resource, NY; 51 (bl), Borromeo/Art Resource, NY; 51 (cl), akg-images; 51 (cr), ©DEA/A. DAGLI ORTI/Getty Images; 54-55 (b), ©Reuters/Corbis; 58 (t), ©Nik Wheeler/CORBIS; 58 (b), ©Carmen Redondo/CORBIS; 59 (r), ©Lowell Georgia/CORBIS ; 59 (l), ©CORBIS; 64 (t), ©The Trustees of the British Museum/Art Resource, NY; 66 (tl), ©Gianni Dagli Orti/Corbis; 67 (r), ©Bob Krist/CORBIS; 67 (l), Scala/Art Resource, NY; 68 (tr), Erich Lessing/Art Resource, NY; 68 (tl-both), ©The Art Gallery Collection/Alamy; 69 (tc), Ronald Sheridan @ Ancient Art & Architecture Collection Ltd.; 69 (tr), Ronald Sheridan @ Ancient Art & Architecture Collection Ltd.; 71, Erich Lessing/Art Resource, NY; 74-75 (br), ©Gianni Dagli Orti/Corbis.

Chapter 4: 82-83 (t), ©Richard Passmore/Stone/Getty Images; 83 (b), ©La Venta Museum, Villahermosa, Mexico/Yoshio Tomii/SuperStock; 83 (c), DEA PICTURE LIBRARY/Getty Images; 88 (l), Erich Lessing/Art Resource, NY; 88 (r), ©Reza/Webistan/Sygma/Corbis; 92-93 (t), ©Musee du Louvre, Paris/Peter Willi/SuperStock; 93 (tc), ©The Trustees of The British Museum/Art Resource, NY; 93 (tr), British Museum, London, UK/The Bridgeman Art Library; 99 (r), ©Gianni Dagli Orti/Corbis; 99 (tc), ©Gianni Dagli Orti/Corbis; 99 (l), Ashmolean Museum, University of Oxford, UK /The Bridgeman Art Library; 101 (br), HIP/Art Resource, NY; 103 (tr), ©Robert Harding Picture Library; 107, Robert Caputo/Aurora Photos; 108 (tr), ©De Agostini Editore/Photolibrary.com.

Chapter 5: 120-121 (t), ©Gavin Hellier/Taxi/Getty Images; 120 (b), DEA/A. Dagli Orti/Getty Images; 121 (br), ©The Art Archive/Corbis; 121 (cr), Réunion des Musées Nationaux/Art Resource, NY; 121 (bl), DEA/G. Dagli Orti/Getty Images; 121 (cl), ©The Trustees of the British Museum/Art Resource, NY; 128 (l), Borromeo/Art Resource, NY; 128 (r), ©Anders Blomqvist/Alamy; 132, ©Burstein Collection/Corbis; 133 (l), Borromeo/Government Museum and National Art Gallery India/Art Resource, NY; 133 (r), Victoria & Albert Museum, London/Art Resource, NY; 134 (br), ©Najlah Feanny/Corbis; 134 (cl), ©Flip Schulke/Corbis; 134 (tr), ©Bettmann/Corbis; 137, ©Gilles Mermet/akg-images; 138-139 (c), age fotostock/Dinodia Photo Library; 140-141 (tr), ©Sena Vidanagama/AFP/Getty Images; 145, SEF/Art Resource, NY; 146 (br), ©Christophe Boisvieux/Corbis; 148 (tr), ©Lindsay Hebberd/CORBIS; 148 (tl), ©Sheldan Collins/CORBIS; 149, ©Philadelphia Museum of Art/CORBIS; 150 (tl), ©C. M. Dixon Colour Photo Library/Ancient Art & Architecture Collection Ltd.; 150 (tr), ©PARIS PIERCE/Alamy; 151 (tr), M.H.S Oxford; 151 (tl), ©Dinodia Picture Agency.

Chapter 6: 156-157 (t), ©Joel Santos/Aurora Photos/Corbis; 156 (b), Erich Lessing/Art Resource, NY; 156 (c), Réunion des Musées Nationaux/Art Resource, NY; 157 (cl), The Granger Collection, New York; 157 (br), ©The Trustees of The British Museum/Art Resource, NY; 157 (cr), Victoria & Albert Museum, London/Art Resource, NY; 162 (r), ©Julia Waterlow; Eye Ubiquitous/Corbis; 162-163 (l), ©Michael S. Yamashita/Corbis; 163 (r), ©Craig Pershouse/Lonely Planet Images; 164, DEA/G. Dagli Orti/Getty Images; 165 (tc), ©Museum of East Asian Art/Photolibrary.com; 174-175, ©FSG FSG/age fotostock/Photolibrary; 175 (r), Doug Stern/National Geographic Image Collection; 175 (c), ©O. Louis Mazzatenta/National Geographic Image Collection; 176, ©Christopher Arnesen/Stone/Getty Images; 177 (r), Snark/Art Resource, NY; 180, ©Asian Art & Archaeology, Inc./Corbis; 181, ©The Trustees of the British Museum/Art Resource, NY; 182 (l), ©SSPL/Getty Images; 183 (r), Erich Lessing/Art Resource, NY; 183 (l), ©Wellcome Library, London; 185, Snark/Art Resource, NY; 186-187 (b), Attributed to: Emperor Huizong, Chinese, 1082-1135, Court ladies preparing newly woven silk (detail), Chinese, Northern Song dynasty, early 12th century, Ink, color, and gold on silk, 37 x 145.3 cm (14 9/16 x 57 3/16 in.) Museum of Fine Arts, Boston Special Chinese and Japanese Fund, 12.886; 187 (inset), ©Wardene Weisser/Ardea.com; 187 (br), ©Michael S. Yamashita/Michael S. Yamashita Photography; 189, ©Charles & Josette Lenars/CORBIS; 190 (b), ©Tiziana and Gianni Baldizzone/CORBIS; 190 (cr), ©Araldo de Luca/CORBIS; 190 (cl), ©Elio Ciol/CORBIS; 191 (cr), ©Reza/Webistan/CORBIS; 191 (tl), ©Asian Art & Archaeology, Inc./CORBIS; 191 (cl), ©Bettmann/CORBIS; 195 MC1-MC2 (c), © Ilya Terentyev/Getty Images.

Chapter 7: 198-199 (t), ©Paul A. Souders/Corbis; 199 (bc), ©Michael Holford Photographs; 199 (br), ©Araldo de Luca/Corbis; 199 (bl), HIP/Art Resource, NY; 199 (cr), Erich Lessing/Art Resource, NY; 199 (cl), ©San Pietro in Vincoli, Rome, Italy/Mauro Magliani/SuperStock; 204 (r), ©Chiesa della Certosa di San Martino, Naples/SuperStock; 204 (l), ©SuperStock/SuperStock; 205 (br), akg-images; 205 (tl), ©Rabatti-Domingie/akg-images; 205 (tr), Erich Lessing/Art Resource, NY; 209, Cameraphoto Arte, Venice/Art Resource, NY; 210, ©Israel images/Alamy; 211 (l), Ronald Sheridan @ Ancient Art & Architecture Collection Ltd.; 211 (r), ©Ted Spiegel/Corbis; 212 (r), ©West Semitic Research/Dead Sea Scrolls Foundation/Corbis; 212 (l), ©Remi Benali/Corbis; 216, ©Bill Aron Photography; 217, ©Peter Guttman/Corbis; 218 (b), Richard T. Nowitz/Photo Researchers, Inc.; 218 (t), ©British Library Board. All Rights Reserved/Bridgeman Art Library.

Chapter 8: 224-225 (t), ©Rob Matheson/Corbis; 224 (b), ©Kevin Schafer/Corbis; 225 (bl), ©La Venta Museum, Villahermosa, Mexico/Yoshio Tomii/SuperStock; 225 (cr), akg-images; 225 (cl), ©Araldo de Luca/Corbis; 225 (br), Snark/Art Resource, NY; 228-229, ©StTphane MarTchal/Photolibrary.com; 230 (tr), Scala/Art Resource, NY; 230-231 (t), Erich Lessing/Art Resource, NY; 231 (r), Scala/Art Resource, NY; 235 (tl), NASA/GSFC/METI/ERSDAC/JAROS, and U.S./Japan ASTER Science Team; 236, Erich Lessing/Art Resource, NY; 237 (r), akg-images; 237 (l), ©Bettmann/Corbis; 240, ©The Art Gallery Collection/Alamy; 244, Erich Lessing/Art Resource, NY; 245 (r), ©Toshifumi Kitamura/AFP/Getty Images; 245 (l), Detroit Institute of Arts, USA/Founders Society purchase, General Membership Fund/The Bridgeman Art Library; 246-247 (b), National Gallery of Victoria, Melbourne, Australia/The Bridgeman Art Library; 249 (r), Donald Miralle/Getty Images; 249 (l), ©Stocktrek/Corbis; 250, ©Hemis/Alamy; 255 MC1-MC2 (c), ©Goodshoot/Jupiterimages/Getty Images.

Chapter 9: 256-257 (t), ©Anders Blomqvist/Lonely Planet Images; 256 (b), Vanni/Art Resource, NY; 257 (bl), National Museum of India, New Delhi, India/The Bridgeman Art Library; 257 (cr), ©Glyptothek, Munich, Germany/ET Archive, London/SuperStock; 257 (cl), ©Michael Holford Photographs; 257 (br), ©Shai Ginott/CORBIS; 262 (r), ©Gianni Dagli Orti/Corbis; 262 (l), SEF/Art Resource, NY; 263, Erich Lessing/Art Resource, NY; 266-267 (bl), Rolf Richardson/Alamy Images; 267 (br), British Museum, London, UK/The Bridgeman Art Library; 268 (tr), Scala/White Images/Art Resource, NY; 268 (bl), ©Ted Spiegel/Corbis; 269 (r), Erich Lessing/Art Resource, NY; 269 (l), Bildarchiv Preussischer Kulturbesitz/Art Resource, NY; 275 (tr), ©The Art Archive/Corbis; 277, ©Angelo Cavalli/SuperStock.

Chapter 10: 290-291 (t), ©Christopher Groenhout/Lonely Planet Images; 290 (b), Erich Lessing/Art Resource, NY; 291 (br), ©Asian Art & Archaeology, Inc./Corbis; 291 (bl), Erich Lessing/Art Resource, NY; 291 (c), Scala/Art Resource, NY; 291 (cl), Museo Etrusco di Villa Giulia, Rome, Italy/Giraudon/Bridgeman Art Library; 291 (cr), ©The Trustees of the British Museum/Art Resource, NY; 295 (br), ©Hubert Stadler/Corbis; 295 (tr), ©Gavin Hellier/Photographer's Choice RF/Getty Images; 296 (bc), Archive Timothy McCarthy/Art Resource, NY; 300, Scala/Art Resource, NY; 304 (t), ©Stephen Jaffe/AFP/Getty Images; 304 (b), ©PRISMA/Ancient Art & Architecture Collection; 311 (tl), Mary Evans Picture Library.

Chapter 11: 318-319 (t), ©JupiterImages; 318 (b), ©Araldo de Luca/Corbis; 319 (br), Erich Lessing/Art Resource, NY; 319 (bl), Bildarchiv Preussischer Kulturbesitz/Art Resource, NY; 319 (cr), Scala/Art Resource, NY; 319 (cl), ©SuperStock/SuperStock; 323, Bridgeman-Giraudon/Art Resource, NY; 326 (br), ©Steve Vidler/SuperStock; 331 (br), SEF/Art Resource, NY; 333 (b), James L. Stanfield/National Geographic Image Collection; 334, INDEX/The Bridgeman Art Library; 335 (b), AP Photo/The Ironton Tribune, Howie McCormick; 335 (t), ©CuboImages srl/Alamy; 336, Alinari/Art Resource, NY; 337, Johnny van Haeften Gallery, London, UK/The Bridgeman Art Library; 342-343 (c), ©Danny Lehman/CORBIS ; 347 MC1-MC2, ©Images & Stories/Alamy.

Chapter 12: 350-351 (t), ©Kazuyoshi Nomachi/Corbis; 350 (b), Réunion des Musées Nationaux/Art Resource, NY; 350 (c), Scala/Art Resource, NY; 351 (b), ©The Art Gallery Collection/Alamy; 357, age fotostock/Robert Harding Picture Library; 359, ©AFP/Getty Images; 363 (r), ©Vanni Archive/CORBIS; 363 (l),

Ian Dagnall/Alamy Images; 365 (inset), The Granger Collection, New York; 367, Hilarie Kavanagh/Stone/Getty Images; 368, Bibliotheque Nationale de Cartes et Plans, Paris, France/The Bridgeman Art Library; 369, Sheila Terry/Photo Researchers, Inc.; 370 (tl), Christopher and Sally Gable/ Dorling Kindersley/Getty Images; 370 (tr), 1Apix/Alamy; 370 (cl), Florian Kopp/ Imagebroker/Photolibrary.

Chapter 13: 376-377 (t), PhotoDisc; 376 (b), Werner Forman/Art Resource, NY; 377 (cl), Werner Forman/Art Resource, NY; 377 (cr), Erich Lessing/Art Resource, NY; 377 (bl), GK Hart/Vikki Hart/Stone/ Getty Images; 377 (bc), ©Ancient Art & Architecture Collection Ltd/Alamy; 377 (br), ©The Trustees of the British Museum/ Art Resource, NY; 382-383, ©White Star/ Monica Gumm/Photolibrary.com; 384 (tr), ©Nik Wheeler/CORBIS; 384 (bl), Aldo Tutino/Art Resource, NY; 384 (cl), Musee du Quai Branly/Scala/Art Resource, NY; 384 (br), ©B Christopher/Alamy; 385 (tr), ©The Trustees of The British Museum/Art Resource, NY; 385 (br), ©Reza/Webistan/ CORBIS; 387, Dr. Roderick McIntosh; 389, Steve McCurry/Magnum Photos; 391 (tr), Private Collection/Photo © Heini Schneebeli/The Bridgeman Art Library; 392, ©Sandro Vannini/Corbis; 395 (r), The Granger Collection, New York; 396-397, Pascal Meunier/Cosmos/Aurora Photos; 398 (l), Reuters/Corbis; 398 (r), AFP/Getty Images.

Chapter 14: 406-407 (t), ©Free Agents Limited/CORBIS; 406 (b), Itani Images/ Alamy; 407 (br), ©G K & Vikki Hart/ PhotoDisc; 407 (cr), ©Free Agents Limited/CORBIS; 407 (cl), ©The Gallery Collection/Corbis; 407 (bl), ©The Trustees of the Chester Beatty Library, Dublin/ The Bridgeman Art Library; 414-415 (b), Keren Su/China Span; 415 (cr), ©Keren Su/Corbis; 416-417 (bl), ©Carl & Ann Purcell/Corbis; 416-417 (cr), ©Keren Su/China Span/Alamy; 418 (t), Private Collection/Paul Freeman/The Bridgeman Art Library; 418 (c), ©China Photo/ Reuters/Corbis; 418 (b), ©Liu Liqun/ Corbis; 419 (l), Private Collection/The Bridgeman Art Library; 419 (r), ©Tom Stewart/CORBIS; 420-421, Traditionally attributed to: Yan Liben, Chinese, about 600û673, Northern Qi scholars collating classic texts (detail), Chinese, Northern Song dynasty, 11th century, Ink and color on silk, 27.5 x 114 cm (10 13/16 x 44 7/8 in.), Museum of Fine Arts, Boston, Denman Waldo Ross Collection, 31.123; 422-423, Snark/Art Resource, NY; 431 (r), National Palace Museum, Taipei, Taiwan/ The Bridgeman Art Library; 435, ©Peter Harholdt/CORBIS.

Chapter 15: 436-437 (t), Spectrum Colour Library; 436 (b), ©Royalty Free/CORBIS; 437 (br), Erich Lessing/Art Resource, NY; 437 (bl) (Detail) Bibliotheque Nationale, Paris, France/The Bridgeman Art Library; 437 (cr), ©National Museum, Tokyo/A.K.G., Berlin/SuperStock; 437 (cl), Erich Lessing/ Art Resource, NY; 442, Erich Lessing/ Art Resource, NY; 443 (r), ©Royalty Free/ CORBIS; 443 (c), The Granger Collection, New York; 443 (b), Ronald Sheridan @ Ancient Art & Architecture Collection Ltd.; 444 (tr), ©Bettmann/Corbis; 444 (b), ©Kenneth Hamm/Photo Japan; 445, age fotostock/Iréne Alastruey; 447, (Detail) Musee des Beaux-Arts, Angers, France/ Giraudon/The Bridgeman Art Library; 448-449, The Tale of Genji, c12th (drawing), Takayoshi, Fujiwara (c.1127-1179)/ Tokugawa Reimeikai Foundation, Tokyo, Japan/Photo ©AISA/Bridgeman Art Library; 449 (l), ©Sakamoto Photo Research Laboratory/Corbis; 449 (r), ©Burstein Collection/Corbis; 450, ©Catherine Karnow/Corbis; 451 (r), ©The Trustees of the Chester Beatty Library, Dublin/ Bridgeman Art Library; 453, Mary Evans Picture Library; 456 (c), Fitzwilliam Museum, University of Cambridge, UK/ The Bridgeman Art Library; 456 (l), Roger Viollet/Getty Images; 457 (l), ©Kenneth Hamm/Photo Japan; 457 (r), Werner Forman/Art Resource, NY; 463 MC1-MC2, ©Burstein Collection/CORBIS.

Chapter 16: 464-465 (t), ©Angelo Cavalli/ SuperStock; 464 (b), ©Gianni Dagli Orti/ Corbis; 465 (br), Freer Gallery of Art, Smithsonian Institution, Washington D.C.: Purchase F1932.28; 465 (cr), Werner Forman/Art Resource, NY; 465 (bl), Erich Lessing/Art Resource, NY; 465 (cl), ©The Trustees of the British Museum/ Art Resource, NY; 469 (r), Erich Lessing/ Art Resource, NY; 469 (l), ©Justin Kerr; 471 (tr), Scala/Art Resource, NY; 472 (l), Charles & Josette Lenars/Corbis; 472 (r), ©The Trustees of the British Museum/Art Resource, NY; 475 (tr), Mexican National Museum, Mexico City 9-2256/D.Donne Bryant/DDB Stock Photography; 477 (l), ©The Trustees of the British Museum/ Art Resource, NY; 479, Frederic Soreau/ Photolibrary; 480, ©Collection of the New-York Historical Society, USA/The Bridgeman Art Library; 481, The Granger Collection, New York; 482 (r), Museo del Banco Central del Ecuador - Quito. 0-19224/D. Donne Bryant/DDB Stock Photography; 482 (t), Stuart Franklin/ Magnum Photos; 482 (l), American Museum of Natural History, New York, USA/The Bridgeman Art Library; 483 (t), Bildarchiv Preussischer Kulturbesitz/Art Resource, NY; 483 (b), Réunion des Musées Nationaux/Art Resource, NY; 485 (cr), ©Kevin Schafer/CORBIS; 489 MC1-MC2 (c), ©imagebroker/Alamy.

Chapter 17: 492-493 (t), ©Robert Harding Picture Library; 492 (b), ©The Crosiers/ Gene Plaisted, OSC; 493 (cl), The Granger Collection, New York; 493 (cr), ©World History Cathedral Treasury, Aachen, Germany/E.T. Archive, London/SuperStock; 493 (b), ©Lordprice Collection/Alamy; 498 (l), ©Vittoriano Rastelli/Corbis; 498-499, Stephen Studd/Stone/Getty Images; 499 (r), ©Stefano Scata/Riser/Getty Images; 501, ©The Crosiers/Gene Plaisted, OSC; 504 (tr), ©North Wind Picture Archives; 505 (r), Scala/Art Resource, NY; 511, Bibliotheque Nationale, Paris, France/The Bridgeman Art Library; 513 (r), Alinari/Art Resource, NY; 513 (l), ©Sakamoto Photo Research Laboratory/CORBIS; 514 (r), Freer Gallery of Art, Smithsonian Institution, Washington D.C. Purchase, F1963.5; 514 (l), ©De Agostini/SuperStock; 518, Alinari/ Art Resource, NY.

Chapter 18: 520-521 (t), age fotostock/©Steve Vidler; 520 (b), ©The Trustees of the British Museum/Art Resource, NY; 521 (cr), ©G K & Vikki Hart/PhotoDisc; 521 (cl), HIP/Art Resource, NY; 525 (cr), Erich Lessing/Art Resource, NY; 525 (bl), ©Elio Ciol/CORBIS; 526 (bl), Hulton Archive/ Getty Images; 526 (tr), ©Hulton Archive/ Getty Images; 529 (t), Scala/Art Resource, NY; 530, Mary Evans Picture Library; 531, Scala/Ministero per i Beni e le Attivitα culturali/Art Resource, NY; 533, ©Ben Mangor/SuperStock; 537 (l), ©Jim Cummins/Corbis; 537 (r), Giraudon/ Art Resource, NY; 538 (tr), Erich Lessing/ Art Resource, NY; 539 (tr), ©Gjon Mili// Time Life Pictures/Getty Images Editorial; 539 (tl), Vanni/Art Resource, NY; 540-541 (b), Ronald Sheridan @ Ancient Art & Architecture Collection Ltd.; 541 (t), Dept. of the Environment, London, UK/ The Bridgeman Art Library; 542 (l), ©Bettmann/Corbis; 542 (tr), The Granger Collection, New York; 542 (bkgd), ©Alex Segre/Alamy; 549, Scala/Art Resource, NY; 553 MC1-MC2, ©The Gallery Collection/ Corbis.

Chapter 19: 554-555 (t), ©Ray Manley/ SuperStock; 554 (b), Bridgeman-Giraudon/ Art Resource, NY; 555 (br), Dorling Kindersley Ltd. Picture Library; 555 (bl), Réunion des Musées Nationaux/ Art Resource, NY; 555 (cr), age fotostock/ Heritage; 558-559, ©SuperStock RF/ SuperStock ; 562 (b), ©Rabatti-Domingie/ akg-images; 562 (t), Erich Lessing/Art Resource, NY; 562-563 (bl), ©Bridgeman Art Library, London/SuperStock ; 563 (cl), ©Bettmann/CORBIS; 563 (r), ©Gianni Dagli Orti/Corbis; 563 (t), Scala/Art Resource, NY; 563 (cr), The Granger Collection, New York; 564 (l), Scala/Art Resource, NY; 564 (r), Scala/Art Resource, NY; 566 (l), ©The Bridgeman Art Library/ Getty Images; 566-567 (r), The Granger Collection, New York; 568, National Portrait Gallery, London/SuperStock; 570 (l), akg-images; 570 (r), Erich Lessing/Art Resource, NY; 573, ©Alberto Campanile/ Photolibrary.com; 574, Erich Lessing/Art Resource, NY; 577, ©Mary Evans Picture Library/Alamy.

Chapter 20: 584-585 (t), ©Bill Ross/Corbis; 584 (b), National Maritime Museum, London, UK/The Bridgeman Art Library; 585 (cl), Royal Society, London, UK/The Bridgeman Art Library; 585 (bl), Werner Forman/Art Resource, NY; 585 (cr), Galleria degli Uffizi, Florence, Italy/Bridgeman Art Library; 585 (br), ©Bob Krist/Corbis; 588-589, Erich Lessing/Art Resource, NY; 593, Image courtesy of NASA/Kennedy Space Center; 597, "Trading at Taos Pueblo – 1635" ©1999: "Taos Timeline Murals," Giovanna Paponetti, Taos, New Mexico; 599, Victoria Smith/HRW; 603 (t), Getty Images/PhotoDisc; 605 (tl, tr), akg-images/ Werner Forman; 605 (bl), Courtesy, National Museum of the American Indian, Smithsonian Institution. 3/9547; 606 (tr), The Granger Collection, New York; 606 (t), © Marilyn Angel Wynn/Nativestock.com/ Getty Images; 611MC1-MC2, ©Cummer Museum of Art & Gardens/SuperStock.

Back Matter: R0-R1, Spectrum Colour Library

CREDITS AND ACKNOWLEDGMENTS

Staff Credits

The people who contributed to ***Holt McDougal Middle School World History*** are listed below. They represent editorial, design, intellectual property resources, production, emedia, and permissions.

Lissa B. Anderson, Melanie Baccus, Charles Becker, Jessica Bega, Ed Blake, Gillian Brody, Shirley Cantrell, Erin Cornett, Rose Degollado, Chase Edmond, Mescal Evler, Rhonda Fariss, Marsh Flournoy, Leanna Ford, Bob Fullilove, Matthew Gierhart, Janet Harrington, Rhonda Haynes, Rob Hrechko, Wilonda Ieans, Cathy Jenevein, Kadonna Knape, Cathy Kuhles, Debbie Lofland, Bob McClellan, Joe Melomo, Richard Metzger, Andrew Miles, Cynthia Munoz, Karl Pallmeyer, Chanda Pearmon, Jarred Prejean, Shelly Ramos, Désirée Reid, Curtis Riker, Marleis Roberts, Diana Rodriguez, Gene Rumann, Annette Saunders, Jenny Schaeffer, Kay Selke, Ken Shepardson, Michele Shukers, Chris Smith, Christine Stanford, Elaine Tate, Jeannie Taylor, Joni Wackwitz, Ken Whiteside, Carrie Jones, Jennifer Campbell, Bill Gillis, Ann Gorbett, Treacy Lambert, Carole Rollins, Terri Taylor, Debra O'Shields, Genick Blaise, Tracy King, Christine Devall, Julie Beckman-Key, Michelle Rimsa, Angela Beckmann, Nadyne Wood, Jennifer Rockwood, Stephanie Friedman, Sarah Lee, Paul Provence